SALES FORCE MANAGEMENT

THE IRWIN SERIES IN MARKETING

SALES FORCE MANAGEMENT

GILBERT A. CHURCHILL, JR.
Graduate School of Business, *University of Wisconsin*

NEIL M. FORD
Graduate School of Business, *University of Wisconsin*

ORVILLE C. WALKER, JR.
School of Management, *University of Minnesota*

FOURTH EDITION

Homewood, IL 60430
Boston, MA 02116

Senior sponsoring editor: Stephen Patterson
Managing developmental editor: Eleanore Snow
Marketing manager: Scott J. Timian
Project editor: Paula M. Buschman
Production manager: Ann Cassady
Designer: Mercedes Santos
Art coordinator: Mark Malloy
Compositor: J.M. Post Graphics, Corp.
Typeface: 10/12 Bembo
Printer: R.R. Donnelley & Sons Company

Library of Congress Cataloging-in-Publication Data

Churchill, Gilbert A.
    Sales force management / Gilbert A. Churchill, Jr., Neil M. Ford,
Orville C. Walker, Jr.—4th ed.
        p.   cm. — (The Irwin series in marketing)
    Includes bibliographical references and index.
    ISBN 0-256-10534-0   ISBN 0-256-10822-6 (International ed.)
    1. Sales management.   I. Ford, Neil M.   II. Walker, Orville C.
III. Title   IV. Series.
HF5438.4.C48   1993
658.8′101—dc20   92–18535

Printed in the United States of America
1 2 3 4 5 6 7 8 9 0   DOC 9 8 7 6 5 4 3 2

PREFACE

For the first 70 years of this century, the practice of sales management resembled the practice of medicine by tribal witch doctors. Sales managers had to rely on large doses of folkore, tradition, intuition, and personal experience in deciding how to motivate and direct the performance of their sales forces. Few firms did any research to better understand the motives and behaviors of their own salespeople. And sales managers got little information or guidance from marketing academicians. There was scant published theory and even less empirical research concerning the variables that influence one salesperson to perform better than another.

Fortunately, the situation began to change about 20 years ago. Since the early 1970s, an increasing volume of relatively sophisticated and informative research has focused on understanding why salespeople behave as they do and identifying factors critical to their performance. Today, nearly every issue of the major academic marketing journals contains at least one article of direct relevance to sales management; and one such journal is dedicated to theory and research in sales management and personal selling. Thus, substantial evidence has accumulated about the impact of different variables on a salesperson's job behavior and performance, namely:

1. Personal characteristics.
2. Aptitude.
3. Skill levels.
4. Role perception.
5. Motivation.
6. Environmental and organizational variables.

The sales manager who is familiar with this growing research evidence and best understands how these factors affect a salesperson's behavior has an advantage in planning and directing that behavior toward desired ends and in evaluating the results produced.

WHY WE WROTE THIS BOOK

Although the body of theory and research relevant for improving sales management practice grew dramatically throughout the 1970s, students of sales management had no single source to turn to for a detailed summary and analysis of that research and its implications. The textbooks of the time either failed to keep pace with the advancing knowledge or dealt with the emerging findings in a piecemeal fashion. Thus, our primary purpose in writing the first edition of this text in 1981 was to offer students a thorough, up-to-date, and integrated overview of the accumulated theory and research evidence relevant to sales management, plus the most recent practices and techniques employed by managers in the "real world."

We realized, though, that simply providing a compendium of theories and research findings would not only be deadly dull, but it would also do little to help students understand how a sales manager might perform his or her job most effectively. A second purpose for writing this book, then, was to emphasize the link between the determinants of sales performance on the one hand and the actions that sales managers can take to direct, influence, and control that performance on the other. We believe this objective was all the more important because of our—and our students'—dissatisfaction with existing texts. Many of them lacked structures that organized the discipline in the logical sequence of activities that managers engage in. Thus, some books discussed planning issues at several different places throughout the text, or dealt with evaluation and control before talking about implementation issues, or discussed implementation issues before examining questions of strategy. Unfortunately, some texts still suffer from this same shortcoming.

THE STRUCTURE OF THIS BOOK

We developed a framework that views the spectrum of sales managers' activities as focusing on three interrelated, sequential processes, each of which influences the various determinants of salesperson performance:

1. **The formulation of a strategic sales program.** This involves organizing and planning the company's overall personal selling efforts and integrating these efforts with the other elements of the firm's marketing strategy.

2. **The implementation of the sales program.** This includes selecting appropriate sales personnel and designing and implementing policies and procedures that will direct their efforts toward the desired objectives.

3. **The evaluation and control of sales force performance.** This involves developing procedures for monitoring and evaluating sales force performance so adjustments can be made to either the sales program or its implementation when performance is unsatisfactory.

The structure of this book reflects this framework. The first chapter introduces the subject with an overview of the duties and responsibilities of sales managers and how these activities relate to these three processes. Chapter 1 also outlines in detail the content of the rest of the book, which is divided into three sections corresponding to the three processes:

- **Part One—Chapters 2 through 8**—looks at the major decisions involved in designing a strategic sales program. This section examines the fit between the external environment, the firm's marketing strategy, and its strategic sales program. It also deals with the formulation of account management policies, ways of organizing the sales force, and methods for estimating demand, designing sales territories, and setting quotas.
- **Part Two—Chapters 9 through 15**—addresses issues involved in implementing the sales program. An overview of the determinants of sales performance is presented and the salesperson's role perceptions are discussed. Part Two then examines decisions involving the recruitment and selection of sales personnel, sales training, motivation, and the design of compensation and incentive programs.
- **Part Three—Chapters 16 through 18**—discusses techniques for monitoring and controlling sales force behavior and performance. It examines various approaches for conducting a sales analysis, costs analysis, and behavior analysis.

INTENDED AUDIENCE FOR THIS BOOK

This book is designed for use in an introductory course in sales management at either the advanced undergraduate or graduate level. It is also designed to complement a variety of teaching approaches. Instructors who primarily emphasize the lecture-discussion approach will find ample material for either a one-quarter or a one-semester course in the chapters and end-of-chapter discussion questions. For those who prefer case-oriented instruction, we have included 32 cases. Twenty-eight of the cases can be found at the end of the three sections since they primarily emphasize the issues discussed in the sections. Four of the cases are more encompassing. They contain a variety of issues and can be found in a final section after the epilog. The epilog, which is new, integrates the discussion and serves as an overall summary of the book's contents.

CHANGES AND ADDITIONS TO THE FOURTH EDITION

Those who have used the earlier editions of this text should find the above discussion very familiar. We have adhered to the admonition, "if it ain't broke, don't fix it." But while we have preserved the basic organization and other features of the book that have proved popular and useful in the past, we have also made many changes and additions to incorporate recent advances in sales management research and practice and to make it an even more effective aid to learning. For example, there is increased emphasis on international issues.

The emphasis is manifested both in terms of the conceptual discussion as well as the examples used to illustrate the points.

Another major change involves ethics, which is given much more prominence in this edition. For example, a section discussing ethical philosophies and frameworks for viewing ethical choices has been added to a new chapter. Moreover, ethical scenarios that students are asked to analyze have been added to the other chapters where appropriate. This organization resolves the problems of how to treat the topic of ethics. It is difficult to treat it early because students do not yet have the technical sophistication to appreciate alternative ways to approach ethical problems nor even the ethical issues involved. Treating the conceptual foundations early in the book and then interweaving ethical dilemmas with managerial issues allows students to more readily appreciate the social consequences of proceeding in particular ways.

Another major emphasis has been to make the book more interesting and easier to read. This has meant a number of changes. First, material has been reorganized, particularly in the first part of the book. Second, each chapter now begins with an introductory scenario, which involves students in the issues. Third, the writing style has been simplified wherever possible. There are many more headings and subheadings. The exhibits have been reworked and simplified where necessary. The art has also been redone so it is more modern looking. The footnotes have been moved to the end of each chapter so they are less intrusive. More Thorny Issues—ethical dilemmas or emerging problems for which there are as yet no clear-cut or generally accepted solutions—have been added to each chapter. The Thorny Issues allow students to come to grips with some of the more difficult issues facing modern sales managers and to apply the concepts they have just learned. The end-of-chapter discussion questions have been upgraded to provide more meaningful vehicles for student exercises or class discussions. Several chapters contain application questions for computer analysis. The combination of changes has produced a manuscript that is much more user friendly and interesting than previous versions.

There has also been a major revision of the cases. Almost one third of the cases are new. Further, several of the old cases have been revised and updated. Nine of the cases are now available on computer disc. The computerized cases also have been reworked so students can perform more sophisticated analyses. The Instructor's Manual contains several additional computerized cases.

In addition, all the chapters have been subjected to thorough scrutiny and rewrite. There has been a major updating of examples, for instance. There are many more in-text examples than were found in the third edition, and the examples are as up-to-date as possible. These changes help the book reflect the current practice of sales management. The discussion in some chapters has been expanded and in others it has been streamlined, always with the intention of making it as clear as possible. Some of the more significant chapter-by-chapter changes including the following:

- **Chapter 1.** This chapter has been shortened by moving the discussion of the characteristics of sales jobs to Chapter 2. Chapter 1 now concentrates on the role of personal selling and sales management in market-driven companies. It also outlines the structure of the remainder of the text.

- **Chapter 2.** This chapter also has been reorganized. It combines material from old Chapters 1 and 3, on organizational buying processes, selling activities, the selling process, types of sales jobs, and characteristics of sales careers. The new chapter provides a much better overview of personal selling, with respect to activities, challenges, and career opportunities.

- **Chapter 3.** This new chapter focuses on external and internal environments that affect marketing and sales programs and the envrionmental variables that influence the performance of individual salespeople. This chapter also contains the discussion of ethical frameworks that can serve as a basis for deciding what to do when faced with difficult ethical choices.

- **Chapter 4.** This chapter consists largely of a reorganization of material that used to be in Chapters 2 and 3. The chapter now ties together the marketing planning process, the role of personal selling under various strategic conditions, and account management policies in a more organized and integrated fashion than before.

- **Chapter 5.** Among the changes to this chapter has been expansion of the discussion of when firms are likely to use independent sales agents versus company salespeople. Moreover, an entire section on organizing global sales forces has been added, drawing primarily on recent research findings.

- **Chapter 7.** This chapter has been revised to capture the modern uses of computers to manage sales territories. Moreover, the section discussing the incremental method for determining sales force size has been reworked.

- **Chapter 16.** This first of three chapters on evaluating the personal selling effort has been revised to capture the increasingly important role played by decision support systems in salesperson evaluations.

A CKNOWLEDGMENTS

A book like this is never the work of a single author or even a small group of authors; rather, there are many people and institutions whose contributions need to be acknowledged. We wish to thank the many scholars and sales managers who have labored so diligently over the last 20 years to move the study of sales management out of the dark ages and into the mainstream of marketing thought. We would also like to acknowledge the special contributions of the Marketing Science Institute, which supported much of the recent research, and especially Steve Greyser, Alden Clayton, and Diane Schmalensee for their willingness to commit MSI's energies and resources to the study of sales management before it became a fashionable topic. Their visionary interest helped produce the critical mass of effort necessary to move the study of the topic forward.

Academicians—even those in marketing—are sometimes not very customer-oriented, particularly when it comes to writing textbooks. We have made a concerted effort to avoid such a heresy. Consequently, we offer special thanks to the more than 60 professors who responded to our questionnaire about their attitutdes toward the previous editions of this book. The information they provided was very helpful in our effort to make the fourth edition a more useful tool for teaching and learning.

A number of unexciting, but nevertheless critical, tasks are associated with the production of a book such as this. The following students all made significant contributions to the competent completion of these tasks: Beth Bubon, Katherine Cheney, Regina Downey, Mary Flanagan, Kiersten Foget, Kelly Granholm, Joseph Kuester, Greg Martin, Erika Matulich, Margaret McCabe, William Murphy, Ravi Sohi, Karen Ryan, and Kevin Dowd. Also, Jonlee Andrews not only prepared new test questions, but she also reviewed and classroom-tested many of the new cases. We gratefully acknowledge their efforts. We also thank our many students over the years for their comments and suggestions. The book is better because of their insights.

Our thanks also go to Professor Raymond LaForge of Oklahoma State University for providing the data base used to develop the Calendar Coffee Company case, Professor Erin Anderson of the Wharton School for permission to use the Barro Stickney case, and Professor Roger Kerin of Southern Methodist University for permission to use the Wilkinson Sword case.

K. Richard Berlet of TRIAD Consultants, Inc., was the driving force behind the development of the Associated Directories case. In addition, he has been a frequent classroom visitor and has shared many insights with us.

Jerome A. Colletti, president of the Alexander Group, Inc., has also contributed to this book in many ways. We particularly thank him for permitting us to use materials from his firm's seminars and publications on sales compensations and incentive programs.

Elmer C. Meider, Jr, president of Highlights for Children, Inc., spent much time helping to develop the Highlights for Children case. Development of that case was supported by a grant from Marlene Futterman and the Direct Selling Education Foundation.

John Verwiel, In-Sink-Erator Division of Emerson Electric, provided data and guidance to develop the In-Sink-Erator case.

A number of sales managers, sales representatives, and others have shared their insights and suggestions with us over the years. They include Dierdre Berns; Peggy Hill of Oscar Mayer Foods; Scott Sklare of Persoft, Inc.; John Shabino of Permatech, Inc.; Christopher Gilmore, lecturer and consultant; Tom Hartley of Union Carbide, Inc., and Delal Makensie, Dow USA.

We hope we haven't forgotten anyone, and we apologize to those whose suggestions we failed to implement. Needless to say, we assume full responsibility for any errors or omissions in this book.

Janet Christopher typed the major part of the manuscript and the Instructor's Manual, and her willingness to operate under tight deadlines and the quality of her output are sincerely appreciated.

Finally, we wish to thank our families, and each of their many members, for their encouragement and support while this book was being written. It is with love we dedicate it to them.

Gilbert A. Churchill, Jr.
Neil M. Ford
Orville C. Walker, Jr.

CONTENTS IN BRIEF

CONTENTS

C h a p t e r 8

Sales Quotas 262

Cases for Part One 289

P a r t T w o   IMPLEMENTATION OF THE SALES PROGRAM   369

C h a p t e r   9
Model of Salesperson Performance   370

C h a p t e r   10
The Salesperson's Role Perceptions   388

PART THREE EVALUATION AND CONTROL OF THE SALES PROGRAM

C h a p t e r   16
Sales Analysis

Chapter 17

Cost Analysis 727

Chapter 18

Behavior and Other Performance Analyses 760

An Overview of Sales Management

XEROX: AN EXAMPLE OF SALES MANAGEMENT'S ROLE IN A CUSTOMER-DRIVEN COMPANY[1]

During the late 1970s and early 1980s, Xerox's preeminent position in the office equipment industry was threatened from several directions. Its competitors in the copier industry—particularly the Japanese—were using their greater efficiency to underprice Xerox's copiers while simultaneously leapfrogging ahead in copier technology. While Xerox managed to maintain its market share lead in the copier business, the firm watched that leading share shrink to only about 10 percent of the market in 1985.

At the same time, rapidly evolving electronic technology was changing the face of the office equipment industry. New office products and systems, such as networks of computer workstations, electronic mail, desktop publishing systems, and fax machines, threatened to reduce the importance of simple plain-paper copiers. Xerox feared it might become an anachronism, particularly in the eyes of its largest, most sophisticated customers, if it continued to focus primarily on its copiers. Weak capital spending levels by American businesses during the early 1980s caused stagnation in the office products industry, flattened Xerox's revenue growth, and squeezed its profits.

A Change in
Strategy

Xerox's leading position in the copier industry had allowed the firm to become a somewhat complacent competitor. But the many threatening changes in its market and competitive environments forced it to reassess the needs of its potential customers and its own competitive strengths and weaknesses. As a result Xerox's top management decided to change several aspects of the firm's competitive strategy. First, to help meet the price competition of its foreign competitors, the company took steps to improve the efficiency of its operations, to make the firm "leaner and meaner." Xerox sought to improve product efficiency by increasing product performance and decreasing cost of components. It also moved to increase efficiency of manufacturing operations. Attention was also focused on finding ways to reduce marketing costs.

A more fundamental change in strategy was to reposition the company as a technological leader in the office automation industry. Management decided to expand on Xerox's strong foundation in the copier business by developing a more complete line of integrated information processing equipment. To this end, the firm greatly increased its research and development budgets and new-product development efforts. The company was also officially dubbed "The Document Company" to communicate to customers it could provide them with equipment to help create, manipulate, distribute, and print—as well as copy—a variety of documents.

To help achieve the strategic goal of becoming a leading innovator in the office automation industry, Xerox's top managers encouraged employees to become more attuned and responsive to the evolving needs of customers. As Paul Allaire, the company's chief executive officer, remarked, "We have to change the company substantially to be more market-driven. If we do what's right for the customer, our market share and our return on assets will take care of themselves." To that end, frequent customer satisfaction surveys were instituted to help managers measure how well they were meeting customer desires. Internal bureaucracy was reduced and decision making was decentralized to enable lower level managers to respond quickly to competitive threats or market opportunities.

The New Marketing Strategy

As a first step toward gaining a better understanding of—and being more responsive to—customer needs, customers and potential customers were grouped into five segments according to their size, operational needs, and buying procedures. The first segment consists of custom system users—the largest commercial firms with multiple branch offices and specialized information processing needs. Other segments include standard commercial accounts (made up of a cross section of medium-size businesses), small businesses, third parties (consisting of dealers and distributors that handle some of the firm's products plus original equipment manufacturers), and institutional customers such as federal and state governments and educational institutions.

When Xerox's marketing managers examined the needs and purchase criteria of each customer segment, they discovered several segments are very price sensitive. This is particularly true for smaller commercial accounts and for institutional customers, which commonly purchase from the lowest bidder. Because the firm's costs were not low enough to always beat the prices of its foreign competitors, Xerox adopted a strategy of providing good value. It focused on developing high-quality, reliable products—backed up by expert and timely service—that would minimize customers' total operating costs over the life of the equipment.

Xerox's examination of each customer segment found more complicated desires among larger commercial customers. They prefer to deal with suppliers that can provide customized information processing systems—integrated networks of computer workstations, word processors, copiers, and communications equipment. To meet the needs of these customers and to reposition itself as a full-line "document processing" manufacturer, Xerox launched a major product development effort to fill the gaps in the product line. This effort had already started when the firm began producing computers and word processors in the late 1970s, but the pace quickened with the introduction of the "memorywriter" electronic typewriter in the early 1980s and has proceeded with the development of computer workstations, facsimile systems, and the Docutech office printing system.

To communicate the firm's new strategy and competitive positioning to prospective customers, Xerox substantially increased its promotional efforts. The company spent more than $95 million on advertising in 1990, placing it among the top 200 advertisers in the United States. The television campaign for the Docutech system attempts to give the soulless document a human face by arguing that behind every great achievement is a great document. The ads show, among other things, documents created, printed, and distributed by Xerox equipment guiding the restoration of a church painting. Some of the firm's recent print ads, like the one shown in Exhibit 1.1, stress Xerox's commitment to high-quality products and service; an appeal strengthened by the fact that the firm has won the Baldrige award for quality. Both TV and print ads feature the tag line "We document the world" to reflect the firm's position as a full-line document processing manufacturer.

Another critical promotional tool Xerox relied on to implement its new marketing strategy was its large sales force. Changes in the firm's marketing strategy, however, also necessitated changes in the activities, organization, and management of its salespeople.

The Role of the Sales Force

Historically, Xerox had maintained separate sales forces for its various product lines. In the mid-1980s, the firm had 3,500 sales reps dedicated to selling its copier-duplicator equipment. Several other 75-to-200-person sales forces (totaling 500 to 1,000 reps) were focused on selling information processing systems, printing systems, office systems, and sales engineering.

In 1985, the firm began to meld all of its separate sales forces into a single, integrated full-line sales force. One reason for this move was to improve sales productivity. As Xerox's product line expanded, it made sense to have existing reps handle more products rather than adding more specialized salespeople. "That way," one manager said, "we get greater coverage for individual products without an increase in total costs because we are already paying their salaries." This view was supported by the company's earlier experience with the memorywriter. Rather than creating another dedicated sales force for the new product, it was added to the lines handled by copier reps. And, as one manager pointed out, "Sales revenue per rep doubled when we added the

EXHIBIT 1 ● 1

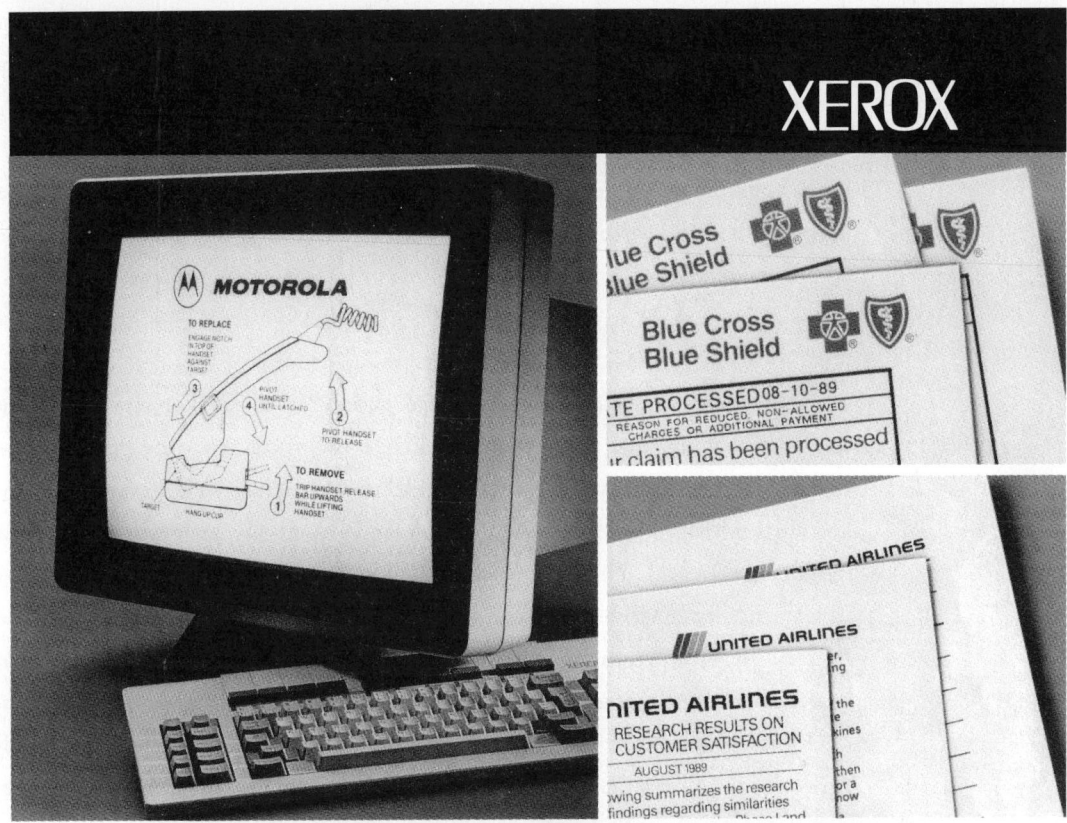

At Xerox our dedication to quality is well documented.

To us, quality isn't simply a matter of providing better products. Or better service. Quality is our corporate culture. Six years ago we found a name for it: "Leadership Through Quality."

Leadership Through Quality means that everything we do, from answering the phone to our most innovative new technology, is done with one thing in mind. 100% customer satisfaction.

For Blue Cross and Blue Shield of North Carolina, we created a system that lets them print and place claim explanations and matching MICR-encoded checks in the same envelope. Improving customer

service, and saving over $350,000 a year in postage and handling.

For Rich Graphics, Leadership Through Quality meant a system that lets them deliver documents to their client Motorola in one-fifth the time and at one-half the cost (a system that has helped Rich Graphics double their printing business every year since coming to Xerox).

For United Airlines, it meant careful analysis to provide solutions and support that greatly improved the cost-effectiveness of their more than 300 offices coast-to-coast.

You see, at Xerox, we work with our customers as partners. We listen to their problems, always looking for new ways to meet their requirements. New ways to provide them with documents superior in both look and content.

At Xerox, quality is a process that never ends. Because we know we can't be a leader in our business unless we help our customers be leaders in theirs.

Team Xerox
We document the world.

XEROX® is a trademark of XEROX CORPORATION.

The Blue Cross and Blue Shield marks are registered marks of the Blue Cross and Blue Shield Association.

This ad appeared in *Fortune,* September 25, 1989.

electronic typewriter. Adding related products to a copier rep's line dramatically increased his ability to satisfy customer needs."

The desire of many larger customers for integrated document processing systems—and the firm's attempt to reposition itself as a full-line manufacturer of such systems—provided another reason for reorganizing the sales force. A Xerox marketing vice president concluded that an increasing number of potential customers "want us to take a coordinated, long-term approach. They want to sit down with one rep and strategize about where they're going and where we're going."

The new sales force organization

The new Xerox sales force is organized according to market segments, with sales reps responsible for selling a full line of products to the customers in their designated segment, within a geographic area. The 350 largest commercial accounts with multiple locations are serviced by about 250 national account managers (NAMs). They are responsible for becoming an expert on the needs of a particular customer and for coordinating the efforts of local Xerox sales reps and service people in dealing with that customer. Recently, some of these national account managers became global account managers in an attempt to deal with some of the unique problems that arise from the increased globalization of the firm's major customers. The rationale for this move is discussed in greater detail in Thorny Issues in Sales Management 1.1.

Lower level account reps and marketing reps within the Xerox sales force focus on medium-sized and small commercial accounts in particular geographic territories. Two other groups of reps focus on specialized customer segments. One group of 100 to 150 reps deals with third-party channels, and another group of 50 to 70 reps sells to governments and large institutions.

Training

One obvious concern in expanding the product lines handled by a salesperson, particularly in a high-tech business, is that the rep may lack the product and technical knowledge to fully assess and satisfy a customer's requirements. To overcome this, Xerox assembled a systematic three-tier training program that extends over three to four years. The first tier consists of two weeks of class-

Thorny Issues in Sales Management 1 • 1

Coordinating Sales to Multinational Customers

The increasing globalization of many businesses poses two problems for sales managers. First, managers in firms that sell products or services in multiple countries must decide how best to organize their sales forces to coordinate and control marketing and sales efforts in the various markets. This organizational problem is examined in more detail in Chapter 5.

A second problem faces firms that sell to global customers. How can a firm coordinate the selling efforts and services it directs at a given customer when that customer has a variety of plants or subsidiaries—and perhaps separate buying offices or purchasing executives—in multiple countries? One solution to this problem is illustrated by a program recently launched at Xerox. Beginning as a pilot program focused on seven key accounts in 1989, this program has evolved into what Xerox calls its Global Accounts Marketing Program. It involved the expansion of roles of some members of the domestic sales force to create global account managers, who are responsible for providing comprehensive account support for the company's Fortune 500 multinational customers on a unified, worldwide basis.

The purpose of Xerox's Global Accounts Marketing Program is illustrated by the activities of Mike Wagoner, global account manager responsible for working with AlphaGraphics Printshops. AlphaGraphics is a print-for-pay franchisor based in Tucson, Arizona, with over 300 stores in the United States, 51 stores in foreign countries, and a satellite communications network that allows documents to be moved electronically from store to store around the world. Wagoner works with AlphaGraphics' top management to help them plan company expansion and the upgrading of document processing equipment, and then he coordinates the sales, delivery, and service efforts of Xerox employees in various countries to carry out those plans. For instance, when AlphaGraphics decided to upgrade 22 of its stores in the United Kingdom by installing new Xerox document processing systems, Wagoner coordinated the delivery, installation, and service activities of employees at Rank Xerox, the firm's British subsidiary, to make sure AlphaGraphics' plan was carried out in a timely and satisfactory manner.

Source: *The Xerox Corporation 1990 Annual Report* (Stamford, Conn.: The Xerox Corporation, 1991), p.15.

room instruction at the firm's training facility in Leesburg, Virginia, aimed at providing basic product and technical information. The second tier of training is done in each district office. Monthly district staff meetings were extended for an additional two hours for this purpose, and the firm created a library of videocassettes on various topics and added new area training managers. The district training covers sales techniques appropriate for selling to different types of customers as well as product knowledge. Finally, Xerox's sales reps receive

EXHIBIT 1 • 2   *Xerox's Revenues and Earnings per Share, 1986–90*

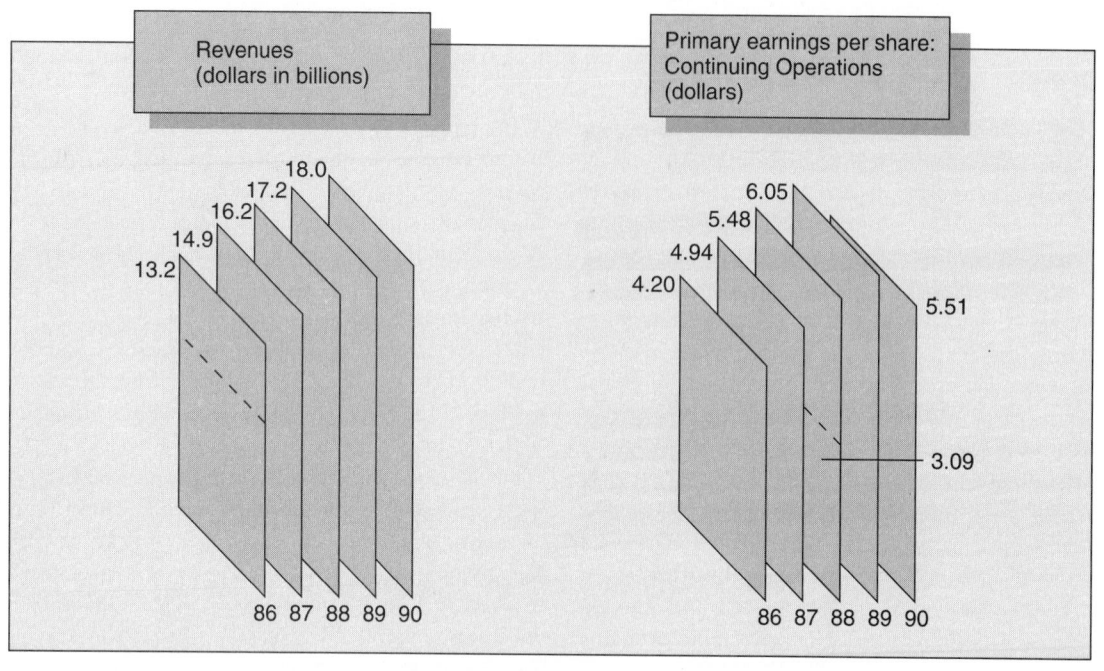

Source: *Xerox Corporation 1990 Annual Report* (Stamford, Conn.: The Xerox Corporation, 1991), p. 1.

periodic updates on product changes and product introductions, which they are expected to learn on their own.

Sales support systems

Another way to help the firm's reps knowledgeably sell all of the firm's products is by providing them with ready access to information. Consequently, the company developed an internal office information system to help its reps perform more productively. Workstations are installed in all district offices for use by the reps, and all NAMs have personal computers. The system provides immediate access to all information in the company concerning a potential account's current equipment and possible needs, competitor characteristics and prices, technical data about the company's products, and other information necessary to prepare and obtain approval for written proposals.

Compensation and incentives

To ensure that reps at different levels gear their activities to the specific needs of their customers, Xerox tailors different compensation and incentive systems for each of its sales groups. Because the NAMs must concentrate on maintaining long-term relationships with their accounts and coordinating the sale of customized systems that may require months or years of planning, their compensation consists of 80 percent salary and only 20 percent commissions and other incentives. To motivate the firm's account and marketing reps calling on smaller customers that buy standardized equipment and require little engineering service, Xerox pays these reps commissions and other incentives that can amount to as much as 40 percent of their total compensation.

The incentive component of Xerox's compensation system is also flexible and can be redesigned to enable the company to direct special selling efforts toward particular products or activities as the market situation changes. Recently, for instance, the NAMs' incentives were changed to shift their focus away from revenues brought in and toward increasing customer satisfaction. Part of their incentive payment was tied to a customer satisfaction measurement system built on periodic customer surveys.

The Current Situation

As Exhibit 1.2 indicates, Xerox has experienced steady revenue growth since reorienting its competitive and marketing strategies and sales programs. While earnings dipped in 1990, the problem rested entirely with the firm's insurance and other financial services businesses. The document processing unit produced profits of $599 million in 1990, up 23 percent from the year before, and a 14.6 percent return on assets. In view of these results, Xerox's managers feel confident they are moving in the right direction.

WHAT IS INVOLVED IN SALES MANAGEMENT?

The Xerox example illustrates several recurring themes in this book. First, sales management programs do not exist in a vacuum. They must respond to a firm's environmental circumstances, and they must be consistent with the business's competitive and marketing strategies. At the same time, good sales management policies and practices are essential to successfully implement a firm's competitive and marketing strategies. No matter how wise Xerox's managers were in deciding to reposition the firm as a producer of high-quality, integrated document processing systems, their new competitive strategy would not have been as effective without the adoption of appropriate policies concerning the organization, training, motivation, compensation, and control of the sales force.

Xerox's actions in recent years provide some useful clues about what is involved in managing an effective sales force. But the full range and complexity of the activities salespeople engage in, and of the decisions involved in managing those activities, cannot be captured in only a few pages. The following is a more detailed look at what sales management—and the rest of this book—is all about.

The Selling Process

It is difficult to manage something without a solid understanding of what it is you're trying to manage. Unfortunately, many people have a number of misconceptions about the selling process, the activities carried out by salespeople, and the personal characteristics necessary for a successful sales career. To complicate matters even more, various selling jobs can involve very different tasks and require different skills and abilities from the people who do them. Xerox's national account reps, for instance, not only need superior system engineering and planning abilities, but they must also have the interpersonal skills necessary to build and maintain long-term relationships with their large customers. And they must be patient because it can take months or years for a customer to approve the purchase of an extensive new document processing system. The firm's marketing reps must have the high motivation levels and self-confidence necessary to make a large number of calls on a variety of small accounts day after day, even though most of those calls do not produce an immediate sale.

To reduce misconceptions about personal selling, and to establish a solid foundation of knowledge for our subsequent discussion of sales force management, Chapter 2 examines the selling process in more detail. It begins with an examination of how organizational buyers make purchase decisions and how salespeople can facilitate and influence those decisions. It then explores the variety of activities, tasks, and decisions involved in different types of selling jobs and situations. Finally, it discusses some unique features of a career in personal selling and sales management and the kinds of career paths typically followed by successful salespeople.

Sales Management Processes

The effective management of a company's sales force involves three interrelated sets of decisions or processes.

1. *The formulation of a strategic sales program.* The strategic sales program should consider the environmental factors faced by the firm. It should organize and plan the company's overall personal selling efforts and integrate these with the other elements of the firm's marketing strategy.

E X H I B I T 1 ● 3 *An Overview of Sales Management*

| The Environment | Marketing Strategy | Sales Management Activities | Determinants of the Salesperson's Performance | Outcomes | Control |

The external environment

Potential customers
Competition
Legal restrictions
Technology
Natural resources
Social

The organizational environment

Objectives
Human resources
Financial resources
Production capabilities
R & D capabilities

Target markets
Products
Pricing policies
Distribution channels
Promotion policies
Personal selling
Advertising
Sales promotion

Account management policies

Sales force organization

Sales planning

Demand forecasts
Quotas and budgets

Deployment
Territory design
Routing

Supervision

Selection of sales personnel

Sales training

Motivating the sales force

Compensation systems
Incentive programs

Salesperson's view of job requirements, role perceptions

Accuracy
Ambiguity
Conflict

Aptitude

Skill levels

Motivation level

Performance

Sales volume
Percent of quota
Selling expenses
Profitability
Customer service
Reports

Evaluation and control of sales force performance

Sales analysis
Cost analysis
Personal evaluations

Feedback

11

2. *The implementation of the sales program.* The implementation phase involves selecting appropriate sales personnel and designing and implementing policies and procedures that will direct their efforts toward the desired objectives.

3. *The evaluation and control of sales force performance.* The evaluation phase involves developing methods for monitoring and evaluating sales force performance. This facilitates adjusting the sales program or the way it is implemented when performance is unsatisfactory.

The specific activities involved in these three processes, along with the variables that influence those activities, are summarized in the model of sales management in Exhibit 1.3. While this book explores the components of this model in detail, here we will briefly discuss the variables and sales management activities involved in each of the three processes.

Formulating a Strategic Sales Program

The activities and influences involved in formulating a company's strategic sales program are shown in Exhibit 1.4. The design of a sales program requires five major sets of decisions.

1. How can the personal selling effort best be adapted to the company's environment and integrated with the other elements of the firm's marketing strategy? In sum, what should be the firm's personal selling strategy?

2. How can various types of potential customers best be approached, persuaded, and serviced? In other words, what account management policies should be adopted?

3. How should the sales force be organized to call on and manage various types of customers as efficiently and effectively as possible?

4. What level of performance can each member of the sales force be expected to attain during the next planning period? This involves forecasting demand and setting quotas and budgets.

5. In view of the firm's account management policies and demand forecasts, how should the sales force be deployed? How should sales territories be defined? What is the best way for each salesperson's time to be allocated within a territory?

The policies and plans involved in such a program must take into account the influences and constraints imposed by the external environment. The demands of potential customers and the actions of competitors are two obvious environmental factors. For example, the efficiency and technical advances made by Xerox's foreign competitors and their customers' demands for custom-designed, integrated office automation systems forced the company not only to rethink its competitive and marketing strategies but also to reorganize its sales force.

E X H I B I T   **1 ● 4**   *Activities and Influences Involved in Formulating a Strategic Sales Program*

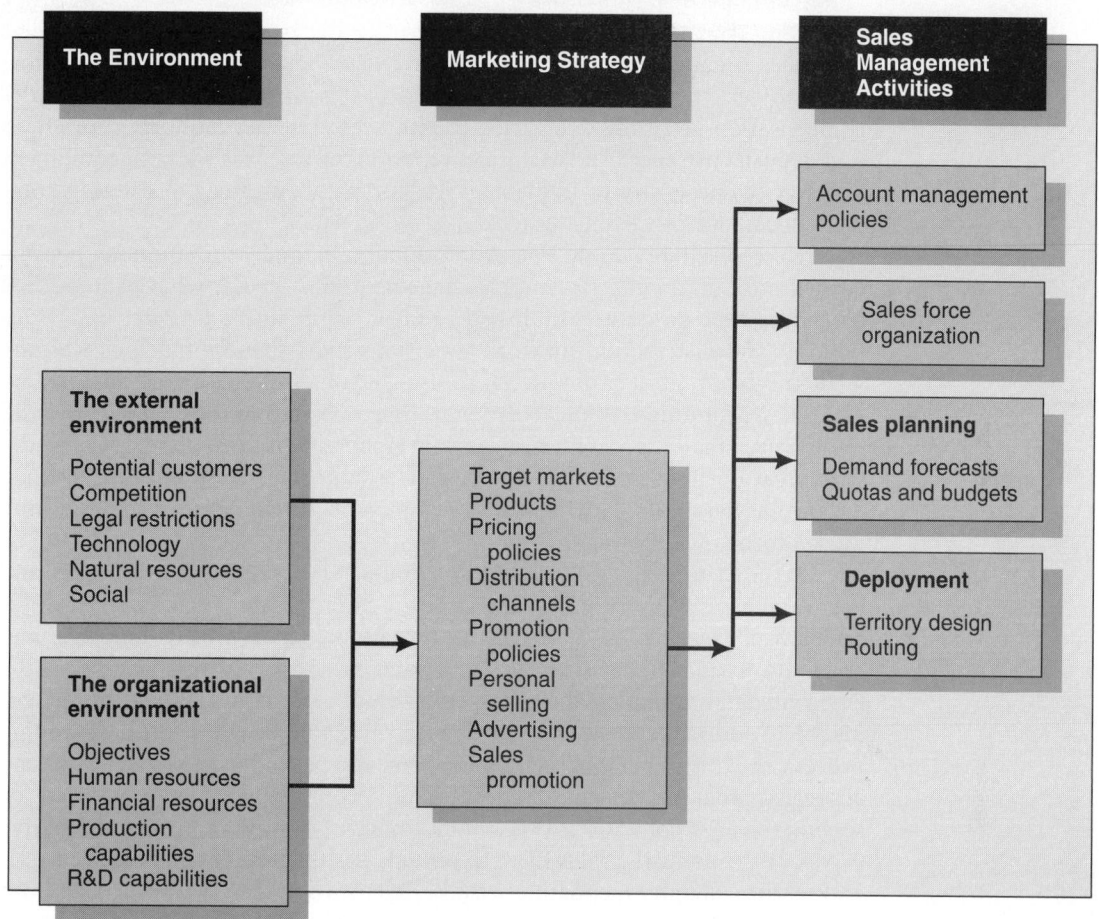

In addition to customers and competitors, other environmental factors such as energy shortages, technical advances, government regulations, and social concerns can affect a company's sales policies and plans. A few years ago, for instance, a large paper products manufacturer told its salespeople not to exceed their quotas because a shortage of pulpwood supplies prevented the company from filling more orders.

A firm's internal environment also helps determine sales programs. Human and financial resources, the firm's production capacity, and its expertise in research and development can either help or hinder the company's ability to pursue particular types of customers or to expand its market share. In Xerox's case, an extensive and competent sales training staff and development of an excellent sales support information system helped make it easier to implement the change to a single, integrated, full-line sales force.

A sales program must be carefully integrated with the rest of the firm's marketing strategy. Again, Xerox's experience illustrates this integration. The new sales organization focuses different types and amounts of selling effort on customers in those segments identified in the firm's marketing plan. Sales compensation programs are varied to reinforce activities most appropriate to each type of customer. And each sales rep can now offer the range of equipment and services necessary to implement the company's strategy of offering complete document processing systems.

Personal selling is only one promotional tool, and promotion is only one element of a marketing strategy. Management must decide what promotional objectives need to be accomplished in view of the firm's product line, price policies, and distribution network. Decisions must then be made concerning what combination of promotional tools—personal selling, media advertising, and sales promotion—can accomplish those objectives most efficiently and effectively. Finally, account management policies and sales plans must be devised that spell out the firm's personal selling objectives, and appropriate organizational and deployment policies must be developed for accomplishing those objectives.

Part 1 of this book (Chapters 3 through 8) examines the decisions and activities involved in formulating a strategic sales program. Chapter 3 explores how a firm's external and internal organizational environments influence and constrain its marketing strategies and sales programs. It also discusses how environmental variables, including ethical and legal issues, affect the performance of individual salespeople. Chapter 4 examines the strategic planning process, the role of personal selling in different types of business and marketing strategies, and the design of appropriate account management policies for serving the needs of various types of customers. Chapter 5 looks at alternative ways of organizing the sales force to provide desired levels of customer contact and service. Chapter 6 examines two key elements in the development of both marketing and sales plans: the conduct of a marketing opportunity analysis and methods for forecasting demand. Finally, Chapters 7 and 8 examine deployment decisions, including designing sales territories, determining how many salespeople are needed to provide adequate market coverage, allocating a salesperson's effort within his or her territory, and establishing sales quotas.

IMPLEMENTING THE SALES PROGRAM

As with any kind of management, implementing a sales program involves motivating and directing the behavior of other people—the members of the sales force. To be effective, the sales manager must understand why the people in his or her sales force behave the way they do. Then policies and procedures can be designed to direct that behavior toward the desired objectives.

E X H I B I T **1 • 5** *Activities Involved in Implementing a Sales Program*

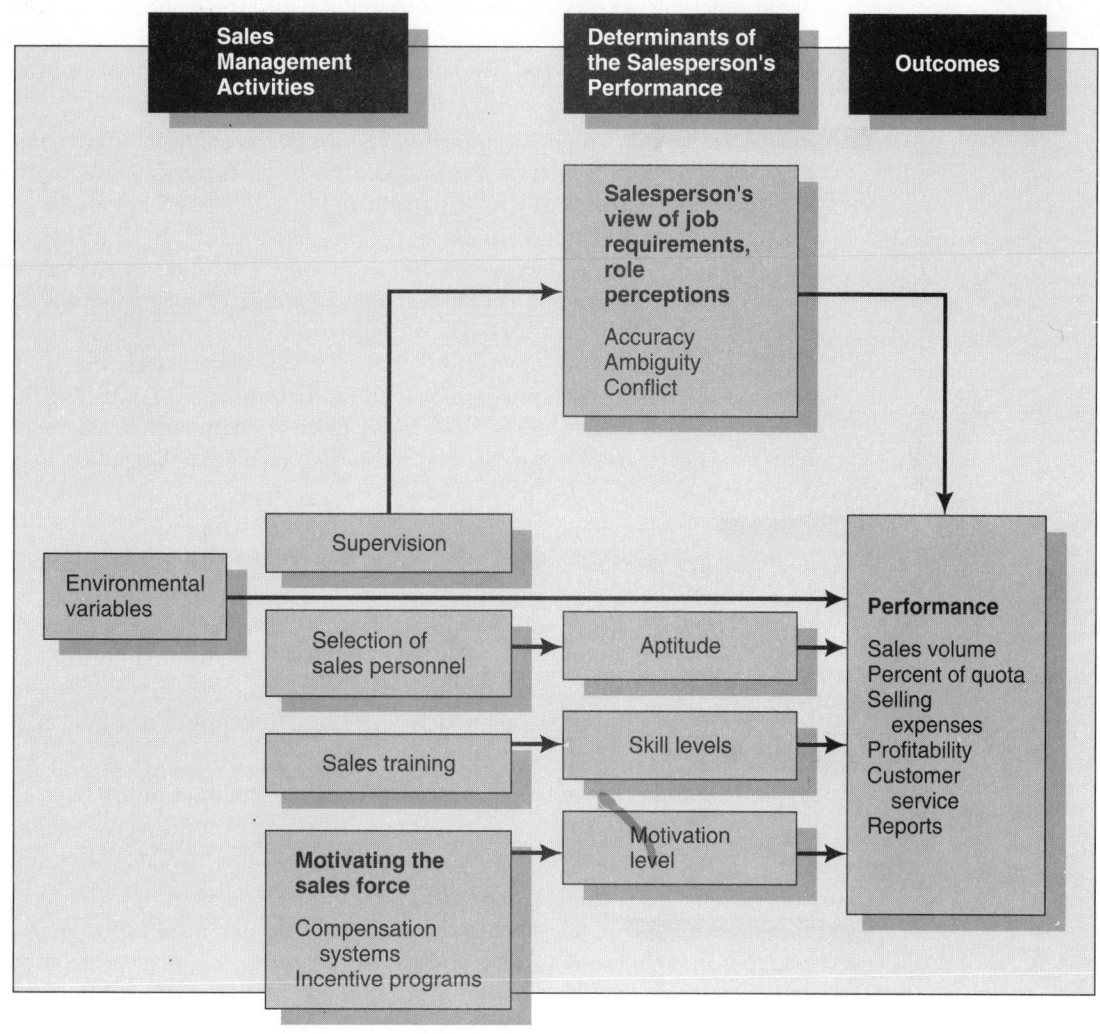

The model of the activities involved in implementing a sales program, shown in Exhibit 1.5, suggests that five factors influence a sales rep's job behavior and performance.

1. *Environmental variables.* Regardless of how highly motivated or competent salespeople are, their ability to achieve a particular level of job performance is influenced—and sometimes constrained—by environmental

factors. The ability to reach a given sales volume, for instance, can be affected by such things as the market demand for the product being sold, the number and aggressiveness of competitors, and the health of the economy. Similarly, other elements of a firm's marketing mix, such as the quality of its products and the effectiveness of its advertising, can affect a salesperson's ability to reach a high level of sales performance.

2. *Role perceptions.* To perform adequately, a salesperson must understand what the job entails and how it is supposed to be performed. The activities and behaviors associated with a particular job are defined largely by the expectations and demands of other people, both inside and outside the organization. Thus, a salesperson's job (or *role*) is defined by the expectations and desires of the customers, sales manager, other company executives, and family members. The salesperson's ability to do the job well is partly determined by how clearly the sales rep understands those role expectations. Also, the salesperson may sometimes face conflicting demands, as when a customer wants a lower price but company management refuses to negotiate. The salesperson's ability to resolve such conflicts helps determine success or failure on the job.

3. *Aptitude.* A salesperson's ability to perform the activities of the job is also influenced by the individual's personal characteristics, such as personality traits, intelligence, and analytical ability. No matter how hard they try, some people are never successful at selling because they do not have the aptitude for the job. Of course, different kinds of sales jobs involve different tasks and activities, so a person with certain characteristics may be unsuited for one selling job but tremendously successful at another one.

4. *Skill levels.* Even when salespeople have the aptitude to do their jobs and an understanding of what they are expected to do, they must have the skills necessary to carry out the required tasks. For instance, a salesperson must have a thorough knowledge of the product and how it works, how to make an effective sales presentation, and other sales skills.

5. *Motivation level.* A salesperson cannot achieve a high level of job performance unless motivated to expend the necessary effort. A person's motivation is determined by the kind of rewards expected for achieving a given level of performance—such as more pay or a promotion—and by the perceived attractiveness of those anticipated rewards.

A sales manager can use several policies and procedures to influence the aptitude, skill levels, role perceptions, and motivation of the sales force. Implementing a sales program involves designing those policies and procedures so that the job behavior and performance of each salesperson are shaped and directed toward the specified objectives and performance levels.

The sales manager must decide what kinds of aptitude are required for the firm's salespeople to do the kind of selling involved and to reach the program's objectives. *Recruiting techniques and selection criteria* can then be developed to ensure salespeople with the required abilities are hired.

A person's selling skills improve with practice and experience. In most cases, though, it is inefficient to let the salesperson simply gain skills through on-the-job experience. Good customers might be lost as the result of mistakes by unskilled sales personnel. Consequently, most firms have a formal training program to give new recruits some of the necessary knowledge and skills before they are expected to pull their own weight in the field. The sales manager must determine what kinds of selling skills are required by the salespeople. The manager can then design training programs that develop those skills as effectively as possible.

Even after completing a training program, salespeople may run into unusual situations where they face conflicting demands or are uncertain about what to do. Supervisory policies and procedures are needed so salespeople can obtain advice and assistance from management with no undue restriction on their freedom to develop innovative approaches to customers' problems.

Finally, a salesperson's motivation to expend effort on the job is largely a function of the amount and desirability of the rewards expected for a given job performance. The sales manager should determine what rewards are most attractive to the sales force and design compensation and incentive programs that will generate a high level of motivation. Compensation programs involve monetary rewards. Incentive programs can also include a variety of nonfinancial rewards, such as recognition programs, promotions to better territories or to management positions, or opportunities for personal development.

Part 2 of this book explores the policies and procedures involved in implementing a firm's sales program. Chapter 9 discusses the determinants of a salesperson's performance and job behavior in more detail. Chapter 10 describes the kinds of role expectations and demands salespeople receive from their customers, managers, and families. It also discusses how supervisory policies can be designed to help them deal with ambiguous and conflicting demands. Chapters 11 and 12 examine the personal characteristics related to selling aptitude and how recruiting and selection procedures can be designed to build an effective sales force. The objectives of sales training and a variety of training techniques are examined in Chapter 13. Chapters 14 and 15 discuss rewards that motivate people to expend efforts on various aspects of their jobs and how those rewards can be incorporated into effective sales compensation and incentive programs.

EVALUATION AND CONTROL OF THE SALES PROGRAM

For a salesperson to be appropriately rewarded for job performance, that performance must first be measured and evaluated. Xerox's compensation plan, for example, provides salespeople with salary and incentives based on the achievement of specific goals, for example, customer satisfaction. At a minimum, the firm must monitor and record customer satisfaction to know how much compensation the person deserves.

E x h i b i t 1 • 6 *Evaluation and Control of Sales Force Performance*

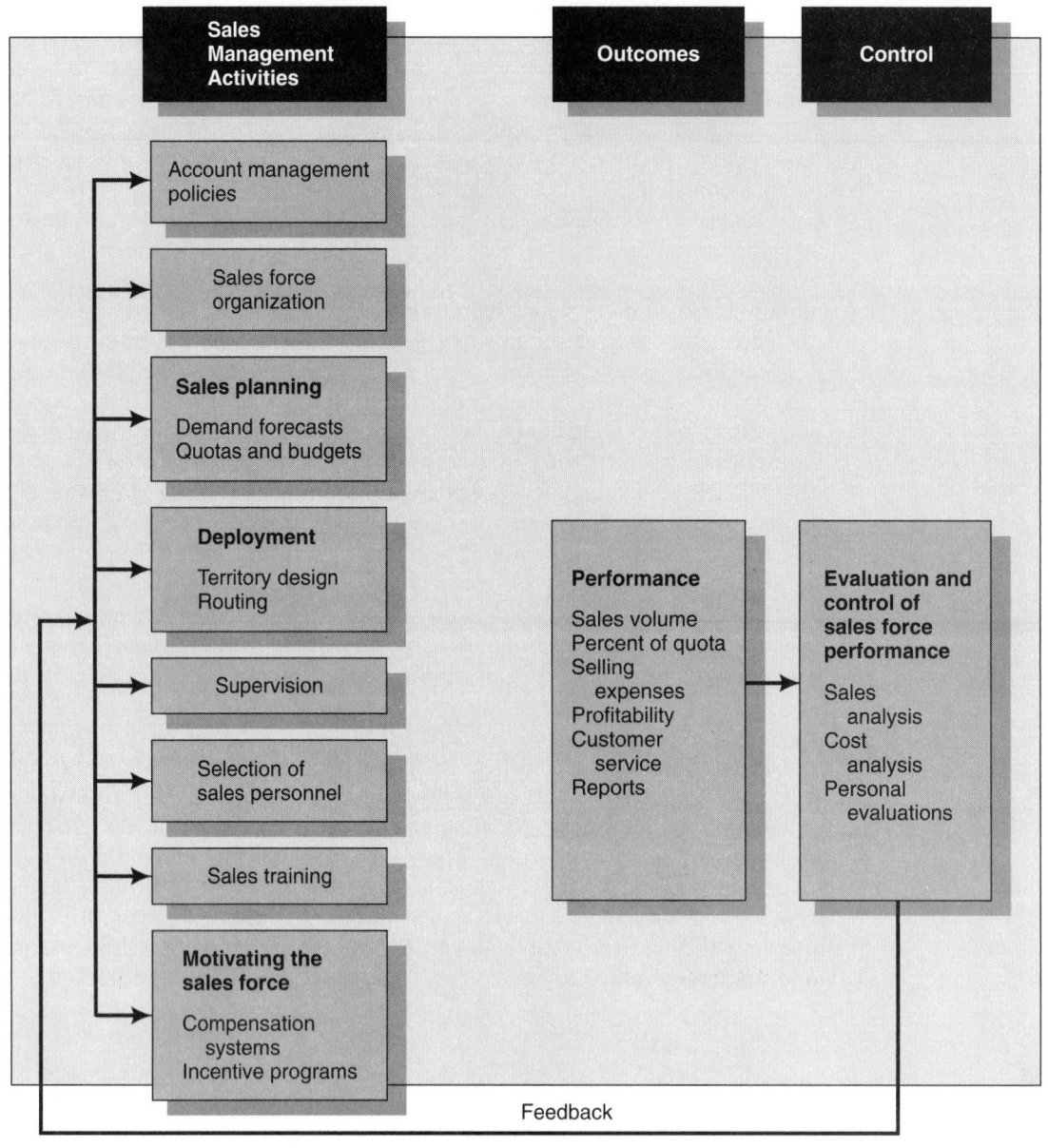

From a sales manager's view, it is equally important to monitor the aggregate performance of the sales force to evaluate and control the firm's strategic sales program and the way it is implemented. Although this is particularly true when new programs or policies are instituted, even a successful program should be carefully monitored. Changes in economic conditions, customer needs, competitors' actions, or other parts of the firm's marketing mix can cause successful programs and policies to suddenly become inappropriate and ineffective. Thus, overall performance should be measured frequently and compared with the planned performance levels specified in the sales program so that any deviations can be quickly identified. Then timely changes in the strategic program or in specific implementation policies and procedures can be made.

As the model of sales evaluation and control activities outlined in Exhibit 1.6 shows, several performance dimensions can be measured and evaluated. Data can be collected not only on sales volume and attainment of quotas but also on selling expenses, the profitability of sales, the quality of services provided to customers, and the timeliness and completeness of call reports and other kinds of information requested from the firm's sales personnel.

A company might utilize three major approaches in evaluating and controlling the sales force to monitor sales program performance:

1. *Sales analysis.* Sales volume can be monitored for each salesperson. In addition, sales figures are often broken down by geographic district, by each product in the line, and by different types of customers. Sales results can then be compared with the quotas and forecasts specified in the firm's sales plans.

2. *Cost analysis.* The costs of various selling functions can be monitored. These might also be examined across individual salespeople, districts, products, and customer types. When combined with the data from sales analysis, this procedure allows a firm to judge the profitability of various products and customer types. However, cost analysis presents some difficult technical questions concerning how certain costs—such as administrative salaries and overhead—should be allocated among salespeople or products.

3. *Behavioral analysis.* A salesperson's ability to achieve a certain sales volume is sometimes constrained by factors beyond the rep's control, such as competition or economic conditions. Therefore, some managers believe it is necessary to evaluate the actual behavior of salespeople as well as their ultimate performance in terms of sales volume. A number of techniques attempt to measure and evaluate various aspects of a salesperson's job behavior, including self-rating scales, supervisor ratings, field observations, and—as in Xerox's case—surveys of customer satisfaction.

Although sales analysis is the most common method of control, a growing number of firms use a combination of all three methods to identify shortcomings in the design or implementation of their sales programs and to help decide on appropriate changes.

Part 3 of this book discusses control procedures. Chapter 16 examines the techniques of sales analysis, and Chapter 17 focuses on cost analysis. Finally, Chapter 18 discusses behavioral analysis and explores corrective measures a sales manager can take when performance falls short of planned levels.

S UMMARY

Sales management programs and activities do not exist in a vacuum. Thus, as was illustrated by the Xerox example, effective sales management programs must be designed to respond to a firm's environmental circumstances, and they must be consistent with the objectives and content of the business's competitive and marketing strategies. Sales management also plays a crucial role in implementing those higher level strategies. Good sales management policies and practices are essential ingredients for ensuring the success of a firm's competitive and marketing strategies.

Effective management requires a solid understanding of the activities one is trying to manage. Unfortunately, many people have misconceptions about the selling process, the activities carried out by salespeople, and the personal characteristics necessary for a successful career in professional sales. In part, these misconceptions arise because different types of selling jobs involve different kinds of tasks and require different skills and abilities from the people who do them. Consequently, Chapter 2 examines the selling process and the activities involved in different types of selling jobs in more detail to establish a solid foundation of knowledge for our subsequent discussion of sales management policies and procedures.

Sales management involves three interrelated processes: (1) the formulation of a strategic sales program, (2) the implementation of the sales program, and (3) the evaluation and control of sales force performance. It is the purpose of this book to describe the variables and sales management activities involved in each of these processes. Each major section of the book elaborates one process: Part 1, the formulation of the sales program; Part 2, its implementation; and Part 3, evaluation and control.

Discussion Questions

1. Marketing is being introduced into organizations that at one time paid little attention to the subject. Most medical organizations have become marketing oriented. Most public accounting firms now advertise, and some have hired marketing directors. What selling activities do these organizations have to consider? What kinds of selling activities might such organizations want to avoid? Why?

2. Recently, more women have entered the field of industrial selling. What unique problems might an industrial saleswoman face as opposed to a woman accountant? What problems might a woman accountant face that the industrial saleswoman would not encounter?

3. In the 1970s, worldwide shortages of gasoline prompted most companies to change their methods of marketing. What changes occurred in the field of selling?

4. Determining which salesperson will make the best manager is a problem confronted by all sales organizations. When a sales management position opens, conventional wisdom suggests the logical candidate to fill it is the company's best salesperson. That seems to be the proper reward for a job well done. Comment.

5. How does the job of selling differ for the following situations? What are the most important activities for each job?

   a. A Procter & Gamble sales representative selling soap and laundry products to grocery stores.
   b. An Eastman Kodak sales rep selling cameras to retail camera stores.
   c. A Scott Paper Company sales rep selling paper towels to manufacturers.
   d. A Phillips Petroleum sales rep selling lubricating greases to manufacturers.
   e. An Abbott Laboratories pharmaceutical representative calling on the medical profession.
   f. An Ohio Medical Products sales rep selling respiratory equipment to hospitals.

6. What type of sales training would be needed for the selling situations described in question 5?

7. Is the sales management task different for those selling situations listed in question 5?

8. Two concepts that will capture the attention of senior management in the 1990s are quality and customer satisfaction. The quality movement gained prominence about 10 years ago and is associated with such names as Deming and Juran. The customer satisfaction movement gained attention in 1982 with the publication of the Peters and Waterman book, *In Search of Excellence*. The recently enacted Malcolm Baldrige National Quality Improvement Act promotes quality awareness and quality achievement of U.S. companies. The Baldrige Award focuses senior management's attention on quality and customer satisfaction.

   These concepts are just beginning to have an impact on sales force management. Some companies, such as Xerox, are exploring how sales managers can reward the sales force for achieving customer satisfaction. Should customer satisfaction be evaluated by sales managers? How would they measure this construct? How can sales managers reward salespeople who achieve high levels of customer satisfaction?

9. The Barrister Corporation decided an office located in London would greatly improve service to Barrister's U. K. market. What precautions should be considered before opening the office and assigning U.S. personnel to London?

10. As Xerox added more related products, individual sales increased as sales reps were able to better satisfy their customer's needs. Is there a danger asking sales reps to carry too many related products? Is there a danger asking sales reps to carry unrelated products? What evidence would you examine to answer these questions?

Endnotes

[1]This example is based on material found in Thayer C. Taylor, "Xerox's Makeover," *Sales & Marketing Management* (June 1987), p. 68; Thayer C. Taylor, "Xerox: Who Says You Can't Be Big and Fast?" *Sales & Marketing Management* (November 1987), pp. 62–65; Jon Berry, "Vickers 'Puts It Together' for Xerox with a Mystical Flair," *Adweek's Marketing Week,* October, 15, 1990, p. 5; Brian Dumaine, "The Bureaucracy Busters," *Fortune,* June 17, 1991, pp. 36–50; and *The Xerox Corporation 1990 Annual Report* (Stamford, Conn.: The Xerox Corporation, 1991).

The Selling Process: Sales Activities and Careers

PILOT AIR FREIGHT LANDS A MAJOR NEW ACCOUNT[1]

Late-night travelers in the Philadelphia airport were startled one recent evening when a well-dressed man at one of the pay phones on the concourse suddenly began shouting and jumping up and down. Another stressed-out executive gone round the bend? No, just Frank Perry celebrating a hard-won victory for Pilot Air Freight.

Perry, who heads a fledgling national accounts program at the small (about $85 million in revenue) freight forwarder, had just called his closest contact on the traffic council of GTE, the giant electronics manufacturer. The council had just spent three days hearing proposals from more than a dozen freight forwarders, and Perry's contact had good news: After nearly three years and more than 100 sales calls on GTE plants and offices around the country, Pilot had won a three-year contract from the huge corporation.

A few hours earlier, Perry, accompanied by Pilot President John Edwards and Dick Morris, vice president of sales and marketing, had presented their case to the GTE group in Kansas City. "You get four minutes, so we could only show six slides," recalls Morris. "It was the shortest time I've ever talked in my life." After answering some questions and making minor adjustments to their proposal, the three headed home with their fingers crossed.

Four minutes doesn't sound like much time, but—as is the case in the sale of many big-ticket products and service systems—most of the real work was done before the final presentation. The process started when Frank Perry determined that GTE had a need Pilot could fill. When he first targeted the GTE account, traffic people at the giant firm weren't in the mood to talk with a potential new supplier. They had just signed three-year contracts with a number of other freight forwarders, and they thought they had all the bases covered. To complicate matters further, major decisions on buying freight services at GTE are made by a traffic council involving 25 decision makers from the company's installations around the country. Nevertheless, Perry thought Pilot had something unique to offer. To differentiate itself from its many competitors, Pilot offers very flexible service. It will pick up and deliver freight 24 hours a day, seven days a week. And Perry believed such flexible service would prove valuable to GTE, whose plants worked two and sometimes three shifts.

It took more than a year and dozens of sales calls before anyone at GTE took much notice of Pilot's unique offering. Expending so much effort on one account is a calculated risk, especially for a small company with limited marketing resources. "(But) we put a lot of effort into it," says Morris, "because Frank Perry just wasn't going to let go of it." Finally, traffic managers at two GTE plants agreed to give Pilot a tryout, and Perry's selling effort gained momentum. Once Pilot established a reliable track record at the first two plants, Pilot's salespeople around the country used it to open other GTE doors. By the decisive meeting in Kansas City, Pilot's case had been presented to all the buying influences within GTE, and a four-minute presentation was sufficient to land a major companywide contract.

AN OVERVIEW OF SELLING AND BUYING PROCESSES

Frank Perry's experience in selling freight services to GTE illustrates some important points about the selling process, particularly the sale of complex products or services to organizational customers. First, it can take a long time and a lot of effort before the final sale is made. Although there is constant pressure on both customers and suppliers to shorten the selling cycle, companies that sell capital equipment, high-tech gear, or other complicated or high-priced goods and services often must work months or years to win an order. Consequently, selling such products and services involves many activities in addition to simply making a sales presentation and writing a contract.

The salesperson must first gather information about the prospective customer's operations to determine whether there is a need for the products or services the rep has to offer, and the salesperson must learn about the concerns of various personnel within the customer organization who might influence the final purchase. Then, many low-key sales calls may be necessary to educate the various purchase influencers about the seller's offerings and to establish credibility. Even after a sale is made, the rep may have a lot of work to do supervising the installation of the product, training the customer's personnel to use it, and providing other post-sale services to ensure the customer will be satisfied and to increase the chances for future sales. A later section of this chapter provides a more detailed examination of the variety of activities involved in the selling process and the various roles those activities can play in establishing and maintaining successful relationships with customers.

Not every sale requires the effort and patience Frank Perry expended in his pursuit of GTE. Different sales jobs can involve different kinds and numbers of activities, depending on the complexity of the product or service being sold, the nature of the firm's relationship with a particular customer, the role of personal selling within the firm's overall marketing strategy, and other factors. We will also examine how the importance of different selling activities varies across different types of sales jobs and situations.

Frank Perry's boisterous dance in the Philadelphia airport suggests that—from his perspective, at least—winning the GTE contract made his great expenditure of time and effort worthwhile. But the thrill of victory is not the only kind of satisfaction good salespeople get from their jobs. A sales career offers a number of attractive rewards. Managers should understand what attracts good salespeople to their jobs, what rewards motivate them, and what career paths they aspire to follow so managers can develop effective selection criteria, incentive programs, and promotion policies. Consequently, the last section of this chapter explores attributes associated with sales jobs, and some of the rewards and career opportunities available to successful salespeople.

To truly understand the selling process, why successful salespeople do what they do, and how to most effectively manage their efforts, however, it is useful to first understand how customers make purchase decisions. After all, marketing strategies, sales programs, and the efforts of individual sales reps should all be aimed at influencing and facilitating those decisions. Therefore, the next section examines how the buying process works and what members of a customer organization are likely to influence that process at various stages.

THE ORGANIZATIONAL BUYING PROCESS

Many topics in this book are appropriate to all kinds of selling, but the primary emphasis is on commercial or industrial selling. Therefore, we focus on the buying process engaged in by organizations—both industrial users and intermediaries.[2]

One way to appreciate the complexity of many organizational purchasing decisions is to examine the variety of activities and the number of people involved. In Exhibit 2.1, a purchasing agent responsible for buying integrated circuits for a computer manufacturer describes the process.

Who Makes Organizational Buying Decisions?

As the buying process described in Exhibit 2.1 illustrates, organizational purchases often involve people from different departments within the firm. These participants in the buying process can be grouped into six categories: initiators, users, influencers, gatekeepers, buyers, and deciders.[3]

Initiators

Initiators are the people who perceive a problem or opportunity that may require the purchase of a new product or service and thereby start the buying process. The initiator can be almost anyone at any level in the firm. Complaints from the secretarial pool about outmoded and inefficient equipment, for instance, might trigger the purchase of new word processors. Or the decision to contract for the construction of a new plant might be initiated by top management's strategic planning deliberations.

Users

The people in the organization who must use or work with the product or service often influence the purchase decision. For example, drill-press operators might request that the purchasing agent buy drills from a particular supplier because they stay sharp longer and reduce downtime in the plant.

Influencers

Influencers provide information for evaluating alternative products and suppliers, and they often play a major role in determining the specifications and criteria to use in making the purchase decision. They are usually technical experts from various departments. In the integrated circuits example in Exhibit 2.1, the buyer relied on people in the engineering and manufacturing departments to help determine the specifications of the circuits to be purchased, and the materials engineering department helped identify and evaluate potential suppliers.

E XHIBIT 2 • 1 *A Purchasing Agent Describes the Activities and People Involved in Buying Integrated Circuits for a Computer Manufacturer*

My job starts when I get a requisition from Manufacturing or Engineering. I look at the specifications for the item and the quantity requested. I also look at the item's cost, the frequency with which the same item has been purchased in the past, the number in inventory, and its effect on inventory costs. We also try to forecast whether larger quantities of the same item will be needed in the future. Finally, if several requisitions are made for similar but slightly different items, I contact Engineering or Production Control to determine whether minor modifications can be made. All of these things are done so we can place the largest possible order to increase leverage with the supplier and gain the lowest possible price.

The most important factors to be considered in buying integrated circuits are quality, price, and delivery time. There are at least six different quality levels. My biggest problem is finding the right quality level to fit the specifications at the lowest price. I also have to consult with Manufacturing to work out delivery requirements so we can gain the lead times necessary to build our computers on schedule.

We usually consider at least two alternative suppliers. I check with Materials Engineering to put together a list of potential suppliers, and we review each of them on the basis of their past performance with regard to quality and meeting delivery schedules. Finally, we make a decision and place the order.

Source: From an interview conducted as part of the research for Joanne M. Klebba, *The Structure of Purchasing Function as Determined by Environmental Uncertainty,* unpublished Ph.D. dissertation, Graduate School of Business Administration. University of Minnesota, 1978.

Gatekeepers

Gatekeepers control the flow of information to other people involved in the purchasing process. They include the organization's purchasing agent and suppliers' salespeople. Gatekeepers influence a purchase by controlling the kind and amount of information that reaches the other decision makers.

Buyers

The buyer is usually referred to as a purchasing agent or purchasing manager. In most organizations, buyers have the authority to contact suppliers and negotiate purchases. In some cases, they are given wide discretion. In other instances, they are constrained by technical specifications and other contract requirements determined by technical experts and top administrators.

Deciders

The decider is the person with the final authority to make a purchase decision. Sometimes buyers have this authority, but often it is retained by higher executives in the organization. When a company buys a large computer installation, for instance, the final decision is likely to be made by the chief executive or a top management committee.

The Organizational Buying Center

All the people who participate in buying a particular product or service can be referred to as a buying center. Estimates of the number of people in the buying center for a typical purchase range from 3 to 12. Different members of the buying center may participate—and exert different amounts of influence—at different stages in the decision process.[4] For example, people from engineering and R&D often exert the greatest influence on the development of specifications and criteria that a new product must meet, while the purchasing manager often has more influence when it comes time to choose among alternative suppliers. The makeup of the buying center also varies with the amount of past experience the firm has in buying a particular product. The buying center tends to be smaller—and the relative influence of the purchasing manager greater—when reordering products the firm has purchased in the past than when buying an entirely new product.

These variations in the relative influence of different members of the buying center across types of purchase decisions and stages in the buying process are illustrated in Exhibit 2.2. The exhibit summarizes the results of a survey of 231 manufacturing firms where managers were asked to indicate the relative influence of various departments at different stages in the purchase of component parts. The influence of each department not only varied across stages in the buying process but also depended on whether the purchase was a "new buy" or a reorder.

Sales planning implications

Since different employees of a customer's organization may be active at different stages of the purchase process, an important part of sales planning involves trying to determine who the salesperson should contact, when each contact should be made, and what kinds of information and appeals each participant is likely to find most useful and persuasive. Unfortunately, the answers to such questions are likely to be different for each potential customer, making information gained from past experience with an organization—and from customer surveys or other market research—useful for planning individual sales calls.

In many cases, however, the roles played by various members of the buying center are sufficiently consistent across similar types of firms that a company can establish policies to guide its salespeople. For example, a study of 140 commercial construction companies found that in smaller firms (defined as those with annual sales volumes under $25 million), presidents and vice presidents exert significantly more influence at all stages in the decision process than purchasing agents or construction engineers, while the situation is reversed in large firms, reflecting increased job specialization and decentralization of purchasing in bigger companies.[5] A firm selling to this industry might adopt a policy of encouraging its salespeople to seek appointments with the top executives when calling on smaller customers, but to initiate contacts through the purchasing department in larger organizations.

EXHIBIT 2 • 2   *The Relative Influence of Representatives from Various Functional Departments at Different Stages in Two Types of Organizational Purchase Decisions*

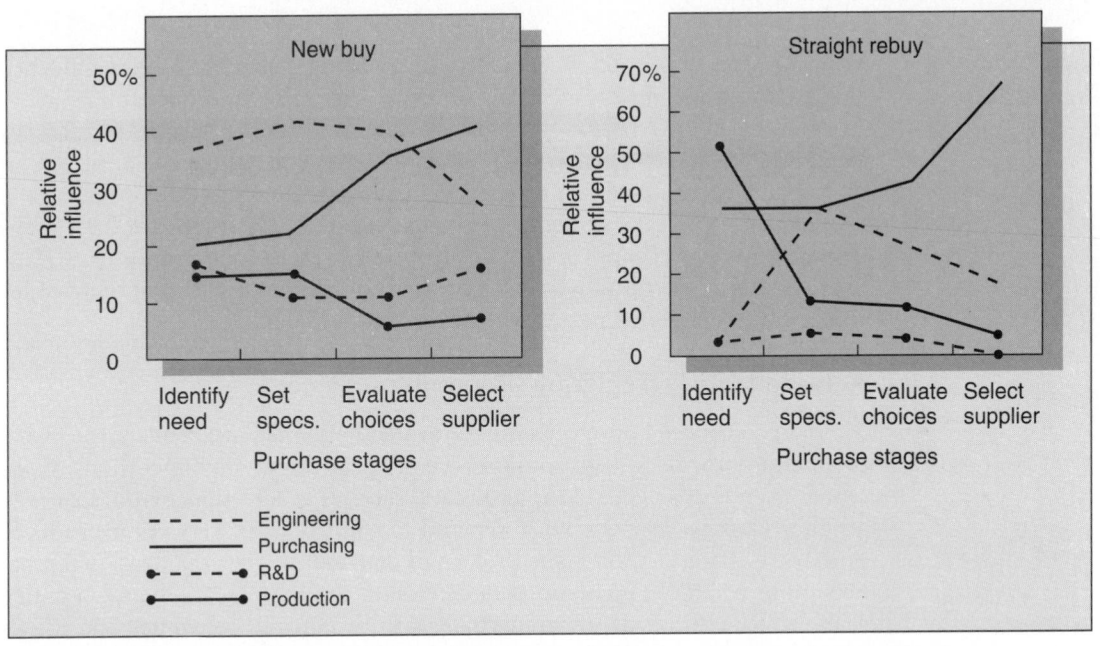

Source: Based on E. Naumann, D. J. Lincoln, and R. D. McWilliams, "The Purchase of Components: Functional Areas of Influence," *Industrial Marketing Management*, May 1984, pp. 113–22. Reprinted by permission of the publisher. Copyright 1984 by Elsevier Science Publishing Co., Inc.

Similarly, customers' buying centers are likely to involve a wider variety of participants when they are considering the purchase of a technically complex, expensive product—such as a computer system—than when the purchase involves a simpler or less costly product. Consequently, firms that sell technically complex capital equipment sometimes organize their salespeople into "sales teams," or utilize "multilevel" selling, with different salespeople calling on different members of the customer's buying center to reach as many decision participants as possible and to give each participant the kinds of information that person will find most relevant. These team approaches to selling are examined in more detail in Chapter 4.

When a firm develops policies or organization structures to guide its salespeople in dealing with customers' buying centers, however, managers must periodically review their assumptions about the roles and influence of the participants. For instance, for years, Eastman Kodak's strategy for selling X-ray film to hospitals was to sell through lab technicians. The company was slow to notice that, as more and more hospitals struggled to control costs, this decision was becoming increasingly centralized and professional administrators were exerting more influence. As its sales declined, Kodak finally grasped the change in buying practices and hurriedly changed its sales strategy.

Stages in the Organizational Buying Process

We have seen that different members of a buying center may exert influence at different stages in the decision process. This raises the question of what "stages" are involved. One widely recognized framework identifies seven steps that organizational buyers take in making purchase decisions: (1) anticipation or recognition of a problem or need, (2) determination and description of the characteristics and the quantity of the needed item, (3) search for and qualification of potential suppliers, (4) acquisition and analysis of proposals or bids, (5) evaluation of proposals and selection of suppliers, (6) selection of an order routine, and (7) performance evaluation and feedback.[6]

Anticipation or recognition of a problem or need

Most organizational purchases are motivated by the requirements of the firm's production processes, merchandise inventory, or day-to-day operations. Consequently, a firm's demand for goods and services is derived demand. Its needs are derived from its customers' demand for the goods or services it produces or markets. This characteristic of derived demand makes organizational markets quite volatile. Fluctuations in economic conditions can change a firm's sales, which can result in rapid changes in production schedules and in accumulations or depletions of inventories. As a result, the organization's requirements for goods and services can change dramatically in a short time.

Many different situations can lead someone to recognize a need for a particular product or service. In some cases, need recognition may be almost automatic, as when a computerized inventory control system reports that the stock of an item has fallen below the reorder level. In other cases, a need may arise when someone identifies a better way of operating. New needs might also evolve when the focus of the firm's operations changes, as when top management decides to make a new product line. In all these situations, needs may be recognized—and the purchasing process may be initiated—by a variety of people in the organization, including users, technical personnel, top management, or purchasing managers.

Determination and description of the characteristics and quantity of the needed item

The kinds and quantities of goods and services to be purchased are usually dictated by the demand for the firm's outputs and by the requirements of its production process and operations. Consequently, the criteria used in specifying the needed materials and equipment must usually be technically precise. Similarly, the quantities needed must be carefully considered to avoid excessive inventories or downtime caused by lack of needed materials. For these reasons, a variety of technical experts, as well as the people who will use the materials or equipment, are commonly involved in this stage of the decision process.

It is not enough for the using department and the technical experts to develop a detailed set of specifications for the needed item, however. They must also communicate a clear and precise description of what is needed, how much is needed, and when it is needed to other members of the buying center and to potential suppliers.

Since organizational buyers tend to use precise and explicit technical and economic criteria when deciding what to buy, organizational buying is often described as being more "rational" than consumer purchasing. Consumers, after all, sometimes buy things for social or emotional reasons. Although this generalization may be largely true, organizational buyers can also be influenced to some extent by social and emotional considerations.

Search for and qualification of potential suppliers

Once the organization has clearly defined the kind of item needed, a search for potential suppliers begins. If the item has been purchased before, this search may be limited to one or a few suppliers that have performed satisfactorily in the past. Organizational buyers, like consumers, often develop loyalties to their old and trusted suppliers. In such circumstances, it can be difficult for new suppliers to "get a piece of the action" unless they offer something unique. If the purchase involves a new item, or if the item is complex and expensive, organizational buyers often search for several potential suppliers to ensure they can select the one with the best product and most favorable terms.[7]

Acquisition of proposals or bids

After potential suppliers are identified, the buyer may request specific proposals or bids from each. When the item is a frequently purchased, standardized, or technically simple product (e.g., nails or typewriter ribbon) this process may not be very extensive. The buyer might simply consult several suppliers' catalogs or make a few phone calls. For more complicated and expensive goods and services, lengthy and detailed sales presentations and written proposals may be requested from each potential vendor.

Evaluation of offerings and selection of suppliers

During this stage of the purchasing process, various members of the buying center examine the acceptability of the various proposals and potential suppliers. Also, the buying organization and one or more potential vendors may negotiate about prices, credit terms, and delivery schedules. Ultimately, one or more suppliers are selected, and purchase agreements are signed.

The people in the buying organization's purchasing department are usually responsible for carrying out this phase of the process. Technical and administrative personnel may also play a role in supplier selection, however, especially when the purchase is complex and costly.

E X H I B I T **2 ● 3**   *Relative Importance to Building Contractors of Criteria Used in Choosing Suppliers*

Importance Ranking	Factor Influencing the Choice of Supplier
1	Service
2	Quality of product
3	Supplier stands behind product
4	Low price
5	Supplier's reputation for fair dealing
6	Nearness of supplier
7	Friendship with supplier
8	Salesperson's personality
9	Availability of credit
10	Prestige of supplier
11	Reciprocity

Source: Guy R. Banville and Ronald J. Dornoff, "Industrial Source Selection Behavior—An Industry Study," *Industrial Marketing Management*, June 1973.

What criteria do members of the buying center use in selecting a supplier? Because organizational buying is largely a rational decision-making process, we would expect "rational" criteria to be considered most important—such as the quality of the product, the price, and the service offered by the supplier. However, social and emotional factors can also influence this decision. For example, Exhibit 2.3 shows the relative importance attached to various supplier selection criteria by people who buy materials and equipment for building contractors and construction firms. Service, product quality, and price are considered important, but social and emotional factors were also mentioned— such as the reputation and prestige of the supplier, friendship with the supplier, and the personality of the supplier's sales representative.

In the study reported in Exhibit 2.3, Professors Banville and Dornoff also found that the relative importance of different supplier selection criteria varies with the organization making the purchase and the kind of product being purchased. Larger contractors attached more importance to attaining the lowest price, whereas smaller contractors were more concerned with selecting a supplier that would stand behind the product. Also, service and price were more important to contractors choosing a supplier for such standardized, nontechnical items as concrete. Product quality was more important in buying technically complex items such as kitchen appliances.[8]

Selection of an order routine

Until the purchased item is delivered, it is of no use to the organization. Consequently, after an order has been placed with a supplier, the purchasing department often tries to expedite the delivery of the goods. Other internal activities also must occur when the order is delivered. The goods must be received, inspected, paid for, and entered in the firm's inventory records.

Performance evaluation and feedback

When the goods have been delivered, evaluation begins. This evaluation focuses on both the product and the supplier. The goods are inspected to determine whether they meet the specifications described in the purchase agreement. Later, the using department judges whether the purchased item performs according to expectations. Similarly, the supplier's performance can be evaluated on such criteria as promptness of delivery, quality of the product, and service after the sale. In many organizations, this evaluation is a formal process, involving written reports from the user department and other persons involved in the purchase. The information is kept by the purchasing department for use in evaluating proposals and selecting suppliers the next time a similar purchase is made.

Repeat purchase behavior

The steps described above apply only to "new task" purchases, where a customer is buying a relatively complex and expensive product or service for the first time (e.g., a custom-built office building or a new computer system). At the other extreme is the "straight rebuy" where a customer is reordering an item it has purchased many times (e.g., office supplies, bulk chemicals). Such repeat purchases tend to be much more routine than the new task situation.[9]

Straight rebuys are often carried out by members of the purchasing department with little influence from other employees, and many of the steps described above (involved with searching for and evaluating alternative suppliers) are dropped. Instead, the buyer chooses from those suppliers on an "approved" list, giving weight to the company's past satisfaction with those suppliers and their products.

From the seller's viewpoint, being an "in" or approved supplier can provide a significant competitive advantage, and policies and procedures should be developed to help maintain and enhance such favored positions with current customers. As we shall see later in this chapter, many firms have developed "major account management" policies to help preserve the long-term satisfaction of their largest customers.

Also, suppliers are offering new technologies—such as computerized reordering systems—to their customers to help them make their reordering process more efficient while simultaneously increasing the likelihood they will continue to reorder from the same supplier. For example, customers of American Hospital Supply Corp. can enter purchase orders into their computers, have them contact American Hospital's mainframe, find out instantly what is available and when it can be shipped, and place the order automatically. This system increases the probability that existing customers will reorder from American Hospital, and it frees the firm's sales rep to spend more time contacting potential new accounts and informing existing customers about new products.

For potential suppliers not on a buyer's approved list, the strategic selling problem is more difficult. An "out" supplier's objective must be to move the customer away from the automatic reordering procedures of a straight rebuy toward the more extensive evaluation processes of a "modified rebuy" purchase decision—where the buyer is interested in modifying the product specifications, prices, or other terms it has been receiving from existing suppliers and is willing to consider dealing with new suppliers.

Since the need to consider a change in suppliers can be identified by a variety of members of a firm's buying center, an out supplier might urge its salespeople to bypass the customer's purchasing department and call directly on users or technical personnel and try to convince them the firm's products offer advantages on some important dimension—such as technical design, quality, performance, or financial criteria—over the products they are currently using.

SELLING ACTIVITIES

Sales Jobs Involve a Variety of Activities

Given the complexity of the purchasing process in many organizations, it is not surprising that sales reps like Frank Perry of Pilot Air Freight spend much of their time collecting information about potential customers, planning, co-ordinating the activities of other functional departments, and servicing existing customers. It is difficult to specify the full range of activities because only a few researchers have systematically investigated those activities or attempted to uncover the underlying dimensions of the typical sales job. In one reasonably extensive study, Professor William Moncrief used a variety of secondary sources, personal interviews, and focus groups to identify 121 activities commonly involved in sales jobs across a number of industries. A sample of 1,393 sales-people from 51 firms then rated each of the activities on a seven-point scale according to how frequently they performed that activity during a typical month. These responses were examined using factor analysis to identify the underlying dimensions or categories of salesperson behavior represented by the 121 activities.[10]

Ten dimensions—or job factors—were identified. These are shown in Exhibit 2.4, along with some of the specific activities involved in each dimension.

One obvious conclusion from Moncrief's study is that a salesperson's job often involves a variety of activities beyond simply calling on customers, making sales presentations, and taking orders. While the first two factors in Exhibit 2.4 are directly related to selling and order taking, factors 3 and 5 focus on servicing customers after a sale. Similarly, factors 4, 6, and 7 incorporate administrative duties, such as collecting and communicating information about customers to sales and marketing executives in the company, attending periodic training sessions, and helping recruit and develop new sales reps. Finally, some salespeople also expend much effort helping build distribution channels and maintain reseller support (factor 10).

EXHIBIT 2 • 4 *Job Factors and Selected Activities Associated with Each*

1. **Selling function**
   Plan selling activities
   Search out leads
   Call potential accounts
   Identify decision makers
   Prepare sales presentation
   Make sales presentation
   Overcome objections
   Introduce new products
   Call new accounts

2. **Working with others**
   Write up orders
   Expedite orders
   Handle back orders
   Handle shipping problems
   Find lost orders

3. **Servicing the product**
   Learn about the product
   Test equipment
   Supervise installation
   Train customers
   Supervise repairs
   Perform maintenance

4. **Managing information**
   Provide technical information
   Receive feedback
   Provide feedback
   Check with superiors

5. **Servicing the account**
   Stock shelves
   Set up displays
   Take inventory for client
   Handle local advertising

6. **Attending conferences/meetings**
   Attend sales conferences
   Attend regional sales meetings
   Work at client conferences
   Set up product exhibitions
   Attend periodic training sessions

7. **Training/recruiting**
   Recruit new sales reps
   Train new salespeople
   Travel with trainees

8. **Entertaining**
   Entertain clients with golf and so forth
   Take clients to dinner
   Take clients out for drink
   Take clients out to lunch
   Throw parties for clients

9. **Traveling**
   Travel out of town
   Spend nights on the road
   Travel in town

10. **Distribution**
    Establish good relations with distributors
    Sell to distributors
    Handle credit
    Collect past due accounts

Source: Adapted from William C. Moncrief III, "Selling Activity and Sales Position Taxonomies for Industrial Salesforces," *Journal of Marketing Research,* August 1986, pp. 266–67, published by the American Marketing Association.

The Rising Costs of Personal Selling

The increasing number of nonselling and administrative activities means sales-people spend only a small portion of their time actually selling. For example, the results of a recent survey of 192 companies employing nearly 10,000 salespeople in a variety of industries are diagrammed in Exhibit 2.5. The survey found, on average, sales reps devote less than half their time to direct contact with customers, either face to face or over the telephone.[11] In firms that sell complicated or customized products or service systems to large customers, the proportion of selling time can be even lower. For instance, a few years ago, management at Hewlett-Packard discovered the 200 reps in the firm's personal computer sales force spent an average of only 31 percent of their time on customer contact activities.[12]

The increasing involvement of sales reps in nonselling activities is one major reason the average cost of a sales call has risen dramatically in recent years. While the cost of a sales call was estimated to be about $100 at the end of the 1970s, that cost more than doubled during the 1980s. The most con-servative estimate placed the cost of an average industrial sales call at $239 in 1990, while other estimates ranged from $250 to nearly $300. To make matters worse, respondents in a *Sales & Marketing Management* survey re-ported an average of three calls were necessary to close a sale with an existing account, and seven calls were required to win a sale from a new customer. Using the most conservative estimate of the cost per call, selling expenses average $717 per sale to existing customers and a whopping $1,673 per sale to new accounts.[13]

This rapid escalation of selling costs helps explain why the search for ways to improve sales force efficiency has become increasingly urgent. Some ap-proaches to resolve this issue, including the increased use of computers to hasten or improve the effectiveness of sales activities, are discussed in Thorny Issues in Sales Management 2.1.

Different Types of Sales Jobs

Not every salesperson engages in all the activities listed in Exhibit 2.4. Nor does every rep devote the same amount of time and effort to the same kinds of activities. The many different kinds of selling jobs involve widely different tasks and responsibilities, require different kinds of training and skills, and offer varying levels of compensation and opportunities for personal satisfaction and advancement.

Retail selling versus industrial selling

Most salespeople are employed in various kinds of **retail selling**. These jobs involve selling goods and services to ultimate consumers for their personal use, such as door-to-door salespeople, insurance agents, real estate brokers, and retail store clerks. A much larger volume of sales, however, is accounted for by **industrial selling**—the sale of goods and services at the wholesale level. Industrial selling involves three types of customers.

EXHIBIT 2 • 5 *How Salespeople Spend Their Time*

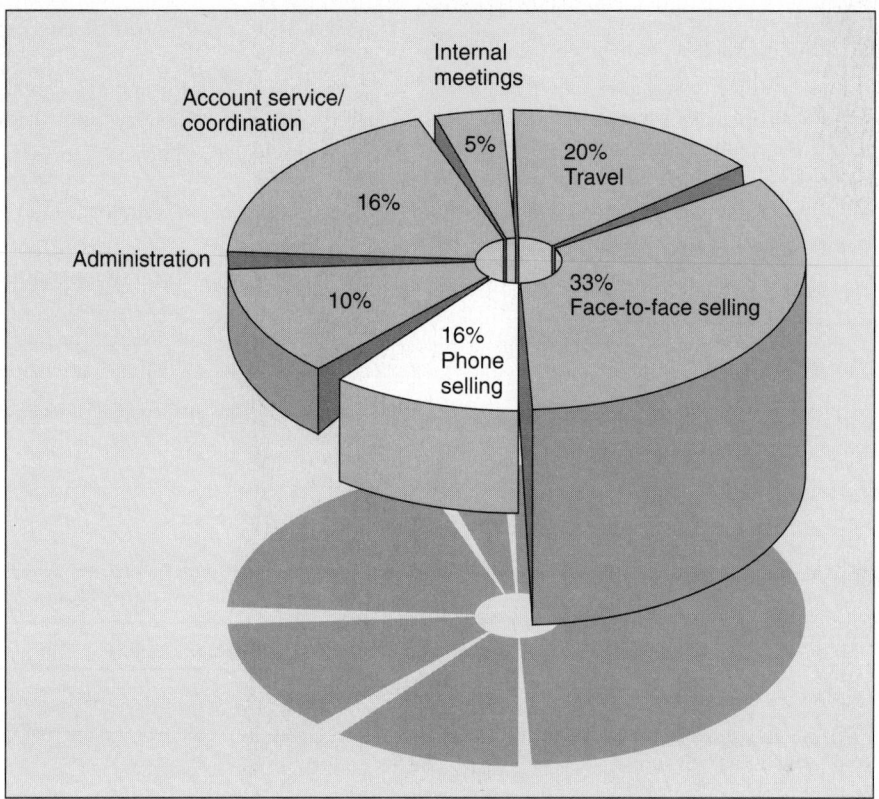

Source: William A. O'Connell and William Keenan, Jr., "The Shape of Things to Come," *Sales & Marketing Management,* January 1990, pp. 36–41. Reprinted by permission of *Sales & Marketing Management.* Copyright © January 1990.

1. *Sales to resellers*—as when a clothing manufacturer's sales rep sells merchandise to a retail store, which resells the goods to its customers.
2. *Sales to business users*—as when manufacturer X sells materials or parts to manufacturer Y, which uses them to produce another product, or when a Xerox salesperson sells a law firm a copier to be used in conducting the firm's business.
3. *Sales to institutions*—as when an IBM salesperson sells a computer or typewriters to a hospital or a government agency.

In many ways, the activities involved in both retail and industrial selling, and in managing the two types of sales forces, are very similar. Success in either type of selling requires interpersonal and communications skills, solid

Thorny Issues in Sales Management 2 • 1

IMPROVING SELLING EFFICIENCY

The expanding marketing role of many industrial sales forces, and the resulting increase in nonselling activities demanded of them, has contributed to a rapid increase in selling costs. Consequently, sales managers are seeking ways to improve sales force efficiency, either by cutting the time required to perform nonselling activities, increasing the effectiveness of activities related directly to sales (e.g., analysis of customer requirements, preparation of proposals, etc.), or both.

Managers are pursuing greater selling efficiency down a variety of avenues, many of which we will discuss in greater detail in other parts of this book. Some promising approaches include the following.

• Many firms have adopted account management policies that classify customers according to their potential and specify how frequently each type of account should be called on. Such policies help ensure salespeople will not spend too much

Current and Planned Use of Computerized Sales Support Systems in Sales Management

Application	Currently Used in: Manufacturing	Services	Planned Use in: Manufacturing	Services
Analyzing customer needs	73%	60%	16%	24%
Budgeting	46	43	18	13
Checking inventory	51	9	23	†
Checking orders	64	34	22	9
Communications/E-mail	66	57	24	11
Competitive intelligence	22	20	27	24
Customer account management	66	60	22	26
Database activity	63	71	26	15
Entering orders	52	37	*	17
Forecasting	55	43	24	7
Graphics	40	37	18	17
Preparing presentations	45	66	22	17
Preparing proposals	43	69	†	†
Pricing	46	54	15	15
Product information	40	49	22	15
Prospecting	26	49	16	24
Reporting expenses	30	20	24	15
Reporting sales calls	42	43	21	19
Spreadsheets	54	40	15	13
Time management/scheduling	31	26	24	22
Word processing	62	57	14	15

*Combined with "checking orders."

†Not included.

(continued)

time on customers with low potential, and they will not devote too little effort to more potentially profitable accounts.

- Because the costs of calling on smaller customers can exceed the revenues they generate, some firms treat such accounts differently than their large customers. They may impose minimum order quantities to discourage business from very small customers. More commonly, firms rely on telemarketing for making sales to smaller customers. This and other ways in which telemarketing is being used to improve sales productivity are discussed further in Chapter 5.
- Some firms, particularly in consumer package-goods industries, have created new positions (e.g., trade merchandisers or customer service specialists) to assist with some of the sales force's nonselling activities. This allows salespeople to

spend more time making sales calls while the service specialists, who often have less training and smaller salaries, concentrate on such activities as stocking shelves, setting up displays, or servicing the company's products.

- The approach that has shown the greatest promise for improving sales efficiency is the greater use of personal computers and computerized sales support systems to help salespeople complete a variety of tasks more quickly and effectively. While we discuss specific computer applications throughout this book, the accompanying table, which is based on the findings of a survey conducted by the Conference Board, provides an overview of how firms in both manufacturing and service industries are using and planning to use personal computers and computerized sales support systems to assist salespeople.

Source: *Computer-Based Sales Force Support*, Report No. 953 (New York: The Conference Board, 1991). See also Thayer C. Taylor, "From Selling Aid to Taskmaster," *Sales & Marketing Management*, May 1991, pp. 69–73.

knowledge of the products being sold, an ability to discover the customer's needs and problems, and the creativity necessary to show the customer how a particular product or service can help satisfy those needs and problems. Similarly, managers must recruit and train appropriate people for both types of sales jobs, provide them with objectives consistent with the firm's overall marketing or merchandising program, supervise them, motivate them, and evaluate their performance.

Retail and industrial selling also differ in some important ways. Many of the goods and services sold by industrial salespersons are more expensive and technically complex than those in retailing. Similarly, industrial customers tend to be larger and to engage in extensive decision-making processes involving many people. Consequently, the activities and skills involved in selling to industrial buyers are often quite different from those in retail selling. Furthermore, the decisions made in effectively managing an industrial sales force are broader than those required for a retail sales force. Consequently, although many topics in this book apply to the management of both types of salespersons (selection and training), others apply only to the management of industrial salespeople (sales territory design).

Types of industrial sales jobs

Even within the broad area of industrial selling, there are many different kinds of jobs requiring different skills. Various authors have described more than 100 ways in which industrial sales jobs might be classified.[14] The availability of so many classification schemes—and the changes in common types of sales jobs and their content as the market environment shifts—presents a thorny issue for both sales managers and researchers, an issue explored further in Thorny Issue 2.2.

One of the most commonly used, and useful, classifications of selling jobs was developed by Derek Newton.[15] Because of its popularity and the fact that it has been the subject of empirical research, we will refer to this scheme occasionally. Newton's scheme identifies four types of industrial selling found across a variety of industries.

1. *Trade selling*—the sales force's primary responsibility is to increase business from current and potential customers by providing them with *merchandising and promotional assistance*. A Procter & Gamble salesperson selling soap and laundry products to chain-store personnel is an example of trade selling.

2. *Missionary selling*—the sales force's primary job is to increase business from current and potential customers by providing them with *product information* and other personal selling assistance. Missionary salespeople often do not take orders from customers directly but persuade customers to buy their firm's product from distributors or other wholesale suppliers. Examples include representatives of brewers, who call on bar owners and encourage them to order a particular brand of beer from the local distributor, and medical "detailers," who call on doctors as representatives of pharmaceutical manufacturers.

3. *Technical selling*—the sales force's primary responsibility is to increase business from presently identified customers and potential customers by providing them with technical and engineering information and assistance. Sales engineers for machine-tool and computer manufacturers are examples of people engaged in technical selling.

4. *New business selling*—the salesperson's primary responsibility is to identify and obtain business from *new customers*.

Each type of sales job involves somewhat different activities and requires different skills and training. Therefore, although most of this book focuses on managing industrial selling in general, from time to time special attention will be paid to unique problems encountered in managing people in these specific types of sales jobs.

Steps in the Selling Process   While a variety of analytical and administrative duties may be important components of a sales rep's job, the primary focus of most sales jobs is on those

Thorny Issues in Sales Management 2 • 2

CLASSIFYING TYPES OF SALES JOBS

The development of a generalizable classification scheme is important for both sales managers and researchers because such a scheme can help them (*a*) make comparisons across different types of jobs, and (*b*) draw conclusions concerning what types of salespeople and management policies are most appropriate for a particular type of sales job. While a number of people have developed classification schemes—or taxonomies—of sales jobs over the years, those schemes differ in various ways, as shown in the table below.

Comparison of Sales Taxonomies

Moncrief (1986)	Newton (1973)	McMurray (1961)
1. Missionary	1. Missionary	1. Missionary
2. Trade servicer	2. Trade servicer	2. Delivery
3. Trade seller	—	—
4. Order taker	—	3. Order taker
—	3. Technical	4. Technical
—	4. New business	5. Create demand
5. Institutional seller	—	—

One reason sales job classifications have changed over the years is because the nature and requirements of the jobs have adapted to changing environmental conditions. Support for this view is provided by William Moncrief's recent empirical study. He examined the frequency of occurrence of 121 different sales activities across a sample of 800 firms as a basis for identifying different types of selling jobs. Three of Moncrief's five job categories correspond closely to Newton's earlier categories of missionary selling and trade selling. However, Moncrief's taxonomy includes both "trade sellers," who are primarily concerned with making sales to new retail or wholesale accounts, and "trade servicers," who primarily deal with the merchandising needs of existing trade customers.

Two other types of sales jobs were also identified by Moncrief: "institutional sellers," who sell primarily to end-users (e.g., other manufacturers or institutions); and "order takers," who perform the kind of routine order writing and account maintenance activities that are increasingly being taken over by telemarketing programs. Because many types of products have become more technically complex over the years, Moncrief did not find a separate "technical selling" category. Instead, technical sales activities were associated with several different types of sales jobs.

Moncrief's findings clearly suggest that sales jobs have changed over the years, and new types of sales jobs will undoubtedly emerge in the future. Thus, we will have to continue updating our taxonomies of selling jobs in order to make meaningful comparisons and managerial prescriptions.

Source: From William C. Moncrief III, "Selling Activity and Sales Position Taxonomies for Industrial Salesforces," *Journal of Marketing Research* 23 (August 1986), pp. 261–70; Derek A. Newton, *Sales Force Performance and Turnover* (Cambridge, Mass. Marketing Science Institute, 1973); and Robert N. McMurray, "The Mystique of Super-Salesmanship," *Harvard Business Review,* March–April 1961, pp. 113–22. For speculation about how categories of sales jobs may change in the future, see William A. O'Connell and William Keenan, Jr., "The Shape of Things to Come," *Sales & Marketing Management,* January 1990, pp. 36–41.

E X H I B I T   2 • 6   *Stages in the Selling Process*

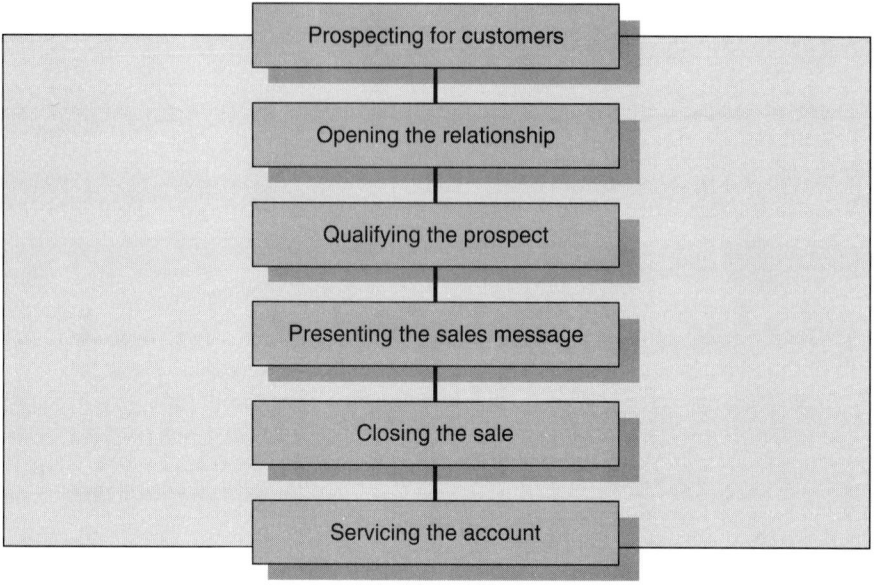

tasks involving direct interaction with customers or potential customers. A number of observers have suggested conceptual schemes that outline various stages in the selling process and indicate the kinds of activities occurring at each stage.[16] The essence of most of these conceptual schemes can be summarized by viewing the selling process as consisting of the six stages diagrammed in Exhibit 2.6: (1) prospecting for customers, (2) opening the relationship, (3) qualifying the prospect, (4) presenting the sales message, (5) closing the sale, and (6) servicing the account.

Although the selling process involves only a few distinct steps, the specific activities involved at each step—and the way those activities are carried out—can vary greatly from one salesperson to the next. Consequently, a firm's strategic sales plan should incorporate *account management policies* to guide each salesperson and ensure that all selling efforts are consistent with the firm's marketing strategy. We will examine the rationale and content of account management policies in more detail in Chapter 4. The following discussion of the stages in the selling process also mentions some of the more common account management policies used to direct sales representatives.

Prospecting for customers

In many types of selling, prospecting for new customers is critical. It can also be one of the most disheartening aspects of selling, especially for beginning salespeople. Prospecting efforts are often met with rejection, and immediate payoffs are usually minimal. Nevertheless, the ability to uncover potential new customers often separates the successful from the unsuccessful salesperson.

A story is often told in selling circles about a recent graduate who became an insurance salesman. In the first year, he received several sales awards for bringing new business to his company. Two years later, he quit and switched to a career outside the sales field. What happened? He exhausted his list of friends and relatives. He was successful as long as he was selling to a select list of prospects, but when that list dwindled, he was unable to generate any new customers. A more successful salesperson would have been seeking new prospects continuously.

In some consumer goods businesses, prospecting for new customers simply involves cold canvassing—going from house to house knocking on doors. In most cases, though, the target market is more narrowly defined, and the salesperson must identify prospects within that target segment. Salespeople use a variety of information sources to identify relevant prospects, including trade association and industry directories, telephone directories, other salespeople, other customers, suppliers, nonsales employees of the firm, and social and professional contacts.

New technologies—particularly telemarketing systems—can also help salespeople identify and qualify potential new accounts. Many firms set up incoming Wide-Area Telecommunication Service (WATS) phone lines and publicize toll-free 800 numbers in their media advertising and other promotional material. When prospects call for more information about a product or service, an operator attempts to determine the extent of interest and whether the prospect meets the company's qualification for new customers. If so, information about the caller is passed on to the appropriate salesperson or regional office.

A firm's account management policies should address how much emphasis salespeople should give to prospecting for new customers versus servicing existing accounts. The appropriate policy for a firm depends on the nature of its product and its customers. If the firm's product is in the introductory stage of its life cycle, if it is an infrequently purchased durable good, or if the typical customer does not require much service after the sale, sales reps should devote substantial time to prospecting for new customers. This is the case in industries such as insurance and residential construction. Such firms may design their compensation systems to reward their salespeople more heavily for making sales to new customers than for servicing old ones, as we shall see in Chapter 15.

Firms with large market shares or those that sell frequently purchased nondurable products or products that require substantial service after the sale to guarantee customer satisfaction should adopt a policy that encourages sales reps to devote most of their efforts to servicing existing customers. Food manufacturers that sell products to retail supermarkets and firms that produce component parts and supplies for other manufacturers fall into this category.

Some very large customers may require so much servicing that a sales rep is assigned to do nothing but cater to that customer's needs. In such circumstances, firms have specialized their sales positions so that some representatives service only existing accounts, while others spend all their time prospecting for and opening relationships with new customers.

Opening the relationship

In the initial approach to a prospective customer, the sales representative should try to accomplish two things: (1) determine who within the organization is likely to have the greatest influence and/or authority to purchase the product and (2) generate enough interest within the firm to obtain the information needed to qualify the prospect as a worthwhile potential customer.[17] An organizational buying center often consists of individuals who play different roles in making the purchase decision. Thus, it is important for the salesperson to identify the key decision makers, their desires, and their relative influence.

Selling organizations can formulate policies to guide sales reps in approaching prospective customers. When the firm's product is inexpensive and routinely purchased, salespeople might be instructed to deal entirely with the purchasing department. For more technically complex and expensive products, the sales representative might be urged to identify and seek appointments with influencers and decision makers in various functional departments and at several managerial levels. When the purchase decision is likely to be very complex, involving many people within the customer's organization, the seller might adopt a policy of multilevel or team selling.

Qualifying the prospect

Before salespeople attempt to set up an appointment for a major sales presentation or spend much time trying to establish a relationship with a prospective account, they should first determine whether the prospect qualifies as a worthwhile potential customer. If the account does not qualify, the sales rep can spend the time better elsewhere.

Qualification is difficult for some salespeople. It requires them to put aside their eternal optimism and make an objective, realistic judgment about the probability of making a profitable sale, as Pilot's Frank Perry did before deciding to spend three years pursuing the GTE account.

As one authority points out, the qualification process involves finding the answers to three important questions:

1. Does the prospect have a need for my product or service?
2. Can I make the people responsible for buying so aware of that need that I can make a sale?
3. Will the sale be profitable to my company?[18]

To answer such questions, the sales representative must learn about the prospect's operations, the kinds of products it makes, its customers, its competitors, and the likely future demand for its products. Information also must be obtained concerning who the customer's present suppliers are and whether there are any special relationships with those firms that would make it difficult for the prospect to change suppliers. Finally, the financial health and the credit rating of the prospect should be checked.

Because so many different kinds of information are needed, nonselling departments within the company—such as the credit and collections department—often are involved in the qualification process. Also, company policies should be formulated to guide the salesperson's judgment concerning whether a specific prospect qualifies as a customer. These policies might spell out minimum acceptable standards for such things as the prospect's annual dollar value of purchases in the product category or credit rating. Similarly, some firms specify a minimum order size to avoid dealing with very small customers and to improve the efficiency of their order-processing and shipping operations.

Presenting the sales message

The presentation is the core of the selling process. The salesperson transmits information about a product or service and attempts to persuade the prospect to become a customer. Making good presentations is a critical aspect of the sales job. Unfortunately, many salespeople do not perform this activity very well. Past studies have discovered that 40 percent of purchasing agents perceive the presentations they witness are less than good. In a recent survey of about 70 purchasing executives, the following 5 presentation-related complaints were among the top 10 complaints the managers had about the salespeople they deal with:

- Running down competitors.
- Being too aggressive or abrasive.
- Having inadequate knowledge of competitors' products or services.
- Having inadequate knowledge of our business or organization.
- Delivering poor presentations.[19]

One decision that must be made in preparing for an effective sales presentation concerns how many members of the buying firm should attend. Since more than one person is typically involved in making a purchase decision, should a sales presentation be given to all of them as a group? The answer depends on whether the members of the buying center have divergent attitudes and concerns, and whether those concerns can all be addressed effectively in a single presentation. If not, scheduling a series of one-to-one presentations with different members of the buying group might be more effective.

In many cases, the best way to convince prospects of a product's advantage is to demonstrate it. This is particularly true if the product is technically complex. Two rules should be followed in preparing an effective product demonstration. First, the demonstration should be carefully rehearsed to reduce the possibility of even a minor malfunction. Second, the demonstration should be designed to give members of the buying center hands-on experience with the product. For example, Xerox's salespeople learn about their clients' office operations so they can demonstrate their products actually doing the tasks they would do after they are purchased.

Different firms have widely varying policies concerning how sales presentations should be organized, what selling points should be stressed, and how forcefully the presentation should be made. Encyclopedia companies commonly train their door-to-door salespeople to deliver the same memorized, forceful presentation to every prospect. A person selling computer systems may be trained in very low-key selling in which the salesperson primarily acts as a source of technical information and advice and does little "pushing" of the company's particular computers.

A firm's policy on sales presentations should be consistent with its other policies for managing accounts. To formulate intelligent sales presentation policies, a sales manager must know about alternative presentation methods and their relative advantages and limitations. Unfortunately, the space limitations of this chapter make it difficult to present a lengthy discussion of such issues. The interested student is urged to examine the appendix at the end of the chapter where a variety of sales presentation methods are discussed and evaluated in more detail.

Closing the sale

Closing refers to obtaining a final agreement to purchase. All the salesperson's efforts are wasted unless the client "signs on the dotted line"; yet this is where many salespeople fail. It is natural to delay making purchase decisions. But as the time it takes the salesperson to close the sale increases, the profit to be made from the sale goes down, and the risk of losing the sale increases. Consequently, the salesperson's task is to speed up the final decision. Often, this can best be done by simply asking for an order. "May I write that order up for you?" and "When do you want it delivered?" are common closings. Another closing tactic is to ask the client to choose among two alternative decisions, such as, "Will that be cash or charge?" or "Did you want the blue one or the red one?"

Servicing the account

The salesperson's job is not finished when the sale is made. Many kinds of service and assistance must be provided to customers after a sale to ensure their satisfaction and repeat business. This is another area in which some salespeople do not perform well. One consultant estimates that when a customer stops buying from a company, about 60 percent of the time it's because the customer thinks the seller's salespeople developed an indifferent attitude after the product was delivered.[20]

The salesperson should follow up each sale to make sure there are no problems with delivery schedules, quality of goods, or customer billing. In addition, the salesperson often supervises the installation of the equipment, trains the customer's employees in its use, and ensures proper maintenance. In most cases, the salesperson must work closely with other departments in the firm to make sure the customer's interests are represented and no problems lead to customer dissatisfaction.

This kind of service can pay great dividends for both the salesperson and the firm. For one thing, satisfied customers are more likely to be repeat purchasers. Also, good service can lead to the sale of other related products and services. For instance, in many capital equipment lines, service contracts—along with supplies and replacement parts—account for greater dollar sales revenue and higher profit margins than the original equipment.

A firm's account management policies should provide its sales representatives with clear guidelines concerning the kinds and extensiveness of customer service they should provide. When service after the sale is critical in determining the future of a firm's relationship with its major customer, the firm might organize its sales force to include "major account managers" who specialize in providing continuing service to the company's largest customers.

WHY SALESPEOPLE SELL: THE ATTRACTIVENESS OF SALES CAREERS

The complexity and competitiveness of most industrial sales jobs makes successful performance a daunting challenge for even the most well-managed sales force. This challenges sales managers to recruit and select the best qualified salespeople, train and supervise them well, keep them highly motivated, and focus their efforts with appropriate sales strategies and account management policies. The challenge of recruiting talented new salespeople is made an even thornier problem for many firms, particularly those who seek recruits with college degrees or MBAs, because many college students hold somewhat negative attitudes toward selling as a potential career. This problem, along with some of its potential causes and solutions, is examined in Thorny Issues 2.3.

For most industrial salespeople, it is the complexity and challenge of their jobs that motivates them and makes them satisfied with their choice of careers. A number of satisfaction surveys have found high levels of job satisfaction among industrial salespeople across a broad cross section of firms and industries. While these surveys did find some areas of dissatisfaction, that unhappiness tended to focus on the policies and actions of the salesperson's firm or sales manager, not on the nature of the job.[21]

Why are so many industrial salespeople so satisfied with their jobs? Different analysts have offered a variety of answers. Some attractive aspects of selling careers include (1) freedom of action and opportunities for personal initiative, (2) a variety of challenging activities, (3) financial rewards, (4) fa-

Thorny Issues in Sales Management 2 • 3

STUDENT ATTITUDES TOWARD CAREERS IN SALES

It is no bed of roses for sales recruiters on college campuses. A number of student surveys over the years, summarized in the accompanying table, indicate that a majority of students perceive sales jobs as involving frustrating work that demands a lot of travel, interferes with leisure time and home life, and contributes relatively little to society. More critically, the majority of students would

Summary of College Students' Perceptions and Attitudes toward Sales Jobs

Perceptions and Attitudes	Findings of Surveys Conducted by			
	Sales Management (1962)	Paul and Worthing (1970)	Dubinsky (1980)	Cook and Hartman (1986)
1. Students associate personal selling with:				
a. Frustration	Agree	DNI	DNI	Agree
b. Insincerity and deceit	Agree	Disagree	DNI	Disagree
c. Low status/low prestige	Agree	Agree	Agree	Disagree
d. Much traveling	Agree	Agree	Agree	Agree
e. Salespeople are "money hungry"	Agree	DNi	DNI	Neutral
f. High pressure/forces people to buy unwanted goods/little contribution to society	Agree	DNI	Agree	Neutral
g. Low job security	Agree	DNI	Agree	Neutral
h. Just a "job," not a "career"/little professionalism	Agree	DNI	Disagree	Disagree
i. Uninteresting/no challenge	Agree	DNI	Disagree	Disagree
j. No need for creativity	Agree	Disagree	Disagree	Disagree
k. Personality is crucial	DNI	Agree	DNI	Agree
l. Too little monetary reward	Agree	Agree	Disagree	Disagree
m. Intereferes with home life/little leisure time	Agree	DNI	Agree	Agree
2. Students prefer nonsales positions much more than sales positions	Agree	Agree	DNI	Agree
3. Students' contact with salespeople largely limited to door-to-door and retail store personnel	Agree	Agree	DNI	Neutral

Sources: In 1962, a study involving 919 undergraduates and graduate students was reported in "Selling Is a Dirty Word," *Sales Management,* October 5, 1962, pp. 44–47.Professors Paul and Worthing interviewed 200 undergraduates at a southern university and reported the results in Gordon W. Paul and Parker Worthing, "A Student Assessment of Selling," *Southern Journal of Business* 5 (July 1970), pp. 57–65. A survey of 219 undergraduates at a midwestern university in a major metropolitan area was discussed by Alan J. Dubinsky in "Recruiting College Students for the Salesforce," *Industrial Marketing Management* 9 (February 1980), pp. 37–45. Finally, the results of a survey of 160 male and 136 female business students at three midwestern universities were reported by Robert W. Cook and Timothy Hartman in "Female College Student Interest in a Sales Career: A Comparison," *Journal of Personal Selling and Sales Management* 6 (May 1986), pp. 29–34.

(continued)

prefer to take a nonsales job over a sales position when they graduate; an attitude that poses an obvious problem for sales recruiters.*

Why do these negative attitudes exist? They probably reflect the limited exposure most students have had to industrial salespeple and the kind of work they do. Consequently, students ignore or underestimate some positive characteristics of selling careers, like those discussed in this chapter, that make them attractive to millions of workers. A survey comparing the perceptions of students with those of salespeople from a variety of firms found that the salespeople rated sales jobs significantly more positive than did the students on such dimensions as status and prestige, security, contributions to society, financial rewards, professionalism, and feelings of accomplishment.†

Many sales managers believe that more accurate information and education will help improve student attitudes toward sales careers. To this end, professional associations and individual firms encourage and support student organizations focused on sales and marketing interests, such as Mu Kappa Tau and Pi Sigma Epsilon, and courses in sales and sales management at colleges and vocational schools. These educational efforts may be having some affect. The table indicates student attitudes toward sales jobs have become more favorable. Students responding to the most recent surveys tend to view sales jobs as more challenging, requiring greater creativity and professionalism, and offering better financial rewards than students in earlier studies.

*Interestingly, while the Cook and Hartman study found that the attitudes of male and female students toward sales jobs were largely the same on most dimensions, females were significantly less likely to perfer a career in sales than males. On the other hand, another recent student survey found that women had more positive attitudes toward some aspects of personal selling than men. See Darrel D. Muehling and William A. Weeks, "Women's Perceptions of Personal Selling: Some Positive Results," *Journal of Personal Selling and Sales Management* 8 (May 1988), pp. 11–20. We will say more about women in selling in Chapter 11.

†Alan J. Dubinsky, "Perceptions of the Sales Job: How Students Compare with Industrial Salespeople," *Journal of the Academy of Marketing Science* 9 (Fall 1981), pp. 352–67.

vorable working conditions, and (5) good opportunities for career development and advancement.[22]

Freedom of Action

A common complaint among workers in many professions is that they are too closely supervised. They complain about superiors "breathing down their necks" and about rules and standard operating procedures that constrain their freedom to do their jobs as they see fit. Salespeople, on the other hand, spend most of their time in the field calling on customers where there is no one to supervise their every move. They are relatively free to organize their own time and to get the job done in their own way as long as they show satisfactory results.

The freedom of a selling career appeals to people who value their independence, who are confident they can cope with most situations they will encounter, and who like to show some personal initiative in deciding how to get their job done. However, this freedom brings responsibilities and pressures. Salespeople are responsible for their territory. Although no one closely supervises the salesperson's behavior, management usually keeps close tabs on the results of that behavior—sales volume, quota attainment, expenses, and the like.

To be successful, salespeople must be willing and able to manage themselves, to organize time wisely, and to make the right decisions about how to do the job. Not everyone wants such responsibilities. For example, one survey found that some sales representatives were dissatisfied with their supervisors, not because they were being supervised too closely but because they believed they were not being supervised enough.[23] These people were uncomfortable about having to take so much responsibility for determining their own job behavior and performance.

Variety and Challenge

People soon become bored doing routine tasks. Consequently, many companies have instituted job enrichment programs to expand the variety in and challenge of their employees' jobs. Boredom is seldom a problem among industrial salespeople, however. Each potential customer has different needs and problems for the salesperson to solve. Those problems are often anything but trivial, and a salesperson must display insight, creativity, and analytical skill to close a sale. For example, a six-person selling team from IBM spent four years studying patient care and handling procedures in a large hospital before designing and selling a data processing system that fit the hospital's needs.

Many analysts expect this kind of creative problem solving to become even more common in the future. New technologies—like telemarketing and electronic reordering systems—are making what was a primary function of the salesperson, order taking, almost obsolete. As a result, the salesperson of the future will be "more of a trainer, a technical adviser, and consultant as opposed to an order-taker."[24]

To make the job even more interesting, conditions in the marketplace are constantly changing. Salespeople must frequently adjust their sales presentations and other activities to changing economic and competitive conditions.

For many people in the selling profession, variety and challenge are the most rewarding aspects of their jobs. In one study, industrial salespeople rated the "sense of accomplishment" and the "opportunities for personal growth" provided by their jobs second only to financial compensation as the most attractive rewards they received.[25]

Compensation

As the preceding suggests, selling can be a very lucrative profession. As Exhibit 2.7 indicates, starting salaries for sales trainees are quite high. They are comparable to those paid in other functional areas of business.

More important, the growth rate of a salesperson's earnings is determined largely by performance. A salesperson's compensation can grow more rapidly and reach higher levels than that of personnel in other departments at comparable levels in an organization. Often, no arbitrary limits are placed on the maximum earnings of a salesperson. Exhibit 2.8 shows the average compensation for industrial salespeople with various amounts of experience and selling responsibilities. These averages fail to show, however, that the most successful

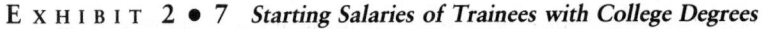

E X H I B I T   **2 • 7**   *Starting Salaries of Trainees with College Degrees*

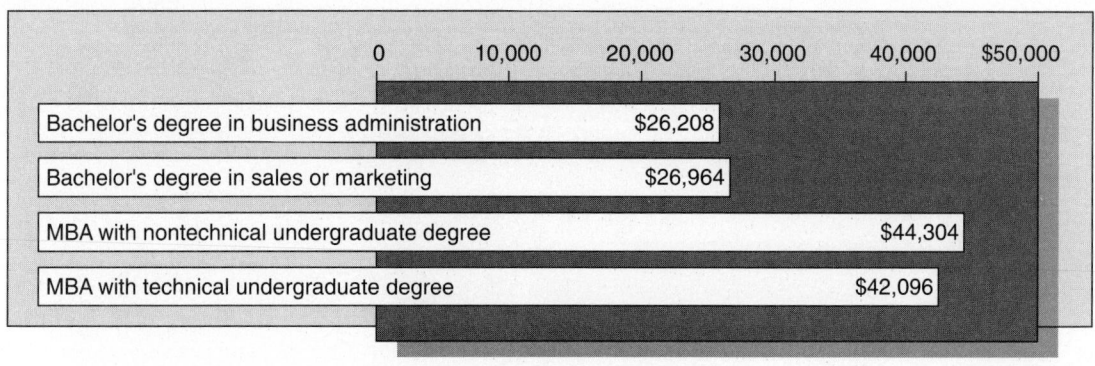

Source: Reprinted with permission from "Compensation," in *Sales & Marketing Management,* June 17, 1991, p. 75. © 1991 by Bill Communications, Inc. Reprinted by permission of *Sales & Marketing Management.* Copyright © June 17, 1991.

salespeople commonly have much higher earnings. For example, at Wells Fargo Bank, a commission structure based on the profits generated by new accounts enables some members of the bank's commercial lending sales force to earn more money than its commercial loan officers and even some of its vice presidents.[26]

Although salespeople are sometimes reluctant to give up their high-paying jobs to move into managerial positions, most firms recognize the importance of good managerial talent and reward it appropriately, particularly as a person reaches the top executive levels of the sales organization. Total compensation of over $250,000 a year is not unheard of for national sales managers or vice presidents of sales in large firms.

**Working
Conditions**

According to the stereotype, salespeople travel extensively, live on big expense accounts, spend much of their time entertaining potential clients, and consequently have little time for home and family life. Again, this is not an accurate description of the working conditions encountered by most salespeople.

Some selling jobs require substantial travel, but most salespeople can sleep at home nearly every night. As we shall see, a major determinant of the size of sales territories is the density of potential customers. In many lines of trade, customers are sufficiently concentrated that firms must define relatively small sales territories to gain adequate customer contact. Also, smaller territories are the trend in many industries as the number of customers has grown and as firms attempt to provide better customer service. Consequently, people who sell such things as office equipment, cleaning supplies, or grocery products commonly have territories limited to a single city or a fraction of a single state.

E X H I B I T   2 • 8   *Average Compensation for Different Sales Positions*

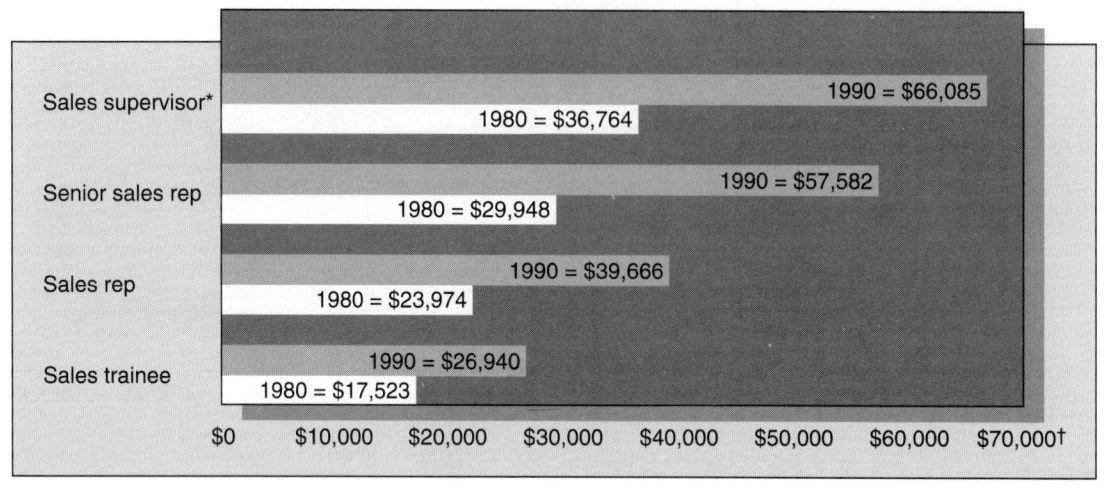

*A "senior sales representative" is at the highest level of selling responsibility in a firm, usually has years of experience, and is assigned to major accounts and territories. A "sales supervisor" is a veteran salesperson whose primary function is to train and direct the activities of other salespeople although the supervisor may also sell to selected key accounts.

†Includes salaries plus commission incentives. Figures are based on consumer goods and industrial goods firms as well as insurance companies, services, transportation companies, and utilities.

Source: Adapted from "Compensation," with permission of *Sales & Marketing Management,* June 17, 1991, p. 73. © 1991 by Bill Communications, Inc. Reprinted by permission of *Sales & Marketing Management.* Copyright © June 17, 1991.

Although some sales jobs still require extensive traveling, modern sales managers are usually aware of the problems such travel can cause for both the salesperson and the firm. Many companies attempt to design their larger territories and schedule calls in such a way that the salesperson reaches home every couple of days. Where necessary, some firms fly their salespeople home every weekend regardless of the distance.

Opportunities for Career Development and Advancement

Many businesspeople believe that an executive must "know the territory" to do an effective job managing. What better way is there to learn about a company's customers, products, and competitive strengths and weaknesses than to spend time in the field calling on customers and meeting the competition? Many companies require managerial trainees to spend time in the sales force in preparation for executive positions in marketing or other functional departments.

The knowledge gained through sales experience is also enhanced by formal training programs. As indicated in Exhibit 2.9, such training involves months of effort (and thousands of dollars in expense) for each trainee. Firms in some

EXHIBIT 2 • 9   *Length of Sales Training by Industry*

Industry Group	Average Training Period (months)	Industry Group	Average Training Period (months)
Agriculture	5.7	Insurance	5.5
Amusement/recreation services	2.0	Lumber/wood products	2.7
Business services	4.1	Machinery	5.6
Chemicals	4.5	Manufacturing	3.3
Communications	4.2	Office equipment	2.8
Construction	5.0	Paper/allied products	6.0
Electronic components	1.5	Primary metal products	4.5
Electronics	3.4	Printing/publishing	5.5
Fabricated metals	3.5	Rubber/plastics	6.5
Food products	2.8	Wholesale (consumer)	1.5
Instruments	2.7	Wholesale (industrial)	3.9
Average	**4.0**		

Note: Industry groups reflect categories selected and reported by Dartnell Corporation. The overall average has been calculated by *Sales & Marketing Management* based on data from the 22 industries listed.

Source: Dartnell Corporation, *26th Survey of Sales Force Compensation* © 1990; Dartnell Corporation.

service industries have longer training programs on average than firms in many manufacturing industries because some service organizations, such as those selling insurance or financial services, have relatively complicated product lines. In many high-tech industries, such as computers or plastics, manufacturers also have relatively extensive and costly training programs. Such programs can last up to two years and cost as much as $100,000 per trainee before a new recruit is prepared to become a productive member of the marketing team.

Given the wealth of knowledge about a firm's customers, competitors, and products—and the experience at building effective relationships—that a sales job can provide, it is not surprising that more corporation presidents come from sales and marketing backgrounds than from any other functional area.[27] Many managerial opportunities are available to successful salespeople at lower levels of the corporate hierarchy as well in sales management and marketing management. Exhibit 2.10 illustrates an ideal and reasonably common career path for a successful salesperson.

Promoting top salespeople into management can sometimes cause problems. Successful selling often requires different personal attributes and skills than does successful management. There is no guarantee that a good salesperson will also be a good sales manager. Also, successful salespeople have been known to refuse promotion to managerial positions. Often this is because they simply enjoy selling, but in some cases it is because they can earn more money selling than they can in a middle-management position.

Finally, while it is common for successful salespeople to follow a career

EXHIBIT 2 • 10   *A Common Career Path for Industrial Salespeople*

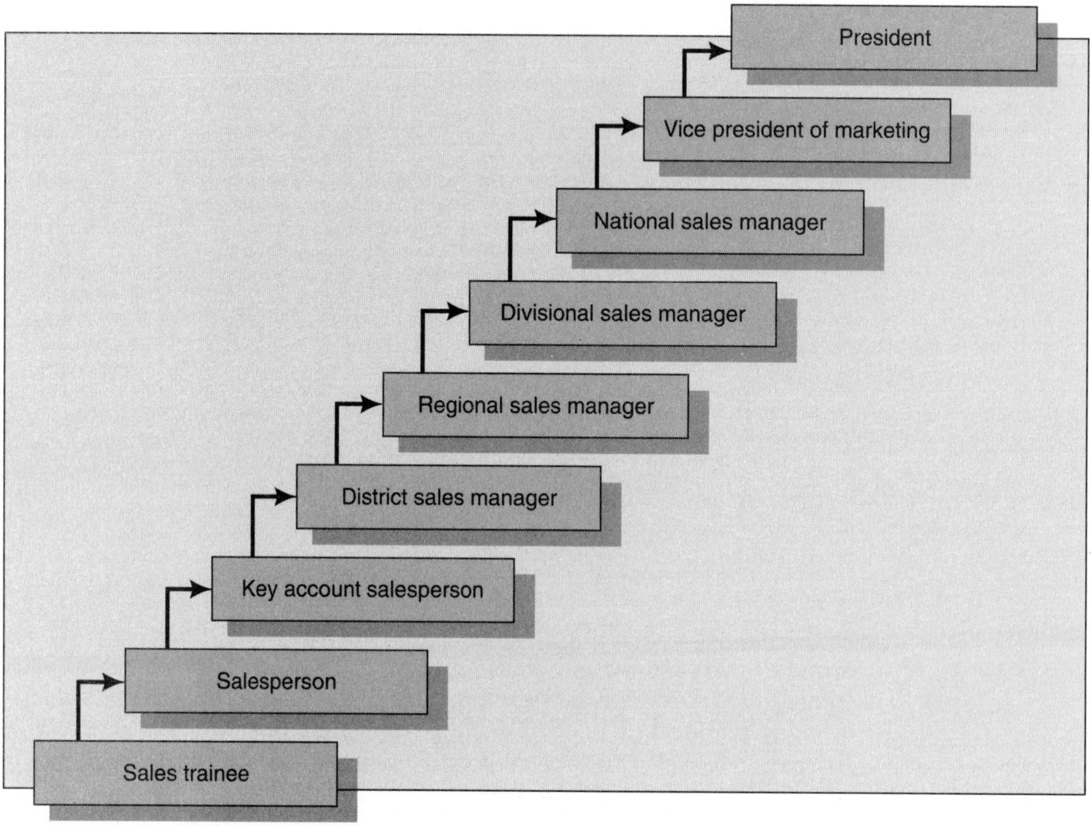

President
Vice president of marketing
National sales manager
Divisional sales manager
Regional sales manager
District sales manager
Key account salesperson
Salesperson
Sales trainee

path like the one in Exhibit 2.10, not all sales recruits are successful. Some are fired, others quit and seek different careers, and some simply languish on the lower rungs of the sales hierarchy. Not everyone has the characteristics and abilities necessary for success in selling. Determining what these personal characteristics and abilities are is difficult because different types of sales jobs require different personal skills and attributes. We will examine this issue in detail in Chapter 11 when we discuss the criteria for selecting sales recruits with the potential to be successful salespeople.

 **S UMMARY**

Many people can be involved in an organizational buying decision, and their roles are those of initiator, user, influencer, gatekeeper, buyer, and decider. The stages in the buying process can include the following:

1. Anticipation or recognition of a problem or need.
2. Determination and description of the characteristics and quantity of the needed item.
3. Search for and qualification of potential buyers.
4. Acquisition of proposals or bids.
5. Evaluation of offerings and selection of suppliers.
6. Selection of an order routine.
7. Performance evaluation and feedback.

The exact structure and time spent at each stage in the process depend on what is being bought and the firm's experience with it.

Effective sales management requires recognition of the various roles and how they operate at different stages of the buying process. These considerations help the sales manager determine the mix of activities in which salespeople should engage. Those activities can be diverse, involving such things as developing distribution channels, servicing the company's products, collecting and communicating market information to management, and servicing customers as well as selling and order taking. The company's view of the purchasing process and the roles played by the members of a prospect's buying center affect the account management policies it adopts. Many firms have explicit policies on what salespeople are to do at each stage in the buying process.

The broadest distinction among sales jobs is between retail selling and industrial selling. Retail selling is concerned with the sale of goods and services to ultimate consumers for their own personal use. Industrial selling involves the sale of goods and services to customers for the production of other goods and services. It includes sales to resellers, business users, and institutions. Some advantages associated with industrial selling as a career are (1) freedom of action and opportunities for personal initiative, (2) variety of challenging activities, (3) attractive opportunities for career development and advancement, (4) substantial financial rewards, and (5) working conditions that are often much better than those perceived by the general public.

APPENDIX

A

Alternative Selling Techniques

Many of the issues sales managers must deal with—including the development of account management policies, the choice of selection criteria for hiring new salespeople, and the design of effective training programs—require an understanding of alternative selling techniques and their advantages and limitations. There are probably as many variations in the way sales presentations are made as there are salespeople. But most selling techniques conform to one of four broad philosophical orientations toward dealing with customers: (1) the stimulus-response approach, (2) the mental-states approach, (3) the need-satisfaction approach, and (4) the problem-solution approach.[28]

Stimulus-response approach

The stimulus-response approach to selling is based on the notion that every sensory stimulus produces a response. Sales recruits thus learn what to say (the stimulus) and what buyers are likely to say in most circumstances (the response). In a well-planned stimulus-response model, most of the unfavorable buying responses are known. This allows the company the opportunity to train representatives to respond appropriately. If the prospect responds, "I can't afford to buy this product now," the sales representative has memorized not one but several responses to overcome this objection. One answer might be, "Well, we have an excellent financing program that you should be able to afford. Let me explain it to you." The emphasis in training is thus on the standardized sales presentation, the likely responses by customers, and the possible rejoinders to overcome their objections.

There are some advantages to this approach. A well-developed "canned" sales presentation ensures that the salesperson will give a smooth, complete talk that covers all the important selling points in a logical order. The stimulus-response approach also enables a firm to hire inexperienced salespeople and get them ready for the field with only minimal training.

The stimulus-response approach has some major disadvantages that limit its appropriateness for many types of personal selling. It ignores differences in the needs and interests of different customers. Since customers differ, they will not all respond in the same way to a canned sales talk. Also, when salespeople memorize their presentations, they cannot adjust them to the feedback provided by the customer, particularly when the customer's response is not one for which the representative has been trained. One story about such problems involves a pot-and-pan salesperson who insisted on going through the entire memorized presentation even though the couple had already decided to buy the product.

Salespeople can be allowed some freedom to adjust their canned presentation to the specific demands of a given selling situation. One way is to provide the salesperson with a standardized presentation printed on flip charts or slides but then instruct the individual to add comments where necessary. The results of a survey of sales executives—in Exhibit A—reveal that such "semiautomated" presentations are thought to be more effective than a completely memorized sales pitch.[29]

Due to its rigidity, the stimulus-response approach is seldom employed in

E X H I B I T   A   *Sales Executive Rankings of Sales Presentation Effectiveness*

Objective	Fully Automated	Semiautomated	Memorized	Organized	Unstructured
Conserves the prospect's time	3	2	5	1	4
Tells the complete story	2	3	4	1	5
Delivers an accurate, authoritative, and ethical message	1	2	4	3	5
Persuades the prospect	4	3	5	1	2
Anticipates objections	3	2	5	1	4
Facilitates training of salespeople	3	2	5	1	4
Increases salesperson's self-confidence	4	2	5	1	3
Facilitates supervision of salespeople	3	2	4	1	5

Notes:

Fully automated: Sound movies, slides, or filmstrips dominate the presentation. The salesperson's participation consists of setting up the projector, answering simple questions, and writing up the order. Many audiovisuals are available.

Semiautomated: The salesperson reads the presentation from copy printed on flip charts, readoff binders, promotional broadsides, or brochures. The salesperson adds comments when necesary.

Memorized: The salesperson delivers a company-prepared message that he has memorized. Supplementary visual aids may or may not be used.

Organized: The salesperson is allowed complete flexibility in wording; however, she does follow a company pattern, checklist, or outline. Visual aids are optional.

Unstructured: The salesperson is on his own to describe the product any way he sees fit. Generally, the presentation varies from prospect to prospect.

Source: From Marvin A. Jolson, "Should the Sales Presentation Be 'Fresh' or 'Canned'?" *Business Horizons,* October 1973, p. 85.

the sale of complex industrial goods where buyers' needs and product applications are likely to vary from one customer to the next. Its primary application today is when a relatively simple, standardized product is being sold to large numbers of potential customers who are likely to respond favorably to a standardized appeal, as in selling encyclopedias and other consumer goods door to door.

The survey results in Exhibit A suggest, however, that sales presentations are much more effective when management provides salespeople with guidelines to help organize their approach than when presentations are entirely unstructured. The mental-states approach is one means for providing such organization.

Mental-states approach

This sales approach is based on the idea that a buyer's mind passes through several successive stages before deciding to make a purchase. It is based on the AIDA theory of persuasion, which stresses that promotional messages must attract the prospect's attention, gain interest, create desire, and stimulate action to complete a sale successfully.

Firms that use the mental-states approach emphasize the use of a selling "formula" in designing a presentation that organizes selling points to coincide with the buyer's movement through the stages of attention, interest, desire, and action. One major advantage of this approach over a strictly memorized presentation is that the salesperson can tailor the sales pitch to each individual prospect. Most companies that use the mental-states approach have found that salespeople can be trained to control the direction of a sales interview by carefully observing the responses of the prospect. They then modify the presentation to stress those points most relevant to the prospect's current state of mind.

This type of selling strategy is used most commonly by firms with products or services that are complicated and difficult for prospective customers to understand. It is particularly appropriate when repeat calls on a long-run basis are likely to be required to close a sale. Consequently, this kind of selling approach is more common in industrial markets than in retail or consumer goods markets.[30]

As with the stimulus-response approach, one disadvantage of a selling formula aimed at moving a prospect through successive mental states is that it is a salesperson-oriented rather than a customer-oriented method. In an effort to move the prospect from one mental state to the next, the salesperson tends to dominate the interview, and the customer may have little chance to participate. Little attention is paid to variations in needs or circumstances among customers. Companies that use this approach tend to emphasize the sales presentation itself at the expense of those steps in the selling process that precede and follow the presentation.

Perhaps the most serious difficulty with the mental-states approach, however, is that there is no general agreement among psychologists that mental states exist in the minds of potential buyers or that all buyers proceed through the same states in the same sequence. Even if such states do exist, however, it can be difficult to train the salespeople to figure out which state a prospect is in at the moment. It is also hard to know when to leave the selling points related to one mental state and move on to the next.

Need-satisfaction approach

Compared with the previous two selling strategies, the need-satisfaction approach is much more compatible with the modern marketing philosophy that emphasizes the customers to be served rather than the product to be sold. Under this approach, the customer's needs are the starting point in making a sale. The salesperson's task is to identify the prospect's needs, make the prospect aware of that need, and then convince the prospect that the rep's product or service will satisfy that need better than any other alternative.

Firms that utilize this approach emphasize the importance of the early stages in the selling process, such as opening the relationship and qualifying the prospect. The salesperson must become familiar with the prospect's business, industry, and even customers and competitors to tailor a sales presentation to the prospect's unique needs and concerns.

One major advantage of the need-satisfaction approach is that it is customer-oriented and flexible. Proponents contend it provides the basis for a friendly buyer-seller relationship with two-way communication. Because the salesperson concentrates on discovering each prospect's needs and developing presentations that demonstrate how the product can satisfy those needs, this approach helps to minimize sales resistance. Over time, salespeople may become a trusted source of information, and their advice and counsel may be sought and accepted by the customer.

The advantages of the need-satisfaction approach outweigh the disadvantages in most selling situations. But the approach does have some practical limitations. It demands highly qualified sales personnel who have an excellent understanding of their potential customers. They must have the training and experience to adjust their selling methods to the needs and concerns of each individual prospect.[31]

Also, this approach requires a lot of time for the salesperson to become familiar with the prospect. Consequently, it is an expensive method, and it should be used only when the value of the potential sale justifies the expense. Finally, firms are likely to adopt this philosophy only when their overall business philosophy is customer-oriented rather than product-oriented. Thus, the need-satisfaction approach is more common in the sale of consumer durables than in the sale of industrial goods. This is gradually changing, however, as more industrial goods producers embrace a customer-oriented philosophy of marketing.

Problem-solution approach

The problem-solution theory of selling is a logical extension of the need-satisfaction approach. Both are customer-oriented approaches where the sales rep focuses on the prospect's individual needs. Under the problem-solution method, however, the salesperson goes one step further to help the prospect identify several alternative solutions, analyze their advantages and disadvantages, and select the best solution. The salesperson deemphasizes the product offering and concentrates on providing expert advice to the prospect much like a true business consultant. The problem-solving approach may lead a sales representative to suggest that a prospect buy a competitor's product, for example. The primary objective is to form long-term relationships with customers in which the sales rep is seen as a trusted source of technical information and advice.

As with the need-satisfaction approach, the problem-solution method requires extremely competent, well-trained, and experienced sales representatives. It also requires that the salesperson spend a great deal of time with each prospect. Consequently, it is a very expensive selling method.[32] In view of these limitations, this approach is seldom used in consumer goods markets. It is used primarily in selling technically complex and expensive industrial goods, such as computer systems and production machinery.

Discussion Questions

1. The organizational buying center varies as a function of size of company and product or service being purchased. How does size of the company influence the composition of the buying center? How would the composition of the buying center differ for each of the following products?

   a. Purchasing a new computer.
   b. Purchasing a new copying machine.
   c. Selecting a different public accounting firm.
   d. Selecting a new textbook for an industrial marketing course.
   e. Choosing a different source for industrial oils and lubricants.
   f. Purchasing a new cardiology machine.
   g. Choosing a marketing research firm.

2. The Kimberly Clark Corporation of Neenah, Wisconsin, requires newly hired product managers to spend six months in the field working as sales representatives before returning to Neenah for assignment to a product line. An occasional objection is "I didn't go to college for four years and then go on for an MBA to end up selling." Why would a company require six months of field selling experience as part of its training program? How would you handle the objection?

3. How do you account for the finding that, despite the negative image of a sales career, most salespeople like their jobs?

4. Sales transactions, especially those made to industrial customers, have been known to last as long as several years. In one situation, a sales rep called on one customer for eight years just to get on the approved supplier lsit. Two years later, the sales rep received the first order. What implications does this situation have on compensation, motivation, and maintaining morale?

5. In 1975, the Allied Bridge Construction Company of New York purchased its first mainframe computer. Ten years later, Allied replaced its original computer with a new system. Would this purchase be classified as a straight rebuy, modified rebuy, or new task purchase situation? How can you explain that two companies buying the same computer would treat the process differently?

6. Just-in-time purchasing procedures have been widely adopted by most major firms. An example comes from Permatech, a subsidiary of ALCOA. ALCOA, using a special product produced by Permatech, ships molten aluminum to Briggs & Stratton to be poured immediately into engine molds. What are the implications of just-in-time purchasing procedures on selling and sales management activities?

7. A report by McGraw-Hill's Laboratory of Advertising Performance notes that fewer than 10 percent of the people who make buying decisions are reached by a salesperson during a typical two-month period. What are the implications of this finding for sales managers? For the marketing mix?

8. Laptop personal computers have been referred to as the answer to a sales rep's desire for more selling time. Others contend that management now wants more and more reports, so many that selling time has been reduced. What has been the impact of laptops on the activities of sales representatives?

9. Over the past 15 years, two major events have changed how purchasing agents view their jobs. Inflation has pushed purchasing costs upward, resulting in companies paying close attention to profits. In addition, the evolution and proliferation of computers have allowed companies to better understand manufacturing costs and determine which parts and components they should be making or buying. How have these changes affected the relationship between purchasing agents and the sales reps calling on them?

10. Many of the activities sales representatives are expected to perform—as described in the Moncrief study summarized in Exhibit 2.4—are not directly related to sales. As a result, reps are sometimes hesitant to devote much time to such activities. What can sales managers do to ensure that such activities are performed adequately?

11. When a firm, such as Pilot Air Freight, adopts the major account management approach for dealing with its largest customers, it typically assigns only one or a few customers to a national account manager or team. This involves substantial selling costs per account. How can such costs be justified? What is the rationale for the major account management approach? Under what conditions is it justified?

12. The purchasing agent was adamant in stating: "Under no circumstances are you to go over my head. I know this contract means a lot to you, but your contacts are to be with me, and no one else!" Should salespeople go over the heads of purchasing agents? How should this approach be handled?

Endnotes

[1] This case example is based on material found in Martin Everett, "This Is the Ultimate in Selling," *Sales & Marketing Management* (August 1989), pp. 28–38.

[2] For more comprehensive reviews of the literature concerning organizational buying behavior for goods and services, see Robert R. Reeder, Edward G. Brierty, and Betty H. Reeder, *Industrial Marketing: Analysis, Planning, and Control* (Englewood Cliffs, N.J.: Prentice Hall, 1987); Michael D. Hutt and Thomas W. Spech, *Industrial Marketing Management,* 2nd ed. (Chicago: Dryden Press, 1985); James R. Stock and Paul H. Zinszer, "The Industrial Purchase Decision for Professional Services," *Journal of Business Research,* February 1987, pp. 1–16; and Rowland Moriarity, *Industrial Buying Behavior* (Lexington, Mass.: D.C. Health, 1983).

[3] Thomas V. Bonoma, "Major Sales: Who Really Does the Buying?" *Harvard Business Review* (May–June 1982), pp. 111–19. Also see Susan Lynn, "Identifying Buying Influences for a Professional Service: Implications for Marketing Efforts," *Industrial Marketing Management,* May 1987, pp. 119–30.

[4] For a comprehensive review of buying center research, see Morry Ghingold and David T. Wilson, "Buying Center Structure: An Extended Framework for Research," in *A Strategic Approach to Business Marketing,* ed. Robert Spekman and David T. Wilson (Chicago: American Marketing Association, 1985), pp. 18–93.

[5] Joseph A. Bellizzi, "Organizational Size and Buying Influences," *Industrial Marketing Management* 10 (1981), pp. 17–21.

[6]Patrick J. Robinson, Charles W. Faris, and Yoram Wind, *Industrial Buying and Creative Marketing* (Boston: Allyn & Bacon, 1967). See also Gary L. Lilien and M. Anthony Wong," An Exploratory Investigation of the Structure of the Buying Center in the Metalworking Industry," *Journal of Marketing Research*, February 1984, pp. 1–11.

[7]Anita M. Kennedy, "The Complex Decision to Select a Suppler: A Case Study," *Industrial Marketing Management* 2 (1983), pp. 45–56. Also see Morry Ghingold, "Testing the 'Buygrid' Buying Process Model," *Journal of Purchasing and Materials Management*, Winter 1986, pp. 30–36; and Erin Anderson, Wujin Chu, and Barton Weitz, "Industrial Buying: An Empirical Exploration of the Buyclass Framework," *Journal of Marketing*, July 1987, pp. 71–86.

[8]Guy R. Banville and Ronald J. Dornoff, "Industrial Source Selection Behavior—An Industry Study," *Industrial Marketing Management* (June 1973). In addition, Donald R. Lehman and John O'Shaughnessy, "Differences in Attribute Importance for Different Industrial Products," *Journal of Marketing*, April 1974, pp. 36–42, studied 35 U.S. and British corporations and also found that the relative importance of different criteria used to make purchase decisions varied with the type of product being purchased. See also Christopher P. Puto, Wesley E. Patton III, and Ronald H. King, "Risk Handling Strategies in Industrial Vendor Selection Decisions," *Journal of Marketing*, Winter 1985, pp. 89–98; and I. Fredrick Trawick, John E. Swan, Gail W. McGee, and David R. Rink, "Influence of Buyer Ethics and Salesperson Behavior on Intention to Choose a Supplier," *Journal of the Academy of Marketing Science* 19 1991), pp. 17–23.

[9]E. J. Wilson, "A Case Study of Repeat Buying for a Commodity," *Industrial Marketing Management* (August 1984), pp. 195–200. See also Ronald P. LeBlanc, "Insights into Organizational Buying," *Journal of Business and Industrial Marketing*, Spring 1987, pp. 5–10.

[10]William C. Moncrief III, "Selling Activity and Sales Position Taxonomies for Industrial Salesforces," *Journal of Marketing Research* (23 August 1986), pp. 261–70. For an earlier study of activities involved in the sale of building materials, see Lawrence M. Lamont and William J. Lundstrom, "Defining Industrial Sales Behavior: A Factor Analytic Study," *1974 Combined Proceedings* (Chicago: American Marketing Association, 1974), pp. 493–98.

[11]William A. O'Connell and William Keenan, Jr., "The Shape of Things To Come," *Sales & Marketing Management* (January 1990), pp. 36–41.

[12]Thayer C. Taylor, "Reduction in Selling Time Underscores Computer Need," *Sales & Marketing Management* (October 7, 1985), pp. 59–60.

[13]William A. O'Connell and William Keenan, Jr., "The Shape of Things," p. 38.

[14]For a brief summary of some of these classification schemes, see Alan J. Dubinsky and P. J. O'Connor, "A Multidimensional Analysis of Preferences for Sales Positions," *Journal of Personal Selling and Sales Management*, November 1983, pp. 31–41.

[15]Derek A. Newton, *Sales Force Performance and Turnover* (Cambridge, Mass.: Marketing Science Institute, 1973), p. 3.

[16]For example, see Charles Futrell, *Fundamentals of Selling*, 4th ed. (Homewood, Ill.: Richard D. Irwin, Inc., 1993, chaps. 7–11.

[17]Benson P. Shapiro, *Sales Program Management: Formulation and Implementation* (New York: McGraw-Hill, 1977), p. 159.

[18]Ibid., p. 160.

[19]Milt Grassell, "What Purchasing Managers Like in a Salesperson . . . And What Drives Them Up the Wall," *Business Marketing*, June 1986, pp. 72–77. See also Edith Cohen, "The View from the Other Side," *Sales & Marketing Management* (June 1990), pp. 108–10.

[20]Milt Grassell, "What Purchasing Managers Like." Also see Barry Farber and Joyce Wycoff, "Customer Service: Evolution and Revolution," *Sales & Marketing Management* (May 1991), pp. 44–51.

[21]Gilbert A. Churchill, Jr., Neil M. Ford, and Orville C. Walker, Jr., "Organizational Climate and Job Satisfaction in the Salesforce," *Journal of Marketing Research*, November 1976, pp. 323–32; and Alan J. Dubinsky, "Perceptions of the Sales Job: How Students Compare With Industrial Salespeople," *Journal of the Academy of Marketing Science*, Fall 1981, pp. 352–67. These findings seem to be equally true for both male and female sales representatives. See John E. Swan, Charles M. Futrell, and John T. Todd, "Same Job—Different Views: Women and Men in Industrial Sales,"

Journal of Marketing, January 1978, pp. 92–98; Darrell D. Muehling and William A. Weeks, "Women's Perceptions of Personal Selling: Some Positive Results," *Journal of Personal Selling and Sales Management,* May 1988, pp. 11–20; and Bill Kelley, "Selling in a Man's World," *Sales & Marketing Management* (January 1991), pp. 29–35.

[22]For example, see Barton Weitz, Stephen Castleberry, and John Tanner, Jr., *Personal Selling: Transactions and Relationships* (Homewood, Ill.: Richard D. Irwin, Inc., 1992), chap. 1; and Charles Futrell, *Fundamentals of Selling,* 4th ed (Homewood, Ill.: Richard D. Irwin, 1993), chap. 1.

[23]Churchill et al., "Organizational Climate."

[24]"Rebirth of a Salesman: Willy Loman Goes Electronic," *Business Week,* February 27, 1984, p. 104. See also Thayer C. Taylor, "Meet the Sales Force of the Future," *Sales & Marketing Management* (March 10, 1986), pp. 59–60; and William A. O'Connell and William Keenan, Jr., "The Shape of Things."

[25]Neil M. Ford, Orville C. Walker, Jr., and Gilbert A. Churchill, Jr., "Differences in the Attractiveness of Alternative Rewards Among Industrial Salespeople: Additional Evidence," *Journal of Business Research,* April 1985, pp. 123–38.

[26]Al Urbanski, "Wells Fargo's Sales Force Tames the Wild West," *Sales & Marketing Management* (January 1987), pp. 38–42.

[27]"Marketing Newletter," *Sales & Marketing Management* (February 1987), p. 27.

[28]R. Gwinner, "Base Theories in the Formulation of Sales Strategy," *MSU Business Topics,* Autumn 1968, pp. 37–44. See also G. M. Grikscheit, H. C. Cash, and W. J. E. Crissy, *Handbook of Selling: Psychological, Managerial and Marketing Bases* (New York: John Wiley & Sons, 1981).

[29]Marvin A. Jolson, "Should the Sales Presentation Be 'Fresh' or 'Canned'?" *Business Horizons,* October 1973, pp. 80–86.

[30]Gwinner, "Base Theories," p. 40.

[31]For a more detailed discussion of some of the selection, training, and compensation implications of the kind of adaptive selling required by both the need-satisfaction and problem-solution approaches, see Barton A. Weitz, Harish Sujan, and Mita Sujan, "Knowledge, Motivation, and Adaptive Behavior: A Framework for Improving Selling Effectiveness," *Journal of Marketing* 50 (October 1986), pp. 174–91. See also David M. Szymanski, "Determinants of Selling Effectiveness: The Importance of Declarative Knowledge to the Personal Selling Concept," *Journal of Marketing* 52 (January 1988), pp. 64–77.

[32]Dan T. Dunn, Claude A. Thomas, and James L. Lubawski, "Pitfalls of Consultative Selling," *Business Horizons,* September–October 1981, pp. 59–65.

Suggested Readings

Aspects of the Organizational Buying Process

Anderson, Erin, Wujin Chu, and Barton Weitz. "Industrial Buying: An Empirical Exploration of the Buyclass Framework." *Journal of Marketing,* July 1987, pp. 71–86.

LeBlanc, Ronald P. "Insights into Organizational Buying." *Journal of Business and Industrial Marketing,* Spring 1987, pp. 5–10.

Stock, James R. and Paul H. Zinszer. "The Industrial Purchase Decision for Professional Services." *Journal of Business Research,* February 1987, pp. 1–16.

Trawick, I. Fredrick, John E. Swan, Gail W. McGee, and David R. Rink. "Influence of Buyer Ethics and Salesperson Behavior on Intention to Choose a Supplier." *Journal of the Academy of Marketing Science* 19 (1991), pp. 17–23.

Selling Activities and Types of Sales Jobs

Moncrief, William C., III. "Selling Activity and Sales Position Taxonomies for Industrial Salesforces." *Journal of Marketing Research,* August 1986, pp. 261–70.

O'Connell, William A., and William Keenan, Jr. "The Shape of Things to Come." *Sales & Marketing Management* (January 1990), pp. 36–41.

*Use of Computers and Other Attempts
to Improve Sales Efficiency*

O'Connell and Keenan.

Taylor, Thayer C. "From Selling Aid to Taskmaster." *Sales & Marketing Management* (May 1991), pp. 69–73.

Steps in the Selling Process

Futrell, Charles. Fundamentals of Selling, 4th ed. (Homewood, Ill.: Richard D. Irwin, Inc., 1993), chaps. 7–11.

Weitz, Barton, Stephen Castleberry, and John Tanner, Jr. *Personal Selling: Transactions and Relationships.* (Homewood, Ill.: Richard D. Irwin, Inc., 1992), chaps. 6–12.

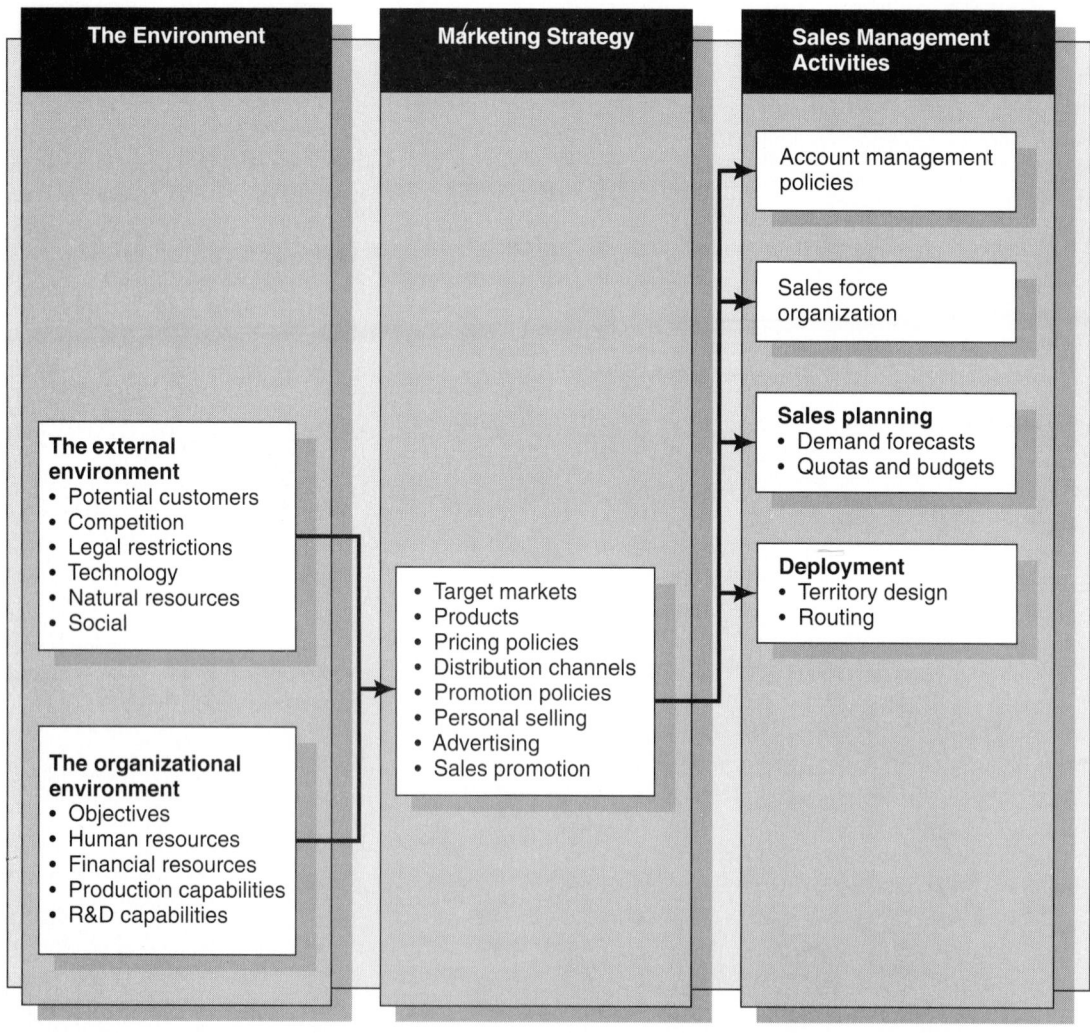

The Environment	Marketing Strategy	Sales Management Activities

The external environment
- Potential customers
- Competition
- Legal restrictions
- Technology
- Natural resources
- Social

The organizational environment
- Objectives
- Human resources
- Financial resources
- Production capabilities
- R&D capabilities

- Target markets
- Products
- Pricing policies
- Distribution channels
- Promotion policies
- Personal selling
- Advertising
- Sales promotion

Account management policies

Sales force organization

Sales planning
- Demand forecasts
- Quotas and budgets

Deployment
- Territory design
- Routing

Formulation of a Strategic Sales Program

Part 1 examines the decisions and activities involved in formulating a strategic sales program. Chapter 3 examines how factors in a firm's external and internal environments influence and constrain its marketing and sales strategies as well as salespeople's performance. Chapter 4 explores the strategic planning process, the role of personal selling in different types of business and marketing strategies, and the design of appropriate account management policies. Chapter 5 examines alternative ways of organizing the sales force. Chapter 6 discusses the conduct of a market opportunity analysis and forecasting methods—two key ingredients in the development of strategic marketing and sales plans. Chapters 7 and 8 examine deployment decisions, including the design of sales territories, the determination of how many people are needed to provide adequate market coverage, methods of allocating a salesperson's effort within a territory, and establishment of sales quotas.

Environmental Influences on Sales Programs and Performance

CAMPBELL SOUP STIRS UP ITS SALES FORCE[1]

John T. Dorrance, a research chemist, invented condensed soup in the late 1800s. The firm he created to manufacture the product—the Campbell Soup Company—quickly became one of the first of a new breed of national consumer package-goods manufacturers. Campbell and other such firms as Procter & Gamble, Quaker Oats, and H. J. Heinz increased their productivity by manufacturing standardized products with new mass production processes and machinery. But they needed a national customer base to exploit the resulting economies of scale.

To attract those customers, these firms devoted substantial portions of their revenues to sales and marketing activities, and they developed highly centralized national sales and marketing organizations. Campbell began advertising on New York City streetcars in 1899, and by 1911 its soup was being marketed across the country. By the 1950s, Campbell was advertising to half of all American households just by sponsoring "Lassie" on TV, and the firm's share of the soup market reached a high of almost 83 percent in 1954.

As Campbell grew, it expanded its product line beyond the familiar red-and-white label condensed soups. Through a combination of internal product development and acquisition, the company added new grocery lines, such as Pepperidge Farm cookies and crackers and V8 Vegetable Juice. The firm also expanded and diversified its sales force. By the early 1980s, Campbell had over 1,200 salespeople organized into four sales forces. As shown in the top half of Exhibit 3.1, each sales force was responsible for a different part of Campbell's product line (e.g., one handled canned foods, another dealt with frozen foods, etc.), and each was organized geographically across 38 sales districts.

Despite the company's expansion efforts, however, it earned a reputation as a rather stodgy marketer that made good returns but relatively little sales growth from soup and a few other products. While Campbell's sales grew 8 percent annually through the 1970s, the food industry's growth averaged 12 to 13 percent. Worse, Campbell's share of the crucial soup market fell to about 63 percent by 1980. Part of the problem was that while the firm clung to its "tried and true" mass marketing strategy, its external environment was changing dramatically.

Campbell's Changing Environment

The mass market that Campbell pursued so successfully during the first two thirds of the century began to fragment during the 1970s. Increasing numbers of working women, minorities, and single-parent households, the "aging" of America, and other demographic and lifestyle changes shattered the domestic market into many different segments, each with its own preferences and concerns.

At the same time, several other environmental changes increased the impact of this market fragmentation on national manufacturers like Campbell. The new demographic and lifestyle segments not only had unique tastes concerning the products they purchased, but they also preferred different types of entertainment and watched different media. This made it more difficult for national manufacturers to reach a large proportion of potential customers with a single national advertising campaign.

Changing technology also increased the impact of market fragmentation. Computerized sales data from supermarket scanners made it clear that con-

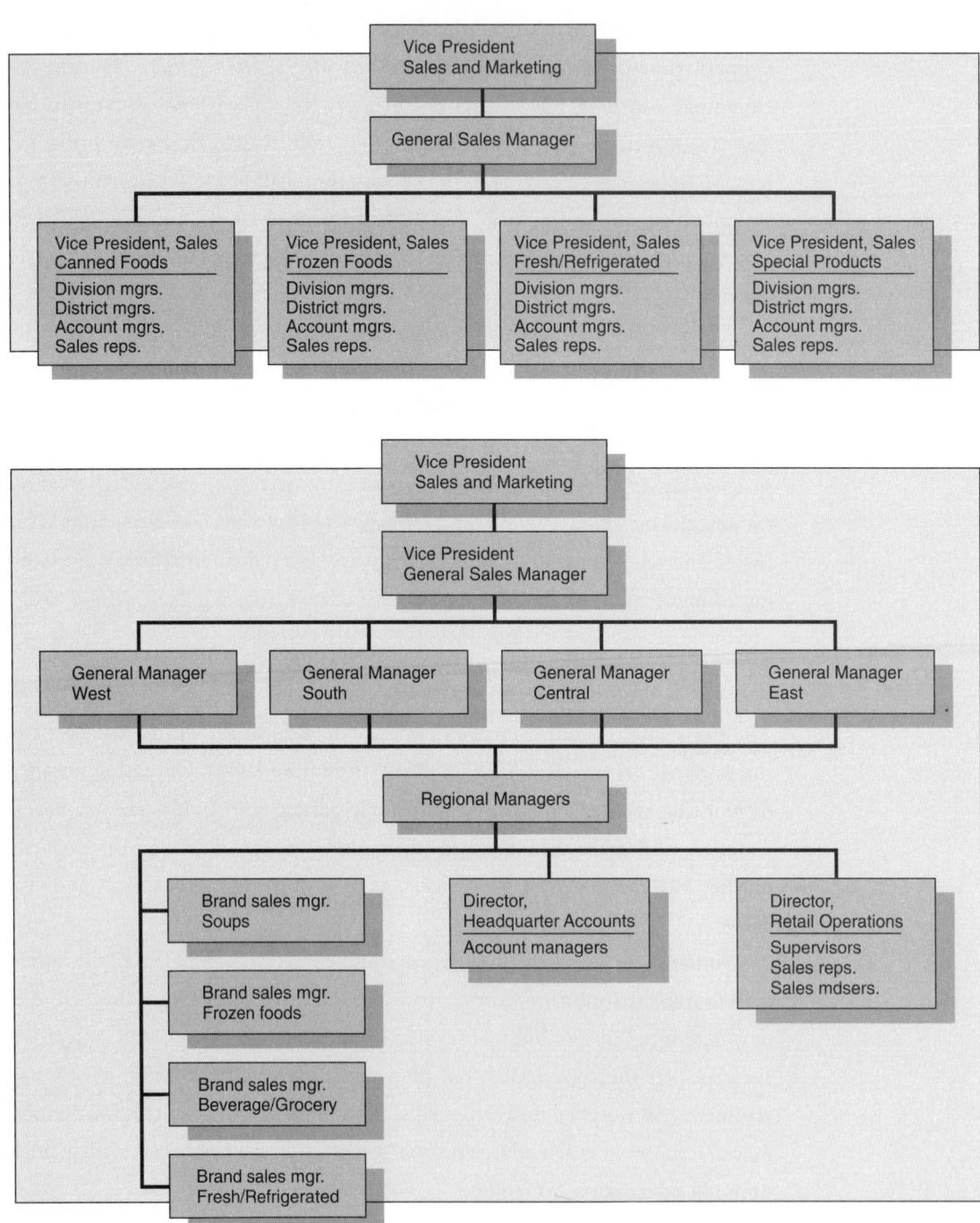

sumption differences across demographic groups and geographic regions were greater than many firms had realized. Retailers made very effective use of the new information technology, increasing their power in the distribution channel. Immediate access to scanner data, coupled with fast computer analysis, enabled retailers to know daily which brands were moving and which were not. The retailers used that knowledge to pressure manufacturers for increased local promotions or more attractive trade deals for their slower-moving brands.[2]

Campbell Changes Its Marketing Strategy

When R. Gordon McGovern took over as Campbell's chief executive in 1980, he moved quickly to adapt the firm's business and marketing strategies to its changing environment to improve volume growth. First, he divided the company's four large divisions (canned foods, frozen foods, fresh foods, and specialty products) into 50 strategic business units (SBUs), each with an average annual sales volume of about $50 million. Each SBU's general manager was given bottom line responsibility and was encouraged to aggressively seek opportunities for new product and market development.

McGovern's admonition to seek faster growth through new product development served as the cornerstone for new marketing strategies in most of Campbell's SBUs. To appeal to newly emerging demographic, lifestyle, and regional consumer segments, the company introduced a variety of line extensions (e.g., a red bean soup for Hispanic markets, a creole soup for the South, etc.) and new products (e.g., Prego spaghetti sauce, Le Menu frozen dinners, etc.). All told, the company introduced more than 400 new products and line extensions from 1981 through 1985 and 214 more from 1985 through 1989. To support those products, the firm more than doubled its sales and marketing expenditures during the same period. And the firm began to focus more of those expenditures on distinct regional and demographic segments by using more local media and by designing different consumer and trade promotion programs for different regions.

Campbell's New Marketing Strategy Leads to a Change in the Sales Force

Although Campbell's new marketing strategy made sense in light of the environmental changes, it was difficult for the firm to implement that strategy effectively within the confines of its old organizational structure and management processes. For one thing, the marketing managers at company headquarters were not always aware of the differences in consumer tastes, media availability, or competitive pressures across geographic regions or demographic segments.

While the sales managers of the various districts could propose product modifications or promotional campaigns uniquely suited to the conditions in their regions, those suggestions had to be reviewed, approved, and implemented by headquarters managers. Since the firm's marketing staff was already stretched thin by the rapid introduction of new products and line extensions, the firm was slow to react to some attractive regional opportunities.

Campbell's sales force was also stretched to the limit by the rapid expansion of the company's product line. Worse, it had increasing difficulty winning shelf space and promotional support for the company's many new products from the powerful retail chains. Since separate sales forces represented different parts of the firm's line, as many as four or five Campbell salespeople would call on the same retailer, each with his or her own unique and uncoordinated requests.

To better implement its new marketing strategy and react more effectively to the changes occurring in its environment, Campbell undertook a major restructuring of its sales organization and procedures in 1986. It combined its four separate sales forces into a single unit organized by customer type and geography. Because each member of the new sales force represents all of Campbell's products, a given retail store is now called on by only one salesperson. As the lower half of Exhibit 3.1 indicates, some of Campbell's salespeople now call only on the headquarters of major retail chains. They report to a director of headquarters accounts in each region. Others call on smaller independent stores; and they, along with sales merchandisers who stock shelves and arrange in-store displays, report to regional directors of retail operations. The company has also consolidated its 38 sales districts into 22 regions, which are overseen by four general managers.

In addition, each region is assigned four "brand sales managers." These people continue to specialize in different Campbell product lines. They serve as a direct link between headquarters product managers and the field sales force. These brand sales managers work with regional managers and salespeople to develop local advertising, sales promotion, and trade programs tailored to the customers and competitive conditions in a specific region. Each regional sales team is now given its own advertising and promotion budget—usually amounting to about 10 to 15 percent of the total advertising and promotion dollars to be spent in its region—and has the authority to decide how that money is used, so long as the spending conforms to brand and corporate objectives.

Results of the New Strategy—Hearty Sales Growth but Thin Profits

As planned, Campbell's new strategy produced robust volume increases. The firm's sales revenues more than doubled from $2.5 billion in 1980 to $5.7 billion in 1989. Unfortunately, the firm's financial performance was not as good. Its earnings-growth rate, return on shareholders' equity, and return on invested capital were all below the food industry's averages for most of the 1980s.

Part of the problem was simply that Campbell encountered unanticipated problems in implementing its new marketing strategy and sales program. For instance, because the firm viewed its new sales organization and regional marketing program as a radical departure from the past, it decided to make the change quickly and all at once. But a lack of past experience and the decision to forgo formal training programs meant many of the salespeople had no clues about how to perform their new responsibilities, and many mistakes were made. As one of the new brand sales managers said,

> We had local TV, radio, and magazine salespeople banging on our doors because they had read that we had marketing money and they all wanted a piece of it. That first year, luckily the amount of money we had wasn't enough to get into trouble with. Some people did things that, if they were getting paid to be in the marketing department, they wouldn't have kept their jobs very long.

Such problems, together with other shortcomings in Campbell's operations and control systems, continuing changes in its market and competitive environment, and the fact that its strategy focused more on growth from new products than on the profitability of established products, all contributed to the firm's lackluster financial results.

But stay tuned. We will examine Campbell's problems, and some adjustments the firm's managers have made in their strategies, policies, and programs, in more detail at the beginning of Chapter 4.

Relationships among Environmental Factors, Marketing Strategy, and the Sales Program

Campbell's experiences illustrate three important points about how factors in the environment influence marketing and sales management decisions and programs.

1. To be successful, a firm's marketing plans must be adapted to the influences and constraints imposed by both the external and internal corporate environments. As those environments change, appropriate adjustments must be made in the firm's marketing strategy.

In Campbell's case, changes in the external environment during the 1970s clearly dictated a change in the firm's marketing strategy. Fragmenting markets, the increasing costs and declining effectiveness of national media, and the growing power of major retail chains all helped make the firm's national mass market strategy obsolete. So the firm changed to a regional strategy emphasizing the development of new products aimed at more narrowly defined user segments, the use of local media and promotions targeted at those segments, and a consolidated sales force with more authority to negotiate with individual retailers.

But factors in Campbell's internal environment, such as the inexperience of the new brand sales managers, hindered the firm's ability to implement its new strategy effectively. As we shall see in the next chapter, Campbell has had to adjust both its strategy and its internal policies and programs to make them more consistent with one another and thereby improve its overall performance.

2. A firm's sales program is only one part of an integrated marketing strategy. As changes are made in other parts of the marketing strategy, the sales program must be adjusted if it is to remain effective.

Campbell found it difficult to implement its new marketing strategy within the confines of its old sales force organization and procedures. Consequently, the company consolidated the sales force, and headquarters account specialists were developed to help the firm negotiate more effectively with the powerful retail chains in different parts of the country. Account management policies were also changed to give the district salespeople more autonomy to design trade promotions tailored to the desires and demands of individual retail chains. Finally, brand sales managers were added and advertising and promotion budgets were allocated to each district to help the field salespeople take a more active role in developing marketing programs tailored to local customer preferences and interests.

3. Regardless of how well conceived a sales program is or how well it is integrated into a firm's overall marketing strategy, its implementation depends on the willingness and ability of individual members of the sales force to carry out its policies and procedures. Factors in the external and corporate environments can directly influence a salesperson's actions in the field and the rep's ability to achieve the desired level of performance.

Because Campbell decided to institute its new sales organization and policies quickly without retraining its salespeople, it took longer than anticipated to effectively implement its new marketing and sales strategies. Many of the firm's salespeople were uncertain about what roles they were expected to play and about how those roles could best be carried out.

To make matters worse, the competitive pressures they face have continued to intensify, partly as the result of the ongoing trend toward consolidation of the food industry through mergers and acquisitions. For example, Pet Inc.'s acquisition of Progresso gave it the marketing resources it needed to pose a major challenge to Campbell in the soup business. These and other influences and constraints in both the internal and external environment made it difficult for some of Campbell's salespeople to achieve desired levels of sales performance and profitability.

Each of the above relationships may seem self-evident, but all must be carefully considered when planning a firm's marketing strategy and sales program. The next two chapters examine the planning process in more detail. The remainder of this chapter explores factors in both the external and internal corporate environments that influence development of effective marketing strategies and sales plans. We also discuss how environmental factors can constrain the ability of individual salespeople to implement a sales program effectively. In Chapter 4, we examine the planning process for developing a marketing strategy, the role of the sales force within different strategies, and the design of account management policies that are appropriate for implementing a firm's strategy.

A HIERARCHY OF STRATEGIES

A sales program constitutes only one part of a marketing plan, and the marketing plan is only one element of the total strategic planning process in most firms. This is particularly true for companies with multiple divisions and those that have divided their operations into strategic business units to improve planning and the allocation of company resources across related groups of products or markets. Since such firms involve multiple "businesses," their overall strategic planning process typically occurs in several stages and involves a series of different plans to guide activities at different levels of the organization. This hierarchy of strategic plans—as diagrammed in Exhibit 3.2—commonly includes the corporate strategic plan, the strategic business unit plan, marketing plans, and programs for individual marketing functions.

E X H I B I T   3 • 2   *A Hierarchy of Strategic Plans*

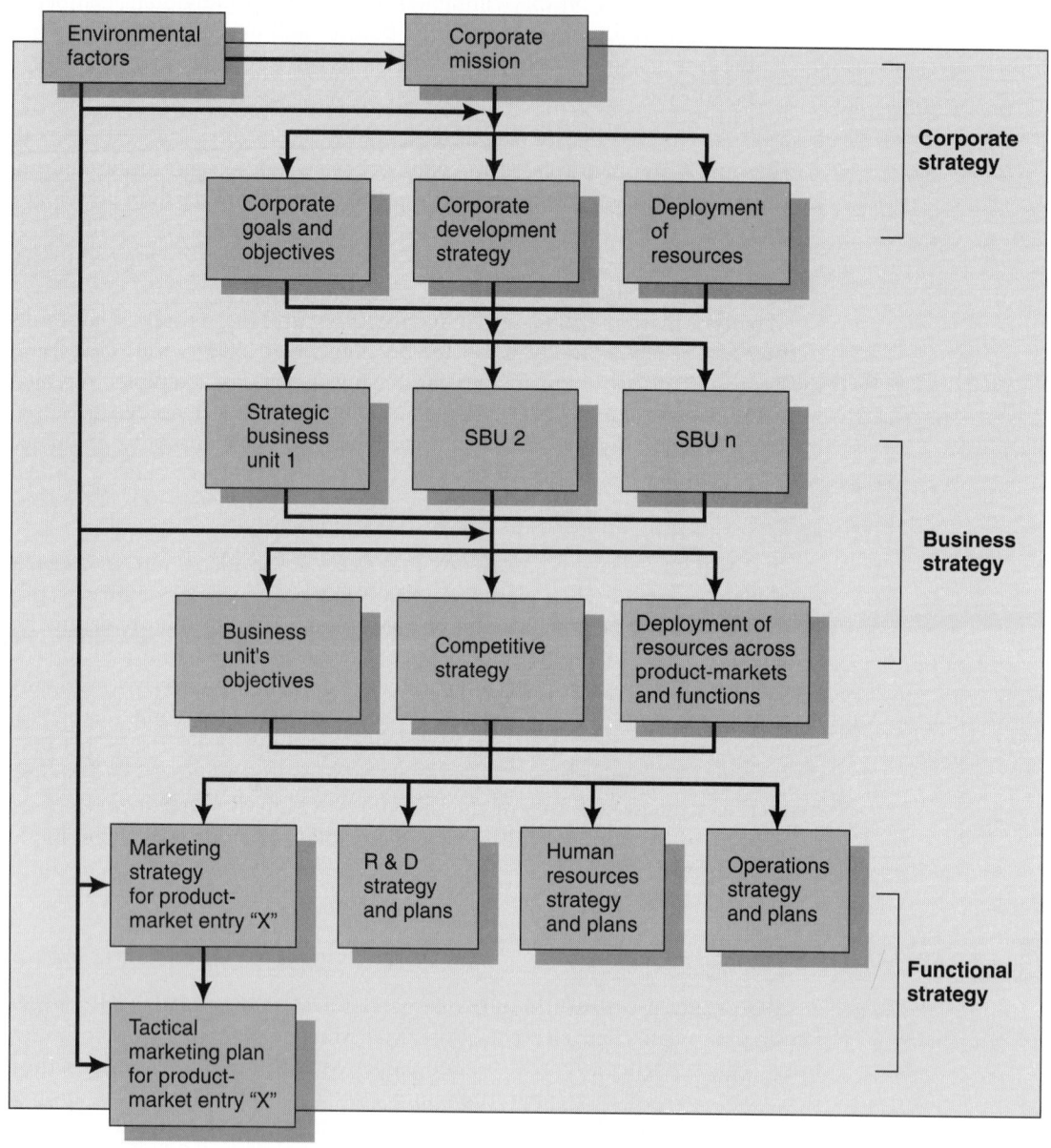

Source: Adapted from Orville C. Walker, Jr., Harper W. Boyd, Jr., and Jean-Claude Larréché, *Marketing Strategy: Planning and Implementation* (Homewood, Ill.: Richard D. Irwin, 1992), p. 11.

The Corporate Strategic Plan

This plan specifies the range of activities to be included in the firm's mission, spells out corporate objectives—such as targets for revenue growth and return on investment—and establishes broad strategies for new business development, acquisitions, and divestitures. Financial analyses and projections are also an important part of the corporate strategic plan because they typically spell out how corporate resources are to be allocated across the firm's various divisions or business units.

Strategic Business Unit Plans

Included here are the specific objectives of the SBU and how the unit plans to compete in its business, or the way it plans to achieve a sustainable competitive advantage. For example, an SBU might plan to be the technology leader in its industry and compete by being the first to introduce new products, or it might try to maintain a low cost position and compete on the basis of low price. The SBU plan should also coordinate the various functional plans—usually including finance, operations, and marketing plans—that spell out how the unit will implement its competitive strategy and achieve its objectives.

Marketing Plans

These plans outline specific marketing objectives for each product or product line, analyze marketing opportunities, identify target markets, and integrate the various elements of the marketing mix into a consistent marketing strategy.

Programs for Individual Marketing Functions

These include the strategies, policies, and activities to be followed by each functional area in implementing a marketing plan. This is where a strategic sales program, such as Campbell's program of using headquarter's account specialists to help the firm negotiate with the more powerful retail chains, fits into a firm's overall strategic planning process.

How firms assign responsibilities for developing these plans varies considerably according to company size, the complexity of its formal planning procedures, and management's preferences. While the specifics of the total corporate planning process are beyond the scope of this book,[3] we will explore formulating marketing and sales strategies in the next chapter.

It is important to remember, however, that marketing plans and sales programs are only component parts of a larger whole. Strategies developed at the corporate and business unit levels are an important part of the internal organizational environment that influences the content of marketing and sales programs. As Exhibit 3.2 indicates, those higher-level strategies help define the mission and objectives to be accomplished and determine the amount and kinds of resources allocated to the marketing of individual products.

IMPACT OF THE ENVIRONMENT ON MARKETING AND SALES PLANNING

Exhibit 3.2 also shows that environmental factors affect every level of strategy. Thus, marketing or sales managers must carefully consider the influences and constraints imposed by environmental factors beyond their control when developing strategic plans for a product or service. Internal and external environmental factors influence marketing strategies and programs in four basic ways.

1. Environmental forces can constrain the organization's ability to pursue certain marketing strategies or activities. An example is when the government declares the sale of a product to be illegal or when a well-entrenched competitor makes it unattractive for the firm to enter a new market.

2. Environmental variables, and changes in those variables over time, help determine the ultimate success or failure of marketing strategies. The rapid growth in the number of women in the labor force in recent years, for instance, helped ensure the success of Campbell's new Le Menu line of convenient frozen entrées.

3. Changes in the environment can create new marketing opportunities for an organization, as when a new technology allows development of new products. For instance, the proliferation of microwave ovens in American kitchens created opportunities for Campbell to develop and market many new convenience-oriented products, like Le Menu frozen entrées and microwave soups.

4. Environmental variables are affected and changed by marketing activities, as when new products and promotional programs help to change lifestyles and social values. In view of the increased activity by consumer groups, environmentalists, and other public-interest groups and agencies, marketers today must consider how proposed programs will affect the environment as well as how the environment will affect the programs.

Consequently, one of the most important—but increasingly difficult—parts of a marketing manager's job is to monitor the environment, predict how it might change, and develop marketing strategies and plans suited to environmental conditions. Because it is one part of the overall marketing plan, the strategic sales program must be adapted to the environmental circumstances faced by the firm as a whole. Specific environmental factors to be considered when developing marketing plans in general, and strategic sales programs in particular, are examined below.

THE EXTERNAL ENVIRONMENT

Factors in the external environment are beyond the control of the individual manager; however, companies do try to influence external conditions through

EXHIBIT 3 • 3 *Components of the External Environment*

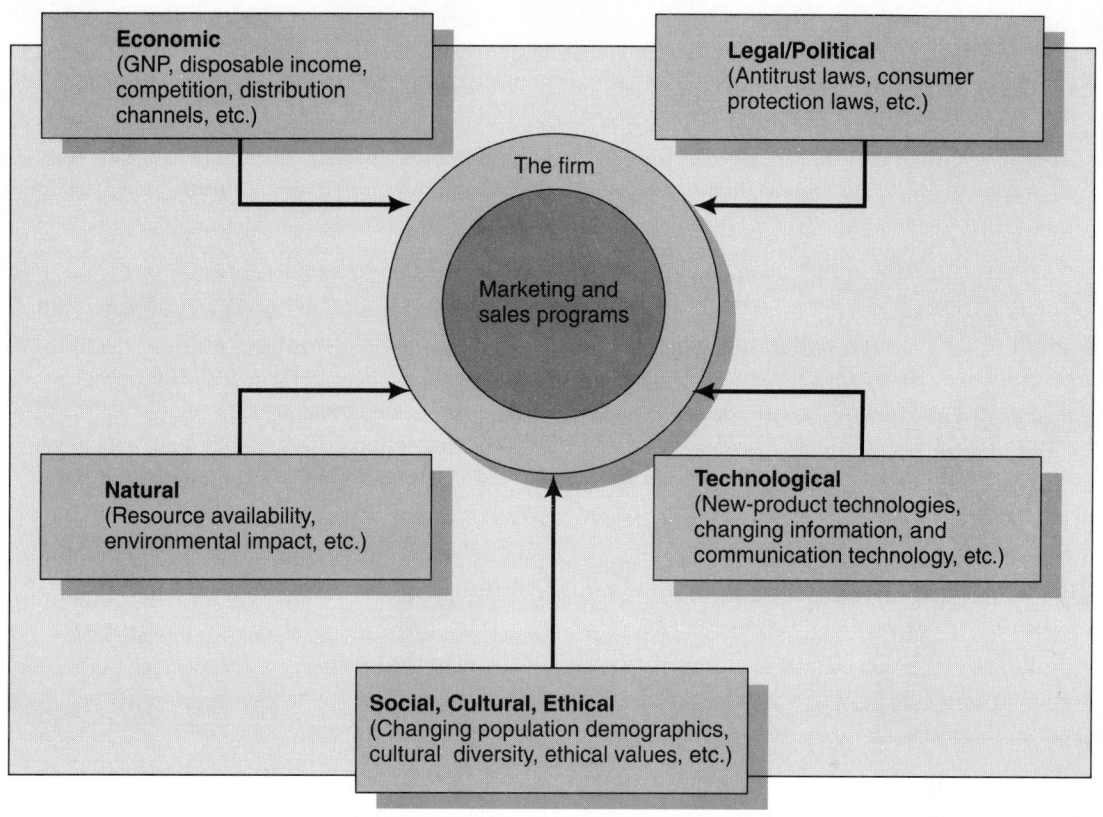

political lobbying, public relations campaigns, and the like. But for the most part, the marketing or sales manager must take the environment as it exists and adapt strategies to fit it. As indicated in Exhibit 3.3, variables in the external environment that affect marketing and sales programs can be grouped into five broad categories: (1) economic, (2) social/cultural/ethical, (3) legal/political, (4) natural, and (5) technical.

The Economic Environment   People and organizations cannot buy goods and services unless they have the money. The total potential demand for a product within a given country depends on that country's economic conditions—the amount of growth, the unemployment rate, and the level of inflation. These factors must be considered when analyzing market opportunities and developing sales forecasts. Keep in mind, though, that different categories of goods and services are affected dif-

Thorny Issues in Sales Management 3 • 1

THE INCREASED POWER OF RETAILERS IN DISTRIBUTING CONSUMER GOODS

The growth of large corporate retail chains such as Wal-Mart Stores and Safeway; voluntary and cooperative chains (e.g., those administered by a wholesaler or a confederation of independent retailers) such as Super-Valu, IGA, and Our Own Hardware; and the improved information that scanners and computers provide about the volume and profitability of specific brands have all helped increase the power of retailers in the distribution channels for many consumer packaged goods.

To maintain retailer cooperation and support, manufacturers have had to reallocate more of their promotion dollars to trade promotion (for example, one-time "slotting fees" to gain shelf space for new products and frequent price discounts on established brands). This practice has caused many manufacturers to reduce their expenditures on such items as brand advertising and product improvements. As a result, many producers worry they may be weakening the equity of their brands in the minds of consumers and damaging their long-term competitive positions.

Larger manufacturers are attempting to offset the new power of the retailers and reestablish some control over their distribution channels in a variety of ways. Some firms, such as Campbell Soup, are regionalizing their market research and sales analysis efforts to provide their sales and marketing people with more timely and detailed information about how various brands are perform-

ing in different geographic areas. Campbell makes this information available through hand-held computers carried by each of its salespeople to reduce their informational disadvantage relative to the retailers they call on. This new information can also be used to tailor product variations and consumer promotions to local markets, thereby improving a brand's sales and making it more attractive to local retailers.

Some manufacturers have also consolidated their sales force across the SBUs or divisions to better coordinate trade promotion efforts for their various brands and to present a more united front to major retailers. This tactic can help a firm use its stronger brands to gain better support for its new or weaker products. When Nabisco introduced its new Almost Home cookies, for instance, its integrated sales force was authorized to offer a 10 percent discount on any other cookie or cracker promoted by the company through the end of the year to any retailer that agreed to give Almost Home the requested four feet of shelf space.

Unfortunately, many of these actions are viable only for large, multibrand manufacturers. The environmental changes that have increased retailers' economic power are likely to make the attainment of strong retail support a more difficult and costly task for smaller consumer goods manufacturers for many years into the future.

Source: Reprinted with permission from Thayer C. Taylor, "The Great Scanner Face-Off," *Sales & Marketing Management*, September 1986, pp. 43–46. © 1986 by Bill Communications, Inc.

ferently by economic conditions. For example, the recession in the United States at the beginning of the 1990s reduced demand for some of Campbell's higher priced products, like Pepperidge Farm cookies. But it stimulated demand for some of the company's more basic and economical foods, such as soup.

Another critical economic variable is the amount of competition in the firm's industry—both the number of competing firms and their relative strengths in the marketplace. Ideally, a company's marketing and sales programs should be designed to gain a differential advantage over competitors. For example, rather than trying to compete with the low prices of foreign competitors— such as Komatsu—Caterpillar has been successful in the heavy construction equipment business by providing superior product quality and excellent service, while charging prices as much as 10 to 20 percent higher than its competitors.

A third aspect of the economic environment is the existing distribution structure in an industry. This includes the number, types, and availability of wholesalers, retailers, and other intermediaries a firm might use to distribute its product. Much of a firm's personal selling effort may be directed at trying to persuade such intermediaries to stock and provide marketing support for the company's products. As we saw in the Campbell Soup example, however, this task has become more difficult in recent years, particularly in consumer package-goods industries. Retail chains have gained increased power in the distribution channels for such products. The reasons underlying this change, and some manufacturers' responses to it, are discussed in Thorny Issues in Sales Management 3.1.

The Social, Cultural, and Ethical Environment

Markets consist of people. As the demographic, educational, and other characteristics of the population change, market opportunities change. This also affects opportunities in industrial markets, since an organization's demand for goods and services is derived from the demand for its own products.

The way potential customers think is an even more important determinant of whether a marketing strategy or sales program will succeed. Changes in social values and lifestyles influence what people buy and their reactions to various marketing activities and promotional appeals.

Ethical dilemmas

The values of a society also affect marketing and sales programs in a variety of ways. Social values set standards for ethical behavior. Ethics is more than simply a matter of complying with the laws and regulations we will discuss in the next section. A particular action may be legal but not ethical. For instance, when a salesperson makes extreme, unsubstantiated statements such as, "Our product runs rings around Brand X," the rep may be engaging in legal "puffery" to make a sale, but many salespeople (and their customers) view such "little white lies" as unethical.

Ethics is concerned with the development of moral standards by which actions and situations can be judged. It focuses on those actions that may result in actual or potential harm of some kind (e.g., economic, mental, physical) to an individual, group, or organization. Thus, ethics is more proactive than the law. Ethical standards attempt to anticipate and avoid social problems, whereas most laws and regulations emerge only after the negative consequences of an action become apparent.[4]

Two sets of ethical dilemmas are of particular concern to sales managers. The first set is embedded in the manager's dealings with the salespeople. Ethical issues involved in relationships between a sales manager and the sales force include such things as fairness and equal treatment of all social groups in hiring and promotion, respect for the individual in supervisory practices and training programs, and fairness and integrity in the design of sales territories, assignment of quotas, and determination of compensation and incentive rewards. Ethical issues pervade nearly all aspects of sales force management. Consequently, such problems are discussed throughout the text, often as "Thorny Issues" managers must wrestle with.

The second set of ethical issues arises from the interactions between salespeople and their customers. These issues only indirectly involve the sales manager because the manager cannot always directly observe or control the actions of every member of the sales force. But managers have a responsibility to establish standards of ethical behavior for their subordinates, communicate them clearly, and enforce them vigorously. Consequently, the remainder of this section focuses on the ethical issues salespeople face in their dealings with customers and on the actions managers can take to help salespeople resolve such issues appropriately.

The consequences of unethical selling practices

One might ask why a manager should be responsible for providing moral guidance to subordinates. One might even question whether setting and enforcing standards of ethical conduct for the sales force infringes on the freedom of its individual members and their right to make their own moral choices. While such questions may be legitimate topics for philosophical debate, there is a compelling and practical organizational reason for a firm to impose ethical standards to guide employees' dealings with customers. Unethical selling practices make buyers reluctant to deal with a supplier and are likely to result in the loss of sales and profits over time.

Exhibit 3.4 reports the findings of a recent survey of 135 purchasing managers from a variety of industries. The first column in the exhibit indicates how the respondents perceived the ethicality of a variety of selling behaviors. The second column shows the correlation between the perceived ethicality of a given selling behavior and the purchasing manager's intention to purchase from a supplier. In all but one instance, the more unethical a salesperson's behavior was perceived to be, the lower the buyer's intention to purchase from the firm employing that salesperson.[5]

The findings presented in Exhibit 3.4 and those from similar studies suggest that ethical behavior by salespeople can help develop norms of cooperation and trust between a firm and its customers and thereby improve customer loyalty and sales volume.[6] As firms strive to become more market-oriented and target improved customer satisfaction as a marketing objective, the promotion of high ethical standards among members of the sales force is likely to become an even more important component of marketing strategy.

Pressures leading to unethical behavior

Not all customers or competing suppliers adhere to the same ethical standards. As a result, salespeople sometimes feel pressure to engage in actions that are inconsistent with what they believe to be right—either in terms of personal values or formal company standards. Such pressures arise because the sales reps, or sometimes their managers, believe a questionable action is necessary to close a sale or maintain parity with competition. This point was illustrated by a survey of 59 top sales executives concerning commercial bribery—attempts to influence a potential customer by giving gifts or kickbacks. While nearly two thirds of the executives considered bribes unethical and did not want to pay them, 88 percent also felt that *not* paying bribes might put their firms at a competitive disadvantage.

Such attitudes help explain why the U.S. Chamber of Commerce estimates that, of the annual $40 billion in white-collar crime, $7 billion takes the form of bribes and kickbacks.[7] Uncertainty about what to do in such situations—often due to a lack of direction from management—may lead to job stress, poor sales performance, and unhappy customers.

The value of formal ethical policies

The results of a survey of 160 sales representatives from 30 companies illustrate the range of ethical questions faced by salespeople and indicate what managers might do to help their subordinates deal with such questions.[8] Respondents were presented with 12 selling situations and asked whether (1) they thought the situation posed an ethical question, (2) their company had an existing policy about how to deal with such situations, and (3) they would like a stated company policy concerning the issue. The percentage of respondents who answered "definitely yes" or "probably yes" to the three questions are shown in Exhibit 3.5.

The survey's results suggest that the more subjective the situation, the greater the proportion of salespeople who thought it posed an ethical problem. For example, the two cases where a majority of respondents agreed that an ethical question existed involved whether to let personalities affect the terms of sale and whether to offer less competitive prices or terms when the salesperson's firm is the customer's sole source of supply.

E X H I B I T   **3 • 4**   *The Impact of Unethical Selling Behavior on Buyers' Intentions to Purchase*
from a Supplier

Salesperson Behavior	Perceived Ethicality of the Behavior*	Correlation between Perceived Ethicality and Intention to Purchase from the Supplier†
Gifts to current customers		
1. Give purchaser who was one of best customers a gift worth $50 at Christmas	1.87	.53†
2. Gave one of best customers a $25 Christmas gift	2.26	.65†
3. Buys lunch for a purchasing agent	3.77	.25†
4. Gives very good customer present worth $10 at Christmas	2.77	.55†
5. Provides entertainment for purchasing agent such as tickets to sporting events	2.63	.55†
Puts own interest first		
1. Quotes higher than normal price for product during temporary shortage situation	1.75	.52†
2. Lets it be known he has information about a competitor if purchasing agent is interested	1.90	.61†
3. Hints if order is placed, price might be lower on next order, when it is not so	1.29	.22
4. Only stresses positive aspects of product, omitting possible problem purchasing agents' firm might have with it	1.97	.43†
5. Grants price concession to purchasing agent of company he owns stock in	1.80	.64†
6. Attempts to sell product to purchasing agent that has little or no value to buyer's company	2.06	.40†
7. Uses "back-door" selling instead of going through purchasing department	1.67	.44†

Respondents were least likely to see ethical dilemmas in practices that could be justified as merely "good ways of doing business," such as circumventing the purchasing department to increase the chances of a sale (backdoor selling) or asking purchasers for information about competitors.

The findings in Exhibit 3.5 also suggest that many situations salespeople see as involving ethical questions are not addressed by management directives, and many sales personnel want more explicit guidelines to help them resolve such issues. Management can help salespeople avoid the stress and inconsistent performance associated with ethical dilemmas by developing written policies that address problem situations. In 1990, more than 90 percent of the Fortune 1,000 companies had formal codes of ethical conduct, up from 75 percent in 1985.[9] Unfortunately, some of those formal codes are overly broad and fail

E X H I B I T 3 • 4 *(concluded)*

Salesperson Behavior	Perceived Ethicality of the Behavior*	Correlation between Perceived Ethicality and Intention to Purchase from the Supplier†
Gifts to prospects		
1. Gave purchaser who had done business before Christmas present worth $10	2.13	.54†
2. Gave purchaser who had not bought from purchaser's firm a Christmas gift worth $25	1.72	.61†
3. A $50 Christmas gift sent to purchaser who has been called on but had not placed order	1.63	.41†
Pressure or coercion		
1. In reciprocal buying situation, salesperson hints unless order is forthcoming, prospect's sales to firm might suffer	1.61	.50†
2. Attempts to use economic power of firm to obtain concessions from the buyer	1.99	.57†
3. Attempts to get purchasing agent to competitor's bid in low bid buying situation	1.64	.36†
4. Exaggerated how quickly order will be delivered to get sale	1.68	.51†
Preferential treatment		
1. In shortage situation allocates product shipments to purchasing agent he personally liked	1.91	.67†
2. Grants concessions to purchasing manager depending on how much he likes manager	2.24	.55†
3. Gives preferential treatment to customers who are also good suppliers	2.97	.68†

*5 = very ethical; 1 = very unethical
†Significant at, 0.01 level

Source: Adapted from I. F. Trawick, J. E. Swan, G. W. McGee, and D. R. Rink, "Influence of Buyer Ethics and Salesperson Behavior on Intention to Choose a Supplier," *Journal of the Academy of Marketing Science* (Winter 1990), p. 10. Copyright © 1990 *The Journal of the Academy of Marketing Science.*

to provide clear guidance for salespeople in specific situations. Many smaller firms still have no formal guidelines.

A manager might use two different philosophical traditions or frameworks for evaluating the ethics of a given action. These different traditions can lead to different conclusions concerning whether an act is ethical or not, causing a thorny problem for managers. Thorny Issues in Sales Management 3.2 discusses the two philosophical traditions along with some of their implications for the development of formal codes of ethical sales conduct.

The important thing, however, is not just to have a formal policy but to have one that is *helpful* to the sales force. Such policies should provide clear guidelines for decision making and action so that employees facing similar situations will handle them in a way consistent with the organization's goals.

E X H I B I T   3 • 5   *Ethical Evaluations of 12 Sales Situations or Practices*

| | Respondents Replying "Definitely Yes" or "Probably Yes" | | | | | |
| | An Ethical Question? | | Have Stated Policy Now? | | Want a Stated Policy? | |
Situation or Practice	Rank	Percent	Rank	Percent	Rank	Percent
1. Allowing personalities— liking for one purchaser and disliking for another—to affect price, delivery, and other decisions regarding the terms of sale.	1	52	3	47	3	57
2. Having less competitive prices or other terms for buyers who use your firm as the sole source of supply than for firms for which you are one of two or more suppliers.	2	50	2	52	1	61
3. Making statements to an existing purchaser that exaggerate the seriousness of his problem in order to obtain a bigger order or other concessions.	3	49	7	31	6	44
4. Soliciting low-priority or low-volume business that the salesperson's firm will not deliver or service in an economic slowdown or periods of resource shortages.	4	42	6	34	5	46
5. Giving preferential treatment to purchasers whom higher levels of the firm's own management prefer or recommend.	5	41	10	28	8	40
6. Giving physical gifts, such as free sales promotion prizes or "purchase-volume incentive bonuses," to a purchaser.	6	39	1	56	2	60
7. Using the firm's economic power to obtain premium prices or other concessions from buyers.	7	37	5	37	7	42
8. Giving preferential treatment to customers who are also good suppliers.	8	36	8	30	10	33
9. Seeking information from purchasers on competitors' quotations for the purpose of submitting another quotation.	9	34	9	29	9	39
10. Providing free trips, free luncheons or dinners, or other free entertainment to a purchaser.	9	34	3	47	4	55
11. Attempting to reach and influence other departments (such as engineering) directly rather than go through the purchasing department when such avoidance increases the likelihood of a sale.	11	29	12	22	11	30
12. Gaining information about competitors by asking purchasers.	12	27	11	29	11	30

Source: Alan J. Dubinsky, Eric N. Berkowitz, and William Rudelius, "Ethical Problems of Field Sales Personnel," *MSU Business Topics*, Summer 1980. p. 14.

Also, the firm's marketing and sales goals should be set with ethical conduct in mind. "Corporations must go beyond merely educating their employees and look at the motivations that cause a person to make a wrong choice," says Lori Tansey, director of advisory services for the Ethics Resource Center in Washington, D.C. "Setting unrealistic quotas is a perfect example. This situation, probably more than any other, leads to problems."[10]

Thorny Issues in Sales Management 3 • 2

Two Perspectives for Evaluating Ethical Behavior

Two philosophical traditions are commonly used as bases for evaluating the ethics of a given action: **deontology** and **teleology.*** Unfortunately, these two traditions can lead managers to conflicting conclusions about whether a given action is ethical or about what ethical standards are appropriate for a firm's salespeople.

Deontology

Deontological ethics focuses on the welfare of the individual and emphasizes means and intentions for justifying an act. Deontologists believe that features of the act itself make it right or wrong. Deontological thinking rests on two fundamental principles—the rights principle and the justice principle. The rights principle focuses on two criteria for judging an action: (1) universality, which means every act should be based on principles that everyone could act on; and (2) reversibility, which means every act should be based on reasons that the actor would be willing to have all others use, even as a basis for how they treat the actor.

The rights principle is the philosophical source of specific, generally acknowledged rights in society, such as the "right to know." With its emphasis on the notion that every individual has the right to be treated in ways that ensure the person's dignity, respect, and autonomy, the deontological model is sometimes referred to as the rights or entitlements model.

* For more detailed discussions of the differences between the two perspectives, see Robert A. Cooke, *Ethics in Business: A Perspective* (Chicago: Arthur Andersen & Co., 1988); O. C. Ferrell and Larry G. Gresham, "A Contingency Framework for Understanding Ethical Decision Making in Marketing," *Journal of Marketing* (Summer 1985), pp. 87–96; Shelby D. Hunt and Scott Vitell, "A General Theory of Marketing Ethics," *Journal of Macromarketing* (Spring 1986), pp. 5–16; and Donald P. Robin and R. Eric Reidenbach, "Social Responsibility, Ethics, and Marketing Strategy: Closing the Gap between Concept and Application," *Journal of Marketing* (January 1987), pp. 44–58.

The *justice principle* reflects three categories of justice: (1) distributive, whereby resources are distributed according to some evaluation of just desserts; (2) retributive, whereby the wrongdoer is punished proportionally to the wrongdoing provided it was committed knowingly and freely; and (3) compensatory, whereby the injured party is restored to his or her original position. An example of the justice principle applied to a sales situation would be a firm offering a rebate to a customer to compensate for missing a delivery schedule promised by its sales representative.

Teleology

The most well-known branch of teleological ethics is utilitarianism, which focuses on society as the unit of analysis and stresses the consequences of an act in evaluating its ethical status rather than the intentions behind it. The utilitarian model emphasizes the consequences an action may have on all those directly or indirectly affected by it. The utilitarian perspective holds that the correct action is the one that promotes "the greatest good for the greatest number."

Utilitarianism requires that a social cost/benefit analysis be conducted for the contemplated action. All benefits and costs to all persons affected by the particular act need to be considered to the degree possible and summarized as the net of all benefits minus all costs. If the net result is positive, the act is morally acceptable; if the net result is negative, the act is not.

To assess the net benefits of an action, however, the manager must be able to answer the following questions.

What are the viable courses of action available?

What are the alternatives?

What are the harms and benefits associated with the course of action available?

Can these harms and benefits be measured? Can they be compared?

How long will these harms and benefits last?

When will these harms and benefits begin?

Who is directly harmed? Who is indirectly harmed?

Who is directly benefited? Who is indirectly benefited?

What are the social and/or economic costs attached to each alternative course of action?

Which alternatives will most likely yield the greatest net benefit to all individuals affected by the decision? Or, if no alternative yields a net benefit, which one will lead to the least overall harm?

Conflicts between the Two Perspectives

Suppose a firm charges higher prices to loyal customers for whom it is the sole supplier than it does to other organizations where it must compete with other suppliers. Is such an action ethical? The deontological view, with its emphasis on fairness and justice for the individual, would suggest it is not. But the utilitarian or teleological perspective, with its focus on the greatest good for the greatest number, might conclude such a practice is ethical *if* the higher wages and increased returns to shareholders enabled by the action more than offsets the economic harm done to a few customers.

The above illustration not only demonstrates how different ethical traditions can lead to different standards, but it also exposes a potential problem inherent in the utilitarian perspective. When a firm bases its ethical standards solely on utilitarian analysis, individuals (either persons or firms) or small groups may suffer major harm because their costs are averaged with small gains to a large number of other people with the result that the net benefit of the act appears positive.

Partly because of this potential problem, some analysts argue utilitarianism is appropriate only for very general planning where no specific harm to individuals is expected, and marketing activities having a foreseeable and potentially serious impact on individuals should be regulated by deontological reasoning.† Given that customers are identifiable individuals or organizations and that the effects of most questionable sales practices on them can be anticipated, these analysts would argue that the criteria of universality and reversibility provide a better basis for formulating ethical standards for the sales force than a broad cost-benefit analysis.

Neither framework can provide precise or mechanistic answers to ethical questions. In a utilitarian analysis, for instance, one must wrestle with the difficult problem of quantifying costs and benefits. While in a deontological analysis, one needs to judge the seriousness of a right's infringement. What constitutes ethical conduct in the eyes of a firm's managers and employees—or in the eyes of the selling profession as a whole—will ultimately be a matter of consensus. But such consensus can be reached only if individual salespeople and sales managers think about ethical issues and exchange views.

---

† Robin and Reidenback, "Social Responsibility, Ethics, and Marketing Strategy."

To further reduce uncertainty, policies must be clearly communicated to both sales personnel and customers. Periodic review sessions, perhaps involving the company's legal staff, can help salespeople remember the policies and can provide an opportunity to discuss any new or unusual situations that might arise. Such communication can be particularly important for newer employees, both because they are likely to have less experience in dealing with ethical dilemmas and because recent studies indicate employees aged 21 to 40 are likely to be significantly more permissive in their ethical attitudes than their older colleagues.[11]

The most effective way for management to influence the ethical performance of their salespeople, however, is to lead by example. Formal policies do not have much impact when top management gives lip service to one set of standards while practicing another. This problem was evident in the comments of a purchasing manager in another study of business ethics: "Our management doesn't want my buyers influenced by the very things they're telling our sales force to do to make sales."[12] Sales managers who expect ethical behavior from their employees should apply high ethical standards to their own actions and decisions.

The Legal/Political Environment

Many of the changes in society's values are eventually reflected in new laws and government regulations. Throughout this century, the number of laws regulating the conduct of business—including personal selling—has increased dramatically at all levels of government. Two broad categories of laws are particularly relevant to sales programs: (1) antitrust laws and (2) consumer protection legislation.

The antitrust laws are aimed primarily at preserving and enhancing competition among firms in an industry. They restrict marketing practices that would tend to reduce competition and give one firm a monopoly through unfair competition. Antitrust law provisions of great relevance to sales management are outlined in Exhibit 3.6.

The restrictions on anticompetitive behavior spelled out in the antitrust laws apply to firms selling goods or services to intermediaries, business users, or ultimate consumers. When a firm sells to consumer markets, however, it faces additional restrictions imposed by federal, state, and local consumer protection laws. These laws are aimed more directly at protecting consumer welfare by setting standards of quality and safety. They also require that consumers be provided with accurate information to use in making purchase decisions. Since personal selling is one means of providing consumers with information, many laws requiring full disclosure and prohibiting deceptive or misleading information have a direct impact on selling activities.

Misrepresentation of a company's product by a salesperson can have both ethical and legal consequences, whether the salesperson is dealing with consumers or organizational customers. Many salespeople are unaware they assume legal obligations every time they approach a customer. By making certain statements, they can embroil their companies in a lawsuit and ruin the very business relationship they are trying to establish. But recent court cases around the United States have held firms liable for multimillion-dollar judgments for misrepresentation or breach of warranty due to statements made by their salespeople, particularly when the sale involved big-ticket, high-tech products or services. This issue is examined further in Thorny Issues in Sales Management 3.3.

E x h i b i t   3 ● 6   *Selected Antitrust and Consumer Protection Laws Relevant to Formulating*
Sales Programs and Policies

- **Antitrust Provisions**

  Conspiracies among competing firms to *control their prices,* or to *allocate markets* among themselves, are *per se* illegal under the Sherman Act.

  The Robinson-Patman Act prohibits a firm and its representatives from *discriminating in the prices or services* offered to competing customers. The major purpose of this law is to protect smaller customers from being placed at a competitive disadvantage by "key account" programs or price promotions that offer special incentives to larger buyers. However, the law does allow a marketer to grant discounts to larger buyers based on savings in the costs of manufacturing or distributing the product. Thus, some quantity discounts are legal.

  Tying agreements, where a seller forces a buyer to purchase one product to gain the right to purchase another, are illegal under the Clayton and Sherman Acts. A computer manufacturer, for example, cannot force a customer to agree to buy cards, paper, and other supplies needed to run a computer as a precondition for buying the computer itself.

  Reciprocal dealing arrangements, the "I'll buy from you if you buy from me" type of agreements, are illegal where the effect is to injure competition. Such arrangements do tend to be anticompetitive because large companies—which are large buyers as well as large suppliers—tend to have an advantage over smaller firms.

  The Federal Trade Commission Act prohibits *"unfair methods of competition"* in general. Thus, deceptive product claims, interfering with the actions of a competitor's sales representative, and other unfair acts are all illegal.

- **Consumer Protection Provisions**

  The Fair Packaging and Labeling Act makes *unfair or deceptive packaging* or labeling of certain consumer commodities illegal.

  The Truth-in-Lending Act requires *full disclosure of all finance charges* on consumer credit agreements.

  State "cooling-off" laws allow consumers to cancel contracts signed with door-to-door sellers within a limited number of days after agreeing to such contracts.

  The Federal Trade Commission requires that door-to-door salespeople who work for companies engaged in interstate commerce clearly announce their purpose when making calls on potential customers.

  Many cities and towns have so-called Green River Ordinances, which require all door-to-door salespeople to obtain a license.

One other type of legislation has a direct effect on sales managers as they attempt to implement their sales programs: the equal employment opportunity laws. It is unlawful to discriminate against a person in either hiring or promotion because of race, religion, nationality, sex, or age. For this reason, certain types of aptitude tests are illegal if they are culturally or sexually biased or if they are not valid predictors of a person's job performance. The legal aspects of recruiting and selecting sales representatives, as well as other issues related to the increasing cultural diversity of the labor force, are examined in Chapter 12.

Thorny Issues in Sales Management 3 • 3

Avoiding Legal Claims for Misrepresentation or Breach of Warranty by the Sales Force

Buyers often depend on the technical knowledge of salespeople and on their professional integrity. However, salespeople sometimes "oversell." They exaggerate the capabilities of their products or services to win a sale. But when a customer relies on a salesperson's statements, purchases the product or service, and then finds it does not perform as promised, the supplier can be sued for misrepresentation and/or breach of warranty.

Misrepresentation and breach of warranty are two distinct causes of action for which an injured party may seek damages. They differ in terms of the proof required and the type of damages awarded by a judge or jury. However, both can arise in a selling context when a salesperson makes erroneous statements or offers false promises regarding a product's characteristics or capabilities.

Not all statements have legal consequences, however. When salespeople loosely describe their offering in glowing terms ("Our product is great!" "Our service is the best around!"), such statements are considered opinions and generally cannot be relied on by a customer, supplier, or wholesaler. Thus, a standard legal defense in misrepresentation and breach of warranty lawsuits is that the purchaser should not have relied on a salesperson's "puffery."

But when a salesperson makes a claim of a factual nature regarding a product's or service's inherent capabilities (e.g., the results, profits, or savings that will be achieved, how it will perform, what it will do for the customer, etc.), the law treats these comments as statements of fact and warranties.

To help avoid legal problems due to misstatements by salespeople, the following guidelines should be followed. The first set guides the behavior of salespeople. The second set suggests actions sales managers might follow to train and educate their salespeople concerning the legal dangers of misrepresentation.

Selling Guidelines for Avoiding Misrepresentation

* Be sure all specific product claims (technical characteristics, useful life, performance capabilities) can be accomplished.
* Be certain all specific positive statements about offerings can be verified. In addition, any strong positive statement about offerings that cannot be demonstrated should be very general (e.g., "high quality" or "great value").
* Customers should be reminded to read warnings, particularly if they seem to be paying little attention to them. Never suggest to customers that warnings can be ignored or even taken lightly.
* Immediately caution customers who appear to be contemplating any improper product use. Cautionary statements should be very specific and related to each customer's product usage situation.
* Assess each customer's level of sophistication—the more inexperienced the customer, the greater the salesperson's legal obligations to deal cautiously with the customer.
* Be able to verify all negative statements about competitors' products, business conduct, and financial condition. Salespersons should try to avoid saying anything negative about competitors, particularly on topics that could be construed as rumors.

(Continued)

Sales Management Programs to Help Salespeople Comply with Legal Guidelines

- Include detailed modules on legal guidelines in training schools for beginning salespersons. Training should focus on both declarative and procedural knowledge.
- Routinely provide updated information to salespersons about the most recent judicial and statutory developments related to communications with prospects and customers.

- Develop incentive compensation packages that encourage and reward salespersons for avoiding or forestalling litigious situations.
- Review salesperson performance to identify quickly and decisively salespersons who engage in practices that might lead to legal problems.
- Manage by example. Always follow the legal guidelines when accompanying salespersons in the field, and hold salespersons to the same standards when reviewing their performance.

Source: Karl A. Boedecker, Fred W. Morgan, and Jeffery J. Stoltman, "Legal Dimensions of Salespersons' Statements: A Review and Managerial Suggestions," *Journal of Marketing*, January 1991, pp. 70–80. Reprinted by permission of the American Marketing Association.

The Natural Environment

The natural environment is an important consideration in the development of marketing and sales plans. It is the source of all the raw materials and energy resources needed to make, package, promote, and distribute a product. Over the past 15 years, firms in many industries—such as steel, aluminum, plastics, and synthetic fibers—have encountered resource or energy shortages that forced them to limit sales of their products. One might assume that sales representatives could take life easy under such circumstances, letting customers come to them for badly needed goods. But the sales force often has to work harder during product shortages, and well-formulated account management policies become even more crucial for the firm's success.

During such periods, the sales force is often required to help administer rationing programs, which allocate scarce supplies according to each customer's purchase history. Since shortages are usually temporary, though, sellers have to be sensitive to their customers' problems so they will not lose customers when the shortage is over. Consequently, account management policies must treat all customers fairly, minimize conflict, and maintain the firm's competitive position for the future.

Increasing social concern about the possible negative impacts of products and production processes on the natural environment also have important implications for marketing and sales programs. This is increasingly true for firms that sell to organizations as well as for manufacturers of consumer goods. For instance, the European Economic Community is considering legislation requiring all manufacturers to take back—and either reuse or recycle—all materials used in packaging and shipping their products.

The Technical Environment

The most obvious impact of the technical environment on marketing is in providing opportunities for product development. Technical advances have been occurring at a rapidly increasing rate, and new products are accounting for an increasing percentage of total sales in many industries. In some divisions of the 3M Company, for example, more than half of current sales volume is generated by products that were not in existence five years ago. Most analysts believe the importance of new products and services to the marketing success of many firms will continue to accelerate.[13]

Rapid development of new products requires adjusting a firm's sales programs. New sales plans must be formulated, the sales representatives must be retrained, and, in some cases, new reps must be hired.

Advancing technology also affects sales management in more direct ways. Improvements in transportation, communications, and data processing are changing the way sales territories are defined, sales reps are deployed, and sales performance is evaluated and controlled in many companies. New communications technologies—together with the escalating costs of a traditional field sales call—are changing how the personal selling function is carried out. The sample case is giving way to the videocassette; and telemarketing, teleconferencing, and computerized reordering systems are replacing the face-to-face sales call in a growing number of situations. The impact of these new technologies and the conditions under which they are most likely to improve sales efficiency and effectiveness are examined in Chapter 5.

Problems in Environmental Scanning and Forecasting

Keeping a close watch on—and attempting to forecast changes in—the external environment as a basis for formulating marketing and sales plans is easier said than done. There are many examples of well-executed marketing and sales programs that came to grief because one or more elements of the environment changed unexpectedly.

A classic example was experienced by Seagate Technology, the leading manufacturer of compact hard-disk drives for personal computers. During the mid-1980s, the firm's 5 1/4-inch hard-disk drive set the standard for the industry, and Seagate maintained a leading share by being the lowest cost producer. The firm, confident demand for its product would continue to grow, spent heavily to expand production in 1987. But the very next year, a competitor introduced a 3 1/2-inch hard disk, and computer manufacturers—interested in producing ever-smaller laptop and notebook models—quickly switched to the smaller drive. Consequently, Seagate took a $53 million loss in 1988 as it wrote off part of its investment.[14]

Part of the reason for such failures to predict changes in the environment is that many corporations do not use sophisticated techniques for environmental scanning and forecasting. A study involving 48 organizations found that business corporations tend to be less sophisticated in their approach to environmental analysis than either consulting firms or government agencies. Environmental scanning and forecasting within business firms occur primarily in response to current crises rather than in an attempt to identify future threats and opportunities.

Responsibility for environmental analysis usually rests with line managers or the corporate planning staff rather than with people specially trained in

EXHIBIT 3 • 7 *Frequency of Consideration Given to Environmental Factors in Developing Strategic Marketing Plans (N = 149 firms)*

Factor	Frequency of Consideration (Percentage of Respondents)		
	Frequent	Occasional	Seldom/ Never
External Environment			
Competition for customers	90	5	5
Implementing new technology	80	16	4
Update technology	75	20	5
Final customers	72	12	16
Distributors as customers	59	14	27
Government controls/inflation	50	36	28
Raw material supplier	44	26	14
Competition for distributor	35	25	40
Public/political attitudes	34	26	40
Internal Organization Environment			
Organization goals and objectives	78	20	2
Nature of products/services	68	27	5
Existing managerial skills	50	35	15
Employee involvement and commitment	48	34	18
Interdepartmental dependency	45	35	20
Interdepartmental procedures	45	40	15
Manpower availability	40	40	20
Different technological characteristics	40	16	44
Education and technological skills	40	35	25
Interdepartmental conflicts	28	30	42

Source: Joel E. Ross and Ronnie Silverblatt, "Developing the Strategic Plan," *Industrial Marketing Management* 16 (1987), pp. 103–8. Reprinted by permission of the publisher. Copyright 1987 by Elsevier Science Publishing Co., Inc.

long-range forecasting. Efforts rely primarily on quantitative analysis of past trends and extrapolation of those trends, rather than on the use of more qualitative methods to help identify "discontinuities" or major changes that may occur.[15]

A recent study of 149 Fortune 500 firms also revealed that many firms do not pay adequate attention to major factors in their external environment. The study asked top marketing executives how much consideration their firms gave to a variety of external and internal environmental factors in developing strategic marketing plans. As you can see from the results reported in Exhibit 3.7, the vast majority of respondents give frequent consideration to trends affecting their customers, competitors, and technology. But less than half the respondents reported giving frequent consideration to such environmental influences as government controls, political trends, or suppliers.[16]

THE ORGANIZATIONAL ENVIRONMENT

The policies, resources, and talents of the organization also make up a very important part of the marketer's environment. Marketing and sales managers may have some influence over organizational factors due to their participation in making policy and planning decisions; however, in the short run, marketing and sales programs must be designed to fit within organizational limitations. Once again, the variables in the organizational environment can be grouped into five broad categories: (1) goals, objectives, and culture; (2) personnel; (3) financial resources; (4) production capabilities; and (5) research and development capabilities.

Organizational Goals, Objectives, and Culture

Formulating marketing plans—and the sales programs that are part of those plans—begins with top management's specification of a company mission and objectives for each functional area within the firm. As the company mission and objectives change, marketing and sales programs must be adjusted.

In some firms, a well-defined mission together with a successful corporate history and top management's values and beliefs lead to development of a strong **corporate culture.** Such cultures shape the attitudes and actions of employees and help determine the kinds of plans, policies, and procedures managers can implement.

The Travel Related Services Division of American Express, the unit responsible for marketing the American Express card and other services, provides a good example of how a company's culture and its marketing and sales programs can influence one another.[17] For years, the division's primary competitive strategy has been to offer superior service to its cardholders. CEO James Robinson communicates top management's commitment to that theme by hammering on the importance of customer service every chance he gets. For example, in one 25-minute tour of an American Express travel agency in Manhattan he uttered the words "service quality" 10 times. And he constantly promotes his vision of American Express as one of the world's premier service providers by preaching homilies like "Quality is the only patent protection we've got" to nearly every gathering of employees.

Over the years, this strategic vision has permeated the company culture to the extent that nearly every employee is committed to serving customers as well as possible. That culture is both reflected in and reinforced by a number of sales and service programs and policies. For instance, the division has had a formal system for measuring service quality for two decades. Managers review how long it takes operators in service centers to answer the phone (the standard is seven seconds) and how long it takes to replace lost cards (48 hours is the goal). A management committee convenes periodically to devise new ways to improve and measure customer service. The division even maintains a "Quality University" to provide regular training for sales reps, customer service people, and their managers to ensure that new ideas for improving customer service are instituted.

Personnel	The number of people in the organization, together with their skills and abilities, constrains marketing strategies and sales programs. In view of the difficulties involved in recruiting highly qualified people for sales positions and the often lengthy training programs needed to teach new sales reps necessary skills, it is often difficult to expand a sales force rapidly to take advantage of new products or growing markets. In some cases, however, it may be possible for a firm to compensate for a lack of knowledgeable employees by utilizing outside agencies or specialists on a fee-for-service or commission basis, such as agent intermediaries.
Financial Resources	An organization's financial strength influences many aspects of its marketing programs. It can constrain the firm's ability to develop new products as well as the size of its promotional budget and sales force. Companies sometimes must take drastic measures, such as selling out to larger firms, to obtain the financial resources needed to realize their full potential in the marketplace.
Production Capabilities	The organization's production capacity, the technology and equipment available in its plants, and even the location of its production facilities can influence its marketing and sales programs. A company may be prevented from expanding its product line or moving into new geographic areas because it does not have the capacity to serve increased demand. Coors Brewing Company, for example, produces a beer that is in demand throughout the country. Because of limited production capacity, however, Coors beer was sold for many years in only about 25 to 30 percent of the United States. The company was reluctant to expand its production facilities because of the difficulty of finding water of the same quality as that at the plant in Colorado. However, such expansion ultimately became necessary for Coors to remain competitive with other major brewers.
Research and Development Capabilities	An organization's technical and engineering expertise is a major factor in determining whether it will be an industry leader or follower in product development. Excellence in engineering and design can also serve as a major promotional appeal in the firm's sales program, as it is for BMW and Mercedes-Benz. As the experience of American Express shows, a firm can find ways to satisfy customer needs and compete effectively even when it is not the technological leader or when it competes in a low-tech industry.
Consideration of Organizational Factors in Marketing Planning	Because all of the above organizational factors influence a firm's ability to implement a given marketing strategy effectively, all should be considered by managers when developing marketing and sales plans and programs. Unfortunately—as the survey results in Exhibit 3.7 indicate—this is not always the case. Although most firms pay frequent attention to defining specific objectives and specifying the kinds of products and services they will offer, less than half

pay the same kind of attention to their personnel or technical capabilities. The danger is that such firms may develop marketing programs that look good on paper but are difficult to implement successfully, a problem that Campbell Soup continues to wrestle with.[18]

ENVIRONMENTAL CONSTRAINTS ON SALES FORCE PERFORMANCE

A firm's marketing plan and sales program should be adapted to the general environmental conditions throughout the market. The problem is that some environmental factors vary among regions. Consequently, even when two salespeople work for the same company, sell the same products, and have similar aptitudes, skills, and motivation, one may outperform the other because the environment in that rep's territory is more favorable.

Researchers have identified factors in both the organizational and the external environments that account for at least part of the variation in productivity within a firm's sales force.[19] Organizational variables that can cause differences in performance include (1) regional variations in the expenditure of money and effort on other elements of the firm's marketing and promotional mix, (2) variations in the firm's past experience in different territories, and (3) regional variations in sales management practices—particularly in the number of sales personnel supervised by different field sales managers.

External factors that may vary from one region to another include (1) intensity of competition, (2) total market potential, (3) concentration of potential sales—the proportion of customers who are relatively large purchasers, and (4) geographic dispersion of customers. The impact of variations in each factor on a sales representative's productivity is summarized in Exhibit 3.8.

The Effects of Organizational Factors on Sales Productivity

The following three organizational variables can influence salesperson productivity.

Variations in company marketing efforts

Since personal selling is only one element of a firm's marketing mix, the success of personal selling efforts is strongly influenced by the intensity of the company's other marketing and promotional activities. When the firm's marketing efforts are more intensive in one region than in others, salespeople in that region have an advantage. Consider a firm that concentrates a large portion of its advertising expenditures in local media on the West Coast. It should be easier for sales representatives in those territories to gain access to purchasing agents and to close sales successfully than for reps in the East or Midwest. Similarly, a salesperson in a territory located near a company warehouse may be able to offer customers quicker delivery and better service than one in a more distant territory.

E x h i b i t 3 • 8   *The Impact of Variations in Environmental Factors on the Productivity of Individual Salespeople*

Environmental Factors	Impact on Salesperson's Productivity
Organizational Variables	
1. Relatively high expenditures on marketing and promotional efforts	Positive
2. A positive sales history within a territory	
a. A relatively high market share in recent years	Positive
b. An increasing market share in recent years	Positive
3. A large span of control—field sales manager supervises a relatively large number of salespeople	Negative
External Environmental Variables	
1. Relatively intense competitive activity	Negative
2. Relatively high total market potential within the territory	Positive
3. Concentration of potential—relatively large proportion of big customers	Positive
4. Geographic dispersion of accounts—relatively large distances between customers	Negative

Source: Based on a summary of research findings presented in Adrian B. Ryans and Charles B. Weinberg, "Sales Productivity: A Multiple Company Study," in *Sales Management: New Developments from Behavioral and Design Model Research*, ed. Richard P. Bagozzi (Cambridge, Mass.: Marketing Science Institute, 1979), pp. 92–129.

Variations in past experience

Many firms enjoy a stronger market position in certain geographic regions. This is particularly true for smaller firms that often start out producing for a local or regional market and then attempt to expand into new markets. Sales representatives in territories where their company is well established should have an easier job. They can more readily maintain old customers and gain access to new ones than salespeople who must work to establish an awareness of their company and its products.

Variations in sales managers' span of control

Ideally, sales management policies and practices should be consistent throughout the company and affect all members of the sales force similarly. In practice, this is not always the case. One policy that often varies from one sales region to another is span of control—the number of sales personnel directly supervised by a field sales manager. Because of variations in the density of potential customers and the quality of transportation networks, some sales managers are responsible for more salespeople than others. The more subordinates a manager must supervise, the less time can be spent training, advising, and monitoring the performance of each salesperson. As discussed later in this book, a large span of control can cause salespeople to feel uncertain about how to do their jobs. This can lead to lower levels of job satisfaction and productivity in the sales force.

Effects of the External Environment on Sales Productivity

The following external environmental factors can affect salesperson performance.

Variations in the intensity of competition

A firm may be more firmly established and have a larger market share in some regions than in others, and the intensity of its marketing efforts also may vary across geographic areas. Obviously, the same may be true for the firm's competitors. Consequently, salespeople in different territories often face competitive efforts of varying intensity. Those who face well-entrenched and aggressive competitors are likely to have a more difficult time attaining a given sales volume than those with weaker competition.

Variations in territory characteristics

Since population density varies among geographic regions, the **total sales potential** for some consumer goods and services is greater in some areas than in others. This is even more true for industrial goods and services because manufacturers often tend to locate close to one another. This is true of automobile manufacturers in Detroit and aerospace firms on the West Coast. Consequently, some of a firm's sales territories may contain more potential customers and total sales volume than others.

Even when the total market potential of two territories is about the same, however, differences in customer characteristics can cause variations in sales productivity. In a territory where potential demand is concentrated among a small number of large customers, a representative should produce a given dollar volume of sales with less traveling, fewer presentations, and fewer orders than in a territory where there are many small customers. When potential customers are widely dispersed geographically, travel time increases, and the number of accounts that a single representative can call on will be smaller than in a territory with a cluster of many potential customers.

Implications for Sales Managers

Regional variations in the preceding factors can lead to substantial differences in sales productivity among a firm's sales representatives. Research indicates such factors account for between 30 and 80 percent of the variation in the dollar sales volumes produced by a firm's sales force.[20] Therefore, it is important for sales managers to consider these differences when developing sales plans and evaluating the performance of sales representatives.

Regional variations in the firm's promotional expenditures, its past market share, the intensity of competition, market potential, and the concentration and dispersion of potential customers should be carefully considered when deciding how to divide the market into sales territories and when determining sales forecasts and quotas for each territory.

Also, environmental differences make the sales representative's job more difficult and less productive in some regions than in others. Thus, it is not sufficient to evaluate a salesperson's performance solely on the basis of sales volume or selling expenses. Such evaluations can lead to unfair comparisons of performance among representatives. Consequently, many firms supplement sales volume and cost analyses with more qualitative behavioral evaluations of selling performance—items to be discussed in more detail later.

S UMMARY

The environmental factors that can severely affect a marketing plan can be grouped into the two broad categories of external and organizational environments. The external environment includes the (1) economic, (2) social, cultural, and ethical, (3) legal/political, (4) natural, and (5) technological environments. The organizational environment includes the firm's (1) goals and objectives, (2) personnel, (3) financial resources, (4) production capabilities, and (5) research and development capabilities.

The values of society set standards for ethical behavior. Ethics is concerned with the development of moral standards by which actions and situations can be judged. It focuses on those actions that may result in actual or potential harm of some kind (e.g., economic, mental, physical) to an individual, group, or organization. Thus, ethics is more proactive than the law, and behaving ethically sometimes means going beyond mere adherence to the law.

Two sets of ethical dilemmas are of particular concern to sales managers. The first set is embedded in the manager's dealings with salespeople. Ethical issues pervade nearly all aspects of the management of a sales force, and such problems will be discussed throughout this text.

The second set of ethical issues arise from the interactions between individual salespeople and their customers. Sales managers must establish standards of ethical behavior for their subordinates, communicate them clearly, and enforce them vigorously. There is mounting evidence that unethical selling practices make buyers reluctant to deal with a supplier and are likely to result in the loss of sales and profits over time.

As part of the firm's marketing program, the company's personal selling program must also be adapted to the external and organizational environments. Some important organizational variables that can cause differences in performance among salespeople are (1) regional variations in the expenditure of money and effort on other elements of the firm's marketing and promotion mix, (2) variations in the firm's experience in different territories, and (3) regional variations in sales management practices—particularly in the number of sales personnel supervised by field sales managers. External factors that can vary from one region to another include (1) intensity of competition, (2) total market potential, (3) concentration of potential sales—the proportion of customers who are relatively large purchasers—and (4) geographic dispersion of customers.

Discussion Questions

1. Kelly Noland, sales manager of Keystone Financial, just completed her review of sales expenses and was concerned about the limited expenses incurred by one of Keystone's financial consultants. In particular, she noted that Martin Gregory did not follow Keystone's gift-giving guidelines. When asked about this, Martin replied: "I know I can give gifts and that my expenses will be covered. But I don't like this. It smacks of bribery, and besides, I don't think it helps one bit." Kelly Noland felt differently and wondered if Martin's less-than-spectacular sales results might be improved if he followed Keystone's recommendations. What is the role of gift giving in business relations?

2. Jon Baker was flabbergasted. Collette Lamour, purchasing agent for Colonial Enterprises, indicated to Jon what she thought might be a nice gift. She opened a gift catalog to a page displaying fur coats and circled one she thought would look great on her. She said, "In case you were wondering what kind of gift to get me, here's an idea." Jon saw the $3,000 price and knew this represented a small part of the $600,000 annual sales made to Colonial. In addition to the dilemma of gift giving on such a large scale, Jon faced another problem. He was opposed to the fur industry's practice. What should Jon do in this situation? What would you do?

3. The chapter illustrates how environmental changes can alter a firm's marketing program and cites three important points. Using these points, what changes have occurred in how AT&T competes in the market today? What changes have occurred in the public accounting industry? In the legal industry?

4. As a result of changes in their code of ethics, public accounting firms can now advertise publicly and engage in other marketing activities. According to some authorities, public accounting firms must first engage in *internal marketing* before they engage in *external marketing*. What do these terms mean?

5. In an attempt to increase the number of sales calls salespeople can make per day, a firm is planning to install radar detectors in company cars. What implications does this have?

6. Karen Coenen, sales rep for Midway Corporation, manufacturer of electronic instruments, has been told to pad her expense account. She has been told everyone else does it, so she should too. She thinks that since everyone else is doing it, she might as well go along with the group. Do you approve, somewhat approve, somewhat disapprove, or disapprove? If you were confronted with this situation, would you pad your account?

7. Dave Nevin was in a quandary. One of his better customers had asked Dave for a contribution to a political campaign for a candidate who had a rather shady reputation. The request was for $50, which represented a small sum compared with the commissions Dave had earned last year. Dave made out a personal check

for $50, thinking that if he did not, he might lose the account. What would you have done in such a situation? Do you approve or disapprove?

8. "There's a limit to honesty," said the district sales manager. "I want all questions answered honestly, but don't volunteer information that will have a negative effect on sales. If the customer doesn't ask, don't talk about it." Comment.

9. The increased power of retailers is the subject of the Thorny Issues in Sales Management. The headline in an article that recently appeared in *Sales & Marketing Management,* March 1987, pp. 41–43, read, "Wal-Mart's War on Reps." The subheadline read, "There have been other attempts at removing manufacturer's reps from the sale, but none so determined, or as secret, as Wal-Mart's. And none so successful. At last, reps are fighting back." Why is Wal-Mart trying to eliminate manufacturers' reps from its buying process? If you were a manufacturer and employed reps, what steps would you take to deal with Wal-Mart's demands?

Endnotes

[1] This example is based on material found in Rayna Skolnik, "Campbell Stirs Up Its Sales Force," *Sales & Marketing Management* (April 1986), pp. 56–58; Bill Saporito, "The Fly in Campbell's Soup," *Fortune,* May 9, 1988, pp. 67–70; Joseph Weber, "From Soup to Nuts and Back to Soup," *Business Week,* November 5, 1990, pp. 114–16; Joseph Weber, "Campbell Is Bubbling, But for How Long?" *Business Week,* June 17, 1991, pp. 56–57; and Bill Saporito, "Campbell Soup Gets Piping Hot," *Fortune,* September 9, 1991, pp. 142–48.

[2] The increased power of large retailers as a result of the new information technology is a problem facing nearly every manufacturer of consumer packaged goods. Consequently, we examine this issue—and how manufacturers and their sales forces are reacting to it—in greater detail later in this chapter.

[3] The interested reader might turn to a number of sources for more information about the strategic planning process and its impact on marketing and sales management. These include Orville C. Walker, Jr., Harper W. Boyd, Jr., and Jean-Claude Larréché, *Marketing Strategy: Planning and Implementation* (Homewood, Ill.: Richard D. Irwin, Inc., 1992), and David A. Aaker, *Strategic Market Management,* 3rd ed. (New York: John Wiley & Sons, 1992).

[4] Robert A. Cooke, *Ethics in Business: A Perspective* (Chicago: Arthur Andersen & Co., 1988).

[5] I. Fredrick Trawick, John E. Swan, Gail W. McGee, and David R. Rink, "Influence of Buyer Ethics and Salesperson Behavior on Intention to Choose a Supplier," *Journal of the Academy of Marketing Science* 19 (Winter 1991), pp. 17–23.

[6] For example, see F. Robert Dwyer, Paul H. Schurr, and Sejo Oh, "Developing Buyer-Seller Relationships," *Journal of Marketing* (April 1987), pp. 11–27; Shay Sayre, Mary L. Joyce, and David R. Lambert, "The Relevance of Ethical Salesperson Behavior on Relationship Quality: The Pharmaceutical Industry," *Journal of Personal Selling and Sales Management* (Fall 1991), pp. 39–48; and Jan Heide and George John, "Do Norms Matter in Marketing Relationships?" *Journal of Marketing* (1992, forthcoming).

[7] "White Collar Crime Cost Increases," *USA Today,* January 8, 1987, p. A1. See also Dawn Bryan, "Using Gifts to Make the Sale," *Sales & Marketing Management* (September 1989), pp. 48–53; and "Do the Right Thing," *Sales & Marketing Management* (August 1990), p. 65.

[8] Alan J. Dubinsky, Eric N. Berkowitz, and William Rudelius, "Ethical Problems of Field Sales Personnel," *MSU Business Topics,* Summer 1980, pp. 11–16. For a comprehensive review of recent research concerning factors that influence ethical behavior in selling situations, see Thomas R. Wotruba, "A Comprehensive Framework for the Analysis of Ethical Behavior, with

a Focus on Sales Organizations," *Journal of Personal Selling and Sales Management* (Spring 1990), pp. 29–42.

[9]Betsy Weisendanger, "Doing the Right Thing," *Sales & Marketing Management* (January 1991), pp. 82–83.

[10]Ibid., p. 83.

[11]Ibid., p. 82.

[12]William Rudelius and Rogene A. Buchholz, "Ethical Problems of Purchasing Managers," *Harvard Business Review* (March–April 1979), p. 8. See also Alan J. Dubinsky, "Studying Field Salespeoples' Ethical Problems: An Approach for Designing Company Policies," in *Marketing Ethics: Guidelines for Managers,* ed. Gene R. Laczniak and Patrick E. Murphy (Lexington, Mass.: Lexington Books, 1985); Michael R. Hyman, Robert Skipper, and Richard Tansey, "Ethical Codes Are Not Enough," *Business Horizons,* March–April 1990, pp. 15–22; and K. Douglas Hoffman, Vince Howe, and Donald W. Hardigree, "Ethical Dilemmas Faced in the Selling of Complex Services: Significant Others and Competitive Pressures," *Journal of Personal Selling and Sales Management* (Fall 1991), pp. 13–26.

[13]For a discussion of the accelerating pace of new product development, the advantages of being a new product pioneer, and some marketing strategies for new products, see Walker, Boyd, and Larréché, *Marketing Strategy,* chap. 8.

[14]Andrew Kupfer, "America's Fastest Growing Company," *Fortune,* August 13, 1990, pp. 48–54.

[15]Liam Fahey, William R. King, and Vadake K. Narayanan, "Environmental Scanning and Forecasting in Strategic Planning—The State of the Art," *Long-Range Planning,* February 1981, pp. 32–39. However, recent evidence suggests the kind and amount of environmental scanning that firms do also depends on the

volatility of their environments. See Richard L. Daft, Juhani Sormunen, and Don Parks, "Chief Executive Scanning, Environmental Characteristics, and Company Performance: An Empirical Study," *Strategic Management Journal* 9 (1988), pp. 123–29.

[16]Joel E. Ross and Ronnie Silverblatt, "Developing the Strategic Plan," *Industrial Marketing Management* 16 (1987), pp. 103–8.

[17]John P. Newport, Jr., "American Express: Service That Sells," *Fortune,* November 20, 1989, pp. 80–94.

[18]For a more detailed discussion of the organizational factors that affect the implementation of marketing and sales strategies, see Walker, Boyd, and Larréché, *Marketing Strategy,* chap. 12.

[19]For example, see David W. Cravens, Robert B. Woodruff, and Joe C. Stamper, "An Analytical Approach for Evaluating Sales Territory Performance," *Journal of Marketing* 36 (January 1972), pp. 31–37; David W. Cravens and Robert B. Woodruff, "An Approach for Determining Criteria of Sales Performance," *Journal of Applied Psychology* 57 (June 1973), pp. 242–47; Henry C. Lucas, Charles B. Weinberg, and Kenneth W. Clowes, "Sales Response as a Function of Territorial Potential and Sales Representative Workload," *Journal of Marketing Research* 12 (August 1975), pp. 198–305; Charles A. Beswick and David W. Cravens, "A Multistage Decision Model for Sales Force Management," *Journal of Marketing Research* 14 (May 1977); and Adrian B. Ryans and Charles B. Weinberg, "Sales Productivity: A Multiple Company Study," *Sales Management: New Developments from Behavioral and Decision Model Research,* ed. Richard P. Bagozzi (Cambridge, Mass.: Marketing Science Institute, 1979), pp. 92–129.

[20]See the summary of results of empirical sales force productivity studies in Ryans and Weinberg, "Sales Productivity."

Suggested Readings

The Impact of Environmental Factors on Marketing and Sales Strategies

Ross, Joel E., and Ronnie Silverblatt. "Developing the Strategic Plan." *Industrial Marketing Management* 16 (1987), pp. 103–8.

Walker, Orville C., Jr., Harper W. Boyd, Jr., and Jean-Claude Larréché. *Marketing Strategy: Planning and Implementation.* Homewood, Ill.: Richard D. Irwin, Inc., 1992, chaps. 4, 12.

Walker, Orville C., Jr., and Robert W. Ruekert. "Marketing's Role in the Implementation of Business Strategies: A Critical Review and Conceptual Framework." *Journal of Marketing,* July 1987, pp. 15–33.

Legal and Ethical Issues

Hoffman, K. Douglas, Vince Howe, and Donald W. Hardigree. "Ethical Dilemmas Faced in the Selling of Complex Services: Significant Others and Competitive Pressures." *Journal of Personal Selling and Sales Management* (Fall 1991), pp. 13–26.

Stern, Louis W., and Thomas L. Eovaldi. *Legal Aspects of Marketing Strategy: Antitrust and Consumer Protection Issues.* Englewood Cliffs, N.J.: Prentice Hall, 1984, pp. 447–74.

Trawick, Fredrick, I., John E. Swan, Gail W. McGee, and David R. Rink. "Influence of Buyer Ethics and Salesperson Behavior on Intention to Choose a Supplier." *Journal of the Academy of Marketing Science* 19 (1991), pp. 17–23.

Weisendanger, Betsy. "Doing the Right Thing." *Sales & Marketing Management* (January 1991), pp. 82–83.

Wotruba, Thomas R. "A Comprehensive Framework for the Analysis of Ethical Behavior, with a Focus on Sales Organizations." *Journal of Personal Selling and Sales Management* (Spring 1990), pp. 29–42.

Marketing Planning, Sales Programs, and Account Management Policies

CAMPBELL SOUP REFOCUSES ITS MARKETING STRATEGY[1]

As we saw in Chapter 3, changes in the external environment during the 1970s dictated changes in Campbell's marketing strategy and sales programs during the 1980s. Fragmenting markets, the increasing costs and declining effectiveness of national advertising media, and the growing power of major retailers all helped make the firm's earlier national mass market strategy ineffective. The company changed to a regional strategy emphasizing development of new products aimed at more narrowly defined user segments and increased use of local media and promotions targeted at those segments. To help implement the new strategy, Campbell also reorganized its sales force and changed some sales policies. The firm gave its salespeople more authority to negotiate with individual retailers and to institute promotions geared to local market environments.

Problems with the New Strategy

Campbell's new strategy accomplished its primary objective of stimulating the firm's lackluster sales growth. Largely as the result of more than 600 line extensions and product introductions, the firm's sales revenues rose from $2.5

billion in 1980 to $5.7 billion in 1989. Unfortunately, the firm's financial performance did not keep pace with its revenues. Campbell's earnings-growth rate, return on shareholders' equity, and return on invested capital were all below average for its industry during most of the 1980s.

Worse, competitors were still making inroads into some of Campbell's most profitable core businesses. For example, Pet Inc.'s Progresso soups enjoyed 20 percent annual volume increases during the late 1980s, and new types of soup, especially the inexpensive, dry ramen noodle soups from Japan, gave consumers new choices to which Campbell was slow to respond.

What went wrong? Many analysts believe the firm's strategy of using new products and line extensions to stimulate volume growth was pushed too far. Not all of the new entries could be adequately researched, intelligently positioned, or adequately supported with sales and marketing resources. Consequently, while there were some major successes, such as the Le Menu line of frozen entrées, there were also many costly failures, like the firm's attempts to sell branded fresh vegetables and salads. Given the vast amounts of managerial and financial resources focused on product introductions, too little attention and money was devoted to improving the efficiency of existing operations and lowering costs.

Some analysts also believe Campbell's strategy of developing and positioning products to appeal to specific consumer segments was not implemented well. For example, while different flavors and types of soup are used by different segments for different purposes (e.g., an ingredient in cooking, lunch for the kids, etc.) Campbell's national advertising stressed "soup is good food," an umbrella appeal that treated all soup as a generic product. Also, the large number of line extensions, many of which were only marginally different products with the same brand name, may have cannibalized the sales of older products, confused consumers, and injured Campbell's brand equity.

As we saw in Chapter 3, the firm also had problems implementing its new regional sales organization and marketing policies. Because the changes were made quickly with little preparation or retraining, Campbell's salespeople had no clues about how to perform their new responsibilities and made many mistakes. The change also created internal conflict. As one general manager admitted, "We had a lot of people in the marketing end resisting this because they thought there was a loss of autonomy associated with it. Or, they were just confused by what was going on."

A Sharpening of Focus

Despite the rapid volume growth Campbell attained during the 1980s, the firm's below-average financial performance—and the resulting dissatisfaction of the Dorrance family, which still owns 58 percent of the company's stock—resulted in Gordon McGovern's resignation as CEO in 1989. He was replaced by David Johnson, who immediately refocused more attention on improving the efficiency of the firm's core businesses in heat-processed and frozen foods. Johnson sold some of the firm's less profitable businesses (e.g., mushroom farms), yanked many unprofitable product lines (e.g., refrigerated salads), closed 20 old plants (including the original soup factory in Camden, New Jersey), reduced the work force by about 15 percent, and required the remaining plants to compete for the available business, thus forcing them to find new ways to lower costs.

The new CEO also fine-tuned Campbell's marketing strategies. He imposed zero-based budgeting, which forced marketing managers to justify every dollar spent on each brand. Overall marketing expenditures were reduced more than 10 percent. Funds were shifted away from costly consumer promotions in commodity categories where Campbell had no competitive advantage (e.g., frozen fried chicken) and focused on share-building advertising and trade promotions in categories where the firm had strong brand equity (e.g., soups and frozen dinners).

Advertising and promotion efforts for individual products were also targeted more precisely at specific user segments. Within the soup line, new ads were developed to promote low-sodium soups, children's soups, microwave soups, family-sized cans for budget buyers, and "cooking" soups such as cream of broccoli. Finally, new product development efforts were cut back, focused on a smaller number of projects less likely to cannibalize established brands, and subjected to more intense research before gaining approval.

Finally, the firm's internal structure and procedures were also changed to reduce turf battles and improve coordination and control across brands and functional departments. The number of SBUs and general managers were

E x h i b i t **4 ● 1**   *Campbell's Recent Performance*

A. Sales Growth and Profit Margins

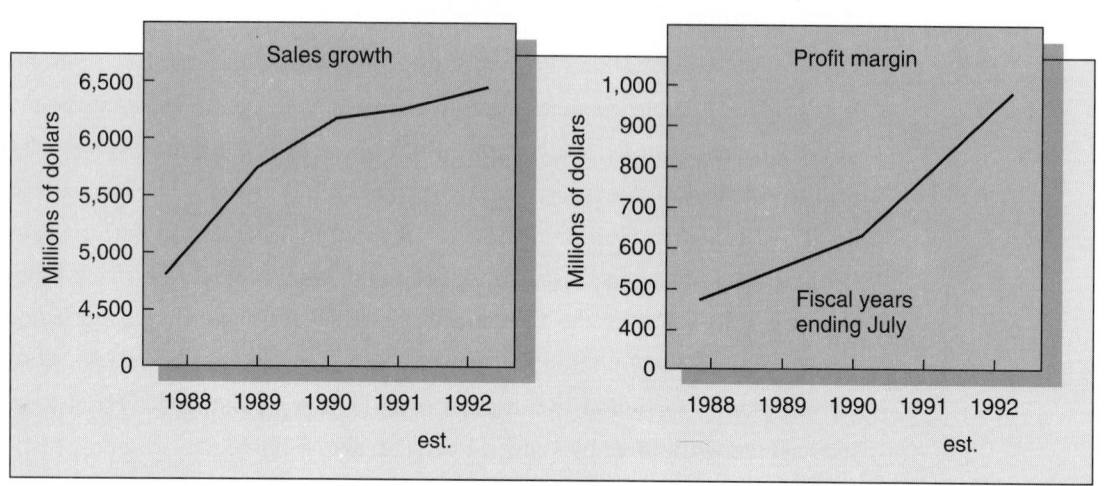

B. Earnings per Share and Stock Price

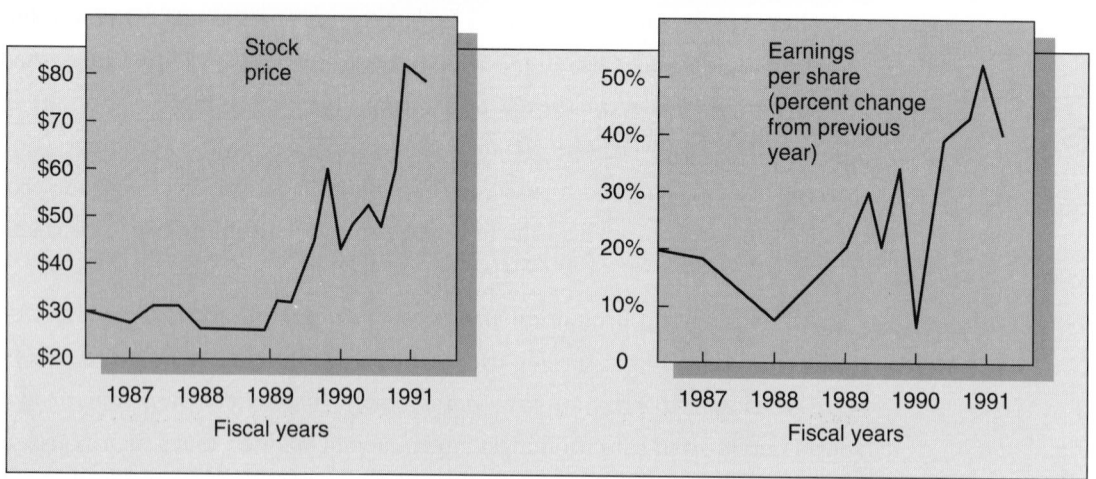

Source: Company reports.

Source: Bill Sapporito, "Campbell Soup Gets Piping Hot," *Fortune*, September 9, 1991, p. 144.

reduced, but this was offset by an increase in the number of lower level product managers responsible for planning and coordinating marketing and sales programs for individual products or product lines. Clearer procedures were also developed to ensure that local sales and marketing efforts are consistent with national objectives and quality standards. And the firm instituted a system of regional performance reviews that set specific marketing goals for each region and then evaluate the performance of that region with local household and store data.

The financial effects of the new CEO's efforts to sharpen Campbell's competitive focus have been dramatic. As Exhibit 4.1 indicates, operating margins, earnings per share, and the firm's stock price all increased substantially from 1988 through 1991. But revenue growth slowed to less than a 2 percent annual rate by 1991. By increasing its focus on profitability, is Campbell mortgaging its future? Will its more cautious approach to new product development and tighter controls on marketing expenditures limit the firm's ability to grow beyond its maturing core businesses? Only time will tell.

MARKETING PLANNING

The changes made at Campbell during the 1980s and 1990s illustrate how a firm's managers must adjust their corporate, business, marketing, and sales strategies and programs in response to the environmental factors discussed in Chapter 3. How are those strategic decisions made? How does the strategic planning process work? And how can strategic sales programs be integrated with the rest of a business's marketing strategy? These questions are the focus of this chapter.

The Importance of Planning

Planning is deciding what to do in the present to achieve what is desired in the future. Planning requires decisions concerning the firm's goals and objectives for the future and the actions that should be taken to accomplish them.

Planning involves an analysis of where the organization is and how it got there and a projection of where the organization will end up if it continues to move in the same direction. Given such an analysis, the company can compare where it wants to be with where it is likely to be. Management can then formulate a strategy for moving closer to what is desired. Thus, a **strategy** is a statement of the fundamental pattern of present and planned objectives, resource deployments, and interactions with markets, competitors, and other environmental factors that indicate how an organization intends to survive and prosper over time.[2]

A strategy provides a broad blueprint to guide the firm's efforts; however, more detailed programs or **tactics** must be developed to spell out how resources are to be allocated and what actions are to be taken, by whom, and when. To use a football analogy, the overall game plan formulated by the coaching staff is a strategy. It is a broad statement of what the team should do to win the game, given its strengths and weaknesses and those of the opponent. One such strategy might be to keep the ball on the ground and run at the tackles. The specific plays designed and practiced by the team are the tactics. Although the quarterback's selection of plays should be guided by the game plan, the tactics used must be adapted to the specific situations encountered during the game, such as an occasional pass to keep the defense honest.

In today's changing environment, planning is crucial to the success of the enterprise. Yet, because things change so rapidly, some managers argue planning is a waste of time. They say changing conditions may force management to revise its plan or scrap it in favor of a new one. But without a clearly stated plan, the firm may overreact to short-lived disruptions in the environment, and erratic changes in direction can cause confusion among both employees and customers.

Campbell provides a good example of a firm that adjusted its tactics to changing external and internal circumstances without abandoning its basic strategy. When it became obvious the firm's managers had overemphasized new product development at the expense of profitability, Campbell took steps to improve efficiency and refocused much of its marketing effort on strengthening its established brands. But its actions were still guided by the basic strategy of tailoring product offerings and marketing programs to the unique preferences of more narrowly defined regional and demographic customer segments.

The Planning Process

As we saw in Chapter 3, most companies, particularly those with multiple divisions or SBUs, develop a hierarchy of strategies. That hierarchy typically incorporates strategic plans at the corporate and business unit levels, as well as marketing strategies for individual product-market entries and plans for functional activities, such as sales. While the specifics of the total corporate planning process are beyond the scope of this book, the essential steps involved in developing strategic marketing and sales plans for a product or service are outlined in Exhibit 4.2 and discussed in the following sections.

Company mission and goals

A statement of an organization's mission attempts to answer the most basic questions about its reason for being. What is our business? What should it be? These seem like simple questions, but they are often difficult for management to answer. Many organizations never define or communicate their mission

EXHIBIT **4 ● 2**   *The Marketing Planning Process*

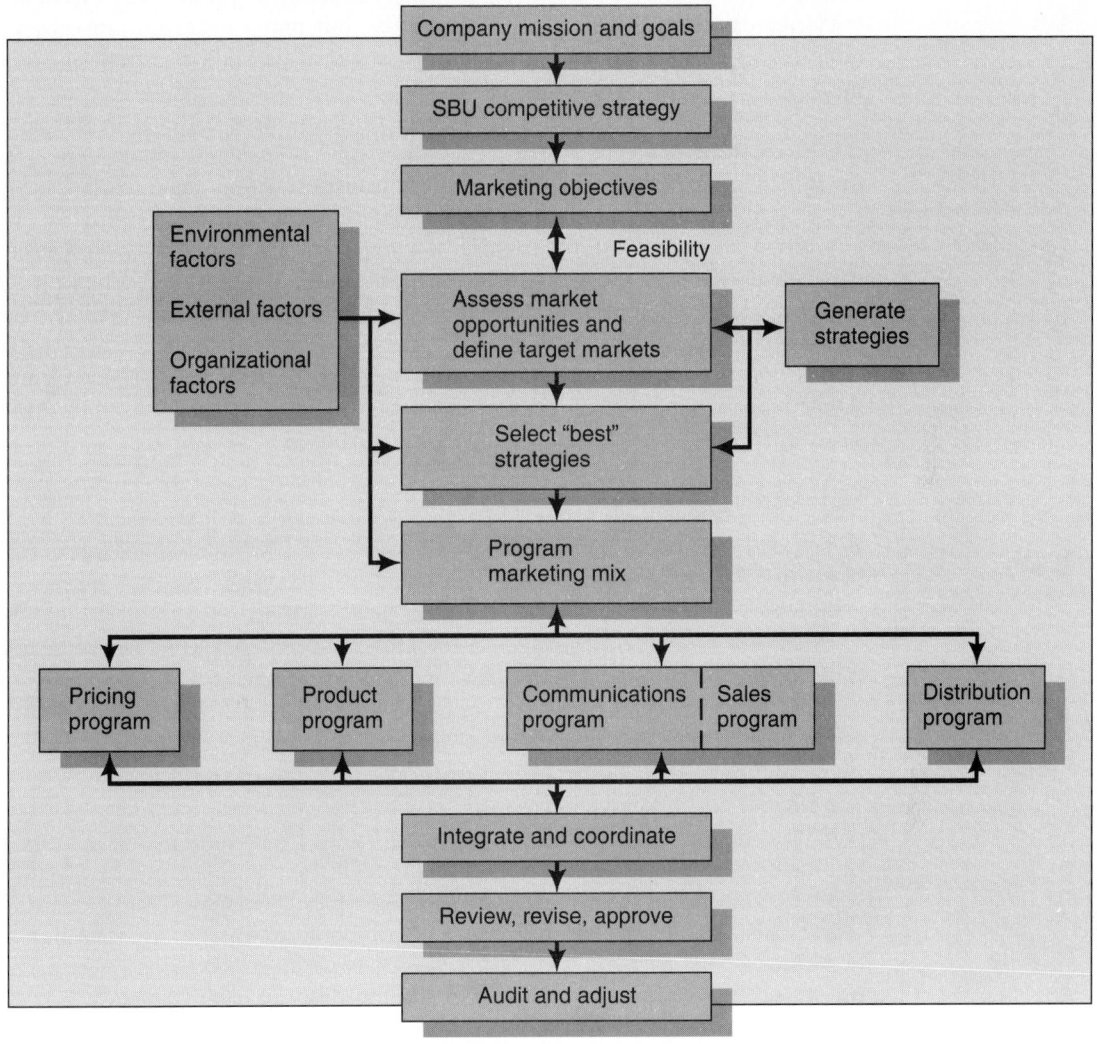

Source: Adapted from Harper W. Boyd and Orville C. Walker, Jr., *Marketing Management: A Strategic Approach* (Homewood, Ill.: Richard D. Irwin, 1990), chap. 1.

clearly. Others state their missions too broadly. For example, some managers say their purpose is simply to make a profit. As a statement of mission, however, this says nothing about how that profit is to be earned, so it provides no guidance for selecting marketing opportunities and alternative strategies.

Many organizations define their missions too narrowly by focusing on the production of a particular product or service. As technology and customer needs change, specific products and services become obsolete, and firms that define their mission in narrow terms can become obsolete as well. There are few streetcar companies today, for instance, but many organizations are attempting to satisfy the need for urban mass transit through a variety of other means.

The most appropriate way for a firm to define its mission is in terms of the broad human needs it will try to satisfy. Volkswagen might define its mission as providing economical private transportation, while Walt Disney Co. describes its mission as providing family entertainment.

When an organization's mission is defined in terms of satisfying a need, it becomes easier to identify attractive marketing opportunities. When an oil company defines its mission as satisfying people's energy needs, it is then clear the company should be exploring a variety of energy sources, such as solar power, in addition to locating new sources of petroleum. Similarly, a clearly defined mission helps management evaluate available opportunities and avoid those that are inconsistent with the firm's purpose.

SBU strategy

In organizations with multiple divisions or strategic business units, each SBU is likely to have its own objectives and a distinct strategy for accomplishing them. As mentioned earlier, the keystone of a business-level strategy is a decision about how the business will compete in its industry to achieve a sustainable competitive advantage. Although an SBU may contain a number of different products or brands, its competitive strategy will influence and constrain the marketing objectives, strategies, and functional programs—including the activities of the sales force—appropriate for each of those products.

Several authors have developed classification schemes that identify a few common, or "generic," strategies pursued by business units across a variety of industries. The best known of these schemes is the one developed by Michael Porter. He defined three basic competitive strategies: Low Cost, Differentiation, and Niche.[3] Another popular typology of competitive strategies was developed by Miles and Snow. They classified strategies according to the emphasis placed on growth through new product and market development, and they labeled the resulting categories Prospector, Defender, and Analyzer strategies.[4] Brief definitions of these six generic business strategies are provided in Exhibit 4.3.

For an SBU to effectively implement its competitive strategy, the marketing strategies and functional programs for each of its products should be tailored to the requirements of that strategy. For example, in the early 1980s when Campbell's soup division changed from its earlier conservative Defender strategy to a more aggressive Analyzer strategy—emphasizing new product and market development—it also had to change its marketing strategies, its advertising and promotion programs, and the role and structure of the sales force. Some specific implications of different competitive strategies for a business's sales programs and activities are also summarized in Exhibit 4.3.[5]

E X H I B I T 4 • 3 *Generic Business Strategies and Their Implications for the Sales Force*

Porter's Typology	Sales Force Implications
Low-Cost Supplier Aggressive construction of efficient-scale facilities, vigorous pursuit of cost reductions from experience, tight cost and overhead control, usually associated with high relative market share.	Servicing large current customers, pursuing large prospects, minimizing costs, selling on the basis of price, and usually assuming significant order-taking responsibilities.
Differentiation Creation of something perceived industrywide as being unique. Provides insulation against competitive rivalry because of brand loyalty and resulting lower sensitivity to price.	Selling nonprice benefits, generating orders, providing high quality of customer service and responsiveness, possibly significant amount of prospecting if high growth industry, selecting customers based on low price sensitivity. Usually requires a high-quality sales force.
Niche Service of a particular target market, with each functional policy developed with this target market in mind. Although market share in the industry might be low, the firm dominates a segment within the industry.	To become experts in the operations and opportunities associated with the target market. Focusing customer attention on nonprice benefits and allocating selling time to the target market.

Miles and Snow's Typology	Sales Force Implications
Prospector Attempt to pioneer in product/market development. Offer a frequently changing product line and be willing to sacrifice short-term profits to gain a long-term stronghold in their markets.	Primary focus is on sales volume growth. Territory management emphasizes customer penetration and prospecting.
Defender Offer a limited, stable product line to a predictable market. Markets are generally in the late growth or early maturity phase of the product life cycle. Emphasis is on being the low-cost producer through high volume.	Maintain the current customer base. Very little prospecting for new customers is involved. Customer service is emphasized along with greater account penetration.
Analyzer Choose high growth markets while holding onto substantial mature markets. Analyzers are an intermediate type of firm. They make fewer and slower product-market changes than prospectors, but are less committed to stability and efficiency than defenders.	Must balance multiple roles: servicing existing customers, prospecting for new customers, uncovering new applications, holding onto distribution of mature products, and supporting campaigns for new products.

Source: Adapted from William L. Cron and Michael Levy, "Sales Management Performance Evaluation: A Residual Income Perspective," *Journal of Personal Selling and Sales Management*, August 1987, p. 58.

Although a clear sense of mission is a necessary first step in planning, the overall mission must be translated into specific objectives for each business unit and each functional area of the firm, including marketing. For example, while Campbell's overall corporate objectives for 1992 were largely financial (e.g., to achieve a 20 percent growth in earnings and a 20 percent return on equity), it assigned marketing objectives to some of its core brands that were much more volume- and growth-oriented. Thus, Swanson's frozen dinner business was given the goal of achieving a two percentage point increase in market share to bring the brand even with Banquet, the market leader. And the business's marketing budget was increased to help it to realize its objective. Such detailed functional objectives guide the planning of each department within the organization, ensure that the plans of each functional area will be reasonably consistent, and motivate the personnel in each functional area by providing them with specific goals. Specifying marketing objectives is one thing, however; determining whether they are feasible is another. The latter involves assessing the available market opportunity.

Market opportunity analysis

In the broadest sense, a market opportunity exists whenever some human need is unsatisfied. However, an unsatisfied need represents a viable and attractive opportunity for a firm only if:

1. The opportunity is consistent with the mission and objectives of the firm.
2. There are enough potential customers for the needed product or service so the total potential sales volume is, or will be, substantial.
3. The firm has the necessary resources and expertise to capture an adequate share of the total market.

Evaluating market opportunities involves first evaluating the environmental factors affecting the market and estimating the total market potential for a good or service. Next, the firm must evaluate its capabilities and strengths compared with those of competitors to estimate the share of the total market potential it can reasonably hope to secure. Later, after a specific marketing strategy has been determined, the firm can develop sales forecasts of the actual sales volume it expects to attain over a specified time.

These estimates of total market potential, company sales potential, and sales forecasts are critical to the firm's sales plans. They provide the basis for defining sales territories, deploying salespeople, and setting sales quotas. Methods for analyzing market opportunities and generating sales forecasts are examined in more detail later in this book.

Market opportunities usually do not involve every consumer or organizational buyer in the marketplace. Market opportunities should be defined—and marketing strategies developed—for specific target markets, which usually consist of only one or a few customer segments with relatively homogeneous preferences and characteristics.

Generate strategies

Strategy generation is a creative task. Typically, several strategies will achieve the same objective. For example, a firm interested in increasing its share of the market might attempt to acquire new customers by either (1) positioning itself head to head against major competitors and attempting to establish a sustainable competitive advantage on some dimension, such as product quality or low price, or (2) differentiating itself from competitors by focusing on a unique market niche where the competition does not have a strong position. Exhibit 4.4 outlines a number of possible marketing strategies. It also summarizes a variety of functional programs—including adjustments in the amount and emphasis of personal selling efforts—that would be appropriate for implementing each strategy.[6]

The key at this stage is to be as creative as possible. The idea is not to evaluate strategies but to generate them. Listing some far-out strategies is not only acceptable at this stage, it is desirable. Later stages in the process will reduce this original list to a more reasonable set; however, generating as many ideas as possible to begin with will ensure that the better strategies are entertained when evaluating alternatives. Even the most sophisticated evaluation procedure cannot select the optimal strategy if no one has thought of it.

Select strategies

The criteria used to select the most promising marketing strategy should be directly related to the objectives to be accomplished. For example, if the major marketing objective is to increase market share, then those strategies likely to yield high share increases should be scrutinized. Typically, however, a business will have several marketing objectives, and the strategy that is best for one might be detrimental in achieving another. Thus, the best overall strategy may not be the best for any single objective.

Program marketing mix

As mentioned, a marketing program reflects a particular allocation of financial and human resources. The decision involves three questions: (1) How much is going to be spent on the total marketing effort? (2) How is that expenditure going to be allocated among the elements of the marketing mix? (3) How are the dollars and effort allocated to an element going to be divided among the possible activities? This is where the formation of the firm's strategic sales program enters the planning picture; it is one part of the firm's communications program. As suggested by Exhibit 4.4, both the amount of resources that should be devoted to the sales function and the activities to be emphasized are shaped by the overall marketing strategy and the communication tasks necessary to implement that strategy.

Review and revision

Those in charge of the functional areas of the business are typically charged with generating plans for the functions they supervise. This raises the possibility that the marketing plan prepared by a product manager may be incompatible with the business unit's financial or production plans. For example, the cash flows generated by projected product sales might be insufficient or provide too low a return on capital to produce the product. The various functional plans, therefore, must be reviewed and integrated into a cohesive whole at the business unit and corporate level.

EXHIBIT 4 ● 4 *Some Appropriate Marketing Strategies and Functional Programs for Achieving Various Marketing Objectives*

Marketing Objective	Potential Marketing Strategies	Functional Programs for Implementing Strategies
Achieve viable level of sales volume (for new product type; introductory stage of life cycle)	Stimulate primary demand—increase number of potential users by: 1. Increasing willingness to buy	a. Increase awareness through heavy advertising of product benefits b. Focus sales efforts on potential new accounts; demonstrate superior benefits of new product c. Expand variety of offerings through development of product-line extensions
	2. Increasing customers' ability to buy	a. Penetration pricing b. Attractive credit terms c. Introductory sales promotions d. Use sales efforts and trade promotion to attain more extensive distribution e. Use sales engineering and installation services to increase compatibility of new product with customers' existing operations
Market share growth (for products with low shares in growing markets)	Stimulate selective demand—acquisition of new customers by: 1. Head-to-head positioning	a. Develop superior product features b. Reduce price (if costs are lower than competitors') c. Spend more than competitors on advertising, sales force, sales promotion d. Use sales effort and trade promotion to attain broader/better distribution than competitors
	2. Differentiated positioning	a. Identify market segment with unique needs not being satisfied by competitors b. Design unique product benefits/services to satisfy target segment c. Develop unique distribution channels d. Focus sales effort on target customers and stress unique benefits/comparisons in presentations

Marketing Objective	Potential Marketing Strategies	Functional Programs for Implementing Strategies
Market share maintenance (for products with a high current share of growing markets)	Stimulate selective demand—acquisition of customers new to the market (e.g., late adopters) by: 1. Head-to-head positioning 2. Differentiated positioning Retention of current customers by: 1. Maintaining satisfaction	 (See above) (See above) a. Product improvement/quality control b. Reminder advertising to maintain familiarity c. Sales efforts focused on service and maintenance of current accounts.
	2. Simplifying the purchase process	a. Improve logistics/delivery time b. Develop complete product lines c. Price protection contracts d. "Sole-source" selling e. "Systems" selling
	3. Reducing attractiveness of switching	a. Develop brand extensions; multiple brands b. Competitive prices and promotions c. "Key" account or national account services d. Automated reorder system
Cash flow maximization (for products with a high share of mature markets)	Retention of current customers by: 1. Maintaining satisfaction 2. Simplifying purchase 3. Reducing attractiveness of switching Increase rate of purchase by current users	 (See above) (See above) (See above) a. Identify and promote alternative uses b. Reduce price; quantity discounts c. "Sole-source" selling d. Increase frequency of sales calls on major accounts
Harvesting (for products in mature or declining markets)	Retention of customers with minimum effort	a. Maintain quality of existing products b. Minimize product improvement/line extension efforts c. Competitive pricing d. Reduce advertising and sales promotion to maintenance levels e. Concentrate sales force efforts on maintenance of profitable accounts

Source: Parts of this exhibit were adapted from material found in Joseph P. Guiltinan and Gordon W. Paul, *Marketing Management: Strategies and Programs* (New York: McGraw-Hill, 1988), chap. 6. For a more detailed discussion of marketing strategies appropriate for different life-cycle stages of a product, see Orville C. Walker, Jr., Harper W. Boyd, Jr., and Jean-Claude Larréché, *Marketing Strategy: Planning and Implementation* (Homewood, Ill.: Richard D. Irwin, 1992), chaps. 8–11.

Audit and adjust

Today's volatile environment makes planning crucial and also necessitates periodic evaluations of these plans. As competitors adjust their strategies and other environmental conditions change, it may be necessary to revise the firm's plans and programs.

When goals and objectives have been spelled out in specific and measurable terms during the planning process, controlling the marketing plan is rather straightforward. It involves periodic comparisons of actual results with the sales volume, market share, expense budgets, and other objectives specific in the plan. When the results deviate from planned levels, management can attempt to find out why and, if necessary, take corrective action. This could involve adjusting specific elements of the marketing mix, adopting a new marketing strategy, or possibly reevaluating market opportunities.

The sales manager, as we have seen, plays a major role in this evaluation and control process since the manager is responsible for evaluating the results of the sales program. Part 3 of this book is devoted to a discussion of this control and adjustment process.

THE ROLE OF PERSONAL SELLING IN A FIRM'S MARKETING STRATEGY

The promotion component of a business's marketing strategy communicates information about, and stimulates demand for, its products or services among potential customers in the target market. Personal selling is only one of several promotional tools a marketing manager might use. Most textbooks categorize promotional activities into four basic types: (1) personal selling, (2) advertising, (3) sales promotion, and (4) publicity. These types are briefly defined in Exhibit 4.5.

Each of these promotional tools has certain advantages for communicating certain kinds of information to certain customers under specific conditions. The emphasis given personal selling relative to the other promotional tools depends on its suitability to the communications tasks.

Advantages of Personal Selling as a Promotional Tool

The advantages of personal selling as a promotional tool stem largely from its face-to-face communication with a potential customer. Personal sales messages are often more persuasive than advertising or publicity in the mass media. In a face-to-face setting, the potential buyer is more likely to feel obliged to pay attention to the sales representative's message. Also, since the salesperson communicates with only one potential customer at a time, the rep can tailor the message to fit the needs and interests of that specific customer. In addition, communication flows in both directions during a sales call. The sales representative receives immediate feedback from the customer in the form of questions, objections, and nonverbal communication such as yawns and shrugs. Thus, the representative often knows immediately when a particular sales approach is not working and then can try a different tack.

EXHIBIT 4 ● 5   *Types of Promotional Activities*

Personal selling
    Oral communication with a potential customer on a person-to-person basis.

Advertising
    Nonpersonal communication the organization pays to have transmitted to a target
    audience through a mass medium, such as television, radio, newspapers, magazines,
    direct mail, transit cards, billboards, catalogs, or directories.

Sales promotion
    Activities and materials that induce potential customers to purchase the firm's product
    or service, usually by drawing the customer's attention to the product or by offering an
    added incentive for purchase. Sales promotion methods are usually classified into two
    types based on the audience they are directed toward. *Consumer sales promotion
    activities* are designed to produce short-run sales increases among ultimate
    consumers by offering such things as "cents-off" coupons, free samples, and contests.
    Trade sales promotion activities encourage wholesalers or retailers to stock and
    aggressively market the firm's product by offering such things as quantity discounts,
    free goods, display materials, and sales contests.

Publicity
    Nonpersonal communication of information about a firm or its products is transmitted
    through a mass medium at no charge to the firm. Examples include magazine,
    newspaper, radio, or television news stories about new products, new stores or
    personnel, or policy changes in an organization.

Another advantage of face-to-face contact in personal selling is that the sales representative can communicate a larger amount of complex information than can be transmitted with other promotional tools. The salesperson can demonstrate the product or use visual aids. And since the salesperson is likely to call on the same client many times, the rep can devote a great deal of time to educating that client about the advantages of a product. The long-term contact in personal selling is particularly important when the product can be customized to fit the needs of an individual customer—as in the case of computer systems and insurance policies—or when the terms of the sale are open to negotiation.

The primary disadvantage of personal selling is that a sales representative can communicate with only a small number of potential customers. Consequently, personal selling is much more costly per person reached than the other promotional tools. An advertisement in *Reader's Digest* costs less than a penny per reader, but the cost of an average industrial sales call is estimated to be between $235 and $300.

Determinants of Personal Selling's Appropriate Strategic Role

Economists argue a business should budget additional financial resources for personal selling only if two conditions are met:

1. The firm receives a greater profit return from the last (marginal) dollar invested in personal selling than it would by spending that dollar on any other part of the marketing program or on any other company activity.

2. Each dollar spent on personal selling produces at least one dollar of marginal income.

Lack of information and uncertainties in costs and revenues make it impossible for a marketing manager to apply this kind of marginal analysis explicitly in deciding how much emphasis to give personal selling. Nevertheless, the concept is valid, and it suggests an important point. Since the costs of communicating with a potential customer through personal selling are high relative to other promotional tools, the sales force should be emphasized only in those marketing situations where the advantages of personal selling outweigh its high costs.

In other words, personal selling should play a substantial role in the firm's marketing mix only when the communications tasks involved are performed better by face-to-face selling than any other method. Such communications tasks include the following:

1. Transmitting large amounts of complex information about the firm's products or policies.

2. Adapting product offerings and/or promotional appeals to the unique needs and interest of specific customers.

3. Convincing customers that the firm's products or services are better on at least some dimensions than similar offerings of competitors.

As Exhibit 4.6 indicates, the communications tasks actually faced by a business—and the appropriate amount of personal selling effort to be used in the marketing strategy—depend on the business's objectives, marketing strategy, and resources; the number and kind of customers in its target market; and the nature of the other elements of its marketing mix.

Company resources, objectives, and marketing strategy

Although the costs per person reached are high for personal selling, a successful personal selling effort may require a smaller total financial outlay than either an advertising or a sales promotion campaign. One major advertising agency refuses to represent consumer goods manufacturers unless they are willing to spend at least $5 million annually on their advertising campaigns. The agency believes an effective national advertising campaign cannot be undertaken for less. The high costs involved in extensive advertising and sales promotion efforts limit their use by smaller firms. Such firms must often rely on personal selling—perhaps supplemented with less expensive local, regional, or cooperative advertising—as their primary promotional tool.

As we saw earlier, formulating a marketing plan involves setting specific objectives for a particular product in a chosen target market and then developing a marketing strategy to accomplish those objectives. Those objectives and strategies help determine the kinds of communications tasks that must be accomplished and the most appropriate promotional tools to use.

For example, if a firm is introducing a new product to the market or

EXHIBIT 4 ● 6 *Factors Influencing the Role of Personal Selling in a Firm's Marketing Strategy*

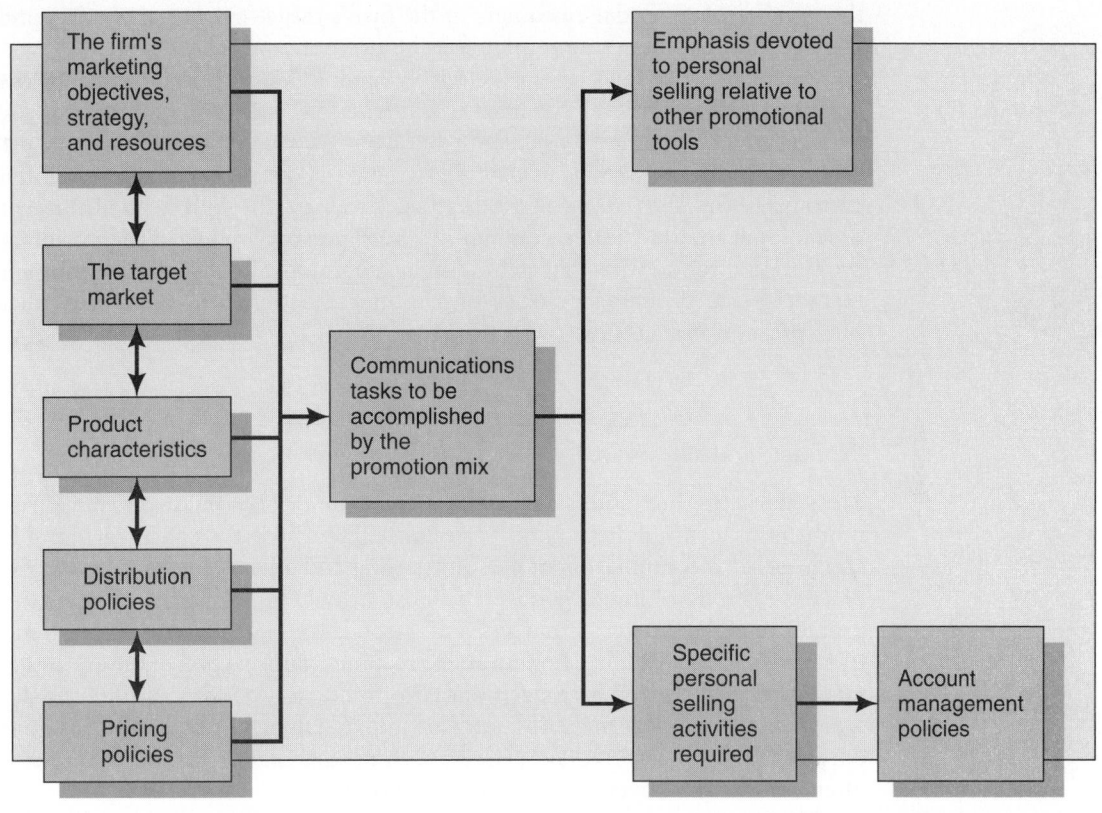

entering an existing product into new markets, marketing objectives might be to stimulate primary demand and to generate awareness of the product among potential customers. Media advertising and sales promotion are the best tools to accomplish such an objective because they can communicate basic information about the product to many potential buyers with great efficiency.

If the firm's objective is to expand distribution by persuading more wholesalers or retailers to carry the product, then a strong personal selling effort and perhaps a trade promotion program are indicated. The highly persuasive nature of personal selling also makes it an appropriate tool when the objective is to take market share away from established competitors, especially if the product is a relatively complex industrial or consumer durable good. Finally, if the objective is simply to maintain the market share of a well-established product, "reminder" advertising should play the primary role in the promotional mix.

Characteristics of the target market

Because various promotional tools differ greatly in their costs per person reached, the number of potential customers in the firm's target market, their size, and their geographic distribution influence the promotional mix.

Since costs per sales call are relatively high, personal selling is most often emphasized when the target market contains relatively few customers, the average customer is likely to place a relatively large order, and customers are clustered close together. Firms that sell to industrial markets with few potential customers, and those that distribute their products through a small number of wholesale intermediaries, commonly rely on personal selling as their primary promotional tool. Firms that sell to large, geographically dispersed, consumer markets place primary emphasis on the more cost-efficient advertising and sales promotion methods.

Product characteristics

Most marketing textbooks suggest that the promotional mixes for industrial products concentrate heavily on personal selling; those for consumer durable goods utilize a combination of personal selling and advertising; and producers of consumer nondurable goods rely most heavily on advertising and sales promotion. The reason is that industrial goods and consumer durables tend to be more complex than nondurables, so potential buyers need more information to make a purchase decision. Also, industrial goods can often be designed or modified to meet the needs of individual customers, and consumer durables (as well as complex services, such as financial or insurance services) often present the buyer with a range of options.

These generalizations are largely supported by the information in Exhibit 4.7, which shows personal selling costs as a percent of sales across a variety of industries. Note that sales force expenses account for a much larger proportion of total revenue in industrial products and service industries (e.g., construction, chemicals, paper products, insurance, etc.) than in consumer nondurable industries, such as food and recreation.

But these generalizations should be viewed with caution. Industrial goods producers usually stress personal selling, but they might also do extensive advertising to build awareness of the company and its products so the sales force can gain access to potential customers more easily. As we saw in Chapter 1, for example, Xerox relies heavily on broadcast and print advertising, as well as a variety of sales promotion programs, to back up its personal selling efforts. Similarly, although a consumer goods producer like Campbell might spend large sums on media advertising, it is also likely to field a sales force to call on retailers and build reseller support in its distribution channels. Some consumer firms, like Campbell, give their salespeople authority to develop and implement local consumer and trade promotion programs.

EXHIBIT 4 • 7   *Sales Force Costs across Selected Industries*

Industry Group	Sales Force Costs as a Percent of Total Sales	Industry Group	Sales Force Costs as a Percent of Total Sales
Agriculture	4.7%	Instruments	5.4%
Amusement/recreation services	2.5	Insurance	4.0
Apparel/other textile products	3.0	Machinery	3.8
Business services	4.2	Manufacturing	3.0
Chemicals	4.0	Office equipment	2.8
Communications	3.8	Paper/allied products	4.8
Construction	5.0	Primary metal products	3.8
Electronic components	4.3	Printing/publishing	3.2
Electronics	4.2	Rubber/plastics	3.0
Fabricated metals	3.8	Wholesale (consumer)	2.2
Food products	1.7	Wholesale (industrial)	3.2
Average	**3.7%**		

Note: Industry groups reflect categories selected and reported by Dartnell Corporation. The overall average has been calculated by *Sales & Marketing Management* based on data from the 22 industries listed.

Source: Dartnell Corporation, *26th Survey of Sales Force Compensation* © 1990; Dartnell Corporation. As reported in "Compensation & Expenses," *Sales & Marketing Management*, June 17, 1991, p. 76.

Distribution policies

As mentioned, personal selling is often necessary to build reseller support and develop adequate distribution for a product, regardless of whether it is a consumer or an industrial good. The importance of the sales force's role in building a distribution channel is influenced by the firm's strategy for inducing resellers to buy its product. When a firm follows a **pull strategy,** it attempts to build strong customer demand for its brand. This encourages wholesalers and retailers to carry the product to satisfy their customers and reap the resulting sales and profits. A strong advertising program is a key to such a strategy.

When a firm uses a **push strategy** to build reseller support, it offers direct inducements to potential wholesalers and retailers to encourage them to stock the product. When consumers see the product in the store, it is hoped that they will like it and buy it. A wide range of inducements can be offered to resellers, including larger-than-average margins, various trade sales promotion offerings, contests for the reseller's salespeople, cooperative advertising programs, sales aids, and point-of-purchase promotion materials. The manufacturer's sales force plays a principal role in implementing a push strategy. The sales force must explain the advantages of carrying the firm's products to potential channel members and persuade them to stock and aggressively merchandise those products.[7]

EXHIBIT 4 ● 8   *Marketing Strategy Characteristics and the Relative Importance of Personal Selling as a Promotional Tool*

Advertising relatively important		Personal selling relatively important
	Number of customers	
Large ←		→ Small
	Buyers' information needs	
Low ←		→ High
	Size and importance of purchase	
Small ←		→ Large
	Postpurchase service required	
Little ←		→ Much
	Product complexity	
Low ←		→ High
	Distribution strategy	
Pull ←		→ Push
	Pricing policy	
Pre-set ←		→ Negotiated
	Resources available for promotion	
Many ←		→ Few

Source: Adapted from David W. Cravens, *Strategic Marketing* (Homewood, Ill.: Richard D. Irwin, 1987), p. 508.

Pricing policies

A firm's pricing policies can also influence the composition of its promotion mix. "Big-ticket" items, both industrial goods and consumer durables, typically require substantial amounts of personal selling. Such expensive products are often technically or aesthetically sophisticated, and customers perceive substantial risk in purchasing them. Therefore, potential buyers usually want the kind of detailed information and advice they can get only from a salesperson before making their decisions.

Also, personal selling is essential in marketing products or services where the ultimate selling price is open to negotiation. Price negotiations can occur only when there is face-to-face contact between a salesperson and a potential buyer. Although negotiated pricing policies are most commonly found among marketers of industrial goods and services, they are also followed in the sale of some consumer durables, such as automobiles.

The importance of personal selling relative to other promotional tools depends on various characteristics of the marketing strategy, including the size and nature of the target market, the complexity and service requirements of the product, and the other elements of the marketing mix. The impact of these factors on the relative importance of personal selling is summarized in Exhibit 4.8.

ACCOUNT MANAGEMENT POLICIES

Simply budgeting the money necessary to fund a large sales force is no guarantee it will effectively perform its role. Selling success depends on how the members of the sales force do their jobs—the kinds of selling activities they engage in and the manner in which those activities are carried out. Salespeople must know the basics of salesmanship—gained through training, experience, or both—before they can make an effective sales call.

But such knowledge alone is not sufficient for outstanding selling performance. As one authority points out, the salesperson "must have guidelines to help decide such things as which specific activities are the key to selling success . . . what selling strategy to use with various customers . . . and how to divide his or her time between servicing existing accounts and prospecting for new ones."[8] Therefore, as a first step in designing a strategic sales program, the sales manager should develop clearly defined account management policies to guide the efforts of the sales representatives.

As we saw in Chapter 1, strategic sales planning is concerned with allocating the firm's sales efforts across different types of potential customers. Account management policies specify which individuals within each type of customer organization the salesperson should attempt to contact, what kinds of selling and service activities should be engaged in, and how those activities should be conducted. Some companies have explicit policies concerning such things as (1) whether salespeople should work through customers' purchasing departments or attempt to call directly on higher level decision makers, (2) the amount of effort and detail to be included in preparing proposals for different types of accounts, and (3) the kinds of information to be reported back to the home office after a sales call.

The Account Management Planning Process

The major steps in formulating sales programs and account management policies are outlined in Exhibit 4.9. The process should begin with careful consideration of the objectives and target markets specified in the marketing plan and analysis of the sales potential represented by various customers and potential customers within the targeted segments. The tools and techniques for estimating sales potential are discussed in Chapter 6.

Next, the sales manager must plan a basic sales program—determining the number of salespeople needed, how they are to be organized, and the design of sales territories—as a first step toward directing appropriate amounts of effort toward target customers.

In some firms, sales planning stops here. Once salespeople are assigned to territories, it is up to them to decide how frequently to call on customers. While this gives the salesperson maximum flexibility to adjust efforts to situations in a specific territory and minimizes the time and expense involved in formal planning, individual salespeople do not always match their selling efforts to the sales or profit potential of the accounts in their territory.

EXHIBIT 4 ● 9   *The Sales Program and Account Management Planning Process*

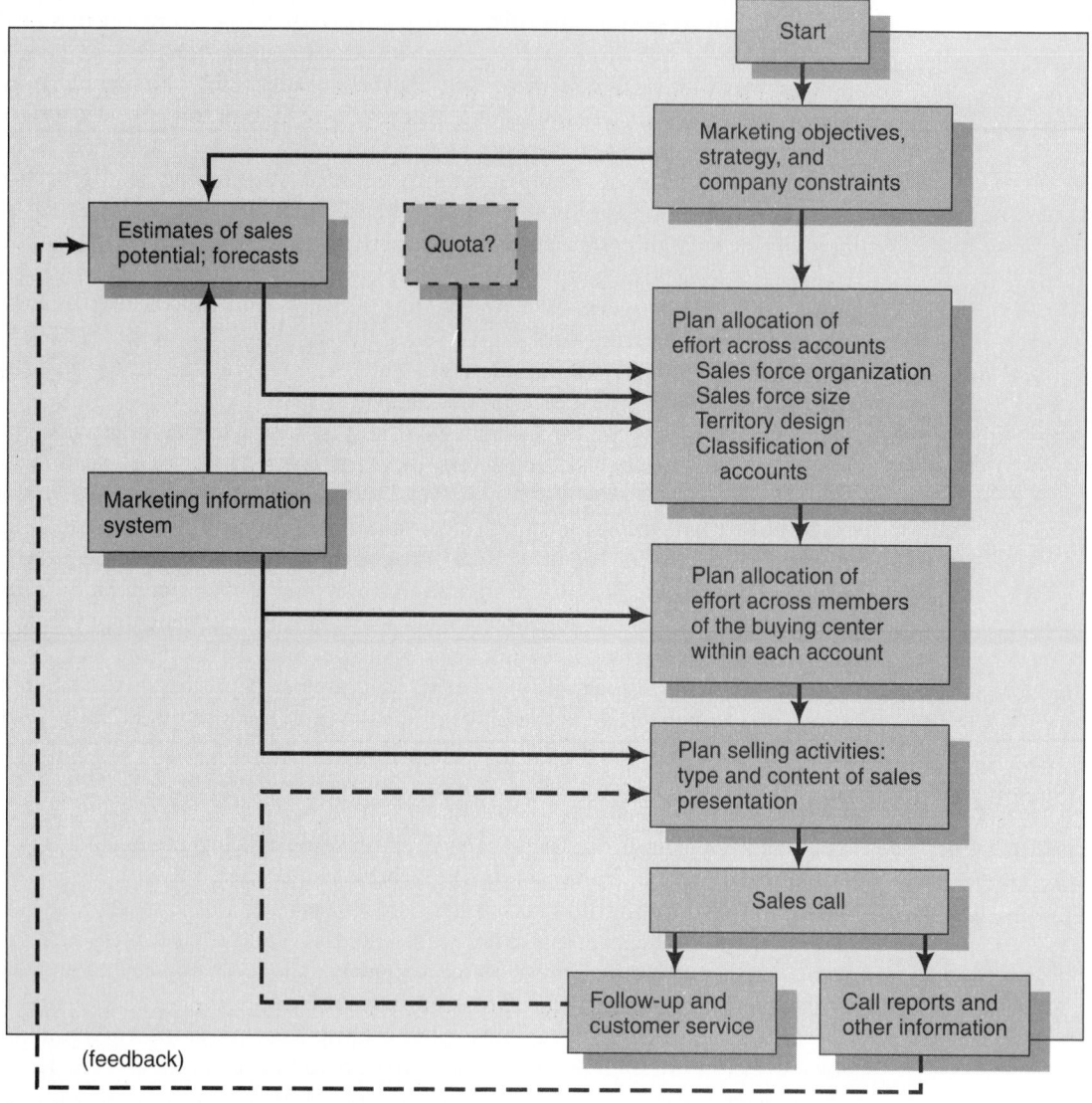

Source: Adapted from John M. Gwin and William D. Perreault, Jr., "Industrial Sales Call Planning," *Industrial Marketing Management* 10 (1981), p. 229.

Some salespeople are "cherry pickers" who spend an inordinate time with current customers where there is a high probability of getting an order, rather than working to develop new customers—even though they may offer greater long-run potential. Other salespeople are simply reluctant to call on certain companies or types of accounts because of negative past experiences, personality conflicts, or a dislike for the procedures involved. In the fashion industry, for example, some salespeople are said to be "plate glass shy" because they are reluctant to call on large department stores where they have to deal with sophisticated buyers and compete with many other sellers. The point is that salespeople often concentrate on those accounts where there is a high probability of attaining reasonable sales volume with reasonable effort, without regard to long-run potential or profitability.

While many salespeople pursue "easy" sales from established customers, they do not always spend enough time and effort strengthening their relationships with—or increasing their share of the purchases made by—such customers. But the maturing of many industries, and the increased concentration of those industries due to mergers and acquisitions, is prompting many firms to focus more of their marketing and sales efforts on satisfying, retaining, and winning increased sales from established accounts. Recent research indicates such efforts can be crucial for improving a firm's sales productivity.[9] This important problem is discussed in Thorny Issues in Sales Management 4.1 (pp. 128–29), together with some of its implications for account management policies.

To overcome problems like those described above, some firms classify the accounts in each territory—or the various products handled by their sales force—into several categories according to their relative sales potential, profitability, or importance to accomplishing the objectives specified in the marketing plan. Policies can then be formulated concerning the amount of effort each salesperson should devote to each class of customers or products.[10] For example, salespeople might be instructed to call on all high-potential type A accounts at least once a month, while less important B accounts are visited only once every two months.

Such policies are often further formalized through developing separate volume or activity quotas for each category of customers or products and reinforced by tying incentive bonuses or other rewards to meeting those quotas. These approaches for detailed planning of sales efforts according to the relative potential or profitability of different types of customers or products are explored in more detail in Chapters 7 and 8.

The next step in sales planning is to decide how individual sales calls will be carried out. As Exhibit 4.9 indicates, this involves two sets of decisions: (1) what individuals within the customer's organization should be contacted, and (2) what selling activities should be engaged in and how should they be carried out? While this kind of sales call planning is primarily the responsibility of the individual salesperson, this stage in the planning process is often the manager's last real opportunity to actively and constructively affect what the salesperson does in the field. Consequently, the manager should ensure the sales rep assumes responsibility for this aspect of planning and provide appropriate account management policies to guide the salesperson's activities before, during, and after the sales call.[11]

Thorny Issues in Sales Management 4 • 1

Productivity Indicators for Those Who Rate Themselves Highly Effective vs. Overall Survey Average

Practice	Percent Who Consider Themselves Very Effective or Quite Effective	Profitability			Cost of Sales		
		Overall Survey	Effective Firms	Percent Difference	Overall Survey	Effective Firms	Percent Difference
Systems selling to major accounts	18%	11.8%	15.2%	28.8%	14%	11.8%	(15.7%)
Determining the profitbility of sales to each account	20	11.8	21.8	84.7	14	13.6	(2.9)
Selling at higher prices	27	11.8	8.4	(28.8)	14	12.8	(8.6)
Gaining share within existing accounts	37	11.8	32.7	177	14	12.5	(10.7)
Selling new products	32	11.8	34.4	192	14	16.3	16.4
Retaining existing accounts	62	11.8	22.6	91.5	14	13.1	(6.4)

Note: Profitability is given as the ratio of profits to total sales; cost of sales as the ratio of reported sales costs to total sales.

THE INCREASING IMPORTANCE OF ESTABLISHED CUSTOMERS

Sales to established customers are usually less costly to obtain, and therefore more profitable, than sales to new accounts. As we saw earlier, respondents in a recent survey reported it took an average of seven sales calls to make a sale to a new customer compared to only three calls per sale to established accounts.

As many industries mature and as more global competitors enter regional markets, competition for available sales dollars is intensifying. The most successful firms in many industries are those that can take customers away from the competition while keeping their own. Firms that do an excellent job of servicing and satisfying established customers, and can capture an increasing share of those customers' purchases, usually enjoy greater growth and profitability than firms that take their customers for granted.

This conclusion is reflected in the results of a recent survey of 192 firms in a variety of industries. As the results in the following table indicate, respondents who considered their company to be effective at such things as retaining existing accounts, increasing their share of purchases made by such customers, focusing on profitable customers, and selling integrated systems to their major accounts had substantially higher profitability and lower selling costs than the average for all respondents.

Note, however, that only two thirds of the respondents considered themselves *effective* at retaining existing customers, and only about a third believed they were doing a good job of gaining share or selling new products to established accounts. This indicates many companies perceive a need to improve their account management policies concerning established customers and key accounts. Thus, more firms are adopting the kinds

(continued)

of account management and key account policies discussed in this chapter to improve their customer service and sales performance among existing cus- tomers. And they are seeking new ways to improve customer service and satisfaction; some of which we will discuss in more detail throughout this text.

Source: William A. O'Connell and William Keenan, Jr. "The Shape of Things to Come," *Sales & Marketing Management* (January 1990), pp. 36–41. See also Barry Faber and Joyce Wycoff, "Customer Service: Evolution and Revolution," *Sales & Marketing Management* (May 1991), pp. 44–51.

Policies Concerning Major or Key Accounts

One account management policy becoming increasingly critical to effective sales management is the firm's posture with respect to winning and keeping major accounts—those very large customers that represent a disproportionate share of the firm's total sales volume. Environmental changes are forcing both industrial goods producers and consumer goods firms in many industries to place greater emphasis on such accounts.

The major account is becoming more important to many firms for several reasons. For one thing, industrial concentration and growth have produced some extremely large organizations with equally large purchasing requirements. The 195-unit Jeans West chain, for instance, makes much larger purchases, demands a more sophisticated selling approach, and expects better service than a single-unit, neighborhood sportswear store.

Also, large organizations have moved toward centralized purchasing to gain greater buying efficiency. Consequently, it is no longer easy for several suppliers to split a prospect's business by making separate sales to different divisions. Another trend has been the increasing complexity—and price—of many products. The sale of a single computer system to one large customer can represent millions of dollars in revenue.

In response to the growing importance of major accounts, some firms are adopting a major account management selling philosophy. This philosophy stresses the dual goals of making sales and developing long-term relationships with large customers. Selling is part of major account management, but this approach also stresses that salespeople can perform other functions for the customer that make them a valuable adjunct to the customer's organization. The salesperson can provide expert advice and counsel to the customer, including advice on the engineering, design, and installation of complete product systems.

Purchasing total systems originated with the government's practices in buying major weapons and communications systems. Instead of making all of the individual decisions involved in purchasing and putting together the various components of such systems, the government solicits bids from prime contractors, who are then responsible for assembling the entire package or system—either by making the components or buying them from subcontractors.

Many nongovernment organizations have also turned to integrated systems to reduce the costs and uncertainties associated with buying technically complicated and interrelated products. Consequently, sellers are engaging in **systems selling** more frequently as one way to provide better service and satisfaction to major customers.

Systems selling involves two components: (1) the design of well-integrated groups of interlocking products (which is likely to involve negotiations with other subcontractors or original equipment manufacturers) and (2) the implementation of a system of production, inventory control, distribution, and other services to meet a major customer's needs for a smooth-running operation.

Major account management policies also often emphasize activities to be performed by the salesperson *after* a sale is made. These activities typically include such routine servicing as expediting credit approval and delivery. They can also include more extensive service where the salesperson acts as the *customer's representative* to the selling company and attempts to ensure that the company is adequately meeting the needs of the buyer.

Because major account management requires that a salesperson devote almost constant attention to the needs of a single customer, firms that use this approach typically have two separate sales forces. One calls on smaller customers, and one is a force of account managers who devote all their time to one or a few major accounts.

Some national accounts are so large and important that a firm may assign a team of representatives (consisting of people from various functional departments of the company) to a single customer. The sales team may include representatives from different levels in the company's management hierarchy, too. Each deals with purchase influencers and decision makers at corresponding levels in the customer's organization. In other words, implementing a major account management program can have important implications for the way a firm organizes its sale force. These and other organizational considerations involved in strategic sales planning are examined in Chapter 5.

S UMMARY

Planning is deciding what to do in the present to achieve what is desired in the future. The planning process begins with a statement of the company's mission and goals. Marketing goals that result from these corporate goals are best achieved through a marketing plan.

The marketing plan logically includes (1) the assessment of market opportunities available and an estimation of the resources necessary to capture an adequate share of the market, (2) the generation of possible strategies, (3) the selection of a strategy that best achieves the stated objectives, and (4) the programming of the marketing mix or allocation of resources to the marketing effort, including the sales function. The plans prepared by each functional area need to be reviewed and integrated at the corporate level. This may entail some revision to make them compatible. Once adopted, the plans must be continually monitored and adjusted as conditions warrant.

The advantages of personal selling as a promotional tool stem largely from the fact that it involves face-to-face communication with a potential customer. For many products and in many industries, advertising is viewed as more effective than personal selling in creating awareness and in reinforcing already held opinions. Personal selling is viewed as the more effective in changing opinions and behaviors. The role personal selling should play in the firm's marketing strategy is logically a function of (1) company resources and objectives, (2) characteristics of the target market, (3) product characteristics, (4) distribution policies, and (5) pricing policies.

The company's view of the purchasing process and the roles played by the members of a prospect's buying center affect the account management policies it adopts. Many firms have explicit policies on what salespeople are to do at each stage in the buying process.

In response to the growing importance of major accounts—those very large customers that represent a disproportionate share of the firm's total sales volume—many firms are also developing explicit policies regarding how such customers should be handled. Often these policies dictate that salespeople should perform functions for the customer's organization that make them more valuable to the customer. These functions might involve designing complete systems, which include components not manufactured by the representative's employer, or assisting in the installation of such systems. Sometimes the salesperson is told to act as the customer's representative to make sure the customer's needs are satisfied.

Discussion Questions

1. As a new employee of an organization, you have become aware of an obvious need for more planning on the organization's part. However, your superiors believe planning is a waste because of the rapidly changing environment of the organization. Present a persuasive argument advocating more extensive planning.

2. If you were in top management in the following organizations, how would you most appropriately define your organization's mission?
   a. McDonald's restaurants.
   b. Pittsburgh Pirates baseball club.
   c. A local parent-teacher association.
   d. Allstate Insurance Company.

3. The chapter discusses various typologies useful for classifying the competitive strategies of strategic business units (SBU). Using the Miles and Snow typology, how would the marketing strategies and tactics of a *prospector* SBU vary from those adopted by a *defender* SBU? Which would be the best option for a *prospector* SBU? A sales force that sells only for the *prospector* SBU? Or a sales force that is *shared* with a *defender* SBU that sells products for both SBUs? What are the relevant issues to consider?

4. In the last 15 years, economic ups and downs occurred frequently. Downturns usually lead to broad, sweeping corporate edicts to become "lean and mean" or "tighten your belts" by eliminating all fat. Such a "wartime" mentality has led firms such as Xerox, IBM, Kodak, Coca-Cola, Heinz, and Wrangler Jeans to reduce "too rich" programs. Carried to the extreme, such cutbacks can reduce an organization's ability to rebound when the economy improves. How can a corporation become "lean and mean," and what symptoms would indicate that cutbacks have gone too far?

5. "Hard times and changing business conditions are pushing a growing number of top corporate officers into the front lines of the sales wars." (*The Wall Street Journal*, August 6, 1991, pp. B1, B8). What are the advantages of having top corporate officers, presidents in some cases, becoming involved in direct sales activities? What are the disadvantages?

6. Team selling has received considerable attention. More and more companies are teaming salespeople, technical experts, and others to work with high-potential customers and prospects. This combination, called a cross-functional sales team, raises several questions. Is cross-functional selling the best way to sell to major accounts? Who benefits from this approach? Under what conditions should a company adopt the team selling approach?

7. "The Sound of No Dealers Selling," is the title of an article that appeared in *Forbes*, February 19, 1990, pp. 122, 124. Nissan's entry into the luxury car market, the Infiniti, relies on a new sales strategy best expressed as: "High pressure is out; Zen is in." High-pressure language, "I slam dunk the mooch" (translated: "I do whatever it takes to keep the customer (mooch) from getting off the lot without buying a car"), is no longer acceptable. The Infiniti dealer welcomes customers Japanese style, as "honored guests" not mooches. Many old-line dealers scoff at Nissan's Zen-sell for the $38,500 Infiniti. Why did Nissan adopt this marketing strategy? Will it succeed?

8. Collaborative marketing is an old strategy that has been the subject of considerable recent thought. Collaboration between Apple Computer and IBM and Ford and Mazda are examples of newly formed cooperative marketing ventures. What trends have contributed to these recent developments? In what ways can companies collaborate? What are the dangers of collaboration?

Endnotes

[1] As was the case in Chapter 3, this example is based on material found in Rayna Skolnik, "Campbell Stirs Up Its Sales Force," *Sales & Marketing Management* (April 1986), pp. 56–58; Bill Saporito, "The Fly in Campbell's Soup," *Fortune*, May 9, 1988, pp. 67–70; Joseph Weber, "From Soup to Nuts and Back to Soup," *Business Week*, November 5, 1990, pp. 114–16; Joseph Weber, "Campbell Is Bubbling, But for How Long?" *Business Week*, June 17, 1991, pp. 56–57; and Bill Saporito, "Campbell Soup Gets Piping Hot," *Fortune*, September 9, 1991, pp. 142–48.

[2] Orville C. Walker, Jr., Harper W. Boyd, Jr., and Jean-Claude Larréché, *Marketing Strategy: Planning and Implementation* (Homewood, Ill.: Richard D. Irwin, Inc., 1992), chap. 1.

[3] Michael E. Porter, *Competitive Strategy* (New York: Free Press, 1980), chap. 2.

[4] Raymond E. Miles and Charles C. Snow, *Organizational Strategy, Structure and Process* (New York: McGraw-Hill, 1978). Miles and Snow also identified a fourth category of businesses, which they called Re-

actors. However, because Reactors are businesses with no clearly defined or consistent competitive strategy, we will ignore this group.

[5]For a more detailed discussion of how a business's competitive strategy influences its marketing and sales strategies and programs, see Orville C. Walker, Jr., and Robert W. Ruekert, "Marketing's Role in the Implementation of Business Strategies: A Critical Review and Conceptual Framework," *Journal of Marketing* (July 1987), pp. 15–33. See also Walker, Boyd, and Larréché, *Marketing Strategy,* chap. 3.

[6]See also William Strahle and Rosann L. Spiro, "Linking Market Share Strategies to Salesforce Objectives, Activities, and Compensation Policies," *Journal of Personal Selling and Sales Management* (August 1986), pp. 11–18.

[7]For a more detailed discussion of the role of personal selling and other promotional tools in gaining reseller support, see Benson P. Shapiro, "Improve Distribution with Your Promotional Mix," *Harvard Business Review* (March–April 1977), pp. 115–23; James A. Narus and James C. Anderson, "Turn Your Industrial

Distributors into Partners," *Harvard Business Review* (March–April 1986), pp. 66–71; and F. Robert Dwyer, Paul H. Schurr, and Sejo Oh, "Developing Buyer-Seller Relationships," *Journal of Marketing* (April 1987), pp. 11–27.

[8]B. Charles Ames, "Build Marketing Strength into Industrial Selling," *Harvard Business Review* (January–February 1982), p. 52. See also William Strahle and Rosann Spiro, "Linking Market Share Strategies"; and Kate Reilly and Eric Baron, "Teaching Salespeople the Five W's and H of Sales Call Planning," *Business Marketing,* August 1987, pp. 62–66.

[9]William A. O'Connell and William Keenan, Jr., "The Shape of Things to Come," *Sales & Marketing Management* (January 1990), pp. 36–41.

[10]Donald L. Brady, "Determining the Value of an Industrial Prospect: A Prospect Preference Index Model," *Journal of Personal Selling and Sales Management* (August 1987), pp. 27–32.

[11]John M. Gwin and William D. Perreault, Jr., "Industrial Sales Call Planning," *Industrial Marketing Management* 10 (1981), pp. 225–34.

Suggested Readings

Strategic Marketing and Sales Planning

Strahle, William, and Rosann L. Spiro. "Linking Market Share Strategies to Salesforce Objectives, Activities, and Compensation Policies," *Journal of Personal Selling and Sales Management* (August 1986), pp. 11–18.

Walker, Orville C., Jr., Harper W. Boyd, Jr., and Jean-Claude Larréché. *Marketing Strategy: Planning and Implementation.* Homewood, Ill.: Richard D. Irwin, Inc., 1992, chaps. 1, 2.

Account Management Policies

Brady, Donald L. "Determining the Value of an Industrial Prospect: A Prospect Preference Index Model." *Journal of Personal Selling and Sales Management* (August 1987), pp. 27–32.

Gwin, John M., and William D. Perreault, Jr. "Industrial Sales call Planning." *Industrial Marketing Management* 10 (1981), pp. 225–34.

O'Connell, William A. and William Keenan, Jr. "The Shape of Things to Come." *Sales & Marketing Management* (January 1990), pp. 36–41.

Reilly, Kate, and Eric Baron. "Teaching Salespeople the Five W's and H of Sales Call Planning." *Business Marketing,* August 1987, pp. 62–66.

Organizing the Selling Effort

NOVELL, INC., REORGANIZES FOR BETTER CUSTOMER SERVICE[1]

As a firm's markets mature and its customers' needs evolve, the sales manager should periodically ask a tough question: "Is our sales force organized to serve customers as well as possible?" The managers at Novell, Inc., recently answered, "No."

Novell, based in Provo, Utah, makes and markets software designed to link different types and brands of computers into networks. With sales of $422 million in fiscal 1989, the firm reported it was the industry leader, accounting for about 70 percent of the installed base of local-area-network operating systems.

Novell sells its software primarily through major computer retailers (e.g., ComputerLand Corp.), distributors, original equipment manufacturers (OEMs) that incorporate it into computer systems they market to their own customers, and other resellers. Its direct sales force is primarily responsible for supporting the sales efforts of those intermediaries, although Novell salespeople also deal directly with about 300 large corporate and government customers.

In the firm's early years, Novell's sales force was organized solely on a geographic basis. Each sales rep was assigned a rather small geographic territory and was responsible for servicing all of the local major accounts, OEMs, distributors, and retailers in that area.

But as network computing became more widespread among corporations and government agencies during the 1980s, and as customers became more sophisticated and began to identify specific problems and unique needs for their computer networks to address, Novell's generalist approach lost its effectiveness. A single sales rep could no longer be knowledgeable about all the applications necessary to solve the different problems and needs of the various customers.

The company reorganized its sales force into three distinct groups, each focused on servicing a different segment of the market. James C. Bills, Novell's executive vice president of sales, reports the reorganization has improved the firm's national account marketing by helping the company better serve its major customers' increasingly sophisticated needs, and it has facilitated joint sales calls with resellers. "By dividing our business along logical and clearly defined market segments," says Mr. Bills, "we've put specialists in charge of areas where they can use their expertise more effectively. It also adds to the support we give to our resellers and distributors, because we've dedicated entire sales groups specifically to serve their needs."

As diagrammed in Exhibit 5.1, Novell's reorganized sales force serves three core market segments: major users, OEMs/systems integrators, and resellers. The major users are further divided into four subsegments. The top 60 Fortune 500 companies are categorized as national accounts. The next 240 corporations are considered major accounts. Federal, state, and local governments are treated as a third subsegment because their purchasing procedures, as well as their needs, tend to be different from those of major corporations. And the fourth customer group consists of large educational institutions.

Novell's new OEM/systems integrator sales team works with vendors that incorporate the firm's software into their own hardware and software applications. Among the customers in this segment are firms such as NCR Corp., Wang Laboratories, and Electronic Data Systems.

The salespeople serving the reseller segment cater to distributors and major retailers, such as Businessland, Inc. This group controls dealer inventories, implements dealer incentive programs, helps train dealer salespeople, and accompanies them on sales calls to potential customers.

A fourth group of people in Novell's sales organization, field management, consists of regional sales managers who coordinate the efforts of the three

EXHIBIT **5 • 1** *Novell's New Sales Organization*

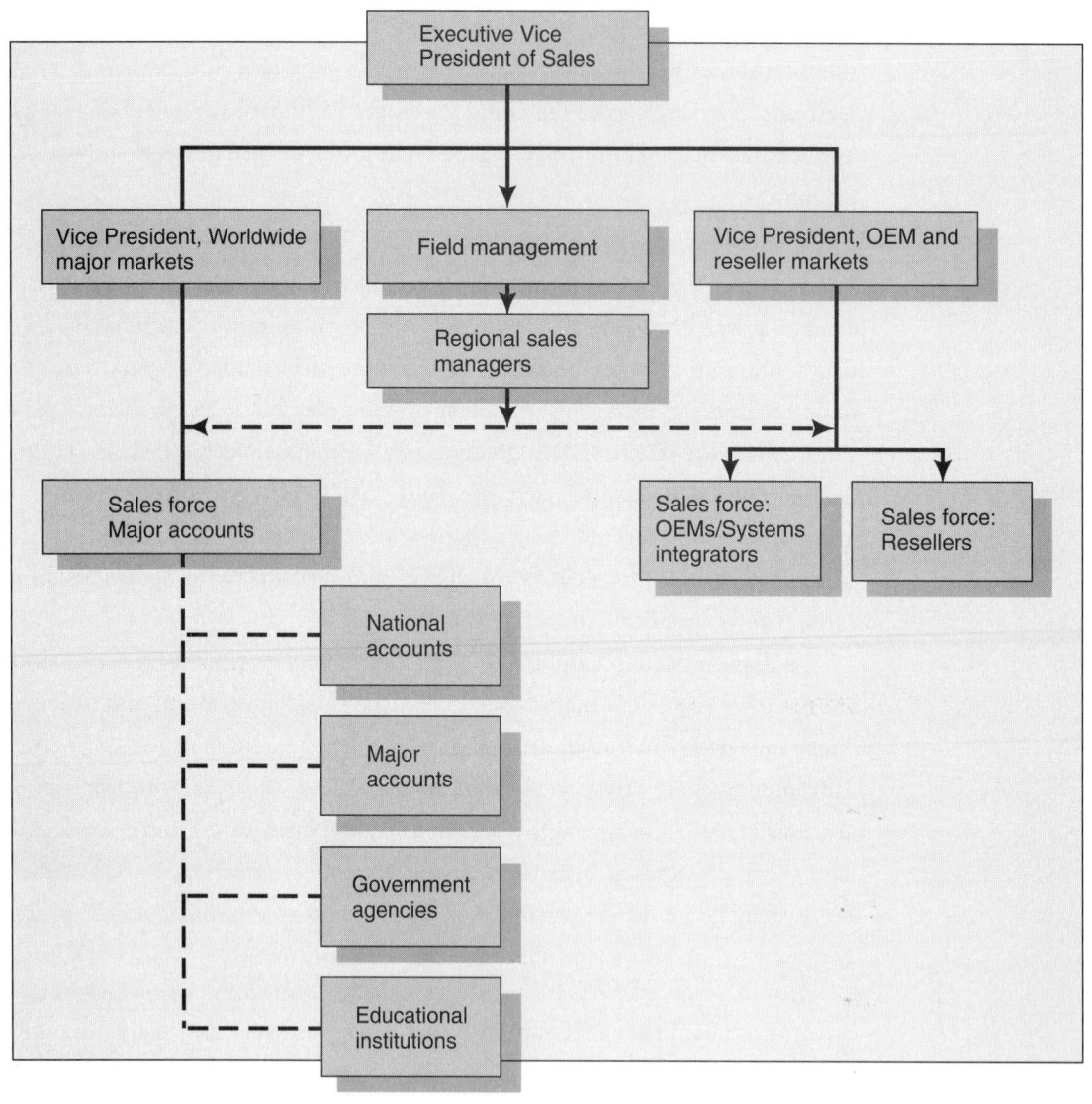

Source: Adapted from Kate Bertrand, "Reorganizing for Sales," *Business Marketing*, February 1990, p. 30.

sales groups within assigned geographic territories. These managers identify opportunities for each of the segment-specific sales groups, plan joint marketing promotions, and provide local support. They are also responsible for planning sales training programs and seminars.

THE INCREASING IMPORTANCE OF SALES ORGANIZATION DECISIONS

Organizing the activities and management of the sales force is a major part of strategic sales planning. Also, as discussed in Chapter 4, certain organizational issues must be resolved before specific account management policies can be implemented effectively. For example, a firm may decide—as Novell did—to assign specialists to handle major national customers. Novell's experience illustrates how a well-conceived sales organization can help focus a firm's sales efforts on its most important target markets.

Until recently, however, the kind of organizational restructuring undertaken by Novell has not been common among either industrial or consumer goods marketers. Once a firm had an organization structure in place, its managers tended to take it for granted—at least until performance problems became apparent. But in the past few years, increasing rates of change in markets, technology, and competition have stimulated managers to pay closer attention to their sales organizations and to be more proactive in restructuring those organizations when necessary. Consider, for instance, the recent organizational changes made by Xerox and Campbell, which were described earlier.

This chapter stresses the importance of designing an appropriate organizational framework for the sales force as an integral part of a firm's strategic sales plan and examines issues involved in developing such a framework. It begins with a discussion of the purposes of organization—the things a good organizational plan should accomplish. Next, issues related to the horizontal organization of the sales effort are explored. Horizontal organization is concerned with how specific selling activities are divided among various members of the sales force. Questions related to horizontal organization include the following:

1. Should the company employ its own salespeople, or should some or all of its selling efforts be contracted to outside agents—such as manufacturer's representatives?

2. How many different sales forces should the company have, and how should they be arranged? Should separate sales representatives be assigned to different products, types of customers, or sales functions?

3. Who should be responsible for selling to major national accounts?

4. How should firms organize their sales and marketing efforts when they enter foreign markets and become global competitors?

Finally, the *vertical* structuring of the sales organization is discussed. Vertical structuring refers to organizing a firm's sales managers and their activities rather than the personnel in the sales force. Vertical organization issues include:

1. How many levels of sales management are appropriate? What span of control is best?

2. Should sales-related functions—such as order entry, credit, or repair and maintenance—be integrated into the sales organization? If so, at what level?

3. What management functions should each sales manager perform? Should staff specialists be hired to perform certain functions? To what level of management should such specialists report?

4. How can the activities of specialized sales forces, staff specialists, and related departments be integrated and coordinated?

An understanding of these issues should provide greater appreciation for the crucial role organizational decisions play in developing an effective strategic sales program.

PURPOSES OF SALES ORGANIZATION

An organizational structure is simply an arrangement of activities involving a group of people. The goal in designing an organization is to divide and coordinate activities so the group can accomplish its common objectives better by acting as a group than by acting as individuals. The starting point in organizing a sales force is determining the goals or objectives to be accomplished; these are specified in the firm's overall marketing plan. The selling activities necessary to accomplish the firm's marketing objectives must then be divided and allocated to members of the sales force so the objectives can be achieved with as little duplication of effort as possible. An organizational structure should serve the following purposes:

1. Activities should be divided and arranged in such a way that the firm can benefit from the *specialization of labor.*

2. The organizational structure should provide for *stability and continuity* in the firm's selling efforts.

3. The structure should provide for the *coordination* of the various activities assigned to different persons in the sales force and different departments in the firm.

Division and Specialization of Labor

Two centuries ago, Adam Smith pointed out the efficiency with which almost any function is performed can be increased by dividing it into its component activities and assigning each activity to a specialist. Division and specialization of labor increase productivity because each specialist can concentrate efforts and become more proficient at the assigned task. Also, management can assign individuals only to those activities for which they have aptitude.

In some cases, the personal selling function is so simple and straightforward a firm could gain few, if any, benefits by applying the principles of division and specialization of labor to its sales force. Salespeople in such companies are expected to carry out all the activities necessary to sell all the products in the company's line to all types of customers within their territories. But in many firms, the selling function is sufficiently complicated that efficiency and effectiveness can be increased by dividing the necessary selling activities. Different activities are assigned to various specialists, creating two or more specialized sales forces.

Management must decide the best way to divide the required selling activities to gain the maximum benefits of specialization within the sales force. Should independent agent intermediaries be used to perform some or all of the firm's selling efforts? Should selling activities be organized by product, by customer type, or by selling function (for example, prospecting for new accounts versus servicing old customers)? As discussed later in this chapter, each basis for horizontally structuring the sales organization has its own advantages and disadvantages. Which one is best depends on the firm's objectives, target market, product line, and other internal and external factors.

Division and specialization of labor can benefit managerial functions as well as selling functions. Some firms use a simple "line" form of vertical organization in which the chain of command runs from the chief sales executive down through levels of subordinates. Each subordinate is responsible to only one person on the next higher level, and each is expected to perform all the necessary sales management activities relevant to his or her own level.

The most common form of vertical organization structure—especially in medium- and large-size firms—is the "line and staff" organization. In this form, several sales management activities—such as personnel selection, training, and distributor relations—are assigned to separate staff specialists. This kind of specialization, however, raises some questions concerning organizational design, such as what specific functions should be assigned to staff executives, how can staff activities be integrated with those of line sales managers, and to what level of sales management should staff executives report? These questions are examined further later in this chapter.

Stability and Continuity of Organizational Performance

Although many companies use division and specialization of labor in designing their sales organizations, they sometimes ignore a related caveat concerning good organizational design: organize activities, not people. In other words, activities should be assigned to positions within the sales organization without regard to the talents or preferences of current employees.

Once an ideal organizational structure has been designed, people can be trained or, if need be, recruited to fill positions within the structure. Over time, those in lower positions should be given the experience and training necessary to enable them to move into higher positions. In athletic terms, the organization should build *depth* at all positions. This provides stability and continuity of performance for the organization. The same activities are carried out at the same positions within the firm even if specific individuals are promoted or leave.

It can be difficult to avoid building an organization around specific individuals. Sometimes the vitality and effectiveness of an organization can be increased by adapting activities to take advantage of the strengths and talents of individuals. For example, a district sales manager may be given a disproportionate share of sales training duties because the manager is recognized as a particularly effective and inspiring developer of young talent. As a rule, however, such "people adaptations" should be kept to a minimum. The organization should not become so dependent on the abilities of specific people that it is impossible to find replacements when those individuals leave the organization.

Coordination and Integration

The advantages of the division and specialization of labor are clear, but specialization also causes a problem for managers. When activities are divided and performed by different individuals, those activities must be coordinated and integrated so all efforts are directed at accomplishing the same objective. The more an organization's tasks are divided among specialists, the more difficult integrating those tasks becomes. The problem is even worse when outside agents—such as manufacturers' representatives—are used, because the manager has no formal authority over them and cannot always control their actions.

Sales managers must be concerned about the coordination and integration of the efforts of their salespeople in three ways. First, the activities of the sales force must be integrated with the needs and concerns of customers. Second, the firm's selling activities must be coordinated with those of other departments, such as production, product development, logistics, and finance. Finally, if the firm divides its selling tasks among specialized units within the sales force, all those tasks must be integrated.

Consequently, the primary function of the vertical structure of a firm's sales organization is to ensure these three kinds of integration. Questions of vertical organization—such as how many levels of sales management the firm should have, the appropriate span of control for each sales executive, and the most effective use of staff specialists—should be examined with an eye toward effective integration of the firm's overall selling efforts.

HORIZONTAL STRUCTURE OF THE SALES FORCE

There is no best way to divide selling activities among members of the sales force. The best sales organization varies with the objectives, strategies, and tasks of the firm. Furthermore, as the firm's environment, objectives, or marketing strategy change, its sales force may have to be reorganized.

There are several common bases used for structuring the sales effort, and each has unique advantages that make it appropriate for a firm under certain circumstances. The first issue to be decided is whether the firm should hire its own salespeople or use outside agents. When a company sales force is used, alternative approaches include (1) geographic organization, (2) organization by type of product, (3) organization by type of customer, and (4) organization by selling function.

A Company Sales Force or Independent Agents?

This book focuses primarily on issues associated with managing an internal company sales force, where all of the salespeople and their managers are employees of the firm. In many cases, though, the use of independent agents instead of company salespeople is an important option.

Exhibit 5.2 summarizes the results of a survey of over 200 firms. Nearly

E x h i b i t 5 • 2 *Customer Contact Methods Used by Manufacturers (n = 214)*

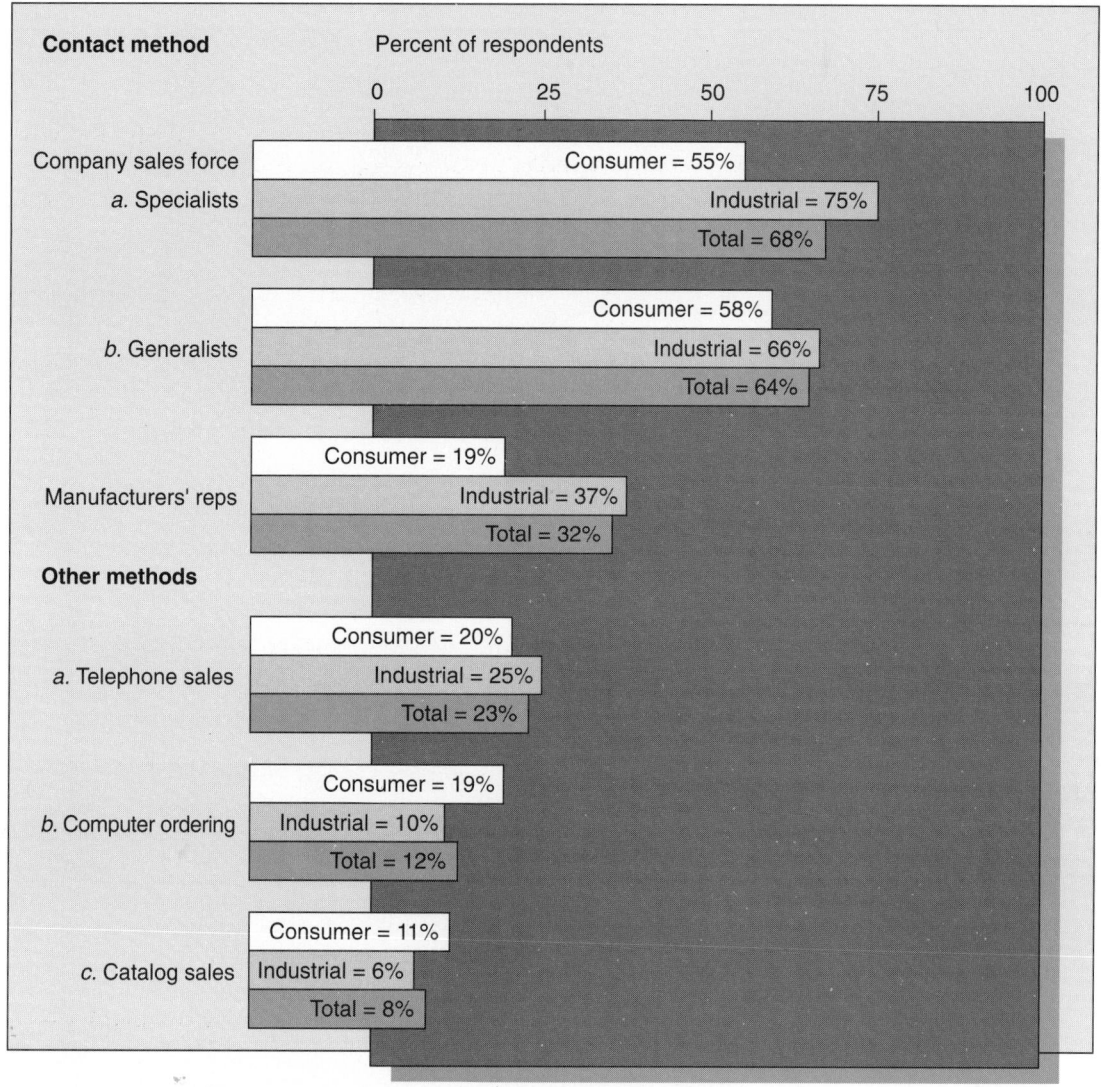

Source: Howard Sutton, *Rethinking the Company's Selling and Distribution Channels* (New York: The Conference Board, 1986), p. 2.

one third of the respondents reported using manufacturers' representatives (one type of intermediary) to contact customers. A larger percentage of industrial goods producers use agents (37 percent) than consumer goods firms (19 percent). The use of agents varies even more widely across different industries. While less than 5 percent of grocery products are sold through man-

E X H I B I T **5 ● 3**   *Percent of Manufacturers Who Expect to Increase Their Dependence on Each Contact Method during the 1990s*

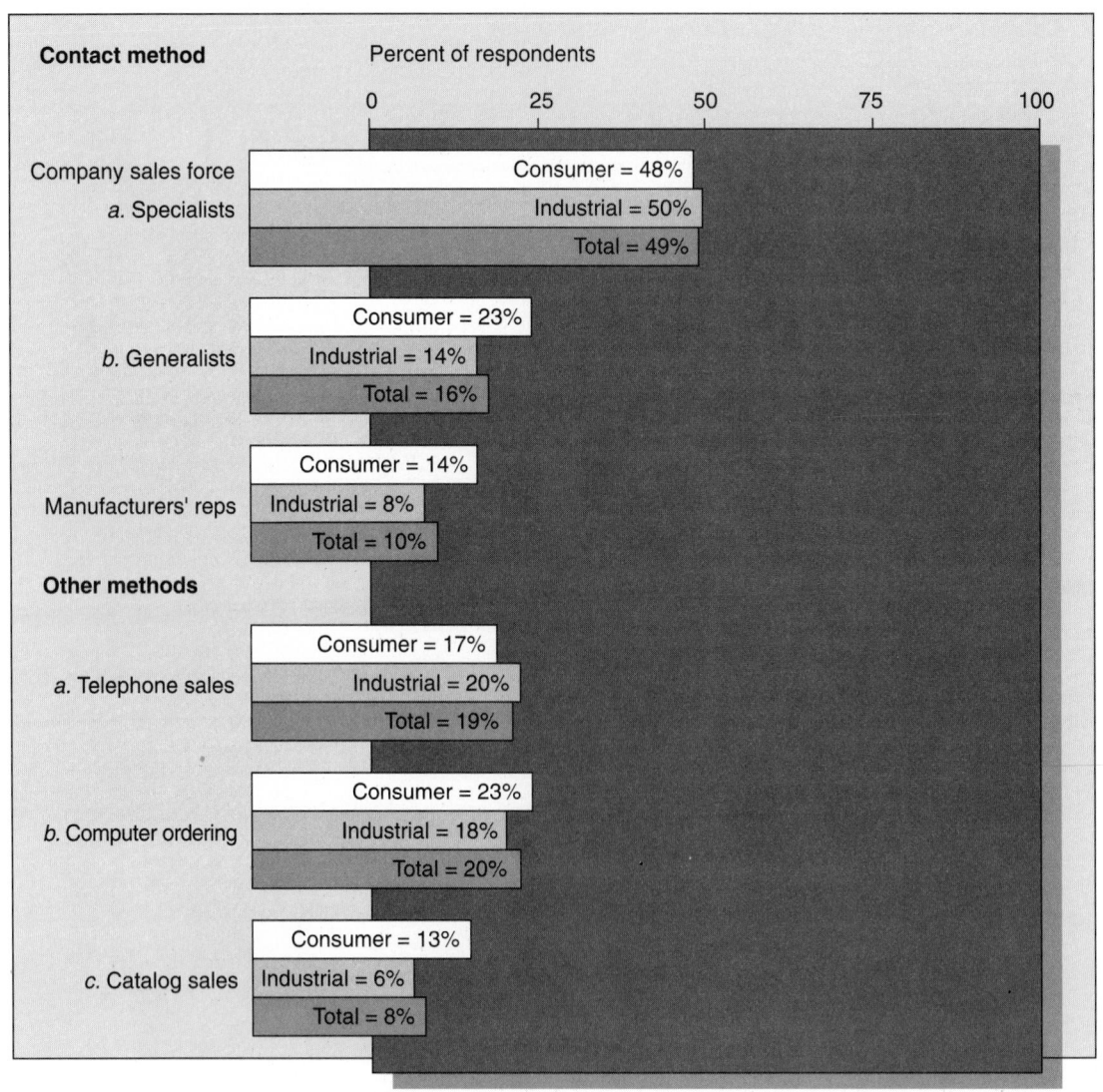

Source: Howard Sutton, *Rethinking the Company's Selling and Distribution Channels* (New York: The Conference Board, 1986), p. 3.

ufacturers' reps, for example, nearly half of all electrical goods are distributed through such intermediaries.

Notice, too, that the percentages in Exhibit 5.2 add up to far more than 100 percent. Some respondents use more than one method to contact customers. It is not unusual, for instance, for a firm to use *both* company salespeople and independent agents.[2] In such cases, firms usually rely on agents to cover geographic areas with relatively few customers or low sales potential—territories that may not justify the cost of a full-time company salesperson.

The use of intermediaries may not grow as fast in the future as other forms of customer contact. As indicated in Exhibit 5.3, when asked whether they expected to become more dependent on manufacturers' reps during the 1990s, only 10 percent of the survey respondents said yes. In comparison, nearly half of all respondents indicated they expect to become more dependent on specialized company salespeople (i.e., salespeople who focus their efforts on only selected product lines, industries, or customer types), and about 20 percent expect to depend more on telephone selling and computerized ordering.[3]

Types of agents

The two most common types of intermediaries a manufacturer might use to perform the selling function are manufacturers' representatives and selling (or sales) agents.[4] **Manufacturers' representatives** are intermediaries who sell part of the output of their principals—the manufacturers they represent—on an extended contract basis. They neither take ownership nor physical possession of the goods they sell, but concentrate instead on the selling function. They are compensated solely by commissions.

Reps have no authority to modify their principals' instructions concerning the prices, terms of sale, and so forth to be offered to potential buyers. Manufacturers' reps cover a specific and limited territory and specialize in a limited range of products, although they commonly represent several related but noncompeting product lines from different manufacturers.

These characteristics give reps the advantages of having (1) many established contacts with potential customers in their territories, (2) familiarity with the technical nature and applications of the types of products they specialize in, (3) the ability to keep expenses low by being able to spread fixed costs over the products of several different manufacturers, and (4) the appearance as a totally variable cost item on their principals' income statements, since the reps' commissions vary directly with the amount of goods sold.

Selling agents are also intermediaries who do not take title or possession of the goods they sell and are compensated solely by commissions from their principals. They differ from reps, however, in that they usually handle the entire output of a principal (operating as the entire sales force for the manufacturer rather than as a representative in a single, specified territory). Selling agents are usually granted broader authority by their principals to modify prices and terms of sale, and they actively shape the manufacturer's promotional and sales programs.

Deciding when outside agents are appropriate

The decision about whether to use independent agents or a company sales force to cover a particular product/market involves a variety of considerations and trade-offs. In general, though, the two most important sets of factors for a manager to consider are (1) economic criteria and (2) control and strategic criteria.[5]

Economic criteria

In a given selling situation, a company sales force and independent agents are likely to produce different levels of costs and sales volume. A first step in deciding which form of sales organization to use is to estimate and compare the costs of the two alternatives. A simplified example of such a cost comparison is illustrated in Exhibit 5.4.

The fixed costs of using external agents are lower than those of using a company sales force because there is usually less administrative overhead, and agents do not receive a salary or reimbursement for field selling expenses. But costs of using agents tend to rise faster as sales volume increases because agents usually receive larger commissions than company salespeople. Consequently, there is a break-even level of sales volume (*Vb* in Exhibit 5.4) below which the costs of external agents are lower but above which a company sales force becomes more efficient. This helps explain why agents tend to be used by smaller firms or by larger firms in their smaller territories where sales volume is too low to warrant a company sales force.

Low fixed costs also make agents attractive when a firm is moving into new territories or product lines where success is uncertain. Since the agent does not get paid unless sales are made, the costs of failure are minimized.

The other side of the economic equation is sales volume. The critical question is whether company salespeople are likely to produce a higher volume of total sales than agents in a given situation. Most sales and marketing managers believe they will because company salespeople concentrate entirely on the firm's products, they may be better trained, they may be more aggressive since their future depends more on the company's success, and customers often prefer to deal directly with a supplier. On the other hand, agents' contacts and experience in an industry can make them more effective than company salespeople—particularly when the company is new or is moving into a new geographic area or product line.

Control and strategic criteria

Regardless of which organizational form produces the greatest sales in the short run, many managers argue that an internal sales force is preferable to agents in the long run due to the difficulty of controlling agents and getting them to conform to their principals' strategic objectives.

Agents are seen as independent actors who can be expected to pursue their own short-run objectives. This makes them reluctant to engage in activities with a long-run strategic payoff to their principal, such as cultivating new accounts or small customers with growth potential, performing service and support activities, or promoting new products. Some research supports this argument, suggesting manufacturers' representatives are more dissatisfied with

E x h i b i t **5 ● 4** *Cost Comparison between a Company Sales Force and Independent Agents*

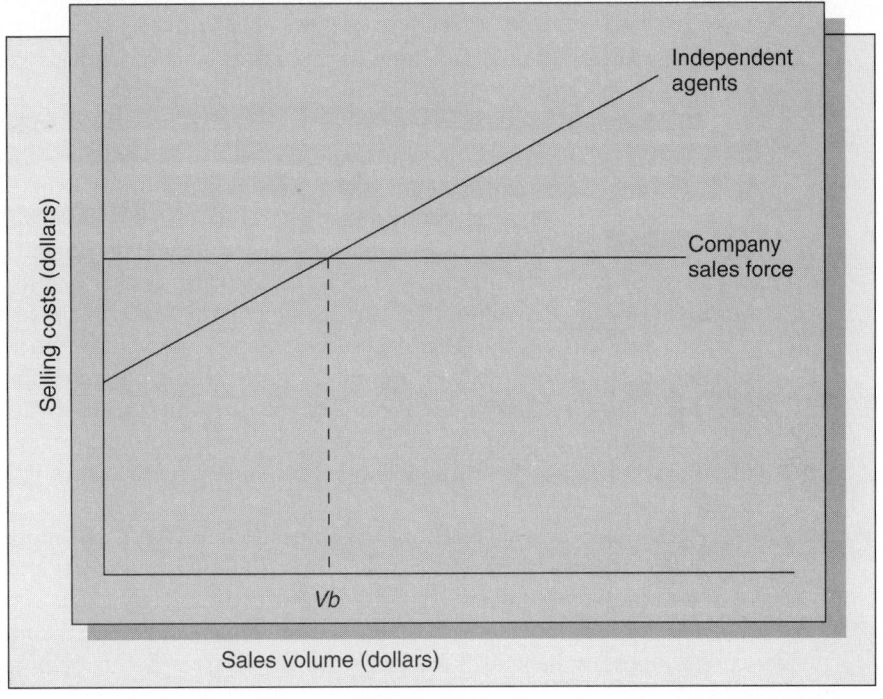

close supervision and attempts to control their behavior than are company salespeople.[6]

Managers can control a company sales force in many different ways—through the selection, training, and supervision of personnel; establishment of operating procedures and policies; formal evaluation and reward mechanisms; and ultimately by transferring or firing salespeople whose performance is not satisfactory.

Independent agents can also be replaced if their performance falls below the manufacturer's expectations. But in many cases, it is difficult for the manufacturer to tell whether an agent's poor performance is due to lack of effort or to factors beyond the agent's control, such as difficult competitive or market conditions. While company salespeople can be monitored on a regular basis, it is usually more difficult and costly—and sometimes impossible—to monitor the behavior of independent agents.[7]

Transaction costs

Even when a manufacturer decides a poor-performing agent should be replaced, it may be difficult to find an acceptable replacement. This is particularly likely when an intermediary must invest in specialized (or *transaction-specific*) assets, such as extensive product training or specialized capital equipment, to sell the manufacturer's product or service effectively. It might take a new manufacturer's rep months to learn enough about a technically complex product and its applications to do an effective selling job. The difficulty of finding acceptable replacements for poor-performing agents under such circumstances makes it even harder for the manufacturer to control those agents.

The theory of **transaction cost analysis** (**TCA**) states that when substantial transaction-specific assets are necessary to sell a manufacturer's product, the costs of using and administering independent agents (i.e., the manufacturer's transaction costs) are likely to be higher than the costs of hiring and managing a company sales force. This is because TCA assumes independent agents will pursue their own self-interests—even at the expense of the manufacturer they represent—when they think they can get away with it. For instance, they might provide only cursory post-sale service or expend too little effort calling on smaller accounts because they are unlikely to earn big commissions from such activities. Because agents are most likely to be able to get away with such behaviors when it is difficult for the manufacturer to monitor or replace them, the transaction cost of using agents under such circumstances is likely to be high.[8]

Recently, however, analysts have questioned TCA's assumption that independent agents will always put their own short-term interests ahead of those of the manufacturer when they can avoid getting caught and replaced. The analysts argue that when both manufacturer and agent believe their relationship can be mutually beneficial for years, norms of trust and cooperation can develop.[9]

Strategic flexibility

Another important strategic issue to consider when deciding whether to use agents or company salespeople is flexibility. Generally, a vertically integrated distribution system incorporating a company sales force is the most difficult to alter quickly. Specialized agent intermediaries can often be added or dismissed at short notice, especially if no specialized assets are needed to sell the manufacturer's product and the firm does not have to sign long-term contracts to gain agents' support.

Firms facing uncertain and rapidly changing competitive or market environments or those in industries characterized by shifting technology and short product life cycles are often best advised to rely on independent agents to preserve the flexibility of their distribution channels.[10] This is a major reason firms in the highly volatile toy industry extensively use manufacturers' representatives.

Most marketing executives argue it is best to use agents in volatile environments, to represent a small company, or for territories with low sales potential where the benefits from scale economies outweigh the difficulties of motivating and controlling the agent's behavior. It is usually preferable to switch to direct salespeople as soon as a company or territory can support the higher fixed costs or when specialized knowledge or other assets are required to do an effective selling job.

Geographic Organization

The simplest and most common method of organizing a company sales force is to assign individual salespeople to separate geographic territories. In this kind of organization, each salesperson is responsible for performing all the activities necessary to sell all the products in the company's line to all potential customers in the territory, as was the case at Novell, Inc., before its sales force was reorganized. A geographic sales organization is illustrated in Exhibit 5.5.

The geographic sales organization has several strengths. Most important, it tends to have the lowest cost. Because there is only one salesperson in each territory and territories tend to be smaller than they are under other forms of organization, travel time and expenses are minimized. Also, fewer managerial levels are required for coordination. Thus, sales administration and overhead expenses are kept relatively low.

The simplicity of a geographic organizational structure leads to another advantage involving the firm's relationships with its customers. Because only one salesperson calls on each customer, there is seldom any confusion about who is responsible for what or about whom the customer should talk to when problems arise.

The major disadvantage of a geographic sales organization is that it does not provide any benefits of the division and specialization of labor. Each salesperson is expected to be a jack-of-all-trades. Each must sell all the firm's products to all types of customers and perform all the selling functions.

Also, this organizational structure provides the individual salesperson with freedom to make decisions concerning which selling functions to perform, what products to emphasize, and which customers to concentrate on. Unfortunately, salespeople are likely to expend most of this effort on the functions they perform best and on the products and customers they perceive to be most rewarding, whether or not such effort is consistent with management's objectives and account management policies.

For instance, many salespeople concentrate on obtaining routine orders from long-standing customers rather than pursuing new prospects where the likelihood of obtaining a sale and commission is lower.

Management can try to direct the efforts of salespeople through close supervision, well-designed compensation and evaluation plans, and clearly defined statements of policy, but the basic problem remains. Since each salesperson is expected to perform a full range of selling functions, the sales rep—rather than management—can control the way that selling effort is allocated across products, customers, and selling tasks.

Although a geographic approach to sales organization has its limitations, its basic simplicity and low cost make it very popular among smaller firms, particularly those with limited, uncomplicated product lines. Also, while it is unusual for larger organizations to rely exclusively on geographic organization, they do commonly use it in conjunction with other organizational forms. For

EXHIBIT 5 • 5   *Geographic Sales Organization*

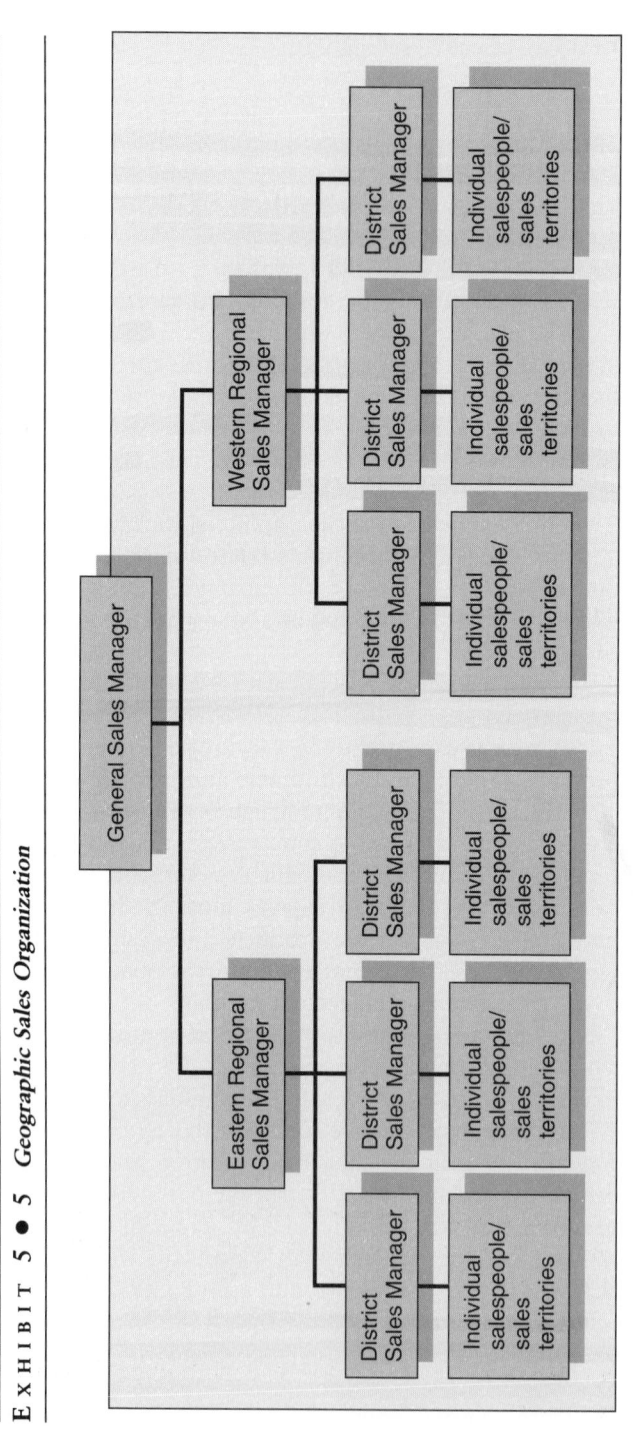

E X H I B I T   5 ● 6   *Sales Force Organized by Product Type*

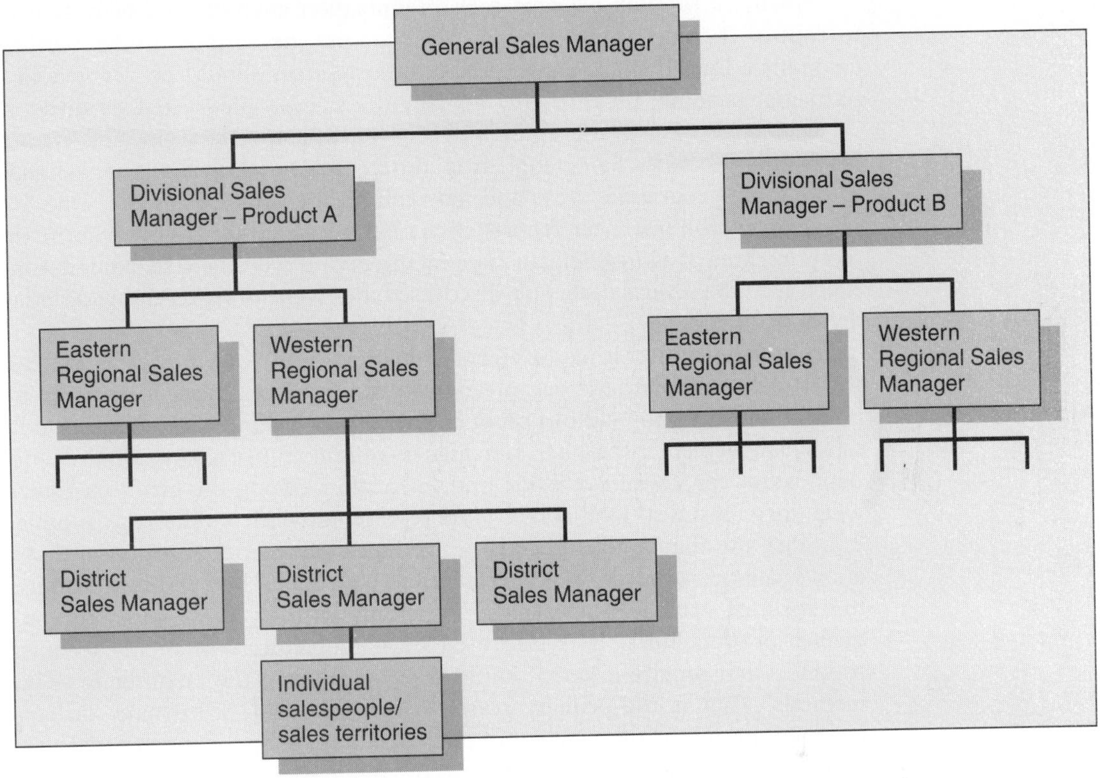

example, a firm may have two separate sales forces for different products in its line, but each sales force is likely to be organized geographically.

Product Organization

Some companies have separate sales forces for each product (or related group of products) in their product line, as shown in Exhibit 5.6. The 3M Company, for example, has more than 40 divisions manufacturing a diverse collection of products ranging from Scotch™ tape to abrasives to medical equipment, and nearly every division has its own separate sales force.

The primary advantage of organizing the sales force by product is that individual salespeople can develop familiarity with the technical attributes, applications, and the most effective selling methods associated with a single product or related products. Also, when the firm's manufacturing facilities are organized by product type—as when separate factories produce each product—a product-oriented organization can lead to closer cooperation between sales and production. This can be very beneficial when the product is tailored to fit the specifications of different customers or when production and delivery schedules are critical in gaining and keeping a customer.

Finally, a product-oriented sales organization enables sales management to control the allocation of selling effort across the various products in the company's line. If management decides more effort should be devoted to a particular product, it can simply assign more salespeople to that product.

The major disadvantage of a sales force organized by product type is duplication of effort. Salespeople from different product divisions are assigned to the same geographic areas and may call on the same customers. One 3M salesperson, for instance, reports encountering six other salespeople in the reception area of a large Belgian manufacturer while waiting to see a purchasing executive. The seven salespeople discovered they were *all* representing different divisions of 3M.

Such duplication leads to higher selling expenses than would be the case with a simple geographic organization. It also creates a need for greater coordination across the various product divisions, which, in turn, requires more sales management personnel and higher administrative costs. Finally, such duplication can cause confusion and frustration among the firm's customers when they must deal with two or more representatives from the same supplier.

Since the major advantage of a product-oriented organization is that it allows salespeople to develop specialized knowledge of one or a few products, this form of organization is most commonly used by firms with large and diverse product lines. It is also used by manufacturers of highly technical products that require different kinds of technical expertise or different selling methods. That is the primary reason a firm like 3M, with many different product lines based on widely differing technologies, continues to organize its sales force by product despite the cost disadvantages.

Organization by Customers or Markets

It has become increasingly popular for firms to organize their sales forces by customer type, as Novell, Inc., did when it reorganized its sales force into three distinct groups serving three different customer segments. Another example is provided by IBM. In its recent reorganization aimed at making the company more responsive to the increasingly fragmented and specialized computer market, IBM assigned many of its salespeople to specific industries.[11] Some of these sales specialists call only on automobile manufacturers while others deal only with the financial institutions on Wall Street. Another example of a customer-oriented sales organization is shown in Exhibit 5.7.

Organizing a sales force by customer type is a natural extension of the "marketing concept" and a strategy of market segmentation. When salespeople specialize in calling on a particular type of customer, they gain a better understanding of such customers' needs and requirements. They can also be trained to use different selling approaches for different markets and to implement specialized marketing and promotional programs.

A related advantage of customer specialization is that, as salespeople be-

EXHIBIT 5 • 7 *Sales Forces Organized by Customer Type*

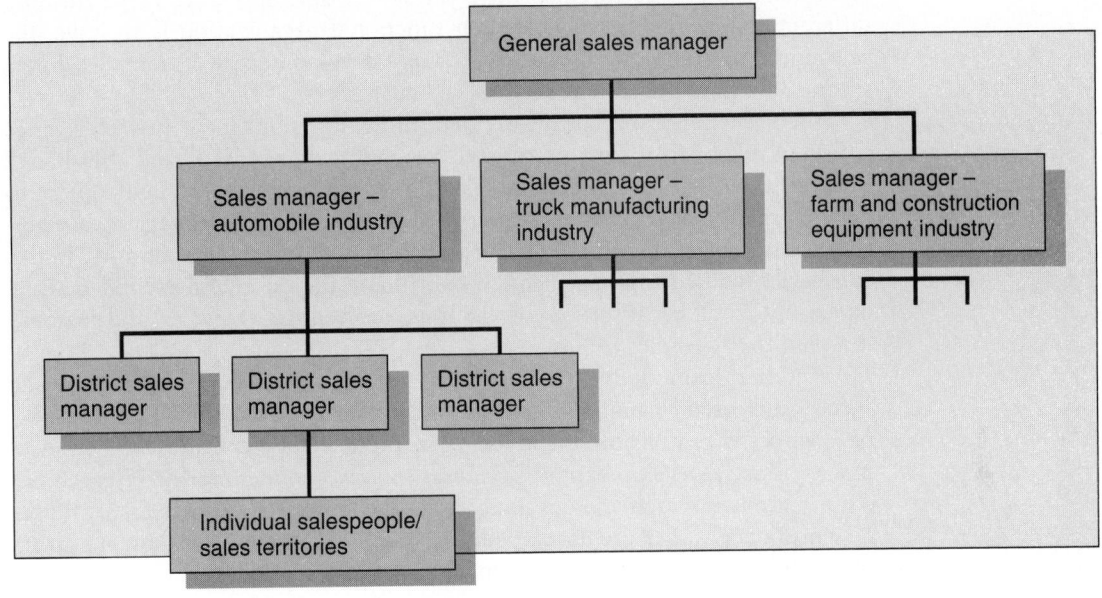

come familiar with their customers' specific businesses and needs, they are more likely to discover ideas for new products and marketing approaches that will appeal to those customers. This can be a definite advantage in rapidly changing, highly competitive markets. Finally, this organizational structure allows marketing managers to control the allocation of selling effort to different markets by varying the sizes of the specialized sales forces.

The disadvantages of a customer-oriented sales organization are much the same as those of a product-oriented structure. Having different salespeople calling on different types of customers in the same territory can lead to higher selling expenses and administrative costs. Also, when customer firms have different departments or divisions operating in different industries, two or more salespeople may call on the same customer. This can cause confusion and frustration among customers.

Many firms must believe the advantages of a customer-oriented sales organization outweigh its limitations because it is growing in popularity as an organizational approach. This is particularly true for firms with products that have widely different applications in different markets or firms that must use different approaches when selling to different types of customers, as when a company sells to the government as well as to private industry. Also, specialization by customer type is a useful form of organization when a firm's marketing objectives include the penetration of previously untapped markets.

Organization by Selling Function

Different kinds of selling tasks often require different abilities and skills on the part of the salesperson. Thus, it may be logical under some circumstances to organize the sales force so different salespeople specialize in performing different selling functions. One such functional organization is to have one sales force specialize in prospecting for and developing new accounts, while a second force maintains and services old customers.

Such functional specialization can be difficult to implement, however. Since a firm is likely to assign its most competent, experienced, and "flashiest" salespeople to the new-accounts sales force, new customers might object to being turned over from the salesperson who won their patronage to a maintenance salesperson with a personality better suited to mundane tasks. It also can be difficult for management to coordinate the development and maintenance functions because there is likely to be feelings of rivalry and jealousy between the two sales forces.

Another form of functional specialization, however, is commonly and successfully used by many industrial product firms: "developmental salespeople" who are responsible for assisting in the development and early sales of new products. Developmental specialists usually conduct market research, assist the firm's research and development and engineering departments, and sell new products as they are developed. These specialists are often part of a firm's research and development department rather than in the regular sales force. Such specialists can help ensure development of successful new products, particularly when they are experienced and knowledgeable about customers' operations and needs as well as about their own firm's technical and production capabilities.

Telemarketing and the Organization of "Inside" and "Outside" Sales Forces

One form of specialization by selling function that has gained great popularity in recent years is the use of inside telephone salespeople and outside field salespeople to accomplish separate selling objectives. Obviously, not all selling functions can be performed over the phone, but telemarketing has proven useful for carrying out selected activities, including the following:

Prospecting for and qualifying potential new accounts, which can then be turned over to field salespeople for personal contact. This function can often be facilitated by including a toll-free 800 phone number in all of the firm's promotional materials so interested potential customers can call to obtain more information about advertised products or services.

Servicing existing accounts quickly when unexpected problems arise, such as through the use of technical-assistance "hot lines."

Seeking repeat purchases from existing accounts that cannot be covered efficiently in person, such as small or marginal customers and those in remote geographic locations.

Gaining quicker communication of newsworthy developments, like the introduction of new or improved products or special sales programs.[12]

The popularity of telemarketing to supplement the activities of the field sales force is growing for two reasons: (1) customers like it, and (2) it can increase the productivity of a firm's sales efforts. From the customers' view, the increased centralization of purchasing together with growing numbers of product alternatives and potential suppliers in many industries have increased demands on the time of purchasing agents and other members of organizations' buying centers. Consequently, they like sales contacts over the phone—particularly for routine purposes, such as soliciting reorders or relaying information about special sales programs and price promotions—because they take less time than personal sales calls.

According to a study of trends in the wholesale-distribution industry conducted by Arthur Andersen & Co., customers say personal contact with a salesperson is becoming less important to them than contact with a capable inside sales force. The study predicts eventually half of the average wholesale distributor's sales force will be inside and the role of the outside salesperson will shift toward greater emphasis on promotion and customer instruction and service.[13]

From the seller's viewpoint, a combination of inside and outside salespeople—together with an appropriate mix of other promotional media, such as targeted advertising, direct mail, and toll-free 800 telephone lines—offers a way of improving the overall efficiency of the sales force.[14] Moving some salespeople inside and using them in conjunction with other promotional efforts allows the firm to lower the costs of routine sales activities substantially. At the same time, it enables the more expensive outside sales force to concentrate on activities with the highest potential long-term payout, such as new-account generation and servicing major accounts.

The efficiency of telemarketing makes it particularly useful for implementing an account management policy that directs different amounts of effort toward classifications of customers based on differences in size or potential. In the past, some firms prohibited sales forces from calling on very small customers—or told them to visit such accounts infrequently—because their purchase volume was not large enough to cover the cost of a sales call and still contribute to profit. But an inside sales force can call on such customers regularly with much lower costs.

The A. B. Dick Co. uses telemarketing to service its smaller accounts. With more than 100,000 of its customers buying less than $200 of office supplies per year, the company realized it was not economically sound to have its field salespeople visiting those accounts regularly. By adopting telephone direct marketing to service low-volume customers, the firm was able to focus its field selling efforts on the larger institutional market. Coordinated with special mail promotions to maximize response, the telephone was used to sell and record orders directly. A first call to each small customer sought permission for later, regular phone contact.

The initial results of the program were impressive. Ten percent of the companies contacted by phone placed an order at the time of the initial call. Another 8 percent of these "small" customers were discovered to have the potential for larger equipment and supply purchases. These accounts were qualified over the phone and passed along to the field sales force for future follow-up. Finally, 60 percent of all the customers contacted asked to become part of the continuing telephone sales program.[15]

As we discuss later in this book, however, implementing two or more specialized sales forces—as in the case of inside and outside salespeople—can cause additional problems for sales managers. Since each specialized sales force focuses on different types of selling activities, separate policies and procedures are often required. For example, some authorities suggest an effective tele-marketing program requires the development of standardized "scripts" for the salesperson to follow, even though their counterparts in the field might have much more flexibility to tailor their presentations to the needs of individual customers. Such differences in policies and procedures may require recruitment of different types of salespeople for the two sales forces and development of different training and compensation programs.[16]

ORGANIZING TO SERVICE NATIONAL AND KEY ACCOUNTS

Regardless of how their sales forces are organized, many firms are developing new organizational approaches to deliver the customer service necessary to attract and maintain large and important customers—their national or key accounts. As discussed in Chapter 4, the increasing technical complexity of products, industrial concentration, and the trend toward centralized purchasing make a few major accounts critical to the marketing success of many firms in both industrial and consumer goods industries. A recent survey confirmed that, on average, 50 percent of a firm's sales volume is accounted for by only 10 percent of its customers.[17] And the importance of major accounts is increasing as large multinational firms seek to coordinate their purchasing across subsidiaries operating in many different countries.[18]

To provide the kinds of service demanded by such key customers, many firms adopt a selling philosophy of major account management. This stresses the dual goals of making sales and developing long-term relationships with major customers. Firms believe national account management policies will lead to improved coordination of selling activities and improved communications with key customers. This should enable the seller to capture a larger share of the purchases made by those customers and to improve profitability. As Exhibit 5.8 indicates, respondents from 23 large industrial firms agree that such expectations were achieved through national account programs.

EXHIBIT 5 • 8 *Perceived Advantages to the Selling Company of Using National Account Marketing*

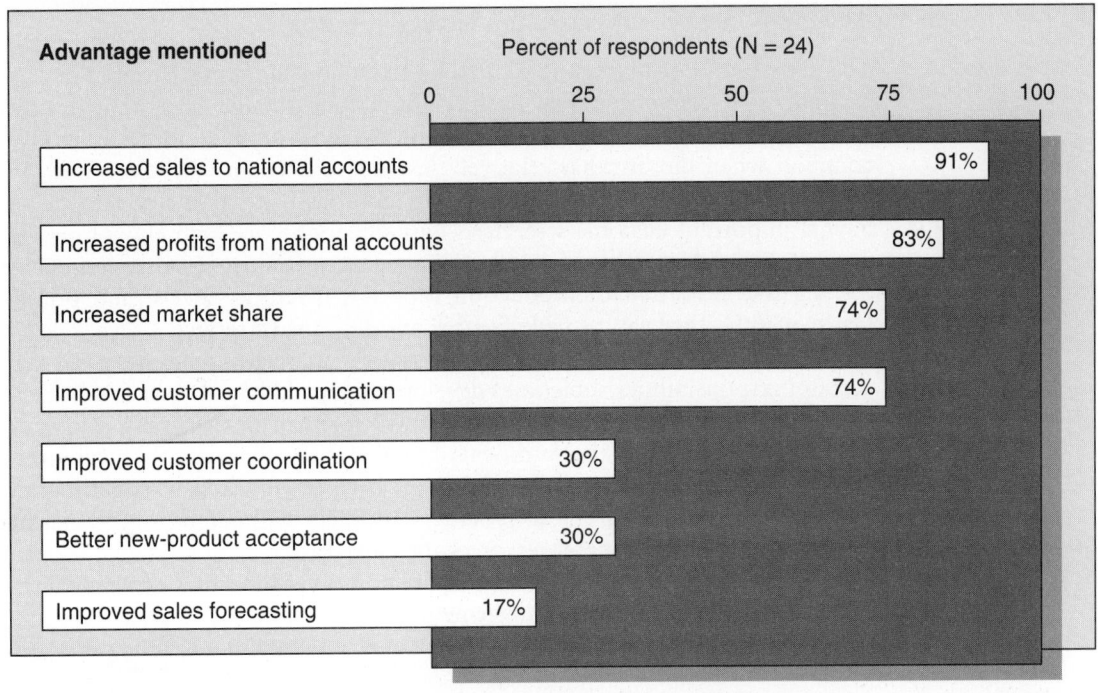

Advantage mentioned	Percent of respondents (N = 24)
Increased sales to national accounts	91%
Increased profits from national accounts	83%
Increased market share	74%
Improved customer communication	74%
Improved customer coordination	30%
Better new-product acceptance	30%
Improved sales forecasting	17%

Source: From Thomas H. Stevenson, "Profits from National Account Management," *Industrial Marketing Management* 10 (January 1981), p. 120. Reprinted by permission of the publisher. Copyright 1981 by Elsevier Science Publishing Co., Inc.

Alternative Organizational Approaches for Dealing with Key Accounts

When a firm decides to implement a national account program, a major question to be resolved is: Who in the organization should be responsible for the functions of national account management? Some firms have no special organizational arrangements for handling their major customers; they rely on members of their regular sales force to sell to national and key accounts. This requires no additional administrative or selling expense.

The disadvantage is that major accounts often require more detailed and sophisticated treatment than smaller customers. Consequently, servicing major accounts may require more experience, expertise, and organizational authority than the average salesperson possesses. Also, if the sales force is compensated largely by commission, there can be difficult questions about which salesperson should get the commissions for sales to national accounts when one person calls on a customer's headquarters while others service its stores or plants in other territories.

In view of these difficulties, many firms have adopted special organizational arrangements for the major account management function. These arrangements include (1) assigning key accounts to top sales executives, (2) creating a separate corporate division, and (3) creating a separate major accounts sales force.[19]

Assigning key accounts to sales executives

The use of sales or marketing executives to call on the firm's national or key accounts is a common practice, especially among smaller firms that do not have the resources to support a separate division or sales force. It is also common when the firm has relatively few major accounts to be serviced. In addition to the relatively low cost of the approach, it has the advantage of having important customers serviced by people who are high enough in the organizational hierarchy to make—or at least to influence—decisions concerning the allocation of production capacity, inventory levels, and prices. Consequently, they can provide flexible and responsive service.

One problem with this approach is that the managers who are given key account responsibilities sometimes develop a warped view of their firm's marketing objectives. They sometimes allocate too much of the firm's resources to their own accounts to the detriment of smaller, but still profitable, customers. In other words, such managers sometimes become obsessed with getting all the business they can from their large customers without paying sufficient attention to the sales, operating, or profit impact.

Another problem is that assigning important selling tasks to managers takes time away from their management activities. This can hinder the coordination and effectiveness of the firm's overall selling and marketing efforts.

A separate key account division

Some firms create a separate corporate division for dealing with major accounts. For example, some apparel companies have separate divisions for making and selling private-label clothing to large general-merchandise chains, such as Sears, Wards, and J. C. Penney. This approach allows for close integration of manufacturing, logistics, marketing, and sales activities. This can be important when one or a few major customers account for such a large proportion of the firm's total sales volume that variations in their purchases have a major impact on the firm's production schedules, inventories, and allocation of resources.

The major disadvantages of this approach are the duplication of effort and the tremendous additional expense involved in creating an entire manufacturing and marketing organization for only one or a few customers. It is also risky because the success or failure of the entire division is dependent on the whims of one or a few customers.

A separate sales force for major accounts

Rather than creating an entire separate division to deal with major customers, it is more common for companies to create a separate national or key account sales force. As indicated in Exhibit 5.9, there are four common ways to organize

EXHIBIT 5 ● 9 *Four Ways to Organize National Account Sales Forces and the Percentage of Survey Respondents Using Each Approach*

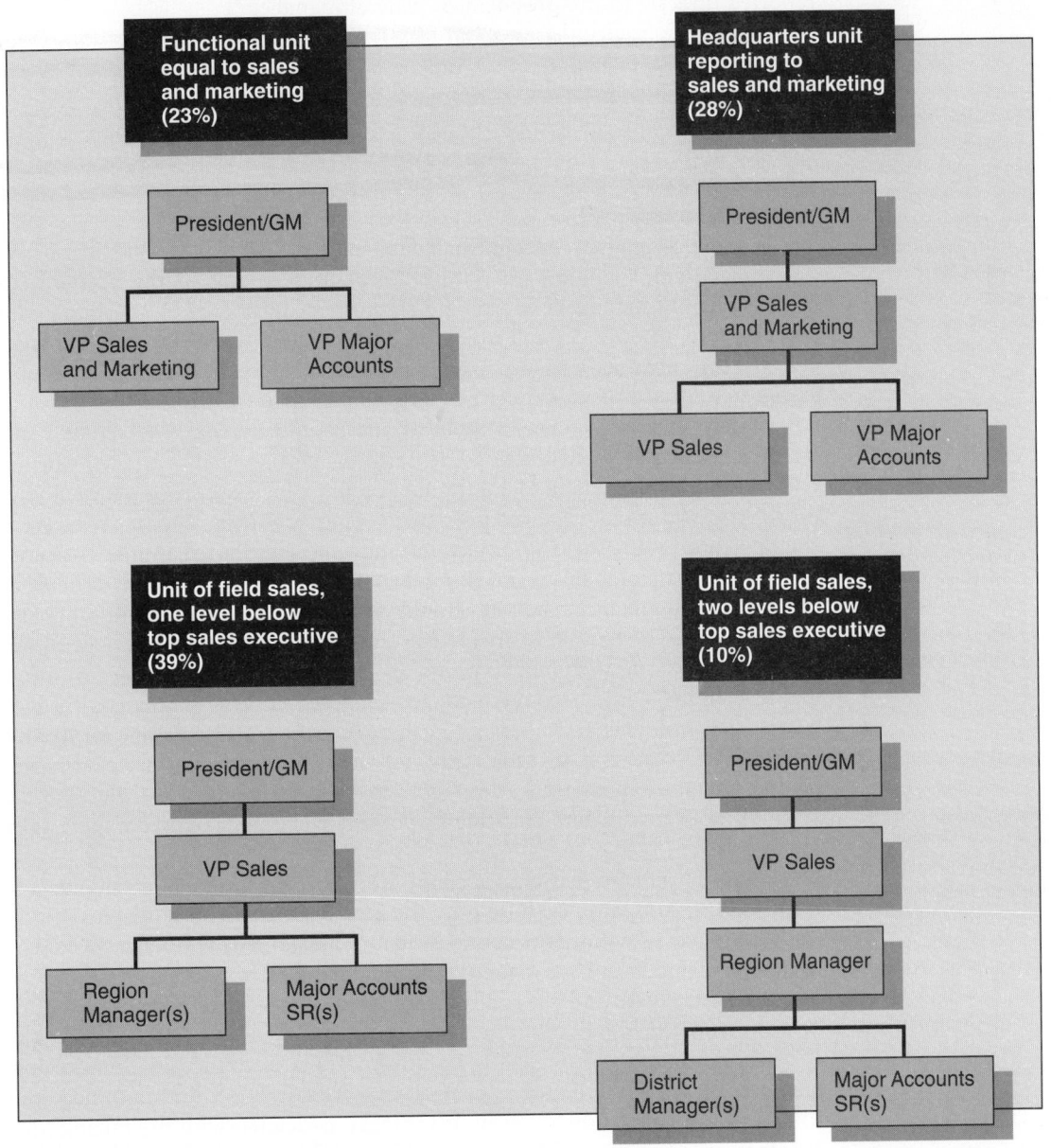

Source: Adapted from Jerome A. Colletti and Gary S. Tubridy, "Effective Major Account Sales Management," *Journal of Personal Selling and Sales Management*, August 1987, p. 4.

such separate sales forces. In nearly one quarter of the cases reported in a recent survey, the national account sales operation was treated as a separate functional area on a par with the firm's marketing and sales department and reported directly to the president or general manager.

More commonly, the national account force and the regular sales force are treated as equal headquarters units reporting to a single sales or marketing executive who is responsible for coordinating their efforts. Novell, Inc., adopted this approach when it reorganized the sales force. The most popular organizational approach, though, is to treat major account executives as equal to regional managers in the regular sales force and have both groups report to the top sales executive.

In some companies, account managers perform all necessary selling activities themselves, including in-store or in-plant servicing of the account. In others, account managers coordinate an entire selling team of assistants who work on the account. In still other situations, the national account manager calls on the customer's headquarters, while field salespeople from the regular sales force service the customer's facilities in their territories.

Under this arrangement, if the field salespeople are compensated by commission, they are usually given some portion—perhaps half—of their normal commission of sales made to a national account's local stores or plants. However, this arrangement can cause bookkeeping problems. When an order is shipped to a central distribution point and then distributed by the customer to its plants or stores in several different sales territories, it can be difficult to determine how much of the sale should be credited to each field salesperson.

Regardless of how it is organized, a separate sales force has several advantages in dealing with key accounts. By concentrating on only one or a few major customers, the account manager can become very familiar with each customer's problems and needs and can devote the time necessary to provide a high level of service to each customer. Also, the firm can select its most competent and experienced salespeople to become members of the national account sales force, thus ensuring important customers receive expert sales attention.

Finally, a separate national account sales force provides an internal benefit to the selling company. Because only the most competent salespeople are typically assigned to national accounts, such an assignment is often viewed as a desirable promotion. Thus, promotion to the national accounts sales force can be used to motivate and reward top salespeople who are either not suited for or not interested in moving into sales management.

In addition to the problem of allocating national account sales to individual members of the field sales force, using a separate sales force for major accounts suffers from many of the other disadvantages associated with organizing sales efforts by customer type. The most troubling problems concern the duplication of effort within the sales organization and the resulting higher selling and administrative expenses.

Team Selling

As mentioned, in some firms, the account manager is responsible for working with an entire team in selling to and servicing major customers. The customer's buying center is likely to consist of people from different functional areas with different viewpoints and concerns. Those concerns can best be understood and met by people from equivalent functional areas of the selling firm. For instance, if the customer's treasurer is concerned about financing and credit arrangements, someone from the seller's finance department is probably best able to address those concerns.

One major disadvantage of a team selling approach is its high cost in time and personnel. It also presents a major coordination problem. Unless the selling efforts of all team members are carefully integrated, various members of the customer's organization may get conflicting impressions.

Team selling is most appropriate for the very largest customers, where the potential purchase represents enough dollars and involves enough functions to justify the high costs. Although team selling is usually used to win new accounts, it is sometimes also used with lower level personnel for maintenance selling. Production schedulers, expeditors, and shipping personnel may join the sales team to keep an existing account satisfied.[20]

Multilevel Selling

Multilevel selling is a variation of team selling. In multilevel selling, the sales team consists of personnel from various managerial levels who call on their counterparts in the buying organization. Thus, the account manager might call on the customer's purchasing department while the selling firm's vice president of finance calls on the buyer's financial vice president.

This approach represents proper organizational etiquette—each member of the selling team calls on a person with corresponding status and authority. Also, it is useful for higher level executives to participate in opening a relationship with a major new prospect, since they have the authority to make concessions and establish policies necessary to win and maintain that prospect as a customer.

Computer-to-Computer Ordering

Another recent technological change under way in some industries needs to be mentioned here because it may change the role of salespeople and ultimately the organization structures most appropriate for managing the selling function. The growth in computerized ordering allows a customer to place an order directly through a dedicated telephone link to a supplier's computer. As we saw in Exhibits 5.2 and 5.3, 12 percent of the firms in one survey already use computerized systems to contact at least some of their customers, and another 20 percent plan to increase their dependence on such systems in the future.

Although such systems have been most widely adopted by manufacturers of relatively simple, standardized consumer products, a substantial proportion of industrial manufacturers are also moving toward computerized ordering.

This is particularly true for firms that customize their products to a customer's order. By having orders sent directly to its computer, the supplier can rely on the computer to organize production schedules and speed up the production process.[21]

From the customer's point of view, computerized ordering is more convenient, flexible, and less time-consuming than placing orders through a salesperson. From the supplier's perspective, linking major customers to a dedicated reorder system can help "tie" those customers to the firm and increase the proportion of purchases they make from a single source.

In the mid-1970s, American Hospital Supply, a wholesaler of medical suppliers, offered to install the industry's first computerized reorder terminals in the stockrooms of major hospitals. Since hospitals were accustomed to ordering supplies from salespeople making regular rounds, they at first accepted the system only as a hedge against emergencies. But stock clerks found the terminals more convenient than waiting for a salesperson to call, and they turned to American Hospital Supply for everything from tongue depressors to blood analyzers. Rival distributors filed an antitrust suit, claiming the system represented an attempt to establish exclusive supply arrangements with major hospitals, but they lost the suit on appeal. By the mid-1980s, American Hospital Supply had become a $3.4 billion-a-year operation and was purchased in a friendly acquisition for nearly $4 billion by drug maker Baxter Travenol.[22]

One question that is yet to be answered is how computerized reorder systems might change the role of the sales force. Will salespeople become largely redundant, or will being freed from the more routine order-taking activities enable firms to refocus personal selling efforts on more complex communications, problem solving, and customer servicing tasks? Some hints concerning how this "thorny" sales management issue may ultimately be answered are provided by Inland Steel's experience with computerized order systems as described in the accompanying Thorny Issues in Sales Management 5.1.

ORGANIZING TO SERVICE GLOBAL MARKETS

As firms expand their marketing and sales efforts into other countries, they face a critical decision concerning how to organize their selling efforts across national boundaries. While globalization obviously adds complexity to a firm's organizational design, the basic questions to be answered are the same as those faced in domestic markets. First, should the firm rely on independent agents to represent its interests in a foreign market or hire its own company salespeople? If the firm decides to establish its own subsidiary or sales office with a dedicated company sales force in a foreign country, a second question arises concerning the appropriate horizontal structure for that sales force. Should it be organized geographically, by product line, by type of customer, or some other way? The following sections review recent research that describes how

Thorny Issues in Sales Management 5 • 1

How Will Computerized Ordering Systems Affect the Selling Function?

Inland Steel Company set up a computer-to-computer ordering system in the spring of 1985. About 15 of the firm's largest customers—including Ford, A. O. Smith, and Emerson Electric—are participating. As described below by Mr. William Sanders, general manager of systems, Inland's experience with computerized ordering suggests such systems may actually free salespeople to focus on more critical tasks and enhance—rather than threaten—their role in a firm's marketing strategy.

In our business, we try to maintain as strong a customer relationship as we can, and service is a major area of company differentiation. We try to make it as administratively easy to order as we can.

We are in a job-shop business. Each order is custom manufactured. We have a fairly long lead time—five to six weeks. The sooner we know what the customer wants, the sooner we can get the order to him. If the customer mails the order in, that takes an extra four or five days.

So we have an electronic link from the customer to our sales department and on to the mill. Once the order is placed, the customer wants to know how the order is progressing. We have a customer-order status system, and he can check his order at any point. When we actually ship it, we transmit that information to the customer and tell him what truck or railroad it is on.

We see a good deal of enthusiasm on the part of our customers. Since there is a lot of technology involved, it does take a little time for them to understand what they can do, and how they go about doing it. We have just gone through a major streamlining of our sales and production planning groups, to make sure we can offer the best service.

Our salespeople are also very enthusiastic. It gives them another service to offer. It is not so much a productivity improvement for them, because they never really were order takers. The salespeople focus on presenting our products and services.

This system can give you a competitive edge if you do it right. Anything you can do to differentiate yourself in the mind of the customer is an advantage. I think Inland has more such services right now, but I am sure all of our competitors are thinking about doing the same thing.

Source: Howard Sutton, *Rethinking the Company's Sales and Distribution Channels* (New York: The Conference Board, 1986), p. 26.

major multinational corporations (MNCs) are resolving these organizational issues.

The Use of Company Salespeople versus Independent Agents

A recent survey of 14 large MNCs examined their sales organization practices across 135 subsidiaries located in 45 countries.[23] As Exhibit 5–10 indicates, about 25 percent of the MNC's subsidiaries use independent agents, either alone or in combination with company salespeople. This is a somewhat lower percentage than found in the U.S. domestic market, where about one third of all firms use manufacturers' reps (see Exhibit 5.2). Note, however, that agents are used somewhat more frequently in developing markets than in more de-

EXHIBIT 5 ● 10   *Type of Sales Organization: Analyses by Industry, Level of Market Development, Region, Sales Level, Sales Force Size, and Country*

	Own Sales Force	Sales Force and Independent Sales Organization
Industry		
General consumer goods	15	9
Pharmaceutical	54	7
Industrial goods	19	14
EDP	13	2
Level of market development		
Developed market	58	14
Developing market	39	14
Region		
Canada, Australia, and New Zealand	11	3
Central, South America	16	4
Europe	44	10
Africa	9	1
Far East, Southeast Asia	17	10
Sales level		
Less than $25 million	62	22
Over $25 million	37	10
Sales force size		
Under 50 persons	66	18
Over 50 persons	35	12

Source: John S. Hill and Richard R. Still, "Organizing the Overseas Sales Force: How Multinationals Do It," *Journal of Personal Selling and Sales Management,* Spring 1990, p. 61.

veloped countries and in markets where the firm's sales volume is relatively small. Both of these findings are consistent with our earlier discussion of the conditions under which firms are most likely to use independent reps.

Industry factors are also related to the use of agents versus company salespeople. Firms selling complex, high-tech products, such as computers and pharmaceuticals, are significantly more likely to rely solely on their own salespeople than firms in other industrial or consumer goods industries. This finding is also consistent with our earlier discussion. The higher levels of product knowledge and post-sale service (transaction-specific assets) required to sell such high-tech products make it relatively more desirable for firms to employ their own salespeople. By doing so, they can maintain better control over the marketing and sales efforts devoted to their products and reduce their transaction costs.

Horizontal Structure of Subsidiary Sales Forces	Slightly more than half (51.5 percent) of the surveyed MNC's subsidiaries report using simple geographic territories to organize their selling efforts within a given country. The rest use more specialized organizational structures, with different salespeople assigned to specific products and/or customer types. As you might expect from our earlier discussion, subsidiaries are most likely to employ specialized structures when they are selling relatively complex products (e.g., pharmaceuticals), when their product lines are broad, when they are operating in highly developed markets, and when their sales volumes are relatively large.

While globalization makes the organization of the sales force more complicated, firms tend to resolve organizational issues in international markets in largely the same way as they do in the United States. The situational and strategic factors that influence firms' organizational decisions appear to be similar in both types of markets, and those factors seem to affect organizational choices in similar ways both at home and abroad.

VERTICAL STRUCTURE OF THE SALES ORGANIZATION

The beginning of this chapter stressed that the sales organization must be structured vertically as well as horizontally. The vertical organizational structure defines clearly what managerial positions have the authority for carrying out specific sales management activities. This vertical structure also provides for the effective integration and coordination of selling efforts throughout the firm.

The Integration of Sales and Marketing	One vertical organization issue that affects both the authority and the autonomy of sales managers is whether the sales function should be integrated within a firm's marketing department or be organized as a separate unit. While good coordination of sales and marketing activities is important for a firm to service its customers and compete effectively, different companies attempt to achieve such coordination in different ways. Thorny Issues in Sales Management 5.2 discusses the various approaches American firms follow in attempting to resolve this coordination problem. The rest of our discussion focuses on issues relevant to the vertical arrangement of the sales organization, regardless of whether it is a subunit of a larger marketing department or a stand-alone organizational unit.

Number of Management Levels and Span of Control	Two questions that must be answered in designing an effective vertical structure for a sales organization are (1) How many levels of sales managers should there be? and (2) How many people should each manager supervise (span of control)? These questions are related. For a given number of salespeople, the

Thorny Issues in Sales Management 5 • 2

SHOULD MARKETING AND SALES FUNCTIONS BE INTEGRATED WITHIN A SINGLE DEPARTMENT?

As many firms strive to become more customer-oriented and market-driven, one might expect them to integrate all of their marketing-related activities, including sales, into a single functional department to improve coordination and increase responsiveness to customer needs and changing market conditions. As one observer asserts, "The closest possible coordination of all facets of a marketing job will ultimately require all phases of [marketing] activity in one centrally and closely coordinated unit."*

But casual observation indicates many organizations do not assign responsibility for all their marketing activities to a single unit. Many treat sales as a separate function, and some also have separate advertising or corporate communications departments. It is also common for other departments to be assigned responsibility for selected marketing activities, as when engineering or R&D is responsible for overseeing new product development. The question, then, is which kind of organizational arrangement of marketing activities—integrated or dispersed—works best? Which is most common?

A random sample of U.S. corporations was recently surveyed to answer these questions. As Table A indicates, only about one third of the 668 responding companies report having *totally integrated* marketing organizations where a single department has responsibility for a full range of marketing activities. In two thirds of the firms, other departments have responsibility for at least one major marketing function. While there is no significant difference between the responses of con-

*S. Bernstein, "A Pair of Problems," *Advertising Age,* February 13, 1989, p. 16.

TABLE A   *Integrated* versus Dispersed Marketing Organizations in Small and Large Companies*

	Total		Small Companies†		Large Companies	
	Number	Percent	Number	Percent	Number	Percent
Integrated	188	32.9	138	39.9	50	22.2
Dispersed	383	67.1	208	60.1	175	77.8
Total	571	100.0	346	100.0	225	100.0

*To qualify as an integrated marketing organization, the responsibility for the following marketing activities had to be assigned to a single organizational unit: new product planning, new product introduction, ongoing product management, recommending price levels or making price decisions, sales, sales support/application engineering, advertising, sales promotion, public relations, consumer relations, channel management, strategic marketing planning, operational marketing planning, marketing research, and sales forecasting.

†Small companies are companies with annual sales of less than $100 million.

TABLE B   *Assignments of Responsibilities of Marketing Activities within Companies*

Organizational Unit with Primary Responsibility	Marketing Activitiy									
	New Product Planning	New Product Introduction	Product Management	Recommend Prices	Set Prices	Sales	Sales Support	Channel Management	Advertising	Sales Promotion
Marketing	84.7%	92.6%	87.9%	90.6%	81.0%	76.6%	79.6%	68.0%	85.9%	86.8%
Corporate marketing/ marketing research	0.3	1.5	1.2	0.6	0.2	0.3	0.4	1.1	2.4	1.9
Product marketing	2.8	1.7	2.3	1.0	0.8	0.3	0.7	1.3	0.8	0.5
Sales and service	1.0	1.5	2.1	3.6	6.0	20.6	16.1	10.5	2.2	4.4
Advertising and public relations	0.0	0.0	0.0	0.0	0.0	0.0	0.0	0.2	5.7	3.0
Finance	0.2	0.0	0.0	1.7	3.0	0.2	0.0	0.0	0.2	0.0
R & D and engineering	6.7	0.9	3.3	0.3	0.2	0.2	0.8	0.2	0.0	0.0
Manufacturing and purchasing	0.3	0.3	0.9	0.3	0.5	0.5	1.1	13.9	0.3	1.7
Senior management	3.1	1.5	1.9	1.8	8.1	1.3	1.3	4.3	2.5	1.7
Other	0.9	0.0	0.5	0.2	0.2	0.0	0.0	0.5	0.0	0.0
Total	100.0%	100.0%	100.0%	100.0%	100.0%	100.0%	100.0%	100.0%	100.0%	100.0%

(continued)

sumer and industrial goods producers, large firms are less likely to have integrated marketing departments than smaller firms (less than $100 million in sales). The primary reason for this difference, according to the survey respondents, is span of control. As firms get very large, it becomes more difficult for a single marketing executive to oversee the full range of marketing activities.

However, as Table B indicates, while only one third of firms integrate all marketing activities in a single department, the vast majority of firms do integrate most marketing activities—including sales—within the marketing organization. Only 20 percent of respondents report having a separate, independent sales department, while more than three quarters incorporate sales within their marketing organization.

Perhaps the major conclusion is that, while marketing activities must be well-coordinated to serve customers effectively, there is more than one viable means for achieving such coordination. While most firms coordinate many of their marketing and sales efforts by organizing them in a single department, other departments also have responsibility for at least some marketing activities in a majority of companies. Many analysts argue that, in a truly market-oriented firm, marketing should be *everyone's* responsibility, so perhaps this is the way it should be.

Source: Donald S. Tull, Bruce E. Cooley, Mark R. Philips, Jr., and Harry S. Watkins, "The Organization of Marketing Activities of American Manufacturers," *Report #91-126* (Cambridge, Mass.: The Marketing Science Institute, October 1991).

greater the span of control, the fewer the levels of management, and the fewer the managers needed.

There are major differences of opinion about the best policy concerning span of control and the number of vertical levels for a sales organization. Some managers think they have greater control and attain greater responsiveness when the sales force has a "flat" organization with few management levels. They argue that few levels between the top sales executive and the field salespeople facilitates communication and more direct control. But some managers argue that such flat organizations actually limit communication and control because they necessitate large spans of control.

The flat organization with large spans of control has lower administrative costs because of the relatively small number of managers involved. Others argue, however, that such cost savings are an illusion because the lower quantity and quality of management can lead to less effectiveness and productivity.

In view of these disagreements, it is difficult to generalize about the most appropriate number of management levels and span of control for a specific organization. However, managers have a few guidelines to follow. The span of control should be smaller and the number of levels of management should be larger when (1) the sales task is complex, (2) the profit impact of each salesperson's performance is high, and (3) the salespeople in the organization are well paid and professional. In other words, the more difficult and important the sales job, the greater the management support and supervision that should be provided to the members of the sales force.

Two empirical studies appear to support this generalization. One study examined the relationship between the span of control and sales force perfor-

EXHIBIT 5 • 11 *Optimal Spans of Control for Field Sales Managers for Different Types of Selling*

Type of Sales Job	Optimal Span of Control for Field Sales Managers
Trade selling	12–16
New business selling	10
Missionary selling	10
Technical selling	7

Source: Reprinted by permission of the *Harvard Business Review.* Adapted form Derek A. Newton, "Get the Most Out of Your Sales Force," September–October 1969, pp. 130–43. Copyright © 1969 by the President and Fellows of Harvard College; all rights reserved.

mance and morale across different types of selling. It found that the optimal span of control was smaller for more complex and difficult types of sales jobs. The findings of this study are summarized in Exhibit 5.11.

Another survey of the organizational practices of firms in different industries found that the median span of control of field sales managers is generally smaller in firms that sell relatively complex and expensive industrial goods than it is in firms that sell consumer products or services. The results of this survey are shown in Exhibit 5.12.

Another general rule is that the span of control should usually be smaller at higher levels in the sales organization because top-level managers should have more time for analysis and decision making. Also, the people who report to them typically have more complicated jobs and require more organizational support and communications than persons in lower level jobs.

Management Roles and Staff Support

In addition to deciding how many subordinates sales managers should supervise, another question is how much authority each manager should be given in managing subordinates. Where should the authority to hire, fire, and evaluate field salespeople be located within the organization? In some sales organizations, first-level field or district sales managers have the authority to hire their own salespeople. In other organizations, the authority to hire and fire is located at higher management levels.

As a general rule of organization, the more important a decision is for the success of a firm, the higher the level of management that should make that decision. In firms that hire many low-paid salespeople who perform relatively routine selling tasks and have only a small impact on the firm's overall profit performance, hiring and evaluation authority is usually given to first-level sales managers. Firms that have professional salespeople who perform complex selling tasks and have a major profit impact usually place the authority to hire and fire at higher levels. This is particularly true when the sales force is viewed as a training ground for future sales or marketing managers.

EXHIBIT 5 • 12   *Median Spans of Control for Field Sales Managers in Different Types of Industries*

Industry	Median Reported Span of Control for Field Sales Managers
Services	10
Consumer products	8
Industrial products	6

Source: Morgan B. MacDonald, Jr., and Earl L. Bailey, "The Field Sales Supervisor," *Conference Board Record* 5 (July 1968), p. 34.

Selling responsibilities

In addition to their supervisory and policy-making roles, many sales managers—particularly those at the field or district level—continue to be actively involved in selling activities. Since many sales managers are promoted to their positions only after proving to be competent and effective salespeople, their employers are often reluctant to lose the benefit of their selling skills. Consequently, sales managers are often allowed to continue servicing at least a few of their largest customers after they join the ranks of management.

Some firms rely on their sales managers for selling and servicing key accounts. Sales managers often prefer this kind of arrangement. They are reluctant to give up the opportunities for commissions and direct contact with the marketplace that they gain by being actively involved in selling. On average, sales managers continue to devote nearly one third of their time to sales activities, as indicated in Exhibit 5.13.

The danger is that sales managers sometimes spend too much time selling and not enough time managing their subordinates. Consequently, some firms limit the amount of actual selling in which managers can engage. This is particularly true in larger firms where coordinating and supervising a vast sales force require greater attention by management personnel.

Sales-related functions

Many firms face markets that demand high levels of service. Firms that sell capital equipment, for instance, must provide their customers with installation and maintenance service; fashion manufacturers must provide rapid order processing and delivery; and firms that sell electronic components must offer special product design and engineering services. These services must be integrated with the rest of the firm's marketing and selling activities for the company to compete effectively.[24]

The question from an organizational viewpoint, though, is whether sales managers should be given the authority to control such sales-related functions. The answer depends on the function and the characteristics and needs of the

Exhibit 5 • 13   *How Sales Managers Spend Their Time*

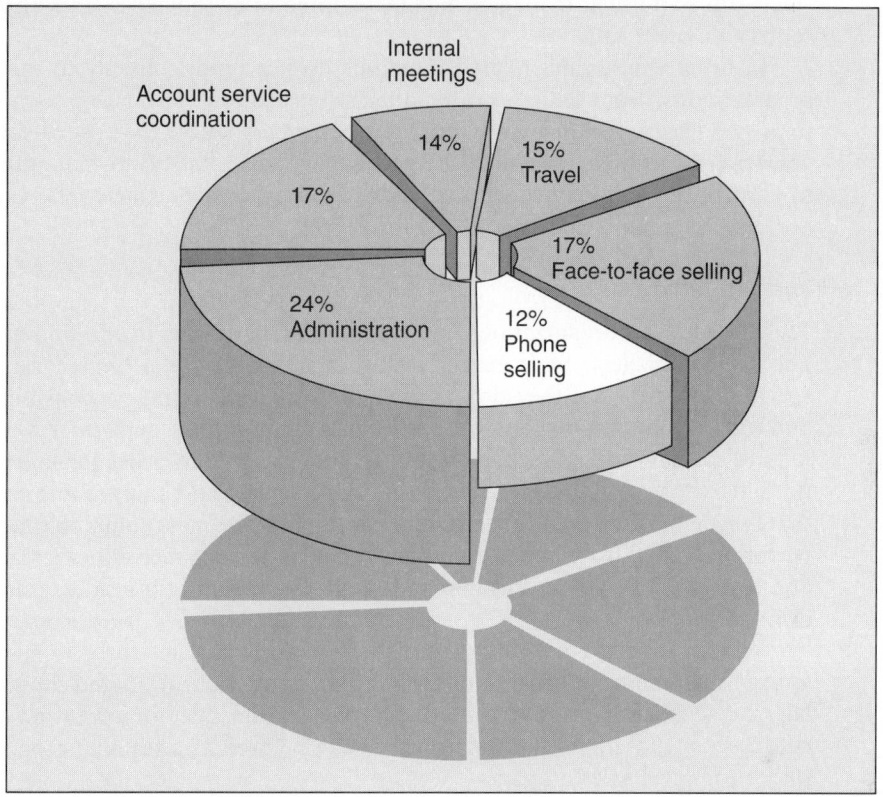

Source: William A. O'Connell and William Keenan, Jr., "The Shape of Things to Come," *Sales & Marketing Management,* January 1990, p. 39.

firm's customers. Order processing and expediting are the least visible but most important sales-related functions. In some firms, persons responsible for order processing report to top-level sales management, whereas in other firms they report to operations management, perhaps as part of an inventory control or data processing department. Usually, the more important rapid order processing and delivery are for keeping customers satisfied, the more appropriate it is for sales management to have authority over this function.

Repair and engineering services tend to be responsible to the sales organization in some firms and to the manufacturing or operations department in others. Again, such functions are most likely to be attached to the sales organization when they play a critical role in winning and maintaining customers. This is particularly true when the product must be designed or modified to meet customer specifications before a sale can be made.

The credit function is almost always the responsibility of the firm's controller or treasurer, and it seldom reports to the sales organization because salespeople and their managers may be tempted to be too generous with credit terms to close a sale.

In firms where sales-related functions do not report directly to the sales organizations, team selling is often a useful means of coordinating such functions—at least when dealing with major customers where the cost of such an approach is justified. Although the account manager has no formal authority to control the actions of team members from other departments, he can coordinate the team's activities at the field level.

Staff support

Most larger sales organizations utilize some staff personnel in addition to their line sales managers. Staff executives are responsible for a limited range of specific activities, but they do not have the broad operating responsibility or authority of line managers. Staff executives commonly perform tasks that require specialized knowledge or abilities that the average sales manager does not have the time to develop. They must also collect and analyze information that line managers need for decision making. Thus, the most common functions performed by staff specialists in a sales organization are recruitment, training, and sales analysis. A typical line and staff sales organization is diagrammed in Exhibit 5.14.

The creative use of staff specialists can enable a sales force to function with fewer managers because of the benefits of specialization and division of labor. It can also improve the effectiveness of the sales organization while cutting costs. In addition, staff positions can be used as a training ground for future top-level sales managers.

On the other hand, staff positions are justified only when the sales organization is large enough so staff specialists have enough work to keep them busy. A staff specialist in sales training, for instance, would not be justified if the firm hires only three or four trainees each year.

S OME ADDITIONAL QUESTIONS

Although many issues concerning the strategic organization of the sales force have been examined, some related questions have yet to be explored. How many salespeople should a firm hire? How should those people be deployed? How should sales territories be defined? What quota, if any, should be assigned to each sales territory?

The answers to these questions depend on the markets to be served, the potential sales volume in those markets, and the selling effort necessary to capture a desired share of that potential volume. In the next chapter, methods of market analysis and sales forecasting are discussed before the questions of sales force size, deployment, and quotas are brought up again in Chapters 7 and 8.

EXHIBIT **5 ● 14**   *Line and Staff Sales Organization*

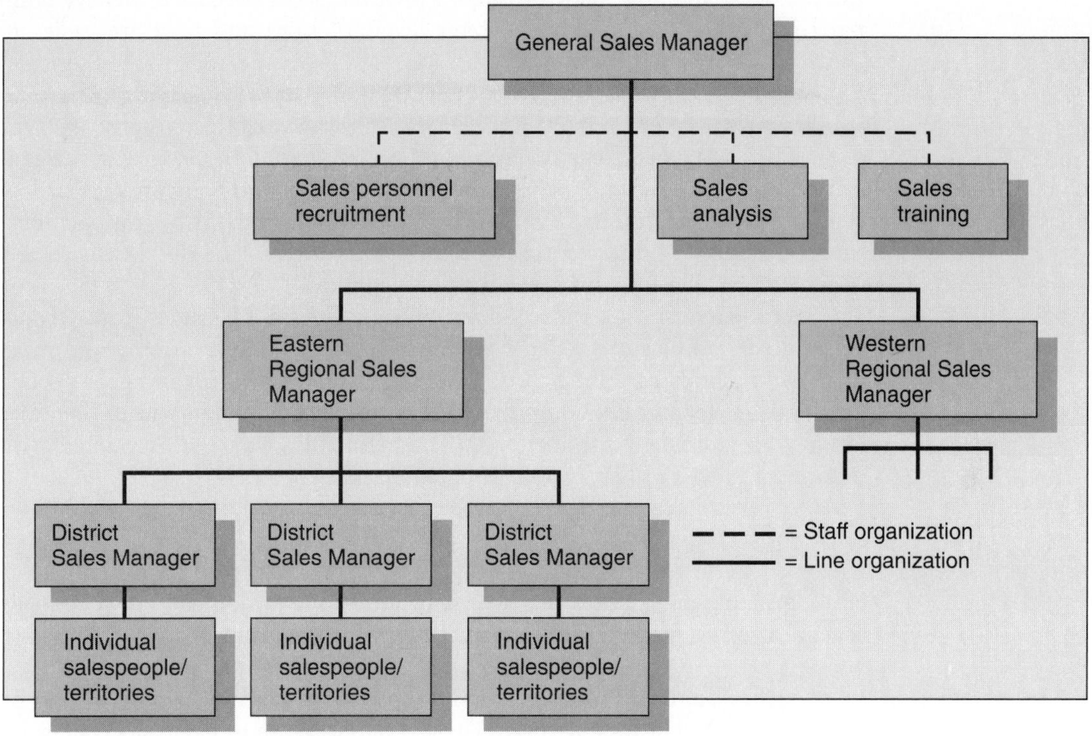

General Sales Manager

Sales personnel recruitment

Sales analysis

Sales training

Eastern Regional Sales Manager

Western Regional Sales Manager

District Sales Manager

District Sales Manager

District Sales Manager

– – – – = Staff organization
————— = Line organization

Individual salespeople/ territories

Individual salespeople/ territories

Individual salespeople/ territories

S UMMARY

This chapter examined important issues regarding the organization of the sales force. It looked at the benefits a good organizational plan can provide and at the major issues involved in deciding on the horizontal and vertical organization of the sales effort.

A good organizational plan should satisfy three criteria. First, it should allow the firm to realize the benefits that can be derived from the division and specialization of labor. Second, it should provide for stability and continuity in the firm's selling efforts. This can best be accomplished by organizing *activities* and not people. Third, it should produce effective coordination of the various activities assigned to different persons in the sales force and different departments in the firm.

Questions of horizontal organization revolve around how specific selling activities are to be divided among members of the sales force. The first issue to be resolved is whether to use company employees to perform the sales function or to rely on outside manufacturers' representatives or sales agents. The cost of using outside agents is usually lower than those of a company sales force at relatively low sales volumes. However, most executives believe company employees will generate greater levels of sales and they are easier to control than agents.

When a firm employs its own sales force, four types of horizontal organization are commonly found, structured according to (1) geography, (2) type of product, (3) type of customer, and (4) selling function. Geographic organization is the simplest and most common. It possesses the advantages of low cost and clear identification of which salesperson is responsible for each customer. Its primary disadvantage is that it does not provide the firm with any benefits from division and specialization of labor.

Specializing the sales force along product lines allows salespeople to develop great familiarity with the technical attributes, applications, and most effective methods of selling those products. This can be advantageous when products are technically complex or when the firm's manufacturing facilities are also organized by product type. The major disadvantage associated with organization by product type is duplication of effort.

Organizing the sales force by type of customer or market serviced allows salespeople to understand the needs and requirements of the various types of customers better. Salespeople are more likely to discover ideas for new products and marketing approaches that will appeal to those customers. However, this scheme also produces duplication of effort, which tends to increase selling and administrative expenses.

A selling function organizational philosophy holds that people should be allowed to do what they do best. Thus, it makes sense to have, say, one sales force specializing in prospecting for and developing new accounts while another maintains and services old customers. These arrangements are often difficult to implement because of coordination problems. A variation, which is much less difficult to implement, is to have developmental salespeople who assist the regular sales force in selling new products the specialists also had a hand in researching and developing. A newer form of this organizational approach that is rapidly growing in popularity is the use of inside telephone salespeople to handle reorders from smaller customers and other routine selling tasks, while outside field salespeople concentrate on new accounts and customer service.

In addition to deciding on a basic structure, a firm needs to specify how it intends to service national and key accounts in its horizontal organizational plans. Three arrangements are most commonly found: (1) assigning key accounts to top sales executives, (2) creating a separate corporate division, and (3) creating a separate major accounts sales force.

Two key questions must be addressed in deciding on an effective vertical structure of the sales organization: (1) How many levels of sales managers should there be? and (2) How many people should each manager supervise? The answers are related; for a given number of salespeople, greater spans of control produce fewer levels of management. Although it is difficult to unequivocally state the optimal span of control for a firm, it is true generally that the span of control should be smaller in those firms where (1) the sales task is complex, (2) the profit impact of each salesperson's performance is high, and (3) the salespeople in the organization are well paid and professional.

In sum, the more difficult and important the sales job, the smaller the span of control should be to allow for greater management support and supervision. The span of control should also be smaller at higher levels in the sales organization than at lower levels to allow increased time for analysis and decision making required by the higher level sales positions.

Another question that must be addressed in designing the vertical structure of the sales organization is how much authority should be given each manager in the sales management hierarchy, particularly with respect to hiring, firing, and evaluating subordinates. As a general rule, the more important such decisions are to the firm, the higher the level of management that should make such decisions.

Discussion Questions

1. In 1975, the national sales manager of Pilot Pen Corporation decided he wanted to set up his own direct sales force. Lack of control over Pilot's network of roughly 100 manufacturer agents prompted Ronald G. Shaw to want the change. The change, unfortunately, did not occur until late 1987. Similar situations exist with other companies that have delayed moving from manufacturers' agents to a company sales force. What factors discouraged Pilot Pen, and others, from making the conversion?

2. Intronics Corporation, a manufacturer of electronic circuit boards, reaches the market through the services of 75 manufacturers' agencies. Most of the agencies average two sales agents who call on Intronics' customers. The agents represent seven to eight other manufacturers that produce noncompetitive products. Intronics wants to eliminate the agents and develop its own company sales force. How many salespeople will Intronics have to hire? What issues affect how many salespeople are needed?

3. The BMC Company, unlike other firms manufacturing similar products, uses the services of 22 manufacturers' agents. The other firms in the industry have their own company sales forces, although a few use both systems. What conditions would lead to a company using manufacturers' agents? What are the advantages and disadvantages of using manufacturers' agents?

4. "Our product line now numbers 75 different products. Moreover, the recently added products are more technical than those that have been around for some time. We need to split up our sales force to allow product line specialization." These views were stated by Don Berceau, product manager for Arcade Electric. Arcade's sales manager, Kevin Hunt, believed otherwise and stated, "That's the last thing we need—having a customer called on by two Arcade sales representatives instead of only one. What we need to do is to expand our sales force and cut back on the number of customers assigned to each representative." What would you suggest?

5. Regardless of how the field sales force is organized, many companies are under pressure to develop organizational approaches to service their very large and im-

portant customers. Why is this subject of interest to sales managers? What are the alternative ways of organizing to serve major accounts?

6. LaMarche's Enterprise manufactures both technical and nontechnical products. Its sales forces are organized in the same manner. The technical sales force has 175 people, and the nontechnical group numbers 128. To what extent would such a division affect the following?
   a. Recruiting.
   b. Sales training.
   c. Compensation.
   d. Supervision.
   e. Span of control.

7. The chapter mentions the theory of transaction cost analysis. What role does transaction cost analysis play in the decision to use a company sales force rather than independent manufacturers' agents?

8. Telemarketing has resulted in the development of inside sales forces. Some companies assign sales trainees to the inside or telephone sales force as part of the training program. Other companies view the two positions as separate. What functions would an inside (telephone) sales force perform? How would these functions differ from those performed by the external sales force? How would compensation plans differ if at all?

9. Just-in-time relationships between suppliers and their customers have become popular arrangements, especially in industrial or business-to-business marketing. How will just-in-time relationships affect the sales organization of suppliers using this approach?

10. Despite introduction of the marketing concept, which should affect how a company organizes the marketing effort, we still see organizations that have separate marketing and sales functions. At a recent executive development seminar, one of the authors spent considerable time arguing that sales should be part of marketing. Why would a firm that supposedly has adopted the marketing concept have the sales function separate from the rest of the marketing function?

Endnotes

[1] This example is based in material found in Kate Bertrand, "Reorganizing for Sales," *Business Marketing*, February 1990, p. 30.

[2] Martin Everett, "When There's More Than One Route to the Customer," *Sales & Marketing Management* (August 1990), pp. 48–56.

[3] See also William A. O'Connell and William Keenan, Jr., "The Shape of Things to Come," *Sales & Marketing Management* (January 1990), p. 38.

[4] Louis W. Stern and Adel I. El-Ansary, *Marketing Channels*, 3rd ed. (Englewood Cliffs, N.J.: Prentice Hall, 1988), chap. 3.

[5] Ibid., chap. 5. See also Edwin E. Bobrow, "The Question of Reps," *Sales & Marketing Management* (June 1991), pp. 33–35.

[6] Jayashree Mahajan, et al., "A Comparison of the Impact of Organizational Climate on the Job Satisfaction of Manufacturers' Agents and Company Salespeople: An Exploratory Study," *Journal of Personal Selling and Sales Management* (May 1984), pp. 1–10.

[7] Bernard J. Jaworski, "Toward a Theory of Marketing Control: Environmental Context, Control Types, and Consequences," *Journal of Marketing* (July 1988), pp. 23–39.

[8] Transaction cost analysis was first developed in Oliver E. Williamson, *Markets and Hierarchies: Analysis and Antitrust Implications* (New York: Free Press, 1975). For empirical evidence that largely supports TCA's predictions about the conditions under which firms will employ independent agents versus company salespeople, see Erin Anderson, "The Salesperson as Outside Agent or Employee: An Transaction Cost Analysis," *Marketing Science* 4 (1985), pp. 234–54; Erin Anderson and Barton Weitz, "Make or Buy Decisions: Vertical Integration and Marketing Productivity," *Sloan Management Review,* Spring 1986, pp. 1–19; and Jan B. Heide and George John, "The Role of Dependence Balancing in Safeguarding Transaction-Specific Assets in Conventional Channels," *Journal of Marketing* (January 1988), pp. 20–35.

[9] For example, see James C. Anderson and James A. Narus, "A Model of Distributor Firm and Manufacturer Firm Working Partnerships," *Journal of Marketing* (January 1990), pp. 42–58; and Jan B. Heide and George John, "Do Norms Matter in Marketing Relationships?" *Journal of Marketing,* 1992 (forthcoming).

[10] Robert W. Ruekert, Orville C. Walker, Jr., and Kenneth J. Roering, "The Organization of Marketing Activities: A Contingency Theory of Structure and Performance," *Journal of Marketing* (Winter 1985), pp. 13–25.

[11] Carol J. Loomis, "Can John Akers Save IBM?" *Fortune,* July 15, 1991, pp. 40–56.

[12] For a more detailed discussion of the variety of objectives and activities that telemarketing can accomplish, see Denise Herman, "Telemarketing Success: A Tough Act to Follow," *Telemarketing,* March 1987, pp. 25–28.

[13] "Rebirth of a Salesman: Willy Loman Goes Electronic," *Business Week,* February 27, 1984, p. 104.

[14] Programs that coordinate the efforts of outside salespeople with the use of telemarketing, direct mail, and other promotional efforts are often refered to as "integrated direct marketing" programs. See Ernan Roman, "Integrated Direct Marketing: Managing the Mix," *Sales & Marketing Management* (May 1991), pp. 83–87.

[15] Murray Roman, "Reach Out and Sell Someone with Business Telemarketing," *Industrial Marketing,* August 1982, pp. 78–79. Additional examples of successful telemarketing and integrated direct marketing programs can be found in Howard Sutton, *Rethinking the Company's Selling and Distribution Channels* (New York: The Conference Board, 1986), pp. 23–26; and Ernan Roman, "Integrated Direct Marketing."

[16] For a more detailed discussion of the sales management problems involved in administering effective telemarketing programs, see William C. Moncrief, Charles W. Lamb, Jr., and Terry Dielman, "Developing Telemarketing Support Systems," *Journal of Personal Selling and Sales Management* (August 1986), pp. 43–49.

[17] William A. O'Connell and William Keenan, Jr., "The Shape of Things to Come," p. 36.

[18] O. E. McDaniel, "The New Name of the Game: Global Account Marketing," *National Account Marketing Association Journal,* Fall 1990, pp. 1–5.

[19] Benson P. Shapiro and Rowland T. Moriarity, *Organizing the National Account Force* (Cambridge, Mass.: The Marketing Science Institute, 1984), pp. 1–37. See also Jerome A. Colletti and Gary S. Tubridy, "Effective Major Account Sales Management," *Journal of Personal Selling and Sales Management* (August 1987), pp. 1–10.

[20] Dan T. Dunne, Jr., and Claude A. Thomas, "Strategy for Systems Sellers: A Team Approach," *Journal of Personal Selling and Sales Management* (August 1986), pp. 1–10. See also Cynthia R. Cauthern, "Moving Technical Support into the Sales Loop," *Sales & Marketing Management* (August 1990), pp. 58–61.

[21] For examples, see Tom Murray, "Just-In-Time Isn't Just for Show—It Sells," *Sales & Marketing Management* (May 1990), pp. 62–67.

[22] Peter Petre, "How to Keep Customers Happy Captives," *Fortune,* September 2, 1985, pp. 42–46.

[23] John S. Hill and Richard R. Still, "Organizing the Overseas Sales Force: How Multinationals Do It," *Journal of Personal Selling and Sales Management* (Spring 1990), pp. 57–66.

[24] Barry Farber and Joyce Wycoff, "Customer Service: Evolution and Revolution," *Sales & Marketing Management* (May 1991), pp. 44–51.

Suggested Readings

Sales and marketing organizational structures

Anderson, Erin, and Barton Weitz. "Make or Buy Decisions: Vertical Integration and Marketing Productivity." *Sloan Management Review*, Spring 1986, pp. 1–19.

Ruekert, Robert W., Orville C. Walker, Jr., and Kenneth J. Roering. "The Organization of Marketing Activities: A Contingency Theory of Structure and Performance." *Journal of Marketing*, Winter 1985, pp. 13–25.

Tull, Donald S., Bruce E. Cooley, Mark R. Philips, Jr., and Harry S. Watkins. "The Organization of Marketing Activities of American Manufacturers." *Report #91-126.* Cambridge, Mass.: The Marketing Science Institute, October 1991.

Telemarketing/integrated direct marketing programs

Moncrief, William C., Charles W. Lamb, Jr., and Terry Dielman. "Developing Telemarketing Support Systems." *Journal of Personal Selling and Sales Management* (August 1986), pp. 43–49.

Roman, Ernan. "Integrated Direct Marketing: Managing the Mix." *Sales & Marketing Management* (May 1991), pp. 83–87.

National or key account selling

Cauthern, Cynthia R. "Moving Technical Support into the Sales Loop," *Sales & Marketing Management* (August 1990), pp. 58–61.

Colletti, Jerome A., and Gary S. Tubridy. "Effective Major Account Sales Management." *Journal of Personal Selling and Sales Management* (August 1987), pp. 1–10.

Global sales organization

Hill, John S., and Richard R. Still. "Organizing the Overseas Sales Force: How Multinationals Do It." *Journal of Personal Selling and Sales Management* (Spring 1990), pp. 57–66.

Demand Estimation

A MPERIF TOLERATES NO SURPRISES

If there's anything worse than a no-sale at Amperif, a Chatsworth, California, manufacturer of data storage systems for mainframe computers, it's an unexpected sale. Salespeople there can get in just as much trouble for a sale that wasn't forecast as for not saying they are going to lose a sale.

The unforecasted sale throws a curve in projections and skews the company's five-year plan, the heartbeat of its operations, says Amperif management. The plan, which details everything from market conditions to projected sales, inventory, production, shipping dates, and cash flow, is analyzed on a daily basis, reviewed monthly, revised quarterly, and rewritten annually.

For 1984, 1985, and 1986, the company came within 3 percent of its objectives. Revenues grew 70 percent from 1985 to 1986, and Amperif Chief Operating Officer Donald Orr projected sales of $175 million by 1990.

The realization of this goal would be determined by the company's basic operating rule—no surprises—which is why sales progress is closely monitored

Source: "Amperif Tolerates No Surprises," *Sales & Marketing Management,* 138 (February 1987), pp. 18–19.

and unanticipated sales are frowned upon. Unfortunately, forecasting is a weak area for most new sales hires, according to Orr.

To ensure against exaggeration, salespeople file a monthly report that lists prospects, expected closing and shipping dates, and the value and probability of a sale based on a percentage scale.

If a salesperson predicts a 90 percent chance of closing a sale, the chance is probably somewhat lower, according to Peter Zinsli, director of strategic programs. "We drill into them," he says, "that 90 percent means the contract is already signed."

If sales reps suddenly list sales that haven't been tracked on prior reports, an alarm goes off, says Zinsli, because it means one of several things: the sales reps weren't making the calls they should have been making; they weren't watching prospects for opportunities; or they have been minimizing prospects so they won't have to track so many.

"Some people think we're nuts to be so fine-tuned, but look what it has done for us," says Orr. "If you constantly analyze, you overcome surprises before they happen."

As this scenario suggests, firms often emphasize producing accurate estimates of demand and identifying the most viable market opportunities. The identification of market opportunities fundamentally affects how firms plan, staff, and operate.

There seems to be confusion over the terms used to describe a firm's marketing opportunities. This chapter reviews the main terms and discusses the interrelationships among these concepts. The rest of the chapter explores the various ways demand estimates can be developed and the advantages and disadvantages of each method.

CLARIFICATION OF TERMS

Market opportunity analysis requires an understanding of the differences in the notions of market potential, sales potential, sales forecast, and sales quota.

Market potential is an estimate of the possible sales of a commodity, a group of commodities, or a service for an entire industry in a market during a stated period under ideal conditions. Note several things about this definition. First, *market potential* is defined for a particular market during a specified time period. The *market* refers to a specific customer group in a specific geographic area. Thus the statement,

> "The market potential for portable air compressors (commodity) to the construction industry (specific consumer group) in the Chicago metropolitan area (specific geographic area) in 1997 (specific time period) is 10,000 units or $10 million (maximum sales),"

is a complete specification of market potential. The omission of any of the items would make the statement incomplete.

Sales potential refers to the portion of the market potential that a *particular firm* can reasonably expect to achieve. Market potential represents the maximum possible sales for *all sellers* of the good or service under ideal conditions and sales potential reflects the maximum possible sales for an individual firm.

The **sales forecast** is an estimate of the dollar or unit sales for a specified future period under a proposed marketing plan or program. The forecast may be for a specified item of merchandise or for an entire line. It may be for a market as a whole or for any portion of it. Note that a sales forecast specifies the commodity, customer group, geographic area, and time period and includes a specific marketing plan as an essential element. If the proposed plan is changed, predicted sales are also expected to change.

Forecasted sales are typically less than the company's sales potential. The firm may not have sufficient production capacity to realize its full potential, or its distribution network may not be sufficiently developed, or its financial resources may be limited. Likewise, forecast sales for an industry are typically less than the industry's market potential.

The distinctions among *market potential, sales potential,* and *sales forecast* are captured in Exhibit 6.1. Historical sales are shown because they often play a key role in determining the sales forecast. Note that an industry forecast is often developed before a company forecast is generated. The industry forecast presumes a specific level of marketing effort by all the firms that serve the industry. As the company's marketing plan becomes more effective, realized sales and then forecasted sales should come closer to sales potential. The same occurs for industry sales and market potential as the marketing efforts of the competitors become more effective.

Exhibit 6.2 shows the relationship between potentials and forecasts. Typically the process begins with an assessment of the economic environment. Sometimes this is simply an implicit assessment of the immediate future. Is the outlook bright or gloomy? Then, given an initial estimate of industry potential and the company's competitive position, the firm's sales potential can be estimated. This in turn leads to an initial sales forecast, often based on the presumption that the marketing effort will be similar to what it was last year. The initial forecast is then compared with objectives established for the proposed marketing effort. If the marketing program is expected to achieve the objectives, both the program and the sales forecast are adopted. That is rare,

E X H I B I T   6 • 1   *Relation among Market and Sales Potentials and Sales Forecast*

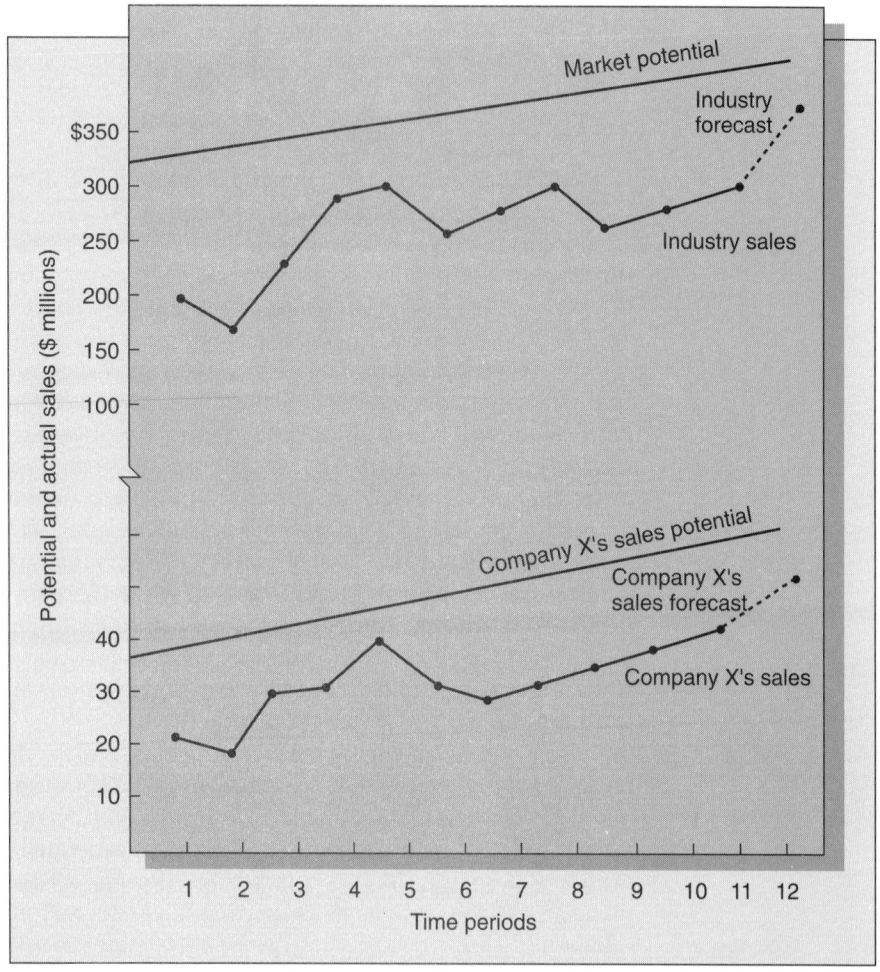

Source: Adapted from Douglas J. Dalrymple and Leonard J. Parsons, *Marketing Management: Strategy and Cases,* 5th ed. (New York: John Wiley & Sons, 1990), p. 234. Used by permission.

however. Usually it is necessary to redesign the marketing program and then revise the sales forecast—often several times.

The objectives may also need revising; but eventually the process should produce agreement between the forecasted or expected sales and the objectives. The sales forecast then becomes a basic input in establishing budgets for the various functional areas. Note that *the sales forecast presumes a specific marketing program.* This is the key to understanding some of the advantages and

EXHIBIT 6 • 2   *Market Potential, Sales Potential, and Sales Forecasting Process*

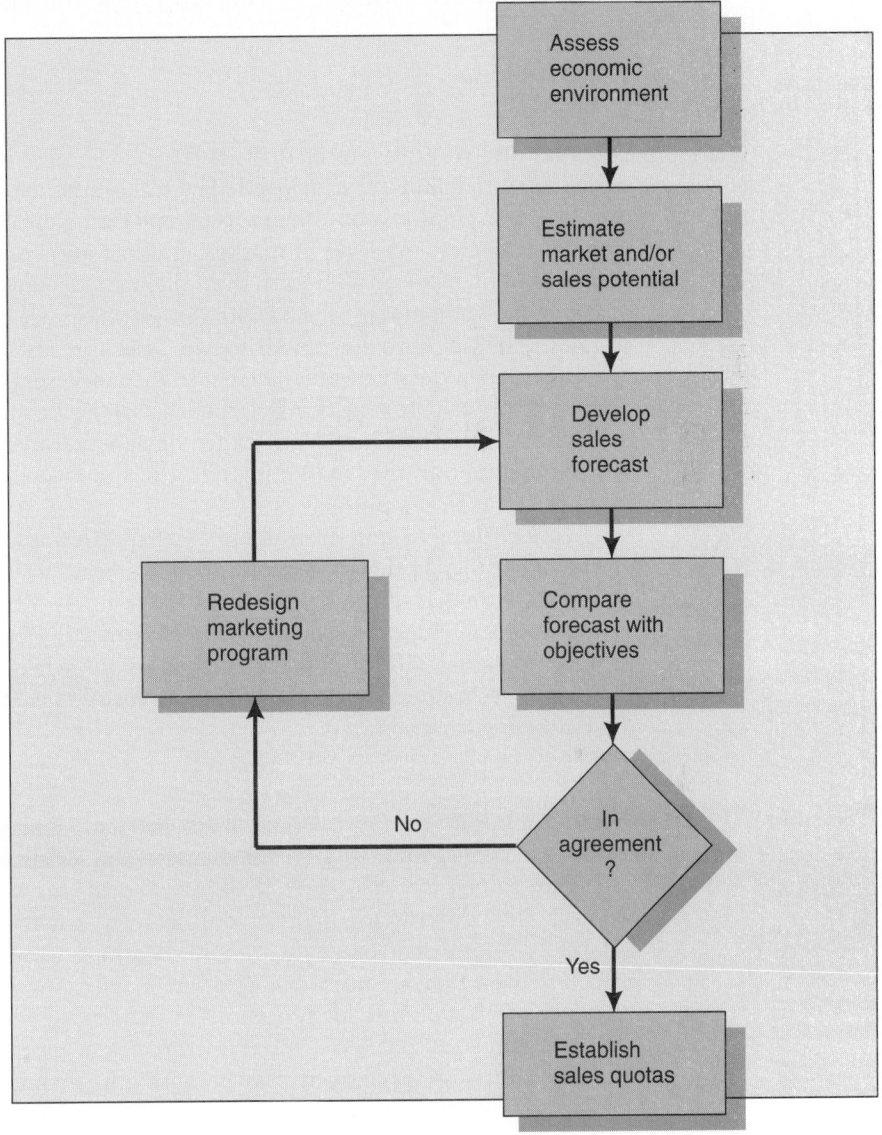

disadvantages of the various sales forecasting methods discussed later in the chapter.

Note, finally, the idea of a sales quota. A **sales quota** is a sales goal or objective assigned to a marketing unit. Sales quotas are typically a key measurement used to evaluate the personal selling effort. They apply to specific periods and can be specified in great detail—for example, sales of a particular item to a specified customer by sales rep J. Jones in June.

E STIMATION OF DEMAND

Potential and forecast are distinct concepts, but they become blurred when estimates of demand are developed. The techniques used to estimate demand differ in their emphasis on the proposed marketing effort. For example, some techniques neglect the level of marketing effort and concentrate on the maximum amount of the commodity that might be demanded from an industry or company. Estimates produced with this emphasis are closer to being market or sales potential estimates than they are sales forecasts.

Other techniques give great weight to the marketing effort planned for the period and are sales forecasts in the true sense of the word. Still other techniques use historic sales as a basis for future demand estimates. They rely on the implicit assumption that marketing effort in the future period will be similar to what it was in the past.

The key thing to note from a user's perspective is where on the spectrum one is operating. Is the projection based on near ideal conditions and thus represents *potential* in the true sense of the term? Is it based on historic marketing effort? Or does it reflect a level of marketing effort and a particular program for that effort? We will find it useful when comparing the sales forecasting techniques later in the chapter to focus on what they presume about the marketing program.

Determine Who Uses the Product or Service

The starting point for any analysis of demand is to determine who uses or will use the product by specifying the important characteristics of users. The market for figure salons like Women's Workout World, for example, is limited to women. They do not equally attract all women, however; those between the ages of 18 and 40 patronize them more. Working women are more likely to patronize them than are nonworking women, and nonworking women without young children are more likely customers than those with young children.

For established products, specifying important user characteristics or factors that affect use is relatively easy because of the company's experience and research. New products may rely on an analogy with similar products—or it might require a survey of potential users or even a small market test.

Determine Rate of Use

It is necessary to determine not only who uses the product but also the rate at which the product is likely to be consumed. A manufacturer of riding lawn mowers might specify that its potential market consists of all households with more than one-third acre of yard and an income of at least $50,000. The firm could not expect to sell every such household a new riding lawn mower every year, however. In estimating market potential, the firm would probably want to estimate new demand and replacement demand, considering the expected life of lawn mowers. This technique is used to estimate the market potential for major appliances and other consumer durables.

The usage estimate is much different for a frequently consumed product such as toothpaste, of which a household uses several tubes each year, and for soft drinks, of which a household might be expected to use a six-pack each week. Both users and rates of usage must be determined to derive the estimates of demand. Furthermore, the manager must understand the basis on which the demand estimate rests. For example,

> One manufacturer considered making stoves for use on boats. A brief analysis clearly indicated that these stoves would be used only on boats with enclosed cabins. The market analyst assigned the job of determining the market potential for these stoves came up with a rather substantial figure for the total number of boats in the United States. With such a sizable market potential, the manufacturer went into production. When sales results were disappointing, an investigation showed that the figure for the number of boats included everything from an eight-foot, flat-bottom rowboat to sea-going yachts.[1]

Determine Who Buys the Product or Service

The analysis of demand might also consider who buys the product. This is particularly important when the purchaser is different from the user. While the number of users and their likely rate of use will determine the total potential for the product, buyers and their motivations for buying will affect how much of that potential is likely to be realized. Thus, although an individual firm might choose to direct a major portion of its promotional efforts to buyers, it might also channel a portion of that effort to users. For example, software manufacturers often address part of their advertising effort to purchasing agents as well as potential users of the software.

Determine the Market Motivations for Purchase

A final factor to consider when analyzing demand is market motivations. Why do customers buy the product? What might influence prospective customers to buy it? Some products have naturally induced causes of sales. For example, when people first set up a household, they typically buy major appliances and furniture. Some manufacturers of these products use the marriage rate as a basis for estimating the size of their markets. Similarly, a manufacturer of baby furniture may base its entire market analysis on birthrates. Likewise, a manufacturer of office furniture might base its estimate of demand on the number of new businesses formed in the firm's market area. Or the firm might use the number of new businesses as an indicator of new demand and use other indicators to estimate replacement demand. For example, manufacturers of pumps for the pulp and paper industry often break the demand for pumps into three components—(1) exchange demand, (2) demand for minor investments, and (3) demand for major investments—and develop separate prediction equations for each of the components using different factors as input.

IMPORTANCE OF SALES FORECAST

The sales forecast is one of the most important pieces of data used by management and lies at the heart of most companies' planning efforts. As the Amperif scenario shows, top management uses the sales forecast to allocate resources among functional areas and to control the operations of the firm. Finance uses it to project cash flows, to decide on capital appropriations, and to establish operating budgets. Production uses it to determine quantities and schedules and to control inventories. Human resources uses it to plan personnel requirements and also as an input in collective bargaining. Purchasing uses it to plan the company's overall materials requirements and also the schedule for their arrival. Marketing uses it to plan marketing and sales programs and to allocate resources among the various marketing activities.

The sales forecast is also of fundamental importance in planning and evaluating the personal selling effort. Sales managers use it to set sales quotas, as input to the compensation plan, and to evaluate the field sales force, among other things. The sales manager thus should be familiar with the techniques used to develop sales forecasts. The subjective and objective methods discussed in this chapter are listed in Exhibit 6.3.[2]

USERS' EXPECTATIONS

The **users' expectations method** of forecasting sales is also known as the **buyers' intentions method** because it relies on answers from customers regarding their expected consumption or purchases of the product. The customers may be surveyed in person, over the telephone, by mail, or perhaps by computer. The Chevrolet Division of General Motors, for example, uses computer interviewing at trade shows to assess attendees' reactions to its new models as a way to forecast how well each model is likely to sell. A major benefit of the microcomputer administration of the questionnaire is that the results are available the day after the trade show ends. As respondents tap in their answers on the keyboard, the results are transmitted by phone lines to a central computer for processing.[3]

The respondents in a users' expectations survey do not necessarily have to be the ultimate consumers. Rather, the firm may find it advantageous to secure the reactions of wholesalers and retailers that serve the channel. For example, Persoft, Inc., a Madison, Wisconsin-based software publisher, typically talks with dealers when trying to gauge demand for its new software packages.[4] The surveys typically are conducted with the ultimate customers, however. Boeing Company, for example, contacts major airlines about their purchase plans for new aircraft when planning its production requirements.

E x h i b i t   6 • 3   *Classification of Sales Forecasting Methods*

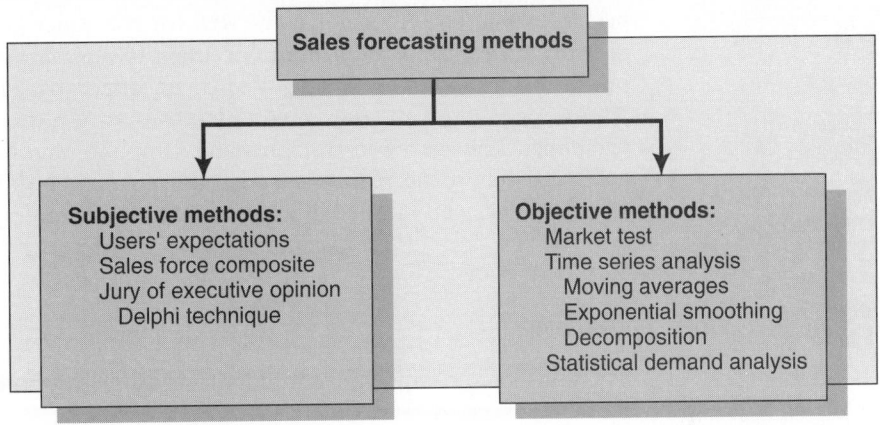

The users' expectations method of forecasting sales may provide estimates closer to market or sales potential than to sales forecasts. In reality, user groups would have difficulty anticipating the industry's or a particular firm's marketing efforts. Rather, the user estimates reflect their anticipated needs. From the sellers' standpoint, they provide a measure of the opportunities available among a particular segment of users.

Advantages

The users' expectations method offers several advantages to a firm. First, the forecast is based on estimates obtained directly from firms whose buying actions will actually determine the sales of the product. Second, the way the information is collected—projected product use by customer—allows the preparation of forecasts in great detail (by product, by customer, or by sales territory). Third, the method often provides some insight into the buyer's thinking and plans. This is helpful in planning the marketing strategy. Finally, this technique can be used when other techniques may be impossible, as when forecasting sales of a new product.

Disadvantages

The users' expectations method is limited to situations in which the potential customers for the product are few and well defined. The technique becomes difficult to implement and can result in serious error when there are many customers and they cannot be readily identified. Thus, the technique works well in forecasting sales for a product such as compressors for natural gas transmission where there are probably no more than two dozen potential customers in the whole world. It would not work well for a company that manufactures paper clips. The technique also depends on the sophistication of potential customers in anticipating their needs. Buyer intentions are subject to change, particularly when the buyer is the household; thus the users' expectations method does not work well for consumer goods.[5] It is sometimes difficult to determine the firmness of intent to purchase, particularly when the person being queried is uninformed or uncooperative. Finally, the users' expectations method requires a considerable expenditure of money, time, and personnel. The survey instruments and sampling plan have to be designed; a field staff has to be recruited and trained; and the data must be collected, edited, coded, and tabulated before the forecast can be prepared.[6]

SALES FORCE COMPOSITE

The sales force composite method of forecasting sales is so named because the initial input is the opinion of each member of the field sales staff. Each person states how much he or she expects to sell during the forecast period. These estimates are typically adjusted at various levels of sales management. They are likely to be checked, discussed, and possibly changed by the branch manager and on up the sales organization chart until the figures are finally accepted at corporate headquarters.

Ex-Cell-O Corporation relies on the sales force composite method of sales forecasting. Ex-Cell-O manufactures a variety of industrial items, including machinery, precision parts and assemblies, aerospace and electronic parts, and expendable tools and accessories. The company manufactures machine tools that range in price from a few thousand dollars to a half-million dollars or more. The products are sold by the machine tool group's own sales force, which consists of approximately 50 salespeople and 100 independent distributors. Each salesperson and distributor is required to forecast the proposals that are outstanding that he or she expects will be converted into orders during each of the upcoming five quarters. The process is repeated every three months. The regional manager reviews the forecasts with the individual salesperson or distributor and secures agreement on any necessary adjustments. When the manager is satisfied that all of the individual forecasts in the region are as realistic as can be, the manager forwards them to the marketing staff at group headquarters, where they are once again reviewed and sometimes adjusted through phone conversations between marketing management and the regional manager submitted the forecast.[7]

Advantages

A primary advantage of the sales force composite method of forecasting sales is that it uses the specialized knowledge of the people closest to the market. The final sales forecast often becomes one basis for establishing quotas for individual sales reps. The sales force composite method puts the responsibility for those forecasts in the hands of those who will eventually have to produce the results. When the sales force understands how the quotas were established, they are much less likely to view them with disdain and distrust. Commitment to the sales forecast and quota can benefit performance. The size of the sample used to develop the forecast tends to produce estimates that are fairly accurate. Individual sales reps may err in producing estimates, with some forecasting high or low; but the errors should cancel to produce a reasonably accurate forecast when the judgments of 20, 50, 100, or more salespeople are combined. Finally, the method lends itself to the easy development of customer, product, or territory breakdowns, which are a distinct plus in controlling the sales effort.

Disadvantages   A main complaint of those opposed to the sales force composite method is that sales reps are notoriously poor estimators. They tend to be overly optimistic when the economy is booming and overly pessimistic when things are not so good. Furthermore, they tend to be unaware of broad economic conditions that shape the demand for the product, and they may even be unaware of the firm's planned marketing program when preparing their estimates. If their sales forecast is to be an input in setting their quotas, they have a vested interest in estimating low. This makes the quota easier to achieve, which makes them look good. Some companies pay bonuses to all who meet or exceed their quotas, so forecasting low can have monetary advantages as well.[8] Thus, elaborate schemes are sometimes necessary to keep the estimates realistic and free from bias. Such schemes can be expensive; they require a good deal of time from highly paid, highly placed people. Therefore, the cost of the sales force composite method is typically higher than that of other methods. Thorny Issue 6.1 identifies major goals of the sales force composite method.

JURY OF EXECUTIVE OPINION

The **jury of executive** or **expert opinion method** informally or formally polls the top executives of the company for their assessment of sales possibilities. The separate assessments are combined into a sales forecast for the company. Sometimes this is done by simply averaging the individual judgments; but other times disparate views are resolved through group discussion. The initial views may reflect no more than the executive's hunch about what is going to happen, or the opinion may be based on considerable factual material, sometimes even an initial forecast prepared by other means.

For example, each group product manager at Rubbermaid's Home Products Division prepares 30-, 60-, 90-day, and annual forecasts for each item for which he or she is responsible. Two upper-level managers provide the managers with the best possible forecasting tools and information to make their forecasts as accurate as possible. Rubbermaid also uses a high-level operating committee to prepare a similar forecast. The separate forecasts are subsequently reconciled using several statistical criteria.[9]

Thorny Issues in Sales Management 6 • 1

Don't Let Sales Forecasting Spook You*

As the title suggests, sales forecasting spooks sales managers, salespeople, and others as well. It seems that once a forecast has been made, regardless of the process used, the figures somehow become engraved in stone only to be used later to evaluate performance. No wonder the sales forecasting process spooks people.

Stewart A. Washburn depicts the sales forecasting process:

> In most sales forces, forecasts are a big deal. Sales representatives panic, and their supervisors become tyrants. Everything comes to a halt as the numbers get filled in. Asking for a best-guess assessment of what each account will buy and of what each account could buy is better than a formal forecast in that it gets sales representatives to review their accounts in terms of future sales.

In fact, Washburn contends that salespeople ought to assess the buying potential for all accounts, not just annually but once a quarter or every six months. This process, referred to as the sales force composite method, should not be so traumatic. "Formidable forms and enormous pressure are unnecessary," claims Washburn. But forms are necessary if the sales force is to provide the information.

---

*The following discussion is based to a large extent on Stewart A. Washburn, "Don't Let Sales Forecasting Spook You," *Sales & Marketing Management*, September 1988, pp. 118, 121.

Two major goals can be achieved when the sales force participates in the forecasting process. The first goal is to provide management with valuable planning information. Often management will use forecasts derived from the field to supplement forecasts derived from the top. Some managers feel that the sales force cannot provide useful sales projections. A second goal, according to Washburn,

> is the more important of the two: The forecasting exercise helps the sales force view a territory as any manager must look at a market. Whether anyone else uses their assessments of territory potential, salespeople need them for planning purposes.

How the sales force uses the information collected is more important. The emphasis should be on this point, argues Washburn. Once sales representatives realize that successful management of a sales territory requires good information, the quality of their forecasts should improve, as will the usefulness of their forecasts to top management.

To facilitate the process, sales representatives need to use easy-to-understand forms. Today, many sales forecasting software packages are available to salespeople. These packages contain not only the forms but also the equations necessary to make various calculations. As a result, the sales force composite method of sales forecasting should prove to be a more reliable technique.

Advantages   Some advantages of this method of forecasting are the ease and quickness with which it may be made. Although preparing elaborate statistics may improve the accuracy of the forecast, this method does not require them. Furthermore, the method brings together a variety of specialized viewpoints. The "collective wisdom" that results reflects the thinking of the top people in the company—

EXHIBIT 6 • 4   *Operation of Delphi Process*

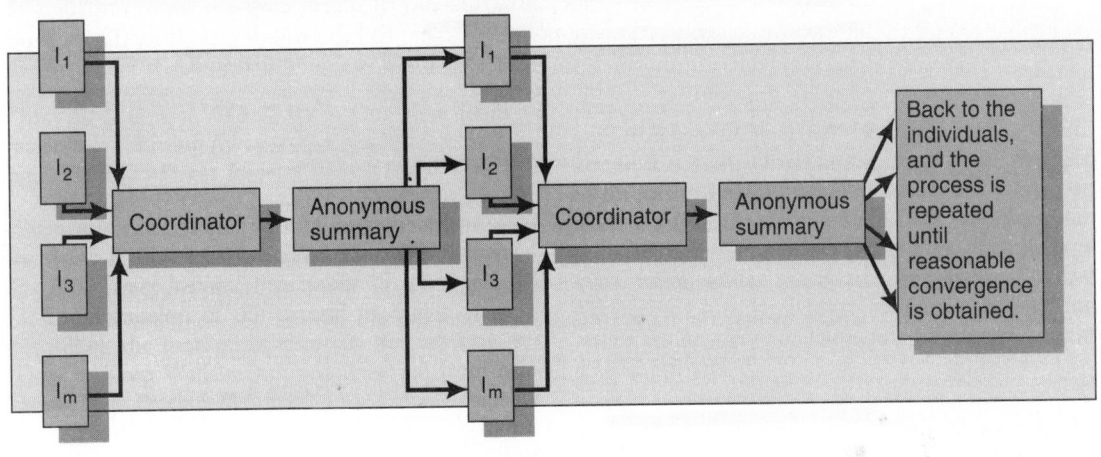

those most aware of company plans and external forces affecting those plans and the consequent impact on them. Finally, when adequate data or experience are absent, as with innovative products, this may be the only means of sales forecasting available to the company.

Disadvantages   One important disadvantage of the jury of executive opinion is that it produces an aggregate forecast that often must be broken down by product and by time to plan production and financing. It also must be broken down by territory and by salesperson to schedule and control the personal selling effort. Generating these breakdowns is extremely difficult, sometimes impossible, and usually expensive. The method is also expensive because of the large amounts of highly paid executives' time it consumes. Furthermore, the pooling of opinion disperses the responsibility for the forecast. If the forecast proves to be grossly inaccurate, it is hard to pinpoint exactly what went wrong and who is at fault.

Also, the forecast may not properly weight the expertise of those most informed. Group dynamics do operate. Those who have most intensively studied the available statistics and facts may not have their judgment weighted more than another executive whose "best guess" has been much more casually derived but who is more eloquent in the discussion or higher in the management hierarchy.

Delphi
Technique

One increasingly popular method for controlling group dynamics to produce a more accurate forecast is the Delphi technique. Delphi uses repeated measurement and controlled feedback instead of direct confrontation and debate among the experts preparing the forecast.[10] Exhibit 6.4 depicts how the method operates. Each individual prepares a forecast using whatever facts, figures, and general knowledge of the environment he or she has available. Then, the forecasts are collected, and an anonymous summary is prepared by the person supervising the process. The summary is distributed to each person who participated in the initial phase. Typically, the summary lists each forecast figure, the average (median), and some summary measure of the spread of the estimates. Often, those whose initial estimates fell outside the midrange of responses are asked to express their reasons for these extreme positions. These explanations are then incorporated in the summary. The participants study the summary and submit a revised forecast. The process is then repeated. There will typically be a number of these iterations. The method is based on the following two premises:

1. The range of responses will decrease, and the estimates will converge with repeated measurements.

2. The total group response or median will move successively toward the "correct" or "true" answer.

The Delphi technique seems to have advantages over the jury of executive opinion, in which group discussion and interaction are used to produce the forecast. The experience of TRW, where the Delphi technique has been used extensively for technological forecasting, is insightful in this regard.

> This method seeks to take full advantage of the "committee" approach to forecasting, while avoiding some of the disadvantages of the typical brainstorming session. Our approach permitted us to circumvent group activity altogether and to deal with each member of our team of predictors directly and individually. Thus, we were able to eliminate the negative factors associated with group action—for example, the "aggressive expert" who feels called upon to defend his publicly stated opinions, the senior executive with whom subordinates are reluctant to differ, and the silver-tongued salesman who can sell refrigerators to Eskimos.[11]

Forcing those whose forecasts lie at the extreme ends of the distribution to justify their estimates means that "informed" experts have greater opportunity to influence the final forecast. Those who might have a deviant opinion, but with good reason, can defend that position, rather than giving in to group pressure. Those who feel strongly about their estimates tend to feel more comfortable with Delphi because of the anonymity it provides. Since their forecasts are not necessarily revised, this can help produce more accurate estimates.

The Delphi technique seems to be an increasingly popular way of handling committee approaches to forecasting. For example, tourism is the third most important sector in Singapore's economy, amounting to over $2 billion per year. Tourism's future after the reunification with China is thus a critical issue, but one hard to judge. A Delphi panel of 23 experts was formed to develop estimates for the year 2000 and beyond. The panel was made up of respondents from the hotel, retail, and airline industries, travel agencies, governing bodies of tourist attractions, and government ministers and statutory boards.[12]

One problem with the Delphi technique is that the iteration and feedback can take a long time. For example, Corning Glass Works used the Delphi method to develop a 10-year market forecast for certain electronic components using three waves of estimation. The study took nine months to complete.[13] IBM uses an interesting variation of the Delphi technique that virtually eliminates the time lag between ballots to estimate "how ripe" a market is for new equipment the company is considering introducing. The Delphi panel is composed of IBM experts with diverse backgrounds who are isolated from interruption so they can concentrate fully on the project. The panelists' judgments are typed directly into a computer where the summary statistics are prepared. With the instant feedback provided by the system, the panelists are often able to reach near consensus in a few hours.[14]

MARKET TEST

Market tests to assess the demand for new products were rare before 1960. They have grown significantly in popularity since then; now the expenditures for test marketing total more than $1 billion per year.

The typical market test involves placing the product in several "representative" cities to see how well it performs and then projecting that experience to the United States as a whole. Often this is done for a new product or an improved version of an old product. For example, Exhibit 6.5 describes Wendy's experience in developing the "Big Classic" hamburger.

Advantages

Many firms consider the test market to be the final gauge of consumer acceptance of a new product and the ultimate measure of market potential.

A. C. Nielsen data, for example, indicate that roughly three out of four products that have been test marketed succeed, while four out of five that have not been test marketed fail.[15] An example of the benefits to be gained from test marketing is provided by the experience of Green Giant in developing Oven Crock baked beans, which came already sweetened in the can. On the basis of blind taste tests, the executives at Green Giant thought they had a certain success:

> "We did a series of blind taste tests and had a significant winner over bland pork and beans by a three-to-one or four-to-one preference margin," said

---

E X H I B I T   6 • 5   *Research Conducted by Wendy's for the "Big Classic" Hamburger*

To find out what people want, Wendy's spent $1 million over nine months doing taste tests with 5,200 people in six cities. They tested:

- Nine different buns: some hard, some soft; with sesame seeds or poppy seeds; cold, toasted, or warmed; square or round; and even croissants.
- Forty special sauces, including steak sauce, hot sauce, mustard, and salad dressing.
- Three types of lettuce: chopped, shredded, and leaf.
- Two sizes of tomato slices.
- Four boxes in 10 earth-tone colors.

Source: "Wendy's Discovers—Old Burger," *The Wisconsin State Journal,* September 19, 1986, p. 6. Reprinted with permission.

The final product is a quarter-pound square beef patty topped with leaf lettuce, two tomato slices, raw onion rings, dill pickles, and extra dabs of ketchup and mayonnaise on a corn-dusted, hearth-baked kaiser bun. It comes in an almond-colored styrofoam box with a dome sculpted to resemble the bun's top. It can cost up to 10 cents more than the old burger, which is still on the menu.

The big news research showed was that the order of the condiments "makes a tremendous difference to consumers," Denny Lynch, a spokesperson for Wendy's, said. "Which is why the Big Classic will taste different rightside up or upside down, depending on the way the toppings hit your taste buds."

Wendy's came up with a color code to help its employees remember the correct order: white, red, green, white, red, green (mayonnaise, ketchup, pickle, onion, tomato, lettuce).

John M. Stafford, an executive vice president at Pillsbury. But Oven Crock was a disaster in a test market. Surveys later showed that people who ate heavily flavored baked beans added their own fixings to the bland variety and didn't want somebody to do it for them. "Our beans were terrific, but they were a solution to no known problem," Mr. Stafford said.[16]

Disadvantages   Test marketing to assess market potential is used much more by manufacturers of consumer products than by makers of industrial products. Many of the latter do not test market at all. There are fewer potential customers for industrial products and producers are more intimately familiar with their customer's needs, likes, and dislikes due to more direct contact in industrial transactions. Although the test market may be the ultimate gauge of consumer reaction to a new product, it is not without its disadvantages.

As Larry Gibson, former director of corporate marketing research for General Mills comments, "It costs a mint, tells the competition what you're doing, takes forever, and is not always accurate. . . . For the moment, it's the only game in town."[17] As his comment suggests, three of the more important disadvantages are cost, time, and control.

Cost has always been a major consideration in test marketing. There are the costs of the experiment itself. These costs include the normal research costs of designing the data-collection instruments and the sample and the wages paid to the field staff that collects the data. Other costs must be borne as well. For instance, the test market should reflect the marketing strategy to be used on the national scale; so the test also includes marketing costs for advertising, personal selling, displays, and so on.

New-product introductions also include costs associated with producing the merchandise. To produce the product on a small scale is typically inefficient. Yet to gear up immediately for large-scale production can be tremendously wasteful if the test market indicates the product is a failure. Given these various expenses, the typical cost of $3.1 million to take a new product from research and development through test marketing in only 2 percent of the United States should not be too surprising.[18]

The time required for an adequate test market can be substantial. For example, it took Procter & Gamble nine years to go national with Pampers disposable diapers after they were first introduced in Peoria, Illinois.[19] One reason for extending the length of test markets is that the empirical evidence indicates their accuracy increases directly with time. Consequently, a year is often recommended as a minimum before any kind of go/no-go decision is made to account for seasonal sales variations and repeat purchasing behavior. Experiments continued over long periods are costly and raise additional problems of control and competitive reaction; yet short-term experiments do not allow for the cumulative impact of the marketing actions.

The problems of control show up in several ways. First, there are the control problems in the experiment itself. What specific test markets will be used? How will product distribution be organized in those markets? Can the firm elicit the necessary cooperation from wholesalers? From retailers? Can the test markets and control cities be matched sufficiently to rule out market characteristics as the primary determinant of the different sales results? Can the rest of the elements of the marketing strategy be controlled to avoid unwanted aberrations in the experimental setting?

A common problem in test marketing products is too much control. Because the product is being test marketed, it receives more attention in the test market—always-stocked shelves, extra effort from the sales force, and so on—than can ever be given to it on a national scale. One reason given for the failure of Pringles potato chips, which was very successful in the test market but bombed nationally, is that quality slipped when the product was mass produced on the larger scale.[20]

There are control problems associated with competitive reaction, also. Although the firm might be able to coordinate its own marketing activities and even those of intermediaries in the distribution channel so as not to contaminate the experiment, it can exert little control over its competitors. Competitors can, and do, sabotage marketing experiments. Thorny Issue 6.2 shows how sabotage occurs and raises two questions: (1) When does legitimate competition end and unethical behavior begin? and (2) Are market tests, even if they are the ultimate measure of market potential, worth the risks?

Thorny Issues In Sales Management 6 • 2

Test Market Sabotage

Example 1: When Campbell first test marketed Prego spaghetti sauce, Campbell marketers say they noticed a flurry of new Ragu ads and cents-off deals that they believe were designed to induce shoppers to load up on Ragu and to skew Prego's test results. They also claim Ragu copied Prego when it developed Ragu Homestyle spaghetti sauce, which was thick, red, flecked with oregano and basil, and which Ragu moved into national distribution before Prego.

Example 2: Procter & Gamble claims competitors stole its patented process for Duncan Hines chocolate chip cookies when they saw how successful the product was in test market.

Example 3: A health and beauty aids firm developed a deodorant containing baking soda. A competitor spotted the product in test market, rolled out its own version of the deodorant nationally before the first firm completed its testing, and later successfully sued the product originator for copyright infringement when it launched its deodorant nationally.

Example 4: When Procter & Gamble introduced its Always brand sanitary napkin in test market in Minnesota, Kimberly-Clark Corporation and Johnson & Johnson countered with free products, lots of coupons, and big dealer discounts, which caused Always to not do as well as expected.

Assume each of the claims is true. Do you

Approve _____
Somewhat approve _____
Somewhat disapprove _____
Disapprove _____

Source: Example 1—Betsy Morris, "New Campbell Entry Sets Off a Big Spaghetti Sauce Battle," *The Wall Street Journal*, December 2, 1982, p. 31; Example 2—Eleanor Johnson Tracy, "Testing Time for Test Marketing," *Fortune* 110 (October 29, 1984), pp. 75–76; Example 3—Kevin Wiggins, "Simulated Test Marketing Winning Acceptance," *Marketing News* 19 (March 1, 1985), pp. 15 and 19; Example 4—Damon Darden, "Faced with More Competition, P&G Sees New Products as Crucial to Earning's Growth," *The Wall Street Journal*, September 13, 1983, pp. 37 and 53.

Time Series Analysis

Time series approaches to sales forecasting rely on the analysis of historical data to develop a prediction for the future. The sophistication of these analyses can vary widely. At one extreme, the forecaster might simply forecast next year's sales to be equal to this year's sales. Such a forecast might be reasonably accurate for a mature industry that is experiencing little growth. If there is growth, however, the forecaster might allow for it by predicting the same percentage increase for next year that the company experienced this year. Still further along the spectrum, the forecaster might attempt to break historical sales into basic components by isolating that portion due to trend, cyclical, seasonal, and irregular influences. The trend, cyclical, and seasonal components could all be forecast separately and then combined to produce the aggregate

EXHIBIT 6 • 6   *Annual and Forecasted Sales for a Manufacturer of Pens and Pencils*

Year	Actual Sales	Forecasted Sales	
		Two-Year Moving Average	Four-Year Moving Average
1980	4,200		
1981	4,410		
1982	4,322	4,305	
1983	4,106	4,366	
1984	4,311	4,214	4,260
1985	4,742	4,209	4,287
1986	4,837	4,527	4,370
1987	5,030	4,790	4,499
1988	4,779	4,934	4,730
1989	4,970	4,905	4,847
1990	5,716	4,875	4,904
1991	6,116	5,343	5,128
1992	5,932	5,916	5,395
1993	5,576	6,024	5,684
1994	5,465	5,754	5,835
1995		5,520	5,772

forecast. There are a number of time series approaches to sales forecasting, but only the moving average, exponential smoothing, and decomposition methods are discussed here.[21]

Moving Averages   The method of moving averages is conceptually quite simple. Consider the forecast that next year's sales will be equal to this year's sales. Such a forecast might be subject to large error if there is much fluctuation in sales from one year to the next. To allow for such randomness, we might consider using some kind of average of recent values. For example, we might average the last two years' sales, the last three years' sales, the last five years' sales, or any number of other periods. The forecast would simply be the average that resulted. The number of observations included in the average is typically determined by trial and error. Differing numbers of periods are tried and the number of periods that produces the most accurate forecasts on the trial data is used to develop the forecast model. Once determined, it remains constant. The term *moving average* is used because a new average is computed and used as a forecast as each new observation becomes available.

Exhibit 6.6 presents 15 years of historical sales data for a manufacturer of pens and pencils and also the resulting forecasts for a number of years using two-year and four-year moving averages. Exhibit 6.7 displays the results graphically. The entry 4,305 for 1982, under the two-year moving average method,

---

E X H I B I T 6 • 7 *Actual and Forecasted Sales Using Moving Averages*

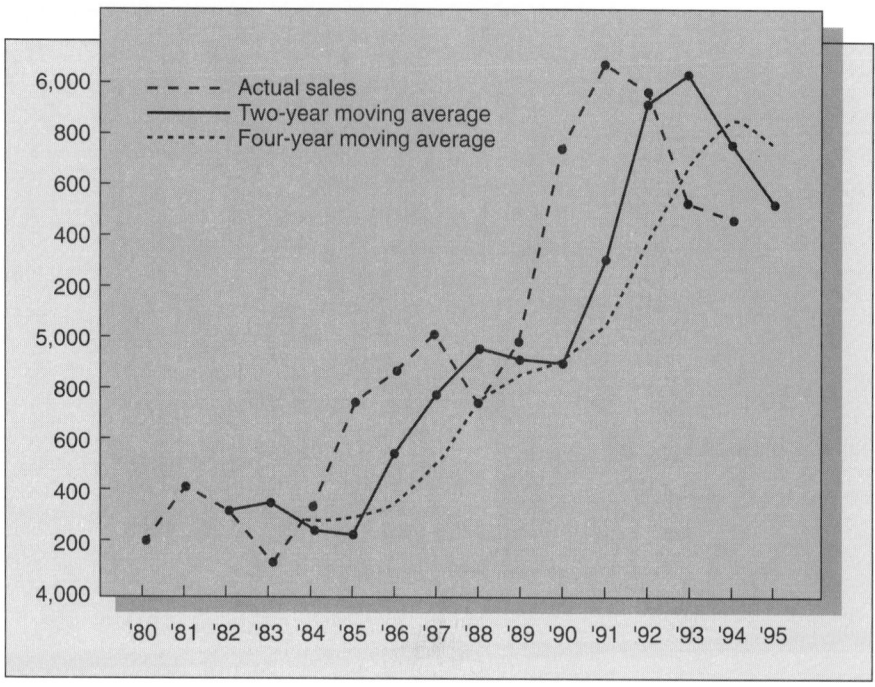

for example, is the average of the sales of 4,200 units in 1980 and 4,410 units in 1981. Similarly, the forecast of 5,520 units in 1995 represents the average of the number of units sold in 1993 and 1994. The forecast of 5,772 units in 1995 under the four-year moving average method, on the other hand, represents the average number of units sold during the four-year period 1991–94. It takes more data to begin forecasting with four-year than with two-year moving averages. This is important when starting to forecast sales for a new product.

Observe also the impact of the number of periods on the fluctuations in the forecasted series. The larger the number of observations included, the greater is the smoothing of the forecasts. Thus, whereas the range of forecasted values is 1,815 (6,024 − 4,209) with the two-year moving average, it is only 1,575 (5,835 − 4,260) with the four-year moving average—a difference of 240 units. When we desire a smoother value because we think there is little change in the underlying pattern and we are observing mainly random fluctuations, we should use many periods to determine the moving average. Conversely, when we think the series is changing rapidly or when there is little randomness in sales, we would use fewer periods to compute the moving average so the forecast can react more quickly to the changes that are occurring.

*Exponential
Smoothing*

The method of moving averages gives *equal* weight to each of the last n values in forecasting the next value. Thus, when $n = 4$ (the four-year moving average is being used), equal weight is given to each of the last four years' sales in predicting the sales for next year. No weight is given to any sales five or more years previous. The forecasting equation, in other words, is

$$\hat{X}_{t+1} = \frac{X_t + X_{t-1} + X_{t-2} + X_{t-3}}{n}$$

$$= \frac{X_t + X_{t-1} + X_{t-2} + X_{t-n+1}}{n}$$

$\hat{X}_{t+1}$ = forecasted value for next year or next period

X_t = actual sales that resulted in year or period t

Exponential smoothing is a type of moving average. However, instead of weighting all observations equally in generating the forecast, exponential smoothing weights the most recent observations heaviest, for good reason. The most recent observations contain the most information about what is likely to happen in the future, and they should logically be given more weight. The general form of the exponential smoothing model is

$$\hat{X}_{t+1} = \alpha X_t + (1 - \alpha)\hat{X}_t$$

where the caret again indicates a forecasted value, and an X without a caret indicates an actual value. The exponential smoothing model thus suggests next year's sales will be equal to this year's sales, X_t, times the constant, α, plus the forecasted value of this year's sales, $\hat{X}_t$, times the constant $(1 - \alpha)$. It can be shown by successive substitution that the second term in this equation implicitly recognizes older values, thereby overcoming a second limitation of the moving average method, which ignores all those values more than n periods old.

The key decision affecting the use of exponential smoothing is the choice of α, which is known as the smoothing constant, and which is constrained to be between 0 and 1. High values of α give great weight to recent observations and little weight to distant sales; low values of α, on the other hand, give more weight to older observations. If sales change slowly, low values of α work fine. When sales experience rapid changes and fluctuations, however, high values of α should be used so that the forecast series responds to these changes quickly. The value of α is normally determined empirically; various values of α are tried, and the one that produces the smallest forecast error when applied to the historical series is adopted. Exhibits 6.8 and 6.9 show what happens to forecasted values when α is set at 0.2, 0.5, and 0.8. Note two things. First, when the forecast is initialized, the first forecast value is simply set equal to the prior year's actual sales.[22] Second, note the impact of α on the speed with which forecasted sales respond to changes in actual sales.

EXHIBIT 6 • 8   *Annual Sales and Forecasted Sales Using Exponential Smoothing and Various Values for the Smoothing Constant α*

Year	Actual Sales	Forecasted Sales		
		α = 0.2	α = 0.5	α = 0.8
1980	4,200			
1981	4,410	4,200	4,200	4,200
1982	4,322	4,242	4,305	4,368
1983	4,106	4,258	4,314	4,332
1984	4,311	4,228	4,210	4,151
1985	4,742	4,244	4,260	4,279
1986	4,837	4,343	4,501	4,649
1987	5,030	4,441	4,669	4,800
1988	4,779	4,559	4,849	4,984
1989	4,970	4,603	4,814	4,820
1990	5,716	4,676	4,892	4,940
1991	6,116	4,883	5,304	5,561
1992	5,932	4,129	5,710	6,005
1993	5,576	5,289	5,821	5,947
1994	5,465	5,346	5,699	5,650
1995		5,370	5,583	5,502

Decomposition

The decomposition method of sales forecasting is typically applied to monthly or quarterly data where a seasonal pattern is evident and the manager wishes to forecast sales not only for the year but also for each period in the year. For example, Coleman Cable Systems of Chicago, a manufacturer of wire and cable products, analyzes sales by quarter to determine what portion of the sales change represents an overall, fundamental change in demand and what portion is due to seasonal aberrations.[23]

The decomposition method attempts to isolate four separate portions of a time series: the *trend, cyclical, seasonal,* and *random* factors.

- The trend reflects the long-run changes experienced in the series when the cyclical, seasonal, and irregular components are removed. It is typically assumed to be a straight line.

- The cyclical factor is not always present because it reflects the waves in a series when the seasonal and irregular components are removed. These ups and downs typically occur over a long period—perhaps two to five years. Some products experience little cyclical fluctuation (canned peas), whereas others experience a great deal (housing starts).

- The seasonal factor reflects the annual fluctuation in the series due to the natural seasons. The seasonal factor normally repeats itself each year, although the exact pattern of sales may be different from year to year.

EXHIBIT 6 • 9   *Actual and Forecasted Sales Using Expotential Smoothing*

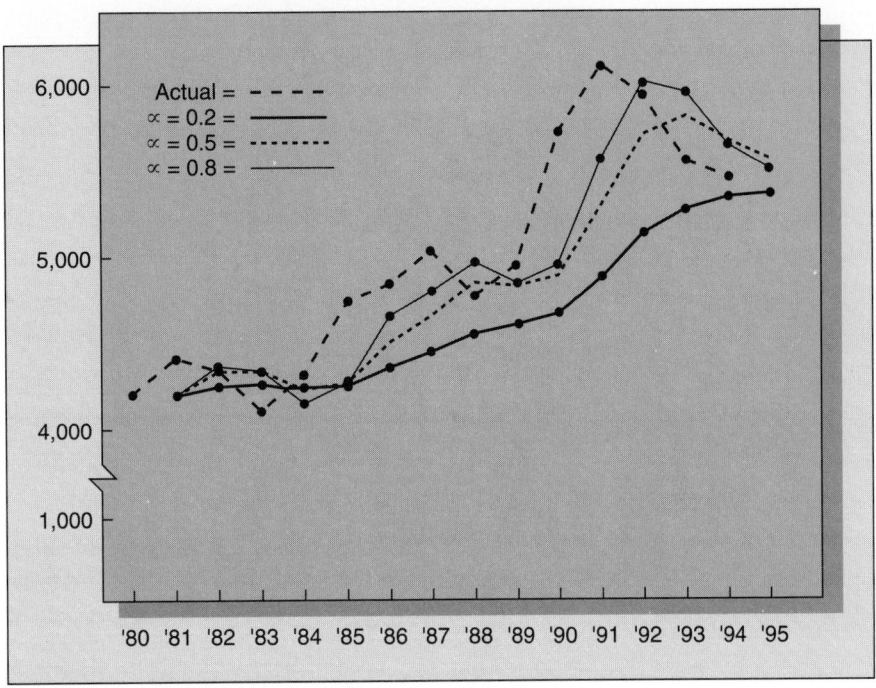

- The random factor is what is left after the influence of the trend, cyclical, and seasonal factors is removed.

Exhibit 6.10 shows the calculation of a simple seasonal index based on five years of sales history. The data suggest definite seasonal and trend components in the series. The fourth quarter of every year is always the best quarter; the first quarter is the worst. At the same time, sales each year are higher than they were the year previous. One could calculate a seasonal index for each year by simply dividing quarterly sales by the yearly average per quarter. It is much more typical, though, to base the calculation of the seasonal index on several years of data to smooth out the random fluctuations that occur by quarter.

The exhibit shows five years of sales history. To calculate the index, first determine the average sales for each quarter for the five years. For example, the average sales for the first quarter over the five-year period were 96.7. Then divide these numbers by the average sales per quarter for the entire period, namely 131.1, to give the seasonal index for each quarter.

The calculations suggest the seasonal indexes for the first and fourth quar-

E X H I B I T   6 • 10   *Calculation of a Seasonal Index*

		Quarter				
Year	1	2	3	4	Total	Quarter Average
1990	82.8	105.8	119.6	151.8	460.0	115.0
1991	93.1	117.6	122.5	156.9	490.1	122.5
1992	92.0	122.4	132.6	163.2	510.2	127.6
1993	95.3	129.0	151.3	185.0	560.6	140.2
1994	120.1	138.1	162.2	180.2	600.6	150.2
5-year average	96.7	122.6	137.6	167.4	524.3	131.1
Seasonal index*	73.8	93.5	105.0	127.7		

*The seasonal index equals the quarterly average divided by the overall quarterly average times 100; for the first quarter, for example, the seasonal index equals (96.7 ÷ 131.1) × 100 = 73.8.

ters, for example, are 73.8 and 127.7. This means sales in the first quarter are typically 26.2 percent less, and those in the fourth quarter are 27.7 percent more than normal because of seasonal factors. A manager should not be upset therefore if the company experiences a 40 percent drop in sales from, say, 200 units in the fourth quarter of last year to 120 units in the first quarter this year. That is natural because of the seasonal pattern to the business.

Rather, the appropriate way to interpret the figures is to deseasonalize them—by dividing the actual sales figures by the appropriate seasonal index. The deseasonalized fourth quarter sales are 200 ÷ 127.7 × 100 = 156.6 while the deseasonalized first quarter sales are 120 ÷ 73.8 × 100 = 162.6. The deseasonalized sales per quarter times four gives the expected yearly sales if sales were to continue at the same rate. While the first inclination was to suggest that the company's sales performance was worse in the first quarter than it was in the prior fourth quarter, the first quarter, in fact, was better. After accounting for the normal seasonal fluctuations in sales by comparing the deseasonalized values, the results suggest that sales in the first quarter were actually up.

In using the decomposition method, the analyst typically first determines the seasonal pattern and removes its impact to identify the trend. Then the cyclical factor is estimated. After the three components are isolated, the forecast is developed by applying each factor in turn to the historical data.[24]

Advantages

The time series approach to sales forecasting provides a systematic means for making quantitative projections of sales—and this is both its major advantage and disadvantage. The method is objective in that two analysts working on the same data series using the same forecasting technique and the same model should produce the same forecast. This is not necessarily true with the subjective sales forecasting schemes discussed earlier. The time series approach allows the forecaster to take advantage of the repetitive patterns exhibited by historical sales. If there are trend, cyclical, or seasonal patterns, the analyst can attempt to isolate them. Such knowledge is often useful when developing company plans.

Disadvantages   Forecasts based on time series methods assume the factors that produced the historic fluctuations in sales will continue to operate. But conditions often change. New factors emerge; old ones diminish in importance. The competitor that was so vital a force in the marketplace several years ago may no longer have that same market clout. And the new entrant two to three years ago may now be a potent force. In sum, even the most regular sales series are likely to vary because of changes in the economic environment, technology, or competition. The adage that "the only constant in life is change" applies here; and to blindly extend the past to the future can be dangerous.

The method may be difficult or even impossible to use when the series is very irregular because of aberrations induced by external shocks. It also requires a good deal of technical skill and judgment, depending on the type of time series forecasting method used. The technical knowledge required has decreased in the past few years as time series models have been programmed for microcomputers. One big disadvantage of time series models for sales managers though is that it is hard to break down the forecasts into estimates for individual salespeople and territories.

STATISTICAL DEMAND ANALYSIS

Time series analysis attempts to determine the relationship between sales and time as the basis of the forecast for the future. Statistical demand analysis attempts to determine the relationship between sales and the important factors affecting sales to forecast the future. Typically, regression analysis is used to estimate the relationship. The emphasis is not to isolate all factors that affect sales but simply to identify those that have the most dramatic impact and then to estimate the magnitude of the impact. For example, Exhibit 6.11 illustrates the use of regression analysis to estimate U.S. monthly demand of natural gas by household. Note that the predictor variables were successful in accounting for variations in demand by household; they explained 99 percent of the variation as indicated by R^2.

Sometimes firms attempt to relate their sales to one or more aggregate indicators of economic activity. For example, a major durable goods manu-

---

E X H I B I T   6 • 1 1   *Use of Regression Analysis to Forecast Demand of Natural Gas by Household*

$$Y_t = 74{,}111X_1 + 752X_2 + 251X_3 + 30X_4 + 41{,}942X_5 - 136{,}747X_6$$
$$R^2 = .99$$

where

Y_t = monthly reported deliveries of natural gas to residential customers in 1,000s of cubic feet

X_1 = index of changes in total personal income in constant dollars received by gas customers and changes in the number of gas customers

X_2 = heating degree days weighted by gas residential space-heating customers

X_3 = cooling degree days weighted by population

X_4 = household wealth in constant dollars

X_5 = price index of natural gas in constant dollars

X_6 = seasonal shift in residential gas demand for the one-month period from mid-December to mid-January

Source: John H. Herbert and Erik Kreil, "Specifying and Evaluating Aggregate Monthly Natural Gas Demand by Households," *Applied Economics* 21 (October 1989), pp. 1369–81.

facturer found the following equation adequately accounted for its factory-to-distributor parts sales:

$$S_t = \$2{,}032{,}243 + 11{,}595X_t$$

where

S_t = parts sales

X_t = composite index of six economic indicators published

in *Business Conditions Digest*

This simple forecast equation accounted for almost half the dramatic variations in sales of parts.[25]

Advantages

The use of statistical demand analysis to generate a sales forecast has many advantages. First, it has great intuitive appeal. It forces the forecaster and the manager to consider the major forces that affect sales. The analyst must identify these factors and accurately model the relationship between the factors and sales. This can be a definite plus in understanding what is happening in the market and in planning future strategy. Second, the technique forces the forecaster to quantify the assumptions underlying the future sales estimates. This makes it easier for management to check the results. Third, this method may discover factors affecting sales that intuitive reasoning may not uncover. The analyst may try suggested variables in the regression equation to see how well they work, since the method contains some statistics that can be used to assess whether the factor makes a "significant" difference. Furthermore, the method is objective. The results can be reproduced by different analysts using the same model and variables.

Disadvantages   One fundamental weakness in using statistical demand analysis is that it presumes that historical relationships will continue. Furthermore, the analyst may have a false sense of security in this regard. Typically, an equation is adopted only after several variables have been tried and a number of equations estimated. The fit of the equation to the data, as measured by the proportion of variation explained, should then be good. Thus, it can prove extremely disconcerting when the forecast is badly in error. If the basic relationship between sales and the factor has changed, however, this is exactly what can happen. The method can prove troublesome in other ways, too. This occurs whenever the equation contains predictor variables with the same time specification as sales.

For instance, in the demand for natural gas by household example in Exhibit 6.11, the analyst would have to predict the future value of several variables, including personal income (X_1), heating degree days (X_2), cooling degree days (X_3), household wealth (X_4), and the price of natural gas (X_5), to estimate likely demand in any given month. Errors in predicting any of these quantities will affect the accuracy of the sales forecast, as will errors in predicting any quantities in a forecasting equation with the same time specification as sales.

Similarly, the durable goods manufacturer needs a forecast of the composite index of economic indicators to forecast factory-to-distributor parts sales. Unless this is readily available, the manufacturer would first have to forecast the index before using it to forecast the sale of parts. There is no problem, of course, when the relationship is between current sales and some *prior* level of the predictor variable, because the value of the predictor is then known. Statistical demand analysis requires technical skill and judgment. Some managers do not possess the necessary expertise and are reluctant to use what they do not understand.

CHOOSING A FORECASTING METHOD

The sales manager faced with a forecasting problem has a dilemma: Which forecasting method should be used and how accurate is the forecast likely to be? The dilemma is particularly acute when several methods are tried and the forecasts don't agree, a common happening, as Thorny Issue 6.3 suggests.

Each method has advantages and disadvantages (which are summarized in Exhibit 6.12), and the decision of which to use will not always be clear.[26] In a typical company, the decision will more than likely depend on its level of technical sophistication and the existence of historic sales data. It will also

EXHIBIT 6 • 12   *Summary of Advantages and Disadvantages of Various Forecasting Techniques*

Sales Forecasting Method	Advantages	Disadvantages
User Expectations	1. Forecast estimates obtained directly from buyers 2. Projected product usage information can be greatly detailed 3. Insights gathered aid in the planning of marketing strategy. 4. Useful for new-product forecasting	1. Potential customers must be few and well defined 2. Does not work well for consumer goods. 3. Depends on the accuracy of user's estimates 4. Expensive, time-consuming, labor intensive
Sales force composite	1. Involves the people (sales personnel) who will be held responsible for the results 2. Is fairly accurate 3. Aids in controlling and directing the sales effort 4. Forecast is available for individual sales territories	1. Estimators (sales personnel) have a vested interest and therefore may be biased 2. Elaborate schemes sometimes necessary to counteract bias. 3. If estimates are biased, process to correct the data can be expensive
Jury of executive opinion	1. Easily done, very quick 2. Does not require elaborate statistics 3. Utilizes "collective wisdom" of the top people 4. Useful for new or innovative products	1. Produces aggregate forecasts 2. Expensive 3. Disperses responsibility for the forecast 4. Group dynamics operate
Delphi technique	1. Minimizes effects of group dynamics 2. Can utilize statistical information	1. Can be expensive and time-consuming

likely depend on the use to which the forecast will be put. A forecasting system designed to estimate production scheduling and inventory requirements may rely on a completely different set of procedures than one designed to plan marketing strategy. One guide a manager might find useful when choosing a forecasting method is what other companies have done.

What Companies Use

Exhibit 6.13 summarizes the results of a survey of U.S. firms. While there is not perfect agreement between the categories used in the survey and the clas-

E X H I B I T   6 • 12   *(concluded)*

Sales Forecasting Method	Advantages	Disadvantages
Market test	1. Provides ultimate test of consumer's reactions to the product 2. Allows the assessment of the effectiveness of the total marketing program 3. Useful for new and innovative products	1. Lets competitors know what firm is doing 2. Invites competitive reaction 3. Expensive and time-consuming to set up 4. Often takes a long time to accurately assess level of initial and repeat demand
Time series analysis	1. Utilizes historical data 2. Objective, inexpensive	1. Not useful for new or innovative products 2. Factors for trend, cyclical, seasonal, or product life-cycle phase must be accurately assessed and included 3. Technical skill and good judgment required 4. Final forecast difficult to break down into individual territory estimates 5. Ignores planned marketing effort
Statistical demand analysis	1. Great intuitive appeal 2. Requires quantification of assumptions underlying the estimates 3. Allows management to check results 4. Uncovers hidden factors affecting sales 5. Method is objective	1. Factors affecting sales must remain constant and be accurately identified to produce an accurate estimate 2. Requires technical skill and expertise 3. Some managers reluctant to use method due to its sophistication

sification used to frame our discussion, the empirical evidence suggests there is heavier reliance on the subjective methods versus the quantitative, objective methods. The sales force composite method and jury of executive opinion seem particularly popular. Both of these findings mirror the situation that existed 15 years previously.[27]

One might wonder why the situation did not change much in 15 years in light of the greater sophistication of the quantitative techniques, managers' increased exposure to them, and the advances in computer technology that have made these techniques more readily available. Part of the answer seems

Thorny Issues In Sales Management 6 • 3

RECONCILING INCONSISTENT FORECASTS

May Building Systems manufactures self-storage or miniwarehouse buildings. The buildings are sold primarily to those who rent space to individual households for storage, typically on a month-to-month basis. May's management has found that its business tends to lag behind the general economy. Its sales tend to decline after the country has gone into recession and recover after the economy has improved. Management has also determined that sales correlate closely with commercial construction and other lagging series of the general economy.

The company, in using statistical demand analysis, found that the number of construction contracts awarded for industrial building was the best predictor variable for warehouse sales 10 months in advance. Using current information on this series found in *Business Conditions Digest,* the company has developed a one-year sales forecast for its self-storage buildings that it hopes to use in preparing budgets. However, management is concerned that the statistical demand-based forecast does not agree with the forecasts prepared using both sales force composite and jury of executive opinion. It is 25 percent higher than the forecast prepared by the salespeople using the sales force composite and 18 percent higher than the sales forecast by a panel of company executives.

Which system should management use when developing its budget plans and budgets? How should it reconcile the differences?

to lie in the benefits to be gained from involving line people in the forecasting process.

> The process of forecasting is stimulating to the committeemen [the company's forecasting committee] who participate. It forces them to think ahead, to evaluate opportunities for improving performance, and to mesh plans in a coordinated way. *These things are more important than the accuracy of the figures that emerge from the process.* [emphasis added].[28]

These sentiments were shared by a vice president of an equipment company, who stated: "We do not want to substitute a procedure which may be more accurate but would reduce the present in-depth involvement of the line and staff personnel."[29]

Accuracy

Another consideration in the choice of forecasting technique is the accuracy of the approach. A number of studies have attempted to assess forecast accuracy using the various techniques. Some studies have been conducted within individual companies; others have used selected data series to which the various forecasting techniques have been systematically applied. One of the most ex-

EXHIBIT 6 • 13   *Various Sales Forecasting Methods Used by U.S. Firms (in percent)*

Forecasting Method	Firms That Use Regularly	Firms That Use Occasionally	Firms That No Longer Use
Subjective Methods			
Users expectations			
Intention to buy survey	16%	10%	19%
Industry survey	15	21	18
Sales force composite	45	17	13
Jury of executive opinion	37	22	8
Objective Methods			
Time series analysis			
Naive	31	21	9
Moving average	21	10	16
Exponential smoothing	11	12	19
Statistical demand analysis			
Simple regression	6	13	20
Multiple regression	12	9	21

Source: Developed from the data in Douglas J. Dalrymple, "Sales Forecasting Practices: Results from a United States Survey," *International Journal of Forecasting* 3, no. 3–4 (1987), pp. 379–91. The percentages are based on the 134 firms that responded to the survey.

tensive comparisons involved 1,001 time series from a variety of sources in which each series was forecasted with each of 24 extrapolation methods. The general conclusion was that the method used made little difference with respect to forecast accuracy.[30] Similarly, comparisons of forecast accuracy of objective versus subjective methods gave no clear conclusion as to which method is superior. Some of the comparisons seem to favor the quantitative methods,[31] but others found that the subjective methods produce more accurate forecasts.[32]

In general, the various forecast comparisons suggest that no method is likely to be superior under all conditions. Rather, a number of factors are likely to impact the superiority of any particular technique, including the stability of the data series, the time horizon, the degree of structure imposed on the process, the degree to which computers were used, and deseasonalization of the data, which is perhaps the most important factor affecting forecast accuracy.[33]

The various forecast comparisons do suggest several important conclusions that are helpful when choosing a forecasting method. First, a technique that works well for one series may not work on another. Managers need to be flexible in their approach, although the quantitative approaches seem to do best when the forecast is short term, frequent, lower level, easy to correct, and where the data base is rich with observations and not subject to major changes. The subjective methods, on the other hand, seem to work best when the forecast is long term, infrequent, hard to correct, and where the data base is skimpy but forecast errors are likely to cause large losses. Thus, the choice of technique should depend partially on the use of the forecast and the consequences if it is in error.

A second major conclusion from the forecast comparisons is that more accurate forecasts can be generated by combining forecasts developed from different techniques, than can be generated by searching for the one "best" technique. Accordingly, the literature has recently switched emphasis from identifying the optimal method of forecasting across all situations toward better ways of combining forecasts developed by different schemes. Invariably, this seems to improve overall forecast accuracy.[34]

A third important conclusion is that forecast accuracy can be overemphasized.

> Forecasts are not always wrong; more often than not, they can be reasonably accurate. And that is what makes them so dangerous. They are usually constructed on the assumption that tomorrow's world will be much like today's. They often work because the world does not always change. But sooner or later forecasts will fail when they are needed most, in anticipating major shifts in the business environment that make whole strategies obsolete.[35]

To cope with the revolutionary changes that can especially affect the business and to better understand the critical sensitivities of the business, firms are increasingly turning to scenario planning when developing sales forecasts. Scenario planning involves asking those preparing the forecast a series of "what if" questions, where the "what ifs" reflect different environmental changes that could occur. Some very unlikely changes are considered along with more probable events. The key idea is "not so much to have one scenario that 'gets it right' as to have a set of scenarios that illuminate the major forces driving the system, their interrelationships, and the critical uncertainties."[36]

DEVELOPING TERRITORY ESTIMATES

Not only must firms develop global estimates of demand, but most also develop territory-by-territory estimates. Territory estimates recognize the condition that the potential for any product may not be uniform by area. Awareness of the differences in territory demand allows the firm to do a better job in designing marketing strategy. For example, S. C. Johnson became "concerned that its dominant share of the household insecticide market had plateaued just above 40 percent . . . Johnson figured out where and when different bugs were about to start biting, stinging, and otherwise making people's lives miserable. The company promoted cockroach zappers in roach capitals such as Houston and New York and flea sprays in flea-bitten cities such as Tampa and Birmingham." This approach increased the company's share of the overall $450 million market for insecticides by some five percentage points.[37] Territory estimates of demand are particularly important to the sales manager who must deal with a geographically dispersed sales force. Territory demand estimates allow more effective planning, directing, and controlling of salespeople in that the estimates affect the following:

1. The design of sales territories.
2. The procedures used to identify potential customers.
3. The establishment of sales quotas.
4. Compensation levels and the mix of components in the firm's sales compensation scheme.
5. The evaluation of salespeople's performance.

In subsequent chapters, particularly in the chapters on territory design, quotas, motivation, and the three chapters on evaluation and control, we will see how territory demand estimates allow sales managers to more effectively manage their salespeople. For the moment, however, simply accept the fact that good territory demand estimates are a key ingredient to effective sales management.

This begs the question, of course, of how territory estimates can be derived. Some of the sales forecasting schemes provide them naturally. A survey of users or salespeople provides detailed estimates of demand, often by product by customer. These estimates can easily be combined into larger aggregates to produce demand estimates by product by territory. Similarly, the use of the sales history for a particular product in a particular territory in, say, a time series approach produces a forecast with the desired geographic detail. Some other forecasting schemes—such as the jury of executive opinion—produce only aggregate forecasts, which then must be broken down by appropriate geographical boundaries. Statistical demand analysis also typically produces aggregate estimates that have to be apportioned to areas.

The use of market factors or market indexes is the basic way aggregate estimates of demand are broken out by territory. A **market factor** is a feature or characteristic in a market that is related to the demand for the product. For example, the number of households in an area is one market factor influencing the demand for microwave ovens. A **market index** is a mathematical expression that combines two or more market factors into a numerical index. For instance, the market for microwave ovens might also be affected by income levels and whether both spouses work. Thus, when assessing the likely demand for microwave ovens in a particular geographic area, we might wish to combine the number of households and the income level in the area and the proportion of households with both spouses working. Typically this would be done by forming a linear combination of the factors where the weights assigned each factor would reflect their expected relative importance in affecting demand for microwave ovens. The amount of total demand apportioned to the territory would reflect the relative size of the index versus the national total. Typically, this means treating the national total as 100 percent and assessing the portion of it that lies within the geographic boundaries being considered.[38]

Industrial Goods   Territory demand estimates for industrial goods are typically developed by relating sales to some common denominator. The common denominator or market factor might be the number of total employees, number of production employees, value added by manufacture, value of materials consumed, value of products shipped, or expenditures for new plant and equipment. Say the ratio of sales per employee is developed for each of several identifiable markets. By then looking at the number of employees in a particular geographic area within each of those identifiable markets, one can estimate the total demand for the product within the area.

The identifiable markets are usually defined using Standard Industrial Classification (SIC) codes, a system developed by the U.S. Census Department for organizing the reporting of business information, such as employment, value added in manufacturing, capital expenditures, and total sales. Each major industry in the United States is assigned a two-digit number, indicating the group to which it belongs. The types of businesses making up each industry are further identified by additional digits. Exhibit 6.14 displays a partial breakdown of the construction industry.

Consider a firm that wants to estimate the demand for its portable air compressors (those typically used on construction sites to power pavement breakers and other equipment) in Kent County, Rhode Island. A priori, sales of portable air compressors are logically related to the number of employees working in the industry, and the number of employees is a direct indicator of the amount of construction activity in the area. At the same time, sales per employee would not be the same across the three major SIC construction categories shown in Exhibit 6.14. Firms in road building (SIC 16) have much greater need for portable air compressors than firms in building construction (SIC 15), which in turn have greater need than special contractors (SIC 17). Suppose the historical evidence suggests dollar sales of portable air compressors per employee are $90, $28, and $13 for the SIC codes 16, 15, and 17, respectively. By knowing the number of construction employees of each type, one can estimate total market demand for portable air compressors in Kent County, Rhode Island. Exhibit 6.15 illustrates the calculations. By considering its competitive position in the Kent market, the firm could develop estimates for sales of its own brand. Alternatively, the firm could use total market demand to assess how well it is doing in the Kent market and could plan its marketing strategy accordingly.

For example, a manufacturer of plumbing equipment categorized its 47 different types of products into 11 product groups. It then analyzed published construction award data to determine the usage pattern by item. Exhibit 6.16 displays the overall product group usage factors for a typical year. Using these ratios, the company developed sales potential estimates and market penetration indexes for each area in which it sold, and it devised its marketing strategy accordingly.[39]

A big advantage of a market factor such as number of employees or square feet for breaking down total demand is that territory demand is derived ob-

E X H I B I T 6 • 14 *Partial Breakdown of Standard Industrial Classification Codes*

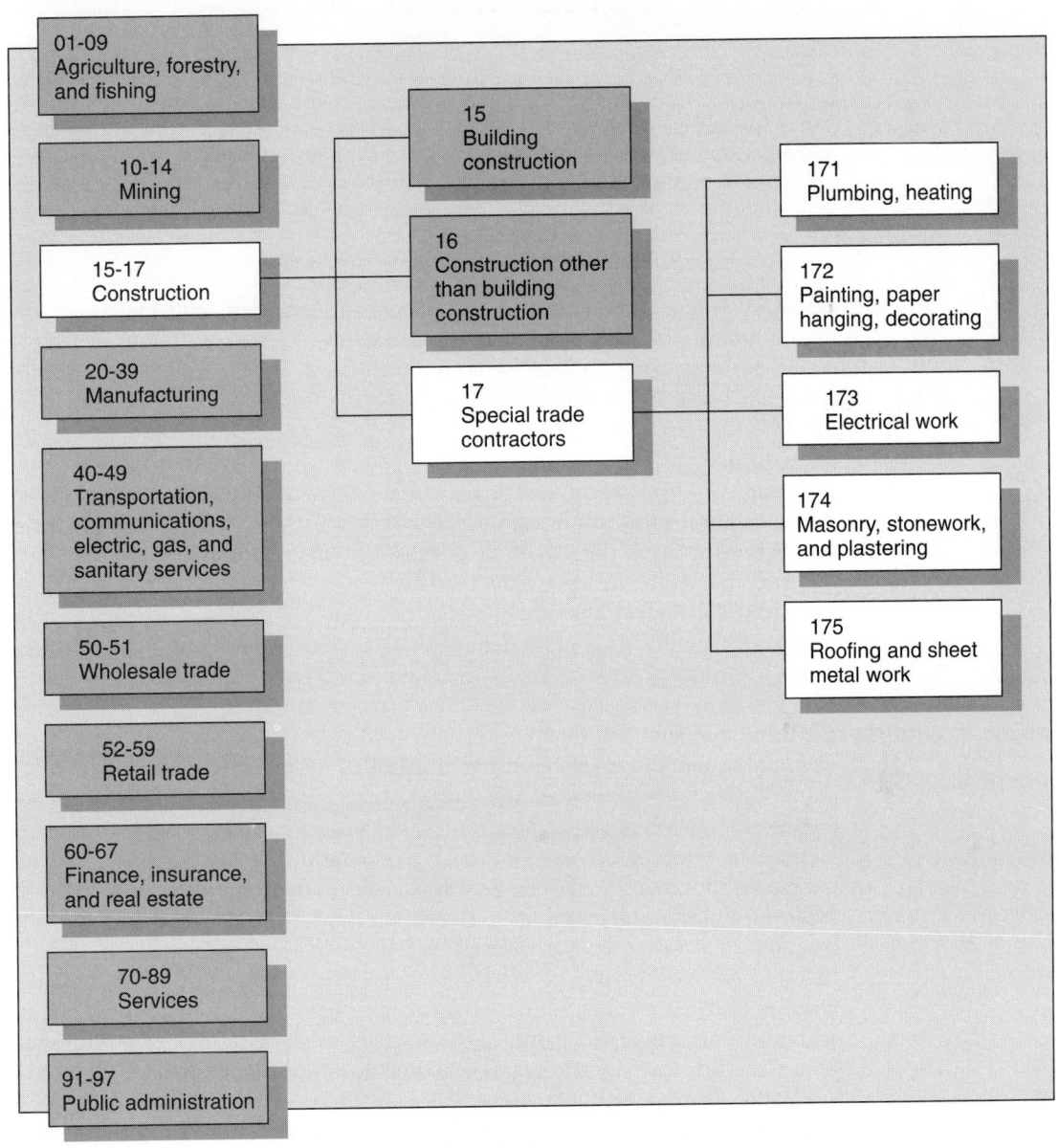

E X H I B I T **6 • 15**   *Estimation of Market Demand for Portable Air Compressors by the Construction Industry in Kent County, Rhode Island*

Industry	Number of Employees	Sales per Employee	Estimated Demand
15—Building construction	551	28	15,428
16—Construction other than building	172	90	15,480
17—Special trade contractor	1,128	13	14,664

jectively. The assumptions and calculations are obvious, and managers can readily follow the development of the estimates. They are likely to feel more confident with something they totally understand. Furthermore, the assumptions can be varied in systematic ways, and the impact on estimated demand can be calculated. For example, the portable air compressor estimates might allow for the fact that the size of a firm affects potential by taking into account the number of firms of different sizes in Kent County. Thus, the method allows the calculation of not only area potentials but also customer potentials if the firm wishes to push the calculations that far. The methods require that data are available in the necessary detail. This is a primary reason firms selling to industrial consumers base their calculations on SIC codes, since the Census Department publishes a great deal of detailed area data by SIC code.[40]

Consumer Goods   We have seen that firms selling to industrial consumers rely most heavily on identifiable market segments using SIC codes when estimating territory demand. Sellers of consumer goods, however, are more apt to rely on aggregate conditions in each territory. Sometimes this will be a single variable or market factor like the number of households, population, or perhaps the level of income in the area. In other instances, the firm attempts to relate demand to several variables combined in a systematic way. The demand for washing machines, for example, has been shown through regression analysis to be a function of (1) the level of consumers' stock of washing machines, (2) the number of wired dwelling units, (3) disposable personal income, (4) net credit, and (5) the price index for house furnishings. Since these statistics are published by area, a firm can use the regression equation to estimate demand by area.

Many firms are willing to expend the effort necessary to develop an expression for the relationship between total demand for the product and several variables that are logically related to its sales. Many other firms, however, are content to base their estimates of territory demand on one of the standard multiple-factor indexes that have been developed.

One of the most popular standard indexes is the buying power index (BPI), which is generated and published by *Sales & Marketing Management* maga-

EXHIBIT 6 • 16   *Use of Various Plumbing Supplies in Commerical Construction*

Product Group	Dollar Usage per 1,000 Square Feet of Nonresidential Construction
1	$2.40
2	9.30
3	4.60
4	.40
5	9.00
6	1.50
7	3.60
8	1.40
9	.40
10	.40
11	1.60
Total for all product groups	$34.60

zine. The index considers income, population, and retail sales. These are weighted by the factors 5, 2, and 3, respectively, to generate a single number for a geographic region. This number is used to estimate the share of total market demand in the area. More specifically, the BPI for an area can be calculated using the formula

$$BPI = \frac{5I + 2P + 3R}{10}$$

where *I* is the percentage of disposable personal income in the area, *P* is the percentage of U.S. population, and *R* is the percentage of total retail sales.

Exhibit 6.17 shows the basic statistics and the BPI for the Atlanta, Georgia, area. Statistics are provided for the city, the county in which it is located, and the total metropolitan area. These statistics, as well as some category details such as how retail sales break out by store group, are published each year in *Sales & Market Management's* "Survey of Buying Power." Firms using the BPI would concentrate their analysis on the total percentage of the BPI found in the territory in question. The Atlanta metropolitan area, for example, has a BPI of 1.2563—(1.2564 × 5 + 1.1274 × 2 + 1.3420 × 3)/10. This means that slightly more than 1 percent of the total potential for the product could be expected to be within the Atlanta metropolitan area. If the total demand for hair spray, for example, was anticipated to be $400 million, the BPI suggests the demand within the Atlanta metropolitan area would be $5,025,000(400,000,000 × .012563).

EXHIBIT 6 ● 17   *Basic Components and BPI for the Atlanta, Georgia Area*

	Area			
	Atlanta	**Fulton County**	**Atlanta Metro Area**	**Total U.S.**
Total effective buying income ($000)	5,795,053	9,715,076	41,303,037	3,287,489,252
Percentage of U.S.	(.1763)	(.2955)	(1.2564)	(100.0)
Total population (000)	448.2	652.0	2,816.6	249,840.3
Percentage of U.S.	(.1794)	(.2609)	(1.1274)	(100.0)
Total retail sales ($000)	3,192,381	5,573,113	23,109,814	1,722,085,523
Percentage of U.S.	(.1854)	(.3236)	(1.3420)	(100.0)
Buying Power Index $(5I + 2P + 3R)/10$	.1797	.2970	1.2563	

Source: "1990 Survey of Buying Power," *Sales & Marketing Management,* August 13, 1990, pp. C-47 and C-50, © 1990 by Bell Communications, Inc.

As one might expect, the BPI is not especially useful for estimating territory potentials for industrial products. Nor is it especially useful for infrequently purchased, high-priced consumer goods. It is very popular, though, when estimating territory potential for frequently purchased, lower-priced convenience goods. One strategy for a firm selling consumer goods is to determine empirically if the BPI correlates with industry sales by area. A firm is fortunate when it does because the BPI index is convenient—it is updated annually and is available by small geographic area. If the index does not correlate well with sales of the product, then the firm is probably better off (1) using a single market factor or (2) developing its own index using factors logically related to sales and some a priori or empirically determined weights regarding their relative importance, rather than blindly using the BPI to develop territory demand estimates.

S UMMARY

This chapter reviewed the analysis of market opportunity, a pivotal ingredient in the design of marketing plans in general and sales plans in particular. Market opportunity analysis involves (1) estimation of market potential or the expected sales of a commodity by the entire industry serving the market during a stated period, (2) estimation of sales potential or the share likely to be realized by the company, and (3) preparation of the sales forecast or the estimate of sales for a specified future period under an assumed marketing plan. The difference between potential estimates and forecasts is that potential estimates reflect maximum demand under ideal conditions, while a forecast reflects a specific marketing plan. Thus, potential reflects opportunities while a forecast reflects expectations.

The notions of potential and forecast are conceptually distinct, but they become blurred when estimates of demand are actually developed as the various techniques available for estimating demand treat the proposed marketing effort differently. Although all are called *sales forecasting methods,* some ignore the marketing plan when estimates are developed, while others incorporate the proposed effort directly.

The main methods for preparing sales forecasts are users' expectations, sales force composite, jury of executive opinion, market test, time series analysis, and statistical demand analysis. The users' expectations method is also known as the buyers' intentions method because it relies on answers from customers regarding their expected consumption or purchases of the product. The sales force composite method requires estimates of expected sales from each member of the sales force. These estimates are typically discussed, revised, and then pooled to form estimates for other levels of the sales organization hierarchy—for example, salesperson, branch, region, district, and overall. The jury of executive or expert opinion polls top executives of the company for their assessment of sales possibilities for the coming period. The forecast may be developed using face-to-face discussion or through anonymous interaction using Delphi procedures, in which each person in the group submits a forecast to the group coordinator. The coordinator prepares a summary of these estimates, which is distributed to all those who submit forecasts. They then have the opportunity to revise their estimates. The process continues until a reasonable consensus is reached. The market test is a controlled experiment in which the product is placed in several representative cities, where its performance is monitored; the results are then projected to the area in which the firm operates. Time series analysis relies on the analysis of historical sales data to isolate the underlying pattern and the use of that pattern to predict the future. Statistical demand analysis rests on determining the relationship between sales and the important factors affecting sales. That relationship is then used to forecast the future.

Evidence indicates the subjective methods, particularly the jury of executive opinion and the sales force composite, are currently used more than the quantitative techniques, time series and statistical demand analysis. The evidence also indicates that no method is superior under all conditions and that greater forecast accuracy can be achieved by systematically combining forecasts developed by different schemes.

It is quite common to divide the total estimate of demand among the geographic areas the company serves. Typically this is done using a market factor or a market index. A market factor is a feature or characteristic in a market that is related to the demand for the product. An often-used market factor for estimating territory demand for industrial goods, for example, is the number of employees in each of several industries (denoted by their SIC codes) the company serves. A market index is a mathematical expression that combines two or more market factors into a numerical index. The buying power index, for example, which combines income, population, and retail sales in an area into a single number, is often used to estimate territory potentials for frequently purchased, lower-priced consumer goods.

Discussion Questions

1. The Amperif Company, discussed in the chapter, does not want to face unexpected orders; forecasts must be accurate. The accuracy of forecasts is a function of the quality of information provided by the sales force. What steps can a sales manager take to substantiate the credibility of a forecast received from a sales rep? What can a sales manager do when the forecast is not supported by good evidence or sound logic?

2. A survey of local business firms to determine how they forecast sales will produce a variety of answers. Some will claim they do not use any formal techniques to forecast sales. You know they must be using some approach, no matter how loosely defined. How do you know the business firm is making a sales forecast? What are the implications of not making a sales forecast?

3. For the following products, indicate what factor(s) you would use to estimate market potential.
   - a. Yoplait yogurt.
   - b. Rolex watches.
   - c. Personal computers.
   - d. Power riding lawnmowers.
   - e. Ektelon racquetball racquets.
   - f. Calvin Klein designer jeans.
   - g. SWATCH watches.
   - h. Tylenol.
   - i. Industrial lubricants.

4. Komplete Kable TV offers movies to home viewers for showing on television. To obtain a movie on a given night, the viewer dials a number, which then allows the movie to be shown on the television set. The cost is $4.50 and is added to the telephone bill. How would you estimate the market potential for this service?

5. To estimate market potential for the garden tractor division of the M-F Implement Co., Mark Haynes, the statistician, estimated the following relationship using multiple regression analyses:

$$Y = a + b_1X_1 + b_2X_2 + b_3X_3 + b_4X_4$$

where

   Y = unit sales of U.S. garden tractors

   X_1 = number of single-family homes

   X_2 = disposable personal income

   X_3 = index of food prices

   X_4 = family size

Using data for 1978–88, $R^2 = 65$ was obtained. Should this method be used to predict market potential?

6. A new cake mix is to be introduced by Miracle Foods. To develop territory potentials, a corollary index has been proposed. The index contains several factors, such as income, population, and retail food sales. Can you justify these factors? Does it make sense to use retail food sales, which means cake sales are a function of food sales?

7. The PTF Corporation, a manufacturer of lawn and garden equipment, relies on trend analysis for determining future sales. Historically, the cost of marketing has been 58 percent of sales. Thus, with 1995 sales predicted to be $750,000, the resulting marketing budget will be $435,000. Comment.

8. The sales manager of a large manufacturer of photographic equipment stated, "The sales forecast is the most important document in the corporate planning process." How can you justify this statement?

9. If you ask a dozen sales managers what method they use to develop a sales forecast, you are likely to hear 12 different answers. What are the implications of such variety of answers? Does this suggest sales forecasting methods are too unreliable to be used with any degree of confidence?

10. Once a quarter, every six months, or annually, each salesperson should estimate the buying potential of each account for each major product or product line. Such a request usually causes the sales force to panic. What goals are likely to be achieved by having the sales force participate in sales forecasting?

Application Questions

A1. The Crystal Pure Bottled Water Company has experienced explosive growth in recent years, unlike the steady trend in earlier years. What would you suggest as a forecasting technique using the following sales data?

Year	Sales	Year	Sales
1977	$ 2,843	1985	10,054
1978	3,523	1986	11,256
1979	4,507	1987	16,074
1980	5,576	1988	19,831
1981	6,462	1989	28,764
1982	7,115	1990	34,093
1983	7,928	1991	39,420
1984	9,371	1992	47,325

A2. The Flambeau Corporation manufactures plastic parts for a variety of customers. Past attempts at sales forecasting have not met with success. Sales patterns display considerable fluctuations. Using the data below, develop a sales forecast for the first quarter of 1993.

	1988	1989	1990	1991	1992
Quarter 1	202	367	576	520	607
Quarter 2	75	158	278	295	309
Quarter 3	157	287	353	326	437
Quarter 4	476	659	901	1007	988

A3. The APCO Division manufactures electric motors used by the parent company, a manufacturer of small household appliances. To plan production for 1995, the sales manager must develop a forecast for one of the models. The following data reflect monthly sales of the product using the particular model. What does the data base reveal?

Small Appliance Sales ($000)

Month	1991	1992	1993	1994
January	68.3	88.9	104.9	156.9
February	107.1	97.9	155.8	228.4
March	107.3	128.9	172.1	308.7
April	69.7	113.8	180.8	198.1
May	78.5	114.2	192.9	281.0
June	127.7	78.0	246.4	272.8
July	151.1	151.3	245.3	225.5
August	187.7	133.5	227.9	194.2
September	157.9	159.7	224.2	348.0
October	142.2	201.8	209.4	308.7
November	141.1	115.9	245.4	315.7
December	142.7	134.5	314.7	306.0

A4. RapidStream, manufacturer of aerodynamic mobile homes, wants to test two different moving average approaches, a three-month versus a five-month approach. Which method provides the most accurate forecast?

Mobile Home Unit Sales (000)

Month	1990	1991	1992	1993	1994
January	15.9	13.9	18.2	20.0	18.6
February	17.4	17.3	19.7	22.2	19.7
March	21.6	22.1	25.4	25.6	24.0
April	24.1	22.3	25.1	25.8	26.2
May	22.9	21.9	26.9	29.0	28.0
June	23.1	23.7	29.5	27.8	25.1
July	21.8	19.5	23.4	24.6	24.3
August	22.4	22.3	30.2	30.0	27.7
September	21.6	21.3	28.1	24.4	24.5
October	20.3	20.4	26.9	27.7	27.7
November	15.7	18.9	23.5	21.9	20.9
December	14.2	16.0	18.8	16.6	16.9

A5. The management of the Farnsworth Corporation, specialists in automobile detailing, wants to expand the number of franchises, currently 10, into new market areas. Management strongly believes sales are related to household income and population over 25 years. Sales for the 10 metropolitan areas along with associated household income and population over 25 years are:

Area	Farnsworth Sales (FS)	Household Income ($000) (HI)	Population Over 25 (000) (PO)
1	$185,792	$23,406	133.17
2	85,643	19,215	110.86
3	97,101	20,374	68.04
4	100,249	16,107	99.59
5	527,817	23,432	289.52
6	403,916	19,426	339.98
7	78,283	18,742	89.53
8	188,756	18,553	155.78
9	329,531	21,953	248.95
10	91,944	16,358	102.13

a.   What are the estimates for the Fransworth sales model?

$$FS = b_0 + b_1(HI) + b_2(PO)$$

b.   Farnsworth is considering establishing a franchise in a new location that has a population over 25 of 128.07 and household income of $23,175. Approximately how much sales can Farnsworth expect?

A6. The number of orders received at Grainger Wholesale for the last four months is presented below:

Month	Number of Orders Received
March	19
April	31
May	27
June	29

a.   Forecast the number of orders for July using simple exponential smoothing with a smoothing constant of 0.1. (You have to assume April's forecast was 21.)

Endnotes

[1]William J. Stanton and Richard H. Buskirk, *Management of the Sales Force,* 6th ed. (Homewood, Ill.: Richard D. Irwin, 1983), p. 412.

[2]For a discussion of some other, less common forecasting techniques, see one of the many excellent books on the subject, such as Frank H. Eby, Jr., and William J. O'Neill, *The Management of Sales Forecasting* (Lexington, Mass.: D.C. Heath, 1977); Spyros Makridakis and Steven C. Wheelwright, *Forecasting: Methods and Applications* (New York: John Wiley & Sons, 1978); Douglas Wood and Robert Fildes, *Forecasting for*

Business: Methods and Applications (New York: Longment Group Limited, 1976); and Spyros Makridakis, *Handbook of Forecasting: A Manager's Guide,* 2nd ed. (New York: John Wiley & Sons, 1987).

[3]Bernie Whalen, "On-Site Computer Interviewing Yields Research Data Instantly," *Marketing News* 18 (November 9, 1984), pp. 1, 17. For a comparison of the various software packages for personal computer assisted interviewing, see Edwin H. Carpenter, "Software Tools for Data Collection: Microcomputer Assisted Interviewing," *Applied Marketing Research* 29 (Winter 1988), pp. 23–32.

[4]"Sales Forecasts: Getting There From Here," *Business Marketing* 73 (October 1988), pp. 36–37.

[5]Manohar U. Kalwani and Alvin J. Silk, "On the Reliability and Predictive Validity of Purchase Intention Measures," *Marketing Science* 1 (Summer 1982), pp. 243–86. Those organizations that collect purchase intentions data regularly often adjust the data based on their past experience as to how much bias intention data might contain. For discussion of some popular adjustment procedures, see Linda F. Jamieson and Frank M. Bass, "Adjusting Stated Intention Measures to Predict Trial Purchase of New Products: A Comparison of Models and Methods," *Journal of Marketing Research* 26 (August 1989), pp. 336–45.

[6]Most introductory marketing research texts discuss what is involved in each of these tasks. The effort can be substantial, and it is not unusual for a market survey to take two or three months. See, for example, Gilbert A. Churchill, Jr, *Marketing Research: Methodological Foundations,* 5th ed. (Hinsdale, Ill.: Dryden Press, 1991).

[7]David Hurwood, Elliott S. Grossman, and Earl L. Bailey, *Sales Forecasting* (New York: The Conference Board, 1978). The empirical evidence indicates about 50 percent of the consumer goods companies and 70 percent of the industrial goods companies among the Fortune 500 firms used the sales force composite to forecast sales. See Robin T. Peterson, "Sales Force Composite Forecasting—An Exploratory Analysis," *Journal of Business Forecasting* 8 (Spring 1989), pp. 23–27.

[8]For sales managers' reports on the accuracy of forecasts prepared by their sales force, see Thomas R. Wotruba and Michael L. Thurlow, "Sales Force Partici-

pation in Quota Setting and Sales Forecasting," *Journal of Marketing* 40 (April 1976), pp. 11–16.

[9]Richard B. Barrett and David J. Kitska, "Forecasting System at Rubbermaid," *Journal of Business Forecasting* 6 (Spring 1987), pp. 7–9.

[10]The technique was originally devised at the Rand Corporation to assist in forecasting the likely state of technology in the future. See Norman C. Dalkey, *The Delphi Method: An Experimental Study of Group Opinion* (Santa Monica, Calif.: The Rand Corporation, 1969). The method has been adopted for sales forecasting. See C. L. Jain, "Delphi-Forecast with Experts' Opinion," *The Journal of Business Forecasting* 4 (Winter 1985–86), pp. 22–23.

[11]Harper Q. North and Donald L. Pyke, "Probes of the Technological Future," *Harvard Business Review* 417 (May–June 1969), p. 70. For a study of the impact of various "experts" on the quality of managerial judgments, see Jean Claude Larréché and Reza Moinpour, "Management Judgment in Marketing: The Concept of Expertise," *Journal of Marketing Research* 20 (May 1983), pp. 110–21.

[12]Yeong Wee Yong, Kau Ah Keng, and Ten Len Leng, "A Delphi Forecast for the Singapore Tourism Industry: Future Scenario and Marketing Implications," *European Journal of Marketing* 23, no. 11 (1989), pp. 15–26. Delphi is frequently used to develop tourism forecasts. For a review of the tourism forecasting literature, see Roger J. Calantone, Anthony Di Benedetto, and David Bojanic, *Journal of Travel Research* 26 (Fall 1987), pp. 28–39.

[13]Jeffrey L. Johnson, "A Ten-Year Delphi Forecast in the Electronics Industry," *Industrial Marketing Management* 5 (March 1976), pp. 45–55.

[14]Hurwood, Grossman, and Bailey, *Sales Forecasting,* pp. 16–17.

[15]"Test Marketing: What's in Store," *Sales & Marketing Management* 128 (March 15, 1982), pp. 57–85.

[16]Lawrence Ingrassia, "A Matter of Taste: There's No Way to Tell If a New Food Product Will Please the Public," *The Wall Street Journal,* February 26, 1980, pp. 1, 23.

[17]"To Test or Not to Test Seldom the Question," *Advertising Age* 55 (February 20, 1984), pp. M10–M11.

[18]Eleanor Johnson Tracy, "Testing Time for Test Marketing," *Fortune* 110 (October 29, 1984), pp. 75–76.

[19]Julie B. Solomon, "P&G Rolls Out New Items at Faster Pace, Turning Away from Long Marketing Testing," *The Wall Street Journal,* May 11, 1984, p. 25.

[20]Damon Darden, "Faced with More Competition, P&G Sees New Products as Crucial to Earnings Growth," *The Wall Street Journal,* September 13, 1983, pp. 37, 53. For discussion of the general problems of over-controlling the marketing effort in test markets, see "How to Keep Well-Intentioned Research from Misleading New-Product Planners" and "How to Improve Your Chances for Test-Market Success," *Marketing News* 18 (January 6, 1984), pp. 1 and 8, and pp. 12 and 13, respectively.

[21]Those who wish a more comprehensive coverage of forecasting with time series should see one of the books specifically devoted to forecasting methods in general, such as Steven C. Wheelwright and Spyros Makridakis, *Forecasting Methods for Management,* 4th ed. (New York: John Wiley & Sons, 1985), or time series forecasting methods in particular, such as C. Chatfield, *The Analysis of Time Series: Theory and Practice* (New York: John Wiley & Sons, 1975) or Douglas C. Montgomery and Lynwood A. Johnson, *Forecasting and Time Series Analysis* (New York: McGraw-Hill, 1976).

[22]The exponential smoothing approach to forecasting can be shown to be a subset of Box-Jenkins methods of forecasting. That approach involves (1) postulating a model that might fit the data, (2) estimating the parameters in the model, (3) checking the adequacy of the model and repeating steps 1 and 2, if necessary, and (4) using the fitted model to generate forecasts. Box-Jenkins models are richer than exponential smoothing models in that they can be fitted to more complex data series. However, they are also more complicated for the manager to understand. See G. E. Box and G. M. Jenkins, *Times Series Analysis,* 2nd ed. (San Francisco: Holden-Day, 1976). For an elementary introduction, see George Kress and John Snyder, "ABC of Box-Jenkins Models," *Journal of Business Forecasting* 7 (Summer 1988), pp. 2–8.

[23]"Sometimes All It Takes Is a Smart Idea," *Manufacturing Systems* 6 (July 1988), pp. 18–19.

[24]The entire process is illustrated in Wheelwright and Makridakis, *Forecasting Methods for Management.* The best-known decomposition method is the technique developed by Julius Shiskin, "Electronic Computers and Business Indicators," National Bureau of Economic Research, Occasional Paper 57, which is used in forecasting many national statistics. It is also possible to adjust for trading day effects or sales patterns with heavier volumes in certain days, such as weekends, using similar procedures. See Arthur J. Adams, "Using the Calendar to Improve Sales Forecasts," *Journal of the Academy of Marketing Science* 12 (Summer 1984), pp. 103–12.

[25]Dick Berry, "Inside the Art of Regression-Based Sales Forecasting," *Business Marketing* 69 (June 1984), pp. 100–11.

[26]See also David M. Georgoff and Robert Murdick, "Manager's Guide to Forecasting," *Harvard Business Review* 64 (January–February 1986), pp. 110–20, which contains a chart in which 20 forecasting techniques are rated on 16 evaluative dimensions.

[27]Stanley J. PoKempner and Earl L. Bailey, *Sales Forecasting Practices: An Appraisal* (New York: National Industrial Conference Board, 1970). See also J. Scott Armstrong, Roderick J. Brodie, and Shelby H. McIntyre, "Forecasting Methods for Marketing: Review of Empirical Research," *International Journal of Forecasting* 3, nos. 3–4, pp. 355–76.

[28]PoKempner and Bailey, *Sales Forecasting Practices,* p. 32.

[29]Ibid.

[30]Spyros Makridakis et al., "The Accuracy of Extrapolation (Time-Series) Methods: Results of a Forecasting Competition," *Journal of Forecasting* 1 (April–June 1982), pp. 111–53. See also Spyros Makridakis et al., *The Forecasting Accuracy of Major Time Series Methods* (New York: John Wiley & Sons, 1984).

[31]Spyros Makridakis and Michele Hibon, "Accuracy of Forecasting: An Empirical Investigation," *Journal of the Royal Statistical Society* 142, pt. 2 (1979), pp. 97–145, and R. M. Hogarth and Spyros Makridakis,

"Forecasting and Planning: An Evaluation," *Management Science* 27 (February 1981), pp. 115–38.

[32]Mark M. Moriarity and Arthur J. Adams, "Management Judgment Forecasts, Composite Forecasting Models, and Conditional Efficiency," *Journal of Marketing Research* 21 (August 1984), pp. 239–50.

[33]Steven P. Schnaars, "Situational Factors Affecting Forecast Accuracy," *Journal of Marketing Research* 21 (August 1984), pp. 290–97; Steven W. Hartley and William Rudelius, "How Data Format and Problem Structure Affect Judgmental Sales Forecasts: An Experiment," in Terrence A. Shimp et al., *AMA Educator's Conference Proceedings* (Chicago: American Marketing Association, 1986), pp. 297–302; and Douglas J. Dalrymple, "Sales Forecasting Practices: Results from a United States Survey," *International Journal of Forecasting* 3 (November 1987), pp. 379–91.

[34]For reviews of the literature on combining forecasts, see Robert Clemens, "Combining Forecasts: A Review and Annotated Bibliography," *International Journal of Forecasting* 5, no. 4 (1989), pp. 559–88. C. W. J. Granger, "Invited Review: Combining Forecasts—Twenty Years Later," *Journal of Forecasting* 8 (July–September 1989), pp. 167–73.

[35]Pierre Wack, "Scenarios: Unchartered Waters Ahead," *Harvard Business Review* 63 (September–October 1985), p. 73.

[36]Pierre Wack, "Scenarios: Shooting the Rapids," *Harvard Business Review* 63 (November–December 1985), p. 146. See also Peter W. Beck, "Debate over Alternate Scenarios Replaces Forecasts at Shell U.K.," *Journal of Business Forecasting* 3 (Spring 1984), pp. 2–6.

[37]Thomas Moore, "Different Folks, Different Strokes," *Fortune* 112 (September 16, 1985), p. 68. This article describes what several companies are doing to take advantage of regional variations in demand.

[38]The Buying Power Index (BPI) discussed below provides an example of a market index-based allocation of total estimated demand to a territory.

[39]See Richard D. Rosenberg, "Forecasting Derived Product Demand in Commercial Construction," *Industrial Marketing Management* 11 (February 1982), pp. 39–46, for details regarding the development and use of the indexes.

[40]For an overview of useful secondary data published by the Census Bureau and other public and private agencies, see Churchill, *Marketing Research,* pp. 287–303.

Suggested Readings

Makridakis, Spyros. *Handbook of Forecasting: A Manager's Guide.* (New York: John Wiley & Sons, 1987).

Georgoff, David M., and Robert Murdick. "Manager's Guide to Forecasting." *Harvard Business Review* 64 (January–February 1986), pp. 110–20.

Sales Territories

DECISION BASES FOR SALES FORCE SIZE AND DEPLOYMENT CHANGED AT SYNTEX LABORATORIES

Syntex Corporation began in 1940 with typical steroid preparations prescribed by dermatologists. The company next introduced birth control products prescribed by gynecologists. By the mid-1980s, Syntex Corporation was an international company that developed, manufactured, and marketed a wide range of health and personal care products. Syntex Laboratories, the U.S. human pharmaceutical and largest Syntex subsidiary, found itself groping with problems common to many organizations: determining how large its sales force should be and how it should be deployed.

Determining the appropriate amount to spend on the sales force is difficult. Theoretically, money should be invested in the sales force as long as marginal returns on that investment are greater than other alternative places for corporate investment. However, determining the rate of return on different sales force investments is very difficult. The biggest determinant of investment in the sales force is the number of people. The size and deployment of the sales force can dramatically affect profitability. Relating incremental sales to changes in sales force size and then relating those sales to profitability is not easy. It is hard to isolate the effect of the sales force from all other effects in the marketplace, e.g., pricing, advertising, changes in distribution, changes in market needs, and changes in competitive behavior.

For ethical pharmaceutical firms, the sales force investment decision is crucial because the sales force is the prominent way of marketing products. The sales force at Syntex Laboratories visits physicians and encourages them to prescribe Syntex drugs. Other marketing elements include advertising in medical journals, direct mail, giving physicians samples of products, and other specialized forms of product promotion such as medical symposia and convention booths.

When a physician prescribes a Syntex drug for a patient, the prescription can be filled at any pharmacy, not necessarily in the same area as the physician. The pharmacies, in many cases, buy through large wholesalers instead of directly from Syntex. Thus, it is very difficult to isolate sales that are influenced by the salesperson's calls on a particular physician. The salesperson does not know whether a sale is made or its amount.

When discussing why Syntex changed its approach to determining sales force size and sales territory design, the senior vice president for sales and marketing at Syntex Laboratories commented:

> Our history had been one of increasing the sales force size in relatively small steps. I've never been really satisfied that there was any good reason why we were expanding by 30 or 40 representatives in any year other than that was what we were able to get approved in the budget process. Over the years, I'd become impatient with the process of going to the well for more people every year with no long-term view of it. I felt that if I went to upper management with a more strategic, or longer term viewpoint, it would be a lot easier to then sell the annual increases necessary to set up a previously established objective in sales force size and utilization.

The old system was abandoned and a new system installed. The new system involved the use of a formal, computerized decision model to determine sales force size, sales territory design, and assignment of sales reps to sales territories. Using the model helped Syntex increase sales force size and change its deployment. These decisions resulted in a documented continuing $25 million, 8 percent annual increase in sales.

Source: Adapted from Leonard M. Lodish, Ellen Curtis, Michael Ness, and M. Kerry Simpson," Sales Force Sizing and Deployment Using a Decision Calculus Model at Syntex Laboratories," *Interfaces* 18 (January–February 1988), pp. 5–20.

As the introductory scenario suggests, the number of salespeople and the design of the individual sales territories can have important sales and profit implications for firms. Poorly designed territories can increase the cost of doing business and produce other negative consequences. These impacts are reviewed in the first part of this chapter. The remainder of the chapter looks at how a sales manager can determine how many sales territories the firm needs and what each territory should be like.

THE NEED FOR SALES TERRITORIES

A sales territory is a group of present and potential customers assigned to a salesperson, branch, dealer, or distributor for a given period. The key word in this definition is *customers*. "Good" sales territories are made up of customers who have money to spend and the willingness to spend it.

While the key to sales territory design is customers, geographical boundaries determine territories in many firms. The salesperson might be assigned the state of Pennsylvania or the city of Philadelphia because geographically defined territories yield certain advantages, discussed below. There are exceptions, though, when firms are unlikely to realize advantages from geographic territories.

When the firm is small or just getting started, for example, management can plan and control the sales operation without using territories. As a firm grows and its markets expand geographically, the advantages of geographically defined sales territories become clearer.

Sometimes firms forgo geographic territories when their products are highly technical and sophisticated, choosing instead to rely on product specialists. Rather than using salespeople who might not be able to answer the customer's technical questions, the firm uses technical specialists who have the necessary expertise. The disadvantage of this scheme is that several field salespeople might call on the same account. An alternative is to have a single salesperson responsible for the account, and the salesperson can call in home-office technical specialists when needed.

Sales territories also are not geographically specified when personal relationships and friendships have a bearing on the sale, such as with the sale of securities or real estate. It would be dysfunctional to tell a customer that he or she had to deal with a salesperson other than the one the customer knew and liked.

Other than these exceptions, geographically defined sales territories are the norm in most companies, and sales territory design is one of the most critical decisions for sales managers. The problems with poorly designed sales territories are illustrated by the experiences of the consumer goods manufacturer depicted in Exhibit 7.1. The firm's experience is not unusual.

The design of sales territories can affect sales force morale, the firm's ability to serve the market, and the firm's ability to evaluate and control the selling effort.

E X H I B I T 7 • 1   *Experiences of a Consumer Durable Good Manufacturer with Territory Design*

Andy and Sally are two members of this firm's sales force. They were hired at about the same time, have attended similar training programs, and have participated in the same motivational programs. The accompanying table compares each salesperson's present allocation of selling effort to trading areas with that recommended by the deployment analysis.

Deployment Analysis for Two Territories

	Trading Area*	Present Effort	Recommended Effort (percent)†
Andy	1	10	4
	2	60	20
	3	15	7
	4	5	2
	5	10	3
Total		100	36
Sally	1	18	81
	2	7	21
	3	5	11
	4	35	35
	5	5	11
	6	30	77
Total		100	236

*Each territory is made up of several trading areas.

†The percentage of salesperson time spent in the trading area (100% = 1 salesperson). Thus, the deployment analysis suggests that Andy's territory requires only 0.36 salespeople, while Sally's territory needs 2.36 salespeople for proper coverage.

The deployment analysis has identified a major problem in the assignment of trading areas to Andy and Sally. Sally's territory has enough opportunity to support more than two salespeople, yet she is expected to provide the desired sales coverage to all of the trading areas in her territory. In contrast, Andy's territory does not offer sufficient opportunity for even one salesperson. Nevertheless, Andy is expected to perform well within this territory.

In this case, management's deployment of selling effort is counterproductive. The firm is not achieving the sales and profits it should expect from its investment in Andy and Sally. Because the trading areas are not receiving enough selling effort, sales opportunities are being lost in Sally's territory. Because selling effort is wasted on trading areas with limited opportunity, profits are being lost in Andy's territory. The net result is that the firm is not obtaining proper market coverage of trading areas. Expensive sales resources are being wasted.

This situation also has different but adverse effects on each salesperson. The high level of opportunity in Sally's territory makes it possible for her to earn desired incentive compensation by merely "skimming" the trading areas. She has little motivation to develop fully her territory's opportunities. Andy, on the other hand, is frustrated. He is overcovering his territory and spends much of his time making sales calls in low-opportunity trading areas. Andy's motivational level is so low that he may consider resigning.

Many sales managers would detect that sales and profits from Sally's and Andy's territories are not what they might be and that both salespeople are not highly motivated.

Source: Reprinted from Raymond W. LaForge, David W. Cravens, and Clifford E. Young, "Improving Salesforce Productivity," *Business Horizons* 28 (September–October 1985), pp. 50–51. Copyright 1985 by the Foundation for the School of Business at Indiana University. Used with permission.

Sales Force Morale

A salesperson's territory can dramatically influence the individual's interest and morale. While companies must adequately cover their accounts, salespeople must also have the opportunity to earn an adequate living. Obviously, a salesperson's territory can have great influence on his or her success. Few salespeople will be content with what they consider to be inferior assignments while their colleagues can make more money with less effort because of superior territories. In short, unequal sales territories are a prime cause of poor morale.

Just as poor sales territory design can hurt morale, good territory design can improve it. There are advantages for salespeople who have their own territories; in some ways, they are in business for themselves. Since they have responsibility for the accounts in their district, they can take pride in what their customers buy and how their customers are served.

Clearly defined territories lead to clarified responsibilities. Sales reps can more readily appreciate the goals assigned them and can better visualize the effort necessary to achieve those goals. Delineating responsibilities by territories can reduce conflicts among salespeople over who is responsible for a given account, and who is entitled to the commission from the sales to a particular customer. If disputes arise, as they always do among customers who transact business in more than one territory, they can be more amicably settled when sales territories are clearly defined. Many firms have very standard divisions; for example, half the commission goes to the sales representative serving the account's national office, and half goes to the representative serving the plant to which the merchandise is shipped. Salespeople understand these ground rules. Although the home office may have no influence on a particular sale, it may be very important on another. Thus, salespeople can appreciate the necessity and desirability of such division of compensation.

Market Coverage

Soundly designed sales territories can improve how the market is served. For example, the Variable Annuity Life Insurance Company was able to realize savings of $8.8 million by redesigning its sales territories.[1]

It is much easier to pinpoint customers and prospects and to determine who should call on them and how often when the market is geographically divided than when the market is considered a large aggregate of potential accounts. Salespeople who are restricted to a geographic area are more likely to get more out of that territory than when they can roam at will. Instead of simply skimming the cream off the top, they are more likely to develop small accounts that have the potential to become important accounts. When sales territories are designed to force such effort, salespeople cannot meet their performance goals calling on only "easy accounts."

Customer service can also be improved with properly designed sales territories. Because sales reps call on the accounts in their territory on a regular basis, they can develop in-depth understanding of their customers' problems and needs. They can better anticipate products that will help the customer.

They also understand the account better and learn who is involved in the purchasing decision. This helps the representative sell more effectively and service the account better, thereby producing greater long-term customer satisfaction.

Good territory design allows better integration of the personal selling effort with other elements in the marketing program, particularly the communications program. In territories that have little potential, the manager may emphasize advertising and supplement that with a telephone sales program; he or she may place only minimal emphasis on personal visits by field representatives. In a territory that has good potential and a concentration of customers, the manager may forgo the telephone-call program, relying instead on personal sales calls while committing fewer dollars to advertising. Before launching a new product, salespeople may be instructed to call on distributors and dealers and to supply them with sufficient point-of-purchase display materials and other marketing aids. Sales representatives could also help to assure that intermediaries have adequate inventories of the product and they know how the product operates and should be serviced.

Evaluation and Control

Effective territory design can improve management's evaluation and control of field selling. Geographically defined sales territories allow sales and cost data to be collected and analyzed by geographic area. This permits area comparisons—an important benefit because the strength of the competition often varies by area. One can compare market shares across areas in total and by product; thus, companies can more accurately pinpoint competitive strengths and weaknesses. In one metropolitan area, the company may be doing poorly because of a dominant distributor that handles a competitor's product. The remedy might involve committing more resources to assist the distributor handling the firm's product. In a territory where the problem is awareness of the company and its products, the remedy could be different.

Managers can also evaluate the sales force better with geographically defined sales territories. Salespeople can be compared with respect to their sales versus potential, and those who may need training can be spotted. The problem may be knowing how to sell to a particular type of account, or it may be linked to less than satisfactory sales of a product. In any case, a more effective cure can be formulated when the exact nature of the problem can be pinpointed. How much help a salesperson should need to manage a territory is the topic of Thorny Issues 7.1.

The experience of Bindicator, a supplier of instruments that measure the levels of wheat, cement, plastic pellets, and numerous other raw materials in the bins of process industries, illustrates a benefit of area comparisons. When Bindicator found its sales were off sharply, the company attempted to determine the extent of the problem by developing marketing potential estimates by territory for the first time in its history. It then compared its sales to potential

Thorny Issues in Sales Management 7 • 1

How Much Help Does a Salesperson Need to Manage a Territory?

This question poses a common dilemma for most sales managers. How much time should sales managers spend helping salespeople manage their territories?

A recent article highlights the practices of several companies.*

> At any given time, Turner Warmack, vice president of sales and marketing at Ziegler Tools, an Atlanta industrial distributor, has a pretty good idea what his 18 salespeople are up to. Each week, they fill out detailed itineraries and call reports, which are compared to quarterly itineraries completed earlier in the year.
>
> Rick Horn, president of Stahl Co., a Worcester, Ohio, specialty truck body manufacturer, has a much looser management style. When he was head of sales and marketing at another manufacturer, he required nothing more from his 45 salespeople than a weekly itinerary. Anything else, he felt, got in the way of their selling.
>
> Bob Cavorsi, national sales manager for Cablec Corp., a manufacturer of high-volume cable in Marion, Ind., plays a strong role in helping salespeople manage their territories. Cablec has about 25 sales people who cover

the entire country. Because of the long buying cycle (as long as two years in some cases) much of their time is spent making follow-up calls. To help guide and keep track of his salespeople, Cavorsi requires a monthly report that he categorizes as a combination itinerary and call report. Cavorsi then reviews the report to be certain that the salespeople are calling on the right people in what can be a fairly complex buying chain.

These few examples illustrate that there is no simple answer. How much time to spend helping salespeople manage their territories will depend on many factors such as company size, experience of the sales force, and individual managerial style. What works for one sales manager may not work for another.

There are trade-offs to consider. Too much involvement from a sales manager may crimp the creativity needed to be a top sales performer. On the other hand, too little involvement may lead to major problems that could have been corrected when they were small. Or, as Kelley contends, "Why wait to the end of the quarter to find out a salesperson hasn't been calling on a key account?" Most sales managers try to be flexible and regulate their involvement according to the territory.

*Bill Kelley, "How Much Help Does a Salesperson Need?" *Sales & Marketing Management*, May 1989, pp. 32–35.

and looked at the number of sales leads by territory. Bindicator found that smaller territories received a higher proportion of sales leads than larger territories and that two of its highest potential areas were being starved for sales leads generated by national advertising. The company consequently revised its advertising schedule, and sales more than doubled in one of the starved high-potential areas and increased substantially in the other.[2]

Cost-control advantages also accrue to the firm with defined sales terri-

---

E X H I B I T   7 • 2   *Using Sales Force Automation to Improve Sales Force Productivity*

Hewlett-Packard equipped all its salespeople with laptop computers backed up by customer-prospecting and relationship-tracking systems at headquarters. The result was a 33% growth in sales, a 31% increase in sales force productivity, and a 40% drop in the attrition rate of sales personnel.

Fina Oil and Chemical, a more than $1 billion division of PertoFina Corp., had salespeople who were handling only 50 accounts, on average, but the dollar magnitude of business could be over $100 million. Salespeople needed to know everything that was happening relative to their account and had to be able to tell a customer the progress of an order on a day-to-day basis to ensure just-in-time delivery.
   Fina turned to laptop computers. The computers were tied into corporate mainframes and downloaded daily to monitor the manufacturing progress of each order and communicate the information via modem to salespeople anywhere in the world.
   To overcome a previous problem in computerizing the sales force, the salesperson was not required to type in data. Only five commands were necessary to gain access to the corporate mainframe and access all data efficiently.

Source: Shawn Clark, "Sales Force Automation Pays Off," *Marketing News,* 24 (August 6, 1990), p. 9.

tories. Again, comparing sales representatives in terms of number of calls they make, their travel and other expenses, and proportion of time spent in face-to-face customer contact versus other related selling activities can provide important insights into doing the job more efficiently. Slight, incremental differences can have important profit implications for the firm. In 1990, the median cost of an industrial sales call was $250.54, while the number of calls per day was approximately 4.[3] Furthermore, industrial salespersons spend only 39 percent of their typical nine-hour, 32-minute workday, or 3.72 hours, in face-to-face selling,[4] the remainder is spent driving to interviews, waiting for interviews, making service calls, attending meetings, and making reports. If one considers face-to-face time as the real "productive" time of the salesperson, the average industrial sales representative's productive time costs its firm $269 per hour (4 calls/day × $250.54/call × 1 day ÷ 3.72 hours)—comparable to that of a $538,000-a-year executive. Of course, some of this other time is also productive time—for example, planning a sales presentation. Reducing the unproductive portions through more effective coverage of accounts and more efficient routing within territories can achieve substantial cost economies. Small incremental cost improvements for each salesperson for a firm that employs 50 to 100 or more representatives can significantly boost profits. For example, one small grocery products firm, "with only 34 salespeople, estimated savings of $250,000 from changes in the allocation of sales calls to existing grocery products accounts."[5] One way firms are helping their salespeople cover their accounts more effectively and improve their productivity is by equipping them with laptop computers. Exhibit 7.2 describes the experiences of Hewlett-Packard Co. and Fina Oil and Chemical.

SALES FORCE SIZE

Salespeople are among the most productive assets of a company; they are also among the most expensive. Determining the optimal number to employ presents several fundamental dilemmas. On the one hand, increasing the number of salespeople will increase sales; on the other hand, it will also increase costs. Achieving the optimal balance between these considerations, although difficult, is vitally important.

The optimal number of territories depends on the design of the individual territories. Different assignments to salespeople and even different call patterns can product different sales levels. Of course, the number of calls the sales force must make directly affects the number of salespeople the firm needs. In sum, the number of sales territories and the design of individual territories must be looked at as interrelated decisions whose outcomes affect each other.

The decisions need to be made jointly and not sequentially. Deployment models are available that simultaneously consider the three interrelated decisions of (1) sales force size or the number of territories, (2) design of the individual territories, and (3) allocation of the total selling effort to accounts. Use of these deployment models is promising, as Exhibit 7.3 suggests. At the same time, it is useful for discussion purposes to separate the issues so as to throw the underlying considerations into bolder relief. Consequently, the subsequent discussion first addresses the issue of sales force size and then the issue of sales territory design. However, the size of the sales force may need to be revised as a result of the sales territory design.[6]

There are several techniques for determining the size of the field sales force. Three of the more popular are the (1) breakdown, (2) workload, and (3) incremental methods.

Breakdown Method

The breakdown method is conceptually one of the simplest. An average salesperson is treated as a salesperson unit, and each salesperson unit is assumed to possess the same productivity potential. To determine the size of the sales force needed, divide total forecasted sales for the company by the sales likely to be produced by each individual. Mathematically,

$$n = \frac{s}{p}$$

where

n = number of sales personnel needed

s = forecasted sales volume

p = estimated productivity of one salesperson unit

Thus, a firm that had forecast sales of $5 million and in which each salesperson unit could be expected to sell $250,000 would need 20 salespeople.

EXHIBIT 7 • 3   *Some Company Experiences Redeploying Sales Forces across*
Geographic Areas or Accounts

Type of Product	Redeployment Basis	Consequence
Medical X-ray film	Redeployment of salespeople across sales districts	$131,000 increase in gross profits
Advertising	Redeployment of selling effort and reassignment of salespeople to accounts	17–21 percent profit increase
Appliances	Redeployment of selling effort across trading areas	$830,000 sales increase
Airline travel and cargo	Redeployment of selling effort to accounts	8.1 percent sales increase
Consumer products	Reduction in sales force size and redeployment of selling effort to accounts	Maintain current sales levels with nearly 50 percent reduction in selling effort
Consumer products	Redeployment of salespeople across regions and distribution channels	7 percent sales increase
Grocery products	Redeployment of selling effort to accounts	8–30 percent sales improvement
Transportation services	Reduction in sales force size and redeployment of selling effort	Maintain current sales levels with 10–20 percent reduction in sales force size

Source: Adapted from Raymond W. LaForge, David W. Cravens, and Clifford E. Young, "Using Contingency Analysis to Select Selling Effort Allocation Methods," *Journal of Personal Selling and Sales Management* 6 (August 1986), p. 23. The original table also lists the sources in which each of the experiences was reported.

Although conceptually simple, the breakdown method is not without its problems. For one thing, it uses reverse logic. It treats sales force size as a consequence of sales. Yet the logical causation is in the opposite direction. As discussed in Chapter 6, the level of sales expected should depend on the level of the marketing effort. The number of sales people in the field is an important part of that marketing effort—in some companies the most important part. Determining the number of sales representatives to cover the market in a given year should logically precede forecasting final sales.

A second problem with the breakdown method is that it depends on the estimate of productivity per salesperson. The firm can compute the average of what each salesperson sold, say, in the previous year. However, such averages can obscure important facts. They fail to account for different ability levels of salespeople, differing potentials in the markets they service, and different levels of competition in sales territories. Perhaps the "most productive" salesperson had lower sales than average because the market area had below-average potential and intense competitive pressure. The technique fails to allow for such differences.

Also, this simple expression of the formula does not allow for turnover in the sales force. New salespeople are usually not as productive as those who have been on the job for several years. The formula can be modified to allow for sales force turnover, but it loses some of its simplicity and conceptual appeal.

One alternative for smoothing out person-to-person differences in productivity due to ability, market potential, and experience differences is to use industry-average productivity estimates in the formula. Unfortunately, an industry-average productivity estimate tends to ignore the market position of the firm trying to determine the best size of its sales force.[7]

Finally, a key shortcoming of the breakdown method is that it does not allow for profitability. It treats sales as the end in itself rather than as the means to an end. The number of salespeople is determined as a function of the level of forecast sales, not as a determinant of targeted profit.

Workload Method

The basic premise underlying the workload approach (or, as it is sometimes called, the buildup method) is that all sales personnel should shoulder an equal amount of work. Management estimates the work required to serve the entire market. The total work calculation is treated as a function of the number of accounts, how often each should be called on, and for how long. This estimate is then divided by the amount of work an individual salesperson should be able to handle, and the result is the total number of salespeople required.[8] More specifically, the method consists of the six steps shown in Exhibit 7.4.

1. **Classify all the firm's customers into categories.** Often the classification is based on the level of sales to each customer. The ABC Rule of Account Classification holds that the first 15 percent of a firm's customers will account for 65 percent of the firm's sales, the next 20 percent will yield 20 percent, and the last 65 percent will produce only 15 percent.[9] The top group is categorized as A accounts, the middle group as B accounts, and the bottom group as C accounts.

Classification could be based on other criteria also. One firm, for example, rates each customer by the prospect's type of business, credit rating, and product line.[10] Fansteel, a maker of milling cutters and other machine tool products, considers each account's sales potential and need for technical advice in forming its classification of A, B, and C accounts, which determines the mix of its sales force and its distribution when selling the account. General Telephone of Florida classifies present customers by their potential for additional services using revenue per employee in each SIC code. Marion/Merrell Dow classifies accounts strictly by sales potential. It considers the top 20 percent of physicians its salespeople call on A accounts and the other 80 percent B accounts. All noncustomers or physicians with low sales potential are considered C accounts.

Any classification system should reflect the different amounts of selling effort required to service the different classes of accounts and consequently

EXHIBIT 7 • 4 *Steps to Determine Sales Force Size by the Workload Method*

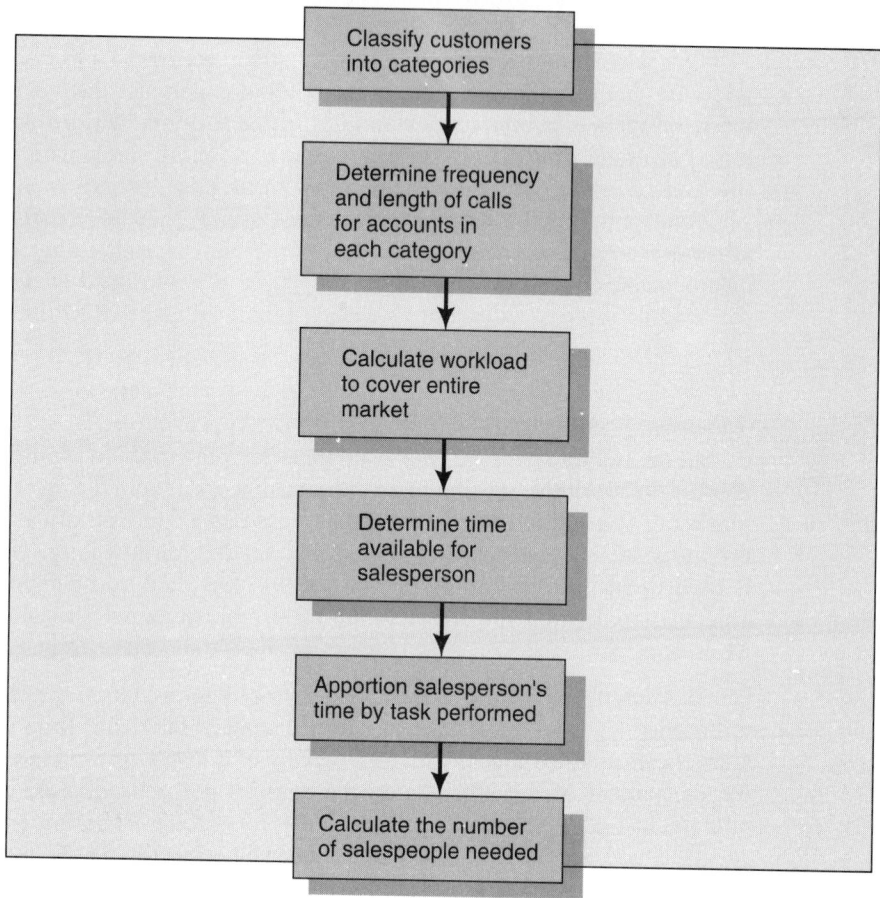

the attractiveness of each class of accounts to the firm. Suppose, for example, the firm had 1,030 accounts that could be classified into three basic types or classes, as follows:

Type A.   Large or very attractive—200
Type B.   Medium or moderately attractive—350
Type C.   Small, but attractive—480

2. **Determine the frequency with which each type of account should be called upon and the desired length of each call.** These inputs can be generated in several ways. They can be based directly on the judgments of management. For example, management at Marion/Merrell Dow wants its salespeople to call on A physicians every two weeks, B physicians every six weeks, and C

physicians only when there is nothing else to do, which is rare. The inputs can also be based on the judgments of experienced salespeople. Alternatively, the firm may conduct controlled experiments in which the frequency of contact and the length of each contact are systematically varied to determine what is optimal. Still another possibility is to analyze historical data using appropriate statistical methods such as regression analysis.

Suppose the firm, using one of these methods, estimates Class A accounts should be called on every two weeks, Class B accounts once a month, and Class C accounts every other month. It also estimates the length of the typical call should be 60 minutes, 30 minutes, and 20 minutes, respectively. The number of contact hours per year for each type of account is thus calculated as:

Class A.   26 times/year × 60 minutes/call = 1,560 minutes, or 26 hours
Class B.   12 times/year × 30 minutes/call =   360 minutes, or 6 hours
Class C.   6 times/year × 20 minutes/call =   120 minutes, or 2 hours

3. Calculate the workload involved in covering the entire market. The total work involved in covering each class of account is given by multiplying the number of such accounts by the number of contact hours per year. These products are summed to estimate the work entailed in covering all the various types of accounts.

Class A.   200 accounts × 26 hours/account = 5,200 hours
Class B.   350 accounts × 6 hours/account = 2,100 hours
Class C.   480 accounts × 2 hours/account =   960 hours
Total   = 8,260 hours

4. Determine the time available per salesperson. For this calculation, estimate the number of hours the typical salesperson works per week and then multiply that by the number of weeks the representative will work during the year. Suppose the typical workweek is 40 hours and the average salesperson can be expected to work 48 weeks during the year, after allowing for vacation time, sickness, and other emergencies. This suggests the average representative has 1,920 hours available per year—that is,

40 hours/week × 48 week/year = 1,920 hours/year

5. Apportion the salesperson's time by task performed. Unfortunately, not all the salesperson's time is consumed in face-to-face customer contact. Much of it is devoted to nonselling activities such as making reports, attending meetings, and making service calls. Another major portion is spent traveling. Suppose a time study of salespeople's effort suggested the following division:

Selling   40 percent =   768 hours/year
Nonselling   30 percent =   576 hours/year
Traveling   30 percent =   576 hours/year
               100 percent = 1,920 hours/year

6. **Calculate the number of salespersons needed.** The number of salespeople the firm will need can now be readily determined by dividing the total number of hours needed to serve the entire market by the number of hours available per salesperson for selling—that is, by the calculation

$$\frac{8{,}260 \text{ hours}}{768 \text{ hours/salesperson}} = 10.75$$

or 11 salespeople.

The workload or buildup method is a common way to determine sales force size. It has several attractive features. It is easy to understand, and it explicitly recognizes that different types of accounts should be called on with different frequencies. The inputs are readily available or can be secured without much trouble.

Unfortunately, it also possesses some weaknesses. It does not allow for differences in sales response among accounts that receive the same sales effort. Two Class A accounts might respond differently to sales effort. One may be content with the products and services of the firm and continue to order even if the salesperson does not call every two weeks. Another, which does most of its business with a competitor, may willingly switch some of its orders if it receives more frequent contact. Also, the method does not explicitly consider the profitability of the call frequencies. It does not take into account such factors as the cost of servicing and the gross margins on the product mix purchased by the account.[11]

Finally, the method assumes that all salespeople use their time with equal efficiency—for example, that each will have 768 hours available for face-to-face selling. This is simply not true. Some are better able to plan their calls to generate more direct selling time; those in smaller geographic territories can spend less time traveling and more time selling. Some simply make better use of the selling time they have available; the quality of time invested in a sales call is at least as important as the quantity of time spent. Yet the buildup method does not explicitly consider this dimension. The workload method to determine sales force size is popular though.

Incremental Method

The basic premise underlying the incremental method of determining sales force size is that sales representatives should be added as long as the incremental profit produced by their addition exceeds the incremental costs.[12] The method recognizes that there will be decreasing returns associated with the addition of salespeople. Thus, while one more salesperson might produce $300,000, two more might produce only $550,000 in new sales. The incremental sales produced by the first salesperson is $300,000, while that for the second salesperson is $250,000. Suppose the addition of a third salesperson could be expected to produce $225,000 in new sales and a fourth, $200,000. Adding all four would increase sales by $975,000. Suppose further that the company's

E X H I B I T 7 • 5   *Illustration of Incremental Approach*

Number of Additional Salespeople (1)	Total Additional Revenue (2)	Incremental Revenue Due to Additional Salesperson (3)	Total Additional Profit* (4)	Incremental Profit Due to Additional Salesperson (5)	Total Additional Cost (6)	Incremental Cost Due to Additional Saleperson (7)
1	$300,000	$300,000	$ 60,000	$60,000	$ 50,000	$ 50,000
2	550,000	250,000	110,000	50,000	100,000	50,000
3	775,000	225,000	155,000	44,500	150,000	50,000
4	975,000	200,000	195,000	40,000	200,000	50,000

*Based on assumption of 20 percent profit margin.

profit margin was 20 percent, and placing another salesperson in the field cost $50,000 on average.

Exhibit 7.5 summarizes the situation. The analysis suggests that two salespeople should be added. At that point, the incremental profit from the additional salespeople equals the incremental cost. Adding more than two salespeople would cause profits to go down as is seen by subtracting column (6) "total additional cost" from column (4) "total additional profit."

The incremental approach to determining sales force size is conceptually correct. Also, it is consistent with the empirical evidence that decreasing returns can be expected with additional salespeople. Decreasing returns can also be expected with other territory design features such as the number of buyers per salesperson, the number of calls the salesperson makes on an account, and the actual time the representative spends in face-to-face contact.[13]

The disadvantage of the incremental approach is that it is the most difficult of the three to implement. While the cost of an additional salesperson can be estimated with reasonable accuracy, estimating the likely profit is difficult. It depends on the additional revenue the salesperson is expected to produce, and that depends on how the territories are restructured, who is assigned to each territory, and how effective they might be. That is not always an easy question to answer as Thorny Issue 7.2 suggests. To compound things further, the profitability of the new arrangement also depends on the mix of products generating the sales increase and how profitable each is to the company.

S ALES TERRITORY DESIGN

After the number of sales territories has been determined, the sales manager can address territory design questions. The general issues involved and the process to follow are shown in Exhibit 7.6 (p. 239). The sales manager strives

Thorny Issues in Sales Management 7 • 2

Assigning Salespeople to Sales Territories

As assistant to the vice president of sales, David was in a quandary. His boss had just handed him the job of developing tentative sales territory assignments for the college recruits that had just completed the company's training program. The company's philosophy was to assign each new rep to the smaller trade accounts in the area. Reps who performed exceptionally well in serving the smaller, independent outlets in the area could be expected to be promoted to better territories— territories that meant calling on regional headquarter offices of larger, national accounts. These offices typically ordered for all the stores in the area and thus placed much larger orders.

Reps were evaluated on the basis of the sales potential of each account. The company used square foot per outlet as its yardstick to assess potential. It had previously established that was a good measure of the size and volume of the account. It had also established some historic standards as to the average amount of each client's potential it could reasonably expect to secure. Those salespeople that consistently beat the standard could expect early promotions.

In making the assignments, David was trying to balance what he thought to be the best interests of the sales reps and the company. At the same time, he was trying to be sensitive to discrimination issues. He believed that by assigning the black sales reps to those areas in which the greatest proportion of the outlets were managed by black managers and Hispanic reps to those areas that had the largest concentration of Hispanic owners, he could maximize their chances for early promotion. The reps might feel more comfortable in operating in these territories, and he was also familiar with empirical evidence that indicated salesperson-customer similarity can affect the likelihood of a sale and its size. If his sense of things was correct, assigning salespeople on this basis would also improve company performance, thereby enhancing his own position. He did not want to be charged in a racial discrimination suit though.

Do you

Approve   _____

Somewhat approve   _____

Somewhat disapprove   _____

Disapprove   _____

of David's thinking to assign salespeople to territories based primarily on racial considerations?

for the ideal of making all territories equal with respect to the amount of sales potential they contain and the amount of work it takes a salesperson to cover them effectively. When territories are equal in potential, it is easier to evaluate each representative's performance and to compare salespeople. Equal workloads tend to improve sales force morale and diminish disputes between management and the sales force. While considering these questions, the sales manager should take into account the impact on market response of particular territory structures and call frequencies. Obviously, it is difficult, if not im-

E X H I B I T 7 • 6   *Stages in Territory Design*

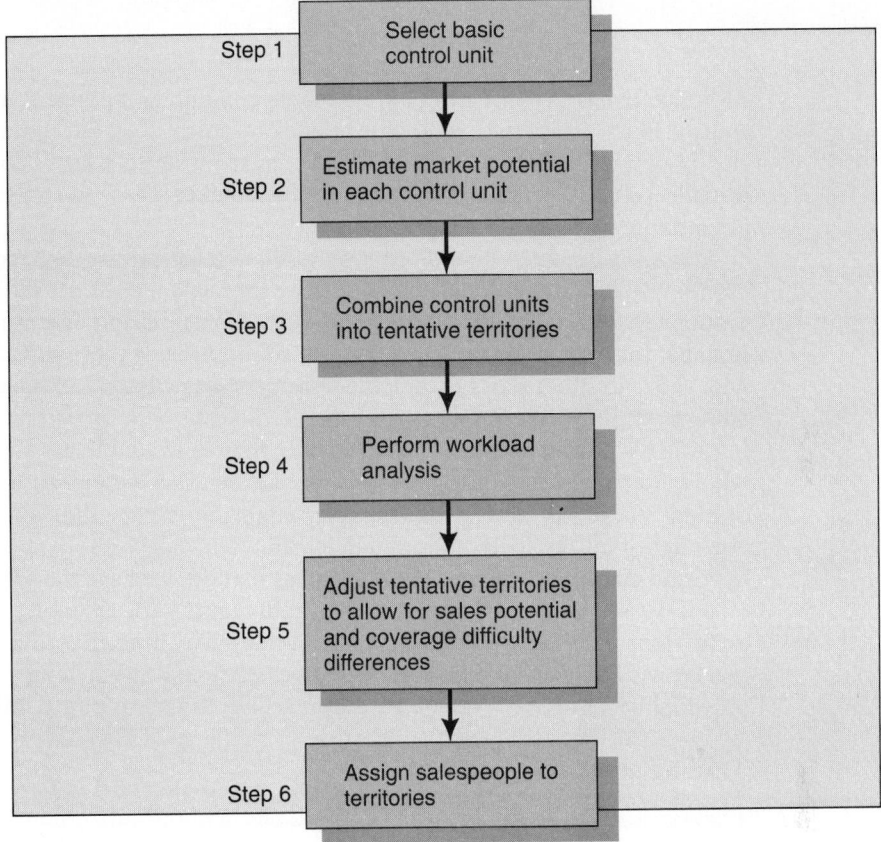

possible, to achieve an optimal balance with respect to all these factors. The sales manager should constantly strive for the proper balance, however.

*Select Basic
Control Unit*

The basic control unit is the most elemental geographic area used to form sales territories—county or city, for example. As a general rule, small geographic control units are preferable to large ones. With large units, areas with low potential may be hidden by their inclusion in areas with high potential, and vice versa. This makes it difficult to pinpoint geographic potential, which is a primary reason for forming geographically defined sales territories in the first place. Also, small control units make it easier to adjust sales territories when conditions warrant. It is much easier to reassign the accounts in a particular county from one salesperson to another, for example, than it is to reassign all the accounts in a state. Some commonly used basic control units are states, trading areas, counties, cities or MSAs, and ZIP code areas.

States

Although it has become less popular, some companies still use states as basic control units. There are some advantages in doing so. State boundaries are clearly defined and thus are simple and inexpensive to use. A good deal of statistical data is accumulated by state, which makes it easy to analyze territory potential.

One primary weakness of using states as control units is that buying habits do not reflect state boundaries. The state represents a political rather than an economic division of the national market. Consumption patterns in Gary, Indiana, for example, may have more in common with those in Chicago than with those in other parts of Indiana. Also, the size of states makes it difficult to pinpoint problem areas. A problem in Ohio may be localized in Cincinnati, but it is hard to determine that if the only figures available are for Ohio as a whole. States also contain great variations in market potential; the potential in New York City alone, for example, might be greater than the combined potential of all the Rocky Mountain states.

State units are sometimes used by firms that do not have the sophistication or staff to use counties or smaller geographic units—for example, firms at the early stages of territory design. States are also used by firms that cover a national market with only a few sales representatives, particularly when they can specify potential accounts by name (e.g., a firm selling dryers to paper mills).

Trading areas

Trading areas are made up of a principal city and the surrounding dependent area. A trading area is an economic unit that ignores political and other non-economic boundaries. Trading areas recognize that consumers who live in New Jersey, for example, may prefer to shop in New York City rather than locally. The trading area for a food processor in western Iowa might be wholesalers located in the upper Midwest rather than those in nearby Kansas.

Trading areas reflect economic factors and are based on consumer buying habits and normal trading patterns. Thus, they facilitate sales planning and control and diminish the likelihood of disputes among sales representatives. For example, after a manufacturer's sales rep does considerable missionary work with retailers, there is little danger they will buy the product from a wholesaler in another person's territory because the retailers ordinarily will be in the same wholesale trading area served by the sales rep.

A major disadvantage of using trading areas as basic control units is that they vary from product to product and must be referred to in terms of specific products. To see this, compare the wholesale Grocery Trading Area Map put out by Rand McNally. The boundaries for two products may not coincide, and this can prove awkward and cumbersome for a multiproduct company. Another difficulty is that it is often hard to obtain detailed statistics for trading areas. This in turn makes them expensive to use as geographic control units, although some firms adjust the boundaries of the trading areas so they coincide with county lines. Whether or not a firm formally uses trading areas as basic control units, it should consider the logical trading areas for the products it produces when specifying the boundaries of each sales territory.

Counties

Counties are probably the most widely used basic control unit. They permit a more fine-tuned analysis of the market than do states or trading areas, given that there are 3,133 counties and only 50 states and a varying number of trading areas depending on the product. One dramatic advantage of using counties as control units is the wealth of statistical data available by county. The county is the smallest geographic unit for which many data series are available. The *County and City Data Book,* published biennially by the Bureau of the Census, provides statistics by county on such things as population, education, employment, income, housing, banking, manufacturing output and capital expenditures, retail and wholesale sales, and mineral and agricultural output. Another advantage of counties is that their size permits easy reassignment from one sales territory to another. Thus, sales territories can be altered to reflect changing economic conditions without major upheaval in basic service. Furthermore, potentials do not have to be recalculated before doing so.

The most serious drawback to using counties as basic control units is that for some purposes they are still too large. Los Angeles County or Cook County (Chicago), for example, may require several sales representatives. In such cases, it is necessary to divide these counties into even smaller basic control units.

Cities and MSAs

Historically, when most of the market potential was within city boundaries, the city was a good basic control unit. Cities are rarely satisfactory anymore, however. For many products, the area surrounding a city now contains as much or more potential than the central city. Consequently, many firms that formerly used cities now employ metropolitan statistical areas (MSAs) as basic control units.

MSAs, which replace the former standard metropolitical statistical area (SMSAs) designation,[14] are integrated economic and social units with a large population nucleus. An area can qualify as an MSA in either of two ways:

1. If it contains a city of at least 50,000 people.
2. If it includes a census defined urbanized area of 50,000, with a total metropolitan population of at least 100,000 people (75,000 in New England).

E X H I B I T   7 • 7   *25 Largest MSAs in Decreasing Order of Size*

Rank	Area	Estimated 1990 Population (in 000s)
1	Los Angeles-Long Beach	8,813.6
2	New York	8,602.1
3	Chicago	6,214.4
4	Philadelphia	4,934.9
5	Detroit	4,385.4
6	Washington	3,778.2
7	Boston-Lawrence-Salem-Lowell-Brockton	3,736.4
8	Houston	3,244.6
9	Atlanta	2,816.6
10	Nassau-Suffolk	2,669.9
11	San Diego	2,486.5
12	St. Louis	2,484.9
13	Dallas	2,481.9
14	Riverside-San Bernardino	2,434.1
15	Minneapolis-St. Paul	2,402.8
16	Baltimore	2,383.1
17	Anaheim-Santa Ana	2,314.0
18	Phoenix	2,108.6
19	Pittsburgh	2,105.4
20	Tampa-St. Petersburg-Clearwater	2,080.8
21	Oakland	2,049.4
22	Newark	1,896.4
23	Miami-Hialeah	1,885.9
24	Seattle	1,866.9
25	Cleveland	1,839.6

Source: "1990 Survey of Buying Power," *Sales & Marketing Management,* 142, August 13, 1990, p. B7.

An MSA includes the county containing the central city and any counties having close social and economic ties to the central county. MSAs always include entire counties except in New England. Exhibit 7.7, which ranks MSAs in order of size, shows the concentration of population within the 25 largest MSAs. The concentration of economic activity matches the concentration of people. As a group, the 320 largest MSAs account for the following percentages of U.S. totals:

77 percent of the population.

83 percent of the effective buying income.

83 percent of total retail sales.

79 percent of food store sales.

85 percent of eating and drinking place sales.

85 percent of general merchandise store sales.

88 percent of furniture/home furnishing/appliance store sales.

83 percent of automotive dealer sales.

77 percent of gasoline service station sales.

87 percent of apparel and accessories store sales.

78 percent of building materials/hardware store sales.

81 percent of drugstore sales.[15]

The heavy concentration of population, income, and retail sales in the MSAs explains why many firms are content to concentrate their field selling efforts on MSAs. Some assign all their field representatives to such large areas. Such a strategy minimizes travel time and expense, because of the geographic concentration of MSAs (see Exhibit 7.8).

ZIP code areas

Some firms, for which city or MSA boundaries are too large, use ZIP code areas as basic control units. The U.S. Postal Service defined more than 36,000 five-digit ZIP code areas.

An advantage of ZIP code areas is that they are relatively homogeneous with respect to basic socioeconomic data. Whereas residents within an MSA might display great heterogeneity, those within a ZIP code area are likely to be relatively similar in age, income, education, and so forth and to even display similar consumption patterns. While the Census Bureau typically does not publish data by ZIP code area, it does provide data from the census and surveys of population and housing to individual companies on computer tape or optical disk. An industry has developed to tabulate such data by arbitrary geographic boundaries. The "geodemographers," as they are typically called, combine census data with their own survey data or data they gather from administrative records, such as motor vehicle registrations or credit transactions, to produce customized products for their clients.

A typical product involves the cluster analysis of census-produced data to produce homogeneous groups that describe the American population. For example, Claritas (the first firm to do this and still one of the leaders in the industry) used over 500 demographic variables in its PRIZM (Potential Ratings for Zip Markets) system when classifying residential neighborhoods. This system breaks the 25,000 neighborhood areas in the United States into 40 types based on consumer behavior and lifestyle. Each of the types has a name that theoretically describes the type of people living there, such as Urban Gold Coast, Shotguns and Pickups, Pools and Patios, and so on. Claritas and the other suppliers will do a customized analysis for whatever geographic boundaries a client specifies. Alternatively, a client can send a tape listing the ZIP

E x h i b i t   **7 • 8**   *Map of Metropolitan Statistical Areas*

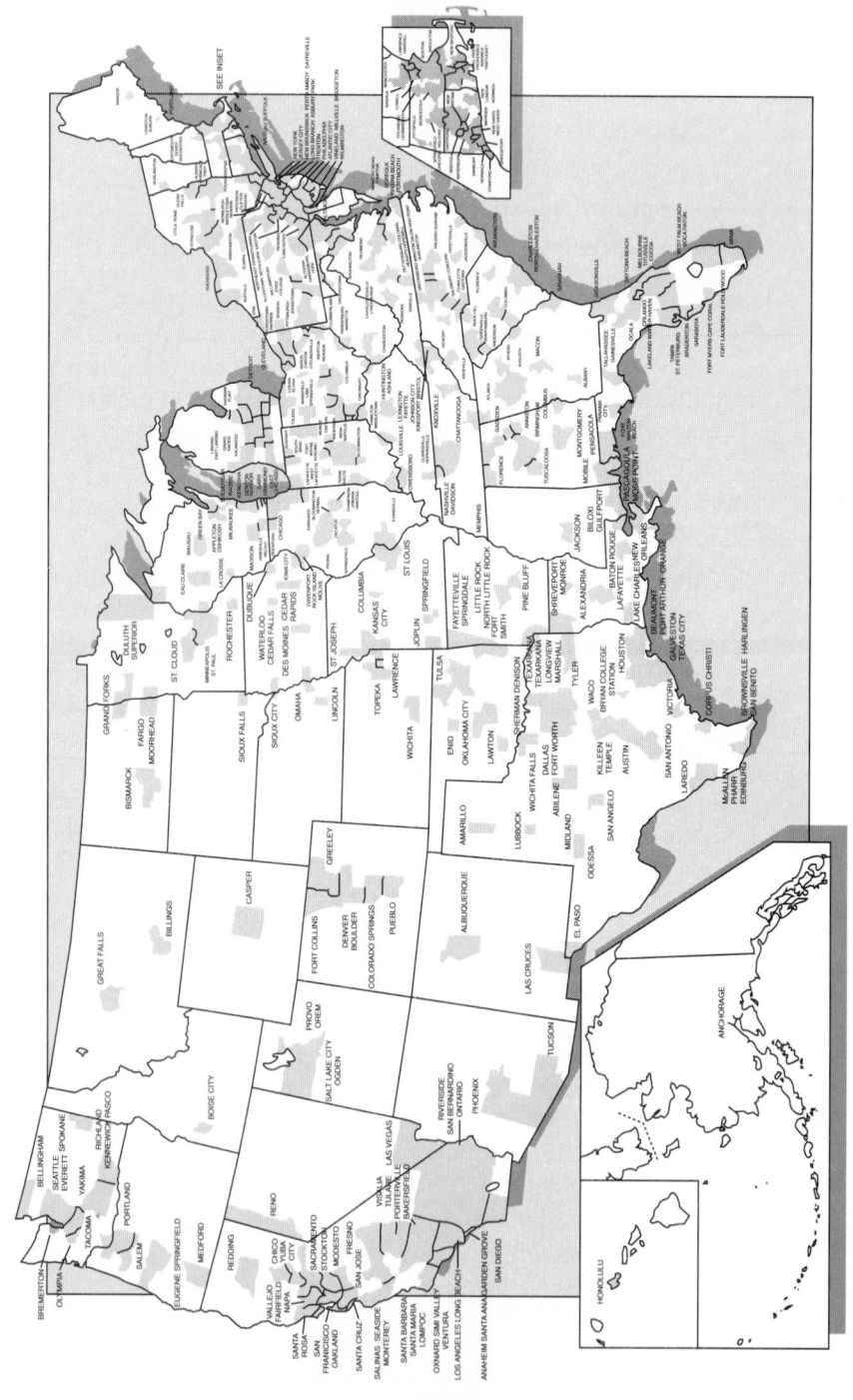

E X H I B I T   7 • 9   *DMI Sales Prospecting Record*

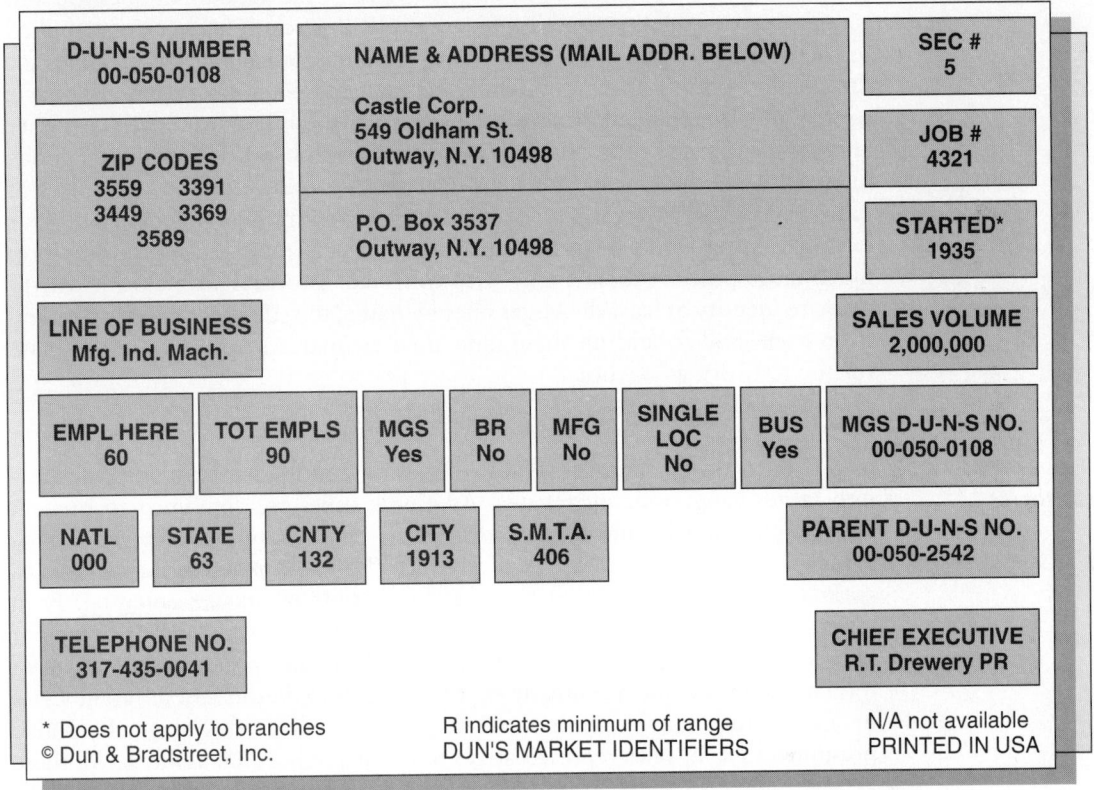

D-U-N-S NUMBER 00-050-0108	NAME & ADDRESS (MAIL ADDR. BELOW) Castle Corp. 549 Oldham St. Outway, N.Y. 10498	SEC # 5

ZIP CODES
3559 3391
3449 3369
3589

P.O. Box 3537
Outway, N.Y. 10498

JOB #
4321

STARTED*
1935

LINE OF BUSINESS
Mfg. Ind. Mach.

SALES VOLUME
2,000,000

| EMPL HERE
60 | TOT EMPLS
90 | MGS
Yes | BR
No | MFG
No | SINGLE
LOC
No | BUS
Yes | MGS D-U-N-S NO.
00-050-0108 |

| NATL
000 | STATE
63 | CNTY
132 | CITY
1913 | S.M.T.A.
406 | PARENT D-U-N-S NO.
00-050-2542 |

TELEPHONE NO.
317-435-0041

CHIEF EXECUTIVE
R.T. Drewery PR

| * Does not apply to branches
© Dun & Bradstreet, Inc. | R indicates minimum of range
DUN'S MARKET IDENTIFIERS | N/A not available
PRINTED IN USA |

Source: Reprinted with permission from Dun's Market Identifiers, © Dun & Bradstreet, Inc.

code addresses of some customer data base, and the geodemographer will attach the cluster codes.

One of industrial marketers' major sources of market data, Dun's "Market Identifiers" (DMI), contains ZIP code information. DMI is a special name given by Dun & Bradstreet to its marketing information service. DMI is a roster of U.S. and Canadian firms updated daily so that the record of each company is accurate and current. Exhibit 7.9 is an example of a card record, which is available on each industrial establishment—an establishment is a single physical location such as a manufacturing plant or a nonmanufacturing headquarters address. Records are also available as printed tabulating cards or magnetic tape. The ability to locate establishments by geographic area can greatly facilitate estimating market potential in planning territory design.

One disadvantage of using ZIP code areas as basic control units is that the boundaries change over time.

Estimate Market Potential

Step 2 in territory design involves estimating market potential in each basic control unit. This is done using one of the schemes suggested in Chapter 6. If a relationship can be established between sales of the product in question and some other variable or variables, for example, this relationship can be applied to each basic control unit. Data must be available for each of the variables for the small geographic area, though. Sometimes the potential within each basic control unit is estimated by considering the likely demand from each customer and prospect in the control unit. This works much better for industrial goods manufacturers than it does for consumer goods producers. The consumers of industrial goods are typically fewer in number and more easily identified—for example, using Dun's "Market Identifiers." Furthermore, each typically buys much more product than is true with consumer goods. This makes it worthwhile to identify at least the larger ones by name, to estimate the likely demand from each, and to add up these individual estimates to produce an estimate for the territory as a whole.

Form Tentative Territories

Step 3 in territory design involves combining contiguous basic control units into larger geographic aggregates. Adjoining units are combined to prevent salespeople from having to crisscross paths while skipping over geographic areas covered by another representative. The basic emphasis at this stage is to make the tentative territories as equal as possible in market potential. Each territory should provide an opportunity for the same standard of living for sales representatives. Differences in workload or sales potential (the share of total market potential a company expects to achieve) because of different levels of competitive activity are not taken into account at this stage. It is also presumed that all sales representatives have relatively equal abilities. All these assumptions are relaxed at subsequent stages of the territory planning process. The attempt at this stage is simply to develop an approximation of the final territory alignment. The total number of territories defined equals the number of territories the firm has previously determined it needs. If the firm has not made such a calculation, it needs to do so now.

Perform Workload Analysis

Once tentative initial boundaries have been established for all sales territories, it is necessary to determine how much work is required to cover each. Ideally, firms like to form sales territories equal in both potential and workload. Although Step 3 should produce territories roughly equal in potential, the territories will probably be decidedly unequal with respect to the amount of work necessary to cover them adequately. In Step 4, the analyst tries to estimate the amount of work involved in covering each.

Example account analysis

Typically, the workload analysis considers each customer (most assuredly, the larger ones) in the territory. The analysis is often conducted in two stages.

EXHIBIT 7 • 10   *Sample Account Analysis*

Account Name	Potential by Product			Estimated Share			Sales Potential			Total	Classi-fication
	X	Y	Z	X	Y	Z	X	Y	Z		
Helen Crosby Manufacturing	$200,000	$140,000	$300,000	0.15	0.30	0.10	$ 30,000	$ 42,000	$ 30,000	$102,000	C
Pelton Industries	420,000	310,000	100,000	0.20	0.40	0.10	84,000	124,000	10,000	218,000	B
The Blattner Company	650,000	180,000	480,000	0.20	0.30	0.25	130,000	54,000	120,000	304,000	A

Classification	Number of Accounts
A	20
B	60
C	150

First, the sales potential for each customer and prospect in the territory is estimated. This step is often called an account analysis. The sales potential estimate derived from the account analysis is then used to decide how often each account should be called on and for how long. The total effort required to cover the territory can be determined by considering the number of accounts, the number of calls to be made on each, the duration of each call, and the estimated amount of nonselling and travel time.

Exhibit 7.10 contains an account analysis for a small sample of accounts in a single territory. Note several things in the table. First, the analysis is carried out customer by customer. Although the firm may not want to do this for every customer in the territory, it would for the potentially larger ones. Second, the potentials in the "Potential by Product" columns are market potentials. Thus, they represent the expected sales of each product to the customer for the entire industry for the period in question. While the analysis here is broken out by product, it is sometimes simply computed in aggregate. Third, the "Estimated Share" columns show the firm's competitive positions with each customer. The firm is particularly entrenched with respect to product Y to Pelton Industries in that it expects to get a 40 percent share, but it has a reasonable share of sales of all three products to all three customers. The multiplication of market potential by product by the firm's estimated share produces an estimate of the firm's sales potential for each product for each customer. The sum of sales potentials by product is the total sales potential of the account.

In the example, the firm uses sales potential by account to classify accounts. Accounts with potential sales greater than $300,000 are classified as A accounts, those with expected sales of $200,000 to $300,000 as B accounts, and those whose potential is less than $200,000 as C accounts. Thus, the Blattner Company is classified as an A account, Pelton Industries as a B account, and Helen Crosby Manufacturing as a C account. The table also indicates that applying a similar analysis to all accounts indicates the firm has 20 A accounts, 60 B accounts, and 150 C accounts.

Criteria for classifying accounts

Total sales potential is one criterion used to classify accounts into categories dictating the frequency and length of sales calls. A number of other criteria have been suggested as well for determining the attractiveness of an individual account to the firm. The key is to identify those factors likely to affect the productivity of the sales call. Some of these other factors include competitive pressures for the account, the prestige of the account, how many products the firm produces that the account buys, and the number and level of buying influences within the account.[16] The factors that affect the productivity of an individual sales call are likely to change from firm to firm.

Determining account call rates

Once the specific factors affecting the productivity of a sales call have been isolated, they can be treated in various ways. One way is to use the ABC Rule of Account Classification discussed earlier and illustrated in Exhibit 7.10.
    Another way is to employ a variation of the matrix concept of strategic planning, which suggests that accounts, like strategic business units or markets, can be divided along two dimensions reflecting the overall opportunity they represent and the firm's abilities to capitalize on those opportunities. In the case of accounts, the division should reflect (1) the attractiveness of the account to the firm and (2) the likely difficulties to be encountered in managing the account.[17] The accounts are then sorted into either a four- or nine-cell strategic planning matrix. For example, Exhibit 7.11 uses the criteria of account potential and the firm's competitive advantage or disadvantage with the account to classify accounts into four cells. It would use different call frequencies in each cell. The heaviest call rates in the sample matrix depicted in Exhibit 7.11 would be on accounts in cells 1, 2, and possibly 3, depending on the firm's abilities to overcome its competitive disadvantages. The lowest planned call rates would be on accounts in cell 4.

Determining call frequencies account by account

Accounts do not have to be divided into classes and call frequencies set at the same level for all accounts in the class. Rather, the firm might want to determine the workload in each tentative territory on an account-by-account basis. There are several ways of doing this. The firm can rate each account on each factor deemed critical to the success of the sales call effort and then develop a sales effort allocation index for each account.[18] The sales effort allocation index is

EXHIBIT 7 • 11 *Account Planning Matrix*

		Strong — Competitive Strength — Weak
Account Potential — High	**Opportunity** Account offers good opportunity. It has high potential and sales organization has a differential advantage in serving it. **Strategy** Commit high levels of sales resources to take advantage of the opportunity.	**Opportunity** Account may represent a good opportunity. Sales organization needs to overcome its competitive disadvantage and strengthen its position to capitalize on the opportunity. **Strategy** Either direct a high level of sales resources to improve position and to take advantage of the opportunity or shift resources to other accounts.
Account Potential — Low	**Opportunity** Account offers stable opportunity since sales organization has differential advantage in serving it. **Strategy** Allocate moderate level of sales resources to maintain current advantage.	**Opportunity** Account offers little opportunity. Its potential is small and the sales organization is at a competitive disadvantage in serving it. **Strategy** Devote minimal level of resources to the account or consider abandoning the account altogether.

Source: Adapted from Raymond LaForge and David W. Cravens, "Steps in Selling Effort Deployment," *Industrial Marketing Management* 11 (1982), pp. 183–94; Renato Fiocca, "Account Portfolio Analysis for Strategy Development," *Industrial Marketing Management* 11 (1982), pp. 53–62; and Raymond W. LaForge, David W. Cravens, and Clifford E. Young, "Improving Salesforce Productivity," *Business Horizons* 28 (September–October 1985), pp. 50–51.

formed by multiplying each rating score by its factor importance weight, summing over all factors, and then dividing by the sum of the importance weights. The resulting sales effort allocation index reflects the relative amount of sales call effort that should be allocated to the account in comparison to other accounts—the larger the index, the greater the number of planned calls on the account.

E X H I B I T   7 • 1 2 *Hypothetical Sales Response Function*

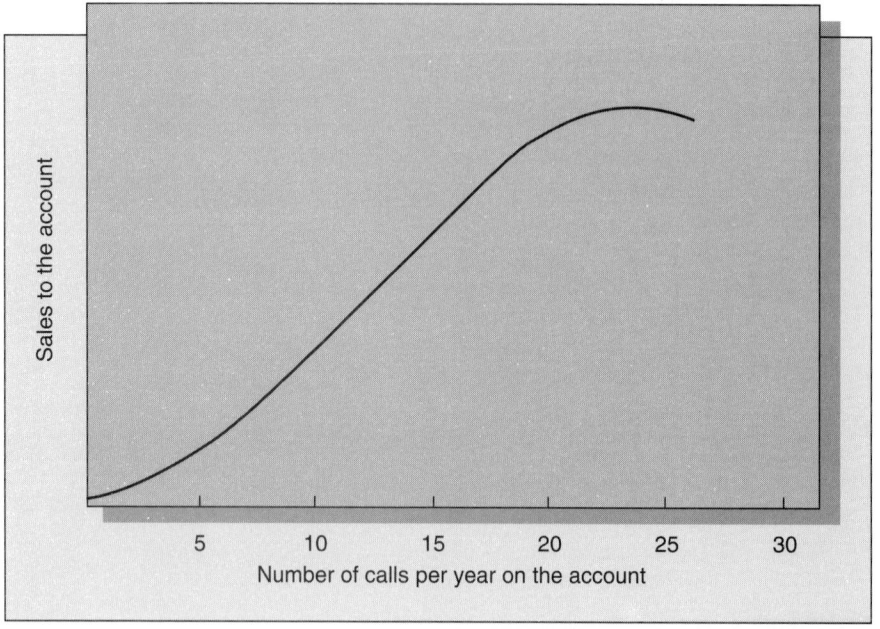

Still another scheme is to estimate the likely sales to be realized from each account as a function of the number of calls on the account. The actual sales response function is the key in determining the optimal number of sales calls to be made on any account and the workload in each tentative territory. A typical sales response function is shown in Exhibit 7.12. The figure shows that there are first increasing, then diminishing, and finally decreasing returns to the number of sales calls. The increasing returns are realized at low levels of sales force effort. The account, never having been contacted previously or only on rare occasions, responds positively and places orders with the salesperson as the number of salesperson calls increases. At first, the rise in sales is swift but then begins to flatten as the number of sales calls is increased. Decreasing returns set in when the number of calls becomes excessive, and the salesperson becomes a nuisance to the account. In the hypothetical example in Exhibit 7.12, this occurs when the salesperson calls on the account more than twice a month. The costs associated with calling on the account are directly proportional to the number of calls. The firm must balance sales/cost considerations to determine the optimal call level on each account taking into consideration the sales response functions of all the accounts in the territory.

There are two popular ways of estimating the function relating sales to the number of calls on an account—empirical-based methods and judgment-based methods.[19] The former use regression analysis to estimate the function relating historical sales in each territory to an a priori set of predictors likely to affect sales, including the number of calls. The function so determined represents the line of average sales relationship across all planning and control units.[20]

The judgment-based approaches require that someone in the sales organization, typically the salesperson serving the account but sometimes the sales manager, estimate the sales–sales call function so that the optimal number of calls to be made on each account can be determined. One of the original, but still popular, judgment-based approaches relies on the interactive computer program CALLPLAN, in which the response function for each account is generated from the salesperson's own inputs.[21] The program operates in the following way. The salesperson assigned to the territory is asked the sales that will result from each current customer and prospect in the following situations:

- No calls are made.
- One half the present calls are made.
- The present level of calls is continued.
- 50 percent more calls are scheduled.
- A saturation level of calls is made.

The salesperson is also asked the probabilities that prospects will be converted into customers with different call frequencies. CALLPLAN then fits curves to these data points and prints out the expected sales for all feasible call frequencies and the optimal number of calls and the length of each call to be made on each client and prospect during an average effort period. In one experiment designed to test CALLPLAN, 20 representatives from United Airlines were matched and then one from each pair was randomly assigned to one of two groups. The 10 control group salespeople were asked to manually estimate their optimal call frequency on each account. The 10 experimental group salespeople were asked their inputs via the CALLPLAN interactive system, and their optimal call levels were determined by the program. Both groups then called on their accounts at these predetermined levels during the experiment. "After six months, the average CALLPLAN salesperson had sales 8.1 percent higher than his matched counterpart."[22] Syntex Laboratories, in the opening scenario, used CALLPLAN to justify increasing its sales force. A modified version of CALLPLAN, which considers the probability that a principal would pull the account from a sales agent if no effort were directed toward its products, has been used to estimate how much selling effort should be allocated to various principals by independent sales agencies.[23] CALLPLAN seems best suited to repetitive selling situations where the amount of time spent with an account is an important factor in the amount of sales generated.

Determine total workload

When the account analysis is complete, a workload analysis can be performed for each territory. The procedure parallels that discussed previously for determining the size of the sales force using the workload method. The total amount of face-to-face contact is computed by multiplying the frequency with which each type of account should be called on by the number of such accounts. The products are then summed. This figure is combined with estimates of the nonselling and travel time necessary to cover the territory to determine the total amount of work involved in covering that territory.[24] A similar set of calculations is made for each tentative territory.

5. Adjust Tentative Territories

Step 5 in territory planning adjusts the boundaries of the tentative territories established in Step 3 to compensate for the differences in workload found in Step 4. It is likely, for example, that Washington, Oregon, Montana, Idaho, Wyoming, and Utah together might contain the same sales potential as Ohio. Since considerably less travel time would be necessary to cover the Ohio territory, the workload in the two territories would be far from equal and adjustments will need to be made.

While attempting to balance potentials and workloads across territories, the analyst must keep in mind that the sale potential per account is not fixed. It is likely to vary with the number of calls made. While computer call allocation models like CALLPLAN consider this, it is not taken into account when, for example, the firm uses the ABC Rule of Account Classification and relies exclusively on historic sales when making account classifications. Clearly there is reciprocal causation between account attractiveness and account effort.

Account attractiveness affects how hard the account should be worked. At the same time, the number of calls and length of the calls affect the sales likely to be realized from the account. Yet, this reciprocal causation is only implicitly recognized in some schemes used to determine workloads for territories. The firm needs a mechanism for balancing potentials and workloads when adjusting the initial territories if it is not using a computer model.

There are several ways to accomplish this balance. One way is to formally estimate the function that relates sales in a territory to the potential and workload in the territory, using regression-based or judgment-based methods discussed previously. An alternative is to use the subjective judgment of executives to decide on all changes in call frequency to achieve some specific objective. For example, a midwestern wholesaler of farm machinery used this approach: It classified all accounts into three categories (A, B, and C) according to potential. It then changed the frequency with which salespeople called on farm equipment dealers and almost doubled sales per territory within three years.[25] Another subjective method restructures the tentative territories so that each territory involves relatively equal amounts of work, since the tentative areas already reflect equal amounts of potential, and to continue adjusting by trial and error until achieving the proper balance.

Whether an analytical, objective-and-task, or trial-and-error approach is taken, some realignment of the tentative territories should be expected, and those involved should allow for this when planning territories. Because of the many ways sales territories can be altered, firms increasingly are using computers to investigate potential realignments. For example, Exhibit 7.13 describes the experience of Perdue Frederick Company in using computer software, specifically Territory Planner Plus, to align territories.

Assign Salespeople to Territories

After territory boundaries are established, the analyst can determine which salesperson should be assigned to which territory. Up to now, it has generally been assumed there are no differences in abilities among salespersons or in the effectiveness of different salespeople with different accounts or different products.[26] Such differences do arise, however. All salespeople do not have the same ability, nor are they equally effective with the same customers or products. At this stage in territory planning, the analyst should consider such differences and should attempt to assign each salesperson to the territory where his or her relative contribution to profit is the highest.

Unfortunately, the ideal cannot always be met. It would be too disruptive to an established sales force with established sales territories to change practically all account coverage. As Thorny Issue 7.3 indicates, changing territory assignments can upset salespeople. If the firm is operating without assigned sales territories, then the realignment might be closer to the ideal. The firm with established territories typically must be content to change assignments on a more limited basis.

One way of allowing for differences in general ability among salespeople is by converting each representative's ability to index form. The best salespersons may be rated 1.0, for example, and all other sales people rated relative to them. One such relative scheme is to consider that a salesperson with a rating of 0.8 could secure 80 percent of the business in the territory that a representative with a rating of 1.0 could obtain. One can then systematically vary the assignments of salespeople to territories to determine which assignment maximizes the company's return.

The actual assignment of salespeople to sales territories also incorporates personal considerations. The firm may not want to change salesperson call assignments for particular accounts because of the potential for lost business. It may not want to reduce sales force size even if the analysis suggests it should because of morale problems associated with downsizing. Even increasing sales force size can be disruptive. More salespeople mean more sales territories, which means redrawing existing boundaries. In sum, sales managers will want to reflect people considerations when they redraw territory boundaries. They will want to minimize disruptions to existing personal relationships between salespeople and customers.

E X H I B I T   7 • 1 3 *Using Computer Software to Realign Sales Territories*

Problems with Manual System

Divvying up sales territories is a monumental, headache-filled job for most companies.

Marketers at Perdue Frederick Co., a pharmaceutical maker in Norwalk, Connecticut, spent up to a day defining the boundaries for a single territory. "We used to sit down with our district managers for days and do a ton of manual calculations to put together our territories," says Stephanie Thompson, manager of marketing programs.

Even after all that work, Perdue Frederick's marketers weren't absolutely sure a revamped territory's sales potential balanced with that of other regions. Rapid sales growth between 1985 and 1987, when the company added more than 100 salespeople, only made the process more unmanageable.

"It was getting to be so much of a monster," especially after the company realigned 40 territories in 1987, says James Shriver, executive director of sales.

Perdue Frederick now employs about 240 salespeople. The privately held company had sales of more than $100 million in 1988, according to its figures.

Deciding that the firm could no longer manage its sales territories manually, Perdue Frederick turned to a microcomputer software package.

Benefits of Computer System

The mapping software helped Perdue Frederick complete a major territory realignment more easily in late 1988, when it added 60 territories. And it allows Ms. Thompson, who operates the system, to reconfigure regions in just a half day, instead of the days she previously needed.

But one of the software's biggest benefits is Perdue Frederick's improved ability to determine whether a salesperson can handle a given territory, and whether a rep is calling on all potential physician customers in an area.

"We wanted to give all our salespeople ample and fair opportunities for sales," Ms. Thompson says. When the company revamped its ZIP code-based territories manually, "it was difficult to visualize" whether it was accomplishing that goal.

For example, the old, manual system might not have revealed that a salesperson didn't call on a prospect physician because the doctor was in an isolated, mountainous area. The newer computer-generated maps let managers see which routes salespeople drive to their sales calls—and then make adjustments when drawing up territories.

The territory planning software also links spreadsheet and mapping functions so marketers can examine both sets of data. When a user changes a map, corresponding changes take place in the spreadsheet, and vice versa.

Role of Judgment

Mr. Shriver says, "The software is a wonderful thing, but nothing takes the place of a district manager's knowledge."

For example, Perdue Frederick made some adjustments so that salespeople with long-established customer relationships would retain that business. The company also reworked the quarterly bonus plans for salespeople who lost business after the realignment.

The new plan took effect in October 1988, with more changes occurring in 1989. Changes go more smoothly, Ms. Thompson says, because the software makes it easy to enter ZIP code changes that shift customer histories and potential prospects from one territory to another. Other data that Perdue Frederick enters into the system, such as the sales revenue and the number of sales calls, shift automatically when the company reassigns ZIP codes.

Although glitches cropped up, Ms. Thompson believes the computerized system works better than the old manual method. Salespeople can see that new assignments are fair, she says, because the company consistently uses objective criteria to change a territory. It no longer makes the arbitrary decisions it sometimes did about who should get certain physicians.

Using the System with Salespeople

It's too early to say whether the new territories will directly contribute to additional sales growth, Ms. Thompson says. Developing a relationship with physicians so they'll readily purchase or prescribe the company's products can take a salesperson a long time. However, Ms. Thompson points out that the software-designed territories are more manageable, so that salespeople can spend more time building those relationships.

All salespeople receive maps of their territories and a list of physicians in those areas. That lets them see where they'll make calls and what the most effective routes are—something they couldn't do with a list of ZIP codes.

Perdue Frederick's sales and marketing managers have gained other benefits from the new system.

For example, managers can enter call reporting data into the software's spreadsheet and map out where a salesperson spends time.

"It's a supportive thing," Mr. Shriver says. "We can say, 'Look at this. You're not taking advantage of this potential,' " he says. Or the company's managers can

(cont'd)

Exhibit 1

District 23 before realignment. Colors represent the starting territory assignments (by 5-digit Zip code). Gray areas are those not currently assigned to any territory. Note the irregular shapes of the territories.

Exhibit 2

The spreadsheet displays totals for current sales, total potential, and target sales calls. In this case, a measure of market potential will be used as the primary variable selected to initially balance the territories. Note the imbalance in territory market potential. For example, Territory #9 has 84% more potential than average. Through realignment imbalances will be reduced.

Exhibit 3

After identifying market potential by Zip code and "asking" the software to reassign Zip codes to different territories, the spreadsheet reflects the changes. The potential in Territory #9 has been reduced significantly from 84% above average to 14% above average.

Exhibit 4

All territories are now balanced to within a few percentage points of average based on potential. Next, additional changes to the territory design will be implemented in an attempt to balance sales and target calls.

Exhibit 5

The final territory assignments for District 23. All territories are closely balanced, unassigned areas are assigned and accessibility by the sales representatives is optimal.

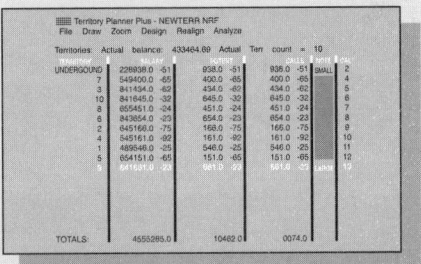

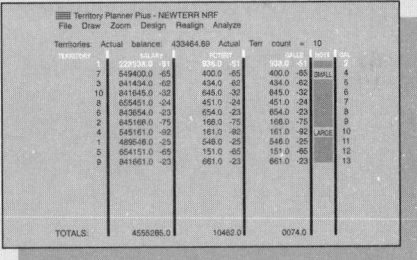

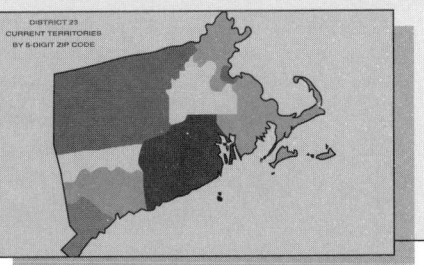

(cont'd)

E X H I B I T   7 • 13   *Concluded*

---

overlay highway maps to determine whether a salesperson lives close to customers and prospects.

In the future, Ms. Thompson adds, Perdue Frederick would like to use Territory Planner Plus to conduct more sophisticated analyses. For example, the company might load in data on retail outlets to determine where retail sales are concentrated. In addition to helping the company devise its retail strategy, that information also would help determine whether a salesperson should receive credit for prescribed products bought outside a physician customers's ZIP code.

Source: Tom Eisenhart, "Drawing a Map to Better Sales," *Business Marketing* 75 (January 1990), pp. 59–61.

S UMMARY

This chapter reviewed the important sales management planning decisions involving the number of sales territories needed and the process that can be used to decide on the design of each. A sales territory represents a group of present and potential customers assigned to a salesperson, branch, dealer, or distributor for a given time. Although territories are often defined by their geographic boundaries, the key distinguishing component is customers. Good territory design can positively influence sales force morale and the firm's ability to serve the market and to evaluate the selling effort, whereas poorly designed territories can have the opposite effect.

The administrative decisions regarding the number of sales territories or the size of the sales force, the design of the individual territories themselves, and the allocation of the total selling effort to accounts are closely intertwined. For purposes of understanding though, it is useful to treat the issues of sales force size before addressing the other issues.

The three primary methods for determining how many territories there should be are the breakdown, workload, and incremental methods. The breakdown method relies on an estimate of what an average salesperson could be expected to sell; the number of salespeople required is then determined by dividing forecasted sales by this average. The workload method rests on the premise that all sales personnel should shoulder an equal amount of work. Management estimates the total amount of work required to serve the market, taking into account the number of customers, how often each should be called on, and for how long. This estimate is then divided by the amount of work an individual salesperson should be able to handle to determine the total number of salespeople required. The basic premise underlying the incremental method of determining the sales force size is that sales representatives should

Thorny Issues in Sales Management 7 ● 3

REDESIGNING SALES TERRITORIES

Carol was furious! She had just come out of a meeting with her sales manager where she had been told her territory size was being reduced. The company believed assigning two people to the territory would increase its penetration and sales. Her sales manager had not only outlined the benefits to the company from the realignment, but he also tried to sell her on the personal benefits she stood to obtain from the smaller territory. She would have to travel less, she would spend very few nights away from home, she could get to know her accounts better because she would have fewer of them and could consequently serve them better, and so on.

For every advantage the sales manager tried to advance, she had a counterargument. And she felt with good reason! The territory was very special to her. It had been her first assignment with the company. The territory was one of the company's three worst when it had been given to her. Through long hours and hard work, careful planning, and going the extra mile for customers, she had developed the territory into one of the company's best. And now the company was going to "reward her" for her efforts by dividing the territory. Her assignment to the western half would give her the two largest metropolitan areas in the territory. While that would cut her travel time, it would also cut her income! Not only would she lose some of her most productive accounts—accounts she had spent years nurturing and developing—but she also would no longer have the same amount of travel time between calls to plan her next sales presentation and general strategies. She would miss that almost as much as the income.

Do you

Approve	_____
Somewhat approve	_____
Somewhat disapprove	_____
Disapprove	_____

of the company's decision to divide Carol's territory?

be added so long as the incremental profit produced by their addition exceeds the incremental cost. While conceptually correct, this is the most difficult method to implement.

Once the number of territories is determined, the sales manager can design the individual territories. The general process he or she might be expected to follow is (1) select the basic control unit, (2) estimate market potential in each control unit, (3) combine control units into tentative territories, (4) perform a workload analysis for each territory, (5) adjust tentative territories to allow for sales potential and coverage difficulty differences, and (6) assign salespeople to territories.

Discussion
Questions

1. Most sales managers hesitate to modify sales territories unless supported by compelling reasons. Likewise, sales managers are reluctant to make major changes in the sales compensation package. On the other hand, reassigning salespeople from one territory to another is fairly common and often reflects a form of promotion. One expert contends that if a company's sales force knows the territory too well, then it's time to reassign territories. Why would a company reassign all or most of the territories? What are the advantages/disadvantages of this approach?

2. What are the advantages and disadvantages of the workload approach to determining sales force size? How would you change the technique to overcome the disadvantages? For example, the workload method does not consider the time spent calling on prospective customers. Could this limitation be incorporated into the method?

3. Many sales managers dislike changing either territories or compensation plans unless it is absolutely necessary. Why is this so? What evidence does a sales manager need to determine if a territory change is needed?

4. Some companies have developed computer models, such as CALLPLAN, for determining the call patterns to be used by their sales personnel. Determining call patterns (routing plans) is very much like deciding how you would visit the 10 largest cities in your state while traveling the least amount of miles or time. In what situations would computer-determined call patterns be appropriate? Have you ever had a job where routing plans were applicable?

5. Referring to the last question, identify the 10 largest cities in your state and develop a routing plan that visits all cities while traveling the least number of miles. Do time of day for traveling or customer preferences affect your routing plan?

6. You have been hired as a sales representative by Interconics, Inc., and assigned to the Ohio territory. The customers are located in the following cities: Columbus, Newark, Springfield, Marion, Findlay, Toledo, Mansfield, Cleveland, Akron, Youngstown, and Warren. Prepare a routing plan that will minimize the number of driving miles. One possible approach is described in John P. Norback and Robert F. Love, "Geometric Approaches to Solving the Traveling Salesman Problem," *Management Science* 23 (July 1977), pp. 1,208–33.

7. The ABS Company uses 25 manufacturers' agents. The sales manager believes circumstances are right for ABS to have its own company sales force. Since 25 manufacturers' agents have met ABS's sales goals, the sales manager thinks ABS needs to hire 25 sales reps. Do you agree?

8. The John Deere Company is a multiproduct manufacturer of farm implements, machinery, snowmobiles, and home lawn and garden machinery. What problems are the Deere Company likely to experience in establishing sales territories? Should it establish the same territories for each product line?

9. The marketing manager of JHP, Incorporated, took issue with the suggestions made by JHP's sales manager, who argued that JHP's sales force was inadequate. The sales manager noted that a successful competitor recently increased its sales force by 25 percent; JHP to stay competitive must follow suit. The marketing manager contended that how the sales force was allocated across products and territories is more critical than size of the sales force. Which position is correct?

10. The sales manager of Coastal Plastics, located in Norfolk, Virginia, had just completed an extensive territory revision. The process took a relatively short time, a result of a new computer allocation procedure used for the first time. The sales manager's feeling of relief was short lived when one of Coastal Plastic's district managers noted that three of her sales representatives would average $6,500 less in total compensation under the new allocation. The sales manager's pleas that the sales reps could still make their previous compensation levels by working harder failed to convince the district manager. What should be done to solve this problem?

Endnotes

[1]Betsy D. Gelb and Basckeer M. Khumawala, "Reconfiguration of an Insurance Company's Sales Regions," *Interfaces* 14 (November–December 1984), pp. 87–94.

[2]Karsten Hellebust, "Bindicator Finds a Fair Measure for Sales Territory Performance," *Sales & Marketing Management* 135 (November 11, 1985), pp. 45–48.

[3]The average number of calls per day is somewhat lower for salespeople selling industrial goods than it is for salespeople selling consumer goods or services, where the averages are 4.5 and 6 calls per day respectively. See "1991 Sales Manager Budget Planning," *Sales & Marketing Management* 143 (June 17, 1991), p. 6.

[4]This percentage has remained relatively constant over time. See *Allocating Field Sales Resources, Experiences in Marketing Management* (New York: National Industrial Conference Board, 1970), p. 92; and Richard Clucas, "Powering Up Your Sales Force," *Personal Computing* 8 (May 1984), pp. 98–99, 101, 103, 105. The insurance industry estimates the average salesperson is actually selling only 1 1/2 hours a day; the rest of the time is spent in preparation and travel. See "Training Agency Salespeople #2: How to Make Every Sales Minute Count," *Agency Sales Magazine* 19 (May 1989), pp. 42–45.

[5]Raymond W. LaForge, David W. Cravens, and Clifford E. Young, "Improving Salesforce Productivity," *Business Horizons* 28 (September–October 1985), p. 50. For an empirical examination of the relationship between use of time and performance, see William A. Weeks and Lynn R. Kahle, "Salespeople's Time Use and Performance," *Journal of Personal Selling and Sales Management* 8 (August 1988), pp. 9–20.

[6]Several of the computer models that try to treat simultaneously the complex interactions that arise between the decisions of sales force and sales design incorporate other variables as well, such as the allocation of selling effort to customers or products. See, for example, Charles A. Beswick and David W. Cravens, "A Multistage Decision Model for Salesforce Management," *Journal of Marketing Research* 14 (May 1977), pp. 135–44; and Leonard M. Lodish, "A User-Oriented Model for Sales Force Size, Product and Market Allocation Decisions," *Journal of Marketing* 44 (Summer 1980), pp. 70–78. For an overview of the thrust of the various sales territory computer decision models, see David W. Cravens, "Salesforce Decision Models: A Comparative Assessment," in *Sales Management: New Developments from Behavioral and Decision Model Research,* ed. Richard P. Bagozzi (Cambridge, Mass.: Marketing Science Institute, 1979), pp. 310–24; and Raymond W. LaForge, David W. Cravens, and Clifford E. Young, "Using Contingency Analysis to Select Selling Effort Allocation Methods," *Journal of Personal Selling and Sales Management* 6 (August 1986), pp. 19–28.

[7]For use of industry productivity estimates, including sources of data for calculating them, for determining sales force size, see Thayer C. Taylor, "Is Your Sales Force Pulling Its Weight?" *Sales & Marketing Management* 135 (August 12, 1985), pp. 58–59.

[8]The method was first proposed by Walter J. Talley, Jr., "How to Design Sales Territories," *Journal of Marketing* 25 (January 1961), pp. 7–13. See also Richard R. Still, Edward W. Cundiff, and Norman A. P. Govoni, *Sales Management: Decisions, Policies, and Cases,*

4th ed. (Englewood Cliffs, N.J.: Prentice Hall 1981), pp. 99–101.

[9]Porter Henry, "The Important Few—The Unimportant Many," *1980 Portfolio of Sales and Marketing Plans* (New York: Sales and Marketing Management, 1980), pp. 34–37.

[10]For these examples, see Jeffrey H. Wecker, "An Approach to Higher Profits with Reduced Selling Costs," *Industrial Marketing* 62 (December 1977), pp. 57–58; Jack Pangrazio, "How to Sell through Independent Distributors . . . and Improve Channel Strategy," *Business Marketing* 69 (September 1984), pp. 118, 120, 122, 124, 126; Philip Maker, "Marketers Find New Muscle in Decision Modeling," *Industrial Marketing* 67 (July 1982), pp. 41–47; Barton A. Weitz, Stephen B. Castleberry, and John F. Tanner, *Selling: Building Partnerships* (Homewood, Ill. Richard D. Irwin Inc., 1992), pp. 46–49. For a general discussion on how to identify attractive accounts, see John Morton, "How to Spot the Really Important Prospects," *Business Marketing* 75 (January 1990), pp. 62–67.

[11]It is possible to calculate the net present value of an account by considering these and other factors. See Donald L. Brady, "Determining the Value of an Industrial Prospect: A Prospect Preference Index Model," *Journal of Personal Selling and Sales Management* 7 (August 1987), pp. 27–32.

[12]The method was first proposed by Semlow, although Weinberg and Lucas subsequently demonstrated there was a flaw in Semlow's procedure for operationalizing the notion. See Walter J. Semlow, "How Many Salesmen Do You Need," *Harvard Business Review* 37 (May–June 1959), pp. 126–32; Charles B. Weinberg and Henry C. Lucas, Jr., "Semlow's Results Are Based on a Spurious Relationship," *Journal of Marketing* 41 (April 1977), pp. 146–47.

[13]Zarrell Lambert and Fred W. Kniffen, "Response Functions and Their Applications in Sales Force Management," *Southern Journal of Business* 5 (January 1970), pp. 1–9.

[14]The Office of Management and Budget adopted the new designation and new standards for defining MSAs in 1980 although the changes did not go into effect until June 30, 1983. See "OMB Revises Metropolitan Statistical Area Definitions," *Data User News* 18 (April 1983), p. 3. While the definition of SMSAs and MSAs was determined strictly on the basis of statistical data through the early 1980s, political considerations now seem to play a role. See Eugene Carlson, "What's a Metropolitan Area? Whatever Congress Says It Is," *The Wall Street Journal,* September 22, 1987, p. 37. For discussion of the advantages that can accrue from MSA status, see David Shribman, "Census '90 Indicates a New Megalopolis," *The Wall Street Journal,* February 6, 1991, pp. B1, B6.

[15]"1990 Survey of Buying Power," *Sales & Marketing Management* 142 (August 13, 1990), pp. B7–B40.

[16]A. Parasuraman, "An Approach for Allocating Sales Call Effort," *Industrial Marketing Management* 11 (1982), pp. 75–79; Renato Fiocca, "Account Portfolio Analysis for Strategy Development," *Industrial Marketing Management* 11 (1982), pp. 53–62. For an empirical assessment of the factors that affect the call frequency of a sample of salespeople representing 34 different firms, see Rosann L. Spiro and William D. Perreault, Jr., "Factors Influencing Sales Call Frequency of Industrial Salespersons," *Journal of Business Research* 6 (January 1978), pp. 1–15.

[17]Fiocca, "Account Portfolio Analysis." La Forge and Cravens argue similarly that it is useful to classify all PCUs (planning and control units, in this case, accounts) according to two criteria: (1) PCU opportunity reflecting the potential available to all firms from the PCU, and (2) sales organization strength or the ability of the sales organization to take advantage of the opportunity. See Raymond La Forge and David W. Cravens, "Steps in Selling Effort Deployment," *Industrial Marketing Management* 11 (1982), pp. 183–94; or David W. Cravens and Raymond W. LaForge, "Salesforce Deployment Analysis," *Industrial Marketing Management* 12 (July 1983), pp. 179–92. Dubinsky and Ingram suggest the cells of the matrix should be defined using the criteria present profit (high/low) and profit potential (low/high). See Alan J. Dubinsky and Thomas N. Ingram, "A Portfolio Approach to Account Profitability," *Industrial Marketing Management* 13 (February 1984), pp. 33–41.

[18]Parasuraman, "An Approach for Allocating."

[19]The empirical evidence suggests the two approaches yield similar guidelines regarding the amount of effort that should be allocated to accounts. See Raymond W.

La Forge and David W. Cravens, "Empirical and Judgment-Based Sales-Force Decision Models: A Comparative Assessment," *Decision Sciences* 16 (Spring 1985), pp. 177–95.

[20]The evidence seems to suggest these functions are relatively stable over time. See Adrian B. Ryans and Charles B. Weinberg, "Territory Sales Response Models: Stability over Time," *Journal of Marketing Research* 24 (May 1987), pp. 229–33.

[21]Leonard M. Lodish, "CALLPLAN: An Interactive Salesman's Call Planning System," *Management Science* 18 (December 1971), pp. 25–40. For a general discussion regarding the estimation and use of judgment-based marketing decision models, see Dipankar Chakravarti, Andrew Mitchell, and Richard Staelin, "Judgment-Based Marketing Decision Models: Problems and Possible Solutions," *Journal of Marketing* 45 (Fall 1981), pp. 13–23.

[22]William K. Fudge and Leonard M. Lodish, "Evaluation of the Effectiveness of a Model Based Salesman's Planning System by Field Experimentation," *Interfaces* 8 (November 1977), p. 104.

[23]See Erin Anderson, Leonard M. Lodish, and Barton A. Weitz, "Resource Allocation Behavior in Conventional Channels," *Journal of Marketing Research* 24 (February 1987), pp. 85–97.

[24]Some writers suggest that the travel time involved in servicing each account should be estimated from the location of the account and its proximity to other accounts. See Robert F. Vizza and Thomas E. Chambers, *Time and Territorial Management for Salesmen* (New York: The Sales Executives Club, 1971), pp. 11–15, for the details as to how such an analysis would be conducted. See Also Robert Vizza, "Managing Time and Territories for Maximum Sales Success," *Journal of Business Research* 1 (March 1972), pp. 18–23. There are computer programs that formally incorporate the time it takes to service each account by considering distances as well as natural obstacles like mountains and rivers. See Andres Zoltners and Prabhakant Sinha, "Sales Territory Alignment: A Review and Model," *Management Science* 29 (November 1983), pp. 1,237–56; Probha Sinha and Andres Zoltners, "Matching Manpower and Markets," *Business Marketing* 73 (September 1988), pp. 95–98; Leon A. Wortman, "STARmanager Makes Big Promises: Does It Deliver?" *Business Marketing* 76 (April 1991), p. 59.

[25]William P. Hall, "Improving Sales Force Productivity," *Business Horizons* 18 (August 1975), pp. 32–42.

[26]Some of the computer call allocation models allow for product and customer mix considerations. They determine the optimal number of sales territories, which salespeople should cover, which customers, and which products salespeople should emphasize, in addition to determining how often and for how long each account should be called on. For a review of the models as to their basic differences, see David W. Cravens, "Sales Force Decision Models: A Comparative Assessment," in *Sales Management: New Developments from Behavioral Decision Model Research,* ed. Richard Bagozzi (Cambridge, Mass.: Marketing Science Institute, 1979), pp. 310–24; and R. S. Howick and M. Pidd, "Sales Force Deployment Models," *European Journal of Operational Research* 48 (October 1990), pp. 295–310.

Suggested Readings

La Forge, Raymond W., and David W. Cravens, "Empirical and Judgment-Based Sales Force Decision Models: A Comparative Analysis." *Decision Sciences* 16 (Spring 1985), pp. 177–95.

La Forge, Raymond W., David W. Cravens, and Clifford E. Young. "Improving Salesforce Productivity." *Business Horizons* 28 (September–October 1985), pp. 50–59.

La Forge, Raymond W., David W. Cravens, and Clifford E. Young. "Using Contingency Analysis to Select Selling Effort Allocation Methods." *Journal of Personal Selling and Sales Management* 6 (August 1986), pp. 19–28.

Sales Quotas

AMBITIOUS SALES GOALS CAUSE TROUBLE AT DUN & BRADSTREET

The decision made Dun & Bradstreet Corp. an information giant—and may haunt it for years. In 1975, Richard F. Schmidt, a former McKinsey & Co. consultant whom D&B had hired as a top executive, was assigned to analyze D&B's strategy. After a year, Schmidt devised a plan. He believed D&B could profit immensely from new products developed by repackaging the vast credit records it maintained on American businesses. Harrington Drake, D&B's chief executive at the time, agreed. He ordered that all information sprinkled throughout D&B be rounded up and stored in a central computer—the key to the new approach.

The plan worked. Spurred by the credit unit, D&B's overall sales doubled by 1980, to $1.4 billion. Sales have climbed about 15 percent a year since. But the strategy also put unrelenting pressure on the credit unit, creating distortions in a 148-year-old culture that traced its roots to such former employees as Abraham Lincoln. "We became a cesspool," says a 30-year D&B West Coast salesman.

Tarnished Image

The new strategy set off a chain of events that could hurt D&B well into the 1990s. About three dozen lawsuits, plus articles in *The Wall Street Journal,* have alleged that D&B salespeople cheated customers and misled them into buying more reports and services than they needed. Without admitting guilt, the company has quietly settled many of these suits out of court and has made a number of other changes in the way it conducts its business.

Impact of Sales Goals

In the late 1970s, D&B's management had begun to pressure the credit division for 15 percent annual gains. "We were told that was a key to D&B's expansion plans," says a former West Coast regional vice president.

The credit division responded. First, it changed the way it billed. For decades, customers had paid up front each year for reports they predicted they would need. In 1977, D&B switched to selling voucher-like units—like carnival tickets for rides. One unit bought a basic report. Two bought the report delivered via computer. A more thorough analysis could run nine units. The system wasn't devious initially, says Harold T. Redding, former senior vice president and still a D&B consultant. It was "the most efficient way to price" D&B's varied line.

But it was also the most confusing. Before long, D&B had more than 200 services, each with a different price. Customers that underestimated the number of units they would need were charged big premiums to buy more in midcontract. And, incredibly, D&B never told customers how many units they had left. It let a management obsessed with growth "make sure that revenue goals were met," says a former D&B manager.

Salespeople had to book 18 percent more revenues each year for commissions to kick in—and those were 60 percent of pay. "The unit system and the pressure on salespeople were a one-two punch intended to increase sales, not cheat customers," says a former D&B vice president. "But the feeling was, if the salesman got a little aggressive and the customer suffered, so what?"

So salespeople turned up the heat. They sold subscribers expensive supplemental units they didn't need. They forged customers' signatures on rewritten, higher priced contracts and even charged customers for thousands of credit reports without authorization. D&B critics say such tactics cost customers tens of millions of dollars. Salespeople who objected were "told to mind their own business," says a 30-year D&B veteran in the Midwest.

Corrective Actions

Besides paying back customers, D&B is easing the pressure on salespeople by making their compensation depend less on commissions. It has developed a simpler pricing system and has set up hot lines for customers. It has rewritten job descriptions so that salespeople spend more time advising customers than selling. And now, D&B employees take classes in ethics. Moreover, sales quotas are gone. Commissions are based on how much customers use and, uniquely, on the results of a new market research program that measures customer satisfaction.

Source: Jeffrey Rothfeder and Stephen Phillips, "Damage Control at Dun & Bradstreet," *Business Week,* November 27, 1989, pp. 187–90. Ambitious quotas were also responsible for the preparation of sloppy and inaccurate credit reports, one of the mainstays of D&B's operations, during this period. See Johnnie L. Roberts, "Dun's Credit Reports, Vital Tool of Business Can Be Off the Mark," *The Wall Street Journal,* October 5, 1989, pp. A1, A10.

The last major element in sales management planning is establishing goals for each sales representative. As the introductory scenario suggests, goals can have a profound impact on what salespeople do and how they do it. The goals assigned to salespeople are called **quotas.** Quotas are one of the most valuable devices sales managers have for planning the field selling effort, and they are indispensable for evaluating the effectiveness of that effort. Quotas help managers plan the amount of sales and profit that will be available at the end of the planning period. They also help managers better anticipate the activities of the sales team.

As defined previously, a sales quota is a sales goal assigned to a marketing unit for use in managing sales efforts. The marketing unit in question might be an individual sales representative, a sales territory, a branch office, a region, a dealer or distributor, or a district, to name a few. Each salesperson in each sales territory might be assigned a sales volume goal for the next year, for example. This quota is not the sales forecast or the estimate of potential for the territory. While it stems from potential, it is typically less than potential.

Sales potential reflects what the company could sell in the territory under ideal conditions. Yet conditions are rarely ideal. The territories may not have been designed optimally, or a firm may not be able to assign the best person for a particular territory to that territory because the individual is needed elsewhere. Differences in salesperson characteristics such as age, experience, energy, initiative, and physical condition should and do make a difference in the quotas assigned to the territory.

Nor is the sales quota equal to the sales forecast for the territory. The sales forecast is the best estimate of what the company can sell with a particular planned level of marketing effort. It is an aggregate estimate that may or may not be broken down by product line, customer, or territory. The ideal forecast is one that is perfectly accurate because that facilitates planning. Thus, while a firm would not want to reward salespeople for exceeding their forecasts, it would want to reward them for exceeding their quotas.

Quotas are management devices and not planning tools. They are typically used to motivate salespeople, and as such must be reasonable. Volume quotas are typically set to a level that is less than the sales potential in the territory and equal to or slightly above the sales forecast for the territory, although they also can be set less than the sales forecast if conditions warrant.

Sales quotas apply to specific periods and may be expressed in dollars or physical units. Thus, management can specify quarterly, annual, and longer-term quotas for each of the company's field representatives in both dollars and physical units. It might even specify these goals for individual products and customers. The product quotas can be varied systematically to reflect the profitability of different items in the line, and customer quotas can be varied to reflect the relative desirability of serving particular accounts.

The full set of quota assignments is called the quota plan.[1] The full specification of the quota plan requires decisions about the types of quotas that will be used, the relative importance of each, and the target levels for each salesperson or other marketing unit.

PURPOSES OF QUOTAS

Quotas facilitate the planning and control of the field selling effort in a number of ways. One useful way of viewing the benefits is by assessing their contribution in (1) providing incentives for sales representatives, (2) evaluating salespeople's performance, and (3) controlling salespeople's efforts.

Provide Incentives for Salespeople

Quotas serve as incentives for sales in several ways. At an elementary level, they are an objective to be secured, a challenge to be met. For example, the definite objective of selling $200,000 worth of product X this year is more motivation to most salespeople than the indefinite charge to go out and do better. It seems one can always do better, but what standard is a reasonable goal? How hard should one push product X in relation to other products in the line? Sales quotas provide an answer to these questions. As one source put it, "Without a standard of measurement, a football team cannot tell whether it made a first down, golfers cannot tell whether they shot par, and sales reps cannot be certain their performance is satisfactory."[2] Evidence suggests most sales personnel are "quota achievers" rather than "dollar maximizers," and salespeople's motivation tends to decline when they have easily attainable goals.

Quotas also influence salespeople's incentive through sales contests. A key notion underlying such contests is that those who perform "best" will receive the contest prizes. Unfortunately, not all salespeople have the same opportunity to win unless some allowance is made for differences in sales abilities and in territorial potential and workload. These differences exist despite the company's best efforts to the contrary. Thus, the company needs to design the sales contest so that all sales reps have a chance to win. Sales quotas provide a common denominator by which territory and personal differences can be neutralized, so all sales representatives have a relatively equal chance.

Quotas can also create incentive via their key role in the compensation systems of most firms. More will be said about compensation in later chapters, but it should be noted here that many firms use a commission or bonus plan, sometimes in conjunction with their base salary plan. In such schemes, salespeople are paid in direct proportion to what they sell (commission plan), or they receive some percentage increment for sales in excess of target sales (bonus plan). Typically, such plans are tied directly to sales quotas. Even when salespeople are compensated with salary only, quotas can provide incentive when salary raises are tied to quota attainment in the previous year.

Evaluate Sales Performance

Quotas provide a quantitative standard against which the performance of individual sales representatives or other marketing units can be evaluated. They allow management to pinpoint the marketing units that are performing above average and those that are experiencing difficulty. They can be used relatively easily and lend themselves to management by exception.

Salespeople who miss their quotas by some appreciable amount, either above or below, can be singled out for more intensive investigation. Perhaps salespersons who perform far above quota are doing something especially right from which all salespeople might profit. Alternatively, perhaps others are having difficulty selling one type of product or to one type of customer.[3] There may be something the company can do to assist them. Maybe they are facing some intense competition from a regional competitor that is not being experienced elsewhere. Perhaps the firm needs to assume a more aggressive price posture in this region or to increase its advertising effort to neutralize the competitor's impact. Quotas localize spots that need more intensive investigation; this would be hard to do without these quantitative standards.

Control Sales Efforts

Quotas can be used not only to evaluate salespeople's performance but also to evaluate and control their efforts. As part of their job, salespeople are expected to engage in specific activities. Although the activities and the time

Thorny Issues in Sales Management 8 • 1

CAN QUOTAS BE DISCRIMINATORY?

Mary Mestousis, the sales manager for Custom Design Office Furniture, was wondering what she should do. She had just completed analyzing the annual performance of each of the 12 sales reps she supervised. While 8 of the 12 had made their quotas, 4 had not.

Mestousis was troubled because three of the four had not made their quotas last year either. At that time, she had met with each salesperson. They had discussed each person's performance in detail, going over the territory account by account for the larger accounts. All three salespeople had argued that their quotas were unrealistic.

Mestousis had reviewed her calculations. She had used the same criteria and indexes for potential in establishing all quotas. She was confident they had been determined correctly, but she knew she was going to hear the same arguments this year.

She was undecided as to what she should do when she met with each sales representative to go over the most recent performances. One option would be to let the three go. That would be consistent with how she had historically handled things when a salesperson had not made quota in two successive years. She was concerned though that such an action could lead to a discrimination suit being filed against her and the company because two of the reps in question were women and one was black. That represented two thirds of all of the female reps in the company and the only black salesperson.

After deliberating, Mestousis decided not to let any of them go. Rather, she would meet with them again and discuss the situations, just like last year.

Do you

Approve   _____

Somewhat approve   _____

Somewhat disapprove   _____

Disapprove   _____

of Mary Mestousis's decision?

---

devoted to them vary by company and industry, typical ones include calling on new accounts, collecting past-due accounts, and planning and developing sales presentations. Activity quotas allow the company to monitor whether sales reps are engaging in these activities to the extent desired. If they are not, corrective action can be taken early rather than waiting for these small activity problems to become large sales and profit problems.

Problems with Quotas

There are many advantages to using quotas, but there are also some problems. For one thing, they sometimes prove to be a difficult comparative yardstick. See Thorny Issue 8.1 for one example of the types of problems they can cause. Many sales are the result of several people. One salesperson may call on corporate headquarters and another on the plant where the equipment will be installed. Both may play important but different roles in securing the order. In such cases, it is hard to decide what share of the total sale should be allocated to each salesperson; thus, it is hard to decide how well the salesperson did in relation to quota. It is equally troublesome when a salesperson's influence is relatively minor in obtaining a sale. Finally, quotas can be costly to establish, particularly if they are to be done well.

CHARACTERISTICS OF A GOOD QUOTA PLAN

For a quota to be effective, the quotas must be (1) attainable, (2) easy to understand, and (3) complete.

Quota Level

There is a great deal of controversy regarding the level at which quotas should be set. Some argue quotas should be set high so they can be achieved only with extraordinary effort. Although most salespeople may not reach their quotas, the argument is that they are spurred to greater effort than they would have expended in the absence of such a "carrot." Although perhaps intuitively appealing, high quotas can cause problems. They create irritation among salespeople. They can also cause salespeople and others in the organization to cheat to make their quotas, sometimes with disastrous consequences for the firm as the opening scenario and the example in Exhibit 8.1 indicate.

The use of very high "carrot" quotas seems to be the exception rather than the rule. The prevailing philosophy is that quotas should be realistic. They should represent attainable goals that can be achieved with normal or reasonable, not Herculean, efforts. That seems to motivate most salespeople best.

To take advantage of the small percentage of salespeople who might be challenged more by high "carrot" quotas, firms can consider two-tier quota systems. For example, Ramtek Corporation, a pioneer in the color computer graphics business, devised a two-level quota system. Level 1 quotas are based on realistically attainable revenue targets. Level 2 quotas are set higher, and salespeople can secure considerably higher bonuses for meeting them. Ramtek allows salespeople to pick the level they want to be measured by. However, those picking the higher level (about one in five) need to get their sales manager's approval so they do not take on more than they can handle and get discouraged.[4]

Quota Complexity

Quotas should not only be realistic but also easy to understand. Complex quota plans may cause suspicion and mistrust among sales representatives and thereby discourage rather than motivate them. It helps when salespeople can be shown exactly how their quotas were derived. They are much more likely

EXHIBIT 8 • 1   *Example of What Can Happen with Very High "Carrot" Quotas*

Itel Corp.'s 1979 junket to Acapulco feted its hottest marketing personnel with fireworks and bugle fanfares, champagne, and showers of rose petals. "It was like *Fantasy Island,*" recalls a former Itel man, who says he was so moved by the splendor and tequila that he tipped Mexican bartenders $600 for a company disco party.

And that was but a flourish in a extravaganza that wined and dined some 1,300 employees and spouses at a month-long show that cost the company some $3 million.

For this was Itel in January 1979, the champagne of West Coast companies, buoyant, elegantly packaged, and giddy with its success. Investors were giddy, too. The stock of the computer and transportation-leasing company had soared to $39 from $18 in a six-month period of 1978, and the company saw 1979 as its first billion-dollar year in volume.

But 1979 proved to be the year Itel's bubble burst. Today, the company is a sober, stripped-down shell. Its shareholder equity has been dissipated by losses totaling $226 million in the nine months ending September 30, 1979. Its employee rolls have been slashed by layoffs and divestitures from 1979's high of 7,000 to an estimated 1,000 in 1980. Its shares led the list of New York Stock Exchange glamour losers in 1979, plunging 79 percent to $5.375. In addition, there are almost a dozen security-holder lawsuits and an investigation by the Securities and Exchange Commission. Vulnerable and debt-ridden, Itel is carefully negotiating its survival with the company's creditors.

The reasons for Itel's swift and stunning collapse will be debated from boardrooms to barrooms for years to come. Probably most important was the supremacy of marketing in the power centers at Itel. In confrontations between the freewheeling marketing people and the more conservative legal and financial staffs, marketing almost always won.

"The salesman at Itel was exalted," a former employee says. "A good one could make $100,000 a year, a great one $150,000. So long as he was productive, he was a demigod." Itel's fabled perks—the bonuses, cruises, and junkets (called "marketing-incentive trips")—were all designed to fuel the marketing machine, to inspire salesmen to meet and exceed *ambitious growth quotas* [emphasis added].

Given these high incentives, the pressure to produce, and the laxity of controls, some sources contend that sleight of hand was inevitable and that it helped undo the company in the end. "If you couldn't meet your sales quota, you might as well submit your resignation," a former Itel attorney close to Itel's lease business says. "So at some point, somebody starts showing a profit that doesn't exist. The guy at the top accepts it. Where the duplicity comes in, I don't know." There isn't any indication that top management knew of such activity before Itel's collapse.

The attorney says salespeople in Itel's complex third-party lease business began to enter false or exaggerated profits. He recalls, "I had salesmen tell me, 'I don't care how you close this deal, just close it. By the time it's discovered the money's not there, I'll be gone. I've got my commission.' "

Source: Adapted from Marilyn Chase, "How a Red-Hot Firm in Computer Business Overheated and Burned," *The Wall Street Journal,* February 22, 1980, p. 1. For another example of how very high quotas led to salespeople cheating to make them, see Andy Zipper, "Cooking the Books: How Pressure to Raise Sales Led MiniScribe to Falsify Numbers," *The Wall Street Journal,* September 11, 1989, pp. A1, A8.

to accept quotas that are related to market potential when they can see the assumptions used in translating the potential estimate into sales goals.

Quotas should also be easy to understand definitionally. If a salesperson's quota is 50 calls on new accounts within a quarter, it is important for the representative to be told exactly what customers qualify as new accounts. Does a call on a customer who has not placed an order within the past year qualify as a new-account call? How about a company that has not placed an order within the past three years but before that was a steady customer? What about a call this quarter on an account that placed its first small order the previous quarter? Does the call qualify if an account makes only a partial payment? To avoid conflicts, the sales manager and all sales personnel must understand the quota and the conditions.

Quota Items   A third desirable feature of a quota plan is that it is complete. It should cover the many criteria on which sales reps are to be judged. Thus, if all sales representatives are supposed to engage in new-account development, it is important to specify how much. Otherwise that activity will likely be neglected while the salesperson pursues volume and profit goals. Similarly, volume and profit goals should be adjusted to allow for the time the representative has to spend identifying and soliciting new accounts.

Carlisle Tire and Rubber, for example, develops quotas for each salesperson using both bottom-up and top-down sales forecasts as a basis. The bottom-up sales forecast requires each district manager "to make a detailed, account-by-account analysis, which is the basis for establishing account sales objectives with specific plans and strategies for their achievement."[5] The top-down forecast is prepared at the same time by the product management group, and any differences in the two forecasts are reconciled by the national sales manager who then negotiates a final quota with each district manager in line with the company total. Salespeople receive 80 percent of their bonuses for achieving their sales volume quotas. "The remaining 20 percent can be earned through the completion of various nonsales quotas. These nonsales quotas are not standard but tailored to each district manager to encourage specific growth."[6]

THE QUOTA-SETTING PROCESS

Quota setting actually involves the three-step process shown in Exhibit 8.2.[7] First, the sales manager or someone else must decide on the types of quotas the firm will use. Next the person must determine the relative importance of each type of quota. Finally, the sales manager needs to determine specific quota levels.

Select Types of Quotas   There are three basic types of quotas: (1) those emphasizing sales or some aspect of sales volume, (2) those that focus on the activities in which sales representatives are supposed to engage, and (3) those that examine financial criteria such as gross margin or contribution to overhead. Sales volume quotas are the most popular.[8] All types seemed to be used more by large firms than small firms (see Exhibit 8.3 on page 272).

Sales volume

The popularity of quotas that emphasize dollar sales or some other aspect of sales volume is understandable. They can be related directly to market potential and thereby be made more credible. They are easily understood by those who must achieve them. They are consistent with what most salespeople envision their jobs to be—that is, to sell. Furthermore, they are consistent with the old adage, "Someone must sell something before the other functions of business

E X H I B I T   8 • 2   *Quota-Setting Process*

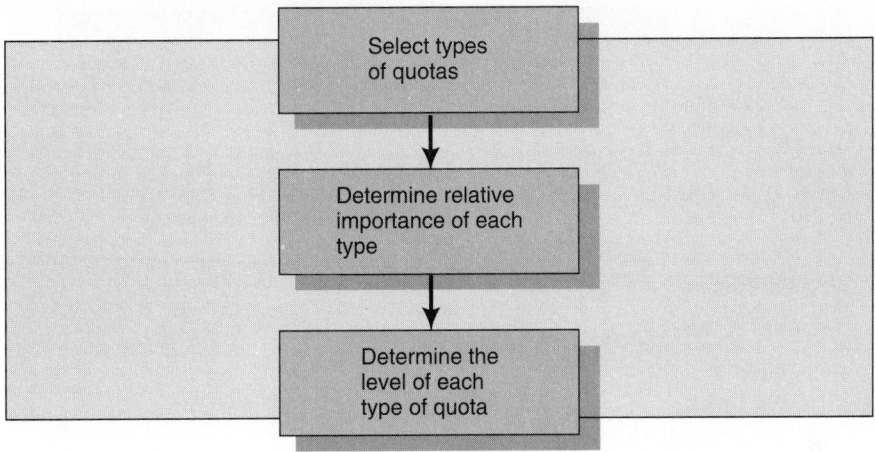

Select types
of quotas

Determine relative
importance of each
type

Determine the
level of each
type of quota

Source: Adapted from Thomas R. Wotruba, *Sales Management: Planning, Accomplishment, and Evaluation* (New York: Holt, Rinehart & Winston, 1971), p. 201.

can be brought to bear." The production, finance, and personnel functions depend on a certain amount of the product being sold.

Sales volume quotas can be expressed in dollars, physical units, or points.

Dollar quotas.   Dollars provide a common measure for all products. This helps to reduce communication problems when each sales representative handles a variety of products. In such instances, establishing physical volume quotas for each product for each sales rep can be very complex.

Dollar volume quotas permit a more direct analysis of salespeople's expenses in relation to quota. The ratio of expenses to sales for each salesperson can be calculated directly, and salespeople can be compared in terms of these expense ratios. Dollar volume quotas are also advantageous when sales reps have some discretion over price. Sales managers can see immediately whether they are using the discretion wisely or whether they are cutting prices so drastically that it cuts into profits. To accomplish the same kinds of analyses with physical volume quotas, it would be necessary to estimate the total dollars of targeted sales by assuming some average price per sale.

Physical volume quotas.   Physical volume quotas express a salesperson's goals in some physical unit of measurement such as number of specific items, weight in pounds or tons, or some volume measure such as gallons.

EXHIBIT 8 • 3   *Firms That "Extensively Use" the Various Types of Quotas*

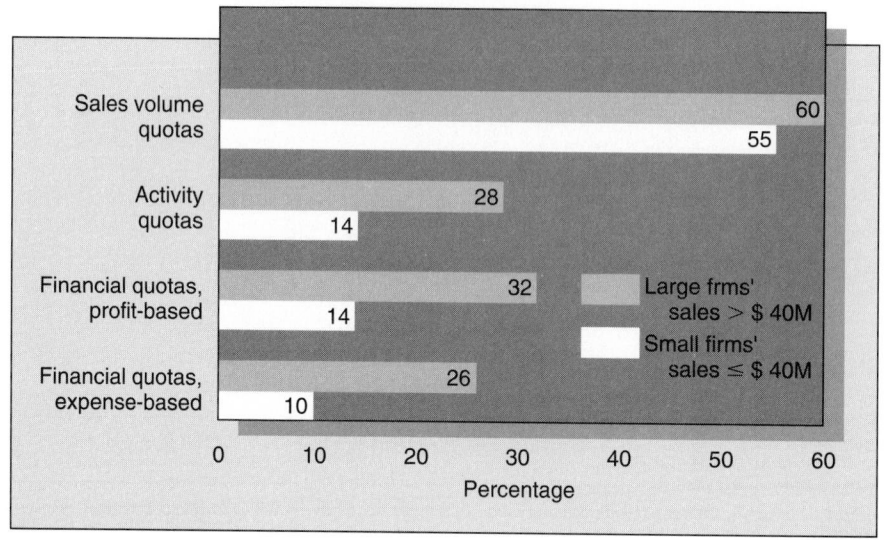

Source: Developed from the information in Alan J. Dubinsky and Thomas E. Barry, "A Survey of Sales Management Practices," *Industrial Marketing Management* 11 (April 1982), pp. 133–41. For discussion of the factors considered when developing these quotas, see David J. Good and Robert W. Stone, "How Sales Quotas Are Developed," *Industrial Marketing Management* 20 (February 1991), pp. 51–55.

Physical volume quotas are especially attractive when sales representatives handle only a few products. Thus, a sales quota for a salesperson who works for a chemical manufacturer might be expressed as so many gallons of toluene, whereas that for a cement manufacturer might be expressed so as many pounds of cement, and that for a steel sales rep as so many tons of carbon steel and so many tons of stainless.

Physical volume quotas are also attractive when prices fluctuate widely because of cyclical and competitive factors. In a price-intensive, competitive market, it may not be unusual for a normal $100 drum of chemicals to sell for $75. Whereas before the salesperson might have had to sell 500 barrels to reach the quota of $50,000, the sales rep would now have to sell 667 drums. The change, however, could not be controlled personally by the representative. Dollar quotas in such situations can demoralize salespeople.

Physical volume quotas are also attractive when unit prices are high. A dollar quota of $2 million, for example, might be psychologically overwhelming to a salesperson, whereas a quota of 20 units might not seem nearly so imposing even though each unit sells for $100,000.

Point quotas.   Point quotas are another variation of sales volume quotas. A certain number of points is given for each dollar or unit sales of particular products. For example, each $100 of sales of product X might be worth three points; of product Y, two points; and product Z, one point. Alternatively, each ton of steel tubing sold might be worth five points, while each ton of bar stock might be worth only two points. The total sales quota for the salesperson is expressed as the total number of points he or she is expected to achieve. The point system is typically used when a firm wants to emphasize certain products in the line. Those that are more profitable, for example, might be assigned more points.

Porter-Cable Machine Company, for instance, once used dollar volume quotas exclusively. On analysis, however, management found that sales personnel often attained most of their quotas through selling only one or two easy-to-sell products. Management initiated a program whereby Porter-Cable products were put into eight different categories according to their relative profitability. Then, individual point volume quotas were set for each product category, and bonus points were awarded for sales over quota in each category. Sales personnel were required to meet all the point volume quotas before becoming eligible for any bonus points. Furthermore, in appraising performance, management regarded a 150 percent total point volume attainment with four points as poorer than a 120 percent point volume attainment with five bonus points. This quota system led to the selling of a considerably more profitable mixture of products.[9]

Point quotas can also be used to promote selective emphases. New products might receive more points than old ones to encourage sales representatives to push them. A given dollar of sales to new accounts might be worth more points than the same level of sales to more established accounts. Point quota systems allow sales managers to design quota systems that promote certain desired goals; yet, point quotas can be easily understood by salespeople.

Activity

Activity quotas attempt to recognize the investment nature of a salesperson's efforts. For example, the letter to a prospect, the product demonstration, and the arrangement of a display may not produce an immediate sale. On the other hand, they may influence a future sale. If the quota system emphasizes only sales, however, salespeople may be inclined to neglect these activities. Left unchecked, sales volume quotas can become an obsession with salespeople and can result in a breakdown in control of other activities. Activity quotas provide such a counterbalance.

Activity quotas are directly related to factors that sales representatives can actually control. As David Fields, vice president of sales for Zellerbach, a distributor of paper products, says, "(Salespeople) can't do sales. (They) do activities that generate sales."[10] Although salespeople may be able to influence sales volume, they cannot control it. Economic conditions and competitive behavior may thwart the salesperson's best efforts. Yet salespeople can control the number of new accounts they call on, the number of service calls they make, the call reports they complete, and so on. Thus, it is reasonable to judge their performance on these activities. Furthermore, if these activities are im-

EXHIBIT 8 • 4   *Common Types of Activity Quotas*

Number of
1. Calls on new accounts.
2. Letters to potential customers.
3. Proposals submitted.
4. Field demonstrations arranged.
5. Service calls made.
6. Equipment installations supervised.
7. Displays arranged.
8. Dealer sales meetings held.
9. Meetings and conventions attended.
10. Past-due accounts collected.

portant to the success of the company, it is reasonable to judge salespeople on whether their performance meets or exceeds these criteria.

Some common types of activity quotas are listed in Exhibit 8.4. Measuring a salesperson's efforts in each activity takes much effort. The number of proposals a salesperson develops or the number of demonstrations he or she arranges is not recorded in the normal accounting cycle. This information has to be developed by requiring salespeople to complete activity reports. This increases paperwork and represents time away from the sales reps' primary activity of face-to-face selling. Furthermore, since sales representatives complete the activity report themselves, there is opportunity for sloppiness and misrepresentation unless this function is closely supervised. The activity report reflects only the amount of effort expended on various activities; that the salesperson called on 20 new accounts in the period says nothing about the quality of these calls. They may have represented nothing more than a salesperson spending five ineffective, or perhaps even detrimental, minutes with a new customer.

All these problems are reduced when a sales volume measure is used for quotas. The normal accounting cycle reveals the figures necessary to compare performance with the established standard. The amount of sales produced, although not perfect, is a somewhat direct measure of the quality of the effort expended on the client. A sales volume quota decreases the amount of paperwork necessary and increases the amount of time sales representatives have available for selling.

Financial

Financial quotas make salespeople conscious of the cost and profit implications of what they sell. Being human, sales representatives left to their own devices often take the easy way out. They emphasize products that are easiest to sell or concentrate on customers with whom they feel most comfortable. Unfortunately, these products may be costly to produce and have a lower-than-average return. Similarly, the customers with whom the representative feels comfortable may not purchase much and may be less profitable than other potential accounts. Financial quotas attempt to make salespeople aware of these conditions so that they direct their efforts to more profitable products and customers.

Financial quotas are often stated in terms of direct selling expenses, gross margin, or net profit. They are most applicable when the firm's market penetration approaches saturation levels. In such instances, it is hard to increase sales or market share, and an emphasis on selling efficiency and cost control becomes a logical mechanism for increasing profit.[11]

Expense quotas. A key to improving profits is to control the field selling expenses incurred in generating a given level of sales. Expense quotas are typically stated as a certain percentage of sales, although they are sometimes expressed in absolute dollar amounts.

Although expense quotas force sales representatives to recognize the costs of what they are doing and to be aware of their responsibilities for controlling expenses, they can also have dysfunctional effects. They may cause salespeople to do other than what they should because they are worried about expenses. Instead of calling four times in a quarter, for example, the salesperson may call only twice because he or she believes the chances for purchase are low. Thus, he or she loses the opportunity to secure a big equipment purchase. Field sales expenses, on the other hand, contribute substantially to the difference in profitability of firms in the same industry, and their control is important.

Gross margin quotas. Gross margin quotas are useful when there are significant differences in gross margins by product, since they can be set so salespeople concentrate on items with higher returns. Unfortunately, gross margin quotas are somewhat difficult to administer. Some firms simply do not wish to disclose production cost information to sales representatives.[12] Even among those that do, it is hard for salespeople to tell how they are doing with respect to their gross margin quotas at any given time, and thus the quotas do not produce the desired motivation effects. In one study among medical supply wholesalers, it was found that firms using gross margin commissions were less efficient than firms using other compensation programs.[13]

Margin information is typically not provided in the normal accounting cycle by a unit of analysis so small as a salesperson. At the same time, the same objective can be accomplished with a well-designed point quota system. Products that bear higher gross margins can simply carry more points. Point quota systems are much easier for salespeople to understand and thereby make it easier for them to monitor their progress.

Net profit quotas. Some managers believe net profit quotas are the ultimate because they emphasize what the selling effort should be—profitable sales volume and not sales volume for its own sake. Net profit quotas are tied directly to a major goal of top management. Also, net profit quotas can be superior to gross margin quotas when products with high gross margins require extensive effort and thereby produce higher field selling expenses and lower net profit.

Net profit quotas also have some disadvantages. First, they are harder than the other types for salespeople to understand, making it difficult for them to monitor their progress. The net profit they produce depends on the product mix they sell, the margins on these products, and the expenses they incur. At any given time, it is difficult for sales representatives to determine how they are doing. This can prove frustrating and stifle motivation.

Second, net profit quota schemes are difficult to administer. Again, the information required to operate them—net profit produced by a given salesperson in a given period—is not produced in the normal accounting cycle in most firms. It can be acquired, but it is typically very expensive to do so.

Finally, the profit a salesperson produces is affected by many factors beyond his or her control—competitive reaction, economic conditions, and the firm's willingness to negotiate on price, for example. Some would argue that it is unreasonable to hold the individual salesperson responsible for all these external influences.

Determine Relative Importance of Each Type

As the preceding discussion indicates, each main type of quota system has advantages and disadvantages. In some situations, the firm may believe the advantages of one scheme outweigh the disadvantages and so may use it without even considering other options. Although quota schemes with a single basis can work well in relatively stable situations, they can prove disastrous in dynamic environments. For example, a sales volume quota may work well for an established product with an established market. That same scheme, however, can lead to an overconcentration of calls on existing accounts and the neglect of new accounts with new products for which new uses are being discovered. In such instances, the sales manager may want to use a combination of criteria that produces the best balance of goals for each salesperson. Furthermore, the conditions from territory to territory and from customer to customer may be different, and the sales manager might wish to reflect such differences in the quota plan. A key question that must be addressed is how the various quotas should be combined to produce a single criterion by which performance can be evaluated.

The problem is illustrated in Exhibit 8.5. The example assumes there are three criteria, one of each of the three main types, on which each salesperson should be evaluated. Note that each sales rep performed best with respect to a single criterion. Thus, if sales volume quota attainment were emphasized,

EXHIBIT 8 • 5   *Performance Evaluation with Multiple Quotas*

Salesperson/Quota Basis	Quota	Actual	Percent Quota	Weight	Percent Quota × Weight
Leslie Curtain:					
Sales volume	$150,000	$150,000	100.0%	3	300.0%
New account calls	22	20	91.0	1	91.0
Gross margin	$ 50,000	$ 40,000	80.0	2	160.0
Average			90.3		91.8
David Michael:					
Sales volume	$200,000	$180,000	90.0	3	270.0
New account calls	20	24	120.0	1	120.0
Gross margin	$ 66,000	$ 70,000	106.1	2	212.2
Average			105.4		100.4
Carol Suchomel:					
Sales volume	$170,000	$160,000	94.0	3	282.0
New account calls	18	21	117.0	1	117.0
Gross margin	$ 56,000	$ 60,000	107.1	2	214.2
Average			106.0		102.2

Curtain would be considered the top salesperson. She is the only one who made her sales volume quota. On the other hand, if the activity measure, number of new account calls were emphasized, Michael would be rated best. Suchomel would be rated best if the emphasis were on the financial measure, gross margin. The example illustrates Finagle's rule of management, which holds "that if you look long enough, you can find a ratio which makes any performer look good—or bad."[14] Rather than simply "looking hard enough" and becoming confused as to who truly performed best, management needs some objective mechanism for determining which representatives satisfied their quota responsibilities.

Simple average

One way is simply to average the ratios reflecting percent quota achievement. Suchomel performed best using the simple average; her performance was 106.0 percent of quota, while Michael's was 105.4 percent, and Curtain's was 90.3 percent.

One problem with the simple average is that it weights all three performance criteria equally when they might not be equally important to the firm. While the firm may want to emphasize the number of new account calls a salesperson makes by including it in the quota system, for example, it may not want to place as much emphasis on this activity as it does on actual sales volume produced by the salesperson.

Weighted average

In situations where the firm may want to give unequal emphasis to the different quota bases, a linear combination can provide a useful summary measure of each representative's overall performance. A linear combination is a weighted average of the results on the individual dimensions, where the weights reflect the importance of each component to management. In the example in Exhibit 8.5, a weight of 3 was assigned to sales volume *(SV)*, a weight of 2 to gross margin *(GM)*, and a weight of 1 to new account calls *(C)*. Thus, the weighted average for overall performance *(OP)* is:

$$OP = \frac{3SV + 1C + 2GM}{6}$$

The sum is divided by the sum of the weights, 6, to reduce the weighted combination to a basis of 100. Using the weighted criterion, Suchomel performed best and Curtain worst. Michael was almost right on target, with an aggregate index of 100.4 versus a 100.0 if he had simply met quota.

Although the weights 3, 2, and 1 were used in the example, other weights could be used. The weights should reflect the importance of performance on each component. The weights can be determined in a number of ways. They might simply be set by the sales manager using his or her own best judgment. They might reflect the collective opinion of a group of top managers, or they might be based on some objective analysis of the importance of each component to the firm's long-run goals. One attractive feature of the linear combination as a measure of overall performance versus quota is that it allows differential weights to reflect unique territory or customer differences. Another advantage is that it can be easily explained to salespeople.

Determine Level of Each Type

The final stage in determining the quota plan assigned to each marketing unit is to decide the level for each type of quota. In establishing these levels, the sales manager must balance a number of factors, including the potential available in the territory, the impact of the quota level on the salesperson's motivation, the long-term objectives of the company, and the impact on short-term profitability. When discussing quota levels, it is useful to separate sales volume, activity, and financial quotas.

Sales volume quotas

As mentioned, sales volume quotas are the most commonly used. Unfortunately, some firms do not use them very intelligently. See Thorny Issue 8.2.

Using historical sales.   Some firms, for example, simply set sales volume quotas on the basis of past sales. Each marketing unit is exhorted to "beat last year's sales." Sometimes the standard is the average of sales in the territory

Thorny Issues in Sales Management 8 • 2

USING QUOTAS TO MAKE SALESPERSON RETENTION DECISIONS

The heat was on at Portfolio Growth Investments! The stock market was down, and small investors were staying away in droves, opting to put their money in money market and savings accounts or in certificates of deposit. Portfolio Growth Investments was particularly hurt by the shift. Individual investors were the lifeblood of its business. It did a much higher proportion of all trades with individual investors and a lower proportion with institutional investors than the average brokerage firm.

To reverse the declining revenue trend, the sales manager has turned up the heat. At a recent meeting, she gave each salesperson a sales and commission goal equal to what each person achieved last year, when the market was robust, commenting: "I don't care how you achieve these goals. That's up to you. The only thing I can tell you for sure is that those who don't reach their quotas will be gone from this firm by next year at this time."

Do you

    Approve   _____

    Somewhat approve   _____

    Somewhat disapprove _____

    Disapprove   _____

of the sales manager's actions?

over some past time period—five years, for example. Sometimes the admonition is expressed more concretely. If the company's sales forecast suggests a 7 percent sales increase this year, each marketing unit is assigned a quota 7 percent higher than last year's or the average of the past five years' sales.

The most attractive feature of this quota-setting scheme is that it is easy to administer. One does not have to engage in an extensive analysis to determine what the quotas should be. This makes it inexpensive to use. Also, salespeople readily understand it.

Unfortunately, such schemes forgo many potential advantages of using sales volume quotas. For one thing, such quotas ignore current conditions. A territory may be rapidly growing, and the influx of new potential customers could justify a much larger increase than the 7 percent established by the overall company's sales forecast. Alternatively, the territory might be so intensely competitive or depressed that any increase in the assigned sales quota is not justified.

A quota based solely on past sales ignores territory potentials and provides a poor yardstick for evaluating individual sales reps. Two salespeople, for example, might each have generated $300,000 in sales last year. It clearly makes a difference in what one can expect from each of them this year if the market potential in one territory is $500,000 while that in the other is $1 million. The firm may be forgoing tremendous market opportunities simply because it is unaware of them.

A quota based solely on past years' sales can also demoralize salespeople and cause undesirable behaviors. For example, a salesperson who has realized quota for one year may be tempted to delay placing orders secured at the end of the year until the new accounting cycle begins. This accomplishes two things: It makes his or her quota for the next year lower, and it gives him or her a start on satisfying that quota.

Although sales quotas should not be based solely on sales in prior years, historic sales should be considered when quotas are established. Historic sales provide some indication of how competitive a firm is within a territory. By comparing historic sales with potential sales, one can localize trouble spots and determine the problem and what action should be taken.

Using territory potential.   Territory potentials provide a useful start for establishing quotas for territory sales volume. However, the firm should not adhere strictly to a formula relating quota to potential, but it should attempt to reflect the special situations within each territory. For example, Haworth, Inc., an office equipment marketer, develops its territory quotas by explicitly considering its three biggest customer industries in each local market. When developing quotas for its Boston, New York, Philadelphia, and Washington, D.C., offices, for instance, it takes special note of what is happening to the insurance industry because the Northeast is such a hotbed of insurance.[15]

Determining how to set territory quotas that reflect the special situations within each territory is often difficult. On one hand, the sales representative who serves the territory should be involved in setting the territory quota, because he or she should have the most intimate knowledge of the conditions in the territory. On the other hand, since the representative will be affected by the quota established, he or she may not be impartial. One might expect sales representatives to understate potential to generate lower, easier-to-reach quotas.

Some firms have resolved the problem of potential bias when salespeople are used to help set their own quotas by tying their compensation into the process. For example, IBM of Brazil established a system that considers territory potential differences and company objectives for the territory. It also encourages good forecasts by rewarding sales representatives according to how close their actual results are to the company's objectives. The system rewards good planning because it simultaneously incorporates the company objectives, O; a salesperson's forecast, F; and the results the salesperson actually achieves, A, in a compensation grid. Exhibit 8.6 describes how the system works. The system seems to work best when the salespeople possess more information about their own prospects than central office personnel and when significant costs are linked to under- and overfulfillment of sales forecasts.[16]

Activity quotas

The levels for activity quotas are most likely to be set according to the territory conditions. They require a detailed analysis of the work required to cover the territory effectively. Activity quotas are affected by the size of the territory and by the number of accounts and prospects the salesperson is expected to call on. The size of the representative's customers can also make a difference, as can their purchasing patterns. These factors affect the number of times the salesperson needs to call on them in the period, the number of service calls or calls to demonstrate the use of the firm's equipment he or she must make, and so on.

The inputs for activity quotas can come from at least three sources: (1) discussions between the sales representative serving the territory and the sales manager, (2) the salesperson's reports, and (3) marketing research.

The sales manager and territory salesperson can use past experience as a basis for determining what activities are necessary to cover the territory effectively. Such a discussion typically revolves around key accounts and what needs to be done to serve them better. It may mean more frequent calls or fewer calls. The specification for a potential account might be simply to bid on three equipment installations during the next year. These assessments are then combined with estimates of other activities—for example, traveling—to determine the total activity level in the territory, from which a judgment can be made as to whether that level is reasonable. If not, some modification is warranted.

The iterative process ceases when reasonable activity levels have been determined. They must be reasonable in the sense of being consistent with the objectives of the firm for the territory and with the time available from the salesperson.

Sometimes activity quotas can be established from salespeople's reports. Suppose, for example, one main duty of field representatives is erecting displays in retail outlets. An analysis of historic call reports can often indicate how long it takes to set up a display on average and for various sizes of displays. Suppose further that different sizes of accounts typically receive different size displays. It is then relatively easy to determine the number of displays and the time required to erect them by analyzing the number of accounts of each class size in the salesperson's territory.

The firm might also rely on marketing research to determine activity level quotas. The firm might systematically vary the number of calls per account to determine the optimal number to be made on each account in any time period. Alternatively, it might study past bid behavior to establish rules as to when the firm should bid on some equipment request.

EXHIBIT 8 • 6   *Systems Used by IBM of Brazil to Reduce Salesperson Bias*
When Helping to Set Own Quotas

After receiving his objective, *O*, a salesman, must turn in his forecast, *F*; *F* divided by *O* determines the column in which the salesman's bonus percentage will fall. For instance, the 1.0 column represents a forecast equal to the quota, the 0.5 column means the forecast is half the objective, and the 1.5 column indicates a forecast 50 percent larger than the objective. The letter *A* stands for actual sales results. Thus, *A* divided by *O* and multiplied by 100 is the percentage of the objective achieved by the salesperson; 100 percent means full achievement of the company's objective, not of the saleperson's forecast.

Now let us see how it works. John sells photographic equipment. His quota is 500 cameras. Let us assume that John fully agrees to his quota and turns in a 500-units forecast. (On the grid, *F/O* equals 1.0.) If John sells 500 cameras, he makes 100 percent of his objective and is entitled to 120 percent of his bonus. In other words, he gets a 20 percent premium for his good planning capability. How much that represents in dollars depends on John's personal value, namely, his experience, time with the company, and merit.

If John sells 750 cameras, which is 150 percent of his objective, he is entitled to 150 percent of his bonus; the more he sells, the more he earns. But now John realizes that if his forecast had been 750 instead of 500 units (1.5 on the grid), then he would have received 180 percent of his bonus instead of 150 percent. Bad planning on his part has deprived him of a good chunk of money. If John had sold 250 units, half of his objective, he would have earned

just 30 percent of his incentive. Here again, John sees that it would have been better to have forecasted 250 instead of 500, for his earnings would have been 60 percent.

In other words, the best earnings lie in the diagonal that goes down from left to right in the grid. For a given result, *A*, the more precise John's forecast is, the higher his earnings. But John will always earn most if his forecast is perfect.

After being introduced to the grid, John goes back to study his territory. This time he does not want to return a faulty forecast—his earnings are at stake. He may still complain that the objective set up by his manager is too high—there is no solution to that—but for the first time he can enhance his earnings through a good work plan. If he comes in with a low forecast, he may damage his earnings in exchange for safety. On the other hand, a high forecast may plunge him into trouble if his sales are too low. John understands that he must be precise. This is exactly what his manager is waiting for.

From that moment on, John becomes committed to the number he forecasts. The grid tells him his sales should be equal to or higher than the forecast in order for his earnings to increase. Soon, John sees that, because of the new interactive approach, the headquarters staff begins to really understand the market and sets sales objectives that approach his own forecast. Total accuracy will never happen, but for practical purposes the three main objectives of the system—sales volume, payment for performance, and good field information for planning—will be brought about.

Financial quotas

The levels of financial quotas are typically set to reflect the financial goals of the firm. For example, a firm may want a particular net profit or gross margin on all sales in a territory. Suppose the potential for a representative is basically concentrated on two products—one with a gross margin of 30 percent and one with a gross margin of 40 percent. The sales manager could shift the relative attention given to one versus the other by assigning a gross margin goal of 37 percent. The salesperson would then have to sell a greater proportion of the products with 40 percent margin to achieve that goal than if the goal were 34 percent.

A field selling expense quota may be based on last year's ratio of field selling expenses to sales. The sales manager might analyze these ratios across territories and establish a target for the territory given the potential in the

EXHIBIT 8 • 6 (concluded)

A/O × 100 (actual results divided by objective, then multiplied by 100)	F/O (forecast divided by objectives)										
	0	0.5	1.0	1.5	2.0	2.5	3.0	3.5	4.0	4.5	5.0
0	—	—	—	—	—	—	—	—	—	—	—
50	30	60	30	—	—	—	—	—	—	—	—
100	60	90	120	90	60	30	—	—	—	—	—
150	90	120	150	180	150	120	90	60	30	—	—
200	120	150	180	210	240	210	180	150	120	90	60
250	150	180	210	240	270	300	270	240	210	180	150
300	180	210	240	270	300	330	360	330	300	270	240
350	210	240	270	300	330	360	390	420	390	360	330
400	240	270	300	330	360	390	420	450	480	450	420
450	270	300	330	360	390	420	450	480	510	540	510
500	300	330	360	390	420	450	480	510	540	570	600

Calculation of grid numbers:
If F equal to A, then $OFA = 120 \times FO$
If F smaller than A, then $OFA = 60 \times (A + F)/O$
If F bigger than A, then $OFA = 60 \times (3A - F)/O$

Source: Reprinted by permission of the *Harvard Business Review*. Exhibit and excerpt from "Tie Salesmen's Bonuses to Their Forecasts" by Jacob Gonik (May–June 1978), p. 119. Copyright © 1978 by the President and Fellows of Harvard College. All rights reserved. See also Murali K. Mantrala and Kalyan Raman, "Analysis of a Sales Force Incentive Plan for Accurate Sales Forecasting and Performance," *International Journal of Research in Marketing 7* (December 1990), pp. 189–202.

territory. Although it is tempting to use the historic average across territories as the target, the unique conditions of the territory should be considered. Perhaps the field selling expense target should be less than the average because of the geographic concentration of customers. Perhaps it should be higher than average because of the intense competition in the territory. Perhaps the accounts require more entertaining at first-class restaurants and social events if the firm is going to have any chance of remaining competitive.

SUMMARY

The last major element in sales management planning is establishing sales quotas. A sales quota is the sales goal assigned to a marketing unit in a specified period. Sales quotas may be expressed in aggregate or broken down by customers and products. The full set of quota assignments is called the quota plan.

Sales quotas are used to motivate salespeople, evaluate their performance, and control their efforts. For a quota plan to produce its potential benefits, the quotas must be attainable with normal effort, easy to understand, and complete.

Setting quotas involves a three-step process. First, the sales manager must decide on the types of quotas the firm will use. This choice entails determining whether the firm will use quotas that emphasize (1) sales or some aspect of sales volume, (2) the activities in which salespeople are supposed to engage, or (3) financial criteria such as gross margin or contribution to overhead. These are known as sales volume, activity, and financial quotas, respectively. Typically, firms use some combination of these quotas rather than relying exclusively on one type because each has advantages and disadvantages.

The second step in the process involves specifying the relative importance of each type of quota. Then most firms seek some mechanism for combining the individual quotas into a single summary measure that serves as the standard for each representative's performance. Often a linear combination or weighted average is used in which the weights reflect the importance of each component to management.

The final step in determining the quotas assigned to each marketing unit is to determine the level at which each type of quota is to be set. In establishing these levels, the sales manager must balance a number of factors, including the potential available in the territory, the impact of the quota level on the salesperson's motivation, the long-term objectives of the company, and the impact on short-term profitability.

Discussion Questions

1. A recent study attempted to determine which factors are important in the development of quotas. Generally, those factors deemed most important included the nature of the territory and the products sold. Factors deemed least important

included the sales representative's traits, past sales forecasts, and past sales experience. Do you agree with these findings? What are the implications of these findings?

2. Some companies start to pay bonuses when sales reps reach 75 percent of quota rather than when 100 percent of quota is reached. Is this evidence that quota setting is an art and not a science?

3. Sales representatives for the Feminique Cosmetic Company are paid a 40 percent commission on sales volume. To date, management has not been able to convince the sales force of the value of putting up store displays and encouraging retailers to utilize Feminique's cooperative advertising. What do you suggest?

4. Quotas at the Acme Feed Corporation are set equal to the average of sales for the last three years plus 5 percent. Sales reps who exceed quota are paid bonuses according to the following schedule:

Percent of Quota	Bonus Percent
106–110	5%
111–115	7
116–120	10
121–125	12
Over 125	15

What are the advantages and disadvantages of this approach? What is likely to happen? How would you change the method?

5. The sales manager of the Clearline Paper Company has tried unsuccessfully to develop a quota system for the sales force. To simplify the procedure, sales volume for the last five years will be averaged for each representative, and a flat percentage increase—10 percent, for example—will be added to this average to determine next year's quota. The process will be repeated for future years by changing the five-year base. What is your opinion of this approach?

6. According to one sales manager, "The sales force should not participate in quota-setting activities. The typical sales representative is either overly optimistic or pessimistic and, as a result, is ill equipped to set quotas." Comment.

7. Sales reps and their district sales manager from the Minneapolis office of the Standard Computer Corporation recently persuaded the national sales manager to adjust the unit volume quota for their district. Word of this has spread to other districts, causing unrest. Personnel from these districts are requesting similar adjustments. How would you respond if you were the national sales manager?

8. One approach for handling sales representatives who fail to make their quotas is to add to next year's quota the amount by which they fell short. The opposite approach deducts this amount from next year's quota. Which approach is the most reasonable?

9. The recent and well-deserved emphasis on total quality programs (TQP) has prompted many sales managers to consider how to include customer satisfaction in the sales compensation package. Linking customer satisfaction to the sales force's compen-

sation package is evidence of commitment to total quality programs. How would a sales manager include customer satisfaction as part of a sales rep's quota?

10. Although top management of Hartford Paper Company was pleased with its recent shift to a national account marketing program, Jack Bastien, national field sales manager, was concerned how quotas of field sales representatives would be affected. He knew the national account manager would have a quota for each national account, but he was also aware that sales reps with national accounts in their territory would be expected to service these same accounts. Jack raised several questions. If the sales rep's quota does not reflect national accounts, then how do you persuade the rep to provide account service? Who gets credit for sales to national accounts? The national account manager? The sales rep? What happens to a sales rep's compensation when an account is designated to be a national or house account?

Endnotes

[1]Thomas R. Wotruba, *Sales Management: Planning, Accomplishment, and Evaluation* (New York: Holt, Rinehart & Winston, 1971), p. 195. See also Thomas R. Wotruba and Edwin K. Simpson, *Sales Management; Text and Cases* (Boston: PWS-Kent Publishing Company, 1989), pp. 193–224.

[2]William J. Stanton and Richard H. Buskirk, *Management of the Sales Force*, 7th ed. (Homewood, Ill.: Richard D. Irwin, 1987), p. 535.

[3]We will have more to say about how sales quotas pinpoint potential marketing strategy deficiencies in the chapter on sales analysis.

[4]Thayer C. Taylor, "Ramtek Sharpens Its Marketing Picture," *Sales & Marketing Management* 131 (September 12, 1983), pp. 45–48.

[5]Benjamin G. Ammons, "Get Greater Commitment by Letting Salespeople Help Set the Quotas," *Sales & Marketing Management* 124 (April 7, 1980), p. 90.

[6]Ibid., p. 93.

[7]Exhibit 8.2 and much of the surrounding discussion is adapted from Wotruba, *Sales Management,* pp. 201–23, which provides an excellent discussion of the subject.

[8]Alan J. Dubinsky and Thomas E. Barry, "A Survey of Sales Management Practices," *Industrial Marketing Management* 11 (April 1982), pp. 133–41.

[9]Richard R. Still, Edward W. Cundiff, and Norman A. P. Govoni, *Sales Management Decisions, Strategies,* and Cases, 4th ed. (Englewood Cliffs, N.J.: Prentice Hall, 1981), p. 598. Reprinted by permission.

[10]Barton A. Weitz, Stephen B. Castleberry, and John F. Tanner, *Selling: Building Partnerships* (Homewood, Ill.: Richard D. Irwin, 1992), p. 445.

[11]Wotruba, *Sales Management*, p. 205.

[12]One of the authors worked for a firm whose policy was not to disclose any price or other sales information to the production people or cost information to field sales personnel, but rather to restrict the possession of both types of information to a few selected people in the company. Top management felt that this arrangement provided some strong advantages when the company was forced to compete on price to secure a major installation.

[13]Douglas Dalrymple, R. Ronald Stephenson, and William Cron, "Gross Margin Sales Compensation Plans," *Industrial Marketing Management* 10 (July 1981), pp. 219–24.

[14]Richard I. Levin, "Who's on First?" *Sales Management: The Marketing Magazine* No. 93, July 17, 1964, p. 56.

[15]Haworth Pegs Quotas to Local Markets," *Sales & Marketing Management* 135 (December 9, 1985), pp. 68, 70.

[16]See Jacob Gonik, "Tie Salesmen's Bonuses to Their Forecasts," *Harvard Business Review* 56 (May–June 1978), pp. 119–20, for a more detailed explanation of

the system, which has also been used by the St. Regis Paper Company, which tied salespeople's compensation to potential quota differences. See "Managing By- and With-Objectives," *Studies in Personnel Policy,* No. 212 (New York: The National Industrial Conference Board, 1968), pp. 43–45. See also Murali K. Mantrala and Kalyan Raman, "Analysis of a Sales Force Incentive Plan for Accurate Sales Forecasting and Performance," *International Journal of Research in Marketing* 7 (December 1990), pp. 189–202.

Suggested Readings

Dubinsky, Alan J., and Thomas E. Barry. "A Survey of Sales Management Practices." *Industrial Marketing Management* 11 (April 1982), pp. 133–41.

Good, David J., and Robert W. Stone. "How Sales Quotas Are Developed." *Industrial Marketing Management* 20 (February 1991), pp. 51–55.

CASES FOR PART ONE

Case 1-1*
THE VALLEY WINERY

Pat Waller, recently hired as sales manager of the San Francisco region's chain division, was lamenting the problems he inherited. Despite favorable sales results for the San Francisco region, turnover was so severe Waller could not understand how sales increased during the past several years. He was surprised to learn the average sales rep had been with the San Francisco division of Valley Winery for only seven months and sales force turnover neared 100 percent a year. In fact, only one sales rep had more than two years' experience. Waller had heard that high turnover was a problem nationwide but did not expect such high figures for San Francisco.

Waller supervises two area managers, who in turn direct nine district managers. District managers supervise 5 to 6 sales reps, of which there are 50 in the San Francisco division. Approximately 50 new sales reps are hired each year, but the sales force size remains relatively constant. Waller knew the increased competitiveness in the market would make it more difficult to continue to obtain future sales increases. The excessive turnover problem would command immediate attention.

The Company

The Valley Winery, founded in 1933 in Napa, California, is the largest domestic producer of wine in the United States. Started with only a $7,500 investment at the end of Prohibition, it has become the leading producer of low-priced, consistent-quality wines. Favorite brands include Santo Rey and Valley premium table wines, Astral sparkling wines, Valley brandy, and most recently the Cool Valley line of wine coolers. As is true with most other wineries, Valley produces a low-grade, fortified sherry known in the streets as "sneaky pete." This product appeals to a small market niche and receives virtually no marketing support. The Valley name does not even appear on the label, a practice followed by other wineries as well. Brand names for this low-end product include Snake-Eye, 20/20, and Acey-Duecy. Valley also bottles a line of pop wines, which have never achieved high sales. Brands in the pop line are California Dream and Mile-High. The Valley Winery sells over 40 percent of all wine produced in the United States each year.

The Valley Winery is also one of this nation's largest privately held companies. As such, it is not required to disclose any financial information. However, according to financial analysts who specialize in the wine and distilled

---

*Jeffrey J. Ertel, MBA—Marketing, University of Wisconsin-Madison, assisted in preparing this case.

spirits industry, 1991 sales were believed to have exceeded $1.5 billion. Of the various producers of wine and distilled spirits, the Valley Winery is believed to be the best managed and most innovative.

Valley's phenomenal growth and success can be traced to two broad factors. As already stated, it produces wines of consistently high quality at relatively low prices. Second, Valley's sales force, using a push strategy, is considered by many to be the most aggressive and innovative in the industry. As the manager of a San Francisco liquor store states, "Turn your back on a Valley sales rep, and your store becomes a Valley warehouse." Heading up the sales force is Carl Roman, whose passion for detail and success is well known.

Valley Winery distributes nationwide through liquor and beer distributors located in metropolitan areas. Valley owns roughly 50 percent of these distributors, mostly those that are larger and more profitable. Valley's field representatives call on noncompany liquor and beer wholesalers across the country. Valley uses a major account system with reps calling on the headquarters of large chain stores.

The organization of the San Francisco division is typical, especially in those market areas where Valley owns the distributor. There are three sales groups. The first group calls on liquor stores and bars. Career-type salespeople dominate this group and most are older. These sales reps are paid a straight commission of 6 percent on sales. Almost all, 95 percent, are male. The second group calls on restaurants, resorts, hotels, and motels. This predominately female sales group is paid a straight salary ($19,500 to $23,500) plus a company car. The third group is the chain division. This group, 99 percent male, receives a straight salary plus car and a year-end bonus. Their salary ranged from $22,000 to $27,000. The chain group is considered the major source of future sales managers.

The San Francisco chain division sales organization has experienced numerous changes. Early in 1987, the company had a wine division and a wine cooler division. Exhibit 1 illustrates this organization. Early in 1987, Carl Roman revamped the structure and created a product line division reflecting premium and vintage products. Within the Premium Division were the Valley wines, the aperitif wines, and the Astral sparkling wines. The Vintage Division carried the Estate wines, Santo Rey wines, the Cool Valley line of wine coolers, and the Valley brandy. Exhibit 2 shows this organization. Less than six months later, Carl Roman introduced yet another modification reflecting the importance of key customers, which were classified as major accounts. Exhibit 3 (page 294) illustrates this change. Sales reps calling on major accounts represented the entire Valley line of wines and distilled spirits. The San Francisco division is responsible for sales to all of the major grocery headquarters, such as Safeway, Lucky, and Alpha Beta.

Forward integration decisions are a function of how well the independent distributor covers the market and the size of the market potential. Carl Roman had been very concerned with the chain store sales performance in the San Francisco area for some time. The previous distributor assigned 15 sales reps

E X H I B I T   1   *San Francisco Division: Chain Store Division Organizational Chart (May 1987)*

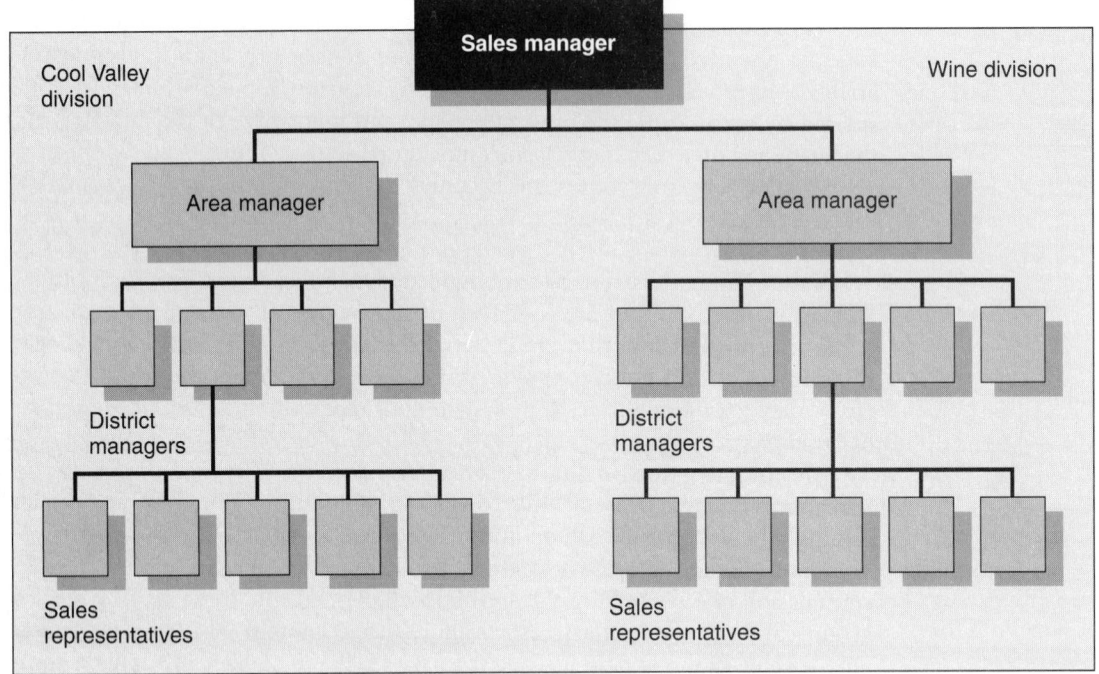

to call on the chain outlets and had resisted Valley's pleas to increase the sales force to 30 to 35 reps. After Valley Winery bought out the San Francisco distributor, sales of Valley Wines increased dramatically, primarily due to the increased number of sales reps calling on chain stores—from 15 up to 50. None of the 15 reps who worked for the previous owner was retained after Valley purchased the distributorship.

The buying process for these major chain accounts is fairly standard. Each sales rep is personally responsible for a specific number of stores taken from all major grocery chains. Thus, a sales rep will call on Safeway, Lucky, and Alpha Beta stores. The total number of outlets constitutes the sales rep's territory.

The sales rep is responsible for reaching monthly display quotas on each line of products. For instance, one month the representative is responsible for displaying 50 cases of Santo Rey wine in 1.5- and 4.0-liter sizes. The next month the rep may have a display quota of 50 cases of Santo Rey in 3.0-liter sizes. This pattern repeats itself throughout the year. Exhibit 4 (page 295) illustrates monthly quota patterns for different display results by sales rep and the extent of the turnover problem.

EXHIBIT 2   *San Francisco Division: Chain Store Division Organizational Chart (January 1988)*

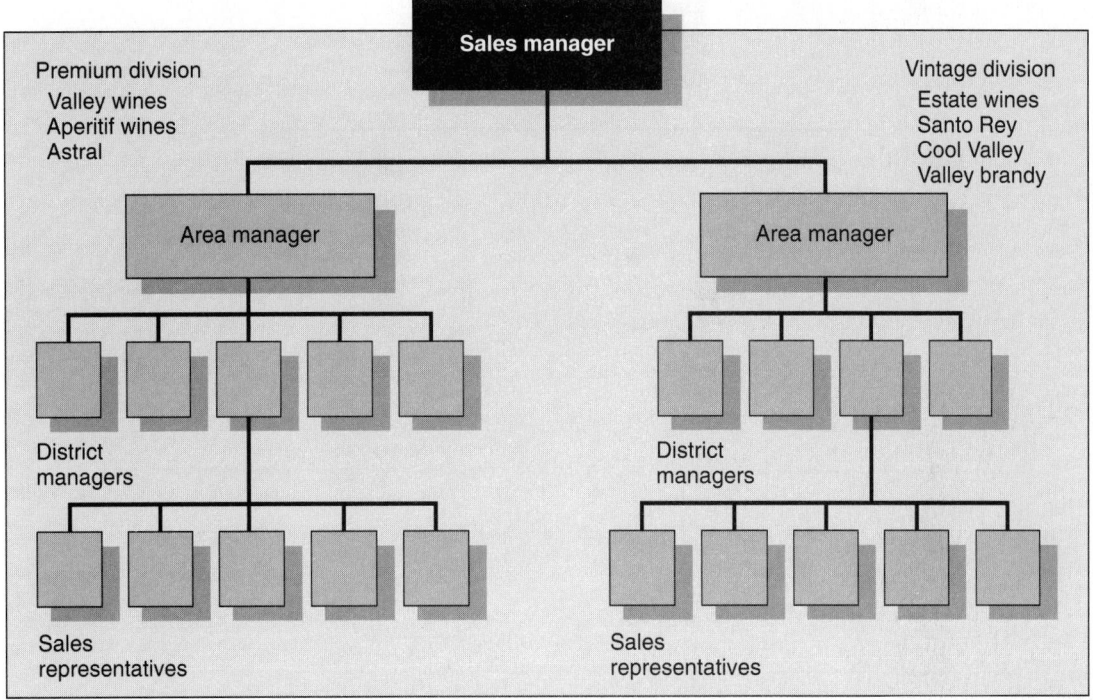

Premium division
Valley wines
Aperitif wines
Astral

Vintage division
Estate wines
Santo Rey
Cool Valley
Valley brandy

Sales manager

Area manager

Area manager

District managers

District managers

Sales representatives

Sales representatives

Sales reps call on either the store manager or the wine clerk, using pre-prepared sales sheets. The store manager or wine clerk must then order the beverages from the chain's warehouse, where all wines and distilled spirits are stored. The sales rep is responsible for all merchandising, service, and anything else related to Valley Winery that is needed in the chain outlet.

Rumors are abundant about the aggressiveness displayed by sales reps in the wine and liquor industry, especially Valley sales reps, who have been accused of relocating competitive displays and products to obtain the best space for Valley wines. Sales reps from other wineries dislike the "competitive spirit" shown by Valley reps, who have also been accused of such tactics as spraying hair spray on competitive displays and bottles so that they will gather dust and so discourage sales. Other so-called tricks of the trade have sales reps dumping bags of ice into the cardboard boxes supporting the display so they will collapse after the ice melts. Occasionally, bottles and even cases are "accidentally" broken by sales reps from competitive producers.

Waller's concern about the turnover problem led to a series of conclusions. First, recruiting and training costs approached $20,000 per year per represen-

E X H I B I T 3   *San Francisco Division: Chain Store Division Organizational Chart (June 1988)*

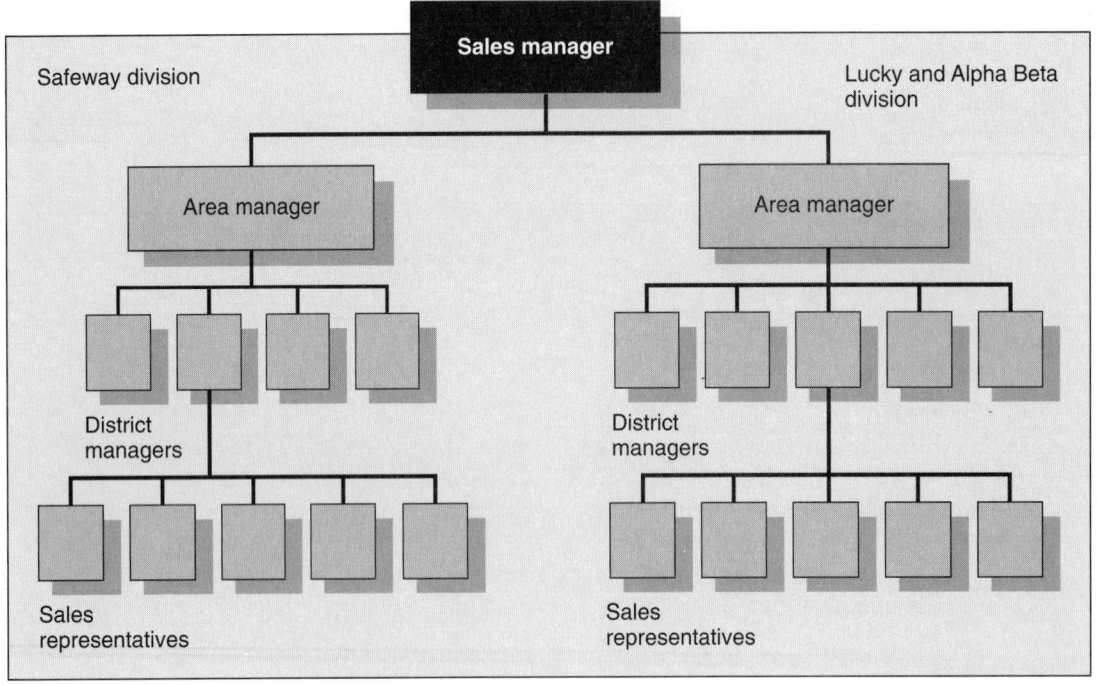

tative. Waller knew that with less turnover, Valley Winery and the San Francisco division profitability would improve. Second, Waller believed sales would improve. The $20,000 figure does not include opportunity costs associated with lost sales resulting from not having accounts called on. And, these costs do not include the time it would take for a new rep to adequately develop rapport with the accounts. Considering all these factors, Waller felt confident that decreasing turnover would improve sales and company profits. On the other hand, Waller knew Carl Roman was pleased with the division's improving performance.

Pat Waller decided at least to investigate the situation. As a start, Waller examined two possible sources to see if they were the crux of the problem. These included the recruiting and hiring process and the nature of the position. To research the recruiting and hiring process, Waller contacted the personnel office. To learn about the nature of the position, Waller traveled with a number of the sales reps.

Mike Wehner, personnel manager for the San Francisco division, was responsible for hiring all personnel for the division, including warehouse workers, truck drivers, office personnel, and the sales force. Wehner used a variety

EXHIBIT 4   Cases on Display Quota *verus* Actual Results by Sales Representative

Product: Cool Valley
Store: Safeway 711

Month	J	F	M	A	M	J	J	A	S	O	N	D	J	F	M	A	M	J	J	A	S
Quota	40	15	40	75	75	100	125	125	75	25	25	40	40	0	50	75	100	110	125	125	115
Mike Fisk	28	15	32	50	0	0	(terminated)														
Tom Rhea							22	45	39	25	30	27		45	62	94	94	96	100	120	70

Product: Santo Rey
Store: Lucky 42

Month	J	F	M	A	M	J	J	A	S	O	N	D	J	F	M	A	M	J	J	A	S
Quota	30	0	75	0	75	0	60	0	80	0	90	0	30	0	75	0	75	0	60	0	80
Stan Smith	0	0	12	0	50	0	60	(terminated)													
John Mahorn								0	21	0	28	(terminated)									
Steve Anderson												0	18	42	0	0	(terminated)				
Neil Johnson																	50	0	50	0	85

Product: Valley Wines
Store: Alpha Beta 572

Month	J	F	M	A	M	J	J	A	S	O	N	D	J	F	M	A	M	J	J	A	S
Quota	50	0	60	0	75	0	50	0	80	0	90	0	50	0	60	0	75	0	50	0	80
Paul Barling	30	0	27	0	60	0	45	0	45	0	50	0	33	(terminated)							
Mark Beringer															45	0	50	0	50	0	75

of methods to attract sales candidates. Recruiting college graduates from a number of area universities was common. This generally resulted in 10 to 15 new sales reps a year. Open newspaper advertisements usually produced 10 hires per year. The use of six local employment agencies, with fees of approximately $2,000 per hired individual, resulted in 15 to 20 new reps per year. Last, any employee recommending a friend or an acquaintance who was subsequently hired received a $200 finder's fee. This practice typically cost the company $2,000 per year. Wehner claims not to recruit personnel from competitors or customers. Wehner said he thought those hired through employment agencies were the most successful, but he was not positive.

The hiring process generally followed a similar pattern. The selected applicant completes a simple application form and is then interviewed by Wehner or his assistant for approximately 30 minutes. During that time, if the candidate seems motivated, enthusiastic, and asks for the sales job, the applicant is asked back for additional interviews.

The candidate then interviews with the distributorship's top manager for no more than 10 minutes. The San Francisco distributor is owned by Valley, and the new sales rep works for the distributor. Valley can reassign the sales rep to wholly owned distributors. All sales reps interact with the area distributor and often participate in training programs with the distributor's other two sales groups. Waller learned the distributor's top manager regards youth and physical characteristics as the most important traits an applicant should have to pass this stage.

The next step involves an interview with Waller's predecessor, John Ruppert, who was promoted to a home office assignment as a major account manager. The recruit is then whisked off to spend a day in the field with an experienced sales rep. Waller questioned whether this day in the field, during which the recruit is "wined and dined," is an accurate representation of the job. If all of these hurdles are passed, the applicant is then offered the job.

Pat Waller's work with the sales reps provided useful information. Waller traveled with two sales reps and discovered many new things about the sales job. Before being promoted to the sales manager position for the San Francisco division, Waller had moved through the ranks, starting as a sales rep in the Seattle division. As a sales rep, Waller served primarily in a missionary capacity, calling on liquor stores and taverns. Waller then advanced to district manager for the Seattle division. Next, Waller moved to the Phoenix division where he served as area manager before accepting a home office assignment as a product manager assistant. This itinerary was typical for a person selected to move into sales management, except that most sales managers are promoted from the chain store sales force. Waller's new assignment represented his first exposure to major account management.

On September 8, 1992, Waller traveled with Marv Flanigan, a nine-month veteran. Although scheduled to meet at 7 A.M, Marv was late, stating his hour-long drive was delayed by a terrible accident. Flanigan said the latest territory change created a longer commute for him. Since he was late, they started to work immediately, forgoing the customary cup of coffee Waller intended to buy as a warm-up tactic to learn about Flanigan's plans for the day. Waller and Flanigan spent nearly the entire morning at an Alpha Beta store (#561) building a 50-case display for Valley wines, resetting the cold box, and servicing the shelves. After a 15-minute presentation to the wine clerk, Flanigan and Waller left for the next call. When Waller congratulated Flanigan on the 50-case display, Flanigan quipped. "Thanks, but unfortunately it's not enough to make quota. Nobody, but *nobody*, ever makes quota. That's 25 cases short, and that store is one of my best accounts. And, did you see my Santo Rey quota—90 cases—no way!"

During their afternoon together, Waller observed a very aggressive sales promotion that Flanigan presented to a wine clerk at a Safeway store (#724). Afterward, Waller questioned the tenuous sales figures Flanigan quoted to the wine buyer. He responded by claiming, "John [the division's previous sales manager] and Rick [Marv's current area manager] told me to stretch the sales estimates." Continuing, he revealed, "They said it's the only way to make my numbers. Rick even told me to pump up the numbers on the recap I send to Napa."

Pumping up the numbers meant a sales rep would claim a 50-case display had been installed when the store manager or wine clerk would only order a 25 to 30-case display. The display would only look like a 50-case display; center boxes in the display would be empty.

On September 23, 1992, Waller worked with Bill Murphy. Murphy, a six-month veteran, arrived grumbling. He said his district manager called him at 10:30 the night before complaining about the condition of Safeway #507. After 30 minutes of specific instructions and other messages, Murphy had agreed to visit the store early that morning to correct the deficiencies. He mentioned that he received calls at night from his district manager about two to three times a week, often to check his progress on winery directives. These usually occurred, he claimed, during the hour or two he spent on preparation each night.

During lunch, Murphy discussed his desire to move into management. He said, "Although district managers are often considered to be no more than baby sitters for the new reps, I really think that I can do a great job. The pay doesn't even bother me. [District managers received $3,000 to $4,000 more.] I mean, with all the cases I've sold, if I were paid on commission, I'd already be rich. I think I can really train those new reps just as the manual says."

At this point, Waller thought he was starting to get a good sense of the situation.

Case 1-2
OMEGA MEDICAL PRODUCTS, INC.*

Omega Medical Products (OMP), located in Denver, Colorado, is one of the top manufacturers of life-support medical equipment and surgical pharmaceuticals. In fiscal year 1992, OMP recorded sales of $380 million (see Exhibit 1). Over the past three years, sales have increased at an annual rate of 18 percent. The company currently employs 175 sales reps, including a separate sales force of 40 that handles the company's anesthesia line exclusively. As the result of a recent staff organization, a decision was made to realign the sales and marketing department to better meet the future goals of the company.

Five years ago, Omega's president retired, and the top position was filled by the executive vice president, Christopher John. Subsequently, several other major changes occurred in the executive staff hierarchy. The most important were elimination of the executive vice president position and creation of the position of vice president, marketing and sales. Reporting to the new vice president would be the current vice president of international sales; the general manager of medical equipment marketing; the general manager of distribution, customer services and gases; the direct of market research and strategic planning; the director of communications; and the marketing manager of architectural products (see Exhibit 2 on page 300).

The vice president of marketing and sales, destined to be one of the most powerful positions at OMP, was filled by Earl Callahan. Callahan had previously held the top marketing job in a firm that manufactured medical products unrelated to those sold by Omega. Filling this position with an outsider generated noticeable discontent among several executives who had been considered top contenders. Soon after he began to work, Callahan was pressured by John to have a revised sales organization chart completed before Omega's new fiscal year, beginning July 1. After reviewing Omega's current organization charts, sales figures, and marketing plans for new products, Callahan realized there were several major problems.

Marketing Activities

Omega's marketing function was divided into four product areas. The patient care group consisted of anesthesia equipment and disposables, nursing equipment, and infant care supplies. The anesthesia equipment and disposables line accounted for the greatest dollar volume with 1992 sales of almost $100 million. With new products as the primary growth factor in the portable patient

---

*Bonnie J. Queram, MBA—Marketing, University of Wisconsin-Madison, assisted in preparing this case.

E x h i b i t 1   *1992 Sales ($000)*

Patient care		$139,045
Anesthesia equipment	$66,165	
Anesthesia disposables	33,742	
Nursing products	22,638	
Infant care	16,500	
Respiratory therapy		66,690
Architectural products		59,367
Anesthesia (gases)		82,591
Other (government, OEM, service, military)		32,424
Total		$380,117

monitoring area, sales were expected to be $191 million by 1996. Product prices ranged from a few cents for disposables to several thousand dollars for equipment.

The respiratory therapy line accounted for $66 million sales in 1992. The line had experienced only slight growth over the last few years but was expected to generate $97 million by 1996 with the introduction of one major new critical care ventilator, priced as high as $35,000 with all accessories. The prime market for this do-everything machine was the small- to medium-size hospital. Although Omega was the leader in the anesthesia field, it did not enjoy the same position in respiratory care. Because of several major failures with new products during the past 10 to 15 years, the Omega name was still associated by many therapists with inferior quality, poor product design, and inadequate service.

The architectural product line, composed of pipelines and gas outlets, had sales of $59 million in 1992 while the anesthesia line (gases), sold by a separate sales organization, accounted for $82 million. The major product was a liquid that, when converted to gas, was used to anesthetize patients for surgery.

Sales Activities

The general sales force, consisting of 135 representatives in the United States and Canada reporting to 16 district managers and six regional vice presidents (see Exhibit 3 on page 301), were expected to call on four major departments in each hospital: operating room, recovery room, emergency room, and nursery. Additionally, they were expected to keep in contact with purchasing and, if one existed, with the biomedical engineering department. The latter, usually present only in larger hospitals, was often responsible for reviewing and testing potential new equipment. Biomedical engineers were becoming instrumental in the purchase of sophisticated electronic monitoring devices.

Also, the sales force was expected to sell bulk oxygen and nitrous oxide as well as Omega's architectural product line equipment to new hospitals or those being remodeled. This required that sales reps work closely with architects and construction contractors, usually a very time-consuming endeavor, ranging from several months to over one year.

Exhibit 2

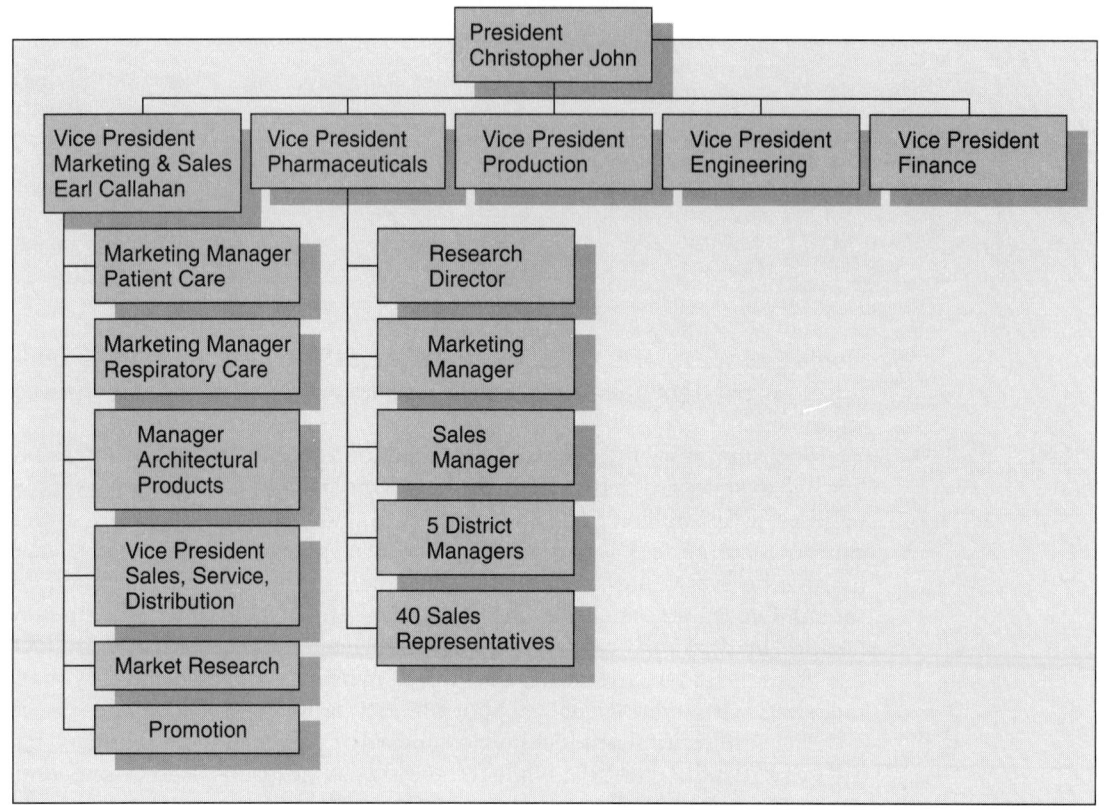

The anesthesia sales force called on the anesthesia staff exclusively. Close and frequent contact was necessary in most cases. The members of the sales force, all with chemical backgrounds, were expected to keep abreast of technological developments in the field. Some sales reps were formerly anesthetists.

Although Omega's products covered a variety of medical applications and necessitated sales calls to many different departments, the general line sales force had handled the lines very well. Callahan thought one primary reason they had done so well was that the majority of Omega's products were not particularly complicated and the sales force could be adequately trained by product managers when new products were introduced. Additionally, although Omega sold several thousand items, which realistically is too much for a sales rep to handle effectively, Callahan knew many products sold with little or no sales effort because of the Omega name and strong dealer network. Most dealers handled low-cost, easy-to-sell products, although some of the very large dealers sold high-priced equipment.

EXHIBIT 3

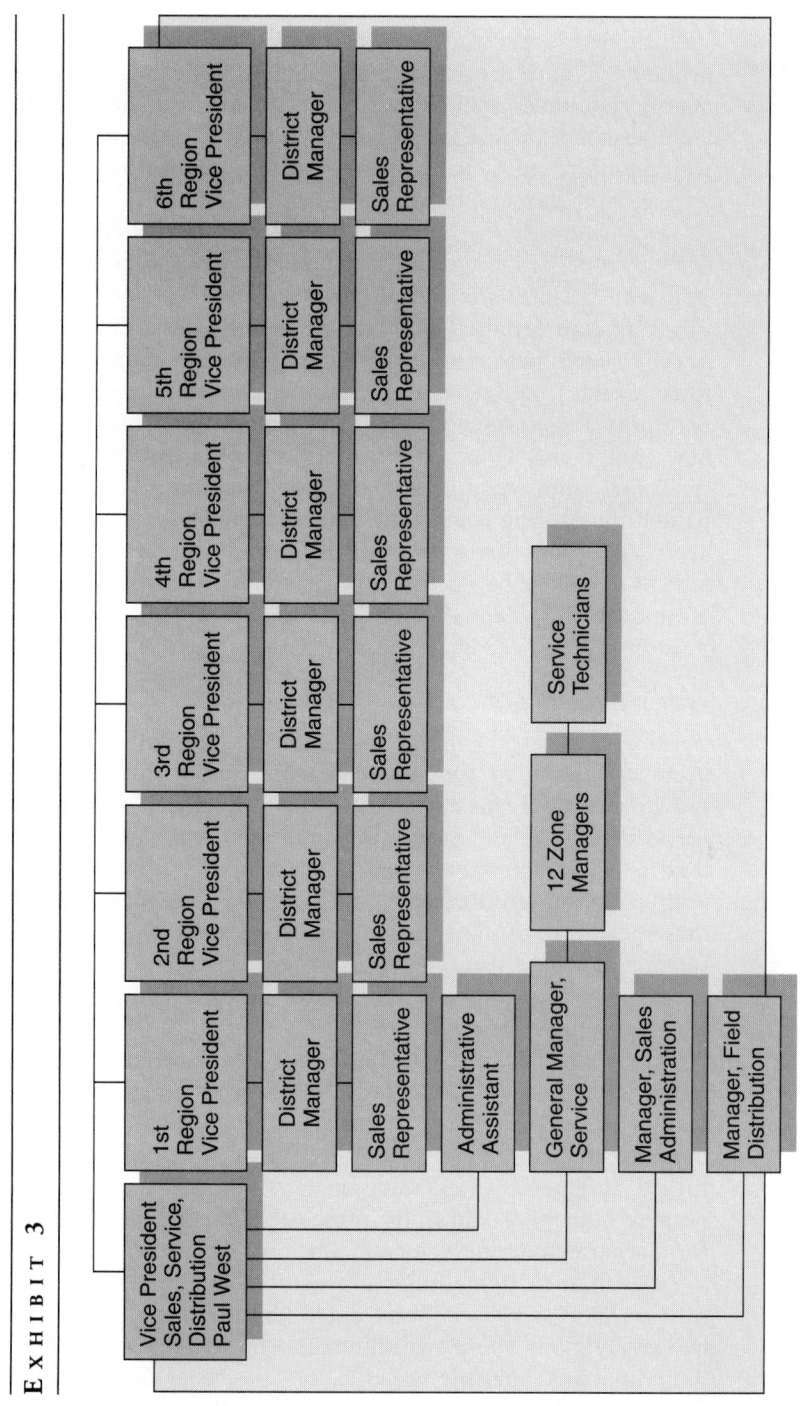

Callahan believed, however, that this would not continue because many products planned for market introduction in the next five years were state-of-the-art electronic monitoring equipment. Most of these products were in the anesthesia line. Omega's lack of experience in the medical electronics field would require an intensive sales effort to enter the market profitably, as there were several formidable competitors.

Unfortunately, as many as half of Omega's sales reps did not have the training or experience to sell these kinds of products. In view of the need to deal with hospital biomedical engineers on a very technical level, in the long run, Callahan surmised, it would be better to use only sales personnel experienced in selling electronic equipment rather than attempt to train the entire force. Besides, he knew from personal conversations that no more than 10 percent of the representatives had any interest in learning about or selling the new equipment. Thus, he wondered about augmenting the sales force with specialists who would be able to provide technical assistance to sell portable patient monitoring equipment. But, since there were already general line and anesthesia sales representatives calling on hospital personnel, he did not want a third party calling on the same personnel. Callahan thought this would be more confusing than advantageous.

Other Information

For the past year, the marketing manager of respiratory care, Bill Griese, had been attempting to convince Callahan that, despite the line's history, real growth potential existed in respiratory therapy. He wanted the company to spend more time and money pursuing this market. Griese had also indicated that to sell and service the products adequately—particularly the new critical care ventilator—the line should be handled by a separate sales force. He argued that because most of Omega's products were in the anesthesia field, the representatives were spending a disproportionate amount of sales time in that area. Thus, Omega's relatively poor sales and image in respiratory therapy were perpetuated.

Callahan knew that Jeff Hardy, marketing manager for patient care, would lobby for a separate sales group for anesthesia products since that line represents one quarter of the company's sales. Apparently this request had been made several times over the past five years. One proposal had included plans for the anesthesia (gases) sales force to handle the anesthesia equipment also because both were sold to the same department. Another proposal had called for a separate anesthesia equipment force altogether.

Callahan thought drugs and equipment required substantially different sales techniques and one force could not adequately handle both. But he also had reservations about two different representatives calling on the same customer, as was currently the case. On the other hand, a separate anesthesia equipment force would result in substantially more sales time spent on respiratory products by the general line sales force.

EXHIBIT 4   *Sales Compensation Plans*

	General Line Representatives	Anesthesia Representatives
Base salary	$3,500–$3,850	$3,650–$4,100
Commission on sales up to quota (percent)	1%	1%
Commission on sales over quota (percent)	2–5%	2–5%
1991 salary range	$46,200–$57,800	$51,800–$64,750
Average salary	$50,100	$54,000

Anesthesia Sales Organization

About 10 years ago, Omega's chemical research department discovered a revolutionary new drug (a gas) to anesthetize patients safely for surgery. After two years of testing for the Food and Drug Administration, the drug was approved and successfully introduced to the marketplace. It is currently used on 60 percent of all surgical patients, and it continues to capture market share. The drug has a very high gross margin, and in 1992, it had profits of $35 million on sales of $83 million. Its patent runs through 1996.

To develop the surgical drug market fully and lead the marketing and sales activities, a vice president position was created at the time of the discovery of the new drug. Ronald Hagen was hired for this position. He put together a separate sales organization with 40 persons by 1991. Most of the sales reps were hired away from pharmaceutical companies and thus demanded and were paid salaries and commissions somewhat above those paid to Omega's general line sales force (see Exhibit 4).

Hagen is very proud of his organization, believing his sales representatives are a cut above the general line organization. Consequently, he wants no part of any plans to join the two forces. Besides, other new drugs are scheduled for introduction in the 1993–94 period and will provide the drug sales group with a sufficient product load for several years.

General Line Sales Organization

The general line sales organization, reporting to Paul West, consisted of 135 representatives, 16 district managers, and six regional vice presidents. The service department, also under West, consisted of 172 technicians reporting to 16 zone managers. Also reporting to West were the managers of sales administration, the manager of field distribution, and an administrative assistant.

West was initially upset about the apparent demotion of his position as a result of the reorganization; he had reported directly to John before Callahan was hired. Knowing that further reorganization was imminent, West believed he would ultimately lose control of the service and distribution areas. Although this would narrow his responsibilities somewhat, West was not concerned. Because of the need to update both the service organization and the distribution organization to handle the new portable patient care monitoring products, those areas had been commanding a disproportionate amount of his time for the past few months. West would prefer to hire a general manager for service and distribution and have that new individual, reporting to him, handle most of the responsibility in those two crucial areas. He intended to propose this to Callahan.

In the meantime, West was most interested in studying the sales force reorganization and conveying his ideas to Callahan. West had always been interested in developing a separate sales force for anesthesia equipment and disposables. He thought there was sufficient sales volume to support it, and customers would be receptive to the extra attention and service. When selling this equipment, the rep would call on the anesthesia staff, a group typically more difficult to deal with and more technically oriented than personnel from other hospital departments. Often the sale also involved the hospital's biomedical engineers, which was not true of Omega's other products. A separate force could be more intensely trained, thus ensuring better customer service.

West also believed a strong case could be made for putting architectural products under the mandate of a small but specialized sales force. General line sales reps tended to ignore architectural products because their sales consumed too much time and involved contact with nonhospital personnel.

If a separate anesthesia equipment force were developed, the remaining general line would be left with nursing, infant care, respiratory therapy, and architectural products. This seemed reasonable because many of these products were sold in the same hospital departments even though they were categorized in different product lines. West also thought the dealers should be encouraged to handle more low-cost products, giving the general line sales force more time for other products.

The real problem with splitting out the anesthesia products, West thought, was that each group would remain responsible for the new portable patient monitoring equipment. West further believed that since each force would be responsible for a smaller number of the new products, they could be sufficiently trained to do this work. Since most of the new portable monitoring equipment was in the anesthesia area, this group would be selected from those with the most training and experience with electronics products. Additionally, West thought there was a strong case to be made for having "monitoring specialists" in both sales groups. These persons would handle all the products of their groups but would emphasize the new equipment and would be available for dual sales calls with their colleagues who were not so well versed in the items.

At a recent convention, West briefly discussed his ideas with Tom Reinke, the western regional vice president and one of West's closest friends. Reinke had, at one time, worked for a company that manufactured sterilization equipment for hospitals. Following the development of a new, very sophisticated unit, it had divided the sales organization into two groups. One handled the existing line, and the other group specialized in the new equipment. Reinke indicated the sales force division proved disastrous, leading to duplicate sales calls, customer confusion, and increased expenses. He thought the same would occur with West's monitoring specialists. He recommended that Omega hire more technically qualified personnel for the general line sales force. West left the convention somewhat less enthusiastic about his sales force proposal.

Case 1-3
OLSEN SEED FARMS*

After graduating from Iowa State University with degrees in agronomy and business, Jon Olsen assumed responsibility for the management and marketing of Olsen Seed Farms, a family business, located in Mount Horeb, Wisconsin. Founded by Jon's grandfather 76 years ago, Olsen Seed Farms now produces and sells a full line of agriculture seeds including corn, alfalfa, beans, and sorghum. As shown in Exhibit 1, sales of seed corn, which is Olsen's main product, totaled $2 million or 39,803 bushels in 1992.

In 1990, under Jon's direction, Olsen Seed Farms embarked on an expansion. The production facilities were upgraded, and production acreage was expanded by 60 percent to 3,500 acres.

After improvements to the production facilities were completed, Jon focused on the marketing function. Olsen's market share has remained unchanged for the past six years. In contrast, the market share of the three dominant national seed companies—Pioneer, DeKalb, and Jacques—has increased steadily.

Jon believes Olsen's lack of growth is primarily due to inefficiencies within the sales organization. In addition, he has identified three conditions in the environment that affect demand for Olsen's products. First, the seed corn industry is in the mature stage of its life cycle and saturated with competitors. In Wisconsin, for example, more than 35 firms sell agriculture seeds. Consequently, Olsen's sales can increase only at the expense of the competitors. Second, while the number of acres planted to corn has stabilized, acreage planted to soybeans and alfalfa is rapidly increasing. Third, acreage planted to crops depends on government and export programs.

Sales Territories

In 1981, Olsen Seed Farms expanded outside its home state. Jon's father, Joseph, logged over 60,000 miles in one year establishing new territories. As a result, Olsen seed is available in seven states—Illinois, Iowa, Michigan, Minnesota, Nebraska, South Dakota, and Wisconsin. Exhibit 2 on page 308 details Olsen's distribution area. However, market share in 1992 varies widely from a high of 11.26 percent in Olsen's home county to less than 0.52 percent in several counties in Michigan and Nebraska.

To improve operations, Jon established market share and profitability

---

*Regina Downey and Linda Drew, MBAs—Marketing, University of Wisconsin-Madison, assisted in preparing this case.

EXHIBIT 1   *Unit Sales of Seed (in bushels)*

Year	Corn	Soybeans	Alfalfa	Total Sales
1988	30,665	4,657	1,066	36,388
1989	31,956	4,175	1,130	37,261
1990	32,873	6,075	1,122	40,070
1991	38,914	5,815	1,053	45,782
1992	39,803	7,120	1,210	48,133

objectives for each territory. In developing the objectives, he considered the higher costs of servicing and delivering to areas outside Wisconsin. Because the areas south and west of Wisconsin differ in soil conditions and length of growing season, Jon concluded that seed more suitable to those regions needs to be developed to obtain significant share improvement. However, he is uncertain whether the existing research and production facilities can accommodate these changes.

Sales Force

Olsen Seed Farms employs a sales manager and 18 district supervisors who manage 576 dealers in seven states. Jon believes poor organization and control of the sales force contributes to Olsen Seed Farm's marketing problems.

Dealers

Like other agriculture seed companies, Olsen Seed Farms sells seed through the company dealer organization. More than 50 percent of the dealers are located in Wisconsin, as shown in Exhibit 3 on page 309.

The dealers are farmers who agree to sell Olsen Seed to their friends and neighbors in exchange for a discount based on the number of bushels sold. The 1992 dealer discount schedule is shown in Exhibit 4 on page 310.

A dealership audit revealed that, although the dealers' associations with Olsen Seed Farms varies from less than 1 year to over 19 years, the majority of dealers have been with the company for 3 to 4 years. Over 60 percent of the dealers are over 50 years old and are full-time farmers. The chief reasons cited for becoming dealers were:

"I was asked."

Free seed (sample bags).

Liked the supervisor and/or Joseph Olsen.

Olsen Seed Farms is a small family operation.

As shown in Exhibit 5 on page 310, categorizing the dealers by number of bushels sold confirmed Jon's suspicion that most of the dealers do not sell

EXHIBIT **2**   *Distribution of Olsen Seed*

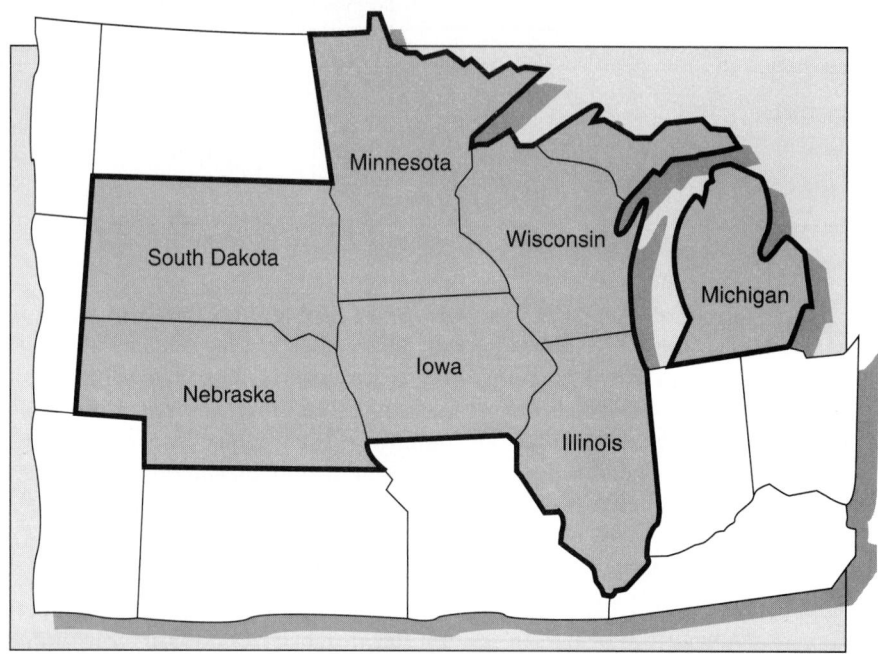

seed. Since over half of the dealers sell less than 49 bushels of seed, some farmers are becoming dealers to get the discount on their own seed rather than to sell seed.

The audit also showed that, while some dealers use Olsen seed for 100 percent of their total requirements, most plant only 30 to 50 percent of their total seed requirements with Olsen seed. When questioned, dealers said they purchase the remaining 50 to 70 percent of their seed from other companies for comparison purposes. Others said they purchase seed from other companies because they are unaware that crop seed, besides corn, is available from Olsen Seed Farms. Many dealers, for example, do not know that Olsen Seed Farms sells alfalfa seed.

A breakdown of the size of the dealers in relation to company sales, as shown in Exhibit 6 on page 310, indicated to Jon that a small percent of the dealers account for more than half of total sales.

Jon is considering reclassifying the small dealers who account for only 20 percent of total sales and probably purchase seed only for their own planting needs.

EXHIBIT 3   *Location and Size of Current Dealers*

Sales Area*	Number of Dealers	Bushels Sold by Dealers	Average Dealer Size (bushels)
1	27	300	11
2	22	1,086	49
3	15	759	51
4	18	320	18
5	92	2,970	32
6*	124	10,851	88
7	25	2,340	94
8*	91	4,014	44
9*	39	2,243	58
10*	21	1,544	74
11	5	110	22
12*	47	2,123	45
13	5	109	22
14	4	204	51
15	9	634	70
16	20	498	25
17	12	308	26
18	—	—	—
Total	576	30,413	53

*Wisconsin territories.

Supervisors

Eighteen district supervisors manage territories in Olsen Seed Farms' seven-state market area, as detailed in Exhibit 7 on page 311.

After a careful analysis of the supervisor structure at Olsen Seed Farms and competing seed companies, Jon identified four major problems.

First, a lack of contact exists between the dealers and supervisors. In 1992, 70 percent of the dealers had not seen their supervisors in six months. One dealer had not been contacted by his supervisor for two years. In the seed industry, close communication between supervisors, dealers, and customers is critical, especially during the growing season, so timely information about the crop can be conveyed to farmers.

For example, in 1991, disease affected most of the corn crop in Wisconsin. The stalk disease hurt the standability of the corn during the later harvesting weeks. Olsen supervisors and dealers were able to warn their customers with longer maturing hybrids to harvest early. Thus, although the hybrids were

EXHIBIT 4   *1992 Dealer Discount Schedule*

Number of Bushels	Discount (percent)
1–24	9%
25–49	14
50–99	16
100–199	18
200–349	20
350–499	21
500–999	22
1,000–1,499	23
1,500+	24

EXHIBIT 5   *Dealer Size*

Bushels Sold	Number of Dealers
0–24	169
25–49	203
50–99	169
100–199	88
200+	41

EXHIBIT 6   *Dealer Sales as a Percent of Company Sales*

Bushels Sold	Percent of Dealers	Percent of Total Sales
1–49	55%	20%
50–99	25	24
100+	19	55

EXHIBIT 7   *Supervisor Territories*

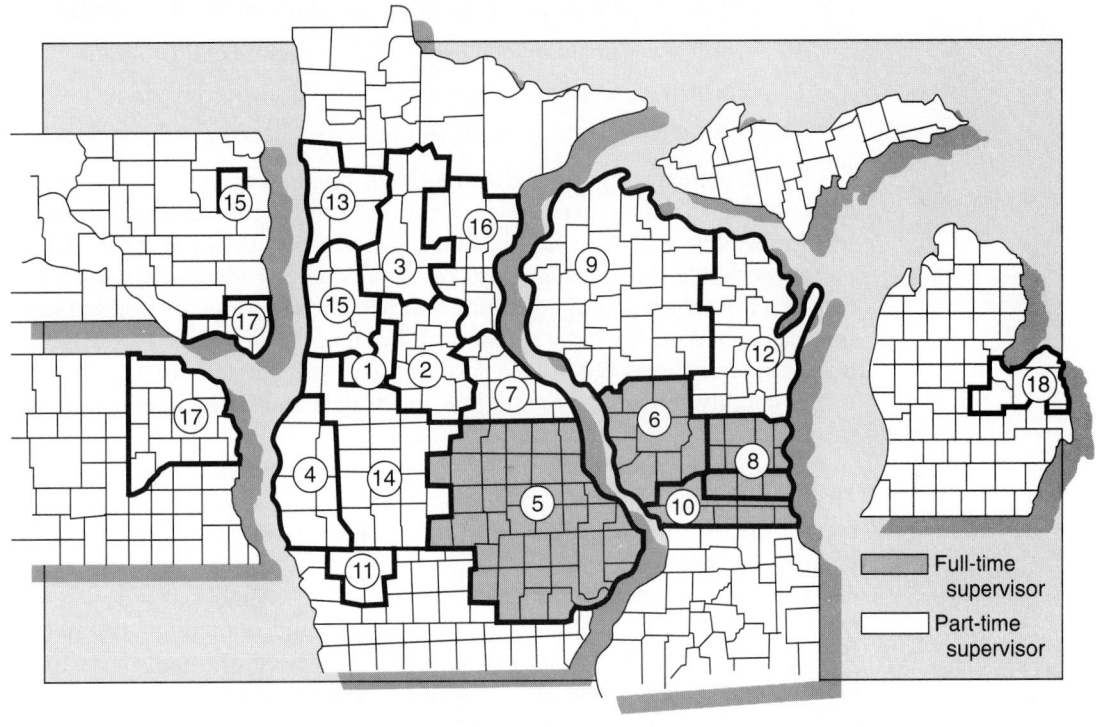

harvested at less than their maximum yield potential, the farmers avoided harvesting a crop that had fallen over and was rotting in the field. Because Olsen's supervisors are typically not very involved with their dealers and customers, Jon feels extremely fortunate that Olsen had been able to catch this problem in time. He thinks a more formal communication channel between the dealers, supervisors, and customers should be implemented to guarantee this timely communication.

Second, the supervisors have varying abilities and commitments to selling Olsen seeds. Unlike the Pioneer Seed Company's sales force, whose supervisors are primarily full-time managers with agronomy degrees, 14 of Olsen's supervisors are part-time supervisors and full-time farmers. Because the supervisors' main source of income is farming, not selling, Jon is having trouble starting a formalized sales structure based on goals and objectives as well as motivating the supervisors to sell and work with their dealers. Many promotional and sales programs are never implemented because unless a supervisor is "sold" on an idea, the supervisor will not pass it on to the dealer. As a result, the supervisors do not inform the dealers, and the dealers cannot inform their customers. Of the dealers Jon surveyed, he found the following:

40 percent were unaware of Olsen's PEN (special deal) program.

20 percent were unaware of the early order discount program.

Most requested information on soil tests, fertilizers, and herbicides.

Third, company figures show that Olsen's highest market share is in counties in which the supervisors reside. Other counties in the supervisors' assigned territories have very low market share. Jon suspects the sales territories may be too large for the supervisors to cover adequately. He also wonders if the lack of a formal agronomy education hampers the supervisors' efforts to service the dealers beyond the basic sale of seed. Because the company is a small family business, Jon believes Olsen Seed Farms' distinct advantage over its competitors is high-quality service and seed. Thus, the dealers and supervisors contact with the customers is critical to Olsen's image.

Finally, the supervisor commission structure encourages the formation of "front dealerships," especially among the part-time supervisors. Dealers can receive up to 24 percent discount, while supervisors can receive only a 14 percent discount.

Part-time supervisors designate another family member as a dealer. Then the supervisor concentrates efforts on servicing and obtaining customers for the dealership rather than on servicing and attracting new customers for the existing dealers. Front dealerships also prevent Jon from gaining an accurate picture of Olsen Seed Farms' customer base.

Based on his analysis of the company's sales force, Jon believes reorganization of the force is necessary to gain greater market share. He is wondering how to develop a plan to meet the market share objectives established.

Case 1-4
BARRO STICKNEY, INC.*

Introduction

With four people and sales of $5.5 million, Barro Stickney, Inc., (BSI) had become a successful and profitable manufacturers' representative firm. It enjoyed a reputation for outstanding sales results and friendly, thorough service to both its customers and principals. In addition, BSI was considered a great place to work. The office was comfortable and the atmosphere relaxed but professional. All members of the group had come to value the close, friendly working relationships that had grown with the organization.

Success had brought with it increased profits as well as the inevitable decision regarding further growth. Recent requests from two principals, Franklin Key Electronics and R. D. Ocean, had forced BSI to focus its attention on the question of expansion. It was not to be an easy decision, for expansion offered both risk and opportunity.

Company Background

John Barro and Bill Stickney established their small manufacturers' representative agency, Barro Stickney, Inc., 10 years ago. Both men were close friends who left different manufacturers' representative firms to join as partners in their own "rep" agency. The two worked very well together, and their talents complemented each other.

John Barro was energetic and gregarious. He enjoyed meeting new people and taking on new challenges. It was mainly through John's efforts that many of BSI's eight principals had signed on with BSI. Even after producing $1.75 million in sales this past year, John still made an effort to contribute much of his free time to community organizations in addition to perfecting his golf score.

Bill Stickney liked to think of himself as someone a person could count on. He was thoughtful and thorough. He liked to figure how things could get done, and how they could be better. Much of the administrative work of the agency, such as resource allocation and territory assignments, was handled by Bill. In addition to his contribution of $1.5 million to total company sales,

*This case was prepared by Tony Langan, B. Jane Stewart, and Lawrence M. Stratton, Jr., under the supervision of Professor Erin Anderson of the Wharton School, University of Pennsylvania. The writing of the case was sponsored by the Manufacturers' Representatives Educational Research Foundation. The cooperation of the Mid-Atlantic Chapter of the Electronic Representatives Association (ERA) is greatly appreciated.

Bill also had a Boy Scout troop and was interested in gourmet cooking. In fact, he often prepared specialties to share with his fellow workers.

A few years later, as the business grew, J. Todd Smith (J.T.) joined as an additional salesperson. J.T. had worked for a nationally known corporation, and he brought his experience dealing with large customers with him. He and his family loved the Harrisburg area, and J.T. was very happy when he was asked to join BSI just as his firm was ready to transfer him to Chicago. John and Bill had worked with J.T. in connection with a hospital fund-raising project, and they were impressed with his tenacity and enthusiasm. Because he had produced sales of over $2 million this past year, J.T. was now considered eligible to buy a partnership share of BSI.

Soon after J.T. joined BSI, Elizabeth Lee, a school friend of John's older sister, was hired as office manager. She was cheerful and put as much effort into her work as she did coaching the local swim team. The three salespeople knew they could rely on her to keep track of orders and schedules, and she was very helpful when customers and principals called with requests or problems.

Most principals in the industry assigned their reps exclusive territories, and BSI's ranged over the Pennsylvania, New Jersey, and Delaware area. The partners purchased a small house and converted it into their present office located in Camp Hill, a suburb of Harrisburg, the state capitol of Pennsylvania. The converted home contributed to the familylike atmosphere and attitude that was promoted and prevalent throughout the agency.

Over the years, in addition to local interests, BSI and its people had made an effort to participate in and support the efforts of the Electronics Representative Association (ERA). A wall of the company library was covered with awards and letters of appreciation. BSI had made many friends and important contacts through the organization. Just last year, BSI received a recommendation from Chuck Goodman, a Chicago manufacturers' rep who knew a principal in need of representation in the Philadelphia area. The principal's line worked well with BSI's existing portfolio, and customer response had been quite favorable. BSI planned to continue active participation in the ERA.

Each week, BSI held a 5 o'clock meeting in the office library where all members of the company shared their experiences of the week. It was a time when new ideas were encouraged and everyone was brought up to date. For example, many customer problems were solved here, and principals' and members' suggestions were discussed. An established agenda enabled members to prepare. Most meetings took about 60 to 90 minutes, with emphasis placed on group consensus. It was during this group meeting that BSI would discuss the future of the company.

Opportunities for Expansion

R. D. Ocean was BSI's largest principal, and it accounted for 32 percent of BSI's revenues. Ocean had just promoted James Innve as new sales manager, and he felt an additional salesperson was needed for BSI to achieve the new sales projections. Innve expressed the opinion that BSI's large commission checks justified the additional effort, and he further commented that J.T.'s expensive new car was proof that BSI could afford it.

BSI was not sure an additional salesperson was necessary, but it did not want to lose the goodwill of R. D. Ocean or its business. Also, while it was customary for all principals to meet and tacitly approve new representatives, BSI wanted to be very sure that any new salesperson would fit into the close-knit BSI organization.

Franklin Key Electronics was BSI's initial principal and had remained a consistent contributor of approximately 15 percent of BSI's revenues. BSI felt its customer base was well suited to the Franklin line, and it had worked hard to establish the Franklin Key name with these customers. As a consequence, BSI now considered Franklin Key relatively easy to sell.

A few days previously, Mark Heil, Franklin's representative from Virginia, perished when his private plane crashed, leaving Franklin Key without representation in its D.C./Virginia territory. Franklin did not want to jeopardize its sales of over $800,000 and was desperate to replace Heil before its customers found other sources. Franklin offered the territory to BSI and was anxious to hear the decision within one week.

BSI was not familiar with the territory, but it did understand that there were many military accounts. This meant there was a potential for sizable orders, although a different and specialized sales approach would be required. Military customers are known to have their own unique approach to purchase decisions.

Because of the distance and the size of the territory, serious consideration was needed as to whether a branch office would be necessary. A branch office would mean less interaction with and a greater independence from the main BSI office. None of the current BSI members seemed eager to move there, but it might be possible to hire someone who was familiar with the territory. There was, of course, always the risk that any successful salesperson might leave and start his or her own rep firm.

In addition to possibilities of expanding its territory and its sales force, BSI also wanted to consider whether it should increase or maintain its number of principals. BSI's established customer base and its valued reputation put it in a strong position to approach potential principals. If, however, BSI had too many principals, it might not be able to offer them all the attention and service they might require.

Preparation for the Meeting

Each member received an agenda and supporting data for the upcoming meeting asking them to consider the issue of expansion. They would be asked whether BSI should or should not expand its territory, its sales force, and/or its number of principals. In preparation, they were each asked to take a good hard look at the current BSI portfolio and to consider all possibilities for

EXHIBIT 1   *Return versus Difficulty in Selling*

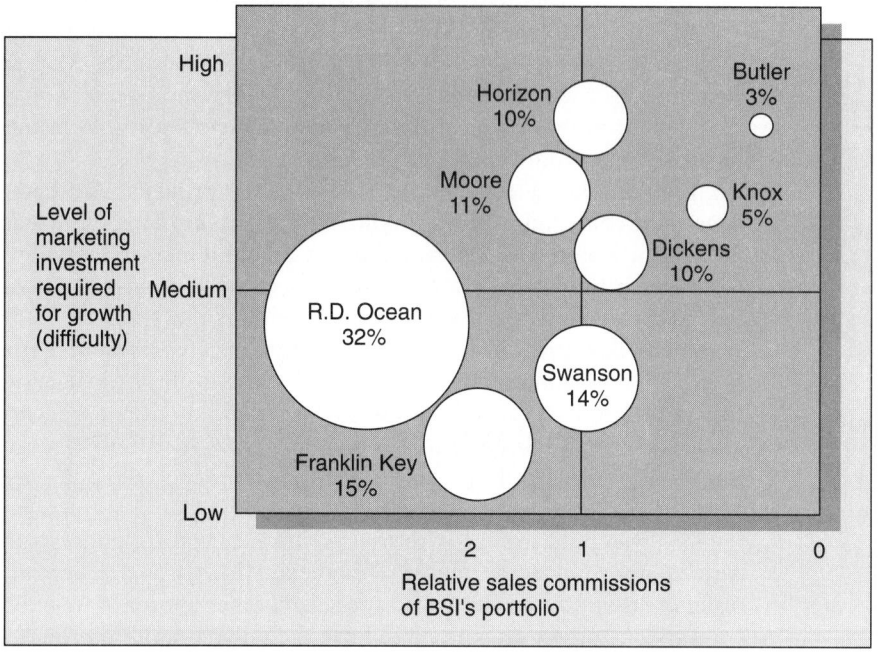

growth, including the effect any changes would have on the company's profits, its reputation, and its work environment.

It was an ambitious agenda: one that would determine the future of the company. It would take even more time than usual to discuss everything and reach consensus. Consequently, this week's meeting was set to occur over the weekend at Bill Stickney's vacation lodge in the Poconos starting with a gourmet dinner served at 7 P.M. sharp.

Before the meeting, Bill Stickney examined the sources of BSI's revenue and the firm's income for the previous year. He also estimated the future prospects for each of BSI's lines, considering each line's market potential and BSI's level of saturation in each market. Finally, he estimated the costs of hiring a new employee both in the current sales territory and in the Washington/Virginia area. Immediately before the meeting, Elizabeth finished compiling Bill's data into four exhibits.

Exhibit 1 evaluates the amount of sales effort (difficulty in selling) necessary to achieve a certain percentage of sales in BSI's portfolio (return). Difficulty in selling is measured by the level of marketing investment required for growth. Stickney's estimate is shown on the vertical axis. Return for this investment is measured by the relative sales commissions as a percent of BSI's portfolio

EXHIBIT 2   *Barro Stickney, Inc., Estimation of Cost of Additional Sales Representative*

Compensation costs for new sales representative:

Depending on the new sales representative's level of experience, BSI would pay a base salary of $15,000–$25,000 with the following bonus schedule:

 0% firm's commission revenue up to $500,000 in sales

20% firm's commission revenue first $.5 million in sales over $500,000

25% firm's commission revenue for the next $.5 million in sales

30% firm's commission for the next $.5 million in sales

40% firm's commission sales above $2 million

Estimate of support costs[1] for new representative.[2]

Search applicant pool, psychological testing, hiring, training,[3] flying final choice to principals for approval.[4]	$28,000
Automobile expenses, telephone costs, business cards, entertainment promotion.	$22,000
Insurance, payroll taxes (social security, unemployment compensation)	$16,000
Total expenses	$66,000
Incremental expenses for new territory	
Transportation (additional mileage from Camp Hill to Virginia)	$ 2,000
Office equipment and rent (same regardless of headquarter's location)	$ 4,000
Cost of hiring office manager[5]	$18,000
Total incremental expenses	$24,000

[1]Rounded to the nearest thousand.
[2]In current territory.
[3]Excludes the lost revenue from selling instead of engaging in this activity (opportunity cost).
[4]Although rep agencies are not legally required to show prospective employees to principals, it is generally held to be good business practice.
[5]Discretionary.

EXHIBIT 3   *Barro Stickney, Inc., Statement of Revenue Total Sales Revenue 1991, $5.5 million*

Principal	Estimated Market Saturation	Product Type	Sales/ Commission Rate	Share of BSI's Portfolio	Commission Revenue
R. D. Ocean	High	Components	5%	32%	$96,756
Franklin Key	High	Components	5	15	45,354
Butler	Low	Technical/computer	12	3	9,070
Dickens	Low	Components	5	10	30,236
Horizon	Medium	Components	5.5	10	30,237
Swanson	High	Components	5.25	14	42,331
Moore	Medium	Consumer/electronics	5.25	11	33,260
Knox	Low	Technical/communications	8.5	5	15,118

EXHIBIT 4   *Barro Stickney, Inc., Statement of Income (for the year ending December 31, 1991)*

Revenue	
Commission income	$302,362
Expenses	
Salaries for sales and bonuses (includes Barro Stickney)	130,250
Office manager's salary	20,000
Total nonpersonnel expenses[1]	128,279
Total expenses	$278,529
New Income[2]	**$23,833 (7.9% of revenue)**

[1]Includes travel, advertising, taxes, office supplies, retirement, automobile expenses, communications, office equipment, and miscellaneous expenses.

[2]Currently held in negotiable certificates of deposits in a Harrisburg bank.

shown on the horizontal axis. If BSI's time were evenly divided among its eight principals, each would receive 12.5 percent of the agency's time. The X axis shows each principal's time allocation as a proportion of 12.5 percent, the "par" time allocation. The area of each ellipse reflects each principal's share of BSI's commission revenue.

Bill Stickney presented the following additional comments as a result of his research:

1. Swanson's products are being replaced by the competition's computerized electronic equipment, a product category the firm has ignored. As a result, the company is losing its once prominent market position.

2. Although small amounts of effort are required to promote Ocean's product line to customers in the current sales territory, Ocean is extremely demanding of both BSI and other manufacturers' representative firms.

3. According to a seminar at the last ERA meeting, the maximum safe proportion of a rep firm's commissions from a single principal should be 25 to 30 percent. Also, at the meeting, one speaker indicated that if a firm commands 80 percent of a market, it should focus on another product or expand its territory rather than attempt to obtain the remainder of the market.

4. The revenue for investment for the manufacturers' representative firm comes from one or more of several sources. These sources include reduced forthcoming commission income, retained previous income, and borrowed money from a financial institution. Most successful firms expand their sales force or sales territory when they experience income growth and use of the investment as a tax write-off.

Case 1-5
Flambeau Plastics, Inc.*

Todd Levin, president of Flambeau Plastics, and Abby Hutchinson, vice president of marketing, faced a critical issue at an inopportune time. Both Levin and Hutchinson had completed plans to introduce a new toy line that would utilize Flambeau's production line capabilities along with its technical expertise in plastics. The new toy line would be distributed through manufacturers' reps who specialize in toys. Now, because of recent developments involving one of Flambeau's more important customers, plans for the new toy line would need to be revised, maybe even scrapped.

Flambeau Plastics produces a broad line of products distributed through manufacturers' agents throughout the country. Flambeau prides itself on being a major producer of plastic products purchased for resale by the nation's leading chain stores. Flambeau produces plastic products that are found in all households.

The critical issue centered on a recent development involving Wal-Mart Stores, Inc. Hutchinson had heard rumors indicating Wal-Mart's intentions to squeeze manufacturers' agents and brokers out of its buying process. She had not given much thought to these rumors, but now she had to face the issue directly. Marlow & Dretzka, Flambeau's manufacturers' rep agency, informed Hutchinson that its attempts to contact buyers at Wal-Mart had failed. A telephone conversation with Craig Marlow revealed Wal-Mart would no longer do business with Flambeau indirectly; all future business deals would have to be direct. For Marlow & Dretzka, such a move would be disastrous; Wal-Mart accounts for about 16 percent of the agency's approximately $6 million in sales. For Flambeau, sales to Wal-Mart account for roughly 42 percent of its household plastic sales volume of $2.3 million. Marlow informed Hutchinson that Flambeau would receive an "official" notification by mail from Wal-Mart's CEO, David D. Glass.

The Household Plastics Market

The household plastics market is dominated by five manufacturers that account for 80 percent of total sales. The market has hundreds of smaller manufacturers that account for the remaining 20 percent. Entry into the household plastics market is relatively easy. Firms with excess capacity often enter this market

---

*This case is based on published information found in Andrea Harter, "Factory-Direct Dealing to Save Wal-Mart Money," *USA Today,* December 4, 1991, pp. 1D,3D; Andrea Harter, "Salesmen Fight Wal-Mart," *Capital Times,* December 4, 1991, p. C2; Karen Blumenthal, "Wal-Mart Set to Eliminate Reps, Brokers," *The Wall Street Journal,* December 2, 1992, pp. A3, A5; and Zina Sawaya, "Cutting Out the Middleman," *Forbes,* January 6, 1992, p. 169. This case was prepared by Professor Neil M. Ford as a basis for class discussion and was not designed to illustrate effective or ineffective handling of an administrative situation.

on a short-term basis. None of the manufacturers relies on consumer advertising; brand loyalty is virtually nonexistent. The one exception is Rubbermaid®, a major producer of household rubber and plastic products.

Household plastic products are sold primarily through supermarkets, department stores, drugstores, and mass (discount) merchandisers. Although the dollar volume sold through these types of retail outlets varies, it is estimated the mass merchandisers account for 45 percent, department stores for 25 percent, supermarkets for 17 percent, and drugstores and other outlets for 13 percent of sales. Catalog stores account for a small, but growing percent of sales.

The five dominant manufacturers secure market distribution using manufacturers' agents. The smaller firms typically rely on brokers. Commissions paid to manufacturers' agents and brokers amounted to about 2 to 3 percent of sales at manufacturers' prices. Using other means of representation, such as a direct company sales force, was not considered to be economically feasible. Most manufacturers believed their lines of household plastic products, although broad, would not justify the costs associated with having a direct sales force.

The typical manufacturers' agent or agency represented 7 to 10 manufacturers that produced noncompetitive but complementary product lines. Most manufacturers have established long-term relationships with their agents and rely on them for market information.

The Company

Flambeau Plastics, Inc., was incorporated in 1953. As one of the five dominant producers of plastic products of all types, Flambeau has enjoyed steady growth. Executives have always been growth oriented and have developed new products and new markets regularly. Flambeau has four manufacturing facilities located throughout the Midwest. Its main office is in Chicago. Corporate sales total $9.2 million, with the bulk of the business coming from OEM sales. Sales by category are:

Automobile industry	$4.1 million
Appliance industry	1.6 million
Electronics industry	0.7 million
Household products	2.3 million
Aerospace industry	0.5 million
Total sales	$9.2 million

Flambeau's original products were custom designed for the automobile industry. Chrysler Corporation accounts for the bulk of its sales in the automobile industry. Whirlpool Corporation is a significant account in the appliance industry. Flambeau's position in the electronics industry is a recent development. Currently, Flambeau sells to this market using manufacturers' reps.

Levin is highly regarded and viewed as a leader in the plastics industry. Levin, along with Jack Russo, vice president of production, instituted quality control procedures long before the concept became poplar. Levin is also considered to be very independent and not likely to adopt procedures unless he is convinced of their merit. Hutchinson has many of these same traits. The trio has become a formidable team and has been largely responsible for Flambeau's success in the plastics industry.

The Wal-Mart Problem

Hutchinson and Levin discussed the recent developments with Wal-Mart with several other Flambeau executives. Gene Manchester, manager of the household products line, was indignant about the news from Marlow & Dretzka. He commented, "We have worked with Marlow & Dretzka from the beginning. Their agency has been largely responsible for our position in this market. We need them for market coverage. Besides, it's our decision as to how we sell to the market, not Wal-Mart's." Hutchinson added, "Our household plastics line is broad, but it is not a high-tech product and does not require a direct sales force. We have reviewed this issue before and feel that the costs associated with a direct sales force would be prohibitive."

Levin commented that before Flambeau makes any decisions, it should wait until the executives read the letter from Wal-Mart's CEO.

The Wal-Mart Story

Wal-Mart was the creation of Sam Walton who started Wal-Mart Stores in Rogers, Arkansas, in 1962. From the beginning, Wal-Mart developed its own distribution system stemming partly from the absence of wholesalers in small towns. Today, Wal-Mart is the nation's largest retailer with an estimated $40 billion in sales provided by almost 1,600 Wal-Mart stores and 150 Sam's Wholesale Club stores. While most retailers view expansion cautiously, Wal-Mart plans to add another 150 stores within the next 12 months.

Wal-Mart's view about manufacturers' agents (reps) and brokers is not new, nor is it alone in its desire to eliminate these intermediaries from the distribution channel. Other retailers, such as Sears, Roebuck & Co., have dealt directly with manufacturers for some time. Wal-Mart has been most aggressive within the industry in trying to eliminate reps and brokers. Since the mid-1980s, Wal-Mart has been asking manufacturers to send only their executives to the Bentonville, Arkansas, headquarters.

Many manufacturers and their reps contend Wal-Mart not only wants to eliminate reps and brokers but it also expects a price cut equal to the 2 to 3 percent commission for an account like Wal-Mart. Wal-Mart executives take issue with this accusation and have denied ever asking for the broker or rep's commission.

The official Wal-Mart position was contained in a November 6 letter sent to vendors. The letter stated Wal-Mart intends to deal only with the vendor's executives and would no longer conduct business with manufacturers' reps or brokers. David Glass claimed the move continued a trend started in the mid-1980s and was necessary to enable Wal-Mart to react quickly to changes in the marketplace and to ensure steady streams of merchandise. Glass also noted the new relationships would be mutually beneficial because Wal-Mart and the manufacturer could coordinate business to eliminate seasonal swings and to provide more stability to the manufacturer. Finally, the letter attempted to provide assurance to smaller manufacturers that Wal-Mart would continue to do business with them if they felt direct contact through executives or a direct sales force was not affordable.

Flambeau's Reaction

The reaction at Flambeau was negative. Hutchinson noted Flambeau's entire sales coverage for the household plastics line was through manufacturers' reps. Levin indicated he was not keen on people telling him how to run his business. Russo was even more adamant: "Why shouldn't manufacturers be free to decide who takes their products to the market based on what is economically feasible rather than have it dictated by an intimidating buyer?" Gene Manchester saw the issue as nothing more than an attempt by Wal-Mart to eliminate a layer of costs and wondered if Flambeau should offer Wal-Mart a 2 to 3 percent discount in place of commissions. Manchester pointed out that this would be in line with Wal-Mart's everyday low prices.

Hutchinson suggested Flambeau invite its manufacturers' rep agency in to discuss the problem. Levin agreed with her and indicated a meeting with Marlow & Dretzka should be scheduled as soon as possible.

The Marlow & Dretzka Meeting

Craig Marlow, Geoff Dretzka, and one of their reps, Anne Mitby, attended the Chicago meeting. They were aware of the problem and knew of other agencies that had been hurt by Wal-Mart's tactics. Marlow identified Anne Mitby as one rep who had worked very hard to develop business with Wal-Mart only to be fired by the agency after Wal-Mart pressured the manufacturer to eliminate her from the process. Mitby, hired two months earlier by Marlow & Dretzka to work on a new account, identified one Texas agency that closed its doors after Wal-Mart forced the manufacturer to deal directly or not at all. The Wal-Mart account represented roughly 50 percent of the agency's commissions.

Dretzka took issue with Wal-Mart's claim that eliminating reps and brokers will lead to price stability. He commented Wal-Mart is "all wet if they think this will eliminate price increases from manufacturers. Manufacturers will have to hire staffs that cost up to $200,000 a year to do the same job they are contracting out to us." He noted reps do not consider themselves to be outsiders or third parties to a transaction, but rather an extension of the principals they represent.

Marlow & Dretzka asked Levin and the others at the meeting what Flambeau intended to do about Wal-Mart's demands. Levin indicated the problem was very serious and they would not treat the issue lightly. Marlow stated one group of manufacturers' agents and brokers is raising money to fight Wal-Mart and legal actions are being considered. He also mentioned a 1988 lawsuit against catalog retailer Fingerhut. The lawsuit charged Fingerhut with illegally interfering with contracts between manufacturers and reps by asking the manufacturers to sell directly to the company.

Dretzka cited an earlier protest that had been reported in a December 1986 issue of *The Wall Street Journal*. The Organization of Manufacturers Representatives (OMR) ran an ad depicting Thomas Jefferson, Benjamin Franklin, and others as founding fathers who symbolize free enterprise. People dressed like the founding fathers picketed at Wal-Mart Stores to protest the company's practice of bypassing reps. Unfortunately, as Dretzka noted, what was intended as a battle only amounted to a brush war.

Flambeau's Decision

Levin asked Hutchinson to carefully review the issues and to arrive at a decision that would be equitable to all parties. Hutchinson knew the task would be difficult. To compound matters, she had heard another rumor that K-Mart and Target Stores, Wal-Mart's prime discounting competitors, were considering similar moves to lower operating costs. "These are difficult times for the nation's retailers," she noted, "that is, except for Wal-Mart, which hopes to top $100 billion in sales by the end of the decade."

Case 1-6
Business Research Associates

Scott Carpenter and Jack Wallman had completed their first year of business as consultants who specialize in providing market potential and sales forecast estimates. Most of their clients were small to medium business firms that lacked the personnel needed for estimating market potential and sales forecasts.

Business Research Associates (BRA) had established a reputation for quality work. The influx of new projects described below indicated Scott and Jack would be busy for several months. They were considering hiring a full-time consultant to aid them with the numerous projects.

Project One

The first project involved a manufacturer of corrugated and solid fiber boxes. The company, California Box, wanted BRA to estimate the total market potential for its line of boxes for a specific county in California. California Box wanted to intensify the company's efforts in Fresno County, one of the areas the firm served. In the Fresno SMA, the company's sales totaled $1,500,000 in 1991 of which $1,275,000, or 85 percent, went to firms within the food and kindred products industry. The remaining $225,000, or 15 percent, went to firms manufacturing stone, clay, and glass products. Nancy Mitchell, president of California Box, indicated to Scott and Jack that she was concerned about the concentration in only two industries. Her sales manager contended this was poor sales performance, considering the diversity of industry in the Fresno area.

Initial discussions with Business Research Associates prompted California Box to retain BRA. BRA management indicated that determining market potential for the Fresno SMA would be necessary before sales quotas could be determined. Nancy Mitchell inquired as to BRA's method, saying she had had little success in locating any statistics that would help determine market potential for Fresno County. Scott informed her that one of their first tasks would be to measure "end use" consumption estimates, using data provided by several sources. He told her several governmental and trade association publications were available for this purpose.

Project Two

Sun-Ray Manufacturing Company was dissatisfied with its quota-setting process and had requested the assistance of Business Research Associates. Sun-Ray, a medium-size producer of television sets, wanted BRA to help develop a method for establishing sales quotas for television sets on a state-by-state basis. Sun-Ray's sales analyst indicated a past project revealed such factors affecting the level of demand on TV sets as population, number of housing units, consumer income, sales of television sets, number of household units with sets, and others. Jakki Mohr, Sun-Ray's sales analyst, also informed BRA that management considered $30 million a realistic national sales quota.

Project Three

Sharper Images supplies rental laundered or dry-cleaned work uniforms to the manufacturing sector in Wayne County, Michigan. The owners of Sharper Images, Russ and Kathy Jamison, contacted Jack Wallman for help. Russ and Jack had been college classmates and had kept in touch since graduation. The Jamisons informed Jack and Scott that Sharper Images had been supplying uniforms only to the manufacturing sector, but now, to increase sales, they wanted to explore the potential market for uniforms in the retail and service industries.

During preliminary discussions, Russ and Kathy indicated not all retail and service industries use uniforms, but they were sure some companies could be persuaded to use them. They identified present user industries as automotive dealerships and repair operations, building maintenance services, and beauty and barber shops. Prospective users might include restaurants and taverns, fast-food outlets, supermarkets, and possibly hotels and motels. Uniform usage would vary by type of business. Jack suggested the size of the business might also be a factor. He recommended restricting the investigation to those establishments with 20 or more employees since he doubted if smaller establishments represented a potential market for Sharper Images.

Project Four

Late last year, Scott and Jack had been contacted by Mark McKinstry, owner of Mark's Save-U Food, a local chain in the Albany, New York, area. Mark had inquired if Business Research Associates was interested in retail location analysis. Scott and Jack indicated this would be in line with their available data bases and they would be willing to work with Mark. Save-U Food was interested in expanding into the Syracuse, New York, SMA and wished to know which of the three counties would offer the best market potential for a new outlet. Specifically, Mark McKinstry not only wanted to select the county that had experienced the fastest economic growth rate but also wanted to know which county appeared to have the strongest development potential.

Initial discussions with Mark revealed the most important growth market indicators are population, income, housing, car ownership, and grocery store sales. When questioned about his source for this information, Mark identified an article that had appeared in *Chain Store Age*.

Project Five

The most demanding project facing the two principals of Business Research Associates involved a request from the new owners of a tire manufacturing company. Past records were not very useful to the new owners, who desired to increase market share for their line of passenger automobile tire replacements.

Past attempts to estimate market potential by state had not been satisfactory since many of the company's regional and district sales managers believed their assigned quotas were disproportionate to the potential of their territory.

Scott and Jack had informally investigated the subject with the new owners and some of the sales managers to identify which market factors influenced the sales of replacement tires. Numerous factors emerged, but the company did not have any data or sources of data for these factors.

Factors identified included averaging life span of radial tires influenced by miles driven, road conditions, speed, age of driver, and number of automobiles scrapped each year. Fuel availability was suggested as well. BRA executives indicated they would need to know the factory value of replacement automobile tires and what market share the company hoped to achieve. Company officers estimated their most recent share was 14 percent but their objective was 18 percent. Finally, Scott and Jack knew they would need an estimate of new car sales or registrations for future years. Company executives were unable to offer Jack and Scott any data or sources to allow them to estimate market potential or to determine quotas by states.

Future Directions

After reviewing these various projects, Scott and Jack were even more convinced they would need to hire a new associate. They had committed to these projects, and more inquiries were arriving weekly.

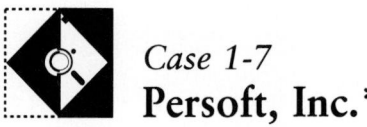

Case 1-7
Persoft, Inc.*

Pat Alea, Persoft's director of marketing, faced two difficult decisions. The first concerned the outlook for Persoft's new software package, IZE. An information management package launched last year, IZE represents a radically different program compared to Persoft's other software programs. Forecasting 1989 sales for IZE will be difficult since Pat does not have a data base available to use time series methods.

The second problem related to Persoft's more mature products—for example, the SmarTerm terminal emulation and communications software. For these products, Persoft combines statistical and qualitative techniques, including analyses of past sales data and a bottom-up approach based on the sales force and contact with customers. Even for the more mature products, Pat Alea hopes to improve the accuracy of their forecasts.

The Company

Persoft, Inc., was formed late in 1982 almost by accident when John Swenson, cofounder, noticed a void in the marketplace. Microcomputers had just begun to multiply in the business community, and Swenson saw a need to design software to emulate the terminals that communicated with the bigger and faster minicomputers made by Digital Equipment Corporation and Data General Corporation. The result of Swenson's efforts was a highly popular series of products called SmarTerm.

Swenson started Persoft on $4,000 and two IBM PCs, all out of his basement. Today, Persoft operates out of a 26,000-square-foot building and employs 85 people. Sales for its first fiscal year, 1983, were $169,000. In 1987, sales reached $4.6 million and rose to $5.9 million in 1988, although 1988 sales were $1.1 million under projections. Projected sales for 1989 of $12 to $15 million have been revised downward to exceed $7 million. These revisions reflect changing market conditions and difficulty in forecasting sales of IZE.

The Products

Until the introduction of IZE, Persoft's major product was a series of software packages produced under the SmarTerm name. Company literature describes the product:

> SmarTerm: a family of powerful, flexible, easy-to-use terminal emulation products. With SmarTerm, you can link your PC to powerful minicomputer

---

*This case is based on information obtained from *Venture*, December 1988; *State Journal*, January 10, 1989; *Newsweek*, December 14, 1987; and Persoft company literature and personnel. Names and unit sales data have been changed.

IZE® provides the user with four major environments in which to work. Most of IZE's functions are available for groups of texts in outlines and the workspace, as well as for individual texts.

1. Word processing allows the user to create texts within IZE or to manipulate information that has been imported into IZE. It contains such features as block copy, delete, and print, as well as on-screen page breaks and "search and replace" operations.

2. The Workspace allows the user to quickly work with and switch between texts in memory without making new search requests. Texts remain in memory until they are released. The workspace is similar to a desktop with a number of different documents and folders on it. Operations such as cutting and pasting between texts are fast and easy using the workspace.

3. Outlines provide a summary of all information requested by the user. A new outline is generated each time the user makes a search request. It always reflects the nature of the request and the current contents of the textbase. It is based on an analysis of the frequency of all the keywords in all texts that meet the initial search criteria. Groups within an outline can be expanded to deeper and deeper levels of detail.

4. Guidelines are custom-made forms that allow the user to control the shape of outlines. These are important if the user wants the outline to be different than the one that IZE would provide automatically.

and mainframe systems—and do everything on your PC that you can do on an expensive and cumbersome dedicated hardware terminal. SmarTerm is offered by Persoft, the leader in terminal emulation software.

Persoft's newest entry in the software market is IZE, a $445 program that achieved critical acclaim in trade publications. The new program is part of a new generation of text-based office management programs. IZE can pull together research reports and search volumes of text, using a powerful and sophisticated word search rather than a complicated pathway, dictated by the program, that a user must learn. Early reviews have been enthusiastic. According to one reviewer, "text-based programs on PCs are so new that no one can predict their potential market size with any accuracy." The *Newsweek* article describes IZE as another way to "take arms against a sea of data. It builds ingeniously detailed indexes." A Chicago attorney "uses IZE to help associates pinpoint thousands of paragraphs from contracts, giving them a guide for their own work." A computer consultant says, "the program reminds him of computers in science fiction, which figure out what you mean when you ask them a simple question." Despite these glowing reviews, Swenson and Alea are aware that the history of software is littered with good ideas that never caught on, a situation they hope to avoid.

The preceding excerpt, taken from Persoft's promotional literature, describes the capabilities of IZE.

Swenson and Alea acknowledge that it may take a year for text-based programs to catch on and establish a market. Persoft is not alone in the market and faces competition from Apple's HyperCard, which is given away with each new Macintosh to get around having to explain it, and Lotus's Agenda, which sells for $400. These new programs have been referred to as *software Erector sets*.

To help market its new product, Persoft obtained $2 million financing from a venture capital firm, Frontenac, of which $750,000 to $1 million will be used to help launch IZE.

The Marketing Program

Persoft's software programs are available nationwide and overseas. About 13,000 value-added resellers (VARS), value-added dealers (VADS), and computer specialty stores (CSS) such as ComputerLand, ValCom, and Inacomp carry Persoft products. These resellers receive Persoft software from a distributor (SoftSell) that provides other programs and peripherals.

Persoft employs five salespeople who call on major value-added resellers and major end-user customers and prospects. In addition, the sales force works with Persoft's wholesaler and its sales force. Persoft provides backup support for all of its software programs. Currently, the sales force directs its efforts on the new IZE product to calling on end-users. The sales force is responsible for obtaining information from SoftSell and key resellers as to the identity of end-users. Current users of IZE are asked to identify other potential end-users as well.

Persoft management wanted IZE to be the dBase III of information management. This line of reasoning influenced the pricing of IZE, which was set at $445.

Pat Alea faced two problems. The first concerned development of a new forecasting procedure for one of the SmarTerm software packages. She had not been satisfied with previous results and wanted to learn if an improved technique would be feasible. Sales data by units for the last three years are in Table 1. Exhibit 1 shows actual versus forecast sales of the SmarTerm product line. As illustrated, the accuracy of the forecasting method has diminished rather markedly since late 1987. Forecasts are made using simple exponential smoothing at the beginning of the year. Because of accuracy problems, Persoft has had production problems meeting demand. Recently, revised forecasts on a quarterly basis have been necessary to help overcome the problem. Alea has relied on qualitative methods to make the revised forecasts.

Her second problem constituted a major challenge: estimating the market potential and resulting sales forecast for IZE. She knew the sales forecast would be a critical factor in determining the feasibility of the marketing plan. Moreover, since IZE was so revolutionary, she knew it would be questionable to rely on past sales growth patterns experienced with the SmarTerm line as an indicator of future sales of IZE.

T A B L E 1   *Monthly Unit Sales of SmarTerm 1985–88*

Month/Year	Unit Sales	Month/Year	Unit Sales
January 1985	206	March	172
February	245	April	210
March	185	May	205
April	169	June	244
May	162	July	218
June	177	August	182
July	207	September	206
August	216	October	211
September	193	November	273
October	230	December	248
November	212	January 1988	262
December	192	February	258
January 1986	162	March	233
February	189	April	255
March	244	May	303
April	209	June	282
May	207	July	291
June	211	August	280
July	210	September	255
August	173	October	312
September	194	November	296
October	234	December	307
November	156	January 1989	281
December	206	February	308
January 1987	188	March	280
February	162	April	345

EXHIBIT 1   *Actual versus Forecast SmarTerm Sales*

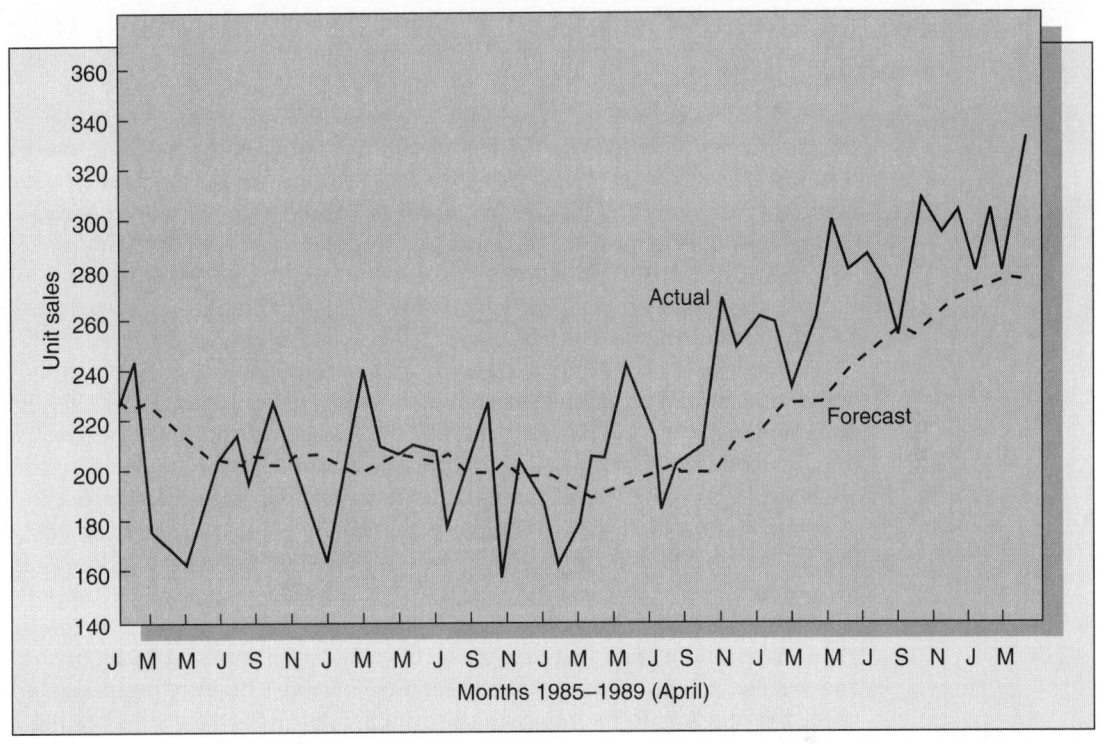

Case 1-8
Delaware Paint and Plate Glass Industries, Inc.

The Strategic Forecasting and Planning Committee had just completed its review of the company's activities for all of its divisions for the past 24 years. The committee was reasonably pleased with its ability to prepare sales forecasts, recognizing how important forecasts are to division heads for planning cash flows, production scheduling, personnel planning, budgeting, inventory control, purchasing, and other purposes. However, the committee was perplexed by problems in the Glass Division.

The Glass Division has confronted rather uncertain times due mainly to fluctuations in the economic environment. As a result, inventories are bloated, and the division is operating at less than 60 percent of capacity. Karl Backes, president of the Glass Division, is concerned about these problems and has asked his forecasting and planning group to review past forecasting procedures and develop new methods that offer greater accuracy. Jackie Vandenberg heads the forecasting and planning group. Although she was transferred recently from another division, she has managed to impress her peers in the Glass Division with her knowledge of the industry and of the various forecasting methods available. Her first activity involved a careful review of past methods and results. It was very apparent that the division's forecasting procedures needed revamping to be more useful to the numerous departments relying on the forecasts for planning and scheduling activities.

The Company

Delaware Paint and Plate Glass incorporated in Delaware in 1895. Delaware P&PG wholly owns a variety of companies, which have been integrated into four basic business segments. In addition, Delaware P&PG has entered several joint ventures with other corporations in such areas as oil and gas exploration, iodine production, and ethylene glycol production.

The company is concentrated in four basic business segments: glass, chemicals, coatings and resins, and fiber glass. The diversity of Delaware's markets helped to soften the effects of the economic downturn that started in 1980. Major markets are transportation and construction, which are served in varying degrees by the business's four segments. Other industrial and agricultural markets are served by the basic business lines. Foreign markets comprise the same categories as the domestic mix.

Domestic sales in 1980 were divided about equally among Delaware's major markets: transportation, primarily automotive; residential and commercial construction, including building and remodeling; chemical processing and refining; and other industrial and agricultural areas.

The previous slump in the automobile industry had had a substantial impact on the glass and fiberglass business segments. Manufacture of original equipment glass parts was affected by the decline in U.S. car production, falling to one of the lowest levels in recent years. Sales of fiberglass products declined due to poor economic conditions and affected the recreational vehicle and pleasure boat markets. The low level of domestic auto production also affected Delaware's factory-applied automotive finishes business. The company's leading position in several areas of technology, which provided superior products, helped offset some of this effect. The recent reversal of this trend improved Delaware's sales, but automobile production declined again in 1986.

Delaware's strong position in the aircraft market remained fairly stable. Sales were strong for windshields and other transparencies for business aviation and military aircraft. The company also provides coatings for specialty ballistics glazing.

In 1982 housing starts were at their lowest level in 35 years, reducing demand for Delaware P&PG's insulating glass units and fiberglass products for such items as bathtubs and shower enclosures. However, in 1983 housing starts increased by almost 60 percent, and the use of fiberglass roofing products and shingles increased dramatically in 1984 but housing starts declined 8 percent from 1987 to 1988.

In contrast to the depressed residential construction market, commercial construction continued strong in the early '80s. Demand grew for Delaware's energy-efficient architectural glass products.

Because of weak economic conditions, demand for most of Delaware's chemical products was down. Sale of farm fertilizers declined along with most industrial chemicals. However, demand was strong for the company's line of chemicals used in the oil-and gas-exploration markets.

The Glass Division

Delaware P&PG is one of the nations's largest producers of flat glass, manufacturing about one third of total domestic industry output. The company's major markets are automotive original equipment, automotive replacement, residential construction, commercial construction, and aircraft transparencies. Delaware also supplies the furniture industry and other markets. Most glass products are sold to other manufacturing and construction companies, although some are sold directly to independent distributors and to consumers through Delaware's franchised distribution centers.

The Forecasting and Planning Group

In addition to Jackie Vandenberg, the group was composed of Clair Voyance, sales analyst; Gregg O. Strander, national sales manager; and Scott Wilson, production planning. The group could rely on a staff statistical group that reported to corporate headquarters for technical assistance, if needed.

The group was expected not only to come up with an overall sales forecast of division sales but also to break down this forecast by market, product, quarter, and major account. Its first task concerned developing a sales forecast for the glass division.

Some differences over what methods to use arose within the group. Gregg thought the group should rely on the sales force composite method, arguing that the end result would be more receptive to the sales reps because of their involvement in its preparation. Scott thought sales force input should be minimal since they have little impact on OEM contracts. These contracts are determined at the top. Clair felt that, regardless of method used, the group must provide forecasts for each major market. Then, by adding up the forecasts, a total estimate of dollar sales for the division would result.

Despite these differences, Jackie thought the group would be able to work together without any major problems. She was aware that numerous techniques existed for making forecasts and was pondering which would be most appropriate. Believing that simplicity is an advantage, she hoped the group would not allow the process to become overly complicated. For example, she knew that trend analysis, using either simple regression analysis or exponential smoothing, would be easier than more complicated methods.

At their first meeting, she initiated the discussion by asking the group members to identify factors they thought would have a significant effect on glass sales. Gregg's immediate response was that sales were dependent on sales force efforts. Although the rest of the group agreed, Jackie pointed out that external variables were desired to develop a sales forecasting model.

To illustrate, she suggested that some national economic variables would be appropriate, such as gross national product, personal income, per capita income, employment, and so on. Clair suggested variables that would closely reflect activities in the division's major markets, such as automobile production, automobile repair, and construction. Scott said construction is too broad and this variable needs to be separated into types of construction, such as residential, nonresidential, and nonbuilding. Housing starts would be useful as well. Jackie suggested accident rates as a proxy for automobile repair. Buildings are remodeled and repaired, and some index reflecting this might be useful. In addition, since weather causes various kinds of damage, some measure of weather, such as the incidence of tornadoes, could be of value.

Realizing the group was headed in the right direction, Jackie suggested they attempt to use these variables and then examine the results for their forecasting effectiveness. She proposed that regression analysis be used at first along with trend analysis over time and exponential smoothing. She thought multiple methods were more effective than trying to rely on a single approach.

Collecting data for the suggested variables was relatively simple. Exhibit 1 contains information for division sales and for per capita income, auto production, housing starts, accidents, residential construction, nonresidential construction, nonbuilding construction, and tornadoes. In case these variables were not useful, Jackie instructed the group to be prepared to discuss the addition of extra variables. This, she hoped, would not be necessary, since more variables violated her principles of parsimony.

EXHIBIT **1**   *Statistical Series for Delaware Paint and Plate Glass Industries, Inc. (1965–1988)*

Year	Automobile Production Units[1] (thousands)	New Housing Units started[2] (thousands)	Per Capita Personal Income[3] (dollars)	Motor Vehicle Accidents[4] (millions)	Residential Construction[5] (billions)	Nonresidential Construction[6] (billions)	Nonbuilding Construction[7] (billions)	Tornadoes[8] (units)
1965	9,306	1,510	$2,773	13.2	$21.20	$17.20	$10.80	899
1966	8,598	1,196	2,987	13.6	17.8	19.4	12.9	570
1967	7,437	1,322	3,167	13.7	21.2	20.1	13.2	912
1968	8,822	1,545	3,433	14.6	24.8	22.5	14.4	661
1969	8,224	1,500	2,705	15.5	25.6	25.9	16.7	604
1970	6,547	1,434	4,056	16.0	24.8	24.6	19.0	649
1971	8,585	2,052	4,305	15.9	31.3	26.7	20.7	888
1972	8,824	2,357	4,676	16.3	42.4	29.8	21.3	741
1973	9,658	2,045	5,198	16.6	45.7	31.4	22.1	1,102
1974	7,331	1,338	5,657	15.6	33.6	33.2	27.0	947
1975	6,713	1,160	6,081	16.5	31.3	31.6	29.8	920
1976	8,500	1,538	6,655	16.8	44.2	30.0	35.9	835
1977	9,201	1,987	7,297	17.6	62.0	35.1	42.6	852
1978	9,165	2,020	8,141	18.3	74.9	45.0	39.9	788
1979	8,419	1,745	9,036	18.1	74.6	50.2	43.7	852
1980	6,376	1,292	9,916	17.9	63.7	52.5	32.2	866
1981	5,049	1,084	10,952	18.0	60.2	60.1	33.2	783
1982	5,073	1,062	11,485	18.4	59.2	59.5	37.4	1,046
1983	6,781	1,703	12,088	18.3	93.6	62.2	37.8	931
1984	7,773	1,750	13,114	18.8	101.4	74.4	35.5	907
1985	8,185	1,742	13,895	19.3	106.8	83.2	40.5	684
1986	7,829	1,805	14,592	17.7	122.9	83.8	42.0	784
1987	7,099	1,620	15,483	20.8	121.1	91.0	45.9	656
1988	7,111	1,488	16,497	n/a	120.9	86.8	45.5	702

[1]*Statistical Abstract of the United States; 1990,* 110th ed. (Washington, D.C., U.S. Bureau of the Census, 1990), p. 602.
[2]Ibid., p. 1260.
[3]Ibid., p. 695.
[4]Ibid., p. 1017.
[5]Ibid., p. 1266.
[6]Ibid.
[7]Ibid.
[8]Ibid., p. 208.

Before scheduling another meeting with her group, she met with Karl Backes to discuss progress. He was pleased with her efforts and expressed confidence that the group's results would be useful in helping to improve some of the Glass Division's problems. Karl mentioned other factors the group may want to consider. For example, Karl suggested the following data series and/or sources: *Business Conditions Digest, Standard & Poor's Index of Stock Prices, The Conference Board's Index of Help-Wanted Advertising, The Federal Reserve Board's Index of Industrial Production,* and several of the indexes from *Forbes* and *Business Week.* He indicated these sources have been useful as predictors of sales for other Delaware P&PG divisions.

Case 1-9
In-Sink-Erator Division*

In July 1991, John Hammond, operations research manager, was reviewing market projections derived from the In-Sink-Erator Division's industry forecasting models. It was clear that In-Sink-Erator's (ISE) forecasting methods needed modification given the discrepancies between forecasted values and actual values. In-Sink-Erator is the leading producer of food waste disposers, producing nearly 70 percent of the disposers sold in America.

The In-Sink-Erator Division's forecasting procedures begin with predictions of industry demand for such segments as new housing starts, replacement demand, first-time installation, and U.S. exports. The Association of Home Appliance Manufacturers provides member companies, which includes ISE, with industry shipment data for a broad range of home appliances, including food waste disposers, commonly known as garbage disposers. The operations research function also collects information from a variety of other external and internal sources.

Company History

The multimillion-dollar In-Sink-Erator Company and a major industry began in 1927 when John W. Hammes, a Racine, Wisconsin, architect, created the world's first garbage disposer. This first garbage disposer was not much to look at; but it did the job, as Exhibit 1 illustrates.

In 1938, Hammes founded In-Sink-Erator Manufacturing Company. Fifty disposers were made and sold that first year. Early growth was hampered by the reluctance of municipal officials to approve the appliance's installation. Various studies pointed out that disposers reduce the incidence of vermin and insects in a home environment and reduce the cost of garbage collection and processing. This led many municipal officials to pass ordinances recommending or requiring the use of household food disposers in all new construction.

During the 1950s, industry disposer sales grew dramatically. In-Sink-Erator had to share the market with competitors that included some of the nation's largest home appliance manufacturers. In-Sink-Erator's market share ranked only third in disposer production at one time in the 1950s.

By 1960, the disposer industry was selling more than 750,000 disposers a year. To meet this tremendous increase in demand, ISE designed and built a 114,300-square-foot manufacturing facility. This facility is the world's largest

*This case was made possible through the cooperation of the In-Sink-Erator Division. It was prepared by Professor Neil M. Ford, School of Business, University of Wisconsin-Madison, as a basis for class discussion and is not designed to illustrate effective or ineffective handling of an administrative situation. Certain names and data have been disguised. Copyright © 1992.

EXHIBIT 1   *In-Sink-Erator*

It all started with a great idea, a pair of tin snips and a soldering iron!

The multi-million-dollar In-Sink-Erator Company and a major industry began very simply overnight back in 1927 when founder John W. Hammes, a Racine, Wisconsin architect, watched his wife grab the garbage and carry it outside to the garbage can.

He felt that there had to be a better way and struck upon an idea. Armed with ingenuity, determination, a soldering iron and a pair of tin snips, he worked in his basement that night to create the world's first garbage disposer.

Not much to look at. But it did the job.

A food shredder in the sink drain.

The operating principle of Hammes' shredder was basically simple; put a power source and grinding mechanism in the kitchen sink drain to shred waste into particles small enough to be easily carried away by drain water into the regular sewerage lines. Hammes correctly assumed that at treatment plants, as well as in septic tanks, those tiny food particles would be broken down along with the regular sewage.

Here was a highly practical, workable idea for helping homeowners eliminate a disagreeable and time consuming task. Yet it took Hammes eleven long years of constant refining and testing to develop a disposer that would do the job quickly and conveniently.

World's first garbage disposer. Created by In-Sink-Erator founder John W. Hammes in 1927 in his basement workshop.

---

of its kind devoted exclusively to the production of garbage disposers. By 1966, expansion increased facilities to 242,900 square feet.

In 1968, In-Sink-Erator was acquired by the Emerson Electric Company. Emerson provided new capital and management disciplines that created a solid base for additional growth of the new division. Within five years, the division almost doubled its sales volume and nearly doubled it again by 1975.

After the acquisition by Emerson, ISE expanded its product line to include trash compactors, hot water dispensers, dishwashers, point-of-use water heating systems, and disposer adaptor rings, which permit the installation of an In-Sink-Erator model to replace competitive brands.

By 1974, ISE had regained its position as the leading producer of garbage disposers with 33 percent of the industry, which had grown to over 2.5 million units annually. Today, nearly 70 percent of all food waste disposers sold in America are manufactured by In-Sink-Erator in an industry that sells an average of 4 million garbage disposers a year. In-Sink-Erator also manufactures disposers under private-label arrangements for Whirlpool, Sears/Kenmore, KitchenAid, Maytag, Magic Chef, Jennair, Ace, True Value, and Grainger. ISE warrants its disposers for five years and backs the warranties with 2,500 independent service agencies. Other disposer manufacturers have similar long-term warranty programs. Disposers have an estimated average life of nine years.

Although the In-Sink-Erator Division leads the industry in the production of food disposers, it competes with three other manufacturers. The largest is Anaheim Manufacturing of Anaheim, California, which has a market share of approximately 19 percent, followed by Watertown Manufacturing of Watertown, Wisconsin, with 6 percent, and Waste King of Vernon, California, with 5 percent market share.

Market Distribution and Saturation

Although ISE's primary marketing commitment has consistently been through the plumbing wholesaler to the plumbing-heating-cooling contractor, other manufacturers obtain market coverage using different channels.

Appliance market saturation rates for refrigerators, clothes washers, garbage disposers, and dishwashers vary considerably. The saturation rate for refrigerators is almost 100 percent, but slightly less than half of households have dishwashers. Disposers are found in 52 percent of households, although regional saturation rates differ substantially. Except for New York, few major cities restrict garbage disposers. Estimates show only 14 percent saturation in New York, whereas disposers are commonly accepted in California. Exhibit 2 illustrates regional saturation estimates based on data provided by the Association of Home Appliance Manufacturers.

Exhibit 3 shows U.S. appliance saturation rates for fiscal years 1960 to the present with ISE-derived estimates for disposers to fiscal year 1993. The division's fiscal year begins October 1.

Division Forecasting Approach

The marketing of food disposers has three segments—new housing, existing houses (involving both replacement and first-time installation), and exports.

To study the new housing market, the operations research department uses government statistics and estimates from the F. W. Dodge National Information Services Division. Exhibit 4 presents new housing starts by fiscal year

EXHIBIT 2   *Regional Disposer Saturation Estimates*

Region	Percent Saturation
New England	45
Middle Atlantic	22
East north central	52
West north central	57
South Atlantic	45
East south central	25
West south central	53
Mountain	85
Pacific	73
Total	52

Sources: Association of Home Appliance Manufacturers and ISE estimates.

EXHIBIT 3   *Appliance Market Saturation Rates (Fiscal year 1960 to fiscal year 1993)*

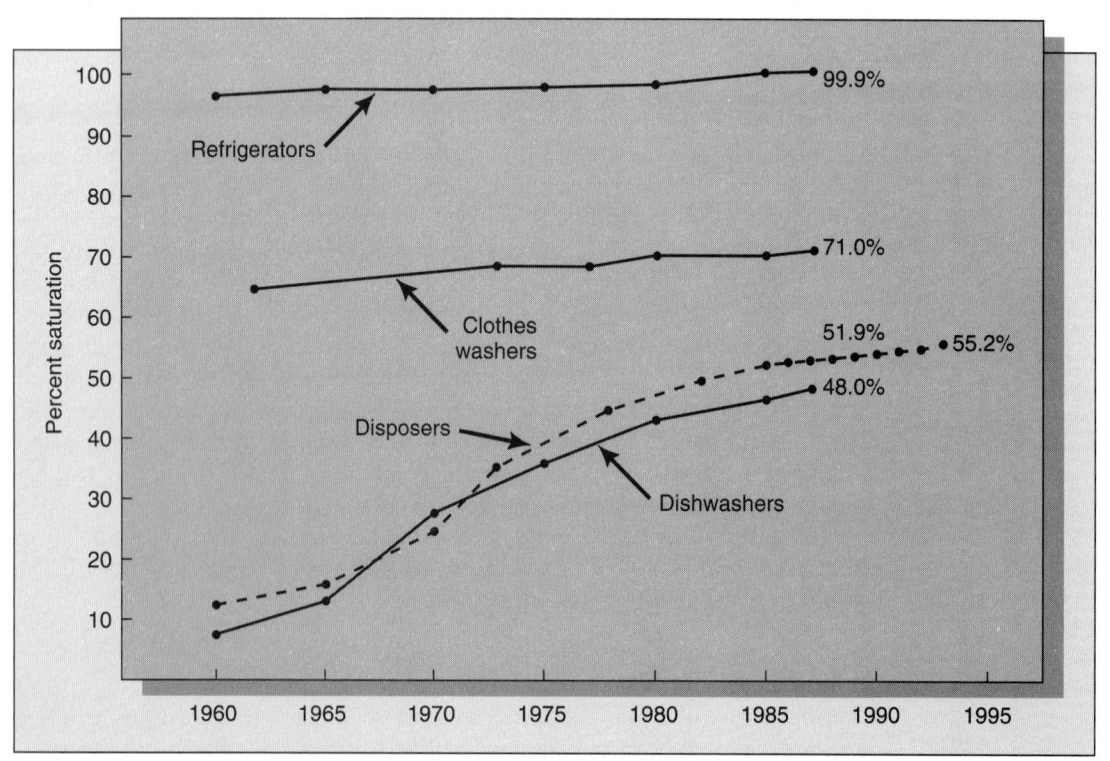

Source: Disposers—ISE Estimates. Other Products—*Appliance,* October 1987.

from 1976 to 1989 and an inclusion rate that reflects the number of new houses with garbage disposers. As Exhibit 4 shows, the inclusion rate rose steadily from 70 percent in 1981 to 82 percent in 1988.

Installation of garbage disposers in existing houses has been a difficult segment to manage. Demand in this segment is twofold: replacement of existing food disposers and first-time installation. Hammond and his associates are confident the majority of households with a disposer will replace it with a new one. Their estimates range from 80 to 90 percent. But it is difficult to forecast when disposers will wear out.

Manufacturers report total sales to the association monthly. The association reports the combined results for the industry, and In-Sink-Erator estimates its replacement and first-time installations from survey cards returned by purchasers.

Exhibit 5 presents factory shipments for garbage disposers from 1961 to 1989, first-time installation sales from 1982 to 1989, and U.S. exports form 1980 to 1989. The association also provides monthly industry shipments of food disposers, as shown in Exhibit 6.

With this data base, John Hammond and his associates faced the problem of developing industry forecasts for the new housing market, the replacement and first-time installation market in existing houses, and the U.S. export market. In addition, industry forecasts would have to reflect regional variations.

E X H I B I T   4   *Estimated Sales of New Housing Disposers (1976–1989)*

Year	Housing[1] Starts (000)	Inclusion[2] Rate Percent	New Housing[2] Disposers (000)
1976	1,448		
1977	1,866		
1978	2,010		
1979	1,835		
1980	1,316		
1981	1,254	70%	878
1982	962	75	722
1983	1,594	75	1,196
1984	1,791	75	1,343
1985	1,693	75	1,270
1986	1,840	75	1,380
1987	1,678	79	1,326
1988	1,486	82	1,211
1989	1,435	78	1,119

Sources: [1]U.S. Bureau of the Census, Construction Reports, series C20.
[2]Assocation of Home Appliance Manufacturers.

E x h i b i t   5   *Total Industry Shipments, Estimated First-Time Installation Sales in Existing Houses,*
and U.S. Export Sales (000s)

Year	Total Industry Shipments	First-Time Installation	U.S. Export Sales
1961	775		
1962	849		
1963	1,041		
1964	1,256		
1965	1,351		
1966	1,427		
1967	1,319		
1968	1,682		
1969	1,976		
1970	1,956		
1971	2,135		
1972	2,701		
1973	2,929		
1974	2,741		
1975	2,077		
1976	2,456		
1977	2,814		
1978	3,281		
1979	3,359		
1980	2,953		117
1981	3,265		150
1982	2,690	344	108
1983	3,411	318	84
1984	4,006	299	125
1985	4,146	302	124
1986	4,182	351	152
1987	4,440	388	192
1988	4,210	394	219
1989	4,380	393	229

Source: Association of Home Appliance Manufacturers.

EXHIBIT 6   *Monthly Industry Shipments*

Month	Industry Shipments	Month	Industry Shipments
October 1986	364,134	November	380,778
November	334,372	December	342,841
December	303,354	January	391,193
January	384,685	February	380,296
February	339,917	March	413,600
March	345,431	April	334,729
April	300,503	May	335,776
May	317,943	June	331,337
June	410,142	July	285,379
July	296,311	August	362,772
August	363,881	September	434,261
September	421,049	October 1990	425,729
October 1987	404,347	November	369,105
November	346,772	December	298,599
December	337,978	January	361,961
January	449,258	February	359,840
February	367,239	March	394,330
March	364,870	April	296,681
April	352,019	May	346,918
May	347,386	June	430,554
June	357,003	July	306,464
July	343,509	August	348,293
August	357,795	September	419,348
September	411,635	October 1991	346,690
October 1988	436,938	November	265,003
November	324,408	December	262,028
December	325,706	January	361,902
January	361,279	February	308,781
February	360,084	March	362,450
March	361,530	April	281,621
April	301,620	May	306,507
May	323,580	June	360,286
June	335,694	July	294,058
July	345,172	August	355,285
August	353,593	September	440,544
September	369,214	October 1992	312,409
October 1989	387,246	November	279,484

Source: Association of Home Appliance Manufacturers.

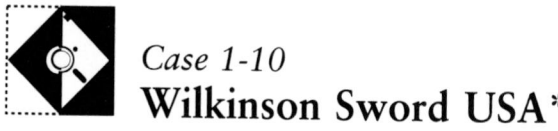

Case 1-10
Wilkinson Sword USA*

Norman R. Proulx, president, and Ronald E. Mineo, vice president of sales for Wilkinson Sword USA, were faced with a decision of strategic importance. They had to decide whether or not Wilkinson Sword USA should establish its own sales force in 1985. In the past, the company had used manufacturers' representatives, brokers, and/or the sales forces of other companies to represent its line of razors and blades in the United States. If they decided to form a company sales force for Wilkinson Sword USA, they would reverse a policy that had existed for 30 years dating back to the creation of the U.S. arm of the London-based Wilkinson Sword Ltd.

Wet-Shave Market

The shaving market is broadly divided into two segments: the dry-shave (electric) market and the wet-shave (razor) market. The wet-shave market accounts for the majority of sales volume. In the United States it is variously estimated at $450 to $500 million annually, at manufacturers' prices. The Gillette Company is recognized as the worldwide leader in the production and marketing of razors and blades. It is estimated that 6 out of 10 U.S. men and women who shave use Gillette products.

Four other companies are major competitors in the wet-shave market: Schick, American Safety Razor, Wilkinson Sword USA, and Bic (leader in the disposable-razor segment). These four competitors, coupled with private (store) brands, capture the great majority of the wet-shave market.

Distribution

Razors and blades are sold primarily through supermarkets, drugstores, and mass (discount) merchandisers. Although the dollar volume sold through each type of retail outlet varies over time, it is estimated that supermarkets account

---

*This case is based on published information found in R. Skolnik, "The Birth of a Sales Force." *Sales & Management,* March 10, 1986 pp. 42–44; Donald B. Thompson, "Can Close Shaves Cut Off Slump for Allegheny Unit?" *Industry Week* (September 16, 1985), p.24; "Gillette: When Being No. 1 Just Isn't Enough." *Business Week* (August 13, 1984), pp. 126, 131; "Wilkinson's Second Safety Match," *Management Today* (September 1983), pp. 50–55ff; "100 Leaders Advertising as a Percent of Sales," *Advertising Age* (September 8, 1983), p. 166; "Daisy (A): The Women's Shaving Marketing," HBS 9-582-152; Allegheny International 10-K Reports; 1985 *Sales and Marketing Management Survey of Selling Costs* (February 18, 1985); Kevin Higgins, "Japanese Buyout Fuels Scripto's Campaign for Dominance in Lighter, Writing Instrument Markets," *Marketing News* (February 15, 1985), pp. 1, 15; and T. J. McNichols, "Wilkinson Sword Limited (A) and (B)," *Policy-Making and Executive Action,* 5th ed. (New York: McGraw-Hill Book Co., 1977). This case was prepared by Professor Roger A. Kerin, Edwin L. Cox School of Business, Southern Methodist University, as a basis for class discussion and is not designed to illustrate effective or ineffective handling of an administrative situation.

for 45 percent, drugstores for 30 percent, and mass merchandisers for 25 percent of razor and blade sales. Catalog and department stores also account for a small percentage of razor and blade sales in any given year.

Advertising and sales

Advertising and consumer promotions play an important role in the marketing of razors and blades. For example, in 1983 Gillette was reported to have spent $205 million in advertising all company products. A sizable percentage was presumably earmarked for razors and blades, since these products account for almost 80 percent of Gillette's total sales. Consumer promotions typically take the form of premium offers, coupons, cents-off deals, and on-package premiums such as a free razor with a cartridge of blades.

Similarly, personal selling is important in the marketing of razors and blades. Salespeople typically call on retail buyers responsible for purchasing items for the health and beauty aid sections of supermarkets, drugstores, and mass-merchandise stores. Salespeople introduce new products and special promotions and generally work with buyers to gain shelf space and adequate display for their products. They also assist with joint advertising programs. Industry practice indicates that salespeople call on retail buyers an average of 10 times per year, with an average sales call lasting three hours including travel and waiting time. Industry standards suggest that a salesperson spends an average of 190 eight-hour days selling per year. In addition, some firms, like Gillette, employ retail merchandisers who make sure that store displays are adequately stocked. Firms differ in terms of how the selling function is performed. Gillette, American Safety Razor, Bic, and Schick have their own company sales forces, whereas Wilkinson Sword USA relies on manufacturers' agents, brokers, and the sales forces of other companies.

Technological innovation and product development

Technological innovation plays an instrumental role in the marketing of razors and blades. According to Dr. J. F. Sackman, research chief at Wilkinson Sword's Technical Center in London, "The objective is closeness without pain." Accordingly, product development is an ongoing process that involves studying hair growth and razor and blade technology. This research has shown that there are approximately 310 hairs per square inch on a man's face, that 15,000 hairs are cut during an average shave, and that facial hair grows at a rate of 0.4 millimeter per day. Cutting this hair without pulling under-the-skin hair roots and damaging nerve fibers has been the purpose of razor and blade product development since the first blade was produced.

Each advance in product technology has rewarded its investor. For example, Wilkinson Sword developed the first safety razor in 1898 and revolutionized the shaving industry. Gillette developed the Super Blue Blade (which significantly reduced the force necessary to cut facial hair) in 1958, the Techmatic shaving system in 1966, and Trac II and Atra razors in the 1970s. Each technological advance improved Gillette's sales volume and market share. Bic introduced the first disposable razor in 1975, an innovation that literally changed the face of the wet-shave industry.

The Company

Wilkinson Sword Ltd. traces its origins back to 1772, when it was a major producer of guns and bayonets. The company began manufacturing cavalry swords in 1820. At the close of the 19th century, Wilkinson Sword's production of cavalry swords was between 30,000 and 60,000 units annually.

The company produced its first straight-edged razor in 1890 and the first safety razor in 1898. In 1956 the company introduced its Teflon-coated Wilkinson Sword Blade. Consumer response to this innovation was phenomenal. The company's market share in Great Britain increased from 20 percent in 1962 to 45 percent in 1966. During the same period, Wilkinson Sword's market share increased from 3 percent to 15 percent in the United States.

Wilkinson Sword U.S. operations

Wilkinson Sword's competitive position in the United States through the late 1960s and mid-1970s was continually buffeted by product innovation and aggressive marketing efforts on the part of Gillette, American Safety Razor, Schick, and Bic. Nevertheless, Wilkinson's market share in the United States remained at a respectable level throughout the 1970s. By the end of 1984, however, Wilkinson Sword's market share for razors and blades had fallen to less than 1 percent. Actual sales were about $4 million at manufacturers' prices. Industry observers cited three factors that contributed to Wilkinson Sword's decline in market share. First, Wilkinson Sword elected to stop advertising in the United States in 1974 and focus advertising and promotional efforts on European markets. This practice was scheduled to change in 1985, with a plan to invest heavily in advertising and sales promotion for Wilkinson Sword products. Second, Wilkinson Sword's product innovation had not kept pace with that of its United States-based competitors. Recent development efforts, however, had resulted in several new products, which were to be introduced in 1985. A third factor was the lack of a company sales force. In the late 1960s and early 1970s, Wilkinson Sword's product line was sold by the sales force of Colgate-Palmolive, a large Fortune 500 manufacturer and marketer of personal care products. Wilkinson Sword parted with Colgate-Palmolive in the mid-1970s. In its place, Wilkinson Sword used manufacturers' agents to call on and service drugstores and brokers for supermarkets. According to industry sources, the commissions paid to manufacturers' agents and brokers amounted to about 10 percent of sales at manufacturers prices.

Acquisition by Allegheny International

In late 1980, Wilkinson Sword was acquired by Allegheny International Holdings, Inc., a wholly owned subsidiary of Allegheny International, a Pittsburgh-based conglomerate. Allegheny International also owned or had major equity positions in such well-known consumer product firms as Scripto, Inc., and

Sunbeam Appliance Company. Scripto, Inc., was engaged in the production and marketing of writing instruments and components and the marketing of disposable lighters. Sunbeam Appliance Company manufactured and marketed a broad line of portable electric products, including hair dryers, curling irons, and electric razors.

In the early 1980s, Wilkinson Sword's sales, marketing, and administrative functions in the United States were integrated with those of Scripto, Inc., but this action failed to arrest the decline in Wilkinson Sword's market share in the United States. Then, in 1984, Allegheny International sold Scripto, Inc., to Tokai Seiki Company Ltd., a Japanese lighter manufacturer. This action left Wilkinson Sword without the sales, marketing, and administrative support that had been provided by Scripto.

At the time of Scripto's acquisition by Tokai Seiki, Norman R. Proulx was vice president and general manager of Scripto, Inc. When it became apparent that Proulx was not going to stay with Scripto, top management at Allegheny International offered him the presidency of Wilkinson Sword USA. Proulx accepted, and he asked Ronald E. Mineo, who had been vice president of sales for Scripto, to serve in that same capacity at Wilkinson Sword USA.

Sales Force Decision

One of the major issues facing Norman Proulx and Ronald Mineo was whether Wilkinson Sword USA should change its sales program in the United States. Wilkinson Sword USA had historically relied on manufacturers' agents, brokers, or the sales forces of other companies to represent its product line in the United States. To recruit, train, organize, and manage its own sales force would be a major undertaking. For example, the cost of recruiting and training one salesperson was as high as $20,000 in 1985. The decision also had a time dimension to it. For a fee, the Scripto sales force would continue to represent Wilkinson Sword USA for two months following the acquisition. After that, Wilkinson Sword USA would assume responsibility for its sales and marketing function. Furthermore, if Wilkinson Sword USA elected to recruit its own sales force, these salespeople would also represent the company's line of cutlery products. Like razors and blades, this product line had been sold by manufacturers' agents and brokers. Cutlery product sales in the United States were about $3.3 million at manufacturers' prices.[1]

If Proulx and Mineo decided to form a Wilkinson Sword USA sales force, then a sales plan would be necessary. This plan would have to include the policies and procedures for recruiting, training, organizing, and managing a sales force. The first step in the decision process was account identification. Mineo identified 25 key accounts from among the supermarkets, drugstores, and mass merchandisers that carried razors and blades. Key accounts repre-

---

[1]For analysis purposes, the commissions paid to salespeople or agents and the channels are the same for cutlery sales as for razors and blades.

sented very large customers whose accounts could be managed from Wilkinson Sword's Atlanta headquarters. Four hundred additional accounts were identified that could be serviced by a sales force.

An experienced salesperson's salary plus expenses would be about $42,000 per year. The sales organization would include two key-account managers to handle the 25 key accounts. A key-account manager's salary plus expenses would be about $40,000 per year. In addition, salespeople and key-account managers would be paid a commission of 5 percent of sales.

Alternatively, Proulx and Mineo could contract with manufacturers' agents, brokers, or another company's sales force to represent the Wilkinson Sword USA product line in return for a commission or fee. This approach would be consistent with past policies.

Case 1-11
Calendar Coffee Company

Joan Russler, Calendar's national sales manager, had completed her review of sales results for the 1991 fiscal year. Although coffee sales had increased by 10 percent, she believed most of this was due to price increases rather than improved market conditions or a more effective marketing effort. The sales productivity of Calendar's 34 salespeople concerned Russler, especially when she considered the money and time that went into such efforts as recruiting, training, and motivating. She knows strong personnel management is important to sales management. She also knew that several salespeople were unhappy and were threatening to leave Calendar. Complaints about territory inequities were frequently heard from sales representatives. Weak territory design can undo the attention Calendar had given to recruiting, training, and motivating.

To better understand the territory issues, Russler selected two sales reps for a detailed analysis of their sales efforts. The two territories selected provided opposite situations. The first territory is represented by Bill Murphy. His territory received excellent coverage according to the quarterly sales and cost analyses. A recent contest designed to attract new customers was criticized by Murphy who said that in his territory any retail outlets not already customers of Calendar were not worth calling on. Russler suspected Murphy was already spending too much time calling on accounts with very limited potential. A performance review with Murphy's district manager revealed Murphy was overcovering his territory and making too many calls on customers of all types, including those with very little potential. His district manager noted that Murphy's motivational level was low and the sales rep had been heard to say he was looking for a new position that would provide more challenge.

The second sales rep reviewed by Russler was Kate Cheney, who had three years' experience. Cheney's problem was the opposite of Murphy's. Russler suspected Cheney's territory was too large, and her review of the sales and cost analysis data confirmed this. Specifically, account penetration in Cheney's territory was low, suggesting that she was "skimming" the best accounts from each trade area within her territory. Russler thought too many medium-size accounts were not producing adequate sales volume due to Cheney not spending enough time on them. These efforts were providing Cheney with a satisfactory level of earnings, and she was not willing to spend the extra effort to meet company objectives for the territory.

Russler discussed the above situation with Scott Wilson, Calendar's CEO, who abruptly dismissed the situation as one that involved lack of effort and nothing more. Wilson even suggested that Russler should examine Calendar's training programs and possibly introduce new motivational programs. Russler believed the training and motivation programs were satisfactory but improve-

| EXHIBIT 1 | | Territory Analysis: Present versus Recommended Time Allocation | |

Sales Representative	Trading Area	Present Allocation (percent)	Recommended Allocation (percent)
Bill Murphy	1	15%	8%
	2	50	25
	3	10	5
	4	10	4
	5	15	6
		100	48
Kate Cheney	1	15	45
	2	5	12
	3	10	22
	4	25	30
	5	5	15
	6	40	85
		100	209

ments are always possible. This was not a time for more "bells and whistles and rah-rah programs," although she did recognize that motivation levels for both Murphy and Cheney were low. Furthermore, changes in the training and motivation programs would produce only short-term benefits, especially if their territories are poorly designed. Russler suspected the territory problems experienced by Murphy and Cheney existed with other sales reps as well.

Next, Russler reviewed time spent in each trading area for both Bill Murphy and Kate Cheney. These results appear in Exhibit 1 along with Russler's estimate of recommended effort. She derived recommended effort estimates using suggested call frequencies based on market potential.

It was obvious to Russler that the two territories need realignment. Exhibit 1 indicates that Murphy's territory is too small and only half of a sales representative is needed to provide adequate coverage. Cheney's territory, on the other hand, is too large, and two sales reps should be assigned. Russler lamented that it was unfortunate the two territories were not conterminous since this would simplify realignment.

The Calendar Coffee Company employs 34 sales reps who are expected to call on approximately 4,000 accounts. Each of the 34 sales reps made an average 2,000 calls last year. Cost of a sales call averages $125. With these figures in mind, Russler knew profits would be seriously affected by poor territory design, leading to a misallocation of sales efforts.

Russler's next step was a meeting with Scott Wilson and Rick Berlet, Calendar's vice president of marketing. She reviewed her findings and discussed

E X H I B I T 2   *Industry Attractiveness*

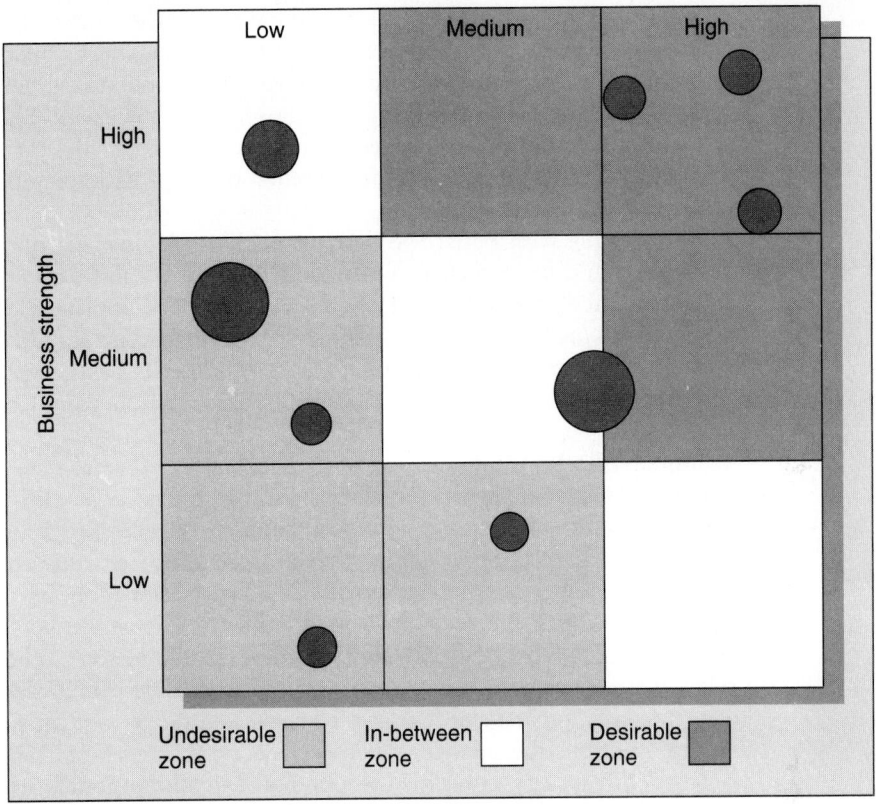

Source: David W. Cravens, *Strategic Marketing* (Homewood, Ill.: Richard D. Irwin, 1982), p. 73.

their implications. She identified three areas that needed attention. First, she noted Calendar must identify how many sales reps are needed to provide strong market coverage. Second, Calendar must determine how to organize the sales reps into territories, meeting two objectives: secure adequate market coverage and provide reasonable earnings opportunities for the sales reps. And, third, Russler indicated that within territories, time allocation decisions are needed by trade areas and specific accounts.

Rick Berlet, convinced that territories needed realigning, asked Russler to meet with him to discuss how the task should be handled. Before their first meeting, Berlet suggested Russler should review some of the materials he had received at a recent seminar on strategic planning. Specifically, he wanted her to review the business screen materials developed by General Electric. Exhibit 2 shows GE's business screen and multifactor assessment.

Russler carefully reviewed the materials provided by Berlet. Initially, she questioned how the voluminous data could be collected since she was well aware of the difficulties she has experienced getting the sales force to return call reports on time. The sales reps would have to be the source of information about each account since they were closest to their customers. Just how much information each sales rep could provide was of major concern. She knew that asking each sales rep to answer questions implied by the General Electric screen was not likely. She did not believe, as do some of her cohorts from other companies, that the sales force can be relied on to provide reliable and valid market research data.

The meeting with Berlet was very productive. He, too, did not believe the sales force could be expected to provide reliable and valid data for all of the points suggested in Exhibit 1. They discussed the GE approach and decided that the terms *business strength* and *industry attractiveness* should be changed to *account opportunity* and *strength of position*. Berlet agreed with Russler's contention that the best source of account information would be the sales force.

Initially, Berlet wanted each sales rep to answer several questions about each account, including account size, growth rate, and competitive intensity, when they were evaluating *account opportunity*. Strength of Calendar's position with each account would be derived from answers to such questions as the firm's current product distribution, shelf space allocation, and Calendar's trade relations with the account. Russler believed this would be a mammoth data-collection process and she would need a research analyst to help with the project. Berlet suggested Russler could obtain an analyst from Calendar's marketing research department. Berlet then suggested the two of them attempt to develop questions the sales reps would answer about each of their accounts.

Russler was very concerned about not only the amount of data to be collected but also the quality of the data. Each item mentioned by Berlet times the number of accounts equaled 24,000 data items. Russler scheduled a meeting with Debra Valine, analyst from Calendar's marketing research department, to discuss the project and her concerns about the sales force's ability to collect the needed data.

Valine shared Russler's concern and suggested a simpler approach would be to ask each sales rep to "consider" the account's size, growth rate, and competitive intensity when evaluating account opportunity. Likewise, the sales rep would "consider" the firm's current product distribution, shelf space allocation, and trade relations with the account when evaluating Calendar's strength of position with each account. Russler indicated she did not understand how this would help. Valine commented, "Look, each sales rep answers just two questions about each account; one assesses account opportunity and one assesses strength of position. We will ask them to 'consider' each attribute before they make their judgment." Valine sketched two questions to show Russler what she had in mind:

Account	Account Opportunity						
	Low						High
1	1	2	3	4	5	6	7
2	1	2	3	4	5	6	7
3	1	2	3	4	5	6	7
.							
.							
.							

Account	Strength of Position						
	Weak						Strong
1	1	2	3	4	5	6	7
2	1	2	3	4	5	6	7
3	1	2	3	4	5	6	7
.							
.							
.							

Valine indicated she had two concerns that needed to be resolved. She asked Russler, "Just what are you going to do with this information? Why do you want to collect these data?" Second, she was concerned about the size of the sample. She pointed out that two data points for 4,000 accounts would provide 8,000 observations. Russler's answer was lengthy and revealed uncertainty on her part as to how the data would be used to resolve the territory problems. She said, "Calendar's sales territories need realignment. To do this we need to know how often each account should be called on based on the sales rep's estimate of account opportunity and strength of position. With this information we can then determine how many accounts a sales rep can adequately handle and end with an estimate of territories."

Russler indicated she did not have any problems with accounts where Calendar's position is strong and the account has high opportunities. She knew more calls should be made on this kind of account than on accounts with low opportunity and where Calendar's position is weak. She indicated some concern about how often to call on accounts that fell between the two extremes. She told Valine the General Electric business screen looked rather formidable.

Valine tried to reassure Russler that the task was not that difficult. She said, "We'll collect the data and then see what happens. Maybe the data will be such that only three or four segments result. I understand that since you want to determine how often each account is to be called on that you think the sales reps must make these assessments for all accounts. Isn't that right?" Russler agreed but did a quick mental calculation and noted that each rep calls on about 120 accounts. She asked, "Can each rep provide good information about this many accounts?" Valine agreed with Russler that asking each rep to assess approximately 120 accounts was very demanding but not impossible. She thought all accounts should be assessed but only a sample of accounts would be used to test the method.

To help improve the quality of the data, Valine recommended that Russler meet with her regional and district sales managers to discuss the project. Meetings with sales reps would be needed as well, Valine noted, to train them on how to identify account opportunity and strength of position.

Russler's next meeting with Rick Berlet ended with him giving his approval to secure the account information. He cautioned Russler that the project might not be successful. He noted, however, that the approach had three advantages. "First, it forces you, your regional and district sales managers, and the sales force to think carefully about Calendar's customers. Second, you will obtain information from people who are closest to our customers. Finally, if the project is successful, the results will be better accepted by the sales reps since they were actively involved in the project's development. The process resembles participative management."

With approval granted, Russler met again with Debra Valine to help get the project under way. The collection process presented few problems due primarily to the careful planning that occurred early in the project. Debra Valine indicated to Russler that she could provide her with data from a sample of 50 accounts so that she could start her analysis. Before doing this, Russler requested two additional pieces of information for each account: number of sales calls made last year and cases of coffee sold last year. Calendar's management information system contained this additional information, and the results appear in Exhibit 3.

The task ahead of Joan Russler was very difficult. Based on her previous reasoning, she decided against nine segments and hoped to end with three or four. She knew that for each segment it would be necessary to develop a strategy and to indicate an average number of times an account in each segment should be called on. She also knew that eventually she would have to consider that accounts contained within a given segment should not receive identical calls due to differences in account opportunity and strength of position.

EXHIBIT 3   *Sample of Account Data (N = 50)*

Account Number	Account Opportunity	Strength of Position	Sales Calls	Sales
1	5	5	50	1,745
2	5	4	25	1,409
3	6	4	25	1,409
4	3	4	25	462
5	5	4	25	654
6	3	4	25	872
7	4	7	26	780
8	4	7	50	780
9	4	7	13	780
10	1	1	50	32
11	7	1	26	156
12	7	1	26	156
13	6	7	50	3,894
14	6	5	50	4,200
15	3	7	20	866
16	2	5	20	156
17	6	7	25	1,376
18	2	7	20	156
19	7	7	12	2,600
20	7	7	49	1,114
21	7	7	49	1,733
22	3	7	49	1,733
23	5	7	49	2,600
24	3	6	12	288
25	7	6	49	1,404
26	5	6	49	1,075
27	3	3	49	430
28	1	1	21	72
29	1	1	6	142
30	1	1	25	72
31	5	7	18	958
32	7	7	9	958
33	7	7	26	2,236
34	2	5	9	395
35	4	6	9	559
36	2	4	6	248
37	5	3	10	196
38	5	2	10	196
39	5	2	10	196
40	6	7	12	1,964

EXHIBIT 3   *(concluded)*

Account Number	Account Opportunity	Strength of Position	Sales Calls	Sales
41	4	4	12	196
42	7	7	10	1,768
43	6	7	25	2,946
44	6	7	24	2,400
45	6	7	25	2,946
46	5	5	20	1,543
47	5	2	23	189
48	3	2	19	635
49	6	7	25	6,037
50	5	7	25	6,037

Case 1-12
Norsk Kjem A/S*

In the summer of 1984, Mr. Johan Sunde, product manager at Norsk Kjem A/S, commented, "Although Nick, Per, and I spend many weeks visiting distributors and customers around the world, it is difficult to feel that we really know what is going on in the promotion and the many different applications of our products. It is difficult to make our distributors put any effort behind our products as we have very little control over what they do. However, our product group broke even for the first time last year and we would like to start making our 20 percent target return."

Norsk Kjem A/S (NK) was an integrated chemical company situated in Larvik, Norway. The company had been in business for 25 years and it had an excellent reputation throughout the world. The company was organized into three major divisions as shown in Exhibit 1. The NK Chemicals Division marketed more than 100 different chemicals and each chemical had many different applications. The division was organized into five product groups according to basic input chemicals such as polymers, alcohols, and sulphates.

Sulphates

In 1978, NK had taken out a license from an American company on a process for converting a by-product from one of the main processes into a salable chemical usually employed as a wetting agent. A wetting agent is used in many processes to promote the retention and even distribution of liquids.

Prior to taking out the 1978 license and inventing in the necessary plant and equipment, the market for wetting agents had been thoroughly researched by Mr. Nick Deveny. Mr. Deveny had visited many applicators in Europe and they had said, "Give us a product equal to what we get from the United States and we will be interested." Mr. Deveny's estimates of demand by industry and country are shown in Exhibit 2.

In 1978, a product manager and two technical salespeople had been hired to launch the wetting agents. Mr. Nick Deveny, who had made the original market survey, was one of the two salespeople employed. All three people held university degrees in chemistry or engineering. Together, they named the original product and subsequent offshoots, prepared technical literature, designed packages, and established a distribution system.

*The case was prepared by Professor Kenneth G. Hardy. The case was supported by the Research Associates Plan for Excellence. Any use or duplication of the material presented in this case is prohibited except with the written consent of the School of Business Administration. The author thanks the North European Management Institute for its cooperation. Copyright © 1974. The University of Western Ontario. Reprinted by permission. Revised 1976, 1986.

EXHIBIT 1   *Simplified Organization Chart*

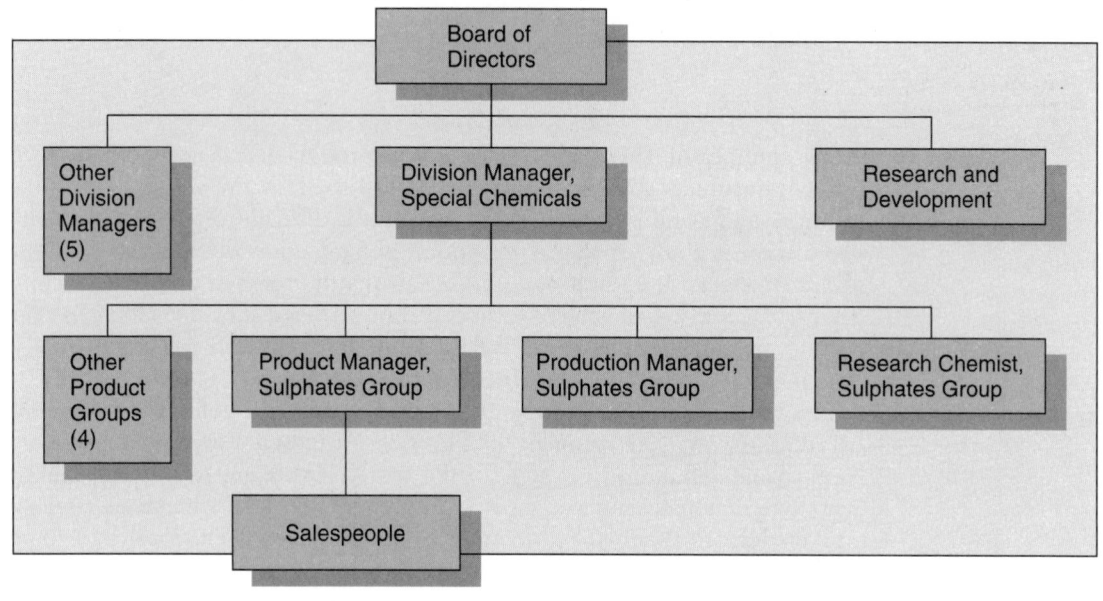

In setting up distributors, the product manager and his salespeople used the following criteria of (1) *establish only one distributor per country, (2) use established chemical distributors owned by nationals, and (3) try to get distributors that serve the concrete, dyeing, and pesticide industries because these end-users seemed to have the largest potential.*Subsequent to establishing the distributors, the product manager discovered that the Norwegian products had to have demonstrable advantages before end-users would risk a switch to a new ingredient. From 1976 to 1980, sales of the two major products were very disappointing.

The original product manager in the Sulphates Group had established distributors on many different arrangements. Some carried inventory and others did not, some took title to the product and others left the transaction between NK and the end-user. For example, the German distributor was wholly owned by NK. The United Kingdom distributor kept inventory, whereas Holland was handled by direct shipments. Distributor margins ranged from 5 to 8 percent of their selling price.

In the establishment of the distributors the original product manager had considered the "hungry" versus the "established" and had gone with the established special chemical distributors because of a bad experience with an overeager distributor and because he felt that a distributor would have to invest three or four years of market development with NK sulphates before he could expect a reasonable financial return.

EXHIBIT 2   *Norsk Kjem A/S Estimated Potential as of 1976 for Chemical Products (by application and country; in tons)*

Country	Textile Dyestuff	Carbon Black and Pigments	Pesticides	Concrete	Plasterboard	Total
Benelux	200–360	0–100	1,000–2,000	1,200–1,600	0	2,400–4,060
England	1,600–3,000	240–320	4,000–6,000	6,000–7,000	0	11,840–16,320
France	2,200–3,000	100–300	4,000–6,000	4,000–8,000	100–600	10,300–16,900
Italy	800–1,600	200–400	4,000–8,000	2,000–4,000	20–100	7,020–15,100
Israel	0	0	200–1,000	400–1,000	0	600–2,000
Scandinavia	0	100–200	200–400	200–600	100–200	600–1,400
Spain	100–300	100–200	200–400	200–400	0	600–1,300
Switzerland	3,000–6,000	100–200	200–1,000	1,000–4,000	0	4,300–11,200
Germany	4,000–6,000	500–1,000	2,000–6,000	2,000–6,000	600–1,000	9,100–20,000
Total	11,900–20,200	1,400–2,800	15,800–30,800	17,000–32,600	800–1,900	46,760–135,100

Most of the distributors were old family-owned companies and all of them carried many other lines, but none that were directly competitive with Sulphates Group products. The margins and required selling effort were the same for NK sulphate products as they were for other manufacturer's products. Special chemical distributors usually had some technical expertise but the wide variety of applications taxed their abilities. The distributors employed from 2 to 100 salespeople and in Mr. Sunde's judgment, all of them needed technical service and backup.

In 1980, NK underwent a major reorganization. A new product manager, Mr. Sunde, was appointed and he reported to Mr. Andreas Hoxmark, general manger for the Chemicals Divisions. Mr. Hoxmark had been one of the two corporate planners at Norsk Kjem and he had excellent education and experience in chemistry.

Just before the reorganization, the previous product manager had decided to buy a second license from the United States company which had sold the rights to the first process. A new series of light-colored wetting agents was launched and the plant was expanded at a cost of $800,000. The new wetting agents were tailor-made for three specific applications: pesticides, concrete, and textile dyestuffs.

Shortly after his appointment, Mr. Sunde decided that he should tell all his customers and potential customers about the many applications of the three new agents as well as the original products. To do this, he prepared a master brochure which showed all five wetting agents and where they applied in 10 different major applications. Then a detailed brochure was prepared for each of the 10 applications and the appropriate brochures were sent to the customers

E X H I B I T 3   *Norsk Kjem A/S Sales, Products, Commission Structure, and Inventory of*
Exclusive Distributors in Each Country in 1983 ($000)

Country	Sales		Commission	Inventory	Industries Served	Notes
	Tons	$ Value‡				
Switzerland*	2,000	$ 450	5% fab	Yes	Textile dyestuff	Small company manager looks after sulphates, good connections in textile dyestuff
Holland	100	400	n.a.	No	Pesticides	
Germany*	2,200	400	3% fob	No	Textile dyestuff, carbon black, concrete and plasterboard	Norsk Kjem Sales Company, Norwegian chemist sells sulphates
U.K.*	800	320	7% cif	Yes	Textile dyestuff, carbon black, pesticides	2 people buy in 20-ton lots
France†	400	160	5% fob	Yes	Pesticides, plasterboard	Large dealer, 100 employees and 8 offices
Japan	300	160	n.a.	No	Textile dyestuff	
Italy†	100	160	n.a.	Yes	Concrete	Medium-size dealer
Eastern Europe	4,400	128	n.a.	No	Animal feed	
Scandinavia	4,246	120	n.a.	Yes	Animal feed, concrete	
Spain†	600	120	n.a.	Yes	Concrete, plaster	Small- to medium-size dealer
Australia	1,200	90	n.a.	No	Pesticides, concrete	
Belgium	1,200	60	n.a.	No	Pesticides	
Kuwait	300	60	n.a.	No	Concrete, plasterboard	
Israel	270	54	n.a.	No	Concrete, plasterboard	
Others	2,000	160	n.a.	No	Miscellaneous	
Total	20,116	$2,834				

*Dependent on Sulphates Group or Norsk Kjem for accounts or financing.
†Mr. Sunde was dissatisfied with the performance of these distributors.
‡Norwegian Kroner have been converted to American dollars at the prevailing rate of exchange.
n.a. = Not available.

EXHIBIT 4   *Norsk Kjem A/S Sales, Costs, and Contribution for 1982 and 1983 ($000)**

	1982		1983	
Sales		$1,852		$2,834
Variable cost		746		1,058
Contribution		1,106		1,776
Fixed manufacturing costs	$914		$1,180	
Promotion costs	212		262	
Corporate and division overhead	104	1,230	150	1,592
Net profit before tax		$ (124)		$ 184

*Norwegian Kroner have been converted to American dollars at the prevailing rate of exchange.

who had been coded according to their current applications. A response card and a letter from Mr. Sunde were sent out with the brochures. The distributors received quantities of all literature in the appropriate language. Mr. Sunde commented, "The response was only fair. The big seller turned out to be one of the new products but mainly to two accounts in Switzerland and Germany, a contract which was arranged even before we bought the license to make the new products."

Between 1980 and 1983, Mr. Sunde and his two salesmen, Mr. Deveny and Mr. Per Wiencke, spent a great deal of time traveling with distributors in order to meet customers and to give out samples. Mr. Sunde called on distributors in Switzerland, France, and Denmark, while Mr. Deveny took Germany, Eastern Europe, Finland, Israel, and Italy. The second salesman, Mr. Wiencke, called on distributors in the United Kingdom, Benelux, Spain, Norway, Sweden, and all others. Exhibit 3 shows the sales volume and arrangement with each distributor in 1983.

In September 1983, Mr. Sunde took a leave in order to study industrial marketing, but he kept in touch with his colleagues at NK. When he returned in the summer of 1984, the research people had redeveloped the product line so that it was more than completely competitive in terms of quality. Exhibit 4 shows sales, costs, and contribution for 1982 and 1983.

Customers

In making any first purchase of a new wetting agent, the technical people in a client company would require samples for testing. In large companies, their recommendation would go to a purchasing agent and production manager, but in small companies, the owner/manager would make the final decision. Mr. Hoxmark considered that it was very important to develop a close rapport with customers. He encouraged contact between customers and R&D people

E X H I B I T   5   *Norsk Kjem A/S Ton Volume per Customer (by application, 1983)*

Applications	Total Number of Customers	Tons per Customer						Total Sales (tons)
		<10	10–19	20–49	50–99	100–499	>500	
Textile dyestuff	17	7	—	6	—	3	1	5,160
Carbon black and pigments	14	8	3	2	1	—	1	480
Pesticides	18	7	2	5	3	1	—	1,176
Concrete	5	1	1	—	1	1	1	2,088
Plasterboard	8	1	2	4	1	—	—	516
Industrial cleaning	2	2	—	—	—	—	—	16
Animal feed	9	1	—	4	—	1	3	9,744
Miscellaneous	37	17	13	7	—	—	—	936
Total	110	44	21	28	6	6	5	20,116

in the Chemicals Division in order that R&D personnel could hear customer wants at first hand. He observed that small companies often preferred small suppliers regardless of nationality. Most customers kept open two sources of supply because delivery was just as important as technical support.

There were 110 end-users buying from Sulphates-Group distributors. Nearly 80 percent of the Sulphates-Group volume was taken by 20 percent of the distributor's customers. Exhibit 5 shows the customers and their annual volume by application for 1983.

Small companies were numerous but not easily identified as potential customers. Compared to larger organizations, small companies tended to have more first-time applications, less information on competitive offerings, less technical expertise, less sensitivity to price, and smaller order quantities. Switching chemicals posed a substantial production risk, especially for large companies.

Differences by industry

There were some differences in purchasing criteria by industry. The *textile dyestuff* manufacturing industry was dominated by large multinational corporations which used a wide variety of auxiliary chemicals. The distributor's salesperson first called on lab and production personnel in the user companies in order to have the NK products tested. If lab and production people approved the products, the distributor's salesperson could discuss price, delivery time, and packaging with the purchasing agent. NK products were priced competitively. The entire process of first visit, discussing test results, and arranging an order could take from six months to more than one year.

The buying procedure in the pesticide and herbicide manufacturing industries was similar to the textile dyestuff industry. However, the manufacture of pesticides and herbicides called for some additional physical criteria of the product. Moreover, multinationals and small formulators were prevalent in these manufacturing industries.

The *industrial cleaning* market was particularly price competitive. The same products were used in the *plasterboard* market where a good wetting agent could reduce water requirements and drying costs. Multinational corporations dominated the manufacture of plasterboard.

In making *concrete,* a good wetting agent could provide better distribution of all particles which could lead to increased compression strength. Small and medium-size companies were prevalent in the manufacture of concrete.

Distributor policies

North Carolina Chemical was Mr. Sunde's toughest competition. Despite having only one distributor for all of Europe, North Carolina Chemical had tied up almost all the big dye houses. As one example of its promotional methods, North Carolina sponsored a technical conference for all the people involved in the textile dyestuff industry.

Mr. Deveny told the casewriter, "We have to support the distributor heavily in the introduction period when a customer is trying our product. After that, there is little maintenance required. Our total sales depend heavily on our marketing effort because we can do research in each market and tell the distributors what to do. We are trying now to work on key users with good volume and fair prices. We are a long way from saturating the market but almost none of our distributors are scanning customers for new end-users. Furthermore, there are a lot of sample requests as a result of our advertising but there is little follow-up from the distributors. We inform them of the sample request and some call on the customer, some do not."

Mr. Sunde had tried to institute a system of field reports from the distributors but they did not fill in the reports. As a result, Mr. Sunde and his salespeople relied on their own observations during their periodic field trips. In each country their itinerary was set up by the local distributor. Mr. Sunde would visit France, for example, two weeks a year and see 20 end-customers in each of those weeks.

Mr. Sunde talked about some experiments with their distributors. First of all, the German subsidiary was developing sales faster than any other distributor. Mr. Sunde ascribed this to the large German market, the German technical sophistication and willingness to try new products, and "the fact that we have a good man there working only with our products." Mr. Sunde had just fired the United Kingdom distributor and shifted the business to two of the distributor's former salespeople. In France, the distributor had hired a product manager who grouped customers, established potentials and sales goals for salespeople and helped the salesperson look for new possibilities and pushed them. The result was a big increase in sales for the French distributor. Mr. Sunde had tried to woo the French pesticide industry with price concessions but the

French distributor would only partly go along with the plan. The distributor would have been obliged to take a small reduction in his margin.

Marketing options

The first option which Mr. Sunde had considered was to drop all the distributors and replace them with either a Norwegian-based sales force or one NK salesperson located in each major market. One field office would cost $100,000 per year for a salesperson's salary, travel expenses, secretarial and other expenses. The extra level and communication expense from Norway would bring the cost of a Norwegian-based force up to the same cost of $100,000 per person.

The second major option was to help the distributors. In major markets, Mr. Sunde would share 50 percent of the cost of a distributor's salesperson if the salesperson would spend half his time on NK sulphates. Most distributor salespeople earned about $50,000 in salary and commissions. In smaller markets, an NK man might do missionary work for part of the year on a split (50—50) commission basis.

Another option would be to delineate selling tasks such as identifying prospects, developing the application, selling the customer, maintaining inventory, and after-sale servicing. Possibly the tasks could be divided between NK and the distributors. To compensate for the performance of these tasks, some sort of commission points or fee structure could be developed.

A fourth option was to assign additional NK salesmen to train the distributor's salespeople. It would take at least a month for one NK salesperson to thoroughly train one of the distributor's people. The likely sales response would vary considerably, depending on the market potential and the skill of the distributor's salespeople.

A fifth option was to work with the distributors, using existing resources. Some sort of management-by-objectives system might serve to motivate and guide the distributors. Mr. Sunde was well aware that the difficult part of a management-by-objectives system was the implementation of the system. The distributor reaction could range from enthusiastic cooperation to rejection of the NK sulphate line. Mr. Sunde had considered hiring more than one distributor per country but generally he felt that the sulphate business was too narrow to support more than one distributor.

In order to get more effort from his distributors, Mr. Sunde had considered the alternative of raising margins from the 5 to 8 percent range up to approximately 15 percent. But he was not sure that this would evoke sufficient extra effort to reach profit targets, given the competitive prices offered by the company.

However, before he could make any of these decisions, Mr. Sunde felt there was a more basic decision of target customers and priority of country/application. He was not sure that Mr. Deveny's 1976 survey of potential sales still held for his products. However, Mr. Hoxmark had asked for a report on distribution strategy and policy by the end of the month.

Case 1-13
Speedway Sales Company, Inc.*

Joe Drake, owner of Speedway Sales, thought about the many issues he would have to address for the upcoming year. While sales had continued strong for 1991, several problems loomed for Speedway Sales Company (SSC). Changes in the basic technology used in catching speeders and questions as to the ethics of using radar detectors worried Drake. Recent articles in several publications caused considerable concern about the future of radar detectors. These articles described new technology that would make radar detectors less effective and even obsolete.

Along with this, the sales volume increase over the past four years was generated more from the novelty of his new company than from competitive advantage. This was beginning to wear off. Additional increases in revenue would have to come at the expense of his competition, and they tended to be much larger and more established than SSC. How could he address these concerns while keeping his small share of the market?

Speedway Sales Company History

In May 1984, Drake graduated from a well-known midwestern university with a business degree, large amounts of energy and enthusiasm, and no job. While his understanding of business concepts, especially marketing, was good, his grades reflected more on his ability to consistently find a Friday night party than to write a good paper. With no companies interested in hiring him, Drake decided to work at his father's gas station while continuing his job search.

While working for his father, Drake's interest in cars, especially fast cars, grew. He noticed the large number of complementary items most well-to-do automobile owners possessed. Some of these items, such as radar detectors, bike racks, and CB radios, were very hard to find in his area. Those who wanted these goods often had to pay a premium price. After speaking with many dissatisfied car owners at the gas station, Drake decided to investigate becoming an upscale auto accessory retailer.

After checking with many manufacturers and distributors of the goods he was interested in carrying, Drake believed there was enough opportunity for success to justify opening his own business. He arranged for shipments of products to be sent directly to him from the manufacturer. While his initial

---

*John P. Schwechel, MBA—Marketing, University of Wisconsin-Madison, assisted in preparing this case.

costs were high due to the small quantity he purchased at a time, he thought he could achieve volume discounts later when sales increased. With $4,000 in personal savings and a $15,000 loan from Drake's father, Speedway Sales was born.

Sales in 1987 were rather sluggish. But, toward the end of the year, word of mouth, the modest newspaper ads he placed, and an aggressive personal sales program paid off. The personal sales program consisted of contacting local businesses and pitching the benefits of using radar detectors to cut salespeople's travel time and expense. This program resulted in sales of $13,500. Sales at year's end totaled $26,000.

Demand and sales grew consistently over the next four years, especially for radar detectors. In 1990, sales totaled $646,000 with a profit of $87,000. Ninety percent of sales and 93 percent of profits came from radar detectors.

Company Goals and Policy

In 1986, when Drake began to contemplate starting his own business, he remembered from his strategic management class that he needed a clear strategy for his company to follow if he was to be successful. Given his interest in cars, Drake studied the auto accessories market in his area for potential opportunities. After much deliberation, Drake decided he could charge a premium price by providing excellent service to customers. He would focus on radar detectors, although other related products would be kept on hand in smaller amounts.

Drake decided he must command a premium price for his product for two reasons. First, he thought this high price was necessary because his costs were high. Since he could not purchase in volume, he was forced to accept the higher prices offered to him by his suppliers. As sales grew over the next three years, Drake was able to purchase radar detectors by the gross at $199.99 each. At this cost, Drake needed to charge $299.99 each, compared with typical competitive prices of $250 to $275. His price was lower, however, than the self-powered SOLO offered at $345 by a major competitor, Cincinnati Microwave.

Second, Drake believed he provided the best service in his area. While people could get these products through mail order or at a department store, he was faster than mail order and had better installation and product training than either of the other two options. He accomplished this high service level through personal, one-on-one attention given by him or his two assistants. While this increased service attracted the wealthier target customers, it also did not come cheap ($45,000 a year for himself and $25,000 a year for his assistants).

Drake focused sales on radar detector for two reasons. The high profit margins achieved through radar detector sales made them very profitable ($100 each versus $50 for CBs and $15 for bike racks). Also, Drake believed this area would be high growth, since the number of cars on the highways was increasing and people always want to speed without getting caught.

Present Situation

While Drake's business had been very successful in comparison to many other small businesses, things were starting to look less rosy. One of the major concerns Drake had was for the continuing demand for radar detectors.

Drake had always assumed radar detectors would be around in one form or another for years. However, several recent developments have led him to question this. First, the increasing tendency of police officers to wait until potential speeders are within radar range before turning the radar gun on has rendered the traditional radar detector obsolete. Second, new devices aid the police by allowing them, at the press of a button, to record the speed of a motorist and place it on a photograph of the speeding auto and driver. This occurs in too short of a time for radar detectors to help speeding motorists. Also, advances in infrared-laser technology have made possible a speed detector that cannot be sensed by radar detectors presently on the market.

To improve SSC's market position, Drake planned to segment the market. A discussion with a neighbor, a sales representative for a wholesale grocery supply firm, revealed there might be a market with his company to install radar detectors in all of the sales reps' cars, a total of 55. The neighbor indicated his sales manager was constantly pushing the sales force to make more calls. The neighbor indicated he had received several speeding tickets and was in danger of losing his license. Drake easily persuaded his neighbor to install a radar detector at a reduced price as a favor for introducing Drake to his sales manager. Drake suspected this situation existed at many other companies as well, although he was not certain how to identify the market.

Another worry was the slowing of revenue growth. Growth for the first five years was fueled largely by the absence of competitors in the upscale radar detector sales niche. Nobody else had challenged Drake for the business of service-hungry customers or those businesses that needed personal attention. Today, however, several new companies, observing the success of SSC, have entered into the market and have begun to steal many key contracts and customers.

Finally, many of Drake's customers have balked at replacing or upgrading their radar detectors for ethical reasons. When asked why they no longer wish to use radar, some clients cited the illegality of speeding and stated their conscience had gotten the best of them. Drake did not know how to address these concerns.

All in all, the year posed many uncertainties for Speedway Sales. Drake will have to consider all the information he had available and make the best possible business decision.

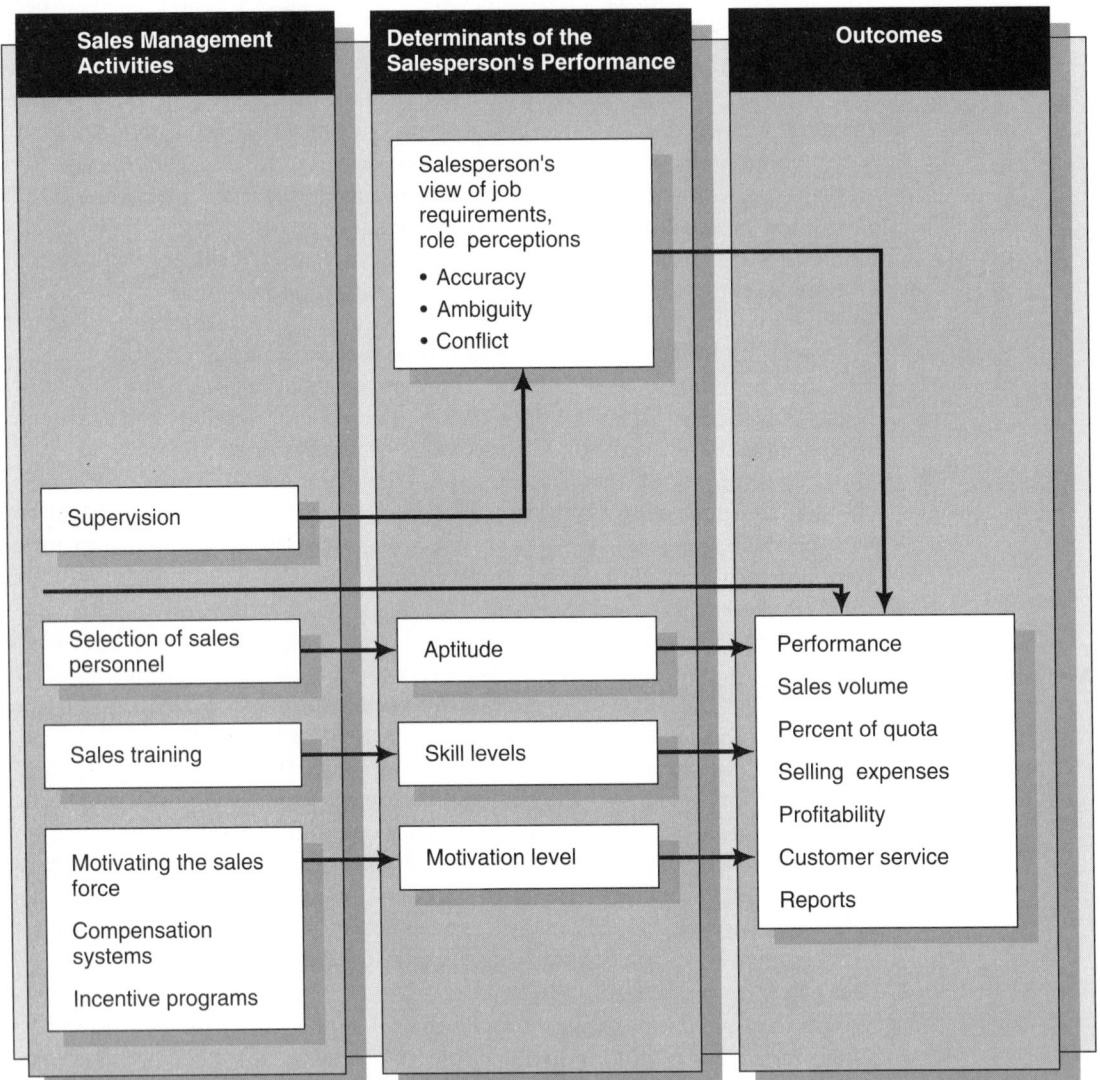

| Sales Management Activities | Determinants of the Salesperson's Performance | Outcomes |

Salesperson's view of job requirements, role perceptions

• Accuracy
• Ambiguity
• Conflict

Supervision

Selection of sales personnel

Aptitude

Sales training

Skill levels

Motivating the sales force

Compensation systems

Incentive programs

Motivation level

Performance

Sales volume

Percent of quota

Selling expenses

Profitability

Customer service

Reports

IMPLEMENTATION OF THE SALES PROGRAM

Chapter 1 suggested that sales management involves three interrelated processes: (1) formulation of a strategic sales program, (2) implementation of the sales program, and (3) evaluation and control of sales force performance. Part 1 of the book concentrated on the first of these processes.

Part 2 concentrates on the second. It explores the policies and procedures involved in implementing a firm's sales program. Chapter 9 provides a model that incorporates the main factors that affect a salesperson's performance and job behavior. The remaining chapters elaborate on the factors and sales management decisions that influence them. Chapter 10 describes the demands salespeople receive from their customers, managers, and families. It also discusses how supervisory policies can help them deal with ambiguous and conflicting demands. Chapters 11 and 12 examine the personal characteristics related to sales aptitude and the ways in which recruiting and selection procedures can be designed to build a sales force with the abilities needed to carry out the required selling tasks and activities. The objectives of sales training and a variety of training techniques are examined in Chapter 13. Finally, Chapters 14 and 15 discuss the kinds of rewards that motivate people to expend effort on various aspects of their jobs and how these rewards can be incorporated into effective sales compensation and incentive programs.

Model of Salesperson Performance

S ALES MANAGER AT OFFICE FORMS WONDERS WHAT TO DO

The sales manager of Stromberg Office Forms of Canada, Helen Crosby, sat at her desk wondering what she should do. She had recently reviewed each salesperson's prior year's sales performance, and the comparisons against quota were disturbing. Fifty-two of the company's 84 salespeople had not made their quota on fax paper, the company's most recent new-product introduction.

The detailed examination of sales versus quota figures by product indicated the problem seemed to be confined to fax paper. All but 7 of the same 52 salespeople had made quota on all of the other business forms the company sells.

Why were sales of fax paper such a problem? The company paid the same commission rate on fax paper that it did on its standard nonpreprinted business forms and supplies. Each salesperson was given the same opportunity to sell fax paper. Each was given the same printed promotional material that described the advantages of Stromberg's fax paper versus the papers made by competitors as well as samples of the paper. Yet only 32 of the reps had made their assigned quota. Moreover, many of the 52 not making quota were some of the company's best salespeople historically. Because of their past sales successes, many of these reps had the best sales territories and largest accounts, a situation that magnified the sales shortfall versus forecast.

At the volume level realized for the past year, the product was clearly unprofitable to Stromberg, and the company would probably never recover its costs in developing it unless the situation could be turned around. But what to do to turn it around, she wondered. A number of thoughts crossed her mind. Do the salespeople need more training on the product's special features? Are the people in the client organization responsible for buying this product the same ones responsible for buying the company's preprinted forms or non-preprinted office paper? Were the sales quotas realistic? Does the product take a disproportionate time to sell? Was it smart to apply the same commission rate to this product as used on the company's other nonpreprinted forms, or should the higher, preprinted form commission rate be used at least during the product's introduction? Were sales of the product hurt by the new generation of fax machines that did not require special paper? The options seemed endless. The more she thought about the issue, the more potential explanations with different implementation implications she developed.

As the introductory scenario suggests, a number of factors can affect a salesperson's performance. When sales managers implement sales programs, they must motivate and direct the behavior of sales representatives toward the company's goals. Sales managers, therefore, must understand why people in the sales force behave the way they do. This chapter offers a model to understand sales force behavior. The model highlights the links between a salesperson's performance and the determinants of that performance. Do not be surprised if you do not completely understand the model after reading this chapter; the purpose of the chapter is only to outline the model and to highlight the various components. Complete understanding of the model should develop as you study the remainder of this section, which discusses the basic components of the model in detail.

THE MODEL

The literature on industrial and organizational psychology suggests a worker's job performance is a function of five basic factors: (1) role perceptions; (2) aptitude; (3) skill level; (4) motivation; and (5) personal, organization, and environmental variables.[1] Exhibit 9.1 presents an overall model of a salesperson's performance that includes these factors as primary determinants.

Although not pictured in the model, there is substantial interaction among the determinants. Much of the published literature, for example, holds that the various factors combine multiplicatively to influence performance. The rationale is that if a worker is deficient in any of these factors, the individual could be expected to perform poorly. If the salesperson had native ability and the motivation to perform but lacked understanding of how the job should be done, for example, he or she could be expected to perform at a low level. Similarly, if the salesperson had the ability and accurately perceived how the job should be performed but lacked motivation, the representative is likely to perform poorly.

The empirical research is somewhat equivocal about whether the factors do combine multiplicatively, but it is fairly certain that the determinants are not independent. There are substantial interaction effects among and between them. Although we know little about the form or the magnitude of those interactions, we need to recognize that they do exist.

THE ROLE PERCEPTIONS COMPONENT

The **role** attached to the position of salesperson in any firm represents the set of activities or behaviors to be performed by any person occupying that position. This role is defined largely through the expectations, demands, and pressures communicated to the salesperson by his or her role partners. These partners include persons both outside and within the individual's firm who have a vested interest in how the salesperson performs the job—top management, the individual's supervisor, customers, and family members. The salesperson's **perceptions** of these expectations strongly influence the individual's definition of his or her role in the company and behavior on the job.

The role perceptions component of the model has three dimensions: role accuracy, perceived role conflict, and perceived role ambiguity. The term **role accuracy** refers to the degree to which the salesperson's perceptions of his or her role partners' demands—particularly company superiors—are accurate. Does what salespeople think their superiors want them to do on the job correspond to their actual expectations and demands?

Perceived role conflict arises when a salesperson believes the role demands of two or more of his or her role partners are incompatible. Thus, he or she cannot possibly satisfy them all at the same time. A salesperson suffers from perceptions of conflict, for example, when a customer demands a delivery schedule or credit terms the sales rep believes will be unacceptable to company superiors.

Perceived role ambiguity occurs when salespeople believe they do not have the information necessary to perform the job adequately. The salespeople may be uncertain about what some role partners expect of them in certain situations, how they should satisfy those expectations, or how their performance will be evaluated and rewarded.

The model indicates the three role perception variables have psychological

EXHIBIT 9 • 1   *Model of the Determinants of Salespersons's Performance*

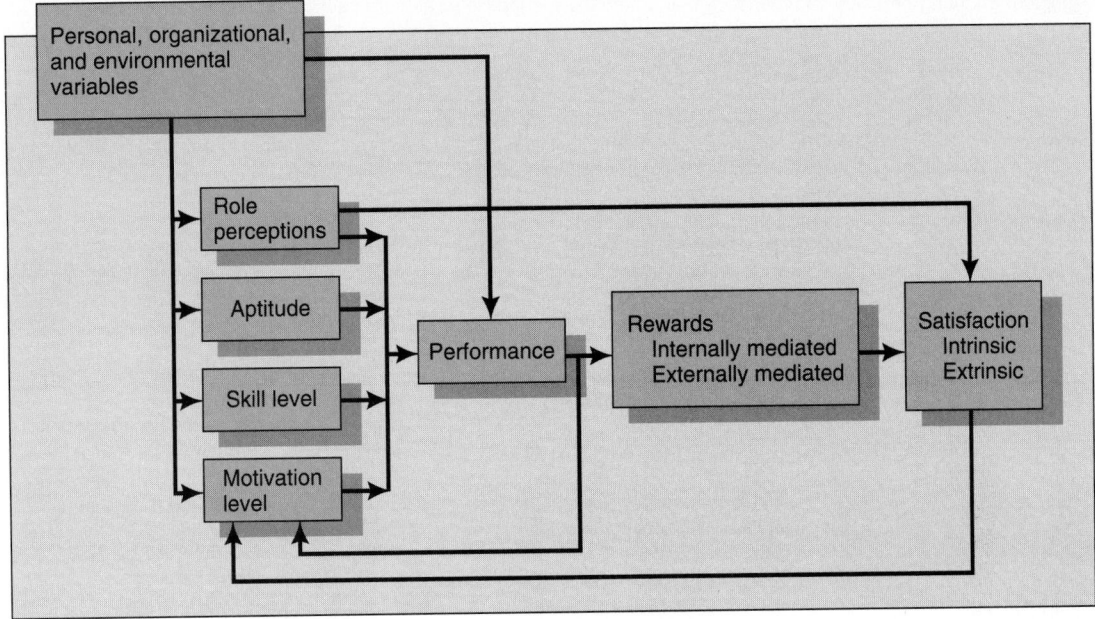

consequences for the individual salesperson. They can produce dissatisfaction with the job. They can also affect the salesperson's motivation.[2] All these effects can produce higher turnover within the sales force and poorer performance.[3]

Industrial salespeople are particularly vulnerable to role inaccuracy, conflict, and ambiguity. Several personal and organizational variables can affect people's role perceptions. Fortunately, many of these variables can be controlled or influenced by sales management policies and methods, thus allowing the sales manager to influence the performance of individual salespeople.[4]

The entire role perceptions component of the model is explored more fully in Chapter 10. That chapter includes a more detailed look at the consequences of inaccuracy, conflict, and ambiguity and the factors that affect these role perceptions.

THE APTITUDE COMPONENT

The overall model of sales performance in Exhibit 9.1 treats the sales aptitude of an individual largely as a constraint on the person's ability to perform the sales job. This assumes there is an adequate understanding of the role to be performed, motivation, and learned skills and an absence of other constraints. In other words, two people with equal motivation, role perceptions, and skills

EXHIBIT 9 • 2   *Common Aptitude Variables Thought to Be Related to Sales Performance*

Aptitude: Enduring personal charcteristics that determine the individual's overall ability to perform a sales job.

Aptitude Variable	Definition	Examples
Intelligence	Summary measures of mental abilities; total scores on multifactor intelligence tests	Wonderlic Personnel Test; Otis Mental Ability Exam
Cognitive abilities	Measures of specific mental processes and abilities, including mental flexibility, ideational fluency, spatial visualization, inductive and logical reasoning, and associative and visual memory	Educational Testing Service's gestalt completion, controlled associations, object number, nonsense, syllogisms, and map memory tests; Kent-Rosanoff associations test; Watson-Glaser critical thinking test
Verbal intelligence	Mental abilities related to the comprehension and manipulation of word; verbal fluency	Educational Testing Service's tests of vocabulary, word fluency, and verbal closure; Adult Placement Test-Verbal; Test of Learning Ability Form S— Vocabulary
Math ability	Mental abilities related to comprehension and manipulation of numbers and quantitative relationships	Educational Testing Service's tests of number facility; Wechsler Adult Intelligence Test—arithmetic subtest; Adult Placement Test—numerical
Sales aptitude	Enduring personal characteristics and abilities thought to be related to performance of specific sales tasks	Life Insurance Marketing and Research Association's Aptitude Index Battery; Aptitudes Associates' Test of Sales Aptitude; Sales Research Associates' Sales Aptitude Checklist

Source: Neil M. Ford, Orville C. Walker, Jr., Gilbert A. Churchill, Jr., and Steven W. Hartley, "Selecting Successful Salespeople: A Meta-Analysis of Biographical and Psychological Selection Criteria," in *Review of Marketing 1987*, ed. Michael J. Houston (Chicago: American Marketing Association, 1987), pp. 103–4.

might perform at very different levels because one has more aptitude or ability than the other.

Aptitude and its impact on sales performance have received much research attention. Sales ability has been thought to be a function of such personal and psychological characteristics as the following:

1. Physical factors, such as age, height, sex, and physical attractiveness.

2. Mental abilities, such as verbal intelligence and mathematical ability.

3. Personality characteristics, such as empathy, ego strength, sociability, aggressiveness, and dominance.

Numerous studies have attempted to predict variations in sales performance using one or more of these aptitude variables. Exhibit 9.2 describes some of the more commonly used aptitude variables and Exhibit 9.3 the more commonly used personality variables. Many studies have found statistically significant relationships between the aptitude variables and performance. How-

EXHIBIT 9 ● 3   *Common Personality Variables Thought to Be Related to Sales Performance*

Personality: Enduring personal traits that reflect the individual's consistent reactions to situations encountered in environment.

Pesonality Variable	Definition	Examples
Responsibility	Person is dependable, emotionally stable, punctual, adjusts well to frustration; keeps promises, follows plans	Gordon Personal Profile—responsibility and emotional stability scales; Guilford-Zimmerman stability scale; peer rating of dependability
Dominance	Person takes command, exerts leadership, pushes own ideas, wants power versus being submissive; is egotistic	Personality Research Form—dominance scale; Murray's dominance scale; Bernreuter Personality Inventory—dominance scale; Edwards Personal Preference Schedule—dominance scale
Sociability	Person enjoys social activities and interaction, likes to be around people, is talkative, gregarious, enjoys attention	Gordon Personal Profile—sociability scale; Bernreuter introversion-extroversion scale; Activity Vector analysis—sociability scale
Self-esteem	Person is confident physically, personally, and career-wise; can stand criticism, claims to have abilities and skills, is confident of success, believes others have a positive attitude toward him/her	Bernreuter self-confidence scale; Cattell ego strength scale; Jackson Personality Inventory—generalized and specific self-esteem scales
Creativity/ flexibility	Person is innovative, flexible, ready to entertain new ideas and ways of doing things, individualistic, tolerant of human nature	Gordon Personal Profile—original thinking and cautiousness scales; Remote Associates Test—creativity scale
Need for achievement/ intrinsic rewards	Person works hard, likes to do his/her best, seeks success in competition, wants to produce something "great," gains satisfaction from accomplishment and personal development	Jackson Personality Inventory—need achievement scale; Murray's achievement and endurance scales; Personality Research Form—achievement scale
Need for power/ extrinsic rewards	Person is motivated primarily by desires for money or advancement, has strong need for security, desires increased power and authority	Martin Bruce Sales Motivation Inventory; Jackson need for power over others, need for high financial rewards, and need for job security scales

Source: Neil M. Ford, Orville C. Walker, Jr., Gilbert A. Churchill, Jr., and Steven W. Hartley, "Selecting Successful Salespeople: A Meta-Analsyis of Biographical and Psychological Selection Criteria," in *Review of Marketing 1987,* ed. Michael J. Houston (Chicago: American Marketing Association, 1987), pp. 103–4.

ever, the broad measures of aptitude by themselves have not been able to explain a very large proportion of the variation in sales performance.[5]

Broad measures of aptitude may not predict sales performance for several reasons. Consider first the motivation component of the overall model. Motivation refers to the salesperson's desire to expend effort on specific sales tasks such as calling on new accounts or preparing sales presentations. This effort should lead to improved performance on one or more dimensions. The link between the effort a salesperson expends on any task and the resulting performance is affected by that salesperson's ability to carry out the task successfully.In other words, the *concept of sales ability or aptitude is very task-specific*. Therefore, the appropriate definition of aptitude, and the appropriate measures of the construct, may vary greatly from industry to industry, firm to firm, and product line to product line. It depends on what specific tasks must be performed and what performance dimensions are considered important.[6] Broad measures of aptitude may fail to capture the task-specific nature of the construct.

Second, aptitude may affect performance in more ways than by simply moderating an individual's ability to do the job. It may also affect the salesperson's motivation to perform. It seems, for example, that the salesperson's *perceived* ability to perform a task and general self-confidence influence the individual's perceptions of whether increased effort will lead to improved performance. Furthermore, salespeople's intelligence and feelings as to whether they largely control their own destiny or whether this destiny is largely controlled by outside forces (internal versus external locus of control) affect whether the representatives believe improved performance will lead to improvement in the rewards they desire. Thus, the salesperson's intelligence and perceptions of his or her own ability as a salesperson may strongly influence the individual's motivation to expend effort on various aspects of the job. All this suggests that objective measures of sales aptitude may be insufficient by themselves. Predictions of sales performance could be improved by including measures of perceived aptitude as well.

THE SKILL LEVEL COMPONENT

Role perceptions determine how well the salesperson knows what must be done in performing a job, and aptitude determines whether the person has the necessary native abilities. **Skill level** refers to the individual's *learned proficiency at performing the necessary tasks*.[7] Aptitude and skill level are thus related constructs. Aptitude consists of relatively enduring personal abilities, while skills are proficiency levels that can change rapidly with learning and experience.

Exhibit 9.4 lists skills thought to be related to sales performance. The relative importance of each of these skills, and the necessity of having other skills, depends on the selling situation. Different kinds of skills are needed for different types of selling tasks.

The salesperson's past selling experience and the extensiveness and content of the firm's sales training programs influence skill level. While American companies spend large amounts of money on sales training, there is almost no published research concerning the effects of these training programs on salespeople's skills, behavior, and performance.

There are a number of articles on training in the sales literature, but they are typically how-to-do-it or experiential pieces. Few studies have evaluated the psychological or behavioral effects of alternative training methods.

EXHIBIT 9 • 4   *Common Skill Variables Thought to be Related to Sales Performance*

Skill: Individual's learned proficiency at performing necessary tasks.

Skill Variable	Definition	Examples
Vocational skills	Job- and company-specific skills; technical knowledge and vocabulary related to the firm's product line, knowledge of the company and its policies	A variety of proprietary tests of technical knowledge, engineering skills, knowledge of the industry and company policies
Sales presentation	Skills related to evaluating customer needs, presentation style, ability to handle objections and close the sale	Martin Bruce Sales Comprehension Test; Sales Style Diagnosis Test; assessment center judgments; interviewer/supervisor ratings
Interpersonal	Skills related to understanding, persuading, and getting along with other people	Diplomacy Test of Empathy; interviewer/supervisor ratings of cooperativeness, sensitivity, ability to resolve conflicts
General management	Skills related to organizing, directing, and leading other people	Various paper and pencil tests on measuring supervisory abilities; assessment center judgments
Vocational esteem	Degree of liking or preference for tasks and activities associated with sales jobs	Strong Vocational Interest Blank; Kuder Preference Record

Source: Neil M. Ford, Orville C. Walker, Jr., Gilbert A. Churchill, Jr., and Steven W. Hartley, "Selecting Successful Salespeople: A Meta-Analysis of Biographical and Psychological Selection Criteria," in *Review of Marketing 1987*, ed. Michael J. Houston (Chicago: American Marketing Association, 1987), p. 104.

THE MOTIVATION COMPONENT

Over the years, **motivation** has meant various, and often inconsistent, things in the literature, although some recent consensus seems to be emerging. For our purposes, *motivation* is viewed as the amount of effort the salesperson desires to expend on each activity or task associated with the job. These activities include calling on existing and potentially new accounts, developing and delivering sales presentations, and filling out orders and reports.

The salesperson's motivation to expend effort on any task seems to be a function of the person's (1) expectancies and (2) valences for performance. Expectancies are the salesperson's estimates of the probability that expending effort on a specific task will lead to improved performance on some specific dimension. For example, will increasing the number of calls made on potentially new accounts lead to increased sales? Valences for performance are the salesperson's perceptions of the desirability of attaining improved performance on some dimension or dimensions. For example, does the salesperson find increased sales attractive?

A salesperson's valence for performance on a specific dimension, in turn, seems to be a function of the salesperson's (1) instrumentalities and (2) valences

Thorny Issues in Sales Management 9 • 1

HAT TO DO ABOUT THE GREAT SALESPERSON
WHO IS NO LONGER SO GREAT

Dave Parrett, sales manager for Ace Chemicals, was wrestling with the issue of how to get Kay Powers back on track. Kay had been with the company 20 years. Historically, she had been one of the company's top salespeople, although her performance had fallen off during the past three to five years.

That concerned Dave because Kay called on some of the largest accounts Ace served. She had earned each of those assignments. When she joined Ace Chemicals, Kay had turned heads with her performance. She had secured business in companies the firm had never previously served. Customers were extremely pleased with the service she provided. Ace received more unsolicited compliments on how she serviced her accounts than on any other salesperson. Her call reports indicated she made more calls in a week than almost any other salesperson with the company, and her sales showed it. She regularly exceeded the quotas she was assigned.

All this seemed to change in the last couple of years. She had developed very few accounts in that time. While Ace Chemicals was not getting a disproportionate number of complaints from her customers, it was getting its share. Kay seemed to start later and quit earlier than she had historically. She made fewer calls on average in a week than most of the other salespeople. She barely met her quota in three of the last five years and fell short of it once. Yet she was still a good enough salesperson that her income with salary and commissions exceeded six figures every year.

for rewards. Instrumentalities are the salesperson's estimates of the probability that improved performance on that dimension will lead to increased attainment of particular rewards. For example, will increased sales lead to increased compensation? Valences for rewards are the salesperson's perceptions of the desirability of receiving increased rewards as a result of improved performance. Does the salesperson, say, find an increase in the compensation level attractive?

A salesperson's expectancy, instrumentality, and valence perceptions can all affect the willingness to expend effort on a specific task or to engage in specific behaviors. Sales managers constantly try to find the right mix of motivation elements to direct salespeople in specific directions. The problem is particularly difficult because rewards that motivate one salesperson may not motivate another. Moreover, what motivated a person at one stage in his or her career may not motivate the rep during some other period, as Thorny Issue 9.1 indicates.

The salesperson's expectancy, instrumentality, and valence perceptions are not directly under the sales manager's control. But they can be influenced by things the sales manager does, such as how he or she supervises the salesperson or rewards the individual.[8] Since the salesperson's motivation strongly influences performance, the sales manager must be sensitive to how various factors exert their impact. These issues are explored more fully in Chapter 14.

The Personal, Organizational, and Environmental Variable Component

The sales performance model in Exhibit 9.1 suggests that personal, organizational, and environmental variables influence sales performance in two ways: (1) by directly facilitating or constraining performance, and (2) by influencing and interacting with the other performance determinants, such as the role perceptions and motivation.

Part 1 described how these variables can influence sales performance directly. The discussion of the organization of the sales force and the design of sales territories reviewed much of the evidence and logic supporting the relationship between performance and organizational factors. These factors include company advertising expenditures, the firm's current market share, and the degree of sales force supervision. There is a relationship between performance and environmental factors like territory potential, concentration of customers, the salesperson's workload, and the intensity of competition. The direct impact of the personal, organizational, and environmental variables on performance is thus rather clear.

Unfortunately, there has been less empirical work investigating the interactions among personal, organizational, and environmental variables and other determinants of performance. As discussed, studies have had modest success identifying personal characteristics associated with sales aptitude and relating them to variations in sales performance.

A few studies have found significant relationships between personal and organizational variables—such as job experience, closeness of supervision, performance feedback, influence in determining standards, and span of control—and the amount of role conflict and ambiguity perceived by salespeople.[9] Other studies related personal characteristics to variations in motivation by showing that salespeople's desires for different job-related rewards (e.g., pay, promotion) differ with such demographic characteristics as age, education, family size, career stage, or organizational climate.[10] Overall, though, many questions concerning the effects of personal, organizational, and environmental variables on the other determinants of sales performance remain unanswered.

Rewards

The performance model in Exhibit 9.1 indicates that the salesperson's job performance affects the rewards the representative receives. The relationship between performance and rewards is very complex, however. For one thing, a firm may choose to evaluate and reward different dimensions of sales performance. A company might evaluate its salespeople on total sales volume, quota attainment, selling expenses, profitability of sales, new accounts generated, services provided to customers, performance of administrative duties, or some combination of these. Different firms are likely to use different dimensions. Even firms that use the same performance criteria are likely to have different relative emphases.

A company can also bestow a variety of rewards for any given level of performance. The model distinguishes between two broad types of rewards—extrinsic and intrinsic.[11] **Extrinsic rewards** are those controlled and bestowed by people other than the salesperson, such as managers or customers. These include such things as pay, financial incentives, security, recognition, and promotion—rewards that are generally related to lower-order human needs. **Intrinsic rewards** are those that salespeople primarily attain for themselves. They include such things as feelings of accomplishment, personal growth, and self-worth—all of which relate to higher-order human needs.

As the model in Exhibit 9.1 suggests, salespeople's perceptions of the rewards they will receive in return for various types of job performance, together with the value they place on those rewards, strongly influence their motivation to perform.

S ATISFACTION

The **job satisfaction** of salespeople refers to all the characteristics of the job that representatives find rewarding, fulfilling, and satisfying, or frustrating and unsatisfying. As Exhibit 9.5 indicates, there seem to be seven different dimensions to sales job satisfaction: (1) the job itself, (2) fellow workers, (3) supervision, (4) company policies and support, (5) pay, (6) promotion and advancement opportunities, and (7) customers. Salespeople's total satisfaction with their jobs is a reflection of their satisfaction with each of these elements.[12]

As Exhibit 9.1 suggests, the rewards received by a salesperson have a major impact on the individual's satisfaction with the job and the total work environment. The seven dimensions of satisfaction can be grouped, like rewards, into two major components—intrinsic and extrinsic. Extrinsic satisfaction is associated with the extrinsic rewards bestowed on the salesperson, such as satisfaction with pay, company policies and support, supervision, fellow workers, chances for promotion, and customers. Intrinsic satisfaction is related to the intrinsic rewards the salesperson obtains from the job, such as satisfaction with the work itself and with the opportunities it provides for personal growth and accomplishment.

The amount of satisfaction salespeople obtain from their jobs is also influenced by their role perceptions. Salespeople who perceive much conflict in the demands placed on them tend to be less satisfied than those who do not. So do those who experience great uncertainty in what is expected from them on the job.

EXHIBIT 9 • 5 *Components of Job Satisfaction and Sample Items*

Component	Number of Items	Sample Items
The job	12	My work is challenging. My job is often dull and monotonous. My work gives me a sense of accomplishment. My job is exciting.
Fellow workers	12	The people I work with get along well together. My fellow workers are selfish. My fellow workers are intelligent. My fellow workers are responsible.
Supervision	16	My sales manager is tactful. My sales manager really tries to get our ideas about things. My sales manager doesn't seem to try too hard to get our problems across to management. My sales manager sees that we have the things we need to do our jobs.
Company policy and support	21	Compared with other companies, employee benefits here are good. Sometimes when I learn of management's plans, I wonder if they know the territory situation at all. The company's sales training is not carried out in a well-planned program. The company is highly aggressive in its sales promotional efforts. Management is progressive.
Pay	11	My pay is high in comparison with what others get for similar work in other companies. My pay doesn't give me much incentive to increase my sales. My selling ability largely determines my earnings in this company. My income provides for luxuries.
Promotion and advancement	8	My opportunities for advancement are limited. Promotion here is based on ability. I have a good chance for promotion. Regular promotions are the rule in this company.
Customers	15	My customers are fair. My customers blame me for problems that I have no control over. My customers respect my judgment. I seldom know who really makes the purchase decisions in the companies I call on.

Source: Gilbert A. Churchill, Jr., Neil M. Ford, and Orville C. Walker, Jr., "Measuring the Job Satisfaction of Industrial Salesmen," *Journal of Marketing Research* 11 (August 1974), p. 258, published by the American Marketing Association.

Thorny Issues In Sales Management 9 • 2

ARE SOME WORKERS BOUND TO BE UNHAPPY?

Traditional thinking holds that companies can increase employee job satisfaction if they do things like give a worker more autonomy. But in recent years many academic researchers have concluded that sometimes an unhappy worker is inherently an unhappy worker—and little can change that.

In a 1985 study, for instance, researchers at the University of California at Berkeley found the job satisfaction of 5,000 middle-age men changed little in five years, regardless of changes in job, pay, or job status.

A study there a year later examined the personality characteristics and job attitudes of people who had been followed over a 50-year period. Those who had unhappy dispositions early in life tended to report the least job satisfaction; those with happy dispositions, the most satisfaction.

Going a step further, Richard D. Arvey, a University of Minnesota management professor, recently found that genetics may play a part. In his study, identical twins who were reared separately had similar scores on certain job-satisfaction measures, like how much feeling of accomplishment they got from their jobs.

Researchers caution that the studies don't suggest companies should abandon efforts to improve job satisfaction; environmental factors—quality of a boss, for instance—clearly play a role. But, says Barry Staw, a management professor at the University of California at Berkeley, "what it means is that influencing job attitude is a hell of a lot harder than we thought it was. You can't put in a weekend program and expect the world to change."

To be sure, many human resources managers aren't sold. "I take this with a grain of salt," says Ronald Pilenzo, president of the American Society for Personnel Administration. Job-enrichment programs, he adds, have "turned on" a lot of workers.

Source: Larry Riebstein, "Are Some Workers Bound to Be Unhappy?" *The Wall Street Journal,* April 18, 1988, p. 31.

As Thorny Issue 9.2 suggests, satisfaction with the job may be part and parcel of the person, an issue that has important implications for sales managers as they seek to motivate and retain productive salespeople.

Finally, a salesperson's job satisfaction is likely to affect the individual's motivation to perform, as suggested by the feedback loop in Exhibit 9.1. The relationship between satisfaction and motivation is, however, neither simple nor well understood. It is explored more fully in Chapter 14.

IMPORTANCE FOR SALES MANAGEMENT

Understanding the model of salesperson performance in Exhibit 9.1 can be extremely important to the sales manager. As mentioned in Chapter 1, sales management involves three interrelated processes:

1. The formulation of a strategic sales program.
2. The implementation of the sales program.
3. The evaluation and control of sales force performance.

Almost everything the sales manager does can influence sales performance. For example, the way the sales manager organizes and deploys the sales force can affect salespeople's perceptions of the job. How the manager selects salespeople and the kind of training they receive can affect the aptitude and skill of sales personnel. The compensation program and the way it is administered can influence motivation levels and overall sales performance. The model offers the sales manager a tool for visualizing the effects of his or her activities and for appreciating the interrelated roles of the options under his or her command.

As mentioned earlier, do not be surprised if you have difficulty comprehending the full implications of the model or the suggested links. This chapter outlined the model and highlighted the various components. The remaining chapters in this section elaborate on the components. Chapter 10 discusses the role component and the evidence supporting its effects and the influences on it. Chapter 11 on aptitude and Chapter 12 on selection provide background on aptitude and its implications for effective sales management. Chapter 13 delves into sales training programs; these directly affect skill levels but can also influence the role component. Chapters 14 and 15 look in more detail at motivation, rewards, and the design of compensation systems. These key elements under the sales manager's control can profoundly affect the motivation level of the sales force.

SUMMARY

This chapter, the first on implementing the sales program, sought to present a model for understanding the performance of salespeople. This chapter was an overview of the model and the important links; the emphasis in the remaining chapters in this section is on detailing the components of the model.

The model suggests that a salesperson's performance is a function of five basic factors: (1) role perceptions; (2) aptitude; (3) skill level; (4) motivation; and (5) personal, organizational, and environmental variables. There is substantial interaction among the components. A salesperson who is deficient with respect to any one could be expected to perform poorly.

The role of the salesperson is defined largely through the expectations, demands, and pressures communicated by his or her role partners. Role partners are people both within and outside the company who are affected by the way the salesperson performs the job. The three major variables in the role perception component are role accuracy, perceived role ambiguity, and perceived role conflict. *Role accuracy* refers to the degree to which the salesperson's perceptions of his or her role partners' demands are accurate. *Perceived role ambiguity* occurs when the salesperson does not believe he or she has the information to perform the job adequately. *Perceived role conflict* arises when a salesperson believes that the demands of two or more of his or her role partners are incompatible.

Aptitude refers to the salesperson's native ability to do the job and includes such things as physical factors, mental abilities, and personality characteristics. Aptitude is a constraint on the person's ability to perform the sales job given an adequate understanding of the role to be performed, motivation, and learned skills and the absence of other constraints.

Skill level refers to the person's learned proficiency at performing the necessary tasks. It is different from aptitude. Whereas aptitude consists of relatively enduring personal abilities, skills are proficiency levels that can change rapidly with learning and experience.

Motivation refers to the effort the salesperson desires to expend on each activity or task associated with the job. These include calling on potential new accounts, developing sales presentations, and the like. The motivation to expend effort on any particular task depends on (1) expectancy—the salesperson's estimate of the probability that expending effort on the task will lead to improved performance on some dimension, and (2) valence for performance—the salesperson's perception of the desirability of improving performance on that dimension. The valence for performance on any dimension is, in turn, a function of (1) instrumentality—the salesperson's estimate of the probability that improved performance on that dimension will lead to increased attainment of particular rewards, and (2) valence for rewards—the salesperson's perception of the desirability of receiving increased rewards as a result of improved performance.

The personal, organizational, and environmental variables influence sales performance in two ways: (1) by directly facilitating or constraining performance, and (2) by influencing and interacting with other performance determinants, such as role perceptions and motivation.

The performance of the salesperson affects the rewards the individual receives. There are two basic types of rewards: extrinsic rewards, which are controlled and bestowed by people other than the salesperson, and intrinsic rewards, which are those that people primarily attain for themselves.

The rewards received by a salesperson have a major impact on the individual's satisfaction with the job and the total work environment. Satisfaction can also be of two types. Intrinsic satisfaction is related to the intrinsic rewards the salesperson obtains from the job, such as satisfaction with the work and the opportunities it provides for personal growth and sense of accomplishment. Extrinsic satisfaction is associated with the extrinsic rewards bestowed on the salesperson, such as pay, chances for promotion, and supervisory and company policies.

*Discussion
Questions*

1. The president of Part-I-Tyme, manufacturer of salty snack foods, was dismayed over the dismal sales results reported for the first six months. A new product, a deluxe cookie, had been taste tested and consumers' response was very positive. Part-I-Tyme's sales force consists of over 5,000 truck driver distributors who had developed an excellent reputation with their customers. Part-I-Tyme's president was convinced the existing sales force of 5,000 would enthusiastically support the new product line. It was obvious something was wrong. How would you determine the nature of the problem? Can you use the model of salesperson performance in this situation?

2. The sales manager of a nationwide corporation commented, "There's no such thing as a sales representative who can't be motivated by money." Do you agree or disagree? Why?

3. Is it possible for a sales rep to want rewards that are not provided by the employer? What impact does this have on motivation? Performance? Satisfaction?

4. Although many aptitude tests exist, their ability to predict sales performance has been weak. How do you account for this?

5. Is it possible for a person to be highly motivated, possess the necessary aptitude, have a high skill level, and still not be able to sell?

6. Frequently, sales managers use contests and recognition rewards to motivate the sales force. If sales managers understand salesperson performance, then why is it necessary to employ these additional techniques?

7. The national sales manager of the C&N Bearing Corporation believes poor sales performance is the reason for the recent decline in sales. It has been recommended that sales commission be raised as a solution to the problem. Comment.

8. A well-known computer manufacturer uses a variety of aptitude tests as part of its recruiting and selection procedures. Personnel from the company's human resource development function claim the tests are used not to predict how well a person will perform on the job but how well a person will do in the training program. What is the rationale for adopting this view? Do you agree with this approach?

9. Sales management involves three interrelated processes: formulation, implementation, and evaluation and control of sales performance. What are the essential points a manager must consider and work with if the sales program, once formulated, is to be effectively implemented?

10. "I don't understand," lamented Bob Coates. "We spend $10,000 to bring in Harold Hill, a highly successful NFL coach, to motivate the sales force and what happens? Nothing! And I thought he would really get the troops all charged up to go out and really hustle. They liked the program. He had them laughing in the aisles, telling jokes, and he even had the sales reps stand up and shout that they were motivated. This guy's a real charmer, a dynamo, and he came to me highly recommended. Sure he charges a high fee, $10,000 for a 30-minute presentation, but I thought he would be able to turn things around. He had great visuals, and his astronaut's uniform was clever. This memo from the CEO wants to know what we got in return for our $10,000. What went wrong?" Comment.

Endnotes

[1]This chapter borrows heavily from the following articles: Orville C. Walker, Jr., Gilbert A. Churchill, Jr., and Neil M. Ford, "Motivation and Performance in Industrial Selling: Present Knowledge and Needed Research," *Journal of Marketing Research* 14 (May 1977), pp. 156–68; and Orville C. Walker, Jr., Gilbert A. Churchill, Jr., and Neil M. Ford, "Where Do We Go from Here? Selected Conceptual and Empirical Issues Concerning the Motivation and Performance of the Industrial Salesforce," in *Critical Issues in Sales Management: State of the Art and Future Research Needs*, ed. Gerald Albaum and Gilbert A. Churchill, Jr. (Eugene: University of Oregon, 1979), pp. 10–75.

[2]For studies of how role perceptions can affect salespeople's job satisfaction and performance, see Douglas N. Behrman, William B. Bigoness, and William D. Perreault, Jr., "Sources of Job Related Ambiguity and Their Consequences upon Salesperson's Job Satisfaction and Performance," *Management Science* 27 (November 1981), pp. 1,246–60; Douglas N. Behrman and William D. Perreault, Jr., "A Role Stress Model of the Performance and Satisfaction of Industrial Salespeople," *Journal of Marketing* 48 (Fall 1984), pp. 9–21; Alan J. Dubinsky and Steven W. Hartley, "A Path-Analytic Study of a Model of Salesperson Performance," *Journal of the Academy of Marketing Science* 14 (Spring 1986), pp. 36–46; and Kenneth R. Bartkus, Mark F. Peterson, and Danny N. Bellenger, "Type A Behavior Experience and Salesperson Performance," *The Journal of Personal Selling and Sales Management* 9 (Summer 1989), pp. 11–18.

[3]For discussions of the hidden costs of salesperson turnover and the factors affecting turnover, see Charles M. Futrell and A. Parasuraman, "The Relationship of Satisfaction and Performance to Salesforce Turnover," *Journal of Marketing* 48 (Fall 1984), pp. 33–40; George H. Lucas, Jr., et al., "An Empirical Study of Salesforce Turnover," *Journal of Marketing* 51 (July 1987, pp. 34–59; Marvin A. Jolson, Alan J. Dubinsky, and Rolph E. Anderson, "Correlates and Determinants of Sales Force Tenure: An Exploratory Study," *Journal of Personal Selling and Sales Management* 7 (November 1987), pp. 9–27; Lynn G. Coleman, "Sales Force Turnover Has Managers Wondering Why," *Marketing News* 23 (December 4, 1989), pp. 6, 21; and Thomas N. Ingram and Keun S. Lee, "Sales Force Commitment and Turnover," *Industrial Marketing Management* 19 (May 1990), pp. 149–54.

[4]R. Kenneth Teas, "Supervisory Behavior, Role Stress, and the Job Satisfaction of Industrial Salespeople," *Journal of Marketing Research* 20 (February 1983), pp. 84–91; Ajay K. Kohli, "Some Unexplored Supervisory Behaviors and Their Influence on Salespeople's Role Clarity, Specific Job Esteem, Job Satisfaction, and Motivation," *Journal of Marketing Research* 22 (November 1985), pp. 424–33; Ronald E. Goldsmith, Kevin M. McNeilly, and Fredrick A. Russ, "Similarity of Sales Representatives and Supervisors' Problem-Solving Styles and the Satisfaction-Performance Relationship," *Psychological Reports* 64 (June 1989), pp. 827–32.

[5]For summaries of the results of these studies, see Edwin E. Ghiselli, *The Validity of Occupational Aptitude Tests* (New York: John Wiley & Sons, 1966), pp. 41–43; Barton A. Weitz, "A Critical Review of Personal Selling Research: The Need for Contingency Approaches," in Albaum and Churchill, Jr., *Critical Issues in Sales Management*, pp. 76–126; Neil M. Ford et al., *Selecting Successful Salespeople: A Meta-Analysis of Biographical and Psychological Selection Criteria*, ed. Michael J. Houston (Chicago: American Marketing Association, *Review of Marketing, 1987*), pp. 90–131. For an example, see Lawrence M. Lamont and William J. Lundstrom, "Identifying Successful Industrial Salesmen by Personality and Personal Characteristics," *Journal of Marketing Research* 14 (November 1977), pp. 517–29.

[6]Ramon A. Avila and Edward F. Fern, "The Selling Situation as a Moderator of the Personality-Sales Performance Relationship: An Empirical Investigation," *Journal of Personal Selling and Sales Management* 6 (November 1986), pp. 53–63.

[7]Siew Meng Leong, Paul S. Busch, and Deborah Roedder John, "Knowledge Bases and Salesperson Effectiveness: A Script-Theoretic Analysis," *Journal of Marketing Research* 26 (May 1990), pp. 164–78.

[8]R. Kenneth Teas, "An Empirical Test of Models of Salespersons' Job Expectancy and Instrumentality Perceptions," *Journal of Marketing Research* 18 (May 1981), pp. 209–26; Thomas L. Quick, "The Best-Kept Secret for Increasing Productivity," *Sales & Marketing Management* 141 (July 1989), pp. 34–38.

[9]Orville C. Walker, Jr., Gilbert A. Churchill, Jr., and Neil M. Ford, "Organizational Determinants of the Industrial Salesman's Role Conflict and Ambiguity," *Journal of Marketing* 39 (January 1975), pp. 32–39; Teas, "Supervisory Behavior, Role Stress;" Lawrence B. Chonko, Roy D. Howell, and Danny N. Bellenger, "Congruence in Sales Force Evaluations: Relation to Sales Force Perceptions of Conflict and Ambiguity," *Journal of Personal Selling and Sales Management* 6 (May 1986), pp. 35–48; and Gary A. Schroeder, "Using an Attitude Survey to Increase Sales Effectiveness," *Personnel* 66 (February 1989), pp. 51–55.

[10]Gilbert A. Churchill, Jr., Neil M. Ford, and Orville C. Walker, Jr., "Motivating the Industrial Salesforce: The Attractiveness of Alternative Rewards," *Journal of Business Research* 7 (1979), pp. 25–50; William L. Cron and John W. Slocum, Jr., "The Influence of Career Stages on Salespeople's Job Attitudes, Work Perceptions, and Performance," *Journal of Marketing Research* 23 (May 1986), pp. 119–29; and Pradeep K. Tyagi, "Organizational Climate, Inequities, and At-tractiveness of Salesperson Rewards," *Journal of Personal Selling and Sales Management* 5 (November 1985), pp. 31–37.

[11]For a study investigating the impact of organizational conditions on salespeople's valences for the various types of rewards, see Pradeep K. Tyagi, "The Effects of Stressful Organizational Conditions on Salesperson Work Motivation," *Journal of the Academy of Marketing Science* 13 (Winter/Spring 1985), pp. 290–309.

[12]See Gilbert A. Churchill, Jr., Neil M. Ford, and Orville C. Walker, Jr., "Measuring the Job Satisfaction of Industrial Salesmen," *Journal of Marketing Research* 11 (August 1974), pp. 254–60, for a description of the procedures used to construct the scale. For an empirical example of its use, see Louis W. Fry et al., "An Analysis of Alternate Causal Models of Salesperson Role Perceptions and Work Related Attitudes," *Journal of Marketing Research* 23 (May 1986), pp. 153–63.

Suggested Readings

Walker, Orville C., Jr., Gilbert A. Churchill, Jr., and Neil M. Ford. "Motivation and Performance in Industrial Selling: Present Knowledge and Needed Research." *Journal of Marketing Research* 14 (May 1977), pp. 156–68.

Walker, Orville C., Jr., Gilbert A. Churchill, Jr., and Neil M. Ford. "Where Do We Go from Here? Selected Conceptual and Empirical Issues Concerning the Motivation and Performance of the Industrial Salesforce?" In *Critical Issues in Sales Management: State of the Art and Future Research Needs,* ed. Gerald Albaum and Gilbert A. Churchill, Jr. (Eugene: University of Oregon, 1979), pp. 10–75.

10

The Salesperson's Role Perceptions

RAMON PONDERS HIS STRATEGY

Ramon Valesquez, a sales engineer in the Caracas, Venezuela, office of Ingersoll Rand, was extremely frustrated as he pondered what to do next. He had been working almost two years to land the pump and compressor order for the new refinery. He had been involved in the refinery's design from the beginning.

Ingersoll Rand was one of the largest pump and compressor manufacturers in the world. Headquartered in the northeastern United States, it had sales offices in many major cities throughout the world. The offices were staffed by engineers of all types, although most of the sales representatives had degrees in mechanical engineering. The company believed engineering training was necessary for salespeople to be successful because they often had to assist customers in designing the systems that would use the company's pumps and compressors.

Ramon had joined Ingersoll Rand soon after completing his undergraduate degree in mechanical engineering at Purdue University. After completing the company's formal six-month training program, he had been assigned to the Chicago office as an inside sales engineer to complete his training. This assignment, in which he serviced two outside sales representatives, lasted 20 months. His duties included selecting equipment for applications, preparing formal proposals for customers, handling unsolicited inquiries, and responding to technical and service questions.

Ramon's promotion to outside sales engineer had been relatively swift, and he was delighted to have been assigned to the Caracas office. He was even more pleased when he heard soon after arriving in Venezuela about the new refinery that was to be built by one of his assigned accounts. He knew that meant a large potential order because refineries were intensive users of pumps and compressors.

Ramon had consulted with the refinery's design engineers to select the best volume and pressure conditions for the output at each stage of the refinery process. He had helped choose the corrosion-resistant materials from which the internal workings of the equipment should be made. His work had paid off when the construction contract was put out for bids. Many of the specifications for pumps and compressors stated "Ingersoll Rand model number so-and-so or equivalent."

This is why the latest developments were so frustrating. When the bids were opened, the quoted price for the Ingersoll Rand pumps and compressors was slightly less than 2 percent higher than that of the leading competitor—a $60,000 difference on a $3 million bid. The general contractor on the project, with whom Ramon had also worked closely, indicated the contract was his if Ingersoll Rand would meet the competitor's price. When Ramon approached headquarters with his dilemma, he received some relief but not as much as he needed. The product manager for compressors indicated she would go along. The product manager for pumps indicated he would not. That left Ramon's bid still $43,000 higher than that of the competitor's.

Moreover, while agreeing that Ramon's decision to quote stainless steel impellers for the pumps handling liquids during one particularly corrosive phase of the refining process was best, the product manager suggested Ramon could meet the competitor's price by substituting impellers made from a less expensive material. That is what the competition had done. Maintenance costs on the pumps would go up with the less expensive impellers, but their substitution would allow Ramon to beat the competitor's price.

What should he do now, Ramon wondered? Should he substitute the less expensive impellers? Should he tell the client about the substitution? Or should he try to convince the client that the use of the less expensive impellers was being penny-wise and pound foolish? Would the client even believe him since the competitor in question was very well respected in the industry? Should he go over the product manager's head and ask the group process equipment manager for permission to meet the competitor's price, still using pumps with stainless steel impellers?

Ramon knew he had to do *something*. He had just spent two years laying the groundwork for the largest sale of his relatively short career—a sale that would mean $45,000 to him in commission.

As this scenario suggests, salespeople are often caught in the middle. The very nature of their jobs often places them in a position in which the expectations and demands of their customers conflict with the expectations of those in the firm for whom they work. In such instances, it is not always clear how they should proceed. Yet as we saw in Chapter 9, the model of salesperson performance suggests a primary influence on how salespeople perform is their perceptions of the demands placed on them (see Exhibit 10.1). Are these perceptions accurate? Are salespeople fairly certain about what they should do? Are the demands of different people consistent?

This chapter elaborates on the role perceptions variable in the model. The chapter first reviews the concept of role and the process that defines the salesperson's role. The second part highlights key aspects of the salesperson's role that make it susceptible to conflicts, ambiguities, and inaccurate perceptions. The chapter then focuses on role conflict and ambiguity. It discusses some common demands salespeople receive and the consequences and causes of the conflict and ambiguity they feel. The fourth part of the chapter takes a similar approach with respect to role accuracy. It reviews the specific nature of the effort-performance and performance-reward linkages salespeople perceive and the consequences and causes of their expectancy and instrumentality estimates.

THE SALESPERSON'S ROLE

Every employee within the firm occupies a position to which a **role** is attached. This role represents the activities and behaviors that are to be performed by *any person* who occupies that position. The salesperson's role is defined through a three-step process.[1]

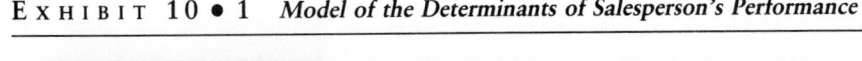

E X H I B I T 10 • 1   *Model of the Determinants of Salesperson's Performance*

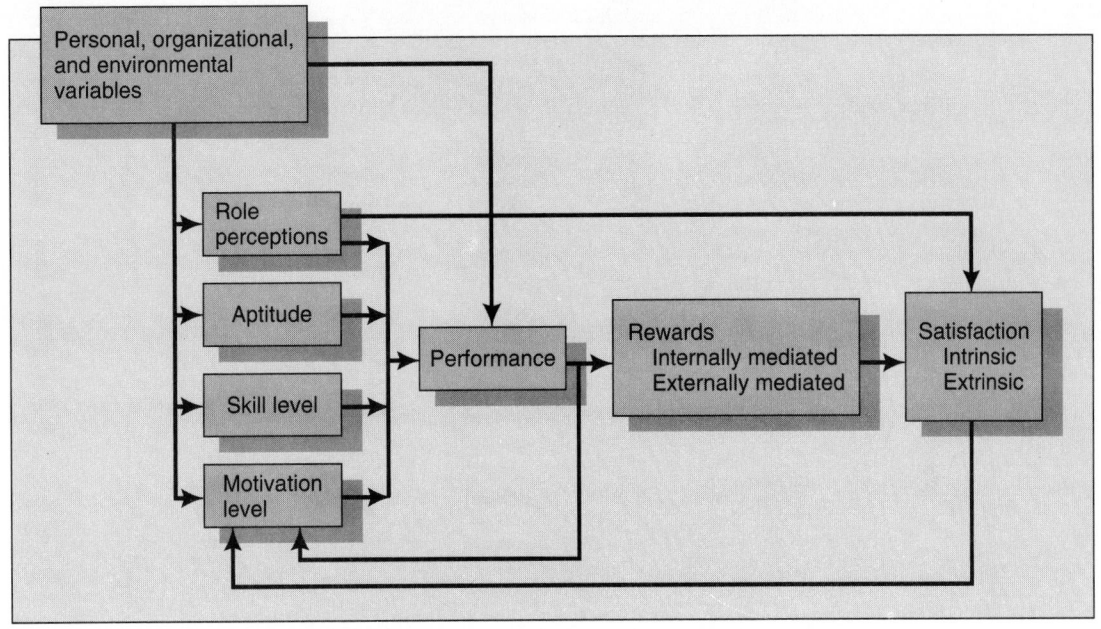

Stage 1:
Role Partners
Communicate
Expectations

First, expectations and demands concerning how the salesperson should be-have, together with pressures to conform, are communicated to the salesperson by members of that person's **role set.** The salesperson's role set consists of people with a vested interest in how the representative performs the job. These people include the individual's immediate superior, other executives in the firm, purchasing agents and other members of customers' organizations, and the salesperson's family. They all try to influence the person's behavior, either formally through organizational policies, operating procedures, training pro-grams, and the like, or informally through social pressures, rewards, and sanc-tions.

Stage 2:
Salespeople
Develop
Perceptions

The second part of the role definition process involves the perceived role. This is salespeople's perceptions of the expectations and demands communicated to them by their role-set members. Salespeople perform according to what they *think* the role-set members expect, even though their perceptions of those expectations may not be accurate. To really understand why salespeople per-

EXHIBIT 10 • 2   *Salesperson's Perceptions of the Job*

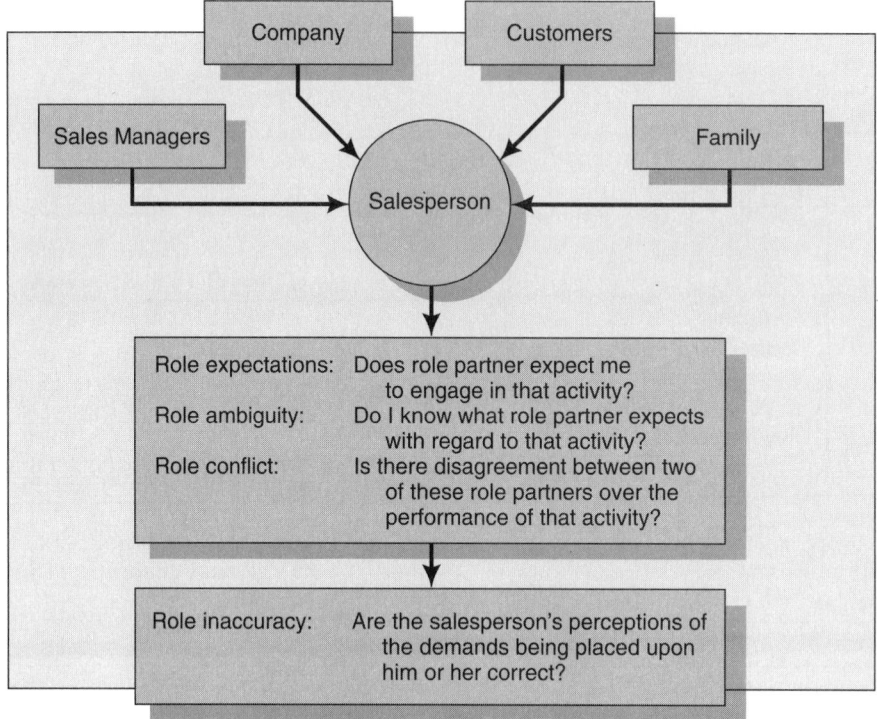

form the way they do, it is necessary to understand what salespeople *think* the members of the role set expect.

At this stage of the role definition process, three factors can wreak havoc with a salesperson's job performance and mental well-being. As Exhibit 10.2 suggests, the salesperson may suffer from perceptions of role ambiguity, role conflict, or role inaccuracy.

Perceived role ambiguity occurs when representatives do not think they have the necessary information to perform the job adequately. They feel uncertain about how to do a specific task, what the members of the role set expect in a particular situation, or how their performance is evaluated by members of the role set.

Perceived role conflict exists when a salesperson believes the role demands of two or more members of the role set are incompatible.[2] A customer, for example, may demand unusually liberal credit terms or delivery schedules that are unacceptable to the salesperson's superiors. The representative's perception that it is not possible to simultaneously satisfy all members of the role set creates conflicting role forces and psychological conflict within the salesperson.

Perceived role inaccuracy arises when the salesperson's perceptions of the role partners' demands are inaccurate. Does the salesperson's idea about what the role partners desire correspond to their actual expectations? Role inaccuracy differs from role ambiguity in that, with role inaccuracy, the salesperson feels fairly certain what should be done—except that the sales rep is wrong. It differs from role conflict in that the salesperson does not see any inconsistencies in the expectations and demands communicated. Furthermore, it differs from both in that it is unrealized. The representative does not know that the perceptions held are inaccurate.

Stage 3: Salespeople Convert Perceptions into Behaviors	The final step in the role definition process involves the salesperson's conversion of these role perceptions into actual behavior. Both the salesperson's job behavior and psychological well-being can be affected if there are perceptions of role ambiguity or conflict or if these perceptions are inaccurate. There is a good deal of evidence, for example, that both perceived ambiguity and conflict are directly related to high mental anxiety and tension and low job satisfaction.[3] Also, the salesperson's feelings of uncertainty and conflict and the actions taken to resolve them can have a strong impact on ultimate job performance.[4] At a minimum, the salesperson's performance is less likely to be consistent with management's expectations and desires when the representative is uncertain about what those expectations are, or believes that the customers or family hold conflicting expectations, or has inaccurate perceptions of those expectations.

S USCEPTIBILITY OF THE SALESPERSON'S ROLE

Several characteristics of the salesperson's role make it particularly susceptible to role conflict, role ambiguity, and the development of inaccurate role perceptions. (1) It is at the boundary of the firm. (2) The salesperson's performance affects the occupants of a large number of other positions. (3) It is an innovative role.

Boundary Position	Salespeople are likely to experience more role conflict than most other organization members because they occupy positions at the boundaries of their firms. Some members of each salesperson's role set—the customers—are in external organizations. As a result, the salesperson receives demands from organizations that have diverse goals, policies, and problems. Since each role partner wants the salesperson's behavior to be consistent with the partner's own goals, their demands are diverse and often incompatible.

A customer, for example, might request that a product be modified to suit her or his company's specific needs. The representative's company, however, may balk at making the modification because of additional design and production costs.[5] The salesperson gets caught in the middle. To satisfy the demands of one role partner, the rep must ignore or attempt to change the demands of the other.

Another problem that arises from the salesperson's boundary position is that the role partners in one organization often don't appreciate the expectations and demands made by role partners in another. A customer, for example, may not know company policies or the constraints under which the salesperson must operate. Or the sales rep's superiors may formulate company policies without understanding the particular needs of some customers. Even a role partner who is aware of another's demands may not understand the reasoning behind them and consider them arbitrary or illegitimate.

A boundary position also increases the likelihood that the salesperson will experience role ambiguity or form inaccurate perceptions. Contact with many of the salesperson's role partners, though regular, is probably infrequent and often brief. Under such conditions, it is easy for the salesperson to feel uncertain about what the customers really expect in delivery, service, or credit or how they really feel about how well the representative services the account. Furthermore, the salesperson's perceptions with respect to these issues may be inaccurate.

Large Role Set

The salesperson's role set includes many diverse individuals. The representative may sell to hundreds of customers, and each expects his or her own particular needs and requirements to be satisfied. In addition, people within the firm rely on the rep to execute company policies in dealings with customers and for the ultimate success of the firm's revenue-producing efforts. The specific design-performance criteria a product is supposed to satisfy, and the delivery and credit terms the salesperson quotes, can directly influence people in the engineering, production, and credit departments, for example. All these people may hold definite beliefs about how the salesperson should perform the job, and they will all pressure the individual to conform to their expectations.

Salespeople for a Fortune 500 subsidiary that manufactured automotive components, for example, were once caught up in such disagreement. Engineering wanted sales to emphasize the technical consistencies in the product line as a prelude to redesigning the line to make it simpler and more consistent. At the same time, marketing wanted sales to downplay the consistencies to maintain some technical mystique, which marketing believed was needed for product differentiation.[6]

The large number of people from diverse departments and organizations who depend on the salesperson increases the probability that at least some role demands will be incompatible. It also increases the probability that the

Thorny Issues in Sales Management 10 • 1

To Give or Not to Give

Due to increasing reports of unethical behavior on the part of its sales force, top management of a manufacturing firm recently held a meeting to denounce some of the alleged practices. Frank Harris has been a salesman for the company for several years. His recent performance has been less than what both he and the company had hoped. Frank believes his future with the company rests on his performance in the next few months. Frank has the opportunity of landing a large customer account, provided he presents certain expensive gifts to the purchaser. This is one of the practices that was just condemned by the firm. However,

Frank believes this large sale will secure his job, so he provides the gifts, charging them against his expense account disguised as other expenses. Do you

Approve   _____

Somewhat approve   _____

Somewhat disapprove   _____

Disapprove   _____

---

salesperson's perceptions of some demands will be inaccurate and that the rep will be uncertain about others.

Innovative Role The salesperson's role is frequently innovative in that the rep is often called on to produce new solutions to nonroutine problems. This is particularly true when the salesperson is selling highly technical products or engineered systems designed to the customer's specifications, as Ramon Velasquez did at Ingersoll Rand. Even the salesperson who sells standardized products must display some creativity in matching the company's offerings to the customer's particular needs. With potential new accounts, this is an extremely difficult, but critical, task. Thorny Issues 10.1 indicates another way in which salespeople can be caught in the middle between the demands of their customers and the expectations of their employers.

Occupants of innovative roles tend to experience more conflict than other organization members because they must have flexibility to perform their roles well. Such people must have the authority to develop and carry out innovative solutions.[7] This need for flexibility often brings the salesperson into conflict with the standard operating procedures of the firm and the expectations of the organization members who want to maintain the status quo. The production manager, for example, may frown on orders for nonstandard products because of their adverse effects on production costs and schedules, although marketing, and particularly the salespeople, might desire flexible production schedules and the ability to sell custom-designed products.

Occupants of innovative roles also tend to experience more role ambiguity and inaccurate role perceptions than occupants of noninnovative roles because they frequently face unusual situations where they have no standard procedures or past experience to guide them. Consequently, they are often uncertain about how their role partners expect them to proceed. The perceptions they do have are more likely to be inaccurate because of the nonroutine nature of the task. The flexibility that is needed to fulfill an innovative role can consequently have unforeseen, negative consequences.

> A salesman of a major manufacturer of heating, ventilating, and air conditioning equipment was recently embarrassed during a sales demonstration. Since the product was higher priced than the competition, the salesman decided to prove that there would be less labor costs for installation. On the field demonstration day, engineering sent the prototype with a last-minute design change without notifying the salesman. The alteration made the product similar to the competition. Thus, the customer was indifferent during the sales installation demonstration, and more importantly, because of the last-minute engineering change, there was no labor advantage. Besides experiencing a demeaning demonstration, the salesman lost the potential sale.[8]

R OLE CONFLICT AND AMBIGUITY

In discussing the causes and consequences of the various role perceptions, it is useful to separate the concepts of role conflict and role ambiguity, on the one hand, and inaccurate role perceptions, on the other. This section concentrates on role conflict and role ambiguity, and the next section emphasizes role accuracy. More particularly, this section looks at common expectations of industrial salespeople, the consequences of perceived conflict and ambiguity, and the primary organizational factors that affect the amount of conflict and ambiguity salespeople feel. Thorny Issues 10.2 discusses environmental variables that have the potential to affect role conflict and ambiguity.

Common
Expectations and
Key Areas of
Conflict and
Ambiguity

Different sales jobs require different tasks and place different demands on salespeople. The person selling dresses to a woman's fashion store may be most concerned with follow-up service to make sure the reorders for styles, colors, or sizes arrive in time for the current selling season. The rep selling pumps to a refinery may have to be most concerned with making sure the equipment can handle the load, chemicals, and other harsh conditions to which it will be subjected. Thus, it is next to impossible to develop one set of expectations common to all sales jobs. Even firms within the same industry often place different demands on their salespeople. Nevertheless, to develop a feel for some common expectations that are important sources of conflict and

Thorny Issues in Sales Management 10 • 2

Changing the Game: The New Way to Sell

This Thorny Issues title is also the title of a book by Larry Wilson, veteran sales training expert. In Chapter 3, Wilson lists and explains six new rules of selling that appear below.* A related publication, "Sales and Marketing Strategies for the 1990s," prepared for Learning International by Yankee Group Consulting Division, presents similar findings.

The fact that both sources identify the changing nature of selling relates to the subject of this chapter: The Salesperson's Role Perceptions. Wilson's identification of more decision makers leads to an expanded role set for industrial salespeople. Demands for specific, custom-made solutions instead of generic ones will affect how sales reps plan their sales presentations. An increase in random events can lead to only more role ambiguity and conflict.

1. *More decision makers.* Wilson believes buyers will be getting advice for more expensive, risky decisions. In fact, he foresees the typical selling scenario as a single salesperson sitting across from several buyers or other influencers.
2. *Longer sales cycles.* More decision makers means more meetings, more presentations, and, ultimately, more time.
3. *An increase in random events.* More decision makers and longer sales cycles increase the likelihood of unpredictable events and changes. People get fired, departments get reorganized, priorities change.
4. *Demands for specific, custom-made solutions instead of generic ones.* Many companies today have a new commitment to quality. Generic, "mass market" solutions generally can't fit the needs of such companies.
5. *A change in the selling relationship from vendor to partner.* More and more companies today are looking for long-term business partnerships with salespeople that can better serve their commitment to quality. This partnership should be on a philosophical as well as a financial level.
6. *The death of the product solution.* "Salespeople are selling products and customers are buying relationships," says Wilson. Because the products of one company in an industry are becoming more and more similar to those of the competition, much more has to go into selling strategy today.

The Learning International study identifies seven sales challenges for the 1990s. They are:

1. Distinguishing between similar products and services.
2. Putting together groups of products to form a business solution.
3. Handling the more educated buying population.
4. Mastering the art of consultative selling.
5. Managing a team selling approach.
6. Knowing the customer's business.
7. Adding value through service.

All of these challenges have the potential to affect the role perceptions of salespeople. For example, salespeople who interact with more educated customers will have to change their sales presentations accordingly. Managing a team selling approach will add to the sales rep's role set. Finally, adding value through service will increase the activities salespeople are expected to perform. Role conflict and ambiguity are susceptible.

ambiguity, we will review one extensive study aimed at measuring the demands placed on salespeople.

The study was conducted among 265 salespeople from 10 companies in seven different industries.[9] All the firms manufactured relatively technical equipment and materials, ranging from computers and machine tools to cleaning supplies. Each participating salesperson completed a questionnaire that listed the various activities in which she might be expected to engage by each role partner. The activities were organized into four groups, reflecting each primary role partner: (1) sales manager, (2) the company (other organizational superiors), (3) customers, and (4) family. The salesperson was asked to indicate whether he thought the role partner expected the salesperson to engage in each activity by checking one of five points on a scale from "strongly agree" to "strongly disagree."

Perceived role conflict was measured by the difference in the salesperson's response between each pair of role partners on each common activity item. For example, the salesperson might "agree strongly" (score 5) that the customers expected her to expedite orders but "disagree strongly" (score 1) that the sales manager held the same expectations. Then the perceived role conflict score for that activity would be $5 - 1$. Similarly, if the salesperson agreed (score 4) with a statement that customers expected the company to tailor delivery schedules to fit their needs but disagreed (score 2) that her company superiors felt the same, the perceived role conflict score for that item would be 2 ($4 - 2$). All possible conflicts between all possible pairs of role partners were examined in this way, and total role conflict was the sum of the absolute differences between the various role partner expectations.

Each salesperson's role ambiguity was measured with another scale that included 41 items regarding the requirements of the salesperson's job. The representative was asked to indicate his level of confidence or ambiguity concerning the expectations and evaluations of the various role partners on a six-point scale from "absolutely certain" (score 1) to "absolutely uncertain" (score 6). Thus, if the salesperson was slightly uncertain (score 4) about the rules and procedures customers expected him to follow in dealing with them and quite uncertain (score 5) about how satisfied customers were with his job performance, the salesperson would have a role ambiguity score of 9 for those two items. The total role ambiguity score was generated by summing the responses to all 41 items.

Role expectations

Exhibit 10.3 presents salespeople's perceptions of what each group of role partners expects of them on the job. It shows the proportion of salespeople in the sample who "agree" or "agree strongly" that the role partner expects them to engage in each activity. Because of the large number of activities examined, Exhibit 10.3 displays only those that a relatively large proportion of salespeople

E X H I B I T   10 • 3   *Salespeople's Perceptions of Role Partners' Expectations*

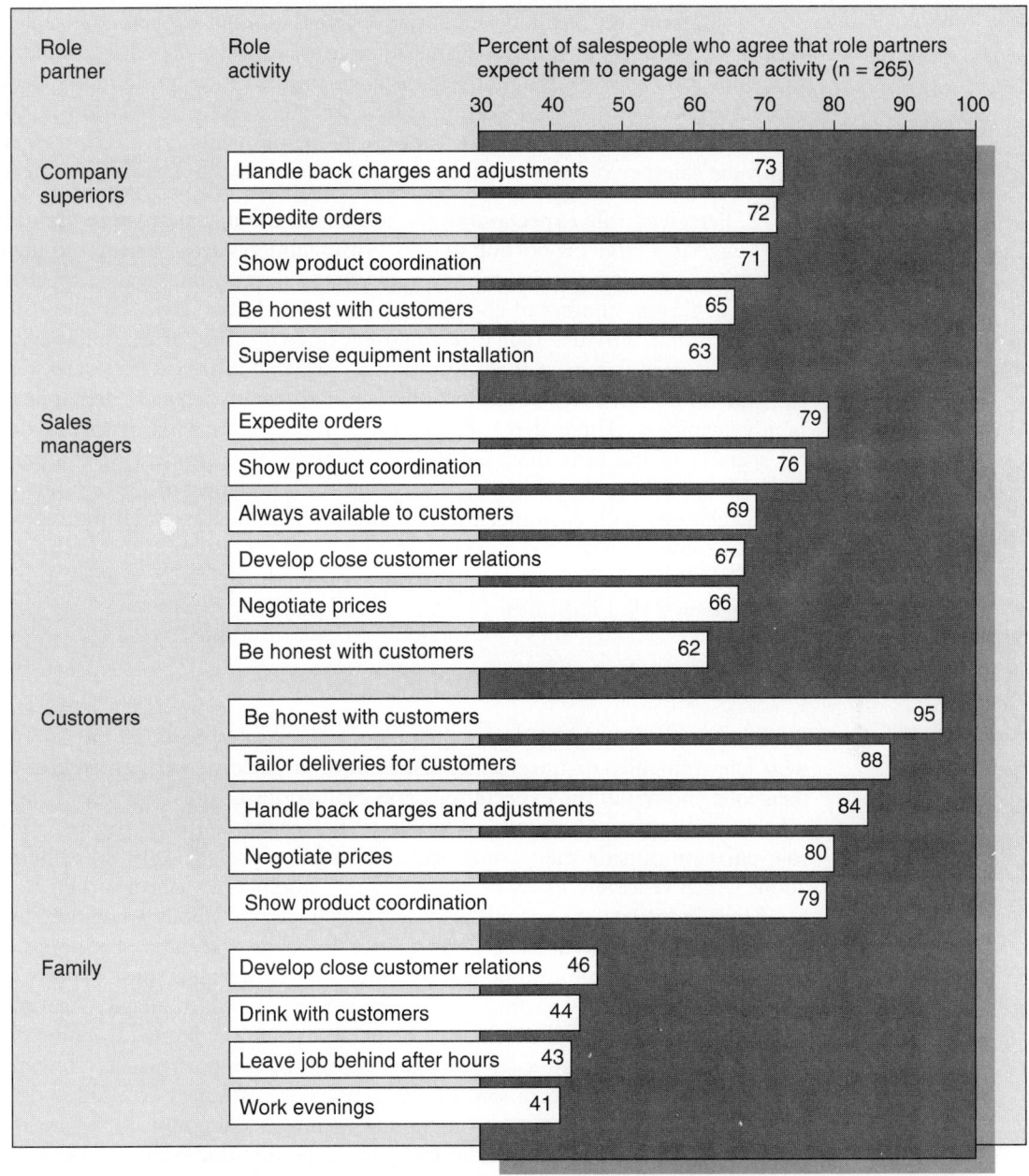

Role partner	Role activity	Percent of salespeople who agree that role partners expect them to engage in each activity (n = 265)
Company superiors	Handle back charges and adjustments	73
	Expedite orders	72
	Show product coordination	71
	Be honest with customers	65
	Supervise equipment installation	63
Sales managers	Expedite orders	79
	Show product coordination	76
	Always available to customers	69
	Develop close customer relations	67
	Negotiate prices	66
	Be honest with customers	62
Customers	Be honest with customers	95
	Tailor deliveries for customers	88
	Handle back charges and adjustments	84
	Negotiate prices	80
	Show product coordination	79
Family	Develop close customer relations	46
	Drink with customers	44
	Leave job behind after hours	43
	Work evenings	41

feel they were expected to perform. The figure prompts the following two major conclusions.

1. Different role partners emphasize different types of expectations. Salespeople see some role partners as being concerned with what they do—company superiors focus on the functional aspects of the job such as handling back charges and adjustments, expediting orders, and supervising installations. Others are more concerned with how they do it—family members are concerned about the salesperson's hours of work and personal relations with customers.

2. Perceived role expectations are consistent among salespeople. Exhibit 10.3 suggests a large proportion of sales representatives are consistent in their perceptions of what their company superiors and sales managers expect of them. The largest number of common perceptions relate to style, but there are also functional activities that three quarters or two thirds of the salespeople say their superiors expect them to perform. The major area where sales representatives do not perceive similar role expectations involves the demands of family members. These demands are much more likely to differ from one salesperson to the next than are the expectations of customers or company superiors. This suggests that no matter what the company expects in hours of work, relations with customers, travel, and the like, a substantial number of its salespeople are likely to be in conflict with the expectations of their families. That is becoming an increasingly serious problem for today's workers, as Thorny Issues 10.3 indicates.

Role ambiguity

Exhibit 10.4 on page 402 shows the proportion of salespeople in the sample who felt ambiguity or uncertainty about how to perform various aspects of their jobs and about the expectations and evaluations of the members of their role set within their companies. Exhibit 10.5 on page 403 does the same for role partners outside their companies. The figures present only those items about which relatively many or unusually few salespeople feel uncertain.

Most industrial salespeople do not seem uncertain about what they are expected to do or how their performance is being evaluated. However, a substantial proportion are plagued by ambiguity concerning some aspects of their job and some role partners. Sales reps say they are particularly uncertain about company policies, how their performance is being evaluated by company superiors, and what their sales managers expect. In comparison, very few are uncertain about the expectations or evaluations of customers or family members. This suggests customers and family members communicate their role expectations more effectively than company superiors do. Perhaps this is not surprising since a representative faces customers and family members almost daily, whereas company policies are communicated through infrequent sales meetings, written memos, and other less effective means.

Thorny Issues in Sales Management 10 • 3

Measuring the Impact When Job, Family Collide

Work-family conflicts take a greater toll on the family than on an employee's job performance, research shows.

Employers are increasingly worried about productivity problems among workers with conflicting job and family responsibilities. But recent research by the Families and Work Institute, a nonprofit research and planning group, shows the family also bears a heavy burden.

The institute found that more than 25 percent of 1,000 headquarters employees of a Fortune 1,000 corporation said they refused overtime because of their families. More than 10 percent said they refused promotions; 24 percent, travel; and 10 percent, relocations.

Though these are serious problems for employers, families are paying an even higher price, says Ellen Galinsky, co-president of the institute. More than 60 percent of those surveyed said their jobs robbed them of adequate energy and time to do things with their families. More than 80 percent said they were only sometimes, rarely, or never able to completely fulfill their personal responsibilities.

The findings, which echo those of similar studies by the institute, have major implications, Ms. Galinsky says. Other studies show that "when parents have demanding and hectic jobs and report [the effects] spilling over on the family, you can see the repercussions" in the quality of family life and the way children develop cognitively and socially.

Source: Sue Shellenbarger, "Measuring the Impact When Job, Family Collide," *The Wall Street Journal*, July 22, 1991, p. B1.

Role conflict

Exhibit 10.6 on page 404 shows the proportion of salespeople who believe the expectations of their role partners are in conflict. Again, the figure includes only those activities where either very many or unusually few salespeople experienced conflict.

A comparison of Exhibit 10.6 with Exhibits 10.4 and 10.5 suggests that many more industrial salespeople experience role conflict than role ambiguity. Compared with other conflicts, intraorganizational conflict—where the role demands of the sales managers are incompatible with those of other organizational superiors—is experienced by few salespeople. Still, as many as one quarter of all representatives perceive conflicts between the demands of their sales managers and other company executives.

Most salespeople perceive conflicts between some company policies or expectations and their customers' demands. Customers are usually seen as demanding more functions performed by the salesperson, more services, more honesty, more liberal use of the expense account, and so forth. Sales managers and other company executives are seen as demanding that the salesperson hold down selling expenses and customer concessions.

EXHIBIT 10 • 4   *Salespeople's Feelings of Role Ambiguity about Internal Demands Placed on Them*

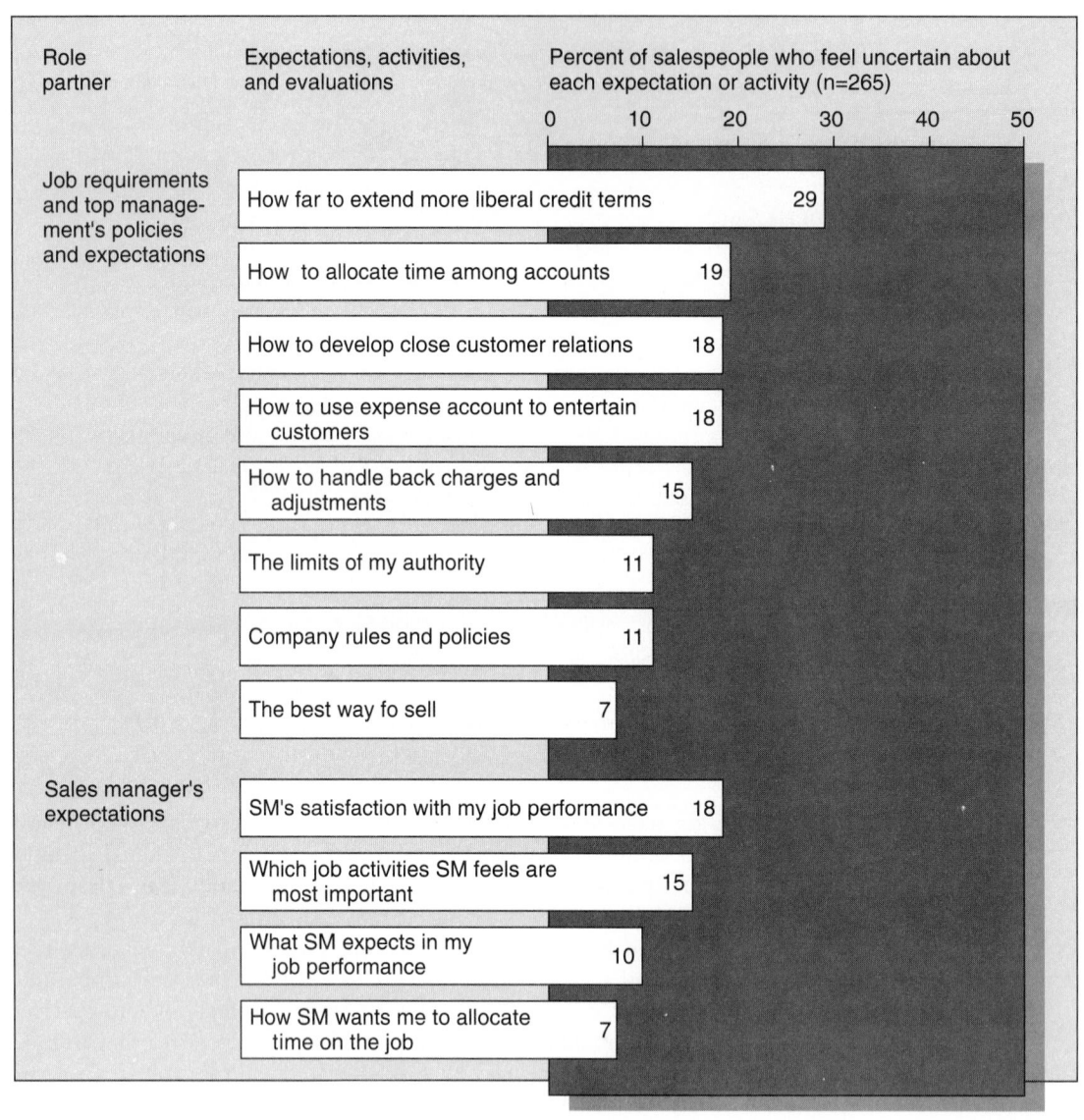

Role partner	Expectations, activities, and evaluations	Percent of salespeople who feel uncertain about each expectation or activity (n=265)
Job requirements and top management's policies and expectations	How far to extend more liberal credit terms	29
	How to allocate time among accounts	19
	How to develop close customer relations	18
	How to use expense account to entertain customers	18
	How to handle back charges and adjustments	15
	The limits of my authority	11
	Company rules and policies	11
	The best way fo sell	7
Sales manager's expectations	SM's satisfaction with my job performance	18
	Which job activities SM feels are most important	15
	What SM expects in my job performance	10
	How SM wants me to allocate time on the job	7

Most salespeople agree that their company superiors and customers expect them to travel, work flexible hours, and be available to customers in the evenings and on weekends. Unfortunately, more than half the representatives in the sample believe these expectations conflict with the desires of their families. Although job-family conflicts are not unique to salespeople, their per-

EXHIBIT 10 • 5   *Salespeople's Feelings of Role Ambiguity with Respect to External Demands Placed on Them*

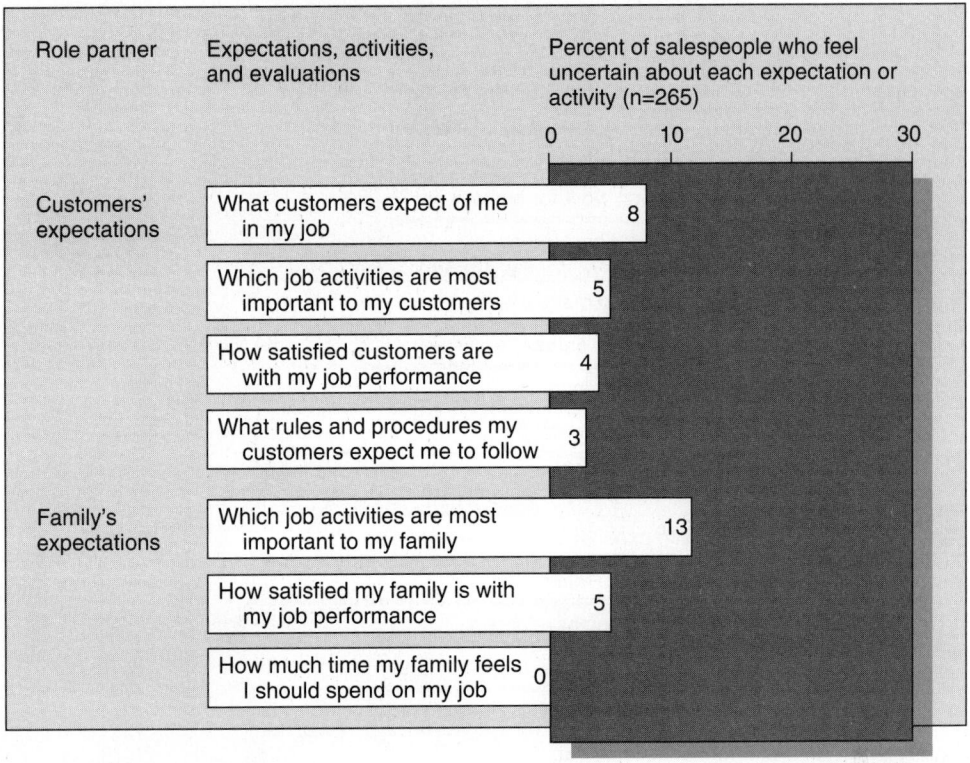

Role partner	Expectations, activities, and evaluations	Percent of salespeople who feel uncertain about each expectation or activity (n=265)
		0 10 20 30
Customers' expectations	What customers expect of me in my job	8
	Which job activities are most important to my customers	5
	How satisfied customers are with my job performance	4
	What rules and procedures my customers expect me to follow	3
Family's expectations	Which job activities are most important to my family	13
	How satisfied my family is with my job performance	5
	How much time my family feels I should spend on my job	0

vasiveness in the sales force should be recognized as a major influence on job satisfaction and performance.

Consequences of Conflict and Ambiguity

Most people experience some occasional role conflict and ambiguity. In small doses, role conflict and ambiguity may be good for the individual and the organization. When there are no disagreements and no uncertainty associated with a role, people can become so comfortable in the position that they constantly strive to preserve the status quo. Some role stress, therefore, can lead to useful adaptation and change. In sum, there is a level of hostility below which conflict and ambiguity may be benign but above which they will be malign. Excessive role stress can have dysfunctional consequences, both psychological and behavioral, for the individual and the organization, as Exhibit 10.7 indicates. Consider first the psychological consequences.

EXHIBIT 10 ● 6 *Salespeople's Perceptions of Role Conflict*

Pair of role partners	Role expectations	Percent of salespeople who perceive some conflict between the two role partners on each expectation

0   20   40   60   80   100

Company management versus sales manager

"Stretch the truth" to make a sale	29
Be honest with customers	29
Be a technical "trouble-shooter"	29
Do product design work for customers	29
Tailor deliveries for customers	24

Company management versus customers

"Stretch the truth" to make a sale	57
Hold normal delivery dates	54
Be honest with customers	54
Use the "hard sell" approach	46
Negotiate prices	42

Sales manager versus customers

Be liberal with expense account entertaining	57
"Stretch the truth" to make a sale	56
Develop close customer relations	54
Be honest with customers	54
Call on customers unlikely to place an order	53
Hold normal delivery dates	51

Sales manager versus family

Always available to customers	60
Leave job behind after hours	56
Work on weekends	52
Include spouse when entertaining customers	49
Develop close customer relations	45

Customers versus family

Always available to customers	60
Work on weekends	53
Work evenings	53
Spend little or no time socializing with customers	44

E X H I B I T 10 • 7   *Causes and Consequences of a Salesperson's Role Perceptions*

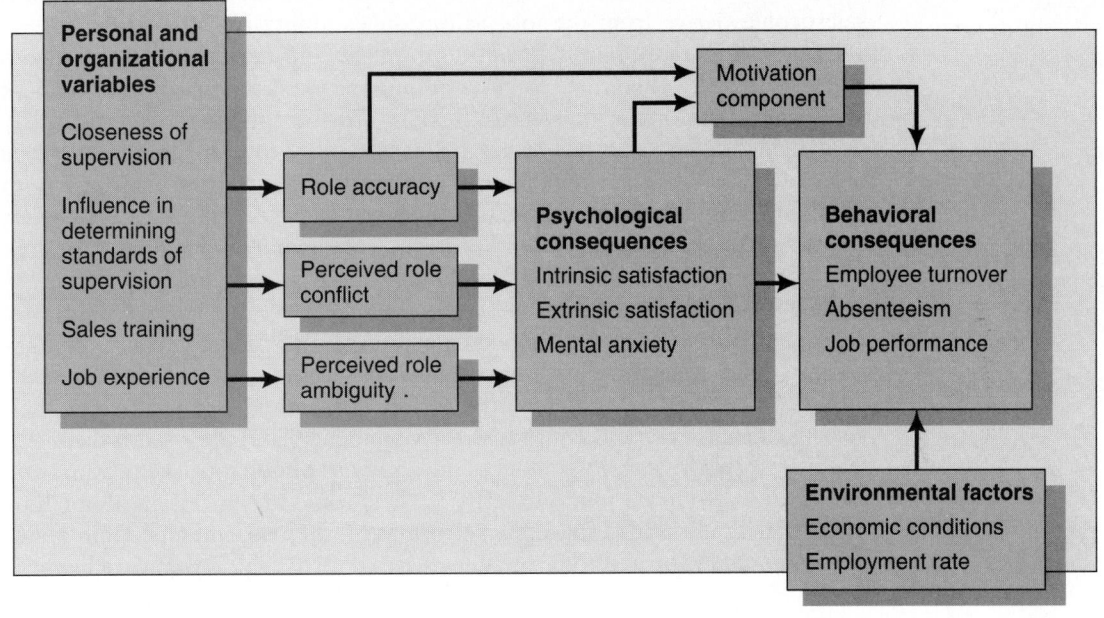

Psychological consequences

When a salesperson perceives that role partners have conflicting expectations about how the job should be performed, the salesperson becomes the "person in the middle." How can the rep satisfy the demands of one role partner without incurring the wrath or disappointment of others? This situation can produce psychological conflict, which is uncomfortable for the individual and can produce various kinds of emotional turmoil. Job tensions increase, and the salesperson tends to worry more about conditions and events at work than usual. The salesperson's overall feelings of anxiety increase, and the rep is likely to become less satisfied with role partners, the company, and the job.[10]

Perceived role ambiguity can have similar negative consequences. When salespeople feel they lack the information necessary to perform the job adequately, when they don't know what role partners expect of them or are uncertain about their ability to perform, they likely lose confidence in the ability to perform the sales role successfully. Salespeople tend to worry more about whether they are doing the right thing and about how role partners will react to their performance. Representatives may also lose confidence in role partners and blame them for failing to communicate their expectations and evaluations adequately. Like conflict, then, perceived role ambiguity is likely to increase a salesperson's mental anxiety and decrease job satisfaction.[11]

Although both conflict and ambiguity affect job satisfaction negatively, they affect it somewhat differently.[12] Perceived role conflict primarily affects extrinsic job satisfaction, but has little or no effect on the intrinsic satisfactions salespeople derive from the job. Salespeople's ability to obtain extrinsic rewards, such as more pay, a promotion, praise, and recognition is influenced by role partners. Therefore, conflicts among the expectations and demands of those role partners not only make it more difficult for salespeople to satisfy their demands but also jeopardize the reps' ability to earn desired extrinsic rewards.[13] On the other hand, such conflicts may not restrain their ability to obtain intrinsic satisfactions from the job. Even when two or more role partners cannot agree on how reps should perform, salespeople may still gain a sense of accomplishment from working or improving personal abilities.

Unlike perceived conflict, ambiguity has a negative impact on the intrinsic components of salespeople's job satisfaction as well as the extrinsic components.[14] When salespeople are uncertain about how they should be doing the job, whether they are doing it right, and how others are evaluating their performance, they are likely to lose self-confidence, and their self-esteem suffers.[15] Ambiguity, therefore, reduces the ability to obtain intrinsic rewards and satisfactions from the job. Similarly, if salespeople are uncertain about how role partners are evaluating their performance, they become uncertain about their chances for promotion or pay increases. Finally, salespeople are likely to be dissatisfied with role partners who fail to make clear their expectations and evaluations, thus causing emotional discomfort in the sales force.

Behavioral consequences

Perceived role conflict and ambiguity can produce dysfunctional behavioral consequences among the sales force. It is naive to think that a happy worker is invariably a productive worker; but evidence collected from a variety of occupations suggests that a worker's satisfaction influences job behavior. For instance, a negative relationship consistently appears between job satisfaction and absenteeism and employee turnover. Low satisfaction is also related to turnover among salespeople, although the relationship is moderated by economic conditions and the availability of alternative jobs.[16]

Another relationship that appears in studies of other occupations is a positive correlation between satisfaction and performance, although there is controversy over the nature of the relationship. Some theorists argue that high satisfaction leads to good performance; others argue that good performance makes workers more satisfied with their jobs. The available sales management literature seems to suggest a salesperson's job satisfaction is directly related to performance on the job[17] and that conflict and ambiguity are negatively related to sales performance.[18] Role ambiguity and role conflict even affect whether sales managers and salespeople agree on how well the salesperson is doing the job.[19]

*Causes of
Conflict and
Ambiguity*

Given that conflict and ambiguity produce dysfunctional psychological and behavioral consequences for salespeople, the next question is: Can sales management do anything to hold conflicts and ambiguities at a manageable level or help the salesperson to deal with them when they occur? Evidence suggests that experienced salespeople perceive less conflict than less experienced representatives.[20] Perhaps this is because salespeople who experience a great deal of conflict become dissatisfied and quit, whereas those who stay on the job do not perceive much conflict.

On the other hand, sales reps may learn with experience how to deal with conflict. They may learn that demands that initially appear to be in conflict may turn out to be compatible. They may learn how to resolve or cope with conflicts so they are no longer so stressful. Finally, they may build up psychological defense mechanisms to screen out conflicts and ease the tension. If these hypotheses are correct, perhaps sales training programs can prepare new salespeople to deal with the conflicts they will encounter on the job. Training, after all, attempts to compress the learning and experience curve into a shorter time period.

Perceived role conflict also seems to be affected by how closely salespeople are supervised. When their sales managers structure and define their roles, salespeople seem to experience more conflict.[21] Perhaps close supervision decreases flexibility in dealing with the diverse role expectations with which salespeople must contend. Another way to reduce role conflict, then, would be to give salespeople a greater voice in what they do and how they do it.

There also seem to be things management can do to reduce role ambiguity. It too depends on experience, and thus sales training should help salespeople cope with it. Perhaps more important, it also depends on the manager's supervisory style. Less ambiguity is experienced when salespeople are closely supervised and have some influence over the standards used to control and evaluate their performance.[22] Closely supervised salespeople are more aware of the expectations and demands of their supervisors, and inconsistent behaviors can be more quickly brought to their attention.

Similarly, salespeople who have an input in determining the standards by which they are evaluated are more familiar with these standards, which tends to reduce role ambiguity. One direct way of affecting the closeness with which salespeople feel supervised is by alternating the sales manager's span of control by changing the number of people the sales manager directly supervises. An increase in the span of control tends to increase salespeople's perceived role ambiguity. Reducing it tends to allow closer supervision, which tends to make job-related issues clearer to salespeople.[23]

Close supervision can thus be a two-edged sword. While it can reduce ambiguity, supervision that is too close can increase a salesperson's role conflict and job dissatisfaction when the rep no longer feels enough latitude to deal effectively with the customer or enough creativity to service the account. The problem is particularly acute when sales managers use coercion and threats to direct the salespeople under them.[24] Sales managers must walk a very fine line in how closely and by what means they supervise the people under them.

ROLE ACCURACY

The role component of the model contains three variables: role conflict, role ambiguity, and role accuracy. It is convenient to highlight role accuracy for separate discussion for two reasons. First, role accuracy can be viewed both generally and from the standpoint of specific linkages. When it is viewed generally, its impact and antecedents are similar to those for role conflict and ambiguity. But additional insight is gained by looking at role accuracy with respect to specific linkages. Second, role accuracy specifically influences the motivation component of the model and to understand role accuracy, it is necessary to assess its impact on the salesperson's motivation to perform.[25]

Nature of Role Accuracy

A salesperson has accurate role perceptions when he correctly understands what role partners expect when performing the job. Role inaccuracy can be either *general* or *linkage*-specific. *General* role inaccuracy involves such considerations as whether salespeople correctly think they can negotiate on price, promise shorter delivery times than normal, and handle back charges and adjustments for customers. General role inaccuracy can occur on almost any job dimension that also gives rise to role ambiguity and conflict. Its antecedents and consequences are also similar.

Linkage role inaccuracy arises when the salesperson incorrectly perceives the relationships between the activities and performance dimensions, or between the performance dimensions and the rewards. In terms of the model in Exhibit 10.1, linkage role inaccuracy relates to the motivational component and more particularly to the expectancy and instrumentality estimates. For example, a salesperson who does not accurately perceive how making more calls leads to more sales has linkage role inaccuracy with respect to this expectancy, or activity-performance, linkage. If the rep does not accurately perceive the relationship between more sales and a promotion, the person has linkage role inaccuracy with respect to this instrumentality, or performance-reward, linkage.

There is great potential for linkage role inaccuracy among salespeople because all three components—activities, performance dimensions, and rewards—are multidimensional. There are consequently a great many linkages, which increases the chances a salesperson will have inaccurate perceptions about at least some of them. Some common activities salespeople are expected to engage in, the criteria used to evaluate their performance, and the rewards typically used to motivate them are listed in Exhibit 10.8.[26] Not all salespeople in every firm are expected to engage in all these activities, nor are they evaluated on each performance dimension. Neither do all firms provide the same rewards

Activities*

1. Selling: plan selling activities, search out leads, identify person in authority, select products for calls, prepare sales presentations, call on accounts, make sales presentations, overcome objections.

2. Working with orders: correct orders, expedite orders, handle back orders, handle shipment problems.

3. Servicing the product: supervise installation, test equipment, train customers to use product, teach safety instructions, order accessories, perform maintenance.

4. Information management: receive feedback from clients, provide feedback to superiors, provide technical information, read trade publications.

5. Servicing the account: set up point-of-purchase displays, assist with inventory control, stock shelves, handle local advertising.

6. Conferences/meetings: attend sales conferences, attend regional sales meetings, set up exhibitions and trade shows; work client conferences, attend training sessions, fill out questionnaires.

7. Training/recruiting: look for new sales representatives, train new representatives, travel with trainees, help company management plan selling activities.

8. Entertaining: take clients to lunch, drink with clients, have dinner with clients, party with clients, go golfing, fishing, or play tennis with clients.

9. Out of town traveling: travel out of town, spend night on road.

10. Working with distributors: establish relations with distributors, sell to distributors, extend credit, collect past-due accounts.

Performance Criteria

1. Total sales volume and increase over last year.

2. Degree of quota attainment.

3. Selling expenses and decrease versus last year.

4. Profitability of sales and increase over last year.

5. New accounts generated.

6. Improvement in performance of administrative duties.

7. Improvement in service provided customers.

Rewards

1. Pay
   a. Increased take-home pay.
   b. Increased bonuses and other financial incentives.

2. Promotion
   a. Higher-level job.
   b. Better territory.

3. Nonfinancial incentives (contests, travel, prices, etc.).

4. Special recognitions (clubs, awards, etc.).

5. Job security.

6. Feeling of self-fulfillment.

7. Feeling of worthwhile accomplishment.

8. Opportunity for personal growth and development.

9. Opportunity for independent thought and action.

*The list of activities in which salespeople commonly engage is developed from the articles by William C. Moncrief, "Selling Activity and Sales Position Taxonomies for Industrial Salesforces," *Journal of Marketing Research* 23 (August 1986), pp. 261–70, and William C. Moncrief, "Ten Key Activities of Industrial Salespeople," *Industrial Marketing Management* 15 (November 1986), pp. 309–17.

to the same degree. This makes it very difficult to discuss linkage inaccuracy in a way that is useful to sales managers in general. One has to get down to the level of the individual firm and the linkages operating there to discuss the concept.

One common salesperson activity is an emphasis on new-account calls. Similarly, the number of new accounts generated is often used to evaluate how salespeople performed. Despite this, it is not unusual to find that salespeople do not spend enough time calling on new accounts, even when they recognize there are many such opportunities in their territories and know their sales managers want them to spend more time on such accounts. One study that investigated the question using reasonably large samples of salespeople and sales managers (over 400 of each) found (1) salespeople fail to see the payoff to themselves in new-account development, and (2) they did not know what it takes to perform these activities successfully.[27] Further:

> the difference in priorities between sales representatives and sales managers appears to start very early in the sales planning process. At the very basic step of classifying accounts, 80 percent of sales managers state that this should be done on the basis of potential volumes, whereas only 54 percent of sales representatives indicate that they do so. The other 46 percent, if they classify their accounts at all, prefer to utilize other factors such as historic volumes or geography.[28]

Clearly, the sales managers in the study did not effectively communicate the linkages between activities and performance, and performance and rewards to the sales force. Yet the accuracy of a salesperson's expectancy and instrumentality estimates, as well as their magnitude, can influence performance and consequently have important implications for sales managers. The next section reviews some causes and consequences of inaccurate role perceptions and highlights what this implies for sales managers.

Causes, Consequences, and Management Implications of Perceived Linkages

For discussion purposes, we will separate expectancy and instrumentality estimates and consider the accuracy and magnitude of each category. Exhibit 10.9 outlines some questions and management implications surrounding a salesperson's expectancy estimates, and Exhibit 10.10 does the same for instrumentality estimates.[29]

Accuracy of expectancies

As we have seen, it is possible for a salesperson to misjudge the true relationship between the effort expended on a particular task and resulting performance. When this happens, the salesperson misallocates efforts. The rep spends too much time and energy on activities that have relatively little impact on performance and not enough on activities with greater impact.

Most industrial psychology literature concerning work expectancies assumes that a worker's immediate superior, by virtue of greater knowledge and

E X H I B I T   10 ● 9   *Important Questions and Management Implications of*
Salespeople's Expectancy Estimates

Question	Management Implications
Accuracy of Expectancy Estimates	
• Are salespeople's views of the linkage between activities and performance outcomes consistent with those of sales managers?	• If substantial variation exists, salespeople may devote too much effort to activities considered unimportant by management, and vice versa. This might indicate a need for the following: –More extensive/explicit sales training. –Closer supervision –Evaluation of salesperson's effort and time allocation as well as performance.
• Are there large variations in expectancy perceptions between high performers and low performers in the sales force?	• If high-performing salespeople hold reasonably consistent views concerning which activities are most important in producing good performance, those views might be used as a model for sales training/professional development programs.
Magnitude of Expectancy Estimates	
• All other things equal, the higher the salesperson's expectancy estimates, the greater the individual's motivation to expend effort. –Do personal characteristics of salespeople influence the size of their expectancies? 　Overall self-esteem? 　Perceived competence? 　Mental ability? (Intelligence?) 　Previous sales experience? –Do perceptions of uncertainty or constraints in the environment (e.g., materials shortages, recession, etc.) reduce salespeople's expectancy estimates?	• If such relationships are found, they may suggest additional criteria for recruitment/selection. • During periods of economic uncertainty, management may have to change performance criteria, evaluation methods, and/or compensation systems to maintain desired levels of effort from the sales force (e.g., lower quotas, reward servicing rather than selling activities, etc.).

experience, will more accurately perceive the linkages between effort and performance in the worker's job than the worker will. If this is also true in the selling profession, then inaccurate expectancy perceptions in the sales force can be improved through closer contact between salespeople and their super-

EXHIBIT 10 • 10   *Important Questions and Management Implications of*
Salespeople's Instrumentality Estimates

Questions	Management Implications
Accuracy of Instrumentality Estimates	
• Are salespeople's views of the linkage between performance on various dimensions and the rewards they will receive consistent with those of sales managers?	• If substantial variation exists, salespeople may concentrate on aspects of performance considered relatively unimportant by management, and vice versa. This might indicate the need for the following: –More extensive/explicit sales training. –Closer supervision. –More direct feedback to salespeople concerning how performance is evaluated and how rewards are determined.
Magnitude of Instrumentality Estimates	
• How are salespeople's instrumentality estimates influenced by their compensation system (salary versus commission)? –Do salespeople on commission have higher instrumentality estimates for performance dimensions related to short-term sales volume? –Do salaried salespeople have higher instrumentalities for performance dimensions not directly related to short-term sales volume?	• If such relationships are found, managers should select the type of compensation plan that maximizes instrumentality estimates for those peformance dimensions considered most crucial.
• Do personal charcteristics of salespeople influence the size of their instrumentality estimates? –Feelings of internal control? –Mental ability? –Sales experience?	• If such relationships are found, they may suggest additional criteria for recruitment/selection.

visors. Expanded sales training programs, closer day-to-day supervision of the sales force, and periodic review of each salesperson's time and effort allocation by the supervisor might improve the accuracy of expectancy estimates.

Salespeople often complain that their supervisors have an unrealistic view of conditions in the field and do not realize what it takes to make a sale.[30] If these complaints are valid, managers' perceptions of the linkages between effort and performance may not be appropriate criteria for judging the accuracy of salespeople's expectancies. It may be better to use the expectancy estimates of the highest performing salesperson in the company as a model for sales training and supervision.

Magnitude of expectancies

The magnitude of a salesperson's expectancy estimates reflects the rep's perceptions of his or her ability to control or influence his or her own job performance.

Several individual characteristics are likely to affect these expectancies. Some psychologists suggest that a worker's overall level of self-esteem and perceived ability to perform necessary tasks are positively related to the magnitude of the person's expectancy estimates.[31] Similarly, the salesperson's general intelligence and previous sales experience may influence the individual's perceived ability to improve performance through personal efforts. If these relationships are also true for salespeople, the characteristics may be useful supplementary criteria for the recruitment and selection of salespeople.

Environmental characteristics also influence a salesperson's perceptions of the linkages between effort and performance. How the rep perceives general economic conditions, territory potential, the strength of competition, restrictions on product availability, and so forth are all likely to affect his thoughts on how much sales performance can be improved by simply increasing efforts. The greater the environmental constraints a salesperson sees as restricting performance, the lower the rep's expectancy estimates will be. Therefore, managers may find it desirable to change performance criteria and/or evaluation methods during periods of economic uncertainty to maintain desired levels of effort from the sales force.

Accuracy of instrumentalities

The true linkages between performance on various dimensions and the attainment of rewards are determined by management practices and policies on sales performance evaluation and rewards for levels of performance. These policies and practices may be misperceived by the salesperson. The rep may concentrate on improving performance in areas that are less important to management and ultimately become disillusioned with her ability to attain rewards.

Thus, it is important to compare salespeople's instrumentality perceptions with stated company policies and management perceptions of the true or desired linkages between performance and rewards. If salespeople misperceive how performance is rewarded in the firm, management must improve the accuracy of those perceptions. This can be done through closer supervision and more direct feedback about evaluation and the determination of rewards.

Magnitude of instrumentalities

One variable that has a notable impact on the magnitude of a salesperson's instrumentality estimates is the firm's compensation plan. A salesperson compensated largely or entirely by commission is likely to perceive a greater probability of attaining more pay by improving performance on the dimensions directly related to total sales volume (increase in total sales dollars or percentage of quota). On the other hand, the salaried salesperson is more likely to perceive a greater probability of receiving increased pay for improving performance on dimensions not directly related to short-term sales volume (new-account generation, reduction of selling expenses, or performance of administrative duties).

The salesperson may also be rewarded with promotion, recognition, and feelings of accomplishment. The rep may value these other rewards more highly than an increase in pay. In any case, the company's compensation plan is unlikely to affect the rep's perceptions of the linkages between performance and these nonfinancial rewards. Therefore, a compensation plan by itself is inadequate for explaining differences in motivation among salespeople.

The salesperson's personal characteristics may also influence the magnitude of instrumentality estimates. One such characteristic is the individual's perception of whether the rep controls life's events or whether these events are determined by external forces beyond the individual's control. Specifically, the greater the degree to which a salesperson believes he has internal control over life, the more likely the rep is to feel that an improvement in performance will result in the attainment of rewards. Similarly, some evidence in industrial psychology suggests a worker's intelligence is positively related to the individual's instrumentality estimates. Once again, if such relationships hold true for industrial salespeople, these personal characteristics may be useful criteria for the recruitment and selection of salespeople.

THE ROLE COMPONENT AND THE SALES MANAGER

As this chapter suggests, the role component of the model has important implications for sales managers. Feelings of ambiguity, conflict, and inaccurate role perceptions can cause psychological stress and job-related anxiety for salespeople. These, in turn, can lead to lowered performance. All are dysfunctional consequences as far as sales managers are concerned. Thus, sales managers have a vested interest in keeping salespeople's role perceptions within tolerable limits.

Fortunately, there are things the sales manager can do to accomplish that goal. The kind of salespeople that are hired, the way they are trained, the incentives used to motivate them, the criteria used to evaluate them, and the way they are supervised can all affect perceptions of role. These factors can also determine whether these perceptions are ambiguous, in conflict, or inaccurate. That is why the role component of the salesperson performance model was discussed first. Its early discussion allows a fuller appreciation of the significance of the sales manager's primary duties, which were outlined in Chapter 1 and discussed more fully in subsequent chapters.

S UMMARY

This chapter elaborated on the role perceptions variable in the model of a salesperson's performance. A person's role represents the set of activities and behaviors that are to be performed by anyone who occupies that position. The role of salesperson is defined through a three-step process: (1) Expectations and demands concerning how the salesperson should behave in various situations, together with pressures to conform, are communicated to the salesperson by members of the individual's role set. (2) The salesperson perceives these expectations and demands that are communicated by members of the role set. (3) The salesperson converts these perceptions into actual behavior.

Perceived role ambiguity arises when the salesperson is uncertain about the expectations and demands being communicated. Perceived role conflict exists when a representative believes the role demands of two or more members of the role set are incompatible. Perceived role inaccuracy arises when the salesperson's perceptions of the role partner's demands are inaccurate.

The role of salesperson is particularly susceptible to feelings of ambiguity and conflict and to forming inaccurate perceptions. There are three reasons for this: (1) It is at the boundary of the firm, (2) the salesperson's relevant role set includes many other people both within and outside the firm, and (3) the position of sales rep often requires a good deal of innovativeness.

Important managerial consequences are associated with salespeople experiencing feelings of ambiguity or conflict or having inaccurate perceptions. Such feelings can cause psychological stress, produce low satisfaction, and lead to poorer performance. Fortunately, the sales manager can affect these consequences through decisions on the type of salespeople that are hired, the way they are trained, the incentives used to motivate them, the criteria used to evaluate them, and the way they are supervised and controlled.

Discussion Questions

1. Maria Gomez-Simpson, a customer service rep with MAR-JON Associates, spends considerable time traveling to various customer offices. As a result, she often arrives home late. Maria asked her manager if she could rearrange her Thursday work schedule to allow her to attend an evening class at a local college.

   Which of the following statements best reflects how to manage the conflict created by Maria's request?

   a. "Since we're talking about only one night, go ahead, sign up for the course, and we'll work out the details."

   b. "We need to discuss this first to see if there is some way you can be back most of the Thursdays in time for your course and still get the job done as well."

   c. "We know that you get home late on certain days, but it is part of the job. Maybe you can take the course some other time."

2. "I want sales representatives who can stand on their own. Once a representative has been through training and shows how to apply this knowledge, it shouldn't

be necessary for me to constantly tell them how they are doing. The stars always shine; it's the other sales representatives that need my attention." Comment on this statement. Do you agree or disagree?

3. Salespeople are likely to experience more role conflict than most other organizations' members because they occupy positions at the boundaries of the firm. Is this true? Explain.

4. "In small doses, role conflict and ambiguity may be good for the individual—and therefore the organization—since stress is often associated with adaptation and change." Do you agree? Explain why or why not.

5. Some sales managers tell married applicants that they would like to interview their spouses before making the hiring decision. Why would a sales manager make such a request? Do you approve?

6. A sales representative for the Railroad Equipment Corporation is faced with a demand from an important customer that is in direct conflict with company policies. The customer wants several product modifications with no change in price. What can the sales rep do to handle this conflict?

7. Most sales representatives are expected to complete a variety of reports—some daily, some weekly, and some annually. However, research indicates most sales reps perceive that very few rewards result from having timely and carefully prepared written reports. Why is this so? What are the implications of this result?

8. Sales reps for the Ansul Company, a manufacturer of fire prevention systems for industrial applications, has been told they will now have to sell small fire extinguishers to the retail market. What role problems are likely to occur?

9. "I don't understand," lamented the national sales manager for the Kardill Corporation. "This sales contest cost us a bundle. Just look at these results for Jim Sugar's territory: no new accounts opened and that's what the contest was all about. Even worse is the fact that his call reports do not indicate that he made any plans or attempts to call on new accounts." Comment. What role do expectancies, instrumentalities, and valences for rewards play in this situation?

10. The chapter suggests role ambiguity can be reduced through closer supervision and training. Role conflict is a different matter. Is there anything a sales manager can do to reduce role conflict? Would it help to ask customers (often a major source of conflict) not to ask for conditions that conflict with company policy? What role, if any, does sales training play in handling role conflict?

Endnotes

[1] The definition of the salesperson's role is a continuous process. The definition process begins when the individual is first socialized into the organization and continues through the person's employment with the company. See Alan J. Dubinsky et al., "Salesforce Socialization," *Journal of Marketing* 50 (October 1986), pp. 192–207, for discussion of the socialization process.

[2] We are restricting our discussion to intersender conflict. For discussion of the other types of conflict that can affect a salesperson, see Janina C. Latack, "Person/Role Conflict: Holland's Model Extended to Role Stress Research, Stress Management, and Career Development," *Academy of Management Review* 6 (January 1981), pp. 89–104.

[3]Robert L. Kahn et al., *Organizational Stress* (New York: John Wiley & Sons, 1964), pp. 57–71; Alan J. Dubinsky and Francis J. Yammarino, "Differential Impact of Role Conflict and Ambiguity on Selected Correlates: A Two-Sample Test," *Psychological Reports* 55 (December 1984), pp. 699–707. For a review of this literature, see Mary Van Sell, Arthur P. Brief, and Randall S. Schuler, "Role Conflict and Role Ambiguity: Integration of the Literature and Directions for Future Research," *Human Relations* 34 (January 1981), pp. 43–71.

[4]Henry O. Pruden and Richard M. Reese, "Interorganizational Role-Set Relations and the Performance and Satisfaction of Industrial Salesman," *Administrative Science Quarterly* 17 (December 1972), pp. 601–9; Cynthia D. Fisher and Richard Gitelson, "A Meta-Analysis of the Correlates of Role Conflict and Ambiguity," *Journal of Applied Psychology* 68 (May 1983), pp. 320–33; and Rosemary Ramsey Lagace, "Role Stress Differences between Salesmen and Saleswomen: Effect on Job Satisfaction and Performance," *Psychological Reports* 62 (June 1988), pp. 815–25.

[5]Product design is only one of the areas where there is often conflict between marketing and engineering departments with respect to how best to serve customers' needs. See J. Donald Weinrauch and Richard Anderson, "Conflicts between Engineering and Marketing Units," *Industrial Marketing Management* 11 (October 1982), pp. 291–301. Product managers also serve as boundary spanners, which creates role conflict for them. See Steven Lysonski and Arch G. Woodside, "Boundary Role Spanning Behavior, Conflicts and Performance of Industrial Product Managers," *Journal of Product Innovation Management* 6 (September 1989), pp. 169–84.

[6]Weinrauch and Anderson, "Conflicts between Engineering and Marketing Units," pp. 291–301.

[7]Kahn et al., *Organizational Stress,* pp. 125–36.

[8]Weinrauch and Anderson, "Conflicts between Engineering and Marketing Units," p. 292.

[9]Actually, 479 salespeople were mailed questionnaires, but only 265 returned both questionnaires used in the study—a response rate of 55 percent. For details of the study and the data collection instrument that was used, see Neil M. Ford, Orville C. Walker, Jr., and Gilbert A. Churchill, Jr., "Expectation-Specific Measures of the Intersender Conflict and Role Ambiguity Experienced by Industrial Salesmen," *Journal of Business Research* 3 (April 1975), pp. 95–112. For another study that attempted to develop an understanding of the salesperson's role in a building materials sales situation, see Lawrence M. Lamont and William J. Lundstrom, "Defining Industrial Sales Behavior: A Factor Analytic Study," in *1974 Combined Proceedings,* ed. R. C. Curhan (Chicago: American Marketing Association, 1974), pp. 493–98. As described below, role conflict was measured by looking at the differences in the expectations held by the various role partners on the same item. The recent evidence indicates that is a poor way to measure the construct, and a better way would be to ask salespeople directly if they perceive a difference in the expectations between two role partners. See J. Paul Peter, Gilbert A. Churchill, Jr., and Tom J. Brown, "Caution in the Use of Difference Scores in Marketing Research," working paper #91-2, University of Wisconsin-Madison, 1991.

[10]Neil M. Ford, Orville C. Walker, Jr., and Gilbert A. Churchill, Jr., "The Psychological Consequences of Role Conflict and Ambiguity in the Industrial Salesforce," in *Marketing: 1776–1976 and Beyond,* ed. Kenneth L. Bernhardt (Chicago: American Marketing Association, 1976), pp. 403–8; Douglas N. Behrman and William D. Perrault, Jr., "A Role Stress Model of the Performance and Satisfaction of Industrial Salespeople," *Journal of Marketing* 48 (Fall 1984), pp. 9–21; R. Kenneth Teas, "Supervisory Behavior, Role Stress, and the Job Satisfaction of Industrial Salespeople," *Journal of Marketing Research* 20 (February 1983), pp. 84–91.

[11]Kahn et al., "Organizational Stress, pp. 72–95; Ajay K. Kohli, "Some Unexplored Supervisory Behaviors and Their Influence on Salespeople's Role Clarity, Specific Self-Esteem, Job Satisfaction and Motivation," *Journal of Marketing Research* 22 (November 1985), pp. 424–33; Louis W. Fry, Charles M. Futrell, A. Parasuraman, and Margaret Chmielewski, "An Analysis of Alternate Causal Models of Salesperson Role Perceptions and Work Related Attitudes," *Journal of Marketing Research* 23 (May 1986), pp. 153–63. The negative effects of role ambiguity on job satisfaction and job tension also occur among service salespeople and sales managers. See John Hafer and Barbara A. McCuen, "Antecedents of Performance and Satisfaction in a Ser-

vice Sales Force as Compared to an Industrial Sales Force," *Journal of Personal Selling and Sales Management 5* (November 1985), pp. 7–17; and James Comer, "Industrial Sales Managers: Satisfaction and Performance," *Industrial Marketing Management 14* (November 1985), pp. 239–44.

[12]Ford, Walker, and Churchill, "Psychological Consequences."

[13]Pruden and Reese, "Interorganizational Role-Set Relations."

[14]James H. Donnelly, Jr., and John M. Ivancevich, "Role Clarity and the Salesman," *Journal of Marketing 39* (January 1975), pp. 71–74; and Eric N. Berkowitz, "Role Strain and Ambiguity: Performance Implications in a Sales Organization," working paper, Graduate School of Business Administration, University of Minnesota, 1978; R. Kenneth Teas, John G. Wacker, and R. Eugene Hughes, "A Path Analysis of Causes and Consequences of Salespeople's Perceptions of Role Clarity," *Journal of Marketing Research 16* (August 1979), pp. 355–69.

[15]Richard P. Bagozzi, "The Nature and Causes of Self-Esteem, Performance, and Satisfaction in the Sales Force: A Structural Equation Approach," *Journal of Business 53* (1980), pp. 315–31.

[16]Charles M. Futrell and A. Parasuraman, "The Relationship of Satisfaction and Performance to Salesforce Turnover," *Journal of Marketing 48* (Fall 1984), pp. 33–40; George H. Lucas, Jr., et al., "An Empirical Study of Salesforce Turnover," *Journal of Marketing 51* (July 1987), pp. 34–59.

[17]Richard P. Bagozzi, "Salesforce Performance and Satisfaction as a Function of Individual Difference, Interpersonal, and Situational Factors," *Journal of Marketing Research 15* (November 1978), pp. 517–31.

[18]Pruden and Reese, "Interorganizational Role-Set Relations"; Donnelly and Ivancevich, "Role Clarity"; Berkowitz, "Role Strain"; Bagozzi, "The Nature and Causes"; and Douglas N. Behrman, William J. Bigoness, and William D. Perreault, Jr., "Sources of Job-Related Ambiguity and Their Consequences upon Salesperson Job Satisfaction and Performance," *Management Science 27* (November 1981), pp. 1246–60.

[19]Lawrence B. Chonko, Roy D. Howell, and Danny N. Bellenger, "Consequence in Sales Force Evaluation: Relation to Sales Force Perceptions of Conflict and Ambiguity," *Journal of Personal Selling and Sales Management 6* (May 1986), pp. 35–48.

[20]Orville C. Walker, Jr., Gilbert A. Churchill, Jr., and Neil M. Ford, "Organizational Determinants of the Role Conflict and Ambiguity Experienced by Industrial Salesmen," *Journal of Marketing 39* (January 1975), pp. 32–39.

[21]Teas, "Supervisory Behavior, Role Stress."

[22]Walker, Churchill, Ford, "Organizational Determinants"; Kohli, "Some Unexplored Supervisory Behaviors."

[23]Lawrence B. Chonko, "The Relationship of Span of Control to Sales Representatives, Experienced Role Conflict and Role Ambiguity," *Academy of Management Journal 25* (June 1982), pp. 452–56.

[24]Paul Busch, "The Sales Manager's Bases of Social Power and Influence upon the Sales Force," *Journal of Marketing 44* (Summer 1980), pp. 91–101; and Ronald E. Michaels, William L. Cron, Alan J. Dubinsky, and Erich A. Joachimsthaler, "Influence of Formalization on the Organizational Commitment and Work Alienation of Salespeople and Industrial Buyers," *Journal of Marketing Research 25* (November 1988), pp. 376–83.

[25]Role ambiguity and role conflict can also influence a salesperson's motivation to work. See Pradeep K. Tyagi, "The Effects of Stressful Organizational Conditions on Salesperson Work Motivation," *Journal of the Academy of Marketing Science 13* (Winter/Spring 1985), pp. 290–309.

[26]For studies investigating the frequency with which salespeople engage in various activities and the importance of these activities to their success, see Moncrief, "Selling Activity and Sales Position Taxonomies," pp. 261–70; Moncrief, "Ten Key Activities of Industrial Salespeople," pp. 309–17; Robert E. Hite and Joseph A. Bellizzi, "Differences in the Importance of Selling Technques between Consumer and Industrial Salespeople," *Journal of Personal Selling and Sales Management 5* (November 1985), pp. 19–30.

[27]Terry Deutscher, Judith Marshall, and David Burgoyne, "The Process of Obtaining New Accounts," *Industrial Marketing Management 11* (July 1982), pp. 173–81. See also Douglas M. Lambert, Howard Mar-

morstein, and Arun Sharma, "The Accuracy of Salespersons' Perceptions of Their Customers: Conceptual Examination and an Empirical Study," *Journal of Personal Selling and Sales Management* 10 (Winter 1990), pp. 1–9.

[28]Deutscher et al., "The Process of Obtaining New Accounts," p. 175.

[29]The tables and much of the discussion are taken from Orville C. Walker, Jr., Gilbert A. Churchill, Jr., and Neil M. Ford, "Measuring and Improving Salesmen's Motivation and Performance," in *Marketing Looks Outward: 1976 Proceedings of International Marketing Conference,* ed. William Locander (Chicago: American Marketing Association, 1977), pp. 25–32. See also Pradeep K. Tyagi, "Perceived Organizational Climate and the Process of Salesperson Motivation," *Journal of Marketing Research* 19 (May 1982), pp. 240–54; and Gary A. Schroeder, "Using an Attitude Survey to Increase Sales Effectiveness," *Personnel* 66 (February 1989), pp. 51–55.

[30]The argument is often advanced, for example, that salespeople should be given pricing flexibility in that they are closest to the customers and have the best perspective on the price that will be needed to make

the sales. Interestingly, one study that investigated the admonition found that among a sample of 108 firms those firms that gave salespeople the highest degree of pricing authority generated the lowest sales and profit performance. See P. Ronald Stephenson, William L. Cron, and Gary L. Frazier, "Delegating Pricing Authority in the Sales Force: The Effects on Sales and Profit Performance," *Journal of Marketing* 43 (Spring 1979), pp. 21–28. See also Richard Kern, "Letting Your Salespeople Set Prices (Sort Of)," *Sales & Marketing Management* 141 (August 1989), pp. 44–49.

[31]Abraham K. Korman, "Expectancies as Determinants of Performance," *Journal of Applied Psychology* 55 (1971), pp. 218–22; Edward E. Lawler III, "Job Attitudes and Employee Motivation: Theory, Research and Practice," *Personnel Psychology* 23 (1970), pp. 223–37; T. J. Newton and A. Keenan, "Role Stress Reexamined: An Investigation of Role Stress Prediction," *Organizational Behavior and Human Decision Processes* 40 (December 1987), pp. 346–68; and Roy D. Howell, Danny N. Bellenger, and James B. Wilcox, "Self-Esteem, Role Stress, and Job Satisfaction among Marketing Managers," *Journal of Business Research* 15 (February 1987), pp. 71–84.

Suggested Readings

Ford, Neil M., Orville C. Walker, Jr., and Gilbert A. Churchill, Jr. "Expectation-Specific Measures of the Intersender Conflict and Role Ambiguity Experienced by Industrial Salesmen." *Journal of Business Research* 3 (April 1975), pp. 95–112.

Moncrief, William C. "Selling Activity and Sales Position Taxonomies for Industrial Salesforces." *Journal of Marketing Research* 23 (August 1986), p. 261–76.

Walker, Orville C., Jr., Gilbert A. Churchill, Jr., and Neil M. Ford. "Organizational Determinants of the Role Conflict and Ambiguity Experienced by Industrial Salesmen." *Journal of Marketing* 39 (January 1975), pp. 32–39.

Personal Characteristics and Sales Aptitude: Criteria for Selecting Salespeople

DOW CHEMICAL: BUILDING THE CHEMICAL INDUSTRY'S TOP-RATED SALES FORCE[1]

Every year, *Sales & Marketing Management* magazine surveys top sales executives in a number of industries (such as chemicals, computers and office equipment, and so on) to determine which company in each industry is perceived to have the best sales force. Respondents rate each firm in their industry on a variety of sales management practices and performance dimensions, such as ability to recruit and retain top salespeople and the sales force's performance at winning new customers and retaining existing accounts.

Throughout the 1980s, Dow Chemical was a perennial chemical industry bridesmaid in the survey. The firm's sales force was consistently rated second behind E.I. du Pont de Nemours & Co. But in the 1991 survey, Dow, whose 500 salespeople produced $19.8 billion in sales, finally edged out Du Pont for the highest-rated sales force in its industry.

The Recruiting and Selection Process

Contributing to Dow's improved reputation was its ability to select and recruit top-quality salespeople. "We're number one because we recruit good people," says Robert Baughman, Dow's vice president of human resources. Executives of other chemical firms apparently agree because Dow was rated as the best recruiter in its industry in *S&MM*'s survey.

During the 1980s, Dow built a strong recruiting and selection system based on developing close relationships with about 35 colleges and universities where the firm obtains most of its new technical and sales talent. Dow treats these target schools like business partners. "We 'penetrate' the account," Baughman explains. "We make sure that our relationship to each school is like our relationship with a supplier. For instance, we get to know the president and vice president of the school. We learn what their needs and goals for the institution are." The firm then contributes money, expertise, or both to help each school attain specific objectives consistent with Dow's interests. This helps improve awareness and the image of the company among each school's faculty and students.

Dow's recruiters also establish contacts with individual departments and faculty at each target school. This gives them valuable sources of information to help identify promising members of each graduating class and to evaluate the intellectual abilities, work habits, leadership qualities, and other personal characteristics of each candidate. This information is combined with more common inputs from résumés, personal interviews, and tests of sales aptitude and various personality traits to evaluate each candidate and decide who will be given job offers.

Training and Career Development

Dow's new hires tend to be evenly split between people with technical backgrounds and those with business or liberal arts degrees. But once they join the company, all new recruits are processed through the same training program, which is also rated number one in the chemical industry. "What makes it so special," says Richard Sosville, vice president of sales and marketing for U.S. Dow Plastics, "is that it aims to produce a fully balanced seller, not just someone trained in product knowledge alone."

During the yearlong program, trainees spend equal time in classroom situations and on training projects involving such things as working the phones in Dow's customer service center or producing in-depth marketing studies of potential new markets. Trainees also spend time in the field interacting with and selling to actual customers and prospects. By the time a recruit is assigned to one of its 23 U.S. sales offices, Dow has made a substantial investment in training and development. "We've calculated that after about four years with the company, our investment is in the hundreds of thousands of dollars," Baughman says.

Career Opportunities

Finally, Dow works hard to keep its investment intact—and out of the hands of raiding competitors—by offering its salespeople a clear career path and plenty of opportunity. "Dow has a good, solid career ladder for people who want to sell as a career," explains John Tysse, vice president of sales and marketing for chemical and performance products. There are many steps between an entry-level sales position and a senior sales executive, including jobs managing national and global accounts. While salespeople are on their way up the ladder, Dow also tries to keep them motivated and informed through the use of structured evaluations and frequent feedback from managers. "We believe in rigorous goal setting," Tysse points out. "As managers, we try to make sure our people meet their personal goals and their business goals. The aim is to make our people feel challenged throughout their careers."

ARE GOOD SALESPEOPLE BORN OR MADE? THE DETERMINANTS OF SUCCESSFUL SALES PERFORMANCE

Stable, self-sufficient, self-confident, goal-directed, decisive, intellectually curious, accurate—these are personal traits one major personnel testing company says an individual should have to be a successful salesperson. A crucial question, though, is whether the presence or absence of such traits is determined by a person's genetic makeup and early life experiences or whether they can be developed through training, supervision, and experience after the person is hired for a sales position. In other words, are good salespeople born or made?

Dow Chemical appears to believe that successful salespeople are *both* born and made. The firm spends an unusual amount of time and energy developing relationships with colleges and faculty members to help identify promising recruits. And it gathers large amounts of information about potential new hires through interviews, references, and tests to determine which candidates have the traits and characteristics the firm believes are important determinants of future sales success. But Dow also devotes substantial resources to training and supervisory programs aimed at further developing each new salesperson's skills, knowledge, and motivation.

Like the managers at Dow, many sales executives seem to have somewhat ambivalent feelings concerning what it takes to become a successful salesperson. When forced to make an explicit choice, a majority of managers say they believe good salespeople are made rather than born that way. For instance, by a margin of 7 to 1, the 2,000 respondents in a survey of sales and marketing executives said training and supervision are more critical determinants of selling success than the inherent personal characteristics of the individual.[2] But many of those respondents also described men and women they knew as being "a born salesperson." And a minority argued that personal traits were critical determinants of good sales performance. For example, one executive asked, "Can they teach ego, train it into an individual? Can they teach personal drive or persistence that gets the sale? Hardly. The best salespeople acquired what it takes to excel when they were kids. . . . Training won't do it. Yet a lot of companies try and waste a lot of money in the process."[3]

Thus, while most managers believe the things a firm does to train and develop its salespeople are the most critical determinants of their future success, many also believe a firm cannot make a silk purse out of a sow's ear, that certain basic personal traits—such as a strong ego, self-confidence, decisiveness, and a need for achievement—are necessary requirements. Is it possible that both sets of factors play crucial roles in shaping a salesperson's performance? A review of past empirical research on this issue can help provide a more definitive answer.

A Review of Past Research

A research technique known as *meta-analysis* has been used to integrate and evaluate the findings of a large number of past research studies examining relationships between the performance of individual salespeople and a variety of personal and organizational factors that might influence that performance.[4] The review examined more than 400 published and unpublished studies conducted between 1918 and 1983, 116 of which reported some statistical evidence regarding the strength of the relationship between one or more variables and differences in performance. Since most of those studies investigated more than one variable, the review actually summarized 1,653 reported relationships between various individual and organizational characteristics and individual sales performance.

For purposes of analysis, variables were grouped into the six categories shown in Exhibit 11.1. The exhibit also shows the actions a sales manager or top executive might take to influence or control each group of determinant variables. Note that two of the categories—aptitude and personal characteristics—contain enduring personal traits and past experiences of the salesperson. These variables are impossible for the manager to influence or change, except by choosing salespeople with desirable traits. A third category—skill levels—

EXHIBIT 11 • 1   *Variables that Cause Differences in Performance across Individual Salepeople and the Actions Management Can Take to Influence Them*

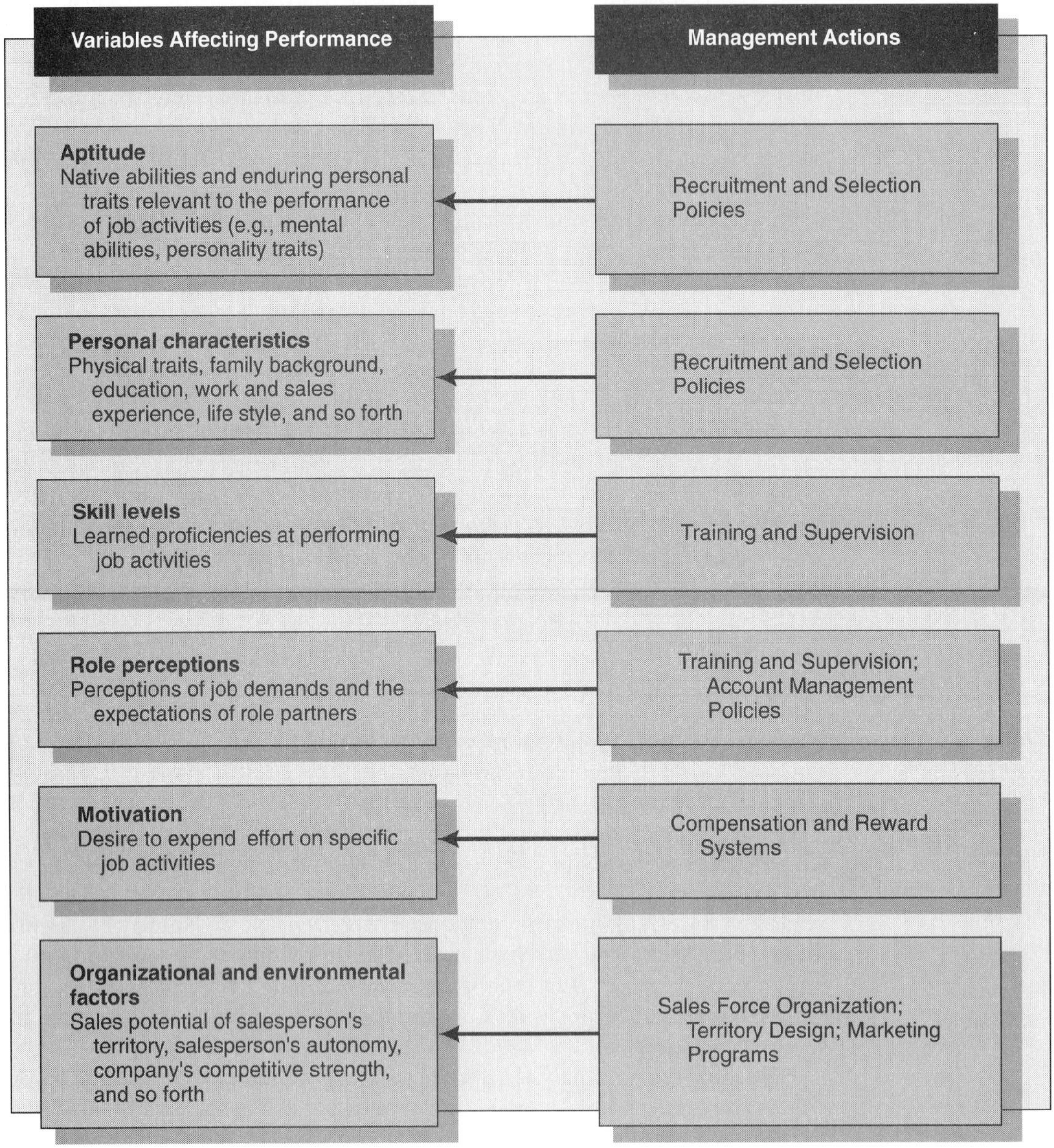

Variables Affecting Performance	Management Actions
Aptitude Native abilities and enduring personal traits relevant to the performance of job activities (e.g., mental abilities, personality traits)	Recruitment and Selection Policies
Personal characteristics Physical traits, family background, education, work and sales experience, life style, and so forth	Recruitment and Selection Policies
Skill levels Learned proficiencies at performing job activities	Training and Supervision
Role perceptions Perceptions of job demands and the expectations of role partners	Training and Supervision; Account Management Policies
Motivation Desire to expend effort on specific job activities	Compensation and Reward Systems
Organizational and environmental factors Sales potential of salesperson's territory, salesperson's autonomy, company's competitive strength, and so forth	Sales Force Organization; Territory Design; Marketing Programs

EXHIBIT 11 • 2   *Average Correlations between Types of Determinant Variables and Variations in Salesperson Performance*

Variables Affecting Performance	Number of Correlations Reported	Weighted Mean Correlation Coefficient (R)	Percent of Variance in Performance Explained (R²)
1. Aptitude	820	.138	.019
2. Personal characteristics	407	.161	.026
3. Skill levels	178	.268	.072
4. Role perceptions	59	.294	.086
5. Motivation	126	.184	.034
6. Organizational/ environmental factors	51	.104	.011

Source: Adapted from Gilbert A. Churchill, Jr., Neil M. Ford, Steven W. Hartley, and Orville C. Walker, Jr., "The Determinants of Salesperson Performance: A Meta-Analysis," *Journal of Marketing Research,* May 1985, p. 107, published by the American Marketing Association.

includes personal abilities that can change and improve as the salesperson gains knowledge and experience. Thus, skill variables can be influenced by management through effective training programs and supervision. The remaining three categories of determinant variables—role perceptions, motivation, and organizational characteristics—are also directly influenced by management through such means as supervision, compensation and reward systems, and other company policies and programs.

Exhibit 11.2 shows the number of correlations reported in past studies for each of the six categories and the average correlation (weighted to reflect differences in sample sizes across studies) between the variables in each category and salesperson performance. When the weighted average correlation coefficient is squared, it indicates the percentage of variation in performance across salespeople that can be accounted for or explained, on average, by the variables in each category. Thus, aptitude variables—with a weighted average correlation coefficient of 0.138—explain an average of only about 2 percent of the variation in performance across salespeople.

On the surface, the results reported in Exhibit 11.2 may seem a bit disappointing since no category of variables appears capable of explaining a very large percentage of the variation in salesperson performance. While differences in role perceptions explain a greater share of variance in performance than any other category of variables, they account for an average of only 8.6 percent of that variance. At the other extreme, organizational and environmental factors account for only slightly more than 1 percent of the differences in performance across salespeople.

However, when interpreting these findings, several points should be kept in mind. First, each of the six categories contains a large number of specific variables. The aptitude category, for instance, encompasses many specific personality traits and mental abilities. As we will see later in this chapter, some of the specific variables included in each category explain a larger proportion of the variation in performance across salespeople (and some explain a smaller portion) than does the average reported for the whole category.

Second, different studies have measured the same variable in different ways. Consequently, the low correlations between categories of variables and salesperson performance may be partly due to measurement error. Some studies may have used inaccurate or invalid instruments to measure a given trait or characteristic. As we see in Chapter 12, much controversy surrounds which measurement methods (e.g., personal interviews versus references versus paper-and-pencil tests) are most appropriate for evaluating whether potential sales recruits possess the specific attributes and abilities a firm is seeking.

Finally, in interpreting the findings, consider that the size of the correlations between each type of determinant variable and sales performance varied widely across studies. One reason for the variation was that different studies examined samples of people engaged in different types of sales jobs. The review found that some categories of predictor variables could explain a greater proportion of the variation in performance for salespeople selling certain types of goods or dealing with certain types of customers, but could not explain performance variations as well in other selling situations. For instance, aptitude variables were found to be more positively related to performance for people selling industrial products to organizational customers than for those selling either consumer goods or services.

With the above points in mind, one can draw the following conclusions from the meta-analysis of past studies of the determinants of sales performance:

- While all six categories of personal and organizational variables account for some of the variance in performance across salespeople, no single category accounts for more than about 8.5 percent of the variance by itself. This suggests the performance of a given salesperson is a function of a variety of influences, including both personal traits and organizational factors.

- The strengths of the relationships between some categories of variables and sales performance vary according to the type of customer and the kind of product or service being sold. This suggests that different personal traits, aptitudes, and skills are required for success in different kinds of sales jobs.

- On average, factors that sales managers can control or influence—such as role perceptions, skills, and motivation—account for the largest proportion of the variance in performance across salespeople. But enduring personal characteristics—such as aptitude, personal background, and personality traits—are also related to individual differences in performance.

EXHIBIT 11 • 3 *Median Salesperson Quit Rates and Discharge Rates by Average Age of the Sales Force*

Average Age of Sales Force (years)	Median Quit Rates	Median Discharge Rates
25–34	5.4%	3.0%
35–39	6.0	2.0
40–44	4.0	1.0
45–54	3.0	0.0

Source: Charles A. Peck, "Compensating Field Sales Representatives," Report No. 828 (New York: The Conference Board, 1982), p. 35.

These conclusions suggest that successful salespeople are *both* born and made. Selecting recruits who have personal traits and abilities appropriate for specific selling tasks is an important determinant of their ultimate sales performance. But while *who* is hired is important, *how those salespeople are managed* is even more crucial to their success.

The Costs of Inappropriate Selection Standards

Although personal characteristics may have less influence on a salesperson's long-term performance than do company policies and management actions, firms should pay close attention to hiring the right kinds of people for their sales forces for another reason. People who lack the personal traits and abilities to be truly successful in a given sales job are more likely to become frustrated and to quit—or be fired—before training and experience can turn them into productive employees.

Surveys have found that an average of 15 percent of a firm's salespeople either quit or are fired during their first year and that turnover approaches 50 percent during the first five years of employment. And as the survey results shown in Exhibit 11.3 indicate, both quit and discharge rates are highest in firms where the average age of the sales force is relatively young. All of this suggests companies are not always successful in identifying and hiring people, particularly those who are younger and inexperienced, who have the personal characteristics and abilities to become satisfied and successful salespeople.

Because firms spend much money and time training and supporting new salespeople before they begin to earn their keep, mistakes in recruitment and selection that lead to high early turnover rates can be very costly. As we saw in the Dow Chemical example, firms with high-tech products or broad and complex product lines can spend more than a year and over $100,000 training a new salesperson. Across a broader range of consumer and industrial goods and service industries, firms spend an average of four months and nearly $30,000 training each new sales rep.[5] And as the results of the survey shown in Exhibit 11.4 indicate, in most industries, it takes from three months to a

EXHIBIT 11 • 4   *The Length of Time before a New Salesperson Becomes Productive in Selected Industries (Percent of respondents, N = 2,000)*

Industry	1 Month	3 Months	6 Months	1 Year	More than 1 Year	Don't Know/ No Answer
Textiles	—	14	45	25	11	4
Glass and building materials	5	23	32	25	9	6
Publishing and printing	9	32	30	17	9	3
Metal manufacturing	5	23	42	16	13	1
Telecommunications	—	31	50	16	2	—
Diversified financial services	8	22	42	12	12	3
Rubber products	7	27	37	24	4	1
Transportation services	6	38	39	10	5	2
Soaps and cosmetics	4	20	46	26	4	—
Electronics	3	18	51	16	11	1

Source: Adapted with permission from Arthur Bragg, "Are Good Salespeople Made or Born?" *Sales & Marketing Management,* September 1988, p. 36. © 1988 by Bill Communications, Inc.

year before new sales reps generate enough sales to cover their compensation and expenses.[6] Thus, when a frustrated salesperson quits in the first year or two of employment, the firm can never recoup the costs of recruiting and training that individual.

Because mistakes in recruitment and selection can be both costly in the short term and lead to lower productivity in the long term regardless of how well a firm trains, supervises, and motivates its sales force, many sales managers consider the evaluation and selection of new recruits to be among the most important aspects of their jobs. Thus, the remainder of this chapter examines some of the personal and psychological characteristics related to a person's ability to carry out different types of sales jobs.

CHARACTERISTICS OF SUCCESSFUL SALESPEOPLE

Aptitude and personal characteristics are typically thought to place an upper limit on an individual's ability to perform a given sales job. Two people with equal motivation, role perceptions, and training might perform at different levels because one does not have the personal traits or abilities necessary to

EXHIBIT 11 • 5   *Importance Rankings of 10 Indicators of Sales Aptitude by Top Sales Executives in 44 Major Manufacturing Firms*

Attribute	1 (10)	2 (9)	3 (8)	4 (7)	5 (6)	6 (5)	7 (4)	8 (3)	9 (2)	10 (1)	Total Points
	Rank Assigned by Respondents*										
Enthusiasm	16	5	8	5	1	5	—	1	—	—	338
Well organized	6	8	11	3	5	5	1	2	—	—	304
Obvious ambition	8	6	5	7	4	3	2	3	3	—	285
High persuasiveness	2	10	3	1	10	4	5	3	1	2	254
General sales experience	3	2	4	6	6	2	8	8	5	4	226
High verbal skill	2	3	3	6	2	7	7	6	4	1	215
Specific sales experience	2	4	2	8	6	1	5	4	4	5	214
Highly recommended	1	—	1	4	3	3	7	2	7	2	149
Follows instructions	—	2	—	3	4	4	2	9	9	8	142
Sociability	—	1	1	2	—	7	6	6	8	10	134

*The top numeral in each column is the ranking given by executives, with 1 being most important and 10 least important. Numbers in parentheses are point ratings assigned to each rank. Numbers in the table show the number of respondents who assigned each rank to each attribute.

Source: Stan Moss, "What Sales Executives Look for in New Salespeople," *Sales & Marketing Management*, March 1978, p. 47. See also Thomas Rollins, "How to Tell Competent Salespeople from the Other Kind," *Sales & Marketing Management*, September 1990, pp. 116–17, 145–46.

do the job as well as the other. The questions to consider are these: What specific personal traits and abilities enable a person to achieve good sales performance? What are the determinants of sales aptitude?

Characteristics Sales Managers Look For

One way to answer these questions is to identify the personal characteristics sales managers look for when selecting new salespeople. Imagine you are sales manager for a major manufacturer and you must judge applicants for a position in your sales force. Which of the characteristics listed below would you consider to be most important for your new salesperson to have? Rank the relative importance of those characteristics from 1 to 10. You can then compare your responses with those of 44 top sales executives from major manufacturing organizations, as displayed in Exhibit 11.5.

_____High persuasiveness   _____Follows instructions
_____Sociability   _____Highly recommended
_____Enthusiasm   _____High verbal skill
_____Well organized   _____General sales experience
_____Obvious ambition   _____Specific sales experience

Thorny Issues in Sales Management 11 • 1

ARE DIFFERENT CRITERIA APPROPRIATE FOR SELECTING SALESPEOPLE IN DIFFERENT COUNTRIES?

As we will see in the next chapter, many firms have well-developed and explicit criteria for evaluating potential new salespeople and deciding who to hire. In some cases, those criteria have been validated by comparing the characteristics of high-performing salespeople within the company to those of reps who have performed less well, quit, or been dismissed.

But when such companies expand their operations into foreign markets—particularly those in developing nations—it is often more difficult to find sales recruits who fit the established criteria. More important, cultural differences can cause some personal traits and characteristics to be more critical for selling success in some countries than in others. Consequently, many global companies have had to adapt their salesperson selection criteria to the cultural and social conditions that prevail in different national markets.

This fact is illustrated by a recent study of 14 multinational corporations. The study surveyed recruiting practices in 135 of those firm's subsi-

diaries operating in 45 countries. Table A indicates the percentage of foreign subsidiaries that reported using various salesperson selection criteria. Note that some factors that are unlawful and seldom explicitly used as selection criteria in the United States, such as ethnic and religious background, are used in a large portion of foreign countries. As the ratings shown in Table B indicate, such factors are perceived to be especially important for selecting salespeople in developing markets as compared to the more developed markets of North America and Europe.

Some of the reasons factors American deem inappropriate or irrelevant for choosing good salespeople are considered important in other countries are suggested by the following caveats offered by the study's authors concerning sales force recruitment in Malaysia.

• There are definite tensions between the native Malays (55 percent of the population) and the Chinese (33 percent), who dominate large sec-

T A B L E A	Salesperson Selection Criteria, Rank-Ordered According to Frequency Mentioned	

Criterion	Number of Subsidiaries Using	Percent
Education	130/135	96.3
Interview	122/135	90.4
Previous experience	119/135	88.1
Personal appearance	109/135	80.7
References	90/135	66.7
Psychological tests	62/135	45.9
Social class	43/135	31.8
Ethnic background	42/135	31.1
Religious background	34/135	25.2

TABLE B   *Percent of Subsidiaries Rating Various Salesperson Selection Criteria "Important" in Developing versus Developed Markets*

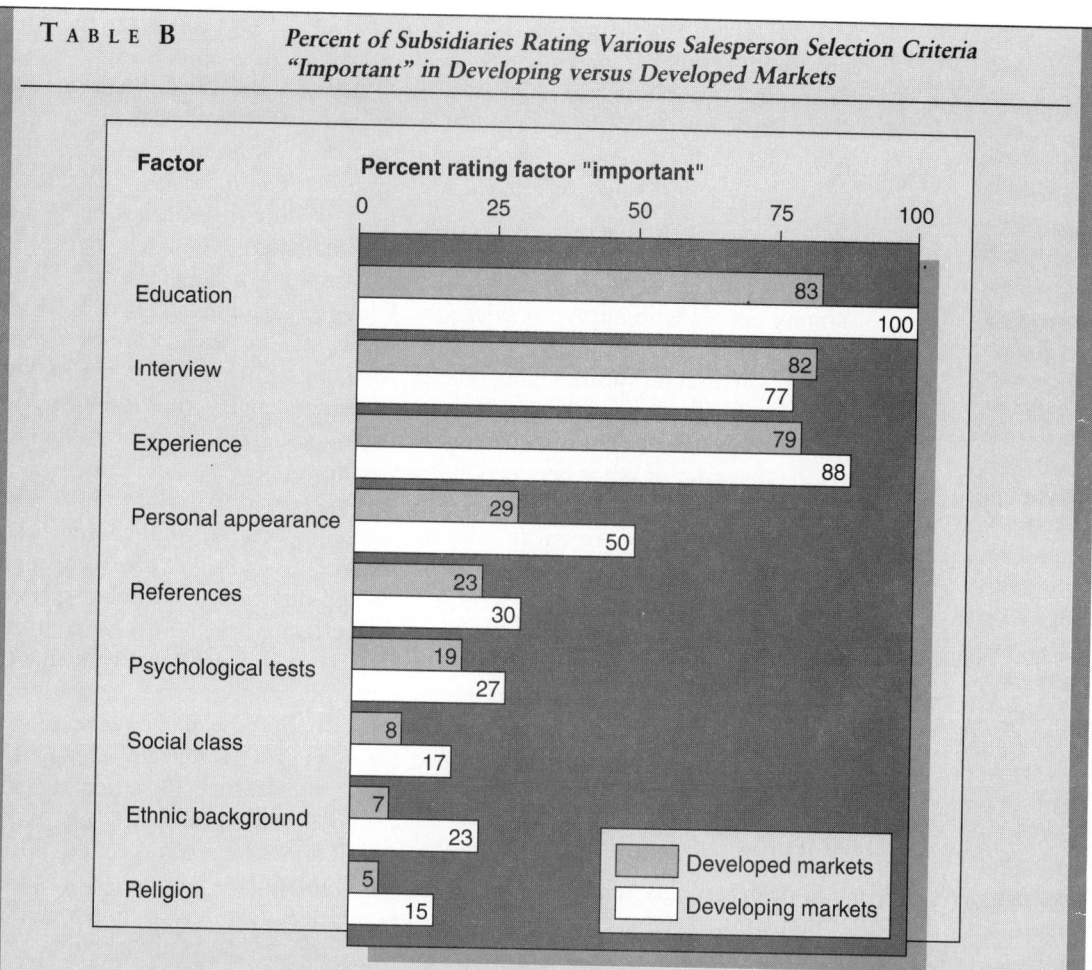

Source: John S. Hill and Meg Birdseye, "Salesperson Selection in Multinational Corporations: An Empirical Study," *Journal of Personal Selling and Sales Management,* Summer 1989, pp. 39–47.

tions of commerce. To correct this, U.S.-style affirmative action laws encourage Malay participation in business.

• Cultural differences are enhanced by religious differences—as Malays are mainly Muslims and Chinese are Buddhists.

• Malay society is highly stratified, and behavior toward individuals depends on the person's background, family, and social position. Malays are not comfortable in situations where social positions have not been defined.

As you can see from the data in Exhibit 11.5, *enthusiasm* ranked as the most important characteristic to look for in new recruits among twice as many sales executives as the next highest trait. Other characteristics the respondents consider relatively important are *well organized, ambition,* and the two related attributes of *high persuasiveness* and *verbal skill.* Although many executives consider previous sales experience to be important in indicating the sales aptitude of new employees, general experience in selling is viewed as being more relevant than specific product or industry experience.

The results of this survey seem to contradict some beliefs widely held among people who apply for sales jobs. Glowing recommendations from previous employers or professors are not seen as relevant indicators of a candidate's potential for future selling success. Also, the highly sociable, "hail-fellow-well-met" type of personality is often not considered a very important attribute.

Surveys like this are instructive, but they do not provide a definitive answer to the question of what personal characteristics make some individuals better salespeople than others. The survey results presented in Exhibit 11.5 reflect only the opinions of American sales managers concerning what characteristics are related to selling success in the U.S. market. As more firms become global competitors, managers must wrestle with the question of whether different characteristics are related to successful sales performance in different countries. This question is discussed further in Thorny Issues in Sales Management 11.1.

Also, such manager surveys merely reflect the opinions and perceptions of those sales executives who responded. Although those perceptions may be based on years of practical experience, they can still be inaccurate, biased, or based on knowledge of only a limited range of industries or types of selling jobs.

A more objective way to determine what specific personal characteristics are most strongly related to selling success is to study a large cross section of salespeople. To this end, it would be very useful to examine in more detail the specific variables included in the "aptitude," "skill levels," and "personal characteristics" categories of the meta-analysis of past research that we discussed earlier. Fortunately, a published study does exactly that.[7]

Research Concerning the Personal Characteristics of Successful Salespeople

One limitation of the initial meta-analysis of factors related to differences in sales performance was that the six categories of variables were very broadly defined. Each category contained a large number of more specific items, some of which may be much more strongly related to differences in sales performance than the average for the whole category. Consequently, a second analysis was done after breaking up the broad aptitude, skill levels, and personal characteristics categories into more narrowly defined subcategories of closely related variables.

First, personal factors related to differences in sales performance were broken down into more precisely defined groupings of physical and behavioral characteristics and psychological traits and abilities. Exhibit 11.6 displays a

EXHIBIT 11 • 6 *Categories of Physical and Behavioral Variables Used as Selection Criteria and Examples of Methods Used to Measure Them*

Variable Category	Definition	Examples of Methods Used
Demographic and physical characteristics Age	**Classifications based on physical traits of an individual**	Self-report on application blank; estimate by interviewer
Sex		Application blank; résumé
Physical appearance	Height, weight, neatness, and general appearance and manner	Self-report on application blank; rating by interviewer or sales manager
Background and experience Personal history and family background	**Developmental education and work experiences of an individual** Father's/mother's occupation; number of siblings, sibling rank; early family responsibilities; extracurricular and athletic activities	Self-report on application blank or résumé; responses from structured interview
Level of educational attainment	Individual's years of schooling; degrees earned; grade average	Self-report on application blank or résumé; reference checks
Educational content	Individual's college major; number of business/sales courses; executive development programs	Self-report on application blank or résumé; reference checks
Sales experience	Individual's years of sales experience; number and type of sales jobs; promotions and career history	Self-report on application blank or résumé; reference checks
Nonsales work experience	Individual's work history, including military service; length of time in past jobs; past occupation most and least enjoyed	Self-report on application blank or résumé; reference checks
Current status and lifestyle Marital/family status	**Individual's present marital, family, and financial status; leisure activities** Individual's current marital status; number and ages of dependents; spouse's occupation	Self-report on application blank or résumé; interviewer estimate
Financial status	Individual's past and current income levels, family income; history of salary increases; assets and liabilities; home ownership; amount of insurance	Self-report on application blank or in interview; reference checks
Activities/lifestyle	Time individual gives to church, clubs, etc.; number of memberships; offices held in organizations; hobbies and interests	Self-report on application blank; interviewer's judgment

Source: Neil M. Ford et al., "Selecting Successful Salespeople: A Meta-Analysis of Biographical and Psychological Selection Criteria," in *Review of Marketing,* ed. Michael J. Houston (Chicago: American Marketing Association, 1988), pp. 90–131.

EXHIBIT 11 ● 7   *Categories of Psychological Traits and Abilities Used as Selection Criteria and Examples of Methods or Instruments Used to Measure Them*

Variable Category	Definition	Examples of Methods Used*
Aptitude	**Enduring personal characteristics that determine an individual's overall ability to perform a sales job**	
Intelligence	Summary measures of mental abilities; total scores on multifactor intelligence tests	Wonderlic Personnel Test; Otis Mental Ability Exam
Cognitive abilities	Measures of specific mental processes and abilities, including mental flexibility, ideational fluency, spatial visualization, inductive and logical reasoning, and associative and visual memory	Educational Testing Service's Gestalt Completion, Controlled Associations, Object Number, Nonsense Syllogisms, and Map Memory tests; Kent-Rosanoff Associations test; Watson-Glaser Critical Thinking test
Verbal intelligence	Mental abilities related to the comprehension and manipulation of words; verbal fluency	Educational Testing Service's test of Vocabulary, Word Fluency and Verbal Closure; Adult Placement Test-Verbal; Test of Learning Ability-Form S-Vocabulary
Math ability	Mental abilities related to the comprehension and manipulation of numbers and quantitative relationships	Educational Testing Service's tests of number facility; Wechsler Adult Intelligence Test-Arithmetic Sub-Test; Adult Placement Test-Numerical
Sales aptitude	Enduring personal characteristics and abilities thought to be related to the performance of specific sales tasks	Life Insurance Marketing and Research Association's Aptitude Index Battery; Aptitudes Associates Test of Sales Aptitude; Sales Research Associates' Sales Aptitude Checklist
Personality	**Enduring personal traits that reflect an individual's consistent reactions to situations encountered in the environment**	
Responsibility	The person is dependable, emotionally stable, punctual, adjusts well to frustration; keeps promises, follows plans	Gordon Personal Profile-responsibility and Emotional stability scales; Guilford-Zimmerman Stability scale; peer ratings of dependability
Dominance	The person takes command, exerts leadership, pushes own ideas, wants power versus being submissive; is egotistic	Personality Research Form-Dominance scale; Murray's Dominance scale; Bernreuter Personality Inventory-Dominance scale; Edwards Personal Preference Schedule-Dominance scale
Sociabilty	The person enjoys social activities and interaction, likes to be around people, is talkative, gregarious, enjoys attention	Gordon Personal Profile-Sociability scale; Bernreuter Introversion-Extroversion scale; Activity Vector Analysis-Sociability scale
Self-esteem	The person is confident physically, personally, and careerwise; can stand criticism, claims to have abilities and skills, is confident of success, believes others have a positive attitude toward him/her	Bernreuter-Self Confidence scale; Cattell-Ego Strength scale; Jackson Personality Inventory-Generalized and Specific Self Esteem scales

EXHIBIT 11 ● 7   *(concluded)*

Variable Category	Definition	Examples of Methods Used*
Personality **(*continued*)**		
Creativity/flexibility	The person is innovative, flexible, ready to entertain new ideas and ways of doing things, individualistic, tolerant of human nature	Gordon Personal Profile-Original Thinking and Cautiousness scales; Remote Associates Test-Creativity scale
Need for achievement/ intrinsic rewards	The person works hard, likes to do his/her best, seeks success in competition, wants to produce something "great," gains satisfaction from accomplishment and personal development	Jackson Personality Inventory-Need Achievement scale; Murray's Achievement and Endurance scales; Personality Research Form-Achievement scale
Need for power/extrinsic rewards	The person is motivated primarily by desires for money or advancement, has strong need for security, desires increased power and authority	Martin Bruce Sales Motivation Inventory; Jackson Need for Power Over Others, Need for High Financial Rewards, and Need for Job Security scales
Skills	**Learned proficiencies and attitudes necessary for effective performance of specific job tasks; skills can change over time with training and experience**	
Vocational skills	Job- and company-specific skills; technical knowledge and vocabulary related to the firm's product line, knowledge of the company and its policies	A variety of proprietary tests of technical knowledge of the industry and company policies
Sales presentation	Skills related to evaluating customer needs, presentation style, ability to handle objections and close the sale	Martin Bruce Sales Comprehension Test; Sales Style Diagnosis Test; assessment center judgments; interviewers/supervisor ratings
Interpersonal	Skills related to understanding, persuading, and getting along with other people	Diplomacy Test of Empathy; interviewer/supervisor ratings of cooperativeness, sensitivity, ability to resolve conflicts
General management	Skills related to organizing, directing, and leading other people	How to Supervise Form M; Sales Aptitude Inventory-Leadership Skills score; assessment center judgment
Vocational esteem	Degree of liking or preference for the tasks and activities associated with sales jobs	Strong Vocational Interest Blank; Kuder Preference Record

*Descriptions of many of the tests of psychological variables and their psychometric properties can be found in Richard C. Sweetland and Daniel J. Keyser, eds., *Tests: A Comprehensive Reference for Assessments in Psychology, Education and Business* (Kansas City: Test Corporation of America, 1983); James V. Mitchell, Jr., ed., *Tests in Print, III* (Lincoln, Neb.: University of Nebraska Press, 1983); and Oscar K. Buros, ed., *The Eighth Mental Measurements Yearbook* (Highland Park, N.J.: Gryphon Press, 1978).

Source: Neil M. Ford et al., "Selecting Successful Salespeople: A Meta-Analysis of Biographical and Psychological Selection Criteria," in *Review of Marketing*, ed. Michael J. Houston (Chicago: American Marketing Association, 1988), pp. 90–131.

variety of the physical and behavioral factors that past research studies have examined in trying to explain individual differences in sales performance. The exhibit defines three subcategories of demographic and physical variables, five groups of background and experience factors, and three groups of variables reflecting a person's current status and lifestyle. It also describes the kinds of methods or tests researchers and sales or personnel managers have used to measure each set of items. Many of these measures rely on subjective or self-report information sources, such as résumés, application blanks, and personal references.

While all of the measurement methods described in Exhibit 11.6 were used in one or more of the past studies whose findings are discussed below, some are no longer legal for use in the selection process. For example, potentially discriminatory information about such demographic characteristics as age, sex, and race cannot be included on application blanks. These and other legal and social concerns related to providing equal employment opportunities and dealing with cultural diversity in the work force are discussed later in this chapter and in Chapter 12.

A number of variables related to salespeople's psychological traits and abilities are described in Exhibit 11.7. The exhibit defines seven subcategories of personality traits, five groups of other enduring aptitude factors or mental abilities, and five groups of skills that past studies have attempted to relate to variations in sales performance. Exhibit 11.7 also describes the kinds of methods and tests used to measure these factors. Note that these kinds of psychological variables are typically measured via more formalized paper-and-pencil tests or assessment techniques.

Overview of the findings

As expected, this more detailed analysis uncovered specific personal characteristics and traits that can better distinguish between high- and low-performing salespeople—and some that are even worse predictors of performance—than the broad categories of variables examined earlier. Although no single trait could account for a majority of the variance in performance across salespeople, Exhibit 11.8 shows that some personal variables (such as an individual's personal history and family background, current marital and family status, and vocational skills) can account for as much as 20 percent of the variance in selling success. Some traits that sales managers commonly rely on to evaluate new recruits (such as educational attainment, intelligence test scores, or sociability) have proven incapable of accounting for much more than 1 percent of the difference in their subsequent sales performance. Thus, the following sections discuss these widely varying relationships between personal variables and sales performance in more depth.

One finding was consistent, however, across both meta-analysis studies. Different types of selling situations appear to require salespeople with different personal traits and abilities. Consequently, the last section of this chapter

EXHIBIT 11 • 8 *The Percent of Variance in Salesperson Performance Explained by Various Personal Factors*

Variables Affecting Performance	Number of Correlations Reported	Percent of Variance in Performance Explained*
I. Demographic and Physical Characteristics		
Age	61	.011
Sex	37	.007
Physical appearance	49	.010
II. Background and Experience		
Personal history and family background	29	.209
Educational attainment	40	.002
Educational content	42	.009
Sales experience	26	.028
Nonsales work experience	54	.014
III. Current Status and Lifestyle		
Marital/family status	32	.119
Financial status	31	.061
Activities/lifestyle	38	.017
IV. Aptitude		
Intelligence	38	.014
Cognitive abilities	21	.067
Verbal intelligence	20	.018
Math ability	41	.023
Sales aptitude	58	.037
V. Personality		
Responsibility	42	.040
Dominance	125	.024
Sociability	94	.011
Self-esteem	106	.019
Creativity/flexibility	51	.014
Need for achievement/intrinsic rewards	81	.024
Need for power/extrinsic rewards	25	.018
VI. Skills		
Vocational skills	28	.094
Sales presentation skills	44	.048
Interpersonal skills	43	.022
General management skills	25	.091
Vocational esteem	115	.010

*As determined by R^2—the square of the weighted mean correlation coefficient.

Source: From Neil M. Ford et al. "Selecting Successful Salespeople: A Meta-Analysis of Biographical and Psychological Criteria," in *Review of Marketing,* ed. Michael J. Houston (Chicago: American Marketing Association, 1988), pp. 90–131.

examines the evidence concerning what personal traits and abilities are best suited to different types of sales jobs.

Demographic and Physical Variables

The meta-analysis results in Exhibit 11.8 indicate that demographic factors, such as sex and age, and physical attributes, such as height and appearance, account for only about 1 percent or less of the difference in performance across salespeople. The *lack* of any strong relationships between these variables and sales performance is a very important finding. It has implications for public policy regarding equal employment opportunities for women and minorities, and it refutes the "conventional wisdom" espoused by some sales managers in the past.

Sex and race

Like many other job categories, industrial selling was predominantly a white male occupation for many decades, and employment opportunities for women and racial minorities were severely limited. The 1980 U.S. Census indicated that while blacks accounted for about 12 percent of the population, only 6 percent of all sales jobs were held by black workers, and the proportion of blacks in more prestigious and rewarding industrial sales positions was even lower. Similarly, women accounted for less than 16 percent of people selling manufactured goods at other than the retail level in 1980.

One major reason for this unequal employment was that many sales managers believed women and racial minorities would not do as well as white men. It was widely believed that some customers would be reluctant to deal with or buy from minority salespeople. Similarly, many sales managers thought women were too emotional and lacking in aggressiveness and self-confidence to be effective salespeople. Some managers thought turnover rates would be higher for women due to marriage and childbirth and women would be less willing to travel and entertain. Consequently, 80 percent of the 180 top sales and marketing executives surveyed by *Sales Management* in the late 1960s admitted they were unwilling to hire women for outside sales positions.[8]

Social changes have improved employment opportunities

Women and minorities have made some inroads into industrial selling, but their progress has been slow. As Exhibit 11.9 indicates, women accounted for an average of more than 22 percent of sales reps across a sample of industries in 1990, and they held nearly 10 percent of the sales management positions in those industries. Note, however, that women have achieved greater acceptance in some industries, such as communications, publishing, apparel, and recreation services, than in more traditionally male-dominated industries such as electronics, chemicals, and agriculture.

The positive trends in the employment of women and minorities in recent years have resulted from a variety of social changes, including pressures exerted

EXHIBIT 11 • 9   *Women in Sales and Sales Management Positions: Percentages by Industry*

Industry Group	Percent of Women Sales Reps	Percent of Women Sales Managers
Agriculture	7.3%	0.0%
Amusement/recreation services	63.2	25.0
Apparel/other textile products	44.4	17.0
Business services	34.9	26.2
Chemicals	4.3	0.0
Communications	39.3	19.5
Construction	12.3	2.3
Electronic components	6.2	4.8
Electronics	2.4	10.7
Fabricated metals	3.6	2.6
Food products	29.7	9.5
Instruments	27.8	21.1
Insurance	14.7	6.6
Lumber/wood products	15.4	0.0
Machinery	5.3	0.0
Manufacturing	15.8	2.0
Office equipment	30.3	24.8
Paper/allied products	28.9	11.0
Primary metal products	18.9	6.7
Printing/publishing	39.7	11.1
Rubber/plastics	12.3	4.8
Wholesale (consumer)	26.2	9.0
Wholesale (industrial)	29.5	12.3
Average	22.3%	9.9%

Source: "1991 Sales Manager's Budget Planner," *Sales & Marketing Management*, July 17, 1991, p. 77.

by the civil rights movement, changing attitudes concerning women's roles, increasing career orientation among women, and legal requirements. The rights of women and minorities to equal employment opportunities in selling, as well as in other occupations, are protected by federal laws. Title VII of the 1964 Civil Rights Act prohibits discrimination in hiring, promotions, and compensation. It covers all private employers of 15 or more persons. The Equal Employment Opportunity Commission administers Title VII. Since 1972, it has had broad enforcement powers. While enforcement policies have fluctuated with political changes in the executive branch of the federal government over the years, the commission's guidelines prohibit withholding jobs or promotions because of either customer preferences for salespeople of a particular race or sex or presumed differences in turnover rates. They also prohibit separate promotional paths or seniority lists. Recently, additional legislation has outlawed discrimination on the basis of age and physical disabilities. These important pieces of employment legislation and their implications for sales force recruitment and hiring decisions are examined in more detail in Chapter 12.[9]

Cultural diversity and changing attitudes

As firms have hired more minorities and women for sales positions, have the old concerns about the possible shortcomings of such individuals been supported or disproved? Have sales managers' attitudes changed as more women and minorities have been added to their sales forces? Do sex and race have anything to do with a person's sales aptitude and ultimate performance?

Unfortunately, the existing research relevant to such questions is neither extensive nor conclusive. Few published studies have compared the job performance of minority salespeople with that of whites, or examined sales managers' attitudes or perceptions of minority salespeople. One reason for this lack of empirical evidence is that still relatively few minorities are employed in industrial selling. As a result, race could not be included as one of the demographic variables examined in the meta-analysis reported in Exhibit 11.8. However, many firms have been active and successful in recruiting minorities for their sales forces in recent years.

The experiences of these companies suggest that, given adequate training and solid company support, minority salespeople have no major difficulties gaining access to customers. Also, their job performance is not systematically different from that of the rest of the sales force. Furthermore, in some selling situations minority salespeople have performed better than whites. For example, some food companies, such as Armour, have found that minority salespeople are more effective than white salespeople in calling on retail stores in minority neighborhoods.

Recent demographic trends in the U.S. population indicate our country's labor force is becoming increasingly culturally diverse. As the discussion in Thorny Issues in Sales Management 11.2 suggests, these trends will present both challenges and opportunities for sales managers over the next decade.

As for saleswomen, the results in Exhibit 11.8 suggest sex is largely irrelevant for explaining differences in performance across salespeople. There is no evidence of consistent differences in the productivity of men and women in industrial sales. The attitudes of sales managers and industrial buyers toward women sales reps have also become more positive over the years.

While both men and women are seen as sharing the potential for sales success, however, both groups are still often perceived to have unique job requirements and concerns and special strengths, which enable them to perform better on different aspects of the sales job. For instance, the etiquette involved in traveling with male colleagues or entertaining male clients can still pose uncertainties for some saleswomen.[10] Similarly, surveys suggest some sales

Thorny Issues in Sales Management 11 • 2

THE IMPLICATIONS OF INCREASING CULTURAL DIVERSITY

The typical salesperson will be a bit more atypical in the years to come, according to a recent study conducted by Towers Perrin, a New York consulting firm, and the Hudson Institute, an Indianapolis research group. The study examined the reactions of 645 U.S. companies across a variety of industries to emerging work force issues such as the decline in the number of entry-level workers, the aging labor pool, and increasing cultural diversity.

According to the survey respondents, American managers in the next decade will be faced with an older, more culturally diverse work force that will be increasingly difficult to recruit and train. And Frank X. Dowd, a principal in the Stamford, Connecticut, office of Towers Perrin, says these trends will also hold true for sales forces. "Sales managers will no longer be able to find someone that fits the demographics of what they view as their ideal candidate," Dowd says. "They need to start taking a much broader view of who'll be working for them."

Even today, managers are facing an increasingly kaleidoscopic work force. One fourth of the surveyed companies reported minority employment of 26 percent or more, and this figure is expected to increase substantially by the year 2000 when nearly one in three Americans will be from a minority group.

To best respond to this trend, Dowd says sales managers should rethink the criteria they use in selecting new sales candidates. "Traditionally, managers selected their sales force so that it would match the demographics of their customers, with the idea that their similar backgrounds would stimulate interaction. Usually—especially in technical fields—this meant that the sales force would be predominantly white and male." Dowd argues

that this rationale has to change. Since the new demographic trends will also affect their customers' work forces and purchasing departments, sales managers who do not anticipate this trend by changing the complexion of their sales forces are likely to find it harder to build close relationships with those customers.

Surprisingly, many firms appear to be slow in responding to these challenges. While 35 percent of the respondents report they are already having difficulty recruiting salespeople, only about one fourth of the respondents are training supervisors in managing ethnically or culturally mixed groups of employees. A quarter of the companies state they are not at all concerned with cultural diversity in their organizations.

Similarly, more than half the respondents said they were unconcerned about the effects the "gray drain" would have on their sales forces. That lack of concern could have serious consequences as today's baby boomers get closer to retirement and the manpower to replace them isn't available. This blind spot is particularly surprising, says Dowd, given that companies could be taking measures now to ease the problem. Nontraditional work patterns, for instance, are one answer to an aging work force—things like using retirees on a part-time basis. Some companies are beginning to get the message. About 30 percent of the study's respondents said they sometimes use retirees as consultants or on special projects. But only 3 percent currently offer retraining programs for older workers or gradual retirement plans to capitalize on older workers' knowledge and skills.

Team selling may also offer at least a partial solution to the problems created by an older and more culturally diverse work force. "Team selling," Dowd says, "reduces the reliance on the sales

(continued)
generalist and allows a company to match the task with available talent. For example, an organiza-

———

Source: Jeffery D. Smith, "Radical Changes in Store for Workforce 2000," *Sales & Marketing Management* (November 1990), pp. 122–23.

tion may have a non-U.S. born employee who is technically superior but who hasn't yet mastered presentation skills. Teaming this person with an outstanding sales type should lead to more productive sales calls."

managers and purchasing agents judge salesmen as being better than saleswomen on some dimensions of job performance, such as product knowledge and technical assistance, but perceive saleswomen to be superior on other attributes, including preparation for sales presentations and follow-through.[11]

One should view such generalizations concerning the comparative strengths and weaknesses of salesmen and saleswomen with caution, however. Both the meta-analysis results and other recent research suggests variations in sales performance are probably much greater *within* each group than between them. For instance, one recent study indicates saleswomen whose selling styles are judged to fit "female" gender stereotypes (e.g., have weak product knowledge, little technical aptitude, low self-confidence, are unaggressive and reluctant to "close," etc.) perform less well in some kinds of selling situations than saleswomen with more "masculine" styles. As the authors point out, many aspects of these gender-specific perceptions, such as product knowledge and self-confidence, can be modified through appropriate training, supervision, and company and peer support.[12] Thus, there appears to be little that is inherently and unalterably either "male" or "female" about any aspect of good sales performance.

Physical characteristics and customer similarity

While demographic and physical attributes are not strongly related to sales performance in general, particular characteristics may enable a salesperson to deal more effectively with some types of customers than with others. Consequently, some research studies have taken a "dyadic" approach to try to explain variations in performance among salespeople.

Most of the studies test a very simple hypothesis: Salespeople are more likely to be successful when they are dealing with prospects who are *similar to themselves in demographic characteristics, personality traits, and attitudes* than when their prospects have characteristics different from their own. We tend to understand, have empathy for, and be attracted to other people more when they are like us. Therefore, a salesperson may be better able to understand a customer's problems and needs, communicate a sales message, and persuade the prospect to make a purchase when the rep has physical characteristics, personality traits, and attitudes similar to those of the prospect.

The first study to explore this "similarity" hypothesis was conducted by Franklin Evans in 1963. He surveyed dyads consisting of life insurance salespeople and their customers. Half the dyads consisted of customers who had purchased insurance from the salesperson, and the other hand included customers who had decided not to purchase. Evans concluded the dyads consisting of salespeople and customers who had purchased life insurance were more similar on the following characteristics:

- Age.
- Height.
- Education.
- Income.
- Religion.
- Political affiliation.
- Smoking habits.

In addition, customers who had purchased insurance were more likely to (1) consider the salesperson as a friend, (2) believe the salesperson liked them, (3) have enjoyed their conversations with the salesperson, and (4) think that the salesperson enjoyed his job.[13]

Evans's findings seem to offer strong support for the similarity hypothesis. Subsequent studies have produced similar results in other types of selling situations, although their findings have usually not been so clear-cut and unequivocal as the original. For instance, many studies have found that other attributes of the salesperson—such as expertise—are more strongly related to selling success than similarity with the customer.

Problems and implications of the similarity hypothesis

The implications of these research findings seem simple and straightforward. Managers should attempt to hire salespeople with demographic and personality characteristics as similar as possible to those of the prospects they will be calling on. Thus, a department store might try to hire young female sales reps for the "juniors" department and people who are experienced in a variety of sports for the sporting goods department. Similarly, an industrial goods firm with salespeople who must call on engineers and technically oriented purchasing agents should seek salespeople with technical educations. They should also implement sales training programs that emphasize the technical attributes of the company's products.

These guidelines seem simple enough; however, they post two fundamental problems. For one thing, they are often impossible to implement. Because buyers and purchasing agents come in all shapes and sizes and vary widely in characteristics, it can be difficult to match a salesperson's attributes with those of all or even most of the potential customers. Matching salesperson and customer characteristics can sometimes be accomplished in retail selling, where different types of consumers tend to patronize different stores or departments within a store. It is much more difficult, however, in industrial or trade selling where purchasing organizations and their buyers are more diverse. And, as we saw in our earlier discussion of the thorny issue of cultural diversity, those organizations and buyers are likely to become even more diverse in the future.

A second problem is that research has cast doubt on the validity of the similarity hypothesis. One authority suggests there is another explanation for the findings that customers who have made a purchase tend to see themselves as more similar to the salesperson than customers who did not make a purchase.[14] Since customers generally were not contacted until *after* they had decided to purchase, their feelings toward the product and toward the salesperson may have been relatively positive as a result of their attempts to reduce postpurchase cognitive dissonance.

Furthermore, people who have positive feelings toward another individual tend to perceive that individual as being similar to themselves. Thus, customers who had decided to purchase may have developed more positive feelings toward the product and the salesperson and, subsequently, came to perceive the salesperson as having the same attitudes and personal characteristics as themselves. Using the same reasoning, customers who did not make a purchase may have developed more negative attitudes toward the product and the salesperson after their decision. As a result, they may have perceived the salesperson as being relatively different from themselves.

One empirical study attempted to eliminate the effects of such potentially biased perceptions. In this study, only *objective* characteristics such as education, religion, political preference, age, height, nationality, sex, and race were measured. Measures of these characteristics were obtained separately from each customer and salesperson rather than relying on one person's perceptions of the other. Four similarity indexes were calculated for dyads composed of retail salesclerks and their customers. *None* of the indexes was significantly related to whether or not the customer in the dyad made a purchase from the salesperson. Two similarity indexes were positively related to the amount customers purchased (that is, customers tended to purchase more from salespeople who were objectively similar to themselves); however, only 2 percent of the variance in the purchase amount could be explained by salesperson-customer similarity.[15]

In view of the conflicting theoretical explanations, research findings, and practical problems involved in implementation, choosing salespeople who have characteristics similar to those of their potential customers does not appear to be a viable method of sales force selection.

Background and Experience

One of the surprises in the findings presented in Exhibit 11.8 is that personal history and family background variables are among the best predictors of sales success, accounting for an average of about 20 percent of the variance in performance across salespeople. This suggests that information about such things as whether a person held part-time jobs or had substantial family responsibilities as a youngster provides a good indication of likely emotional maturity and motivation. These traits, in turn, are important determinants of sales performance, particularly for younger recruits.

Even more surprising, perhaps, is that some of the background factors that sales managers most commonly rely on when evaluating potential recruits—such as the person's educational attainment, course of study, and general work experience—do not show much relationship with sales performance. Even a person's past sales experience—a factor that receives primary emphasis in some firms' recruitment and selection—explains only about 3 percent of the variation in performance across salespeople.

Current Status and Lifestyle Variables	As was the case with personal history and family background, a person's current marital and family status, income level, and financial obligations (e.g., a large mortgage) also appear to reflect emotional maturity and motivation and are relatively good predictors of sales performance. Variables related to marital and family status account for about 12 percent of the variance in performance across salespeople, while those reflecting financial status explain about 5 percent of that variance. As we see later, though, these relationships are much stronger for some kinds of sales jobs than for others.

But the ways in which people spend their time outside of their jobs do not appear to be closely related to their likely performance as salespeople. Lifestyle and activity variables account for less than 2 percent of individual differences in sales performance.

Aptitude Variables	Despite the variety of tests of sales aptitude developed specifically for selecting salespeople, such measures explain an average of only about 4 percent of differences in sales performance. Once again, however, the ability of sales aptitude measures to predict performance varies greatly across different types of sales jobs. We explore this in more detail in the next section of this chapter.

Most tests of general mental aptitude or abilities—such as general intelligence tests, measures of verbal ability and fluency, and tests of math ability—are all relatively uncorrected with sales performance. But a person's ability to think logically and display flexibility in solving problems—an ability measured by tests of cognitive ability—is a relatively good indicator of likely success in selling. Cognitive ability measures explain nearly 7 percent of the variance in performance across salespeople.

Personality Variables	More studies have attempted to explain variations in sales performance across salespeople by examining differences in their personality traits than any other personal characteristic. Also, much of the conventional wisdom adhered to by

sales managers and consultants over the years stressed the importance of such personality traits as self-esteem, sociability, dominance, and a strong need for achievement as determinants of sales success. It is rather disappointing, then, to discover that individual personality traits explain an average of no more than 3 percent of the variation in salespeople's performance. Once again, though, we see later in this chapter that certain personality variables have a stronger relationship with performance in some kinds of selling situations than in others.

Skill Variables   Vocational skills encompass a salesperson's acquired knowledge and abilities directly related to the company, its products, and customers. Not surprisingly, the more skill a salesperson has the better the performance is likely to be. Vocational skills account on average for more than 9 percent of the variance in sales performance. It is also no surprise that differences in salespeople's skill at preparing and delivering good sales presentations can explain as much as 5 percent of the differences in their performance.

A more unexpected finding is that general management skills, such as organizational and leadership abilities, account for about 9 percent of the variance in performance across salespeople. Perhaps this shouldn't come as a surprise, though, given that many field salespeople have much freedom to manage their own time and to organize their own efforts within their territories. Also, some salespeople must work closely and coordinate their efforts with a customer's personnel to carry out such tasks as sales engineering, installation of equipment, and training the customer's employees.

The fact that management skills are related to successful sales performance raises another interesting question. Does the same relationship hold true in the opposite direction? Do successful salespeople necessarily make good sales managers? How to decide who should be promoted into the management ranks is a thorny issue for many companies. We examine it in more detail in Thorny Issues in Sales Management 11.3.

Finally, neither interpersonal skills related to understanding and getting along with people nor the salesperson's vocational esteem—the attitude toward the tasks and activities involved in selling—are strongly related to ultimate sales performance. Both of these findings run counter to the conventional wisdom offered by many authorities.

J OB-SPECIFIC DETERMINANTS OF GOOD SALES PERFORMANCE

Different types of sales jobs require salespeople to perform different tasks and activities under different circumstances. It would seem to make sense, then, to develop task-specific definitions of sales aptitude and ability, since the traits and skills needed to be successful in one type of sales job may be irrelevant to another. As discussed in Chapter 12, this kind of task-specific, or "contingency," approach is the one sales managers *should* use when determining what

Thorny Issues in Sales Management 11 • 3

Deciding Who to Promote into Sales Management

Many firms reward their highest performing salespeople by promoting them into sales management positions. Unfortunately, this sometimes results in the company losing a top-notch salesperson while simultaneously gaining a lousy sales manager. In other words, competence in a selling job is a necessary but not necessarily a sufficient condition for success in sales management. The question, then, is what personal characteristics a firm should look for when deciding which members of its sales force to promote into management.

Unfortunately, no studies have related personal traits or abilities to the relative performance of sales managers. The best we can do is examine the opinions of other sales managers concerning what skills and characteristics are important to look for. The results of a survey of 176 sales executives from a variety of industries are shown in the following table.

Factors Associated with Promotion to Sales Management

Most Important	Least Important
1. Integrity	1. Parent's occupation
2. Dependability	2. Being single
3. Self-motivation	3. Advanced (graduate) degree
4. Positive attitude	4. Upper-management sponsor
5. Good judgment	5. Being married
6. Customer relations	6. Being a workaholic
7. Overall job knowledge	7. Working for successful manager

Note: Results are rank-ordered, with integrity being most important in the survey and parent's occupation being the least important.

Source: Alan J. Dubinsky and Thomas N. Ingram, "Important First-line Sales Management Qualifications: What Sales Executives Think," *Journal of Personal Selling and Sales Management* 3 (May 1983), pp. 18–25.

In the opinion of sales managers, personality traits—such as integrity, dependability, and intrinsic or self-motivation (need for achievement)—are the most important determinants of success among sales managers. However, some respondents noted that factors generally considered less important could, in some cases, be critical for receiving a promotion. For instance, having an upper-management sponsor may be essential for gaining a promotion in some firms, while having

an MBA may enhance promotional opportunities in others.

Keep in mind, though, that the evidence summarized in the table merely represents sales managers' opinions about the characteristics necessary for doing their jobs, opinions that may be inaccurate or self-serving. More objective research is needed to determine what personal traits and abilities differentiate good sales managers from less successful ones.

traits and abilities to look for in new sales recruits. Unfortunately, little published research is available to guide sales managers in deciding what personal characteristics are most important in enabling salespeople to perform well in specific types of sales jobs. Only two published studies have examined this issue across different types of selling jobs.[16] One was carried out as part of the meta-analysis discussed earlier. The other was a survey of a large sample of firms conducted some years ago. Both studies' findings are examined in the following sections.

Selling Different Types of Products and Services

The meta-analysis of previous research discussed in the preceding section found that the strength of the relationships between some personal characteristics and sales performance varied widely across studies. Some of the variation was because different studies examined samples of salespeople engaged in selling different types of products. Thus, a given trait might bear a strong relationship with performance in studies where the respondents were selling industrial goods to organizational customers, but the same trait might have only a weak relationship to performance in studies focused on people selling consumer goods or services.

Overall, seven of the subcategories of personal characteristics described in Exhibit 11.7 were found to be systematically different in their ability to explain variations in sales performance depending on the types of products being sold. Exhibit 11.10 summarizes these seven categories and the strength of their relationship to performance for different types of products.

The findings in Exhibit 11.10 suggest that for people selling industrial goods to institutional customers, "professional" skills and traits—such as sales aptitude, sales presentation skills, interpersonal skills, and self-esteem—are relatively good predictors of successful performance. But for jobs involving the sale of services, such job-related skills appear to be relatively less important. Traits related to aggressiveness and motivation, such as a dominant personality and family obligations, are better indicators of success in selling services than they are for jobs involving either consumer or industrial goods.

Different Types of Sales Jobs

One earlier survey directly compared the characteristics of successful and unsuccessful salespeople in specific sales jobs across a large number of organizations. In this study, responses were obtained from a sample of 1,029 sales executives in a variety of manufacturing, wholesaling, and service firms. These firms were classified according to the type of selling their salespeople were primarily engaged in. The four categories of industrial sales jobs discussed in Chapter 2 were used: (1) trade selling, (2) missionary selling, (3) technical selling, and (4) new business selling. The study then compared personal characteristics of successful and unsuccessful salespeople in each of the four kinds of sales jobs. The results of this survey are summarized in Exhibit 11.11 on page 450 and discussed here.[17]

EXHIBIT 11 • 10 *Strength of Relationships between Selected Personal Characteristics and Salesperson Performance When Selling Different Types of Products* *

Variables Affecting Performance	Type of Product Being Sold		
	Industrial Goods	Consumer Goods	Services†
Personal history and family background	Weak	Weak	Strong
Marital/family status	Weak	Moderate	Strong
Sales aptitude	Strong	Moderate	Weak
Dominance	Weak	Weak	Moderate
Self-esteem	Strong	Moderate	Moderate
Sales presentation skills	Strong	Moderate	Weak
Interpersonal skills	Moderate	Moderate	Weak

*Strong = the variable on average accounts for more than 9 percent of the variance in performance.
Moderate = the variable on average accounts for 4 to 9 percent of the variance in performance.
Weak = the variable on average accounts for less than 4 percent of the variance in performance.

†The services examined in past studies were primarily financial services sold to individual consumers, such as life insurance, banking, and brokerage services.

Source: Neil M. Ford et al. "Selecting Successful Salespeople: A Meta-Analysis of Biographical and Psychological Selection Criteria," in *Review of Marketing*, ed. Michael J. Houston (Chicago: American Marketing Association, 1988), pp. 90–131.

Trade selling

The primary responsibility of the trade sales force is to increase the volume of a firm's sales to its customers (usually wholesalers or retailers). It does this by providing them with merchandising and promotional assistance to help them become more effective at selling to their customers. The trade sales force *sells through,* rather than *sells to,* its customers. Trade selling is common in many industries, but it predominates in such consumer goods fields as food and apparel and in selling to wholesalers in general.

Products sold through trade selling tend to be well established; thus, a company's personal selling effort is often less important than its advertising and promotion efforts. The exception is when a new item is being introduced and the trade must be persuaded to stock it. Trade salespeople are usually not so highly pressured by management as salespeople in other fields, such as new business selling. However, the trade sales job can become dull and repetitious if it involves nothing but stocking shelves or taking orders.

Long-term personal relationships are critical for successful trade selling. The salesperson must have empathy and experience to understand customers. Technical competence is less important than getting along well with customers, and aggressiveness is less important than maturity. Consequently, successful trade salespeople tend to be older on the average than successful salespeople in other types of sales jobs.

EXHIBIT 11 • 11   *Charcteristics Related to Sales Performance in Different Types of Sales Jobs*

Type of Sales Jobs	Relatively Important Characteristics	Relatively Less Important Characteristics
Trade selling	Age, maturity, empathy, knowledge of customer and business methods	Aggressiveness, technical ability, product knowledge persuasiveness
Missionary selling	Youth, high energy and stamina, verbal skill, persuasiveness	Empathy, knowledge of customers, maturity, previous sales experience
Technical selling	Eduation, product and customer knowledge—usually gained through training, intelligence	Empathy, persuasiveness, aggressiveness, age
New business seling	Experience, age and maturity, aggressiveness, persuasiveness, persistence	Customer knowledge, product knowledge, education, empathy

Missionary selling

The primary responsibility of the missionary salesperson is to provide the firm's *direct* customers (wholesalers, retailers) with personal selling assistance. This is done by providing product information to *indirect* customers and persuading them to buy from the firm's direct customers. For example, a brewer's sales rep might call on bar owners and attempt to persuade them to order the company's brand from its local distributor.

Like trade selling, missionary selling is low key and low pressure, but it differs in its primary objective; the missionary force sells for its direct customers, whereas the trade sales force sells through them. This type of selling is common in many industries, particularly foods, pharmaceuticals, chemicals, transportation, and the utilities.

Good coverage of potential indirect customers and the ability to make a succinct, yet persuasive, presentation of product benefits is vitally important in missionary selling. Missionary salespeople tend to be more communicators and persuaders than problem solvers. Consequently, missionary salespeople should be energetic and articulate. They need not be particularly aggressive at closing sales because the people they talk to do not buy directly from them.

Also, while it helps to have a pleasing personality, missionary salespeople need not be particularly empathetic to customers because the development of long-term relationships is not so important. The lack of an opportunity to develop satisfying relationships with customers and the lack of intellectually challenging problem-solving activities are often cited as two unattractive aspects of the missionary sales job. In view of this, successful missionary sales forces tend to consist of young people with the energy and stamina to make a lot of calls. After a few years, such people commonly move into other marketing jobs or more challenging types of sales work.

Technical selling

The major job of the technical sales force is to increase the volume of sales to existing customers by providing them with technical advice and assistance. These salespeople sell directly to the firms that use their products. Technical selling is especially important in industries such as chemicals, machinery, and heavy equipment.

Technical selling is much like management consulting in that the ability to identify, analyze, and solve customer problems is vitally important. Technical competence and knowledge of both product and customer are necessary for such salespeople since they need to discover customer problems and then explain the product's benefits for solving the problems. However, too much aggressiveness can undermine the customer's confidence in the objectiveness of the salesperson. Because of the need for technical competence, the successful technical sales force tends to be relatively young, with a high proportion of recent college graduates. To provide product knowledge, successful firms give technical salespeople extensive training and company support.

New business selling

The primary responsibility of the new business sales force is to seek and persuade new customers to buy from the firm for the first time. Persuasiveness, aggressiveness, and persistence are important attributes for success. The greatest difficulty in new business selling is the frequent rejection, and consequent deflation of the ego, that salespeople experience. Young, inexperienced people typically do not perform well in this kind of selling; they are too easily discouraged and their turnover rate is very high. Consequently, successful new business salespeople tend to be older persons with substantial sales experience. They like the challenge and independence from supervision that goes along with "cold canvassing" potential new accounts.

IMPLICATIONS FOR SALES MANAGEMENT

What has this review of the wisdom accumulated through experience and published research taught us about the personal characteristics that are related to sales aptitude and the potential for selling success? For one thing, no general physical characteristics, mental abilities, or personality traits appear to be consistently related to sales aptitude and performance in all companies and selling situations. Also, the evidence suggests it is probably neither wise nor practical for a sales manager to try to select salespeople with characteristics that match those of their potential customers. (The possible exception is in retail selling.) Instead, the most potentially useful approach to defining sales aptitude and evaluating a person's potential is first to determine the kinds of tasks involved in a specific sales job. Then, one can evaluate the relevance of particular characteristics and abilities for enabling a person to carry out those tasks successfully.

Unfortunately, few published studies have either analyzed the tasks and activities unique to particular types of selling or identified the personal traits and abilities important for success in different sales jobs. For the time being, then, sales executives must develop their own specifications concerning what to look for in new sales recruits. Those specifications should be developed after a careful analysis and description of the tasks and activities involved in selling the firm's products to its target market. There should also be an evaluation of the characteristics and qualifications that new salespeople must have to perform those tasks and activities. Therefore, Chapter 12 examines the methods and procedures involved in sales force recruitment and selection. It begins with a discussion of how to carry out a job analysis and develop a list of qualifications to use in evaluating recruits.

SUMMARY

This chapter, the first of two dealing with salesperson selection, sought to review the evidence regarding what personal and psychological characteristics are related to an individual's likely performance as a salesperson. Personal traits and aptitude are typically thought to place an upper limit on an individual's ability to perform a given sales job.

Several sets of personal factors are thought to affect a salesperson's ability to perform, including the following:

1. **Demographic and physical characteristics**—such as age, sex, and physical appearance.

2. **Background and experience factors**—such as a person's personal history and family background, educational attainment, and sales experience.

3. **Current status and lifestyle variables**—including a person's marital and financial status and activities outside of the job.

4. **Aptitude variables**—enduring mental characteristics such as intelligence, cognitive abilities, and sales aptitude.

5. **Personality traits**—including such characteristics as sociability, dominance, and self-esteem.

6. **Skill levels**—learned proficiencies, such as vocational skills (e.g., product knowledge, etc.), interpersonal skills, sales presentation skills, and general management skills.

Although a number of reasons can be advanced as to why these factors might be related to sales performance, the available evidence suggests that none is consistently related to performance when examined across industries and job settings.

One of the more persuasive reasons for these inconsistent relationships is that particular characteristics of salespeople enable them to deal more effectively with some kinds of customers than with others. Consequently, some studies have used a dyadic approach to explain variations in performance among salespeople. The basic hypothesis is that salespeople are more likely to be successful when they deal with prospects who are similar to themselves in terms of demographic characteristics, personality traits, and attitudes. The implication of the dyadic perspective for sales managers is that they should hire salespeople with characteristics similar to the customers they will call on. But such a strategy can be hard to implement in industrial selling, and it is likely to become even more difficult as both sales recruits and customer organizations become more culturally diverse. Also, the existing research evidence does not consistently support the proposition.

The most important conclusion regarding salespeople selection is that there are many different types of selling jobs. Each type requires the salesperson to perform a variety of different tasks and activities under different circumstances. Consequently, the most useful approach to defining sales aptitude and evaluating a person's potential for future success is, first, to determine the kinds of tasks involved in a specific sales job. Then, one can evaluate the relevance of particular characteristics and abilities for enabling a person to carry out those tasks successfully.

Discussion Questions

1. Mark and Cynthia had just finished a long session that produced a heated discussion concerning hiring people who are overweight. Mark stressed that overweight people are considered lazy, sloppy, and lacking in self-esteem. He insisted no sales manager would overlook these features and hire such a person. "What a waste of money since customers don't want to do business with a tubbo," argued Mark.

   Cynthia countered with equal conviction accusing Mark of stereotyping all people who are overweight. She asked Mark if he knew that for some people the problem was genetic and not overindulgence. "Besides," she stressed, "not hiring someone because of their weight just happens to be illegal." She recited a line from Dickens' *Pickwick Papers,* "You'll find that as you get wider you'll get wiser. Width and wisdom . . . always grows together."

   Is it legal not to hire a person because of his or her weight?

2. An article in *Sales & Marketing Management* (July 1988, p. 80) discusses women in sales. William O'Connell, partner in Personnel Corporation of America, discusses the phenomenal increase of women in sales and attributes part of this increase to the more equitable compensation practices that reward people based on quantitative measures of performance (i.e., sales volume). *S&MM* laments that "women are not enjoying sales success across the board—there is an alarming disparity in their ability to secure sales jobs on an industry basis." O'Connell notes that women are securing jobs where the buyers are predominately female; and where the buyers are predominately male, men are hired. What are the dangers of this situation? Will it lead to a "pink ghetto" in sales for women, similar to the situation where blacks and Hispanics are hired to call only on stores in ghetto neighborhoods?

3. What are the opportunity costs resulting from a firm having a poor recruitment and selection policy? Can these costs be measured?

4. Enthusiasm is one of the more important attributes sales executives look for in new salespeople. How would you measure or determine whether an applicant possessed enthusiasm? If an applicant lacks enthusiasm but shows a positive interest in sales, would it be possible to "teach" enthusiasm?

5. There is evidence that some sales managers prefer to hire tall, good-looking, well-proportioned people for their sales force. How do you justify this practice? Does it constitute discrimination?

6. A study reported in *Sales & Marketing Management* (December 1989, p. 16) notes that: "A very attractive man was likely to receive $2,200 more in starting salary than a man who was not as good looking." What are the implications of this finding? Is it legal to pay attractive people more than those who are considered to be not as attractive? What role should physical appearance play in sales force recruiting?

7. "Sure, I'm willing to hire minorities and women for my sales force," said Marvin C. Procter, "but they'll be treated the same as everybody else; no special training programs or differential treatment." Comment on this statement. Do you agree?

8. The sales manager of a company manufacturing metal castings attempts to hire salespeople based on the personalities of the customers. The sales manager uses the same process when assigning salespeople to customers. In other words, the Evans's similarity hypothesis is being applied. Does this process make sense? Does this procedure agree with Weitz's contingency theory?

9. A few companies have organized their sales forces into two groups. One group calls only on existing customers and the other calls on prospective customers. Are the selling jobs different enough to justify this approach? What differences in traits would you expect to discover between the two groups?

10. The following brief appeared in *Sales & Marketing Management* (February 1987, p. 68):

Selling Is in Their Blood

Some Japanese companies now recruit executives based on their blood type. A new theory suggests that basic personality traits can be linked to the four major blood types. People with Type O are said to be born leaders, Type A are deep thinkers, Type B are creative, and Type AB are problem-solvers. Some job ads now state, "Only those with Type A or B should apply."

What evidence is needed to establish that blood type should be used to determine hiring preferences?

Endnotes

[1]This example is largely based on material found in William Keenan, "Power Selling: America's Best Sales Forces," *Sales & Marketing Management*, September 1991, pp. 41–46.

[2]Arthur Bragg, "Are Good Salespeople Born or Made?" *Sales & Marketing Management*, September 1988, pp. 74–78.
[3]Ibid., p. 74.

[4]Gilbert A. Churchill, Jr., et al., "The Determinants of Salesperson Performance: A Meta-Analysis," *Journal of Marketing Research,* May 1985, pp. 103–18. See also Neil M. Ford et al., "Selecting Successful Salespeople: A Meta-Analysis of Biographical and Psychological Selection Criteria," in *Review of Marketing,* ed. Michael J. Houston (Chicago: American Marketing Association, 1988), pp. 90–131.

[5]"1991 Sales Manager's Budget Planner," *Sales & Marketing Management,* June 17, 1991, p. 77.

[6]Bragg, "Are Good Salespeople Born or Made?" pp. 74–78.

[7]Ford et al., "Selecting Successful Salespeople."

[8]Eleanore Swartz, "Women in Sales: Will the Walls Come Tumbling Down?" *Sales Management,* August 15, 1969, pp. 39–40.

[9]For a detailed review of such issues, see C. David Shepherd and James C. Heartfield, "Discrimination Issues in the Selection of Salespeople: A Review and Managerial Suggestions," *Journal of Personal Selling and Sales Management,* Fall 1991, pp. 67–75.

[10]Bobbi Linkemer, "Women in Sales: What Do They Really Want?" *Sales & Marketing Management,* January 1989, pp. 61–65.

[11]John E. Swan, David R. Rink, G. E. Kiser, and Warren S. Martin, "Industrial Buyer Image of the Saleswoman," *Journal of Marketing,* Winter 1984, pp. 110–16. See also Rayna Skolnik, "A Woman's Place Is on the Salesforce," *Sales & Marketing Management,* April 1, 1985, pp. 34–37; Myron Gable and B. J. Reed, "The Current Status of Women in Professional Selling," *Journal of Personal Selling and Sales Management,* May 1987, pp. 33–39; and Bill Kelley, "Selling in a Man's World," *Sales & Marketing Management,* January 1991, pp. 28–35.

[12]Lucette B. Comer and Marvin A. Jolson, "Perceptions of Gender Stereotypic Behavior: An Exploratory Study of Women in Selling," *Journal of Personal Selling and Sales Management,* Winter 1991, pp. 43–59.

[13]Franklin Evans, "Selling as a Dyadic Relationship—A New Approach," *American Behavioral Scientist,* May 1963, pp. 76–79.

[14]Barton A. Weitz, "Effectiveness in Sales Interactions: A Contingency Framework," *Journal of Marketing,* Winter 1981, pp. 85–103.

[15]Gilbert A. Churchill, Jr., Robert H. Collins, and William A. Strang, "Should Retail Salespersons Be Similar to Their Customers?" *Journal of Retailing,* Fall 1975, pp. 29–42.

[16]While another recent study examines job-specific abilities, it focuses on only one type of sales job—missionary selling. See Dan C. Weilbaker, "The Identification of Selling Abilities Needed for Missionary Type Sales," *Journal of Personal Selling and Sales Management,* Summer 1990, pp. 45–58.

[17]Derek A. Newton, "Get the Most Out of Your Salesforce," *Harvard Business Review,* September–October 1969, pp. 130–43. See also Weilbaker, The Identification of Selling Abilities."

Suggested Readings
Readings concerning the determinants of sales performance

Bragg, Arthur. "Are Good Salespeople Born or Made?" *Sales & Marketing Management,* September 1988, pp. 74–78.

Churchill, Gilbert A., Jr., et al. "The Determinants of Salesperson Performance: A Meta-Analysis." *Journal of Marketing Research,* May 1985, pp. 103–118.

Ford, Neil M., et al. "Selecting Successful Salespeople: A Meta-Analysis of Biographical and Psychological Selection Criteria." In *Review of Marketing,* ed. Michael J. Houston. Chicago: American Marketing Association, 1988, pp. 90–131.

Weilbaker, Dan C. "The Identification of Selling Abilities Needed for Missionary Type Sales." *Journal of Personal Selling and Sales Management,* Summer 1990, pp. 45–58.

Readings concerning women and cultural diversity

Shepherd, C. David, and James C. Heartfield. "Discrimination Issues in the Selection of Salespeople: A Review and Managerial Suggestions." *Journal of Personal Selling and Sales Management*, Fall 1991, pp. 67–75.

Smith, Jeffery D. "Radical Changes in Store for Workforce 2000." *Sales & Marketing Management*, November 1990, pp. 122–23.

Gable, Myron, and B. J. Reed. "The Current Status of Women in Professional Selling." *Journal of Personal Selling and Sales Management*, May 1987, pp. 33–39.

Kelley, Bill. "Selling in a Man's World." *Sales & Marketing Management*, January 1991, pp. 28–35.

Comer, Lucette B., and Marvin A. Jolson. "Perceptions of Gender Stereotypic Behavior: An Exploratory Study of Women in Selling." *Journal of Personal Selling and Sales Management*, Winter 1991, pp. 43–59.

Sales Force Recruitment and Selection

PILOT PEN CORP. BUILDS A NEW SALES FORCE[1]

For decades, Pilot Pen Corp., a subsidiary of Japan's Pilot Corp., relied on manufacturers' reps to sell the firm's writing instruments to commercial stationers, office supply dealers and wholesalers, college bookstores, and variety outlets. While the company's sales had reached $57 million by 1987, Ronald G. Shaw, the firm's president, thought Pilot had gone about as far and fast as it could on the backs of its reps. The reps had grown older and wealthier, he said, and were losing the energy and drive of earlier years. Shaw estimated Pilot was getting only about one eighth of the reps' selling time, and few reps were willing to handle extra sales-building chores such as dropping off new product samples at customer sites. Consequently, the firm decided to replace its 100 manufacturers' reps with a 40-person company sales force to gain increased control over its sales and marketing efforts. As Shaw pointed out, "Control is the key to managing your own future."

Easing Out the Reps

Having reflected on the switch for years, Shaw believed a six-month transition period would be needed to make the change smoothly. His goal was to have a full complement of company salespeople up and running by July 1, 1988.

One of Shaw's chief concerns about the transition was to find a way to ease out the manufacturers' reps without suffering any economic recriminations. He didn't want to create the impression the reps were being replaced because of a failure to deliver the goods, thus damaging their reputations. They had been major contributors to Pilot's rapid growth. And he wanted to make sure the reps would not be so upset with the change that they would damage Pilot's good name and standing, especially among key accounts.

After breaking the news to the reps April 1, Shaw sent letters to all Pilot's customers that announced the change, explaining the reasons for it and emphasizing how the firm could improve its service to clients under the new program. He also stressed the change would occur across the country at the same time, minimizing any adverse effects on individual customers. In addition, he devised a severance package to soften the economic blow to the reps. In return for their agreement not to compete with Pilot for six months, they received a full commission for the first month, gradually declining sums for the next three months, and a full commission for the final month.

Recruiting and Selection Policies

Good planning also helped Pilot through the tricky recruiting and hiring phase of the transition. The firm had already divided the United States into five sales regions with a field sales manager assigned to each to oversee the reps' activities. On May 1, each field manager started recruiting the best sales candidates for the region.

On the basis of a detailed analysis of the firm's marketing strategy and the sales skills and activities necessary to carry out that strategy effectively, Pilot's managers developed selection criteria to evaluate the new recruits. Those criteria were consistent with the firm's mission of being "not the biggest, but the best company in the business." Among other things, the company sought people with substantial office supply sales experience who were highly motivated self-starters, who had a professional appearance and demeanor, and who had a stable work history.

Recruiting began by placing identical want ads in local newspapers. Of the hundreds of applicants in each territory, at least 10 met the basic background requirements. Those people were then subjected to lengthy personal interviews by local sales managers and a battery of tests to further evaluate their personal skills and characteristics.

Training and Motivation

During the planning period, Shaw and his marketing team developed company policy and training manuals for the new recruits. The regional sales managers then used those manuals as a guide during a weeklong classroom training program that concentrated on product knowledge, company policies, reporting and operating procedures, and presentation skills. Then, the field managers accompanied new recruits on their first week of customer calls and on a diminishing proportion of calls during the next month.

To attract the experienced and highly motivated salespeople its strategy demanded, and to keep them fired up after they had joined the company, Pilot offered an attractive combination of salary, benefits, bonuses, and travel incentive contests offering trips to such locales as Monte Carlo and Japan. With average incomes ranging between $38,000 and $42,000 per year, "Our salespeople are earning larger incomes than they ever did." reported Shaw.

Improved Results

Shaw now has Pilot's sales organization under the control he sought for years. He can direct his sales team to focus on projects with longer-term and potentially larger payoffs. For example, not only are his people setting aside one day a month to deliver new product samples, but they are also calling on small-business owners to promote the product line, even though they don't sell directly to such customers. Any orders they take are turned over to Pilot's wholesalers, a step that should strengthen relations with those dealers.

Also, the move has improved the firm's sales efficiency. By eliminating rep commissions, the company cut sales costs by $500,000 through 1990—even while sales were soaring toward $83 million. "Sales came in so fast and at such lower costs," said Shaw, "that I wish I had done this much sooner."

RECRUITMENT AND SELECTION ISSUES

The Pilot Pen example illustrates the variety of important issues that must be resolved when recruiting and selecting new salespeople. Exhibit 12.1 diagrams these issues.

EXHIBIT 12 • 1   *The Decision Process for Recruiting and Selecting Salespeople*

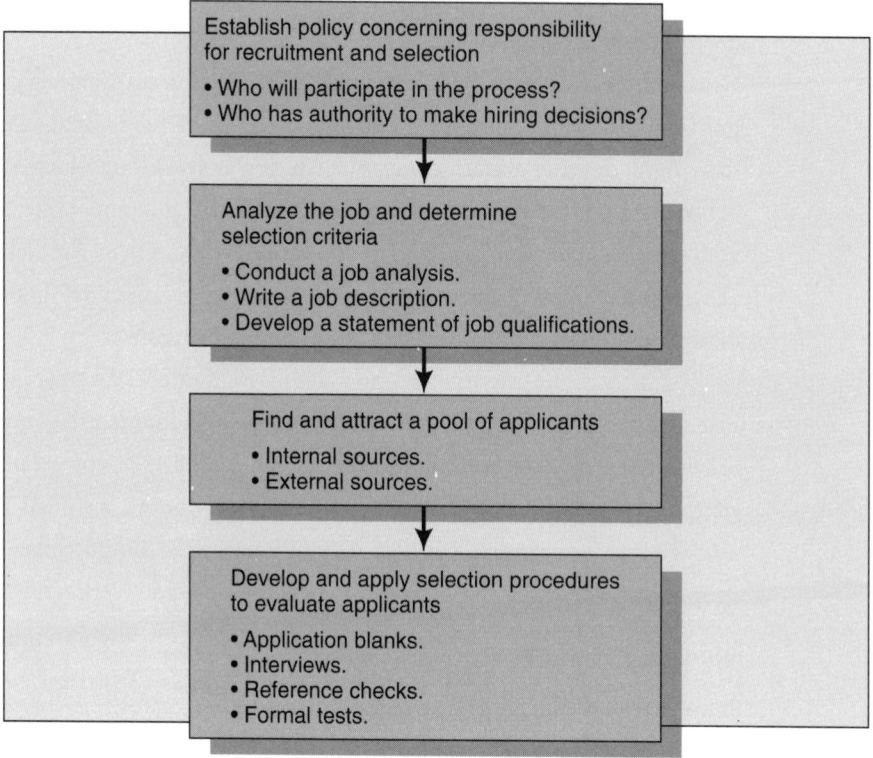

Establish policy concerning responsibility
for recruitment and selection

• Who will participate in the process?
• Who has authority to make hiring decisions?

Analyze the job and determine
selection criteria

• Conduct a job analysis.
• Write a job description.
• Develop a statement of job qualifications.

Find and attract a pool of applicants

• Internal sources.
• External sources.

Develop and apply selection procedures
to evaluate applicants

• Application blanks.
• Interviews.
• Reference checks.
• Formal tests.

The first decision to be made concerns who in the company will be responsible for hiring new salespeople. While it is common to assign this responsibility to field sales managers, as Pilot did, top sales executives or personnel departments play a more active role and bear more of the burden for this important function in some firms.

Regardless of who is responsible for recruitment, certain procedures should be followed to ensure the recruits have the aptitude for the job and the potential to be successful. As discussed in Chapter 11, no general characteristics seem to make people better performers across all types of sales jobs. Therefore, the starting point in the recruitment process should be a thorough analysis of the job to be filled and a description of the qualifications a new hire should have.

The next step is to find and attract a pool of job applicants. The methods used for this should be selective and chosen with an eye to drawing only applicants with the qualifications for which the firm is looking. The objective is not to maximize the number of job applicants but to attract a few *good* applicants because of the high costs of attracting and evaluating candidates. For instance, a large industrial services firm estimates it spent more than $750,000 for want ads, employment agency fees, psychological tests, and the time sales managers spent interviewing and evaluating candidates to hire 50 new salespeople in 1990. And it cost another $1 million to train those new recruits.

The final stage in the hiring process is to evaluate each applicant through personal history information, interviews, reference checks, and formal tests. The purpose is to determine which applicants have the characteristics and abilities most likely to lead to success. During this stage of the evaluation and selection process, managers must be especially careful not to violate equal employment opportunity laws and regulations.

The remaining sections of this chapter discuss the specific methods and procedures managers might use at each stage of the recruitment and selection process. Although the primary focus is on "how to do it" from a manager's point of view, some material in this chapter should be useful for learning what is expected if you ever apply for a sales job.

WHO IS RESPONSIBLE FOR RECRUITING AND SELECTING SALESPEOPLE?

Several years ago, an MBA student at one of the authors' schools was recruited for a sales job with a major manufacturer of outdoor and garden equipment. She was interviewed extensively and "wined and dined," not only by the sales manager, who was her prospective supervisor, but also by higher-level executives in the firm, including the vice president of marketing. All this attention from top-level managers surprised the candidate. "After all," she said, "it's only a sales job. Is it common for so many executives to be involved in recruiting new salespeople?"

The student's question raises the issue of who should have the primary responsibility for recruiting and selecting new salespeople. The way in which a company answers this question typically depends on the size of the sales force and the kind of selling involved. In firms with small sales forces, the top-level sales manager commonly views the recruitment and selection of new people as a primary responsibility. In larger, multilevel sales forces, however, the job of attracting and choosing new recruits is usually too extensive and time-consuming for a single executive. In such firms, authority for recruitment and selection is commonly delegated to lower-level sales managers.

In companies where the sales job is not very difficult or complex, new recruits do not need any special qualifications, and turnover rates in the sales force are high—as in firms that sell consumer goods door to door—first-level sales managers often have sole responsibility for hiring. When a firm must be more selective in choosing new recruits with certain qualifications and abilities, however, a recruiting specialist may assist first-level managers in evaluating new recruits and making hiring decisions. These staff positions are usually filled by sales managers who are being groomed for higher-level executive positions.

In some firms, members of the personnel department assist and advise sales managers in hiring new salespeople instead of assigning such duties to a member of the sales management staff. This approach helps reduce duplication of effort and avoids friction between the sales and personnel departments. One disadvantage is that personnel specialists may not be as knowledgeable about the job to be filled and the qualifications necessary as a member of the sales management staff. When the personnel department is involved in sales recruiting and hiring, it usually helps to attract applicants and aid in evaluating them. The sales manager, however, typically has the final responsibility for deciding whom to hire.

Finally, when the firm sees its sales force as a training ground for sales and marketing managers, either personnel executives or other top-level managers may participate in recruiting to ensure the new hirees have management potential. This was the situation in the firm that interviewed our MBA student. Although they wanted to hire her for "just a sales job," company executives saw that job as a stepping-stone to management responsibilities.

JOB ANALYSIS AND DETERMINATION OF SELECTION CRITERIA

Research relating salespeople's personal characteristics to sales aptitude and job performance suggests there is no single set of traits and abilities sales managers can use as criteria in deciding what kind of recruits to hire. Different sales jobs require the performance of different activities, and this suggests people with different personality traits and abilities should be hired to fill them. The first activities in the recruitment and selection process thus should be the following:

1. *Conduct a job analysis* to determine what activities, tasks, responsibilities, and environmental influences are involved in the job to be filled.
2. *Write a job description* that details the findings of the job analysis.
3. *Develop a statement of job qualifications* that determines and describes the personal traits and abilities a person should have to perform the tasks and responsibilities involved in the job.

Job Analysis and Description

Most companies—particularly larger ones—have written job descriptions for sales force positions. Unfortunately, often those job descriptions are out of date and do not accurately reflect the current scope and content of the positions. The responsibilities of a given sales job change as the customers, the firm's account management policies, the competition, and other environmental factors change. But firms often do not conduct new analyses and prepare updated descriptions to reflect those changes. Also, firms create new sales positions, and the tasks to be accomplished by people in these jobs may not be spelled out. Consequently, a critical first step in the hiring process is for management to make sure the job to be filled has been analyzed *recently* and the findings have been *written* out in *great detail*. Without such a detailed and up-to-date description, the sales manager will have more difficulty deciding what kind of person is needed. In addition, prospective recruits will not really know for what position they are applying.

Who conducts the analysis and prepares the description?

In some firms, analyzing and describing sales jobs are assigned to someone in sales management. In other firms, the task is assigned to a job analysis specialist, who is either someone from the company's personnel department or an outside consultant. Regardless of who is responsible for analyzing and describing the various selling positions within a company, however, it is important that person collect information about the job's content from two sources: (1) the current occupants of the job, and (2) the sales managers who supervise the people in the job.

Current job occupants should be observed and/or interviewed to determine what they actually do. Sales managers at various levels should be asked what they think the job occupant should be doing in view of the firm's strategic sales program and account management policies. It is not uncommon for the person who analyzes a job to discover the salespeople are doing things management is not aware of and they are "slacking off" on some activities management believes are important. Such misunderstandings and inaccurate role perceptions illustrate the need for accurate and detailed job descriptions.[2]

Job descriptions written to reflect a consensus between salespeople and their managers concerning what a job should entail can serve several useful functions in addition to guiding the firm's recruiting efforts. They can guide the design of a sales training program that will provide new salespeople with the skills to do their job effectively and that will improve their understanding of how the job should be done. Similarly, detailed job descriptions can serve as standards for evaluating each salesperson's job performance, as discussed in Chapter 18.

Content of the job description

Good descriptions of sales jobs typically cover the following job dimensions and requirements:

1. The *nature of product(s) or service(s)* to be sold.
2. The *types of customers* to be called on, including the policies concerning the frequency with which calls are to be made and the types of personnel within customer organizations who should be contacted (e.g., buyers, purchasing agents, plant supervisors).

3. The *specific tasks and responsibilities* to be carried out, including planning tasks, research and information collection activities, specific selling tasks, other promotional duties, customer servicing activities, and clerical and reporting duties.

4. The *relationships between the job occupant and other positions* within the organization. To whom does the job occupant report? What are the sales-person's responsibilities to the immediate superior? How and under what circumstances does the salesperson interact with members of other departments, such as production or engineering?

5. The *mental and physical demands* of the job, including the amount of technical knowledge the salesperson should have concerning the company's products, other necessary skills, and the amount of travel involved.

6. The *environmental pressures and constraints* that might influence performance of the job, such as market trends, the strengths and weaknesses of the competition, the company's reputation among customers, and resource and supply problems.

An example of a job description that addresses most of these job dimensions is presented in Exhibit 12.2.

Determining Job Qualifications and Selection Criteria

Determining the qualifications a prospective employee should have to perform a given sales job is the most difficult part of the recruitment and selection process. The sales manager—perhaps with assistance from a manpower planning specialist or a vocational psychologist from the firm's personnel department—should consider the relative importance of all the personal traits and characteristics discussed previously. These include physical attributes, mental abilities and experience, and personality traits.

The problem is that nearly all these characteristics are of at least some importance in choosing new salespeople. No firm, for instance, would actively seek sales recruits who are unintelligent or lacking in self-confidence. It is unlikely that many job candidates will possess high levels of all these desirable characteristics. The task, then, is to decide which traits and abilities are most important in qualifying an individual for a particular job and which are less critical. Also, some thought should be given to trade-offs among the qualification criteria. Will a person with a deficiency on one important attribute still be considered acceptable if he has outstanding qualities in other areas? For example, will the firm be willing to hire someone with only average verbal ability and persuasiveness if that person has an extremely high degree of ambition and persistence?

Methods for deciding on selection criteria

Decisions about the qualifications that should be looked for in selecting new employees can often be made by simply *examining the job description*. If the job requires extensive travel, for instance, management might look for applicants who are young, have few family responsibilities, and want to travel. Similarly, statements in the job description concerning technical knowledge and skill can help management determine the educational background and previous job experience to look for when selecting hirees.

Most larger firms go one step further and *evaluate the personal histories of their existing salespeople* to determine what characteristics differentiate between good and poor performers. As seen in Chapter 11, this analysis seldom produces consistent results across different jobs and different companies. It can produce useful insight, however, when applied to a single type of sales job within a single firm.

Current sales employees might be divided into two groups according to their level of performance on the job—one group of high performers and one group of low performers. The characteristics of the two groups can be compared on the basis of information from job application forms, records of personal interviews and intelligence, aptitude, and personality test scores. Alternatively, statistical techniques might be used to look for significant correlations between variations in the personal characteristics of current salespeople and variations in their job performance. In either case, management attempts to identify personal attributes that differ significantly between high-performing and low-performing salespeople. The assumption is that there may be a cause-and-effect relationship between such attributes and job performance. If new employees are selected who have attributes similar to those of people who are currently performing the job successfully, they also may be successful.[3]

In addition to improving management's ability to specify relevant criteria in selecting new salespeople, a firm should conduct a personnel history analysis for another compelling reason. Such analyses are necessary to validate the selection criteria the firm is using, as required by government regulations on equal employment opportunity in hiring. This issue is discussed later in this chapter.

Besides comparing the characteristics of good and poor performers in a particular job, management might also try to *analyze the unique characteristics of employees who have failed*—people who either quit or were fired. One consulting firm, the Klein Institute for Aptitude Testing, suggests that the following characteristics are frequently found among salespeople who fail:

1. Instability of residence.

2. Failure in business within the past two years.

3. Unexplained gaps in the person's employment record.

4. Recent divorce or marital problems.

5. Excessive personal indebtedness; for example, bills could not be paid within two years from earnings on the new job.

The firm might attempt to identify such characteristics among its own sales failures by conducting exit interviews with all salespeople who quit or are

EXHIBIT 12 • 2   *Job Description*

JOB TITLE SALES REPRESENTATIVE	JOB CODE
ESTABLISHMENT—DEPARTMENT MARKETING BD SALES	DATE

Function

Promotes and consummates the sale of office systems and related equipment, paper, accessories, and other supplies within an assigned geographic territory, for the Business Division.

Major Activities

A. Establishes and maintains close liaison between the company and customers within an assigned geographic territory, for the ultimate purpose of selling Business Division products.

B. Establishes and maintains a working rapport with customers by providing expertise in the analysis of systems problems and the application of BD products and services to the solution of these problems.

C. Provides service to customers by recommending changes in operating procedures, assisting them in planning for office systems applications, recommending equipment purchases and supervising their installation, suggesting methods of quality control, and checking to determine that equipment and systems function properly.

D. Provides accurate and timely information on office products and demonstrates to customers the benefits derived from utilizing these products in his or her business. Keeps customers and prospects updated on new products and office systems.

E. Assists customers in achieving the high-quality capabilities of the company's office products.

F. Prepares a variety of reports and correspondence including data reports on activities, expenses, market acceptance of office products, product problems, market needs, etc.

G. Studies customers' systems needs and formulates written proposals to satisfy these with the general philosophies established by BD. Outlines systems recommendations incorporating products in customer proposals, cites advantages and operating cost reductions resulting from the proposed system.

H. Maintains a thorough familiarity of the products of other manufacturers to deal with questions posed by customers and prospects in daily activities.

I. Participates in and/or originates customer seminars and education programs by instructing customers and their personnel in the capabilities of office systems and the proper application and operation of BD products. Provides information and assistance at trade shows and exhibits to interested persons.

J. Keeps abreast of the new developments and trends in office equipment and systems to be capable of understanding customer needs and to be better prepared to provide workable solutions to customer systems requirements.

K. Handles product complaints and makes recommendations to the marketing center regarding goodwill replacements of products.

L. Advises district, and/or regional, and/or BD management of any information pertinent to BD activities gathered as a result of observations made in the field. Reports include new systems applications, activities of other manufacturers, equipment modifications and improvements, customer needs, etc.

M. Follows up on all sales leads as quickly as possible. Makes new calls on potential customers to stimulate interest in BD products.

N. Plans activities in a manner that provides for adequate territory coverage. Allocates time on the basis of maximum potential yield and/or priorities established by the district sales manager.

E X H I B I T 12 • 2   *(concluded)*

Scope of the Position

A. Accountability

  1. Reports to the district sales manager of the marketing center to which assigned. May direct the activities of less experienced sales representatives assigned to assist on a project basis or for training and development purposes.

  2. Responsible for reviewing unusual complex and/or sensitive problems proposals, or controversial matters with supervision before taking any action. Manages the assigned territory with considerable independence.

  3. The assigned territory is in the middle range in relation to others in the region in overall dollar accountability, and/or customers have complex installations with sophisticated systems and product applications with which the sales representative must be familiar.

  4. Responsible for having a thorough knowledge of all BD products and services and is capable of effectively analyzing, from a systems viewpoint, customers' problems and needs in developing new business by demonstrating the capabilities of Business Division products to satisfy these needs.

  5. Is capable of independently meeting expected sales goals for all categories of products in the assigned territories.

  6. Responsible for submitting knowledgeable reports on emerging trends in the marketplace, market needs, and ideas for new products that demonstrate a thorough understanding of the company's position in the marketplace and the direction it must pursue to maintain and improve this position.

  7. Shows increasing expertise and professionalism in customer contracts, diagnosis of customers needs, analysis of systems, preparation and presentation of proposals for new systems based on sound economic evaluations.

  8. Is expected to exhibit maturity and competence in running the assigned territory with a minimum of direction. Has demonstrated the ability of developing large accounts, multiple sales, etc.

B. Innovation

  1. Has a thorough understanding of the capabilities of other manufacturers' product and effectively uses this information to serve customers' needs.

  2. Demonstrates originality and creativity in solving systems problems and meeting needs of the market.

  3. Responsible for consistently aiding customers by disseminating information on new methods, systems, and techniques that are applicable to their operations.

Job Knowledge

A. Has a college degree or the equivalent in applicable training and experience.

B. Requires completion of the basic BD training program.

C. Requires a thorough knowledge of all billing, credit, and distribution procedures, paperwork, and policies and is capable of resolving complex problems in these areas with a minimum of confusion, frustration, and inconvenience for all parties concerned.

D. This level of activity is generally achieved with four years' selling experience, or the equivalent, with the assigned products where the individual is subjected to all types of problems and challenges covering the entire product line.

WRITTEN BY	APPROVED	DATE	APPROVED	DATE

fired. Although this sounds like a good idea, it seldom works well in practice. Salespeople who quit are often reluctant to discuss the real reasons for leaving a job, and people who are fired are not likely to cooperate in any research that will be of value to their former employer. However, some useful information about ex-salespeople can often be obtained from the application forms and test scores recorded when they were hired. They may also have spoken with the managers who were their supervisors at the time they left the company.

On the basis of these kinds of information, a written statement of job qualifications should be prepared that is specific enough to guide the selection of new salespeople. These qualifications can then be reflected in the forms and tests used in the selection process, such as the interview form in Exhibit 12.3.[4]

RECRUITING APPLICANTS

Some firms do not actively recruit salespeople. They simply choose new employees from applicants who come to them and ask for work. Although this may be a satisfactory policy for a few well-known firms with good products, strong positions in the market, and attractive compensation policies, today's labor market makes such an approach unworkable for most companies.

Firms that seek well-educated people for industrial sales jobs must compete with many other occupations in attracting such individuals. To make matters worse, people with no selling experience often tend to have negative attitudes toward sales jobs. Also, the kinds of people who do seek employment in sales often do not have the qualifications a firm is looking for, particularly when the job involves relatively sophisticated selling, such as technical or new business sales. Consequently, the company may have to evaluate many applicants to find one qualified person.

This is one area where some firms are "penny-wise but pound-foolish." They attempt to hold down recruiting costs on the assumption that a good training program can convert marginal recruits into solid sales performers. As we saw in the last chapter, however, some of the determinants of sales success, such as aptitude and personal characteristics, are difficult or impossible to change through training or experience. Therefore, spending the money and effort to find well-qualified candidates can be a profitable investment.[5]

In view of the difficulties in attracting qualified people to fill sales positions, a well-planned and effectively implemented recruiting effort is usually a crucial part of the firm's hiring program. The primary objective of the recruiting process should not be to maximize the total number of job applicants. Too many recruits can overload the selection process, forcing the manager to use less thorough screening and evaluation procedures. Besides, numbers do not ensure quality. The focus should not be on how many recruits can be found, but on finding a few *good* ones.

Therefore, the recruiting process should be designed to be the first step in the selection process. Self-selection by the prospective employees is the most

EXHIBIT 12 ● 3

Business Division
Applicant Interview Form

Applicant name: _____ Date:_____

Interview with: Time

1. _____   _____

2. _____   _____

3. _____   _____

4. _____   _____

Rating:
5—Excellent
4—Above average
3—Average
2—Fair
1—Poor

Directions: Check square that most correctly reflects characteristics applicable to candidate. An outstanding
candidate would score 95 to 100.

	1	2	3	4	5

General appearance

1. Neatness, dress
2. Business image

Impressions

3. Positive mannerisms
4. Speech, expressions
5. Outgoing personality
6. Positive attitude

Potential sales ability

7. Persuasive communication
8. Aggressiveness
9. Sell and manage large accounts
10. Make executive calls
11. Organize and manage a territory
12. Work with others
13. Successful prior experience
14. Potential for career growth

Maturity

15. General intelligence, common sense
16. Self-confidence
17. Self-motivation, ambition
18. Composure, stability
19. Adaptability
20. Sense of ethics

General comments: _____

_____

Overall rating (total score): _____

Would you recommend this candidate for the position? _____

Why or why not? _____

efficient means of selection. The recruiting effort should be implemented in a way that discourages unqualified people from applying. To accomplish this, recruiting communications should point out both the attractive and unattractive aspects of the job to be filled, spell out the qualifications, and state the likely compensation. This will help ensure that only qualified and interested people apply for the job. Also, recruiting efforts should be focused only on sources of potential applicants where fully qualified people are most likely to be found.

Sales managers can go to a number of places to find recruits or leads concerning potential recruits. *Internal sources* consist of other people already employed in other departments within the firm and *external sources,* include people in other firms (who are often identified and referred by current members of the sales force), educational institutions, advertisements, and employment agencies.

Each source is likely to produce candidates with somewhat different backgrounds and characteristics. Therefore, while most firms seek recruits from more than one source, a company's recruiting efforts should be concentrated on sources that are most likely to produce the kinds of people needed. A recent survey of 113 firms found that companies use different sources for finding recruits depending on the type of sales job they are trying to fill. When the job involves missionary or trade selling, firms rely most heavily on a variety of external sources, such as advertisements, employment agencies, and educational institutions. When the job involves technical selling requiring substantial product knowledge and industry experience, firms focus more heavily on employees in other departments within the company and on personal referrals of people working for other firms in the industry.[6] The relative advantages and limitations of each of these sources of new recruits are discussed in more depth in the following sections.

Internal Sources—People within the Company

People in nonsales departments within the firm, such as manufacturing, maintenance, engineering, or the office staff, sometimes have latent sales talent and are a common source of sales recruits. Past surveys suggest more than half of U.S. industrial goods producers hire at least some of their salespeople from other internal departments.

Recruiting current company employees for the sales force has distinct advantages:

1. Company employees have established performance records, and they are more of a known quantity than outsiders.

2. Recruits from inside the firm should require less orientation and training because they are already familiar with the company's products, policies, and operations.

3. Recruiting from within can bolster company morale as employees become aware that opportunities for advancement are available outside of their own departments or divisions.

E X H I B I T **12 • 4**   *External Source of Sales Recruits*

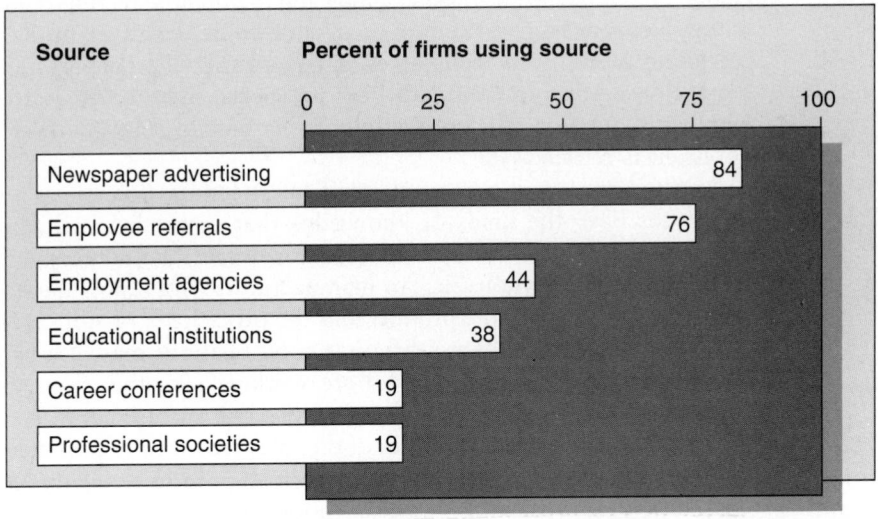

Source	Percent of firms using source
Newspaper advertising	84
Employee referrals	76
Employment agencies	44
Educational institutions	38
Career conferences	19
Professional societies	19

Source: *Recruiting and Selection Procedures,* Personnel Policies Forum Survey No. 146, pp. 7, 9 (May 1988). Copyright 1989 by the Bureau of National Affairs, Inc.

To facilitate successful internal recruiting, the company's personnel department should always be kept abreast of sales staff needs. Because the personnel staff is familiar with the qualifications of all employees and continuously evaluates their performance, they are in the best position to identify people with the attributes necessary to fill available sales jobs.

Internal recruiting has some limitations. People in nonsales departments seldom have much previous selling experience. Also, internal recruiting can cause some animosity within the firm if supervisors of other departments think their best employees are being pirated by the sales force.

External Sources

Although it is often a good idea to start with internal sources when recruiting new salespeople, there may not be enough qualified internal candidates to meet the human resource needs of a firm's sales force. At this time, the search is expanded to cover external sources. Exhibit 12.4 lists a number of commonly used external sources of sales recruits along with the percent of firms that use each source.

Referral of people in other firms

In addition to being potential sales employees themselves, company personnel can provide management with leads to potential recruits from outside the firm. Current salespeople are in a good position to provide their superiors with leads to new recruits. They know the requirements of the job, they often have contacts with other salespeople who may be willing to change jobs, and they can do much to help "sell" an available job to potential recruits. Consequently, many sales managers make sure their salespeople are aware of the company's recruiting needs. Some companies, such as IBM, offer bonuses as incentives for their salespeople to recruit new prospects. Such referrals from current employees must be handled tactfully so as not to cause hard feelings if the applicant is rejected later.

Customers can also be a source of sales recruits. Sometimes a customer's employees have the kinds of knowledge that make them attractive as prospective salespeople. For instance, department store employees can make good salespeople for the wholesalers or manufacturers who supply the store because they are familiar with the product and the procedures of store buyers.

Customers with whom a firm has good relations may also provide leads concerning potential recruits who are working for other firms, particularly competitors. Purchasing agents know what impresses them in a salesperson, they are familiar with the abilities of the sales reps who call on them, and they are sometimes aware when a sales rep is interested in changing jobs.

The question of whether a firm should recruit salespeople from its competitors, however, is controversial. Such people are knowledgeable about the industry from their experience. They also might be expected to "bring along" some of their current customers when they switch companies. This does not happen frequently, however, since customers are usually more loyal to a supplier than to the individual who represents that supplier.

On the other side of the argument, it is sometimes difficult to get salespeople who have worked for a competing firm to unlearn old practices and to conform to their new employer's account management policies. Also, some managers think recruiting a competitor's personnel is unethical. They believe it is unfair for firm B to recruit *actively* someone from firm A after A has spent the money to hire and train that person. Such people may be in a position to divulge A's company secrets to B. Consequently, some firms refuse to recruit their competitor's salespeople, although whether such policies are due to high ethical standards, the expense of retraining, or fear of possible retaliation is open to question.

Advertisements

A less selective means of attracting job applicants is to advertise the available position. When a technically qualified or experienced person is needed, an ad might be placed in an industry trade or technical journal. More commonly, advertisements are placed in the personnel or marketplace sections of local newspapers to attract applicants for relatively less demanding sales jobs where special qualifications are not required. A well-written ad can be very effective for attracting applicants. As suggested, however, this is not necessarily a good thing. When a firm's advertisements attract large numbers of applicants who

Thorny Issues in Sales Management 12 • 1

The Use of "Open" Versus "Blind" Ads to Recruit Sales Applicants

How much information about the company and the available sales job should a firm include in its recruiting ads? Many sales managers argue that "open" ads, which disclose the firm's name, product to be sold, compensation, and specific job duties (see example A below) generate a more select pool of high quality applicants, lower selection costs, and decreased turnover rates than ads without such information. Open ads also avoid any ethical questions concerning possible deception.

However, for less attractive, high-turnover sales jobs, such as door-to-door selling, some sales managers prefer "blind" ads like example B below.

These maximize the number of applicants and give the manager an opportunity to explain the attractive features of the job in a personal meeting with the applicant. One study found that a blind ad for a low-skilled, door-to-door sales position produced three times more applicants than an open ad for the same position. Consequently, the number of successful salespeople hired per ad was higher for the blind compared to the open ad, although selection costs were also higher. In general, though, blind ads are much less attractive when a firm must be selective in recruiting and hiring people who meet a detailed set of job qualifications.

A. Example of an "Open," Full-Disclosure Newspaper Recruitment Ad

> **SALES ENGINEER**
>
> Responsible for the sale of highly engineered materials and components to electronic, computer, and other original equipment manufacturers. Seeks new product opportunities and new applications for present products. BSEE or the equivalent in a combination of schooling and experience, plus 2 years experience in applications engineering or technical sales. Salary plus commission guaranteed in the first year. Car and expenses provided. Will be located in Minneapolis. Send resume, salary history and requirements to: L. D. Schultz, Corporate Personnel Director, Kennesaw Corp., Kennesaw, AL 21940.
>
> Equal Opp. Employer M/F

B. Example of a "Blind" Newspaper Recruitment Ad

> SALES, national company needs 4 salespersons. High income, local territory, paid insurance, fringe benefits. We train. Phone Employment Manager, 689-4112.

Sources: Marvin A. Jolson, "A Comparison of Blind vs. Full-Disclosure Ads for Sales Personnel," *Akron Business and Economic Review* 5 (Winter 1974), pp. 16–18; and Marianne Matthews, "If Your Ads Aren't Pulling Top Sales Talent . . . " *Sales & Marketing Management*, February 1990, pp. 73–79.

are unqualified or only marginally interested, the firm must engage in extensive and costly screening and selection to "separate the wheat from the chaff."[7]

If a firm does use newspaper advertising in recruiting, it must decide how much information about the job should be included in its ads. The arguments concerning the relative merits of "open" versus "blind" recruiting ads—and the conditions where each may be appropriate—are discussed in Thorny Issues in Sales Management 12.1.

Employment agencies

Employment agencies are sometimes used to find recruits, usually for more routine sales jobs such as retail and door-to-door sales. However, some agencies specialize in finding applicants for more demanding sales jobs. Some sales managers have had unsatisfactory experiences with employment agencies. They charge that agencies are sometimes overzealous in attempting to earn their fees, and they tend to send applicants who do not meet the job qualifications. Consequently, many firms turn to employment agencies only as a last resort.

Others argue, however, that when a firm has problems with an employment agency, it is often the fault of the company for not understanding the agency's role and not providing sufficient information about the kinds of recruits it is seeking. When a firm carefully selects an agency with a good reputation, establishes a long-term relationship, and provides detailed descriptions of job qualifications, the agency can perform a valuable service. It locates and screens job applicants and reduces the amount of time and effort the company's sales managers must devote to recruiting.

Educational institutions

College and university placement offices are a common source of recruits for firms that require salespeople with sound mental abilities or technical backgrounds. They are used particularly when the sales job is viewed as a first step toward a career in management. College graduates are often more socially poised than people of the same age without college training, and good grades are at least some evidence the person can think logically, budget time efficiently, and communicate reasonably well.

But college graduates seldom have much selling experience, and they are likely to require more extensive orientation and training in the basics of salesmanship. Also, college-educated sales recruits have a reputation for "job hopping," unless their jobs are challenging and promotions are rapid. One insurance company, for instance, stopped recruiting college graduates when it found that such recruits did not stay with their jobs very long. Such early turnover is sometimes more the fault of the company than of the recruits. When recruiters paint an unrealistic picture of the job demands and rewards of the position to be filled, or when they recruit people who are overqualified for the job, high turnover is often the result.[8]

Junior colleges and vocational schools are another source of sales recruits that has expanded rapidly in recent years. Many such schools have programs explicitly designed to prepare people for selling careers. Thus, firms that recruit the graduates of such programs do not have to contend with the negative attitudes toward selling they sometimes encounter in four-year college graduates. Junior colleges and vocational schools are particularly good sources of recruits for sales jobs that require reasonably well-developed mental and communications abilities, but where advanced technical knowledge or a four-year degree is not essential.

SELECTION PROCEDURES

After the qualifications necessary to fill a job have been determined and some applicants have been recruited, the final task is to determine which applicants best meet the qualifications and have the greatest aptitude for the job. To gain the information needed to evaluate each prospective employee, firms typically use some combination of the following selection tools and procedures.[9]

1. Application blanks.
2. Personal interviews.
3. Reference checks.
4. Physical examinations.
5. Psychological tests.
    a. Intelligence.
    b. Personality.
    c. Aptitude/skills.

A meta-analysis of past research studies that have examined the use of these selection tools found that—on average across all occupations—composites of psychological test scores have the greatest predictive validity for evaluating a potential employee's future job performance, whereas evaluations based on personal interviews have the lowest. In other words, test scores have the highest correlations with candidates' subsequent performance on the job, with an average correlation coefficient of 0.53. Thus, test scores account for about 28 percent of the variance in subsequent performance across hirees. Ratings based on personal interviews, on the other hand, have an average correlation of only 0.14 with (and account for only about 2 percent of variance in) subsequent performance.[10] These findings are shown in more detail in Exhibit 12.5. A bit surprising, though, is that the frequency with which firms actually use the various selection tools for evaluating potential salespeople is not consistent with the demonstrated validity of those tools. As Exhibit 12.6 indicates, a survey of selection procedures followed by 121 industrial firms suggests personal interviews are almost universally employed while psychological tests are the least used selection tools. However, large firms are somewhat more thorough in their use of psychological tests—and the development of detailed job descriptions—than smaller firms.

Why do many firms avoid selection tools that appear to be valid predictors

E X H I B I T   1 2 • 5   *Predictive Validity of Various Selection Criteria*

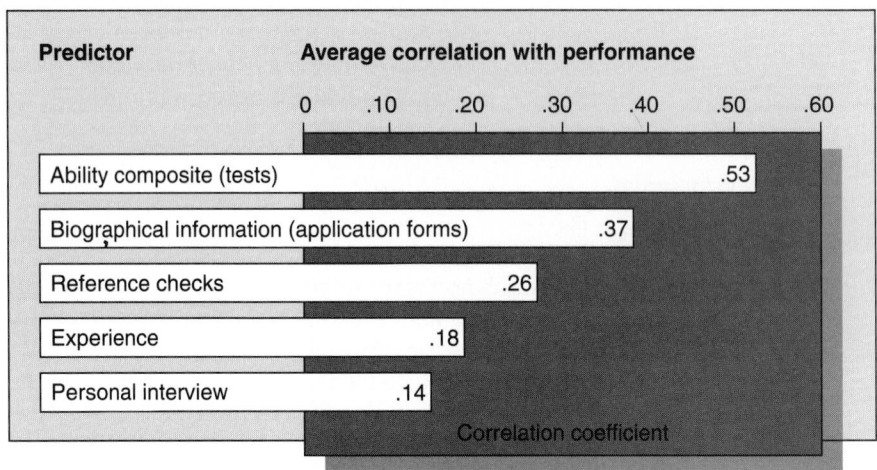

of a candidate's future success while relying on tools with less predictive validity? Some of the practical advantages and limitations of the various tools—and some possible reasons for managers' reluctance to use psychological tests—are discussed in the remaining sections of this chapter.

Application Blanks

Although professional salespeople often have résumés to submit to prospective employers, many personnel experts believe a standard company application form makes it easier to assess applicants. A well-designed application blank helps ensure that the same information is obtained in the same form from all candidates.

The primary purpose of the application form is to collect information about the recruit's physical characteristics and personal history. Forms typically ask for facts about the candidate's physical condition, family status, education, business experience, military service, participation in social organizations, and outside interests and activities. This information can be reviewed to determine whether the applicant is qualified for the job on such dimensions as education and experience.

A second function of the application form is to help managers prepare for personal interviews with job candidates. Often a recruit's responses to items on the application form raise questions that should be explored during an interview. If the application shows that a person has held several jobs within the past few years, for example, the interviewer should attempt to find out the reasons for these changes. Perhaps the interviewer can determine whether the

EXHIBIT 12 • 6   *Percentage of Small and Large Firms that "Extensively Use" Various*
Tools for Selecting Salespeople

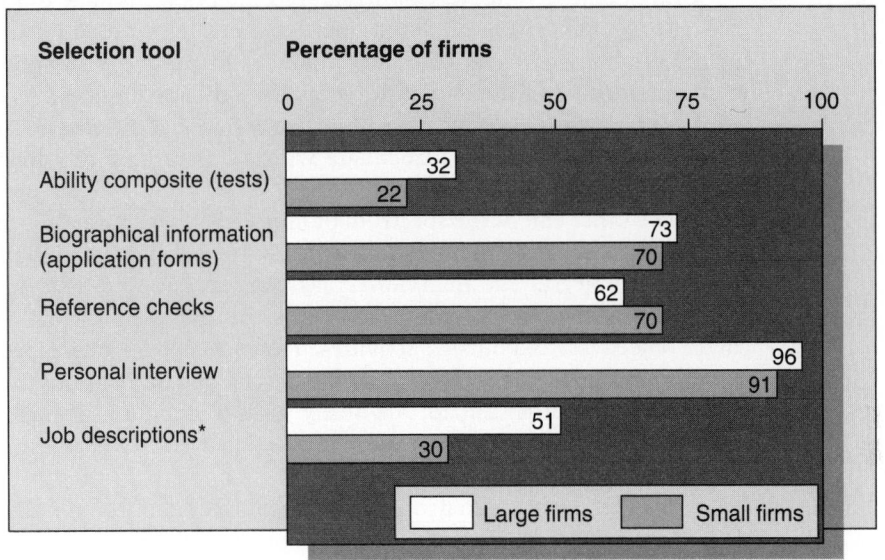

*A statistically significant difference ($p < 0.05$) exists between the percentage of small and large firms that "extensively use" this sales management tool. In this survey, *small* firms were defined as those with annual sales of less than $40 million ($n = 74$), and *large* firms were those with sales over $40 million ($r = 47$)

Source: Alan J. Dubinsky and Thomas E. Barry, "A Survey of Sales Management Practices," *Industrial Marketing Management* 11 (1982), p. 136.

applicant is a "job hopper" who is unlikely to stay with the company very long.

Personal Interviews

In addition to probing deeper into the applicant's history, personal interviews enable managers to gain insight into the applicant's mental abilities and personality. An interview provides a manager with the opportunity to assess a candidate's communication skills, intelligence, sociability, aggressiveness, empathy, ambition, and other traits related to the qualifications necessary for the job. Different managers use many different interviewing approaches to accomplish these objectives. These methods of conducting personal interviews, however, can all be classified as either structured or unstructured.

In *structured interviews*, each applicant is asked the same predetermined questions. This approach is particularly good when the interviewer is inexperienced at evaluating candidates. The standard questions help guide the interview and ensure that all factors relevant to the candidate's qualifications are covered. Also, asking the same questions of all candidates makes it easier to compare their strengths and weaknesses. To facilitate such comparisons, many firms use a standard interview evaluation form on which interviewers rate each applicant's response to each question together with their overall impressions of the candidate.

One potential weakness of structured interviews is that the interviewer may rigidly stick to the prepared questions and fail to identify or probe the unique qualities or flaws of each candidate. In practice, though, structured interviews are often not so inflexible as the criticism implies. As a manager gains interviewing experience, she often learns to ask additional questions when an applicant's response is inadequate without disturbing the flow of the interview.[11]

At the other end of the spectrum of interviewing techniques is the *unstructured interview*. Such interviews seek to get the applicant talking freely on a variety of subjects. The interviewer asks only a few questions to direct the conversation to topics of interest, such as the applicant's work experiences, career objectives, and outside activities. The rationale for this approach is that significant insights into the applicant's character and motivations can be gained by allowing the applicant to talk freely with a minimum of direction. Also, the interviewer is free to spend more time on topics where the applicant's responses are interesting or unusual.

Successful, unstructured interviewing requires interviewers with experience and interpretive skills. Because there is no predetermined set of questions, there is always a danger that the interviewer will neglect some relevant topics. It is also more difficult to compare the responses of two or more applicants. Consequently, since most firms' sales managers have relatively little experience as interviewers, structured interviews are much more common in selecting new salespeople than unstructured approaches.

Within the interview itself, particularly those that are relatively unstructured, some sales managers use additional techniques to learn as much as possible about the applicant's character and aptitude. One such technique is the *stress interview*. The interviewer puts the applicant under stress in one of many ways, ranging from silence or rudeness on the part of the interviewer to constant, aggressive probing and questioning. The rationale for this technique is that the interviewer may learn how the applicant will respond to and deal with the stress encountered in selling situations.

Another approach is for the interviewer to ask the applicant to sell something. "Hand the prospect a stapler, a pencil, or any other object that's handy and ask him to 'sell' it. . . . A pro should be able to sell anything," says one sales manager. "The one thing he's got to do is to ask for the order. Seven of ten fail to do so."[12]

Techniques like these can be useful to assess a candidate's character and selling skills, but they should be used as only one part of the interview. Sometimes sales managers become so obsessed with finding the "one best way" to assess candidates that they allow interviewing gimmicks to get in the way of real communication. After all, another purpose of job interviews is to provide candidates with information about the job and company so they will be interested in taking the job. One real danger with gimmicky interviewing tech-

Thorny Issues in Sales Management 12 • 2

ARE PERSONAL INTERVIEWS A VALID TOOL FOR SELECTING SALESPEOPLE?

Personal interviews are both the most commonly used method of selecting salespeople and the one considered most helpful by sales managers. But assessments of the use of evaluations based on personal interviews across a variety of occupations suggest they are disappointing predictors of future job performance. As we have seen, the meta-analysis conducted by Hunter and Hunter found that evaluations based on interviews have a correlation of only 0.14 with candidates' subsequent performance, and an even lower correlation of 0.08 with candidates' future promotion within the firm.

Professor Richard Arvey and his colleagues have a more favorable opinion of the usefulness of interviews when they are used specifically to select new sales personnel. In one study of the use of structured interviews to select retail salespeople, they found a correlation of 0.44 between interviewers' ratings of candidates and their subsequent job performance. Arvey and his colleagues explain this positive result by suggesting that interviews are a more valid selection tool when the job to be filled requires skills and behaviors similar to those that are on display in a personal interview setting, as is often the case with sales jobs. They also indicate that interviews are most useful when several different people interview the candidate and then compare their evaluations, and when at least some of those interviewers have a detailed knowledge of the requirements of the job to be filled (as sales managers typically do concerning sales positions).

These findings suggest that sales managers should play an active role in interviewing prospective salespeople, rather than rely on employment agencies or members of the personnel department to do all the interviewing. They also indicate the manager should employ interviewing techniques that require the candidate to display product and industry knowledge and selling skills—techniques such as asking the candidate to "sell something." When these guidelines are followed, personal interviews may provide as valid an indication of a candidate's future success as any other selection tool.

Source: Richard D. Arvey and J. E. Campion, "The Employment Interview: A Summary and Review of Recent Research," *Personnel Psychology* 35 (1982), pp. 736–65; Richard D. Arvey et al., "Enhanced Interview Validity: A Sight for Sore Eyes," unpublished working paper (Minneapolis: Carlson School of Management, University of Minnesota, 1985); and E. James Randall and Cindy H. Randall, "Review of Salesperson Selection Techniques and Criteria: A Managerial Approach," *International Journal of Research in Marketing* 7 (1990), pp. 81–95.

niques is that the applicant will be "turned off" and lose interest in working for the firm.

Regardless of what kinds of interviewing techniques are used, more managers rely on interviews as a means of evaluating sales candidates than any other selection tool. Yet as we saw earlier, there is some evidence that evaluations based on personal interviews are among the least valid predictors of subsequent job performance. Does this mean many firms are doing a less than optimal job of evaluating and selecting new salespeople? Are there ways to improve the accuracy of impressions gained from interviews? These questions are explored in more detail in Thorny Issues in Sales Management 12.2.

Reference Checks

If an applicant passes the face-to-face interview, a reference check is often the next step. Some sales managers question the value of references because "they always say nice things." However, with a little resourcefulness, reference checks can be a valuable selection tool.

Checking references can ensure the accuracy of factual data about the applicant. It is naive to assume that everything a candidate has written on a résumé or application form is true. Facts about previous job experiences and college degrees should be checked. The discovery of false data on a candidate's application raises a question about basic honesty as well as about what the candidate is trying to hide.

References can supply additional information and opinions about a prospect's aptitude and past job performance. Although it is important to respect applicants' requests not to prejudice their position with a current employer, useful information can be obtained from previous employers and supervisors. Even though most applicants try to provide only "good references," a resourceful interviewer can probe beyond a reference's positive biases with questions such as, "If you were hiring this individual today, what qualities would you think it most important to develop?" Also, some firms require applicants to supply as many as six or seven references on the theory that it is unlikely so many people will all have strong personal biases in favor of the applicant. Calling a large number of references and probing them in depth can be time-consuming and costly, but it can also produce worthwhile information and protect against making expensive hiring mistakes.[13]

Physical Examinations

One typically does not think of selling as physically demanding, yet sales jobs often require a great deal of stamina and the physical ability to withstand lots of stress. Consequently, even though physical examinations are relatively expensive compared with other selection tools, many sales managers see them as valuable aids for evaluating candidates.

However, managers should be very cautious in requiring medical examinations, including specific tests for such things as drug use or the HIV virus, for prospective employees. Under the Americans with Disabilities Act (discussed in more detail later in this chapter), it is no longer advisable to use a standard physical examination for all positions. If used, the physical exam should focus only on attributes directly related to the requirements of the job to be filled. For example, in many sales positions, conditions such as diabetes or epilepsy would have little or no impact on the candidate's ability to perform. Therefore, questions concerning such conditions should be avoided, and any information collected for emergency situations should be kept confidential. Under the new law's guidelines, a physical examination should be performed only *after* a job offer has been extended. And the job offer cannot be made conditional on the results of the physical exam unless all hirees for a position are subjected to the same physical exam and the results of those exams are treated as confidential medical records.[14]

Tests

A final set of selection tools used by many firms consists of tests aimed at measuring an applicant's mental abilities and personality traits. The most commonly used tests can be grouped into three types: (1) intelligence, (2) aptitude, and (3) personality tests. Within each category, there are a variety of different tests used by different companies.

Intelligence tests

Intelligence tests are useful for determining whether an applicant has sufficient mental ability to perform a job successfully. Sales managers tend to believe these are the most useful of all the tests commonly used in selecting salespeople. General intelligence tests are designed to measure an applicant's overall mental abilities by examining how well the applicant comprehends, reasons, and learns. The *Wonderlic Personnel Test* is one common general intelligence test. It is popular because it is short; it consists of 50 items and requires only about 12 minutes to complete.

When the job to be filled requires special competence in one or a few areas of mental ability, a specialized intelligence test might be used to evaluate candidates. Tests are available for measuring such things as speed of learning, number facility, memory, logical reasoning, and verbal ability.

Aptitude tests

Aptitude tests are designed to determine whether an applicant has an interest in, or the ability to perform, certain tasks and activities. For example, the *Strong Vocational Interest Blank* asks respondents to indicate whether they like or dislike a variety of situations and activities. This can determine whether applicants' interests are similar to those of people who are successful in a variety of different occupations, including selling. Other tests measure skills or abilities that might be related to success in particular selling jobs, such as mechanical or mathematical aptitude.

One problem with at least some aptitude tests is that, instead of measuring a person's native abilities, they measure current level of skill at certain tasks. At least some skills necessary for successful selling can be taught, or improved, through a well-designed training program. Therefore, rejecting applicants because they currently do not have the necessary skills can mean losing people who could be trained to be successful salespeople.

Personality tests

Many general personality tests evaluate an individual on numerous traits. The *Edwards Personal Preference Schedule,* for instance, measures 17 traits such as sociability, aggressiveness, and independence. Such tests, however, contain many questions, require substantial time to complete, and gather information about some traits that may be irrelevant for evaluating future salespeople. Consequently, more limited personality tests have been developed in recent years that concentrate on only a few traits thought to be directly relevant to a person's future success in sales. *The Multiple Personal Inventory*, for example, uses a small number of "forced-choice" questions to measure the strength of two personality traits: empathy with other people and ego drive.

Concerns about the use of tests

During the 1950s and early 1960s, tests—particularly general intelligence and sales aptitude tests—were widely used as selection tools for evaluating potential salespeople. A survey conducted by the National Society of Sales Training Executives in 1964 found that 83 percent of its member companies were using tests as part of the salesperson selection process. A follow-up survey in 1975, however, revealed the proportion of companies using tests had fallen to 22 percent, largely due to concerns over the possible legal problems and restrictions posed by civil rights legislation and equal opportunity hiring practices; we discuss these concerns and restrictions shortly. Recently, however, evidence that properly designed and administered tests are among the most valid selection tools has spurred an increase in their popularity; although as we saw in Exhibit 12.6 they are somewhat more widely used in large firms than in smaller ones.[15]

Despite the empirical evidence, however, many managers continue to be leery of tests, and a majority of firms do not use them as part of their evaluation of sales recruits. There are a number of reasons for these negative attitudes.

For one thing, despite the evidence that tests have relatively high predictive validity *on average,* some managers continue to doubt that tests are valid for predicting the future success of salespeople *in their specific firm.* As discussed in Chapter 11, no mental abilities or personality traits have been found to be positively related to performance across a variety of selling jobs in different firms. Thus, specific tests that measure such abilities and traits may be valid for selecting salespeople for some jobs, but invalid for others.

Also, tests for measuring specific abilities and characteristics of applicants do not always produce consistent scores. Some commercially available tests have not been developed according to the most scientific measurement procedures; as a result, their reliability and validity are questionable. Even when a firm believes a particular trait, such as empathy or sociability, is related to job performance, there is still a question about which test should be used to measure that trait.

A related concern, particularly in the case of personality tests, is that some creative and talented people may be rejected simply because their personalities do not conform to the test norms. Many sales jobs require creative people, particularly when those people are being groomed for future management responsibilities. Yet these people seldom fit an average personality profile because the "average" person is not particularly creative.

Another concern about testing involves the possible reactions of the people who are tested. A reasonably intelligent, "test-wise" person can "fudge" the results of many tests by selecting answers the applicant thinks management will want. These answers may not accurately reflect that person's feelings or behavior. Also, many prospective employees view extensive testing as a burden and perhaps an invasion of privacy. Therefore, some managers fear that requiring a large battery of tests may turn off a candidate and reduce the likelihood of accepting a job with the firm.

Finally, a given test may discriminate between people of different races or sexes, and the use of such tests is illegal. Consequently, some firms have abandoned the use of tests rather than risk getting into trouble with the government.

Guidelines for the appropriate use of tests

To avoid, or at least minimize, the preceding testing problems, managers should keep the following guidelines in mind.

1. Test scores should be considered only one input to the selection decision. Managers should not rely on them to do the work of other parts of the selection process—such as interviewing and checking references. Candidates should not be eliminated solely on the basis of test scores.

2. Applicants should be tested only on those abilities and traits that management, on the basis of a thorough job analysis, has determined to be relevant for the specific job. Broad tests that evaluate a large number of traits not relevant to a specific job are probably inappropriate.

3. When possible, tests with build-in "internal consistency checks" should be used. Then the person who analyzes the test results can determine whether the applicant responded honestly or was faking some answers. Many recently designed tests ask similar questions with slightly different wording several times throughout the test. If respondents are answering honestly, they should always give the same response to similar questions.

4. A firm should conduct empirical studies to ensure the tests are valid for predicting an applicant's future performance in the job. This kind of hard evidence of test validity is particularly important in view of the government's equal employment opportunity requirements.

EQUAL EMPLOYMENT OPPORTUNITY REQUIREMENTS IN SELECTING SALESPEOPLE

The number of federal lawsuits alleging workplace discrimination is large and growing rapidly. There were 7,613 such suits in 1989, up from only 336 in

---

EXHIBIT 12 • 7   *Legislation Affecting Recruitment and Selection*

Legislative Act	Purpose
Civil Rights Act of 1866	Gives blacks the same rights as whites and has since been extended by the courts to include all ethnic groups.
Civil Rights Act of 1964 (Title VII)	Prohibits discrimination in employment based on race, color, religion, national origin, or sex.
Age Discrimination in Employment Act (1967)	Prohibits discrimination against people ages 40 to 70.
Fair Employment Opportunity Act (1972)	Founded the Equal Employment Opportunity Commission to ensure compliance with the Civil Rights Act
Rehabilitation Act of 1973	Requires affirmative action to hire and promote handicapped persons if the firm employs 50 or more workers and is seeking a federal contract in excess of $50,000.
Vietnam Era Veterans Readjustment Act (1974)	Requires affirmative action to hire Vietnam veterans and disabled veterans of any war by firms holding federal contracts in excess of $10,000.
Americans with Disabilities Act (1990)	Prohibits discrimination based on handicaps or disabilities—either physical or mental. Applies to all employers with 25 or more employees beginning July 26, 1992, and extends to employers with 15 or more workers on July 26, 1994.

1970.[16] The primary basis for these suits is Title VII of the 1964 Civil Rights Act, which forbids discrimination in employment on the basis of race, sex, religion, color, or national origin. A number of more recent federal laws have extended this protection against job discrimination to include such factors as age and physical and mental disabilities, as summarized in Exhibit 12.7. Consequently, extreme care should be taken to ensure the selection tools a firm uses in hiring salespeople—especially its interviewing and testing procedures— are not biased against any subgroup of the labor force. Exhibit 12.8 offers guidelines concerning the kinds of illegal or sensitive questions managers should avoid when conducting employment interviews or designing application forms.

Requirements for Tests

Section 703(h) of the 1964 Civil Rights Act approves the use of "professionally developed ability tests," provided such tests are not "designed, intended, or used to discriminate because or race, color, religion, sex, or national origin." Suppose, however, an employer innocently uses a test that does discriminate in that a larger proportion of men than women, or a larger percentage of whites than blacks, receives passing scores. Has the employer violated the law? Not necessarily.

In such cases, the employer must prove the test scores are valid predictors

EXHIBIT 12 • 8 *Illegal or Sensitive Questions that Should Be Eliminated from Employment Applications and Interviews*

Nationality and Race

Comments or questions relating to the race, color, national origin, or descent of the applicant—or his or her spouse—must be avoided. Applicants should not be asked to supply a photo of themselves when applying for a job. If proficiency in another language is an important part of the job, the applicant can be asked to demonstrate that proficiency but cannot be asked whether it is his or her native language. Applicants may be asked if they are U.S. citizens, but not whether they—or their parents or spouse—are naturalized or native-born Americans. Applicants who are not citizens may be asked whether they have the legal right to remain and work in the United States.

Religion

Applicants should not be asked about their religious beliefs or whether the company's workweek or the job schedule would interfere with their religious convictions.

Sex and Marital Status

Except for jobs where sex is clearly related to job performance—as in a TV commercial role—the applicant's sex should not enter the hiring discussion. Applicants should not be asked about their marital status, whether or not their spouse works, or even whom the prospective employer should notify in an emergency. A woman should not be asked whether she would like to be addressed as Mrs., Miss, or Ms. Applicants should not be asked any questions about their children, baby-sitting arrangements, contraceptive practices, or planned family size.

Age

Applicants may be asked whether they are minors or age 70 or over, because special laws govern the employment of such people. With those exceptions, however, applicants should not be asked their age or date of birth.

Physical Characteristics, Disabilities, Handicaps, and Health Problems

In view of the recently passed Americans with Disabilities Act, all such questions are best avoided. However, once an employer has described the job to be performed, applicants *can* be asked whether they have any physical or mental condition that would limit their ability to perform the job.

Height and Weight

While not illegal, such questions are sensitive since they may provide a basis for discrimination against females or Americans of Asian or Spanish descent.

Bankruptcy or Garnishments

Both questions are suspect because the bankruptcy code prohibits discrimination against individuals who have filed bankruptcy.

Arrests and Convictions

Questions about past arrests are barred. Applicants can be asked about past convictions, but the employer should include a statement that the nature and circumstances of the conviction will be considered.

Source: Adapted from C. David Shepherd and James C. Heartfield, "Discrimination Issues in the Selection of Salespeople: A Review and Managerial Suggestions," *Journal of Personal Selling and Sales Management*, Fall 1991, p. 71.

of successful performance on the job in question. In other words, it is legal for a firm to hire more men than women for a job if it can be proven that men possess more of some trait or ability that will enable them to do the job better. This requires that the employer have *empirical evidence* showing a significant relationship between scores on the test and actual job performance. The procedures a firm might use to produce this kind of evidence were described earlier in this chapter when discussing how to determine whether particular job qualifications are valid.[17]

Requirements for Interviews and Application Forms

Because it is illegal to discriminate in hiring on the basis of race, sex, religion, age, and national origin, there is no reason for a firm to ask for such information on its job application forms or during personal interviews. It is wise to avoid all questions in any way related to such factors. Then there will be no question in the applicant's mind about whether the hiring decision was biased or unfair. This is easier said than done, however, because some seemingly innocent questions can be viewed as attempts to gain information that might be used to discriminate against a candidate.

SUMMARY

This chapter reviewed the issues that surround the recruitment and selection of new salespeople. The issues discussed ranged from who is responsible for these tasks to the impact of federal legislation barring job discrimination on selection procedures.

Two factors are primary in determining who has the responsibility for recruiting and selecting salespeople: (1) the size of the sales force, and (2) the kind of selling involved. In general, the smaller the sales force, the more sophisticated the selling task, and the more the sales force is used as a training ground for marketing and sales managers, the more likely it is that higher-level people, including the sales manager, will be directly involved in the recruitment and selection effort. To ensure recruits have the aptitude for the job, it is useful to look at the recruitment and selection procedures as a three-step process. The steps are (1) a job analysis and description, (2) the recruitment of a pool of applicants, and (3) the selection of the best applicants from the available pool.

The job analysis and description phase includes a detailed examination of the job to determine what activities, tasks, responsibilities, and environmental influences are involved. This analysis may be conducted by someone in the sales management ranks or by a job analysis specialist. Regardless of who does it, it is important for that person to prepare a job description that details the findings of the job analysis. Finally, the job description is used to develop a statement of job qualifications, which lists and describes the personal traits and abilities a person should have to perform the tasks and responsibilities involved.

The pool of recruits from which the firm finally selects can be generated from a number of sources, including (1) people within the company, (2) people in other firms, (3) educational institutions, (4) advertisements, and (5) employment agencies. Each source has its own advantages and disadvantages. Some, such as advertisements, typically produce a larger pool. The key question the sales manager needs to address is which source or combination of sources is likely to produce the largest pool of good, qualified recruits.

Once the qualifications necessary to fill a job have been determined and applicants have been recruited, the final task is to determine which applicant best meets the qualifications and has the greatest aptitude for the job. To make this determination, firms often use most, and in some cases all, of the following tools and procedures: (1) application blanks, (2) face-to-face interviews, (3) reference checks, (4) physical examinations, and (5) intelligence, aptitude, and personality tests. Although most employers find the interview and then the application blank most helpful, each device seems to perform some functions better than the other alternatives. This may explain why most firms use a combination of selection tools.

Title VII of the 1964 Civil Rights Act forbids discrimination in employment on the basis of race, sex, color, religion, or national origin. A firm must be careful, therefore, about how it uses tests, how it structures its application form, and the questions it asks during personal interviews so as not to be charged with noncompliance with the act. A firm that uses tests, for example, must be able to demonstrate empirically that the attributes measured are related to the salesperson's performance on the job.

Discussion Questions

1. The following quote from *Marketing News* (March 2, 1992, p. 14) illustrates an application of computers to the recruiting and selection process:

   It doesn't care who you know, what kind of suit you're wearing, or whether you have a firm handshake. Salespeople looking for a job may soon have to face their toughest interview yet—with a computer.

   What are the advantages of using a software program to conduct preliminary job interviews? What problems are a company that uses computer-aided interviewing likely to encounter?

2. The demanding process of recruiting and selecting new sales reps has led many sales managers to search out faster methods. Beyond the traditional tools described in the chapter, other questionable techniques appear such as graphology, astrology, and numerology. Numerology assumes there is a codified relationship between the conscious and the unconscious. The letters used in one's first and last names, along with their values (e.g., $A = 1$, $H = 8$, $N = 5$), when summed produce a value that indicates the individual's personality. How would you test the predictive validity of numerology?

3. The sales manager was flustered at the recent suggestion made by the newly hired sales analyst. The sales analyst thinks the sales force spends too much time on mundane activities, such as stacking cans and taking inventory, that could be better performed by less costly personnel. When asked by the sales manager just where these "less costly" personnel would come from, the sales analyst commented: "Why

not hire temporaries from Manpower, Kelly, or Professional Temporaries?" The sales manager retorted the job was far too important to entrust to a bunch of part-timers. Who is right? How would you determine if hiring temporaries is feasible?

4. The following quote was taken from *The Wall Street Journal* (August 25, 1988, p. 17):

> Thomas Klobucher is looking for employees with the write stuff.
>
> Before someone is hired at Thomas Interior Systems, Inc., the president of the Elmhurst, Ill., office-furniture company has a handwriting analyst examine the candidate's writing to develop a personality profile.
>
> Mr. Klobucher says he believes that ignoring the results can be costly. He was once so impressed with a sales candidate—the man had a pleasant personality, good recommendations, and an MBA—that he dismissed a handwriting specialist's warning that the candidate was argumentative and defiant. It proved true, and within months of being hired the man was out.

The article also mentions, "Handwriting analysis is quietly spreading through corporate America." What accounts for this trend? What are the implications of this trend? How would you design a study to test the reliability and validity of handwriting analysis as a selection tool? Please prepare your answer in writing, not typed.

5. According to one recruiter, "Selling requires skills in being persuasive. The best way to see if a person is persuasive is to ask them to sell me something during the interview, a pen, an ashtray, or even a coffee cup, anything." Do you approve of this tactic? What would you do if you were asked to sell something during the interview?

6. Two college recruiters were discussing some of the students they had interviewed that day. One female applicant with excellent credentials was described by one interviewer as follows: "She looked too feminine, like she would need someone to take care of her, that she was not all that serious about a sales job with us." When asked to explain her comments, the interviewer said: "Under her jacket she wore a flowery blouse with little flouncy sleeves and a lace collar." The other recruiter countered and asked: "What does a flowery blouse, flouncy sleeves, and a lace collar have to do with performance?" Comment.

7. The national sales manager of the Quick-Change Tool Co. recruits people for the position of driver-sales representative. Duties involve calling on service stations, garages, and automobile dealers. To be considered, all applicants must be high school graduates and pass both the Bennett Mechanical Comprehension Test and the Wonderlic Personnel Test, an abbreviated 12-minute IQ test. The personnel manager has advised the national sales manager that this procedure may violate equal employment opportunity regulations. Do you agree?

8. One potential source of applicants for sales positions is sales representatives who work for competitors. One sales manager indicated: "Pirating sales representatives from other companies makes sense. Let them do the training, then we'll hire them." Is this ethical? Does this practice make good business sense?

9. "Nuts to all those scientific tests and theories about how to hire sales reps. With my years of experience I can spot a winner after a 30-minute interview. My sixth sense just tells me who to hire and not to hire." Is this a reasonable approach?

Does it make any difference if the sales manager extolling the sixth sense approach has never had a failure?

10. "Listen, when I hire my next sales rep, I will ask if the candidate is a 'first-born' since evidence proves that first-born children are better suited for selling," claimed the sales manager. The sales manager noted that 21 of the first 23 U.S. astronauts, 65 percent of the members of the U.S. Supreme Court, and 66 percent of Ivy League students were first-born children. Should order of birth be used in the salesperson selection process? Is it legal to ask for this information?

Endnotes

[1] This example is based on material found in Tom Murray, "Starting a Sales Force from Scratch," *Sales & Marketing Management*, April 1991, pp. 51–58. For a detailed discussion of the switching costs involved in changing from manufacturers' reps to a company sales force, see Allen M. Weiss and Erin Anderson, "Converting from Independent to Employee Salesforces: The Role of Perceived Switching Costs," *Journal of Marketing Research,* February 1992, pp. 101–15.

[2] Thomas Rollins, "How to Tell Competent Salespeople from the Other Kind," *Sales & Marketing Management*, September 1990, pp. 116–18; 145–46.

[3] Ibid. See also Timothy J. Trow, "The Secret of a Good Hire: Profiling," *Sales & Marketing Management*, May 1990, pp. 44–55.

[4] For a detailed discussion of critical job dimensions, see Phil Faris, "No More Winging It," *Sales & Marketing Management*, August 1986, pp. 88–91.

[5] Rene Y. Darmon and S. J. Shapiro, "Sales Recruiting—A Major Area of Underinvestment," *Industrial Marketing Management* 9 (1980), pp. 47–51; and Gregory B. Salsbury, "Properly Recruit Salespeople to Reduce Training Costs," *Industrial Marketing Management* 11 (1982), pp. 143–46.

[6] George J. Avlonitis, Kevin A. Boyle, and A. G. Kouremenos, "Matching Salesmen to the Selling Job," *Industrial Marketing Management* 15 (1986), pp. 45–54.

[7] Marianne Matthews, "If Your Ads Aren't Pulling Top Sales Talent. . ." *Sales & Marketing Management*, February 1990, pp. 73–79.

[8] Arthur Bragg, "Shell-Shocked on the Battlefield of Selling," *Sales & Marketing Management*, July 1990, pp. 52–58.

[9] For a detailed review of these—as well as some less commonly used—selection tools, see E. James Randall and Cindy H. Randall, "Review of Salesperson Selection Techniques and Criteria: A Managerial Approach," *International Journal of Research in Marketing* 7 (1990), pp. 81–95.

[10] John E. Hunter and R. F. Hunter, "Validity and Utility of Alternative Predictors of Job Performance," *Psychological Bulletin* 96 (1984), pp. 72–98. For a discussion of the validity of different selection procedures as applied to the evaluation of salespeople, see Neil M. Ford et al., "Selecting Successful Salespeople: A Meta-Analysis of Biographical and Psychological Selection Criteria," in *Review of Marketing,* ed. Michael J. Houston (Chicago: American Marketing Association, 1988), pp. 90–131.

[11] For a discussion of how an interviewer can obtain more detailed information through probing questions, see John H. Rose, *How to Recruit, Interview, and Select Prospective Sales Representatives* (Orlando, Fla.: National Society of Sales Training Executives, 1981).

[12] "How Fredrich's McElveen Finds Super Salesmen," *Sales Management*, August 5, 1974, p. 4.

[13] Arthur Bragg, "Checking References," *Sales & Marketing Management*, November 1990, pp. 68–71.

[14] C. David Shepherd and James C. Heartfield, "Discrimination Issues in the Selection of Salespeople: A Review and Managerial Suggestions," *Journal of Personal Selling and Sales Management*, Fall 1991, p. 71.

[15] Richard Kern, "IQ Tests for Salesmen Make a Come-

back," *Sales & Marketing Management*, April 1988, pp. 42–46; and Richard Nelson, "Maybe It's Time to Take Another Look at Tests as a Selection Tool," *Journal of Personal Selling and Sales Management*, August 1987, pp. 33–38.

[16]Leon E. Wynter, "Would Rights Bill Boost Volume of Job Suits?" *The Wall Street Journal,* August 22, 1991, p. B21.

[17]For a detailed discussion of the procedures required to validate employment tests, see *Principles for the Validation and Use of Personnel Selection Procedures* (College Park, Md.: Society for Industrial and Organizational Psychology, Inc., 1987).

Suggested Readings

Bragg, Arthur. "Checking References." *Sales & Marketing Management*, November 1990, pp. 68–71.

Ford, Neil M., "Selecting Successful Salespeople: A Meta-Analysis of Biographical and Psychological Selection Criteria." In *Review of Marketing*, ed. Michael J. Houston. Chicago: American Marketing Association, 1988, pp. 90–131.

Matthews, Marianne. "If Your Ads Aren't Pulling Top Sales Talent . . . " *Sales & Marketing Management*, February 1990, pp. 73–79.

Nelson, Richard. "Maybe It's Time to Take Another Look at Tests as a Selection Tool." *Journal of Personal Selling and Sales Management*, August 1987, pp. 33–38.

Randall, E. James, and Cindy H. Randall. "Review of Salesperson Selection Techniques and Criteria: A Managerial Approach." *International Journal of Research in Marketing* 7 (1990), pp. 81–95.

Rollins, Thomas. "How to Tell Competent Salespeople from the Other Kind." *Sales & Marketing Management*, September 1990, pp. 116–18; 145–46.

Shepherd C. David, and James C. Heartfield. "Discrimination Issues in the Selection of Salespeople: A review and Managerial Suggestions," *Journal of Personal Selling and Sales Management*, Fall 1991, pp. 67–75.

Sales Training: Objectives, Techniques, and Evaluation

H OW KRAFT BUILDS BUSINESS MANAGERS FROM SALES TRAINEES[1]

Empowerment describes a variety of actions a company can take to give employees a greater sense of control and participation in the events and decisions affecting their business life. Applying empowerment to a sales organization finds sales representatives managing their territory as a business, instead of the business managing them. Kraft USA instills this ability during the initial training stage. Instead of the traditional supervisor-driven training where the trainee takes a passive role, Kraft developed a basic training program that starts on the trainee's first day on the job and ends 12 weeks later with the sales rep ready to take full responsibility for a sales territory as a business manager.

Kraft's training program starts with five weeks of intensive independent and one-on-one development exercises at the trainee's district office, at other district and regional facilities, and on sales routes. This is followed by seven weeks of on-the-job development training in the trainee's new territory.

Next, the trainee learns 17 distinct learning modules that cover every skill needed to perform basic responsibilities. The program is adaptable. A 12-week program is the norm, but adjustments can be made to accommodate the personal training plan developed by the sales manager for each trainee.

Rather than placing total responsibility on the rep's immediate supervisor, Kraft USA adopted the "district support team" concept. Team members are selected based on their specific skills to ensure that trainees master each of the 17 learning modules. To assure continuity, all district support teams work from the same script. The trainee's sales manager controls the process and tries to be flexible during the 12 weeks based on the rep's ability to learn the material.

Kraft USA developed a "learning contract" (see Exhibit 13.1) for each module). The trainee and a support team member review the contract; the support team member identifies available resources and helps the sales rep understand the learning process.

At the end of each training session, the sales rep indicates the "mastery indicators" he is ready to demonstrate. This process continues until all mastery indicators have been completed, the contract is then signed, and the sales rep moves on to the next indicator.

Kraft USA gives trainees a *Kraft USA Sales Representative's Handbook* that lists assignments and activities to complete for each module. Sales reps receive the *Kraft USA Product Manual* and the *Kraft USA Field Sales Manual.* The latter is geared to Kraft's audiovisuals and handouts, needed for interactive training and a computer-based training format.

Considered essential to the empowerment approach is the use of "thought provokers"—questions, problems, suggestions, or activities strategically placed throughout the program. For example, a trainee may be asked, "Why would you want to know the organizational structure of each of the stores you call on? List some specific reasons why and discuss them with a support team member."

Periodic assessments are an important element of the training program. Sales managers and team support members must answer the following questions:

• Is the trainee grasping and integrating the necessary knowledge accurately and with sufficient speed?

E X H I B I T **13 • 1** *Example of Kraft USA Learning Contract*

LEARNING CONTRACT: THE RETAIL SALES CALL

EXPECTATIONS/SKILLS

Upon completing the contract, I shall be able to:

A. Describe the three types of sales calls and the steps involved in each.
B. Accurately demonstrate each type of call.
C. Understand the format of a store call organizer.
D. Explain the job functions of typical store personnel.

RESOURCES & LEARNING ACTIVITIES

I shall be provided with the resources, developmental discussions, and field work necessary for successful completion of this contract, as detailed in the learning module.

ASSESSMENT/MASTERY INDICATORS

I shall meet the expectations described above by successfully completing the following indicators of mastery, as directed by my Support Team:

A. I shall satisfactorily demonstrate a regular, speed, and blitz sales call and give one example of how each call might be used to manage my territory.
B. Given a copy of my current store call organizer, I shall accurately explain the practical use (by myself and others in the district) of the information in that organizer.
C. Given an organizational chart from a local store, I shall describe the job responsibilities of each job function listed.

INITIALS AND DATES FOR THE

	SALES REP	SUPPORT TEAM
A.	_____	_____
B.	_____	_____
C.	_____	_____

This Quality Partnership between myself and my Support Team has been completed this ____ day of _____, 19___.

_____   _____
Sales Representative Signature   Sales Manager Signature

_____
District

SOURCE: Kraft USA.

Source: Suzy Barrett, Richard L. Ranges, and Stuart M. Lasky, "How Kraft Builds Business Managers from Sales Trainees," *Sales & Marketing Management*, May 1991, p. 111.

- Is the trainee demonstrating mastery of the necessary skills and behaviors with sufficient speed?
- Is there a need for any midcourse corrections?

The trainee's sales manager must determine if and when sales reps are ready for assignment. Input for this determination include:

- The rep's evaluation of progress and comfort level with the job.

- The support team's flow of progress reports and recommendations.
- The rep's performance against the assigned thought provokers.
- The completed learning contracts.

Kraft USA continues to assess the impact of the training program after the sales reps are on their own by using sales data and coaching techniques. Sales managers and support team members travel with the sales reps to observe behavior. Advanced training programs are available that include skill development managers for special problems.

The following statement describes Kraft USA's training philosophy:

> We need reps who are able to break through their own learning barriers, and we feel very strongly that we owe each of them the resources and opportunities to learn their roles as business managers.

SALES TRAINING AT AMERICA'S BEST SALES FORCES

Each year since 1985, *Sales & Marketing Management* has published a special report on America's best sales forces.[2] Companies are evaluated on such criteria as recruiting, retention, training, new account penetration, account retention, product/technical knowledge, and reputation among customers. The following examples of training programs are based on the 1991 report.

1. **Dow Chemical.** "We're number one because we recruit good people," according to Robert M. Baughman, vice president of human resources. New hires are split between those who have technical degrees and those who have less specialized degrees. All new hires go through Dow's training program, referred to as one of Dow's "best-kept secrets" by Richard E. Sosville, vice president of sales and marketing. Sosville says, "What makes it so special is that it aims to produce a fully balanced seller, not just someone trained in product knowledge alone."

In Dow's yearlong program, trainees spend equal time in classroom situations and working on projects. These projects involve handling customer calls and orders in Dow's customer service center or producing in-depth studies about customers and new markets. The last stage has trainees selling to and interacting with Dow's customers and prospects.

2. **Hewlett-Packard.** "Our goal is to deploy the best sales force in the industry," says Manuel Diaz, Hewlett-Packard's director of sales and marketing. Diaz cites H-P's sales training efforts as instrumental in achieving this goal. He says the sales training program's "thrust toward providing the best, the fastest, and the most powerful technology" and its "continuing focus on the customer as our number-one priority goal" are contributing factors.

The computer industry's trend toward systems and solutions produces a corresponding evolution in sales training programs. Diaz says: "The new salesperson will have to be able to understand customer requirements and explain solutions in terms the customer can understand. He'll have to deal with a number of partners, including value-added resellers, software vendors, and even competitors whose equipment may also be integrated into a customer's system."

To accomplish these requirements, H-P requires the sales staff to receive training in such areas as strategic selling and account management. H-P uses custom-training videos that provide the latest information about new products and interactive TV/satellite training sessions for its sales groups. The company offers an advanced training course on open systems and client-server technologies and frequently sends customers through these same programs.

3. **Scott Paper.** Major changes in how retailers operate have placed new demands on Scott's sales force. Retailers now insist that suppliers play their games and not vice versa. Salespeople at one time dictated product mix and shelf space allocations. Retailers now ask, "What can *you* do for me?" Salespeople now find themselves serving as financial strategists, category analysts, and marketing researchers.

According to Lee Griffith, vice president of North American consumer marketing at Scott Paper, "It was quite a massive change. It required months of preparation, entirely new systems, and big changes in corporate culture and training." Scott's sales team must now understand brands and how consumers respond to various marketing actions rather than rely on the traditional volume or promotional approach.

To learn the new methods, Scott's salespeople were trained to blend their persuasive skills, market knowledge, and computerized data base to arrive at the most profitable product mix for both company and customer. Scott's salespeople had to learn data processing and financial analysis skills.

4. **Eli Lilly & Co.** Lilly ranks high in recruiting top salespeople and training them in product and technical knowledge. The company offers a defined training program that permits salespeople to study their products and learn how best to promote them. After Lilly's two-year training program, salespeople take a series of psychological tests to teach them more about themselves, to identify their own strengths and weaknesses so they can concentrate on reinforcement and improvement.

As stated by E. M. Cavalier, Lilly's vice president of sales, "We need to communicate the value of innovative products in *controlling* health-care costs as well as increasing productivity and improving the quality of life."

THE CHALLENGES OF SALES TRAINING

In today's economy, companies seeking to develop a differential advantage while selling commodity-type products have found that the role of the sales

EXHIBIT 13 ● 2   *Characteristics of a Successful Salesperson*

Percent of All Characteristics Cited; Multiple Responses Were Possible	
Attitude—committed to quality and customer service, aggressive, persistent, self-confident	48%
Skills—sales, problem-solving, communication, time management	25%
Knowledge—of product, industry, market	13%
Sales record—meets objectives	11%
Other—completes paperwork, political acumen	4%

Source: Meg Kerr and Bill Burzynski, "Missing the Target: Sales Training in America," *Training and Development Journal*, July 1988, p. 68. © 1988, *Training and Development Journal*, American Society for Training and Development. Reprinted with permisson. All rights reserved.

force is preeminent. Even in competitive markets where product differentials exist, the caliber of the sales force often makes the difference. Training has a lot to offer in both situations: Through training, a company can create an outstanding sales force that will differentiate it from competitors.

The criticisms of sales training center on several topics. One is that some companies have no sales training programs. Another criticism concerns the content of sales training. Several critics dislike the emphasis placed on product knowledge, contending selling skills are neglected as a result. Others dislike the content as being too trendy, involving questionable psychological methods or using inappropriate people to conduct the training programs (e.g., professional football players).

One study of 235 participants, people responsible for sales training, revealed a significant discrepancy between the content of their sales training programs and what the participants believe successful salespeople needed.[3] Exhibit 13.2 presents the characteristics of successful salespeople as revealed by the study. Of the characteristics, almost half could be classified as attitude related. Skills make up one quarter with product knowledge, and other factors were mentioned less frequently.

These results are not surprising and agree with findings reported in Chapter 11. The sales training programs in the companies that participated in the study focus primarily on sales skill and knowledge, not attitude as defined in Exhibit 13.2. The discrepancy between what is taught and what is needed is shown clearly in Exhibit 13.3. Note that only 1 percent of the program content for new hires pertains to attitudes, yet this is the characteristic deemed most important by the respondents.

Major weaknesses in sales training, as expressed by Roy Chitwood, president of sales training firm, are more specific.[4] Chitwood states that no sales training is required in some firms that hire only college graduates. He also discredits companies that "try to turn their salespeople into robots" producing people with "no individuality, no personality, no sales."

Chitwood, along with others, criticizes companies that "get involved in

EXHIBIT 13 • 3   *Program Content versus Characteristics of Success**

	Characteristics of Success	Program Content: New Hirees	Program Content: 1–3 Years Seniority
Skills	25%	56%	65%
Knowledge	13%	43%	35%
Attitudes	48%	1%	0%

*See Exhibit 13.2 for additional characteristics.

Source: Meg Kerr and Bill Burzynski, "Missing the Target: Sales Training in America," *Training and Development Journal*, July 1988, p. 69.

all the psychological nonsense that goes under the guise of sales training." He is skeptical of such programs as "TA," "TM," Graphology, Numerology, Astrology, and "hug therapy," arguing they do not belong in sales training. A related criticism comes from Jack Falvey, a sales consultant, who dislikes using football players and coaches as part of the sales training program. Falvey sees little similarity between professional selling and professional football.[5] Thorny Issues 13.1 illustrates a similar problem with motivational speakers.

Using Qualified Trainers

The credibility of sales training suffers when a person who is not successful in sales becomes a sales trainer. Also, turning a senior sales representative into a sales trainer may be a mistake if the person lacks the ability to teach sales training. According to Chitwood, some companies "try to teach nontransferable selling techniques." This can be a problem, especially in high-technology industries, where the new recruit is sent into the field to learn selling skills from a 15-year veteran who is very successful. It is ambitious to expect that the new recruit will learn in a matter of hours what has taken 15 years to acquire. No doubt the veteran has developed a high level of adaptive selling techniques, which consider customer differences. Adaptive selling and its influence on sales training is covered later in the chapter. The veteran probably learned most of the selling skills over time, sometimes referred to as on-the-job training (OJT).

It is naive to think a new recruit can learn in a three-day or a three-week training session what has taken years to accomplish. Falvey comments, "Understanding what has to be done to build selling skills can be mastered in 15 minutes. Doing it takes years of actual, not simulated, practice."[6]

Other critics comment that current sales training practices contribute to the negative image discussed in Chapter 2. Alessandra and Wexler dislike the practice of training salespeople to dominate and control.[7] Salespeople are trained to "ask questions that always get a 'yes,' techniques to handle any objection, 'closing' techniques designed to maneuver the most reluctant buyer

Thorny Issues in Sales Management 13 • 1

MOTIVATIONAL HYPE AND SALES TRAINING: IS THERE A RELATIONSHIP?

A large screen rises in front of the hotel meeting room. Just behind it, cloaked beneath yards of black fabric, are 16 slide projectors, a videotape player, a sound system, and a computer system that will digitally drive a multi-thousand-dollar four minutes of hype.

Silence settles over this chapel of capitalism as a minister of motivation grabs a microphone and, like a Vegas showman, spins his tale, winding his rhythmic rhetoric faster and faster, preaching the salvation of salespeople—motivation. The faces of the converted lean toward him, and their silent refrain fills the room:

We believe! Oh, yes! We believe!

The house lights dim and BAM! The multimedia presentation synchronously beams images of products and company personnel in cadence with crescendoing music driven by a heavy bass.

Hallelujah! That's it! We're saved!

These salespeople are whipped to a frenzy of enthusiasm fortified with an emotional fervor that their company hopes will help them sell.

Do motivational presentations like this have any lasting effect? Do they constitute an entertaining form of sales training? Jack Snader, president of Systema, Inc., says: "These types of meetings create an illusion of team spirit—a feeling that fades on the second Tuesday after the meeting." Snader compares these motivational pitches to "high school pep rallies: They're momentarily inspiring, but without training for the players, the game is lost."

The same philosophy applies to sales meetings. Rather than spend $12,000 on this form of entertainment, companies would be better off spending the money on sales training. After all, with the cost of a sales call now exceeding $300 in many industries, it becomes imperative that companies address ways to become more efficient.

Management is starting to scrutinize the cost of their sales meetings and ask: "What are we getting out of this?" Snader believes "national sales meetings will become wonderful opportunities for a large amount of support for the continued development of salespeople." Sales meetings represent an excellent opportunity for refresher training for the entire sales force and should have one goal: to enhance the ability and reputation of the sales force so they can help customers solve real-world problems.

Source: Joseph Conlin, "The Lowdown on Sales Meetings," *Sales & Marketing Management*, May 1990, pp. 111–12.

into saying 'yes' ('UNCLE!')." Expanding on this point, Alessandra and Wexler note: "Three topics have dominated the sales training field over the years: how to give the 'razzle dazzle' sales pitches, 101 ways to close a sale, and power techniques for overcoming objections.

Obstacles Managers Face

A recent survey by Peterson, reviewed by *Training* magazine, asked sales managers to identify the problems they face when trying to introduce sales training programs. The top five obstacles identified by the 297 respondents are the following:

- Top management is not dedicated to sales training.
- Sales training programs are not adequately funded.
- Salespeople are apathetic about sales training.
- Salespeople resent training's intrusion on their time.
- Salespeople resist changes suggested by training programs.[9]

This rather negative perspective of sales training should raise an important question. What is management doing that allows some of these problems to occur? In evaluating sales training programs, wouldn't management discover that the cost exceeds the benefits? Two problems exist. First, management too often expects that sales training will be a panacea for all of the company's sales problems. If the sales problems are not resolved, budget-cutting activities often start with the sales training program. Or, management fails to understand sales training. Sales training is viewed as a cost of doing business rather than as an investment that pays future dividends. Why are only costs evaluated and not the other half of the operating statement?[10]

The second problem rests within the sales training function: namely, the evaluation of sales training programs. Too many sales training programs are conducted without any thought of measuring the benefits. Evaluation is difficult, but considering the millions of dollars devoted to sales training, it is not unreasonable to expect some attempt to measure the benefits. More is said later about how to evaluate sales training programs.

IMPROVING SALES TRAINING

Many of the problems overlap and can be resolved by adopting a more objective approach. First, sales training often lacks credibility. Programs fail to deliver what they promise and are viewed by many being a waste of time and money. Second, the level of approach assumes too much: "Trainees already know how to listen or to be enthusiastic, so why spend time on such basic areas?" Or, "Sales veterans already know how to sell, so time is not needed on this subject." Third, once techniques have been taught, it is not necessary to worry about the use of reinforcers or rewards to stimulate sales reps to continue to use them.

Creating Credibility in Sales Training[11]

Many sales trainers believe their programs lack credibility. Budget-cutting efforts are too often directed at existing sales training programs. This may reflect management's feeling that these programs are accomplishing little and are expendable. Sales training programs have to be sold, just like any other product or service. Well-designed programs are easier to sell to management than those put together with little thought.

Analyze needs

The starting point in creating credibility is to analyze the needs of the sales force (see Exhibit 13.4). One way to do this is to travel with sales reps, observing them and asking what they need to know that will help them perform more effectively. (Recent research designed to elicit selling procedures is discussed later in the chapter.) Field sales managers are a useful source of information because they are closest to the sales reps. Interviews with key members of management are productive ways to identify training needs. One expert advocates sending anonymous questionnaires to customers asking: What do you expect of a salesperson in the industry? How do salespeople disappoint you? Which company in the industry does the best selling job? In what ways are its salespeople better? Other sources include company records showing turnover data, performance evaluations, and sales and cost analyses. Attitudinal studies conducted with the sales force are useful sources of information. This analysis of needs answers three basic questions: Where in the organization is training needed, what should be the content of the training program, and who needs the training.[12]

Determine objectives

Setting specific, realistic, and measurable objectives adds to the credibility of a sales training program. The objectives may include learning about new products, new techniques, or new procedures. It pays to keep the objectives simple. Management may want a 10 percent sales increase, which then becomes the broad objective of the training program. The specific objective might be to teach sales reps how to call on new accounts, which will help lead to the broad objective. Measurability is critical in sales training. More will be said about this later.

Develop and implement program

At this point, a decision has to be made concerning developing the training program or hiring an outside organization to conduct it. Many companies, both large and small, use outside agencies for sales training. Small companies may farm out most of their training needs. Large companies develop most of their own programs and will use outside agencies to handle specialized needs. Lack of careful investigation of outside suppliers can lead to problems. One sales manager mentioned how embarrassed he was by retaining a company that put on an "entertaining song-and-dance routine" that cost $5,000 but failed to have any lasting effect. Use of outside sources is encouraged if they meet the objectives of the company.

Evaluate and review program

Designing a measurement system is the next step. Questions that need to be asked include: What do we want to measure? When do we want to measure?

EXHIBIT 13 • 4   *Analyzing the Needs of the Sales Force*

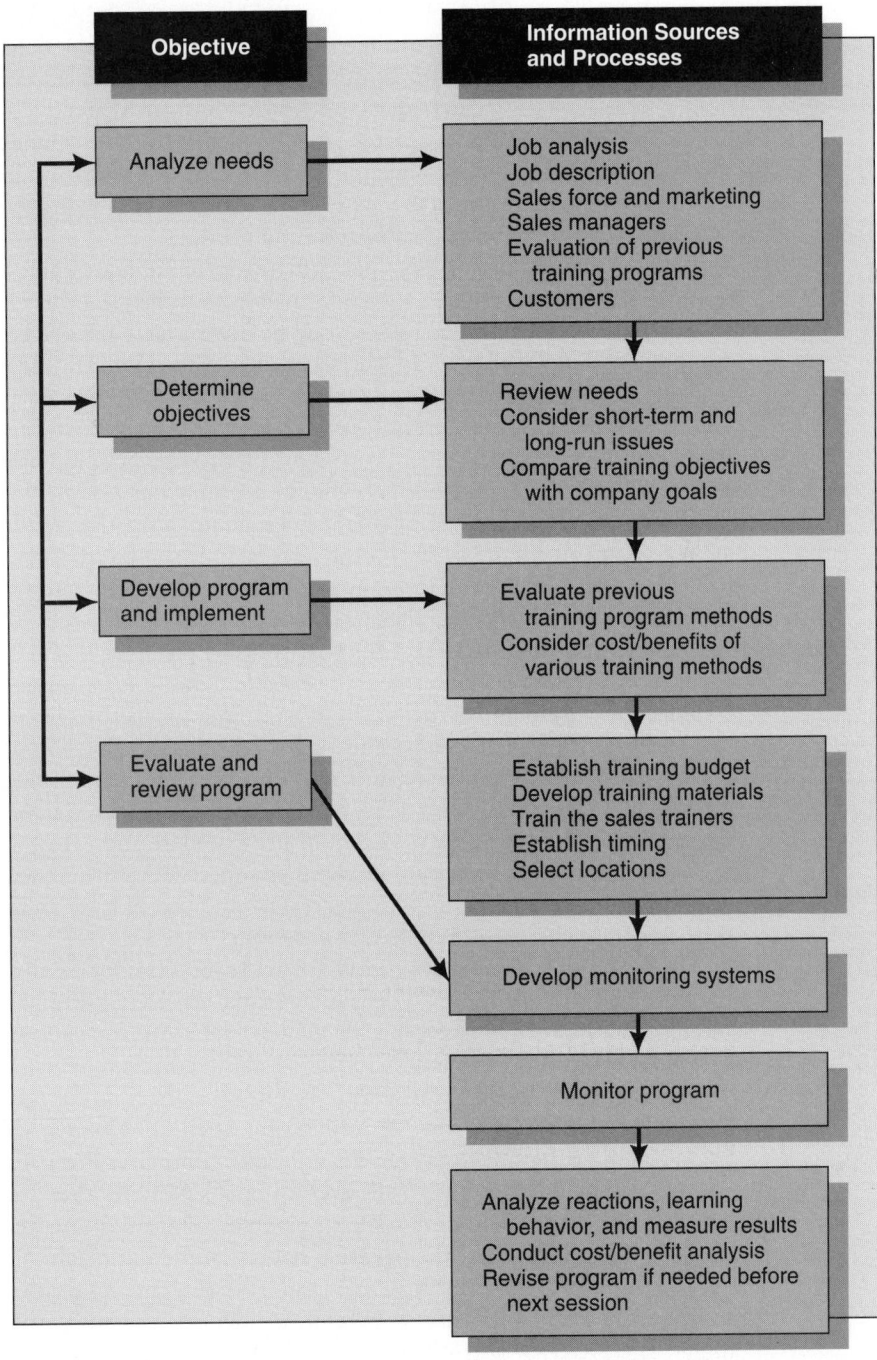

How do we do it? Or, what measuring tools are available? Using tests to measure learning is not difficult; measuring application in the field is difficult. Training a sales rep to demonstrate a product can be evaluated during the training session. But whether the sales rep demonstrates effectively in front of a customer is harder to evaluate. This is why field sales managers are an important link: They can provide follow-up and feedback information on how well the sales rep demonstrates the product. The field sales managers can coach the salesperson on how to demonstrate the product.

Finally, evaluations of sales performance provide additional evidence on the value of training, although such information must be used carefully. Changes in performance, like sales increases, may be due to factors not related to sales training. To claim that they are casts doubt on the sales training efforts.

Larger companies must decide which group to train. Not everyone in the sales force needs training. Certainly, newly hired recruits need training, whether it's on the job at first and then more centralized later or some other arrangement. When procedures or products change, training needs are universal. However, if certain sales reps are having a sales slump, then the training needs to be directed at them and not everybody. To include the entire force may create problems, especially among those not experiencing the sales slump. This latter group may resent being included and let others know as well. When a new training method is being tested, it is wise to use a group that will be receptive. This increases credibility, creating a favorable climate for continuation.

Since measurement is crucial, the sales trainer needs to collect data before training starts. The needs analysis provided relevant information pertaining to program content. For example, if it was observed that some salespeople had difficulty managing their sales calls, then observation by the trainer or the field sales manager after the program should provide data indicating the value of the training. Call reports would be another source of information. Follow-up must continue beyond the initial check since the use of new skills may drop off. If this happens, reinforcement is necessary.

The data-collection process should provide sales trainers with information that will justify the program. Top management wants to know if the benefits exceed or equal the costs. Keeping top management informed about the success of training programs contributes to the overall credibility.

Continuous follow-up and evaluation of all sales training efforts is mandatory. Gene Hahne, manager of training for Shell Oil Company, comments, "We used one program for seven years in our company. We used it because nobody evaluated it. Nobody followed up on it. Nobody ever took the time out to go out in the field and ask participants. 'What did you get out of the program?' "[13] In this case, the program had attempted to teach sales reps how to probe for information during a sales call. Although most sales reps identified the subject matter, very few were able to identify the skills that had been taught. The program was not working and probably had been written off as a poor investment by management.

Sales training programs, whether being sold to the sales manager or to top management, must be credible. Management can always find other alternatives for spending resources.

Needed: A Back-to-Basics Approach

Traditional sales training programs concentrate on teaching factual information about new products or services, new company procedures, and important changes in the market. For the most part, these programs have been successful. They have been less successful in developing sales skills. Characteristics of the firm's superstars are portrayed as the ideal, and all others are told they should try to emulate these high performers. It's as if the goal of the program is to produce clones of the superstars. According to one authority,

> The problem in trying to produce superseller clones is that it just doesn't work. One of the best examples I've encountered in trying to clone a superseller was provided by a mid-sized insurance company. The company's most productive agent was asked to develop a sales presentation. The agent was a fast-paced, quick-witted, distinctively New York, New Yorker. He wrote a presentation that was distributed at a national sales training seminar to other insurance agents who were instructed to "learn it" (i.e., memorize it).[14]

The program failed since it ignored regional, cultural, and personality differences not only of the participants but also of their customers. In a sense, the program was saying a single personality type exists that applies to all salespeople and to all of their customers. Unfortunately, this image is hard to dispel. There is no one type of personality or selling style that works in all cases. People are different, regardless of whether they are selling or buying. To assume otherwise leads to development of meaningless sales training programs.

The back-to-basics approach rests on a key assumption. Selling is a process of influence.[15] The salesperson influences the customer, who in turn influences the salesperson. For salespeople to influence the selling process they must accurately assess the buying situation to determine the approach most likely to work. In some cases, being persuasive works; in others, being quietly persistent and forceful is more effective. No one selling style or personality works in all cases. Successful salespeople alter their approach to meet the needs of specific customers and specific selling situations. Successful selling is situation-specific. This conclusion leads to the development of a more general basis of sales training, namely a behavioral approach or behavior modeling.

Behavior modeling

What is behavior modeling? How does it influence salesperson behavior? How can modeling be used in a sales training program? Psychologists define behavior modeling as a process by which new patterns of behavior can be acquired or existing patterns of behavior altered. The idea is that learning occurs through observation of others, not through actual experiences. Thus, modeling is a vicarious process that takes place through observing others, copying, matching,

EXHIBIT 13 • 5   *Traditional Sales Training Models versus Behavior Modeling*

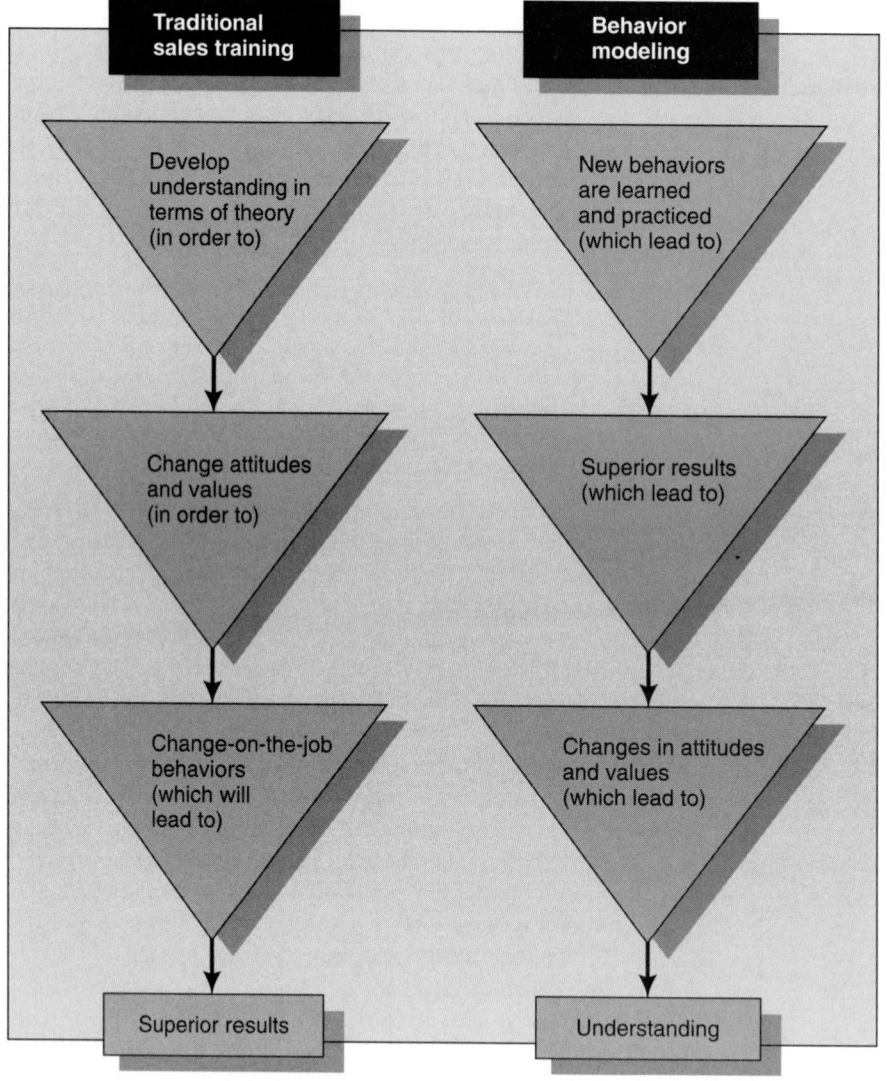

Source: Reprinted with permission from A. J. Kraut, "Developing Managerial Skills via Modeling Techniques: Some Positive Research Findings—A Symposium," *Personnel Psychology,* 1976, p. 326.

or imitation. Exhibit 13.5 contrasts traditional sales training with behavior modeling.

If we can assume that salespeople need to know a variety of selling skills to be successful, then it follows that behavior modeling would be an appropriate method. Behavioral sales training programs should help sales reps acquire a wide range of desirable selling behaviors such as giving information, asking questions, listening, and solving problems. Shaw identifies two basic patterns of behavior: "First, the sales representative may choose to *act* upon the customer . . . in ways which are aimed at shaping the customer's viewpoints, feelings, and reactions. Secondly, the sales representative may *reach* to the customer in ways which are aimed at drawing out the customer's views and demonstrating empathy and responsiveness."[16]

Two choices exist for a salesperson: to *act* or to *react*. In a sales transaction, the rep combines these two resources to influence the transaction. Successful salespeople have been described broadly as being "problem solvers" and narrowly as being "persuasive." Salespeople who are behaving persuasively use gestures, vary the pitch and tempo of their voice, make eye contact, smile, and use positive words and phrases.

There are three tiers of behavior, according to Shaw, who states, "Since problem-solving behavior is a different order of concern than giving information which is, in turn, of a different order than 'making eye contact,' it was found that three tiers were useful in clarifying the relationship between means and ends."[17] They are (1) behavioral strategies, (2) behavioral skills, and (3) behavioral tactics.

Behavioral strategies can be defined as a basic selling approach comprised of a set of skills that, when used together, form an approach for dealing with a specific customer. Different strategies are used with different customers. Behavioral skills are the competencies needed to excuse a specific strategy. To use a **problem-solving strategy**, a term too broad to be meaningful, it is necessary to use specific skills such as listening carefully, asking the right questions, and presenting solutions. Behavioral sales training must concentrate on these. Behavioral tactics are subsets of skills. For example, persuasiveness is a skill requiring tactics such as using gestures, varying voice tempo and pitch, making eye contact, and so forth. Can these tactics be acquired via observation and practice? Behavior modeling assumes they can be learned, as illustrated in Exhibit 13.5.

Skill and tactics can be combined into two categories: "A" or *act* skills and tactics, and "R" or *react* skills and tactics. A partial listing of each class is in Exhibit 13.6.

The sales manager who urges the sales rep to be more persuasive without telling the rep *how* to be persuasive is not providing training. Persuasiveness must be broken down into subsets before training can occur.

Selling strategies consist of (1) interactive or problem-solving strategies using A and R skills, (2) proactive or controlling strategies primarily using A skills, (3) reactive or adaptive strategies primarily using R skills, and (4) mixed or negotiating strategies combining A and R skills. The skilled sales rep acquires skills and tactics and blends them to meet the needs of specific situations. Remember that customers have different needs and personalities, and one selling strategy will not work in all cases.

How can behavior modeling help train sales representatives to acquire the necessary tactics, skills, and strategies? Once desired behaviors have been iden-

EXHIBIT 13 • 6   *Act and React Skills and Tactics*

Act (A) Skills and Tactics	React (R) Skills and Tactics
Give information by: • Being brief and specific. • Making eye contact. • Avoiding apologies or equivocations. *Be persuasive by:* • Talking benefits. • Using affirmative words. • Varying voice dynamics and tempo. • Gesturing. *Be convincing by:* • Being deliberate and emphatic. • Using facts. • Being "grounded."	*Explore the other's view by:* • Asking direct questions. • Asking open-ended questions. • Sustaining eye contact. *Support the other by:* • Summarizing his or her viewpoint. • Reflecting feelings. • Identifying with customer's feelings. *Adapt to other's views by:* • Seeking compromise • Seeking alternatives. • Modifying your behavior.

tified, the next stage is to provide a means whereby sales trainees can observe and experience these activities. Exhibit 13.7 illustrates the process.

The starting point is to present or display the desired behavior using demonstrations or models employing live or filmed presentations, written examples, case problems, exercises, and so forth. Shaw argues that only desired behavior should be demonstrated so negative habits are avoided.[19] This view coincides with a concern expressed by Jack Falvey in "Myths of Sales Training" that it is wrong to "Let Old Joe Train the New Rep." Old Joe has acquired many tactics that work for him, some right and some wrong, and it's erroneous to have him teach bad habits.[20]

The next step in the training process is to have the sales rep experience the desired behavior by doing it alone or with a trainer or manager in a one-on-one setting. This is followed by practice and more practice coupled with coaching. On-the-job practice with a field sales manager present allows for instant feedback and reinforcement.

Reinforcement is critical to the success of all behavior modeling programs and must occur during all phases. Meeting quota provides rewards to salespeople, but incentives must be available during training. The sales rep who learns how to be persuasive by practicing various tactics needs reinforcing as the tactics are learned.[21] Eventually acquiring the necessary skills and tactics will lead to higher order rewards, such as a promotion. In the interim, management needs to provide a support system that reinforces and supports positive behavior. An important ingredient of behavior modeling as a sales training

E X H I B I T   13 • 7   *Modeling Processes and Methods*

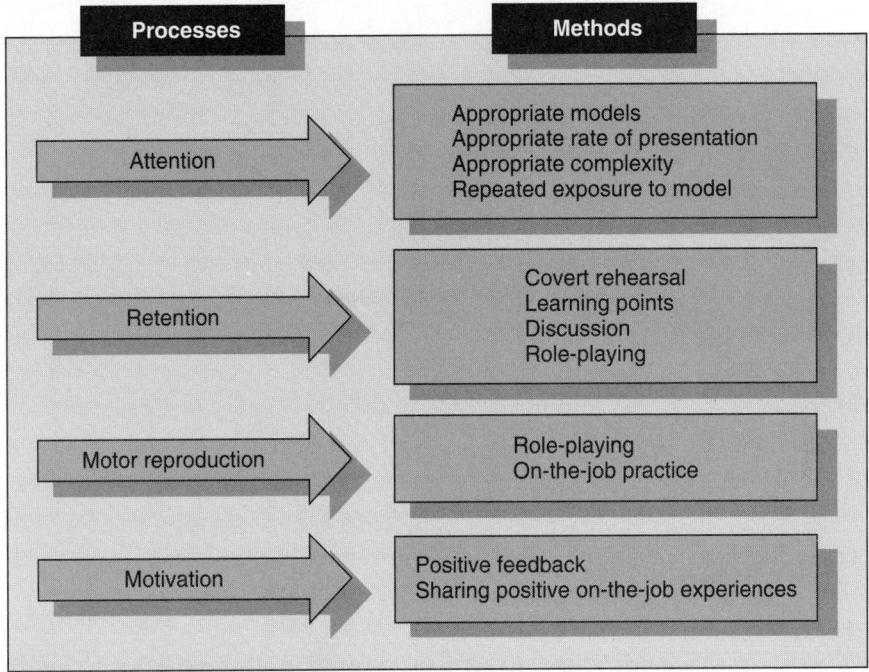

Source: Carl. D. Riegel, "Behavior Modeling for Management Development," *Cornell Hotel and Restaurant Administration Quarterly*, August 1982, p. 79.

method is follow-up and reinforcement. Snader advocates allocating 50 percent of the budget to the training program and 50 percent to reinforcement and follow-up.[22] Without this, sales managers may be inclined to assume that training is over, and they can turn their attention to other issues.

Sales Training Needs

A Learning International study reveals which training topics were considered important to sale success.[23] Of the 1,300 respondents from U.S. and Canadian industrial firms, 43 percent revealed they did not provide training for their sales force, 34 percent relied on internally developed programs, and 23 percent used professional sales training services.

These conclusions were drawn from the study:

1. The outcome of the training seems to be more important than how the training is implemented.

2. Materials that enable management to reinforce what is covered in the

E X H I B I T 13 • 8   *Sales Training Topics Desired by Organizations*

Training Topics Desired Most	Percentage of Respondents
Effective listening	34
Closing and gaining commitment	32
Maintaining self-motivation	27
Time management	25
How to cold call	24
Training Topics Desired Least	**Percentage of Respondents**
Following up with clients	5
Providing service after the sale	5
How to differentiate your product or service	4
Developing workable territory plans	3
Prioritizing accounts	3

Source: Reprinted from "Study Reveals Sales-Training Needs of Business Marketers," *Marketing News,* March 13, 1989, p. 6, published by the American Marketing Association.

training as well as services to conduct post-training evaluations should be included in future programs.

3. To be successful, salespeople need training in many different areas in addition to product knowledge and policies and procedures training.

4. Training can't be a single event.

5. Participants need reinforcement, and most organizations want sales managers to provide any reinforcement necessary for the development of their salespeople.[24]

Respondents evaluated 59 sales training tropics. Exhibit 13.8 profiles both the most desired and least desired topics. The top two most desired topics relate to selling style, not product or service knowledge. The findings also revealed respondents were more interested in the results rather than in "using particular teaching methods—such as new technologies, seminars, self-study, etc." As we shall see, sales training methods have undergone dramatic changes that it is hoped will enhance the learning process.

The study also showed high interest in developing "tracking instruments to measure the impact of training on performance." Cost-effective and modular training programs also received support from the respondents. Multiple buying contacts in the customer's organization, a predominant characteristic of business-to-business marketing, appear to be a determinant of the existence of training programs. In those firms that do not provide training (43 percent), "purchasing agents were significantly more likely to be the primary sales contact."

OBJECTIVES OF SALES TRAINING

Although the specific objectives of sales training may vary from firm to firm, there is some agreement on the broad objectives. Sales training is undertaken to increase productivity, improve morale, lower turnover, improve customer relations, and produce better management of time and territory.

Increase Productivity

One objective of sales training is to provide trainees with the necessary skills so their selling performance makes a positive contribution to the firm. In a relatively short time, sales training attempts to teach the skills possessed by the more experienced members of the sales force. The time it takes for a new member of the sales force to achieve satisfactory levels of productivity is thus shortened considerably.

Improve Morale

How does sales training lead to better morale? One objective of sales training is to prepare trainees to perform tasks so their productivity increases as quickly as possible. If sales trainees know what is expected of them, they will be less likely to experience the frustrations that arise from trying to perform a job without adequate preparation. Without sales training, customers may ask questions that sales representatives cannot answer, leading to frustration and lower morale. Evidence indicates salespeople who are uncertain about their job requirements tend to be less satisfied with their jobs.[25] This same evidence shows that reps who are most aware of the job requirements are also more satisfied with their company's sales training activities.

Lower Turnover

If sales training can lead to improved morale (greater job satisfaction), then this should result in lower turnover. Younger, inexperienced salespeople are more likely to get discouraged and quit as a result of not being prepared for the task. Turnover can also lead to customer problems, since many customers prefer continuity with sales representatives. A customer who is called on by a sales representative who suddenly quits may transfer business to other suppliers rather than wait for a new representative. Sales training, by leading to lower turnover, alleviates such problems.

Improve Customer Relations

One benefit of sales training that accompanies lower turnover is continuity in customer relationships. Having the same sales representative call on customers on a regular basis promotes customer loyalty, especially when the salesperson can handle customer questions, objections, and complaints. Customers place orders for their own benefits. Inadequately trained salespeople are usually not able to provide these benefits, and customer relations suffer.

Manage Time and Territory Better

Time and territory management is a subject in many sales training programs. How much time should be devoted to calls on existing accounts and how much time to calls on potential new accounts? How often should each class of account be called on? What is the most effective way of covering the territory to ensure routes traveled are the most efficient with respect to miles driven and time spent? Many sales training programs provide salespeople with answers to these questions.

THE TIMING OF SALES TRAINING

Although sales training is a continuous process, exactly when firms accept sales trainees into the formal sales training program varies considerably. A common practice is to have sales trainees work in the field calling on accounts before any formal sales training occurs. It is also common to start with formal training followed by a field assignment. In either case, the length of the formal training program can vary from a few days to more than a year, depending on company needs.

Training of experienced sales personnel varies also. Some companies have annual programs, and others have programs only when the need arises. The length of both types of programs varies from firm to firm. Training of experienced sales personnel may be routine, such as when it is associated with an annual sales convention. It may be nonroutine or remedial and may occur because of problems experienced by one or more members of the sales force. The introduction of new products often leads to sales training.

TRAINING NEW SALES RECRUITS

Most larger companies have programs for training new sales recruits. These programs differ considerably in length and content, however. The differences often reflect variations in company policies, nature of the selling job, and types of products and services.[26] Even within the same industry, sales training programs vary in length, content, and technique.

Although a few companies have no preset time for training sales recruits, most firms have embraced the notion of a fixed period for formal training. The time varies from just a couple of days in the office, followed by actual selling combined with on-the-job coaching, to as long as two or three years of intensive training in a number of fields and skills.

What accounts for this variation? First, training needs vary from firm to firm and even within a firm. For example, one manufacturer of drugs has a

EXHIBIT 13 • 9   *Length of Sales Training by Industry*

Industry Group	Average Training Period (months)	Industry Group	Average Training Period (months)
Agriculture	5.7%	Insurance	5.5%
Amusement/recreation services	2.0	Lumber/wood products	2.7
Business services	4.1	Machinery	5.6
Chemicals	4.5	Manufacturing	3.3
Communications	4.2	Office equipment	2.8
Construction	5.0	Paper/allied products	6.0
Electronic components	1.5	Primary metal products	4.5
Electronics	3.4	Printing/publishing	5.5
Fabricated metals	3.5	Rubber/plastics	6.5
Food products	2.8	Wholesale (consumer)	1.5
Instruments	2.7	Wholesale (industrial)	3.9
Average	**4.9%**		

Note: Industry groups reflect categories selected and reported by Dartnell Corporation. The overall average has been calculated by *Sales & Marketing Management* based on data from the 22 industries listed.

Source: Reprinted with permission from "1991 Sales Manager's Budget Planner," *Sales & Marketing Management*, June 17, 1991, p. 77, © by Bill Communications, Inc.

seven-week program for new recruits who will sell conventional consumer products. For those recruits destined to sell more technical products, the training lasts two years.

Second, training needs vary because of differences in the needs and aptitudes of the recruits. Experienced recruits have less need for training than inexperienced recruits, although most large firms require everyone to go through some formal training. One industrial firm requires a one-week program for experienced recruits, but inexperienced recruits may require a two- to three-year program.

A final reason for variation in the length of training programs is company philosophy. Some sales managers believe training for new recruits should be concentrated at the beginning of a sales career, but others think it should be spread over a longer time, including a large dose of learning by doing. Exhibit 13.9 illustrates the differences in the length of sales training programs.

TRAINING PROGRAMS FOR NEW RECRUITS

Training programs for new recruits vary not only in length but also in content and not only among industries but within industries as well. For example, among the 17 manufacturers of food, beverages, and tobacco products that participated in a Conference Board study, the time devoted to teaching product knowledge varied from 10 percent to 50 percent of the total time available

EXHIBIT 13 • 10   *Distribution of Training Time by Subject Matter for*
Newly Hired Sales Personnel

| | Percentage of Time Devoted | | |
Values*	First Quartile	Median	Third Quartile
Company orientation	5	10	20
Market/industry orientation	10	15	20
Selling technique	15	20	30
Product knowledge	30	40	60

*Based on 152 sales units.

Source: Adapted from David S. Hopkins, *Training the Sales Force: A Progress Report* (New York: The Conference Board, 1978), p. 6.

for training. A sales manager from one insurance company revealed that 70 percent of the training program was spent on product knowledge; as little as 10 percent of training was spent in another insurance company.

Exhibit 13.10 shows how companies generally allocate time to various subjects in formal sales training programs. Product knowledge receives the most emphasis, followed by selling techniques, market/industry orientation, and company orientation. The quartiles show that considerable divergence exists, however; 25 percent of the firms spend 5 percent of the time on company orientation, but 75 percent spend 20 percent of the total time on this subject. Individual company differences are even more extreme.

The information most needed by the new salesperson should determine what to teach new recruits. Typically this means at least some information should relate to one of the training objectives cited earlier. Telling recruits about company service policies gives them information for answering customer questions. Training recruits on handling objections from customers can lead to more sales and more satisfied customers.

The four orientations in Exhibit 13.10 do not fully capture the range of issues in modern sales training programs. To overcome the negative image associated with the selling profession and to improve overall effectiveness, many sales managers have modified training programs to develop more well-rounded business professionals who are beyond the stage of being just an inventory counter or an order taker.

A metal producer has upgraded its program to provide what is termed *in-depth training* so that sales personnel will in fact "represent our company and our industry to the highest levels of their customers." On completing the program, trainees are said to be able to comprehend and handle all types of financial, marketing, and operational discussions.

EXHIBIT 13 • 11   *Percentage of Small and Large Firms that "Extensively Use" the Following Sales Training Tools and Practices*

Training Practices	Percentage of Small Firms	Percentage of Large Firms
Type of training program:		
Product knowledge training	74	79
Field/on-the-job training	66	68
Selling skills training	43	64
Market/competition training	28	55
Company information training	14	34
Type of trainer:		
Sales manager	55	55
Senior salesperson	30	33
Full-time (staff) sales trainer	5	38
Outside training consultant	1	9
Training program procedure:		
Establishment of training program objectives	37	64
Evaluation of training program effectiveness	19	53

Note: A statistically significant difference ($p < 0.05$) exists between the percentage of small and large firms that "extensively use" this sales management tool or practice.

Source: Adapted from Alan J. Dubinsky and Thomas E. Barry, "A Survey of Sales Management Practice," *Industrial Marketing Management* 11 (1982), p. 137, copyright by Elsevier Science Publishing Co., Inc.

At a *rubber products company,* training of field personnel has been directed toward business counsel, inventory management, and similar programs to reinforce knowledge of product-line profitability.

For a *railroad,* " . . . the most dramatic and significant improvement in our sales training efforts . . . has been to change the traditional concept of our field personnel selling rail service only, into making them transportation and distribution consultants with knowledge of marketing concepts and advanced distribution techniques that can benefit the customer as well as our company."

At a *tobacco company,* there has been a shift in training emphasis from "selling" to "merchandising." . . . Says the vice president of sales, " . . . those sales representatives who are the most knowledgeable about the customer's whole business, as well as about the category in which his products fit, will be the most successful."[27]

Developing sales representatives with the skills described in these examples places a heavy burden on sales training. Sales training programs must include more topics than just selling skills, but what is the most appropriate mix of subjects? Although this determination must always be made by the individual firm, an appreciation for the "whys" of some general industry techniques should be helpful. Exhibit 13.11 details the training practices of small and large firms.

*Product
Knowledge*

Although product knowledge is one of the most important topics, knowing when and how to discuss the subject in a sales call is probably even more important. More time is typically spent on product knowledge than any other subject, although the time spent varies with the commodity sold.

Companies that produce technical products, such as computer manufacturers, spend more time on this subject than do manufacturers of nontechnical products. One manufacturer of specialized industrial components allocates 90 percent of its sales training program to application engineering and product knowledge for graduate engineers recruited directly from campuses.[28] Producers of personal care products and toiletry preparations spend less time on product knowledge. In the service industry, the complexity of the service influences the amount of time needed to learn the service, such as with various types of insurance.

Product knowledge involves not only knowing how the product is made but also how the product is used and, in some cases, how it should not be used. One producer of machine tools gives newly hired sales engineers extensive in-plant exposure to technical and engineering matters. Before field assignment, they spend time in a customer's plant, where they are taught machine setup and operations under realistic conditions.

Product knowledge is not limited to only those products the sales trainee will eventually sell. Customers often want to know how competitive products compare on price, construction, performance, and compatibility with each other. Customers expect reps to show them how the seller's products can be coordinated with competitive products, such as in a computer installation that involves products made by different manufacturers. One paper products manufacturer that supplies paper towels to industrial firms exposes sales trainees to competitive towel dispensers so they will know which dispensers handle their paper towels.

A major objective in training in product knowledge is to enable a salesperson to provide potential customers with the information needed for rational decision making. Some benefits that accrue to salespeople as they acquire product knowledge include the following:

1. Pride and confidence in product quality.
2. Self-assurance emanating from technical knowledge of product makeup.
3. Communication with customers through the use of the operational vocabulary peculiar to the industry.
4. Understanding of product functioning that allows effective diagnosis of customer problems.[29]

All these benefits contribute to improved salesperson-customer interaction.

*Market/Industry
Orientation*

Sales training in market/industry orientation covers both broad and specific factors. From a broad viewpoint, salespeople need to know how their particular industry fits into the overall economy. Economic fluctuations affect buying behavior, which affects selling techniques. Information about inflationary pressure, for example, may be used to persuade prospective buyers to move their decision dates ahead. If the sales force is involved in forecasting sales and setting quotas, knowledge of the industry and the economy is essential.

From a narrower viewpoint, salespeople must have detailed knowledge about present customers. They need to know their customers' buying policies, patterns, and preferences and the products or services these companies produce. In some cases, sales reps need to be knowledgeable about their customers' customers. This is especially true when sales representatives sell through wholesalers or distributors who often want reps to assist them with their customers' problems. Missionary salespeople are expected to know the needs of both wholesalers and retailers, even though the retailers buy from the wholesalers.

Company Orientation

Sales trainees must be aware of company policies that affect their selling activities. Like all new employees, they need indoctrination in personnel policies on such items as salary structure and company benefits.

Sales representatives can expect customers to request price adjustments, product modifications, faster delivery, and different credit terms. Most companies have policies on such matters arising from legal requirements or industry practices. Too often, however, avoidable delays and possibly lost sales result from inadequate sales training in company policies.

Two practices provide salespeople with knowledge of company policies. The first requires sales trainees to learn about company policies and procedures by working in the home office in various departments, such as credit, order processing, advertising, sales promotion, and shipping. The second approach has the trainee work as a sales correspondent for a time. The trainee processes customer orders, maintains mail and telephone contact with customers, and sometimes serves as the company contact for a group of customers.

Major corporations provide the sales force with sales manuals that cover product line information and company policies. A well-prepared sales manual can give a sales representative a quick answer to a customer's question.

Time and Territory Management

Sales trainees also need assistance in how to manage their time and territories. The recent survey by Learning International suggests that salespeople perceive this as an important problem.[30]

The familiar 20:80 ratio, where 20 percent of a company's customers account for 80 percent of the business, applies to time and territory management in the reverse direction. It is not unusual to find sales representatives who are skilled in all areas except efficient time management, spending 80 percent of their time with customers who account for only 20 percent of sales.

Poor assignment of customers and development of territories contribute to the time management problem. Sales managers need to know how to develop territories to enhance the sales rep's efficiency. Assigning a sales representative too many accounts or a territory that is too large leads to time and territory management problems.

The program for a manufacturer of micrographic equipment and supplies trains salespeople to "plan your work—work your plan." Although some instruction in time management is provided by this company during classroom training, the major responsibility rests with the district sales managers. Effective time management is more likely to be achieved via on-the-job training. Sales representatives turn in their projected activities every two weeks and review their district sales manager's past plans and performance. The district sales manager helps them modify the projected plans for greater efficiency. The desire for more effective time and territory management has led to greater telephone usage and telemarketing sales training courses.

Legal Issues

Statements, or rather misstatements, made by salespeople have legal implications. Thorny Issues in Sales Management 13.2 describes problems companies experience because of legal actions. Companies intending to sell overseas need to include training in cultural differences. How to sell in France is discussed in Thorny Issues 13.3.

Other Subjects

Recent technological developments have led to a new sales training subject: how to use a personal computer. Many companies now require their sales reps to carry personal computers with them to improve productivity. Salespeople use PCs to plan their call activities, submit orders, send reports, check on inventory and price levels, receive messages, and present product and service demonstrations. In some cases, the sales rep can access the company's decision support system (DSS) to learn what products have been selling in an area or for a specific customer. A few companies have found that the use of PCs allows their salespeople more face-to-face customer contact time.

Many companies, like Caterpillar Inc., spend substantial sums of money each year on trade shows. Increasing cost pressures have forced management to be more concerned about the return from trade shows and other similar expenditures. As a result, Caterpillar Inc. personnel selected to staff trade show exhibits undergo a training program designed to handle a trade show's unique features. Most salespeople selected have the "training and experience to make in-depth presentations in their specialties. But even though they're very good at what they normally do, they are not necessarily skilled at working a trade show. They don't always know how to engage and qualify new prospects, handle big crowds, or weed out the buyers from the 'tire kickers.'"[31]

Other subjects in training programs include topics such as body language, eye movement, and attempts to determine if the prospect is right-brained or left-brained. One advocate comments, "Customers come in right- and left-brained thinking styles, and understanding their differences and your own brain

LEGAL DIMENSIONS OF SALESPERSONS' STATEMENTS: A SALES TRAINING SUBJECT?

Salespeople have created liability problems for their companies by making statements that consciously or inadvertently mislead prospects/customers. An enthusiastic salesperson may overstate the capabilities of a product, unaware that the presentation contains impossible-to-meet promises. Although such overstatements may be described as "sales talk" or "harmless puffery," they have been known to lead to expensive litigation. To avoid such problems, sales training programs may need to provide instruction about legal issues.

In one case, *Dunn Appraisal* v. *Honeywell Information Systems, Inc.* (1982), 687 F.2d 877 (6th Cir.), a sales rep overstated that a software program could perform several analyses. The customer, relying on this information, purchased the software program only to learn it could not function as indicated. Even though the salesperson believed he was telling the truth, "innocent misrepresentation," the courts ruled for the plaintiff. The plaintiff received $61,573 actual plus $30,768 punitive damages plus legal fees of $24,628.

Although most companies discourage their sales reps from "knocking the competition," situations occur that lead to negative statements about competitive products/services. In *Systems Operations, Inc.* v. *Scientific Games Development Corp.* (1976), 414 F. Supp. 750 (D. N.J.), the defendant's sales reps suggested the plaintiff's lottery tickets could be "read" without any visible signs of tampering. In court, the defendant's sales reps were not able to demonstrate how the plaintiff's lottery tickets could be "read" during testimony. The court prohibited the defendant's sales force from making such claims.

Overstating product features is a problem. Telling prospects that information printed in company literature is not important is also a problem. Security salespeople in *In re First Commodity Corp. of Boston* (1987), 119 F.R.D. 301 (D. Mass.), told clients that legally mandated information in the securities prospectus was unimportant and should be ignored. Clients who acted on this advice lost substantial sums of money because of rapidly declining securities prices. The court certified the plaintiffs for class action litigation. Damages assessed in prior cases have ranged from $260,000 to $3 million.

Currently, there is little evidence indicating that sales training programs should provide legal instruction. The following indicates how sales management might instruct sales reps as to their legal obligations.

1. Include detailed modules on legal guidelines in training schools for beginning salespersons. Training should focus on both declarative and procedural knowledge.

2. Routinely provide updated information to salespersons about the most recent judicial and statutory developments related to communications with prospects and customers.

3. Develop incentive compensation packages that encourage and reward salespersons for avoiding or forestalling litigious situations.

4. Review salesperson performance to identify quickly and decisively salespersons who engage in practices that might lead to legal problems.

5. Manage by example. Always follow the legal guidelines when accompanying salespersons in the field, and hold salespersons to the same standards when reviewing their performance.

Source: Karl A. Boedecker, Fred W. Morgan, and Jeffrey J. Stoltman, "Legal Dimensions of Salespersons' Statement: A Review and Managerial Suggestions," *Journal of Marketing,* 55 (January 1991), pp. 70–80.

Thorny Issues in Sales Management 13 • 3

How to Sell in France

Global marketing is increasing dramatically. Political changes in Eastern Europe will provide new global market opportunities. Although most companies doing business abroad prefer to hire residents of the country, companies will interact directly with prospects on occasion. In such situations, one must be knowledgeable about cultural differences to avoid committing a faux pas.

Selling in France is no different. According to Jean-Pierre Tricard, who heads his own company, Jean-Pierre Tricard Conseil, there are significant cultural differences between French and American salespeople. Americans consider how much money one makes as a sign of success. The French, on the other hand, are reluctant to talk about how much money they make. People who brag about how much they make are looked on as thieves.

Attitudes toward money affect sales negotiations, especially when price enters the picture. Tricard notes that French salespeople panic when price issues surface. American salespeople, Tricard believes, are better prepared to negotiate price.

Tricard identifies several other problem areas. Business lunches in France should be reserved for an-after-the-sale celebration. Inviting French customers to dinner usually happens after a salesperson has worked with the customer for a long time.

Any tendency for an American salesperson to brag about being the "greatest" or the "biggest" should be stifled. The French view this as subtle aggression, which they instantly reject. Tricard advises American salespeople not to call the executives of a French company by their first names.

Companies that intend to sell in France should be aware of cultural differences and how these differences affect sales transactions. Tricard, who is well known as a sales trainer, identifies 10 negotiation tactics used by French customers. These tactics should be part of the sales training program for companies planning to conduct business in France.

Ten Negotiation Tactics Used by French Customers

French customers are superb actors and many of them play their parts with great flair. To test your skills as a negotiator it is not uncommon for them to set friendly traps. The key to cross-cultural negotiations is patience, understanding, and an attitude that says, "I want your business, but if it doesn't work out, that's fine with me." French customers respect competence, confidence, pride, audacity, and passion. Below are 10 negotiation tactics French customers use. They will:

- Show very little interest in your product.
- Tell you that if you lower your price now, they'll do much more business with you in the future.
- Tell you that French-made products are much better and cheaper in the long run.
- Tell you your competitor offers a superior quality at a better price.
- Shower you with compliments. They'll tell you that they like you. They'll smile a lot and reassure you that they want to do business with you.
- Go along with your proposal and agree with you up until the very last minute. Then they'll tell you that they can't do the deal unless you lower your price significantly.
- Ask you to lower your quality and reduce the service, so you can lower the price. Then they'll reverse their strategy and up the quality and the service, but insist on the lower price.
- Ask you to conclude the deal over an inexpensive lunch. They'll get you to taste four different wines, they'll toast you and your company at

(continued)

every occasion until you are so relaxed that you gladly give in to their demands.

- Sell you on the big picture, the long-term relationship, the great "fit" between your companies, and the fantastic opportunities that will follow. Then when you explain the details of your deal, they'll act as if you had offended and betrayed them.

- Ask you for your timetable and stall you with minor details to wear you down. When you begin to run out of time, they'll shift gears and expect you to decide on the important issues in a matter of minutes.

Negotiation Tip

When negotiating with French customers, always start your negotiations by selling the big picture first, then work your way down to the details. Once you've sold the "big idea," the sale will be easy. If you begin your sale by working your way from the individual parts to the whole, your negotiation strategy will be far less successful.

Companies that plan to sell in the French market should consider how their sales training programs will need to be modified. An investment is required and as Tricard notes: "There are many American companies that could do very well in France; however, they don't make the investment to understand French customs."

Source: Gerhard Gschwandtner, "How to Sell in France," *Personal Selling Power*, July–August 1991, pp. 54–60.

waves can help you make your next sale." Indicators of left- and right-brained people might be whether or not a customer wears a watch or carries a calculator.[32] Evidence supporting the efficacy of this concept as a sales training subject is not available.

Alan J. Zaremba, in a *Business Marketing* article, notes that analyzing body language has received attention since Julius Fast published *Body Language* in 1970. Zaremba states, "Nonverbal gestures do affect how messages are perceived." He cautions, however, that a harmful assumption about body language is that there is not a "finite and universal meaning for all messages transmitted nonverbally."[33] Training salespeople to observe and interpret a customer's body movements may help improve the sales presentation, but it is a skill that would require extensive training to accomplish. As with any training technique, evaluation of the process is mandatory to measure costs and benefits.

SALES TRAINING METHODS

The most commonly used methods of sales training are on-the-job training (OJT), individual instruction, in-house classes, and external seminars. Exhibit 13.12 summarizes industry preferences. Companies use a variety of techniques, recognizing that different subjects require different methods. Overlap exists within a given method. On-the-job training includes individual instruction

EXHIBIT 13 • 12   *Methods Used in Sales Training*

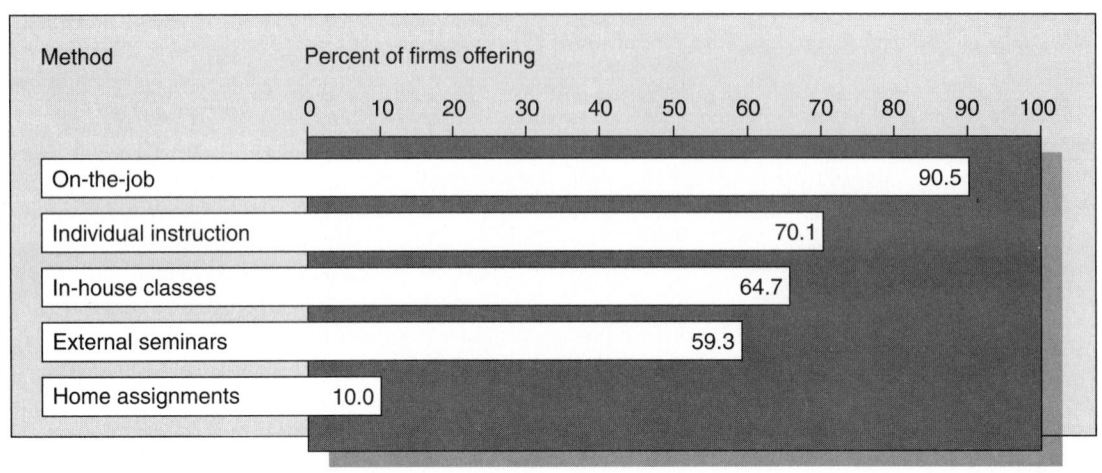

Source: Data, Cartnell Corporation; *26th Survey of Sales Force Compensation.* © 1990; Dartnell Corporation; chart, "1991 Sales Manager Budget Planner," *Sales & Marketing Management,* June 17, 1991, p. 78.

(coaching) and in-house classes held at district sales offices. District sales personnel attend external seminars as well.

The techniques of instruction vary, as Exhibit 13.13 shows. The most prevalent forms of instruction are videotapes, lectures, and one-on-one instruction, and companies combine techniques to achieve the best possible balance.

One source of sales training comes from outside suppliers, which use many of the techniques listed in Exhibit 13.12. As Falvey indicates: "the design, development, and sale of training materials is a big business these days." Companies question if they should spend money on outside sales training. Falvey's answer is: "Only if you have lots of discretionary money to spend and don't know what to do with it."[34]

"Selling," according to Falvey, "is an interactive skill that must be acquired in combination with the knowledge of how both you and your customers do business. It can't be separated out into a generic system that can later be recombined in some way with your business."[35]

On-the-Job Training

The mere mention of OJT sometimes scares new sales recruits. The thought of "learning by doing" is psychologically discomforting to many. Often, this is due to their incorrect perceptions of what is involved in OJT. On-the-job training is not a "sink or swim" approach in which the trainee is handed an order book, maybe a sales manual, and told to "go out and sell." OJT should be a carefully planned process in which the new recruit learns by doing and, at the same time, is productively employed. Furthermore, a good OJT program

EXHIBIT 13 • 13   *Instructional Methods Used in Training*

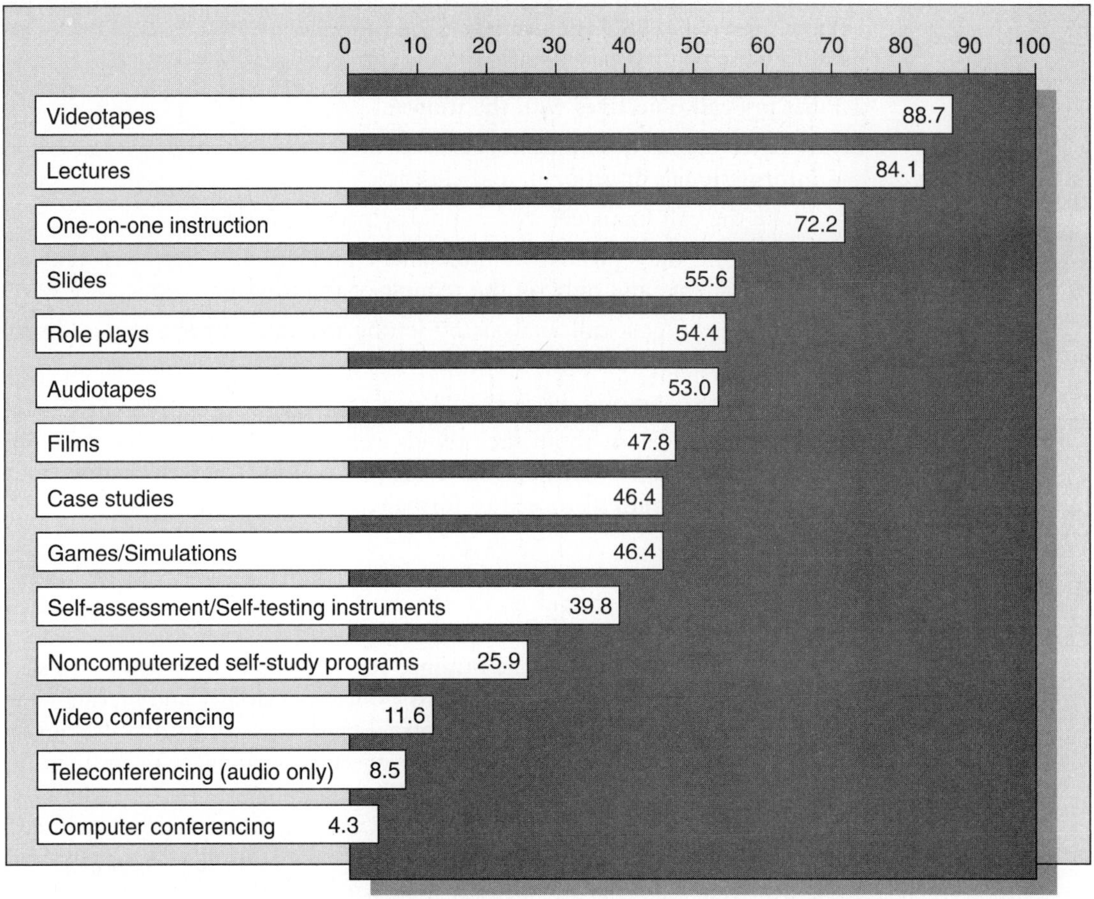

Method	Percent
Videotapes	88.7
Lectures	84.1
One-on-one instruction	72.2
Slides	55.6
Role plays	54.4
Audiotapes	53.0
Films	47.8
Case studies	46.4
Games/Simulations	46.4
Self-assessment/Self-testing instruments	39.8
Noncomputerized self-study programs	25.9
Video conferencing	11.6
Teleconferencing (audio only)	8.5
Computer conferencing	4.3

Note: Responses were gathered from a number of different industries and job types including training, human resources, sales and marketing, and customer service.

contains established procedures for evaluating and reviewing a sales trainee's progress. Critiques should be held after each OJT sales call and summarized daily. The critiques cover effectiveness, selling skills, communication of information in a persuasive manner, and other criteria.

A key aspect of on-the-job training is the coaching sales trainees receive from trainers, who may be experienced sales personnel, sales managers, or personnel specifically assigned to do sales training.

On-the-job training and coaching often occur together; this is referred to as one-on-one training. Observation is an integral part of the process. One-on-one training should not become "two-on-one" selling, where the objective becomes getting the order, not training the recruit. The sales manager or trainer is supposed to be a coach, not a player, and should stay out of the game no matter what the score. When the manager jumps in and says, "Let me take it from here," the recruit knows training has stopped and two-on-one selling has begun.[36] Some suggestions for making one-on-one training most effective are as follows:

1. Set pre-call objectives with the trainee.
2. Practice actual questions to be used to accomplish objectives (such as informational, directional, and closing).
3. Make the call (manager as a nonparticipating observer).
4. Contribute only positive reinforcement and act as a resource only on specific points and only on the request of the trainee.
5. Conduct the post-call analysis by letting the sales representative do the majority of the talking.[37]

OJT often involves job rotation—assigning trainees to different departments where they learn about such things as manufacturing, marketing, shipping, credits and collections, and servicing procedures. After on-the-job training, many sales trainees proceed to formal classroom training.

Classroom Training

For most companies, formal classroom training is an indispensable part of sales training, although very few of them rely solely on it. Classroom training has several advantages. First, each trainee receives standard briefings on such subjects as product knowledge, company policies, customer and market characteristics, and selling skills. Second, formal training sessions often save substantial amounts of executive time because executives can meet an entire group of trainees at once. Third, classroom sessions permit the use of audiovisual materials such as movies and videotape. Lectures, presentations, and case discussions can also be programmed into a classroom setting. The opportunity for interaction between sales trainees is a fourth advantage.

Such interaction is beneficial, since reinforcement and ideas for improvement can come from other sales trainees. Interaction is so important that many companies divide sales trainees into teams for case presentations, which results in interaction and forces trainees to become actively involved.

Classroom training also has its disadvantages. It is expensive and time-consuming. It requires recruits to be brought together and facilities, meals, transportation, recreation, and lodging to be provided for them. Sales managers, who are cognizant of these costs and time demands, sometimes attempt to cover too much material in too short a time. This results in less retention of information: Many sessions become merely cram sessions. Sales managers must avoid the natural tendency to add more and more material because the additional exposure is often gained at the expense of retention and opportunity for interaction.

Role-playing

A popular technique used in most companies has the trainee act out the part of a sales rep in a simulated buying session. The buyer may be either a sales instructor or another trainee. Role-playing is widely used to develop selling skills, but it can also be used to determine whether the trainee can apply knowledge taught via other methods of instruction. Immediately following the role-playing session, the trainee's performance is critiqued by the trainee, the trainer, and other trainees.

Role-playing where a sales trainee performs in front of others and where that performance is subsequently critiqued can be harsh. One sales training expert compares this approach with the guillotine, pointing out that:

> The victims are kept in line and forced to witness the execution of others.
>
> The victims' fates are published and scheduled in advance with much fanfare and an apprehensive countdown.
>
> The method seems to be designed for surgical incisiveness and spectator enjoyment.[38]

Some of these problems disappear if the critique is conducted only in the presence of the sales trainee and then only by the sales instructor. When handled well, most trainees can still identify their own strengths and weaknesses.

Electronic Training Methods

A recent phenomenon in training methods involves the use of computers. IBM uses interactive video to train redeployed technical people to become sales-people. IBM's program, InfoWindow, combines a personal computer and a laser videodisc that provides an interactive TV. A trainee can practice calls with an on-screen actor whose response is a function of the trainee's approach.[39]

IBM is not the only company that uses such a system. Massachusetts Mutual Life Insurance (Mass Mutual) recently implemented an interactive video (IAV) training method for on-site sales training.[40] Mass Mutual retained Performax (a Westport, Connecticut, developer of electronic training systems) to develop a system. Performax's Simulation System Trainer (SST) combines a 640K PC with a videodisc player and a video camera to simulate for novice salespeople the entire sales process and enables them to practice their selling styles by taping their responses to customer objections. Mass Mutual's new program lets trainees sharpen their skills in their offices before meeting with potential customers. Exhibit 13.14 illustrates an interactive video script.

Even before the development of interactive video training methods, also known as *expert systems,* electronic training had been introduced to help trainees learn "soft" selling skills.[41] These earlier programs, known as *artificial intelligence* (AI), include Sales Edge produced by Human Edge Software, Sell Sell Sell from Thoughtware, and more recently SELLSTAR! available from

EXHIBIT 13 ● 14   *Example of an Interactive Video Script*

A beginning video shot has Mr. X answering your telephone call; then a computer screen will ask you several questions about the content of your call and your evaluation of background information on Mr. X.

For example, when starting your qualifying interview with Mr. X, the computer will prompt:

Will you . . . .
  (a) ask him an open question about any changes he may be planning for the future.
  (b) ask him a closed question concerning whether or not he'd like to upgrade his equipment.
  (c) make a statement about what you see as his needs and match them to your product's features.
  (d) introduce yourself and state that you work for Company Y.

If the trainee selected the wrong option, the computer program could remind the trainee of the role model for the sales process.

The interactive video has been designed to respond to the individual style of the trainee. For example, in the meeting after qualifying Mr. X, the computer will show Mr. X greeting you, and then you make a statement that is recorded by the video camera. After the camera has finished recording your response, the computer lets you describe what you did by selecting from the following:

Did you . . . .
  (a) describe a need identified during the qualifying telephone call?
  (b) make a benefit statement?
  (c) make a reference?
  (d) describe need and state purpose of the call?
  (e) make a reference and state purpose of the call?
  (f) state purpose of the call?

The response from Mr. X will depend on the trainee's answer. There are a large number of different combinations of responses, based on the way the trainee handles the call. As a result, one role-play contains many different scenarios.

If the trainee selects option *a*, Mr. X would respond positively if the need had been identified in the qualifying telephone call.

If the need had not been defined, Mr. X would give a negative response.

If the trainee selects option *b*, Mr. X will agree with the benefit statement.

If the trainee selects option *c*, Mr. X will express agreement.

If the trainee selects option *d*, Mr. X will agree with the need and ask to get right down to business.

If the trainee selects option *e*, Mr. X will express agreement and ask to get right down to business.

If the trainee selects option *f*, Mr. X will ask to get right down to business.

If options *a*, *b*, or *c* were selected, one set of prompts on what the trainee would do next is provided.

If options *d*, *e*, or *f* were selected, another set of prompts on what the trainee would do next is provided.

Source: Warren S. Martin and Ben H. Collins, "Sales Technology Applications: Interactive Video Technology in Sales Training: A Case Study," *Journal of Personal Selling & Sales Management* 11 (Summer 1991), p. 65. Adapted with permission.

SELL-STAR! ESPRIT Software Technology. These training programs are based on psychological demographic models that require the salesperson to answer a series of questions about the customer and themselves. The programs provide a strategy report based on the psychological profiles of both parties.[42] The Sales Edge's output is a five-to-seven-page report that tells the salesperson what to expect from the customer and the appropriate response needed to make a sale.

Do these programs work? Can they train salespeople to effectively interact with customers? Answers to these questions have not been well documented. As with all methods, be it understanding body language or eye movements, if they help salespeople to be more sensitive to customer differences, then they may make a contribution. The output of these artificial intelligence programs should not be thought of as the "final word on how to handle any customer."[43]

TRAINING EXPERIENCED SALES PERSONNEL

After sales trainees are assigned to field positions, they quickly become involved in customer relationships, competitive developments, and other related matters. Over time, their knowledge of competitive developments and market conditions becomes dated. Even their personal selling styles may become stereotyped and less effective. Also, because of changes in company policies and product line, sales representatives require refresher or advanced training programs. Few companies halt training after the trainee has completed the basics. Most managements endorse the view that the need to learn is a never-ending process and even the most successful of their sales representatives can benefit from refresher training.

Additional training often occurs when a sales representative is being considered for promotion. In many companies, a promotion is more than moving from sales to district sales manager. A promotion can include being assigned better customers, transferring to a better territory, moving to a staff position, or being promoted to sales management. Whenever salespeople are assigned better customers or better territories, additional sales training acquaints them with their increased responsibilities.

A recent *Sales & Marketing Management* survey investigated company practices concerning the training of experienced salespeople.[44] Respondents were asked to indicate how much money was spent for training. The average amount spent, according to the 1,554 companies responding, was $3,737 per person; the median expenditure was $1,767. Exhibit 13.15 shows median spending by size of company as measured by sales volume.

An important and related issue is how much time to spend training experienced reps. The corollary question is: How long can a company afford to keep experienced salespeople out of the field? The survey indicated a median of 1.7 weeks (8 1/2 days). Larger companies have a median of two weeks. Exhibit 13.16 reveals that time out of the field increases with sales force size.

Some large companies try to reduce training time for experienced salespeople by emphasizing initial training. Hercules, Inc., a chemical industry company, provides new sales reps 26 weeks of training during the first year. Formal training programs for experienced sales reps last one week or less.

Many companies decentralize the training for experienced salespeople.

EXHIBIT 13 • 15   *What You're Spending on Sales Training*

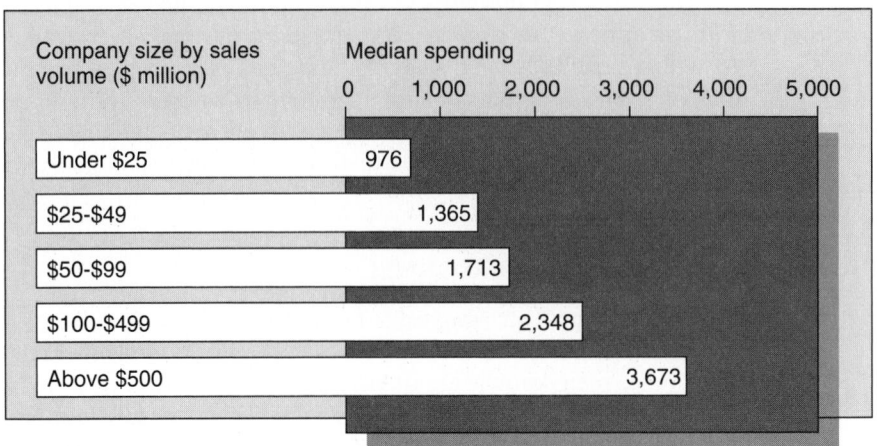

Company size by sales volume ($ million)	Median spending
Under $25	976
$25-$49	1,365
$50-$99	1,713
$100-$499	2,348
Above $500	3,673

Source: William Keenan, Jr., "Are You Overspending on Training?" *Sales & Marketing Management,* January 1990, p. 38.

Hercules, Bergen-Brunswig, and Xerox are among many companies that attempt to get training into the field using self-paced training manuals, videos, and computer-based programs.

Training experienced salespeople is viewed as providing insurance for a company's major asset. David Barousse of Bergen-Brunswig notes: "Find me a company without that insurance, that has stopped training its salespeople, and I'll target that market and that company and have its business by year's end."[45]

Sales Training for New versus Experienced Salespeople

Most new salespeople are exposed to a concentrated training program that features such topics as product knowledge, selling techniques, market/industry orientation, and company orientation. Of these topics, product knowledge receives the most emphasis.

When a company changes procedures, additional training usually results for experienced salespeople. Changes to a company's product line (e.g., new products, modifications, and deletions) usually lead to additional training. Changes in a company's market strategy and market focus/segmentation will also trigger more sales training. Learning how to develop skills that lead to improved selling effectiveness receives the most emphasis for experienced salespeople. Experienced salespeople need additional training to learn how to integrate product knowledge into sales presentations that differ from one setting to the next.

Exhibit 13 • 16   *Time Out of Field*

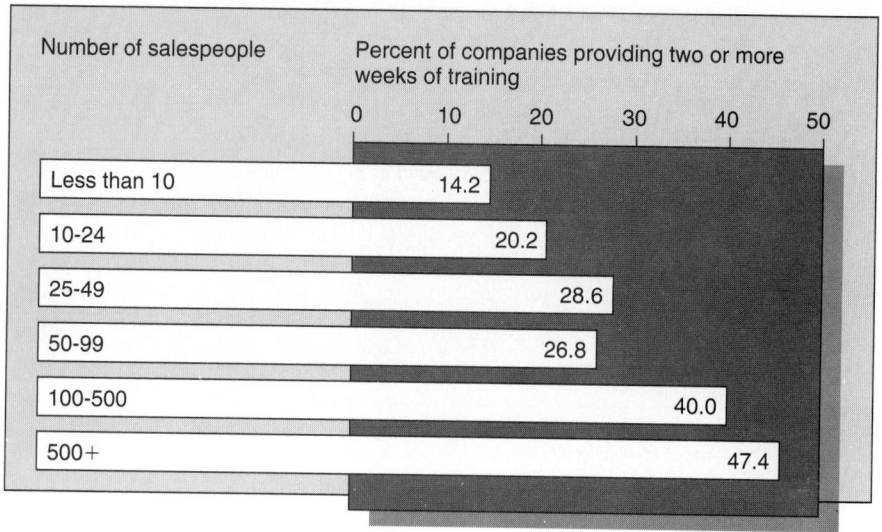

Number of salespeople	Percent of companies providing two or more weeks of training
Less than 10	14.2
10-24	20.2
25-49	28.6
50-99	26.8
100-500	40.0
500+	47.4

Source: William Keenan, Jr., "Are You Overspending on Training?" *Sales & Marketing Management,* January 1990, p. 39.

Adaptive Selling: Knowing How to Sell

Extensive knowledge about products, customers, competitors, company procedures, plus a myriad of other factual items is a necessary but not sufficient condition for successful sales performance. It is like the quarterback who memorizes all of the plays but doesn't know the right play to call at the right time, the novice chess player who knows the basic moves but doesn't understand the various patterns that call for specific strategies. The experienced quarterback or master chess player can assess situations and adapt accordingly. Conveying this ability to adapt is what sales training is all about.

Sales training attempts to teach sales trainees in a relatively short period the skills of the more experienced and successful members of the sales force. Weitz, Sujan, and Sujan stress the potential role of salesperson knowledge, especially as it applies to specific selling situations and the appropriate selling responses, and the salesperson's ability to process customer information as key determinants of sales performance.[46]

Leigh and McGraw contend that experienced and effective salespersons have "sophisticated knowledge structures that enable them to categorize selling situations more effectively and efficiently on the basis of similarity to other 'remembered' situations, then apply the activities and behaviors of an appropriate selling approach to each."[47] This knowledge, known as *declarative and procedural knowledge,* permits an experienced salesperson "to recognize or classify a particular selling situation as an instance of a more general selling

EXHIBIT 13 • 17   *Script Objectives for an Initial Sales Call*

Initial Sales Call Objectives (*n* = 25)	Percent
1. Gather information about buyer needs, objectives	84
2. Develop personal rapport with the buyer	44
3. Create favorable impression of me as a salesperson	44
4. Communicate positive impression of my company	33
5. Determine who are key decision makers	24
6. Assess sales potential	20
7. Assess the buyer's attitude toward my company	20
8. Lay groundwork for follow-up contact	20
9. Set specific follow-up appointment	20
Interjudge reliability = 0.91	

Source: Reprinted from Thomas W. Leigh and Patrick F. McGraw, "Mapping the Procedural Knowledge of Industrial Sales Personnel: A Script-Theoretic Investigation," *Journal of Marketing* 53 (January 1989), p. 22, published by the American Marketing Association.

category." The salesperson, as a result of interacting with the customer, may determine the buyer is task-oriented rather than relationship-oriented and adopt a task-oriented selling approach.

The potential impact of the adaptive selling concept on sales training is significant. Through sales training, novices can be taught how to classify customers, how to determine which approach would be most effective, and how to apply the selected approach. Novices also need to learn that as relationships change so will selling styles change, as governed by the situation. Adaptive selling is an approach that recognizes differences across customers and differences in the salesperson as well.

Do experienced and successful salespeople possess knowledge structures and can these structures be identified and used as a basis for sales training? Research indicates both questions can be answered with a yes. Exhibit 13.17 identifies the script objectives and activities for an initial sales call derived from a sample of 25 salespeople from a major hospital supply corporation. Note that the most common objective (84 percent) is to gather information about buyer needs.

Leigh and McGraw conclude that the procedural knowledge of experienced and effective salespeople can be identified and subsequently used in sales training. Behavior modeling requires that a sales trainee and an experienced salesperson interact to allow the trainee to observe and practice the methods used by the successful salesperson. Over time, the sales trainee develops a customized approach that represents individual traits to be used according to the situation.

In another study, Szymanski found that successful salespeople were more effective at categorizing prospects than unsuccessful salespeople. Successful salespeople not only were able to rely on fewer customer traits, but they also placed different weights or values on these traits.[48]

Furthermore, Szymanski reveals that the effective sales rep has a definite ordering of attributes according to their discriminating power, unlike the random ordering for the ineffective sales rep. And the effective sales rep has better discriminating power, relying on three attributes for classifying the prospect. The ineffective sales rep faces two problems: The first involves having to rely on more attributes, and the second is the greater risk of incorrectly classifying the prospect.[49] Clearly, training salespeople how to correctly classify prospects is a worthy topic of most sales training programs.

MEASURING THE COSTS AND BENEFITS OF SALES TRAINING

Sales training is a time-consuming and very costly activity. Is all this effort worth the cost? Does sales training produce enough benefits to justify its existence?

Sales training and increased profits have an obscure relationship at best. In the beginning of this chapter, we identified some broad objectives of sales training: improved selling skills, increased productivity, improved morale, lower sales force turnover, better customer relations, and better time and territory management. Unfortunately, pinning down the relationship between sales training and these broad objectives is not easy. Very little research has been done to determine what effect, if any, sales training has on the sales force. Most sales organizations simply assume on blind faith that their sales training programs are successful. After all, if a company has high sales and high profits, why should a sales manager assume sales training is anything but effective?

Sales Training Costs

Business firms spend millions of dollars each year on sales training in hopes of improving overall productivity. Exhibit 13.18 shows direct sales training costs for 1988. Exhibit 13.18 suggests that only the largest companies can afford to support a full-scale training program, yet all firms need sales training, regardless of size. The statistics suggest business has a relatively generous attitude toward sales training. It allocates funds for training with minimal regard for the results. Clearly, measuring the benefits of sales training needs some attention.

Is the measurement process that difficult? After all, if sales training is supposed to lead to better productivity, improved morale, and lower turnover, then why not measure the changes in these variables after training has occurred? Some sales managers have done just that. They have assumed: We instituted sales training and shortly after sales increased. Therefore, sales training was the reason. Right? Wrong! Unless appropriate procedures are used to design the research by which the benefits are assessed, it is hard to say what caused

EXHIBIT 13 • 18   *Average Cost of Sales Training per Salesperson*

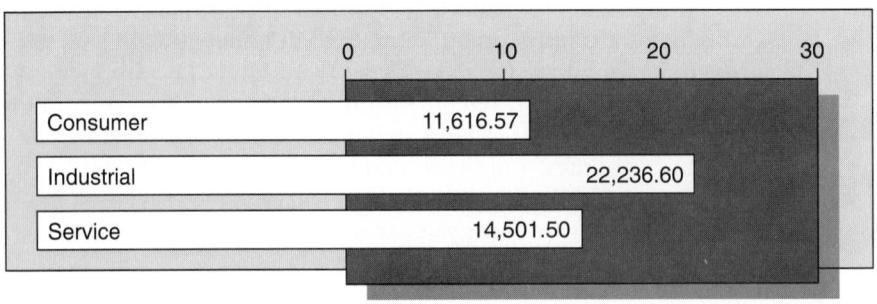

Note: Figures for major industry groups reflect costs from 37 selected industries surveyed by Dartnell Corporation in its *24th Biennial Survey of Sales Force Compensation.* Determinations of industry classifications and the calculation of individual averages were made by *Sales & Marketing Management* based on these data. © 1988 by Dartnell Corporation.

Source: Reprinted with permission from "1989 Survey of Selling Costs," *Sales & Marketing Management,* February 20, 1989, p. 23. © 1989 by Bill Communications, Inc.

the sales increase. Sales may have increased as a result of improved economic conditions, competitive activity, environmental changes, seasonal trends, or other reasons. Consequently, research must be carefully designed to isolate these contaminating effects to identify the benefits directly attributable to training.

Measurement Criteria

Even though intervening variables such as changes in competitive activities make evaluation of sales training programs difficult, some measurement must occur. This raises the question of what characteristics of sales training should be assessed. Exhibit 13.19 illustrates an evaluation options matrix.

One could certainly single out one of the criteria shown in Exhibit 13.19 as the measure of effectiveness, but a strong argument can be made that several criteria should be used in assessing the results of any sales training program. Measuring what was learned, for example, seems inappropriate because the obtained knowledge may not produce desired behavior changes. Not to assess what was learned is inadequate, however, because the program might be considered a failure if nothing was learned or if what was learned is inappropriate. The solution rests in properly specifying the objectives and content of the sales training program, the criteria used to evaluate the program, and the proper design of the research so benefits can be unambiguously determined.

Measuring Broad Benefits

Broad benefits of sales training include improved morale and lower turnover. Morale can be partially measured by studies of job satisfaction. This approach is feasible with experienced sales personnel. Suppose, for instance, a company

EXHIBIT 13 • 19   *Evaluation Options Matrix*

Evaluation Level: What Is the Question?	Information Required: What Information to Collect?	Method: How to Collect?
Reaction Did participants respond favorably to the program?	Attitudinal	Evaluation Questionnaires Comments Anecdotes Interviews with participants
Learning Did participants learn concepts or skills?	Understanding of concepts, ability to use skills	Before-and-after test
Behavior Did participants change their on-the-job behavior?	On-the-job behavior	Behavior ratings, before and after Critical incident technique Time-series analysis
Results What personal or organizational results occurred?	Changes in sales, productivity, or other performance	Cost-benefit methods

Source: Thomas Atkinson and Theodore L. Higgins, "Evaluation Obstacles and Opportunities," from *A Forum Issues Special Report,* February 1988, p. 22.

measured job satisfaction as part of a needs analysis and found evidence of problems. A follow-up job satisfaction study after the corrective sales training program would determine if morale changed noticeably.

Measuring reactions and learning is important in sales training for both new and experienced personnel. Most companies measure reactions by asking those attending the training to complete an evaluation form either immediately after the session or several weeks later. Emotions and enthusiasm may be high right after a session, but sales training effectiveness is much more than a "warm feeling."

Measuring what was learned requires tests. To what extent did sales trainees learn the facts, concepts, and techniques included in the training session? Objective examinations are appropriate.

Measuring Specific Benefits

Liking the program and learning something is not enough. Specific measures to examine behavior and results are needed to assess effectiveness. The effectiveness of a sales training program aimed at securing more new customers, for example, can be partially assessed by examining call reports to see whether more new customers are being called on. Results can be measured by tracking new-account sales to see whether they have increased. If the specific objective of sales training is to increase the sales of more profitable items, evidence that

EXHIBIT 13 • 20   *Group Ranking of Evaluation Approaches by Frequency*

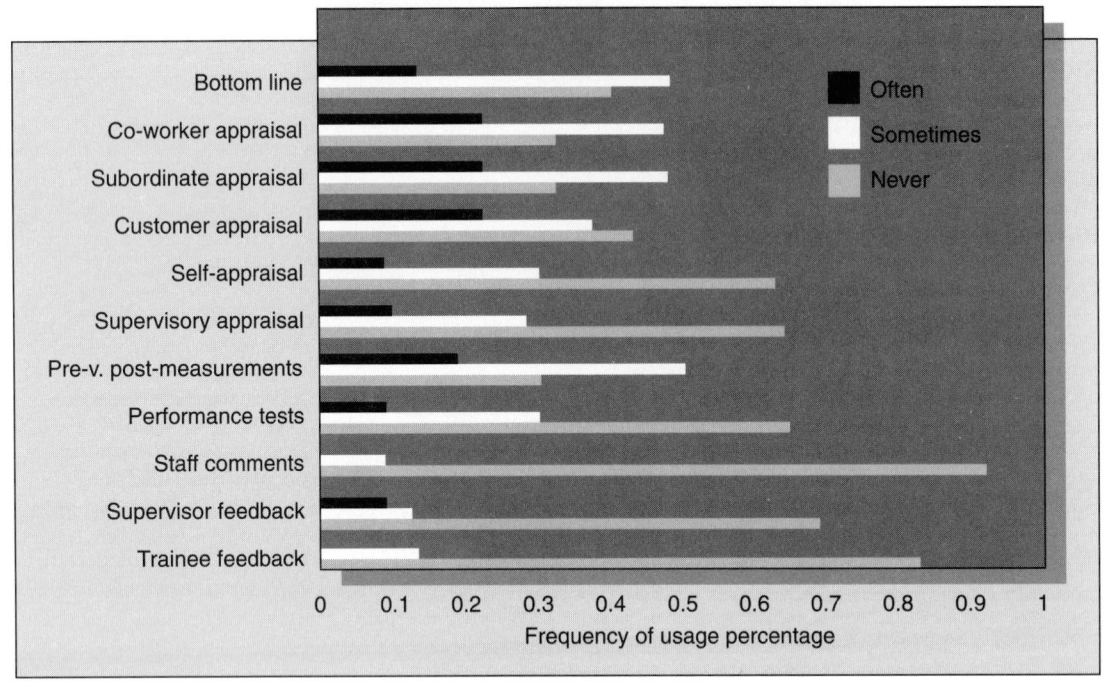

Source: Robert C. Erffmeyer, K. Randall Russ, and Joseph F. Hair, Jr., "Needs Assessment and Evaluation in Sales-Training Programs," *Journal of Personal Selling and Sales Management* 11 (Winter 1991), p. 24.

this has been accomplished provides a partial measure of training effectiveness. Finally, if reducing customer complaints was more objective, then the appropriate specific measure is whether customer complaints decreased.

The measurement of both specific and broad benefits presumes the sales training program is designed to achieve certain goals. The goals should be established before sales training begins. When specific objectives have been determined, the best training program can be developed to achieve these objectives. Most training programs have several objectives. Multiple measurements of the effectiveness of the training program are then a necessary part of evaluating the benefits.

Recent studies reveal that most sales training evaluation measures are simple, consisting primarily of reactions to the program. Meaningful evaluation measures, such as learning, behavior, and results, are used much less frequently.[50] Exhibit 13.20 presents frequency of usage for the different methods of evaluating sales training programs. As can be seen, the weakest or easiest to collect measures—staff comments and feedback from supervisors and train-

E X H I B I T 13 • 21 *Overall Ranking of Evaluation Measures*

Approach	Type	Importance	Frequency
Trainee feedback	Reaction	1	2
Supervisory appraisal	Behavior	2	6
Self-appraisal	Behavior	3	7
Bottom-line measurement	Results	4	9
Customer appraisal	Behavior	5	10
Supervisory feedback	Reaction	6	4
Performance tests	Learning	7	5
Training staff comments	Reaction	8	3
Course evaluations	Reaction	9	1
Subordinate appraisal	Behavior	10	12
Pre- vs. post-training measurements	Learning	11	11
Co-workers appraisal	Behavior	12	13
Knowledge tests	Learning	13	8
Control group	Learning	14	14

Source: Robert C. Erffmeyer, K. Randall Russ, and Joseph F. Hair, Jr., "Needs Assessment and Evaluation in Sales-Training Programs," *Journal of Personal Selling & Sales Management* 11 (Winter 1991), p. 24.

ees—are used the most. Bottom-line evaluation (e.g., changes in sales volume) is relatively limited.

Exhibit 13.21 shows how sales managers rank the various measures by both importance and frequency of use. The rankings are inconsistent. The most frequently used measure is course evaluation, but its importance is ninth out of a list of 14. Course evaluation is a reaction measure that fails to reveal learning, behavioral, and results changes associated with the sales training.

Evaluating the benefits of sales training is difficult. One study asked sales managers to identify the most important restrictions against sales training evaluation. The most common restrictions were time and money and difficulty in either gathering the data and/or gaining access to data.[51]

 **S UMMARY**

Sales training programs have been criticized by emphasizing the wrong subjects and for using techniques that are not effective. The actual process of selling is one of the neglected subjects. Behavior modeling differs from traditional sales training programs and offers significant advantages. A Chinese proverb expresses the concept of behavior modeling well: "Tell me, I'll forget. Show me, I may remember. But involve me and I'll understand." Indeed, behavior modeling involves not only the sales representative but field sales managers as well. An essential ingredient of sales training programs is the follow-up activities required of sales management and sales trainers.

Sales training is a varied and on-going activity that is time-consuming and expensive. Most companies engage in some type of sales training. In fact, most sales managers feel that sales training is such an important activity that they require it for everybody, regardless of their experience. Some common objectives of sales training are to teach selling skills, increase productivity, improve morale, lower turnover, improve customer relations, and improve time and territory management.

Considerable variability exists in the length of sales training programs. Industry differences account not only for variations in length but also variations in program content. Company policies, the nature of the selling job, and the types of products and services offered also contribute to differences in time spent and on topics covered.

Product knowledge receives the most attention followed by selling techniques, market/industry orientation, and company orientation. This allocation is the subject of considerable criticism, as described in the chapter.

As a result of various environmental changes, the content and method of sales training has changed. How to use the telephone in selling is a commonly taught subject. Salespeople receive instruction on how to use a microcomputer to better plan their activities. And, salespeople are now being trained via personal computers and VCR systems. Companies recognize that their technical people need sales training, as shown by the IBM example.

Recent sales training methodology and research provide promising developments. Expert systems allow sales trainees to interact with an actor using a personal computer and a video screen to practice their selling skills. Several companies provide artificial intelligence programs using personal computers that help the sales reps plan their strategies based on customer and sales rep psychological demographics. Research into the existence of declarative and procedural knowledge structures possessed by effective salespeople promises to provide a new source of knowledge needed to train novice sales representatives.

Sales training is very expensive and generally considered beneficial. Accurate measurement of the benefits is difficult. It is hard to isolate the effects produced solely by sales training from those that might have been produced by other factors such as changes in the economy or the nature of competition.

Sales training provides managers with the opportunity to convey their expectations to the sales force. A well-designed training program shows the sales force how to sell. Sales managers can communicate high performance expectations through training and equip the force with the skills needed to reach high performance levels.

*Discussion
Questions*

1. The newly assigned sales representative was perplexed about her inability to learn about customers' needs. She contends her customers are not willing to tell her what problems they are experiencing. After making several joint

calls with her, the district sales manager agreed she was not receiving informative responses to her questions. The manager wondered if it is possible to train salespeople to ask better questions. What are the characteristics of good questions? How can sales reps be trained to ask better questions?

2. Various artificial intelligence (AI) programs such as **Sales Edge, Sell Sell Sell,** and **SELLSTAR!** promise to help sales representatives adapt their selling style to more effectively match the customer's style. The results are based on the psychological demographics of both parties. What do you see as the advantages and disadvantages of these programs? How would you design a research program to test the effectiveness of these AI programs?

3. The sales training manager of I. Klug Co., a manufacturer of office equipment, was debating the merits of the firm's recent decision to add eight women to its sales force. The debate centered on whether the content of the training program should be the same for the women as for the men. I. Klug's sales manager was opposed to any differential treatment, arguing that to do so constituted special treatment. The sales training manager thought otherwise. With whom do you agree? Are there different subjects that should be taught?

4. The sales manager of a large insurance company believes sales training is too expensive and a waste of money. Turnover rates have increased recently, and many of those leaving went to work for other insurance firms. To this, the sales manager replied, "Nuts to sales training. All we're doing is training salespeople for our competitors. What we need to do is hire experienced people." Do you agree?

5. Many times, salespeople are put into conflict situations resulting from customers having expectations that differ from expectations of others. Can sales training reduce the conflict encountered by salespeople?

6. Experimental design, a subject taught in most marketing research courses, has had limited application in measuring the benefits of sales training programs. Why is this? How would you design an experiment to measure the benefits of a sales training program?

7. A consulting organization is trying to persuade the sales manager to use its program for training salespeople. The program's thrust involves transactional analysis. The cost is $250 per salesperson. The company employs 150 sales reps who have been experiencing a decline in sales. How should the sales manager decide whether to adopt the program?

8. Koppers Company of Pittsburgh has developed a new outdoor deck-care line. Koppers was faced with building an entire distribution network to carry the new Wolman Deck Care line. The company is considering using a sales training program as a sales incentive. How can a sales training program be used as an incentive?

9. One expert contends that sales training is not at all complicated as some would claim. He predicts that regardless of the advances in communication, resources, technology, and training tools, the basic selling skills that trainers teach salespeople will change very little from those that have been successful during the past 50 years. What will change, according to the expert, is how salespeople are trained to use these skills effectively. Do you agree with this prediction? What advantages does interactive video (IV) offer to sales training?

10. A quote from the April 1987 issue of *Sales & Marketing Management* (p. 76) reads, "Research now identifies that much eye contact between seller and prospect can be a sign of trouble, visible proof that a person is resisting a sales effort or has little or no interest in the offered product," An associate of yours thinks this idea has merit and wants to train the sales force how to read and interpret eye movements. What would you advise?

Endnotes

[1]This example is based on material found in Suzy Barrett, Richard L. Ranges, and Stuart M. Lasky, "How Kraft Builds Business Managers from Sales Trainees," *Sales & Marketing Management,* May 1991, pp. 110–11

[2]These examples are based on material found in William Keenan, "Power Selling: America's Best Sales Forces," *Sales & Marketing Management,* September 1991, pp. 41–44, 46, 48, 50, 55–57.

[3]The following discussion is based to a large extent on Meg Kerr and Bill Burzynski, "Missing the Target: Sales Training in America," *Training and Development Journal,* July 1988, pp. 68–70.

[4]Roy Chitwood, "Let's Get Back to Basic Training," *Sales & Marketing Management,* September 1988, p. 10.

[5]Jack Falvey, "Compare Football to Selling? Nonsense," *Sales & Marketing Management,* January 1989, pp. 15, 17.

[6]Jack Falvey, "To Develop the Best Salespeople, Let Them Do It Themselves," *Sales & Marketing Management,* November 1988, p. 87.

[7]Anthony Alessandra and Phil Wexler, "The Professionalization of Selling," *Sales and Marketing Training,* February 1988, pp. 37–38, 42–43.

[8]Ibid., p. 38.

[9]"What's the Problem with Sales Training" *Training Today,* March 1990, p. 16.

[10]James F. Evered, "Measuring Sales Training Effectiveness," *Sales and Marketing Training,* February 1988, pp. 9–12, 16–18.

[11]The following discussion is based to a large extent on Gene Hahne, "Creating Credibility for Your Sales Training," *Training and Development Journal,* November 1981, pp. 34–38.

[12]Kenneth N. Wexley, "Personnel Training," *Annual Review of Psychology,* 1984, pp. 519–51.

[13]Alessandra and Wexler, "The Professionalization of Selling" p. 38.

[14]Laura L'Herisson, "Teaching the Sales Force to Fail," *Training and Developmental Journal,* November 1981, p. 78–82.

[15]The following discussion is based to a large extent on Malcolm E. Shaw, "Sales Training in Transition," *Training and Development Journal,* February 1981, pp. 74–83.

[16]Ibid., p. 75.

[17]Ibid., p. 76.

[18]Ibid., p. 78.

[19]Ibid., p. 80.

[20]Jack Falvey, "Myths of Sales Training," *Sales & Marketing Management,* June 1978, p. 80.

[21]For an excellent discussion of behavior modification in marketing, see Robert A. Scott et al., "Organizational Behavior Modification: A General Motivational Tool for Sales Management," *Journal of Personal Selling & Sales Management* 6 (August 1986), pp. 61–70.

[22]Jack R. Snader, "Most Sales Training Doesn't Work," *Sales Report* 1, no. 3 (Chicago: Systema Corporation), p. 4.

[23]The following discussion is based to a large extent on "Study Reveals Sales-Training Needs of Business Markets," *Marketing News,* March 13, 1989, p. 6.

[24]Ibid., p. 6.

[25]Neil M. Ford, Orville C. Walker, Jr., and Gilbert A. Churchill, Jr., "The Psychological Consequences of Role Conflict and Ambiguity in the Industrial Salesforce," in *Marketing 1776–1976 and Beyond,* ed. Kenneth L. Bernhardt (Chicago: American Marketing Association, 1976), pp. 403–8.

[26]David S. Hopkins, *Training the Sales Force: A Progress Report* (New York: The Conference Board, 1978), p. 4. The material in this section has been adapted from this source.

[27]Ibid., p. 13.

[28]Ibid., p. 5.

[29]H. Robert Dodge, *Field Sales Management* (Dallas: Business Publications, Inc., 1973). p. 226.

[30]Study Reveals Sales-Training Needs," p. 6.

[31]Edward Roberts, "Training Trade Show Salespeople: How Caterpillar Does It," *Business Marketing,* June 1988, pp. 70, 72–73.

[32]Priscilla Donovan, "Selling Right and Left," *Sales & Marketing Management,* June 3, 1985, pp. 62–63, 65.

[33]Alan J. Zaremba, "Beyond Body Language," *Business Marketing,* March 1987, pp. 133–34.

[34]Jack Falvey, "Forget the Sharks: Swim with Your Salespeople," *Sales & Marketing Management,* November 1990, p. 8.

[35]Ibid.

[36]Falvey, "Myths of Sales Training," p. 78.

[38]Ibid., p. 64.

[39]Urbanski, "Electronic Training May Be in Your Future," *Sales & Marketing Management,* March 1988, pp. 46, 48.

[40]Patricia Sellers, "How IBM Teaches Techies to Sell," *Fortune,* June 6, 1988, pp. 141–42, 46.

[41]For an excellent discussion of expert systems see Arlyn R. Rubash, Rawlie R. Sullivan, and Paul H. Herzog, "The Use of an 'Expert' to Train Salespeople," *Journal of Personal Selling & Sales Management* 7 (August 1987), pp. 49–55.

[42]Al Urbanski, "Electronic Training May Be in Your Future," p. 46. SELLSTAR! is reviewed by Hubert D. Hennessey, "Microcomputer Applications: Accelerating the Salesperson Learning Curve," *Journal of Personal Selling & Sales Management* 8 (November 1988), pp. 77–82. For the last several years, the *Journal of Personal Selling & Sales Management* has published a special section on microcomputer applications.

[43]Diane Lynn Kastiel, "Psyching Out Buyers with AI," *Business Marketing,* March 1987, pp. 72–74.

[44]The following discussion is based to a large extent on William Keenan, Jr., "Are You Overspending on Training?" *Sales & Marketing Management,* January 1990, pp. 36–40.

[45]Ibid., p. 40.

[46]Barton A. Weitz, Harish Sujan, and Mita Sujan, "Knowledge, Motivation, and Adaptive Behavior: A Framework for Improving Selling Effectiveness," *Journal of Marketing* 50 (October 1986), pp. 174–91.

[47]The following discussion is based to a large extent on Thomas W. Leigh and Patrick McGraw, "Mapping the Procedural Knowledge of Industrial Sales Personnel: A Script-Theoretic Investigation," *Journal of Marketing* 53 (January 1989), p. 16–34.

[48]David M. Szymanski, "Explaining Differences in Selling Effectiveness: A Knowledge Structure Approach to Examining the Ability of Sales Personnel to Prospect for Clients," unpublished doctoral dissertation, School of Business, University of Wisconsin-Madison, 1987.

[49]David M. Szymanski, "Determinants of Selling Ef-

fectiveness: The Importance of Declarative Knowledge to the Personal Selling Concept," *Journal of Marketing* 52 (January 1988), pp. 64–77.

[50]Robert C. Erffmeyer, K. Randall Russ, and Joseph F. Hair, Jr., "Needs Assessment and Evaluation in Sales-Training Programs," *Journal of Personal Selling & Sales Management* 11 (Winter 1991), pp. 17–31.

[51]Earl D. Honeycutt and Thomas H. Stevenson, "Evaluating Sales Training Programs," *Industrial Marketing Management* 18 (August 1989), pp. 215–22.

Suggested Readings

Alliger, George M., and Elizabeth A. Janak. "Kirkpatrick's Levels of Training Criteria: Thirty Years Later." *Personnel Psychology* 42 (1989), pp. 331–42.

Anglin, Kenneth A., Jeffrey J. Stolman, and James W. Gentry. "The Congruence of Manager Perception of Salesperson Performance and Knowledge-Based Measures of Adaptive Selling." *Journal of Personal Selling & Sales Management* 10 (Fall 1990), pp. 81–90.

Catalanello, Ralph F., and Donald L. Kirkpatrick. "Evaluating Training Programs—The State of the Art." *Training and Development Journal* 22 (1968), pp. 2–9.

Honeycutt, Earl D., and Thomas H. Stevenson. "Evaluating Sales Training Programs," *Industrial Marketing Management* 18 (August 1989), pp. 215–22.

Smith, Barry J., and Brian L. Delahaye. *How to be an Effective Trainer,* 2nd ed. New York: John Wiley & Sons, 1989.

Weitz, Barton A., Harish Sujan, and Mita Sujan. "Knowledge, Motivation and Adaptive Behavior: A Framework for Improving Selling Effectiveness." *Journal of Marketing* 50 (October 1986), pp. 174–91.

Motivating the Sales Force

L OTUS BLOSSOMS BY OFFERING DIFFERENT INCENTIVES FOR DIFFERENT MEMBERS OF THE SALES TEAM[1]

Lotus Development Corporation, one of the world's largest producers of computer software, introduced a new product named Lotus Notes in 1990. Lotus Notes is a sophisticated networking program that enables many different personal computers in an organization to communicate and exchange a variety of information.

While Notes is an easy-to-use program, at the time of its introduction, it was a revolutionary product with a variety of potential applications. Consequently, a good deal of customer education—and sometimes systems engineering assistance—was needed to generate sales. Also, with a minimum price of $62,500, Notes was much more expensive than most of Lotus's other software products, making the selling process even more complex and difficult.

In view of Notes' unique characteristics and selling requirements, Daniel P. Doran, Lotus's director of network application sales, created a separate direct sales force devoted to marketing the new product to its primary target market of Fortune 1,000 companies. The Notes sales force consists of six teams, each composed of a salesperson and a systems engineer. The engineer usually accompanies the sales rep on calls to help demonstrate the product, explain its technical details and answer questions, and seek and help develop new applications for the software.

To motivate his new teams to expend the effort needed to successfully introduce Notes, and to help ensure the members of each team would cooperate in the pursuit of a common goal, Doran designed an incentive compensation system that offers each team member a base salary plus a commission based on the team's sales volume. But Doran's experience in managing both sales-people and engineers—and the results of an informal survey of the attitudes and preferences of both sets of team members—led him to conclude his sales reps were more strongly motivated by the risk/reward factor in competitive selling than were his systems engineers. So, he designed a system that provides salespeople with smaller salaries and larger commissions as a proportion of their total compensation, while the engineers receive relatively larger salaries and smaller commissions. According to Doran, "The sales reps like the leverage and the engineers appreciate the security."

To further increase the incentive for his teams to boost their sales volumes and capture as many customers as possible before competitors entered the market, Doran built in a series of "accelerators" that increase the commissions team members earn when they exceed sales quotas. If, for instance, a team hits 150 percent of its quota, Doran rewards it with an extra commission; for 200 percent, yet another, and so on. "There's no cap on how much they can make," he says.

After the first year of operation, both the sales reps and the systems engineers seem very satisfied with Lotus's incentive compensation program. And so far, says Doran, all of the teams have met or exceeded their sales quotas.

FACTORS THAT AFFECT MOTIVATION

On the surface, the incentive compensation system Doran developed to motivate the Lotus Notes sales force seems simple and straightforward. But that system has worked well because its design considered a variety of underlying factors that influence motivation, including (1) market conditions, product characteristics, and the nature of the sales task to be accomplished, (2) related management policies and programs within the company (e.g., the decision to combine sales reps and systems engineers in teams), and (3) the different personal characteristics of the people to be motivated.

Unfortunately, many firms are not so successful in designing compensation systems or incentive programs that are appropriate for the marketing challenges they face and the people they employ. Consequently, their salespeople are either undermotivated or stimulated to expend too much time and effort on the wrong tasks and activities. In either case, sales effectiveness and productivity suffer.

In view of the complicated nature of motivation and its critical role in sales management, the rest of this chapter and all of Chapter 15 are devoted to the subject. This chapter examines what is known about motivation as a psychological process and how a person's motivation to perform a given job is affected by environmental, organizational, and personal variables. Chapter 15 discusses compensation plans and incentive programs sales managers use to stimulate and direct salespeople's efforts.

THE PSYCHOLOGICAL PROCESS OF MOTIVATION

The term *motivation* produces severe stomachaches for many psychologists because of the wide variety of different and often inconsistent meanings attached to the term. In recent years, though, some consensus seems to be emerging. Most industrial and organizational psychologists now view *motivation* as a general label for the choice (1) to initiate action on a certain task, (2) to expend a certain amount of effort on that task, and (3) to persist in expending effort over a period of time.[2]

For our purposes, **motivation** is viewed as the amount of effort the salesperson desires to expend on each activity or task associated with the job. This may include calling on potential new accounts, developing sales presentations, and filling out reports. The psychological process involved in determining how much effort a salesperson will want to expend, and some variables that influence the process, are shown in Exhibit 14.1. The conceptual framework outlined in Exhibit 14.1 is based on a view of motivation known as *expectancy theory*. A number of other theories of motivation exist,[3] and many of them are useful for explaining at least a part of the motivation process. However, expectancy theory incorporates and ties together (at least implicitly) important aspects of many of those theories, it has been the subject of much empirical research in sales management, and it also provides a useful framework for guiding the many decisions managers must make when designing effective motivational programs for a sales force. Consequently, the remainder of this discussion focuses primarily on expectancy theory, although several other theories are mentioned later when we examine how personal characteristics affect the motivation of different individuals.

EXHIBIT **14 ● 1**   *The Psychological Determinants of Motivation*

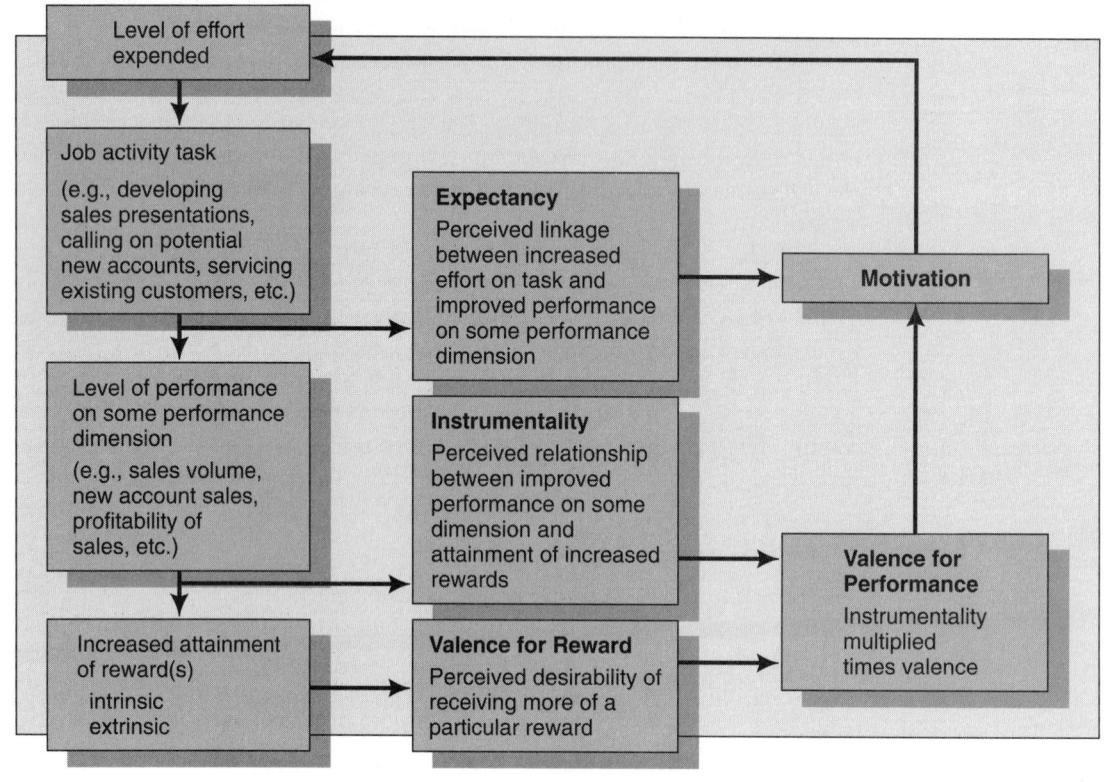

Major Components of the Model

The model in Exhibit 14.1 suggests the effort expended by a salesperson on each task associated with the job will lead to some level of achievement on one or more dimensions of job performance. These dimensions include total sales volume, profitability of sales, and new accounts generated. It is assumed the salesperson's performance on some of these dimensions will be evaluated by superiors and rewarded with one or more rewards. These might be externally mediated rewards, like a promotion, or internally mediated rewards, such as feelings of accomplishment or personal growth. A salesperson's motivation to expend effort on a given task is determined by three sets of perceptions: (1) expectancies—the perceived linkages between expending more effort on a particular task and achieving improved performance, (2) instrumentalities—the perceived relationship between improved performance and the attainment of increased rewards, and (3) valence for rewards—the perceived attractiveness of the various rewards the salesperson might receive.

Expectancies—
Perceived Links
between Effort
and Performance

Expectancies are the salesperson's perceptions of the link between job effort and performance. Specifically, an expectancy is the person's estimate of the probability that expending effort on some task will lead to improved performance on a dimension. The following statement illustrates an expectancy perception: "If I increase my calls on potential new accounts by 10 percent (effort), then there is a 50 percent chance (expectancy) that my volume of new account sales will increase by 10 percent during the next six months (performance level)."

When attempting to motivate salespeople, sales managers should be concerned with two aspects of their subordinates' expectancy perceptions: magnitude and accuracy. The magnitude of a salesperson's expectancy perceptions indicates the degree to which that person believes expending effort on job activities will influence ultimate job performance. Other things being equal, the larger a salesperson's expectancy perceptions, the more willing the sales rep is to devote effort to the job in hopes of bettering performance.

The *accuracy* of a salesperson's expectancy perceptions refers to how clearly the rep understands the relationship between effort expended on a task and the resulting achievement on some performance dimension. When salespeople's expectancies are inaccurate, they are likely to misallocate job efforts. They spend too much time and energy on activities that have little impact on performance and not enough on activities with a greater impact. Consequently, some authorities refer to attempts to improve the accuracy of expectancy estimates as "trying to get salespeople to work smarter rather than harder."[4]

Working smarter requires that the salesperson have an accurate understanding of what activities are most critical—and therefore should receive the greatest effort—for concluding a sale. Of course, a single activity might be carried out in a number of ways. For instance, a salesperson might employ any of several different sales techniques or strategies when making a sales presentation. Therefore, working smarter also requires an ability to adapt the techniques used to the needs and preferences of a given buyer. While methods for improving the accuracy of salespeople's expectancy estimates and their understanding of the effectiveness of different selling techniques and strategies through training and skill development were the primary focus of the last chapter, such issues are also important to consider when designing motivation and compensation programs. Motivating a salesperson to expend more effort on inappropriate activities or approaches can worsen performance and lead to great frustration within the sales force.

As Exhibit 14.2 indicates, personal and organizational characteristics affect the magnitude and accuracy of salespeople's expectancy perceptions. Managers must consider these factors when deciding on supervisory policies, compensation, and incentive plans so their subordinates' expectancies will be as large and as accurate as possible. The factors that affect salespeople's expectancy estimates, along with their managerial implications, are discussed later in this chapter.

E X H I B I T 1 4 • 2   *Factors Influencing the Motivation Process*

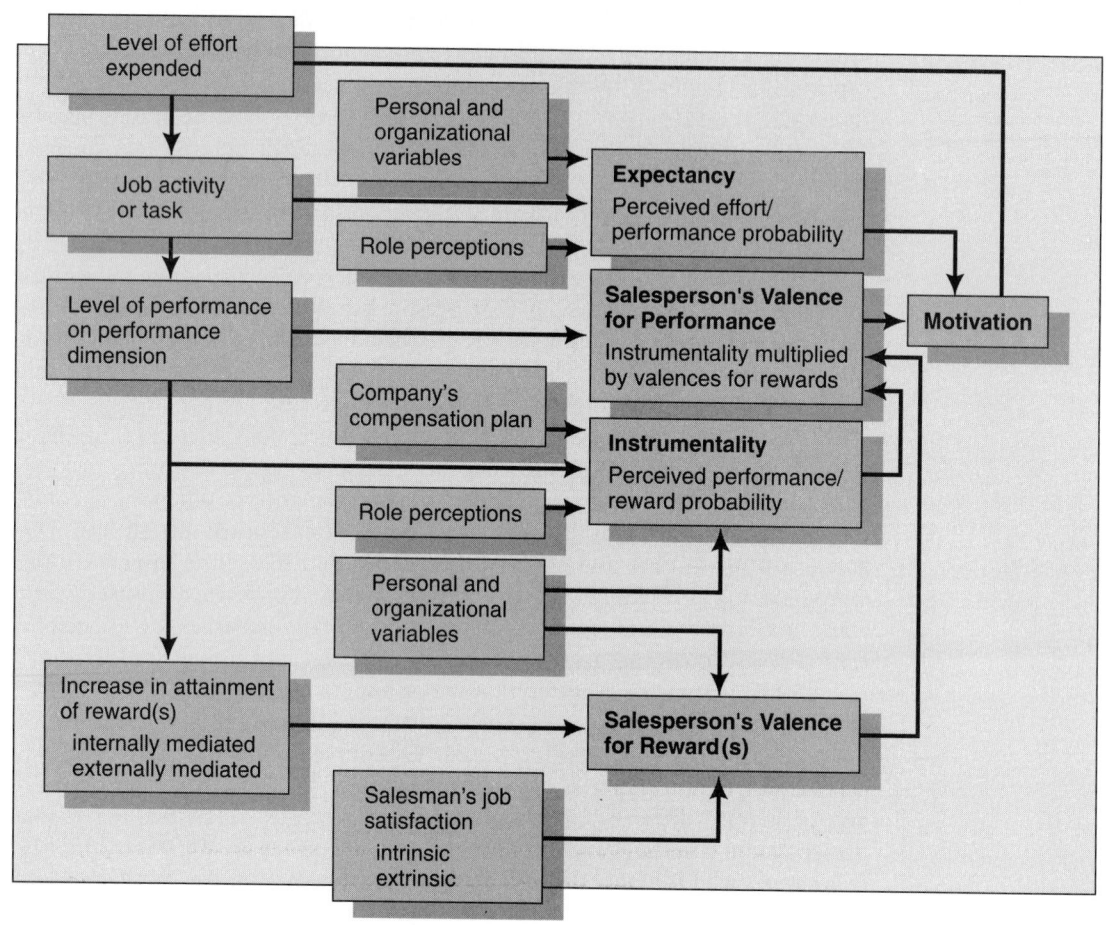

Instrumentalities—
Perceived Links
between
Performance and
Rewards

Like expectancies, instrumentalities are probability estimates made by the sales-person. They are the individual's perceptions of the link between job perfor-mance and various rewards. Specifically, an instrumentality is a salesperson's estimate of the probability that an improvement in performance on some dimension will lead to a specific increase in a particular reward. The reward may be more pay, winning a sales contest, or promotion to a better territory.

As with expectancies, sales managers should be concerned with both the magnitude and the accuracy of their subordinates' instrumentalities. When the magnitude of a salesperson's instrumentality estimates is relatively large, the sales rep believes there is a high probability that improved performance will lead to more rewards. Consequently, the sales rep will be more willing to expend the effort necessary to achieve better performance.

The true link between performance and rewards in a firm are determined by management policies about how sales performance is evaluated and what rewards are conferred for various levels of performance. In the Lotus Notes sales force, for instance, when a team's performance exceeds its sales volume quota, its members are rewarded with increased commissions. Sometimes, however, a firm's evaluation and reward policies may be inaccurately perceived by its salespeople. They may devote too much attention to activities or objectives that are relatively unimportant to management, and they may ultimately become disillusioned with their inability to attain desired rewards.

Besides the firm's compensation policies, other organizational factors and the personal characteristics of the salespeople can influence both the magnitude and the accuracy of their instrumentality estimates. These factors and their managerial implications are explored in a later section of this chapter and in Chapter 15.

Valence for Rewards

Valences are salespeople's perceptions of the desirability of receiving increased amounts of the rewards they might attain as a result of improved performance. One question about valences that has always interested sales managers is whether there are consistent preferences among salespeople for specific kinds of rewards. Are some rewards consistently valued more highly than others?

Historically, many sales managers and most authors of books and articles on motivating salespeople have assumed monetary rewards are the most highly valued and motivating rewards. They believe recognition and other psychological rewards are less valued and spur additional sales effort only under certain circumstances. However, only a few recent studies have empirically tested whether salespeople typically have higher valences for more pay than for other rewards. Thus, the assumption that they do has been based largely on the perceptions of sales managers rather than on any evidence obtained from salespeople themselves.

Surveys conducted among employees in other occupations often find that increased pay is *not* always the most highly desired reward. For example, one psychologist reviewed 43 surveys of nonsales workers in which the importance of more pay was rated relative to other rewards. Pay was ranked most important in only 25 percent of these studies, and its average importance across all studies was third.[5]

In view of this evidence, is the conventional wisdom that salespeople desire money more than other rewards wrong? Or do salespeople simply desire different rewards than workers in other kinds of jobs, as Doran assumed when he designed different incentive compensation systems for the Lotus Notes salespeople and systems engineers? Several studies focused on industrial salespeople generally support the conventional view. Their findings suggest that,

E X H I B I T   14 • 3   *Valence Ratings and Rankings of Alternative Rewards by Salespeople in Two Manufacturers*

	Company A (n = 151)		Company B (n = 76)	
	Valence Rating	Rank	Valence Rating	Rank
More pay	90.8	1	80.9	3
Sense of accomplishment	74.8	2	84.6	2
Opportunities for personal growth	74.7	3	87.9	1
Promotion	64.7	4	74.6	4
Liking and respect	62.2	5	64.8	5
Security	60.3	6	57.4	6
Recognition	50.3	7	53.9	7

Source: Adapted from Gilbert A. Churchill, Jr., Neil M. Ford, and Orville C. Walker, Jr., *Motivating the Industrial Salesforce: The Attractiveness Rewards:* Report No. 76-115 (Cambridge, Mass.: The Marketing Science Institute, 1976), p. 14.

on average, salespeople place a higher value on receiving more pay than any other reward.[6]

But increased pay is not always seen as the most attractive reward by all salespeople in all companies. Exhibit 14.3 illustrates the results of a study conducted some years ago that asked 481 salespeople from two different manufacturing organizations to rate seven different rewards on a 100-point scale according to their relative attractiveness.

More pay was not universally seen as the most desirable reward by all the salespeople in the study. Although more pay was by far the most attractive reward for salespeople in Company A, it ranked only third behind "opportunities for personal growth" and "sense of accomplishment" for those in Company B.

Why did the salespeople in one company value a pay increase more than those in the other? One plausible answer is that the average total compensation received by salespeople in Company B was about $5,000 higher than that of salespeople in A at the time of the study. Also, the proportion of salespeople reaching quota and qualifying for bonuses in Company A in the year preceding the study had declined sharply due to quota increases of as much as 25 percent over the year before. No such changes had occurred in Company B. It is possible, then, that the salespeople in Company A had a higher valence for more pay because they were less satisfied with the financial compensation they were receiving.

No universal statements can be made about what kinds of rewards are most desired by salespeople and most effective for motivating them. Salespeople's valences for rewards are likely to be influenced by their satisfaction with the rewards they are currently receiving. Their satisfaction with current rewards, in turn, is influenced by their personal characteristics and by the compensation policies and management practices of their firm.

CAN THE MOTIVATION MODEL PREDICT SALESPERSON EFFORT AND PERFORMANCE?

Several studies have tested the ability of motivation models such as the one outlined in Exhibits 14.1 and 14.2 to predict the amount of effort workers will expend on various job activities. The findings support the validity of such expectancy models of motivation, explaining as much as 25 percent of the variation in effort among workers.[7]

The salesperson model of performance discussed previously suggests motivation is only one determinant of job performance. Thus, it seems inappropriate to use only motivation to predict differences in job performance among workers. Nevertheless, several studies have attempted to do just that, and with surprising success. Some studies have found that predictions of workers' motivation to expend effort can explain as much as 40 percent of the variation in their overall job performance.[8]

It is nice to know that models like Exhibit 14.1 are valid descriptions of the psychological processes that determine a salesperson's motivation. However, there is a question of even greater relevance to sales managers as they struggle to design effective compensation and incentive programs. The question is how the three determinants of motivation—expectancy perceptions, instrumentality perceptions, and valences for rewards—are affected by (1) differences in the personal characteristics of individuals, (2) environmental conditions, and (3) the organization's policies and procedures. Therefore, the impact of each of these variables on the determinants of motivation is now examined in greater detail.

THE IMPACT OF A SALESPERSON'S PERSONAL CHARACTERISTICS ON MOTIVATION

When placed in the same job with the same compensation and incentive programs, different salespeople are likely to be motivated to expend widely differing amounts of effort. People with different personal characteristics have divergent perceptions of the links between effort and performance (expectancies) and between performance and rewards (instrumentalities). They are also likely to have different valences for the rewards they might obtain through improved job performance. The personal characteristics that affect motivation include (1) the individual's satisfaction with current rewards, (2) demographic variables, (3) job experience, and (4) psychological variables—particularly the salesperson's personality traits and attributions about why performance has been good or bad. The impacts of each of these sets of variables on salespeople's expectancies, instrumentalities, and valances are examined below.

Also, as we see later, many of these personal characteristics change and interact with one another as a salesperson moves through various career stages. For instance, when people begin their first sales job, they are likely to be relatively young and have few family responsibilities, little job experience, and low task-specific self-esteem. Later in their careers, those salespeople will be older and have more family obligations, more experience, and more self-esteem. As a result, their valences for various rewards and their expectancy and instrumentality estimates are all likely to change as their careers progress. Consequently, a later section of this chapter examines how salespeople's motivation is likely to change during their careers, and some managerial implications of such changes.

Satisfaction

Is it possible to pay a salesperson too much? After a salesperson reaches a certain satisfactory level of compensation, does the sales rep lose interest in working to obtain still more money? Does the attainment of nonfinancial rewards similarly affect the salesperson's desire to earn more of those rewards? The basic issue underlying these questions is whether a salesperson's satisfaction with current rewards has any impact on the valence for more of those rewards or on the desire for different kinds of rewards.

The relationship between satisfaction and the valence for rewards is different for rewards that satisfy lower-order needs (e.g., pay and job security) than for those that satisfy higher-order needs (e.g., promotions, recognition, opportunities for personal growth, self-fulfillment). Maslow's theory of a need hierarchy,[9] Herzberg's theory of motivation,[10] and Alderfer's "existence, relatedness, and growth theory"[11] all suggest that lower-order rewards are valued most highly by workers currently dissatisfied with their attainment of those rewards. In other words, the more dissatisfied a salesperson is with current pay, job security, recognition, and other rewards related to lower-order needs, the higher the valence attached to increases in those rewards. In contrast, as salespeople become more satisfied with their attainment of low-ordered rewards, the value of further increases in those rewards declines.

The theories of Maslow, Herzberg, and Alderfer further suggest that high-order rewards are not valued highly by salespeople until they are relatively satisfied with their lower-order rewards. The greater the salesperson's satisfaction with lower-order rewards, the higher the valence of increased attainment of high-order rewards.

Perhaps the most controversial aspect of Maslow's and Alderfer's theories is the proposition that high-order rewards have increasing marginal utility. The more satisfied a salesperson is with the high-order rewards received from the job, the higher the value the sales rep places on further increases in those rewards.

Research in industrial psychology provides at least partial support for these

EXHIBIT 14 ● 4   *The Influence of Demographic Characteristics on Valence for Rewards*

Demographic Variable	Valence for Higher-Order Rewards	Valence for Lower-Order Rewards
Age	+	−
Family size		+
Education	+	

suggested relationships between satisfaction and the valence of lower-order and higher-order rewards. Some of the evidence is equivocal, though, and some propositions—particularly the idea that high-order rewards have increasing marginal utility—have not been tested adequately.

Several studies of valence for rewards conducted among salespeople also provide partial—though mixed—support for the preceding hypotheses. In general, these studies show that salespeople who are relatively satisfied with their current income (a lower-order reward) have lower valences for more pay than those who are less satisfied. Most of these studies also suggest salespeople who are relatively satisfied with their current attainment of higher-order rewards, such as recognition and personal growth, tend to have higher valences for more of those rewards than those who are less satisfied. However, the evidence is mixed concerning whether salespeople who are relatively satisfied with their lower-order rewards have significantly higher valences for higher-order rewards than those who are less satisfied, as the theories would predict.[12]

Demographic Characteristics

Demographic characteristics, such as age, family size, and education, also affect a salesperson's valence for rewards. At least part of the reason for this is that people with different characteristics tend to attain different levels of rewards and are therefore likely to have different levels of satisfaction with their current rewards. Although there is only limited empirical evidence regarding salespeople, some conclusions can be drawn from studies in other occupations.[13] These conclusions are summarized in Exhibit 14.4.

Generally, older, more experienced salespeople obtain higher levels of lower-order rewards (e.g., higher pay, a better territory) than newer members of the sales force. Thus, it could be expected that more experienced salespeople are more satisfied with their lower-order rewards. Consequently, they also should have lower valences for lower-order rewards and higher valences for higher-order rewards than younger and less experienced salespeople.

A salesperson's satisfaction with the current level of lower-order rewards may also be influenced by the demands and responsibilities the sales rep must satisfy with those rewards. The salesperson with a large family to support, for instance, is less likely to be satisfied with a given level of financial compensation than the single salesperson. Consequently, the more family members a salesperson must support, the higher the valence for more lower-order rewards and the lower the valence for higher-order rewards.

Finally, individuals with more formal education are more likely to desire opportunities for personal growth, career advancement, and self-fulfillment than those with less education. Consequently, highly educated salespeople are likely to have higher valences for higher-order rewards.

Job Experience

As people gain experience on a job, they are likely to gain a clearer idea of how expending effort on particular tasks affects performance. Experienced salespeople are also likely to understand better how their superiors evaluate performance and how particular types of performance are rewarded in the company. Consequently, a positive relationship is likely between the years a salesperson has spent on the job and the accuracy of the rep's expectancy and instrumentality perceptions.

In addition, the magnitude of a salesperson's expectancy perceptions may be affected by experience. As they gain experience, salespeople have opportunities to sharpen their selling skills; and they gain confidence in their ability to perform successfully. As a result, experienced salespeople are likely to have larger expectancy estimates than inexperienced ones.

Psychological Traits

An individual's motivation also seems to be affected by psychological traits. Various traits can influence the magnitude and accuracy of a person's expectancy and instrumentality estimates, as well as valences for various rewards, as summarized in Exhibit 14.5. People with strong achievement needs are likely to have higher valences for such higher-order rewards as recognition, personal growth, and feeling of accomplishment. This is particularly true when they see their jobs as being relatively difficult to perform successfully.[14]

The degree to which individuals believe they have internal control over the events in their lives or whether those events are determined by external forces beyond their control also affects their motivation. Specifically, the greater the degree to which salespeople believe they have internal control over events, the more likely they are to think they can improve their performance by expending more effort. They also believe improved performance will be appropriately rewarded. Therefore, salespeople with high "internal locus of control" are likely to have relatively high expectancy and instrumentality estimates.[15]

There is some evidence that intelligence is positively related to feelings of internal control.[16] Therefore, more intelligent salespeople may have higher expectancy and instrumentality perceptions than those less intelligent. Those with relatively high levels of intelligence—particularly verbal intelligence—are especially likely to understand their jobs and their companies' reward policies

EXHIBIT 14 • 5   *The Influence of Psychological Traits on the Determinants of Motivation*

| | Motivational Variables | | | | | |
| | Expectancies | | Instrumentalities | | Valences | |
Personality Trait	Magnitude	Accuracy	Magnitude	Accuracy	High Order	Low Order
High need achievement					+	
Internal locus of control	+		+			
Verbal intelligence	+	+	+	+		
General self-esteem	+				+	
Task-specific self-esteem	+				+	

more quickly and accurately. Thus, their instrumentality and expectancy estimates are likely to be more accurate.

Finally, a worker's general feeling of self-esteem and perceived competence and ability to perform job activities (task-specific self-esteem) are both positively related to the magnitude of expectancy estimates.[17] Since such people believe they have the talents and abilities to be successful, they are likely to see a strong relationship between effort expended and good performance. Also, people with high levels of self-esteem are likely to attach greater importance to, and receive more satisfaction from, good performance. Consequently, such people probably have higher valences for the higher-order, intrinsic rewards attained from successful job performance, although the lone study to examine the impact of self-esteem on salespeople's reward valences failed to support this proposition.[18]

Performance Attributions

People try to identify and understand the causes of major events and outcomes in their lives. A given individual might attribute the cause of a particular event—such as good sales performance last quarter—to the following:

1. **Stable internal factors** that are unlikely to change much in the near future, such as personal skills and abilities.

2. **Unstable internal factors** that may vary from time to time, such as the amount of effort expended or mood at the time.

3. **Stable external factors,** such as the nature of the task or the competitive situation in a particular territory.

4. **Unstable external factors** that might change next time, such as assistance from an unusually aggressive advertising campaign or good luck.

EXHIBIT 14 • 6   *The Influence of Performance Attributions on the Magnitude of a Salesperson's Expectancy Estimates*

Performance Attribution	Impact on Magnitude of Salesperson's Expectancy Estimates
Good performance attributed to:	
Stable internal cause	+
Unstable internal cause	+
Stable external cause	+
Unstable external cause	0
Poor performance attributed to:	
Stable internal cause	–
Unstable internal cause	+
Stable external cause	–
Unstable external cause	0

The nature of a salesperson's recent job performance, together with the kind of causes the rep attributes that performance to, can affect the individual's expectancy estimates concerning the likelihood that increased effort will lead to improved performance in the future.[19] Various attributions' likely effects on the magnitude of a salesperson's expectancy estimates are summarized in Exhibit 14.6.

As Exhibit 14.6 indicates, expectancy estimates are likely to increase if recent successful sales performance is attributed to either stable or unstable internal causes or to stable external causes. For instance, salespeople are likely to attach even higher expectancies to future performance where they take credit for past success, either as the result of superior skill (stable internal cause) or personal effort (unstable internal cause). Salespeople's expectancies are also likely to increase where past success is attributed to a perception that the task is relatively easy (stable external cause). However, if past successful performance is attributed to an unstable external cause that could change in the next performance period—such as good luck—there is no basis for salespeople to revise their expectancy estimates in any systematic way.

Suppose a salesperson performed poorly last quarter. Exhibit 14.6 indicates the impact of that poor performance on the individual's expectancy estimates is influenced by the causal attributions the person makes. If the salesperson attributes poor past performance to stable causes that cannot be changed in the foreseeable future, such as low ability (stable internal cause) or a difficult competitive environment (stable external cause), the sales rep's expectancy estimates are likely to be lower. However, if the poor performance is attributed to an unstable internal cause—such as not expending sufficient effort to be successful—the person's expectancies may actually increase. The person may believe performance can be improved simply by changing the internal factor that caused the problem last time—by expending more effort or by improving selling skills.

Management Implications

The relationships between salespeople's personal characteristics and motivation levels have two broad implications for sales managers. First, they suggest people with certain characteristics are likely to understand their jobs and their companies' policies better. They also should perceive higher expectancy and instrumentality links. Such people should be easier to train and be motivated to expend greater effort and achieve better performance. Therefore, as researchers and managers gain a better understanding of these relationships, it may be possible to develop improved selection criteria for hiring salespeople who are easy to train and motivate.

More important, some personal characteristics are related to the kinds of rewards salespeople are likely to value and find motivating. This suggests sales managers should examine the characteristics of their salespeople and attempt to determine their relative valences for various rewards when designing compensation and incentive programs. Also, as the demographic characteristics of a sales force change, the manager should be aware that salespeople's satisfaction with rewards and their valences for future rewards may also change.

CAREER STAGES AND SALESPERSON MOTIVATION

The previous discussion of the personal factors affecting motivation also suggests that salespeople's expectancy estimates and reward valences are likely to change as they move through different stages in their careers. As a person grows older and gains experience, demographic characteristics and financial obligations change, skills and confidence tend to improve, and the rewards the salesperson receives—as well as satisfaction with those rewards—are likely to change. We have seen that all of these factors can affect an individual's expectancies and reward valences.

Career Stages

Research has identified four stages that salespeople go through during their careers: exploration, establishment, maintenance, and disengagement.[20] Typical paths of progression through these four career stages are diagrammed in Exhibit 14.7. The individual concerns, challenges, and needs associated with each career stage—together with their implications for motivating a salesperson at that stage—are summarized in Exhibit 14.8 and discussed below.

Exploration stage

People in the earliest stage of their careers (typically individuals in their 20s) are often unsure about whether selling is the most appropriate occupation for

E X H I B I T   **14 ● 7**   *Sales Career Path*

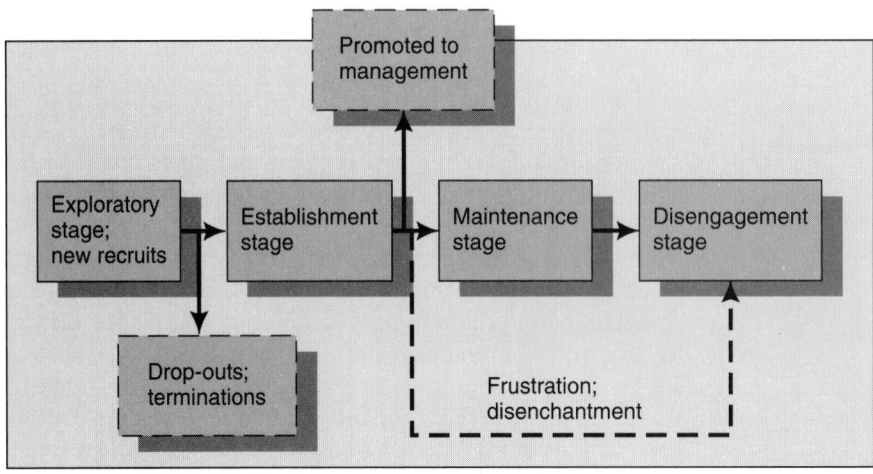

them to pursue and whether they can be successful salespeople. To make matters worse, underdeveloped skills and a lack of knowledge about their roles tend to make people at this early stage among the poorest performers in the sales force. Consequently, people in the exploratory stage tend to have low psychological involvement with their job and low job satisfaction. As Exhibit 14.7 indicates, this can cause some people to become discouraged and quit and others to be terminated if their performance does not improve.

Because salespeople in the exploratory career stage are uncertain about their own skills and the requirements of their new jobs, they tend to have the lowest expectancy and instrumentality perceptions in a firm's sales force. They have little confidence that expending more effort will lead to better performance or that improved performance will produce increased rewards. But they do have relatively high valences for high-order rewards, particularly for personal growth and recognition. They need reassurance that they are making progress and that they will eventually be successful in their new career. Consequently, good training programs, supportive supervision, and much recognition and encouragement are useful for motivating and improving the performance of salespeople at this formative stage of their careers.

Establishment stage

Those in the establishment stage—usually in their late 20s or early 30s—have settled on an occupation and desire to build it into a successful career. Thus, the major concerns of salespeople at this stage involve improving their skills and their sales performance. As they gain confidence, these people's expectancy

EXHIBIT 14 • 8   *Characteristics of Different Stages in a Salesperson's Career*

	Exploration	Establishment	Maintenance	Disengagement
Career concerns	Finding an appropriate occupational field	Successfully establishing a career in a certain occupation	Holding on to what has been achieved Reassessing career, with possible redirection	Completing one's career
Developmental tasks	Learning the skills required to do the job well Becoming a contributing member of an organization	Using skills to produce results Adjusting to working with greater autonomy Developing creativity and innovativeness	Developing broader view of work and organization Maintaining a high performance level	Establishing a stronger self-identify outside of work Maintaining an accceptable performance level
Personal challenges	Must establish a good initial professional self-concept	Producing superior results on the job in order to be promoted Balancing the conflicting demands of career and family	Maintaining motivation though possible rewards have changed Facing concerns about aging and disappointment over what one has accomplished Maintaining motivation and productivity	Acceptance of career accomplishments Adjusting self-image
Psychosocial needs	Support Peer acceptance Challenging position	Achievement Esteem Autonomy Competition	Reduced competitiveness Security Helping younger colleagues	Detachment from organization and organizational life
Impact on motivation	Low expectancy and instrumentality perceptions High valences for high-order rewards, such as personal growth and recognition Supportive supervision is critical	Highest expectancy and instrumentality perceptions High valences for pay, but highest valences for promotion and recognition Must avoid generating unrealistic expectations	Instrumentality and valence for promotion falls Valence for recognition and respect remain high Highest valences for increased pay	Lowest instrumentality perceptions and valences for both high-order and low-order rewards Still desires respect, but that is unlikely to motivate additional effort

Source: Adapted from William L. Cron, "Industrial Salespersons Development: A Career Stages Perspective," *Journal of Marketing,* Fall 1984, p. 40; and William L. Cron, Alan J. Dubinsky, and Ronald E. Michaels, "The Influence of Career Stages on Components of Salesperson Motivation," *Journal of Marketing,* January 1988, pp. 79–92.

and instrumentality perceptions reach their highest level. People at this stage believe they will be successful if they devote sufficient effort to the job and their success will be rewarded.

Because people at this career stage are often making other important commitments in their lives—such as buying homes, marrying, and having children—their valences for increased financial rewards tend to be relatively high. However, their strong desire to be successful—and in many cases the desire to move into management—makes their valences for promotion higher at this stage than at any other. They also have very high valences for recognition and other indications that their superiors approve of their performance and perhaps consider them worthy of promotion.

However, the strong desire for promotion at this stage can have negative consequences. As shown in Exhibit 14.7, some successful people may win promotions into sales or marketing management, but many others will not, at least not as soon as they hoped. Some of these individuals may become so frustrated by what they consider to be slow progress that they quit for jobs in other companies that promise faster advancement or they move prematurely into a "disengagement" stage. To help prevent this, managers should guard against building unrealistic expectations concerning the likelihood and speed of future promotions among their establishment-stage salespeople.

Maintenance stage

This stage normally begins in a salesperson's late 30s or early 40s. The individual's primary concern at this stage is with retaining the present position, status, and performance level within the sales force, all of which are likely to be quite high. For this reason, people in the maintenance stage continue to have high valences for rewards that reflect high status and good performance, such as formal recognition and the respect of their peers and superiors.

By this stage, though, both the opportunity and desire for promotion diminish. Consequently, instrumentality estimates and valences concerning promotion fall to lower levels. But salespeople at this stage often have the highest valences for increased pay and financial incentives of anyone in the sales force. Even though such people are among the highest paid salespeople, they tend to want more money due to both increased financial obligations (e.g., children getting ready for college, large mortgages, etc.) and a desire for a symbol of success in lieu of promotion.

Disengagement stage

At some point, everyone must begin to prepare for retirement and the possible loss of self-identity that can accompany separation from one's job. This usually begins to happen when people reach their late 50s or early 60s. During this disengagement stage, people psychologically withdraw from their job, often seeking to maintain just an "acceptable" level of performance with a minimum amount of effort in order to spend more time developing interests outside of work. As a result, such people have little interest in attaining more high-order rewards—such as recognition, personal development, or a promotion—from their jobs.

Because they tend to have fewer financial obligations at this stage, they are also relatively satisfied with their low-order rewards and have low valences for attaining more pay or other financial incentives. Not surprisingly, then, salespeople at this career stage have average performance levels lower than any others except new recruits in the exploratory stage. And their low valences for either high- or low-order rewards make it difficult to motivate them.

What is most disconcerting about disengagement, however, is that it does not occur only among salespeople at the end of their careers. As mentioned earlier, long before they approach retirement age, people may become bored with their jobs and frustrated by a failure to win promotion. Such people may psychologically withdraw from their jobs rather than search for a new position or occupation. They are commonly referred to as *plateaued* salespeople—people who have stopped developing, stopped improving, and often stopped showing an interest.

The Problem of the Plateaued Salesperson

Plateauing, or early disengagement, is not an isolated phenomenon among salespeople. A recent survey of more than 200 manufacturing and retailing firms suggests an average of about 15 percent of a firm's sales force can be expected to have reached a plateau, and in some companies the percentage is much higher.[21] While this study suggests the average plateaued salesperson is a male in his mid-40s, respondents reported that some salespeople reach plateaus while only in their early 30s, and women are about equally susceptible to early disengagement as men.

Causes of plateauing

Exhibit 14.9 shows managers' perceptions of the relative importance of various causes of plateauing among salespeople. These rankings are broken down according to whether the sales force consists of a majority of men or women and according to the type of compensation plan employed (e.g., salary only, commission only, etc.). Overall, these managerial perceptions are consistent with what was mentioned earlier. The primary causes of early disengagement are the boredom and frustration that arise when a relatively young person is kept in the same job too long and sees little likelihood of a promotion or other expansion in job responsibilities in the near future. Among the top-ranked causes of plateauing are a lack of a clear career path, boredom, and a failure to manage the person effectively. Note, too, that these factors are viewed as important regardless of the gender of the sales force or the compensation system used.

However, the respondents did believe that simple burnout may be a more important cause of plateauing among saleswomen than salesmen, perhaps due to the demands of their multiple roles as mothers and homemakers in addition

EXHIBIT 14 • 9   *Manager's Rankings of the Causes of Plateauing among Salespeople*

	Overall	Mostly Men	Mostly Women	Salary Only	Salary plus Bonus	Salary plus Commission	Salary Commission Bonus	Commission Only
No clear career path	1	1	2	1	2	1	3	4
Not managed adequately	2	2	4	3	1	3	4	1
Bored	3	3	3	2	4	4	2	5
Burned out	4	5	1	5	3	5	1	2
Economic needs met	5	4	7	6	5	2	6	3
Discouraged with company	6	6	5	4	6	6	5	6
Overlooked for promotion	7	7	6	7	7	7	7	8
Lack of ability	8	8	9	8	10	8	8	7
Avoiding risk of management job	9	9	10	10	8	9	9	9
Reluctance to be transferred	10	10	8	9	9	10	10	10

Note: The numbers in each column indicate how early warning signals and causes of plateauing were ranked by *S&MM* survey respondents overall and by several subgroups. (By "mostly men" or "mostly women" we mean sales forces comprised of at least 60 percent men or 60 percent women.)

Source: Reprinted with permission from William Keenan, Jr., "The Nagging Problem of the Plateaued Salesperson," *Sales & Marketing Management*, March 1989, p. 38 © 1989 by Bill Communicatons, Inc.

to those of their jobs. Also, the survey results suggest the opportunity to earn high levels of pay provided by compensation systems made up entirely or substantially of commission payments can exacerbate the plateauing problem. Managers indicate salespeople compensated by commission may more easily earn sufficient pay to meet their economic needs and thereby become less motivated by the chance to earn still higher financial compensation. We explore this issue in more detail in the next chapter.

Possible solutions

All of this suggests that one way of reducing the plateauing problem in a sales force—and of remotivating salespeople who have reached a plateau—is to develop clearly defined career paths for salespeople who are good performers but are not promoted into management early in their careers. Such "alternative" career paths typically involve promotions to positions *within* the sales force that involve additional responsibility and more demanding challenges.

For instance, a firm might develop a career path involving frequent promotions to increasingly lucrative and challenging territories or assignments to larger and more sophisticated accounts. For instance, some firms promote high-performing salespeople into national account management positions. Assignments to new product development teams or staff support positions (e.g., director of sales recruiting or training) might also be part of the sales career path. The idea is to provide opportunities for frequent changes in job duties and responsibilities to increase the variety of salespeople's jobs. Simultaneously, those changes can be used as rewards for good performance to motivate the members of the sales force and to show that they are valued employees even though they do not rise to management positions.

To be effective, however, the promotions along the sales career path must be *real* rather than simply changes in title. They must involve real changes in duties and responsibilities, and they must be offered on the basis of good past performance. Cosmetic promotions—particularly when they are doled out simply on the basis of time-in-rank—do little to stimulate continued effort among a firm's older salespeople.

Another closely related approach to revitalizing plateaued salespeople is to enrich their current jobs by finding ways to add variety and responsibility without developing a complicated system of hierarchical positions and promotion criteria. This is often a more viable approach in smaller sales forces where it is difficult to develop complex career paths for salespeople. For example, plateaued salespeople might be asked to devote time to training and mentoring new recruits, to gathering competitive intelligence, or to working on special task forces. A number of other specific suggestions for dealing with disengaged salespeople offered by respondents in the *Sales & Marketing Management* survey are listed in the accompanying Thorny Issues in Sales Management 14.1.

The Impact of Environmental Conditions on Motivation

Environmental factors such as variations in territory potential and strength of competition can constrain a salesperson's ability to achieve high levels of performance. Such environmental constraints can cause substantial variations in performance across salespeople. In addition to placing actual constraints on performance, however, environmental conditions can affect salespeople's *perceptions* of their likelihood of succeeding and thus their willingness to expend effort.

Although management can do little to change the environment faced by its salespeople (with the possible exception of rearranging sales territories), an understanding of how and why salespeople perform differently under varying environmental circumstances is useful to sales managers. Such an understanding provides clues about the compensation methods and management policies that will have the greatest impact on sales performance under specific envi-

Dealing with the Plateaued Salesperson

Since plateauing or early disengagement is so pervasive among salespeople, finding ways to remotivate such employees represents a thorny issue for nearly every sales manager. The following solutions were suggested by responding managers in the *Sales & Marketing Management* survey discussed in the text. While these suggestions vary a great deal, termination is almost universally viewed as a last resort. Plateaued salespeople often have a past history of successful performance, and they are potentially too valuable to simply dismiss without first trying to find creative ways to rekindle their energy and enthusiasm.

- Confront the problem as soon as there is evidence of it. Talk about what plateauing is about and strategies to avoid cutting back on effort. Challenge them—through new assignments or additional responsibilities.
- Give *true* perquisites—vacations, bonuses, etc.—immediately after landing a new or big account.
- Continually create new challenges by introducing new products, redeploying resources, reassigning accounts.
- Assign the salesperson to a different manager, one who relates well with subordinates.
- Ask the salesperson to help develop a new territory or to survey customers for new product/service ideas. This gives the salesperson an extra objective on sales calls.
- Speak frankly with the person and tell him or her what is expected. Set a time limit in which you expect to see improvement. Advise the salesperson to get back to basics, to do the things that made him or her successful in the first place.
- Offer a transfer or a change of role.
- Have him or her assist newer sales representatives in making new customer presentations.
- Set up special bonus or recognition plans.

- Probe for reasons. Define a plan of action to address each reason. Require a detailed accounting of all the salesperson's activities. Set a probation period and enforce it.
- Make the rep recognize the problem and have him or her come up with possible means of eliminating it.
- Conduct regular training and motivational sessions to serve as a reminder of how exciting sales can be.
- Provide an ongoing goal attainment assessment program that sets and resets goals as they are approached and reached.
- Give them some time off. Increase perks and benefits.
- Reevaluate the relationship between the company and the employee. Clear the air. Redefine goals and set definite schedules for reevaluating the situation.
- Give them a rest and a chance to rethink their life and options while they regenerate their selling juices.
- Make sure the sales *manager* is at least equal to the salesperson in competence and experience.
- Encourage salespeople to be creative. Listen to any ideas that will open new markets—we pay a premium for this and find salespeople to be a good source of new product and packaging ideas.
- Hold personal meetings with the salespeople. Encourage them to explain what they see as the problem. Then, together, decide what is the best course of action.
- Manage, lead, communicate, pay attention, and don't wait until too late to take corrective action.

Source: Reprinted with permission from William Keenan, Jr., "The Nagging Problem of the Plateaued Salesperson," *Sales & Marketing Management,* March 1989, p. 40. © 1989 by Bill Communications, Inc. See also Thomas L. Quick, "Salvaging the Problem Salesperson," *Sales & Marketing Management,* April 1989, pp. 41–44.

EXHIBIT 14 • 10   *Influence of Environmental Factors on the Determinants of Motivation*

| | Motivation Variables | | | |
| | Expectancies | | Instrumentalities | |
Environmental Factors	Magnitude	Accuracy	Magnitude	Accuracy
Stability of product offerings		+		
Output constraints	−		−	
Superiority of competitive position	+			
Territory potential	+			

ronmental conditions. The effects of various environmental factors on sales-people's perceptions and motivations are summarized in Exhibit 14.10.

In some industries, the pace of technological change is very rapid, as recent advances in the computer and office machine industries show. Salespeople in such industries must deal with a constant flow of product innovations, modifications, and applications. Salespeople often look with favor on a constantly changing product line because it adds variety to their jobs, and their markets never have a chance to become saturated and stagnant. However, a rapidly changing product line can also cause problems for the salesperson. New products and services may require new selling methods and result in new expectations and demands from role partners. Consequently, an unstable product line may lead to less accurate expectancy estimates among the sales force.

In some firms, salespeople must perform in the face of output constraints, which can result from short supplies of production factors, including shortages of raw materials, plant capacity, or labor. Such constraints can cause severe problems for the salesperson. In one paper-products firm a few years ago, salespeople were penalized for exceeding quotas. In general, salespeople operating in the face of uncertain or limited product supplies are likely to feel relatively powerless to improve their performance or rewards through their own efforts. After all, their ultimate effectiveness is constrained by factors beyond their control. Therefore, their expectancy and instrumentality estimates are likely to be low.

There are many ways of assessing the strength of a firm's competitive position in the marketplace. One might look at its market share, the quality of its products and services as perceived by customers, or its prices. Regardless of how competitive superiority is defined, though, when salespeople believe they work for a strongly competitive firm, they are more likely to think selling effort will result in successful performance. In other words, the stronger a firm's competitive position, the higher its salespeople's expectancy estimates are likely to be.

Sales territories often have very different potentials for future sales. These potentials are affected by many environmental factors, including economic conditions, competitors' activities, and customer concentrations. Again, though, the salesperson's *perception* of the unrealized potential of the territory can influence that person's motivation to expend selling effort. Specifically, the greater the perceived potential of a territory, the higher the salesperson's expectancy estimates are likely to be.

THE IMPACT OF ORGANIZATIONAL VARIABLES ON MOTIVATION

Company policies and characteristics can directly facilitate or hinder a salesperson's effectiveness. Such organizational variables may also influence salespeople's performance indirectly, however, by affecting their valences for company rewards and the size and accuracy of their expectancy and instrumentality estimates. These relationships between organizational variables and the determinants of motivation are summarized in Exhibit 14.11.

Supervisory Variables and Leadership

According to one highly regarded theory of leadership, a leader attains good performance from the work unit by increasing subordinates' personal rewards from goal attainment and by making the path to those rewards easier to follow—through instructions and training, reducing roadblocks and pitfalls, and by increasing the opportunities for personal satisfaction.[22]

This theory suggests that effective leaders tailor their style and approach to the needs of their subordinates and the kinds of tasks they must perform. When the subordinates' task is well defined, routine, and repetitive, the leader should seek ways to increase the intrinsic rewards of the task. This might be accomplished by assigning subordinates a broader range of activities or by giving them more flexibility to perform tasks. When the subordinate's job is complex and ambiguous, that person is likely to be happier and more productive when the leader provides relatively high levels of guidance and structure.[23]

In most occupations, workers perform relatively well-defined and routine jobs, and they prefer to be relatively free from supervision. They do not like to feel their superiors "breathing down their necks." Industrial salespeople, however, are different. They occupy a position at the boundary of their companies, dealing with customers and other nonorganization people who may make conflicting demands. Salespeople frequently face new, nonroutine problems. Consequently, evidence shows industrial salespeople are happier when they feel relatively closely supervised, and supportive supervision can increase their expectancy and instrumentality estimates for attaining extrinsic rewards.[24] Closely supervised salespeople can learn more quickly what is expected of them and how they should perform their job. Consequently, such individuals should have more accurate expectancies and instrumentalities than less closely supervised salespeople. But close supervision can lead to more role conflict since it can reduce flexibility in accommodating and adapting to customers' demands.

E X H I B I T   14 • 11   *Influence of Organizational Variables on the Determinants of Motivation*

	Motivation Variables					
	Expectancies		Instrumentalities		Valences	
Organizational Variables	**Magnitude**	**Accuracy**	**Magnitude**	**Accuracy**	**High Order**	**Low Order**
Closeness of supervision	+			+		
Span of control	−			−		
Influence over standards				+		
Frequency of communication	+			+		
Opportunity rate					Curvilinear	
Recognition rate					Curvilinear	
Compensation rate						−
Earnings opportunity ratio						+

Another organization variable related to the closeness of supervision is the firm's first-level sales managers' span of control. The more salespeople each manager must supervise (the larger the span of control), the less closely the manager can supervise each person. Therefore, the impact of span of control on role perceptions and motivation variables should be the opposite of the expected impact of close supervision.

Another related supervisory variable is the frequency with which salespeople communicate with their superiors. The greater the frequency of communication, the less role ambiguity salespeople are likely to experience and the more accurate their expectancy and instrumentality estimates should be. Again, however, frequent contact with superiors may increase the individual's feelings of role conflict.

Management by objectives (MBO) is a popular supervisory technique in sales management. Specific procedures vary from firm to firm, but one basic principle of MBO is to give the individual a voice in determining the standards and criteria by which performance will be evaluated and rewarded. Salespeople who believe that they influence such standards are likely to have a clearer understanding of how to perform their jobs and how performance will be rewarded.

Incentive and Compensation Policies

Management policies and programs concerning higher-order rewards, such as recognition and promotion, can influence the desirability of such rewards in the salesperson's mind. For these rewards, there is likely to be a curvilinear relationship between the perceived likelihood of receiving them and the salesperson's valence for them. For example, if a large proportion of the sales force receives some formal recognition each year, salespeople may think such recognition is too common, too easy to obtain, and not worth much. If very few members receive formal recognition, however, salespeople may believe it is not a very attractive or motivating reward simply because the odds of attaining it are so low. The same curvilinear relationship is likely to exist between the proportion of salespeople promoted into management each year (the *opportunity* rate) and salespeople's valence for promotion.[25]

A company's policies on the kinds and amounts of financial compensation paid to its salespeople are also likely to affect their motivation. As seen, when a person's lower-order needs are satisfied, they become less important and the individual's valence for rewards that satisfy such needs, such as pay and job security, is reduced. This suggests that in firms where the current financial compensation is relatively high, salespeople will be satisfied with their attainment of lower-order rewards. They will have lower valences for more of those rewards than people in firms where compensation is lower.

The *range* of financial rewards currently received by members of a sales force also might affect their valences for more financial rewards. If some salespeople receive much more money than the average, many others may feel underpaid and have high valences for more money. The ratio of the total financial compensation of the highest paid salesperson to that of the average in a sales force is the **earnings opportunity ratio.** The higher this ratio is within a company, the higher the average salesperson's valence for pay is likely to be.

Finally, the kind of reward mix offered by the firm is a factor. Reward mix is the relative emphasis placed on salary versus commissions or other incentive pay and nonfinancial rewards. It is likely to influence the salesperson's instrumentality estimates and help determine which job activities and types of performance will receive the greatest effort from that salesperson. The question from a manager's viewpoint is how to design an effective reward mix for directing the sales force's efforts toward the activities believed to be most important to the overall success of the firm's sales program. This leads to a discussion of the relative advantages and weaknesses of alternative compensation and incentive programs—the topic of Chapter 15.

SUMMARY

The amount of effort the salesperson desires to expend on each activity or task associated with the job—the individual's *motivation*—can strongly influence job performance. This chapter reviewed the factors that affect an individual's motivation level. The chapter suggested an individual's motivation to expend effort on any particular task is a function of that person's (1) expectancy, (2) instrumentality, and (3) valence perceptions.

Expectancy refers to the salesperson's estimate of the probability that expending a given amount of effort on some task will lead to improved performance on some dimension. Expectancies have two dimensions that are important to sales managers—magnitude and accuracy. The magnitude of a salesperson's expectancy perceptions indicates the degree to which the individual believes that expending effort on job activities will directly influence job performance. The *accuracy of expectancy perceptions* refers to how clearly the individual understands the relationship between the effort expended on a task and the performance on some specific dimension that is likely to result.

Instrumentalities are the person's perceptions of links between job performance and various rewards. Specifically, an instrumentality is a salesperson's estimate of the probability that a given improvement in performance on some dimension will lead to a specific increase in the amount of a particular reward. A reward can be more pay, winning a sales contest, or promotion to a better territory. As with expectancies, sales managers need to be concerned with both the magnitude and accuracy of their subordinates' instrumentalities.

The salesperson's valence for a specific reward is the individual's perception of the desirability of receiving increased amounts of that reward. This valence, along with the individual's valence for all other attractive rewards and the person's instrumentality perceptions, determines how attractive it is to perform well on some specific dimension.

Several factors influence salespeople's expectancy, instrumentality, and valence perceptions. Three major forces are (1) the personal characteristics of the individuals in the sales force, (2) the environmental conditions they face, and (3) the company's own policies and procedures. The chapter reviewed some major influences and their likely impacts on each of the three categories.

Discussion Questions

1. "What's all this stuff about different pay packages and different incentive plans based on how long a sales rep has been with the company?" demanded the irate sales manager. "Around here, everybody gets the same treatment. We're not offering customized compensation packages." What are the problems associated with motivating sales reps based on their stage in the career cycle?

2. "Can Sports Stars Really Motivate Your Sales Force?" is the title of an article appearing in *Sales & Marketing Management*, December 1987. Fees for these "jocks turned motivators" range from $5,000 to $15,000. Of what value are these motivational speakers to a sales force? Can they really inspire a sales force?

3. What sales manager has not had the problem of motivating the older sales representative? The once-valuable producer has dried up and is not meeting quotas. He or she is a drag on the rest of the district sales team. What do you do? Fire the sales rep? Baby him or her? What can a sales manager do to turn the older sales rep into a valuable asset?

4. A situation different from the above concerns how to motivate the sales representative when money or merchandise is not the question. When ordinary incentives no longer work—commissions, incentives, or cars—what can a sales manager do to motivate the successful salesperson?

5. Most sales reps dislike preparing call reports. They think their time could be spent more profitably, such as calling on accounts. Using Exhibit 14.2, trace the thought

process sales reps would go through as they consider applying more effort to the preparation of call reports. Do the same for applying more effort to calling on accounts.

6. The desirability of an increase in personal growth and development was ranked second by the sales reps of a Fortune 500 corporation. Sales managers ranked this reward eighth. What explains the apparent discrepancy? How can sales managers motivate the sales force that desires personal growth and development?

7. Sales representatives and sales managers from one company were asked to state their valence for earning points in a sales contest. Out of 13 rewards, the sales reps ranked this reward 10th, and the sales managers ranked it 11th. What might explain this relatively low ranking for sales contests, considering their popularity?

8. What assumptions are sales managers making when they claim all the sales force needs is a pat on the back? Thus, they bring in the so-called motivation expert to pep up the sales group to apply more effort. What role do these entertaining experts play in the motivation of the sales force?

9. "If you ask me, there's entirely too much mystique about motivation. This stuff about valences, expectancies, and instrumentalities is nothing more than 'college-knowledge.' Either my sales force will be fired up with enthusiasm, or I'll fire them with enthusiasm." Comment.

10. The March 1992 issue of *Personal Selling Power* published the results of a survey, faxed back to the publisher by an unspecified number of respondents, on motivation. The November/December issue contained the questionnaire, which readers were expected to fax back. Readers were asked: "Who are the top motivators today?" The top 10 are: Zig Ziglar, Dr. Denis Waitley, Tony Robbins, Dr. Norman Vincent Peale, Tom Hopkins, Brian Tracy, Dr. Wayne Dyer, Mary Kay Ash, Lou Holtz, and Rich Wilkins. What role do these motivators play in the motivation process discussed in the chapter? How could a sales manager measure their effectiveness?

Endnotes

[1] This example is based on material found in Tom Murray, "Team Selling: What's the Incentive?" *Sales & Marketing Management*, June 1991, pp. 89–93.

[2] John P. Campbell and Robert D. Pritchard, "Motivation Theory in Industrial and Organizational Psychology," in *Handbook of Industrial and Organizational Psychology*, ed. Marvin D. Dunnette (Chicago: Rand McNally, 1976), p. 65.

[3] Theories of motivation can be classified into two groups: content theories and process theories. Major content theories include Maslow's need hierarchy, Alderfer's ERG theory, Herzberg's hygiene-motivation theory, and McClelland's theory of learned needs. Many of these content theories are briefly discussed later in this chapter. In addition to expectancy theory, other process theories of motivation include equity theory, attribution theory, and reinforcement theory. For a discussion of both sets of theories and their interrelationships, see James L. Gibson, John M. Ivancevich, and James H. Donnelly, Jr., *Organizations: Behavior, Structure, Processes,* 7th ed. (Homewood, Ill.: Richard D. Irwin, 1991).

[4] Baron A. Weitz, Harish Sujan, and Mita Sujan, "Knowledge, Motivation, and Adaptive Behavior: A Framework for Improving Selling Effectiveness," *Journal of Marketing*, October 1986, pp. 174–91. See also Harish Sujan, "Smarter versus Harder: An Exploratory

Attributional Analysis of Salespeople's Motivation," *Journal of Marketing Research*, February 1986, pp. 41–49.

[5]Edward E. Lawler III, *Pay and Organizational Effectiveness: A Psychological View* (New York: McGraw-Hill, 1971).

[6]For example, see Thomas N. Ingram and Danny N. Bellenger, "Personal and Organizational Variables: Their Relative Effect on Reward Valences of Industrial Salespeople," *Journal of Marketing Research,* May 1983, pp. 198–205; Neil M. Ford, Orville C. Walker, Jr., and Gilbert A. Churchill, Jr., "Differences in the Attractiveness of Alternative Rewards among Industrial salespeople: Additional Evidence," *Journal of Business Research,* April 1985, pp. 123–38; and Lawrence B. Chonko, John F. Tanner, Jr., William A. Weeks, and Melissa R. Schmitt, "Reward Preferences of Salespeople," Research Report No. 91-3 (Waco, Texas: The Center for Professional Selling, Baylor University, 1991).

[7]For a detailed discussion of a large number of such studies, see Campbell and Pritchard, "Motivation Theory," pp. 63–130. For a study that tests the mode with a sample of salespeople, see Gilbert A. Churchill, Jr., Neil M. Ford, and Orville C. Walker, Jr., "Predicting a Salesperson's Job Effort and Performance: Theoretical, Empirical, and Methodological Considerations," in *Sales Management: New Developments from Behavioral and Decision Model Research,* ed. Richard P. Bagozzi (Cambridge, Mass.: Marketing Science Institute, 1979), pp. 3–39.

[8]Campbell and Pritchard, "Motivation Theory." For a study focused on industrial salespeople, see Richard L. Oliver, "Expectancy Theory Predictions of Salesmen's Performance," *Journal of Marketing Research,* August 1974, pp. 243–53.

[9]Abraham H. Maslow, *Motivation and Personality,* 2nd ed. (New York: Harper & Row, 1970).

[10]Frederick Herzberg, Bernard Mauser, and Barabara Snyderman, *The Motivation to Work,* 2nd ed. (New York: John Wiley & Sons, 1959). See also Robert Berl, Terry Powell, and Nicholas C. Williamson, "Industrial Salesforce Satisfaction and Performance with Herzberg's Theory," *Industrial Marketing Management,* February 1984, pp. 11–19; and David D. Shipley and Julia A. Kiely, "Industrial Salesforce Motivation and Herzberg's Dual Factor Theory: A U.K. Perspective," *Journal of Personal Selling and Sales Management,* May 1986, pp. 9–16.

[11]Clayton P. Alderfer, "An Empirical Test of a New Theory of Human Needs," *Organizational Behavior and Human Performance* 4 (1969), pp. 142–75.

[12]Gilbert A. Churchill, Jr., Neil M. Ford, and Orville C. Walker, Jr., "Personal Characteristics of Salespeople and the Attractiveness of Alternative Rewards," *Journal of Business Research,* 1979, pp. 25–50; Ford, Walker, and Churchill, "Differences in the Attractiveness of Alternative Rewards"; Ingram and Bellenger, "Personal and Organizational Variables"; and Robert L. Berl, Nicholas C. Williamson, Terry Powell, "Industrial Salesforce Motivation: A Critique and Test of Maslow's Hierarchy of Needs," *Journal of Personal Selling and Sales Management,* May 1984, pp. 33–39.

[13]See ibid., and Lawler, *Pay and Organizational Effectiveness,* especially pp. 46–59.

[14]David C. McClelland, John W. Atkinson, Russell A. Clark, and Edgar L. Lowell, *The Achievement Motive* (New York: Appleton-Century-Crofts, 1953); and John W. Atkinson, *An Introduction to Motivation* (Princeton, N.J.: Van Nostrand, 1964).

[15]See, for example, E. E. Lawler III, "Job Attitudes and Employee Motivation: Theory, Research, and Practice," *Personnel Psychology* 23 (1970), pp. 223–37; or Julian B. Rotter, "Generalized expectancies for Internal versus External Control of Reinforcement," *Psychological Monographs: General and Applied* 80 (1966).

[16]Ibid.

[17]Abraham K. Korman, "Expectancies as Determinants of Performance," *Journal of Applied Psychology* 55 (1971), pp. 218–22; and Lawler, "Job Attitudes," pp. 223–37.

[18]Ingram and Bellenger, "Personal and Organizational Variables," pp. 203–4.

[19]R. Kenneth Teas and James C. McElroy, "Causal Attributions and Expectancy Estimates: A Framework for Understanding the Dynamics of Salesforce Motivation," *Journal of Marketing,* January 1986, pp. 75–86. See also Harish Sujan, "Smarter versus Harder," pp. 41–49.

[20]The following discussion is largely based on material found in William L. Cron, "Industrial Salesperson Development: A Career Stages perspective," *Journal of Marketing*, Fall 1984, pp. 41–52; William L. Cron and John W. Slocum, Jr., "The Influence of Career Stages on Salespeople's Job Attitudes, Work Perceptions, and Performance," *Journal of Marketing Research*, May 1986, pp. 119–29; and William L. Cron, Alan J. Dubinsky, and Ronald E. Michaels, "The Influence of Career Stages on Components of Salesperson Motivation," *Journal of Marketing*, January 1988, pp. 78–92.

[21]William Keenan, Jr., "The Nagging Problem of the Plateaued Salesperson," *Sales & Marketing Management*, March 1989, pp. 36–41.

[22]Robert House, "A Path-Goal Theory of Leadership Effectiveness," *Administrative Science Quarterly*, September 1971, pp. 321–39.

[23]Bill Kelley, "How Much Help Does a Salesperson Need?" *Sales & Marketing Management*, May 1989, pp. 32–34.

[24]Gilbert A. Churchill, Jr., Neil M. Ford, and Orville C. Walker, Jr., "Organizational Climate and Job Satisfaction in the Sales Force," *Journal of Marketing Research*, November 1976, pp. 323–32; and Pradeep K. Tyagi, "Relative Importance of Key Job Dimensions and Leadership Behaviors in Motivating Salesperson Work Performance," *Journal of Marketing*, Summer 1985, pp. 76–86.

[25]Ingram and Bellenger, "Personal and Organizational Variables."

Suggested Readings

Readings concerning motivation and valences for rewards

Ford, Neil M., Orville C. Walker, Jr., and Gilbert A. Churchill, Jr. "Differences in the Attractiveness of Alternative Rewards among Industrial Salespeople: Additional Evidence." *Journal of Business Research*, April 1985, pp. 123–38.

Gibson, James L., John M. Ivancevich, and James H. Donnelly, Jr. *Organizations: Behavior, Structure, Processes*, 7th ed. Homewood, Ill.: Richard D. Irwin, 1991.

Ingram, Thomas N. and Danny N. Bellenger. "Personal and Organizational Variables: Their Relative Effect on Reward Valences of Industrial Salespeople." *Journal of Marketing Research*, May 1983, pp. 198–205.

Sujan, Harish, Barton A. Weitz, and Mita Sujan. "Increasing Sales Productivity by Getting Salespeople to Work Smarter." *Journal of Personal Selling and Sales Management*, August 1988, pp. 9–19.

Teas, R. Kenneth, and James C. McElroy. "Causal Attributions and Expectancy Estimates: A Framework for Understanding the Dynamics of Salesforce Motivation." *Journal of Marketing*, January 1986, pp. 75–86.

Weitz, Barton A., Harish Sujan, and Mita Sujan. "Knowledge, Motivation, and Adaptive Behavior: A Framework for Improving Selling Effectiveness." *Journal of Marketing*, October 1986, pp. 174–91.

Readings concerning leadership and motivation

Kelley, Bill. "How Much Help Does a Salesperson Need?" *Sales & Marketing Management*, May 1989, pp. 32–34.

Tyagi, Pradeep K., "Relative Importance of Key Job Dimensions and Leadership Behaviors in Motivating Salesperson Work Performance." *Journal of Marketing*, Summer 1985, pp. 76–86.

Readings concerning career stages and the problem of plateaued salespeople

Cron, William L. "Industrial Salesperson Development: A Career Stages Perspective." *Journal of Marketing*, Fall 1984, pp. 41–52.

Cron, William L., Alan J. Dubinsky, and Ronald E. Michaels. "The Influence of Career Stages on Components of Salesperson Motivation." *Journal of Marketing*, January 1988, pp. 78–92.

Keenen, William, Jr. "The Nagging Problem of the Plateaued Salesperson." *Sales & Marketing Management*, March 1989, pp. 36–41.

Designing Compensation and Incentive Programs

RETAIL CHAINS FIND SALES INCENTIVES A HARD SELL

John Palmerio, a 25-year veteran of the men's shoe salon at Bloomingdale's Manhattan store, has found working on commission a lucrative proposition. During the first year after his department switched its compensation plan from an hourly wage scale to 10 percent commission on sales, he averaged an extra $175 a week—a 25 percent increase in earnings. And overall sales in the nine-person department increased 22 percent.

Palmerio is one beneficiary of a quiet revolution that swept through department store retailing in the late 1980s and early 1990s. To boost sales and upgrade service, major retail chains converted thousands of hourly sales employees to commissions or other incentives tied to their performance. Department stores always paid some salespeople by straight commission, but typically only in a few departments selling big-ticket items, such as furniture, electronics, and men's suits. Recently, the idea has been applied throughout the store.

Retailers hope to use incentives, and their promise of higher pay, to motivate their sales staffs and attract more skilled salespeople. Many have been inspired by Nordstrom Inc., a Seattle-based department store that has earned a reputation for exceptional customer service and profitability. One ingredient of Nordstrom's success has been its reliance on lucrative commissions to attract and keep skilled salespeople.

But the Nordstrom formula has not been easy for other retailers to duplicate. For one thing, while most stores have designed their commission structures to enable salespeople to make more money for a given volume of sales (as illustrated by the example in Exhibit 15.1), some employees have been unable to match their previous hourly wages. Consequently, many chains have experienced increased sales force turnover and labor unrest after switching to incentive compensation plans. For instance, at Frederick & Nelson, Nordstrom's rival in Seattle, turnover ballooned from under 5 percent annually to 18 percent after the firm switched to commissions in 1987. Part of the increase was due to the loss of longtime employees who could not maintain their earnings. But even some promising new hires soon quit. "It's not a question of age or tenure, but whether people are really cut out to sell," says Robert Presser, Frederick & Nelson's senior vice president.

On the positive side, the switch to incentive compensation has improved the efficiency of many chain's operations. At Frederick & Nelson, for example, selling costs as a percentage of sales fell nearly 1 percent in the year after the firm switched to commissions. But the effect on sales productivity has been uneven. Most store executives say departments offering big-ticket fashion goods such as better apparel, handbags, and towels and linens often enjoy rapid improvements in volume after changing to commissions. But small-ticket staple items, such as stationery and food, show little volume improvement.

It is even harder to judge the effects of incentive programs on customer service. While the chains hope incentives will motivate salespeople to provide better customer service, and thereby increase customer satisfaction and loyalty, some analysts argue they may have the reverse effect. When incentives are tied only to sales volume, salespeople may be more reluctant to spend time providing services that are unlikely to result in an immediate sale. And the aggressive pursuit of sales volume does not always please potential customers. As one store manager points out, "You are less harmed by someone who leaves you alone than someone who is attacking you."

To avoid some of these potential problems, some chains offer compensation systems that incorporate a variety of rewards tied to multiple aspects

EXHIBIT 15 • 1   *A Comparison of Old and New Compensation Plans at Bloomingdales*

As an example, consider a salesclerk in Bloomingdale's women's ready-to-wear department. The clerk's earnings under the old hourly wage plan and the new commission plan are compared below, based on the assumption that the clerk's annual sales volume is a consistent $500,000 under both plans. The new plan guarantees the clerk minimum earnings about equal to the wages paid under the old plan, but that guarantee takes the form of a "draw" against future commissions. Pension benefits also increase under the new plan if the clerk's total compensation increases.

Old Plan		New Plan	
$7 per hour for 1,950 hours	$13,650	5% commission	
0.5% commission of $500,000	2,500	on $500,000	$25,000
Total annual pay	$16,150	Total annual pay	$25,000

of a salesperson's performance. Dayton Hudson Corp., for instance, compensates its sales staff with a combination of hourly wages and a series of bonuses for exceeding sales quotas and meeting a variety of customer service standards. Despite its more flexible system, however, Dayton Hudson has also experienced unrest among its longtime salespeople because of the new program. Among other things, some employees charge that the evaluation of customer service performance is too subjective.

SOME MAJOR COMPENSATION AND INCENTIVE ISSUES

The trials and tribulations of retail chains trying to improve salespeople motivation by switching from hourly wages to incentive systems illustrate some difficult questions involved in designing effective compensation programs. Which compensation method among the variety available—from straight salary to 100 percent commission with many combinations in between—is best for motivating specific kinds of selling activities in specific situations? Are straight commission plans appropriate for motivating retail salespeople to improve customer service? Is the Dayton Hudson program, which ties incentive bonuses to specific aspects of customer service, likely to be a better motivator? Is a single program likely to be equally effective at motivating employees in every department even though they sell different kinds of merchandise?

A related issue concerns the proportion of a salesperson's total compensation that should be determined by incentive pay. At Bloomingdale's and Frederick & Nelson, 100 percent of a salesperson's earnings are determined by incentives based on that person's sales volume. In contrast, the Dayton Hudson program combines incentive bonuses with a stable base of hourly wages. Which approach is more appropriate?

A final question concerns the appropriate mix of financial and nonfinancial incentives for motivating salespeople. The fact that most of the new department store incentive plans rely solely on financial rewards to motivate salespeople is one possible cause of employee dissatisfaction and unrest. Longtime hourly employees worry that the new plans threaten their incomes and job security, fail to provide recognition for the many contributions they have made over the years, and overlook important job activities that may not always produce short-term sales.

Because most salespeople value more than one kind of reward for good performance, and because people with different characteristics have different valences for the same reward, many firms outside the retail industry do not rely on a single type of reward to motivate salespeople. They offer a mix of both financial and nonfinancial incentives, such as formal recognition programs and opportunities for career advancement. The ideal motivation program would perhaps offer different rewards tailored to the unique needs and characteristics of each member of the sales force. Such an approach is usually not practical, though, because of the administrative complexities involved. Nevertheless, many firms offer compensation and incentive programs that are flexible enough, and incorporate a variety of rewards, so all salespeople are offered at least something they consider worth working for.[2]

This chapter discusses the relative strengths and shortcomings of a variety of financial and nonfinancial incentives. The financial rewards examined include the total level of compensation; forms of incentive pay, such as commissions and bonuses; and short-term incentives, such as sales contests. Among the nonfinancial rewards discussed are programs for personal and career development and recognition programs. The most appropriate conditions for using each type of reward are also examined.

One other crucial question addressed is how to choose among such a diverse variety of rewards and integrate them into one effective compensation and incentive program. To answer this question, it is useful to examine the analytical procedures and decisions involved in designing such a program.

PROCEDURES FOR DESIGNING A COMPENSATION AND INCENTIVE PROGRAM

As a number of major retailers have recently discovered, the many complex issues involved make designing and implementing an effective compensation and incentive program difficult. Many managers wonder whether their company's program is as effective as possible in motivating the kinds and amounts of effort they desire from their sales personnel. One survey of more than 400 industrial firms discovered more than a third of the responding managers were unhappy with their companies' compensation and incentive programs.[3]

To make matters worse, even well-designed motivational programs can lose their effectiveness over time. The changing nature of the market environment and evolving characteristics of the sales force can cause motivation programs to lose their balance and power of stimulation. As salespeople become satisfied with the rewards offered by a particular plan, for instance, their valences for more of those rewards may decline.

Recognizing such problems, an increasing number of firms frequently review their compensation and incentive policies. Many firms adjust their total compensation levels at least annually, and they are increasingly willing to make more substantial adjustments in their programs—as many retail chains are doing—when circumstances demand. Some firms have established compensation and incentive committees to regularly monitor sales motivation programs for fairness and effectiveness.

The critical question is this: How should a firm design a new compensation and incentive program? What factors should be considered in designing a program to effectively motivate the sales force to expend effort on activities that are most consistent with the firm's marketing objectives? Exhibit 15.2 diagrams the analytical processes and decisions involved in designing an integrated and effective sales motivation program. The components of this diagram are examined in more detail in the following sections.

Assessing the Firm's Situation and Sales Objectives

A major purpose of any sales compensation program is to stimulate and influence the sales force to do what management wants, how it wants it done, and within the desired time. Before managers can design a program that accomplishes this purpose, though, they must have a clear idea of what they want the sales force to do.

As a first step in deciding what job activities and performance dimensions a new or improved motivation program should stimulate, a manager should evaluate how salespeople are allocating their time. What job activities do they focus on and how much time do they devote to each? How good are their current outcomes on various dimensions of performance, such as total sales volume, sales to new accounts, or sales of particular items in the line? Much of this information can be obtained from job analyses the firm conducts as part of its recruitment and selection procedures, as well as from performance evaluations and company records.

This assessment of the sales force's current allocation of effort and levels of performance can then be compared to the firm's marketing and sales objectives, as outlined in the company's marketing plans, strategic sales program, and account management policies. Such comparisons often reveal that some selling activities and dimensions of performance are receiving too much emphasis from the sales force, while others are not receiving enough.

E X H I B I T   15 • 2   *Procedures for Designing Compensation and Incentive Programs*

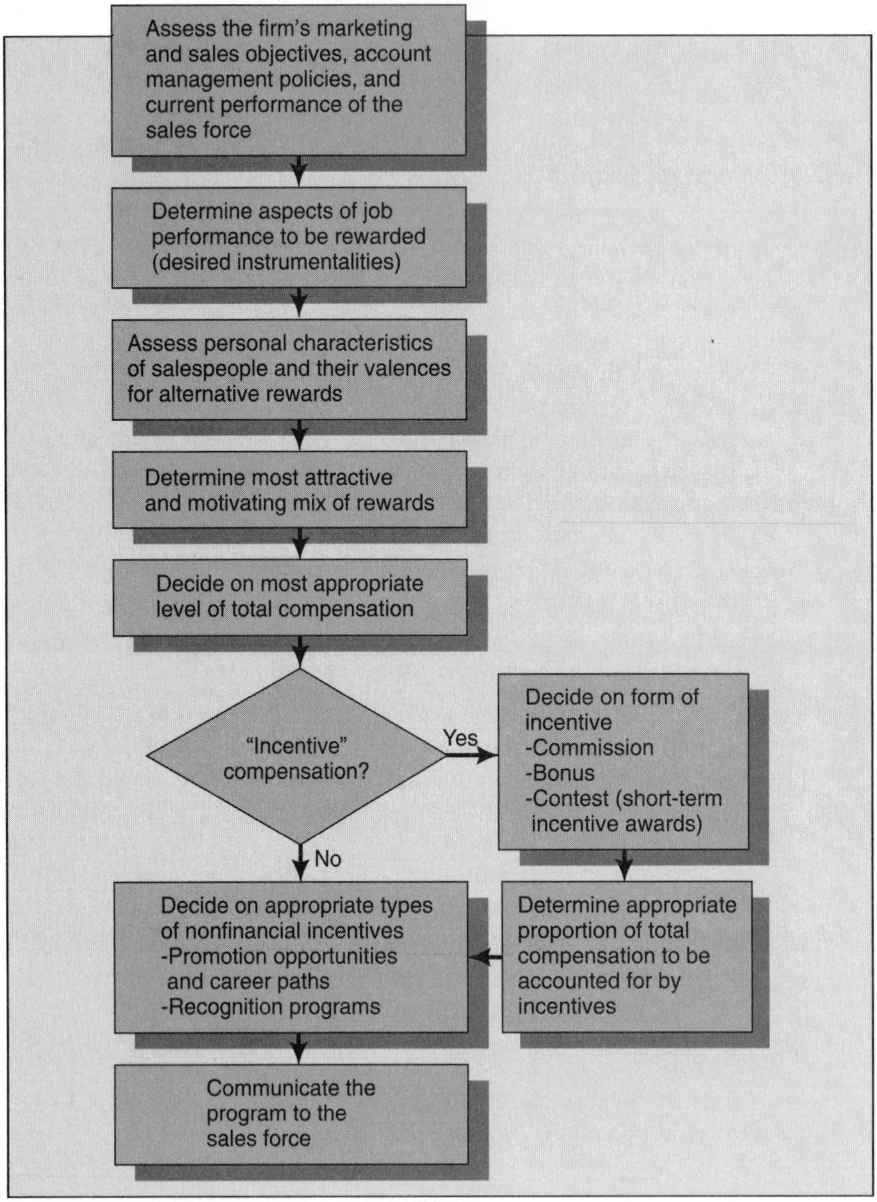

Assess the firm's marketing
and sales objectives, account
management policies, and
current performance of the
sales force

↓

Determine aspects of job
performance to be rewarded
(desired instrumentalities)

↓

Assess personal characteristics
of salespeople and their valences
for alternative rewards

↓

Determine most attractive
and motivating mix of rewards

↓

Decide on most appropriate
level of total compensation

↓

"Incentive"
compensation?   —Yes→   Decide on form of
incentive
-Commission
-Bonus
-Contest (short-term
  incentive awards)

↓ No   ↓

Decide on appropriate types
of nonfinancial incentives
-Promotion opportunities
  and career paths
-Recognition programs   ←   Determine appropriate
proportion of total
compensation to be
accounted for by
incentives

↓

Communicate the
program to the
sales force

EXHIBIT 15 • 3   *Sales Activities and Performance Outcomes That Might Be Encouraged*
by Compensation and Incentive Programs

- Sell a greater overall dollar volume.
- Increase sales of more profitable products.
- Push new products.
- Push selected items at designated seasons.
- Achieve a higher degree of market penetration by products, kinds of customers, or territories.
- Secure large average orders.
- Secure new customers.

- Service and maintain existing business.
- Reduce turnover of customers.
- Achieve full-line (balanced) selling.
- Reduce direct selling costs.
- Increase the number of calls made.
- Submit reports and other data promptly.

DETERMINING WHICH ASPECTS OF JOB PERFORMANCE TO REWARD

When the firm's objectives and how its sales force is allocating its time are misaligned, the compensation and incentive program can be redesigned to reward desired activities or performance outcomes more strongly, thus motivating the sales reps to redirect their efforts. In terms of the motivation model discussed in Chapter 14, management can increase the instrumentalities of desired activities and performance dimensions by increasing the rewards associated with them. For example, Dayton Hudson is trying to improve various dimensions of customer service by offering its sales staff bonuses for good performance on those dimensions.

Exhibit 15.3 lists specific activities and performance dimensions that can be stimulated by a properly designed compensation and incentive program. Of course, managers would like their salespeople to perform well on all of these dimensions. And as we shall see, different components of a compensation program can be designed to reward different activities and achieve multiple objectives.

However, it is a mistake to try to motivate salespeople to do too many things at once. When rewards are tied to numerous different aspects of performance, the salesperson's motivation to improve performance dramatically in any one area is diffused. Also, when rewards are based on many different aspects of performance, the salesperson is more likely to be uncertain about how total performance will be evaluated and about what rewards can be obtained as a result of that performance. In other words, complex compensation and incentive programs may lead to inaccurate instrumentality perceptions by salespeople. Consequently, most authorities recommend that compensation and incentive plans link rewards to only two or three aspects of job performance. They should be linked to those aspects consistent with the firm's highest-priority sales and marketing objectives. Other aspects of the sales force's

Thorny Issues in Sales Management 15 • 1

DESIGNING INCENTIVES FOR CUSTOMER SERVICE AND SATISFACTION

As many markets mature and become more competitive, firms are attaching greater importance to providing excellent service to keep those customers satisfied and loyal and to sustain a competitive advantage. Salespeople often play a crucial role in generating customer satisfaction, particularly in industrial goods and services industries where customers rely on salespeople to act as consultants and problem solvers rather than simply "pushing products," and where postsale services are often important for enabling customers to obtain full value from their purchases.

To motivate salespeople to focus more effort on providing customer service and satisfaction, many firms are trying to incorporate these performance dimensions as an explicit part of their incentive and compensation programs. But this raises two thorny issues. First, how can a salesperson's performance on customer service and satisfaction dimensions be accurately measured to provide a basis for rewarding that performance? And second, how can customer service performance be rewarded without deflecting the salesperson's efforts from the equally important objective of increasing sales volume?

Measurement

One problem with some attempts to reward salespeople for good customer service is that subjective measures, such as the perceptions of the sales manager, are used to evaluate the salesperson's service performance. Such measures frequently are challenged by the sales force, leading to a lack of trust in the program and low instrumentality estimates, a problem reflected in Dayton Hudson's bonus program.

A variety of more objective measures can be employed to measure both customer service and satisfaction. With respect to customer *service*, internal measures are most commonly used. These include such things as percentage of on-time deliveries and/or installations, merchandise returns, customer credits, and the number of customer complaints received. For measuring customer *satisfaction*, companies typically rely on information gained from periodic customer surveys using focus groups, telephone interviews, or mail questionnaires.

Because ongoing customer surveys are expensive, some firms statistically analyze and compare internal measures of customer service with survey-based measures of customer satisfaction. The objective is to identify those internal measures with the strongest relationship to actual customer satisfaction. With this relationship established, service incentives can then be based on internal measures that are both easier to obtain and shown to directly affect customer satisfaction.

Linking Customer Satisfaction and Sales Volume Incentives

Some firms have made the mistake of tying only a small proportion of salespeople's total incentives to performance on customer service or satisfaction dimensions to avoid deflecting too much attention from the pursuit of new customers and increased sales volume. Such an approach is likely to provide little motivation for reps to expend additional effort satisfying customers, and it may signal a lack of management commitment to the program.

A more promising approach is to link incentive rewards for customer satisfaction to the salesperson's overall sales volume performance. This can

(continued)

be done by making the reward for customer satisfaction contingent on the salesperson's sales volume, as illustrated in the example below. Note that the plan establishes bonus awards for various levels of sales quota attainment. Those bonuses are then either increased or decreased by a multiplier determined by a measure of customer satisfaction in the salesperson's territory. Thus, a rep whose sales volume equals 100 percent of quota and who achieves higher than a 96 percent customer satisfaction rating would earn a bonus amounting to $15,000 × 1.75 = $26,250.

Sales Quota Attainment			Customer Satisfaction Performance Multiplier	
Percent of Sales Quota	Target Award	×	Satisfaction Score	Multiplier
<90%	$10,000		<90%	0.75
91%–100%	$15,000		91%–95%	1.25
>100%	$20,000		96%>	1.75

Source: Jerome A. Colletti and Linda J. Mahoney, "Should You Pay Your Sales Force for Customer Satisfaction?" *Perspectives in Total Compensation* no. 11 (Scottsdale, Ariz.: American Compensation Association, November 1991).

behavior and performance should be directed and controlled through effective training programs and supervision by field sales managers.

One objective mentioned in Exhibit 15.3—servicing existing customers—deserves special mention. As more firms work to improve their market orientation and adopt the principles of Total Quality Management (TQM), they are beginning to target customer service and satisfaction as important objectives to be rewarded in incentive programs. But as some department store chains have discovered, effectively tying sales force incentives to customer service is sometimes easier said than done. Rewarding customer service presents some thorny measurement and design issues for the sales manager[4]—issues discussed in more detail in Thorny Issues in Sales Management 15.1.

ASSESSING SALES REPS' VALENCES AND DETERMINING THE MOST ATTRACTIVE MIX OF REWARDS

All salespeople do not find the same kinds of rewards equally attractive. Salespeople may be more or less satisfied with their current attainment of a given reward, and this causes them to have different valences for more of that reward. Similarly, people's needs for a particular reward vary, depending on their personalities, demographic characteristics, and lifestyles. Consequently, no single reward—including money—is likely to be effective for motivating all of a firm's salespeople. Similarly, a mix of rewards that is effective for motivating a sales force at one time may lose its appeal as the members' personal circumstances and needs change and as new salespeople are hired. In view of this, a wise preliminary step in designing a sales compensation and incentive package is for a firm to determine its salespeople's current valences for various rewards. This could be done with a simple survey in which each salesperson is asked to rate the attractiveness of specific increases of various rewards on a numerical scale, say from zero to 100.[5] Also, one of the techniques specifically aimed at assessing a person's preferences could be used, such as conjoint analysis.[6]

Today, few managers actually carry out such surveys when designing motivation programs because they believe they know their salespeople's needs and desires well enough. Yet, when salespeople's actual valences for rewards have been compared with their managers' perceptions of those valences, the managers' perceptions can be very inaccurate. For example, in one large firm, top sales executives believed their recognition program was an important reward in the eyes of their salespeople. In a subsequent survey of those salespeople's actual valences, it was discovered they rated recognition as the least attractive of seven alternative rewards. Rather than offering rewards that managers think their subordinates find attractive, it may be worth the time and trouble to conduct a study of salespeople's actual valences for rewards before designing a motivation program.

DECIDING ON THE MOST APPROPRIATE LEVEL OF TOTAL COMPENSATION

The total amount of compensation a salesperson receives affects satisfaction with pay and with the company, as well as valence for more pay in the future. Thus, the decision about how much total compensation (base pay plus any commissions or bonuses) a salesperson may earn is crucial in designing an effective motivation program. The starting point for making this decision is to determine the gross amount of compensation necessary to attract, retain, and motivate the right type of salespeople. This, in turn, depends on the type of sales job in question, the size of the firm and the sales force, and the sales management policies.

Average compensation varies substantially in different types of sales jobs. In general, more complex and demanding sales jobs, which require salespeople with special qualifications, offer higher pay than more routine sales jobs. To compete for the best talent, a firm should determine how much total compensation other firms in its industry or related ones pay people in similar jobs. Then the firm can decide whether to pay its salespeople an amount average in relation to what others are paying or above average. Few companies consciously pay below average (although some do so without realizing it) because below-average compensation generally cannot attract the right level of selling talent.

The decision about whether to offer average total pay or premium compensation depends on the size of the firm and its sales force. Large firms with good reputations in their industries and large sales forces (more than 75 or 100 salespeople) generally offer only average or slightly below average compensation. Such firms can attract sales talent because of their reputation in the marketplace and because they are big enough to offer advancement into management. Also, such firms can hire younger people (often just out of school) as sales trainees and put them through an extensive training program. This allows them to pay relatively low gross compensation levels because they do not have to pay a market premium to attract older, more experienced salespeople. Smaller firms often cannot afford extensive training programs. Consequently, they must often offer above-average compensation to attract experienced sales reps from other firms.

Dangers of Paying Too Much

Some firms, regardless of their size or position in their industries, offer their salespeople opportunities to make very large amounts of financial compensation. For example, a recent survey found that salespeople working for manufacturers with compensation plans based on straight commission commonly earned six-figure incomes, and the highest paid salesperson in the survey made over a quarter of a million dollars.[7] The rationale for such high incomes is that opportunities for high pay will attract the best talent and motivate members of the sales force to continue working for higher and higher sales volumes. As some managers say, "We don't care how much we pay our salespeople, since their compensation relates to their volume of sales."[8]

Overpaying salespeople relative to what other firms pay for similar jobs and relative to what other employees in the same firm are paid for nonsales jobs can cause major problems, however. For one thing, compensation is usually the largest element of a firm's selling costs. Therefore, overpaying salespeople unnecessarily increases selling costs and reduces profits. Also, it can cause resentment and low morale among the firm's other employees and executives when salespeople earn more money than even top management. It then becomes virtually impossible to promote good salespeople into managerial positions because of the financial sacrifice they would have to make. Finally, it is not clear that offering unlimited opportunities to earn higher pay is always an effective way to motivate continually increasing selling effort. "Need theory," for example, suggests that when salespeople reach a compensation level they consider satisfactory, their valences for still more money are likely to be reduced. One empirical study found that most salespeople tend to work toward a "satisfactory" level of compensation rather than to maximize their pay.[9]

Dangers of Paying Too Little

Overpaying salespeople can cause problems, but it is equally important not to underpay them. Holding down sales compensation may appear to be a convenient way to hold down selling costs and enhance profits, but this is usually not true in the long run. When buying talent in the labor market, a company tends to get what it pays for. If poor salespeople are hired at low pay, poor performance will almost surely result. If good salespeople are hired at low pay, the firm is likely to have high turnover, with higher costs for recruiting and training replacements and lost sales.

The results of a survey of 192 companies in a variety of industries appear to support the wisdom of offering enough compensation to attract good sales talent. The survey found that firms in the top quartile of performance on dimensions such as volume growth and profitability pay their salespeople significantly higher average compensation than firms in the lowest quartile.[10] This raises a question of cause and effect. Do firms perform well because they pay to attract good salespeople, or do they pay better simply because they can afford to? In either case, paying what it takes to attract and keep a competent sales force seems a more likely path to good marketing performance than being overly tightfisted with sales compensation.

FINANCIAL INCENTIVES: CHOOSING THE MOST EFFECTIVE FORM OF FINANCIAL COMPENSATION

Components and Objectives

In most firms, the total financial compensation paid to salespeople comprises several components, each of which may be designed to achieve different strategic sales and personnel management objectives. These components are listed in Exhibit 15.4, along with the specific objectives appropriate for each.

The foundation of most compensation plans is a package of **benefits.** These are designed to satisfy the salesperson's basic needs for security. They typically include such things as medical and disability insurance, life insurance, and a pension plan. The types and amount of benefits included in a compensation plan are usually a matter of company policy and apply to all employees. However, the benefit package a firm offers its salespeople should be reasonably comparable to those offered by competitors to avoid being at a disadvantage when recruiting new sales talent.

The core of sales compensation plans consists of a salary or commissions. A **commission** is a payment based on short-term results, usually a salesperson's dollar or unit sales volume. Since there is a direct link between sales volume and the amount of commission received, commission payments are particularly useful for motivating a high level of selling effort.

A **salary** is a fixed sum of money paid at regular intervals. The amount of salary paid to a given salesperson is usually a function of the salesperson's experience, competence, and time on the job, as well as superiors' judgments about the quality of the individual's performance. As we shall see, salary adjustments are useful for rewarding salespeople for performing activities that may not directly result in sales in the short term, such as prospecting for new customers or providing postsales services. They can also help adjust for differences in sales potential across territories.

Many firms that pay their salespeople a salary also offer additional **incentive payments** to encourage good performance. Those incentives may take the

E X H I B I T 15 • 4 *Components and Objectives of Financial Compensation Plans*

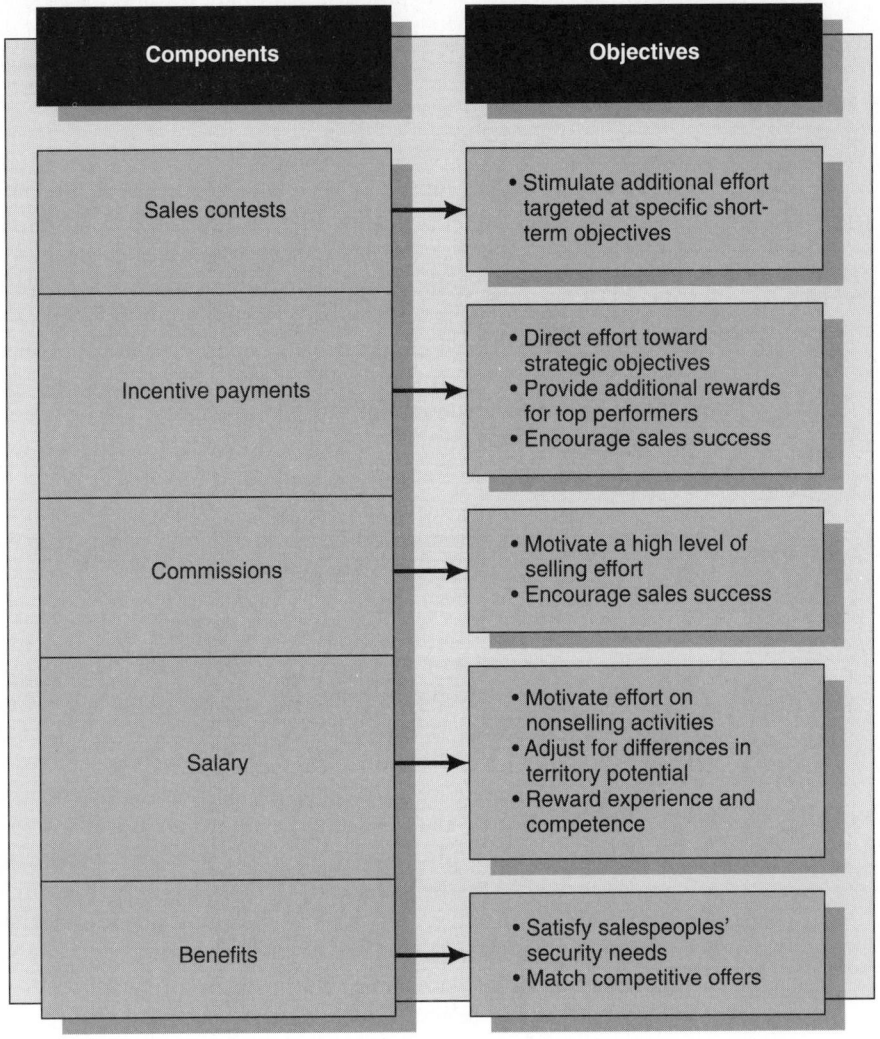

Components	Objectives
Sales contests	• Stimulate additional effort targeted at specific short-term objectives
Incentive payments	• Direct effort toward strategic objectives • Provide additional rewards for top performers • Encourage sales success
Commissions	• Motivate a high level of selling effort • Encourage sales success
Salary	• Motivate effort on nonselling activities • Adjust for differences in territory potential • Reward experience and competence
Benefits	• Satisfy salespeoples' security needs • Match competitive offers

Source: Adapted from *Sales Compensation Concepts and Trends* (New York: The Alexander Group, Inc., 1988), p. 3.

form of commissions tied to sales volume or profitability, or bonuses for meeting or exceeding specific performance targets (e.g., meeting quotas for particular products within the company's line or for particular types of customers). Such incentives are useful for directing salespeople's efforts toward specific strategic objectives during the year, as well as providing additional rewards for the top performers within the sales force.

Finally, many firms conduct **sales contests** to encourage extra effort aimed at specific short-term objectives. For example, a contest might offer additional rewards for salespeople who obtain a specified volume of orders from new customers or who exceed their quotas for a new product during a three-month period. Contest winners might be given additional cash, merchandise, or travel awards.

Types of Compensation Plans

Commissions, salary, and incentive payments constitute the essential building blocks of most financial compensation plans for sales forces. Thus, while nearly all firms provide benefit packages and many run sales contests from time to time, the three primary methods of compensating salespeople are (1) straight salary, (2) straight commission, and (3) a combination of base salary plus incentive pay in the form of commissions, bonuses, or both. Over the past 35 years, there has been a steady trend away from both straight salary and straight commission plans toward combination plans. Today, combination plans are by far the most common form of compensation, as the survey results in Exhibit 15.5 indicate. The data in Exhibit 15.5 also show that individual bonuses are the most popular form of incentive pay found within combination plans, followed by commissions. Bonuses based on the overall performance of a group of salespeople or a sales team are not very common.

Straight Salary

Two sets of conditions favor the use of a straight salary compensation plan: (1) when management wishes to motivate salespeople to achieve objectives other than short-run sales volume, and (2) when the individual salesperson's impact on sales volume is difficult to measure in a reasonable time.

The primary advantage of a straight salary is that management can require salespeople to spend their time on activities that may not result in immediate sales. Therefore, a salary plan or a plan offering a large proportion of fixed salary is appropriate when the salesperson is expected to perform many account servicing or other nonselling activities. These may include market research, customer problem analysis, stocking, or sales promotion. Straight salary plans are also common in industries where many engineering and design services are required as part of the selling function, such as in the aerospace and other high-technology industries.

Straight salary compensation plans are also desirable when it is difficult for management to measure the individual salesperson's actual impact on sales volume or other aspects of performance. Thus, firms tend to pay salaries to their sales force when (1) their salespeople are engaged in missionary selling, as in the pharmaceutical industry; (2) other parts of the marketing program, such as advertising or dealer promotions, are the primary determinants of sales success, as in some consumer packaged goods businesses; or (3) the selling process is complex and involves a team or multilevel selling effort, as in the case of computers or atomic reactors.

EXHIBIT 15 • 5   *Percent of Companies Using Three Types of Compensation Plans*

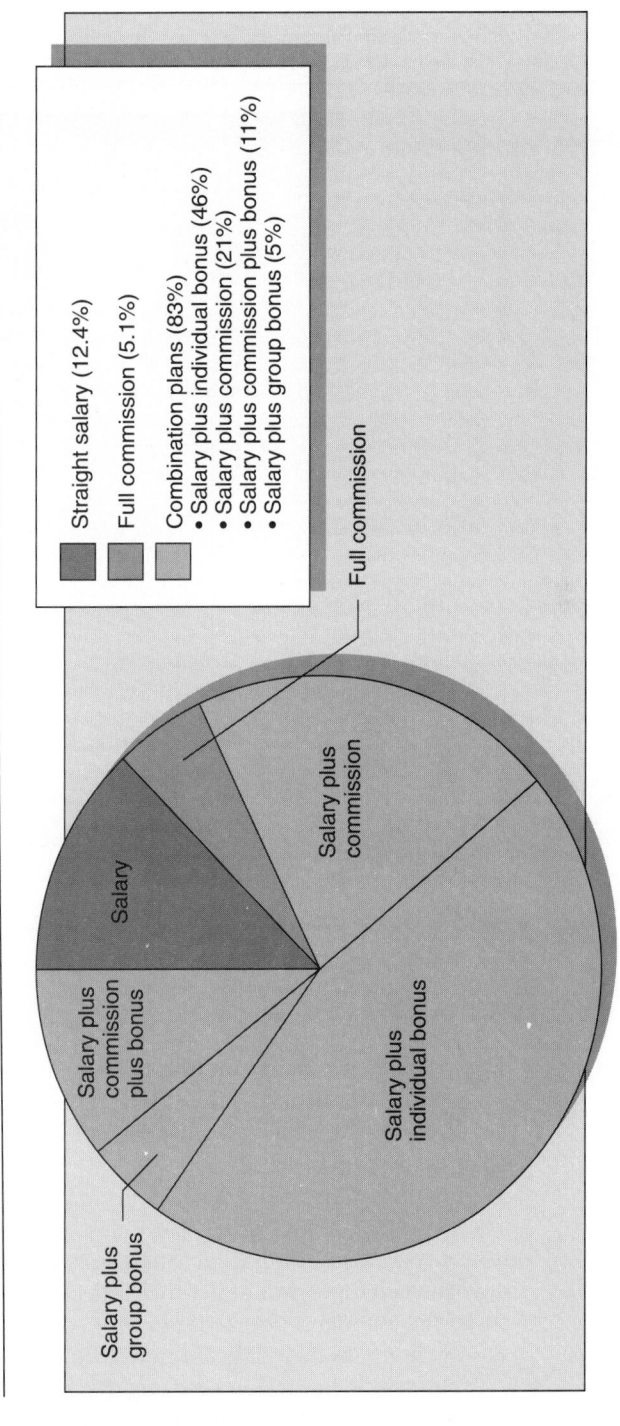

Straight salary (12.4%)

Full commission (5.1%)

Combination plans (83%)
• Salary plus individual bonus (46%)
• Salary plus commission (21%)
• Salary plus commission plus bonus (11%)
• Salary plus group bonus (5%)

Full commission

Salary plus commission

Salary

Salary plus individual bonus

Salary plus commission plus bonus

Salary plus group bonus

Source: *1986/1987 Sales Personnel Report* (New York: The Alexander Group, Inc., 1988).

E X H I B I T   15 • 6   *Relative Costs of Salary and Commission Compensation Plans*

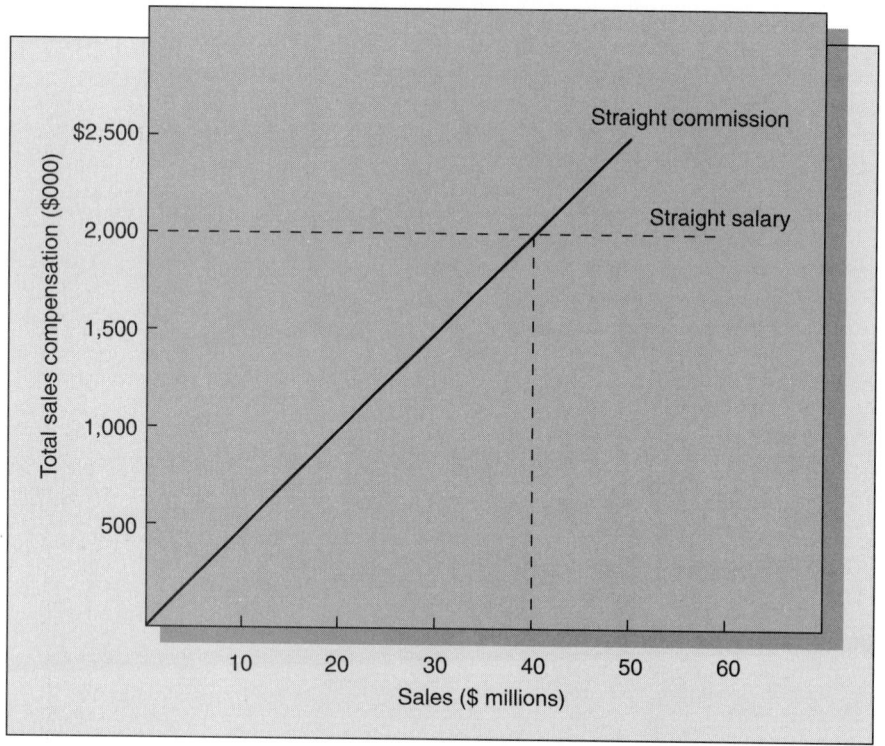

Note: This firm has 50 salespeople, and it has the option of paying each of them a salary of $40,000 per year or a 5 percent commission on net sales. As you can see, the salary plan results in higher compensation costs at sales volumes below $40 million, but lower costs at volumes above $40 million.

Straight salary plans provide salespeople with a steady, guaranteed income. Thus, salary compensation plans are often used when the salesperson's ability to generate immediate sales is uncertain, as in the case of new recruits in a field-training program or when a firm is introducing a new product line or opening new territories.

Finally, salary plans are easy for management to compute and administer. They also give management more flexibility. It is easy to reassign salespeople to new territories or product lines because they do not have to worry about how such changes will affect their sales volumes. Also, since salaries are fixed costs, the compensation cost per unit sold is lower at relatively high levels of sales volume, as shown in Exhibit 15.6.

The major limitation of straight salary compensation is that financial rewards are not tied directly to any specific aspect of job performance. Management should attempt to give bigger salary increases each year to the good performers than those given to the poor ones. However, the amount of those increases and the way performance is evaluated are subject to the whims of the manager who makes the decision. Consequently, salespeople are likely to have lower and less accurate instrumentality perceptions about how much more money they are likely to receive as the result of a given increase in sales volume, profitability, or the like. In other words, salaries do not provide any direct financial incentive for improving sales-related aspects of performance. Consequently, salary plans appeal more to security-oriented rather than achievement-oriented salespeople.

Straight Commission	A commission is payment for achieving a given level of performance. Salespeople are paid for results. Usually, commission payments are based on the salesperson's dollar or unit sales volume. However, it is becoming more popular for firms to base commissions on the profitability of sales to motivate the sales force to expend effort on the most profitable products or customers. The most common way is to offer salespeople variable commissions, where relatively high commissions are paid for sales of the most profitable products or sales to the most profitable accounts. Variable commission rates can also be used to direct the sales force's efforts toward other straight sales objectives, such as introduction of a new product line.

Advantages

Direct motivation is the key advantage of a commission compensation plan. There is a direct link between sales performance and the financial compensation the salesperson earns. Consequently, salespeople are strongly motivated to improve their sales productivity to increase their compensation, at least until they reach such high pay that further increases become less attractive. Commission plans also have a built-in element of fairness (if sales territories are properly defined with about equal potential), because good performers are automatically rewarded, whereas poor performers are discouraged from continuing their low productivity.

Commission plans have some advantages from an administrative view. Commissions are usually easy to compute and administer. Also, compensation costs vary directly with sales volume. This is an advantage for firms that are short of working capital because they do not need to worry about paying high wages to the sales force unless it generates high sales revenues.

Limitations

Straight commission compensation plans have some important limitations that have caused many firms to abandon them. Perhaps the most critical weakness is that management has little control over the sales force. When all their financial rewards are tied directly to sales volume, it is difficult to motivate salespeople to engage in account management activities that do not lead directly to short-term sales. Consequently, salespeople on commission are likely to "milk" existing customers rather than work to develop new accounts. They may overstock their customers and neglect service after the sale. Finally, they have little motivation to engage in market analysis and other administrative duties that take time away from actual selling activities.

Straight commission plans also have a disadvantage for many salespeople. Such plans make a salesperson's earnings unstable and hard to predict. When business conditions are poor, turnover rates in the sales force are likely to be high because salespeople find it hard to live on the low earnings produced by poor sales. And agency theory, a conceptual framework developed in economics, suggests such problems are likely to be even more severe when a firm's salespeople are relatively risk averse; that is, when they prefer a predictable future income stream to one that offers uncertain chances to earn either unusually high or unusually low levels of income.[11]

To combat the inherent instability of commission plans, some firms provide their salespeople with a **drawing account.** Money is advanced to salespeople in months when commissions are low to ensure they will always take home a specified minimum amount of pay. The amount of the salesperson's "draw" in poor months is deducted from earned commissions when sales improve. This gives salespeople some secure salary, and it allows management more control over their activities. A problem arises, however, when a salesperson fails to earn enough commissions to repay the draw. Then the person may quit or be fired, and the company must absorb the loss.[12]

Combination Plans

As indicated by the survey results in Exhibit 15.5, compensation plans that offer a base salary plus some proportion of incentive pay are the most popular. They have many of the advantages but avoid most of the limitations of both straight salary and straight commission plans. The base salary provides the salesperson with a stable income and gives management some capability to reward salespeople for performing customer servicing and administrative tasks that are not directly related to short-term sales. At the same time, the incentive portion of such compensation plans provides direct rewards to motivate the salesperson to expend effort to improve sales volume or profitability.

Combination plans combine a base salary with commissions, bonuses, or both. When salary plus commission is used, the commissions are tied to sales volume or profitability, just as with a straight commission plan. The only difference is that the commissions are smaller in a combination plan than when the salesperson is compensated solely by commission.

A **bonus** is a payment made at the discretion of management for achieving or surpassing some set level of performance. Whereas commissions are typically paid for each sale that is made, a bonus is typically not paid until the salesperson surpasses some level of total sales or other aspect of performance. When the salesperson reaches the minimum level of performance required to earn a bonus, however, the size of the bonus might be determined by the degree to

EXHIBIT 15 • 7   *A Point System for Basing Bonus Payments on Two Performance Dimensions*

An industrial chemical manufacturer pays its salespeople a base salary of $15,000 per year. An annual sales quota is established for each salesperson, and the sum of the quotas equals the firm's annual sales forecast.

The incentive plan is divided into two parts. Part I provides that each sales rep who meets or exceeds quota receives 10 bonus points. In addition, for each 2 percent of sales in excess of quota, each salesperson receives an additional bonus point up to a maximum of 20 points per year on Part I of the plan.

Part II of the plan provides bonus points for bringing in new accounts. A new account is defined as one that has not placed an order during the preceding 36 months. Bonus points are granted to salespeople for new accounts as follows:

Annual Purchase Volume by New Account	Sales Rep Bonus Points
$ 5,000–25,000	1
25,001–50,000	2
50,001–100,000	3
100,001–and up	4

Each salesperson is limited to a maximum of 20 bonus points per year on Part II of the plan.

Bonus earnings are calculated and paid annually. For each bonus point earned, the salesperson receives 1 percent salary. Thus, each salesperson can earn bonus payments up to a maximum of 40 percent of the salary.

Source: Based on a plan described in Richard C. Smyth and Matthew J. Murphy, *Compensating and Motivating Salesmen* (New York: American Management Association, 1969), pp. 127–29.

which the sales rep exceeds that minimum. Thus, bonuses are usually additional incentives to motivate salespeople to reach high levels of performance, rather than part of the basic compensation plan.

Attaining quota is often the minimum requirement for a salesperson to earn a bonus. As mentioned in Chapter 8, quotas can be based on sales volume, profitability of sales, or other account-servicing activities. Therefore, bonuses can be offered as a reward for attaining or surpassing a predetermined level of performance on any dimensions for which quotas are set. Some complex bonus plans use a point system to tie the bonus to the accomplishment of two or more performance objectives. An example of such a point bonus plan is described in Exhibit 15.7.

Other Issues in Designing Combination Plans

Whether base salary is combined with commission payments or bonuses, managers must answer several other questions in designing effective combination compensation plans. These are (1) the appropriate size of the incentive relative to the base salary, (2) whether there should be a ceiling on incentive earnings, (3) when the salesperson should be credited with a sale, and (4) how often the salesperson should receive incentive payments.

Relative proportion of incentive pay

What proportion of total compensation should be incentive pay? One of the most common reasons combination plans are not very effective at motivating salespeople is that the incentive portion is too small to generate much interest. After studying the reasons for the success or failure of 180 compensation plans, two researchers concluded that "if the average successful salesman working under a sales incentive plan cannot make at least 25 percent of his gross earnings as incentive pay in the form of bonus or commissions, the plan will never be truly successful."[13]

The 25 percent figure appears to be not only a good rule of thumb, but also a reasonably accurate reflection of industry practice. A more recent survey of more than 1,600 organizations conducted by the American Productivity Center found that salespeople on combination compensation plans earned an average of slightly more than 20 percent of their total pay from incentive payments.[14] However, the relative size of such payments varies substantially across different industries (e.g., service firms tend to pay a larger proportion of incentive pay than goods producers) and across different types of plans. For instance, another survey found that plans offering a salary plus bonus based on one or more dimensions of total performance contained incentive pay that averaged only 11 percent of total compensation, while "salary plus commission" plans averaged 33 percent incentive pay.[15]

A manager's decision concerning what proportion of the overall compensation package is represented by incentive pay should be based on the company's objectives and the nature of the selling job. When the firm's primary objectives are directly related to short-term sales, such as increasing sales volume, profitability, or new customers, a large incentive component should be offered. When customer service and other nonsales objectives are deemed more important, the major emphasis should be on the base salary component of the plan. This gives management more control over the sales force's account management activities.

Similarly, when the salesperson's selling skill is the key to sales success, the incentive portion of compensation should be large. However, when the product has been presold through advertising and the salesperson is largely an order taker, or when the salesperson's job involves a large proportion of missionary or customer service work, the incentive component should be relatively small.

Incentive ceilings

Should there be a ceiling or cap on incentive earnings to ensure top salespeople do not earn substantially more money than other employees? This is one of those thorny issues in sales management that is dealt with in different ways across companies and industries, and for which strong arguments can be made on both sides.[16] Some of those arguments are summarized in Thorny Issues in Sales Management 15.2 together with an overview of the use of ceilings across industries.

Thorny Issues in Sales Management 15 • 2

THE USE OF CEILINGS ON INCENTIVE PAYMENTS

As the following table indicates, there is a great deal of variation across industries in the prevalence of ceilings or "caps" on incentive payments to salespeople. Part of this variation seems to reflect differences in average compensation levels, with firms in relatively low-paying industries being more likely to impose caps than those in higher paying lines of trade. The use of caps also varies by type of compensation plan. Two out of every three firms with "salary plus bonus" plans impose incentive ceilings, while only one third of firms using "salary plus commission" plans do so.

Arguments in favor of using ceilings include that they ensure top salespeople will not make such high earnings that other employees suffer resentment and low morale. Ceilings also protect against windfalls—such as increased sales due to the introduction of successful new products—where a salesperson's earnings might become very large without corresponding effort. Finally, ceilings make a firm's maximum potential sales compensation expense more predictable and controllable.

A strong argument can be made, however, that

Use of Incentive Caps by Industry

Industry	Prevalence of Caps
Food and beverages	91.7%
Soaps, cosmetics, consumer packaged goods	83.3
Pharmaceuticals	66.7
Telecommunications	42.0
Forest products	40.0
Publishing	20.0
Office equipment/computers	20.0

such ceilings have a bad effect on motivation and dampen the sales force's enthusiasm. Also, some salespeople may reach their earning maximum early in the year and be inclined to take it easy for the rest of the year.

As a compromise, one authority suggests that it might be acceptable to limit incentive earnings to 100 percent of base salary. This should give the firm adequate protection yet offer an attractive enough opportunity to motivate salespeople.

Source: Published with permission from Lesley Barnes, "Finding the Best Sales Compensation Plan," *Sales & Marketing Management*, August 1986, pp. 46–49. © 1986 by Bill Communications, Inc. See also William Keenan, Jr., "Is Your Pay Plan Putting the Squeeze on Top Performers?" *Sales & Marketing Management*, January 1990, pp. 74–75.

Some functions of ceilings can be accomplished without arbitrarily limiting the motivation of the sales force if management pretests any new or revised compensation plan before it is implemented. Managers can do this by applying the plan to the historical sales performance of selected salespeople. Particular attention should be given to the amount of compensation that would have been earned by the best and poorest performers to ensure that the compensation provided by the plan is both fair and reasonable.

When is a sale a sale?

When incentives are based on sales volume or other sales-related aspects of performance, the precise meaning of a sale should be defined to avoid confusion and irritation. Most plans credit a salesperson with a sale when the *order* is accepted by the company, less any returns and allowances. Occasionally, though, crediting the salesperson with a sale only after the goods have been shipped or payment is received from the customer makes good sense. This is particularly true when the time between receipt of an order and shipment of the goods is long and the company wants its salespeople to maintain close contact with the customer to prevent cancellations and other problems. As a compromise, some plans credit salespeople with half a sale when the order is received and the other half when payment is made.

When should the sales rep receive incentive payments?

One survey of over 200 compensation plans found that 31 percent paid salespeople incentive earnings on an annual basis, 8 percent paid semiannually, 28 percent paid quarterly, and 32 percent made monthly payments. In general, plans offering salary plus commissions were more likely to involve monthly incentive payments, while salary plus bonus plans more often made incentive payments on a quarterly or annual schedule.[17]

Shorter intervals between performance and the receipt of rewards increase the motivating power of the plan. However, short intervals add to the computation required, increase administrative expenses, and may make the absolute amount of money received by the salespeople appear so small they may not be very impressed with their rewards. Consequently, many authorities argue that quarterly incentive payments are an effective compromise.

A Summary Overview of Financial Compensation Methods

The above discussion indicates combination plans pose more prickly administrative and control problems than either straight salary or straight commission plans. This may be one reason combination plans are more commonly found in larger firms than in smaller ones. Despite such problems, however, the offsetting advantages offered by combination plans make them the most popular method of compensating salespeople. But as we have seen, all three types of plans have some unique advantages and limitations that make each of them particularly well suited for use in certain circumstances. Those advantages, limitations, and uses are summarized in Exhibit 15.8.[18]

S ALES CONTESTS

Sales contests are short-term incentive programs designed to motivate sales personnel to accomplish specific sales objectives. Although contests should not be considered part of the firm's ongoing compensation plan, they offer salespeople the opportunity to gain financial, as well as nonfinancial, rewards. Contest winners often receive prizes in cash or merchandise or travel. Winners

EXHIBIT 15 • 8   *Characteristics of Compensation Methods for Sales Personnel*

Compensation Method (Frequency of Use)	Especially Useful	Advantages	Disadvantages
Straight salary (12%)	When compensating new sales reps; when firm moves into new sales territories that require developmental work; when sale reps must perform many nonselling activities	Provides sales rep with maximum amount of security; gives sales manager large amount of control over sales reps; easy to administer; yields more predictable selling expenses	Provides no incentive; necessitates closer supervision of sale reps' activities; during sales declines, selling expenses remain at same level
Straight commission (5%)	When highly aggressive selling is required; when nonselling tasks are minimized; when company cannot closely control sales force activities	Provides maximum amount of incentive; by increasing commission rate, sales managers can encourage reps to sell certain items; selling expenses relate directly to sales resources	Sales reps have little financial security; sales manager has minimum control over sales force; may cause reps to provide inadequate service to smaller accounts; selling costs less predictable
Combination (85%)	When sales territories have relatively similar sales potentials; when firm wishes to provide incentive but still control sales force activities	Provides certain level of financial security; provides some incentive; selling expenses fluctuate with sales revenue; sales manager has some control over reps' nonselling activities	Selling expenses less predictable; may be difficult to administer

also receive nonfinancial rewards in the form of recognition and a sense of accomplishment.

Successful contests require the following:

- Clearly defined, specific objectives.
- An exciting theme.
- Reasonable probability of rewards for all salespeople.
- Attractive rewards.
- Promotion and follow-through.

Contest Objectives   Because contests supplement the firm's compensation program and are designed to motivate extra effort toward some short-term goal, their objectives should be very specific and clearly defined. What kinds of objectives do firms

EXHIBIT 15 ● 9   *Managers' Ratings of Sales Contest Objectives*

Contest Objective	Weighted Rating
Stimulate overall sales volume	586
Stimulate specific product sales	521
Increase market penetration	479
Introduce new products	463
Acquire new accounts	460
Get balanced sales	422
Emphasize higher profit products	396
Improve service to accounts	351
Overcome seasonal slump	323
Increase activity in new area	322
Ease unfavorable inventory situation	284
Develop or improve sales skills	254

Source: *Current Practices in Sales Incentives* (New York: The Alexander Group, Inc., 1988), p. 20.

pursue with contests? The weighted ratings shown in Exhibit 15.9 reflect the frequency with which managers in 254 firms reported that each listed objective was either a primary or secondary purpose of their sales contests. Note that while "stimulate overall sales volume" was the number one objective (i.e., most often a primary contest goal), most of the others are much more specific and narrowly focused (e.g., stimulate specific product sales, introduce new products, acquire new accounts, etc.).

The time in which the contest's objectives are to be achieved should be relatively short. This ensures the salespeople will maintain their enthusiasm and effort throughout the contest. But the contest should be long enough to allow all members of the sales force to cover their territories at least once and to have a reasonable chance of generating the performance necessary to win. Therefore, the median duration of sales contests is three months, as shown in Exhibit 15.10.

Contest Themes

A sales contest should have an exciting them to help build enthusiasm among the participants and promote the event. The theme should also be designed to stress the contest's objectives and appeal to all participants. Sports themes, such as "a sales superbowl" or "world series," are popular because they provide a competitive atmosphere.

Probability of Winning

There are three popular contest formats. In some contests, salespeople compete with themselves by trying to attain individual quotas. Everyone who reaches or exceeds quota during the contest period wins. A second form requires that

EXHIBIT 15 • 10   *Average Length of a Sales Contest*

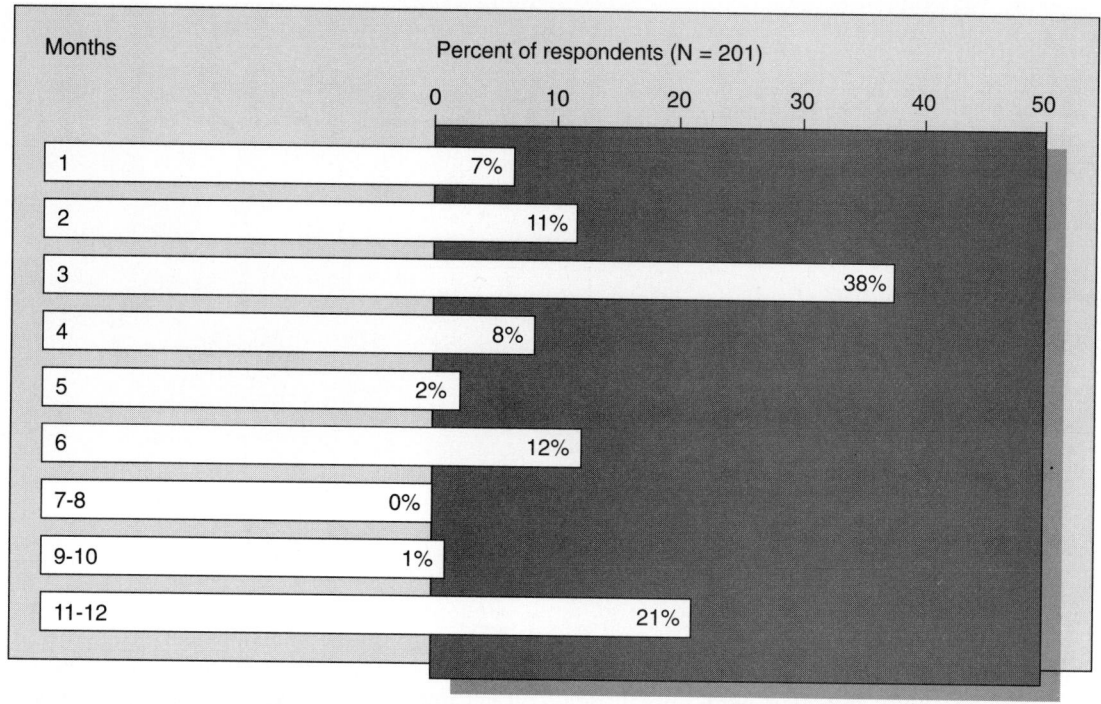

Months

Percent of respondents (N = 201)

Months	Percent
1	7%
2	11%
3	38%
4	8%
5	2%
6	12%
7-8	0%
9-10	1%
11-12	21%

Source: *Current Practices in Sales Incentives* (New York: The Alexander Group, Inc., 1988), p. 18.

all members of the sales force compete with each other. The people who achieve the highest overall performance on some dimension are the winners, and everyone else loses. A third format organizes the sales force into teams, which compete for group and individual prizes.

The results of the survey conducted by the Alexander Group suggest that the assignment of individual quotas is by far the most popular contest format. Eighty-three percent of responding firms reported using quota-based contests, and only 28 percent evaluated the performance of sales teams rather than of individuals.[19] This reliance on individual quotas allows firms to design contests that focus salespeople's effort on specific objectives, do not put representatives in low-potential territories at a disadvantage, and do not undermine cooperation in the sales force by forcing salespeople to compete against each other.

Whichever format is used, every member of the sales force should have a reasonable chance of winning an award. If there are to be only one or a few winners, many salespeople may think their chances of coming out on top are remote. Consequently, their instrumentality perceptions of the likelihood of winning are low, and they are not motivated to expend much effort to win.

EXHIBIT 15 • 11   *The Odds of a Salesperson Being a Contest Winner*

Odds of being a winner	Percent of responding firms (N = 209)
1 in 5 or less	35%
About 2 in 5	31%
About 3 in 5	21%
About 4 in 5	8%
More than 4 in 5	5%

Source: Adapted from *Current Practices in Sales Incentives* (New York: The Alexander Group, Inc., 1988), p. 22

As one sales executive put it, "The percentage of winners you get is very important. If you have only a few winners, the salesmen say, 'See, I told you the goals were unrealistic.' You get much better reaction if you can come in with 40 percent to 50 percent of your men winners."[20] In this respect, contests that provide rewards to everyone who meets quotas during the contest period are desirable. The number of possible winners is not arbitrarily limited, and everyone has a chance for a reward. As the survey results in Exhibit 15.11 indicate, however, the odds of a salesperson being a winner in a majority of sales contests are less than two out of five, with the average percentage of winners falling between 25 and 30 percent.

Types of Rewards

Contest rewards can take the form of cash, merchandise, or travel. All three types of rewards are commonly used, and a company may vary the kinds of rewards offered from contest to contest. In the Alexander Group's survey, for instance, 77 percent of respondents used cash awards in one or more recent contests, 61 percent offered merchandise, and 60 percent gave travel awards.[21]

Whatever form of reward is used, the monetary value must be large enough to be attractive to the participants, given their level of compensation. A portable TV, for example, may be more attractive where the average salesperson makes $25,000 per year than where the average compensation is $60,000. One authority recommends contest awards should be worth the equivalent of at least one week's compensation of the average person in the sales force.[22] As Exhibit

EXHIBIT 15 • 12   *Average Monetary Value of Sales Contest Prizes*

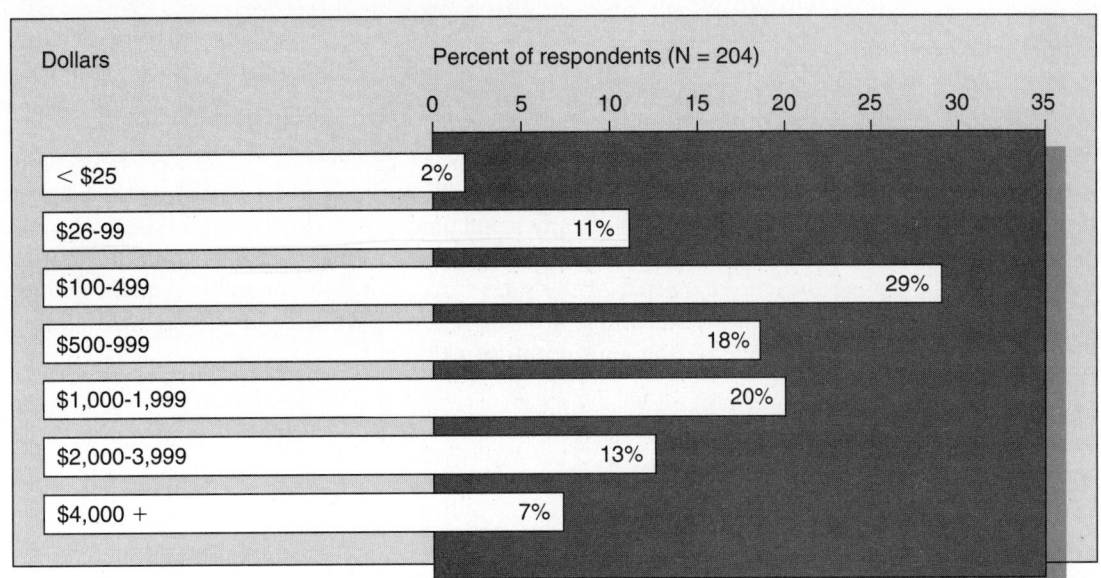

Source: *Current Practices in Sales Incentives* (New York: The Alexander Group, Inc., 1988), p. 25.

15.12 indicates, however, a substantial percentage of sales contests provide rewards with an average monetary value of only $500 or less.

Promotion and Follow-Through

To generate interest and enthusiasm, contests should be launched with fanfare. Firms announce contests at national or regional sales meetings. Follow-up promotion is also necessary to maintain interest throughout the contest period. As the contest proceeds, salespeople should be given frequent feedback concerning their progress so they know how much more they must do to win an award. Finally, winners should be recognized within the company, and prizes should be awarded promptly.

Criticism of Sales Contests

Although many sales managers believe contests are effective for motivating special efforts from salespeople, contests can cause a few potential problems, particularly if they are poorly designed or used.

Some critics argue that contests designed to stimulate sales volume may produce results that are largely illusory, with no lasting improvement in market share. Salespeople may "borrow" sales from before and/or after the contest to increase their volume during the contest. They may hold back orders before the start of the contest and rush orders that would normally not be placed until after the contest. As a result, customers may be overstocked, and sales volume falls off for some time after the contest is over.

Contests may also hurt the cohesiveness and morale of the company's salespeople. This is particularly true when plans force individual salespeople to compete with one another for rewards and when the number of rewards is limited.

Finally, some firms tend to use sales contests to "cover up" faulty compensation plans. Sales personnel should not have to be compensated a second time for what they are already being paid to do. Thus, contests should be used only on a short-term basis to motivate special efforts beyond the normal performance expected of the sales force. If a firm conducts frequent contests to maintain an acceptable level of sales performance, it should reexamine its entire compensation and incentive program.[23]

NONFINANCIAL REWARDS

Promotion and Career Paths

Most sales managers consider opportunities for promotion and advancement second only to financial incentives as an effective sales force motivator. This is particularly true for young, well-educated salespeople who tend to view their jobs as stepping-stones to top management. Unfortunately, salespeople's valences for promotion tend to decline in many companies as they get older. As we saw in the last chapter, one likely reason for this is that many firms do not provide many promotion opportunities for salespeople. The common career path is from salesperson to district sales manager to top sales management. Thus, if a person has been with a firm for several years without making it into sales management, the individual may start to believe such a promotion will never happen. Consequently, older salespeople may concentrate solely on financial rewards, or they may lose motivation and not work as hard at their jobs.[24]

To overcome this problem, some firms have instituted two different career paths for salespeople. One leads to management positions for promising candidates, while the other leads to more advanced positions within the sales force. The latter usually involves responsibility for dealing with key accounts or leading sales teams. In this system, even though a salesperson may not make it into management, the rep can still work toward a more prestigious and lucrative position within the sales force. To make advanced sales positions more attractive as promotions, many firms provide people in those positions with additional perquisites ("perks"), including higher compensation, a better automobile, and better office facilities.

EXHIBIT 15 • 13 *Guidelines for Effective Formal Recognition Programs*

Regardless of its size or cost, any recognition program should incorporate the following features, says consultant Dr. Richard Boyatiz of McBer and Co.:

• The program must be strictly performance-based with no room for subjective judgments. If people suspect that it is in any way a personality contest, the program will not work. Says Boyatiz: "It should be clear to anyone looking at the data that, yes, these people won."

• It should be balanced. The program should not be so difficult that only a few can hope to win, or so easy that just about everyone does. In the first case, people will not try; in the second, the program will be meaningless.

• A ceremony should be involved. If rings are casually passed out, or plaques sent through the mail, a lot of the glamour of the program will be lost.

• The program must be in good taste. If not, it will be subject to ridicule and, rather than motivate people, leave them uninspired. No one wants to be part of a recognition program that is condescending or tacky. Says Boyatiz: " The program should make people feel good about being part of the company."

• There must be adequate publicity. In some cases, sales managers do such a poor job of explaining a program or promoting it to their own salespeople that no one seems to understand or care about it. Prominent mention of the program in company publications is the first step to overcoming this handicap.

Source: Bill Kelley, "Recognition Reaps Rewards," *Sales & Marketing Management*, June 1986, 104.

Recognition Programs

Contest awards and promotions provide recognition for good performance, but many firms also have separate recognition programs to provide nonmonetary rewards.[25] As with contests, effective recognition programs should offer a reasonable chance of winning for everyone in the sales force. But if a very large proportion of the sales force achieves recognition, the program is likely to lose some of its appeal because the winners feel no special sense of accomplishment.

Consequently, better recognition programs often recognize the best performers for several different performance dimensions. For example, winners might include persons with the highest sales volume for the year, the biggest percentage increase in sales, the biggest dollar increase, the highest penetration of territory potential, and the largest sales per account.

Recognition is an attractive reward because it makes a person's peers and superiors aware of the outstanding performance. Communication of the winner's achievements, through recognition at a sales meeting, publicity in the local press, announcements in the company's internal newsletter, or other ways, is an essential part of a good program. Also, firms typically give special awards as part of their recognition program, although these are often symbolic awards with low monetary value, such as trophies, plaques, or rings. Finally, as Exhibit 15.13 points out, objectivity and good taste are also important ingredients of effective recognition programs, as they are for contests and other incentives.

THE REIMBURSEMENT OF SELLING EXPENSES

The cost of a sales call, estimated to be between $230 and $300 in 1990, increased substantially faster than the rate of inflation over the past decade. A large portion of those selling costs are accounted for by the salesperson's compensation and financial incentives. But as Exhibit 15.14 indicates, various expense items incurred by the sales rep in the field—travel, lodging, meals, and entertaining customers—are also substantial. While average selling expenses vary across types of industries and the experience of the salesperson, they generally account for between 20 and 30 percent of the total costs of employing a salesperson, and in some cases they can be much higher.

As mentioned in earlier chapters, the rapid rise in selling costs has caused many sales managers to question the economic viability of having field salespeople make face-to-face calls on smaller customers and to turn to telemarketing and other approaches to reduce the expenses involved in servicing smaller firms. A second response to cost increases has been a search for improved methods of expense control. Many firms have experimented with a variety of expense reimbursement plans. Such plans range from unlimited reimbursement for all "reasonable and allowable" expenses to plans where salespeople must pay all expenses out of their total compensation.

When deciding which form of expense reimbursement to use, sales managers must make trade-offs between tight control aimed at holding down total expenses and the financial well-being—and the subsequent motivation level—of salespeople. Some expense items—such as entertainment expenses, club dues, and the costs of personal services while the salesperson is away from home—can be considered either legitimate business expenses that should be reimbursed by the company or personal expenses that should be paid for by the salesperson. Obviously, company policies and reimbursement plans that treat such costs as business expenses increase the salesperson's total financial compensation but also increase the firm's total selling costs. The issue of expense control and techniques firms might use to improve their control over selling expenses are discussed in more detail in Chapter 17. Since different reimbursement plans have an impact on the effective financial compensation received by, and the motivation level of, a firm's salespeople, however, some of the relative advantages and limitations of alternative plans and policies are discussed now.

Direct Reimbursement Plans

The most popular type of expense reimbursement plan—employed by about 85 percent of all firms—involves direct and unlimited reimbursement of all "allowable and reasonable" expenses.[26] However, reimbursement under such plans is contingent on the salesperson submitting receipts or detailed records justifying expense claims. So the processing and evaluation of expense claims add to the firm's sales administration costs.

The primary advantage is that such plans give the sales manager some

EXHIBIT 15 • 14   *Compensation and Expenses by Industry*   *(1990)*

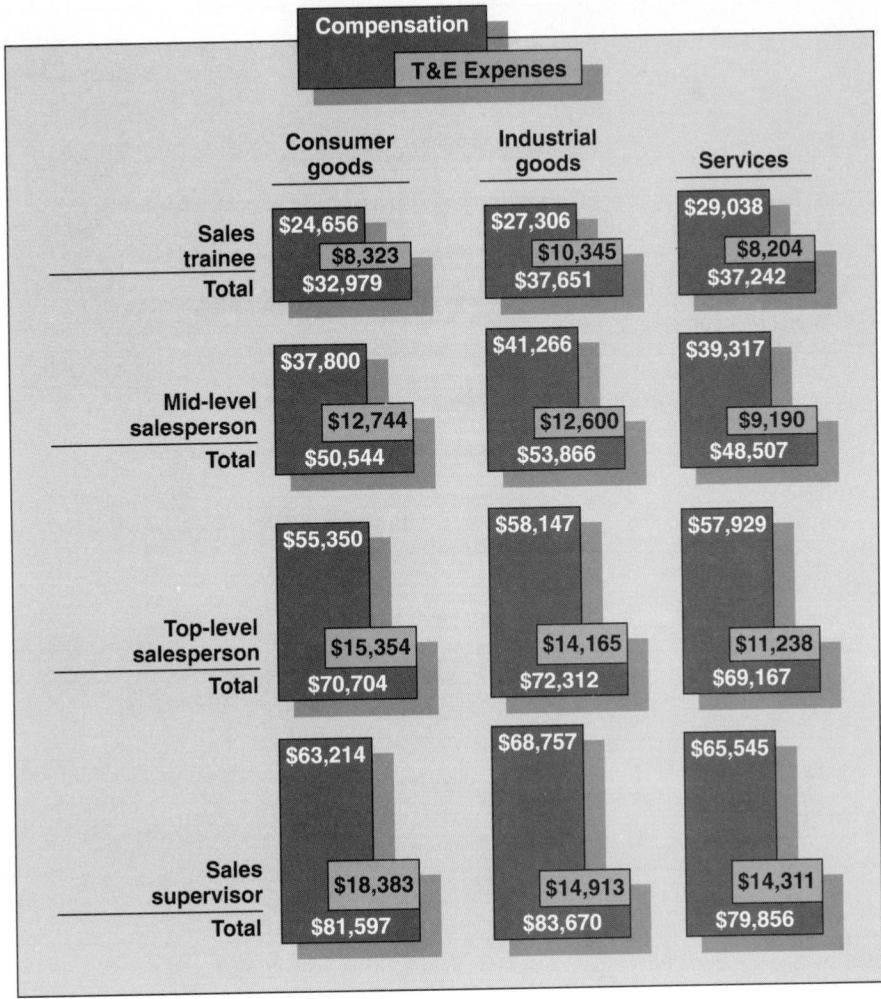

Compensation

T&E Expenses

	Consumer goods	**Industrial goods**	**Services**
Sales trainee	$24,656	$27,306	$29,038
	$8,323	$10,345	$8,204
Total	$32,979	$37,651	$37,242
Mid-level salesperson	$37,800	$41,266	$39,317
	$12,744	$12,600	$9,190
Total	$50,544	$53,866	$48,507
Top-level salesperson	$55,350	$58,147	$57,929
	$15,354	$14,165	$11,238
Total	$70,704	$72,312	$69,167
Sales supervisor	$63,214	$68,757	$65,545
	$18,383	$14,913	$14,311
Total	$81,597	$83,670	$79,856

Notes: Compensation includes base salary, commission, and bonus. T&E Expenses include travel, entertainment, food, and lodging.

Source: "1991 Sales Manager's Budget Planner," *Sales & Marketing Management,* June 17, 1991, p. 72.

control over both the total magnitude of sales expenses and over the kinds of activities salespeople will be motivated to engage in. If a particular activity, such as entertaining potential new accounts, is thought to be an important ingredient of the firm's account management policies, salespeople can be encouraged to engage in that activity by being informed that all related expenses

Exhibit 15 • 15   *Sales Expenses: What Do Companies Pay For?*

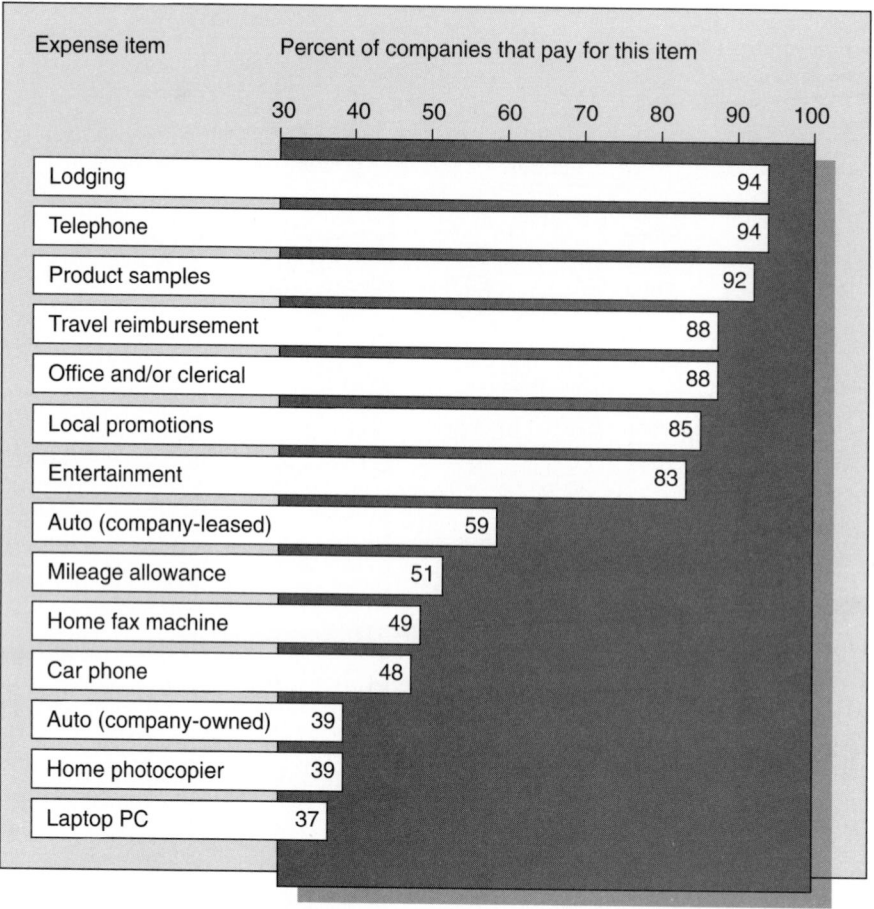

Source: "1991 Sales Manager's Budget Planner," *Sales & Marketing Management,* June 17, 1991, p. 76.

will be reimbursed. On the other hand, managers can discourage their subordinates from spending time on unimportant tasks by refusing to reimburse expenditures for such activities.

Thus, company policies concerning reimbursable expenses can be a useful tool for motivating and directing sales effort. Some firms report they adjusted their expense reimbursement policies according to the differences in the territories covered or the job activities required of different members of their sales forces.[27] For example, some firms reimburse a broader range and higher levels of expenses for their national account managers than for members of their regular field sales force. The results of a survey of company reimbursement policies concerning a variety of different expense items are displayed in Exhibit 15.15.

Limited Reimbursement Plans

Some firms limit the total amount of expense reimbursement, either by setting maximum limits for each expense item (e.g., a policy that limits reimbursement for restaurant meals to $40 per person) or by providing each salesperson with a predetermined lump-sum payment to cover total expenses. This approach keeps total selling expenses within planned limits, limits that are often determined by the sales expense budget set at the beginning of the year. In some cases, budgeted expense amounts may vary across members of the sales force, depending on the past or forecasted sales volume or the requirements of the territories.

Unless the budgeted limits are based on an accurate understanding of the costs associated with successful sales performance in each territory, however, these kinds of plans can hurt motivation and sales performance. Individual salespeople may believe their ability to do a good job is constrained by tight-fisted company expense reimbursement policies. Rather than pay for necessary activities out of their own pockets, salespeople are likely to avoid or cut back on certain expense activities to keep their costs within their budgets.

No Reimbursement Plans

A variation of the advanced lump-sum plan still found in some firms is a policy of requiring salespeople to cover all of their own expenses. Such plans usually involve paying the salesperson a relatively high total financial compensation to help cover necessary expenses. Such plans are most commonly associated with "straight commission" compensation plans involving high percentage commissions. The rationale is that salespeople will be motivated to spend both the effort and money necessary to increase sales volume as long as the resulting financial rewards are big enough to be worthwhile.

Since these plans are simply a variation of the "limited reimbursement" plans discussed previously, they have similar advantages and limitations. They help the firm limit sales expenses or—in the case of commission plans—make them a totally variable cost that moves up and down with changes in sales volume. They also sacrifice management control over the motivation and types of activities engaged in by members of the sales force.

S UMMARY

The sales manager concerned with motivating the members of the sales force needs to be concerned with the firm's compensation system. Which rewards do salespeople value? How much of each is optimum? How should the rewards be integrated in a total compensation system? This chapter sought to provide answers to these questions.

The chapter suggested a framework that sales managers can use when designing compensation and incentive programs. The frame work includes the following steps: (1) assess the firm's marketing and sales objectives, account management policies, and current performance of the sales force; (2) determine the aspects of job performance that are to be rewarded; (3) assess personal characteristics of salespeople and their valences for alternative rewards; (4) determine the most attractive and motivating mix of rewards; (5) decide on the most appropriate level of total compensation; (6) decide whether incentive compensation is to be used and, if the answer is yes, what kind and proportion of total compensation it should represent; (7) decide on the appropriate types of nonfinancial incentives; and (8) communicate the program to the sales force.

A major purpose of any sales compensation program is to influence the sales force to do what management wants, the way they want it done, and within the desired time. These requirements are largely dictated by the firm's marketing and sales objectives and account management policies. The important first two steps, then, are to establish the most important objectives for the personal selling effort and to decide which priorities the compensation system should attempt to address.

The success of any compensation system depends on whether those affected by it find the rewards attractive. Thus, the third and fourth steps in the process involve finding out exactly which rewards the company's salespeople value and what combination of rewards they find most attractive. These often vary by salesperson and can be determined by simple surveys or other research methods that assess a person's performance. Given this determination, the firm is in a position to weight the benefits and costs associated with various combinations of rewards.

The fifth step in the process is determining the total amount of compensation. Here the firm often walks a fine line. If it overpays its salespeople, it incurs increased costs and runs the risk of creating low morale among other employees of the company. If it pays less than its competitors, it generally attracts lower quality recruits and experiences higher turnover and its attendant costs.

In determining the most effective form of financial compensation, the firm must decide whether it should use (1) straight salary, (2) straight commission, or (3) a combination of base salary and incentive pay such as commissions, bonuses, or both. Most companies today use the combination approach. The base salary provides the salesperson with a stable income while allowing the company to reward its salespeople for performing tasks not directly related to short-term sales. The incentive portion of combination plans provides direct rewards to motivate salespeople to expend effort to improve their sales volume or profitability. To be effective, the incentive pay portion of the combination plan has to be large enough to generate the necessary interest among salespeople. Although the opportunity to earn 25 percent of the base salary in incentive has been suggested as a good rule of thumb, the decision should be based on the company's objectives and the nature of the selling job.

Sales contests are often part of the incentive portion of compensation systems. To be successful, a sales contest needs to have (1) clearly defined, specific objectives, (2) an exciting theme, (3) a reasonable probability of rewards for all salespeople, (4) attractive rewards, and (5) the necessary promotion and follow-through.

Nonfinancial incentives can play an important role in a firm's compensation system. In one survey of sales managers, it was found that they consider opportunities for promotion and advancement to be second only to special recognition as effective sales motivators. Because all salespeople cannot possibly move into sales management positions, some companies have dual career paths to maintain the motivating potential of promotion and advancement. One path leads to positions in the sales management hierarchy, while the other leads to greater responsibility in selling itself, such as a better territory or key account sales. For recognition programs to be effective, the salesperson's peers and superiors must be made aware of the representative's outstanding performance. This can be done through a formal recognition program at a sales meeting, publicity in the local press, announcements in the company's internal newsletter, or in other desirable ways.

The last stage in the process is to communicate the compensation program to the sales force. Salespeople need to have a clear understanding of its overall structure and what they have to do to secure the elements in the total package that they find desirable.

Discussion Questions

1. The following quote is from *Sales & Marketing Management*, April 1990, p. 136:

   If the customer isn't satisfied, the sales rep isn't paid. The sales force at Network Equipment Technologies, Redwood City, Cal., tells customers they can bank on being satisfied with its office automation products because NET salespeople are denied their full commission on the sale until customers are satisfied. NET withholds 50% of commissions until the account verifies everything's rosy.

   What is your reaction to this tactic? Do you think it is too severe? What difference would it make if customer satisfaction is beyond the control of the sales rep? Can you think of other ways to accomplish the same objective?

2. The Ruppert Company needed to build market share quickly. To motivate sales growth, Ruppert installed a straight commission compensation plan: the more the sales reps sold, the more they made. This strategy seemed to work; sales volume climbed and the Ruppert Company captured more market share. After two years on this program, sales growth flattened out and Ruppert began to lose market share. Sales reps continued to earn $75,000 to $80,000 on average in commissions through developing and penetrating key accounts in their territories. Studies showed

the sales force was not overworked and further territory penetration was clearly possible. What was happening?

3. When OfficeSolutions, software producer, went into business, it needed to establish market share quickly. To accomplish this, it decided to pay the sales force on a commission basis. After two years, however, the company had a large base business and customers began to complain the salespeople were not spending enough time with them on postsale service and problem solving. The salespeople said they did not make any money on problem solving and they would rather spend their time finding new accounts. What's more, salespeople spent little or no time selling the new products on which OfficeSolutions was staking its future. Salespeople said they could sell the old products more easily and earn more money for both themselves and the company. How can the company resolve this issue?

4. The Walker Company was an established company in a medium growth market with significant competition. The sales force was paid on a salary-plus-commission plan. Fifty percent of expected earnings were commission. Sales rep Victor managed an established territory and consistently earned the target level of total compensation (base salary plus commission). Sales rep Downey faced a different situation in a low-volume territory with stiff competition; after one year, commission earnings were next to nothing with no relief in sight. Discouraged, Downey left Walker, just like the last four reps in that territory. That underpenetrated territory and others like it would stay that way. The best the Walker Company could do was to maintain its current market share. How can Walker Company solve this problem?

5. "Look, Barb, the sales picture right now is not very good. A raise is not likely for the immediate future. For certain, if anyone deserves a raise it's you. Here's a suggestion: Since nobody watches expenses that closely, just add an additional amount to cover for the raise you didn't get, and I'll approve the voucher." What should Barb do in this situation? What would you do?

6. When designing sales compensation plans, it is important to match objectives with the sales environment and at the same time reward appropriately the person who has to meet those objectives. How would you design sales compensation plans to match the following objectives?

   a. Company has a high revenue growth objective in a sales environment characterized by frequent product introductions, "boom" markets, and a loose competitive structure.

   b. Company has a protect-and-grow revenue objective in a sales environment characterized by slow growth, many competitors, and few product introductions; the differentiation is determined by the excellence of the sales force.

   c. Company's objectives are to have an overall revenue growth and balanced product mix sales in an environment with multiple customer markets, many product groups, high-growth and low-growth products, and with high and low sales intensity.

   d. Company's objective is to maintain revenue and have new account sales growth (that is, conversion selling by taking customers from the competition); the environment is a moderate-to-slow-growth marketplace.

7. The MoKay Company recently had its sales compensation program evaluated by a recognized consulting firm that indicated the plan compared favorably with other plans offered by similar companies. The analysis revealed the program is more

than competitive and its mechanics and administration are equitable. Yet, MoKay still experiences a disturbing rate of turnover, and those that stay are not enthusiastic about their pay plan. What factors might be contributing to MoKay's problems?

8. Compensation of field managers involves some rather difficult issues. How should this critically important individual be paid? Should field sales managers participate in an incentive program that is similar to that offered to the sales force? Or should the field sales manager's compensation reflect—to a greater degree than the sales rep's—the overall profitability of the division? Should sales reps have the opportunity to earn more than their field sales manager?

9. West Virginia Paper, a paper distributor in a mature market, currently earns 18 to 20 percent gross margins. Commissions for salespeople are 20 percent of gross profit. Overall, the plan seems to be in line with the paper distributor's goal of improving profitability. Recently, growth in gross profit has been accompanied by a drop in net profit. The sales manager believes the sales reps are concentrating on small orders, which take less time, rather than large accounts, which have longer sales cycles. The larger accounts have lower service and processing costs. The growth in small orders increases overhead costs faster than the increase in gross profit, and net profit margins drop. West Virginia Paper needs a plan that will maintain its high gross profit and increase net profit as well. The problem facing the company is how to reward sales reps who maintain, or come close to, the desired price and how to motivate sales reps to pursue larger orders.

10. Even experienced executives become enthusiastic about planning product introductions. To transmit this enthusiasm to the sales force, it is often necessary to modify the sales incentive compensation plan. There are several questions to consider:
    a. How do you link sales rep performance and incentive payout without a sales history on which to base territory goals?
    b. How do you ensure appropriate sales force attention to the new product?
    c. How do you motivate sales maintenance as well as sales growth after introduction?
    d. How do you know when sales compensation will not be an effective tool in new product launches?

11. Sales contests, although very popular, raise questions concerning their value. Questions asked include: Don't they simply shift into the contest period sales volume that would have occurred anyway? How can everyone be equally motivated when certain territories have a built-in edge because of customer and market characteristics? Won't the contest backfire if people feel they haven't had a fair chance to win? Will all sales reps participate with equal enthusiasm when there can be only a few winners? How would you handle these objections?

12. The sales rep from the premium company was very positive about the benefits of his plan. He claimed past users have experienced sales increases ranging from 15 percent to 25 percent. The sales manager was not so excited about the proposal. She wondered what would happen if the sales increase was less than 15 percent. Variable costs were 40 percent of sales and fixed costs were 50 percent. Added to this would be the cost of the incentive program which would average 7 percent. Should the incentive program be used?

13. Things are tough at Morgan, Inc. For the last several months, sales reps, who are paid on a commission basis, have barely covered their personal monthly expenses. To help the sales force through these tough times, Morgan executives decided to introduce monthly draws. Sales reps whose commission earnings fall below a specified monthly amount receive a special loan, or draw, against commissions. When sales and commissions improve, the sales reps will repay the cash advance from future earnings. Will this plan help Morgan achieve its sales strategy?

14. As scores of companies that have switched to team selling can attest, there are numerous problems to resolve, including who leads the team, team composition, customer reactions, and team cooperation. Perhaps the thorniest issue concerns compensation. Developing a compensation plan for a sales team raises many questions. Should incentive pay be paid to all team members? If so, what kind? What's the best way to determine each member's contribution? A related question is: Should sales support/nonsales employees get incentive pay?

Endnotes

[1]This example is based on material found in Amy Dunkin, "Now Salespeople Really Must Sell for Their Supper," *Business Week,* July 31, 1989, pp. 50–52; and Francine Schwadel, "Chain Finds Incentives a Hard Sell," *The Wall Street Journal,* July 5, 1990, pp. B1, B4.

[2]David M. Gardner and Kenneth M. Rowland, "A Self-Tailored Approach to Incentives," *Personnel Journal,* November 1979, pp. 907–12; and Todd J. Englander, "Let Salespeople Design Your Incentive Plan," *Sales & Marketing Management,* September 1991, pp. 155–56.

[3]There Has To Be a Better Way," *Sales & Marketing Management,* November 12, 1979, pp. 41–43.

[4]Jerome A. Colletti and Linda J. Mahoney, "Should You Pay Your Sales Force for Customer Satisfaction?" *Perspectives in Total Compensation,* Vol. 2, no. 11 (Scottsdale, Ariz.: American Compensation Association, 1991); Alan M. Johnson, "The Incentive Program's Contribution to Quality," *Sales & Marketing Management,* April 1991, pp. 91–93; and Barry Farber and Joyce Wycoff, "Customer Service: Evolution and Revolution," *Sales & Marketing Management,* May 1991, pp. 44–51.

[5]Englander, "Let Salespeople Design Your Incentive Plan."

[6]Rene Y. Darmon, "Setting Sales Quotas with Conjoint Analysis," *Journal of Marketing Research,* February 1979, pp. 133–40.

[7]Gregg Cebrzynski, "Sales Compensation Survey Shows Some 'Dramatic' Findings," *Marketing News,* November 7, 1986, p. 32.

[8]"What Happens When a Salesperson Earns More Than His Manager?" *Sales & Marketing Management,* May 1990, pp. 32–34.

[9]Rene Y. Darmon, "Salesmen's Responses to Financial Incentives," *Journal of Marketing Research,* July 1974, pp. 39–46.

[10]William A. O'Connell and William Keenan, Jr., "The Shape of Things to Come," *Sales & Marketing Management,* January 1990, pp. 36–41.

[11]Amiya K. Basu, Rajiv Lal, V. Srinivasan, and Richard Staelin, "Sales Compensation Plans: An Agency Theoretic Perspective," *Marketing Science,* Fall 1985, pp. 267–91; George John and Barton Weitz, "Salesforce Compensation: An Empirical Investigation of Factors Related to the Use of Salary versus Incentive Compensation," *Journal of Marketing Research,* February 1989, pp. 1–14; and Richard L. Oliver and Barton Weitz, "The Effects of Risk Preference, Uncertainty, and Incentive Compensation on Salesperson Motivation," Report Number 91-104 (Cambridge, Mass.: Marketing Science Institute, 1991). For a more detailed review of agency theory propositions and research concerning the appropriate conditions for the use of salary versus incentive compensation, see Mark Bergen, Shantanu Dutta, and Orville C. Walker, Jr., "Agency Relationships in Marketing: A Review of the Applications and

Implications of Agency and Related Theories," *Journal of Marketing*, (forthcoming, 1992).

[12]For a more detailed discussion of this and other potential problems with drawing accounts, see Rick Dogen, "Don't Be Too Quick on the Draw," *Sales & Marketing Management*, September 1988, pp. 59–62; and Joanne Dahm, "Using Draws Wisely in Your Sales Compensation Plan," *Sales & Marketing Management*, August 1990, pp. 92–93.

[13]Richard C. Smyth and Matthew J. Murphy, *Compensating and Motivating Salesmen* (New York: American Management Association, 1969), p. 58.

[14]Jerry McAdams, "Rewarding Sales and Marketing Performance," *Management Review*, April 1987, pp. 33–38.

[15]Charles A. Peck, *Compensating Field Sales Representatives*, Report No. 828 (New York: The Conference Board, 1982), p. 14.

[16]Lesley Barnes, "Finding the Best Sales Compensation Plan," *Sales & Marketing Management*, August 1986, pp. 46–49; and William Keenan, Jr., "Is Your Pay Plan Putting the Squeeze on Top Performers?" *Sales & Marketing Management*, January 1990, pp. 74–75.

[17]Peck, *Compensating Field Sales Representatives*, p. 10.

[18]For an empirical study that largely confirms the exhibit's summary of conditions favoring the use of different types of compensation plans, see John and Weitz, "Salesforce Compensation: An Empirical Investigation."

[19]*Current Practices in Sales Incentives* (New York: The Alexander Group, 1988), p. 21.

[20]Sally Scanlon, "A New Role for Incentives," *Sales & Marketing Management*, April 7, 1975, p. 43. See also Jack Falvey, "Make 'em All Winners," *Sales & Marketing Management*, June 1991, pp. 8–11.

[21]*Current Practices in Sales Incentives*, p. 23.

[22]Benson P. Shapiro, *Sales Program Management: Formulation and Implementation* (New York: McGraw-Hill, 1977), p. 309.

[23]For a more detailed discussion of some of the pros and cons of sales contests and how management might evaluate the effectiveness of such contests, see Albert R. Wildt, James D. Parker, and Clyde E. Harris, Jr., "Assessing the Impact of Sales Force Contests: An Application," *Journal of Business Research* 15 (1987), pp. 145–55; Richard F. Beltramini and Kenneth R. Evans, "Salesperson Motivation to Perform and Job Satisfaction: A Sales Contest Participant Perspective," *Journal of Personal Selling and Sales Management*, August 1988, pp. 35–42; and William C. Moncrief, Sandra H. Hart, and Dan H. Robertson, "Sales Contests: A New Look at an Old Management Tool," *Journal of Personal Selling and Sales Management*, November 1988, pp. 55–61.

[24]In addition to the discussion of career stages and valence for promotion in Chapter 14, see William L. Cron, Alan J. Dubinsky, and Ronald E. Michaels, "The Influence of Career Stages on Components of Salesperson Motivation," *Journal of Marketing*, January 1988, pp. 78–92.

[25]Bill Kelley, "Recognition Reaps Rewards," *Sales & Marketing Management*, June 1986, pp. 102–5; and Jeanne Greenberg and Herb Greenberg, "Money Isn't Everything," *Sales & Marketing Management*, May 1991, pp. 10–12.

[26]Alan J. Dubinsky and Thomas E. Barry, "A Survey of Sales Management Practices," *Industrial Marketing Management* 11 (1982), p. 137.

[27]Thomas R. Mott and Tom Peiffer, "Should Sales Compensation Be Based on Where Your Salespeople Live?" *Sales & Marketing Management*, December 1990, pp. 116–117.

Suggested Readings

Design of compensation and incentive programs

Barnes, Lesley. "Finding the Best Sales Compensation Plan." *Sales & Marketing Management,* August 1986, pp. 46–49.

Englander, Todd J. "Let Salespeople Design Your Incentive Plan." *Sales & Marketing Management,* September 1991, pp. 155–56.

John, George, and Barton Weitz, "Salesforce Compensation: An Empirical Investigation of Factors Related to the Use of Salary versus Incentive Compensation." *Journal of Marketing Research,* February 1989, pp. 1–14.

Johnson, Alan M. "The Incentive Program's Contribution to Quality." *Sales & Marketing Management,* April 1991, pp. 91–93.

Keenan, William, Jr. "Is Your Pay Plan Putting the Squeeze on Top Performers?" *Sales & Marketing Management,* January 1990, pp. 74–75.

Mott, Thomas R. "Is Your Sales Compensation Plan a De-Motivator?" *Sales & Marketing Management,* February 1989, pp. 61–64.

Oliver, Richard L., and Barton Weitz. "The Effects of Risk Preference, Uncertainty, and Incentive Compensation on Salesperson Motivation." Report Number 91-104. Cambridge, Mass.: Marketing Science Institute, 1991.

Contests and nonfinancial incentives

Cron, William L., Alan J. Dubinsky, and Ronald E. Michaels. "The Influence of Career Stages on Components of Salesperson Motivation." *Journal of Marketing,* January 1988, pp. 78–92.

Greenberg, Jeanne, and Herb Greenberg. "Money Isn't Everything." *Sales & Marketing Management,* May 1991, pp. 10–12.

Kelley, Bill. "Recognition Reaps Rewards." *Sales & Marketing Management,* June 1986, pp. 102–5.

Moncrief, William C., Sandra H. Hart, and Dan H. Robertson. "Sales Contests: A New Look at an Old Management Tool." *Journal of Personal Selling and Sales Management,* November 1988, pp. 55–61.

Cases For Part Two

Case 2-1
GENERAL ELECTRIC APPLIANCES*

Larry Barr had recently been promoted to the position of district sales manager (B.C.) for G.E. Appliances, a division of Canadian Appliance Manufacturing Co. Ltd. (CAMCO). One of his more important duties in that position was the allocation of his district's sales quota among his five salesmen. Barr received his quota for 1992 in October 1991. His immediate task was to determine an equitable allocation of that quota. This was important because the company's incentive pay plan was based on the salesmen's attainment of quota. A portion of Barr's remuneration was also based on the degree to which his sales force met their quotas.

Barr graduated from the University of British Columbia in 1983 with the degree of bachelor of commerce. He was immediately hired as a product manager for a mining equipment manufacturing firm because of his summer job experience with that firm. In 1986, he joined Canadian General Electric (C.G.E.) in Montreal as a product manager for refrigerators. There he was responsible for creating and merchandising a product line, as well as developing product and marketing plans. In January 1989, he was transferred to Coburg, Ontario, as a sales manager for industrial plastics. In September 1990, he became administrative manager (Western Region) and when the position of district sales manager became available, Barr was promoted to it. There his duties included development of sales strategies, supervision of salesmen, and budgeting.

Background

Canadian Appliance Manufacturing Co. Ltd. (CAMCO) was created in 1990 under the joint ownership of Canadian General Electric Ltd. and General Steel Wares Ltd. (G.S.W.). CAMCO then purchased the production facilities of Westinghouse Canada Ltd. Under the purchase agreement, the Westinghouse brand name was transferred to White Consolidated Industries Ltd., where it became White-Westinghouse. Appliances manufactured by CAMCO in the former Westinghouse plant were branded Hotpoint. (See Exhibit 1.)

The G.E., G.S.W., and Hotpoint major appliance plants became divisions of CAMCO. These divisions operated independently and had their own separate management staff, although they were all ultimately accountable to CAMCO management. The divisions competed for sales, although not directly, because they each produced product lines for different price segments.

EXHIBIT 1   *Organization Chart*

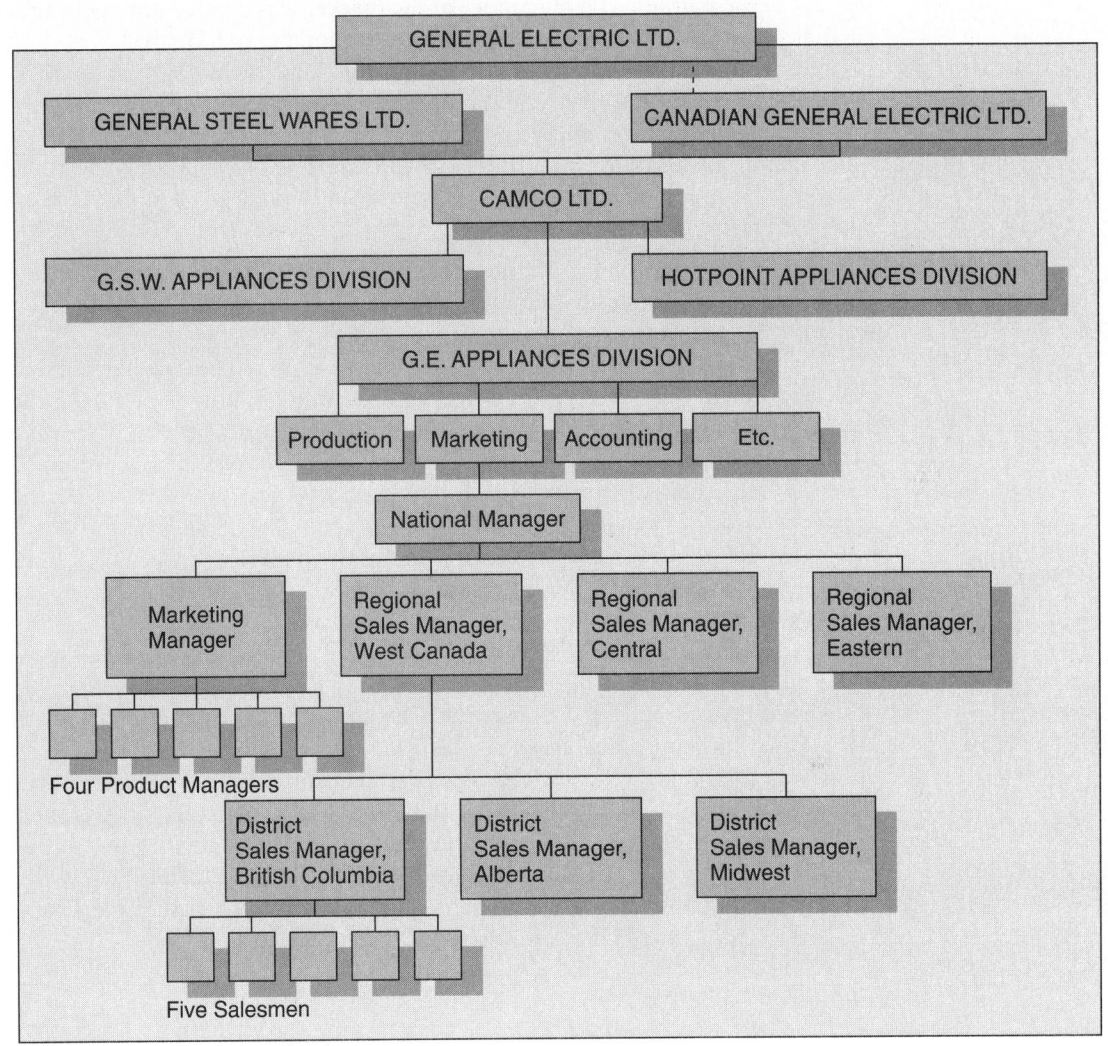

Competition

Competition in the appliance industry was vigorous. CAMCO was the largest firm in the industry, with approximately 45 percent market share, split between G.E., G.S.W. (Moffatt & McClary brands), and Hotpoint. The following three firms each had 10 to 15 percent market share: Inglis (washers and dryers only), W.C.I. (makers of White-Westinghouse, Kelvinator, and Gibson), and Admiral.

These firms also produced appliances under department store brand names such as Viking, Baycrest, and Kenmore, which accounted for an additional 15 percent of the market. The remainder of the market was divided among brands such as Maytag, Roper Dishwasher, Gurney, Tappan, and Danby.

G.E. marketed a full major appliance product line, including refrigerators, ranges, washers, dryers, dishwashers, and television sets. G.E. appliances generally had many features and were priced at the upper end of the price range. Their major competition came from Maytag and Westinghouse.

The Budgeting Process

G.E. Appliances was one of the most advanced firms in the consumer goods industry in terms of sales budgeting. Budgeting received careful analysis at all levels of management.

The budgetary process began in June of each year. The management of G.E. Appliances division assessed the economic outlook, growth trends in the industry, competitive activity, population growth, and so forth to determine a reasonable sales target for the next year. The president of CAMCO received this estimate, checked and revised it as necessary, and submitted it to the president of G.E. Canada. Final authorization rested with G.E. Ltd., which had a definite minimum growth target for the G.E. branch of CAMCO. G.E. Appliances was considered an "invest and grow" division, which meant it was expected to produce a healthy sales growth each year, regardless of the state of the economy. As Barr observed, "This is difficult, but meeting challenges is the job of management."

The approved budget was expressed as a desired percentage increase in sales. Once the figure had been decided, it was not subject to change. The quota was communicated back through G.E. Canada Ltd., CAMCO, and G.E. Appliances, where it was available to the district sales managers in October. Each district was then required to meet an overall growth figure (quota) but each sales territory was not automatically expected to achieve that same growth. Barr was required to assess the situation in each territory, determine where growth potential was highest, and allocate his quota accordingly.

The Sales Incentive Plan

The sales incentive plan was a critical part of General Electric's sales force plan and an important consideration in the quota allocation of Barr. Each salesman had a portion of his earnings dependent on his performance with respect to quota. Also, Barr was awarded a bonus based on the sales performance of his district, making it advantageous to Barr and good for staff morale for all his salesmen to attain their quotas.

The sales force incentive plan was relatively simple. A bonus system is fairly typical for salesmen in any field. With G.E., each salesman agreed to a basic salary figure called "planned earnings." The planned salary varied according to experience, education, past performance, and competitive salaries.

EXHIBIT 2   *Sales Incentive Earnings Schedule: Major Appliances and*
Home Entertainment Products

Sales Quota Realization (Percent)	Percent of Base Salary Total	Sales Quota Realization (Percent)	Incentive Percent of Base Salary Total
70%	0 %	105%	35.00%
71	0.75	106	37.00
72	1.50	107	39.00
73	2.25	108	41.00
74	3.00	109	43.00
75	3.75	110	45.00
76	4.50	111	46.00
77	5.25	112	47.00
78	6.00	113	48.00
79	6.75	114	49.00
80	7.50	115	50.00
81	8.25	116	51.00
82	9.00	117	52.00
83	9.75	118	53.00
84	10.50	119	54.00
85	11.25	120	55.00
86	12.00	121	56.00
87	12.75	122	57.00
88	13.50	123	58.00
89	14.25	124	59.00
90	15.00	125	60.00
91	16.00	126	61.00
92	17.00	127	62.00
93	18.00	128	63.00
94	19.00	129	64.00
95	20.00	130	65.00
96	21.00	131	66.00
97	22.00	132	67.00
98	23.00	133	68.00
99	24.00	134	69.00
100	25.00	135	70.00
101	27.00	136	71.00
102	29.00	137	72.00
103	31.00	138	73.00
104	33.00	139	74.00
		140	75.00

A salesman was paid 75 percent of his planned earnings on a guaranteed regular basis. The remaining 25 percent of salary was at risk, dependent on the person's sales record. There was also the possibility of earning substantially more money by selling more than quota (see Exhibit 2).

The bonus was awarded such that total salary (base plus bonus) equaled planned earnings when the quota was just met. The greatest increase in bonus came between 101 and 110 percent of quota. The bonus was paid quarterly on the cumulative total quota. A holdback system ensured that a salesman was never required to pay back previously earned bonus because of a poor quarter. Because of this system, it was critical that each salesman's quota be fair in relation to the other salesmen. Nothing was worse for morale than one person earning large bonuses while the others struggled.

Quota attainment was not the sole basis for evaluating the salesmen. They were required to fulfill a wide range of duties including service, franchising of new dealers, maintaining good relations with dealers, and maintaining a balance of sales among the different product lines. Because the bonus system was based on sales only, Barr had to ensure the salesmen did not neglect their other duties.

A formal salary review was held each year for each salesman. However, Barr preferred to give his salesmen continuous feedback on their performances. Through human relations skills, he hoped to avoid problems that could lead to dismissal of a salesman and loss of sales for the company.

Barr's incentive bonus plan was more complex than the salesmen's. He was awarded a maximum of 75 annual bonus points broken down as follows: market share, 15; total sales performance, 30; sales representative balance, 30. Each point had a specific money value. The system ensured that Barr allocate his quota carefully. For instance, if one quota was so difficult that the salesmen sold only 80 percent of it, while the other salesmen exceeded quota, Barr's bonus would be reduced, even if the overall area sales exceeded the quota. (See Appendix, "Development of a Sales Commission Plan.")

Quota Allocation

The total 1992 sales budget for G.E. Appliances division was about $100 million, a 14 percent sales increase over 1991. Barr's share of the $33 million Western Region quota was $13.3 million, also a 14 percent increase over 1991. Barr had two weeks to allocate the quota amongst his five territories. He needed to consider factors such as historical allocation, economic outlook, dealer changes, personnel changes, untapped potential, new franchises or store openings, and buying group activity (volume purchases by associations of independent dealers).

Sales force

There were five sales territories within B.C. (Exhibit 3). Territories were determined on the basis of number of customers, sales volume of customers,

EXHIBIT 3   *G.E. Appliances—Sales Territories*

Territory Designation	Description
9961 Greater Vancouver (Garth Rizzuto)	Hudson's Bay, Firestone, Kmart, McDonald Supply, plus seven independent dealers
9962 Interior (Dan Seguin)	All customers from Quesnel to Nelson, including contract sales (50 customers)
9963 Coastal (Ken Block)	Eatons, Woodwards, plus Vancouver Island north of Duncan and upper Fraser Valley (east of Clearbrook) (20 customers)
9964 Independent and Northern (Fred Speck)	All independents in lower mainland and South Vancouver Island, plus northern B.C. and Yukon (30 customers)
9967 Contract (Jim Wiste)	Contract sales Vancouver, Victoria. All contract sales outside 9962 (50–60 customers)

geographic size, and experience of the salesman. Territories were altered periodically to deal with changed circumstances.

One territory was comprised entirely of contract customers. Contract sales were sales in bulk lots to builders and developers who used the appliances in housing units. Because the appliances were not resold at retail, G.E. took a lower profit margin on such sales.

G.E. Appliances recruited M.B.A. graduates for their sales force. They sought bright, educated people who were willing to relocate anywhere in Canada. The company intended that these people would ultimately be promoted to managerial positions. The company also hired experienced career salesmen to get a blend of experience in the sales force. However, the typical salesman was under 30, aggressive, and upwardly mobile. G.E.'s sales training program covered only product knowledge. It was not felt necessary to train recruits in sales techniques.

Allocation procedure

At the time Barr assumed the job of district sales manager, he had a meeting with the former sales manager, Ken Philips. Philips described to Barr the method he had used in the past to allocate the quota. As Barr understood it, the procedure was as follows.

The quota was received in October in the form of a desired percentage sales increase. The first step was to project current sales to the end of the year. This gave a base to which the increase was added for an estimation of the next year's quota.

From this quota, the value of contract sales was allocated. Contract sales were allocated first because the market was considered the easiest to forecast. The amount of contract sales in the sales mix was constrained by the lower profit margin on such sales.

The next step was to make a preliminary allocation by simply adding the budgeted percentage increase to the year-end estimates for each territory. Although this allocation seemed fair on the surface, it did not take into account the differing situations in the territories, or the difficulty of attaining such an increase.

The next step was examination of the sales data compiled by G.E. Weekly sales reports from all regions were fed into a central computer, which compiled them and printed out sales totals by product line for each customer, as well as other information. This information enabled the sales manager to check the reasonableness of his initial allocation through a careful analysis of the growth potential for each customer.

The analysis began with the largest accounts, such as Firestone, Hudson's Bay, and Eatons, which each bought over $1 million in appliances annually. Accounts that size were expected to achieve at least the budgeted growth. The main reason for this was that a shortfall of a few percentage points on such a large account would be difficult to make up elsewhere.

Next, the growth potential for medium-sized accounts was estimated. These accounts included McDonald Supply, K mart, Federated Cooperative, and buying groups such as Volume Independent Purchasers (V.I.P.). Management expected the majority of sales growth to come from such accounts, which had annual sales of between $150,000 and $1 million.

At that point, about 70 percent of the accounts had been analyzed. The small accounts were estimated last. These had generally lower growth potential but were an important part of the company's distribution system.

Once all the accounts had been analyzed, the growth estimates were summed and the total compared to the budget. Usually, the growth estimates were well below the budget.

The next step was to gather more information. The salesmen were usually consulted to ensure that no potential trouble areas or good opportunities had been overlooked. The manager continued to revise and adjust the figures until the total estimated matched the budget. These projections were then summed by territory and compared to the preliminary territorial allocation.

Frequently, there were substantial differences between the two allocations. Historical allocations were then examined and the manager used his judgment in adjusting the figures until he was satisfied that the allocation was both equitable and attainable. Some factors that were considered at this stage included experience of the salesmen, competitive activities, potential store closures or openings, potential labor disputes in areas, and so forth.

The completed allocation was passed on to the regional sales manager for his approval. The process had usually taken one week or longer by this stage. Once the allocations had been approved, the district sales manager then divided them into sales quotas by product line. Often, the resulting average price did not match the expected mix between higher and lower priced units. Therefore, some additional adjusting of figures was necessary. The house account (used for sales to employees of the company) was used as the adjustment factor.

EXHIBIT 4   *Sales Results*

Territory	1989 Budget (× 1,000)	Percent of Total Budget	1989 Actual (× 1,000)	Variance from Quota (V%)
9967 (Contract)	2,440	26.5%	2,267	(7)%
9961 (Greater Vancouver)	1,790	19.4	1,824	2
9962 (Interior)	1,624	17.7	1,433	(11)
9963 (Coastal)	2,111	23.0	2,364	12
9964 (Ind. dealers)	1,131	12.3	1,176	4
House	84	1.1	235	—
Total	9,180	100.0%	9,299	1%

Territory	1990 Budget (× 1,000)	Percent of Total Budget	1990 Actual (× 1,000)	1990 Variance from Quota (V%)
9967 (Contract)	2,587	26.2%	2,845	10%
9961 (Greater Vancouver)	2,005	20.3	2,165	8
9962 (Interior)	1,465	14.8	1,450	(1)
9963 (Coastal)	2,405	24.4	2,358	(2)
9964 (Ind. dealers)	1,334	13.5	1,494	12
House	52	0.8	86	—
Total	9,848	100.0%	10,398	5%

Once this breakdown had been completed, the numbers were printed on a budget sheet, and given to the regional sales manager. He forwarded all the sheets for his region to the central computer, which printed out sales numbers for each product line by salesman, by month. These figures were used as the salesmen's quotas for the next year.

Current situation

Barr recognized that he faced a difficult task. He thought he was too new to the job and the area to confidently undertake an account by account growth analysis. However, due to his previous experience with sales budgets, he did have some sound general ideas. He also had the records of past allocation and quota attainment (Exhibit 4), as well as the assistance of the regional sales manager, Anthony Foyt.

Barr's first step was to project the current sales figures to end-of-year totals. This task was facilitated because the former manager, Philips, had been making successive projections monthly since June. Barr then made a preliminary quota

EXHIBIT 5   *Sales Projections and Quotas, 1991–1992*

			Projected Sales Results 1991		
Territory	Oct. 1991 Year to Date	1991 Projected Total	1991 Budget	Percent of Total Budget	Projected Variance from Quota (V%)
9967	$2,447	$ 3,002	$ 2,859	25.0%	5%
9961	2,057	2,545	2,401	21.0	6
9962	1,318	1,623	1,727	15.1	(6)
9963	2,124	2,625	2,734	23.9	(4)
9964	1,394	1,720	1,578	13.8	
House	132	162	139	1.2	—
Total	$9,474	$11,677	$11,438	100.0	2%

	Preliminary Allocation 1992		
Territory	1991 Projection	1992 Budget*	Percent of Total Budget
9967	$ 3,002	$ 3,422	25.7%
9961	2,545	2,901	21.8
9962	1,623	1,854	13.9
9963	2,625	2,992	22.5
9964	1,720	1,961	14.7
House	162	185	1.3
Total	$11,677	$13,315	100.0

1992 budget = 1991 territory projections + 14% = $13.315.

allocation by adding the budgeted sales increase of 14 percent to each territory's total (Exhibit 5).

Barr then began to assess circumstances that could cause him to alter that allocation. One major problem was the resignation, effective at the end of the year, of one of the company's top salesmen, Ken Block. His territory had traditionally been one of the most difficult, and Barr believed it would be unwise to replace Block with a novice salesman.

Barr considered shifting one of the more experienced salesmen into that area. However, that would have disrupted service in an additional territory, which was undesirable because it took several months for a salesman to build up a good rapport with customers. Barr's decision would affect his quota allocation because a salesman new to a territory could not be expected to immediately sell as well as the incumbent, and a novice salesman would require an even longer period of adaptation.

Barr was also concerned about territory 9961. The territory comprised two large national accounts and seven major independent dealers. The buying decisions for the national accounts were made at their head offices, where G.E.'s regional salesmen had no control over the decisions. Recently, Barr had heard rumors that one of the national accounts was reviewing its purchase of G.E. Appliances. If it were to delist even some product lines, it would be a major blow to the salesman, Rizzuto, whose potential sales would be greatly reduced. Barr was unsure how to deal with that situation.

Another concern for Barr was the wide variance in buying of some accounts. Woodwards, Eatons, and McDonald Supply had large fluctuations from year to year. Also, Eatons, Hudson's Bay, and Woodwards had plans to open new stores in the Vancouver area sometime during the year. The sales increase to be generated by these events was hard to estimate.

The general economic outlook was poor. The Canadian dollar had fallen to 92 cents U.S. and unemployment was at about 8 percent. The government's anti-inflation program, which was scheduled to end in November 1992, had managed to keep inflation to the 8 percent level, but economists expected higher inflation and increased labor unrest during the postcontrol period.

The economic outlook was not the same in all areas. For instance, the Okanagan (9962) was a very depressed area. Tourism was down and fruit farmers were doing poorly despite good weather and record prices. Vancouver Island was still recovering from a 200 percent increase in ferry fares, while the lower mainland appeared to be in a relatively better position.

In the contract segment, construction had shown an increase over 1990. However, labor unrest was common. There had been a crippling eight-week strike in 1990, and there was a strong possibility of another strike in 1992.

With all of this in mind, Barr was very concerned that he allocate the quota properly because of the bonus system implications. How should he proceed? To help him in his decision, he reviewed a note on development of a sales commission plan that he had obtained while attending a seminar on sales management the previous year (see Appendix below).

Appendix: Development of a Sales Commission Plan

A series of steps are required to establish the foundation on which a sales commission plan can be built. These steps are as follows:

A. Determine Specific Sales Objectives of Positions to be Included in Plan

For a sales commission plan to succeed, it must be designed to encourage the attainment of the business objectives of the component division. Before deciding on the specific measures of performance to be used in the plan, the component should review and define its major objectives. Typical objectives might be:

- Increase sales volume.
- Do an effective balanced selling job in a variety of product lines.
- Improve market share.
- Reduce selling expense to sales ratios.
- Develop new accounts or territories.
- Introduce new products.

Although it is probably neither desirable nor necessary to include all such objectives as specific measures of performance in the plan, they should be kept in mind, at least to the extent that the performance measures chosen for the

---

Tailoring Commission Plan Measurements to Fit Component Objectives

Objectives	Possible Plan Measurements
1. Increase sales/orders volume	Net sales billed or orders received against quota.
2. Increase sales of particular lines	Sales against product line quotas with weighted sales credits on individual lines.
3. Increase market share	Percent realization (%R) of shares bogey.
4. Do balanced selling job	%R of product line quotas with commissions increasing in proportion to number of lines up to quota.
5. Increase profitability	Margin realized from sales Vary sales credits to emphasize profitable product lines. Vary sales credit in relation to amount of price discount.
6. Increase dealer sales	Pay distributor *salespeople* or sales manager in relation to realization of sales quotas of assigned dealers.
7. Increase sales calls	%R of targeted calls per district or region.
8. Introduce new product	Additional sales credits on new line for limited period.
9. Control expense	%R of expense to sales or margin ratio. Adjust sales credit in proportion to variance from expense budget.
10. Sales teamwork	Share of incentive based upon group results.

plan are compatible with and do not work against the overall accomplishment of the component's business objectives.

Also, the relative current importance or ranking of these objectives will provide guidance in selecting the number and type of performance measures to be included in the plan.

B. Determine Quantitative Performance Measures to Be Used

Although it may be possible to include a number of measures in a particular plan, there is a drawback to using so many as to overly complicate it and fragment the impact of any one measure on the participants. A plan that is difficult to understand will lose a great deal of its motivation force, as well as be costly to administer properly.

For those who currently have a variable sales compensation plan(s) for their salespeople, a good starting point would be to consider the measures used in those plans. Although the measurements used for sales managers need not be identical, they should at least be compatible with those used to determine their salespeople's commissions.

However, keep in mind that a performance measure that may not be appropriate for individual salespeople may be a good one to apply to their manager. Measurements involving attainment of a share of a defined market, balanced selling for a variety of products, and control of district or region expenses might fall into this category.

Listed on the preceding page are a variety of measurements that might be used to emphasize specific sales objectives.

For most components, all or most of these objectives will be desirable to some extent. The point is to select those of greatest importance where it will be possible to establish measures of standard or normal performance for individuals, or at least small groups of individuals working as a team.

If more than one performance measurement is to be used, the relative weighting of each measurement must be determined. If a measure is to be effective, it must carry enough weight to have at least some noticeable effect on the commission earnings of an individual.

As a general guide, it would be unusual for a plan to include more than two or three quantitative measures with a minimum weighting of 15 to 20 percent of planned commissions for any one measurement.

C. Establish Commission Payment Schedule for Each Performance Measure

1. Determine appropriate range of performance for each measurement

The performance range for a measurement defines the percent of standard performance (%R) at which commission earnings start to the point where they reach maximum.

The minimum point of the performance range for a given measurement should be set so that a majority of the participants can earn at least some incentive pay and the maximum set at a point that is possible of attainment by some participants. These points will vary with the type of measure used and the degree of predictability of individual budgets or other forms of measurement. In a period where overall performance is close to standard, 90 to 95 percent of the participants should fall within the performance range.

For the commission plan to be effective, most of the participants should be operating within the performance range most of the time. If a participant is either far below the minimum of this range or has reached the maximum, further improvement will not affect his or her commission earnings, and the plan will be largely inoperative as far as he or she is concerned.

Actual past experience of %Rs attained by participants is obviously the best indicator of what this range should be for each measure used. Lacking this, it is better to err on the side of having a wider range than one that proves to be too narrow. If some form of group measure is used, the variation from standard performance is likely to be less for the group in total than for individuals within it. For example, the performance range for total district performance would probably be narrower than the range established for individual salespeople within a district.

2. Determine appropriate reward to risk ratio for commission earnings.

This refers to the relationship of commission earned at standard performance to maximum commission earnings available under the plan. A plan that pays 10 percent of base salary for normal or standard performance and pays 30 percent as a maximum commission would have a 2 to 1 ratio. In other words, the participant can earn twice as much (20 percent) for above standard performance as he or she stands to lose for below standard performance (10 percent).

Reward under a sales commission plan should be related to the effort involved to produce a given result. To adequately encourage above-standard results, the reward to risk ratio should generally be at least 2 to 1. The proper control of incentive plan payments lies in the proper setting of performance standards, not in the setting of a low maximum payment for outstanding results that provides a minimum variation in individual earnings. Generally, a higher percentage of base salary should be paid for each 1%R above 100 percent than has been paid for each 1%R up to 100%R to reflect the relative difficulty involved in producing above standard results.

Once the performance range and reward to risk ratios have been determined, the schedule of payments for each performance measure can then be calculated. This will show the percentage of the participant's base salary earned for various performance results (%R) from the point at which commissions start to maximum performance. For example, for measurement paying 20 percent of salary for standard performance:

Percent Base Salary Earned		Percent of Sales Quota
1% of base salary for each + 1%R	0%	80% or below
	20%	100% (standard performance)
1.33% of base salary for each + 1%R	60%	130% or above

D. Prepare Draft of Sales Commission Plan

After completing the above steps, a draft of a sales commission plan should be prepared using the outline below as a guide.

Keys to effective commission plans

1. Get the understanding and acceptance of the commission plan by the managers who will be involved in carrying it out. They must be convinced of its effectiveness to properly explain and "sell" the plan to the salespeople.

2. In turn, be sure the plan is presented clearly to the salespeople so that they have a good understanding of how the plan will work. We find that good acceptance of a sales commission plan on the part of salespeople correlates closely with how well they understood the plan and its effect on their commission. Salespeople must be convinced that the measurements used are factors they can control by their selling efforts.

3. Be sure the measurements used in the commission plan encourage the salespeople to achieve the marketing goals of your operation. For example, if sales volume is the only performance measure, salespeople will concentrate on producing as much dollar volume as possible by spending most of their time on products with high volume potential. It will be difficult to get them to spend much time on introducing new products with relatively low volume, handling customer complaints, and so on. Even though a good portion of their compensation may still be in salary, you can be sure they will wind up doing the things they feel will maximize their commission earnings.

4. One good solution to maintaining good sales direction is to put at least a portion of the commission earnings in an "incentive pool" to be distributed by the sales manager according to his or her judgment. This "pool" can vary in size according to some qualitative measure of the sales group's performance, but the manager can set individual measurements for each salesperson and reward each person according to how well he or she fulfills the goals.

5. If at all possible, you should test the plan for a period of time, perhaps in one or two sales areas or districts. To make it a real test, you should actually pay commission earnings to the participants, but the potential risk and rewards can be limited. No matter how well a plan has been conceived, not all the potential pitfalls will be apparent until you've actually operated the plan for

a period of time. The test period is a relatively painless way to get some experience.

6. Finally, after the plan is in operation, take time to analyze the results. Is the plan accomplishing what you want it do, both in terms of business results produced and in realistically compensating salespeople for their efforts?

Case 2-2
ADAMS BRANDS*

Ken Bannister, Ontario regional manager for Adams Brands, was faced with the decision of which of three candidates he should hire as the key account supervisor for the Ontario region. This salesperson would be responsible for working with eight major accounts in the Toronto area. Mr. Bannister had narrowed the list to the three applicants and began reviewing their files.

The Company

Warner-Lambert Inc., a large diversified U.S. multinational, manufactured and marketed a wide range of health-care and consumer products. Warner-Lambert Canada Ltd., the largest subsidiary, had annual sales exceeding $200 million. Over half the Canadian sales were generated by Adams Brands, which focused on the confectionery business. The major product lines carried by Adams were (1) chewing gum with brands such as Chiclets, Dentyne, and Trident, (2) portable breath fresheners, including Certs and Clorets, (3) cough tablets and antacids such as Halls and Rolaids, and (4) several other products including Blue Diamond Almonds and Sparkies Mini-Fruits. In these product categories, Adams Brands was usually the market leader or had a substantial market share.

The division was a stable unit for Warner-Lambert Canada with profits being used for investments throughout the company. Success of the Adams Brands was built on (1) quality products; (2) strong marketing management; (3) sales force efforts on distribution, display, and merchandising; and (4) excellent customer service.

Adams was organized on a regional basis. The Ontario region, which also included the Atlantic provinces, had 46 sales representatives whose responsibilities were to service individual stores. Five district managers coordinated the activities of the sales representatives. Also, three key account supervisors worked with the large retail chains (e.g., supermarkets) in Ontario and the Atlantic area. The key account supervisor in the Toronto area had recently joined one of Adams' major competitors.

The Market

The confectionery industry included six major competitors that manufactured chocolate bars, chewing gum, mints, cough drops, chewy candy, and other

---

*This case was written by Gordon H.G. McDougall and Douglas Snetsinger. Copyright © 1988 by Gordon H.G. McDougall. Adapted with permission.

EXHIBIT 1   *Major Competitors in Confectionery Industry*

Company	1986 Market Share (Percent)	Major Product Lines	Major Brands
Adams	23	Gum, portable breath fresheners, cough drops	Trident, Chiclets, Dentyne, Certs, Halls
Cadbury/Nielson	22	Chocolate bars	Caramilk, Crunchie, Dairy Milk, Crispy Crunch
Rowntree	15	Chocolate bars	Black Magic, Kit-Kat, Smarties, Turtles
Nabisco/Hershey	14	Gum, chocolate bars, chewy candy	Lowney, Reese's Pieces, Lifesavers
Wrigley's	9	Gum	Hubba Bubba, Extra, Doublemint
Effem Foods Ltd.	9	Chocolate bars, chewy candy	Mars, Snickers, M&Ms, Skittles
Richardson-Vicks	2	Cough drops	Vicks
Others	6		

Source: Company records and industry data.

products. The 1986 market shares of these six companies are provided in Exhibit 1.

In the past few years, total industry sales in the confectionery category had been flat to marginally declining in unit volume. This sales decline was attributed to the changing age distribution of the population (i.e., fewer young people). As consumers got older, their consumption of confectionery products tended to decline. While unit sales were flat or declining, dollar sales were increasing at a rate of 10 percent per annum as a result of price increases.

In the confectionery business, it was critical to obtain extensive distribution in as many stores as possible and, within each store, to obtain as much prominent shelf space as possible. Most confectionery products were purchased on impulse. One study found that up to 85 percent of chewing gum and 70 percent of chocolate bar purchases were unplanned. While chocolate bars could be viewed as an indirect competitor to gum and mints, they were direct competitors for retail space and were usually merchandised on the same display. Retailers earned similar margins from all confectionery products (25 percent to 36 percent of retail selling price) and often sought the best-selling brands to generate those revenues. Some industry executives believed that catering to the retailers' needs was even more important than understanding the ultimate consumers' needs.

Adams Brands had always provided store display racks for merchandising all confectionery items including competitive products and chocolate bars. The advantage of supplying the displays was that the manufacturer could influence the number of prelabeled slots that contained brand logos and the proportion of the display devoted to various product groups, such as chewing gum versus chocolate bars. The displays were usually customized to the unique requirements of a retailer, such as the height and width of the display.

Recently, a competitor, Effem, had become more competitive in the design and display of merchandising systems. Effem was regarded as an innovator in the industry, in part because of its limited product line and new approach to the retail trade. The company had only eight fast-turnover products in its line. Effem had developed its own sales force, consisting of over 100 part-time merchandising sales people and eight full-time sales personnel, and focused on the head offices of A accounts. A accounts were large retail chains such as Mac's, Beckers, Loblaws, A & P, Food City, Miracle Food Mart, K mart, Towers, and Zellers. Other than Adams, Effem was one of a few companies that conducted considerable research on racking systems and merchandising.

The Retail Trade

Within the Adams Brands, over two thirds of confectionery volume flowed through wholesalers. The remaining balance was split between direct sales and drop shipments to retailers. Wholesalers were necessary because, with over 66,000 outlets in food, drug, and variety stores alone, the sales force could not adequately cover a large proportion of the retailers. The percentage of Adams sales through the various channels is provided in Exhibit 2.

The volume of all consumer packaged goods sold in Canada had increasingly been dominated by fewer and larger retail chains. This increased retail concentration resulted in retailers becoming more influential in trade promotion decisions, including dictating the size, timing, and numbers of allowance, distribution, and co-op advertising events. The new power of the retailers had not as yet been fully wielded against the confectionery business. Confectionery lines were some of the most profitable lines for the retailer. Further, the manufacturers were not as reliant on listings from any given retailer as were other food and household product manufacturers.

The increased size of some retail chains also changed the degree of management sophistication at all levels including the retail buyer—those responsible for deciding what products were carried by the retail stores. At one time, the relationship between manufacturers' sales representatives and retail buyers was largely based on long-term and personal associations. Usually the sales representative had strong social skills, and an important task was to "get along well" with the buyers. Often when the representatives and buyers met to discuss various promotions or listings, part of the conversation dealt with making

---

Exhibit   2   *Adams Brand Sales by Distribution Channel*

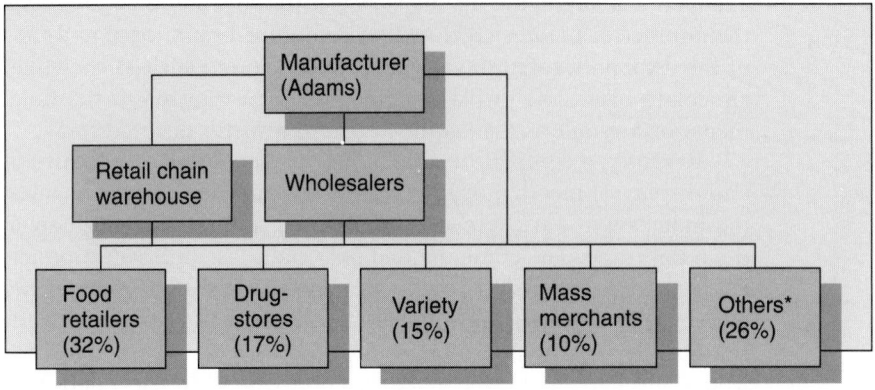

*Consists of a wide variety of locations, including vending machines, restaurants, cafeterias, bowling alleys, and resorts.

---

plans for dinner or going to a hockey game. The sales representative would be the host for these social events.

More recently, a new breed of buyer was emerging in the retail chains. Typically, the new retail managers and buyers had been trained in business schools. They often had product management experience, relied on analytical skills, and used state-of-the-art, computer-supported planning systems. In some instances, the buyer was now more sophisticated than the sales representative with respect to analytical approaches to display and inventory management. The buyers were frequently requesting detailed plan-o-grams with strong analytical support for expected sales, profits, and inventory turns. The buyer would also at times become the salesperson. After listening to a sales presentation and giving an initial indication of interest, the buyer would attempt to sell space—space on the store floor and space in the weekly advertising supplements. For example, the buyer for Shopper's Drug Mart could offer a dump bin location in every store in the chain for a week. In some instances, both the buyer and the representative had the authority to conclude such a deal at that meeting. At other times, both would have to wait for approval from their respective companies.

The interesting aspect of the key account supervisor's position was that the individual would have to feel comfortable dealing with the "old" and "new" school of retail management. The task for Bannister was to select the right candidate for this position. The salary for the position ranged from $25,000 to $48,200, depending on qualifications and experience. Bannister expected the candidate selected would probably be paid somewhere between $32,000 and $40,000. An expense allowance would also be included in the compensation package.

The Key Accounts Supervisor

The main responsibility of the key accounts supervisor was to establish and maintain a close working relationship with the buyers of eight A accounts whose head offices were located in the Toronto area. An important task was to make presentations (15 to 30 minutes in length) to the retail buyers of these key accounts every three to six weeks. At these meetings, promotions or deals for up to five brands would be presented. The supervisor was responsible for all Adams brands. The buyer might have to take the promotions to his buying committee where the final decision would be made. In addition, the supervisor used these meetings to hear from the buyer about any merchandising problems occurring at the store level.

Mid-year reviews were undertaken with each account. These reviews, lasting for one hour, were focused on reviewing sales trends and tying them into merchandising programs, listings, service, and new payment terms. Another important and time-consuming responsibility of the key accounts supervisor was to devise and present plan-o-grams and be involved with the installation of the displays. The supervisor also conducted store checks and spent time on competitive intelligence. Working with the field staff was a further requirement of the position.

Bannister reflected on what he thought were the attributes the ideal candidate would possess. First, the individual should have selling and merchandising experience in the retail business to understand the language and dynamics of the situation. On the merchandising side, the individual would be required to initiate and coordinate the design of customized display systems for individual stores, a task that involved a certain amount of creativity. Second, strong interpersonal skills were needed. The individual had to establish rapport and make effective sales presentations to the buyers. Because of the wide range of buyer sophistication, these skills were particularly important. Bannister made a mental note to recommend that whoever was hired would be sent on the professional selling skills course, a one-week program designed to enhance listening, selling, and presentation skills.

Finally, the candidate should possess analytic skills because many of the sales and performance reports (from both manufacturer and retailer) were or would be computerized. Thus, the individual should feel comfortable working with computers. Bannister hoped he could find a candidate who would be willing to spend a minimum of three years in the job to establish a personal relationship with the buyers.

Ideally, the candidate selected would have a blend of all three skills because of the mix of buyers he or she would contact. Bannister believed it was most likely these characteristics would be found in a business school graduate. He had advertised the job internally (through the company's newsletter) and externally (in the *Toronto Star*). A total of 20 applications were received. After an initial screening, three possible candidates for the position were identified. None were from Warner-Lambert.

EXHIBIT 3

Lydia Cohen

Personal:	Born 1956; 5'6"; 140 lbs.; single.
Education:	B.B.A. (1978), Wilfrid Laurier University; active in Marketing Club and Intramural sports.
Work:	1985–87, Rowntree Mackintosh Canada Inc.—District Manager
	Responsible for sales staff of three in Ottawa and Eastern Ontario region. Establish annual sales plan and ensure that district meets its quota.
	1978–84, Rowntree Mackintosh Canada Inc.—Confectionery Sales Representative
	Responsible for selling a full line of confectionery and grocery products to key accounts in Toronto (1983–84) and Ottawa (1978–82). 1984 Sales Representative of the Year for highest volume growth.
Interests:	Racquet sports
Candidate's comments:	I am interested in working in the Toronto area, and I would look forward to concentrating on the sales task. My best years at Rowntree were in sales in the Toronto region.
Interviewer's comments:	Lydia presents herself very well and has a strong background in confectionery sales. Her record at Rowntree is very good. Rowntree paid for her to take an introductory course in Lotus 1-2-3 in 1984, but she has not had much opportunity to develop her computer skills. She does not seem to be overly ambitious or aggressive. She stated that personal reasons were pre-eminent in seeking a job in Toronto.

John Fisher

Personal:	Born 1960; 6'3"; 195 lbs.; single
Education:	B.A. (Phys. Ed.) (1985), University of British Columbia
	While at U.B.C. played four years of varsity basketball (team captain in 1983–84). Assistant Coach, Senior Basketball at University Hill High School, 1981–1985. Developed and ran a two-week summer basektball camp at U.B.C for three years. Profits from the camp were donated to the Varsity Basketball Fund.
Work:	1980–86, Jacobs Suchard Canada Inc. (Nabob Foods)
	Six years' experience (full-time, 1985–86, and five years part-time, 1980–85 during school terms and full-time during summers) in coffee and chocolate distribution and sales; two years on the loading docks, one year driving truck, and three years as a sales representative. Sales tasks included calling on regular customers, order taking, rack jobbing, and customer relations development.
	1986–87, Scavolini (Professional Basketball)
	One year after completing studies at U.B.C., traveled Western Europe and Northern Africa. Travel was financed by playing professional basketball in the Italian First Division.
Candidate's comment:	I feel the combination of educational preparation, work experience, and my demonstrated ability as a team player and leader make me well suited for this job. I am particularly interested in a job, such as sales, which rewards personal initiative.
Interviewer's comments:	A very ambitious and engaging individual with a good record of achievements. Strong management potential is evident, but interest in sales as a career is questionable. Minored in Computer Science at U.B.C. Has a standing offer to return to a sales management position at Nabob.

In early August 1987, Bannister and a member of the personnel department then interviewed each of the candidates. After completing the interviews, brief fact sheets were prepared (see Exhibit 3). Bannister reviewed the sheets before making the decision.

EXHIBIT 3   (concluded)

Barry Moore

Personal: Born 1947; 5'11"; 185 lbs.; married with two children

Education: Business Administration Diploma (1972), Humber College

While at school was active participant in a number of clubs and political organizations. President of the Young Liberals (1971–72).

Work: 1984–87, Barrigans Food Markets–Merchandising Analyst

Developed merchandising plans for a wide variety of product categories. Negotiated merchandising programs and trade deals with manufacturers and brokers. Managed a staff of four.

1981–84, Dominion Stores Ltd,—Assistant Merchandise Manager

Liaison responsibilities between stores and head office merchandise planning. Responsible for execution of merchandising plans for several food categories.

1980, Robin Hood Multifoods, Inc.—Assistant Product Manager.

Responsible for the analysis and development of promotion planning for Robin Hood Flour.

1975–80, Nestlé Enterprises Ltd.—Carnation Division Sales Representative.
Major responsibilities were developing and maintaining sales and distribution to wholesale and retail accounts.

1972–75, McCain Foods Lt.—Inventory Analyst

Worked with sales staff and head office planning to ensure the quality and timing of shipments to brokers and stores.

Activities: Board of Directors, Richview Community Club
               Board of Directors, Volunteer Centre of Etobicoke
               Past President of Etobicoke Big Brothers
               Active in United Way
               Yachting—C&C34 Canadian Champion

Candidate's comment: It would be a great challenge and joy to work with a progressive industry leader such as Adams Brands.

Interviewer's comments: Very articulate and professionally groomed. Dominated the interview with a variety of anecdotes and humorous stories, some of which were relevant to the job. Likes to read popular books on management, particularly books that champion the bold gut-feel entrepreneur. He would probably earn more money at Adams if hired.

Case 2-3
GOLDEN BEAR DISTRIBUTORS*

John Gray, president of Golden Bear Distributors (GBD), had been pleased with his company's performance, but felt that the lack of an extensive training program for his salesmen might be a limiting factor in the company's growth plans. Thus in November 1992, Gray hired a San Francisco consulting firm to study the GBD sales force and to outline a sales-training program. Specifically, he wanted the consultants to define the training that would be best for his salesmen, to indicate the material which should be covered, and to recommend how it should be presented.

Background

Golden Bear distributed several nationally advertised brands of electrical home appliances as well as a line of home-entertainment equipment through more than 200 dealers in California. The product lines included stereos, automatic washers and dryers, vacuum cleaners, air conditioners, television sets, radios, ranges, refrigerators, garbage disposals, dishwashers, mixers, toasters, and complete kitchen installations.

GBD's sales organization included four product sales managers who reported to a general sales manager (see Exhibit 1). Each product sales manager was assigned to three or four of the company's lines and was held responsible for sales and profits.

The sales force consisted of 25 salesmen, supervised collectively by the product sales managers. Each salesman was assigned a specific geographic territory made up of approximately 4 percent of the total Retail Distribution Index of GBD's trading area.[1] Each time a new man was hired, he was assigned a territory equal in potential to the other 24 salesmen.

There was little *formal* sales training. Whenever a new man was hired, the product sales managers took turns "going the rounds" with him to acquaint him with his territory and to introduce him to his customers. Each salesman sold all of the products in the company's line; if his sales fell off in one product area, that product sales manager usually discussed at regular biweekly meetings any problems the salesmen had encountered.

Each salesman could draw a salary of $350 a week against commissions. Since the average commission rate was $2\frac{1}{2}$ percent, each salesman had to sell

---

*This case was prepared by Professor Robert T. Davis, Stanford University, Graduate School of Business. Reprinted from *Stanford Business Cases 1980* with permission of the publishers, Stanford University Graduate School of Business, © 1980 by the Board of Trustees of the Leland Stanford Junior University.

[1]Taken from *"The Survey of Buying Power," Sales & Marketing Management*, published annually.

E X H I B I T 1   *Organizational Chart*

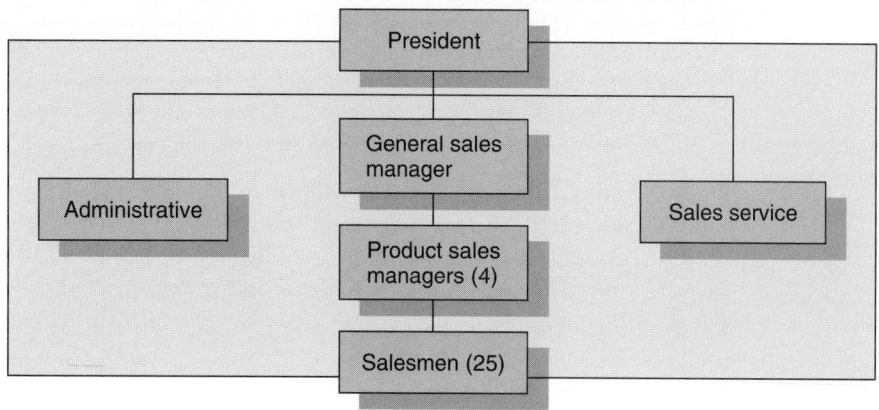

$728,000 of merchandise per year in order to cover his draw. Net annual commissions for the different salesmen varied between $20,000 and $30,000. All selling expenses were paid out of the salesmen's gross, although several salesmen received a mileage allowance when extensive travel was required.

The salesmen filled out detailed weekly route sheets describing all planned activities for the following week. In addition, they made out a daily call report which they mailed in to the home office at the end of each workday.

GBD's 200 outlets consisted primarily of small, independent merchants who account for perhaps one third of the area's total volume. The other two thirds was represented by discounters and mass merchandising chains who typically dealt directly with the suppliers, or bought through large buying groups. Although the discounters continued to grow, their increased share of the market was beginning to slow. The independents were presumably starting to offer a service alternative, as well as more aggressive pricing, which appealed to certain segments of the population. Price cutting, nonetheless, remained a serious problem for the independents.

Mr. Murphy's Interview

The consulting firm assigned the GBD account to one of its top young men, Kelvin Murphy. Murphy received an MBA from a leading western business school in 1988 and had taken a job with a large industrial equipment manufacturer upon graduation. He left his sales management job there four years later to join the consultant.

Shortly after John Gray's initial discussion with the consultants, Murphy contacted GBD's general sales manager, Lynn Philips, at the home office in Oakland. After getting some background data on the sales organization, Murphy asked Lynn for his views on sales training at GBD. He responded:

As far as I'm concerned, the training job has to be two-fold; retail salesmen need training just as much as distributor salesmen. Right now we have a policy whereby we invite dealer personnel to our home office in small groups for meetings to demonstrate and discuss all of the appliances that we carry. On the other hand, as I mentioned earlier, our salesmen's only on-the-job training is by the product sales managers. Such limited training probably isn't sufficient, but I'm not sure what kind of training they do need. That's what I expect *you* to tell *me* after you spend some time with them.

Lynn Philips then arranged for Murphy to "make the rounds" with several of GBD's salesmen. Murphy first met Bob Boatwright, who serviced part of Monterey County, south of San Francisco. Bob was 32 years old and had been with GBD over four years. His initial reaction to Murphy was, "I never hear from the office unless my sales are down"; but when Murphy explained that he was merely interested in learning how he sold as part of a general study on sales training, Bob talked more freely:

> You gotta learn to sell like a retailer sells. New salesmen oughta be given all kinds of product information, and the company should demonstrate the operation of our products to the new men.
>
> Next, you gotta follow up on the new men, so they tell their story to the retailer *every* time they go into a store. The idea is to get 'em to give the story to the retailer and his salesmen so many times that when a customer walks in the store and asks about a dishwasher, the retailer goes into the pitch on our machines automatically.
>
> According to the home office we're supposed to be "sales consultants" to the dealers, but I don't go for that much. I tried to help out a couple of small retailers once by showing 'em how I'd sell our product line, but they both thought I was trying to run their business. I think the best way is to bring the retail salesmen into the home office every once in a while and show 'em how to operate our equipment and explain it thoroughly—just like we do now. That's how to train 'em to sell.

Bob's first stop Friday afternoon was at Harry's TV and Radio Shop. Before he and Murphy went in, Bob explained his sales approach.

> I go in and say hello to the salesmen first because if there's any service problem with any of our stuff, they're sure to know about it. That way, the boss won't surprise me if something's gone wrong. Next, if I have a chance, I slip back into the stock room to see how many TVs they have left. This guy, Harry, sells TVs, and that's about all. Incidentally, most of my sales are on TVs—I can't sell many white goods down in this area.
>
> Well, after that, I usually check with the service manager to make certain that anything I've promised him in the last week or so has been taken care of. Then, of course, I tip my hat to the secretary and ask to see the boss.

When Bob entered the store, he greeted the two retail salesmen, walked over to a quiet corner of the store and conversed with one of the salesmen in low tones. Shortly thereafter, he went downstairs for about 10 minutes. When he came back upstairs, he headed for a desk at the back and motioned for Murphy to follow. He greeted the service manager and introduced Murphy as his helper. The service manager was apparently mad at GBD, and Bob in particular, because Bob had promised him a replacement transmission for an automatic washing machine that had not yet been delivered. After Bob stated that he had relayed the information to GBD's service department a week or so ago, he phoned the GBD service manager and a short, heated argument ensued. When Bob finished the call, he informed Harry's service manager that he would have to "check further." Although Harry's service manager was not satisfied, Bob explained that he wanted to see Harry first and that he would talk with him later.

Bob then knocked on a door marked *Private* and motioned Murphy to follow. As they entered, a man on the telephone looked up and waved them to a seat. After he hung up, Bob introduced Murphy and proceeded to ask Harry if there was anything he wanted in the line of TV sets. Harry answered by questioning Bob about the replacement transmission. When Bob assured him that he was following it up, Harry stated, "That's O.K. for me, Bob."

Bob then began to explain a new window display GBD had designed for its dealers for the Christmas holidays. Harry turned down the display because, "Panasonic pays me 100 bucks a year to put their line in the window during the first three weeks of December, so you can forget about that for me."

Bob glanced at his notepad and informed Harry that he needed to stock up on several models. Harry replied, "I'm OK for now, but I'll give you an order next week." After leaving Harry's office, Bob stopped by the service manager's desk and reviewed the transmission problem. Bob concluded by stating that he would check on the unit the following morning when he reported to the home office. He promised to call the service manager with a report.

As they left the store, Bob remarked, "Harry evidently wasn't in a buying mood today, but I'll definitely get an order from him next week." Since it was then nearly 4:30 P.M., Bob wanted to call it a day, but he offered to take Murphy to visit other stores on Monday if he wished.

The following week Murphy spent most of one day with Walt Warren. Walt was about 40 years old and had sold for GBD about 1½ years. He had left a comfortable job as a feed and seed wholesaler because a back injury prevented him from carrying and stacking the heavy bags of seed and grain. Walt had a large territory north of San Francisco, which covered a number of small towns. Murphy met Walt about 9:00 A.M. and they chatted over a cup of coffee before beginning their calls.

When Murphy explained that he was helping to do a study for GBD on methods of training salesmen, Walt evidently interpreted this to mean that he should talk about his job, for he started explaining his daily call routine. His suggested approach to the retailer was much the same as that voiced by Bob Boatwright.

Walt and Murphy first visited Anderson's Gas and Appliance Company, which sold butane and propane gases, as well as a large line of home appliances.

Walt quickly introduced Murphy to Mrs. Anderson, listened to a complaint about a scratched cabinet on a television set, and checked the company's inventory. After discussing with Mrs. Anderson the aggressive price cutting initiated by a local discounter, Walt took an order for four mixers. The call lasted about 20 minutes.

As they walked toward the second stop several blocks away, Walt stated, "I always try to get on a first-name basis with my retailers as soon as I can because it helps me establish rapport with them. Another thing about calling on a territory that you haven't visited in a week or so is to walk along the main street and window shop and see who's got what bargains displayed. That helps you get a 'feel' for the town. I also buy a local paper most every time I come into these little towns to see who's advertising what. I think that helps me get a feel for my competition, too."

The second call, which lasted about 45 minutes, was at a large home service center. As soon as they entered the store, Walt introduced Murphy to Joe, the owner. The following conversation took place:

Walt: *I see you're leasing a couple of our video recording systems, Joe. Great—that should help to boost your sales.*

Joe: *Yeah, that's true. But the reason I'm renting 'em is that I can't sell 'em. As long as the payments keep coming in, though, I should care.*

Walt: *Joe, portable radios and hi-fi's should be picking up pretty soon now—Christmas, you know. Over half of these sales should come in November and December.*

Joe: *What's good?*

Walt: *Everything, Joe.*

Joe: *[Looking at display] I've got some G.E.'s here, got 'em at a special price. But the last I sold was about three months ago.*
(Walt began to talk about a new warranty program on the food mixer. Joe explained he was aware of it.)

Walt: *Well, we do have a nice gift promotion on the mixers.*

Joe: *I don't need all that stuff. I've got plenty now.*

Walt: *We can send it to you prepaid you know, Joe, plus a 10 percent dating. These mixers will really go well. . . .*

Joe: *I just don't need any.*

Walt: *Well, anything else? How about taking an ad in your local paper on the automatic washer. I've never seen your newspaper feature any of our products. What's the cost over there anyway?*

Joe: *$1.60 a line.*

Walt: *Well, of course, we'd split the cost fifty-fifty with you, Joe, on any ads you'd like to run.*

Joe: *Fifty-fifty?*

Walt: *Yep, on all the lines you run with our mats.*

Joe: *On everything?*

Walt: *That's right. Just send us the tear sheets.*

Joe: *Why don't you mail me some mats then? I can use 'em.*

Walt: *O.K. Now, how about those radios, Joe?*

Joe: *Send me a couple of those new brown FM sets—you know the ones I mean.*

Walt: *The FM-36B? Yeah, that's the popular one, Joe.*

Joe: *O.K. I'll see you next week.*

Walt: *Fine, Joe, see you.*

As they left the store, Walt remarked, "Gee, sure looks like a good day. You know, the personal approach means everything in this business. I'm trying to build goodwill so that when I leave a store, those retailers will want to sell GBD because I'm a good guy. Now Joe there thinks that I'm a nice guy, so he tries to sell my line. Incidentally, the reason I pushed some advertising is that he's got to advertise if he wants to sell. These dealers often look upon advertising as a cost instead of an investment. Or they think the manufacturer should do it all."

The next stop was a new TV dealer. Walt had taken an order from the dealer for a new combination stereo TV and home recording system on the promise that it would be delivered in two days. Three days after taking the order, Walt had received a phone call from the dealer who stated that, unless the set was delivered that very day, Walt was to cancel the order. Walt commented to Murphy, "I checked with our delivery people yesterday after I got the call, and they weren't sure the set would go out. If it isn't there now, I'll be in trouble with him. Seeing as how he's a new dealer, I don't want to rock the boat."

In the TV dealer's window was the system distributed by GBD. "Well," remarked Walt, "I guess it's safe to go in." As soon as they entered the store, a thin man greeted Walt with, "The set arrived just as I was closing last night." Walt explained some of the features of the set to the dealer and gave him some literature on several other models. Then Walt inquired about what other sets the dealer was planning to install. The dealer replied that he wouldn't carry any others until he had sold this one. After a few more words, Walt and Murphy left the store. Several minutes later Walt remarked, "You know, bringing people around with you hurts your sales . . . but he's a tough dealer to sell, anyway."

Murphy and Walt then drove 20 miles to another town further north. During the trip, Walt talked about why he had left his wholesaling business and why he liked selling. When they arrived at the next stop, Walt explained, "I have to try to collect a check from the dealer and report my results back to the home office by telephone." Since the man he wished to see was not in, he made arrangements to call back later that afternoon.

During lunch at a small diner, Walt talked more about the seed and grain business. He also expressed a desire to obtain a territory closer to the city. After lunch, as they began walking toward the next call, they passed a newly renovated hardware store. Walt paused, "This is a new store. I haven't got them for an account. It's just possible they haven't got a kitchen line. I think I'll go in cold and see what I can do." They entered the store and looked around for a clerk. A woman came out, and Walt explained the purpose of his call, stating that his company had just started up with a new line of complete kitchen installations. When he mentioned the brand name, the woman remarked that the store carried that line, and added that she could show it to him. In a corner of the store, a complete kitchen was installed in a little room off the main part of the building. The woman explained that she and her husband had recently purchased the store and were in the process of renovating it. Walt noticed the fixtures that she had and explained that on his next call he would supply her with some promotional material on the line. He also added that the distributor who formerly handled the line had gone out of business and that GBD would gladly provide them with the components from now on. The woman thanked him, and they left the store.

• • • • •

After similar experiences traveling with three other salesmen, Kelvin Murphy felt that he had a good feeling for the GBD selling job and its requirements. Since two men were retiring soon from GBD's sales force, John Gray was very anxious that Murphy complete his recommendations for a sales training program before new men had to be hired to take over the territories. Thus, Murphy began outlining a training program for GBD that would include recommendations for training dealer sales personnel as well as the firm's own salesmen.

Case 2-4
STONE & LEWIS*

Introduction

Tony Grant had just been appointed the new sales manager of the San Diego district in the Health Care Products Division of Stone & Lewis. He was leaving a job as a very successful section sales manager within the Phoenix, Arizona, district of the Personal Care Division of the company. The Personal Care Division produces consumer products, as is true for all of the other divisions of Stone & Lewis except for the new Health Care Products Division. Based on his past performance as a sales rep and section sales manager, he was among the select few who were expected to advance to upper-level management. He had interviewed for the job less than two weeks ago and was now in his second day at his new position. His predecessor, Ken Burns, had left the company suddenly, and Tony had been given very little information as to the circumstances surrounding Ken's decision to leave. Tony had unsuccessfully tried to reach Ken to discuss the situation.

During the interview process, the Southern California regional sales manager of the division, Reed Taylor, had seemed reluctant to talk about the situation. He had emphasized what a great opportunity the new job would be for Tony to add to his experience by learning to deal with the problems of managing a sales force of approximately 25 people. He had seemed intent on selling Tony on the merits of the job and how it would be a necessary step in advancing his career. However, Tony had been unable to get a clear picture of exactly what types of problems he would be facing. The regional manager had seemed very eager to fill the district manager's position and had sidestepped any serious discussion of the job's negative aspects. Tony believed there were more problems than Reed Taylor was willing to discuss. However, after carefully considering what he knew of the situation, Tony decided to accept the job, thinking it would offer interesting challenges.

What little information Tony could gather in the short time before he accepted the job came from talking with the regional manager and through brief contacts with some of the other district sales managers in the Southern California region. He had found out that sales force turnover in the division was much higher than the average for the company as a whole. While the company had experienced a fairly steady annual turnover rate of 15 percent of the sales force over the past five years, the Health Care Products Division had annual turnover rates averaging 65 percent over the last three years. As

---

*Christopher G. Gilmore and Christopher J. Pitts assisted in preparing this case.

if this was not bad enough, the San Diego district had experienced nearly 225 percent turnover in the past 18 months, meaning that on the average, a sales rep would be on the job only eight months before leaving. Tony learned that of all the employees in his district who had left their jobs in the past two years, only five had accepted new positions within the company. The rest had left the company.

After Tony accepted the new job, he talked with his three new section managers, each of whom supervised between six and eight sales and technical support employees. His impressions after these conversations reinforced his growing suspicions that he would be facing serious personnel problems. While it was obvious that turnover was a major problem, he sensed that his section managers were unwilling to admit to the seriousness of the situation. Each of them seemed preoccupied with presenting a picture of stability and convincing Tony they had the situation under control. They were all quick to point out that for the latest year, which had ended four months ago, they had been fairly successful in meeting the sales volume quotas for their respective areas. Only the Los Angeles area had failed to reach its objective, but it had achieved 96 percent of its targeted sales volume. For the San Diego district as a whole, the sales objective had even been exceeded by 1 percent.

Tony had told the section managers that he was impressed with these results. However, he secretly wondered if the sales force was performing as well as it could. Last year's quotas had been set at volumes that were essentially the same as for the year before, but the previous district manager's files indicated he and the division sales management had extensively debated whether to increase quotas. It appeared the district manager had won his case by keeping quota increases to a minimum. This was surprising because the business in which the Health Care Products Division was operating was widely considered to be a growth industry. Aside from the fact that his section managers seemed a little too content with such apparently insignificant sales volume progress, Tony was disturbed by their lack of concern over the high level of turnover among the sales force. He decided a much closer look would be needed to uncover possible causes of the problems facing his district.

Background Information

Stone & Lewis occupies a prominent position as a leading manufacturer and marketer of household consumer goods and personal care products. The majority of the company's products are sold in grocery stores and similar retail establishments. The company was founded over 75 years ago, and it has established a strong marketing tradition of advertising and promoting its products very heavily. Noted for its marketing-driven approach to sales, Stone & Lewis is also known for its conservative approach to innovation, which is usually the result of very extensive product testing and market research. The company has been criticized for being too slow to react to changing markets with the result that it was being beaten by competitors in the introduction of new products.

Seven years ago, Stone & Lewis diversified its line of products by moving into the growing and highly profitable area of health-care products. The company acquired a pharmaceutical manufacturing firm that already produced some very successful nonprescription medicines. At the same time, the company began testing its own new product for adults with incontinence, or the inability to control bowel and bladder function. The new product, known as PRO-TEKS disposable briefs, is a revolutionary concept. It incorporates a patented plastic inner lining containing "mini-sorbs," which is extremely effective in drawing moisture away from the wearer's skin and trapping it in an absorbent fiber padding between the inner and outer linings.

The ability to keep skin drier for longer periods would mean healthier skin for incontinent patients in nursing homes and hospitals. Skin care is a major issue. With proper skin care, bedsores can be avoided. In some surgical cases, without proper skin care the patient may have to return for more surgery. At the same time, nursing staffs would be able to provide proper patient care with less effort and much greater convenience than afforded by other incontinence products, most of which were judged to be highly inferior to PRO-TEKS.

The basic PRO-TEKS brief is available in three sizes: small, medium, and large. The briefs have recently been improved by the addition of refastenable tapes, which allow a nurse to check a patient's condition without having to replace the brief each time. Both briefs and pads also have a pH strip that changes color when urine is present. The strips can be easily viewed by a nurse.

PRO-TEKS has now been on the market for three years and is currently the only product sold by the Health Care Products Division. Exhibit 1 shows the organization of the division. This organization is identical to other divisions of Stone & Lewis. Sales volume is generated primarily through nursing homes, retirement and health-care centers, and rehabilitation centers. Hospitals, clinics, and medical supply stores provide a fair amount of additional sales. The product can be purchased directly from the company, but the majority of sales are made to independent wholesale distributors, which then sell to final customers. Exhibit 2 illustrates the distribution of PRO-TEKS.

PRO-TEKS is easily the most expensive product on the market, but the company and many health-care professionals also believe it is the best product available. Exhibit 3 presents an evaluation of the available products prepared by an independent testing agency. PRO-TEKS currently holds a 24 percent market share. It has achieved its greatest success in Florida and the southwestern states where large numbers of relatively wealthy elderly persons reside.

The two strongest competitors are AmCo and Allied United, which are perceived by the market as having high quality products. They have current market shares of 17 percent and 10 percent, respectively. The choice of 31 percent of the market is reusable cloth diapers that require laundering. The remainder of the market uses lower quality disposable products of various types.

PRO-TEKS are sold by a sales force that includes regular Stone & Lewis

E X H I B I T **1**   *Organization of Health Care Products Division: Stone & Lewis*

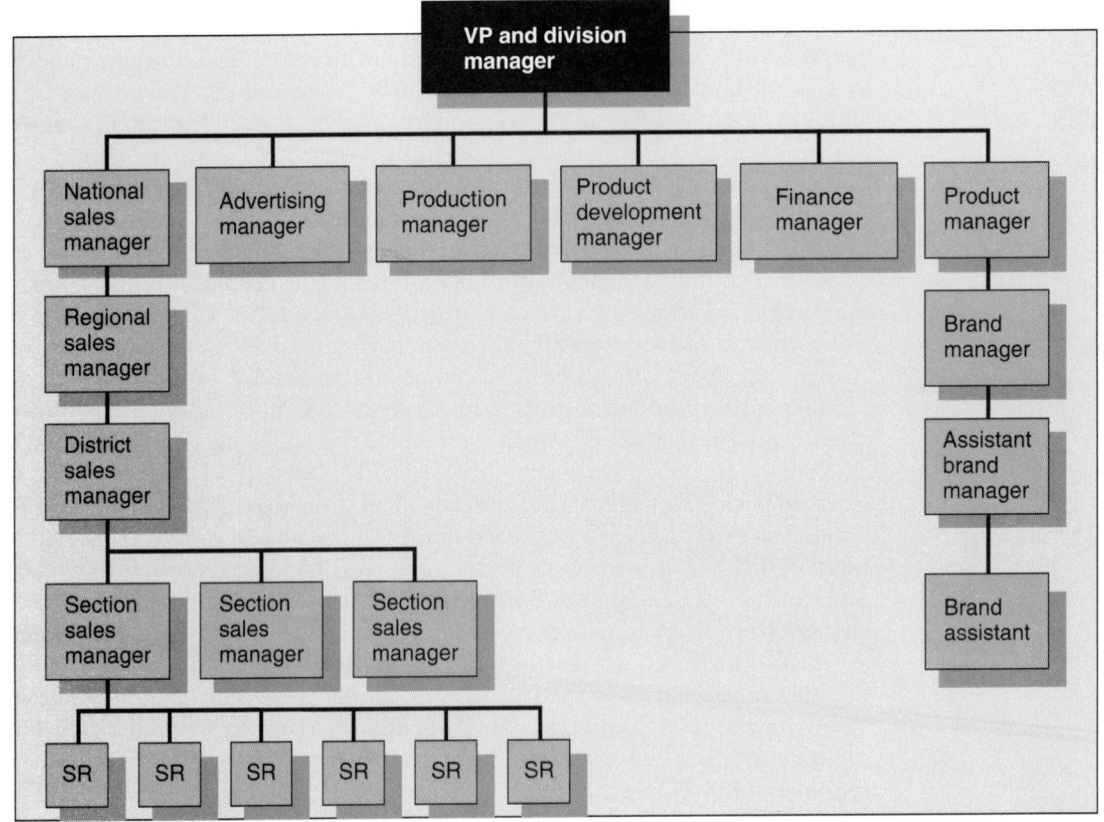

sales representatives of the Health Care Products Division and nurses hired under contract from the HCR Corporation to provide technical selling assistance. The standard selling procedure includes a sales rep presentation to a prospective account. The presentation emphasizes the benefits of the product in keeping patients' skin in better condition, reducing laundry costs and labor, and improving the smell and condition of the living environment within the facility to make a favorable impression on the patients' families and other visitors to the facility.

The account can be further persuaded to try PRO-TEKS by receiving free products for three weeks for all of its incontinent patients. The support nurses are on hand to administer the trial and to instruct the facility's staff on the proper use of the product. At the end of the three-week evaluation period, the sales rep returns to summarize the results, which are expected to include

EXHIBIT 2   *Distribution of PRO-TEKS*

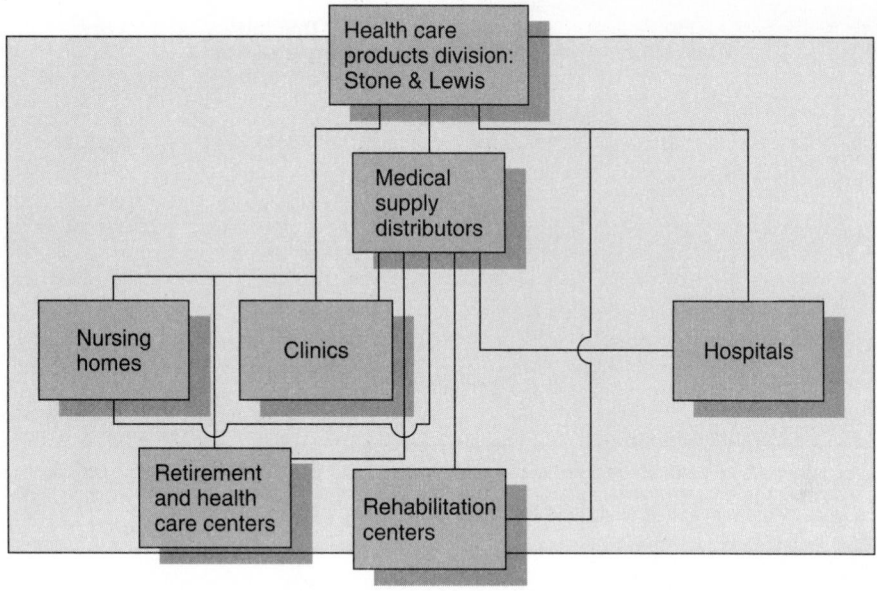

improved patient skin care and actual or potential cost savings due to reduced laundry and labor. Cost savings at times have been very substantial due to a reduced demand for labor. In some cases, positions have been eliminated.

Much cooperation is required from the account and its staff to use the product correctly and to accumulate the necessary information to show cost savings. This type of product and the methods by which it is sold are substantially different from the traditional consumer package goods produced by other business units within Stone & Lewis (with their heavy emphasis on advertising and promotions) in which the company has been traditionally engaged and on which it has built its great strength.

One Week Later

Now that Tony had been on the new job for over a week, he had gathered more information from his sales reps and other district managers that would provide clues as to what actions he would need to take to improve the operation of his district. The following is a summary of his findings.

1. The system of sales rep performance evaluation is based on a measure of the number of accounts that are sold, the number maintained as active customers, and the number of "theoretical" incontinent patients at each of

EXHIBIT 3   *Product Comparison Analysis*

Company/ Brand	Fit/ Wearability	Absorbency/ Leakage Protection	Comfort/ Breathability	Price/ Case	Quantity/ Case
Stone & Lewis PRO-TEKS	8	10	10	$39.17 47.64 42.32	60 60 40
AmCo RE-LYS	7	7	6	46.24 58.50 40.32	96 96 84
Allied United COM-FORTS	10	8	7	51.60 66.48 60.80	120 120 80
AmCo Cloth diapers	2	4	8	36.82 31.12 36.82	300 200 150

Note: All companies produce three sizes. Above prices are for small, medium, and large sizes. Rating scale information is based on a 10-point scale with 1 representing a weak product characteristic and 10 a strong product characteristic. According to MED-TECH, leakage protection and breathability are the most important product features.

Source: MED-TECH Testing Laboratory Analysis.

these accounts. Theoretical users are determined by multiplying the number of beds in a facility by standard demographically based statistical percentages that indicate the expected number of incontinent patients for different types of facilities. Sales reps are given objectives as to the number of theoretical users that are to be added within a given short-run time period, typically monthly or quarterly. Sales reps are then responsible for keeping their own records of which accounts are active buyers and therefore how many theoretical users they can take credit for. The results are reported by the sales reps to their section managers each month.

There is currently no other way for these numbers to be compiled, and the managers have no easy way of assessing their accuracy. The general feeling among the sales force seems to be that there is much cheating going on as to how many accounts reported are actually active buyers. This has created some bitter feelings because pay raises and promotions have been based to some extent on this measure of performance and because some of the more ambitious sales reps have apparently succeeded at reporting inflated results for the number of theoretical users.

The negative effects of this situation are compounded by the fact that the standard "theoretical" percentages used in calculating performance results usually bear little resemblance to the proportion of actual users in any given facility. Therefore, a sales rep may receive too much or too little credit for the actual contribution to the company from any given account.

2. Part of the reason for the inability of managers to check the accuracy

of sales reps' reported results is the method by which the product is distributed. The company has traditionally used independent distributors to make its products available to end consumers, and this method has been carried over into the PRO-TEKS business. The company has tried to make the product as widely available as possible and has therefore recruited a large number of medical supply distributors. Sales reps perform a missionary sales function by persuading end-users to buy the product, but the company generally sells only to the distributors. Because the distributors are often unwilling to disclose who their customers are and how much they are buying, the company has no way of accumulating the information on which to base actual sales results to end-user accounts. This presents a much different situation from the retail store setting in which the company has traditionally done business and for which highly organized methods and services are available for auditing end-user buying.

3. Section sales managers are evaluated on the volume of sales to distributors within their territories. However, the end-users within a given section manager's territory cannot be required to buy from distributors within that territory. Distributors compete against each other on price and order servicing, and it is not unusual for a distributor in one territory to lower its price of PRO-TEKS to lure customers in another area manager's territory. Section managers compete with each other by trying to persuade distributors in their respective territories to adjust prices or service or by "requesting" that their sales reps persuade end-users to buy only from their own distributors. Pushing end-users to buy from a particular distributor, when that distributor consistently fails to match the price or service of a competitor in another territory, may damage the total PRO-TEKS business for the company. Aside from this, sales reps may feel caught in the middle between two battling section managers, with the result that their own performance suffers due to lost accounts.

4. Sales reps report that they often lose sales because the expected cost savings fail to materialize. This is often due to uncooperativeness on the part of the facility staff in providing complete and accurate costs for a before- and after-PRO-TEKS comparison. In addition, the staffs often include a majority of low-paid and unmotivated aides who actually perform the tasks associated with the use of the product. In such a situation, it would be difficult for the sales force to provide the necessary level of training and supervision for using the product and for providing for a well-controlled evaluation.

5. Essentially all prospective accounts have been contacted since PRO-TEKS was introduced. When repeat calls are made to accounts that do not use the product, sales reps report they are often confronted by decision makers who tell them not to come back until they have something new to offer. The price of the product places it beyond the budget of many potential accounts, and they often have very strong preconceived negative impressions about the product. In some cases this results from the fact that PRO-TEKS are made from a plastic material and many of the nurses on facility staffs have been trained on the merits of traditional cloth products. When refastenable tapes

EXHIBIT 4   *Sample Daily Call Plan*

Name	Active Account	Number of Beds	Percent Occupancy	Percent Theoretically Incontinent	People to See*
Alvarado Hospital	Yes	214	58.2	10.0	PA GER DN SW
San Diego P&S Hospital	Yes	156	76.4	10.0	ADM DN
San Diego P&S Retirement Home	Yes	78	64.1	35.0	ADM
Mercy Hospital	No	457	70.3	10.0	PA GER DN SW
Sharp Memorial Hospital & Rehabilitative Center	Yes	415	76.1	10.0	PA DN SW GER ADM
St. Paul's Health Care Center	No	86	95.3	35.0	ADM DN

*ADM = Administrator
 GER = Gerontologist
 DN = Director of Nursing
 PA = Purchasing Agent
 SW = Social Worker

were introduced to PRO-TEKS, many accounts regarded this as insignificant and were therefore unimpressed by sales reps' claims that this was something new.

Sales reps are often told by accounts that they are simply hard-selling over and over again on the same worn out themes, and in doing so they encounter great resistance from potential accounts. In many sales reps' opinions, the company is not responsive enough to the needs of the market and is not providing a sufficient product line to the sales reps. The reps believe the company is failing to meet the needs of customers with different financial constraints or different philosophies toward incontinent care.

6. Most account's facilities are headed by an administrator, who is concerned with overall management and financial considerations. However, there is also typically a director of nursing who is responsible for the facility's patient care operations. In the usual selling situation, the sales rep must persuade both persons to buy the product, although the administrator has the final authority.

The two authorities often have conflicting goals: the director of nursing is interested in providing the best possible care and may be convinced of the product's merits, but the administrator sees only the short-run costs of buying an expensive product. Alternatively, the administrator may be convinced that PRO-TEKS will reduce overall costs of supplies and labor, but the nursing director and/or the rest of the staff may be opposed to using the product. The result is that the sales rep must often contend with selling to more than one decision maker, whose goals are in opposition.

As the size of the facility increases, the sales rep typically must call on more people. In addition to those already mentioned, other people include the director of gerontology, usually a doctor, and the social worker. Social workers are important contacts (influentials) since they are in a position to recommend services and products that patients will need on discharge from the medical center. Exhibit 4 illustrates a daily call plan for one of Tony Grant's sales reps.

7. A final consideration is that while the product may be the best quality available and would be chosen by the patient, the patient usually has no choice in the matter. Budget constraints in some cases render quality considerations unimportant. This is particularly true for the majority of patients in nursing homes who receive varying degrees of governmental assistance to pay for the care they receive. The current economic and fiscal climates have resulted in a reduction in government subsidies for health care of institutionalized patients.

After reviewing the information he had gathered, Tony thought he had some clues about where to find possible causes of his district's high turnover problems. His next task would be to decide what could be done to eliminate or reduce some of these problems. He would have to plan action for his own district and make recommendations to the regional and divisional sales managers to improve performance.

Case 2-5
ASSOCIATED DIRECTORIES, INC.*

When the U.S. Justice Department ordered the splitting up of AT&T, many of the telephone company's side businesses were granted greater freedom to expand the geographic and commercial scope of their operations. They were also immediately exposed to the competitive pressures of the nonregulated world. One of the most profitable of these side businesses was telephone directory publication. Under the protective umbrella of the phone companies, this business flourished and, in essence, subsidized the telecommunications network. Now that these businesses were open to competition, many new entrants, both inside and outside the "Baby Bell" companies, were attracted by the market and its apparent promise of high profits.

Bill Caldwell had long been active in the directory industry. His career included a stint as a salesman for one of the Bell publishing companies, and he subsequently worked for several other directory publishing concerns. At 40, Bill was looking for something more challenging than his present district sales manager's position. Gradually, the concept of a new directory product began to take shape in his mind.

The New Directory

Bill's idea was to create a directory that listed a wide range of travel-related services for a geographic area much broader than the typical Yellow Pages directories. This directory would give families planning vacations a ready source of information on all the services offered along their route. Bill thought that if the geographic scope of the directory was limited to a single state it could be distributed as a natural adjunct to the information provided by the state tourism bureaus and local travel agents.

The total market for this directory in any given state would not be enough to support more than one dominant publisher. Thus, for the venture to succeed, it had to capture a preemptive share of each market entered. The coverage and intensity of the selling effort clearly emerged as *the* critical factor in attaining this objective.

As the concept for this directory was refined, it became clear that there would be three categories of advertising in each edition:

1. *Classified regional services.* This section would include all of the classified, single-line, Yellow Page-type listings broken into logical geographic regions

---

*This case was prepared with the assistance of Professor Jonlee Andrews, Case Western Reserve University, and K. Richard Berlet, TRIAD Consultants.

EXHIBIT 1

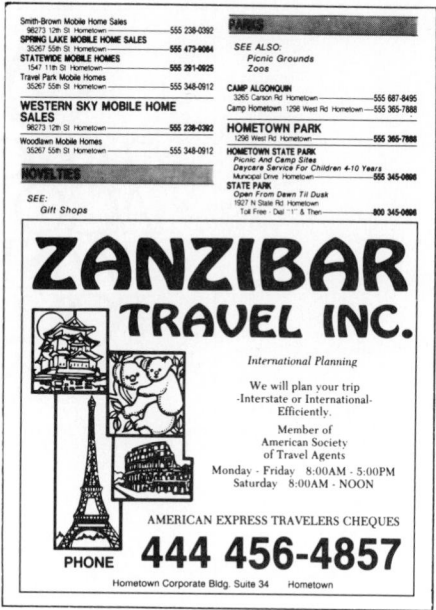

of each state. It would also include display ads of various sizes (see Exhibit 1).

2. *Statewide events and attractions.* Special events or unique attractions in the state would be advertised in the editorial (text) section of the directory in much the same format as a conventional magazine (see Exhibit 2).

3. *National advertising.* Major travelers' services (e.g., car rental agencies, hotels) and general travel-related products (e.g., automobiles, golfing equipment, luggage) would advertise in magazine format and would probably be placed in several state directories at one time (see Exhibit 3).

Bill recognized that the advertising rates and revenues for his new product would, like a conventional magazine, ultimately depend on readership. The more "exposures" each advertisement had to potential buyers, the more an advertiser would pay for the space. The number of exposures would depend on two factors: the utility of the directory as perceived by its intended audience and the effectiveness of the directory's distribution channels.

If the classifications in the directory did not evenly represent the full range of travel services, or if major gaps in geographic coverage emerged, the utility of the directory would be diminished. Since AT&T was required to provide its directory competitors with a list of Yellow Pages advertisers, Bill's new directory could use these listings to help round out the single-line classifications in his directory. These listings would also be used as a source of prospective

OVER 2,000 YEARS AGO THREE WISE MEN FOLLOWED A STAR.

THIS YEAR YOU CAN JOIN THEM.

This year The Adler Planetarium is pleased to present the 56th showing of *Star of Wonder.*

You'll see what the Wise Men saw as we recreate the sky as it was then. And you'll follow them as they follow this brightest of Stars across the heavens.

For a sight and sound spectacular not to be missed, don't miss *Star of Wonder,* December 3rd thru January 2nd. Weekdays at 2 PM. Fridays also at 8 PM. Saturdays and Sundays at 11 AM, 1, 2, 3, and 4 PM.

Also showing thru January 2nd, *Return of Halley's Comet.* For showtimes call 322-0300. Admission to either show is $2.50 for adults, $1.50 for children (6-17).

Children under six are welcome at our Special Children's Sky Show, *Stargazing with Meteor Mouse,* Saturdays at 10 AM. $1.50 for adults and children.

Please join us for any one or all of these informative and engaging shows.

THE ADLER PLANETARIUM
Bringing the Universe Down to Earth.

We are located at 1300 South Lake Shore Drive. If you drive, there's plenty of parking. Or take the #146 Marine/Michigan Avenue bus to the door. For more information, call 322-0300 anytime.

EXHIBIT 3

When Your Travel Plans Expand, So Should Your Garment Bag.

Ah, the bag's packed and you're enjoying that last cup of coffee.
Ring.
"I'll get it."
One phone call, and your three-day trip just became a six-day trip.
A quick zip and your three-day garment bag has just become a six-day garment bag. That's why we call our zipper the FasTrac, and it's on a garment bag where the main clothing compartment can instantly double in size. It's the Lark Expand·Able™ Garment Bag, one of seven Lark Expand·Able™ luggage styles.
And by the way, if you're not as wild about our new Pewter or Classic Black as we are, well, there are seven other colors to choose from.
So, finish the coffee and kiss your family goodbye. They may find the three extra days hard to take, but your garment bag won't.

Lark®

Luggage For Your Expanding Needs.™

© 1985 Lark Luggage Co., P.O. Box 390094, Denver, Co. 80239, (800) 782-7555

Reprinted with permission of Lark Luggage Co., Inc., Denver, Colorado.

advertising customers, and the utility of the directory would be increased further by convincing many of these prospects to purchase display ads that would provide travel directions, hours, and other useful information.

Even if the directory satisfactorily fulfilled the coverage objectives, it would be viewed as a success by the advertisers only if it was broadly circulated on a timely basis. Thus, the state tourism bureaus and the travel agency associations were also critical ingredients to the success of the venture.

The Business Plan

Bill developed a business plan for the first year of operations. He included several assumptions about the pricing of advertising and structure of the first editions of the directory. The assumptions included expectations about the size and mix of black and white and color ads that would be sold. He considered these assumptions to be reasonable for a new venture; however, he wanted to encourage the sales force to sell larger ads and color ads.

Because in most states tourism is highly seasonal, it was projected that there would be a fall and spring edition of each directory. An initial pricing schedule for the classified service and statewide/national advertising space was developed to reflect the relative costs and profitability of the various-sized ads (see Exhibit 4).

| EXHIBIT 4 | Advertising Rates | | |

Ad Size	Black/White	2-Color	4-Color
A. Statewide and National Advertising:			
Full page	$4,700	$5,500	$6,300
$2/3$ page	3,500	4,100	4,700
$1/2$ page	2,800	3,300	3,800
$1/3$ page	2,100	2,500	2,800
$1/6$ page	1,200	1,400	n.a.*
B. Classified Services Advertising:			
Full page	2,700	3,000	3,500
$2/3$ page	2,000	2,300	2,600
$1/2$ page	1,600	1,800	2,100
$1/3$ page	1,200	1,400	1,600
$1/6$ page	700	800	900
$1/12$ page	400	n.a.	n.a.
Boldface	75	n.a.	n.a.

n.a. = not available

The statewide/national section of the directory planned for one state was expected to contribute $120,000 in revenues during the first year. An average page revenue of $4,500 was used to estimate the number of equivalent pages (27) that must be sold to meet the revenue objective of the first two editions. The average page revenue was based on the pricing schedule and several assumptions about the mix of black and white, two-color, and four-color ads of various sizes that would be sold. Each equivalent page was expected to have an average of three advertisements, of sizes varying from one-sixth page to a full page, contributing to the total revenue target.

The classified section of this state's directory was projected to contribute $500,000 in revenues during the first year (split between fall and spring editions). Based on preliminary market research, Bill anticipated that a typical classified page would contain about 40 items, including a mix of display ads, ranging in size from a boldface listing to one-half page, and single-line listings. Furthermore, he expected that 85 percent of the items on a typical page would be single-line listings (which contribute no revenue). Although increasing the average size of display ads would reduce unit production costs, Bill thought the 40-item page—with five or six display ads per page—was an appropriate target. Based on similar assumptions about the size and color mix of a typical ad page, the projected revenue per equivalent page for the classified section was set at $2,500. To meet the targeted revenue, 200 pages of classified ads must be sold.

EXHIBIT 5   *Competitive Compensation Data*

| Position Match (source) | Industry | Survey Medians | |
		Base Salary	Total Compensation
A. Face-to-Face Sales Representatives:			
Sales rep*	Printing and publishing	$23,000	$30,600
Senior sales rep*	Printing and publishing	28,200	38,000
Sales rep†	Publishing		42,200
Retail sales rep‡	Newspaper publishing		28,000
Retail sales rep§	Newspaper publishing	28,000	33,600
B. Telephone Sales Representatives:			
Telemarketing rep*	Consumer products	20,900	24,900
Telemarketing rep*	Other commerce and industry	19,800	21,800

*Executive Compensation Service (ECS) (1985)
†Dartnell Research Institute (1985)
‡Custom survey (1984)
§Custom survey (1984)

Sales Force Decisions

Bill believed the selling effort would differ greatly for the classified and magazine-format advertising categories he had defined. His experience with the Bell publishing units suggested that the most efficient way to sell to the classified section advertisers was through telephone solicitation and follow up by mail. On the other hand, the statewide and national categories would likely be sold to media directors at ad agencies or directly to major advertisers. Bill thought this selling effort would require a relatively sophisticated face-to-face approach. He concluded that two sales forces would be necessary: a telemarketing group for classified ads and a field group for statewide and national ads.

Because of the importance of the selling function, Bill prepared a list of the decisions he had to make and continued to compile information pertaining to these decisions. The initial steps in recruiting the sales forces were to determine the staffing levels for each force and to establish a budget for the related personnel cost. Once these tasks were completed, he had to determine a target level of total compensation for each selling position, specify the goals and corresponding performance measures of the compensation plan, and select the proper mix of salary and incentive pay.

Bill realized the decisions he had before him were crucial. He canceled his lunch engagement and settled in to sift through the information he had collected.

The business plan indicated that, to ensure a profit, personnel costs for the sales forces must be no greater than 25 percent of revenues. For the two sales forces, a total budget of about $160,000 was available. In reviewing published compensation surveys, the data presented in Exhibit 5 could be used to help plan the staffing and compensation levels for the organization.

Bill drew on his prior experience with other directory sales organizations to further evaluate staffing levels. He knew that in each edition's selling cycle there would be approximately 100 selling days to close the directory. He anticipated that the close rate (number of calls required for each sale) for statewide and national advertising would be 1 in every 10 calls; whereas, in the classified section, the rate would be 1 in 5. With these assumptions, the competitive compensation data, the sales personnel cost budget, and the revenue targets in hand, Bill was ready to set staffing levels and productivity targets for each salesperson.

Having established staff levels, Bill then had to analyze the selling jobs to determine what pay systems would work best in the new organization. The newness of the organization would have to be considered in recruiting the sales personnel, since this added insecurity might affect the attractiveness of the jobs.

The Bell publishing companies had used a straight commission pay plan that was tied to total advertising revenue. Bill was convinced this was not appropriate for his new venture. He wanted his compensation program to create a real team spirit among the salespeople and reinforce a keen awareness of their contribution to the success of the venture. He knew he must offer some form of compensation that would offset the risk inherent in joining the new company.

The *telemarketing* job would require a high-intensity effort on the part of the salesperson since each market had a large number of prospects. Also, at least in the initial selling campaign, the product was unknown to the advertiser. On the other hand, the typical customer for the classified ad was a small retail business with a relatively small advertising budget. Often, directory advertising was the only type of advertising used by these customers. Therefore, although intense, the selling effort was not expected to be complex or time-consuming.

As noted earlier, the expected close rate for this sales force was relatively high since the customer's expenditure would be quite small and the decision process simple. Bill was particularly interested in maintaining a consistent and well-directed effort throughout the campaign. This would maximize his coverage and establish a broad base of advertisers for the renewal campaign in subsequent editions. He knew the renewal rate for directory advertising was usually high and recognized that some modification in the compensation programs might be required in the second year, once a customer base was established.

The *field selling* effort (for statewide and national ads) was expected to be somewhat lower in intensity and higher in sophistication. The number of prospects was much smaller than for the classified section, the advertisements were usually more complex in design and production, and the decision process for some ads could include several functions or people within the customer's organization. Bill expected the close rate for this sales force to be about half of that for the telemarketing force, primarily due to the multiple calls required and the more analytical selling approach demanded by the customer.

Case 2-6
OUTDOOR SPORTING PRODUCTS, INC.*

The annual sales volume of Outdoor Sporting Products, Inc., for the past six years had ranged between $6.2 million and $6.8 million. Although profits continued to be satisfactory, Mr. Hudson McDonald, president and chief operating officer, was concerned because sales had not increased appreciably from year to year. Consequently, he asked a consultant in New York City and the officers of the company to submit proposals for improving the salesmen's compensation plan, which he believed was the basic weakness in the firm's marketing operations.

Outdoor's factory and warehouse were located in Albany, New York, where the company manufactured and distributed sporting equipment, clothing, and accessories. Mr. McDonald, who managed the company, organized it in 1956 when he envisioned a growing market for sporting goods resulting from the predicted increase in leisure time and the rising levels of income in the United States.

Products of the company, numbering approximately 700 items, were grouped into three lines: (1) fishing supplies, (2) hunting supplies, and (3) accessories. The fishing supplies line, which accounted for approximately 40 percent of the company's annual sales, included nearly every item a fisherman would need such as fishing jackets, vests, caps, rods and reels of all types, lines, flies, lures, landing nets, and creels. Thirty percent of annual sales were in the hunting supplies line, which consisted of hunting clothing of all types including insulated and thermal underwear, safety garments, shell holders, whistles, calls, and gun cases. The accessories line, which made up the balance of the company's annual sales volume, included items such as compasses, cooking kits, lanterns, hunting and fishing knives, hand warmers, and novelty gifts.

While the sales of the hunting and fishing lines were very seasonal, they tended to complement one another. The January–April period accounted for the bulk of the company's annual volume in fishing items, and most sales of hunting supplies were made from May through August. Typically, the company's sales of all products reached their lows for the year during December.

Outdoor's sales volume was $6.37 million in the current year with self-manufactured products accounting for 35 percent of this total. Fifty percent of the company's volume consisted of imported products, which came principally from Japan. Items manufactured by other domestic producers and distributed by Outdoor accounted for the remaining 15 percent of total sales.

Mr. McDonald reported that wholesale prices to retailers were established

*Adapted from a case written by Zarrel V. Lambert, Auburn University, and Fred W. Kniffin, University of Connecticut, Stamford. Used with permission.

by adding a markup of 50 to 100 percent to Outdoor's cost for the item. This rule was followed on self-manufactured products as well as for items purchased from other manufacturers. The resulting average markup across all products was 70 percent on cost.

Outdoor's market area consisted of the New England states, New York, Pennsylvania, Ohio, Michigan, Wisconsin, Indiana, Illinois, Kentucky, Tennessee, West Virginia, Virginia, Maryland, Delaware, and New Jersey. The area over which Outdoor could effectively compete was limited to some extent by shipping costs, since all orders were shipped from the factory and warehouse in Albany.

Outdoor's salesmen sold to approximately 6,000 retail stores in small- and medium-sized cities in its market area. Analysis of sales records showed that the firm's customer coverage was very poor in the large metropolitan areas. Typically, each account was a one- or two-store operation. Mr. McDonald stated that he knew Outdoor's share of the market was very low, perhaps 2 to 3 percent; and for all practical purposes, he felt the company's sales potential was unlimited.

Mr. McDonald believed that with few exceptions, Outdoor's customers had little or no brand preference and in the vast majority of cases they bought hunting and fishing supplies from several suppliers.

It was McDonald's opinion that the pattern of retail distribution for hunting and fishing products had been changing during the past 10 years as a result of the growth of discount stores. He thought that the proportion of retail sales for hunting and fishing supplies made by small- and medium-sized sporting goods outlets had been declining compared to the percent sold by discounters and chain stores. An analysis of company records revealed Outdoor had not developed business among the discounters with the exception of a few small discount stores. Some of Outdoor's executives felt that the lack of business with discounters might have been due in part to the company's pricing policy and in part to the pressures current customers had exerted on company salesmen to keep them from calling on the discounters.

Outdoor's Sales Force

The company's sales force played the major role in its marketing efforts since Outdoor did not use magazine, newspaper, or radio advertising to reach either the retail trade or consumers. One advertising piece that supplemented the work of the salesmen was Outdoor's merchandise catalog. It contained a complete listing of all the company's products and was mailed to all retailers who were either current accounts or prospective accounts. Typically, store buyers used the catalog for reordering.

Most accounts were contacted by a salesman two or three times a year. The salesmen planned their activities so that each store would be called on at the beginning of the fishing season and again before the hunting season. Certain key accounts of some salesmen were contacted more often than two or three times a year.

Management believed that product knowledge was the major ingredient of a successful sales call. Consequently, Mr. McDonald had developed a "selling formula," which each salesman was required to learn before he took over a territory. The "formula" contained five parts: (1) the name and catalog number of each item sold by the company; (2) the sizes and colors in which each item was available; (3) the wholesale price of each item; (4) the suggested retail price of each item; and (5) the primary selling features of each item. After a new salesman had mastered the product knowledge specified by this "formula" he began working in his assigned territory and was usually accompanied by Mr. McDonald for several weeks.

Managing the sales force consumed approximately one third of Mr. McDonald's efforts. The remaining two thirds of his time was spent purchasing products for resale and in general administrative duties as the company's chief operating officer.

Mr. McDonald held semiannual sales meetings, had weekly telephone conversations with each salesman, and had mimeographed bulletins containing information on products, prices, and special promotional deals mailed to all salesmen each week. Daily call reports and attendance at the semiannual sales meetings were required of all salesmen. One meeting was held the first week in January to introduce the spring line of fishing supplies. The hunting line was presented at the second meeting, which was scheduled in May. Each of these sales meetings spanned four to five days so the salesmen were able to study the new products being introduced and any changes in sales and company policies. The production manager and comptroller attended these sales meetings to answer questions and to discuss problems the salesmen might have concerning deliveries and credit.

On a predetermined schedule, each salesman telephoned Mr. McDonald every Monday morning to learn of changes in prices, special promotional offers, and delivery schedules of unshipped orders. At this time, the salesman's activities for the week were discussed, and sometimes the salesman was asked by Mr. McDonald to collect past due accounts in his territory. In addition, the salesmen submitted daily call reports, which listed the name of each account contacted and the results of the call. Generally, the salesmen planned their own itineraries in terms of the accounts and prospects that were to be contacted and the amount of time to be spent on each call.

Outdoor's sales force during the current year totaled 11 full-time employees. Their ages ranged from 23 to 67 years, and their tenure with the company ranged from 1 to 10 years. Salesmen, territories, and sales volumes for the previous year and the current year are shown in Exhibit 1.

Compensation of Salesmen

The salesmen were paid straight commissions on their dollar sales volume for the calendar year. The commission rate was 5 percent on the first $300,000, 6 percent on the next $200,000 in volume, and 7 percent on all sales over

EXHIBIT   1   *Salesmen: Age, Years of Service, Territory, and Sales*

Salesmen	Age	Years of Service	Territory	Sales Previous year	Sales Current Year
Allen	45	2	Illinois and Indiana	$ 330,264	$ 329,216
Campbell	62	10	Pennsylvania	1,192,192	1,380,240
Duvall	23	1	New England	—	414,656
Edwards	39	1	Michigan	—	419,416
Gatewood	63	5	West Virginia	358,528	358,552
Hammond	54	2	Virginia	414,936	414,728
Logan	37	1	Kentucky and Tennessee	—	447,720
Mason	57	2	Delaware and Maryland	645,032	825,088
O'Bryan	59	4	Ohio	343,928	372,392
Samuels	42	3	New York and New Jersey	737,024	824,472
Wates	67	5	Wisconsin	370,712	342,200
Salesmen terminated in previous year				1,828,816	—
House account				257,384	244,480
Total				$6,478,816	$6,373,160

$500,000 for the year. Each week a salesman could draw all or a portion of his accumulated commissions. Mr. McDonald encouraged the salesmen to draw commissions as they accumulated since he felt the men were motivated to work harder when they had a very small or zero balance in their commission accounts. These accounts were closed at the end of the year so each salesman began the new year with nothing in his account.

The salesmen provided their own automobiles and paid their traveling expenses, of which all or a portion were reimbursed by per diem. Under the per diem plan, each salesman received $70 per day for Monday through Thursday and $42 for Friday, or a total of $322 for the normal workweek. No per diem was paid for Saturday, but a salesman received an additional $70 if he spent Saturday and Sunday nights in the territory.

In addition to the commission and per diem, a salesman could earn cash awards under two sales incentive plans that were installed two years ago. Under the Annual Sales Increase Awards Plan, a total of $10,400 was paid to the five salesmen having the largest percentage increase in dollar sales volume over the previous year. To be eligible for these awards, a salesman had to show a sales increase over the previous year. These awards were made at the January sales meeting, and the winners were determined by dividing the dollar amount

EXHIBIT 2   *Salesmen's Earnings and Incentive Awards in the Current Year*

| Salesmen | Sales | | Annual Sales Increase Awards | | Weekly Sales Increase Awards (Total Accrued) | Earnings* |
	Previous Year	Current Year	Increase in Sales (Percent)	Award		
Allen	$ 330,264	$ 329,216	(0.3%)	—	$1,012	$30,000†
Campbell	1,192,192	1,380,240	15.8	$3,000 (2d)	2,244	88,617
Duvall	—	414,656	—	—	—	30,000†
Edwards	—	419,416	—	—	—	30,000†
Gatewood	358,528	358,552	(0.1)	400 (5th)	1,104	18,513
Hammond	414,936	414,728	—	—	420	30,000†
Logan	—	447,720	—	—	—	30,000†
Mason	645,032	825,088	27.9	4,000 (1st)	3,444	49,756
O'Bryan	343,928	372,392	8.3	1,000 (4th)	1,512	19,344
Samuels	737,024	824,472	11.9	2,000 (3d)	1,300	49,713
Wates	370,712	342,200	(7.7)	—	612	17,532

*Exclusive of incentive awards and per diem.
†Guarantee of $600 per week or $30,000 per year.

of each salesman's increase by his volume for the previous year with the percentage increases ranked in descending order. The salesmen's earnings under this plan for the current year are shown in Exhibit 2.

Under the second incentive plan, each salesman could win a Weekly Sales Increase Award for each week in which his dollar volume in the current year exceeded his sales for the corresponding week in the previous year. Beginning with an award of $4 for the first week, the amount of the award increased by $4 for each week in which the salesman surpassed his sales for the comparable week in the previous year. If a salesman produced higher sales during each of the 50 weeks in the current year, he received $4 for the 1st week, $8 for the 2nd week, and $200 for the 50th week, or a total of $4,100 for the year. The salesman had to be employed by the company during the previous year to be eligible for these awards. A check for the total amount of the awards accrued during the year was presented to the salesman at the sales meeting held in January. Earnings of the salesmen under this plan for the current year are shown in Exhibit 2.

The company frequently used "spiffs" to promote the sales of special items. The salesman was paid a spiff, which usually was $4, for each order he obtained for the designated items in the promotion.

For the past three years in recruiting salesmen, Mr. McDonald had guaranteed the more qualified applicants a weekly income while they learned the business and developed their respective territories. During the current year, five salesmen, Allen, Duvall, Edwards, Hammond, and Logan, had a guarantee of $600 a week, which they drew against their commissions. If the year's cumulative commissions for any of these salesmen were less than their cumulative weekly drawing accounts, they received no commissions. The commission and drawing accounts were closed on December 31, so each salesman began the new year with a zero balance in each account.

The company did not have a stated or written policy specifying the maximum length of time a salesman could receive a guarantee if his commissions continued to be less than his draw. Mr. McDonald believed the five salesmen who currently had guarantees would quit if these guarantees were withdrawn before their commissions reached $30,000 per year.

Mr. McDonald stated that he was convinced the annual earnings of Outdoor's salesmen had fallen behind earnings for comparable selling positions, particularly in the past six years. As a result, he felt that the company's ability to attract and hold high-caliber professional salesmen was being adversely affected. He strongly expressed the opinion that each salesman should be earning $50,000 annually.

Compensation Plan Proposals

In December of the current year, Mr. McDonald met with his comptroller and production manager, who were the only other executives of the company, and solicited their ideas concerning changes in the company's compensation plan for salesmen.

The comptroller pointed out that the salesmen having guarantees were not producing the sales that had been expected from their territories. He was concerned that the annual commissions earned by four of the five salesmen on guarantees were approximately half or less than their drawing accounts.

Furthermore, according to the comptroller, several of the salesmen who did not have guarantees were producing a relatively low volume of sales year after year. For example, annual sales remained at relatively low levels for Gatewood, O'Bryan, and Wates, who had been working four to five years in their respective territories.

The comptroller proposed that guarantees be reduced to $250 per week plus commissions at the regular rate on all sales. The $250 would not be drawn against commissions as was the case under the existing plan but would be in addition to any commissions earned. In the comptroller's opinion, this plan would motivate the salesmen to increase sales rapidly since their incomes would rise directly with their sales. The comptroller presented Exhibit 3, which showed the incomes of the five salesmen having guarantees in the current year as compared with the incomes they would have received under his plan.

From a sample check of recent shipments, the production manager had

EXHIBIT 3   *Comparison of Earnings in Current Year under Existing Guarantee Plan with Earnings under the Comptroller's Plan**

Salesmen	Sales	Existing Plan			Comptroller's Plan		
		Commissions	Guarantee	Earnings	Commissions	Guarantee	Earnings
Allen	$329,216	$16,753	$30,000	$30,000	$16,753	$12,500	$29,253
Duvall	414,656	21,879	30,000	30,000	21,879	12,500	34,379
Edwards	419,416	22,165	30,000	30,000	22,165	12,500	34,665
Hammond	358,552	18,513	30,000	30,000	18,513	12,500	31,013
Logan	447,720	23,863	30,000	30,000	23,863	12,500	36,363

*Exclusive of incentive awards and per diem.

concluded the salesmen tended to overwork accounts located within a 50-mile radius of their homes. Sales coverage was extremely light in a 60- to 100-mile radius of the salesmen's homes with somewhat better coverage beyond 100 miles. He argued that this pattern of sales coverage seemed to result from a desire by the salesmen to spend most evenings during the week at home with their families.

He proposed that the per diem be increased from $70 to $90 per day for Monday through Thursday, $42 for Friday, and $90 for Sunday if the salesman spent Sunday evening away from his home. He reasoned that the per diem of $90 for Sunday would act as a strong incentive for the salesmen to drive to the perimeters of their territories on Sunday evenings rather than use Monday morning for traveling. Further, he believed the increase in per diem would encourage the salesmen to spend more evenings away from their homes, which would result in a more uniform coverage of the sales territories and an overall increase in sales volume.

The consultant from New York City recommended that the guarantees and per diem be retained on the present basis and proposed that Outdoor adopt what he called a "Ten Percent Self-Improvement Plan." Under the consultant's plan, each salesman would be paid, in addition to the regular commission, a monthly bonus commission of 10 percent on all dollar volume over his sales in the comparable month of the previous year. For example, if a salesman sold $40,000 worth of merchandise in January of the current year and $36,000 in January of the previous year, he would receive a $400 bonus check in February. For salesmen on guarantees, bonuses would be in addition to earnings. The consultant reasoned that the bonus commission would motivate the salesmen, both those with and without guarantees, to increase their sales.

He further recommended the discontinuation of the two sales incentive plans currently in effect. He felt the savings from these plans would nearly cover the costs of his proposal.

Following a discussion of these proposals with the management group, Mr. McDonald was undecided on which proposal to adopt, if any. Further, he wondered if any change in the compensation of salesmen would alleviate all of the present problems.

Case 2-7
OPPENHEIMER MANAGEMENT CORPORATION*

The national sales manager of Oppenheimer Management Corporation was confident that the sales contest developed to reward stockbrokers and others who sell Oppenheimer's three new mutual funds would be a strong motivator. Oppenheimer Management offers 18 mutual funds to the public and, like other brokerage houses, frequently uses various incentives to motivate the stock-brokers/sales reps to push certain funds. Oppenheimer Management is a unit of Mercantile House Holdings PLC, a British financial services firm. Mercantile sold Oppenheimer & Company, the securities broker and investment bank, in early 1986.

Mercantile House Holdings PLC

Mercantile House Holdings PLC is a holding company involved in wholesale brokerage, money brokerage, fixed-interest brokerage, investment banking and securities trading, fund management, and financial information services. Established in the United Kingdom, Mercantile House has approximately 2,700 employees. Sales in 1986 were £385 million, which produced a profit of £44.5 million. In April 1986, Mercantile sold 82 percent of Oppenheimer & Company, Inc., and Oppenheimer Capital Corp. for $100 million cash plus $50 million in other assets.

Incentives for the New Mutual Funds

The sales awards for the three new mutual funds have attracted considerable attention. At a recent convention in Chicago's McCormick Place exposition center, a red Porsche 944 Turbo was the star attraction. Financial planners, attending the International Association for Financial Planning convention, heard representatives of Oppenheimer Management promote three new mutual funds with the promise of the sports car to whoever sells the highest amount, exceeding $5 million, and with a minimum of 10 sales. Other cars offered were a Jaguar XJ-S or a Corvette coupe or convertible. Financial planners can win other rewards, as Exhibit 1 illustrates.

Offering sales incentives to financial planners, stockbrokers, insurance agents, and others is not uncommon. What is uncommon, according to some critics, is the size and range of prizes being offered by Oppenheimer.

Other contests sponsored by brokerage houses and fund developers offer

---

*This case is based on published information found in Robert L. Rose, "Incentives vs. Clients: Which Ones Most Concern Financial Planners?" *The Wall Street Journal,* November 24, 1986, pp. C1, C4; *Wiesenberger Investment Companies Service,* 1986 edition; and *Moody's International Manual,* 1986 edition.

EXHIBIT   1   *Sales Awards and Requirements*

Requirements	Sales Awards
$100,000 and 5 sales	Casio pocket color television, or Cobra cordless telephone, or Simac II Gelataio 800 ice-cream maker
$250,000 and 5 sales	Sony compact disc player, or Canon PC 10 personal copier, or Panasonic microwave convection oven
$500,000 and 10 sales	Sony Video 8 camcorder or attaché case with $1,000 cash, or Waterford crystal barware
$1 million and 10 sales	Honda scooter, or IBM PC laptop computer, or Sony rear-projection videoscope TV
$3 million and 10 sales	Blackglama mink coat, or IBM Personal Computer XT, or Sony entertainment system
Grand Prize: highest total over $5 million and 10 sales	Porsche 944 Turbo, or Jaguar XJ-S, or Corvette coupe or convertible

prizes that are just as generous. Trips, for example, are a common incentive. Companies typically will mix business with pleasure. Recently, JMB/Carlyle, a real estate firm, planned a business symposium in Kauai, Hawaii, for top sellers of its real estate partnerships. Winners were to receive five days in an exotic paradise along with an opportunity to expand their business expertise.

Some incentive programs are more modest. First Investors Corporation gave away turkeys for financial planners who sold $5,000 or more of the company's funds during a recent Thanksgiving holiday. Investors range from individuals to institutions such as companies that manage pension programs.

To the critics, however, the issue is when does the financial planner start to think more about the Porsche rather than whether the product is right for the consumer. One critic argues that giving a gift, such as a Gucci handbag, will lead brokers to compromise their ethics.

A supporter of the use of incentives claims they are a normal part of any salesperson's job. He sees incentives as part of the American system: if you produce above-average results, your efforts should be rewarded, within reason.

Others contend the issue is serious enough that disclosure laws are needed to inform prospective investors about these non-cash incentives. This proposal is viewed as being unrealistic by the president of one financial planning firm who claims few brokers would announce that another $5,000 in sales is needed to win a trip somewhere.

The president of a real estate partnership firm disputes the effectiveness of such disclosure laws. He notes that such a statement would represent one paragraph out of several thousand in a 250-page prospectus. Oppenheimer Management's prospectus contains a disclosure about the non-cash sales incentives available for the three new funds.

EXHIBIT 2   *Oppenheimer Mutual Funds*

Name of Fund	Primary Objective*
Oppenheimer A.I.M. Fund	MCG
Oppenheimer Challenger Fund	G
Oppenheimer Directors Fund	G
Oppenheimer Equity Income Fund	I
Oppenheimer Fund	MCG
Oppenheimer Gold & Special Minerals	I
Oppenheimer High Yield Fund	I
Oppenheimer Money Market Fund	I
Oppenheimer N.Y. Tax-Exempt Fund	TF
Oppenheimer Premium Income Fund	I
Oppenheimer Regency Fund	G
Oppenheimer Special Fund	MCG
Oppenheimer Target Fund	G
Oppenheimer Tax-Free Bond Fund	G
Oppenheimer Time Fund	MCG
Oppenheimer U.S. Government Trust	I

*Abbreviations used are MCG—maximum capital gain; G—growth; I—income; S—stability; and TF—tax-free municipal bond.

Oppenheimer's Experience

The prizes offered by Oppenheimer may be having the hoped-for effect. Sales of the three funds are going well. One of them, the GNMA fund, was number four in sales out of the firm's 18 funds and appears to be headed for the number one position. Exhibit 2 details characteristics of 16 Oppenheimer funds.

Oppenheimer's national sales manager insists that all three funds are timely investments. He seriously doubts, given the environment existing today, that anybody could be hurt.

Case 2-8
WBYL/Z108 RADIO STATION*

By the early 1990s, competition in the Gainesville radio market was hot. In a city of about 250,000, nine major radio stations compete for listening audiences and advertising commitments from businesses, local government, and area schools and colleges. Four station competitors sell a combination AM and FM offering, one station sells a simulcast AM/FM offering, and four others sell a single offering (three FM and one AM).

Radio stations in the Gainesville market have developed positioning strategies that focus their efforts on specific target audiences, so program formatting varies by target audience. However, most competing sales representatives find themselves vying for advertising commitments from many of the same sponsors.

WBYL/Z108 Radio

WBYL/Z108 is one of four combination AM/FM competitors in the Gainesville radio market. WBYL-AM is best classified as a sports-news-talk station that features country music. The target audience for WBYL-AM is those over 35. Play-by-play action of both professional and collegiate sports along with several sports talk shows are emphasized. Z108-FM targets 18-to-39-year-olds with its programming focus of Top 40 hits.

Z108-FM held top market share of the Gainesville listening audience until early 1989 when a new competitor entered the market. The new competitor targets the same audience and uses a similar program format. Following a large rating loss, Z108 tightened its programming offering and brought in new disc jockey talent. Z108 also changed program directors and hired a consultant to help direct its efforts. By early 1990, the rating slide was halted and a new, potentially stronger Z108 faced the 1990s with enthusiasm.

Similar to other stations, WBYL/Z108 has commission sales representatives. Sales reps are responsible for both selling, on which they make about 15 percent of sales, and collections. Reps lose a portion of their commissions, up to all of it, if payments are 60, 90, or 120 days late. Sales reps at WBYL-Z108 tend to earn slightly more than at other stations, with annual pay ranging from $17,500 to $38,000.

Bill Bennett, sales manager for WBYL/Z108, works with a sales staff of nine commission-only sales reps. He reports to the station manager but is generally left to his own judgment in focusing sales staff efforts and achieving station sales goals. To focus selling activities and provide incentive for extra efforts (or "recharge" the reps as Bill puts it), sales contests are promoted to

---

*This case was prepared especially for this text by William H. Murphy, marketing doctoral student, University of Wisconsin-Madison.

the sales team two or three times yearly. Bill is convinced by past contest outcomes that they lead to increased sales.

Ever since new competition hit the Gainesville market, station management had been pressing Bill to reduce account losses and to find ways to bring ad revenues back to pre-1989 levels. To Bill, this meant finding ways to increase the efforts of his sales team. In mid-1990, Bill decided a sales contest would provide the sales boost management wanted. With the fall/winter season approaching, Bill spent many hours designing the most extensive and what he hoped would be the most successful sales contest to date.

The WBYL/Z108 Sales Football Scoreboard Contest

Bill reflected on past contests and on articles he had read about contest dos and don'ts before deciding on the final format for the contest. Deciding on an exciting theme was easy, especially since WBYL-AM was dedicated to sports. Bill knew he could get station approval for the awards he wanted since increased revenues from the contest would more than offset contest expenses.

When sales reps arrived at the station for their weekly sales meeting in the last week of September, they were greeted with much fanfare. The station was decorated with a Hawaiian look. Sales reps were told a new contest was about to get under way—and the first person to reach contest goals would receive a trip for two to Hawaii! Pictures were taken with reps holding coconuts, posed in front of exotic posters of the winning destination. At the meeting, Bill passed out a detail sheet of his carefully conceived contest (see Exhibit 1).

During the meeting, Bill discussed the contest and asked for questions from the reps. By the meeting's end, everyone seemed to understand the goals and objectives, and everyone was clearly enthusiastic about the awards. Even so, the contest seemed to get off to a slow start. After the first week, two reps were tied for most yardage gained—at one yard each. By the end of the second week, the yardage leader had 4.5 yards gained. At the same time, four reps still had zero yardage. Bill assumed his reps were "getting the feel of the contest" and "soon things would get rolling."

Each week thereafter, Bill provided his sales representatives enthusiastic updates of their standings. He also made regular announcements of specials that would win extra yards. Examples of these updates and specials are shown in Exhibit 2.

After posting "second-quarter" results (results through November as shown in 12/14 memo), Bill was convinced he had hit on a winning contest. Three reps, Jenny, Mike, and Kurt were in a close race to be first to the 100-yard mark. Bill thought the other reps, though further behind, might be encouraged by the successes of the leaders to push harder for the final two months of the contest.

As with most well-laid plans, the approaching holiday season saw unforeseen delays in getting results tabulated for the "third quarter," due in part to changes in the station computer system and to vacation schedules—including

EXHIBIT 1   *Details of the WBYL/Z108 Sales Contest*

The WBYL/Z108 Sales Football Scoreboard Contest!

Gainesville's newest, most exciting sales contest kicks off today with the grand prize trip for two to . . . where else . . . Hawaii!!! Earn yardage as quickly as you can! Avoid getting penalized! First person to get over the 100 yard goal line wins the trip for two to Hawaii!

1st Quarter—October   2nd Quarter—November
3rd Quarter—December   4th Quarter—January

% Goal Attainment	100%	110%	120%	130%	140%
			Yardage Gained		
Monthly sales goal	4	5	6	7	8
Monthly new business goal	3	4	5	5	6
Monthly sports goal	2	3	3	3	4
Monthly production goal	1	2	2	2	2

26- or 52-week contracts	1	
Highest weekly average	1	
Best-written proposal	1	
Client testimonial letters	.5	(Maximum 5 yards total)
Showing up at station promotions	.5	(Maximum 5 yards total)
Sales committee work	1	
Highest % goal entering month	2	

*Please turn in copy of order, contract, or memo to earn yards. You will be provided weekly yardage summaries. Unreported yardage will not be carried into new month.

Specials—Yardage will vary but opportunities for yardage will at times be posted. Example: "I'll give you 2 bonus yards if you sell a Football Saturday available by 5 P.M. today."

	Negative Yards
Missed monthly goal	2
Missed monthly new business goal	2
Missed monthly sports goal	2
Missed monthly production goal	2
Missed sales meeting	1
Late monitor report	1

1st person to reach 100 yards—Wins a trip for two to Hawaii in February including the additional vacation week ($4,000 value).

2nd person to reach 100 yards—Wins a $500 shopping spree to Spruce Mall.

3rd person to reach 100 yards—Wins a $250 shopping spree to Spruce Mall.

All people that go over 100 yards win a $50 dinner for two gift certificate.

Bill's two weeks away from the station. Postings for the third quarter of the football contest came over a month late, with promises for a rapid posting of final contest results (see Exhibit 3).

As Bill calculated January totals, he realized no sales rep had reached the 100-yard goal. On the positive side, the station would be saving the cost of

EXHIBIT 2   *Contest Updates and Specials*

To: Sales Reps
From: Bill

Date: 10/9/90

Earn extra yards with Spec production.
For the remainder of October we will pay
you 0.5 yards, maximum of 5 yards for all
spec production. Please give me a copy
of the production order to qualify for
yardage!

Think Hawaii!!

To: Sales Reps
From: Bill

Date: 12/14/90

We have summarized all of the
contest points for November. After
two quarters of play here are the
standings!!

Rep	Yardage
Jenny	49.5
Mike	43
Kurt	31
Kaili	19
Toni	9
Ben	6
Tahir	4
Albert	3.5
Connie	3

Don't forget the points you can earn
for testimonial letters, volunteer
work, and Best Written Proposal
each month!!

More bonus point opportunities still
to come!

the awards that had been promised for those attaining 100 yards. On the other
hand, Bill thought his reps had been working hard on the contest. Rather than
jeopardize the credibility of the contest, Bill sent out a closing memo, thanking
the reps for their efforts and promising an even more exciting contest in the
next month or two.

Behind the Scenes

Bill was right; a trip to Hawaii was appealing to the members of his sales
team. What Bill hadn't counted on was the slow start of many of the reps. By
the end of the second quarter (12/14 memo), it was clear that no one besides
Jenny, Mike, and maybe Kurt had a chance at winning. The rest of the sales
team dropped interest in the football contest. Worse yet, several began blaming
Bill for intentionally setting their contest goals beyond reach. Ensuing memos

EXHIBIT 3   *Third-Quarter Contest Posting*

To: Sales
From: Bill

February 11, 1991

Here is the long-lost update on the Scoreboard contest. The computer switchover has delayed end-of-month figures, thus delaying related new business figures, etc.

Closing figures for January are still to come, and final yardage to be awarded. Here are the standings after 3 out of 4 months.

Jenny	73	yards
Mike	59.5	
Kurt	32	
Kaili	27	
Toni	16	
Ben	13	
Tahir	8.5	
Albert	7	
Connie	5	

Good Luck! (It's almost over!)

from Bill, designed to encourage contest enthusiasm and participation, actually became annoyances to most of the sales team.

Meanwhile the top contenders, Jenny and Mike in particular, began to believe they could win the football contest. During the final month, each increased efforts to try to be the first to reach 100 yards. With less than a month remaining, Mike figured out a scheme, a "slight breaking of the rules" as he later called it, to give himself an edge. Some orders were written in advance of a customer's actually placing the order. Other orders were padded, with the intention that after the contest close date Mike would simply write off portions of the orders as nonpayments. Of course, Mike hadn't counted on several of his customers calling the station to complain about being over-billed. Some of these calls came through when Mike was on the road, resulting in others at the station being faced with irate customers. At the same time, Jenny focused her January contest efforts on asking for favors from customers she had close relationships with. Several of these accounts were willing to "buy a little more than they needed to help me out."

After receiving Bill's final memo, announcing no rep had reached 100 yards, Jenny and Mike were furious. As Mike said privately, "To this day it's affecting me in some way . . . in my relationship with the company . . . in my attitude toward future contests." Ben, one of the reps who dropped out of contest pursuit early on, later commented privately, "You lay this big thing down and do this song and dance and then screw the thing up. What does that tell me about our management?"

Closing Thoughts

Not knowing the behind-the-scenes sentiments of the sales team, Bill analyzed contest outcomes. He was pleased to find that improvements were made in most contest-related objectives, and ad revenues in particular showed gains from October through January. Reporting to his superiors, Bill commented on the effectiveness of the football scoreboard sales contest and enthusiastically mentioned several new contest ideas to further motivate his sales team. Given the apparent success of the football scoreboard sales contest, the station manager continued to give Bill a free hand in developing and running sales contests.

Case 2-9
MIDWEST BUSINESS FORMS, INC.*

Sandro Rossi, Midwest Business Forms vice president of marketing, cut right to the point, "We have an excess inventory problem that needs your immediate attention. Our vice president of finance wants to know why our sales force is not doing a better job of selling off the excess inventory of standard forms." Toni Carter, sales director for the firm, defended her sales team. "The inventory problem was not created by the sales force. Our inventory problem is the result of poor sales forecasting," she said. "That may be true," replied Rossi, "but we still have to sell off the inventory and that's the job of the sales force."

On her way back to her office, Carter knew she had to get her salespeople to refocus their efforts on the inventory problem. Even so, she did not like this situation. "Pushing the sales force to solve an inventory problem that they did not create, especially when it would lead to less selling effort for other responsibility areas, could lead to all sorts of problems," she thought. She also considered some recent revelations about the attitudes of her salespeople, furthering her concern about the next steps to take.

Midwest Business Forms, Inc.

Midwest Business Forms, Inc., is a regional printer of a large line of business forms used by companies, institutions, and government agencies. Midwest, located in Des Moines, Iowa, sells business forms throughout the region including North and South Dakota, Minnesota, Wisconsin, Illinois, and Nebraska. Sales are made directly to users by 22 sales representatives who work under sales managers based in either St. Paul or Chicago. Toni Carter directs the sales effort out of the Des Moines headquarters.

At Midwest, a sales rep's compensation consists of 85 percent salary plus 15 percent commission on gross margin for all sales. Most of the business forms are standard and have the customer's name imprinted if needed. In some situations, sales reps help customers design business forms. The average base salary in 1990 was $23,500 and the average commission was $4,600. Midwest's 1990 sales totaled $4,726,000, cost of goods sold averaged 40 percent, and profit before taxes was $661,000.

The inventory problem Rossi voiced was in the company's standard line of legal documents. These are preprinted forms that contain space for imprinting the customer's name and address. The forms meet very specific legal requirements for content and format. Based on 1990 sales of these documents,

*William H. Murphy, marketing doctoral student, University of Wisconsin-Madison, assisted in preparing this case.

EXHIBIT 1   *Pay Component of Job Attitude Index**

	Midwest Mean	Mean across All Companies
1. My pay is high in comparison with what others get for similar work in other companies	2.41	2.51
2. My pay doesn't give me much incentive to increase my sales	2.24	3.59
3. My pay is low in comparison with what others get for similar work in other companies	3.10	2.91
4. In my opinion the pay here is lower than in other companies	3.22	2.97
5. My income provides for luxuries	2.66	2.91
6. My selling ability largely determines my earnings in this company	2.15	3.25
7. I'm paid fairly compared with other employees in this company	3.32	3.38
8. My income is adequate for normal expenses	3.78	3.49
9. I am very much underpaid for the work that I do	3.71	3.43
10. I can barely live on my income	4.12	3.78

*Sales representatives responded to the question, "To what extent do you agree with each of the following statements?" A 5-point response set was used, anchored with "strongly disagree" (1) and "strongly agree" (5).

Midwest has inventory on hand to last well into 1993. Inventory carrying charges are substantial enough to cause real concern among several Midwest executives. Another concern related to impending changes in legislation that would require changes in the forms, likely rendering all inventory worthless. As one Midwest executive said, "We have to get these forms unloaded before the laws change, or they will become candidates for recycling."

Carter had her own concerns. She had recently commissioned an outside consulting agency to conduct a sales force survey. Sitting on her desk were synopses of the survey results, suggesting the sales force's attitudes toward Midwest's compensation program were unfavorable (see Exhibit 1). Carter had thought the sales force was satisfied with the program, yet the findings, which also included the results of surveys to competing sales forces, strongly suggested otherwise.

She was also concerned about another part of the same study. One of the findings suggested the sales force believed they were not being adequately recognized for good performance (see Exhibit 2).

"What do they want?" she wondered. "A pat on the back every time they make a sale?" In any event, Carter now faced a number of problems. She had to find a way to meet the directive to move excess inventory and move it quickly if possible. She was also faced with the awareness that sales force attitudes toward both compensation and recognition issues were unfavorable. She suspected she would have to turn attitudes around in the near future, or the consequences could be severe.

EXHIBIT 2   *Company Policy and Management Support Component of Job Attitude Index**

	Midwest Mean	Mean across All Companies
1. Management keeps us in the dark about things we ought to know	2.78	2.79
2. Our sales goals are set by the higher-ups without considering market conditions ..	2.73	3.15
3. Management really knows its job	3.34	2.88
4. This company operates efficiently and smoothly	2.73	2.46
5. Our home office isn't always cooperative in servicing our customers	3.22	2.65
6. I'm satisfied with the way employee benefits here are handled	3.97	3.26
7. Sometimes when I learn of management's plans, I wonder if they knew the territory situation at all	2.66	2.57
8. I have confidence in the fairness and honesty of management	3.10	3.29
9. Management here is really interested in the welfare of employees	3.39	3.25
10. I feel that the company is highly aggressive in its sales promotion efforts	2.61	2.42
11. Sales representatives in this company receive good support from the home office	2.63	3.09
12. Management here sees to it that there is cooperation between departments	2.85	2.71
13. There isn't enough training for sales representatives who have been on the job for a while	2.90	2.65
14. Management ignores our suggestions and complaints	3.12	3.07
15. Management fails to give clear-cut orders and instructions	3.17	3.08
16. Formal recognition programs compare favorably with those of other companies ...	2.34	None
17. There are not enough formal recognition programs in this company	2.61	None
18. I do not get enough formal recognition for the work I do	2.76	None
19. Formal recognition programs in this company are attractive	2.12	None
20. I am satisfied with the way our formal recognition programs are administered	2.39	None
21. Recognition awards are based on ability	2.44	None
22. Recognition awards are given in an arbitrary manner	2.97	None

*The higher the score, the more the sales representatives are satisfied. This applies to both positive and negative items, since the negative items are reversed scored. The range is from 1 to 5.

Sales reps responded to the question, "To what extent do you agree with each of the following statements?" A 5-point response set was used, anchored with "strongly disagree" (1) and "strongly agree" (5).

Problem Resolution

Carter read several sales publications to gain additional insight about sales force compensation. As a result of this study, the idea of having a sales contest seemed appealing. Moreover, a sales contest, in addition to providing financial rewards, would provide recognition for contest winners. Carter's attention turned to publications and articles dealing specifically with sales contests. Eventually, she developed a sales contest proposal for Rossi to approve.

The proposed sales contest would involve all the sales force and their spouses as well. To increase spouse awareness and interest, contest details would be mailed directly to the sales representatives' homes. The contest would last three months, beginning in April 1991. Cash prizes would be awarded monthly and a grand prize awarded at the end of the contest.

Monthly winners would be the three sales reps who achieved the highest percentage increase in sales compared with their sales for the same months the previous year. Monthly winners would receive cash awards of $500, $400, or $300. The grand prize of $1,000 would be awarded to the sales rep obtaining the highest average increase for all three months in 1991 (April, May, and June), compared to the same three-month period in 1990.

In addition to the cash prizes, merchandise points would be awarded each month to sales reps whose sales for the month exceeded sales for the same month in 1990. Each percentage point over the previous year would be worth $5 of merchandise points. Thus, if a sales representative's sales for April 1991 exceeded April 1990 sales by 18 percent, then $90 of merchandise points would be earned. Carter also proposed that four prize points be awarded for each case of the standardized legal documents sold during the contest. Each case carried a suggested retail price of $40. Merchandise points could be cashed in immediately by selecting items from a prize catalog or saved to be "built up" over the three months.

The prize catalog would contain pictures of merchandise and the points needed to obtain the various items. Carter proposed using a firm specializing in sales contests to design the catalog. The firm, Starr Enterprizes, Inc., would also handle distribution of the merchandise prizes. Midwest would be billed for the retail price of the merchandise. Starr Enterprizes considered the retail markup as its fee.

The final aspect of the sales contest was the opportunity for a member of the sales force to win a merchandise grand prize. In addition to the cash awards and the merchandise opportunities, each point earned during the contest also earned a chance to win a home entertainment center, valued at $750. The drawing would occur at a dinner dance, at which time all cash prize winners would be recognized and the cash awards presented.

Toni Carter presented the contest proposal to Sandro Rossi for approval.

Case 2-10
CALIFORNIA CREDIT LIFE INSURANCE GROUP

Diane Flanagan, vice president of human resources at California Credit Life Insurance Group (CCLI), had just returned to her office after a lengthy conversation with Kevin Stark, vice president of sales. Flanagan and Stark had spent many hours reviewing the results of several reports that described the problems and opportunities experienced by women in sales.

The reports came from a variety of sources and were based on one-on-one discussions between women and men in sales and another person such as a reporter or a human resource manager. In some cases, the information resulted from focus group interviews. Flanagan and Stark hoped to gain a comprehensive understanding of the environment faced by women in sales.

Toward the end of their meeting, Flanagan received a rather urgent telephone call from Shelley Ryan, a lawyer from CCLI's legal staff. Ryan was calling to inform Flanagan that Suzette Renoldi, a sales rep in the southeastern region, had just filed a sexual discrimination suit against James Bradford, CCLI area sales manager from the southeastern region. Ryan called to Flanagan's attention that this was not the first complaint of sexual discrimination involving Bradford. Flanagan was aware of this and, in addition, knew of another situation that could have led to sexual harassment charges being brought against Bradford. The person involved, Ilse Riebolt, declined to pursue the matter for a variety of reasons. Diane Flanagan had been unable to assure Ilse Riebolt that bringing charges would be very reasonable, based on the description of the events. After an excellent start with CCLI, Riebolt quit in 1986 and took a position with a competitor.

California Credit Life prided itself on being an equal opportunity employer and wanted to avoid any adverse publicity. Flanagan was very concerned about the veracity and implications of the suit. On the other hand, she was not interested in any attempts to cover up the situation if the charges were true.

According to company policy and advice provided by Shelley Ryan, the first action to be taken should be a thorough investigation of the charges and of all available data. Ryan urged Flanagan to gather the necessary information as quickly and as quietly as possible.

Initially, Flanagan determined she would need a vast amount of information. CCLI's computerized decision support system (DSS) would be a source of much of the needed data. The DSS contained such files as sales performance, quotas, expenses, salaries, and commissions for all of CCLI's sales reps across the country. The DSS contained the data for the numerous studies conducted by Human Resources on such subjects as job satisfaction, role conflict, role ambiguity, supervisory style, and numerous other subjects.

EXHIBIT 1   *Total Sales and Sales to Quota, 1985–1991**

	1985 Total Sales	Percent to Quota	1986 Total Sales	Percent to Quota	1987 Total Sales	Percent to Quota
Suzette Renoldi	$228,800	101.4	$247,104	102.1	$261,930	101.4
Stuart Pletz	215,600	97.3	219,912	99.4	230,908	99.9
Alvin Polard	100,000	96.7	101,000	97.2	103,020	100.0
Ted Hervington	350,000	100.3	346,500	95.4	343,035	99.6
Tim Hart	264,900	99.8	270,198	100.4	275,602	100.9
Brett Moore	234,000	98.9	231,660	96.7	231,660	99.0
Shari Swaggert	375,000	105.3	397,500	103.5	413,400	102.6
Mark Hoffton	189,000	101.2	192,780	100.6	198,563	101.1
Bob Pizzano	250,100	100.1	257,603	101.0	265,331	101.8
Felicia Abler	289,650	100.8	309,926	104.5	325,422	103.2
Katy Levenhagen	190,000	103.8	209,000	106.2	223,630	103.5
Jeff Birdest	195,640	95.4	205,422	100.4	211,585	102.9
Larry Green	320,000	99.6	326,400	99.7	336,192	102.4
Chris Brackett	296,430	101.3	311,252	102.4	326,815	103.6
Ilse Rieboldt	287,500	102.4	296,125	105.3	T	
Mike Peck					100,412	102.3
Jeff Martin						
Cliff Arlen						
Kim Babler						

*Terminations are noted by *T*.

The Company

California Credit Life Insurance Group was incorporated in Los Angeles in 1955. CCLI's initial product line included all types of life insurance. Since its inception, CCLI has expanded its product line to include all types of insurance such as health, automobile, professional liability, pension and retirement programs, commercial packages, and related financial services.

In 1983, CCLI decided to open an office in the southeastern area of the United States as soon as all staffing and physical details could be resolved. The southeastern region became a reality in 1985, with James Bradford selected to be area sales manager. Bradford had been a sales rep in the Dallas region and had been selected for the new position based on his excellent sales performance and his strong interpersonal skills. Shortly after Bradford accepted the position, it became apparent to Diane Flanagan that Bradford did not wholeheartedly support CCLI's position concerning equal opportunity. In fact, it became necessary to instruct Bradford that one third of his sales force would be female, a figure in line with CCLI's experience in its other regional offices.

E X H I B I T   1   (concluded)

1988 Total Sales	Percent to Quota	1989 Total Sales	Percent to Quota	1990 Total Sales	Percent to Quota	1991 Total Sales	Percent to Quota
$267,169	102.3	$264,340	101.1	$282,844	99.6	$288,500	98.5
242,453	101.1	245,442	101.6	262,623	98.4	288,885	100.2
106,111	100.3	107,500	100.6	115,025	100.3	124,227	100.6
T							
281,114	100.8	282,445	101.2	302,216	102.0	326,395	102.7
232,818	98.1	T					
417,534	102.1	410,890	99.8	T			
204,520	100.8	204,800	100.7	219,136	100.1	230,093	100.4
273,291	101.2	275,364	101.6	294,639	102.1	318,210	102.0
326,724	103.4	322,745	101.9	345,337	102.9	348,790	98.7
230,339	103.9	225,990	102.1	241,809	100.1	265,990	99.0
217,932	101.6	218,500	101.7	233,795	101.4	252,110	101.7
347,959	102.3	348,660	102.0	373,066	103.1	414,103	102.5
339,887	103.0	342,110	103.4	366,057	104.1	406,323	103.8
253,117	101.6	241,553	99.1	281,313	101.8	305,014	102.4
213,419	99.1	235,017	100.2	279,106	101.2	312,844	102.8
		185,442	97.1	214,877	99.3	264,651	98.1
				204,913	98.4	278,228	100.2

California Credit Life Insurance has 15 regional offices and 230 sales representatives. Area sales managers typically supervise 15 people, a large number but manageable given the nature of the selling job. The sales reps work independently and do not need day-to-day supervision or contact with their area sales manager. CCLI requires two performance evaluations each year. Area sales managers have hiring authority and can set base salaries with approval from CCLI. Promotional opportunities are limited, and turnover among the area sales managers has been very low.

Area sales managers can recognize excellent performance by increasing the base salary and modifying a sales rep's territory to cover better accounts. Sales reps receive a 3 percent commission on sales in addition to their base salaries. Yearly bonuses are distributed by the area sales manager based on a sales rep's performance. Records indicated Bradford's bonus allocation did not reflect sales volume and seemed to be determined by taking the total bonus award and dividing it by 15. This process added an average of $1,750 to each sales rep's income.

EXHIBIT 2	*Expense Account Data, 1985–1991**						
	1985	**1986**	**1987**	**1988**	**1989**	**1990**	**1991**
Suzette Renoldi	$1,800	$1,875	$1,820	$1,830	$1,790	$1,933	$1,905
Stuart Pletz	1,100	1,367	1,450	1,690	1,855	2,078	2,210
Alvin Polard	1,250	1,462	1,667	1,723	1,775	1,988	1,995
Ted Hervington	1,790	1,890	1,993	T			
Tim Hart	2,000	2,134	2,177	2,189	2,950	3,304	3,380
Brett Moore	2,500	2,578	2,673	2,774	T		
Shari Swaggert	1,540	1,603	1,615	1,672	1,715	T	
Mark Hoffton	1,778	1,800	1,829	1,950	2,059	2,306	2,384
Bob Pizzano	1,892	1,966	1,998	2,150	2,331	2,611	2,673
Felicia Abler	1,224	1,250	1,282	1,354	1,332	1,439	1,461
Katy Levenhagen	1,452	1,466	1,562	1,432	1,455	1,571	1,543
Jeff Birdest	1,970	1,980	2,155	2,245	2,778	3,111	3,260
Larry Green	2,145	2,256	2,347	2,355	2,679	3,000	3,114
Chris Brackett	2,234	2,457	2,679	2,789	2,887	3,233	3,211
Ilse Rieboldt	1,234	1,423	T				
Mike Peck			1,131	2,046	2,811	2,270	2,413
Jeff Martin				1,548	2,060	2,316	2,385
Cliff Arlen					1,440	2,119	2,376
Kim Babler						1,804	2,223

*Terminations are noted by *T*.

The Suzette Renoldi Matter

Renoldi joined CCLI in 1985 after graduating with a business degree from the University of South Carolina. Her initial performance was strong, and she made quota each year except for the last two years. Quotas are set by the area sales manager based on guidelines handed down from Kevin Stark, vice president of sales, and negotiations between the area sales manager and each sales representative.

Diane Flanagan contacted Shelley Ryan to determine what was behind Renoldi's legal action against CCLI and Bradford. Ryan informed her that she had not seen the actual complaint but knew that Renoldi had asked for territory changes so that her sales opportunities would be greater, a request that Bradford denied. Bradford allegedly told Renoldi that her unwillingness to entertain clients, especially males, was the reason her sales had fallen off and not because of a lack of sales potential. Renoldi refuted this accusation and claims Bradford's territory assignment was discriminatory from the start. Flanagan knew she would need to see the complete complaint and personally discuss the

EXHIBIT 3						*Number of Performance Evaluations, 1985–1991**							
	1985		1986		1987		1988		1989		1990		1991	
	1st	2nd	1st	2nd	1st	2nd	1st	2nd	1st	2nd	1st	2nd	1st	2nd
Suzette Renoldi	Y	—	Y	Y	Y	Y	Y	Y	—	Y	Y	—	Y	Y
Stuart Pletz	Y	Y	Y	Y	Y	Y	Y	Y	Y	Y	Y	Y	Y	Y
Alvin Polard	Y	Y	Y	Y	Y	—	Y	Y	Y	Y	Y	Y	Y	Y
Ted Hervington	Y	Y	Y	Y	Y	Y	T							
Ted Hart	Y	Y	—	Y	Y	Y	Y	Y	Y	Y	Y	Y	Y	Y
Brett Moore	Y	Y	Y	Y	Y	Y	Y	Y	T					
Shari Swaggert	Y	Y	Y	Y	Y	Y	Y	Y	—	Y	T			
Mark Hoffton	Y	Y	Y	Y	Y	Y	Y	Y	Y	Y	Y	—	Y	Y
Bob Pizzano	Y	Y	Y	Y	Y	Y	Y	Y	Y	Y	Y	Y	Y	Y
Felicia Abler	Y	Y	—	Y	Y	Y	Y	Y	Y	Y	Y	—	Y	Y
Kathy Levenhagen	Y	—	Y	Y	—	Y	Y	Y	—	Y	Y	Y	—	Y
Jeff Birdest	Y	—	Y	Y	Y	Y	Y	Y	Y	Y	Y	Y	Y	Y
Larry Green	Y	Y	Y	Y	Y	Y	Y	Y	Y	Y	Y	Y	Y	Y
Chris Brackett	Y	Y	Y	—	Y	Y	Y	Y	Y	—	Y	Y	—	Y
Ilse Rieboldt	Y	Y	—	Y	T									
Mike Peck						Y	Y	Y	Y	Y	Y	Y	Y	Y
Jeff Martin							Y	Y	Y	Y	Y	Y	Y	Y
Cliff Arlen										Y	Y	Y	Y	Y
Kim Babler												Y	—	Y

*Terminations are noted by *T*.

situation with both Renoldi and Bradford. Meanwhile, Flanagan started compiling as much information as possible from company sources.

The first documents received by Flanagan revealed sales volumes for each sales representative (Exhibit 1), expense account data (Exhibit 2), number of performance evaluations (Exhibit 3), and base salaries (Exhibit 4). Her office conducts various personnel studies, and she had available the summary results of a recent job satisfaction survey for the entire company. She requested a breakout based on region and sex, knowing that the small number of women in the southeastern region posed a statistical problem. Exhibit 5 presents job satisfaction scores for the sales representatives by sex for the southeastern region and the entire company. Flanagan was somewhat pleased with the results for the entire company but disappointed with the southeastern region's showing. At this juncture, Flanagan decided to summarize some of the studies she and Stark had been reviewing.

The first study, conducted by HBRS (a research company), was based on

EXHIBIT 4	*Base Salaries for All Sales Reps in the SE Region, 1985–1991**						
	1985	**1986**	**1987**	**1988**	**1989**	**1990**	**1991**
Suzette Renoldi	$25,000	$27,600	$29,200	$29,200	$29,250	$29,300	$30,750
Stuart Pletz	25,000	27,300	28,900	29,150	29,860	30,580	32,750
Alvin Polard	25,000	28,930	29,600	29,990	30,650	31,320	33,850
Ted Hervington	25,000	26,000	26,700	T			
Tim Hart	25,000	25,780	26,750	26,890	26,900	27,000	29,700
Brett Moore	25,000	25,900	26,200	26,750	T		
Shari Swaggert	25,000	29,000	29,500	29,750	29,800	T	
Mark Hoffton	25,000	26,200	27,150	27,450	27,900	28,500	30,500
Bob Pizzano	25,000	27,100	28,450	28,600	28,770	28,900	31,300
Felicia Abler	25,000	28,750	29,200	29,450	29,500	29,750	31,500
Katy Levenhagen	25,000	28,450	28,750	28,950	29,340	29,750	31,500
Jeff Birdest	25,000	25,700	26,500	27,800	29,100	31,000	33,750
Larry Green	25,000	25,900	28,000	28,750	30,100	31,500	34,000
Chris Brackett	25,000	27,000	27,800	28,900	29,900	31,000	33,750
Ilse Rieboldt	25,000	26,200	T				
Mike Peck			26,000	27,500	28,300	28,750	30,000
Jeff Martin				26,500	27,500	28,250	29,500
Cliff Arlen					27,000	27,500	28,250
Kim Babler						27,250	28,000

*Terminations are noted by *T*.

a series of focus group interviews with women sales reps from a variety of selling positions. HBRS also conducted focus group sessions with men. No attempt was made to conduct sessions with both men and women since it was believed this would limit discussion. Flanagan read the following verbatim comments:

Karen R.   *(computer sales): I really enjoy the challenge of selling high-priced, high-tech computers. It feels great to help somebody solve a problem. But, I still get questions from my friends when I tell them about my travel demands.*

Margaret McC.   *(medical equipment sales): I don't mind the travel, but at times it is all lumped together. Making child-care arrangements can be a hassle.*

Sherry W.   *(office equipment sales): This travel thing is bad news at my house. My husband becomes aloof the minute I mention that I have to be gone overnight. He's still aloof after I return. I know he wants me to quit and get a job with no travel.*

EXHIBIT 5   *Job Satisfaction Summary, 1991*

	Southeastern Region			Total Company		
	Male	Female	Total	Male	Female	Total
1. Job	54.06	45.13	52.16	53.84	50.19	53.61
2. Fellow workers	58.35	49.63	55.82	57.98	51.11	57.39
3. Supervisor	59.91	41.24	57.33	54.13	48.54	51.43
4. Company policy and management support	61.58	52.28	60.17	58.91	53.28	56.46
5. Pay	49.31	52.39	50.07	49.88	51.65	49.92
6. Promotion and advancement	59.41	48.37	57.30	58.28	49.87	57.06
7. Customer	53.70	48.44	51.19	54.07	48.56	52.09
Total	59.47	48.14	59.12	58.19	50.23	57.48

*All scores are standardized at a mean of 50. The higher the score, the more sales representatives are satisfied.

Martha W.   *(cosmetics sales): I don't have a husband to contend with, but with my travel schedule I don't have much of a social life either. My biggest problem was deciding what to pack and lost luggage. I'm supposed to carry a sample case that weighs 35 pounds plus a garment bag and my briefcase.*

Deirdre B.   *(insurance sales): I rarely travel outside of the city. My major headache is the guy who thinks that I should be home sewing and cooking or, if I have to work, in the typing pool.*

Karen R.   *(computer sales): I've made quota every year for the last five years only to confront men who say I'm lucky. One guy told me that I make more sales because customers want to see what a female sales rep looks like; then when I'm making my presentation, I rely on my feminine wiles to make the sale.*

Cherie L.   *(aluminum sales): I've had the credibility problem too. One purchasing agent informed me that my predecessor stood 6 feet 2 inches, weighed 195 pounds, and had a beard. I was really flustered with that comment and even more so when he asked me if I was busy in the evening. No doubt he wanted to explain the intricacies of aluminum to me.*

Laura W.   *(advertising sales): Being hassled comes with the territory. And, I don't have to leave the office either. But, I've adapted. I either play naive and ignore the comments, or I told one fellow laughingly that he could do better than me. But I do get tired of the hassle.*

Candace S.   *(commercial lending): The surprises never end. My first attempt at customer entertaining was a shocker. The customer said he would join me* *for dinner if he could bring his wife along. I was dumbfounded. Do I take both and report the expenses? I did, but business talk was very limited. I got the account, but it was weird.*

Laura W.   *(advertising sales): Entertaining has been a problem with me too, especially when it comes to paying the check. Some men must feel threatened by this.*

Brenda S.   *(building supply sales): Remember when we were girls? The boys wouldn't let us join their stupid clubs. Not much has changed has it? Now it's the country club where decisions are made. And, damn it, don't tell me that I have to take up golf. I may get good and win. I remember my boss's reaction when I clobbered him in tennis.*

Roseann S.   *(textbook sales): Speaking of bosses, my manager's evaluation of my performance is an embarrassment. He is absolutely unable to criticize my performance. Most reviews have been late too.*

Karla H.   *(software programs): This is my second sales job. My first put me into a "pioneer" situation, industrial equipment. To succeed with that company you had to be a "superwoman" and become "one of the guys." I was told that I could not succeed without experience. What a catch-22! I can't get experience without succeeding.*

Peggy T.   *(chemical sales): You know, I've experienced a lot. This is my 10th year with _____. And, I've been hassled, rejected, had to cancel a sales call due to a sick child, but I wouldn't trade it for anything. Your sales manager is really key. Mine treats me the same as he treats everybody else, but he does recognize that there are gender differences.*

The male commentators had this to say:

Bill M.   *(computer sales): Well, I can tell you this much. When the first women showed up, I was really surprised. Not that women cannot sell computers, after all many of my customers are women and most of them are really sharp, but we weren't informed that a woman had been hired.*

Joe M.   *(machine tool sales): Yeah, I was surprised too. But this "little thing" wanted to set the pace. You know, be the first woman ever to sell heavy-duty machinery costing $250,000 and up. She just didn't look the part, flowery dresses, heels, perfume. One of her customers called my boss and asked him to send a man the next time.*

Frank C.   *(office furniture sales): We have several women in my district. Like everybody else, some are super, some are average. I think that it has been a good move. We are now selling accounts that we were unable to sell before. And our national sales manager had us attend several company training sessions on how to integrate women into the sales force.*

John R.   *(tractor sales): I know this is going to sound strange, but I don't like it. A woman's place is in the home, not out selling and taking up space that some man could occupy. They have no business selling tractors!*

Mike R.   *(pharmaceutical sales): Talk about problems. We now have the token gal on our sales force. You should have seen the other reps when she was introduced at a sales meeting. You would have thought that she was the first gal these guys had ever seen. But I just about lost it when she comes up to me one day and asks if I would help her carry some boxes to her car. "Carry them yourself" is what I should have said.*

Paul T.   *(building materials sales): The thing that bugs me is the equal rights stuff, or should I say unequal rights. I'd like to see what happens if I call the boss or a customer and tell them I can't keep an appointment because my baby sitter is sick. Not only that, Susan just got back from maternity leave—something I'll never get— and I had to cover her accounts while she was gone.*

Mack H.   *(stockbroker): I don't want to play "Can You Top This," but we have a similar situation. Karen comes back off of maternity leave (this was her second child) and then decides that full-time is too much for her. She asks (and gets it too) to work only from Tuesday to Thursday. And she still gets full benefits but at a reduced salary.*

Calvin H.   *(chemical sales): We have a few women in the sales force, and the problems have been minimal, sort of what you would expect with any change. Management handled it well. They even had discussions with the sales force about how to call on customers who are women. Our purchasing agents, production engineers—they're all men—have had sessions on how to deal with women sales reps.*

Brad M.   *(food product sales): Well, with women in my group we've had the usual mess. Office romance, you know. He was married—was, that is— and now he's divorced, and she is working for another company. I think she was fired, but nobody will admit it.*

Bob R.   *(aluminum sales): Yeah, I can identify with that. It almost caused a divorce in my house. I was expected to travel with Beth and show her the ropes. Well, my wife wanted to know what "ropes" I was going to show her. All I had to do was mention that I was going to travel with Beth, and things went to hell. It's OK now, but it was shaky for a while.*

Todd B.   *(commercial lending sales): I've made joint calls with Katherine, and I've learned a lot. I thought I knew all the answers, but watching Kate interact with customers has been a real treat. She's good and really has a knack for finding out customer needs. My own sales have increased as a result, I'm sure.*

Flanagan finished her review of the HBRS report and thought that most of the comments reinforced what she suspected were the major problems confronting women in sales. Other reports she reviewed supported the findings of the HBRS report. She wondered if she could get the remaining women in the southeastern region to discuss their feelings, attitudes, and problems with her or with a neutral third party. She knew the legal proceedings might prevent her from contacting the women. Shelley Ryan, CCLI's legal staff, suggested she could bring in several women from different regions for a focus group or one-on-one sessions. Ryan told her to bring in some men too since their perceptions will be valuable. Flanagan decided to adopt this strategy. After all, regardless of the outcome of the Renoldi case, CCLI should learn as much as possible about the subject to avoid future incidents.

Flanagan decided to retain a research firm to conduct the focus group interviews with samples of women and men sales reps. Six groups of 10 sales reps each participated in the project. The sessions lasted approximately two hours. Dana Moore and Bill Carson moderated the focus groups and reported to Flanagan that they felt very positive about the process and the results. The report was accompanied with videotapes so Flanagan could see and hear the proceedings. To remain objective, Flanagan did not review the tapes and asked Moore and Carson to prepare their verbatim comments without identifying the respondent.

Flanagan reviewed the report hoping to find some insight as to how CCLI might avoid future problems such as the one existing in the southeastern region. Many of the comments coincided with those from the HBRS report, although a few provided additional insight concerning the problem in the southeastern region. Flanagan read with great interest the following verbatim comments from the women:

Sales rep #1:   *Basically, I like my job a lot. But it has taken me much time to get to that point. And it's been my doing, all the way, especially with the limited support that I get from my manager.*

Sales rep #2:   *Speaking of support, some of the guys I work with view me as a threat to their precious power structure. One guy gold me that I should be home making soup and not taking up space that a man could fill.*

Sales rep #3:   *I can relate to that. My manager at my last sales job was the only woman district sales manager in the company. She was told that she should not take credit for work done by the men who worked for her.*

Sales rep #4:   *It's not just how I relate to my manager but the whole support issue. I don't feel like I'm part of the company. Why just the other day, a customer asked about a new policy that he knew about but nobody told me about. I asked one of the men in our office, and he knew.*

Sales rep #5:   *I had a similar situation just the other day, and I don't like having to say, "I don't know the answer, but I'll find out for you." But I knew that the customer expected an answer then, not later.*

Sales rep #6:   *I'd like to think that if I needed an answer my manager would be the logical source. But in my office I ask one of the other women.*

Sales rep #4:   *I really question the ability of the higher-ups to tell me what's going on. It would be great to have a mentor or someone that I could rely on for the straight scoop.*

Sales rep #7:   *Hey, I don't want to seem odd, but my manager is really supportive. I told him about my problem taking a customer to dinner and getting into the hassle about who pays the bill. The customer just would not let a woman buy him dinner. My manager said I should join the Capital Club and take customers there where the bill doesn't come to the table. It works like a charm.*

Sales rep #8:   *I've had a similar experience. A customer, a good one, sent me a bottle of Passion perfume and a cashmere sweater. I was dumbfounded and asked my manager what to do, since I didn't recall hearing anything about receiving gifts during our training program. He gave me several suggestions, and I decided which one to try. It worked, and I still have the account.*

Sales rep #9:   *My manager is pretty supportive. But he can't eliminate the hassling that goes on with some customers. Do the purchasing agents and others with CCLI treat women sales reps the same?*

Sales rep #10:   *I'd really like a chance to move into sales management. That's why I got into sales to begin with. Now, all I have to do is figure out what it takes to get promoted. It's a big mystery at CCLI. And if something doesn't happen soon, I'll go elsewhere.*

Sales rep #11:   *This whole performance evaluation process is a joke. My manager is usually late, and on top of it the review is so general and vague that I have no idea what I'm supposed to do to better myself. And our annual bonuses show no relation to contribution. We all get the same bonus.*

The comments from the men did not add anything to her understanding of CCLI's problems. They were very similar to those provided by HBRS, plus they duplicated many of the comments made by the women concerning performance evaluations and promotion policies.

The report suggested to Diane Flanagan that CCLI has much work ahead if it is going to avoid problems similar to those in the southeastern region. Although names were not given in the report, Flanagan thought she could associate many of the comments with James Bradford, CCLI's problem sales manager. She did not learn anything from the focus groups that would help with the legal proceedings in the Suzette Renoldi matter. But, for certain, she wanted to change things to avoid future problems.

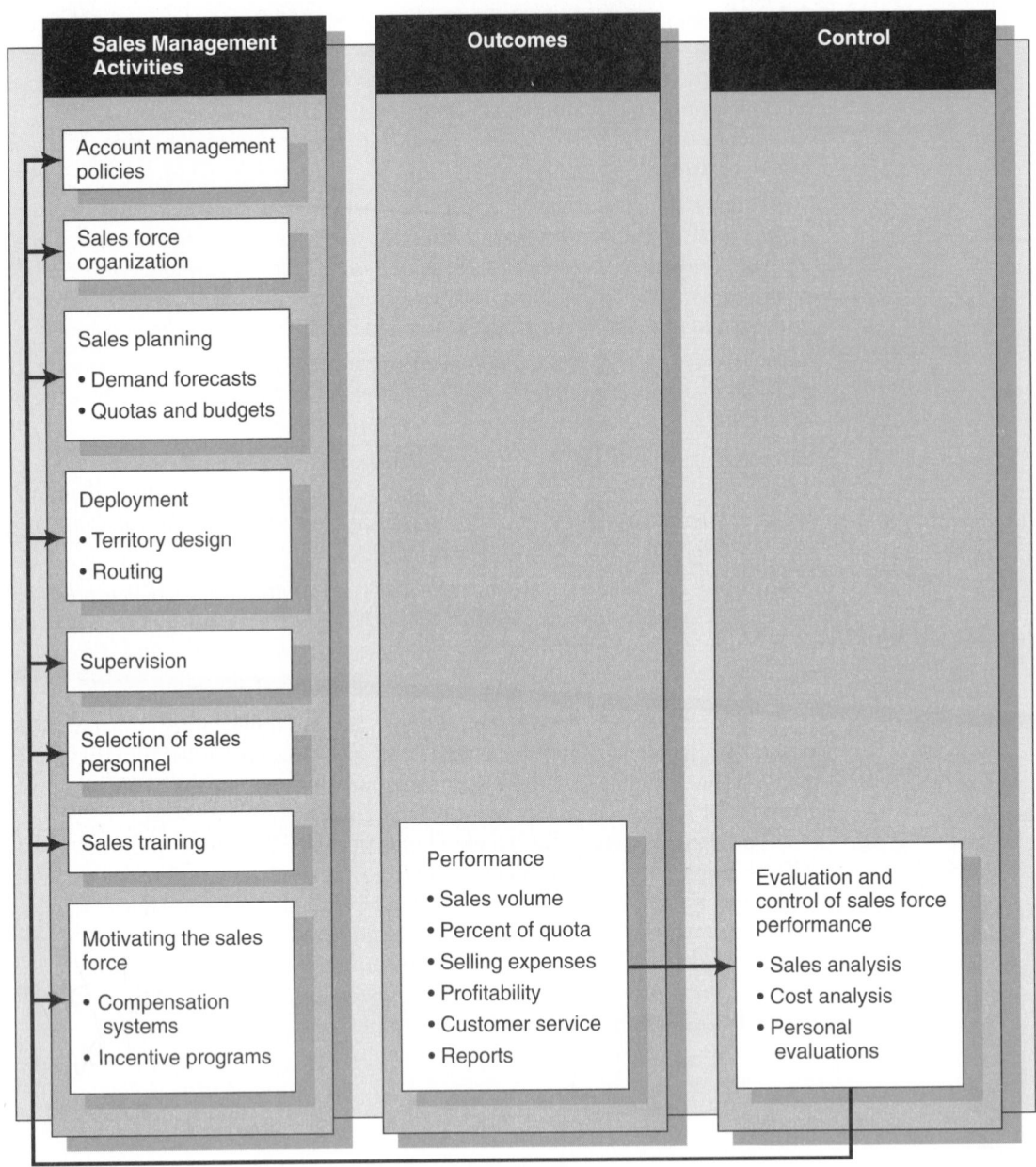

Sales Management Activities

Account management policies

Sales force organization

Sales planning
- Demand forecasts
- Quotas and budgets

Deployment
- Territory design
- Routing

Supervision

Selection of sales personnel

Sales training

Motivating the sales force
- Compensation systems
- Incentive programs

Outcomes

Performance
- Sales volume
- Percent of quota
- Selling expenses
- Profitability
- Customer service
- Reports

Control

Evaluation and control of sales force performance
- Sales analysis
- Cost analysis
- Personal evaluations

Feedback

EVALUATION AND CONTROL OF THE SALES PROGRAM

Three activities are central to the basic process by which sales or any other managers operate: planning, implementing, and evaluating and controlling. Part 3 explores the policies and procedures involved in evaluating and controlling a firm's sales program. Chapter 16 discusses audits, decision support systems, and sales analysis, three primary mechanisms of evaluation. Chapter 17 discusses cost analysis, which focuses on the profitability of the personal selling effort in general and specific salespeople in particular. Chapter 18 looks at other measures for assessing the performance of salespeople, both objective and subjective.

Sales Analysis

S OFTWARE MAKES FOOD SALES A PIECE OF CAKE

Early in 1990, Frito-Lay, Inc., had a problem in San Antonio and Houston. Sales were slumping in that area's supermarkets. So CEO Robert H. Beeby turned to his computer, called up the data for south Texas, and quickly isolated the cause. A regional competitor had just introduced El Galindo, a white-corn tortilla chip. The chip was getting good word of mouth and, as a result, more supermarket shelf space than Frito's traditional Tostitos tortilla chips. Within three months, Beeby had Frito-Lay producing a white-corn version of Tostitos that matched the competition and won back lost market share.

A few short years ago, it might have taken Frito-Lay three months just to pinpoint the problem. But recently the $4.5 billion snack-food division of PepsiCo Inc. finished installing a sophisticated decision support system that gathers sales data daily from supermarkets, scans it for important clues about local trends, and flags executives about problems and opportunities in all of Frito-Lay's markets.

Data Overload

Frito-Lay now has probably the most powerful knowledge-gathering machine in the business, although apparently not for long. Such consumer giants as

Kraft USA, Procter & Gamble, and RJR Nabisco are installing massive systems to track sales blips as current as yesterday and never older than a month ago. These systems allow executives to take advantage of the mountains of sales data from electronic scanners.

For over a decade, scanners at supermarket checkout counters have collected data about which products are being bought at what price. But at first, no software existed to present the information in a form marketing managers could easily use. Consequently, says John D. Little, professor of management at Massachusetts Institute of Technology and a director at Information Resources, Inc., "the first scanner reports were delivered by forklift trucks." And, he adds, they were mostly ignored.

By the mid-1980s, A. C. Nielsen Co. and others had developed systems to sort data by brand. Since then, though, "the amount of scanner information has increased something like five hundredfold," says Danny L. Moore, Nielsen vice president for product development. Weekly, rather than monthly, data are available, providing such specific details as how many cans of 32-ounce Prego tomato sauce with mushrooms were sold in a given store in a particular week.

To manage the rising tide of data, Nielsen and software makers Information Resources and Metaphor Computer Systems have developed "quasi-expert systems." These automatically break down brand performance within regions and detail how competing products are doing, which promotions work, and whether specific store displays are attracting customers. They also generate summary reports with graphs that highlight unusual product performance.

Marketers welcome these systems. Kathleen Mocniak, research and analysis director at Planters LifeSavers Co., recalls how executives had to wade through lists of numbers for relevant figures on regional performance. It was, she says, like "trying to get a drink of water from a fire hydrant."

Frito-Lay's experience shows how useful these systems can be. Updated daily on hand-held terminals by 10,000 Frito-Lay salespeople, information on 100 Frito product lines in 400,000 stores appears on company computer screens in easy-to-read charts. Red means a sales drop, yellow is a slowdown, and green is an uptick.

These daily snapshots have accelerated the information flow. Two years ago, says Michael H. Jordan, president of PepsiCo Worldwide Foods, "if I asked how we did in Kansas City on July 4th weekend, I'd get five partial responses three weeks later." It's still too early to know the system's impact on the bottom line, but Jordan says it eliminates a day of paperwork from each salesperson's weekly schedule.

Local Frito-Lay brand managers have persuaded Beeby and Jordan to tighten relations with parent Pepsico to make even better use of the new information. About 7,000 Pepsi salespeople were scheduled to use the same hand-held input system as Frito-Lay by 1992. Then, the data from the two decision support systems could be combined so managers at both companies can cooperate—possibly on promotions, discounts, and coupon campaigns.

Food companies hope these systems will further strengthen their influence with the supermarkets. Kraft, for instance, uses data from its software system to help such chains as Kroger and Pathmark decide how to stock their refrigerated section most effectively. Michael L. Blyth, Kraft's vice president for trade marketing, wants to increase Kraft's leverage even more by supplying his salespeople with a decision support system that will generate even more details faster on Kraft products and the competition.

Source: "How Software is Making Food Sales a Piece of Cake," *Business Week*, July 2, 1990, pp. 54–55. See also Richard H. Beeby, "Managers' Journal: How to Crunch a Bunch of Figures," *The Wall Street Journal*, June 11, 1990, p. A14, for more discussion of Frito-Lay's information system.

The three steps of planning, implementing, and evaluating and controlling are the basic process by which managers operate. In sales management, planning involves such problems as organizational structure, territory design, and establishment of sales quotas. Implementing includes selecting, training, and motivating sales representatives. All these topics have been treated in this book. Now we turn to evaluating and controlling the field selling effort.

Evaluation and control are vital parts of the management process. As the opening scenario suggests, management needs feedback on the effectiveness of its plans and the quality of their execution to operate more effectively; otherwise it is easy to lose sight of the firm's objectives and how to achieve them. A firm with no effective evaluation and control programs can easily end up under full power and no direction, consuming resources to no effective end, much like a ship that has lost its bearing because of a broken compass.

EXHIBIT 16 • 1   *Basic Management Control Process*

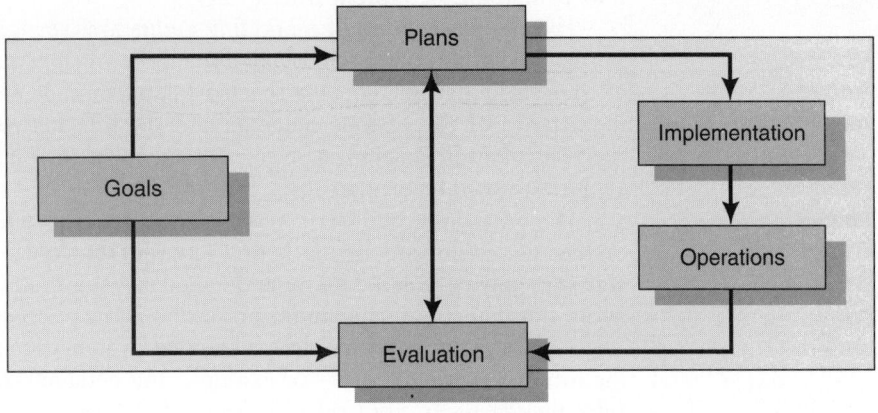

NATURE OF CONTROL

The key role played by evaluation and control in the management process is depicted in the feedback-control loop of Exhibit 16.1. Company goals initiate the process by serving as the targets that guide the formulation of plans. Once designed, the plans need to be implemented to become part of the daily operations. The firm then needs to collect and organize information about its operations so it can compare these data with its goals to determine how well it is doing. This evaluation and comparison provide the control for the enterprise. They allow the assessment of where the firm is now versus where it wants to go so corrective action may be taken.

The situation again parallels that of a ship at sea: By knowing where the ship is now compared with its target destination, the captain can adjust the course to arrive at the destination. It is not impossible for the ship to arrive there without such evaluation. By simply wandering about aimlessly, it may eventually get there by a stroke of good luck. Similarly, the firm may eventually get where it wants to go without proper evaluation and control procedures. But it is much more likely to get there faster and at less cost if it can assess where it is now and compare that with where it wants to go so the appropriate corrective action can be taken, as the opening scenario indicates.

MARKETING AUDIT

The most thorough mechanism for evaluating the marketing effort is a marketing audit. A **marketing audit** is a complete, systematic, objective evaluation of the total marketing effort of a firm. Marketing audits examine the firm's goals, policies, organization, methods and procedures, and personnel. They also assess the firm's current position and its strengths and weaknesses so a new course can be plotted if necessary.

The two basic types of marketing audits are: vertical and horizontal. The horizontal audit is often referred to as a **marketing mix** audit in that it examines all the elements that go into the marketing mix. It emphasizes the relative importance of the various elements and the mix between them. In contrast, the vertical audit singles out selected elements of the marketing operation and subjects them to thorough study and evaluation.

The horizontal audit is a systems level audit in which the focus is more on the relationship among marketing activities than on any one activity. Certain activities may be isolated for more detailed investigation through the horizontal audit, but that is not its main purpose; that is the purpose of the vertical audit. The vertical audit is a complete, objective, systematic analysis of one part of the total marketing effort—for example, the personal selling effort. The term *sales management audit* refers to the vertical audit associated with the sales manager's responsibilities.[1]

Although this book emphasizes sales management audits, all functional audits within the firm must be coordinated so their timing and scope coincide. Suppose, for example, a sales management audit indicated the sales force is encountering unusual difficulty selling one major product line. Information on the advertising effort and its effectiveness must also be available by product line. If the advertising audit analyzes the function only by geographical area and not product line, the available information would not be sufficient to diagnose the reason for the sales problems. A similar problem arises if the two functional audits do not correspond in their timing.

The relation between the vertical sales management audit and the horizontal marketing audit can be discerned by looking at some of the issues addressed under each.

Objectives

The initial step in a horizontal marketing audit is to secure a clear statement of the company's goals and mission. This is often difficult. The goals should be measurable. The goal "to achieve a high rate of sales" is too nebulous to be of value. A marketing audit often uncovers executives operating with different goals and imprecise targets.

The goals for the personal selling effort must be coordinated with those of the firm. The sales management audit attempts to specify goals for the personal selling function and the role personal selling is to play in the total marketing effort of the firm.[2] It also includes a statement of short-run objectives. Two examples are (1) increase the number of salespersons in the southeastern territory by two in the next two years and (2) increase the frequency with which sales reps contact type A accounts by 10 percent within the next year.

Policies

The next audit step is to examine how well the firm's current policies coincide with its goals. Policies can grow obsolete in dynamic economies. Consider these changes of the 1980s. J. C. Penney, with its profits squeezed by competition from fancy department stores at the high end of the retailing scale and mass discounters at the low end, reappraised its policies and decided to move up the scale and drop paint, hardware, and lawn and garden sections from its stores. Timex reduced its dependence on mechanical watches to shed its utilitarian image and it is hoped reverse its declines in profits and market share. Texas Instruments got out of the increasingly price-competitive home computer industry, even though it was one of the pioneers. One primary function of the audit is to stimulate management to consider such policies.

Policies about personal selling might also need revision. Thus, if the firm's policy of promoting from within the sales force prevents it from filling an area manager's position with the type of person needed for that territory, the policy should be changed. Similarly, a policy of frequent assignment changes (even if to bigger and better territories) that produced excessive turnover in the sales force would be questioned.

Any policy made obsolete by a changing external environment should be revised. For example, because of the rapidly increasing costs of salespeople, Mannington Mills, Inc., installed computers in its retail outlets in an attempt to improve their productivity. Instead of the salesperson sorting through samples of vinyl floor covering with the customers, Mannington programmed small computers to digest the answers to eight questions about the decor of a customers' room and then to display the style numbers of between 3 and 10 appropriate Mannington patterns.[3]

The sales management audit similarly might suggest a change in salespeople's compensation scheme or the criteria used in hiring new reps. The important thing is that the spectrum of sales management policies be systematically evaluated and those that need to be changed be identified. After such an analysis, for example, Xerox decided to sell its retail stores despite the fact they were originally planned to complement its direct sales force.[4]

Organization

The marketing audit looks at the organization of the company as a whole and the marketing department in particular. It seeks to determine whether the organization is optimal in terms of the company's resources and talent. Perhaps an organization that is structured by function should be converted to a product-manager basis. Perhaps it should be revamped into strategic business units (SBUs), as has been done recently within a number of firms.

The sales management audit focuses on the organization of the sales force. Is it large enough? Is it organized optimally given the firm's current situation? Take for example, Bantam Doubleday Dell, which comprises the U.S. publishing operations of Bertlesmann AG of Germany. After an organizational audit, it decided to reorganize into four sales forces organized according to

E X H I B I T 16 • 2   *Reorganization of IBM's Operations in Europe*

The planning and implementation of the IBM Europe reorganization began in 1989. The blueprint, developed in a series of Paris management meetings, calls for IBM's European operations to become more centralized in some respects and increasingly decentralized in others within about five years.

IBM's internal affairs—product warehouses, in-house computer systems, the planning of advertising—are being centralized to save money and boost efficiency.

For instance, the managers of IBM France, IBM Germany, and other national organizations currently each run their own slightly different but interconnected computer systems for billing, ordering, and other company data. This arrangement means that across Europe IBM pays 8,000 employees, out of a 108,000-worker European payroll, to tend a variegated, computerized management information system with 150 to 170 data centers. IBM wants to decrease the number of centers to between just three and five big ones within five years.

In contrast, external affairs, the marketing operations that deal directly with customers, are being decentralized so sales decisions get made faster and better locally, rather than by a slow-moving headquarters bureaucracy.

As part of this effort, IBM—beset by customer complaints of red tape at Paris headquarters—is moving many key managers out of Paris and scattering them around the continent.

The result, if the program is succcessful, will produce a structure that simultaneously takes advantage of possible savings from a unified European Community market and also avoids alienating local customers, who will still have parochial tastes. That is the hope, at least, and the plan has received flattering reviews even from a few IBM competitors.

Source: Richard L. Hudson, "IBM Again Revamps European Sector: It Seeks to Find Proper Mix as Market Grows Tougher," *The Wall Street Journal,* April 22, 1991, p. B5.

how its books are distributed (e.g., retail, wholesale), rather than two sales forces, one for Bantam hardcover and paperback titles and Dell paperbacks and another handling Doubleday and Delacorte hard covers.[5]

Perhaps the increasing technical complexity of the firm's products warrants a shift from geographically defined sales territories to the use of product specialists. Perhaps a key national account sales force should be developed to supplement the firm's current area coverage. Or maybe recent growth in the Southwest warrants dividing that region into two areas, each with its own regional manager. Then 7 salespeople would report to each manager, rather than the 14 now reporting to the 1 regional manager.

The dynamic nature of the international environment is causing a number of firms to rethink their organization structures. Exhibit 16.2 describes how IBM is reorganizing its European operations to take better advantage of the changes occurring there with unification.

Methods and Procedures

Methods and procedures are the tactical means by which the firm's policies are carried out. Perhaps the policies are good, but their implementation is inadequate. The marketing audit would attempt to assess the quality of execution of each marketing activity. Have new products been properly test marketed? Have distribution channels evolved to reflect changing consumption patterns? Have pricing policies been adhered to?

The sales management audit attempts to assess how well those activities that directly influence the personal selling function have been carried out. It looks at such issues as how well recent recruits have been trained, how quickly customer orders have been processed, whether salespeople have been given accurate and prompt feedback on their sales and costs, and whether customer requests have been promptly satisfied.

Personnel

The marketing audit does not stop with a review of the goals, policies, organization, and procedures used to carry out the marketing function. It also examines the people involved to determine how well they are performing.

The sales management audit is similar. Most of its attention, however, is directed at individual salespeople and at branch, district, regional, and other area managers. In such audits, determining where people are now versus where they should be if the personal selling effort were on target is emphasized. Three of the more productive and partly overlapping programs for making such assessments are sales analysis, cost and profitability analysis, and individual performance evaluation.

Not all firms use all three, though many are moving in that direction. Sales analysis is the most common, and cost analysis is the least used. The remainder of this chapter concentrates on sales analysis; Chapter 17 focuses on cost and profitability analysis; and Chapter 18 examines performance evaluation of individual salespeople using ratios and subjective supervisor ratings. Increasingly, firms are asking decision support systems for these analyses. Consequently, we shall discuss briefly the purpose and structure of decision support systems before turning to the details of how these analyses can be conducted.

DECISION SUPPORT SYSTEMS

A decision support system (DSS) has been defined as "a coordinated collection of data, systems, tools, and techniques with supporting software and hardware by which an organization gathers and interprets relevant information from business and environment and turns it into a basis for marketing action."[6] A DSS concentrates on the design of data systems, model systems, and dialog systems that can be used interactively by managers (see Exhibit 16.3).[7]

Data Systems

The **data system** in a DSS includes the processes used to capture and the methods used to store data coming from marketing, finance, and manufacturing, as well as information coming from any number of external or internal sources. The typical data system has modules containing customer information, general economic and demographic information, competitor information, and industry information, including market trends.

E X H I B I T 16 • 3   *Components of a Decision Support System*

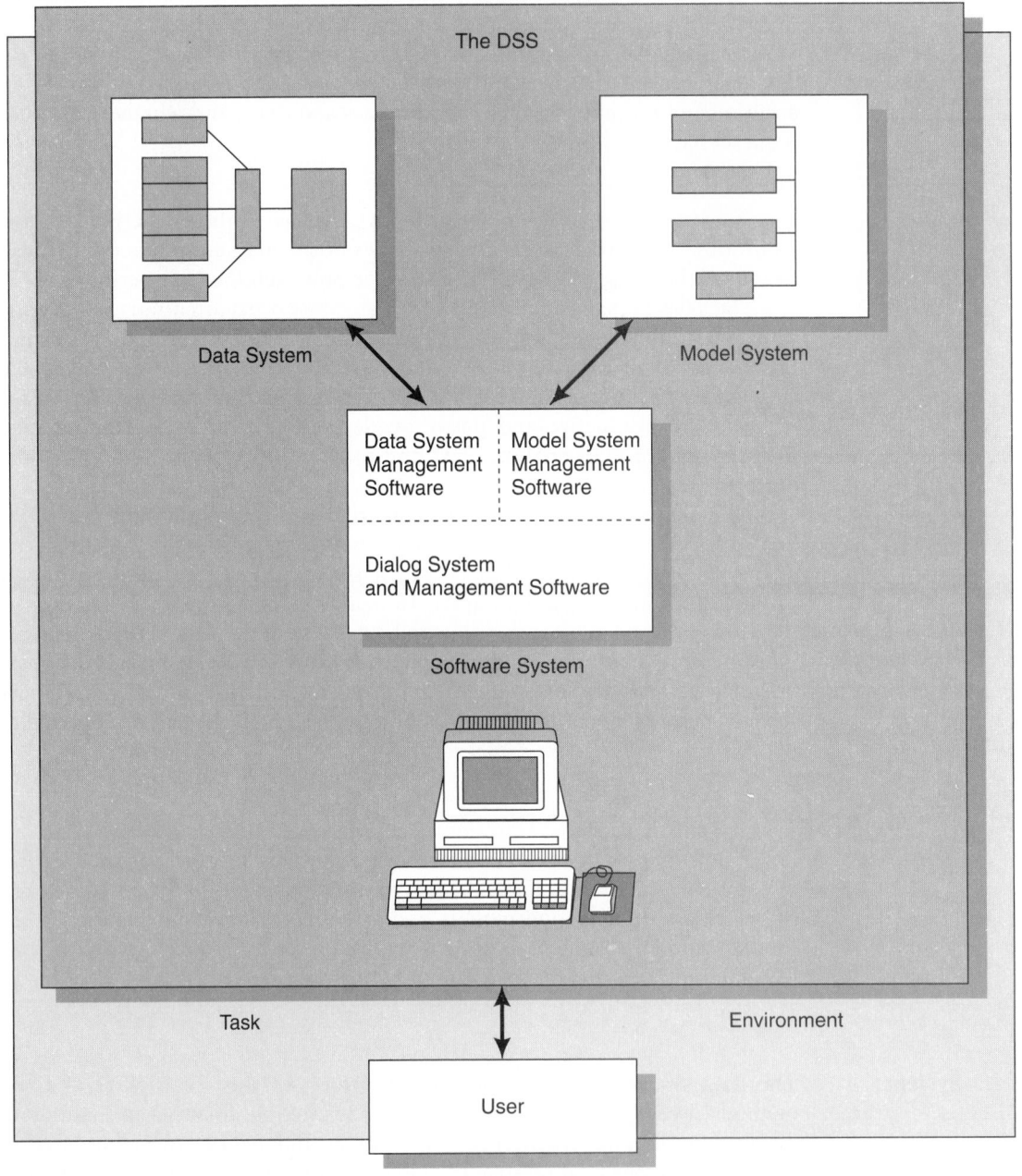

Source: Adapted from Ralph H. Sprague, Jr., and Eric D. Carlson, *Building Effective Decision Support Systems,* © 1982, p. 29. Adpated by permission of Prentice Hall, Inc., Englewood Cliffs, New Jersey.

The customer information module typically contains information on who buys and who uses the product, where they buy and use it, when, in what situations, quantities, and how often. It could also include information on how the purchase decision is made, the most important factors in making that decision, the influence of advertising or some sales promotion activity on the decision, the price paid, and so on. Marketing research would typically supply some of the information input to the customer information module of the data system. Other inputs might come from the purchase of syndicated commercial marketing information.

The module containing general economic and demographic information attempts to capture some of the most relevant facts about what is happening in the external environment. These might be facts on national or international economic activity and trends, or they might concern interest rates, unemployment, or changes in GNP. The demographic facts concern changes in population, changes in the rate of household formation, or any of the other factors that could potentially affect the future success of the firm. Many of these inputs come from government data, primarily from the various censuses.

One module could contain information on specific competitors. What are their names, market shares? In which market niches do they operate? What is their percentage of sales by product? What are their distribution methods? Where are their production facilities located? How big are they? What are their goals? What are their unique capabilities?

The industry information and market trend module contains general information on what is happening in the industry. This might mean financial information about margins, costs, research and development activities, and capital expenditures. It could mean trends in manufacturing or technology, either with respect to raw materials or processes. The industry module could contain information on new technologies that might affect the production process or create new product substitution capabilities. It also contains information on marketing trends, such as changing distribution patterns or product consumption.

The past few years have seen an explosion in data bases that provide information on customers, competitors, industries, or general economic and demographic conditions. More than 3,000 data bases now can be accessed on line via computer as compared to fewer than 900 in 1980. Some 200 to 300 of these apply to the information needs of business.

The fundamental criterion as to whether a particular piece of data might find itself in the data bank is whether it is useful for marketing decision making. The basic task of a DSS is to capture relevant marketing data in reasonable detail and to put that data in a truly accessible form. It is crucial that the data base management capabilities built into the system can logically organize the data the same way a manager does, regardless of the form that organization assumes.

E X H I B I T   16 • 4   *Use of Marketing Decision Models in Fortune 1,000 Companies*

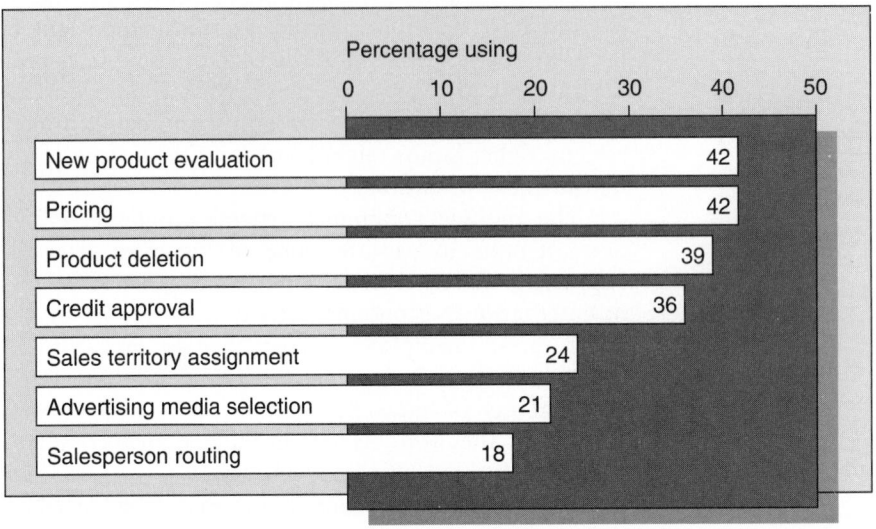

Percentage using

New product evaluation	42
Pricing	42
Product deletion	39
Credit approval	36
Sales territory assignment	24
Advertising media selection	21
Salesperson routing	18

Source: Developed from information in Raymond McLeod, Jr., and John C. Rogers, "Marketing Information Systems: Their Current Status in *Fortune* 1000 Companies," *Journal of Management Information Systems* 1 (Spring 1985), pp. 57–75.

Model Systems

The **model system** includes all the routines that allow the user to manipulate the data to conduct the kind of analysis the individual desires. Whenever managers look at data, they have a preconceived idea of how something works and, therefore, what is interesting and worthwhile in the data. These ideas are called models.[8] Most managers also want to manipulate data to gain a better understanding of a marketing issue. These manipulations are called procedures. The routines for manipulating the data may range from summing a set of numbers to conducting a complex statistical analysis to finding an optimization strategy using some kind of nonlinear programming routine. At the same time, "the most frequent operations are basic ones: segregating numbers into relevant groups, aggregating them, taking ratios, ranking them, picking out exceptional cases, plotting and making tables."[9]

In recent years, there has been an increase in the application of formal decision models to marketing situations. Formal models attempt to capture the issues managers deem most relevant when making particular decisions. Exhibit 16.4 shows the extent to which marketing decisions are being modeled among the Fortune 1,000 companies. Note that two of the seven most frequent modeling applications involve personal selling issues.[10]

Dialog Systems

The dialog systems, also called **language systems,** are most important and clearly differentiate DSSs. The dialog systems permit managers, who are not programmers, to explore the data bases using the system models to produce reports that satisfy their particular information needs. The reports can be tabular or graphical, and the report formats can be specified by individual managers. The dialog systems can be passive, which means the analysis possibilities are presented to the decision makers for selection via menu, a few simple keystrokes, light pen, or a mouse device, or they can be active, requiring the users to state their requests in a command mode.

Instead of funneling their data requests through a team of programmers, managers can conduct their analyses by themselves (or through one of their assistants) sitting at a computer terminal using the dialog system. This allows them to target the information they want and not to be overwhelmed with irrelevant data. Managers can ask a question and, on the basis of the answer, can ask a subsequent question, and then another, and another, and so on.

> With the right DSS, for example, a marketing vice president evaluating the sales of a recently introduced test instrument could call up sales by month, then by year, breaking them out at his option, by say, customer segments. As he works at his CRT terminal, his inquiries could go in several directions, depending on the decision at hand. If his train of thought raises questions about monthly sales last year compared to forecasts, he wants his information system to follow along and give him answers immediately.
>
> He might see that his new product's sales were significantly below forecast. Forecasts too optimistic? He compares other products' sales to his forecasts and finds that the targets were very accurate. Something wrong with the product? Maybe his sales department is getting insufficient leads or isn't putting leads to good use? Thinking a minute about how to examine that question, he checks ratios of leads converted to sales—product by product. The results disturb him. Only 5 percent of the new products' leads generate orders compared to the company's 12 percent all-product average. Why? He guesses that the sales force isn't supporting the new product enough. Quantitative information from the DSS perhaps could provide more evidence to back that suspicion. But already having enough quantitative knowledge to satisfy himself, the vice president acts on his intuition and experience and decides to have a chat with his sales manager.[11]

As the availability of on-line data bases has increased, so too has the need for better dialog systems. The dialog systems are what put data at the managers' fingertips. This is difficult because of the large amount of data that are available, the speed with which they hit a company, and the fact that data come from various sources. Bringing together the data from the disparate data sources into meaningful reports is no small feat.

> Large data base services typically provide their customers with a hard copy of the data (usually the size of a large phone book) and a magnetic tape with the data for loading on a mainframe. (They) give you the tapes in their format. You have to be able to read it and load it, which is not an easy task. The documentation that some of the services give you to load the data is sketchy.
>
> Some of the data comes in basically as flat, sequential files, and it is easy to decode and load that in a day or two. But if you are trying to load it into

a formal data base, that can take several days or weeks because you are trying to figure out all the indexing structures (for efficient retrieval) and are writing custom code.[12]

To compound things, the geographic boundaries used by the data suppliers differ from each other and most often from the firm's own geographic territories. Further, the services typically collect data on different time cycles. Some might provide it weekly, whereas others might provide it twice a month, monthly, or even less often. The discrepancies must be reconciled in a meaningful way if the various inputs are going to be combined into effective decision making.

A relatively recent way to handle these problems is distributed network computing. These systems rely on linked workstations. Because they are linked, users do not have to worry where the information is stored in the network of computers usually found in the largest corporations. More importantly, the systems used to access and manipulate the data make use of a common interface or server. Through that server, the analyst can do data entry, data query, spreadsheet analysis, plots, or statistical analysis or can even prepare reports, all through some very simple commands (see Exhibit 16.5).

For example, one of the more popular systems, Metaphor, uses a mouse-driven graphic front end.[13] Users simply need to point and click the mouse to access the documents they need. Further, they can formulate complex queries through simple instructions. For example, they can join data elements simply by drawing a line between two boxes. Thus, to look at sales in the Southeast, for example, users can simply draw a line between the data element marked "sales" and the box labeled "southeast region." They can build more elaborate routines by flowing data through a series of the available tools (word processing, spreadsheet, and graphics, for instance). They can specify sequences of operations by drawing arrows from one routine to the next. Once created, they can store these routines and launch similar analyses in the future with a single click of the mouse. Once recalled, they can modify and restore them. Thus, managers are able to continuously improve their modeling of the problems they face without becoming computer experts or even very knowledgeable about what goes on behind the scenes.

DSS in Sales Management

As the discussion above indicates, decision support systems are action-oriented. They allow managers to use their own instincts when seeking answers to problems. They are very adaptable to changing environmental circumstances and different management styles.

Decision support systems for managing the personal selling effort promise to be particularly important in the future as the microcomputer revolution continues. Not only is it becoming increasingly likely for branch, regional, and district managers to have microcomputers connected directly to the company's data bases at their desks, but also many companies are outfitting their sales-

EXHIBIT 16 • 5   *Use of Dialog Systems with Common Server or Interface Using Simplified, Standardized Instructions to Perform Multiple Tasks*

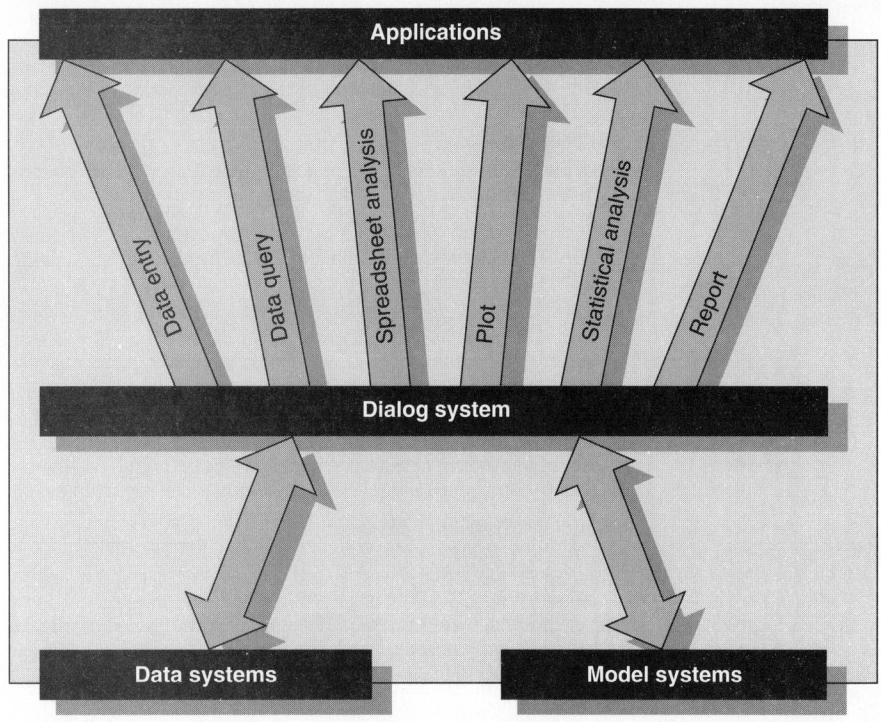

people with them as well and are developing special applications software. Exhibit 16.6, for example, describes Shell Chemical Company's experience in this regard.[14] The most common uses of DSSs in sales and sales management are as follows:[15]

- Customer account management   63%
- Data base inquiries   63
- Word processing   60
- Checking orders   58
- Forecasts   53
- Spreadsheets   51
- Entering orders   50
- Checking inventory   44
- Time management   29
- Prospecting   29
- Reporting expenses   26

EXHIBIT 16 ● 6   *Shell Chemical's Experience with Microcomputers with Special Applications Software for Salespeople*

in 1985, Shell Chemical Company began developing a software system that would improve the effectiveness and productivity of its field sales personnel and provide communication with business functions and administrative offices. Harold L. Cohan, Shell Chemical's manager of systems development, describes the process and its results.

System Detail

"Our Sales Force Automation system is a laptop computer-based 'tool kit' of integrated software applications. Its specific functions are these:

"Electronic mail. This allows our sales reps to create and read mail on their portable PCs. They periodically connect to a host system via an auto-dial phone to send and receive messages.

"Daily sales information. Sales reps can receive reports of sales activities for their customers and products, updated as of the previous day. This application is intregrated with the same connection as electronic mail; both applications were designed to eliminate time spent in front of the computer.

"Account management modules. These integrated applications help the sales force improve the management and information accessibility of their accounts. They include account-specific information such as contacts, phone numbers, addresses, and prices. These modules also include an easy-to-use call reporting system.

"Corporate forms. These incorporate several administrative forms we've automated, of which the company expense statement is the most significant.

"Other features of the system are a word-processing function to let sales reps create letters for direct mail or electronic distribution to the corporate word-processing system; a graphics software package for preparing charts and graphs; an appointment calendar and to-do-list functions."

Successes

After a year, certain applications have proven outstandingly useful. "The expense statement and sales inquiry functions alone were incentive enough for the sales force to learn the necessary technology," Cohan says.

"With the expense statement sales reps not only have a tool that helps them record and manage their day-to-day expenditures but also, because of its ease of use, error reduction, and time-saving features, allows them to receive reimbursement in a more timely manner."

"The sales inquiry function allows reps to better prepare for sales calls, without relying on clerical staff assistance or obsolete data."

Cohan mentions other features that were less convincing at first but now considered useful. "At first reps felt that E-mail merely duplicated Shell's audio mail system. Now they agree that these systems complement each other."

Word-processing functions were also originally rejected by the reps, many of whom couldn't type and who felt this was something their secretaries should do. "They now recognize that word processing is an excellent replacement for earlier methods of providing information to their support staffs. Now, instead of often illegible handwritten drafts that resulted in error and delay, computer-generated drafts can be provided to secretaries to be finished."

Iniitally skeptical about the benefits of graphics capabilities, sales reps have found this an effective tool for portraying data in graphs and charts rather than numbers and words. Using this in conjunction with their word processors, reps are providing impressive presentations to their customers and to Shell management.

Source: "Computer-Based Sales Support: Shell Chemical's System," *Marketing: The Conference Board's Management Briefing* 4 (April–May 1989), p. 4.

SALES ANALYSIS

A sales analysis involves gathering, classifying, comparing, and studying company sales data. It may "simply involve the comparison of total company sales in two different time periods. Or it may entail subjecting thousands of component sales (or sales-related) figures to a variety of comparisons—among themselves, with external data, and with like figures for earlier periods of time."[16]

A major benefit of even the most elementary sales analysis is in highlighting those products, customers, orders, or territories in which the firm's sales are concentrated. A heavy concentration is so common that some have labeled the general phenomenon the *80:20 principle.*[17] This means it is not at all unusual to find 80 percent of the customers or products accounting for only 20 percent of total sales. Conversely, the remaining 20 percent of the customers or products account for 80 percent of the total sales volume. The same phenomenon applies to orders and territories; only a small percentage of the total number of orders or a few of the firm's many territories account for the great percentage of its sales. The 80:20 principle describes the general situation, although the exact concentration ratio varies by company.

In one early study to assess the magnitude of the concentration ratio, 200 questionnaires were mailed to companies listed in the American Institute of Management's *Manual of Excellent Managements*. The companies were asked to rank their products, orders, customers, salespeople, and sales territories according to sales volume and to indicate the percentage of sales generated by the top third of each. Of those contacted, 80 responded. While the results did not yield an 80:20 ratio, they did suggest a heavy concentration. For example, the percentages of sales accounted for by each of the top one-third items in each category were as follows.[18]

Products	72 percent
Orders	73 percent
Customers	74 percent
Salespeople	59 percent
Sales territories	62 percent

To produce these overall percentages, some individual companies had to have concentration ratios much higher than these averages. There are some other interesting examples in this regard.

One manufacturer found that 78 percent of his customers produced only slightly more than 2 percent of his sales volume. In another business, 48 percent of the orders accounted for only 5 percent of the sales. In yet another case, 76 percent of the number of products manufactured accounted for only 3 percent of the sales volume. In another business, 59 percent of the sales reps' calls were made on accounts from which only 12 percent of the sales were obtained.

In a wholesale grocery firm, more than 50 percent of the total number of customers brought in less than 2 percent of the total sales volume. Similarly, 40 percent of the total number of items carried in stock accounted for less than 2 percent of the total sales volume.[19]

The most cursory sales analysis should reveal such concentrations. The Mosinee Paper Company, for example, almost dropped one of its products because of its dismal sales performance. Then an elementary sales analysis found that only a single sales rep was selling the specific grade of industrial paper. On further investigation, Mosinee discovered how the buyers "were using the paper—an application that had been known only to the one salesman and his customers. This information enabled management to educate its other salespeople as to the potential market for the paper and sales rose substantially."[20]

Key Decisions in a Sales Analysis

Those wishing to undertake a sales analysis must decide (1) the type of evaluation system, (2) the sources of information, and (3) the sales breakdowns that will be used. Exhibit 16.7 overviews the nature of these decisions.

Type of Evaluation System

The type of evaluation system determines how the sales analysis will be conducted. Will it be a simple sales analysis or a comparative analysis? When it is to be a comparative analysis, two additional questions arise: (1) What is to be the base for the comparison? (2) What type of reporting and control system is to be used?

In a simple sales analysis, the facts are listed and not measured against any standard. In a comparative analysis or, as it is sometimes called, *a performance analysis,* comparisons are made. Consider, for example, the data in Exhibit 16.8. A simple sales analysis would be restricted to the facts in column (1). These figures suggest Dawson sold the most and Barrington the least. A performance analysis would attempt to go beyond the mere listing of sales to determine where they are greatest and poorest; it would try to make comparisons against some "standard." In Exhibit 16.8, the standard is the quota for each salesman, and column (3) provides a performance index for each. This performance index is calculated as the ratio of actual sales to sales quota ($PI = S/Q \times 100$). It suggests Dawson was not the "best" in 1993, but rather Bendt was; and in fact, Dawson realized the smallest percentage of his total potential as judged by his quota.

Base for comparison

The comparison with quota is only one type of comparison that can be made. It is one of the most common because it is very useful, particularly when quotas have been specified well. That is a big *if,* however. Quotas can be a real problem—as we saw in Chapter 8—when they are done poorly and perhaps

EXHIBIT 16 • 7   *Some Key Decisions when Conducting a Sales Analysis*

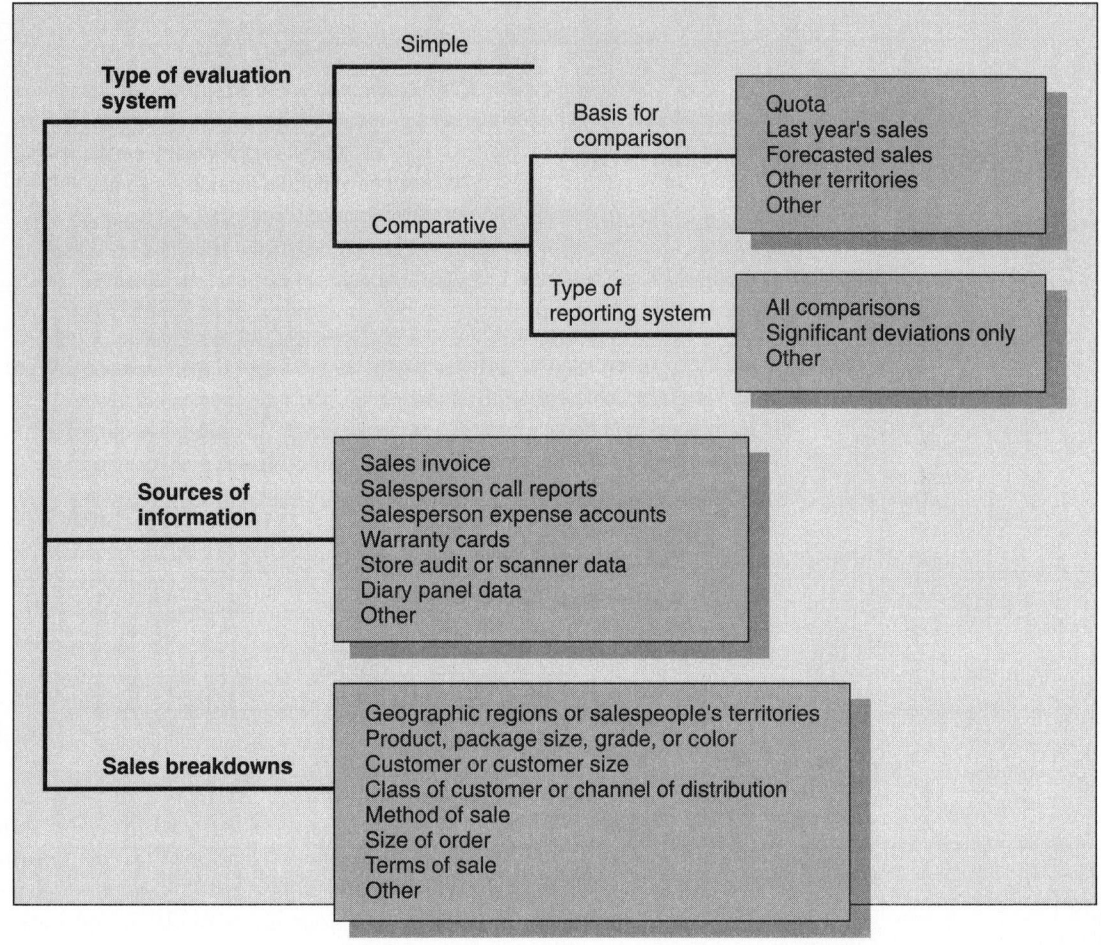

even when they are done well, as Thorny Issue 16.1 suggests. Consequently, some firms resort to other bases of comparison for a sales analysis. These include this year's sales versus last year's sales or the average of a number of prior years' sales; this year's sales versus forecasted sales; sales in one territory versus sales in another, either absolutely or in relation to the ratios in prior years; and the percentage change in sales from one territory to another, as compared with last year.

Such comparisons are certainly better than simply viewing raw sales figures, but they are not generally as productive as a "true" performance analysis. In

EXHIBIT 16 • 8   *Differences between Simple Sales Analysis and Comparative Analysis*

Sales Representative	(1) 1993 Sales ($000)	(2) 1993 Quota ($000)	(3) Performance Index
Duane Barrington	$760.9	$700	108.7
John Bendt	793.5	690	115.0
James Dawson	859.2	895	96.0
George Richardson	837.0	775	108.0
Walter Keyes	780.3	765	102.0

the latter, variations from planned performance are highlighted, and the reasons for such exceptions are isolated.

Type of reporting system

The other major question that arises in a comparative sales analysis is the type of reporting and control system to be used. At one extreme, all comparisons are provided. Thus, if one relevant comparison is to be sales as a percentage of quota, this statistic would be provided for each salesperson, branch, district, region, customer, product, and every other unit by which sales are to be analyzed. The problem with this is that it can inundate the sales manager with information. The manager may be unable to process it effectively, and it becomes a useless pile of unused computer output or a computer screen filled with numbers.

At the other extreme, only "significant" deviations from the norm are highlighted—for example, all those that deviate by at least 10 percent from standard. According to this criterion, the only performance index in Exhibit 16.8 that would be reported to management would be Bendt's. For many sales managers, this "extreme deviation" reporting does not provide the necessary detail for them to operate most effectively. Deviations just short of the significance cutoff go unnoticed.

Probably the most useful reporting system is one in which all comparisons are reported, or at least are available for inspection, while the significant deviations are highlighted. This can be done by a separate listing of those sales units beyond the predetermined boundaries or by simply highlighting on the all-comparisons report those deviations that are excessive, for example, by asterisking them. Sales managers can then concentrate on the exceptions while having the full profile of comparisons for assessing the significance of what happened.

Sources of Information

A second class of major decisions that must be made with respect to sales analysis is what information is to serve as input to the system and how the

Thorny Issues in Sales Management 16 • 1

Crosby Chemical, a manufacturer of industrial cleaning compounds and solvents, had just completed its first marketing audit. On the basis of the audit, the company decided to develop market potentials for each of its sales territories, both domestic and international, and to use these potentials to develop quotas, which would be used to assess each salesperson's performance.

The first year's results are in, and Andrea Parrett is furious. She has complained loudly and continuously to Irma Pelton, Crosby's sales manager, about her most recent performance evaluation. While she had produced a 16 percent sales increase in her Venezuelan territory, she had been given a below-average performance evaluation using the company's new criterion of sales versus quota.

Pelton explained to Parrett that the company used the same criteria—number of establishments and number of employees—to establish the market potential for its products in Venezuela and Parrett's quota that it had used for other territories. Parrett countered that those criteria were inappropriate in Venezuela. Not only was there less manufacturing equipment per person in Venezuela, and thus less cleanup per employee, but also users of the cleaning compounds were more likely to reuse them in Venezuela than in other countries where single use and disposal were the norms.

What would you recommend Pelton do, particularly given the fact that Parrett had been considered one of the company's top young salespeople?

basic source documents are to be processed. To address this question, the firm first needs to determine the types of comparisons to be made. A comparison with sales in other territories will require fewer documents than a comparison against market potential or quota or against the average sales in the territory for the last five years. The firm also needs to decide the extent to which preparing the sales report should be integrated with preparing other types of reports. These may include inventory or production reports or sales reports for other company units such as other divisions.

Generally, the one most productive source document is the sales invoice. From this, the following information can usually be extracted:

- Customer name and location
- Product(s) or service(s) sold.
- Volume and dollar amount of the transaction.
- Salesperson (or agent) responsible for the sale.
- End use of product sold.
- Location of customer facility where product is to be shipped and/or used.
- Customer's industry, class of trade, and/or channel of distribution.
- Terms of sale and applicable discount.
- Freight paid and/or to be collected.

- Shipment point for the order.
- Transportation used in shipment.[21]

Other documents provide more specialized output. Some of the more important of these are listed in Exhibit 16.9. Most companies are likely to use only two or three of these sources of sales information in addition to the sales invoice. Which ones depend on the company and the types of other analyses used to evaluate salespeople.

Sales Breakdowns

The third major decision management must confront when designing a sales analysis is which variables will serve as points of aggregation. Without such categories, the firm would be forced to analyze every transaction in isolation or would need to look at sales in the aggregate. The latter is not particularly informative, and the former is almost impossible. The most common and instructive procedure is to assemble and tabulate sales by some appropriate groupings, such as these:

- Geographic regions such as states, counties, regions, or salespeople's territories.
- Product, package size, grade, or color.
- Customer or customer size.
- Market, including class of customer, end use, or channel of distribution.
- Method of sale, including mail, telephone, or direct salespeople.
- Size of order.
- Financial arrangement such as cash or charge.

The classes of information a company may use depends on such things as the diversity of its product line, the geographic extent of its sales area, the number of markets and customers it serves, and the level of management for which the information is to be supplied. The firm with a product management form of organization, for example, would be interested in sales by product groups. These managers might focus on territory-by-territory sales of their products. The sales manager and regional managers might be much more interested in territory and customer analyses and only secondarily interested in the territory sales broken out by product.

These breakdowns are not necessarily mutually exclusive in that the manager has to choose a breakdown by region or product or customer. Rather, sales analyses are most productive when they are done hierarchically, in the sense that one breakdown is carried out within another category. The categories are treated simultaneously instead of separately. For example, the analysis may end up showing that customer XYZ in the western region purchased so many units of each products A, B, C, and D; this illustrates a territory, customer, and product hierarchical breakdown.

Cash register receipts

Type (cash or credit) and dollar amount of transaction by department by salesperson.

Salesperson's call reports

Customers and prospects called on (company and individual seen; planned or unplanned calls)
Products discussed
Orders obtained
Customers' product needs and usage
Other significant information about customers
Distribution of salespeople's time among customer calls, travel, and office work
Sales-related activities: meetings, conventions, etc.

Salespeople's expense accounts

Expenses by day by item (hotel, meals, travel, etc).

Indivdual customer (and prospect) records

Name and location and customer number
Number of calls by company salesperson (agents)
Sales by company (in dollars and/or units by product or service by location of customer facility)
Customer's industry, class of trade, and/or trade channel
Estimated total annual usage of each product or service sold by the company
Estimated annual purchases from the company of each such product or service
Location (in terms of company sales territory)

Financial records

Sales revenue (by products, geographic markets, customers, class of trade, unit of sales organization, etc.)
Direct sales expenses (similarly classified)
Overhead sales costs (similarly classified)
Profits (similarly classified)

Credit memos

Returns and allowances

Warranty cards

Indirect measures of dealer sales
Customer service

EXHIBIT 16 • 10 *Sales Reports in a Consumer Food Products Company*

Report Name	Purpose	Report Access*
Region	To provide sales information in units and dollars for each sales office or center in the region as well as a regional total	Appropriate regional manager
Sales office or center	To provide sales information in units and dollars for each district manager assigned to a sales office	Appropriate sales office or center manager
District	To provide sales information in units and dollars for each account supervisor and retail salesperson reporting to the district manager	Appropriate district manager
Salesperson summary	To provide sales information in units and dollars for each customer on whom the salesperson calls	Appropriate salesperson
Salesperson customer/product	To provide sales information in units and dollars for each customer on whom the salesperson calls	Appropriate salesperson
Salesperson/ product	To provide sales information in units and dollars for each product that the salesperson sells	Appropriate salesperson
Region/product	To provide sales information in units and dollars for each product sold within the region. Similar reports would be available by sales office and by district.	Appropriate regional manager
Region/customer class	To provide sales information in units and dollars for each class of customer located in the region. Similar reports would be available by sales office and by district.	Appropriate regional manager

*To understand the report access, it is useful to know that salespeople were assigned accounts in sales districts. Sales people were assigned one or, at most, a couple of large accounts and were responsible for all the grocery stores, regardless of geography, affiliated with these large accounts, or they were assigned a geographic territory and were responsible for all of the stores within that territory. All sales districts were assigned to sales offices or sales centers. The centers were, in turn, organized into regions.

The advantage of hierarchical breakdowns is illustrated later. For now, you should know that the typical sales analysis results not in a single report but in a family of reports, each reflecting a different level of aggregation, tailored to the person receiving it. Exhibit 16.10, for example, shows the types of sales reports used in a consumer food products company for which one of the authors served as consultant.

A HIERARCHICAL SALES ANALYSIS

To illustrate some relevant comparisons and the process used in conducting a sales analysis, consider the data in Exhibit 16.11. The figures apply to a national

EXHIBIT 16 • 11 *Sales and Sales Quotas for Kitchenware Company*

Region	BPI (percent of U.S.)	Sales Quota ($ millions)	Sales ($ millions)	Difference ($ millions)	Performance Index (*PI* = *S/Q* × 100)
New England	5.8193%	$ 24.44	$ 25.03	$ 0.59	102.4
Middle Atlantic	18.3856	77.22	78.19	0.97	101.3
East north central	20.1419	84.60	79.48	−5.12	94.0
West north central	7.3982	31.07	30.51	−0.56	98.2
South Atlantic	14.7525	61.96	64.07	2.11	103.4
East south central	5.2571	22.08	23.20	1.12	105.1
West south central	9.2022	38.65	38.42	−0.23	99.4
Mountain	4.2819	17.98	17.73	−0.25	98.6
Pacific	14.7613	62.00	64.60	2.60	104.2
Total United States	100.0000%	$420.00	$421.23	$ 1.23	100.3

manufacturer of small kitchen appliances, though the actual numbers, as well as the identity of the company, have been disguised. The Kitchenware Company previously determined its sales are highly correlated with population, income, and the general level of retail sales. Thus, it has determined market potential by region using the corollary index method. More particularly, it has used the buying power index (BPI) published by *Sales & Marketing Management* to determine each region's market potential and has then multiplied these potentials by the company's expected market share to generate the regional quotas in Exhibit 16.11.[22]

Note that, although the annual quota was $420 million, total sales in all regions were $421.23 million. Not only has the total company met quota, but also so have most of the regions. The performance index, the ratio of sales to quota, is greater than 100 for five regions. Four regions fell short of their targets, but three of those came very close. Only the east north-central region fell short by more than 2 percent, but it still had the highest absolute dollar value of sales of any of the major regions. Many sales managers might be tempted from this to assume all is well. At the most, they might send a letter to the manager of the east north-central region, urging her to push the sales-people in the region to do better.

Fortunately, the sales manager for Kitchenware did neither. Rather he simply interrogated the information system to generate the sales breakdown for the east north-central region, shown in Exhibit 16.12. The state quotas were determined by multiplying the BPI total U.S. percentages for each state by the $420 million total forecasted sales. In many cases, the firm might wish to convert each percentage to a percentage of the region, rather than of the United States as a whole. Thus, the percentage for Illinois would be (6.0037 ÷ 20.1419) × 100 = 29.8; this percentage would then be applied to the

EXHIBIT 16 • 12 *Sales Breakdown for East North-Central Region*

State	BPI (percent of U.S.)	Sales Quota ($ millions)	Sales ($ millions)	Difference ($ millions)	Performance Index ($PI = S/Q \times 100$)
Illinois	6.0037%	$25.22	$24.30	$ −0.92	96.4
Indiana	2.4103	10.12	10.24	0.12	101.2
Michigan	4.6401	19.49	17.77	−1.72	91.2
Ohio	4.9764	20.90	20.43	−0.47	97.8
Wisconsin	2.1114	8.87	6.74	−2.13	76.0
Total region	20.1419%	$84.60	$79.48	$ −5.12	94.0

$8.60 million quota for the region to get the quota for Illinois. Although the result is the same, this second alternative provides a clearer picture of the concentrations of demand in the region; the benefit holds particularly when one works with smaller and smaller units of analysis.

Exhibit 16.12 shows a problem with sales throughout the region. Only the sales representatives in Indiana exceeded quota, and then only slightly. Note that the deviations about quota are larger than they were in Exhibit 16.11. This generally happens as one moves to smaller units of analysis. With larger aggregates—for example, regions versus states—the statistician's law of large numbers seems to apply in that the pluses and minuses about quota tend to balance each other; thus, the performance indexes in the larger analysis tend to be closer to 100. A smaller deviation from quota should initiate further investigation when the analysis is based on large aggregates (regions) than on small ones (salespeople).

Although there is some negative deviation in actual sales from standard in Exhibit 16.12 among four of the five states, the deviation in Wisconsin is most pronounced. Only 76 percent of the quota was realized here.

Again, it would be very easy for a sales manager to take impulsive action. Instead of getting on a plane to Wisconsin, having the east north-central regional manager call the Wisconsin district manager, or calling him himself, the Kitchenware general sales manager looked at the tabulation of sales by sales representatives in the Wisconsin district. The eight areas into which the state is divided are shown in Exhibit 16.13, and the results of the tabulation are shown in Exhibit 16.14 on page 716. Sales are below quota in all sales areas in the state. This suggests there may be something fundamentally wrong. Perhaps economic conditions are poor and unemployment is high; perhaps competition is more intense than in other areas; or there may be a problem with sales force morale and motivation. Although there are many plausible explanations for the sales manager to check, the core problem seems to be Hutchins. If he had done as well as the other sale reps in the state, sales for

E X H I B I T 16 • 13 *Sales Territories in Wisconsin*

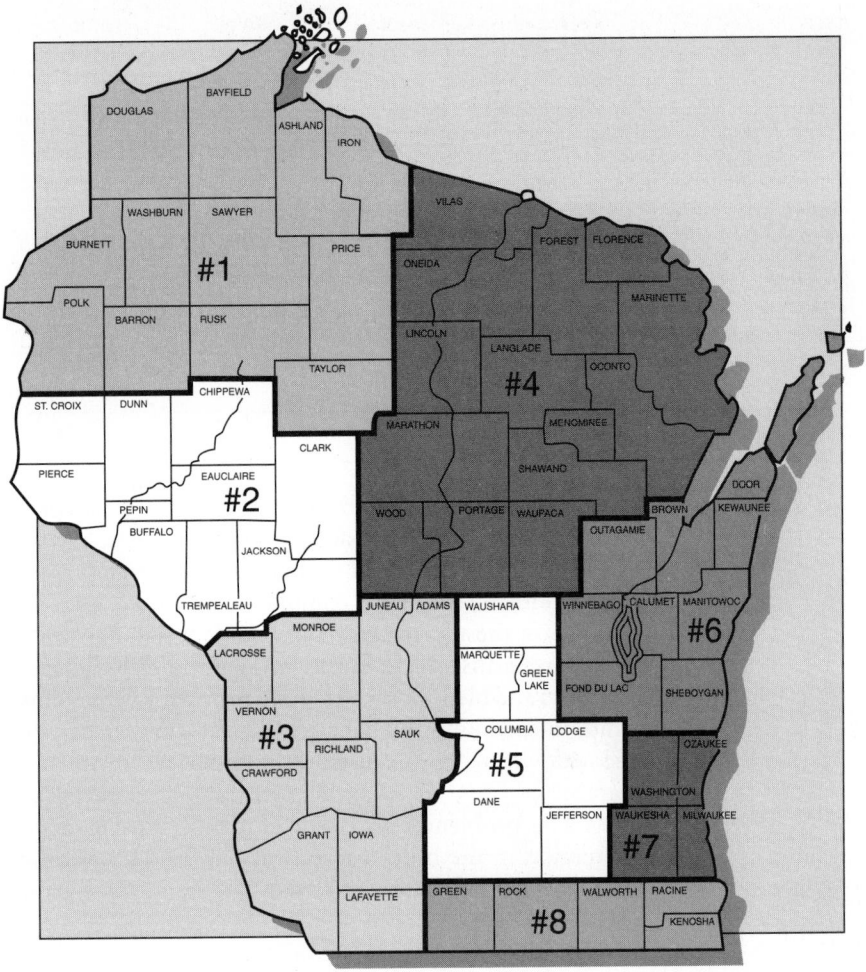

the district would have been much closer to target. The problem is particularly acute because Hutchins has the prime Milwaukee market as his sales territory.

Before taking action about Hutchins, the sales manager wanted more information. Consequently, he requested the tabulation of Hutchin's sales by product, shown in Exhibit 16.15 on page 717. Hutchins is below quota on the entire product line; however, he seems to be having the most problem with coffee makers and blenders/mixers/food processors.

Is the problem Hutchins or these products? A further analysis of sales of these products by customer indicated the problem was concentrated among

EXHIBIT 16 • 14 *Sales by Representative in the Wisconsin District*

Area Representative	BPI (percent of U.S.)	Sales Quota ($000)	Sales ($000)	Difference ($000)	Performance Index (PI = S/Q × 100)
1. T. Tate	0.0953%	$ 400.2	$392.6	$ −7.6	98.1
2. T. Bir	0.1332	559.4	501.0	−58.4	89.6
3. C. Holzem	0.1325	556.5	512.4	−44.1	92.1
4. A. Elliott	0.2021	848.8	768.7	−80.1	90.6
5. P. Martin	0.2596	1,090.3	969.3	−121.0	88.9
6. J. Campbell	0.3384	1,421.3	1,340.3	−81.0	94.3
7. L. Hutchins	0.6975	2,929.5	1,285.0	−1,644.5	43.9
8. B. Lessner	0.2528	1,061.8	970.5	−91.3	91.4
Total Wisconsin	2.1114%	$8,867.8	$6,739.8	$−2,128.0	76.0

large department store buyers. Furthermore, the problem was not unique to Hutchins but was common to all reps in the east and west north-central regions. A major competitor had been attempting to improve its position in the north-central region through a combination of heavy advertising and purchase rebate offers on these products. This problem had been obscured in other sales territories because sales of other products had compensated for lost sales in coffee makers and blenders/mixers/food processors. Hutchins's sales of other products did not make up the deficit. His problem was compounded by the economic slowdown in the metal-working industry, a big employer in the Milwaukee area.

The problem then is not Hutchins. Rather, it is the special competitive situation in the north-central region. This situation would not have come to light without the sales analysis.

Iceberg Principle

One important principle illustrated by the preceding example is that aggregate figures can be deceiving and small, visible problems are often symptoms of large, unseen problems. The phenomenon has been linked to an iceberg. Only about 10 percent of an iceberg's mass is above the water level. The other 90 percent is below the surface, and not always directly below it either. The submerged portion can be very dangerous to ships. So it is with much marketing and business data.

The typical business engages in many varied activities and collects large volumes of data to support these activities. Thus, it is very common for difficulties or problems in one area to be submerged. On the surface, all appears calm and peaceful, but more careful analyses may reveal submerged problems with jagged edges that can "sink the business" if they are not attended to

EXHIBIT 16 • 15 *Hutchin's Sales by Product*

Product	Sales Quota	Sales	Difference	Performance Index ($PI = S/Q \times 100$)
Can openers/knife sharpeners	$ 212,000	$ 124,500	$ − 87,500	58.7
Toasters	468,000	237,000	− 231,000	50.6
Coffee makers	627,000	176,000	− 451,000	28.1
Blenders/mixers/food processors	604,000	159,200	− 444,800	26.4
Griddles/electric fry pans	573,000	340,000	− 233,000	59.3
Other—electric carving knives/popcorn makers/hot trays, etc.	445,500	248,300	− 197,200	55.7
Total	$2,929,500	$1,285,000	$ − 1,644,500	43.9

properly. Those analyzing the information that is collected need to be especially wary that the summaries they produce by aggregating and averaging data do not hide more than they reveal.

The iceberg principle is pervasive. The 80:20 rule or concentration ratio discussed earlier is one manifestation of it. Often, the concentration of sales within certain territories, products, or customers hides specific weaknesses. More than one company has shown satisfactory total sales, but when the total was subdivided by territories, customers, and products, serious weaknesses were uncovered.

Simple versus Comparative Analysis

The preceding example also shows the difference between a simple sales analysis and a comparative sales analysis, as well as the advantages of the latter. The simple sales analysis would have focused on the sales data in Exhibit 16.11; it would not have examined the differences from quota, but simply the raw figures. It probably would not have generated any detailed investigation of the east north-central region because sales there were higher than in any other region. The comparison with quota, however, emphasized that the potential in this region was also greater than in any other and the firm was failing to get its share. The comparative analysis triggered the more intensive investigation and isolated the primary reason for the sales shortfall. The execution of the process depended on having sales quotas available on a very small basis. They had to be available by customer, by product, and by salesperson or the problem would never have come to light.

It is sometimes difficult to generate quotas on such a small basis. In the

Kitchenware Company, it was possible because detailed geographic statistics on the BPI were available. In situations where other data should be used, they need to be available by small geographic area. That is one reason the sales planning and sales evaluation questions are so intertwined. One must keep in mind the questions of evaluation and the comparisons needed when designing sales territories and sales quotas.

A comparative sales analysis has uncovered problems that were not revealed by a simple sales analysis in many other instances. Hansen Manufacturing Company produces quick connective couplings for air and fluid power transmission systems. It found that one distributor that had been a consistent winner of sales performance awards under its old system (no comparisons with potential but simply absolute dollar sales and yearly sales increases) ranked 31st out of the 31 distributors handling the products in a comparative sales analysis.

> Subsequent investigation showed that the distributor did not know how to sell Hansen couplings to some important accounts. Recognition of the problem produced needed changes in the distributor's operations and performance improved.[23]

Isolate and Explode

Another concept the example illustrates is the principle of "isolate and explode," in which the most significant discrepancies between actual and standard are identified, or isolated, and then examined in detail, or exploded. The detail this explosion reveals is then analyzed, the most significant discrepancies are again isolated, and these are exploded. The process continues until the "real" problems are isolated. Thus, in the Kitchenware example, the following were all isolated and exploded in turn: the east north-central region, the Wisconsin district, Hutchins's sales by product, and Hutchins's product sales by customer.

An alternative would have been to have masses of data available to the sales manager initially. For example, the information system could have supplied the sales manager with the detailed tabulations of sales by each salesperson of each product to each customer in the beginning. More than likely, such a tabulation would go unused because of its size and the time it would take to decipher its contents. The isolate-and-explode principle makes the task manageable. The sales manager can quickly localize trouble spots by focusing on the most substantial exceptions from standard and then home in more efficiently on an effective cure.

The principle can also be used to isolate exceptional performances for the clues they might provide to what the firm is doing right. Investigating why the east south-central region was 5.1 percent over quota when the entire company was only 0.3 percent over quota might suggest effective competitive strategies.

The isolate-and-explode principle assumes the company's information system can provide sales data hierarchically. In Kitchenware, the sales manager could secure data broken out by customer, by product, by sales rep, by district, and by region (see Exhibit 16.16). The breakdowns resemble a tree: total U.S.

EXHIBIT 16 • 16 *Hierarchical Sales Analyses Possible in Kitchenware Company*

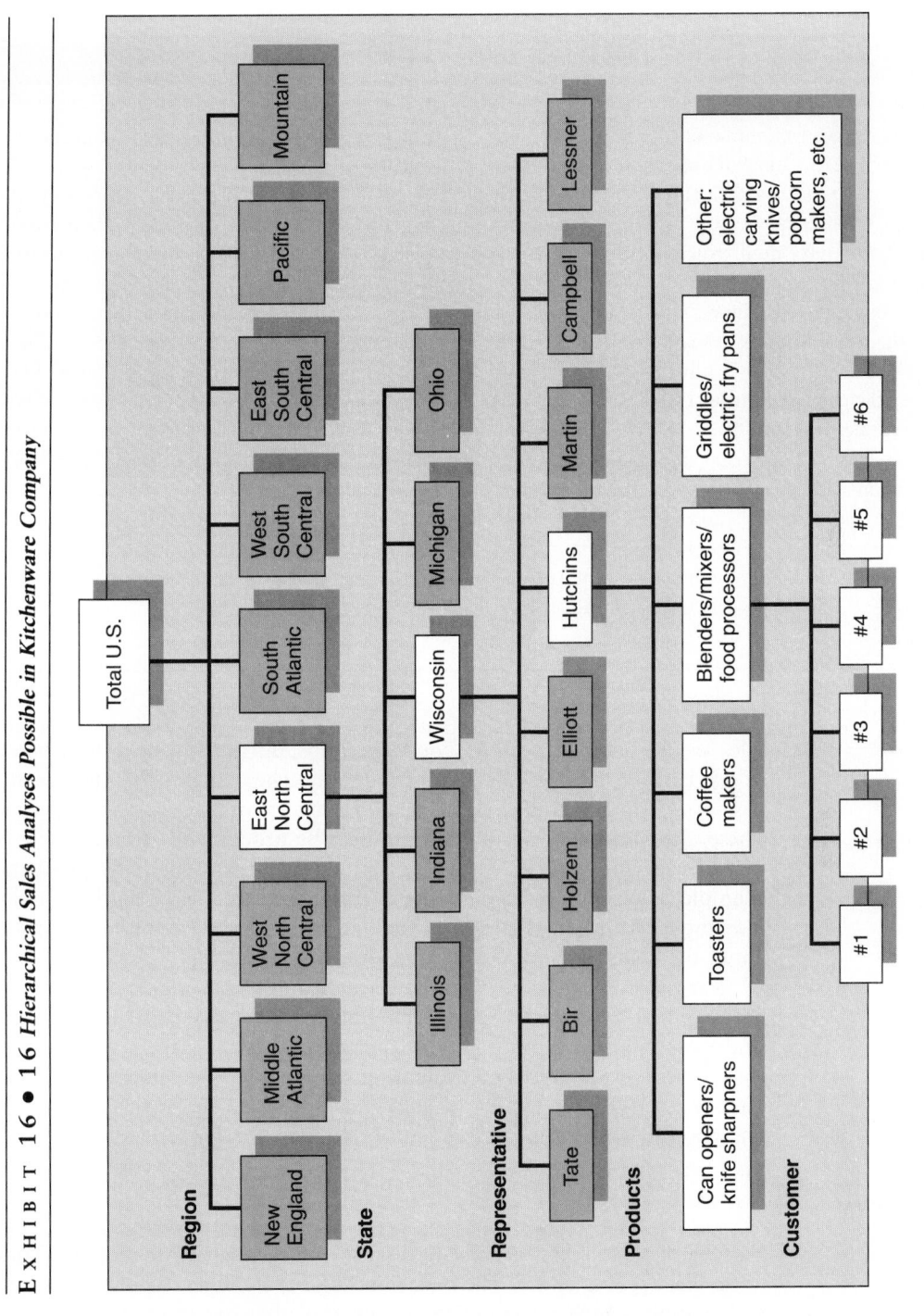

Thorny Issues in Sales Management 16 • 2

Sales of oxygen concentrators have been in a slump for several years. During the recession, home health-care dealers who buy such equipment and lease it to people with respiratory problems for use in their homes have been reluctant to buy new machines and have been repairing their old ones instead. Because of the slump, A-Plus Concentrators is laying off one of its salaried salespeople. Brad Borchert, the company's sales manager, has narrowed the choice to one of two of the company's newest salespeople.

One of them, Arnold, has shown slow but steady growth in sales. Arnold is also a friendly person, loyal to the company, and seems to have high ethical standards. A-Plus has received a number of favorable, unsolicited comments from Arnold's customers about how well they like doing business with him because of his integrity and interest in their welfare.

The other sales rep, Bruce, has shown great promise and seems to be a "natural" salesperson. Since day one, his sales have been consistently higher than Arnold's, and in a couple of quarters they approached the levels achieved by more senior salespeople. At the same time, Borchert believes Bruce is more aggressive, less personal, and less loyal to A-Plus Concentrators than Arnold is. He also receives fewer unsolicited kudos from Bruce's customers, and some of them have volunteered that Bruce is "pushy" and "overly aggressive."

Which representative do you think Borchert should let go? Why?

---

sales are the trunk, regions are the main limbs, districts the next branches, and so on. Further, all combinations of these branches are possible. For example, it is possible to do a study by product and territory, or by customer and product. These alternate types of analysis can also be productive, as can simple one-way categorizing of sales data. The simple tabulation of sales by product, for example, is very useful in showing a firm's product line strengths. Similarly, the simple tabulation of sales by major classes of customers is often informative about the company's market strengths.

Keep in mind that these analyses are diagnostics, not decision rules. They do not tell the manager what to do, but only offer clues as to causes of problems. And sales analyses is only part of the story. Sales managers might want to consider other factors when evaluating salespeople (see Thorny Issues 16.2). That is why cost and other analyses also play a role in the evaluation of salespeople.

SUMMARY

This chapter is the first of three to discuss management evaluation and control of the field selling effort. The most thorough evaluation mechanism is a marketing audit, which is a complete, systematic, objective evaluation of the total marketing effort of the firm. The sales management audit is an example of a vertical audit because it is the detailed analysis of one part of the total marketing effort. The sales management audit should examine objectives, policies, organization, methods, and procedures used in managing the personal selling function, as well as assess how individual personnel are performing.

Decision support systems are increasingly being used to evaluate the personal selling effort in general and the performance of individual salespeople as well. A DSS is a coordinated collection of data, systems, tools, and techniques with supporting software and hardware by which an organization gathers and interprets relevant information from business and the environment and turns it into a basis for marketing action.

A DSS concentrates on the design of data systems. The data systems include the processes used to capture and store information useful for marketing decision making. The model system includes all the routines that allow users to manipulate data to conduct the analyses they desire. The dialog systems are most important and most clearly differentiate DSSs from traditional information systems. They allow managers to conduct their own analyses while they or an assistant sit at a computer terminal. This allows managers to analyze problems using their own personal insight into what might be happening in a given situation.

A sales analysis can be one of the more revealing inputs in a performance appraisal. A sales analysis involves gathering, classifying, comparing, and studying company sales data. The study may simply involve the comparison of total company sales in two time periods, or it may subject thousands of component sales figures to a variety of comparisons. One real benefit of a sales analysis is in highlighting the concentration ratio, or the 80:20 principle, for products, customers, and the like.

Those wishing to make a sales analysis must decide at least three things. First, the sales manager must decide the type of control system to be used. Will it involve simple or comparative sales analyses? Will it be one that provides all relevant comparisons, or one that reports only significant exceptions, or some combination of these schemes? Second, the source documents must be pinpointed or designed. The sales invoice is typically one of the most useful source documents, so great care must go into its design. Third, the sales manager must decide which variables are to serve as points of aggregation—for example, geographic regions, products, or salespeople. Most likely, the manager will want the input records to be maintained disaggregatively, so hierarchical sales analyses can be conducted. A hierarchical sales analysis involves the investigation of sales by several components when the components are considered simultaneously.

One productive way to conduct a sales analysis is via the principle of isolate and explode, in which the most significant discrepancies between actual and standard are isolated and then exploded. The detail this explosion reveals is then analyzed, the most significant discrepancies are noted, and these are exploded. A rather common output of an isolate-and-explode analysis is to find that small, barely visible problems are often underlying symptoms of large, invisible problems, much like an iceberg; thus, the phenomenon has been referred to as the iceberg principle.

*Discussion
Questions*

1. The sales manager of Eastwood Electronics, a Canadian firm located in Toronto, reviewed sales results for the provinces located in the western region, where sales were about 5 percent below quota. To gain a clearer picture, the sales manager examined sales in each province and noted that sales in Vancouver, British Columbia, were well below quota. Sales in the two other provinces in the western region were actually above quota. Murray Eastwood, the owner's nephew, is responsible for the Vancouver area and has reported sales that are 30 percent below quota. How should the sales manager handle this situation? Should Murray Eastwood be given a warning?

2. The use of scanner data collected at the time of checkout in supermarkets has increased dramatically in sales analysis. One company has recruited families nationwide to participate in a panel study. When a shopper enters the checkout lane, he or she gives the clerk a plastic card that is passed over the scanner. All items purchased that are scanned are recorded in the shopper's diary. Oscar Mayer, a Wisconsin-based producer of meat, turkey, and seafood, has used different advertising campaigns in several markets to determine which ad campaign was most effective. How else could Oscar Mayer and other companies use scanner data? Of what value would scanner data be to sales reps? To food retailers?

3. One critic, commenting about sales potential, said, "If you look long enough, and hard enough, you can find ratios that will make anybody look good and anybody look bad." What does this say about the sales analysis process?

4. Typically, management by exception concentrates on ratios that indicate substandard performance. What arguments can be advanced for analyzing ratios that reveal both substandard performance and exceptional performance?

5. The Recall Computer Co. has six sales territories, each represented by one sales rep. After extensive planning, the company determines that each territory would be expected to achieve the following percentages of total company sales for 1993.

Territory 1	27%	Territory 4	12%
Territory 2	15%	Territory 5	20%
Territory 3	18%	Territory 6	8%

These figures are used as the standard for comparing each sales representative's actual 1993 sales. The company projected sales for 1993 of $20,500,000. Determine which sales representatives' territory had the best performance, by using the performance index, if the actual sales for 1993 in each territory were $5,425,000, $3,205,000, $3,710,000, $2,400,000, $3,900,000, and $2,000,000, respectively.

6. The use of personal computers by managers has been viewed as an invasion of privacy by some people. According to one critic, "Sales information is transmitted immediately, and I don't have a chance to explain any strange variations." Another commented, "This is like 'Big Brother' watching me. Before, my sales manager

couldn't care less; now he's on my back constantly." Comment. Are these views justifiable?

7. The Amjoy Corporation has developed a series of ratios to evaluate regional, district, and individual performance. Upper and lower control limits permit quick identification of significant deviations. The accompanying chart shows the sales-expense-to-sales ratio for Barbara Smith. What does this chart reveal? What action, if any, should Barbara's district sales manager take?

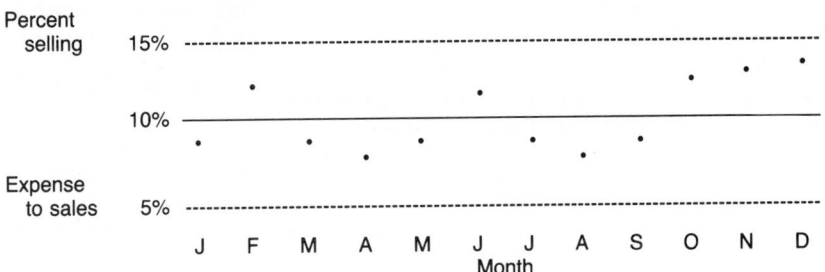

8. How might the results of a sales analysis affect the following activities?
   a. Recruiting.
   b. Sales training.
   c. Compensation.
   d. Sales force motivation.
   e. Sales forecasting.
   f. Pricing.

9. In planning a sales analysis system, one must consider that information needs vary from district sales manager to regional sales manager to national sales manager. Give specific examples of how information needs vary among individuals.

10. The marketing manager of the Kitchenware Company was incensed after seeing the results in Exhibit 16.14 and concluded that L. Hutchins was not devoting sufficient effort to the job. Hutchins's performance was $1.6 million below quota. The marketing manager has asked you, Kitchenware's sales manager, to take disciplinary action and place Hutchins on 90-day probation. How would you handle this situation?

Endnotes

[1] For discussion of the concept and conduct of a sales management audit, see Alan J. Dubinsky and Richard W. Hansen, "The Sales Force Management Audit," *California Management Review* 24 (Winter 1984), pp. 86–95.

[2] For suggestions on how to conduct a sales management audit, see Jim Cook, "Conducting an Audit of the Sales Organization," in *Sales Manager's Handbook,* eds. Edwin E. Bobrow and Larry Wizenberg (Homewood, Ill.: Dow Jones-Irwin, 1983), pp. 467–76.

[3] "Firms Start Using Computers to Take the Place of Salesmen," *The Wall Street Journal,* July 15, 1982, p. 29.

[4] Susan Chase, "Xerox Plans to Sell Most of Its Retail Stores to New Concern Headed by Texas Group," *The Wall Street Journal,* October 25, 1983, p. 60.

[5]Meg Cox, "Marketing & Media: Bantam Doubleday Sales Operations Are Restructured," *The Wall Street Journal,* May 9, 1991, p. B6.

[6]John D. C. Little, "Decision Support Systems for Marketing Managers," *Journal of Marketing,* 43 (Summer 1979), p. 11. See also Martin D. Goslar and Stephen W. Brown, "Decision Support System Models," *Information Processing and Management* 2 (1988), pp. 429–48.

[7]Exhibit 16.3 and the surrounding discussion are adapted from the excellent treatment of the subject by Ralph H. Sprague, Jr., and Eric D. Carlson, *Effective Decision Support Systems* (Englewood Cliffs, N.J.: Prentice Hall, 1982), chap. 1 and 2. See also Jitender S. Deogun, "A Conceptual Approach to Decision Support Systems: Advantage in Consumer Marketing Settings," *Journal of Consumer Marketing* 3 (Summer 1986), pp. 43–50; and Alan J. Greco and Jack T. Hogue, "Developing Decision Support Systems in Consumer Goods Firms," *The Journal of Consumer Marketing* 7 (Winter 1990), pp. 55–64.

[8]John D. C. Little and Michael N. Cassettari, *Decision Support Systems for Marketing Managers* (New York: American Management Association, 1984), p. 14.

[9]*Ibid.,* p. 15.

[10]Raymond McLeod, Jr., and John C. Rogers, "Marketing Information Systems: Their Current Status in Fortune 1000 Companies," *Journal of Management Information Systems* 1 (Spring 1985), pp. 57–75. This article also contains a brief history of the development of marketing information systems. Increasingly, firms are attempting to duplicate the decision processes used by "experts" when developing the DSS's decision models. For discussion of the development of expert systems, see Thomas H. Stevenson, D. Anthony Plath, and Chandler M. Bush, "Using Expert Systems in Industrial Marketing," *Industrial Marketing Management* 19 (August 1990), pp. 243–50; and Robert A. Benfer, Edward E. Brent, and Louanna Furbee, *Expert Systems* (Newbury Park, Calif.: Sage Publications, 1991).

[11]Michael Dressler, Ronald Beali, and Joquin Ives Brant, "What the Hot Marketing Tool of the '80s Offers You," *Industrial Marketing* 68 (March 1983), pp. 51, 54. See also Lindsay Meredith, "Developing and Using a Data Base Marketing System: An On-Line Marketing and Sales System," *Industrial Marketing Management* 18 (November 1989), pp. 245–58.

[12]Bob Goligoski, "Brand Leaders," *Business Computer Systems* 5 (June 1986), pp. 26–33.

[13]Some other popular systems are Express, Marksman, and Decision Master. For a general discussion on the use of these systems, see Valerie Free, "The Marketing War Gets Automated," *Marketing Communications* 13 (June 1988), pp. 40–48, 79.

[14]For discussions of what other companies are attempting to accomplish by equipping their salespeople with microcomputers, see Gilbert Fuchsberg, "Hand-Held Computers Help Field Staff Cut Paper Work and Harvest More Data," *The Wall Street Journal,* January 30, 1990, pp. B1, B6; and Doris C. Van Doren and Thomas A. Stickney, "How to Develop a Database for Sales Leads," *Industrial Marketing Management* 19 (August 1990), pp. 201–8.

[15]Louis A. Wallis, *Computer-Based Sales Force Support,* report no. 953 (New York: The Conference Board, 1990). This report also describes what individual companies are doing.

[16]*Sales Analysis,* Studies in Business Policy, no. 13 (New York: National Industrial Conference Board, 1965), p. 3. This early classic is still one of the best sources on the conduct of a sales analysis.

[17]See, for example, E. Jerome McCarthy and William D. Perreault, Jr., *Basic Marketing: A Managerial Approach,* 10th ed. (Homewood, Ill.: Richard D. Irwin, 1990), p. 546; Charles H. Sevin, *Marketing Productivity Analysis* (New York: McGraw-Hill, 1965), pp. 7–8; another classic, William J. Stanton, Richard H. Buskirk, and Rosann L. Spiro, *Management of the Sales Force,* 8th ed. (Homewood, Ill.: Richard D. Irwin, 1991), pp. 539–40.

[18]Harry D. Wolfe and Gerald Albaum, "Inequality in Products, Orders, Customers, Salesmen, and Sales Territories," *Journal of Business* 35 (July 1962), pp. 298–301. For discussion of how specific firms are increasing profits by attempting to systematically alter the 80:20 principle, see Alan J. Dubinsky and Richard W. Hansen, "Improving Marketing Productivity: The 80/20 Principle Revisited," *California Management Review* 25 (Fall 1982), pp. 96–105; and Richard T. Hise and

Stanley H. Kratchman, "Developing and Managing a 20/80 Program," *Business Horizons* 30 (September–October 1987), pp. 66–73.

[19]Sevin, *Marketing Productivity Analysis* pp. 7–8.

[20]Jon G. Udell and Gene R. Laczniak, *Marketing in an Age of Change* (New York: John Wiley & Sons, 1981), p. 154.

[21]Adopted from *Sales Analysis*, p. 68.

[22]BPI percentages in Exhibits 16.11 through 16.15 were taken from *Sales & Marketing Management's Survey of Buying Power*, which is published each July.

[23]Sales potentials were determined by establishing the functional relationship between Hansen's sales and the number of employees in key SIC codes. It was found that the distributor, who had been increasing his sales of Hansen couplings for 20 years and, thus, had been recognized for good performance under the simple sales analysis scheme, was actually getting only 15.4 percent of the potential in the area. See William E. Cox, Jr., and George N. Havens, "Determination of Sales Potentials and Performance for an Industrial Goods Manufacturer," *Journal of Marketing Research* 14 (November 1977), p. 578.

Suggested Readings

For discussion of how to go about a sales management audit, see:

Dubinsky, Alan J., and Richard W. Hansen. "The Sales Force Management Audit." *California Management Review* 24 (Winter 1981), pp. 86–95.

For useful discussion of the structure and use of decision support systems, see:

Little, John, D. C. "Decision Support Systems for Marketing Managers," *Journal of Marketing* 43 (Summer 1979), pp. 9–27.

Sprague, Ralph H., Jr., and Eric D. Carlson. *Effective Decision Support Systems.* Englewood Cliffs, N.J.: Prentice Hall, 1982, especially chap. 1 and 2.

Wallis, Louis A. *Computer-Based Sales Force Support.* report no. 953. New York: The Conference Board, 1990.

For discussion of the conduct and insights from sales analyses, see the classic treatments:

Sales Analysis Studies in Business Policy, no. 13. New York: National Industrial Conference Board, 1965.

Sevin, Charles H. *Marketing Productivity Analysis.* New York: McGraw-Hill, 1965.

Cost Analysis

NEEDED: A FOCUS ON SALES PROFITABILITY

You're the national sales manager for a medical products giant that sells a broad line of equipment and supplies to hospitals and clinics. Personal selling is crucial to the company's success, and, after four years of fussing with sales compensation, you've finally got a plan that should put the troops in high gear.

It's a bit complicated, but isn't that expected of a plan designed to achieve specific objectives? Salespeople are paid a salary, a bonus for making quota, another bonus when they sign new accounts, and a commission on equipment the product managers want emphasized. Salespeople think the plan is great, and results so far seem to bear them out. They're signing up new accounts at a record rate, and for the first time in years it looks as if you're going to make your volume goals.

Then comes a rude shock. The new CEO has the financial vice president do a detailed analysis of the entire operation, and it contains disturbing news: the domestic business (your turf) is losing money!

Sure, the sales force is landing a lot of new customers, but they're all small ones. The margin contribution on some of these transactions doesn't even cover the cost of processing the orders.

What's more, it looks as if salespeople are leaving money on the table with every deal. Although they have some flexibility to negotiate prices and discounts with customers, there's little incentive for them to take a hard line. The compensation plan rewards them mainly for generating sales volume at any price.

After making calls with a cross section of the sales force, the president is convinced that improved sales profitability holds the key to the company's future.

Source: Jerry Colletti, "Are You Tough Enough to Raise Sales Productivity?" *Sales & Marketing Management* 140 (October 1988), pp. 50–54.

Cost analysis is complementary to sales analysis in the management of the personal selling effort. While sales analysis focuses on the results achieved, cost analysis looks at the costs incurred in producing those results and whether the returns justify the expenditures. As the opening scenario suggests, sales increases do not always produce profit increases. To determine whether the returns justify the expenditures, it is necessary to gather, classify, compare, and study marketing cost data, which is the essence of marketing cost analysis.

Marketing cost analysis can help identify opportunities for increasing the effectiveness of marketing expenditures. Sales are achieved at some cost, and marketing productivity focuses on the sales or profit output per unit of marketing effort input. Unfortunately, it is often difficult for a firm to know what the output/input relationships are without detailed analyses.

Most firms today produce multiple products, which they sell in multiple markets. For each product and market, the mix of marketing elements differs. Only by analyzing specific relationships among these products and markets can the firm hope to identify situations where marketing input should be increased or altered, where it should remain at historic levels, and where it should be decreased. These insights are simply not produced by the information that flows from normal accounting operations. Similarly, to deploy the firm's salespeople most effectively, the sales manager needs to appreciate the output/input relationships by product, territory, customer, channel of distribution, and so on. Marketing cost analysis estimates these relationships.

Cost Analysis Development

Sales management has been somewhat slower to adopt cost (or as it is sometimes called, *profitability*) analysis than sales analysis for managing the sales function. The empirical evidence indicates that if they do it at all, firms are most likely to conduct profitability analyses for products, less likely to do it for sales territories and salespeople, and least likely to do it by customers. Only about half of all companies do it for any one of these bases, and less than a third analyze profits by all four bases of products, territories, salespeople, and customers.[1]

One apparent reason for this neglect seems to be that most accounting systems are still not designed to meet the needs of marketing management, in that they were originally designed to report the aggregate effects of a firm's operations to its creditors and stockholders. They were subsequently modified to provide a better handle on the production operations of the firm, so most accounting systems are currently oriented toward external reporting and production cost analysis. This is unfortunate because a company can realize many benefits from carefully conducted marketing cost and profitability analyses.

To understand the apparent gap between the need for accounting information to measure marketing performance and the supply of that information, one must appreciate the differences between normal accounting costs and marketing costs.

Accounting versus Marketing Costs

One has to recognize at the outset the different purposes that underlie accounting and marketing costs. Accounting costs are computed to provide a historical record of the company's operations. To an accountant, net income is essentially a historical record of the past. In computing net income, for example, the accountant attempts to allocate all the costs of the equipment used to produce the product during the time the equipment was used. This ensures that revenues equal to the original cost of the equipment are not distributed as dividends but are put back into assets, such as more equipment or cash. Whether this amount is enough to replace the asset is not part of the accounting problem.

The marketing perspective is like an economist's perspective because it is future-oriented. To an economist, net income is essentially a speculation about the future, not a historical record of the past. Thus, the economist looks to the future to determine the basic value of today's assets. The real costs of an asset are the opportunity costs forgone by putting the asset to one use versus another.

The past is also irrelevant to the businessperson making a decision except to forecast the future. Thus, although the accountant might classify costs on the basis of object (e.g., plant, equipment, materials) or process (e.g., finishing, assembly), a decision-making perspective requires that costs be classified in terms of *those that will be affected* by a proposed decision and those *that will not be affected*. Similarly, while the accountant looks at the original or outlay cost of an input factor to determine its value, the decision maker needs to look to *future value*. This value should include the full range of *opportunities forgone or sacrifice entailed*.

Although many costs reflect the *result* of some particular activity—such as production—marketing costs are directed at *producing* some benefit. Thus, in controlling production costs, management focuses on the effect of volume on costs. In controlling distribution costs, it looks at the effect of costs on volume. Moreover, there is less certainty about the effects marketing costs have on volume than about the effects volume changes have on production costs.

FULL COST VERSUS CONTRIBUTION MARGIN

Marketing cost analysis can take either a full-cost (or, as it is sometimes called, *net profit*) approach or a contribution margin approach. The argument over which should be used[2] has generated controversy through the years. To appreciate the controversy fully, it is helpful to understand the differences between direct and indirect costs and specific and general expenses.

Direct versus Indirect Costs

A **direct cost** can be specifically identified with a product or a function.[3] The cost is incurred because the product or function exists or is contemplated. If the product or function were eliminated, the cost would also disappear. An example is inventory carrying costs for a product.

An **indirect cost** is a shared cost because it is tied to several functions or products. Even if one of the products or functions were eliminated, the cost would not be. Rather, the share of the cost previously borne by the product or function that was eliminated would shift to the remaining products or functions. An example of an indirect cost is the travel expenses of a salesperson selling a multiple product line. Even if one product the rep sells is eliminated, the travel cost would not be.

Costs versus Expenses

The profit and loss or net income statement typically distinguishes between costs and expenses. The term *costs* is often restricted to the materials, labor, power, rent, and so on used in making the product. The cost of goods sold on the following conceptual net income statement reflects these costs.

$$\text{Less: } \frac{\text{Sales}}{\text{Cost of goods sold}}$$

Sales

Less: $\dfrac{\text{Cost of goods sold}}{\text{Gross margin}}$

Less: $\dfrac{\text{General administrative and selling expenses}}{\text{Profit or net income before taxes}}$

The expenses reflect the other costs incurred in operating the business, such as the cost of advertising and of maintaining branches. Expenses cannot be tied nearly as well as costs to specific products, since they are general expenses associated with doing business. In marketing cost analysis, the distinction between costs and expenses is not nearly so clear, and the terms are often used interchangeably.

Specific versus General Expenses

Just like costs, expenses can be classified into two broad categories: specific and general expenses. A **specific expense** is just like a direct cost—it can be identified with a specific product or function. The expense would be eliminated if the product or function were eliminated. If the product were eliminated, for example, the specific expense of the product manager's salary need not be incurred.

A **general expense** is like an indirect cost—it cannot be identified directly with a specific object of profit measurement such as a territory, salesperson, or product. Thus, the expense would not be eliminated if the specific object were eliminated. The sales manager's salary is an example when the object of measurement is a product in a multiple-product company. The elimination of the product would not eliminate this salary.

Measurement Objective Affects Classification

A particular cost or expense may be direct for some measurement purposes and indirect for others. The object of the measurement determines how the cost should be treated.

> If this is a product line, costs directly associated with the manufacture and sales of the product line are direct. All other costs in the business are indirect. If the object of measurement shifts to a sales territory, some of the costs of product-line measurement, which were direct, will remain direct costs now associated with the territory; some will become indirect; and others that were indirect will become direct. For example:[4]

	Object of Measurement	
Cost	Product	Territory
Sales promotion display	Direct	Direct
Sales rep compensation	Indirect	Direct
Product line manager's salary	Direct	Indirect
Corporate president's salary	Indirect	Indirect

Which to Use

As mentioned, there is controversy about whether one should use a full-cost or contribution margin approach in marketing cost analysis. Proponents of the full-cost or net profit approach argue that all costs should be assigned and

EXHIBIT 17 • 1   *Differences in Perspective between Full-Cost and Contribution Margin Approaches to Marketing Cost Analysis*

Full-Cost Approach		Contribution Margin Approach	
	Sales		Sales
Less:	Cost of goods sold	Less:	Variable manufacturing costs
Equal:	Gross margin	Less:	Other variable costs directly traceable to the segment
		Equal:	Contribution margin
Less:	Operating expenses (including the segment's allocated share of company administration and general expenses)	Less:	Fixed costs directly traceable to products Fixed costs directly traceable to the market segment
Equal:	Segment net income	Equal:	Segment net income

somehow accounted for in determining the profitability of any segment (e.g., territory, product, salesperson) of the business.

> Under this approach, each unit bears not only its own direct costs which can be traced to it, but also a share of the company's cost of doing business, referred to as indirect costs. Full-costing advocates argue that many of the indirect costs can be assigned to the unit being costed on the basis of a demonstrable cost relationship. If a strong relationship does not exist, *the cost must be prorated on as reasonable a basis as possible.* Under the full-costing approach a net income for each marketing segment can be determined by matching the segment's revenue with its direct and *its share of indirect costs.* [Emphasis added.][5]

Contribution margin advocates argue, on the other hand, that it is misleading to allocate costs arbitrarily. They suggest that only those costs that can be *specifically identified* with the segment of the business should be deducted from the revenue produced by the segment to determine how well the segment is doing. Any excess of revenues over these costs contributes to the common costs of the business and thereby to profits. The contribution margin approach does not distinguish where the costs are incurred, but rather simply whether they are variable or fixed. Thus, the difference between sales and all variable costs, whether they originate in manufacturing, selling, or some administrative function, are subtracted from revenues or sales to produce the contribution margin of the segment.

The net profit approach does attempt to determine where the costs were incurred. The difference in perspectives is highlighted in Exhibit 17.1. Not only is segment net income derived differently in the two approaches, but also advocates of the contribution margin approach do not even focus on net income when evaluating the profitability of a segment of the business. Rather, they

EXHIBIT 17 • 2   *Profit and Loss Statement by Departments Using a Full-Cost Approach*

	Totals	Department 1	Department 2	Department 3
Sales	$500,000	$250,000	$150,000	$100,000
Cost of goods sold	400,000	225,000	125,000	50,000
Gross margin	100,000	25,000	25,000	50,000
Other expenses				
Selling expenses	25,000	12,500	7,500	5,000
Administrative expenses	50,000	25,000	15,000	10,000
Total other expenses	75,000	37,500	22,500	15,000
Net profit (loss)	25,000	(12,500)	2,500	35,000

focus on the contribution produced by the segment after subtracting the costs directly traceable to it from its sales.

The contribution margin advocates are winning the controversy. Although the early emphasis in accounting for distribution costs was on full-cost allocation,[6] the recent emphasis is on the contribution margin approach.[7] The contribution margin approach has unmistakable logic. If the costs associated with the segment are not removed with the elimination of the segment, why should they be arbitrarily allocated? That just confuses things and provides a blurred, distorted picture for management decision making. The costs still have to be borne after the segment is eliminated, but they must be borne by other segments of the business. This can simply tax the ability of these other segments to remain profitable. Exhibits 17.2 and 17.3 illustrate this phenomenon.

The example involves a department store with three main departments. The administrative expenses in Exhibit 17.2 are all fixed costs; they were allocated to departments on the basis of the total percentage of sales accounted for by each department. This is a common allocation basis about which more will be said later. Those who embrace the full-cost approach would argue that Department 1 should be eliminated because of the net loss of $12,500 it is producing.

Note what would happen if this were pursued. First, the sales of the department would be lost, but $12,500 of selling expenses would also be eliminated. However, the $25,000 of fixed costs must now be borne by the other departments. Allocating these costs on the basis of percentage of sales suggests that Department 2 is unprofitable (see Exhibit 17.3). If one used the same argument as before, it too should be considered for elimination. Then the $50,000 of administrative expenses would be borne entirely by Department 3. This would make Department 3, which is now the entire store, unprofitable. That would suggest the store be closed, meaning management would close a profitable store simply because one department displayed a small dollar loss—a loss that could be attributed to an arbitrary allocation of fixed costs. De-

EXHIBIT 17 • 3   *Profit and Loss Statement if Department 1 Were Eliminated*

	Total	Department 2	Department 3
Sales	$250,000	$150,000	$100,000
Cost of goods sold	175,000	125,000	50,000
Gross margin	75,000	25,000	50,000
Other expenses			
Selling expenses	12,500	7,500	5,000
Administrative expenses	50,000	30,000	20,000
Total other expenses	62,500	37,500	25,000
Net profit (loss)	12,500	(12,500)	25,000

partment 1, in fact, makes a positive contribution to profits, as the contribution margin statement in Exhibit 17.4 shows.

A contribution margin versus a full-cost profitability analysis is also supported by the recognition that most marketing phenomena are highly interrelated. For example, the demand for one product in a multiproduct company is often influenced by the availability of others, and the absence of a product may cause the sale of another product to decline. The entire product line may be greater than the sum of its parts in terms of sales and profits. The same argument applies to other elements of the marketing mix. They have interdependent effects. The contribution margin approach implicitly recognizes this synergy through its emphasis on the contribution of each segment or part.

In sum, allocations of indirect costs for segment performance evaluation are generally inappropriate. That is, any measure of segment performance that includes allocated shares of indirect costs includes factors that do not really reflect performance in the segment as a separate entity. Hence, indirect cost allocations should not be made if the purpose is to measure true performance.

PROCEDURE

The general procedure followed in conducting a cost or profitability analysis first involves specifying the purpose for which the cost study is being done. This helps to determine the functional cost centers. The next step is to spread the natural account costs to these functional cost centers. Then the functional costs are allocated to appropriate segments using some reasonable basis. Finally, the allocated costs are summed, and the contribution of the segment is determined. Incidentally, *segment* is used here to mean a portion of the business, not in the normal sense of market segment.

The process is shown in Exhibit 17.5 on page 737. Although the diagram is simple, its execution is difficult. It often involves hard decisions about what

EXHIBIT 17 ● 4   *Contribution Margin by Departments*

	Totals	Department 1	Department 2	Department 3
Sales	$500,000	$250,000	$150,000	$100,000
Cost of goods sold	400,000	225,000	125,000	50,000
Selling expenses	25,000	12,500	7,500	5,000
Total variable costs	425,000	237,500	132,500	55,000
Contribution margin	75,000	12,500	17,500	45,000
Fixed costs				
Administrative expenses	50,000			
Net profit	25,000			

costs or expenses are to be treated as fixed, semifixed, or variable, and how various costs should be allocated to segments.

Purpose

As mentioned, the first step in a marketing profitability analysis is to determine the purpose for which it is being done. Is it designed to investigate the profitability of the various products in the line? Or is it designed to determine the profitability of sales branches, customers, or individual salespersons? The decision is essential because the treatment of the various costs and expenses depends on the purpose.

Ideally, the firm would want to break all its costs or revenues into small building blocks or modules. These elements would be as small as possible and yet still be meaningful.[8] This allows the firm to aggregate these building blocks as needed to produce profitability analyses for various segments of the business. An example of a basic building block or module of cost is a regional sales manager's salary. This is a general expense when the profitability of various product lines is at issue. It is a specific expense and needs to be considered when determining the contribution to profit of the region.

Thus, good profitability analyses require that the various costs be partitioned into direct and indirect expenses so the proper aggregations can be made. What is properly treated as direct and what should be treated as indirect or general depend on the study's purpose. Sales managers typically are most concerned with the profitability of various regions, branches, salespeople, and customers; they are only remotely concerned with the profitability of various products. Thus, a salesperson's salary is more likely to be treated as a direct than an indirect expense, whereas a product manager's salary is likely indirect, when the profitability of regions, branches, salespeople, and customers is at issue. Investigation of the profitability of the product line requires just the opposite treatment, which again illustrates the importance of specifying the purpose of the study.

E X H I B I T   17 ● 5   *Steps in Conducting a Marketing Profitability Analysis*

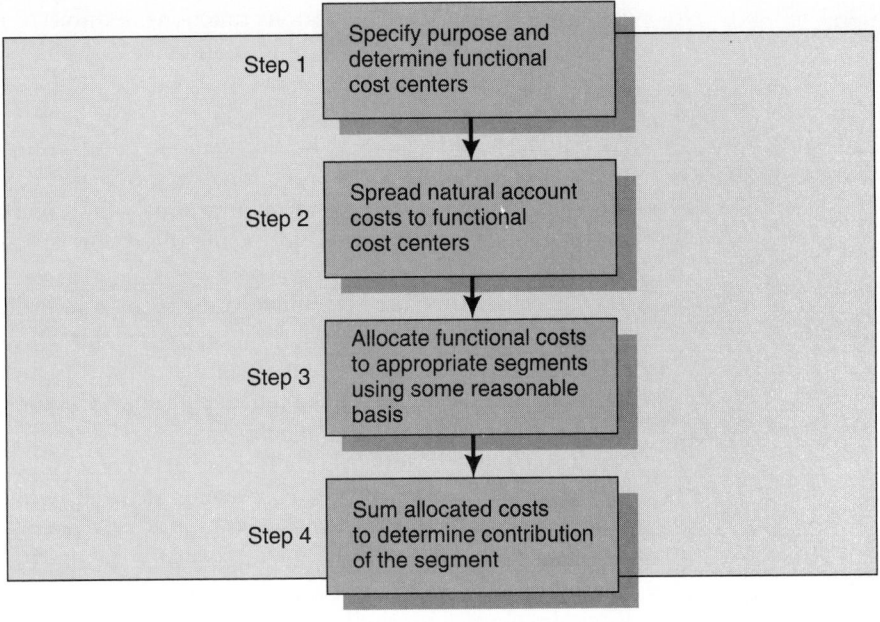

Step 1   Specify purpose and determine functional cost centers

Step 2   Spread natural account costs to functional cost centers

Step 3   Allocate functional costs to appropriate segments using some reasonable basis

Step 4   Sum allocated costs to determine contribution of the segment

Natural Accounts versus Functional Accounts

In the second step of a profitability analysis, natural account costs need to be spread to the functional cost centers. **Natural accounts** are the categories of cost used in the normal accounting cycle. These costs include such things as salaries, wages, rent, heat, light, taxes, auto expenses, raw materials, and office supplies. They are called *natural accounts* because they bear the name of their expense categories.

This is not the only way of classifying costs. In manufacturing cost accounting, for example, costs are often reclassified according to the *purpose* for which they were incurred. Thus, production wages might be broken into the cost categories forging, turning, grinding, milling, polishing, and assembling. These categories are **functional account** categories because they recognize the function performed, which is the purpose for incurring the cost.

Marketing cost analysis has a similar orientation. It recognizes that marketing costs are incurred for some purpose, and it reorganizes general selling and administrative expenses according to their purposes or functions. As Edmund D. McCarry stated so elegantly years ago, "The term *function* should be defined so as to meet the purpose for which it is used. The function of the heart is not simply to beat, which is its activity, but rather to supply the body with a continuous flow of blood."[9]

The salaries paid in a branch office, for example, could go to perform such functions as direct selling, advertising, order processing, and extending credit. A functional cost analysis would involve spreading the total salaries paid in the office to these various functions. Exhibit 17.6 lists the major functional accounts that are useful in marketing cost analyses.

Allocate
Functional Costs

As Exhibit 17.5 indicates, the third step in conducting a cost or profitability analysis is to allocate the functional costs to the various segments of the business. One needs to recognize immediately that the bases for allocation are not fixed. Rather, they depend on the discretion of the decision maker and what she feels are "reasonable" bases.

One basis often used is to divide the expenses according to volume attained. Thus, if a regional sales manager was responsible for six branch offices, and one office produced 25 percent of the sales in the region, it would be charged with one fourth of the sales manager's salary and expenses. This method is often used because of its simplicity.[10]

It is erroneous, however, in that it fails to recognize the purpose for which the regional sales manager's costs were incurred, which is the reason for a functional cost analysis. Maybe the branch was troublesome to manage and consumed 50 percent of the manager's time. In this case, it should bear half his salary. Alternatively, it may have run smoothly. The manager rarely had to get involved with the branch activities, so it consumed only 10 percent of his time and effort. In this case, only one tenth of the regional sales manager's salary should be charged against the branch in determining its profit contribution. As Horngren, the eminent cost accountant, stated years ago, "The costs of efforts are independent of the results actually obtained, in the sense that the costs are programmed by management, not determined by sales. Moreover, the allocation of costs on the basis of dollar sales entails circular reasoning."[11]

If one should not use sales to allocate costs, what should one use? Although there are no unequivocal allocation bases, one generally searches for factors

---

E X H I B I T   17 • 6   *Major Functional Accounts Useful in Marketing Cost Analysis*

- Direct selling
- Advertising and sales promotion
- Product and package design
- Technical product services
- Sales discounts and allowances
- Credit extension
- Warranty costs
- Marketing research

- Warehousing and handling
- Inventory
- Packaging, shipping, and delivery
- Order processing
- Customer service
- Billing and recording of accounts receivable
- Returned merchandise

that are measurable and for which there is a cause-and-effect relationship between the factor used as a basis of allocation and the dollar expenditure in the corresponding functional cost group.

The causal relationships used can, and most likely will, be different for different questions (see Thorny Issues 17.1). Exhibit 17.7 shows some common bases for allocating functional costs to product groups, account size classes, and sales territories.

EXHIBIT 17 ● 7 *Functional Cost Groups and Bases of Allocation*

| Functional Cost Group | Basis of Allocation | | |
	To Product Groups	To Account Size Classes	To Sales Territories
1. **Selling—direct costs:** Personal calls by salespeople and supervisors on accounts and prospects. Sales salaries, incentive compensation, travel, and other expenses	Selling time devoted to each product, as shown by special sales call reports or other special studies	Number of sales calls times average time per call, as shown by special sales call reports or other special studies	Direct
2. **Selling—indirect costs:** Field supervision, field sales-office expense, sales-administration expenses, sales-personnel training, sales management. Market research, new product development, sales statistics, tabulating services, sales accounting	In proportion to direct selling time, or time records by project	In proportion to direct selling time, or time records by project	Equal charge for each sales rep
3. **Advertising:** Media costs such as TV, radio, billboards, newspaper, magazine, etc. Advertising production costs; advertising department salaries	Direct; or analysis of space and time by media; other costs in proportion to media costs	Equal charge to each account; or number of ultimate consumers and prospects in each account's trading area	Direct; or analysis of media circulation records
4. **Sales promotion:** Consumer promotions such as coupons, patches, premiums, etc. Trade promotions such as price allowances, point-of-purchase displays, cooperative advertising, etc.	Direct; or analysis of source records	Direct; or analysis of source records	Direct; or analysis of source records

(cont'd)

E X H I B I T 17 ● 7   *(concluded)*

Functional Cost Group	Basis of Allocation		
	To Product Groups	To Account Size Classes	To Sales Territories
5. Transportation: Railroad, truck, barge, etc., payments to carriers for delivery of finished goods from plants to warehouses and from warehouses to customers. Traffic department costs	Applicable rates times tonnages	Analysis of sampling of bills of lading	Applicable rates times tonnages
6. Storage and shipping: Storage of finished goods inventories in warehouses. Rent (or equivalent costs), public warehouse charges, fire insurance and taxes on finished goods inventories, etc. Physical handling, assembling, and loading out of rail cars, trucks, barges for shipping finished products from warehouses and mills to customers. Labor, equipment, space, and material costs.	Warehouse space occupied by average inventory. Number of shipping units	Number of shipping units	Number of shipping units
7. Order processing: Checking and processing of orders from customers to mills for prices, weights and carload accumulation, shipping dates, coordination with production planning, transmittal to mills, etc. Pricing department. Preparation of customer invoices. Freight accounting. Credit and collection. Handling cash receipts. Provision for bad debts. Salary, supplies, space, and equipment costs (teletypes, flexowriters, etc.)	Number of order lines	Number of order lines	Number of order lines

Sum Allocated Costs   The fourth step in the process is to sum the costs allocated to the segment. Costs for which there is no direct causal relationship remain unallocated in determining the contribution of the segment. A comparison of the contributions of like segments then indicates the remedial action that might be taken, if any.

EXHIBIT 17 • 8   *Example Profit and Loss Statement*

Profit and Loss Statement for
BAITINGER BICYCLE COMPANY
St. Louis Office

Sales		$4,963,500
Cost of goods sold		4,061,000
Gross margin		902,500
Selling and administrative expenses:		
Salaries	$309,000	
Commissions	49,635	
Advertising	254,000	
Postage and office supplies	980	
Packaging materials	60,840	
Transporation charges	182,520	
Travel expenses	76,000	
Rent	130,000	
Total selling and administrative expenses		1,062,975
Net profit (loss)		(160,475)

THE PROCESS ILLUSTRATED

To illustrate the process of conducting a cost or profitability analysis, consider the situation encountered by the Baitinger Bicycle Company, in Exhibit 17.8, which was faced with a loss in its St. Louis branch of more than $160,000. Suppose the sales manager is interested in further analyzing the branch to see whether the loss can be traced to particular sales reps or customers, much as the discrepancy between sales and quota was localized in Chapter 16.

Apportion Natural Account Costs to Functional Accounts

The sales manager has completed the first step in a cost analysis—the manager has decided the purpose of the analysis is to isolate the profit contributions of the various sales representatives in the branch. The next thing the manager must do is spread the general selling and administrative expenses incurred by the branch in the profit and loss statement to the various functional accounts. To keep the example simple, the costs incurred in manufacturing will not be separated, although a more sophisticated contribution margin analysis would reflect such differences. Rather, the cost of goods sold is assumed to be a fixed charge to the St. Louis branch, meaning the manager needs to concentrate on spreading only the selling and administrative expenses of functional cost groups.

Exhibit 17.9 lists the functional cost categories across the top and the natural account categories along the side. The individual entries indicate how a total natural cost is apportioned according to purpose. Note that the sum of all the functional costs in a row equals the natural cost for that row; that is, all natural costs are accounted for in the spread.

The details in the division of costs depend on the operation of the branch. In this case, the branch in the previous year paid $309,000 in salaries. They

Thorny Issues in Sales Management 17 • 1

Carol Suchomel, the sales manager for ArtCraft, a manufacturer and distributor of art and craft supplies, was in the midst of a heavy discussion with representatives from the company's accounting department. The discussion revolved around the new cost system the accounting department was developing so the sales function could be managed more effectively. The topic at the moment was how each salesperson's automobile expenses should be allocated, given the salespeople were handling eight product lines and selling to three different types of outlets—office supply stores, book stores, and arts and crafts specialty supply outlets. The situation was complicated further because sales reps were also expected to prospect for new accounts and attend trade shows in their own and contiguous territories.

How would you recommend the costs be allocated if Suchomel wanted to determine the profitability of each salesperson? Each product line? Each customer?

were distributed in the following way: branch manager—$78,000; four salespeople—$179,000; warehouse clerk—$24,000; and a clerical person handling order processing and billing—$28,000. The salaries of the branch manager and salespeople are charged against direct selling expenses because that is the purpose for which they were incurred. Similarly, the office and warehouse clerk salaries are charged against their main functions. The functional account direct selling is also charged with the commissions earned by the four representatives; in addition to their base salaries, all salespersons were paid a commission equal to 1 percent of sales.

Advertising charges reflect both a natural account cost and a functional account cost. Advertising charges are typically maintained in a separate category in the normal accounting cycle, and their name speaks to their purpose. The same is true of transportation charges.

The postage and supplies the office consumed were used to support the order-processing and billing functions, and thus they are assigned to this category. Similarly, packaging material costs are assigned to warehousing and shipping because that is the function for which they are used. Travel expenses reflect the food, lodging, and other expenses incurred by the sales representatives in carrying out their main function of selling; thus, these costs are so assigned.

Perhaps the one natural account cost that requires the most explanation is rent. The company was paying $70 per square foot for office space and $20 per square foot for warehouse space. These costs are spread to the functional accounts in proportion to the space used by each activity. More particularly, the order-processing and selling functions used 100 of the 500 square feet of office space the company rented; the salespeople and sales manager used the remainder. The $95,000 assignment of rent to warehousing and shipping costs reflects the 4,750 square feet of warehouse space the company rented at $20 per square foot.

EXHIBIT 17 • 9   *Allocation of Natural Accounts to Functional Accounts*

Natural Accounts		Functional Accounts				
		Direct Selling	Advertising	Warehousing and Shipping	Order Processing and Billing	Transporation
Salaries	$309,000	$257,000		$ 24,000	$28,000	
Commissions	49,635	49,635				
Advertising	254,000		$254,000			
Postage and supplies	980				980	
Packaging materials	60,840			60,840		
Transportation charges	182,520					$182,520
Travel expenses	76,000	76,000				
Rent	130,000	28,000		95,000	7,000	
	$1,062,975	$410,635	$254,000	$179,840	$35,980	$182,520

Allocate Functional Costs to Segments

To assess the profit contribution of each salesperson, it is necessary to allocate all "relevant" functional costs to salespeople. Costs that bear some causal relationship to the level of activity should be allocated; these include salaries, commissions, and travel expenses. Conversely, costs that are not affected by the level of activity are not allocated. Office rent is an example. Even if one salesperson were fired, this cost would not change; thus, it should not be allocated.

Exhibit 17.10 provides much of the data on which the allocations to generate the profitability analysis by salesperson in Exhibit 17.11 are based. Exhibit 17.11 lists the gross margin by salesperson. From this, all direct expenses are subtracted to derive the contribution to profit by salesperson. Let us consider each expense category.

Direct selling

The salary and commission items need little explanation; they reflect what each representative is paid and the 1 percent commission each earned on what was sold. Travel expenses per sales rep were determined by dividing total travel expenses by the number of calls to generate the cost per call. This was $190, which was then multiplied by the number of calls each salesperson made. If the branch accounting records allowed the identification of travel expenses by sales representative, these numbers would be used directly. If the office records also specified the amount of time the sales manager spent with each representative, one could allocate a portion of the sales manager's salary to each

EXHIBIT 17 ● 10 *Basic Data Used for Allocations*

A. Information by Product

Products	Selling Price per Unit	Cost per Unit	Gross Margin per Unit	Number Sold in Period	Sales in Period	Advertising Expenditures
A	$230	$180	$50	6,450	$1,483,500	$120,000
B	180	150	30	10,060	1,810,800	80,000
C	120	100	20	13,910	1,669,200	54,000
				30,420	$4,963,500	$254,000

B. Information by Salesperson

Salesperson	Number of Sales Calls	Number of Orders	Number of Units Sold A	B	C	Total
Steve Nicholls	75	50	1,400	2,210	3,410	7,020
Sharon Pogue	125	65	1,725	2,725	3,515	7,965
Paul Vilwock	100	50	1,711	2,609	3,506	7,826
Stan Tucker	100	80	1,614	2,516	3,479	7,609
	400	245	6,450	10,060	13,910	30,420

salesperson. This cost is not allocated in the example because this information was not available, and in its absence, there is no reasonable cause-and-effect basis for making the allocation.

Advertising

Panel A of Exhibit 17.10 lists the amount spent on advertising for each product. When these amounts are divided by the number of units sold, the following advertising charges per unit are generated:

A—$120,000 ÷ 6,450 units = $18.60/unit

B—$80,000 ÷ 10,060 units = $ 7.95/unit

C—$54,000 ÷ 13,910 units = $ 3.88/unit

The advertising expenses borne by each salesperson are determined by multiplying these per-unit advertising charges by the number of bicycles of each model that each rep sold.

The number of units of the product sold is a very common basis for allocating advertising expenses. Two other common bases are the number of prospects secured and the number of sales transactions. The decision to allocate advertising expenses on the basis of the number of units sold is controversial. While the per-unit-of-product-sold approach is popular, it is not hard to develop an argument against it. One could argue, for example, that advertising expenses are fixed for a period, and since they are fixed costs, productive

EXHIBIT 17 • 11 *Profitability Analysis of Salesperson*

	Total	Nicholls	Pouge	Vilwock	Tucker
Sales					
Product A	$1,483,500	$322,000	$396,750	$393,530	$371,220
Product B	1,810,800	397,800	490,500	469,620	452,880
Product C	1,669,200	409,200	421,800	420,720	417,480
Total Sales	4,963,500	1,129,000	1,309,050	1,283,870	1,241,580
Cost of Goods Sold					
Product A	1,161,000	252,000	310,500	307,980	290,520
Product B	1,509,000	331,500	408,750	391,350	377,400
Product C	1,391,000	341,000	351,500	350,600	347,900
Total COGS	4,061,000	924,500	1,070,750	1,049,930	1,015,820
Gross margin	902,500	204,500	238,300	233,940	225,760
Expenses					
Direct selling					
Salary	179,000	40,000	45,000	46,000	48,000
Commissions	49,635	11,290	13,091	12,839	12,416
Travel	76,000	14,250	23,750	19,000	19,000
Advertising					
Product A	120,000	26,047	32,093	31,833	30,028
Product B	80,000	17,575	21,670	20,748	20,008
Product C	54,000	13,238	13,646	13,611	13,506
Warehousing and shipping	60,840	14,040	15,930	15,652	15,218
Order processing	980	200	260	200	320
Transportation	182,520	42,120	47,790	46,956	45,654
Total Expenses	802,975	178,759	213,229	206,837	204,149
Contribution to Profit (Loss)	99,525	25,741	25,071	27,103	21,611

salespeople should not have to assume a larger advertising burden than unproductive salespeople. One could also argue that the per-unit approach treats advertising as a consequence of sales, rather than as a cause, and therefore the scheme violates the control principle alluded to earlier that one should search for factors that control the functional cost.

While both of these arguments have merit, we will use the per-unit-of-product basis for allocating advertising expenses below for three reasons: (1) the per-unit approach is one of the most popular; (2) there is no clearly preferred alternative in the literature; (3) the example is designed to illustrate the cost analysis process, not to provide the last word on all possible nuances. Yet, you should be aware that the decision as to how to allocate advertising expenses or any of the expense categories can change the fundamental conclusions one draws about the profitability of a particular segment.

Warehousing and shipping

The profitability analysis by sales representative does not include an allocation for the warehouseperson's salary because that salary would continue regardless of what any sales rep sold. Rather, all that is allocated to the salespeople are the packaging costs per unit, which amounted to $2 per bicycle.

Order processing

The office clerk's salary is not allocated to salespeople because there is no causal link between an individual representative's sales and that salary. The office rent charged to this activity is similarly not allocated. The order-processing costs that are allocated are the direct expenses for postage and supplies. This is most directly linked to the number of orders, which produces an allocation of $4 per order.

Transportation

Transportation charges amounted to $6 per bike. These are charged against the individual sales representatives according to the number of bicycles each sold.

When all these expenses are aggregated and subtracted from gross margin, it is found that each representative is contributing to profits. This poses a dilemma for the company sales manager. The branch is not profitable, but each salesperson in the branch is contributing to profits. Admittedly, the sales reps may not be making a large enough contribution. If there were a profit standard for each salesperson, this could be assessed. This demonstrates the difference between a performance analysis in which a standard of comparison is established beforehand and a straight cost and profitability analysis.

The company sales manager could compare the contributions to profit of the representatives in the St. Louis branch with those of other sales representatives by doing a similar analysis for other branches. If the St. Louis salespeople were found to be low, it might indicate the payroll in the St. Louis branch was too high for the number of bicycles sold. The sales manager might then consider removing one or more reps from the territory. Alternatively, the manager might consider increasing the number of calls or changing the salary/commission mixture in the salespeople's compensation package. Still other strategies would be to close the warehouse associated with the branch or to close the branch. The profit implications of each strategy would be different. They could be calculated, however, if the company maintains sales and cost records by small units. Conversely, when basic records are aggregated into larger totals and are stored that way in the company's accounting system, such isolate and explode analyses are precluded.

Profitability of Stan Tucker by Customer

Suppose the sales manager felt that for strategic reasons, she did not wish to close the branch or the warehouse. Rather, she wished to consider reassigning one representative in the branch to another office and territory. Since there are typically significant company costs and personal disruptions to the rep in such a switch, the sales manager did not take these reassignments lightly.

EXHIBIT 17 • 12 *Activities of Stan Tucker Broken Down by Account*

Customers of Stan Tucker	Number of Sales Calls	Number of Orders	Number of Units Purchased			
			A	B	C	Total
Allen	50	35	807	1,258	1,567	3,632
Brown	25	20	645	880	1,043	2,568
Cooper	25	25	162	378	869	1,409
Total	100	80	1,614	2,516	3,479	7,609

Suppose, therefore, she wanted to ascertain the profitability of each account to the salesperson and the company.

Exhibit 17.12 and Exhibit 17.13 contain, respectively, the activity levels of Stan Tucker, the "worst"-performing representative in terms of the analysis contained in Exhibit 17.11, broken down by account and the resulting profit contribution of each account based on the same allocation criteria used previously. The analysis illustrates the operation of the iceberg principle.

Although Tucker overall contributes to profit, one of his accounts is generating a loss. The loss can be traced to the number of bicycles ordered by Cooper. While Cooper orders every time Tucker calls, his average order size is very low. Less frequent calls might be the answer; this might produce the same net sales but reduce Stan's travel expenses charged to Cooper. The analysis also reveals that, although Allen purchased the most bikes, Brown was the most profitable account Tucker had. Again these insights would be impossible to generate if Baitinger Bicycle Company did not use modularized marketing cost analyses.

The profitability analyses by marketing segment do not tell the sales manager of Baitinger Bicycle Company or any other manager what to do, as illustrated by Thorny Issues in Sales Management 17.2. They do, however, provide managers with some basic information for making intelligent choices.

PROSPECTS AND PROBLEMS

The preceding example, while basic, reveals both the promise and some of the problems associated with marketing cost analysis. The real benefit is the opportunity it provides managers to isolate segments of the business that are most profitable as well as those that generate losses. This information allows those involved to improve their planning and control of the firm's activities. When combined with proper sales analysis techniques discussed in Chapter 16, it provides sales managers with a formidable analytical weapon for managing the personal selling function.

The example also illustrates the problems associated with the technique. It requires that data be available in the proper detail. Some data can be costly

EXHIBIT 17 • 13 *Profitability Analysis for Stan Tucker Broken Down by Customer*

	Total	Allen	Brown	Cooper
Sales				
Product A	$371,220	$185,610	$148,350	$37,260
Product B	452,880	226,440	158,400	68,040
Product C	417,480	188,040	125,160	104,280
Total Sales	1,241,580	600,090	431,910	209,580
Cost of Goods Sold				
Product A	290,520	145,260	116,100	29,160
Product B	377,400	188,700	132,000	56,700
Product C	347,900	156,700	104,300	86,900
Total COGS	1,015,820	490,660	352,400	172,760
Gross Margin	225,760	109,430	79,510	36,820
Expenses				
Direct selling				
Salary	48,000	24,000	12,000	12,000
Commissions	12,416	6,001	4,319	2,096
Travel	19,000	9,500	4,750	4,750
Advertising				
Product A	30,028	15,014	12,000	3,014
Product B	20,008	10,004	6,998	3,006
Product C	13,506	6,083	4,049	3,374
Warehousing and shipping	15,218	7,264	5,136	2,818
Order processing	320	140	80	100
Transportation	45,654	21,792	15,408	8,454
Total Expenses	204,149	99,798	64,740	39,611
Contribution to Profit (Loss)	21,611	9,632	14,770	(2,791)

to generate and expensive to maintain. Furthermore, the technique requires a sophisticated information system. The system must be able to select and aggregate only those inputs appropriate to the segment of the business being analyzed. As the example indicates, there is often a question as to which costs should be allocated and what bases should be used to allocate these costs. The most appropriate allocation bases can generate spirited discussion among those involved. Allocations cannot be taken lightly because they ultimately affect the profitability of a segment; at the same time, however, there are usually no perfect answers as to how costs should be allocated. Thus, setting up a good marketing cost system can take a good deal of expensive executive time.

The benefits increasingly seem to be higher than the costs, if the literature on the subject is a reliable barometer. Not only has more been written on the subject of late, but the literature also describes an increasing number of companies that have profited from implementing marketing cost analysis.[13]

RETURN ON ASSETS MANAGED

Sales and cost analyses provide the sales manager with two important financial techniques for controlling the personal selling function. The first measures the

Thorny Issues in Sales Management 17 • 2

Bill Watts had been under great pressure from the corporate sales manager to improve the profitability of the branch office he managed. What had started as gentle nudges that the branch needed to do better had become an ultimatum in the past couple of weeks. Watts knew that if the profitability of the branch did not improve in the next quarter, he would be looking for a new job.

In response to the pressure, Watts generated the detailed analysis shown below and on the basis of that analysis he decided to fire Quamme. Do you . . .

Approve _____

Somewhat approve _____

Somewhat disapprove _____

Disapprove _____

			Salesperson			
	Total Branch	Susan Aime	Mary Byram	Richard Leach	Edward Morris	Heath Quamme
Sales	$4,343,063	$903,200	$981,788	$994,999	$869,106	$593,970
Cost of Goods Sold	$3,553,376	$739,600	$803,063	$813,696	$711,074	$485,943
Gross Margin	$789,687	$163,600	$178,725	$181,303	$158,032	$108,027
Expenses						
Direct selling						
Salary	$156,625	$32,000	$33,750	$34,500	$33,600	$22,775
Commissions	$43,431	$9,046	$9,818	$9,949	$8,691	$5,927
Travel	$66,501	$11,400	$17,813	$14,725	$13,300	$9,263
Advertising	$222,266	$45,490	$50,562	$51,302	$44,482	$30,430
Office overhead	$213,797	$45,088	$47,985	$48,676	$42,834	$29,214
Total Expenses	$702,620	$143,024	$159,928	$159,152	$142,907	$97,609
Contribution to Profit	$87,067	$20,576	$18,797	$22,151	$15,125	$10,418

results achieved and the second the cost of producing those results. The important financial ingredient left out of those analyses is the assets needed to produce those results. At a minimum, the company will be committing working capital in the form of accounts receivable and inventories to support the sales function. The return produced on the assets used in each segment of the business provides sales managers with a useful variation of more traditional cost analysis procedures for evaluating and controlling various elements of the personal selling function.

The formula for return on assets managed (ROAM) reflects both the contribution margin associated with a given level of sales and asset turnover.[14] More particularly, it is as follows:

$$\text{ROAM} = \frac{\text{Contribution as a}}{\text{percentage of sales}} \times \frac{\text{Asset turnover}}{\text{rate}}$$

E X H I B I T 17 • 14 *Analysis of Return on Assets Managed*

	Branch A	Branch B
Sales	$2,500,000	$1,500,000
Cost of Goods Sold	2,000,000	1,275,000
Gross Margin	500,000 (20%)	225,000 (15%)
Less variable branch expenses		
Salaries	155,000	80,000
Commissions	25,000	10,000
Office expenses	30,000	20,000
Travel and entertainment	40,000	20,000
	250,000	130,000
Branch contribution to profit	250,000	95,000
Branch investments		
Accounts receivable	500,000	150,000
Inventories	750,000	225,000
	1,250,000	375,000
Earnings as a percent of sales	10.0%	6.3%
Turnover	2.0	4.0
Branch percent return on assets managed	20.0%	25.2%

The formula indicates that the return to a segment of the business can be improved either by increasing the profit margin on sales or by maintaining the same profit margin and increasing the asset turnover rate. The formula can then be used to evaluate segments or to select the best alternative from strategies being considered.

Consider, for example, the use of the concept to evaluate the performance of two sales branches. Exhibit 17.14 contains the basic financial data. Note that Branch A sold more than Branch B and the gross margin on these sales was higher, both in total and as a percentage of sales, because of the mix of products. Furthermore, the contribution to total company profits was higher for Branch A than for Branch B, and earnings as a percentage of sales were 10.0 percent in Branch A and only 6.3 percent in Branch B. By all these standards, Branch A performed better.

These criteria, however, ignore the assets needed to produce these results. When the investment in assets, which in the example consists of accounts receivable and inventories for each branch, is also considered, the picture changes. Branch B required a smaller commitment of the firm's capital. Consequently, Branch B was able to effect an asset turnover twice as large as Branch A, so the return on investment was higher in Branch B than in Branch A.

While the basic ROAM formula can be used to provide useful management information, the managerial insights it affords can be magnified by breaking the basic formula down by its components. The first component—contribution

E X H I B I T 17 • 15 *Expanded Return on Assets Managed (ROAM) Model*

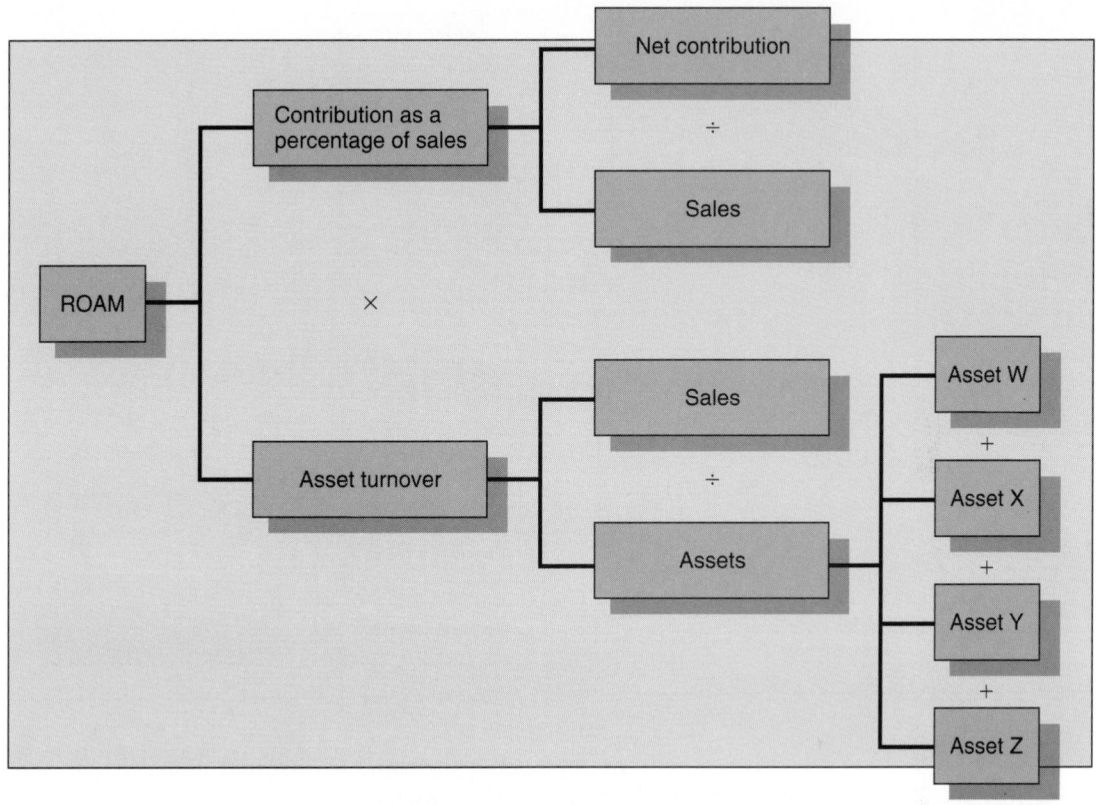

as a percent of sales—equals the ratio of net contribution divided by sales. The second component—the asset turnover rate—equals sales divided by the assets needed to produce those sales. Each of these second-level components could be expanded. One could, for example, break down the sales component by product or salesperson and could similarly break down the assets to assess the impact of each product or salesperson on profitability. Alternatively, one might choose to explode into its detailed elements only one of the second-level components of net contribution, sales, and assets. Exploding one or more of the components of the equation allows management to trace the impact of a number of "what if" scenarios.

Exhibit 17.15, for example, diagrams the return on assets model, with the asset component exploded. Each of the boxes applies to the segment of the business being analyzed. Previously, we saw, for example, that Branch B produced a higher ROAM than Branch A. With the exploded model, management can quickly explore what might be done to bring the returns into line. Exhibit

EXHIBIT 17 • 16 *Impact of a Reduction in Accounts Receivable to $250,000 in Branch A*

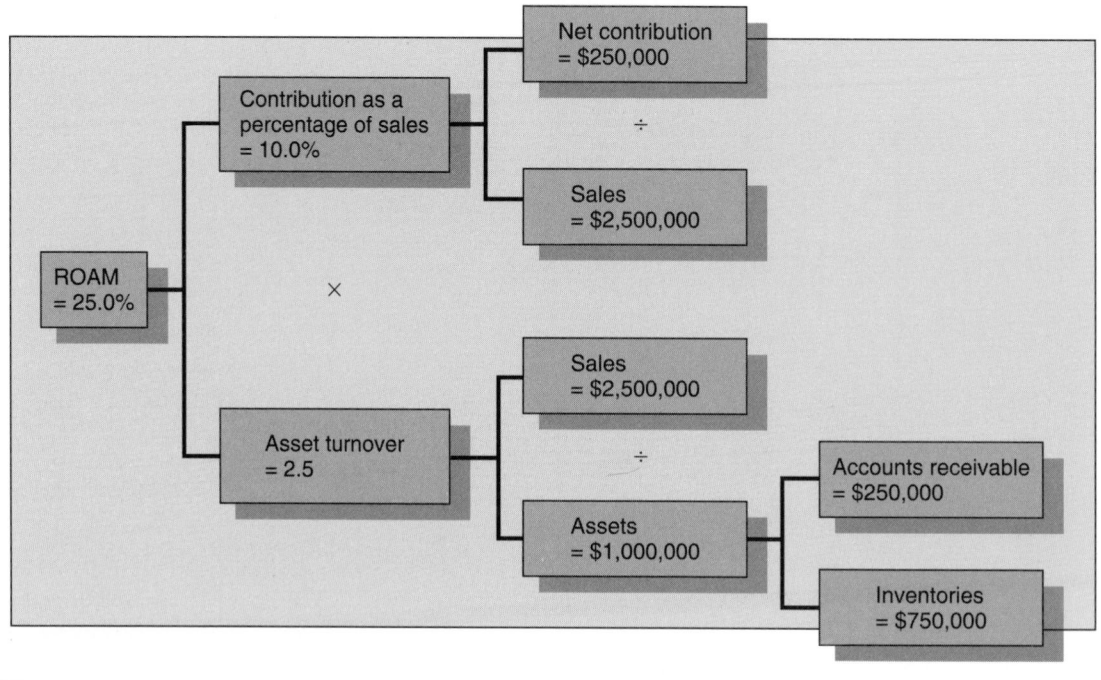

17.14 indicates, for example, that the amount invested in receivables and inventories as a percentage of sales varies across the two branches and that, in particular:

	Branch A		Branch B	
Receivables as a percentage of sales	$\dfrac{500,000}{2,500,000}$	$= 20\%$	$\dfrac{150,000}{1,500,000}$	$= 10\%$
Inventories as a percentage of sales	$\dfrac{750,000}{2,500,000}$	$= 30\%$	$\dfrac{225,000}{1,500,000}$	$= 15\%$

Management might logically ask the question: What would happen to ROAM in Branch A if receivables or inventories as a percentage of sales or both were reduced to the levels existing in Branch B? Exhibit 17.16 traces the implication of what a reduction in accounts receivable to 10 percent of sales or $250,000 in Branch A through better billing and follow-up procedures might do for its profitability. The example, which assumes no lost sales because of these billing efforts, demonstrates the returns could be brought directly in line with this one change. Management could just as easily assess the profit implications of, say, 5, 10, and 15 percent declines in sales to determine how sensitive the branch returns might be to a change in the billing procedures.

EXHIBIT 17 • 17 *Popularity of Sales, Cost, and Asset Return Analysis by Segment*

	Segment			
Description	**Product**	**Customer**	**Salesperson**	**Geographic Area**
Sales analysis:				
Sales volume (units or dollars)	92	91	87	92
Sales volume (versus quota or objective)	54	48	75	70
Cost analysis:				
Expenses	40	18	53	38
Contribution to profit (sales less direct costs)	75	41	32	26
Net profit (sales less direct costs less allocated indirect costs)	57	24	19	12
Return on assets	29	10	10	7

Source: Developed from information provided in Donald W. Jackson, Jr., Lonnie L. Ostrom, and Kenneth R. Evans, "Measures Used to Evaluate Industrial Marketing Activities," *Industrial Marketing Management* 11 (October 1982), pp. 269–74.

In sum, assets managed adds another important dimension to the financial control picture. The investment required for a venture needs to be recognized because long-run profits can be maximized only if the optimal level of investment in each asset is achieved. As Alfred P. Sloan, who was chief executive officer for 23 years at General Motors, comments in his book, *My Years with General Motors,* "No other financial principle with which I am acquainted serves better than rate of return as an objective aid to business judgment."[15]

The point was made earlier that marketers have been slower to embrace cost analysis than sales analysis. The evidence indicates they have been even slower to adopt ROAM. Exhibit 17.17, for example, summarizes the results of a survey among 146 industrial manufacturers in SIC codes 20–39 regarding their use of sales, cost, and ROAM analysis in managing the marketing function in general and the personal selling function in particular. While most of these firms engaged in sales analysis by customer, salesperson, or geographic area, only about one third of them engaged in profitability analysis by these segments, and only one tenth investigated the returns they realized on the assets devoted to these segments.

Clearly, despite their compelling intuitive appeal, cost or profitability analysis and asset return analysis have a way to go before they match the popularity of sales analysis in managing the personal selling function.

SUMMARY

Marketing cost analysis attempts to isolate the costs incurred in producing various levels of sales to determine the profitability of sales by segment of the business. Marketing cost analysis can be used to advantage by sales managers to investigate the profitability of regions, branches, territories, customers, or various channels of distribution.

Most firms have been slower to embrace cost analysis than sales analysis for studying their marketing activities. Part of this lag can be explained by the fact that many costs associated with doing business are not entered in the firm's accounting system in their most useful form for decision making. Thus, it is necessary to rework these costs so they are more useful.

A marketing cost analysis can be conducted using either a full-cost or a contribution margin approach. The full-cost approach allocates all the costs of doing business, even fixed costs, to one of the operating segments. The contribution margin approach holds that only those costs that can be specifically identified with the segment of the business should be deducted from the revenue produced by the segment. The contribution margin approach is more logically defensible from a decision-making perspective.

There are four steps in conducting a marketing cost analysis. First, the purpose of the study must be specified. Second, the natural account costs must be spread to functional cost centers. Next, the functional costs must be allocated to appropriate operating segments using some reasonable bases. Here one looks for those factors that bear a cause-and-effect relationship with the cost. Finally, the allocated costs are summed so the contribution of the segment can be determined.

Return on assets managed provides the sales manager with still another financial tool for controlling the personal selling function. Return on assets managed is the product of contribution to profit as a percentage of sales multiplied by asset turnover. Asset turnover is found by dividing sales by the assets needed to produce those sales. The formula recognizes that the sales manager has only limited assets with which to work. He can maximize the profits produced by the personal selling function only if each asset is put to its highest and best use. Return on assets managed is currently less popular than either sales or cost analysis in managing the personal selling function.

Discussion Questions

1. Amy Wagner, sales analyst for E. Z. Gregory, has completed a marketing cost study to determine the cost of doing business with small accounts and small orders. She has determined a minimum size for both small accounts and small orders. For small accounts, the minimum size is $6,000 yearly sales. For small orders, the minimum size is $185. Accounts and orders above the minimum are profitable. She recommends to Gregory's sales manager that the company should stop dealing with accounts that do not place more than $6,000 annual business and that orders under $185 should not be accepted. Do you agree with this tactic?

2. The Boston territory sales manager was unhappy with the recent report that revealed, although the Boston territory exceeded its sales goals by 20 percent, its contribution to profits was below expectations. In analyzing territorial profitability, the Jamieson Corporation includes rent and utilities as part of each territory's overhead. The Boston sales manager contends this is unfair: "Energy costs are higher here than in any other territory. Besides, the building is old and not insulated

and, furthermore, where we are located in Boston is not my decision, it's made by top management." Top management's response has been: "The location of the Boston office provides us with the most efficient location in terms of distribution costs. Our shipping costs would be too high if we relocated to one of the suburban areas where we could rent an energy efficient building." Whose view is right? What should be done?

3. Advertising has a synergistic effect. For example, in the Baitinger Bicycle Company case, the $254,000 advertising expenditure for product A had a positive impact on products B and C and on the company as well. Besides, dollars spent in one period have a carry-over effect to future periods. What recommendations would you make to handle these situations?

4. The Rite-Way Corporation, a manufacturer of a line of writing instruments, has completed a ROAM analysis for all products. The deluxe model in its line of fountain pens sells for $145.50 but produces a ROAM of 8.3 percent, well below the 23.5 percent average for the other products. Management believes rising raw material costs, such as gold and silver prices, are beyond Rite-Way's control. Should Rite-Way drop its deluxe product? Should Rite-Way eliminate commissions paid to sales representatives for deluxe sales?

5. The midwestern territory manager of the Knickerbocker Corporation disagrees with the allocation of advertising costs. The manager contends it is the sales force that produces sales, not advertising. In any case, according to the manager, "The advertising is wasted and stresses the wrong product features. My profitability suffers when you allocate advertising costs to my territory." What do you think should be done in this situation? What would you tell the midwestern manager?

6. The sales manager of Branch A (Exhibit 17.14) was dismayed with the results. The 20 percent ROAM for the branch was below expectations. The sales manager's response was "OK, they want better results, then we'll increase sales by at least 10 percent. But, we'll have to cut prices by 5 percent to do this." Will this benefit Branch A?

7. Accounts receivables are too high for Branch A, Exhibit 17.14. One sales analyst recommends giving credit and collection responsibilities to the sales force. Sales reps would be provided with delinquency objectives aimed at reducing accounts receivables by 20 percent. Those meeting their objectives would earn an additional 1 percent of sales for commission. Will this work? Another analyst contends that, since the sales force has no training in credits and collections, accounts receivables should be excluded from ROAM calculations. Do you agree? What would happen to Branch A's ROAM if accounts receivables were excluded?

8. Given the following profit and loss statement for the XYZ Company, allocate the natural accounts to the functional accounts:

XYZ Company
Profit and Loss Statement
1989

Sales	$1,676,000
Cost of goods sold	1,003,000
Gross margin	$ 673,000
	(cont'd)

Selling and administrative expenses:
Salaries
Salespeople	120,000
Sales manager	30,000
Office personnel	38,000
Warehouse personnel	30,000
Commissions	16,760
Advertising	93,800
Postage	450

Supplies
Office	200
Warehouse	500
Packaging	30,000
Transportation	80,290
Travel expenses	40,000

Rent
Sales	15,000
Warehouse	35,000
Order processing	10,000

Heat and electricity
Sales	7,000
Warehouse	18,000
Order processing	5,000

Total selling and administrative expenses:	570,000
Net profit (loss)	$ 103,000

9. Some large companies treat the marketing department as a profit center and have created the position of marketing controller. What problems will this approach produce? How would you resolve these problems?

Application Questions

A1. You are given the following information on two salespeople:

Sales-person	Number of Calls	Number of Orders	Units Sold	Total Sales	Cost of Goods Sold
A	200	250	15,000	$750,000	$600,000
B	295	230	18,000	$900,000	$720,000

Salesperson A earns a $22,000 salary compared to $23,000 for salesperson B. Both earn 1 percent commission. Advertising costs $3 per unit. Shipping expenses are $2 per unit. Order processing costs total $1 per order. Travel expenses amount to $0.50 per call. Your task is to calculate the contribution to profit (loss) made by each salesperson.

A2. As the sales manager of the M.N.O. Company, you are trying to evaluate the performance of two districts. You have decided to look at how each district has managed its assets employed in the selling function. From the information below, determine each district's ROAM.

		District 1		District 2
Sales		$800,000		$500,000
Cost of goods sold		624,000		390,000
Gross margin		176,000		110,000
Variable district expenses				
Salaries	$49,600		$31,000	
Commissions	8,000		5,000	
Office expenses	9,600		6,000	
Travel	12,800		8,000	
Total expenses		80,000		50,000
Net profit (loss)		96,000		60,000
District investment in assets:				
Accounts receivable		120,000		45,000
Inventories		200,000		80,000
Earnings as a percent of sales		.12		.12
Turnover		2.5		4.0

A3. Sylvie Faivre, sales analyst for the Bouvre Cheese Company located in Lyons, France, had completed her analysis of one of the southern districts. The district was a candidate for consolidation since management believed sales were not as expected. Sylvie suggested she should first determine the district's return on assets managed before any decisions were made concerning territory modification. The following provides the data needed to calculate ROAM for the district:

Sales	Fr4,500,000
Cost of goods sold	4,000,000
Gross margin	500,000
Less variable branch expenses	
Salaries	175,000
Commissions	30,000
Office expenses	35,000
Travel and entertainment	55,000
	295,000
District contribution to profit	205,000
District investments	
Accounts receivable	750,000
Inventories	900,000
	1,650,000

Determine the ROAM for the district. What would happen if inventories were reduced by 20 percent? How much would sales have to increase to obtain the company average ROAM of 25 percent? Bouvre management believes salaries are too high and is considering a 15 percent reduction. Assuming no impact on sales, how would this affect district ROAM?

A4. Use the following information to determine for the company and for each sales representative:

Market share

Account penetration

Contribution margin

Sales calls per active account

Selling expenses ratio

What problems do your results identify? What additional information or calculations are needed to fully understand the situation?

Territory Sales Analysis, 1993

Sales Represen-tative	Territory	Sales Potential ($000)	Sales Volume ($000)	Potential Accounts	Active Accounts	Sales Calls	Base Salary	Bonus	Sales Expenses
D. Myers	Minneapolis-St. Paul, Rochester, Madison, Milwaukee	$ 6,861	$1,036	433	117	2,192	$ 17,500	$ 2,240	$ 4,375
J. Hester	Washington, D.C., Baltimore, Philadelphia	9,603	864	728	400	2,138	15,000	1,950	3,750
B. Moore	Chicago	11,300	893	685	343	1,855	16,250	1,825	5,125
M. Houston	Chicago	10,468	806	673	370	2,040	13,750	1,740	3,375
W. Reitman	Detroit	6,838	1,087	498	289	2,027	18,750	2,375	4,125
S. Tyler	Dallas–Ft. Worth, Houston, San Antonio, New Orleans	24,230	703	770	208	1,782	13,750	1,600	4,625
D. Nelson	Denver	6,585	1,060	428	205	2,096	15,625	2,200	3,875
T. Sikes	St. Louis, Kansas City, Tulsa, Oklahoma City	9,374	478	455	100	1,514	12,500	1,010	5,375
Totals		$85,259	$6,927	4,670	2,032	15,644	$123,125	$14,940	$34,625

Endnotes

[1] See, for example, Richard T. Hise, "Have Manufacturing Firms Adopted the Marketing Concept?" *Journal of Marketing* 29 (July 1975), pp. 9–12; L. Gayle Rayburn, "Accounting Tools in the Analysis and Control of Marketing Performance," *Industrial Marketing Management* 6 (1977), pp. 175–82; and Alan J. Dubinsky and Thomas E. Barry, "A Survey of Sales Management Practices," *Industrial Marketing Management* 11 (April 1982), pp. 133–41.

[2] For a review of the controversy, as well as a historical perspective on why it exists, see John J. Wheatley, "The Allocation Controversy in Marketing Cost Analysis," *University of Washington Business Review,* Summer 1971, pp. 61–70.

[3] Sanford R. Simon, *Managing Marketing Profitability* (New York: American Management Association, 1969), p. 37. All serious students of marketing cost analysis are urged to read this classic book on marketing profitability analysis. It illustrates the process that should be followed in carrying out a marketing cost analysis and the insights gained from doing so with detailed examples. Much of this and the following section rely heavily on this excellent book.

[4] Ibid., pp. 37–38.

[5] Rayburn, "Accounting Tools," p. 178.

[6] The early "classics" on marketing cost analysis emphasized the full-cost approach. See J. B. Heckert and R. B. Miner, *Distribution Costs* (New York: Ronald Press, 1953); and D. R. Longman and M. Schiff, *Practical Distribution Cost Analysis* (Homewood, Ill.: Richard D. Irwin, 1955).

[7] See, for example, Simon, *Managing Marketing Profitability;* Charles H. Sevin, *Marketing Productivity Analysis* (New York: McGraw Hill, 1965); L. Gayle Rayburn, *Financial Tools for Effective Marketing Administration* (New York: American Management Association, 1976); James M. Fremgen and Shu S. Liao, *The Allocation of Corporate Indirect Costs* 18 (New York: National Association of Accountants, 1981); and Robin Cooper and Robert S. Kaplan, "Measure Costs Right: Make the Right Decision," *Harvard Business Review* 66 (September–October 1988), pp. 96–103.

[8] See Donald W. Jackson and Lonnie L. Ostrom, "Grouping Segments for Profitability Analysis," *MSU Business Topics* 28 (1980), pp. 39–44, for a discussion of the segments that are typically used in a marketing cost analysis.

[9] Edmund D. McCarry, "Some Functions of Marketing Reconsidered," in *Theory in Marketing,* ed. Reavis Cox and Wroe Anderson (Homewood, Ill.: Richard D. Irwin, 1950), p. 267.

[10] It is, in fact, the most frequently used basis. See Douglas M. Lambert and Jay U. Sterling, "What Types of Profitability Reports Do Marketing Managers Receive?" *Industrial Marketing Management* 16 (November 1987), pp. 295–304.

[11] Charles R. Horngren, *Cost Accounting: A Managerial Emphasis,* 2nd ed. (Englewood Cliffs, N.J.: Prentice Hall, 1967), p. 381.

[12] The example is purposely hypothetical to throw the basic process into more bold relief, while at the same time illustrating some common features of such situations. For actual examples, which at times can get quite complex, see Simon, *Managing Marketing Profitability;* Sevin, *Marketing Productivity Analysis;* J. S. Schiff and M. Schiff, *Strategic Management of the Sales Territory* (New York: New York Sales Marketing Executives, 1980); and Robert A. Howell and Stephen R. Soucy, "Customer Profitability—As Critical as Product Profitability," *Management Accounting* 72 (October 1990), pp. 43–47.

[13] In addition to the references previously cited, see Dana Smith Morgan and Fred W. Morgan, "Marketing Cost Controls: A Survey of Industry Practices," *Industrial Marketing Management* 9 (July 1980), pp. 217–21; and Thomas M. Petro, "Profitability: The Fifth 'P' of Marketing," *Basic Marketing* 22 (September 1990), pp. 48–52.

[14] J. S. Schiff and Michael Schiff, "New Sales Management Tool: ROAM," *Harvard Business Review* 45 (July–August 1967), pp. 59–66. For the application of ROAM to evaluating sales territories, see J. S. Schiff, "Evaluating the Sales Force as a Business," *Industrial Marketing Management* 12 (April 1983), pp. 131–37. One problem with the return on assets managed measure for evaluating segment performance is that it neglects the firm's opportunity costs for the capital invested in the assets. Residual income analysis is a preferred alternative on these grounds for evaluating the profitability of the personal selling effort. See William L. Cron and Michael Levy, "Sales Management Performance Evaluation: A Residual Income Perspective," *Journal of Personal Selling and Sales Management* 7 (August 1987), pp. 57–66.

[15] Alfred P. Sloan, *My Years with General Motors* (Garden City, N.Y.: Doubleday, 1964), p. 140.

Suggested Readings

Cooper, Robin, and Robert S. Kaplan. "Measure Costs Right: Make the Right Decision." *Harvard Business Review* 66 (September–October 1988), pp. 96–103.

Rayburn, L. Gayle. "Accounting Tools in the Analysis and Control of Marketing Performance." *Industrial Marketing Management* 6 (1977), pp. 175–82.

Schiff, J. S. "Evaluating the Sales Force as a Business." *Industrial Marketing Management* 12 (April 1983), pp. 131–37.

Simon, Sanford R. *Managing Marketing Profitability.* New York: American Management Association, 1969.

Behavior and Other Performance Analyses

IBM-WISCONSIN ALTERS PERFORMANCE EVALUATION CRITERIA

In the United States, IBM is organized into trading areas. Until 1991, IBM-Wisconsin, one of those trading areas, evaluated and compensated its salespeople primarily on what they sold. Each sales representative was given a quota at the beginning of the year. The primary performance and compensation criterion was how the rep did versus quota, although salespeople were also evaluated on territory management, marketing programs, and professional responsibilities. The latter criteria had little bearing on compensation but were used during performance evaluation. In many cases, sales reps were assumed to have an adequate level of these skills, and their performance evaluation and compensation were based on how their sales compared to the quota assigned them.

Because of this emphasis, salespeople tended to operate as individuals rather than teams. They focused on activities that would enhance their own sales and gave short shrift to activities that might help another representative or the trading area in general but that possessed little potential for personal benefit.

To create more synergy across sales territories, products, industries, and sales reps, IBM-Wisconsin changed its salesperson performance evaluation and compensation systems in 1991. It abandoned individual quotas in favor of a trading area quota. If the trading area makes its sales target, then all sales reps participate in the trading area's bonus. The extent of their participation depends on how well they perform on six performance criteria; (1) business volume, (2) customer satisfaction, (3) leadership/teamwork, (4) opportunity identification/territory planning, (5) professional responsibility or the behavioral characteristics and skills they bring to the job, and (6) market-driven quality.

IBM-Wisconsin has formal systems for measuring business volume and how well representatives are doing in identifying opportunities and managing their territories. It has informal systems to measure the other traits, but it is developing objective measurement systems to assess customer satisfaction among each rep's accounts and the leadership/teamwork the individual displays. For now, it will continue to assess market-driven quality more informally by looking at the number and types of involvement individuals have with respect to improving customer service. Similarly, it will continue to assess professional responsibility or the behavioral characteristics the individual brings to the job through informal monitoring.

Individuals skills will be tracked and measured objectively with the use of an automated skills system. Measurement of skills will be done in the future with a Professional Careers Certification process.

Source: IBM-Wisconsin. Used with permission.

Sales and cost analysis are two very important techniques sales managers can use to assess the overall personal selling effort. They help to measure whether the selling effort is on target with respect to the goals established for this portion of the marketing mix and also provide strong clues of where and how it can be improved.

Although these techniques also provide valuable input for evaluating individual salespeople, relying on them exclusively can produce a distorted picture of what an individual sales rep accomplished. Measures of salesperson sales or profits ignore the goodwill the rep may have generated for the company, the efforts to develop new accounts that offer long-term profit potential, the information brought back from the field, and so on. Recognizing this, most firms supplement sales and cost analyses with other evaluations of how individual salespeople are doing, as the scenario suggests. These firms recognize that what gets measured, gets managed.

This chapter reviews other evaluation measures. The chapter first highlights why they are necessary. It discusses some supplemental objective measures for evaluation and then some subjective or qualitative measures.

PERFORMANCE VERSUS EFFECTIVENNESS

Part 2 of this book was concerned with understanding the individual salesperson. The model used to structure that discussion suggested a sales representative's performance was a function of five factors: the individual's (1) role perceptions, (2) aptitude, (3) skill level, (4) motivation level, and (5) personal, organizational, and environmental variables that influence performance. Exhibit 18.1 depicts a slightly modified form of that model. The main change is the distinction among behavior, performance, and effectiveness.[1] While role perceptions, aptitude, skill level, and motivation level were previously pictured as being directly linked to performance, now they are directly linked to behavior. The modified model is useful for understanding the role of sales and cost analyses in salespeople's evaluation as well as why other measures for evaluating representatives are necessary.

Behavior

Behavior refers to what representatives do—that is, the tasks they expend effort on while working. These tasks might include calling on customers, writing orders, preparing sales presentations, developing formal equipment proposals, and the like.

Performance

Performance is behavior evaluated in terms of its contributions to the goals of the organization. Performance, in other words, has a normative element reflecting whether a salesperson's behavior is "good" or "bad" in light of the organization's goals and objectives. Note that behavior and performance are both influenced by relevant sales activities. These in turn depend on the types of sales jobs in question.

Effectiveness

Exhibit 18.1 also distinguishes between performance and effectiveness. By definition, **effectiveness** refers to some summary index of organizational outcomes for which an individual is at least partly responsible, such as sales volume, market share, or profitability of sales. The crucial distinction between performance and effectiveness is that the latter does not refer to behavior

EXHIBIT 18 • 1   *Sales Behavior, Performance, and Effectiveness*

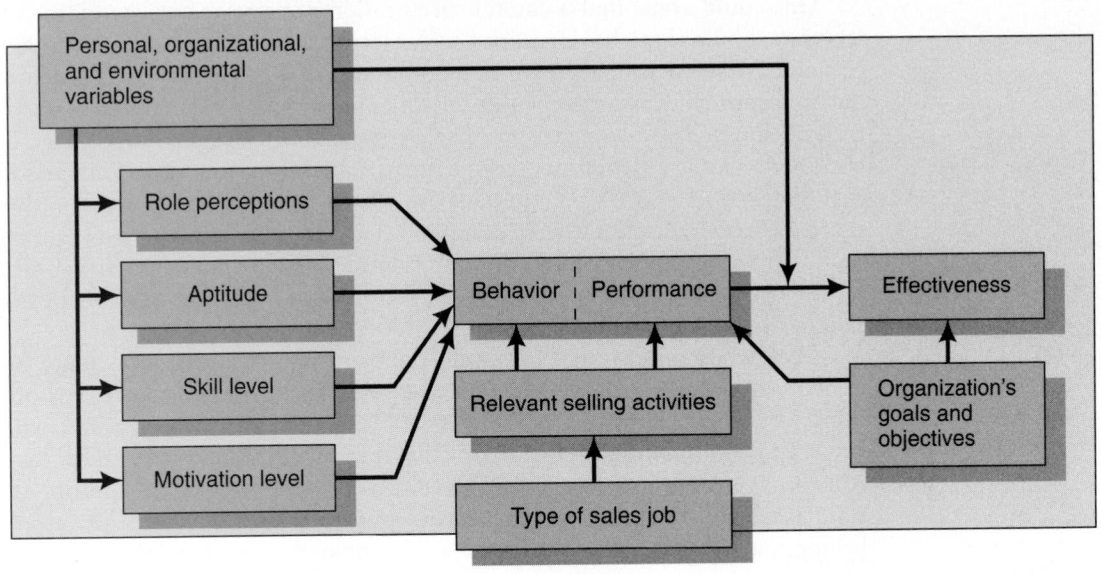

Source: Orville C. Walker, Jr., Gilbert A. Churchill, Jr., and Neil M. Ford, "Where Do We Go from Here? Selected Conceptual and Empirical Issues Concerning the Motivation and Performance of the Industrial Salesforce," in *Critical Issues in Sales Management: State-of-the-Art and Future Research Needs,* ed. Gerald Albaum and Gilbert A. Churchill, Jr. (Eugene: College of Business Administration, University of Oregon, 1979), p. 36.

directly; rather it is a function of additional factors not under the individual salesperson's control. These include top management policies, the sales potential of a territory, and the actions of competitors.

In terms of Exhibit 18.1, sales and cost analyses produce effectiveness measures; that is, the results are partially determined by the performance of the sales reps. However, differences between two salespersons' "performances" are not solely determined in this way. There may be differences in the potential in their territories or in the physical makeup of the territories and consequently in what it takes to service them. There may be differences in the level of company support by territory or the competitive conditions within each. When such differences exist, is it reasonable to say that one salesperson did better than another because his sales, market share, or contribution to profit was higher?

It is generally agreed that salesmen should be judged solely on those phases of sales performance over which they exercise control, and should not be held responsible for results beyond their control. If a company's method of measuring salesmen's performance is to result in valid comparisons, serious consideration must be given to such factors in developing yardsticks for objective or subjective evaluation.[2]

One could argue that a careful specification of performance standards by territory should eliminate inequities across territories. For example, percentage of quota attained should be an acceptable measure of performance because quotas supposedly consider variations in environmental factors across territories. Admittedly, a comparison of salespeople with respect to percentage of quota attained is a better measure of their performance than is a comparison that simply looks at each representative's level of absolute sales or market share, *assuming* the quotas were done well. This is a big *if,* however; sometimes they are not. In some instances, they are arbitrary and are not necessarily based on an objective assessment of all the factors that facilitate or constrain a salesperson's ability to make a sale.

Even when quotas are done well, the measure "percentage of quota attained" still omits much with respect to a salesperson's performance. For one thing, it ignores the profitability of sales. Sales reps can be compared with respect to profitability, or the return they produce on the assets under their control, as shown in Chapter 17. Nevertheless, determining the appropriate standards of profitability for each territory is even more difficult than establishing quotas that accurately consider the many factors that affect the level of sales a representative should be able to produce in a territory.

Even if good sales and profit standards could be developed, the problem of salespeople's evaluation would not be solved because neither measure incorporates activities that may have no short-term payout but still have substantial consequences to the firm long run, as in Thorny Issues 18.1. These include the time devoted to developing a potential large account, to building long-term territorial goodwill for the company, or to developing detailed understanding of the capabilities of the firm's products. That is why many firms supplement sales and cost analyses with other measures that more directly reflect each sales reps performance.

The other measures firms use to evaluate salespeople fall into two broad categories, (1) objective measures and (2) subjective measures. The objective measures reflect other statistics the manager can gather from the firm's internal data. The subjective measures rely on personal evaluations by someone in the organization, typically the salesperson's immediate supervisor, of how individual salespeople are doing.

OBJECTIVE MEASURES

The objective measures that firms use to supplement traditional sales and cost analyses fall into the three subcategories of output measures, input measures, and ratios of output and/or input measures. Exhibit 18.2 on page 764 summarizes the more common output and input measures, and Exhibit 18.3 on

Thorny Issues in Sales Management 18 • 1

How Much is a Customer Worth?

How much does it cost to replace a lost customer? The fact that some companies use "number of lost accounts" as a measure of sales performance indicates their concern with this issue. Consider the impact to service providers:

The cost of replacing a customer can top $400 in the service industry, according to a survey by the Sandy Corporation, a Troy, Mich., training and consulting firm.

Sandy Corp. mailed surveys to 5,400 service company executives to see how they handle customer service—and what it costs them when they don't do it well. Among Sandy's findings were that banks lost about $80 in unrealized revenue every time they lost a customer; lodging and restaurants lost $21; and transportation companies lost $322.

In addition, the study found that it cost $100 in sales and marketing to replace customers in the banking and transportation industries, and $20 in lodging and restaurants. The loss plus replacement costs for banks was $180; lodging and restaurants, $41; and transportation, $422.

The survey also revealed that the major sources of customer dissatisfaction were, in order: a lack of responsiveness or the inability to resolve a problem; delays or interruptions in service; unfriendly employees; and errors in billing or delivery.

As the article reveals, whenever a customer becomes history, revenues and costs suffer. The loss in sales leads to a reduction in revenues. Attempts to bring the ex-customer back will increase costs.

page 765 displays some of the more commonly used ratios. The rationales for why these measures are used are discussed briefly below.

Output Measures The most used output measures for evaluating salespeople are sales statistics. More than 8 of 10 firms evaluate salespeople with respect to their level of sales, and 3 of 4 assess how closely salespeople come to the quota assigned them. At the same time, a number of firms look beyond dollar or unit sales data and focus on order and account data.[3]

Orders

The *number of orders* each salesperson secures is often used to assess the rep's ability to make sales presentations since it reflects the individual's ability to "close." Not only must the timing of the close be right, but also the salesperson must have adequately moved the buyer through the prior stages of the buying process via the sales presentation if the close is going to be successful.[4]

Although the number of orders a salesperson secures is important, the *average size of those orders* is equally so. Having many orders may mean the

EXHIBIT 18 • 2   *Common Output and Input Factors Used to Evaluate Salespeople*

Output Factors	Input Factors
Orders	Calls
Number of orders	Number of calls
Average size of orders	Number of planned calls
Number of canceled orders	Number of unplanned calls
Accounts	Time and time utilization
Number of active accounts	Days worked
Number of new accounts	Calls per day (call rate)
Number of lost accounts	Selling time versus nonselling time
Number of overdue accounts	
Number of prospective accounts	Expenses
	Total
	By type
	As a percentage of sales
	As a percentage of quota
	Nonselling activities
	Letters written to prospects
	Telephone calls to prospects
	Number of formal proposals developed
	Advertising displays set up
	Number of meetings held with
	distributors/dealers
	Number of training sessions held with
	distributor/dealer personnel
	Number of calls on distributor/dealer
	customers
	Number of service calls made
	Number of overdue accounts collected

orders are small and may indicate the person is spending too much time calling on small Type C accounts and not enough time calling on large type A accounts.

Still another measure of a salesperson's presentation effectiveness is the *number of canceled orders*. A salesperson who loses a large proportion of total orders to subsequent cancellation may be using high-pressure tactics in sales presentations.

Accounts

The various account measures provide a perspective on the equity of territorial assignments and also on how the salesperson is handling the territory. One popular measure focuses on the *number of active accounts* in the salesperson's customer portfolio. Various definitions of active accounts are used. It may be any customer that has placed an order in the past six months or in the past year. A salesperson's performance in one year may be compared to performance

EXHIBIT 18 • 3   *Common Ratios Used to Evaluate Salespeople*

Expense ratios

- Sales expense ratio $= \dfrac{\text{Expenses}}{\text{Sales}}$

- Cost per call ratio $= \dfrac{\text{Total costs}}{\text{Number of calls}}$

Account development and servicing ratios

- Account penetration ratio $= \dfrac{\text{Accounts sold}}{\text{Total accounts available}}$

- New account conversion ratio $= \dfrac{\text{Number of new accounts}}{\text{Total number of accounts}}$

- Lost account ratio $= \dfrac{\text{Prior accounts not sold}}{\text{Total number of accounts}}$

- Sales per account ratio $= \dfrac{\text{Sales dollar volume}}{\text{Total number of accounts}}$

- Average order size ratio $= \dfrac{\text{Sales dollar volume}}{\text{Total number of orders}}$

- Order cancellation ratio $= \dfrac{\text{Number of canceled orders}}{\text{Total number of orders}}$

Call activity and/or productivity

- Calls per day ratio $= \dfrac{\text{Number of calls}}{\text{Number of days worked}}$

- Calls per account ratio $= \dfrac{\text{Number of calls}}{\text{Number of accounts}}$

- Planned call ratio $= \dfrac{\text{Number of planned calls}}{\text{Total number of calls}}$

- Order per call (hit) ratio $= \dfrac{\text{Number of orders}}{\text{Total number of calls}}$

in past years by contrasting the number of active accounts. Closely related to this yardstick is a measure that tracks the *number of new accounts* a salesperson develops in a given time. Some companies even establish new-prospect quotas by salespeople that allow a ready comparison of performance to standard.

While not as popular as the number of new accounts, the *number of lost accounts* can be a revealing statistic, since it indicates how successfully the salesperson is satisfying the ongoing needs of the established accounts in the territory. Still other account measures by which salespeople can be compared are the *number of overdue accounts,* which might indicate the salesperson is not following company procedures in screening accounts for their creditworthiness, and the *number of prospective accounts,* which assesses the salesperson's ability in identifying potential target customers.

Input Measures

Many objective measures of performance evaluation focus on the efforts sales representatives expend rather than the results of those efforts. There are at least two good reasons for this. First, efforts or desirable behaviors are much more controllable than results. If a rep's sales fall short of quota, the problem may lie with the person, the quota, or a change in the environment. If the number of calls a salesperson makes falls short of the target, however, the problem lies much more directly with the individual.[5] Second, in many selling situations, there is a time lag between inputs and outputs. A particularly large sale may be the result of several years of efforts.

> At the age of 29, Kim Kelley is already something of a legend around Honeywell, Inc. "He's the one who cried when he made his sale, isn't he?" a fellow Honeywell salesman asks with a chuckle.
>
> Indeed, he is. Kim stood there in his customer's office last June and bawled like a baby. And for good reason. Kim had just shaken hands on an $8.1 million computer sale to the state of Illinois. He had gambled his whole career on making that sale. He had spent three years laying the groundwork for it, and for three solid months he had been working six days a week, often 14 hours a day, competing against salesmen from four other computer companies.
>
> It was a make-or-break situation for Kim Kelley, and, standing there with tears of joy and relief streaming down his cheeks, he knew he had it made. A bright future with Honeywell was assured, and he had made $80,000 commission—more money than he had earned in all four of his previous years with the company. . . .
>
> For three years, he patiently made daily rounds of key state offices, pausing a few minutes in each one to drop off technical documents or just to chat.[6]

In such situations, it seems more reasonable to conclude that performance was good during all three years, rather than it was bad in all years except the one in which the order was finally placed. Sales representatives' efforts are measured in a number of ways.

Calls

The *number of current customer* and/or prospect *calls* is often used to decide whether a salesperson is covering the territory in accord with the company's plan. As discussed previously, the number of calls on each of the various classes of accounts is an important factor in the design of territories. Thus, such information should also be used to evaluate the salesperson assigned to the territory. After all, sales calls are a resource with finite supply. They represent a resource that is time sensitive in that the time available to make them evaporates if it is not used.[7] The number of calls typically can be determined from a salesperson's call reports.

Many companies further distinguish between the *number of planned and unplanned calls*. They would like salespeople to make a lot of calls and also prefer that these are planned. Unplanned calls typically reflect some emergency or breakdown in customer service. While these will always occur, they create inefficiencies in covering the territory; it is a mark of good territory management when they are low relative to the number of planned calls.

Time and time utilization

The *number of days worked* and the *calls per day* (or *call rate*) are routinely used by many companies to assess salespeople's efforts since the product of the two quantities provides a direct measure of the extent of customer contact. If the amount of customer contact by a salesperson is low, one can look separately at the components to see where the problem lies. Perhaps the salesperson has not been working enough because of sickness, extenuating circumstances, or just plain laziness—a situation that would show up in the number of days worked. Alternatively, perhaps the salesperson's total time input was satisfactory, but the salesperson was not using that time wisely and, consequently, had a low call rate.

Comparing salespeople's division of time between sales calls, traveling, and office work offers a useful perspective. For the most part, the firm would want salespeople to maximize the time in face-to-face customer contact at the expense of the other two factors. The company would want representatives particularly to minimize unproductive travel time. Such analyses require detailed input on how each person is spending time and can be expensive. Some companies, however, routinely conduct such analyses because the benefits are deemed to outweigh the costs.

Expenses

The objective inputs discussed so far for evaluating salespeople focus mainly on the extent of the salespeople's effort. Another key emphasis when evaluating them is the cost of those efforts. Many firms keep records detailing the *total expenses* incurred by each salesperson. Some break these expenses down *by type,* such as automobile expenses, lodging expenses, entertainment expenses, and so on. They might look at these expenses in total and/or as a percentage of sales or quotas by salesperson and use these expense ratios to evaluate salespeople (see Thorny Issues 18.2).

Nonselling activities

In addition to assessing the direct contact of salespeople with customers, some firms monitor indirect contact. They use indexes such as the *number of letters*

Thorny Issues in Sales Management 18 • 2

Blattner's Inc. manufactures industrial abrasives used in the machining of metals using grinders and related equipment. An analysis of sales expenses using the company's recently installed decision support system revealed that 6 of the company's 47 salespeople had expenses as a percentage of sales so much higher than the average that they could be considered outliers. The company's sales manager decided to do a more detailed check of each of the six salespersons' expense reports.

The analysis indicated extraordinary circumstances could account for the high expense-to-sales ratio for three of the salespeople. Follow-up interviews with the other three produced a satisfactory explanation for one more of the deviant cases. However, two of the salespeople did not offer sufficiently satisfactory explanations to the sales manager to make him believe all the expenses claimed were legitimate, nor could the salespeople produce adequate receipts. The sales manager was perplexed as to the action he should take. Both people had been with the company for over 10 years and had been good producers along with being good corporate citizens.

If you were the sales manager for Blattner's what would you do? Why?

---

written, the *number of telephone calls made,* and the *number of formal proposals* developed.

In many industries, the sales rep's duties go beyond what might be considered a normal selling emphasis. In such instances, firms often try to monitor the extent of these duties, using such indexes as the *number of promotion or advertising displays set up,* the *number of dealer meetings* and the *number of training sessions for distributor personnel* held, the *number of calls* the salesperson made *on dealer customers,* the *number of service calls made,* the *number of customer complaints received,* and the *number of overdue accounts collected.* Some of this information can be gathered from sales-call reports. The rest of it, such as the number of customer complaints, requires monitoring other correspondence.

There are also other ways to secure feedback. Consider, for example, the lengths to which one company went to assess sales force feedback. The company had always emphasized to its sales force the importance of feedback and prided itself on the amount it secured. Nevertheless, to quantify the amount of information it actually did get, the firm decided to conduct an experiment. Two other firms agreed to supply new products that were strategically placed with customers who would mention to the firm's salespeople that these were superior competitive products. The salespeople's feedback about the new competitive products was then carefully monitored. You can appreciate the firm's dismay when it found that this information was transmitted back to management less than 20 percent of the time.[8]

Ratios   The focus on outputs rather than sales volume can reveal how salespeople are performing. So can an analysis of their efforts. Additional insights can also be gathered by combining the various outputs and/or inputs in selected ways, typically in the form of ratios.[9] Exhibit 18.3, for example, lists some of the ratios commonly used to evaluate salespeople.

Expense ratios

The *sales-expense ratio* combines both salespeople's inputs and the results produced by those inputs in a single number. Salespeople can affect this ratio either by making sales or by controlling expenses. The ratio can also be used to analyze salesperson expenses by type. Thus, a sales/transportation-expense ratio that is much higher for one salesperson than others might indicate the salesperson is covering her territory inefficiently. One does need to recognize territorial differences when comparing these ratios, though; the salesperson who has the out-of-line ratio may simply have a larger, more geographically dispersed sales territory to cover.

The *cost-per-call ratio* expresses the costs of supporting each salesperson in the field as a function of the number of calls the salesperson makes. The ratio can be evaluated using total costs or the costs can be broken down by elements, and ratios such as expenses per call and travel costs per call can be computed. Not only are these ratios useful for comparing salespeople from the same firm, but they can also be compared to those of other companies in the same industry to assess how efficient the firm's personal selling effort is.

Account development and servicing ratios

A number of ratios concern accounts and orders that reflect on how well salespeople are capturing the potential business that exists in their territories. The *account penetration ratio,* for example, measures the percentage of accounts in the territory from which the salesperson secures orders. It provides a direct measure of whether the salesperson is simply skimming the cream of the business or is working the territory systematically and hard.

The *new account-conversion ratio* similarly measures the salesperson's ability to convert prospects to customers. The *lost account ratio* measures how well the salesperson keeps prior accounts as active customers and reflects on how well the representative is serving the established accounts in the territory.

The *sales per account ratio* indicates the salesperson's success per account on average. A low ratio could indicate the salesperson is spending too much time calling on small nonprofitable accounts and not enough time calling on larger ones. One could also look at the sales per account ratios by class of account, which can reveal the strengths and weaknesses of each salesperson. A salesperson who has a low sales per account ratio for class A accounts might need help in learning how to sell when there are multiple buying influences, for example.

The *average order size* ratio can also reveal the salesperson's call patterns. A very low average size might suggest the calls are too frequent and the salesperson's productivity could be improved by spacing them more. The *order-cancellation ratio* reflects on the salesperson's method of selling; a very high ratio could mean the salesperson is using high-pressure tactics to secure orders, rather than satisfactorily handling customer concerns.

Call activity and/or productivity ratios

The call activity ratios measure the effort and planning salespeople put into their customer call activities and the successes they derive from it. The measures might be used to compare salesperson activities in total—such as when using *calls per day* or when using calls per total number of accounts, or by type of account. The *planned call ratio* could be used to assess if the salesperson is systematically planning territory coverage or whether the representative is working the territory without an overall game plan. The *orders per call ratio* bears directly on the question of whether the salesperson's calls on average are productive. This ratio is sometimes called the hit ratio or batting average, since it captures the number of successes (hits or orders) in relation to the number of at-bats (calls).

Caution Is in Order

As Exhibits 18.2, 18.3, and the above discussion indicate, there are many objective outputs, inputs, and ratios by which salespeople can be compared. As you probably sense, many of the measures are somewhat redundant; they provide overlapping information on salespeople's behavior and successes. A number of other ratios could be developed by combining the various outputs, inputs, or ratios in various ways. One combination that is often used to evaluate salespeople, for example, is the equation:

$$\text{Sales} = \text{Days worked} \times \frac{\text{Calls}}{\text{Days worked}} \times \frac{\text{Orders}}{\text{Calls}} \times \frac{\text{Sales}}{\text{Orders}}$$

or

$$\text{Sales} = \frac{\text{Days}}{\text{worked}} \times \frac{\text{Call}}{\text{rate}} \times \frac{\text{Batting}}{\text{average}} \times \frac{\text{Average}}{\text{order size}}$$

The equation highlights nicely what the salesperson can do to increase sales. The representative can increase (1) the number of days worked, (2) the calls made per day, (3) success in securing an order on a given call, and (4) the size of those orders. Thus, the equation can be used to isolate how an individual salesperson's performance could be improved. Such an equation, though, focuses on the results of the salesperson's efforts and ignores the cost of these efforts. Similarly, many of the other measures that have been reviewed and could be combined via similar equations would probably ignore one or more elements of salesperson success.

There are two essential points to this discussion. First, just as sales and cost analyses have advantages and disadvantages, so do all of these other objective measures of performance. Rather than relying on only one or two of the measures to assess performance, the methods are most productively used in combination. Second, and more important, all of the indexes are an aid to judgment, not a substitute for it. The comparisons the indexes allow *should be the beginning not the conclusion* of any analysis aimed at assessing how well individual salespeople are doing.

SUBJECTIVE MEASURES

A useful conceptual distinction exists between the objective measures of effort and performance discussed in the preceding section and the subjective measures discussed here. Quantitative measures of effort focus on what salespeople do, whereas qualitative measures reflect how well they do what they are doing. This subtle difference in what is being measured creates some marked differences in the way the measurements are made.

In many ways, it is more difficult to assess the quality than the quantity of a salesperson's efforts. The quantity measures can require a detailed analysis of salespeople's call reports, an extensive time and duty analysis, or even some experimentation. Once the process is set up, though, it can be conducted with little bias and inconsistency. Not so with quality assessments. Even with a well-designed process that is firmly in place, there is substantial room for bias. Such schemes must invariably rely on the personal judgment of the individual or individuals charged with evaluation. Typically, these judgments are secured by having the appraiser rate the salesperson on each of a number of attributes using some kind of rating scale.

The attributes most commonly evaluated using merit rating forms are these:

1. **Sales results**—volume performance, sales to new accounts, selling the full product line.
2. **Job knowledge**—knowledge of company policies, prices, products.
3. **Management of territory**—planning of activities and calls, controlling expenses, handling reports and records.
4. **Customer and company relations**—standing with customers, associates, and company.
5. **Personal characteristics**—initiative, personal appearance, personality, resourcefulness, and so on.

The emphasis given to each varies by company. The emphasis also seems to depend on the purpose for which the evaluation is being used. For example, sales performance measures seem to be more important in termination and compensation decisions, whereas product knowledge and customer relations seem to be more important in transfer and promotion decisions.[10]

Exhibit 18.4 shows the rating scale used by the Testor Corporation. This sales personnel inventory is completed for every Testor salesperson every six months. These evaluations supplement the computer-generated reports of sales

E x h i b i t   18 • 4   *Sales Personnel Inventory, Used by the Testor Corporation*

SALES PERSONNEL INVENTORY

Employer's Name _____ Territory _____

Position Title _____ Date _____

INSTRUCTIONS (Read Carefully)

1. Base your judgment on the previous six-month period and not upon isolated incidents alone.
2. Place a check in the block which most nearly expresses your judgment on each factor.
3. For those employees who are rated at either extreme of the scale on any factor—for example, outstanding, deficient, limited—please enter a brief explanation for the rating in the appropriate space below the factor.
4. Make your rating an accurate description of the person rated.

FACTORS TO BE CONSIDERED AND RATED:

1. Knowledge of Work (includes knowledge of product, knowledge of customer's business)

☐	☐	☐	☐	☐
Does not have sufficient knowledge of products and application to represent Company effectively.	Has mastered minimum knowledge. Needs further training.	Has average amount of knowledge needed to handle job satisfactorily.	Is above average in knowledge needed to handle job satisfactorily.	Is thoroughly acquainted with our products and technical problems involved in this application.

Comments _____

---

2. Degree of Acceptance by Customers

☐	☐	☐	☐	☐
Not acceptable to most customers. Cannot gain entry to their offices.	Manages to see customers but not generally liked.	Has satisfactory relationship with most customers	Is on very good terms and is accepted by virtually all customers.	Enjoys excellent personal relationship with virtually all customers.

Comments _____

---

3. Amount of Effort Devoted to Acquiring Business

☐	☐	☐	☐	☐
Exceptional in the amount of time and effort put forth in selling.	Devotes constant effort in developing business.	Devotes intermittent effort in acquiring moderate amount of business.	Exerts only minimum amount of time and effort.	Unsatisfactory. Does not put forth sufficient effort to produce business.

Comments _____

EXHIBIT 18 • 4 *(continued)*

4. **Ability to Acquire Business**	☐ Is able to acquire business under the most difficult situations.	☐ Does a good job under most circumstances.	☐ Manages to acquire good percentage of customer's business if initial resistance is not too strong.	☐ Able to acquire enough business to maintain only a minimum sales average.	☐ Rarely able to acquire business except in a seller's market.
	Comments _____				
5. **Amount of Service Given to Customers**	☐ Rarely services his accounts once a sale is made.	☐ Gives only minimum service at all times.	☐ Services accounts with regularity but does not do any more than he is called on to do.	☐ Gives very good service to all customers.	☐ Goes out of his way to give outstanding service within scope of Company policy.
	Comments _____				
6. **Dependability— Amount of Supervision Needed**	☐ Always thoroughly abreast of problems in his territory, even under most difficult Rises to emergencies and assumes leadership without being requested to do so.	☐ Consistently reliable under normal conditions. Does special as well as regular assignments promptly. Little or no supervision required.	☐ Performs with reasonable promptness under normal supervision.	☐ Effort occasionally lags. Requires more than normal supervision.	☐ Requires close supervision in all phases of job.
	Comments _____				
7. **Attitude Toward Company— Support Given to Company Policies**	☐ Does not support Company policy— blames Company for factors that affect his	☐ Gives only passive support to Company policy—does not act as member of a team.	☐ Goes along with Company policies on most occasions.	☐ Adopts and supports Company viewpoint in all transactions.	☐ Gives unwavering support to Company and Company policies to customers even though

(cont'd)

E X H I B I T 18 • 4   *(continued)*

---

				he personally may not agree with them.
customers unfavorably.				

Comments _____

_____

8. Judgment

☐	☐	☐	☐	☐
Analyses and conclusions subject to frequent error and are often based on bias. Decisions require careful review by supervisor.	Judgments usually sound on routine, simple matters but cannot be relied on when any degree of complexity is involved.	Capable of careful analyzing of day-to-day problems involving some complexity and rendering sound decisions. Decision rarely influenced by prejudice or personal bias.	Decisions can be accepted without question except when problems of extreme complexity are involved. Little or no personal bias enters into judgment.	Possesses unusual comprehension and analytical ability. Complete reliance may be place on all judgments irrespective of degree of complexity. Decisions and judgments are completely free of personal bias or prejudice.

Comments _____

_____

9. Resourcefulness

☐	☐	☐	☐	☐
Work is consistently characterized by marked originality, alertness, initiative, and imagination. Can be relied on to develop new ideas and techniques in solving the most diffcult problems.	Frequently develops new ideas of merit. Handling of emergencies is generally characterized by sound decisive action.	Meets new situations in satisfactory manner. Occasionally develops original ideas, methods, and techniques.	Follows closely previously learned methods and procedures. Slow to adapt to changes. Tends to become confused in new situations.	Requires frequent reinstructon. Has failed to demonstrate initiative or imagination in solving problems.

Comments _____

_____

To be more effective on present job, this employee should:

1. Be given additional instruction on _____

_____

EXHIBIT 18 • 4 (concluded)

2. Be given additional experience such as _____

_____

3. Study such subjects as _____

_____

4. Change attitude as follows: _____

_____

5. There is nothing more that I can do for this employee because _____

_____

6. Remarks _____

_____

_____

of each product to each customer to provide an overall evaluation of a sales-person's performance. The Testor inventory form is better than many of those in use because it contains anchors or verbal descriptors for the various points on the scale. Furthermore, it provides room for verbal comments, which enhance understanding of the ratings supplied. The form contains a section where needed improvements and corrective action can be detailed. All in all, the form should help salespeople understand their weaknesses and improve performance.

The worst type of merit rating forms simply list the attributes of interest along one side of the form and the evaluation adjectives along the other. Exhibit 18.5, which is a recast version of the Testor inventory, illustrates such a form. The form can be completed very easily; the evaluator simply checks the adjective that most clearly describes the salesperson's performance on that attribute. While such forms are common, they work very poorly in practice.

Problems in Use   Some common problems with performance appraisal systems that rely on merit rating forms, particularly those using the simple checklist type, include the following.[11]

1. Lack of an outcome focus. The most useful type of performance appraisal highlights areas of improvement and the actions that must be taken to effect such improvements. For this to occur, the key behaviors in accomplishing the tasks assigned must be identified. Unfortunately, many companies have not taken this step. Rather, they have simply identified attributes thought to

EXHIBIT **18 • 5**   *Modified Version of Testor Personnel Inventory*

	Poor	Fair	Satisfactory	Good	Outstanding
Knowledge of work	☐	☐	☐	☐	☐
Degree of acceptance by customers	☐	☐	☐	☐	☐
Amount of effort devoted to acquiring business	☐	☐	☐	☐	☐
Ability to acquire business	☐	☐	☐	☐	☐
Amount of service given to customers	☐	☐	☐	☐	☐
Dependability—amount of supervision needed	☐	☐	☐	☐	☐
Attitude toward company—support given to company policies	☐	☐	☐	☐	☐
Judgment	☐	☐	☐	☐	☐
Resourcefulness	☐	☐	☐	☐	☐

be related to performance, but they have not attempted to assess systematically whether the attributes are key. A recent emphasis in performance appraisal called BARS (behavioral anchored rating scale) overcomes this weakness. A BARS system attempts to identify behaviors that are more or less effective with respect to the goals established for the person. It then secures superior ratings on these behaviors.

2. Ill-defined personality traits. Many merit rating forms contain personality factors as attributes. In the case of salespeople, these attributes might include such things as initiative, personal appearance, and resourcefulness. Although these attributes are intuitively appealing, their actual relationship to performance is open to question.[12]

3. Halo effect. A halo effect is a common phenomenon in the use of any rating form. It refers to the fact that the rating assigned to one characteristic significantly influences the ratings assigned to all others. One experiment that investigated the phenomenon among sales managers found that their overall evaluations could be predicted quite well from their rating of the salesperson on the single performance dimension they felt to be the most important.[13] Different branch or regional managers might have different feelings about what is most important, compounding the problem.

4. Leniency or harshness. Some sales managers rate at the extremes. Some are very lenient and rate every salesperson as *good* or *outstanding* on every attribute, whereas others do just the opposite. This behavior is often a function of their own personalities and their perceptions of what is outstanding performance. There may be no fundamental differences in the way the salespeople under each of the managers are performing. The use of different definitions of performance can seriously undermine the whole performance appraisal system.

5. **Central tendency.** Some managers err in the opposite direction in that they never, or very rarely, rate people at the ends of the scale. Rather, they use middle-of-the-road or play-it-safe ratings. One learns very little from such ratings about differences in performance and such ratings can be particularly troublesome when used as the basis of termination decisions as Thorny Issues 18.3 indicates.

6. **Interpersonal bias.** Interpersonal bias refers to the fact that our perceptions of others and the social acceptability of their behaviors are influenced by how much we like or dislike them personally. Many sales managers' evaluations of sales reps are similarly affected. Furthermore, research suggests a salesperson can use personal influence strategies on the manager to bias evaluations upward.

7. **Organizational uses influence.** Performance ratings are often affected by the use to which they will be put.

> If promotions and monetary payments hinge on the ratings, there is often a tendency for leniency on the part of the manager who values the friendship and support of subordinates who press for higher ratings. It is not difficult to imagine the dilemma of a district sales manager if other district sales teams received consistently higher compensation increments and more promotions than his or her sales group. On the other hand, when appraisals are used for the development of subordinates, managers tend to more freely pinpoint weaknesses, and focus on what is wrong and how it can be improved.[14]

To guard against the distortions introduced in the performance appraisal system by such occurrences, many firms issue admonitions to those completing the forms. Some common instructions issued with such forms are the following:

1. Read the definitions of each trait thoroughly or carefully before rating.
2. Guard against the common tendency to overrate.
3. Do not let personal like or dislike influence your rating. Be as objective as possible.
4. Do not permit your evaluation of one factor to influence your evaluation of another.
5. Base your rating on the observed performance of the salesperson, not on potential abilities.
6. Never rate an employee on several instances of good or poor work, but rather on general success or failure over the whole period.
7. Have sound reasons for your ratings.[15]

Behaviorally Anchored Rating Scales (BARS)

These admonitions probably help, particularly when the evaluator must supply the reasons for ratings. They do not resolve the question of attributes used for the evaluation in the first place, however. A recent emphasis in performance appraisal directed at this question is BARS, which stands for *behaviorally anchored rating scale*.

Thorny Issues in Sales Management 18 • 3

When All Else Fails—Terminating a Sales Representative

As distasteful as it is, terminating a sales representative for poor performance is sometimes unavoidable. Although the objective of a sales performance evaluation is to reward effective performance and to modify behavior to lead to future improvement, termination may be the best solution for both parties if corrective actions have been exhausted.

The right to fire an employee has long been an accepted prerogative of employers. However, a timely article on this subject cautions: "Terminating a salesperson is never pleasant, but if you don't watch it, it can be downright dangerous—to your company and your career."* What can go wrong is dramatically described in the following paragraphs.

> You're vice president of sales. You consider your top salesman an SOB, but because he's your best producer you've put up with him for 10 years. One morning his arrogance and rudeness are too much. You fire him on the spot. Two years later you're in court defending your action in a wrongful discharge suit filed by the salesman. You have to agree that the salesman's job performance was excellent. When asked why you fired him, you say his boorishness and obnoxious manner became too much to handle. While the salesman's behavior didn't affect his own performance, it was disruptive and upsetting to the sales support staff.
>
> The jury finds in favor of the salesman and then awards him $200,000 for lost wages and benefits and even more in punitive damages.

This scenario would not have occurred a quarter of a century ago. Today, however, the nation's courts are jammed with "wrongful termination suits charging everything from broken promises, invasion of privacy, violation of public policy, and, in Montana and California, a failure of good faith and fair dealing." One legal expert contends that even with a carefully documented case involving termination, a lawsuit may still occur. However, companies can reduce the risk.

The first step is to maintain extensive documentation, starting with employee manuals that describe in detail all relevant company policies and procedures. Current job descriptions for each sales position are mandatory, and salespeople must be familiar with the manual's contents and be advised of any changes. Performance reviews should be routine, occur when scheduled, and bear the signatures of both the sales representative and the sales manager(s). During a performance review management must effectively communicate its expectations and identify what actions will be taken when goals are met or not met. Evidence of failure to communicate is obvious when the sales representative, upon being terminated, states: "I didn't know I was supposed to do that. I didn't know anything was wrong." One consultant identifies weak communications as the primary cause of many terminations.

Another source of the problem stems from the performance evaluation process. Sales managers would much rather conduct a positive evaluation than a negative one. Some managers will even delay a negative evaluation, hoping the problem will go away or the sales rep will quit. Another equally undesirable outcome occurs when the manager, trying to avoid a confrontation, rates the sales rep as "average" when "inadequate" would be more appropriate. If termination eventually does result, a lawsuit would not be surprising given the lack of documentation justifying the action. One expert says too many sales man-

---

*The following discussion is based to a large extent on Liz Murphy, "The Art of Firing Smarter," *Sales & Marketing Management*, February 1988, pp. 36–40.

(continued)

agers have not been trained to conduct performance reviews.

Companies can employ other actions to help reduce the likelihood of legal action. Murphy discusses several approaches designed to "defuse the bomb":

> No one likes the business of firing. Often the experience is as traumatic for the manager doing the firing as it is for the person being fired. Today companies do as much as they can to cushion the blow with outplacement services and severance packages. One indication of fairness that helps is the benefit package offered.

During the past several years, the number of companies that provide outplacement services has increased. Outplacement consultants contend that companies using their services are less likely to end up in court.

Attractive severance packages—anywhere from one to four weeks' pay for each year of employment—help to defuse the bomb and the likelihood that a wrongful termination suit will ensue.

The firing process should occur at the beginning of the week, never on Friday or by telephone, and take no more than 10 minutes, argues one consultant. The process should be done in such a way "as to preserve the employee's dignity."

Clearly defined goals that are effectively communicated to salespeople are absolutely mandatory. For most salespeople who have been apprised of their ineffective performance, firing is not a surprise.

Thus, companies can take precautions to avoid wrongful termination lawsuits. These precautions, while not guarantees, lessen the likelihood of legal action.

A BARS system attempts to concentrate on the behaviors and performance criteria that can be controlled by the individual. The system focuses on the fact that a number of factors affect any employee's performance. However, some of these factors are more critical to job success than are others, and the key to evaluating people is to focus on these "critical success factors" (CSFs). For example, Xerox Learning Systems found through an extensive field study three critical behaviors had a direct impact on the selling success of representatives: (1) identifying needs and opportunities, (2) probing for information, and (3) handling objections.[16] Implementing a BARS system for evaluating salespeople requires identifying the behaviors that are key to their performance. Also, the subsequent evaluation of a salesperson's performance must be conducted by rating these key behaviors using the appropriate descriptions.

The whole process is implemented in the following way.[17] First, the key behaviors with respect to performance are identified using critical incidents. *Critical incidents* are occurrences that are critical or vital to performance. To use the critical incident technique, those involved could be asked to identify some particularly outstanding examples of good or bad performance and to detail the reasons why.[18] The performances identified are then reduced to a smaller number of performance dimensions by those working on the BARS development.

Next, the group of critical incidents is presented to a group of sales personnel who are asked to assign each critical incident to an appropriate di-

EXHIBIT 18 • 6 *A BARS Scale with Behavioral Anchors for the Attribute "Promptness in Meeting Deadlines"*

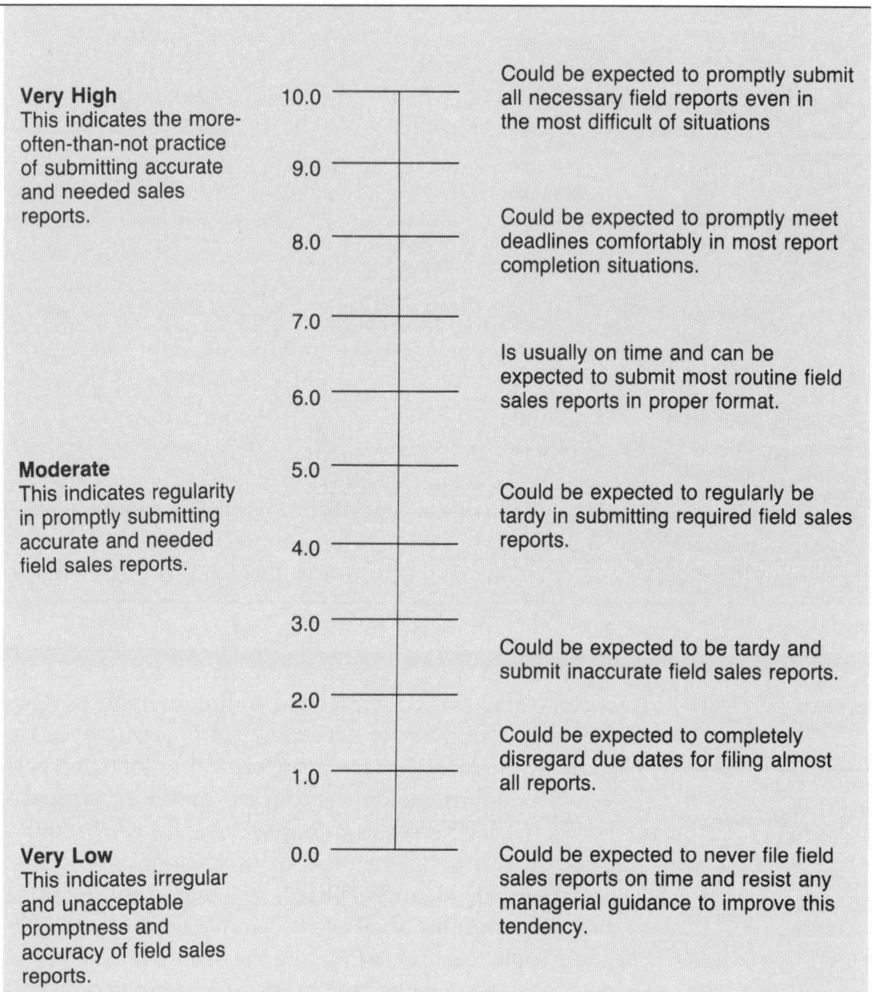

Very High
This indicates the more-often-than-not practice of submitting accurate and needed sales reports.

10.0 — Could be expected to promptly submit all necessary field reports even in the most difficult of situations

9.0 —

8.0 — Could be expected to promptly meet deadlines comfortably in most report completion situations.

7.0 —

6.0 — Is usually on time and can be expected to submit most routine field sales reports in proper format.

Moderate
This indicates regularity in promptly submitting accurate and needed field sales reports.

5.0 —

4.0 — Could be expected to regularly be tardy in submitting required field sales reports.

3.0 —

2.0 — Could be expected to be tardy and submit inaccurate field sales reports.

1.0 — Could be expected to completely disregard due dates for filing almost all reports.

Very Low
This indicates irregular and unacceptable promptness and accuracy of field sales reports.

0.0 — Could be expected to never file field sales reports on time and resist any managerial guidance to improve this tendency.

Source: Reprinted from A. Benton Cocanougher and John M. Ivancevich. " 'BARS' Performance Rating for Sales Personnel," *Journal of Marketing* 42 (July 1978), p. 92, published by the American Marketing Association.

mension. An incident is typically kept in if 60 percent or more of the group assigns it to the same dimension, as did the instrument development group.

The sales personnel group is also asked to rate the behavior described in the critical incident on a 7- or 10-point scale with respect to how effectively or ineffectively it represents performance on the dimension. Incidents that generate good agreement in ratings, typically measured by the standard deviation, are considered for the final scale. The particular incidents chosen are determined by their location along the scale, as measured by the means. Typically, the final scale has six to eight anchors. An example of a BARS scale that resulted from such a process for the attribute "promptness in meeting deadlines" is shown in Exhibit 18.6

The advantage of a BARS system is that it requires appropriate personnel to consider in detail the components of a salesperson's job performance. They must also define anchors for those performance criteria in specific behavioral terms. In terms of the model of Exhibit 18.1, a BARS system tends to emphasize behavior and performance rather than effectiveness. Perhaps that is what a system appraising the performance of salespeople should emphasize, particularly when effectiveness is already assessed through sales and cost analyses.

Bar systems are not without their limitations though.[19] For one thing, the job-specific nature of the scales they produce suggest they are most effective in evaluating salespeople performing very similar functions. They might be effective in comparing one national account rep to another national account rep or two territory representatives against each other, but they could suffer major shortcomings if used to compare a national account representative against a territory salesperson because of differences in their responsibilities. They also can be relatively costly to develop since they require a good deal of time from a number of people.

SUMMARY

Although sales and cost analyses are two important tools in sales management control and evaluation of individual representatives, they do have problems. A main difficulty in using them is that they measure effectiveness rather than performance. The distinction between these notions is important. Performance is directly related to salesperson behavior. Behavior refers to what the representatives do or the tasks on which they expend effort. Performance is behavior evaluated in terms of its contributions to the organization. It focuses on whether the number of calls a salesperson made or the number of proposals the representative developed are good or bad, above expectations or below. Effectiveness includes additional factors not under the individual salesperson's control, such as the potential within the territory and the actions of competitors. Many firms supplement their sales and cost analyses with other measures that assess salesperson performance more directly.

These other measures can be either objective or subjective, and either group can be used to assess inputs or outputs. The objective measures reflect other statistics the manager can gather from the firm's internal data. Some of the most common objective output measures focus on orders or accounts such as the number of orders, the number of canceled orders, the number of active accounts, the number of new accounts, the number of lost accounts, and so on.

The more common objective input measures emphasize calls, time and time utilization, expenses, and nonselling activities. Typical ones from each category would be the number of calls, the number of days worked, the salesperson's total expenses, and the number of service calls made. The input for these objective measures often comes from salespeople's call reports or from time and duty analyses. The data can also be secured from other operating systems within the firm or from special research investigations.

Many firms combine the various outputs and/or inputs to form ratios. The three most common types are expense ratios, account development and servicing ratios, and call activity and/or productivity ratios.

The various measures are most productively used in combination. They are an aid to judgment, not a substitute for it. The comparisons that the indexes allow should be the beginning and not the end of any analysis aimed at assessing how well the personal selling effort is going and how individual salespeople are doing.

Some common performance attributes assessed using subjective measures are job knowledge, management of the territory, customer and company relations, and personal characteristics. Also included are other aspects of sales such as whether the person sold the full product line.

The subjective assessments are typically made using some type of merit rating form in which the evaluator checks the amount of each of a number of predetermined attributes of the salesperson. A severe problem with merit rating forms is their lack of an outcome focus; that is, they often contain many attributes not critical or vital to performance. To get at the more essential attributes, a number of firms are turning to BARS (behaviorally anchored rating scales). The BARS procedure emphasizes the isolation of behaviors most critical to performing the duties assigned. Subsequent evaluations are carried out with respect to these critical behaviors.

Discussion Questions

1. Kimberly's progression as a sales rep for Midland Paper had been very steady. She exceeded quota each of the last four years and earned Midland's Sales Rep of the Year Award her third year. Year five, however, is a different story. Not only have Kimberly's sales lagged, but other activities are suffering as well. What should a sales manager do when a good employee starts having problems?

2. Many companies include the sales rep in the performance evaluation process. Thus, the sales rep and the immediate supervisor discuss the rep's performance. With this process, is there a danger of giving the sales rep too much information?

3. "Our new performance evaluation procedure is so precise—all terms have been defined and all scales have been tested—that we no longer have to train our district sales managers on how to conduct a performance evaluation." Do you agree with this statement?

4. "I'm sorry, Gregg," said Gregg's sales manager, "your performance evaluation is being downgraded. Who you live with is your business, but when you and your lady friend showed up at the recent three-day convention together, it was a source

of embarrassment for many of the wives present." "But I'm the district's top producer," argued Gregg, "and that's what's important." Comment.

5. "In this company, you had better make quota four out of five years or you can start looking for another job. I don't care if you are doing the right things—it's the results that count." Do you agree with this position?

6. A large corporation notices an irregular decrease in the sales of a particular representative. The sales rep, normally in very high standing among other salespeople and quotas, has of late failed to achieve her own quota. What can be done by the corporation to determine whether the slump in the sales curve is the responsibility of the representative or due to things beyond her control?

7. Given the following information from evaluations of the performance of different sales representatives, what possible deductions could be made about the sales reps *not achieving quota?*
   a. Representative 1: Achieved target goals for sales calls, telephone calls, and new accounts; customer relations good, no noticeable deficiencies in any areas.
   b. Representative 2: Completed substantially fewer sales calls than target; telephone calls high in number, but primarily with one firm. Time management analysis shows the sales representative to be spending a disproportionately large amount of time with one firm. New accounts are low; all other areas good to outstanding.
   c. Representative 3: Number of sales calls low, below target; telephone calls, letters, proposals all very low and below target; evaluation shows poor time utilization, very high amount of service-related activities in sales representative's log; customer relations extremely positive, high amount of feedback on product function produced lately.

8. "We have spent many hours establishing our quotas using sophisticated statistical techniques. Thus, we are very confident that these can be used as valid measures of performance for our salespeople." Evaluate this statement in light of the possible problems that this type of policy may cause.

9. The following is based on "When a Kiss Is Not Just a Kiss," *Sales Manager's Bulletin*, February 29, 1992, p. 7. "You overstepped your bounds!" shouted Rich Barrows, district sales manager of the Atlas Corporation's Kansas City office. "It was bad enough with the love notes you left on Claudia's desk. I was shocked when she told me about that faux pas. To avoid trouble, she asked me not to report this to our regional sales manager. You, however, were warned to knock it off. Today she tells me that you tried to kiss her, and that's sexual harassment. Atlas doesn't permit this behavior."

"Hey, come on, Claudia and I are friends. A kiss between friends can't be called sexual harassment," responded Bill angrily.

Barrows retorted, "If she doesn't want your affection, then it's harassment. Besides, she tells me the love notes have started again and that she told you to stop it. You knew you were doing something wrong."

Bill countered, "I absolutely deny that I knew sending those notes was wrong. Remember when I asked you if that was grounds for dismissal and you said you didn't know. Now, I suppose you're going to fire me.

"Atlas' rules about sexual harassment are quite clear. Look Bill, you physically grabbed Claudia and tried to kiss her," Barrows noted. "That's ground for termination."

"What rules about sexual harassment? I've never seen one memo about the subject. Anyway, trying to kiss someone doesn't add up to sexual harassment from my perspective," argued Bill.

"Bill, your own common sense should tell you to stay away from someone who refuses your advances and tells you to stop sending her love notes. Claudia's married, and you know that. I'm sorry, but you're finished at Atlas," Barrows responded.

Do you agree with Barrows's decision? Why? Why not?

10. Jackie Hitchcock, recently promoted to district sales manager, faced a new problem she wasn't sure how to resolve. The district's top sales rep is also the district's number one headache. Barton Coombs traditionally leads the company in sales but also leads the company in problems. He has broken every rule, bent every policy, deviated from guidelines, and has been less than truthful. Jackie knew Barton had never done anything illegal or unethical, but she was worried that something could happen. Other problems with Barton include not preparing call reports on time, failing to show up at trade shows, and not attending sales training programs.

How should Jackie handle this problem? How does a sales manager manage a maverick sales rep?

Application Questions

A1. Bill Smith has just finished performing a cost analysis on his district. The results show that while two salespeople have reached their planned sales goal, two other salespeople have missed their planned sales goals (see Table 1 below). To gain insight into what is happening in his district, Bill has decided to do a ratio analysis. He used the information shown in Table 2 (p. 785) to complete the ratio analysis. Compute the following ratios for each salesperson:

a.   Sales expense ratio.
b.   Account penetration ratio.
c.   New account conversion ratio.
d.   Average order size ratio.
e.   Calls per day ratio.
f.   Orders per call ratio.

TABLE 1

	Sales Representative			
	1	2	3	4
Planned sales	$575,000	$650,000	$640,000	$650,000
Actual sales	550,000	650,000	640,000	620,000
Cost of sales	445,000	530,000	520,000	500,000
Gross margin	105,000	120,000	120,000	120,000
Expenses:				
Salaries	20,000	22,000	21,000	23,000
Commissions	5,500	6,500	6,400	6,200
Travel	7,000	10,000	9,500	9,500
Advertising	27,000	28,000	31,000	31,000
Warehouse	7,000	8,000	8,000	7,600
Order processing	100	140	100	160
Transportation	21,000	24,000	24,000	23,000
Total expenses	87,600	98,640	100,000	100,460
Net profit (loss)	$ 17,400	$ 21,360	$ 20,000	$ 19,540

TABLE 2

	Sales Representative			
	1	2	3	4
Number of calls	90	125	100	100
Number of orders	50	70	50	80
Number of accounts in territory	250	260	240	275
Number of accounts sold	40	70	70	75
Number of new accounts	3	7	6	7
Number of days worked	20	20	20	20

A2. Use the information contained in the following table to evaluate Marsha Jackson's sales performance.

Marsha Jackson
District: New Orleans

	1989	1990	1991	1992
1. Sales class I	339,125	339,288	361,800	352,554
2. Quota class I	354,730	368,791	411,136	419,707
3. Sales class II	529,000	588,528	742,226	752,946
4. Quota class II	439,360	481,216	550,204	575,646
5. Gross margin-class I	67,825	67,858	72,360	70,511
6. Gross margin-class II	52,900	58,853	74,223	75,295
7. Sales expenses	12,750	13,875	14,500	16,500
8. Number of calls	1,685	1,710	1,690	1,670
9. Number of orders	1,011	1,060	1,115	1,119
10. Average number of customers	330	334	338	344
11. Average number of potential customers	577	573	564	562
12. Number of new customers	18	19	20	25
13. Number of lost customers	13	15	16	19
14. Number of days worked	241	246	245	248

Endnotes

[1]This section borrows heavily from the paper by Orville C. Walker, Jr., Gilbert A. Churchill, Jr., and Neil M. Ford, "Where Do We Go from Here: Selected Conceptual and Empirical Issues Concerning the Motivation and Performance of the Industrial Sales force," in *Critical Issues in Sales Management: State-of-the Art and Future Research Needs,* ed. Gerald Albaum and Gilbert A. Churchill, Jr. (Eugene: College of Business Administration, University of Oregon, 1979), pp. 10–75. See also Ramon A. Avila, Edward F. Fern, and O. Karl Mann, "Unravelling Criteria for Assessing the Performance of Salespeople: A Causal Analysis," *Journal of Personal Selling and Sales Management* 8 (May 1988), pp. 45–54.

[2]*Measuring Salesmen's Performance,* Business Policy Study, No. 114 (New York: National Industrial Conference Board, 1965), p. 8. See also G. P. Latham and K. N. Wexley, *Increasing Productivity through Performance Appraisal* (Reading, Mass.: Addison-Wesley,

1981) and; Donald A. Tavers, James B. Hunt, and Ken Bass, "Behavioral Self-Management as a Supplement to External Sales Force Controls," *Journal of Personal Selling and Sales Management* 10 (Summer 1990), pp. 17–28.

[3]Donald W. Jackson, Jr., Lonnie L. Ostrom, and Kenneth R. Evans, "Measured Used to Evaluate Industrial Marketing Activities," *Industrial Marketing Management* 11 (October 1982), pp. 269–74. See Donald W. Jackson Jr., Janet E. Keith, and John L. Schlacter, "Evaluation of Selling Performance: A Study of Current Practices," *Journal of Personal Selling and Sales Management* 3 (November 1983), pp. 42–51; and Michael H. Morris and Sean R. Aten, "Sales Force Performance Appraisal: Contemporary Issues and Practices," in *Progress in Marketing Thought,* ed. Louis M. Capella, Henry W. Nash, Jack M. Starling, and Ronald D. Taylor (Mississippi State, Miss.: Southern Marketing Association, 1990), pp. 413–18.

[4]For a discussion of the steps in the selling process, see Barton S. Weitz, Stephen B. Castleberry, and John F. Tanner, *Selling: Building Partnerships* (Homewood, Ill.: Richard D. Irwin, 1992), or Charles Futrell, *Fundamentals of Selling,* 4th ed. (Homewood, Ill.: Richard D. Irwin, 1993).

[5]The distinction between outcomes and desirable behaviors is an important one. Many performance appraisal systems emphasize the former rather than the latter—a condition that has been labeled the "Achilles heel of the personnel profession." In outcome-based systems, salespeople are held accountable for their results but not for how they achieve the results. However, behavior-based systems address the process of selling rather than simply the outcomes. Behavior-based systems involve much more monitoring and directing of salespeople's activities. See Erin Anderson and Richard L. Oliver, "Perspectives on Behavior-Based versus Outcome-Based Salesforce Control Systems," *Journal of Marketing* 51 (October 1987), pp. 76–88, for a discussion of the differences in philosophy between the systems and what these philosophical differences imply for managing salespeople.

[6]"To Computer Salesmen, the 'Big-Ticket' Deal Is the One to Look For," *The Wall Street Journal,* January 22, 1974, p. 1. For a general discussion of what is involved in selling big-ticket items, see Steve Fishman, "The Longest Sale—What It Takes to Close the Big-Ticket Client," *Success* 36 (May 1989), pp. 48–52.

[7]Because of their finite stock, some people hold that standards for acceptable sales calls should be established, and each call should be measured against these standards. See, for example, Stewart Washburn, "Measuring Sales Effectiveness and Productivity," in *Sales Manager's Handbook,* ed. Edwin E. Bobrow and Larry Wizenberg (Homewood, Ill.: Dow Jones-Irwin, 1983), pp. 233–63; and Henry P. Polly, "Sales Call Reports—A Necessary Tool for Marketing?" *Secured Lender* 45 (May–June 1989), pp. 22, 24.

[8]Dan H. Robertson, "Sales Force Feedback on Competitive Activities," *Journal of Marketing* 38 (April 1974), pp. 69–72. See also Douglas M. Lambert, Howard Marmorstein, and Arun Sharma, "Industrial Salespeople as a Source of Market Information," *Industrial Marketing Management* 19 (May 1990), pp. 141–48.

[9]For general tips on working with ratios, see Charles A. Krueger, "How to Work with Ratios," *1986–87 Personal Planning Guide for Management Development* (Madison, Wis.: Management Institute, University of Wisconsin, 1986). For discussion of the use of ratios to analyze sales person performance specifically, see Dick Berry, "A Method to Portray and Analyze Sales Performance," *Industrial Marketing Management* 16 (May 1987), pp. 131–44.

[10]W. E. Patton III and Ronald H. King, "The Use of Human Judgment Models in Evaluating Sales Force Performance," *Journal of Personal Selling and Sales Management* 5 (May 1985), pp. 1–14.

[11]Benton Cocanougher and John M. Ivancevich, " 'BARS' Performance Rating for Sales Force Personnel," *Journal of Marketing* 42 (July 1978), pp. 87–95; Mark R. Edwards, W. Theodore Cummings, and John L. Schlacter, "The Paris-Peoria Solution: Innovations in Appraising Regional and International Sales Personnel," *Journal of Personal Selling and Sales Management* 4 (November 1984), pp. 26–38.

[12]For an example of one of many studies that have attempted to assess the relationship between personality factors and salespeople's performance, see Lawrence M. Lamont and William J. Lundstrom, "Identifying Successful Industrial Salesmen by Personality and Personal Characteristics," *Journal of Marketing Research* 14 (November 1977), pp. 517–29. For a summary of the results of these studies, see Neil M. Ford et al., "Selecting Successful Salespeople: A Meta-Analysis of Biographical and Psychological Selection

Criteria," in *Annual Review of Marketing,* ed. Michael J. Houston (Chicago: American Marketing Association, 1987), pp. 90–131.

[13]William D. Perreault, Jr, and Frederick A. Russell, "Comparing Multiattribute Evaluation Process Models," *Behavioral Science* 22 (November 1977), pp. 423–31. Similarly it has been discovered that subordinates with whom sales managers have established relatively high levels of acquaintance receive more favorable overall performance ratings and are more likely to be promoted and that salespeople who have similar values to their sales managers are evaluated better. See P. O. Kingstrom and L. E. Mainstone, "An Investigation of the Rater-Ratee Acquaintance and Rater Bias," *Academy of Management Journal* 28 (September 1985), pp. 641–53; William A. Weeks, Lawrence B. Chonko, and Lynn R. Kahla, "Performance Congruence and Value Congruence Impact on Sales Force Annual Sales," *Journal of the Academy of Marketing Science* 17 (Fall 1989), pp. 345–51.

[14]Cocanougher and Ivancevich, " 'BARS' Performance Rating," p. 89. For some suggestions on how ratings of employees can be made more comparable, see Mark R. Edwards, Michael Wolfe, and J. Ruth Sproull, "Improving Comparability in Performance Appraisal," *Business Horizons* 26 (September–October 1983), pp. 75–83; and Jan P. Muczyk and Myron Gable, "Managing Sales Performance through a Comprehensive Performance Appraisal System," *Journal of Personal Selling and Sales Management* 7 (May 1987), pp. 41–52.

[15]*Measuring Salesmen's Performance,* p. 34. Despite such admonitions, there is evidence that there is an attribution bias in sales managers' ratings of salespeople. For example, sales managers do not seem to consider contextual factors like territory differences but do seem to consider effort when evaluating salespeople's performance. See John C. Mowen et al., "Utilizing Effort and Task Difficulty Information in Evaluating Salespeople," *Journal of Marketing Research* 22 (May 1985), pp. 185–91.

[16]John Franco, "Managing Sales Success," *Business Marketing* 69 (December 1984), pp. 48–57. See also Jeff A. Weekley and Joseph A. Gier, "Reliability and Validity of the Situational Interview for a Sales Position," *Journal of Applied Psychology* 72 (August 1987), pp. 484–87.

[17]Cocanougher and Ivancevich, " 'BARS' Performance Rating," pp. 90–99. For a detailed example illustrating the process, see Robert P. Bush, Alan J. Bush, David J. Ortinau, and Joseph F. Hair, Jr., "Developing a Behavior-Based Scale to Assess Retail Salesperson Performance," *Journal of Retailing* 66 (Spring 1990), pp. 119–36.

[18]For sales related application of the critical incident technique, see Mary Jo Bitner, Bernard H. Booms, and Mary Stanfield Tetreault, "The Service Encounter: Diagnosing Favorable and Unfavorable Incidents," *Journal of Marketing* 54 (January 1990), pp. 71–84.

[19]For discussion of some of the limitations of BARS that have restricted its use, see Roger J. Placky, "Appraisal Scales That Measure Performance Outcomes and Job Results," *Personnel* 60 (May–June 1983), pp. 57–65.

Suggested Readings

Anderson, Erin and Richard L. Oliver. "Perspectives in Behavior-Based versus Outcome-Based Salesforce Control Systems." *Journal of Marketing* 51 (October 1987), pp. 76–88.

Ford, Neil M., Orville C. Walker, Jr., Gilbert A. Churchill, Jr., and Steven W. Hartley. "Selecting Successful Salespeople: A Meta-Analysis of Biographical and Psychological Selection Criteria." in *Review of Marketing 1987,* ed. Michael J. Houston, (Chicago: American Marketing Association, 1987), pp. 90–134.

Jackson, Donald W., Jr., Lonnie L. Ostrom, and Kenneth R. Evans. "Measures Used to Evaluate Industrial Marketing Activities." *Industrial Marketing Management* 11 (October 1982), pp. 269–74.

CASES FOR PART THREE

Case 3-1
COMPUTING SYSTEMS LTD.*

"Bob doesn't appear to be too happy. He isn't making money, because he isn't selling. His own self-image is . . . well, he likes to spend money. He likes nice clothes, a nice car, and a nice house, that kind of thing, but he can't afford to live that way." These thoughts passed through Mike Hagen's mind in February 1980, as he reviewed once again the possible courses of action in dealing with one of his salespeople, Bob Nichols. Mike Hagen was the district manager in Winnipeg, Manitoba, for Computing Systems Ltd., a major full-line computer manufacturer. Mike had become increasingly concerned about Bob's performance in the last year. While the other salespeople in the district were having a very successful year, it had become quite clear to Mike that Bob was not even going to achieve his quota. Bob was thus hindering the district in its drive to meet its goals.

The Company

Computing Systems Ltd. was the Canadian subsidiary of Computing Systems, Inc., a major multinational manufacturer of a wide range of computers and peripheral equipment. The Computing Systems product lines were in direct competition with some of the computer lines of other major computer manufacturers.

The head office of Computing Systems was located in Toronto. The vice president of marketing, who was located in the Toronto head office, oversaw all the firm's marketing activities. Reporting were the various marketing staff groups and three regional marketing managers who coordinated the marketing activities in the western, central, and eastern regions. The Winnipeg office was located in the western region, and Mike Hagen reported to the western region marketing manager in Calgary. A partial organization chart of the Computing Systems marketing organization is shown in Exhibit 1.

The Winnipeg District

Mike Hagen had two groups of people reporting to him in the Winnipeg District. Three sales representatives reported directly to him. There were also 10 programmer analysts who reported to him through the district systems manager. A partial organization chart of the Winnipeg Branch is shown in Exhibit 2.

The programmer analysts in each district were responsible for providing systems support to the firm's customers. Many of the programmer analysts

---

*Prepared by Adrian B. Ryans of the University of Western Ontario. © 1983 by the University of Western Ontario. Reproduced by permission.

EXHIBIT 1   *Partial Organization Chart of Computing Systems Marketing Department*

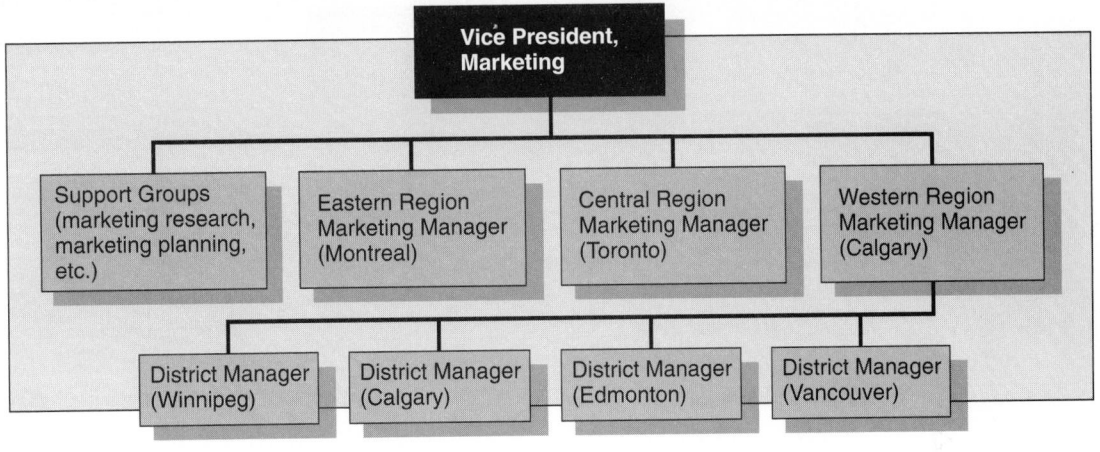

worked exclusively with one customer, while the others acted essentially as systems consultants for several of the firm's smaller customers. The programmer analysts were often involved in the presales evaluation of a customer's systems requirements. In this capacity, one or more systems analysts formed a team with one of the district's sales representatives, and together they evaluated the customer's needs. Programmer analysts were compensated on a salary basis, with raises dependent on job performance.

Sales Activities

When asked to describe and comment on the sales job in the computer business, Mike Hagen said:

> The sales job is broken down into prospecting, qualifying prospects, planning the sales campaign, and all those activities related to closing. Now prospecting, generally speaking, is taken rather lightly by the sales reps, and I think that is a big mistake. It's a very, very difficult activity, and it is closely related to qualifying—they dovetail very closely together. We're in the stage of the computer business where there is enough activity out there that you don't have to create demand. We qualify a prospect by asking, "Are you going to make a computer buying decision within the next 6 to 12 months?" If not, we just keep in touch. We don't really have time to say to a prospect, "Well, why don't you think of making this new application or why don't you think of buying that new equipment?" We may go in and try to develop a need if we see an area where a company could computerize, and then make a proposition and try and get their interest. But if they are not immediately interested, we forget it, because we really don't have the time or the resources to do it. So, the key thing in any salesperson's success is to have a big prospect list, because you don't get 'em all. And the key thing with the prospect list is how well

EXHIBIT 2   *Organization of the Winnipeg District*

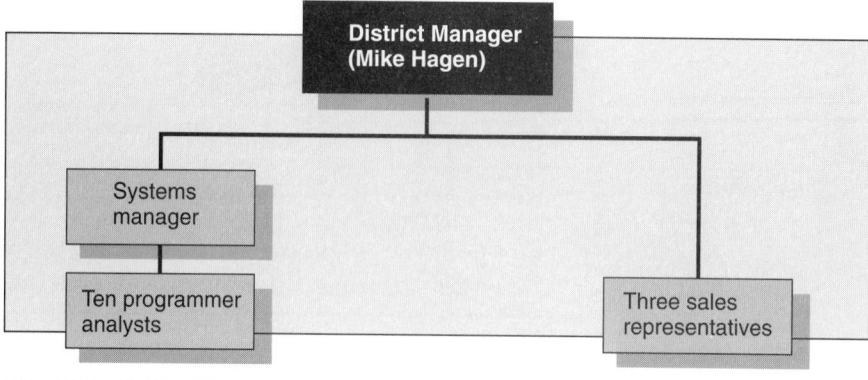

they are qualified. Will the person buy from us? Are we talking to the right person? Are they going to make the decision in the time frame they say? Timing is particularly important. If you peak out in your sales campaign to a prospect too early, you know your competitor is going to pick up the dice. It is very competitive. So the qualifying aspect is whether you are talking to the right person, will they make the decision, and do they have the guts to be the internal salesperson—the person to carry the ball for you in getting others in the company, the boss and so on, to agree to the purchase. All those questions in any sales campaign are very key because the next steps cost a lot of money in terms of time and resources. So once you get the customers to the point where you can say they are a qualified prospect, you can assume they will make a decision within a reasonable period of time. We have to restrict our dealings to qualified prospects because a person has got to make a quota in the 12-month period. That's because, unfortunately, we work on a 12-month planning horizon.

Planning is probably one of the things that most sales-oriented people do worst. They respond to immediate conversations, interactions, and stimuli. The difficult thing is to say, "Well, when are you going to do this? What are you going to do if? What are your contingency plans?" And so on. It's an easy thing really for a manager to get salespeople to put together a plan in terms of putting it down on paper and saying this is what I am going to do. The hard part is to get them to do it, and to discipline themselves to do it when they say they are going to do it. And then they must constantly ask the customer for the order, to go through trial closes to get objections. You see, in a sense, the qualifying process in our business never really ends, you never get to that point unless you have the order. So you are constantly asking questions and directing your campaign to further substantiate your qualification. With one key order we got here in Winnipeg, for example, we didn't qualify until a week before we got the order. We didn't really consider them a prospect until we got very close to the order, because we hadn't been able to get to the top people.

The point at which the systems representative comes in depends on the level of gear. We sell computers anywhere from a $1,000 per month to $100,000 per month. Selling covers such a wide range of activities and such a wide range of customer prospect situations, that you might sell a small computer without ever getting a systems person in. You just go in and you say, "You want to computerize your payroll? No problem, we have just the package for you. It will do a super job for you. Sign here." Generally speaking, customers don't know their own needs well enough to evaluate anything properly anyway, so that after you sell it, anything that you give them is a hell of a lot better than what they currently have. So if you know a little bit about receivables and payables, you don't need a systems person, but you might bring in one or two people to impress the customer. When you get into, say, a large system, you need a host of technical people, not just in systems but in specialized areas of systems, such as data base management, communications, and operations management. With a large system you may have five or six computer operations raising hell, and you've got to coordinate that as a basic management function. When you only have a little main frame, you have a much simpler problem. You have only one person, so it's not really a coordination problem. Thus, the systems support that a salesperson needs varies dramatically from one situation to the next.

Each salesperson in Computing Systems was assigned an annual sales quota. The company used a "top-down" approach in developing sales quotas. Each year the marketing group in Toronto analyzed the anticipated levels of activity in the Canadian economy, the previous years' sales, the trends in the computer industry, and so forth, to develop a reasonable sales forecast for the following year. This forecast was then broken down into sales quotas for the individual districts, and these quotas were communicated to the district managers. It was then the responsibility of the district managers to develop quotas for the individual salespeople. Mike Hagen felt that this method resulted in salespeople receiving reasonable, attainable quotas. In fact, Mike said that if he asked any of his salespeople what was a reasonable quota for the next year, they usually gave him a figure higher than the quota he would assign them.

Salespeople were compensated largely on a commission basis, receiving a commission on each sale related to the profitability of the sale to the company. Generally, total compensation was highly correlated with quota achievement.

The Growth of the Winnipeg Office

Mike Hagen had joined Computing Systems after graduating with an M.B.A. degree from an eastern university in 1976. Mike had spent his first few months with the company in its sales training course in Toronto. On completion of the course he had become a sales representative in Toronto. After one year with Computing Systems, Mike had been transferred to Winnipeg as a sales representative. Initially, he was the only sales representative in Winnipeg, and he reported to the district manager in the Calgary office. In September 1977, two additional experienced salespeople, Jill Cooper and Nick Johnston, were hired from outside the computer business and joined the Winnipeg office. In 1977, Mike met his sales quota, and in 1978, he was one of the top Computing Systems salespeople in Canada. In June 1978, Winnipeg became a separate district, and a district manager was appointed. The district manager then reported directly to the western region marketing manager in Calgary. About six months after moving to Winnipeg, the district manager was promoted and left Winnipeg, and in January 1979, Mike Hagen was promoted to district manager. Mike felt the decision to promote him to district manager had been a difficult one for the company, since he was relatively inexperienced, having been employed by Computing Systems for only two and one-half years. Mike thus felt he had a lot to prove in his new job, and he was anxious to prove that he could do a superior job as district manager.

Shortly before Mike Hagen became district manager, Bob Nichols was transferred to Winnipeg from Vancouver. Bob Nichols had joined the company directly after graduating from college with a B.S. in 1974. Bob spend his initial six months with the company in a training program for systems analysts. After completing the training program in November 1974, Bob became a systems representative in the Vancouver office. He progressed well in the job, and in 1975 he received a President's Award for his outstanding performance as a systems representative. Even though he had spent very little time as a systems representative, Bob's superiors considered him one of the most promising systems people in Canada. The following year Bob requested a move from systems to sales. Bob entered the company's basic sales training program and received part of his training in Toronto, and, in fact, for a couple of months he and Mike worked in the same office in Toronto. Bob's switch into sales was motivated largely by his desire for the higher compensation a successful sales representative could earn. A few of Bob's friends from his undergraduate days, who had been quite successful financially, were also living in Vancouver, and the group of young couples led an active social life. Bob thought that a salesperson's compensation would allow him to lead that type of life.

Within a few months of beginning work as a sales representative, one of Bob's customers purchased a major system, one of the largest systems ever installed by Computing Systems in Canada. The sale of this system was the culmination of a major selling job by Bob and a couple of his superiors in the Vancouver office. Largely as a result of being credited with this sale, Bob won a second President's Award in 1977 for his performance as a sales representative. Bob did not have such a successful year in 1978. In the first nine months of 1978 Bob did not meet his quota, although his performance was considered acceptable. In September 1978, Bob was transferred to Winnipeg because company management felt the change of environment might result in improved sales performance. Although Mike saw very little of Bob and his wife socially after they moved to Winnipeg, he gathered from his conversations with Bob that they were adjusting reasonably well to their new life.

EXHIBIT 3   *Sales Performance as a Percent of Quota—Winnipeg District*

| | | Percentage of Achievement Quota | |
	Salespeople	1978	1979
	Tony Webb	100	81*
	Jill Cooper	105	195
	Nick Johnston	53	205
	Bob Nichols	55*	63

*Quota prorated for the period in Winnipeg.

Mike Hagen as district manager

When Mike Hagen assumed the job of district manager in January 1979, he had four salespeople reporting to him. His first year in the new job was reasonably successful, and the Winnipeg office made quota at a time when several other districts did not.

The quota achievements for the four salespeople in the Winnipeg District for 1978 and 1979 are shown in Exhibit 3. In late 1979, Tony Webb, whose performance had been satisfactory in 1978 but marginal in 1979, was transferred to the Vancouver office. The performance of Jill Cooper and Nick Johnston both showed a significant improvement between 1978 and 1979. In 1979, they were both among the top Computing Systems salespeople in Canada.

Bob, in his short period in Winnipeg in 1978, had not met his quota, which was not surprising, since it took a few months to develop a list of prospects. However, his performance was again marginal in 1979. As Mike Hagen reviewed Bob's performance record and prospect list in February 1980, it appeared very likely to him that Bob would not make his quota again in 1980. From his previous discussions with Bob about his performance, he knew that Bob realized this too, although Bob would probably not openly admit it. Bob seemed uneasy that he, the senior salesperson in the office, was performing much worse than other, less experienced salespeople.

Mike felt that he had developed a good business relationship with Bob in their 18 months together in the Winnipeg office. Shortly after becoming manager Mike had assisted Bob in landing a major order. The order had required a lot of internal selling within Computing Systems, and Mike had spent many hours convincing Computer Systems personnel that the deal he and Bob had worked out with the customer was a good one for Computing Systems. Mike felt that Bob realized that he would not have been able to do the internal selling job himself, and thus, he felt he had gained Bob's respect for his skill and efforts.

The situation in February 1980

As he reviewed the situation in February 1980, Mike Hagen felt there were at least four possible courses of action he could take. The first alternative was simply to ask Bob for his resignation. Mike was personally not very happy with this alternative, since he knew there were several other Computing Systems salespeople in other districts performing less satisfactorily than Bob. However, Bob's performance was inconsistent with Mike's goals for the Winnipeg district. He had also broached the subject of Bob's performance with the western region marketing manager, and he felt his attitude and the attitude of other people in senior management was that Bob was worth saving.

The second alternative was transferring Bob to another district as a sales representative. This was probably the easiest course of action.

The third alternative was for Mike to spend additional time with Bob trying to improve his sales performance. Mike had spent a large amount of time the previous year accompanying Bob and each of the other salespeople on sales calls and critiquing their selling methods. Mike felt that Bob did an excellent job right up to the point of actually trying to close the sale. In Mike's words, "Bob doesn't have that killer instinct—to go for the throat—the real pressure that you have to exert to get some orders—the real pushing-hard, brass-knuckled approach that is sometimes absolutely necessary to get an order." Mike also felt that Bob did not handle risk well and often seemed to want to "give away" the systems when he got close to the sale. Mike also believed that Bob was not very effective in doing the internal selling that had to be done inside Computing Systems. Since the computer systems packages were often customized to an individual customer's needs, the computer salesperson had to convince Computing Systems management that the deal they were proposing to the customer was also profitable from Computing Systems's viewpoint. Mike felt Bob had a very difficult time handling the two sets of conflicting demands.

Mike also knew that one of Bob's goals was eventually to move into sales management, but in Computing Systems a necessary condition for promotion into sales management was a good selling record. For this reason he felt he should consider making further efforts to develop Bob in the sales area. He wondered, however, where he would be able to find additional time to spend with Bob without neglecting the other salespeople and, even if he did spend the time, whether he would be successful.

The final alternative was to try to change Bob's career path from sales back into systems. Mike had checked with senior management about any suitable openings for Bob in other offices in Canada in a systems capacity, but there were none. Thus, any move would have to be made within the Calgary office. Mike thought he might be able to persuade Bob to accept a position as a senior systems analyst, but he knew that it would be a difficult switch for Bob to accept. The salary as a senior systems analyst would be comparable to Bob's total compensation in 1979. However, had he made quota in 1979, his total compensation as a salesperson would have been 50 percent higher than the amount he could earn as a systems analyst. The switch also had other potential problems: Mike felt his systems manager would deeply resent having to take on a "loser" from sales. The personalities of Bob and the systems manager were different, and this was also likely to be an area of further conflict. Furthermore, Mike did not feel he could discuss this alternative with the systems manager before making the decision, since he felt the systems manager would attempt to prevent the change. Mike also felt some of the systems staff would resent a salesperson moving into a senior systems position in the office. If it hadn't been for all these potential problems, Mike felt that Bob would probably do an outstanding job as a senior systems analyst.

As he weighed the pros and cons of the different alternatives in his mind, Mike wondered if there were any other alternatives he had overlooked. He was also concerned about how he should reveal his decision to Bob and to what extent he should involve the western region marketing manager and other senior company personnel. Mike knew he had to come to a decision quickly, since he was flying to Calgary in three days to see the western region marketing manager. He wanted to tell his superior what course of action he planned to follow and to get his approval.

Case 3-2
SUPERSONIC STEREO, INC.

" At this rate, I'll be looking for a new job," thought Bob Basler, sales manager of Supersonic's Atlanta district. "Our sales are stagnant, and what's worse, our profits are down." Sales and profit results for the last five years did not measure up to objectives established for the Atlanta district (see Exhibit 1). Basler knew that soon he would be hearing from Pete Lockhart, Supersonic's national sales manager, and the same question would be asked: "When are you going to turn the Atlanta district around?"

Basler was faced with another problem that added to his worries. One of his sales representatives, Charlie Lyons, was very upset and was threatening to quit unless he received a substantial salary increase. Lyons thought that since he led the district in sales volume, he should be amply rewarded. "I have to find out what's happening in the Atlanta district before I go and make recommendations for salary increases," Basler thought. "Besides, if I make such a recommendation, Pete will think that I have taken leave of my senses. He will not approve any salary increases for anybody as long as the Atlanta district's performance is so weak."

Supersonic Stereo is one of the country's leading manufacturers of stereo equipment. Since its formation in 1962, Supersonic has experienced rapid growth, based largely on its reputation for high-quality stereo products. Prices were competitive, although some dealers engaged in discounting. Supersonic distributed its stereo equipment on a selective basis. Only those dealers who could provide strong marketing support and reliable servicing were selected by Supersonic. Dealers were supported by Supersonic's national advertising campaign. Advertising averaged 5 percent of sales, somewhat more than other stereo manufacturers spent for this item.

Supersonic's sales force was compensated with salary plus commission of 6 percent based on gross margin. Gross margin was used to discourage sales reps from cutting prices. Accounts were assigned to sales representatives based on size. New sales reps were usually assigned a number of small accounts. As they progressed, they were assigned larger accounts. The more experienced sales representatives were assigned the larger, more desirable accounts. In some cases, a sales rep would have only three or four accounts, each averaging $250,000 a year.

The average base salary for the sales force reached $26,500 in 1992 and commissions averaged $9,500. Total average sales force compensation was $36,000 in 1992. Travel expenses were paid by Supersonic. The total package was considered by one executive to be too plush. This executive, Stella Jordan, thought not enough was expected from the sales force. "I know of one sales

EXHIBIT 1	Total Sales and Profits for the Atlanta District, 1988–1992				
	1988	**1989**	**1990**	**1991**	**1992**
Total sales	$2,641,081	$2,445,120	$2,610,029	$2,514,113	$2,638,340
Net profit	13,873	14,050	15,381	16,511	14,383

representative who calls on three accounts and in 1991 earned $38,563," she stated at a recent meeting. "If we want to improve our profits, then we need to either reduce our base salaries or cut back our commission rate."

Jordan's suggestion was not favorably received by Basler, who believed such a move would have a disastrous effect on sales force motivation. Jordan countered by pointing out that motivation must be lacking since the Atlanta district's performance is so poor. "If salaries or commissions cannot be reduced, at least let's not raise them," she suggested. "Maybe we should consider raising quotas and not pay commissions until sales representatives exceed their quotas. Or," she continued, "maybe a management by objectives approach should be developed."

Basler knew that Jordan's comments demanded a response. He also knew she was talking about Charlie Lyons when she mentioned a sales rep with three accounts earning $38,563. Basler suggested he should be allowed time to do a complete cost analysis by sales representative before adopting any corrective action. Jordan agreed and offered her assistance. Salaries for the others were as follows: Sand, $24,500; Gallo, $27,500; and Parks, $26,000.

Basler's first activity was to identify available information for his district. He was able to secure a profit and loss statement for the Atlanta district (see Exhibit 2). Jordan suggested that since Basler was interested in sales force profitability, his next step should be to allocate the natural accounts in Exhibit 2 to their appropriate functional accounts. Exhibit 3 shows the results of this step.

"If we are going to do an analysis by sales representative, we need much more information," Jordan indicated. To help in this regard, she compiled product sales data (see Exhibit 4).

Basler provided data for each sales representative, showing number of sales calls, number of orders, and unit sales by product line (see Exhibit 5). The next step would be to compile the data to develop a profitability analysis by sales representative.

The problem with Charlie Lyons is still there, mused Basler. He wants more money, and Stella Jordan thinks he is overpaid and underworked. Since Charlie Lyons is something of a focal point, we ought to do a profitability analysis for each of his customers. Basler's next step was to compile data by customer. Exhibit 6 presents customer data for each of Lyons's three accounts.

EXHIBIT 2   *Profit and Loss Statement, Atlanta District, 1992*

Sales		$2,638,340
Cost of goods sold		2,014,485
Gross margin		$ 623,855
Expenses:		
Salaries	$177,000	
Commissions	37,431	
Advertising	131,915	
Packaging	43,642	
Warehousing and transportation	76,374	
Travel expenses	59,340	
Order processing	770	
Rent	83,000	
Total expenses		609,472
Net profit (before taxes)		$ 14,383

EXHIBIT 3   *Allocation of Natural Accounts to Functional Accounts, Atlanta District*

		Functional Accounts					
Natural Accounts		Selling Direct Costs	Selling Indirect Costs	Advertising	Order Processing	Warehouse and Transportation	Packaging
Salaries	$177,000	$106,500	$47,500		$12,000		$11,000
Commissions	37,431	37,431					
Advertising	131,915			$131,915			
Packaging	43,642						43,642
Warehousing and transportation	76,374					$ 76,374	
Travel expenses	59,340	57,340	2,000				
Order processing	770				770		
Rent	83,000		18,500		4,500	40,000	20,000
Total expenses	$609,472	$201,271	$68,000	$131,915	$17,270	$116,374	$74,642

EXHIBIT 4   *Product Line Sales and Costs*

Product	Selling Price per Unit	Cost per Unit	Gross Margin per Unit	Number Sold in Period	Sales in Period	Advertising Expenditures	Packaging
Receivers	$250	$212	$38	3,151	$ 787,750	$ 40,000	$ 6,302
Turntables	85	64	21	12,079	1,026,715	50,000	24,158
Speakers	125	87	38	6,591	823,875	40,000	13,182
				21,821	$2,638,340	$130,000	$43,642

EXHIBIT 5   *Sales Calls, Orders, and Units Sold by Salesperson*

Salesperson	Sales Calls	Orders	Number of Units Sold Receivers	Turntables	Speakers	Total
Paul Sand	85	60	668	2,652	1,534	4,854
Diane Gallo	105	85	823	3,270	1,582	5,675
Kathy Parks	110	60	816	3,131	1,578	5,525
Charlie Lyons	170	75	844	3,026	1,897	5,767
	470	280	3,151	12,079	6,591	21,821

EXHIBIT 6   *Customer Activity Analysis for Charlie Lyons*

Customers of Charlie Lyons	Sales Calls	Average Time Spent on Each Call (minutes)	Orders	Number of Units Purchased Receivers	Turntables	Speakers	Total
American TV	65	55	40	422	1,513	854	2,789
Appliance Mart	55	45	15	337	1,058	569	1,964
Audio Emporium	50	45	20	85	455	474	1,014
	170	48	75	844	3,026	1,897	5,767

Preparing guidelines for allocating costs to sales representatives and customers was Basler's next task. Based on his review of several distribution cost and analysis textbooks and further conversations with Stella Jordan, Basler developed the following guidelines:

Functional Cost Item	Basis of Allocation
Direct selling	Number of calls × average time spent with each customer
Commissions	6 percent of gross margin
Travel	Total travel costs by number of calls; this figure is then multiplied by individual salesperson calls or customer calls
Advertising	5 percent of sales dollars
Packaging	Number of units × $2
Warehousing and transportation	Number of units × $3.50
Order processing	Number of orders × $2.75

Basler's next step is developing the necessary accounting statement, which will permit a detailed analysis of each sales rep's profitability. From there he will proceed to a customer profitability analysis for Charlie Lyons's customers.

Case 3-3
NATIONAL TELECOMMUNICATIONS
CORPORATION*

After two years as an account executive in southern Illinois for National Telecommunications, Dan Peters was well on his way to developing a rewarding and challenging career. Although the majority of his experience was in consumer sales, he quickly adapted to a more sophisticated selling environment. He enjoyed the challenge the work offered and discovered that his selling skills were perfectly matched for longer selling cycles and extended customer relations. After five months, he was a consistent top performer within the division, and his monthly sales were steadily increasing.

His second year with National was highlighted by sales to two major accounts that would generate substantial revenue for the company and earnings for himself. Dan invested in a new car and considered starting a family, something he was hesitant to do before going to work for National. The beginning of his third year was accompanied by a serious change at National on a corporate level. Top management perceived the company's sales performance to be substandard, and personnel at even the highest levels were either reassigned or terminated.

Several divisions also began to experience delays in customer service due to equipment failure and only marginal backup and repair. Dan was frustrated by the lack of management and company support he was receiving in the field to service major accounts and their changing demands.

To deal with his major customer's problems, Dan had to spend an increasing amount of time away from his primary selling duties, including the signing of new accounts. Since his monthly quota was based on originating new business, he was unable to reach quota several times. Although his immediate supervisor showed little concern, Dan received a strong written warning concerning his performance.

With upper management threatening termination, Dan became confused as to what his actual responsibilities should include and how he could be expected to actively sell and service accounts at the same time. Dan also thought upper management failed to consider the service disadvantage National had in eastern Illinois. The company's major competitor, AT&T, possessed superior equipment and reliability. This hindered Dan's sales performance.

---

*This case was prepared especially for this text by Dale Humphrey, MBA University of Wisconsin-Madison, under the supervision of Professor Neil M. Ford, University of Wisconsin-Madison.

Company Background

National Telecommunications originated in 1963 when communications expert John Gross formed National Microwave, Inc. The company under Gross's guidance implemented a microwave link between St. Louis and Kansas City to assist trucking firms operating between the two cities. After five years of successful operation, Gross and longtime friend Roger Deane, current National chairman, decided to expand operations by moving headquarters to Kansas City and renaming the company National Communications of America, Inc. Deane, who then owned a substantial portion of the company, agreed to buy Gross's share and pursue other opportunities for expansion.

The early 70s for National was a period of difficult change dictated by legislation governing telecommunications. National and others relied on the government to provide opportunities for expansion. In the wake of Federal Communications Commission approvals for a national network, National Telecommunications Corporation was born. National placed itself against industry giant AT&T which, in conjunction with local Bell operating companies, controlled the vast majority of required interconnects. AT&T used this advantage to discourage and even prevent major competition from entering several markets. The result was 10 years of legal maneuvering between National and AT&T over equipment rights.

Gradually, AT&T lost its complete hold on interconnects and services after several major lawsuits went in National's favor. In 1982, National became a Fortune 500 company and acquired several regionally based communication firms. From 1983 to 1985, legal actions against AT&T by National and others culminated when the government initiated the breakup of AT&T into separate entities. National was then able to develop its own operating system in conjunction with the Bell system.

Following the breakup, National extended its national network and service base. The introduction of National Mail and COMMNET established the company as an innovator in business communication technology and service. In 1988, National purchased Vericom Global Communications, an established market leader in international telex and data transfer services. At the close of 1989, National registered its most profitable year with annual revenue reaching a historic high of $6.4 billion. In 1991, National's market share reached 12 percent, slowly penetrating AT&T's dominant position (see Exhibit 1).

Today, National is truly an international company, providing services in over 10 countries. The company's $6.9 billion network is comprised of systems owned and operated by National and 60 independently operated regional networks. In addition to basic phone line service, National provides over 50 customer service options to the consumer and business markets. Using aggressive advertising, National has directly confronted AT&T, creating a telecommunications war between the two companies. AT&T is now defending its dominant market share as National continues to invest in new equipment and regional networks.

E X H I B I T   1   *National 1991 Market Share*

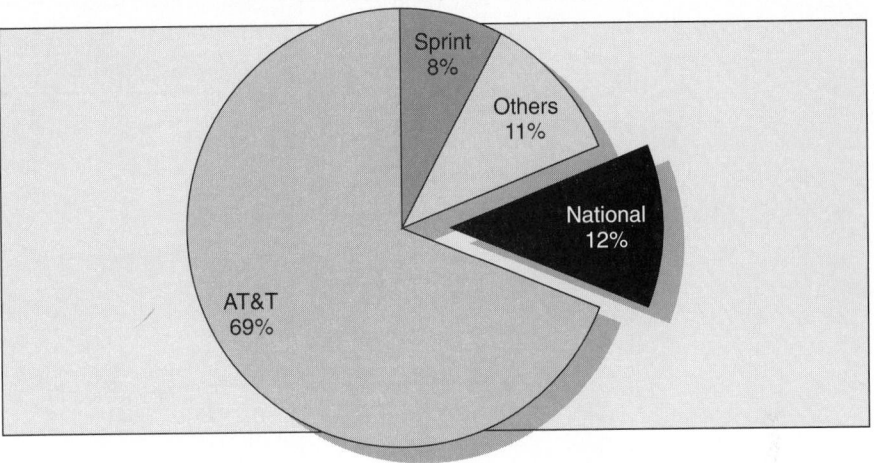

National's Sales Organization

National's selling efforts are directed at consumer and business markets. The consumer market is serviced by the company's media-based promotion efforts and telemarketing division. The advertising campaigns of National and AT&T resemble the "cola war" being waged by Pepsi and Coke. National promotes a cost advantage while AT&T counters with claims of superior customer service. Advertising is direct and openly critical of the other's product. National's telemarketing division contacts consumers directly to promote the company's long-distance service and other products.

National's primary selling effort is carried out by the company's general business sales force. Comprised of over 5,000 sales representatives (account executives) and six levels of management, the general business sales organization is the largest and most profitable division of National. Exhibit 2 outlines the sales organization with detail on the Midwest division.

The other sales divisions are the West, Southwest, Pacific, Mid-Atlantic, Southeast, Northeast, and International. The vertical composition of the Midwest division is reflective of the other national divisions. Many states with larger markets are much larger horizontally to balance the lower level manager's span of control.

State and area sales managers (ASMs) are typically former account executives with the company. Major account representatives (MARs) are responsible for a number of larger National business customers and report di-

E X H I B I T 2   *National Sales Organization*

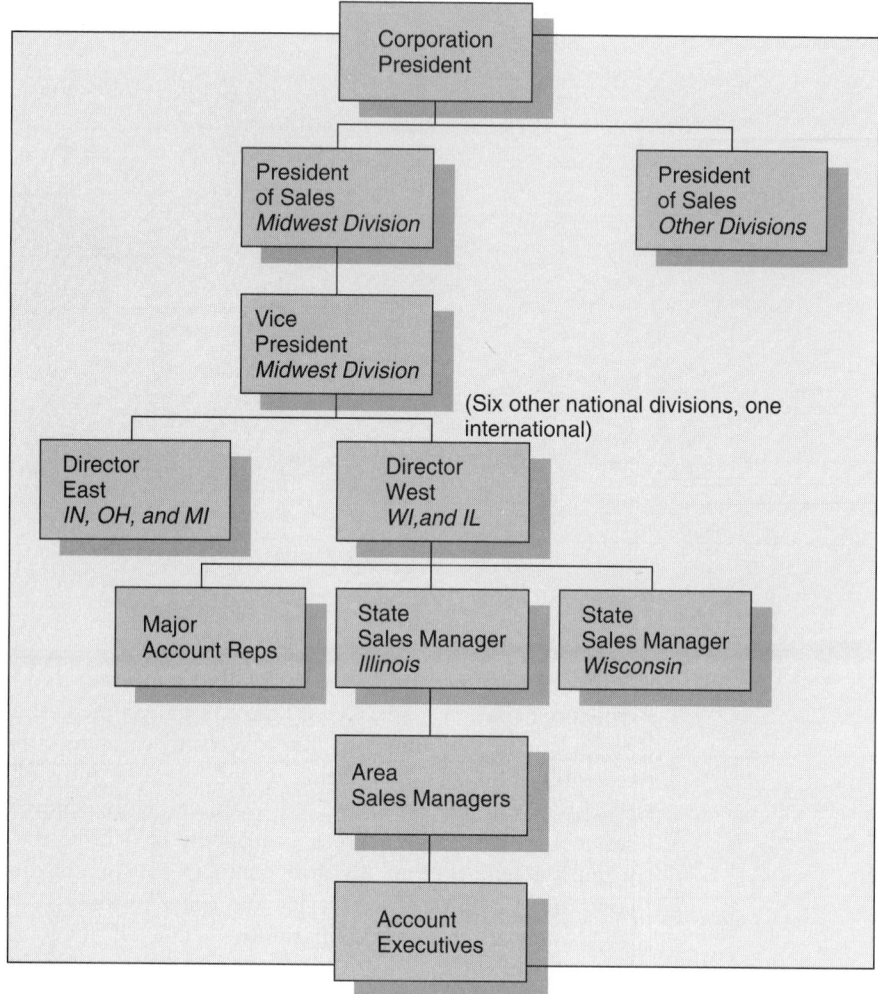

rectly to regional sales directors. Their compensation is on an 80/20 plan with a base salary averaging $26,000 to $32,000 plus a 20 percent commission based on customer billing. Account executives are divided into two classes: AE1 and AE2.

AE2s have typically been with the company over five years or are former AE1s who demonstrated exceptional performance. Their base salary ranges between $20,000 and $24,000 per year plus commissions based on customer billing schedules. AE1s have typically been with the company less than five years and do not have previous experience in the telecommunications industry.

Base salary for AE1s ranges from $18,000 to $22,000 per year in addition to a rolling average commission schedule.

Account Executive Work Analysis

Dan Peters's first six months with National were dedicated primarily to training. He attended various seminars and company workshops that presented operating policies, product knowledge, specialized selling tactics, and information on the telecommunications market. Following several weeks of on-the-job training with another account executive, Dan was officially assigned as an AE1 with National-Illinois. His assigned territory consisted of eastern Illinois, including a portion of the Chicago market.

The product he was assigned to sell is actually a service—custom-designed communication systems. The term *systems* includes any form of wire or optical transmission utilizing existing telephone networks. The complexity of the system varied in proportion to the type and size of the business it was being designed for. For example, a company relying on telemarketing would demand a more complex and customer-driven long distance service than a small business operating in a local market.

Dan was responsible for assessing the long-distance needs of such customers and presenting National systems and services that fulfilled these needs. As discussed earlier, the entrenchment of AT&T and the Bell companies presented Dan with one primary task: offer services that were more flexible, reliable, and cost-effective than those offered by AT&T and Bell. Since the vast majority of prospective customers used AT&T services, Dan was presenting many with a competing service for the first time. For prospecting purposes, Dan was expected to generate his own calling schedule based on company listings of firms not currently using National services. The listings are distributed to each AE based on territory. Each AE is required to compile weekly reports that contain the number of calls made (in person or on the phone) and the number of presentations made during a week. The reports are used to monitor AE activity and provide a written summary for the meeting of calling quotas. The quotas are set at 25 phone calls per day to prospective customers and 10 person-to-person appointments per week.

In addition to activity quotas, AEs are expected to reach monthly dollar quotas based on new customer billing. The monthly long distance revenue a new account will generate is estimated from past billing behavior. If Dan was attempting to sign a customer currently using AT&T, he would examine that company's long-distance usage and then present a competing estimate based on that information. This same estimate was then credited to Dan during the month the new account was signed to National. The quota for AE1s is $4,000 per month and $5,000 per month for AE2s.

Monthly revenue figures are straight dollar amounts, and the actual number of accounts making up the total is not considered critical. Dan could sign 10 smaller accounts that would bill over $4,000 per month or one account

EXHIBIT 3

NATIONAL TELECOMMUNICATIONS
Commission Calculation Statement
Employee SSN: 355-34-4947

OFFICE: 71334200 East Illinois
SALES REPRESENTATIVE: Peters, Daniel
SEPTEMBER ACTIVITY:

TYPE/STATUS: AE AE/ACTV

| | | | | Commissionable Revenue | |
Account Name	Inst Date	Total Account Revenue	Account History Peak	New Growth	Retention
Assigned Accounts:					
The Illinois Press	900605	15.39	13.29	2.10	13.29
Veterans Affairs	881227	109.74	163.05	0.00	109.74
Plastics Inc.	890616	111.84	141.39	0.00	111.84
Illinois Press	890920	2251.01	1594.35	0.00	2251.04
Illinois Physicians	900515	3102.11	394.31	2707.80	394.31
Illinois Physicians	900227	2012.24	6773.18	0.00	2012.24
Illinois Power & Li	881003	157.86	196.84	0.00	157.86
Illinois Power & Li	890808	83.59	100.77	0.00	83.69
Illinois Power & Li	890808	59.53	67.88	0.00	59.53
Illinois Power & Li	890808	157.88	179.27	0.00	157.88
Illinois Power & Li	890808	47.77	79.38	0.00	47.77
Illinois Power & Li	890320	20.99	43.24	0.00	20.99
Illinois Power & Li	890613	35.64	100.70	0.00	35.64
Illinois Power & Li	890712	31.87	52.81	0.00	31.87
Illinois Power & Li	890523	104.42	121.45	0.00	104.42
Illinois Power & Li	890411	10.91	33.32	0.00	10.91
Illinois Power & Li	881025	850.43	1097.07	0.00	850.43
Illinois Power & Li	890821	20.97	26.41	0.00	20.97
Illinois Power & Li	890320	29.10	53.24	0.00	29.10
Illinois Power & Li	900824	0.73 −	0.00	0.00	0.73
Illinois Power & Li	900814	2.29	0.00	2.29	0.00
Illinois Power & Li	890620	97.04	124.32	0.00	97.04
Illinois Power & Li	900718	20.81	9.37	11.44	9.37
IPS	900515	54778.39	40996.29	13783.10	40996.29
Assigned Account Totals:		103704.82		16744.18	86873.81
Total Month's Activity:		103704.82		16744.18	86873.81

that would reach the same level of billing activity. Such a system does not discipline an AE who is able to sign only one large account, although calling schedules (activity quotas) must still be attained. Levels in excess of selling quotas are not candidates for bonuses or incentives. The AE is rewarded through a commission structure discussed next.

Dan's total compensation included a base salary plus two types of commissions. The base or primary commissions are calculated from the billing activity of each account signed by the AE while working for National. Thus, the AE would earn income on a month-to-month basis from the entire account base retained by that AE. Dan, for example, would receive monthly reports that would outline each account he sold National services to and the long-distance charges the account accumulated during the month. Exhibit 3 illustrates a commission statement for Dan.

The statement is totaled and combined with three previous months to arrive at a four-month billing statement. Commissions are set at 22 percent of the average billing over the four months. Commission payments are generally paid one month after the fourth statement is closed. The AE then receives account listings for the final month and a summary sheet displaying previous totals and commissions based on the average. In addition to these commissions, the AE is paid on what National calls "retention revenue." This is based on the percentage of the AE's signed accounts that are still using National services. Payments are calculated from a schedule that initiates payment at a level of 90 percent. Percentages to up to 1,000 percent and commissions range from $16 to $320 per month.

Dan was extremely satisfied with the working conditions and compensation structure at National. He consistently met both his activity and selling quotas from month to month and received a base salary raise at the start of his second year. Unfortunately, his satisfaction with work and his superiors began to change drastically during his third year.

Dan Peters's Difficulties

During the spring of 1990, Dan was concentrating on developing a proposal for two large potential accounts located in his portion of the Chicago sales territory. Due to the size of the accounts and the complexity of their communication needs, Dan spent many hours outside of work analyzing their current long-distance usage and the National services he would propose for replacement. He also worked with technicians from National to provide accurate estimates on hardware requirements and installation times. After making several appointments with the key decision makers in each company, he was confident of securing a sale with at least one of the firms.

After nearly two months of negotiations, Dan closed sales with both of the firms. Combined, the two companies would bill an estimated $70,000 in long-distance charges, nearly exceeding Dan's entire account base. The ac-

EXHIBIT 4

TO:	D. R. Peters
CC:	Karen Sullivan
CC:	Jim Sanders
CC:	Diane Robinson
CC:	Mark Hanusa
SUBJECT:	Congratulations!

Your position as a contender for CIC 100 is outstanding given the top quality of NTC's sales reps! Keep up the great work and you'll be among the first recipients to achieve this new and exclusive distinction. Mark your calendars for Tahiti, May 15–19, 1992!

counts would provide healthy monthly commissions and would put Dan among the top 15 National AEs in the country. His position also put him in contention for a major company sales award that was given to the top 100 representatives in the country (see Exhibit 4).

Dan did not have much time to enjoy his success or compliments from upper management. Following installation, his two major accounts began to experience serious equipment failures. He was constantly at their offices trying to remedy the problems and repair deteriorating relations with his customers. Dan's selling time did not permit such extensive post-sale responsibilities. Following a sale, major technical issues were to be handed over to National-Service, not the AE. In Dan's case, National was slow to react and Dan was pinned down in his customers' offices listening to their concerns and trying to assure them the system merely had to be "broken in."

Most of the technical problems were due to an unexpected degree of incompatibility between National's internal equipment and Illinois Bell's regional network. As Dan explained, "National has experienced problems developing its own regional network here (Chicago), and it has handicapped National's larger installation projects." After a month of inconsistent service, Dan's accounts were moving beyond frustration. One of the accounts refused to pay a National bill and was immediately disconnected.

Dan was voicing his concerns, but his immediate manager only would urge him to continue servicing the accounts to the best of his abilities. During this period, Dan was off his selling quota two months in a row because of the difficulties experienced by his major accounts. Dan's office took little action until the regional office pressured his manager for an explanation of Dan's performance. Dan was shocked when his manager presented him with a written warning (see Exhibit 5).

Dan's explanation went seemingly unheard as he said, "What was I to do? I couldn't possibly make quota while trying to satisfy my largest customers.

EXHIBIT 5

NTC Telecommunications Corporation
NTC Midwest
6300 Exclusive Drive
Suite 333
Champaign, IL 63909
217 304 2222
800 423 6125
FAX 217 304 3333

August 6, 1991

TO: Daniel R. Peters
FROM: Karen Sullivan
SUBJECT: Disciplinary Action/Written Warning

Dan,

As we discussed today, your sales performance as Account Executive has been substandard. The issue discussed pertained to a lack of sales activity. Both reported sales and UCS revenues have been below divisional and corporate standards. Weekly activity and monthly sales funnel are very weak and require immediate attention.

This is your Official Written Warning, which means we (you and I) must bring your abilities in these areas up to speed. You have my commitment to help you develop the skills required to increase sales activity.

If your performance has not met minimum and acceptable levels, there will be additional disciplinary action taken which may include termination.

I have discussed this with my manager, Karen Sullivan, and agree to work diligently to increase my abilities in the areas described above.

_____

Daniel R. Peters
Account Executive I
NTC Midwest Division

_____

Karen Sullivan
Manager I
NTC Midwest Division

KS/bh

EXHIBIT 6

Command: Date: From:	Fri, Sep 28, 1991 10:12 AM CST Sally Hickman/NTC Midwestern Region
To:	Karen Sullivan/NTC Midwestern Region
Subject:	CIC REP RESULTS—AUGUST BILLING

The CIC rep rankings through August Billing were distributed via Fax Broadcast to each office on Wednesday, September 26th. The ranking report is based on National performance listing the top 75 reps in the country qualifying for CIC 100, followed then by all reps performing at 125% or better based on their Revenue Goal qualifying for CIC.

The Midwest Division has 59 CIC contenders as of August Billing! Congratulations to each of those fortunate reps that are vying for positions "In The Sun"! It is not too late to turn up the heat and reserve a lounge chair by the pool in Tahiti or Florida! The rules are such that each rep is in competition with his/her own abilities. Perform at 125% or better and a reservation for a "Place In The Sun" is guaranteed!!!

The following highlights our top performers as of August UCS Billing:

CIC 100 Contenders:

CIC Rank	Div Rank	Name	Rep Type	Branch Name	YTD Rev	% of Goal
3	1	Kevin Hugh	AE2	Chicago North	$240,693	401%
6	2	Collin Cherney	AE2	Chicago North	$160,569	378%
15	3	Belle Starr	AE2	Wisconsin	$107,407	275%
16	4	Theodore Spinks	AE1	Michigan East	$ 87,363	273%
19	5	Tulula Sentry	AE2	NE Ohio	$106,028	272%
21	6	Sandy Tyson	MAR	Chicago North	$319,341	266%
34	7	Brenda Hasse	AE2	Chicago Downtown	$147,036	245%
36	8	Mark Anderson	AE1	Columbus	$ 76,693	230%
39	9	Teddy Johannes	AE1	SW Illinois	$ 73,693	230%
42	10	Jonlee Devlin	AE2	Wisconsin	$ 95,579	225%
55	11	Marv Birdwhistle	AE2	Chicago North	$122,074	203%
57	12	Marge Kenton	AE1	SW Ohio	$ 64,895	203%
58	13	Dan Peters	AE1	Eastern Ilinois	$ 64,762	202%
70	14	Roberta Prancer	AE2	Michigan West	$ 88,221	192%
73	15	Stephen Willey	AE2	Chicago North	$ 94,399	191%
74	16	Michael Dubois	AE1	Chicago Downtown	$ 60,725	190%
75	17	Danielle Morrison	AE1	Wisconsin	$ 60,581	189%

They were ready to go back to AT&T and I was simply trying to make up for my company's dismal reliability." Dan became increasingly frustrated, especially after receiving memos congratulating him for his two largest sales.

Dan learned one month after receiving his written warning that National was dealing with problems at the highest levels of the company. Several division presidents were reassigned, and two decided to leave National for employment at AT&T. The reason was twofold: inconsistent sales in several regions and companywide growth far below forecasted levels. Dan could only relate it to his own experience by stating, "I knew after signing those accounts that National still had network problems in several regions, including eastern Illinois. This damaged the company's reputation and hindered the selling effort. The company was making a big mistake by pointing the finger at the salespeople and not themselves."

Nearly two months after receiving his written warning, Dan got the feeling that his area office was falling apart. Two AEs in the office quit after receiving similar warnings, and his area manager was noticeably concerned about his own future. Dan continued to have problems in the field, but his two largest accounts initiated billing, handing him the largest paycheck of his career. He was also pleased after receiving the national and divisional sales rankings (see Exhibit 6).

Unfortunately, Dan did not get the chance to have his place "in the sun." One week after receiving the rankings, the state sales manager requested his immediate resignation due to his "inconsistent month-to-month performance." Dan was not surprised. He had spent two months trying to deal with his customers and the company, and he got caught in the middle. His area sales manager was not there to help him because he was busy fighting for his own job. Dan put the situation into perspective by stating, "I performed well at National, my sales record proved it. Near the end it was clear everyone was looking out for themselves and not dealing with the real problem. I was labeled as the problem and paid for it with my job."

Case 3-4
COUNTRY ROADS, INC.*

Camille Berggren had just completed a review of a staff report covering the various problems facing the telemarketing program at Country Roads, Inc.— a large, multimillion-dollar direct marketing organization that sells merchandise throughout North America. Although attractive catalogs that contain mail order forms are mailed to customers 13 times a year, approximately 60 percent of Country Roads's sales are made by customers calling the 800 number to place an order.

The telemarketing division was the subject of the staff report. A special committee had been convened to review morale problems and to make recommendations. The relatively high turnover among Country Roads's telemarketing specialists (personal shopping representatives—PSRs) was of considerable concern not only to Camille but also to her superiors. Despite the fact that PSRs were paid a straight salary plus a year-end bonus (unlike conventional telemarketing compensation programs that usually pay a straight commission), morale and turnover problems were serious enough to warrant the special committee's assignment.

The Company

Country Roads, Inc., established in 1971, is located in Burlington, Vermont. Since its inception, Country Roads has experienced rapid growth in catalog sales. The catalogs contain mostly clothing, but other unique items are also available. Country Roads prides itself on high-quality merchandise at reasonable prices. In addition, Country Roads set a trend in the fast-growing catalog mail order business by following a customer complete satisfaction policy. Customers can receive a full refund with no questions asked if they are not completely satisfied with their purchases. Company executives believe this policy has been instrumental in helping Country Roads enjoy unprecedented growth in the direct marketing business. Not only have sales increased dramatically, but employee growth has also been significant.

Country Roads, Inc., provides 24-hour telephone service, hiring people mostly from the Burlington, Vermont, area. Most of the telemarketing reps are full-time, although about one fifth of the PSRs are part-time employees. About two thirds are women. Average compensation including year-end bonuses is $15,000. Turnover among this group in recent years has averaged 60 percent. Company executives realize this is low in comparison with turnover

---

*Katherine Cheney assisted in preparing this case.

rates experienced by other direct marketing companies, but they think the 60 percent rate will cause future problems. In fact, one study recommends that Country Roads, Inc., consider establishing telemarketing operations at other locations away from the Burlington, Vermont, area. The study supported this recommendation by pointing out that unless the turnover problem was resolved, Country Roads would find it difficult to hire more personal shopping representatives from the Burlington area.

The Staff Report

Mike Peck, chairman of the committee, initiated the project by conducting one-on-one interviews with a sample of personal shopping representatives. Interviews were conducted with the PSRs' supervisors and with others at Country Roads, Inc., as well. Mike then held a series of four focus group interviews with 36 of the PSRs. Following these interviews, the committee, with the assistance of Country Roads's personnel manager, administered a series of questionnaires that measured such variables as job satisfaction, role ambiguity, role conflict, and organizational climate. The personnel manager provided a report for the committee to review.

The following comments are based on the information the committee collected:

1. The personal shopping representatives are reasonably satisfied with pay, the nature of the job, their fellow workers, company policies and benefits, and their customers.

2. The PSRs are dissatisfied with promotion, supervision, and company support.

3. Role conflict was a problem, especially between the PSRs' supervisors and their customers. Little conflict existed between customers and Country Roads, Inc., and between their supervisors and Country Roads, Inc.

4. PSRs perceive role ambiguity, especially as it affects promotions and supervision.

5. The one-on-one and focus group interviews were not too productive. The committee thought PSRs did not trust the process, afraid that their comments would reach the wrong people. Despite these reservations, the committee did learn that PSRs were not pleased with their supervisors. One PSR, leaving Country Roads, indicated the performance evaluation system was a joke, but she did not care to elaborate for fear that her cohorts who were still there might suffer. Another PSR indicated that getting promoted was a mysterious process.

The committee suspected that the dissatisfaction with company support was related to supervision and promotion problems. Finally, the committee recommended that Country Roads, Inc., review the performance evaluation process and the promotion procedure.

Camille Berggren met with Mike Peck to discuss the staff report his com-

Exhibit 1

Country Roads, Inc.
Burlington, Vermont

To: Customer Sales
From: Supervisors
Date: September 4, 1989
Subject: Country Roads's philosophy

Country Roads's philosophy is based on friendliness and service to our customers. It is extremely important that this Country Roads's image be projected.

To help develop good performance and ensure that a positive Country Roads's image is being projected, we are going to formalize performance observation.

The attached information will explain the program.

KF/rsp
Attachment

P.S. PSR is the abbreviation for Personal Sales Representative.

mittee had prepared. She was particularly concerned about the criticism of Country Roads's performance evaluation procedure, a relatively recent creation implemented on September 4, 1989. Considerable effort had gone into developing the new system. Mike indicated that maybe the system was fine but the implementation was at fault. He informed Camille that one of his committee members recommended that Country Roads consider using behaviorally anchored rating scales to improve the performance evaluation process. Due to time constraints, this idea was not investigated. Anyway, Mike suggested the process sounded too complicated for Country Roads's supervisors to use.

Next, Camille obtained a copy of the evaluation system implemented in 1989 (see Exhibit 1). She believed the current program's objectives were meaningful: (1) to help develop good performance and (2) to project Country Roads's image of friendliness and service. Fulfilling these objectives was certainly important for Country Roads, Inc., as they would be for any firm. However, Camille thought it would be difficult to measure performance in either of these categories without more specific objectives or intermediate goals.

Using reading materials provided by Country Roads's personnel manager, Camille formulated objectives of performance appraisal procedures. The traditional function of a performance appraisal system is threefold:

1. To provide adequate feedback to employees about their performance.

2. To serve as a basis for modifying behavior to initiate more effective, desirable working habits.

3. To provide data to managers for purposes of sales and cost analysis and promotion.

These goals are simply a more detailed derivation of Country Roads's purposes. For instance, good performance can be developed only when employees first receive proper feedback about their performance and then modify their behavior accordingly. Further, if data are compiled during the procedure, it is possible to ensure that the proper image is being portrayed by rewarding those PSRs with good ratings and working with those who have less than acceptable scores. If these objectives were utilized as intermediate goals, the long-term purpose would be easier to measure and obtain.

In her review of Country Roads's performance evaluation system, Camille noted the following points:

1. The program offers performance observation guidelines the supervisor should follow when monitoring PSRs.

2. The program names eight specific points on which PSRs will be rated; these points take into account most of the performance observation guidelines.

3. Directions are given for the supervisor to follow when filling out the monitoring form.

4. The monitoring form lists attributes on the left-hand side of the form, and leaves space for the evaluation marks; *E* and *N*, respectively, stand for *effective* and *noneffective*.

Although Camille felt that the system had been put together in a hurry, she thought it was better than no system, which was pretty much the situation before the 1989 procedure. If implementation was difficult, then a review of actual performance evaluations should reveal any problems. Next, Camille asked for a sample of completed evaluation forms from Country Roads's personnel function (see pp. 819–23).

Before she had received the completed evaluation forms, Camille discussed the situation with Peter Bylow, Country Roads's public relations director, to determine if any image studies had been conducted. Bylow assured her that Country Roads had a sound image based on company surveys and other sources. In their discussion, Bylow mentioned customer shopping studies that had been conducted at his former place of employment, a bank in Boston. He indicated that tellers, personal bankers, and other bank employees with public contact were observed frequently and evaluated on their customer relations skills, sales skills, and technical skills. These observations were prepared by a consulting firm that had hired people to conduct actual transactions, both in

Observation Dates _____

Employee Name _____

Annual Review Due _____

Supervisor _____

Employment Status _____

Subjects of Evaluation:

Greeting _____

Pleasantries _____

Complete Information Volunteered _____

Understand Customer _____

Overcome Customer Objections _____

Read CRT-Use System _____

Telephone Techniques _____

Closing _____

_____

_____

Comments _____

_____

_____

_____

_____

_____

_____

E = Effective   N = Noneffective

Employee Signature _____ Date _____

CRI: 9/4/89

Observation Dates 4/18 4/29 5/3 5/18 7/11 8/15 9/3 11/14

Employee Name _DEIRDRE BURNS_

Annual Review Due _9/1/92_

Supervisor _DANA MOORE_

Employment Status _PSR-II SECOND SHIFT_

Subjects of Evaluation:

	4/18	4/29	5/3	5/18	7/11	8/15	9/3	11/14
Greeting	E	E	N	E	E	N	N	N
Pleasantries	E	E	N	E	E	N	N	N
Complete Information Volunteered	E	E	N	E	E	N	N	N
Understand Customer	E	E	E	E	E	E	E	N
Overcome Customer Objections	E	E	N	E	E	N	N	N
Read CRT-Use System	E	E	E	E	E	E	N	N
Telephone Techniques	E	E	N	E	E	N	N	N
Closing	E	E	N	E	E	N	N	N

Comments _4/18 GOOD PERFORMANCE 4/29 SOLID RESULTS 5/3 NEEDS TO GET BACK ON TRACK 5/18 MUCH BETTER 7/11 EXCELLENT 8/15 DEIRDRE IS INCONSISTENT AND MUST TRY HARDER 9/3 POOR TREND — SHE IS NOT TRYING 11/14 PLACED HER ON 60 DAYS PROBATION_

E = Effective   N = Noneffective

Employee Signature _Deirdre Burns_ Date _12/15/92_

CRI: 9/4/89

Observation Dates _3/11 3/26 4/3 4/12 5/15 6/10(1) 6/10(2) 6/10(3)_

Employee Name _JACK MURRAY_

Annual Review Due _6/12/92_

Supervisor _JAYNE PERRIN_

Employment Status _PSR III THIRD SHIFT_

Subjects of Evaluation:

	3/11	3/26	4/3	4/12	5/15	6/10(1)	6/10(2)	6/10(3)
Greeting	E	E	E	E	E	N	N	N
Pleasantries	E	E	E	E	E	N	N	N
Complete Information Volunteered	E	E	E	E	E	E	E	E
Understand Customer	E	E	E	E	E	E	E	E
Overcome Customer Objections	E	E	E	E	E	N	N	N
Read CRT-Use System	E	E	E	E	E	E	E	E
Telephone Techniques	E	E	E	E	E	N	N	N
Closing	E	E	E	E	E	N	N	N

Comments _JACK'S EXCELLENT PERFORMANCE CHANGED DIRECTIONS. HE NEEDS TO FIGURE OUT HOW TO GET BACK ON TRACK._

E = Effective   N = Noneffective

Employee Signature _Jack Murray_ Date _6/15/92_

CRI: 9/4/89

Observation Dates _7/1 7/3 8/5 8/16 8/17 10/1 10/5 10/15_

Employee Name _Lisa Daniel_

Annual Review Due _10/17/92_

Supervisor _John Ruppert_

Employment Status _PSR-I first Shift_

Subjects of Evaluation:	7/1	7/3	8/5	8/16	8/17	10/1	10/5	10/15
Greeting	E	E	E	E	N	E	E	E
Pleasantries	E	E	E	E	N	E	E	E
Complete Information Volunteered	E	E	E	E	N	E	E	E
Understand Customer	N	N	E	E	N	E	E	E
Overcome Customer Objections	N	N	N	N	N	E	E	E
Read CRT-Use System	E	E	E	E	N	E	E	E
Telephone Techniques	E	E	E	E	N	E	E	E
Closing	E	E	E	E	N	E	E	E

Comments _Lisa has had problems overcoming objectives and needs to practice. Her poor performance on 8/17 is not significant. She had a bad day._

E = Effective   N = Noneffective

Employee Signature _Lisa Daniel_ Date _11/1/92_

CRI: 9/4/89

Observation Dates	9/1	10/3	11/7	12/18	3/23	5/16	7/1	8/5

Employee Name Gretchen Nelson

Annual Review Due 8/17/92

Supervisor Mary Cable

Employment Status PSR-I First Shift

Subjects of Evaluation:	9/1	10/3	11/7	12/18	3/23	5/16	7/1	8/5
Greeting	E	E	E	E	E	E	E	E
Pleasantries	E	E	E	E	E	E	E	E
Complete Information Volunteered	E	E	E	E	E	E	E	E
Understand Customer	E	E	E	E	E	E	E	E
Overcome Customer Objections	N	N	N	N	N	N	N	N
Read CRT-Use System	E	E	E	E	E	E	E	E
Telephone Techniques	E	E	E	E	E	E	E	E
Closing	N	N	N	N	N	N	N	N

Comments Gretchen needs to learn how to handle objections. Her closing technique is not effective and she is losing sales. I placed her on 90 days probation.

E = Effective   N = Noneffective

Employee Signature Gretchen Nelson Date 9/1/92

CRI: 9/4/89

Observation Dates _6/12 7/18 10/8 10/9 1/17(1) 1/17(2) 4/12(1) 4/12(2)_

Employee Name ___Nancy Luther___

Annual Review Due ___4/12/92___

Supervisor ___Pam Benjamin___

Employment Status ___PSR-I- Third Shift___

Subjects of Evaluation:

	10/12	7/18	10/8	10/9	1/17(1)	1/17(2)	4/12(1)	4/12(2)
Greeting	E	E	N	E	N	N	E	E
Pleasantries	E	E	N	E	N	N	E	E
Complete Information Volunteered	E	E	N	N	N	N	E	E
Understand Customer	E	E	N	N	N	N	E	E
Overcome Customer Objections	E	N	N	N	N	N	E	E
Read CRT-Use System	E	E	N	E	N	N	E	E
Telephone Techniques	E	E	N	E	N	N	E	E
Closing	E	N	N	N	N	N	E	E

Comments ___Nancy needs to improve if she
hopes to be promoted to PSR-II.___

E = Effective   N = Noneffective

Employee Signature ___Nancy Luther___ Date ___4/12/92___

CRI: 9/4/89

person and by telephone. Results of the shopping studies were to be part of the performance evaluation process, but Bylow indicated that this idea was dropped due to lack of acceptance on the part of the supervisors. Bylow indicated the telephone approach might be suitable for Country Roads, Inc. Camille was intrigued with the approach and wondered if it might be appropriate. She liked the idea of the three broad areas of evaluation—customer relations skills, sales skills, and technical skills. Acceptance by the supervisors, however, might be a problem.

Finally, the sample of completed evaluation forms arrived on Camille's desk. She hoped they would provide further insight into Country Roads's morale and turnover problems. She knew her boss was waiting for recommendations on how to resolve the problem.

Customer Sales Performance Observation Guidelines

The following items and their definitions should be used as the criteria for assessing the effectiveness of customer contacts. Each item contains a variety of descriptive definitions based on the type of contact.

Greeting: Was the greeting prompt, cordial, courteous, and friendly? Did the PSR give the impression that he/she was ready to serve the customer? Did the greeting follow the prescribed script?

Overcoming objections: Did the PSR counter negative comments made by the customers? Were positive questions and statements used? Were alternate positive suggestions provided by the operator?

Understand the customer: Did the PSR effectively listen to the customer to avoid unnecessary repetition of conversations? Did the PSR provide correct information? Was there an even exchange of information, thus avoiding a confrontation and an unsatisfied customer?

Voice quality: Did the PSR's conversation contain proper voice inflection or did it appear to be harsh, indifferent, or monotonous?

Ask for the business: Did the PSR suggest alternate merchandise on out-of-stock items? If an item was on back order, did the PSR handle the back-order information in a positive manner? Did the PSR listen to the customer and suggest additional merchandise if the opening was given?

Customer responsiveness: Did the PSR project interest, enthusiasm, friendliness, and courtesy toward the customer? Did the PSR's tone of voice and inflection indicate a positive interaction with the customer, the company, and other employees? Did the PSR appear to be complacent or was a positive friendly feeling projected to the customer? Did the PSR project the Country Roads's image of service to the customer? Did the PSR maintain control of the conversation? Was a sincere desire to serve the customer projected and were the PSR's efforts directed immediately toward answering the customer's questions or resolving a problem, if any? Did the PSR quickly understand the customer's problem? Did he/she understand the steps necessary to solve the problem?

Shipping procedures: Are shipping procedures understood by the PSR? Was the "bill-to" information taken correctly? Was the customer asked if he/she wanted to ship to another address?

Closing: Was the order number given in an appropriate manner? Did the PSR use a suitable expression of appreciation in closing, such as "Thank you for calling Country Roads" or "Thank you and have a pleasant day/evening"?

Returns/refunds: Was proper information provided to the customer regarding return of merchandise and/or refunds?

Credit: Was the proper procedure followed for credit card number and billing address? Was proper information provided the customer concerning his/her account?

Courtesy: Did the PSR use courtesy phrases such as *please* and *thank you* when appropriate during the contact? Did the PSR excuse himself or herself if it was necessary to put the customer on hold to check a reference? Upon return to the telephone, did the PSR thank the customer for waiting? In short, did the PSR provide the customer with positive recognition throughout the contact?

Work habits—on-line system: Does the PSR know how to use the system to take full advantage of its efficiencies, thus providing customer service? Is the information on the screen used effectively to answer customers' inquiries? Are problems with the system reported to management?

Work habits—forms: Are all forms completed as required? Are the forms legible and are they completed quickly or at a time that avoids customer inconvenience?

Control of the conversation: Was the conversation controlled in a positive and effective manner? Did the PSR acknowledge customer comments and move effectively back to business?

Use of time: Is the PSR utilizing time efficiently during a contact while maintaining a friendly and courteous attitude? Is the PSR minimizing unavailable time during contacts? Is time used effectively between calls?

Appearance—personal: Does the PSR dress in an appropriate manner? Did the PSR chew gum during a contact?

Appearance—work area: Did the PSR check the position for material and forms necessary to properly service customers over the telephone, thus avoiding interruptions while on the telephone? Did the PSR maintain the position so that it appeared clean, orderly, and businesslike? Did the PSR report equipment out of service (i.e., desk, telephone, or chair)?

Adjustment—inquiry handling: Did the PSR handle shipment inquiries in the proper manner? Did the PSR provide correct information for general inquiry calls—avoiding inconvenience to our customers? Were proper adjustment procedures followed?

Monitoring Observation

Greeting: Was the greeting prompt, cordial, courteous, and friendly? Did the PSR give the impression that he/she was ready to serve the customer?

Pleasantries: Did the agent use courtesy phrases such as *please* and *thank you* when appropriate during the contact? Did the PSR excuse himself or herself if it was necessary to leave the telephone to check on something? Upon returning to the telephone, did the PSR thank the customer for waiting?

Complete information volunteered: Was proper information provided to the customer regarding return of merchandise and/or refunds? Did the PSR offer alternative merchandise for out of stock items? Did PSR offer information on back-order dates and shipping info?

Understand customer: Did the PSR provide correct information? Did the PSR listen to the customer to avoid unnecessary repetition of conversations?

Overcome customer objections: Did the PSR counter negative comments made by the customer? Were positive questions and statements used by the PSR?

Read CRT-use system fully: Does the PSR know how to use the system to take full advantage of helping the customer? Are problems with the system reported to the supervisor or lead?

Mannerisms: Are irritating mannerisms (i.e., heavy breathing, gum chewing) avoided when speaking on the telephone? Is the headset adjusted properly? When dialing out for another extension, does the PSRS allow sufficient rings or ring too long before hanging up if no answer?

Closing: Did the PSR acknowledge any expression of appreciation for the customer? Did the PSR use a suitable expression of appreciation in closing, such as *thank you for calling Country Roads and have a pleasant day or evening?*

1. Date of observation period.
2. Personal sales rep to be observed.
3. Supervisor, lead, trainer performing the observation.
4. Employment status.
5. Enter an *E* for effective contact or an *N* for a noneffective contact.
6. Record subjective comments and reference each item of noncompliance. Note all positive aspects of an employee's performance.
7. Personal sales rep's signature acknowledging review of the observation.

Case 3-5
ANDERSON DISTRIBUTORS, INC.*

Anderson Distributors, Inc., was a Phoenix corporation that wholesaled a full line of dry groceries. The line included 12,000 items and was sold primarily to independent food retailers in Arizona and parts of southern California. Stocks were held in three warehouses scattered throughout the territory. The company had prospered since it was formed 30 years earlier by three brothers who, before that, had managed a successful small chain of three retail stores. Sales were made by 45 salespeople who operated out of eight district offices. In brief, the sales organization consisted of the following:

45 salespeople

8 district managers

2 regional managers

1 sales vice president

Salesperson compensation ranged from $280 to $370 a week, district managers from $380 to $450. Anderson operated as a voluntary cooperative. That is, the member retailers agreed to concentrate the bulk of their purchases with Anderson in return for quantity discounts, a standard, simplified ordering system, special merchandising and promotional programs, and a convenient delivery system by Anderson trucks. All retailers in the system were allowed to use the co-op logo *Best Stores*. In 1980, Anderson had over 3,000 affiliated retailers, most of whom did concentrate their dry grocery purchases.

As was true with any extensive field sales organization, Anderson experienced most of the routine field management problems concerning salesperson evaluation, compensation, and supervision. A handful of these problems has been summarized on the following pages.

Evaluating Salespeople

District managers were required to make quarterly and annual evaluations of their salespeople. Clark Philbin had been a district manager for one month when he received a memo from Dan Pace, his regional manager, stating that all current quarterly evaluations were due in three weeks. The memo concerned Clark because he felt that he could not honestly evaluate his sales force after such a short time in his new position. He had had no management training or experience in evaluating people, except for the infrequent occasions when his previous boss had asked him to take over a sales meeting.

*This case was prepared by Professor Robert T. Davis, Stanford University, Graduate School of Business. Reprinted from *Stanford Business Cases 1980* with permission of the publisher, Stanford University Graduate School of Business, © 1980 by the Board of Trustees of the Leland Stanford Junior University.

Clark knew that he could accept the recommendations of the former district manager in writing his first quarterly evaluations, but there were several which he considered questionable. He could not easily identify specific reasons for his disagreement, but felt strongly nonetheless. Not wanting to make any serious mistakes, he decided to talk with his regional manager about evaluation techniques and standards before making any recommendations:

Pace: *Well, Clark, what's on your mind?*

Philbin: *Dan, I'm worried about this rating business. I've never evaluated anyone for anything before, and rather than make some real blunder, I wanted to ask you if you could offer me any guides or ground rules to follow.*

Pace: *Well, you've really picked a good question. What's bothering you now has been, and still is, a problem for most managers. As far as I know, there is no effective form or rating chart for evaluating people. This is something you just have to pick up from experience.*

Philbin: *Yes, Dan, but this is quite a responsibility, and I'm afraid of making some big mistakes during the learning process.*

Pace: *True, Clark, but it's hard for me to be specific. It's something all managers go through. You learn by doing, and basically have to develop your own standards. What I find acceptable performance, you might question. There's a lot of "feel" to it.*

Philbin: *O.K., Dan. I'll do the best I can. I have one question, though—this business of looking for people with management potential rather than sales potential. I don't understand why there should be so much emphasis on management. Aren't good salespersons just as important to the company as potential managers? After all, the business is becoming so competitive that we have to have top caliber salespeople. Today most of the buyers are pretty sophisticated, and the old-fashioned drummer has no place anymore. We need people who can read income statements and talk in terms of profits and other customer benefits.*

Pace: *I agree with you on the last part, Clark, and I guess the argument can be made that the best salespeople under these new conditions have to be more like managers. And if we continue to grow, there will always be room for the best young managers. Good luck with your evaluations!*

After returning to his office, Clark began to think over the interview. He realized that experience was undoubtedly a good, if not the best, teacher but he still felt that some effective evaluation technique would be helpful. He decided to try one other approach. He called an old boss, Kelly O'Brien, and asked him for his opinion on the problem. Kelly indicated that he would be glad to help. He said that the same problem had bothered him when he first became a district manager. Consequently, he had attempted to quantify some of the criteria commonly used in determining a person's management and sales potential. He had drawn up a rough chart which was divided into two separate

EXHIBIT 1   *Evaluation of Sales and Management Potential*

Management	Points	Sales	Points
1. Judgment	25–35	1. Aggressiveness	20–25
2. Maturity	15–25	2. Enthusiasm	25–30
3. Aggressiveness	15–20	3. Adaptability	25–35
4. Enthusiasm	20–30	4. Planning (sales calls)	30–40
5. Adaptability	20–30	5. Initiative	20–25
6. Planning		6. Dependability	25–30
(organizing ability)	25–25	7. Promptness	15–18
7. Creativity	15–25		160–203
8. Dependability	10–15	1. Making quota	48–62
9. Report writing	10–15	2. Reports (clean,	
10. Motivating	10–15	concise, and factual)	8–12
11. Controlling	10–15	3. Servicing accounts	14–18
	170–250	4. New account generation	15–25
		5. Calls/day	6–10
		6. Appearance	12–14
		7. Care of company property	10–12
			113–153
Rating scale:	70	80 90	100
	poor	fair good	excellent

areas of recognition: one for people with management potential and one for those with sales potential. The chart had proven useful to him, and he offered it to Clark to use in making his evaluation (see Exhibit 1). Clark, of course, wasn't sure if he could separate the requirements for selling and management, nor was he even sure if an "attribute" approach was reasonable.

Recommending Salary Increases

After Clark had finished making his evaluations, he reviewed the salary levels of the salespeople in his territory. He noticed that one man, Larry Gilbert, had been recommended for an increase six weeks earlier by the former manager. Since Clark had just completed his own evaluation of this man, he was interested in seeing how Gilbert had been rated over the years. Gilbert's file showed that he had been with Anderson as a salesman for 12 years but had only progressed to the middle of the current salary range. He had not been granted a salary increase for 22 months, although most salespeople received increases every 10 to 12 months. The recommendation written by the former district manager stated, "Larry is continually trying to improve, and some progress is noted every so often. He hasn't had an increase for over a year and a half and should be considered for one soon."

In his own evaluation Clark had ranked Gilbert as one of his poorest salespersons—one who had little or no probability of improving and who should possibly be terminated. Clark realized that he had only worked with Larry for a short time and felt he should take a second look at him. However, he felt strongly about his own evaluation in this case and was absolutely against recommending a raise. Although the increase had already been submitted by the former district manager, Clark did not know whether it had been reviewed by the regional manager yet. Clark thought to himself how difficult it would be to give someone an increase and then fire him a month later.

Awarding Salary Increases

The regional manager approved the salary increases that Clark had recommended for his sales staff. Awarding an increase was generally considered fairly routine, but Clark could remember well how, as a young salesman, he had reacted to the way his supervisors had awarded increases to him. Once, his local manager called him long distance and said, "Next week your pay check will be $10 larger. . . ." Before Clark had a chance to say a word his manager had hung up. On another occasion with a different manager, both he and his wife were taken out to dinner by the district manager on the day he had received his raise.

Clark felt that the way in which increases were awarded could make a significant difference in a person's future performance. Moreover, he believed that one should be told why he/she was receiving the raise. However, he was undecided about two things: whether it was a good idea to involve the family in company business by including the spouse, and whether one would be motivated to a greater degree if salary increases were constantly promised.

Compensation Policy

Anderson's policy was to give fairly quick salary increases (perhaps six to nine months apart) up to the median of the salary range. It was more difficult to earn a salary increase over the median; generally, a person did not receive a raise for 10 months or more, depending on his/her efficiency and potential for promotion.

In April, Clark Philbin recommended a salary increase for one of his salespeople, Al Peters. Peters was making $325 per week and had not had a raise in three years. He had been a salesman with the company for about 14 years. Clark wrote the following as a basis for the salary increase: "Peters has demonstrated consistent up-grading of accounts and increased sales to key accounts and has shown marked improvement in establishing better relations with his customers." Philbin indicated that, after working closely with Peters, he was convinced an increase was warranted. He believed that salary administration was a serious responsibility and that increases should be recommended only when merited by performance.

The regional manager, Dan Pace, thought that Peters was about average.

Due to the lapse of time since the last salary increase, however, he approved the recommendation and passed it along to the sales vice president for final approval.

The vice president knew that Al Peters had not had an increase for over 18 months, but from past experience he had also considered Peters an average performer. He believed, however, that Clark Philbin was very conscientious about awarding salary increases solely on a merit basis rather than time elapsed since the last raise.

The incident brought a matter to the vice president's mind which he had been pondering for some time. He wondered whether senior salespeople should be given automatic salary increases (other than cost of living increases) or whether (in line with company policy) increases should be awarded strictly on a merit basis. In the case of Philbin's recommendation on behalf of Al Peters, the vice president was not convinced that Peters deserved a merit increase. Possibly this was a case in which a salesperson should be considered for an automatic annual increase. In either event, Ken was reluctant to turn down the application since it had been passed by the regional manager and district manager, both of whom he considered very capable. Moreover, these people knew Peters and his capabilities far better than he did because of their closer association with him.

Bonus Incentive Plan

Clark Philbin was concerned about unrest exhibited by his sales force. He attributed it to the company's newly instituted bonus incentive plan.

Formerly, Anderson had an individual incentive plan based on each man or woman's sales volume over and above his or her quota. Each person was directly responsible for attaining the individual quota assigned. The percentage by which a salesperson surpassed that quota was applied to his or her base salary for that period, as a bonus.

The new bonus incentive plan was based on the performance of the group rather than the individual. Each district was a team which consisted of the district manager and the salespeople. At the end of a quarter, the district bonus was computed on the basis of combined sales over quotas, and the quota was set so that it would be almost impossible to meet the total requirements unless each team member contributed his/her share. Consequently, if one territory fell short due to a weak salesperson, the whole district could lose its chance for a bonus. It was expected that any staff member would be willing to help out those who were falling behind.

Each individual's share under the new system was based on a "stated percentage" of his/her salary for the preceding quarter (see Exhibit 2). This percentage was determined by the amount by which the district exceeded its budget.

Philbin questioned whether the new plan was better or worse than the old one, and in order to evaluate the two plans he wondered how he could get

EXHIBIT 2   *Computation Table—Quarterly Incentive*

Quarterly Invoiced Sales versus Total Budget	Percent Gross Salary* at End of Quarter
I. 100.0 to 105	7%
II. 106 to 110	8
III. 110 to 115	9
IV. 115 to beyond	10

*Weekly salary rate × 13.

honest opinions from the sales force. Clark decided that a good way to find out what was troubling everyone was to have a post-sales meeting "gripe" session. He had tried this once before, and it had yielded favorable results. The salespeople were asked to participate by writing down any complaints they might have and by bringing them to the "gripe" session. At a previous session Clark had assured them that anything they said would be confidential, and that the point of the meeting was to improve understanding between management and the sales force. Because confidences had been maintained in the past, Clark hoped that the meeting might be beneficial.

At the meeting the following opinions were expressed:

Salesperson 1:   *Clark, this new incentive plan has killed individual effort. Not only is the weakest person boosted up in each territory, but also one weak territory is helped by stronger or harder working ones. . . .*

Salesperson 2:   *Yes, and that brings up something else. I don't mean to offend you (turning to a new man), but under this system you guys get the same share of the bonus as we old timers do. I know that we all had to start from scratch, and I'm not objecting to that. But, and I think everyone will agree, a new man just isn't worth as much to the company as an older man in terms of actual sales volume. Under the old system a guy really got paid for what he was worth. Any extra effort was rewarded by extra pay.*

Salesperson 3:   *You bet. This place is becoming a loafer's paradise!*

Salesperson 4:   *You guys have a point on this "individual effort business," but I still think the team effort idea is good. Everyone works together for the benefit of all. We're all interested in how we do as a district.*

Salesperson 2:   *Sure, that's fine if everyone works together, but how do we know that some guy can't improve his performance?*

Salesperson 4:   *Well, I'm sure we all want the extra cash flow, as much as we did before under the old system, so I think everyone will work just as hard if not harder.*

(Clark Philbin began to wonder if the new system really was better than the old one. Just as the meeting was breaking up one of the men approached Clark.)

Salesperson 5:   *Clark, one of our men puts in about a four-day week but still makes quota. There's something strange about this system if things like that can go on.*

Philbin: *Well, I think we all know that these things can happen in any territory—even in this one—but they happened under the old incentive plan, too. Suppose we have two salesmen. One is a plugger, putting in a 10- to 12-hour day and barely making quota each time. The other is a whiz-kid. Works six to seven hours a day, four days a week, but is way over quota each time. Now, under these conditions, is the second person getting away with anything if the quotas are fairly set? Under the new system that person is really helping the other.*

Salesperson 5:   *Well, I just can't see a guy or gal working only four days a week when everyone else is working five. Somehow, it's different when someone overworks—sort of makes a healthy competitive environment.*

Philbin: *Yes, but don't you resent someone who is always putting in extra time trying to get ahead, especially if he or she is barely making quota?*

Salesperson 5:   *No, as I said, I think it makes a healthier working environment.*

Compensating Managers

The sales training department of Anderson was reviewing its current hiring policy for college graduates and M.B.A.s. In the past few years the company had been hiring more and more well-educated people. There was, however, a problem which involved paying these people the salary required to attract them to Anderson. For example, those hired for the product management group were first sent to the field as sales trainees, and in order to get top caliber people, it was necessary to pay them more than the salesperson scale.

One M.B.A., for example, was hired recently by the product and research department and was assigned to the field as a salesperson for five months as the first phase of his training. His initial salary was well above the maximum that could be earned by a salesperson. Thus, he had been told by the head office not to discuss his salary with anyone, not even his district manager. All went well for about three weeks until, through the grapevine, the others found out that the new hiree was earning more than any of them.

The sales training department was stumped as far as future hiring and salary ranges were concerned. They realized that they had to continue to pay high salaries in order to get top caliber people, but on the other hand, it was risky to continue to antagonize the sales force.

Internal Corporate Politics

The sales vice president was due to visit Clark Philbin after spending a few days with Dan Pace at the regional office. Clark was uneasy about the forthcoming visit because he had heard a number of unpleasant rumors about the vice president from his regional manager. Clark thought highly of Dan, but he felt that it had been poor practice on Dan's part to have passed the rumors down. Clark believed that no matter how well-deserved, remarks such as these should not be transmitted to lower levels in the organization.

The vice president's visit went smoothly except for two incidents. The first concerned Andy Smith, a salesperson whom Clark considered an "average to good" performer. The salesman had recently grown a long handlebar mustache and the vice president commented to Philbin. "Clark, why don't you tell Andy to shave off that damn thing, or at least bring it back to normal size. It's so out of keeping with what our customers are used to."

The second incident concerned a saleswoman, Lee Beckwith. The vice president had previously met Lee at a sales meeting shortly after Lee was hired and had been very impressed with her after this brief contact. Now, after spending a few more hours with Lee, he commented to Clark, "That certainly is an outstanding girl; if she receives the proper training, she'll make a good manager."

After the vice president had left, Clark pondered what had been said. In recalling the mustache situation he remembered that his regional manager had expressed a concern about the vice president interfering in the evaluation of his staff. The promotion record showed that, over the years, many of the vice president's favorites had followed him up the corporate ladder.

With these points in mind, Clark wondered what he should do about Andy and Lee. In the recent evaluations he had recommended Andy both for a salary increase and for a possible promotion. On the other hand, he had characterized Lee as an opportunist with not too much potential for sales or management. Clark felt that Pace was a "fair-shooter" and would back him up, but the fact that the vice president had the final say in approving all recommendations could negate Dan's influence.

Characteristics of a Good Sales Manager

After attending a management training seminar at a nearby university, Dan Pace returned to his office with several ideas in mind for improving the performance of his districts. First, he decided to examine the characteristics of his managers in order to determine what qualities were important.

He summarized his conclusions as follows:

Clark Philbin: Clark is very systematic in his approach to evaluating his staff. He carefully weighs all the important factors which contribute to a person's potential and actual sales ability. So far Clark's recommendations for promotions and increases have been granted exactly as requested. He is neither consistently high nor low in his praise pattern: rather he awards increases as he feels they are due. If someone is worth a $40/week raise, then it is requested; similarly for a $10/week raise. Clark keeps running files on all of his people, so there are few, if any, last minute or "impulse" decisions on a man or woman's value. Clark once commented, "After a framework is outlined, a manager should be permitted to operate autonomously within it." He motivates his staff largely through recognition of jobs well done. On a person's anniversary with the company or on a birthday, he always sends out a card. Also, if someone makes a single outstanding contribution, such as getting a large new account, then in addition to counting it toward a raise or promotion, Clark may take that person out to dinner, give a "pat on the back," or send a letter of commendation.

Jack Steelman: It seems that Jack is always sending in a raise request for one of his staff. He seldom changes the amount; it is always a minimum amount. A number of Jack's raise requests have been turned down because they seem like automatic increases. In many cases the people haven't actually earned them. Jack, however, is a very aggressive guy and an excellent salesman, as well as a good manager. He was once asked whether there was much variance in the quality of his sales force and he commented: "No, they are all great guys and gals who work hard and deserve to be paid well." Jack is sometimes referred to as the "Little King." He tries to maintain self-respect and to motivate salespeople by always doing things for them, such as recommending raises. On the other hand, he usually keeps all but the most general information quite private. This makes his position appear to have a little more prestige.

Ozzie Davidson: Ozzie is sort of impulsive in the way he awards increases and promotions. On several occasions good salespeople have gone without raises for over a year, even though their quality evaluation forms showed excellent progress. In each case, however, when Ozzie worked with someone just before an evaluation, something happened which, in Ozzie's eyes, ruined the person's chances for an increase. He apparently is fairly well-liked by his staff and is always promising one of them a raise or promotion. This was often done before the increase was sent in for approval. In several instances this method of motivation caused difficulties when raises were not sanctioned by senior supervisors.

Jerry Hatch: Jerry does not believe in using pats on the back for jobs well done or any other type of nonfinancial recognition. He thinks that the dollar reward is sufficient, and if his people produce, they get paid for it; if they don't, they get fired. Jerry has always worked hard himself and is very fond of a dollar. He also feels that actual performance is the best measure of whether or not a person deserves an increase or promotion.

In reviewing his findings, Dan Pace found it difficult to decide which techniques or characteristics peculiar to each manager contributed the most to success in the job. He was not thinking solely in terms of an Anderson manager but more of a sales manager in general.

This book suggests there are three essential sales management activities:

1. The formulation of a strategic sales program.
2. The implementation of the sales program.
3. The evaluation and control of sales force performance.

The formulation of the strategic sales program involves the organization and planning of the company's overall personal selling efforts and the integration of these efforts with other elements of the firm's marketing strategy. It includes such considerations as how the sales force should be organized, the appropriate number and design of sales territories, and the proper types and levels of quotas.

Implementation involves selecting appropriate sales personnel and designing and setting in motion policies and procedures that will direct their efforts toward the desired objectives. It includes all the issues surrounding the selection, training, and motivation of the individual representatives.

All these activities are undertaken to produce the results targeted in the sales and marketing plans, which in turn must be consistent with overall corporate goals. In the evaluation and control phase, the sales manager needs to find out what happened and why it happened and then decide what to do about it.

A serious discrepancy between goals and results in any area might suggest a revision of goals, a change in plans, or some alteration of how the plans are implemented. The corrective action called for depends on what the analysis highlights as the fundamental problem or problems. There may have been a serious erosion in economic conditions since the marketing and sales plans were formulated. In this case, all that may be warranted is a lowering of the sales goals to more realistic levels. Alternatively, the goals may be diagnosed as still realistic and the fault traced to the plans and their implementation. Then these need to be changed.

With respect to the job of the sales manager, discrepancies between goals and results might call for restructuring sales territories, reassigning salespeople to territories, or respecifying the frequency with which representatives are to call on different types of accounts. These actions would deserve consideration if there seemed to be some general problems in most of or the entire personal selling effort.

Alternatively, the problems might be traced to an individual representative or perhaps several salespeople. The problem would then be to determine why they did not do as well as they should. Again, there could be a number of reasons. Perhaps the quota assigned them was unrealistic, in that it did not accurately reflect the economic and competitive conditions in their territory.

Or the analysis might reveal the individual sales rep is personally at fault. The task is then to determine why. Does the rep truly possess the necessary aptitude for a personal selling career with the company? Has the person acquired all the necessary skills for success through training? Does the person find the rewards available within the company attractive? Do they motivate the rep? The model used to understand the behavior of individual salespeople—which views a sales representative's performance as a function of the individual's (1) role perceptions, (2) aptitude, (3) skill level, (4) motivation level, and (5) personal, organizational, and environmental variables—can be used to highlight the questions one might pose to get at the root cause of why a particular salesperson's performance was poor. It can also be used to formulate corrective action.

The challenge facing sales managers is how to put it all together. The sales manager who is able to develop good plans, effectively implement them, and determine what corrective action to take when the results are not tracking correctly is a highly valued person in the business world. Thus, not only can sales management be an interesting and intellectually rewarding activity, but it can also be a very financially rewarding one as well.

COMPREHENSIVE CASES

Case 4-1
HIGHLIGHTS FOR CHILDREN, INC.*

Elmer C. Meider, president of Highlights for Children, Inc., had just completed a lengthy meeting involving several of his managers. Each manager had been assigned the task of recommending ways Highlights for Children could more effectively utilize the three marketing channels currently being used. Meider thought the company had not been taking full advantage of the capabilities of direct mail, telemarketing, and direct sales in terms of prospecting, lead distribution, current and new product sales, and overall profitability. Moreover, Meider contends that Highlights for Children needs to capitalize on the continuity of direct mail, the rapid follow-up possible via telemarketing, and the value of face-to-face customer contact available through direct sales.

Although Meider knew he had the authority to eliminate the direct sales force operation, he believed this would not be in the best interests of Highlights. Rumors were abundant about possible legal restrictions on telemarketing programs. Several states were considering legislation that would greatly restrict when telephone calls could be made for sales purposes. One such law would limit telephone calls to specified times and no later than 7 P.M. Meider knew such a limit would sharply curtail Highlights's successful telemarketing program. Moreover, the threat of increases in postal rates caused Meider concern about the future of Highlights's successful direct mail program. These possible environmental changes provided support for Meider's position to keep the direct sales arm intact. Company experience revealed that the direct sales force was in a better position to learn about and resolve customer problems and concerns than either telemarketing or direct mail.

Managers from each of the three distribution methods had been asked to prepare recommendations concerning changes they would implement to improve the overall sales and profitability picture. Meider's task would be to review the various recommendations and prepare a final report to present to Garry C. Myers III, chief executive officer, who was present at the meeting. Also present at the meeting were Richard H. Bell, chairman of the board; Lynn Wearsch, national rep sales service manager; Chuck Rout, vice president—telemarketing; and Gayle Ruwe, mail marketing manager.

Of the various recommendations, the one that provoked the most discussion was that Highlights for Children rely exclusively on telemarketing and direct mail distribution and that the company eliminate the direct sales force. Richard Bell, responding to this suggestion, pointed out that it was the direct sales force that got the company started and would keep the company going well into the future. He commented, "Highlights for Children might as well close its doors if the direct sales force is eliminated." One manager's response to Bell's defense of the direct sales force consisted of referring to the relative sales contributions from each source and how telemarketing and direct mail have grown faster. This manager noted the following:

> Telemarketing and direct sales are in a competitive position from a lead utilization standpoint. Profitability is greatly enhanced when leads are sent directly to telemarketing rather than to the direct sales force. Sure, representatives can sell a bigger package and a longer-term subscription than the other marketing arms, but the reps rely solely on company-generated leads and are not using referrals generated from customers, nor are they doing any local prospecting. The resources assigned to the direct sales force could be more profitably used by telemarketing and direct mail. Our opportunity costs, or losses, have been rising as a result of sending leads to the direct sales group. They cannot handle all of the leads, and by the time telemarketing receives them they are stale and of little value.

Bell agreed in part with these observations but was quick to note that the size of the direct sales force had dropped from an all-time high of 750 to the current level of 265 independent sales reps, which includes 65 area managers. "We need to be more effective recruiting new sales reps. Just doubling the direct sales force would produce significant benefits," noted Bell. After this interchange, Garry Myers suggested that Meider would consider all proposals and attempt to arrive at a recommendation that would combine the best of everything.

The Company

General information

Begun in 1946 as a children's publication, Highlights for Children, Inc., has become a multidivisional company, selling not only magazines but also textbooks, newsletters, criterion referenced tests, and other materials. The consumers include children, parents, and teachers.

The Mission Statement of Highlights for Children, Inc., states:

> Highlights for Children, Inc.'s mission is to create, publish, produce, or distribute on a profitable basis quality products and services uniquely designed for the educational development of children, their parents and teachers, and others with specific educational needs.

Each of the current divisions or subsidiaries operates within these guidelines.

Highlights emphasizes the fair and courteous treatment of its customers. Promotional offers are closely reviewed to ensure prospective customers are not being misled. Highlights is committed to maintaining a "pure" image in the marketplace in terms of marketing efforts as well as quality of its product.

Highlights for Children magazine is circulated to approximately 2 million subscribers. It is marketed through direct selling (via independent contractors), telephone marketing, and direct mail. Parents, teachers, doctors, and gift donors are targeted by the different marketing arms. In addition, Highlights sells various educational products that have been promoted through the introductory-offer school programs.

History

Dr. Garry C. Myers, Jr., and Caroline C. Myers founded Highlights for Children, Inc., in 1946 in Honesdale, Pennsylvania. Based on the belief that learning must begin early to fully develop a child's learning ability, the magazine was geared to challenge children's creative thinking and abilities. Today, the editorial offices are still in Honesdale, although the corporate headquarters are in Columbus, Ohio, and the magazine is printed in Nashville, Tennessee.

At the time Highlights for Children, Inc., was founded, magazines were sold almost exclusively by door-to-door salesmen. *Highlights for Children* followed suit. Today, Highlights continues to use direct selling in conjunction with telephone marketing and direct mail to market the magazine.

In 1955, Myers hit on the idea of putting *Highlights for Children* in doctors' offices with lead cards. At about the same time, his wife came up with the introductory-offer program to be marketed to parents through the schools. This was the beginning of marketing *Highlights for Children* by mail. Both programs met with immediate and resounding success.

Magazine Content

Highlights for Children targets and services a diverse age group from 2 to 12. The material in the magazine ranges from easy to advanced. This conforms to the philosophy of challenging children: Rather than having material graded and directed to a particular age child, children are allowed to work at their own rate and are "encouraged" to achieve and understand more.

The tag line of *Highlights for Children* is "Fun with a Purpose" (see Exhibit 1). The *purpose* of the magazine is to educate and instruct, not merely entertain. The magazine is positioned as supplemental material to be used in the home, rather than in the classroom.

Highlights for Children likes to maintain the image of an educational magazine. No cut-outs or mark-ups are included in the magazine content, enhancing the idea of *lasting* quality. There is no paid advertising in *Highlights for Children,* which is in line with the educational image. Throughout the years, advertising has been considered at various times. Management continues to believe the magazine is more salable as an educational supplement without advertising. Highlights also believes children are already subjected to more than enough advertising pressure through other sources, much of which is resented by parents and teachers. Recently, President Elmer Meider raised the

EXHIBIT 1

advertising issue and suggested that advertising revenues might be a way to improve *Highlight's* profit performance.

The Marketing Program

Highlights for Children, Inc., uses three different marketing arms to sell its products: direct selling, telephone marketing, and mail marketing. Each type is discussed in following sections. Exhibit 2 shows the current organization.

Direct selling

The direct selling organization has two kinds of representatives: the school representatives and regular representatives. Almost all reps receive company-

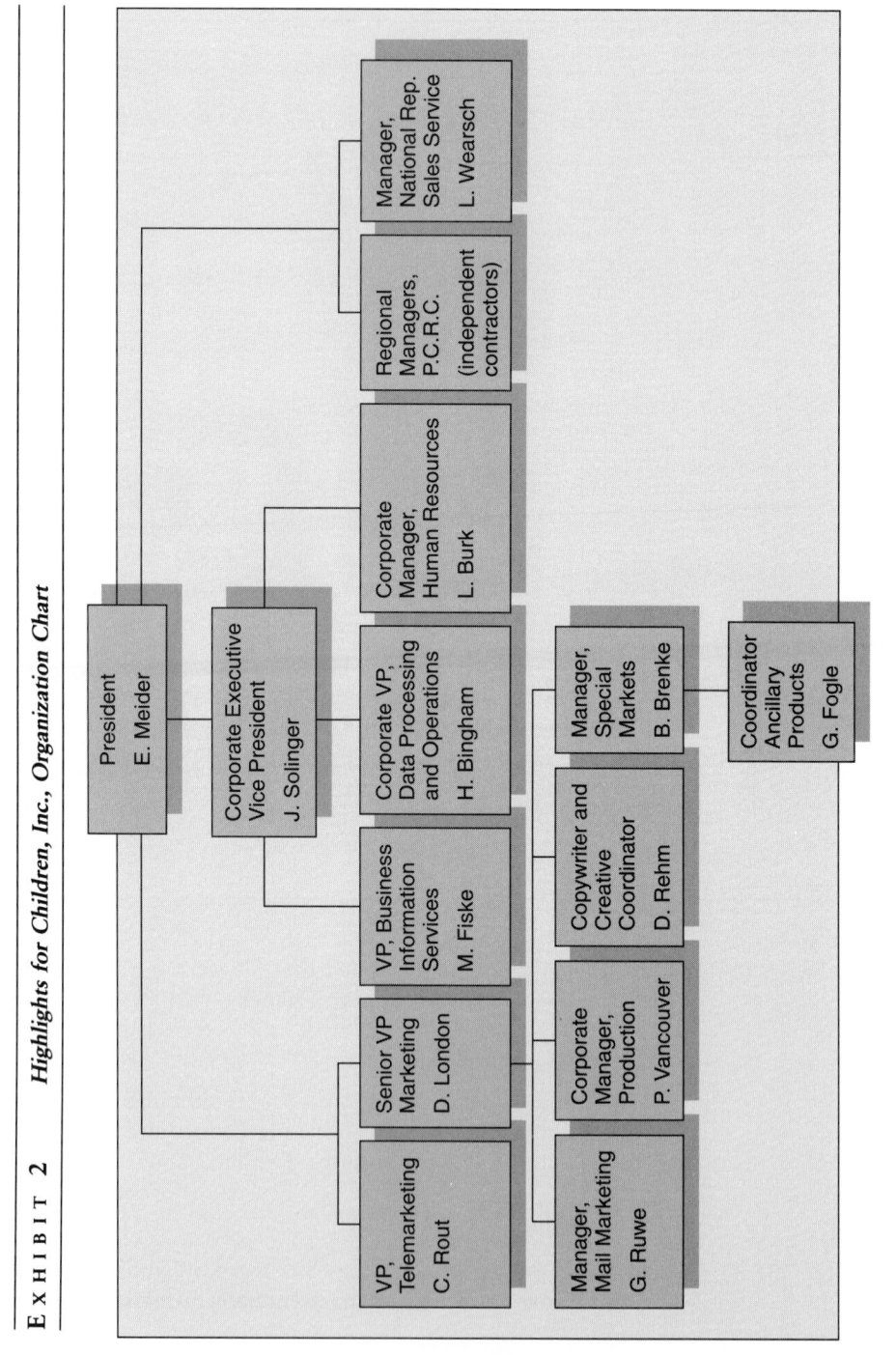

generated leads; however, school reps make most of their sales from self-generated "school drop" leads.

School representatives

Reps make their initial presentation to a school principal or superintendent. The object of the presentation is to gain permission to leave sample copies of *Highlights for Children* in grades K–4. If the school agrees to participate, a sample copy, along with a lead card, is sent home with each child. The child is instructed to return the card to the school if the parents are interested in ordering *Highlights*. Reps then pick up the lead cards from the schools. A school rep usually visits a particular school once every two to three years. Currently *Highlights for Children* has about 70 school reps.

Regular reps

Regular reps contact the following company-generated leads:

1. *Parent inquiries (PI)* and *doctor inquiries (DI)*. These people have not had a subscription but have sent in a card indicating interest.
2. *Introductory-offer renewals (IO)*. These people have been sold the six-month introductory offer through the school and are now up for renewal.
3. *Regular renewals (RR)*. These people have had a regular subscription (11 issues or more) and are up for renewal.
4. *Donor renewals (DR)*. These people have given a gift subscription (11 issues or more) and are up for renewal.

A rep has a set amount of time to work the leads (depending on the type). At the end of that time period, the lead automatically goes to either phone or mail for follow-up. Reps send back the leads marked "no contact" or "no sale" once they have been worked, so the other departments can follow up quickly.

Reps call on parents at home. The increasing number of women working and higher gasoline prices have made the rep's job more difficult over the years. When reps do find someone at home, their presentation hits mainly on what *Highlights for Children* is, how to use it, and its educational value. The rep can sell, on average, a 2.8-year term subscription.

There is a management structure in the regular rep program. Not all reps are under a manager; none reports directly to the home office. Managers receive an override on all area sales (personal and representative's sales).

The current rep structure is composed of about 265 active reps, of which about 65 are managers. The Columbus, Ohio, office has seven employees who are assigned to the direct-selling arm. Reps are independent contractors and as such are not paid a salary, but rather they earn a commission on their sales. Their commission is calculated by commission level times sales units. Units are determined by term sold: (five-year subscription = 1.4 units; three-year subscription = 1.0 unit; two-year subscription = 0.7 unit; and one-year subscription = 0.3 unit). *Highlights for Children* subscription rates are $49.95 for 33 issues (three years) and $79.95 for 55 issues (five years). For example, the commission for a three-year subscription is $24.97 (1.0 unit = .50; $49.95 × .50 = $24.97).

Telephone marketing

Started over 10 years ago in response to the energy crisis and the possibility of the greatly reduced mobility of the representative selling arm, telephone marketing has grown and flourished from a staff of 3 to 190 telemarketing reps, all paid on a commission basis. Telemarketing commissions are about one half (23 percent) of direct sales commissions. Commissions are not paid for sales that are canceled or never paid by the customers. These reps are located in Columbus along with 25 staff employees.

Telemarketing receives basically three types of leads: parent and doctor inquiries, introductory-offer renewals, and regular renewals. Telemarketing reps have a specified time period in which to contact and sell their leads before they go to mail marketing for follow-up. They attempt to contact leads, all types, 10 times before giving up. In one day's time, they can make up to four attempts. On average, telemarketing sells a 2.3-year term.

Mail marketing

The mail marketing department consists of three primary areas: creative, production/analysis, and list rental. Currently, 10 employees work in the mail marketing department. Major responsibilities, in addition to list rental, include acquiring *new customers* (through efforts such as the Christmas mailing and school teacher introductory-offer mailing), acquiring *new leads* (through the doctors' offices, doctor inquiries, and parent inquiries mailings), and converting leads (these leads may be new or renewals) to customers (typically after regular reps and/or phone reps have tried to convert). All activities are conducted through direct mail.

More specifically, all promotion packages (to acquire either a lead or a customer), space ads, package inserts, billing stuffers, preprinted computer forms, and so forth are created and produced through the efforts of this department. The actual mail production (merge/purge, lettershop, etc.) is also coordinated here. Finally, the results are analyzed here as well.

Christmas program

The Christmas program is a multimedia effort to acquire one-year subscriptions targeting a donor. The mail program consists of over 5 million names, mailed from mid-September to mid-October.

Additionally, the Christmas program includes card inserts in the October, November, and December issues of *Highlights for Children* magazine, statement stuffers, approximately 2 million package inserts in outside packages (*Drawing Board, Current,* etc.) and space ads (*The Wall Street Journal, New York Times, Christian Science Monitor,* etc.).

Introductory-offer program

A mailing is made to teachers who hand out "take-home" slips on which the parents can subscribe. The subscription offer to the parents is for six months of *Highlights for Children,* an "introductory offer."

Parent inquiry/doctor inquiry program

Several times a year, *Highlights for Children* purchases doctor lists for an outside mailing to produce doctor inquiries. General practitioners, pediatricians, dentists, any doctors who have children, and/or parents visiting their offices and waiting rooms are targeted. Doctors who subscribe are especially valuable because they provide a vehicle to reach parents, and the primary purpose of the doctor mailing is to eventually reach parents. Highlights for Children can send the magazine, complete with parent inquiry cards, into a doctor subscriber's office on a *monthly* basis, potentially reaching many parents.

Marketing Arm Effectiveness

Background information revealed that mail marketing produced the most revenue for seven years. In 1983, telemarketing surpassed direct marketing in terms of revenue. Exhibit 3 shows sales by marketing arm since 1976. Order-per-lead ratios by marketing arm are as follows:

Telemarketing: over 30 percent.

Direct sales: over 20 percent.

Mail: over 5 percent.

Normally, order-per-lead ratios are higher for direct sales. In fact, for a given number of leads, say 50, the direct sales group will produce more orders than the telemarketing group. However, since the reps are asking for more leads than they can possibly handle, many end up wasted and are not viable by the time they are received by telemarketing and direct mail.

The decline in the number of independent contractors has been of some concern for several years. Various programs have been initiated over the years to increase the number of reps. These programs have not met with much success as evidenced by the size of the direct sales force. Selling low-ticket items, however, limits how much a regular rep can earn. About one half of the regular reps worked part time. Earnings range from as low as $1,000 a year for some reps to as high as six figures for those reps who are managers. Managers earn overrides on the sales of those reps they have recruited into the sales organi-

EXHIBIT 3	*Highlights for Children, Inc.: Annual Gross Sales by Source, 1976–1985 ($000)*		
	Reps	**Telephone**	**Mail**
1976	11,400	860	10,700
1977	11,800	1,500	11,300
1978	12,100	2,300	12,100
1979	10,300	3,300	14,400
1980	10,400	6,400	16,300
1981	11,100	8,400	16,400
1982	12,400	9,000	21,400
1983	12,300	13,400	28,000
1984	10,800	20,400	36,000
1985	10,200	23,800	46,000

zation, a common practice in direct selling programs. Exhibit 4 is typical of the literature used by Highlights to recruit new reps.

Meider and others are aware that this is a problem that others in direct selling have faced. Giants in the direct selling industry such as Avon, Tupperware, Mary Kay, Amway, and so forth have all confronted this problem and have adopted various techniques to alleviate the negative impact that fewer reps have had on sales. A major contributing factor has been the dramatic increase in the number of working mothers.

The ability of people in direct selling to earn a reasonable level of income has been inhibited due to these trends. Many companies have adopted party plan selling programs in an attempt to increase the income-earning opportunities of the reps. Other companies have expanded their product lines to provide their direct sales reps with more commission opportunities. Exhibit 5, a fact sheet published by the Direct Selling Association, provides a summary of the 1985 direct selling industry.

Meider, on the other hand, thinks that despite these trends, the direct sales reps are not working as hard as they should and are not following prescribed and proven methods of selling. Reps are supposed to ask customers who have ordered a subscription to *Highlights for Children* for the names of others who might be interested in subscribing. Since the reps knew they could secure company-generated leads free, there was no financial incentive for them to ask for referrals. This referral process has been the mainstay method of direct selling not only for *Highlights for Children* but other direct selling companies as well. Reps are expected to engage in local prospecting, which involves locating residential areas occupied by parents of young children. These activities have been neglected, and reps today rely solely on company-generated leads.

Sales reps continually ask for more leads than they can process, resulting

EXHIBIT 4   *Sales Opportunity Fact Sheet*

Highlights for Children is an educational magazine for children ages 2 through 12. There are 11 issues published each year, and the December issue includes an annual Resource Index, which turns that year's books into a home reference library for the whole family.

Highlights is available by enrollment only. It is not sold on any newsstand, contains no advertising, and is created primarily for family use. The vast majority of its subscribers are parents. *Highlights* contains a wide range of fiction, nonfiction, thinking and reasoning features, contributions from readers, and things to make and do. The high interest articles include humor, mystery, sports, folk tales, science, history, arts, animal stories, crafts, quizzes, recipes, action rhymes, poems, and riddles.

Dr. Garry Cleveland Myers and Caroline Clark Myers founded *Highlights for Children* in 1946 as the outcome of years of professional work in child psychology, family life, education, and publishing for children. *Highlights* has grown from a first issue circulation of 22,000 to over 1,500,000 in 1982 and is the world's most honored book for children.

Noted educator, psychologist, and author, Dr. Walter B. Barbe, is the editor-in-chief of *Highlights*. Dr. Barbe's books and professional publications have made him nationally renowned in education and in demand as an international speaker. The ongoing production of each issue is coordinated by a talented staff educators, most of whom are parents. The editorial offices are located in Honesdale, Pennsylvania. The marketing arm for *Highlights for Children* is Parent and Child Resource Center, Inc., and the administrative offices are centered in Columbus, Ohio, where a dedicated representative sales staff plans and directs the business of selling and delivering *Highlights* all around the world.

Highlights for Children is sold nationally by authorized independent representatives directly to families, teachers, preschools, daycare centers, doctors' offices, and to any other person or place interested in welfare and development of children. This is a direct, person-to-person sales opportunity.

As independent contractor selling *Highlights'* products, you are free to work the hours you want and earn as much commission as possible. You are in business for yourself with exclusive leads and virtually no product competition. There is no investment required, and you are provided with the information and instruction you need to grow in skill, experience, and earnings. Your business will grow in proportion to the time, skill, and resourcefulness you use in presenting the values of *Highlights* to families, individuals, groups in your community. Your job is to visit with prospective customers, show them how *Highlights* will benefit their children, and write up the order. Statistics show that one out of three contacts will enroll.

You find that selling *Highlights'* products is enjoyable, pleasant, and profitable. The only qualifications necessary are that you enjoy meeting people and have a sincere interest in children.

There is no limit to your earnings. Every home with children aged 2 through 12 is a potential customer. You retain a liberal commission on every enrollment at the time of the sale, plus additional commissions as your sales record grows. You receive bonuses for the quantity of sales you report, bonuses for the quality of the sale you make, and bonuses for recommending others as representatives. Your sales can also make you eligible to win incentive contests with cash and/or merchandise prizes.

If you are interested in a sales career, complete the enclosed Confidential Information form and mail it today!

in lost opportunities. By the time the leads are sent back to Columbus, they are of limited value. Meider was particularly distressed to learn that several reps had established their own telemarketing operations to enhance their earnings opportunities. As a result of this practice, Highlights was paying the reps a commission that was twice the amount normally paid for telemarketing sales. A report prepared by Marilyn Fisk, vice president of business information services, added further to Meider's concern. Her report contained the following points:

- Telemarketing sales in general are for the magazine only; sales of other products are very limited.

- Telemarketing sales do not involve a down payment, hence there are more cancellations.

EXHIBIT 5   *Fact Sheet*

Summary: 1985 Direct Selling Industry Survey	
Total Retail Sales: $8,360,000	
Percent of Sales by Major Product Group:	
Personal care products	34.8%
Home/family care products	50.0%
Leisure/educational products	9.4%
Services/other	5.8%
Sales Approach (method used to generate sales reported as a percent of sales dollars):	
One-on-one contact	81.0%
Groups sales/party plan	19.0%
In the home:	77.0%
In a workplace:	11.8%
At a public event*:	2.5%
Over the phone:	6.9%
Other:	1.8%
Total Salespeople: 2,967,887	
Demographics of Salespeople:	
Independent	97.9%
Employed	2.1%
Full-time (30 + hours per week)	11.7%
Part-time	88.3%
Male	22.0%
Female	78.0%

*Such as a fair, exhibition shopping mall, theme park, etc.
Source: Direct Selling Association, Washington, D.C.

- Recruiting of additional direct sales reps has declined, especially in those situations where the reps, with the assistance or blessing of their managers, have started their own telemarketing operations.

Meider's reaction to Fisk's report further solidified his decision that changes are needed. He could understand why the managers would favor telemarketing conducted by their direct reps. Each subscription netted a $4 override for the manager regardless of how it was secured, although suggestions had been made that the $4 override was not adequate. And, the direct reps received their usual commission. He had previously attempted to persuade the former national sales manager to do something about this practice only to be told the direct reps were independent and would view this as interference. Besides, as the national sales manager indicated, "The reps view the annual Christmas mailing as a direct threat and want the program to be eliminated or at least share in the commissions on sales from their territories."

Some time later, the national sales manager left Highlights for Children, Inc., due to a reorganization that eliminated the position. Meider hired two regional sales managers who work in the field and can provide closer supervision of the direct sales reps and their managers. Meider divided the United States into two regions: east and west. This move greatly reduced the span of control problems experienced by the former national sales manager.

Meider discussed these problems with Garry Myers III and asked for his reactions. Myers noted that it should not be surprising that reps rely totally on company-generated leads. As Myers stated, "Our reps want to make the most sales, and the best avenue is to call on people who have taken the effort to complete a card and mail it in to Highlights. Reps know that these leads are more likely to produce sales than what they are likely to obtain using the referral process." Myers likened the referral process to "cold-call selling" and company-generated leads as "warm-call selling." Regardless, Highlights for Children is losing profits as a result of these practices, and Myers hoped Meider's report would be available soon.

Meider indicated his initial report would contain a series of alternative recommendations that would be used to generate discussion. For example, Meider suggested that one alternative would be to eliminate company-generated leads. Another possibility, suggested by Meider, would limit the number of company-generated leads a rep could receive each month. The number received might be a function of previous referral sales or some other factor. Meider also suggested charging the managers and/or the reps for each company-generated lead. To offset these additional charges, one likely countersuggestion would be to increase commissions paid to the reps. The Fisk report prompted another option: reducing the commission paid to reps for orders received without a down payment. This might curtail the use of telemarketing by the reps, a practice Meider wanted to stop. Finally, one manager suggested the school reps be charged a small fee for all of the sample copies that are left at schools for K–4 distribution. The manager said, "If the regular reps are wasteful of the excessive leads that they receive, then the school reps may be just as guilty when they give away too many free samples."

Eliminating the independent reps is one alternative, as is increasing the number of reps. Meider did not agree with Bell that more reps was the best solution, although he did think it was an alternative to consider. Expanding the product line to give the reps more items to sell and more commission opportunities was another alternative suggested to Meider. Currently, a three-year subscription at $49.95 produces a commission of $24.97. Meider knew no one would suggest replacing the direct sales force with a company sales force. Such a move would increase overhead expenses by at least 15 percent to cover fringe benefits costs plus staff additions needed for purposes of governmental reporting. Eliminating the direct selling arm would be a better solution than creating a company sales force.

Myers thought Meider's suggestions would produce much discussion among his management team. At this juncture, he believed Meider should narrow the alternatives to a final set of recommendations.

Case 4-2
CRESTLIGHT PAPER COMPANY*

The speed of David Farrel's management changes had surprised everyone. Age 33, David was the first of the firm's graduate M.B.A. recruits to reach the divisional general management level. He always seemed quiet and reserved, but interested in and understanding of others' viewpoints, and his promotion from assistant manager in the forms division to general manager of the education division had been a popular one. Three weeks after he took over from the retiring general manager, however, the education division had a new personnel manager, a replacement for the accountant, and two entirely new posts advertised for product managers. Now Farrel was calmly asking Andrew Smythe to take over as divisional sales manager. "Wesley McFarlane expressed his interest in early retirement," said Farrel, "and we agreed that there would be little purpose in a drawn-out handover period. He will formally retire from Crestlight at the end of March, but hand over the reins of the sales force to you as from Friday week, 24th February. Unfortunately, I shall be away at the group conference all next week, but we can go over the situation in detail as soon as I am back—let's say the afternoon of Monday, 27th February."

Farrel's approach was so unexpected and his manner so direct, that in five minutes Andrew found he had accepted the promotion, agreed to clean up his outstanding commitments at group head office within two days and to spend the next week, Wesley McFarlane's last, learning all he could from Wesley. As he walked back to his office, Andrew was elated with his new appointment; but he had a strange feeling of his future vanishing into a vacuum. Farrel had somehow stopped him from asking about where he, Farrel, wished to head the education division and had avoided any discussion at all about Wesley McFarlane's sales achievements. Had Wesley been good, bad, or indifferent? Whatever the answer, this was the sort of opportunity Andrew had been waiting for. In fact, it was beyond his immediate expectations. He had believed his image in Crestlight to be that of a future "comer" who would be given a year or two to prove himself in some assistant sales management post before he would be offered a senior divisional appointment. Farrel had certainly picked Andrew up and put him on the escalator.

---

*This case was prepared by Kenneth Simmonds of the London Business School. © Kenneth Simmonds, 1979.

Andrew Smythe

Andrew Smythe had joined Crestlight 18 months ago, on completing his Master of Business Administration degree at Manchester Business School. He had been based at the group head office as assistant to the group marketing director and given a succession of nonrepetitive problems to sort out—mainly concerned with matching supply and forecasts for Crestlight lines. Off and on over the past six months he had also participated as a member of a team sorting out a new group acquisition. But at 28 he was becoming restless in a staff position. He felt that he should get into some operating post. Operations seemed the only way to the top at Crestlight. At business school he had positioned himself as a finance specialist, but then became disillusioned with capital asset pricing theory and rather low finance grades and, anyway, marketing had seemed from outside the function of the future in Crestlight. From within, he was not so sure. He had come to regard the marketing director as little more than the group's senior salesperson, with the added concern for investigating major foreign orders and new agency possibilities.

Prior to his two years at business school, Andrew had been a sales management trainee with a branded food company. There, too, the position had been a misnomer—probably titled to attract graduates. The post had amounted to two and a half years as a field representative, calling on supermarket buyers and store managers and arranging special promotions. He supposed it was good experience, but he had not really enjoyed the job and he could see that his bachelor's degree in economics from Nottingham was not going to move him along in any way at all—he needed an M.B.A. for that.

Andrew shared a flat in London with two other business school graduates and led an active social life. He still played rugby, turning out for a team in Esher on Sundays, and for the last two years he had taken winter skiing holidays. He had no plans for marriage and the idea of settling into a Wates house in Croydon, as one of his friends had done, did not appeal to him, although he had toyed with the idea of buying a house in order to build up some equity.

Crestlight Education Division

Crestlight had grown from a small beginning in the late 1940s, based on a license from the United States to manufacture and distribute throughout the United Kingdom a coated paper used in industrial drawing offices. Over the years the firm had added a whole range of photographic and reproduction papers and supplies, together with a line of equipment for reproduction of large size drawings. Then in 1964 Crestlight had moved onto the acquisition trail and added a speciality paper merchant and a major form printing house. A divisional organization pattern had emerged almost without planning. There were now five principal divisions—equipment, supplies, paper, education, and forms—and four nonintegrated subsidiaries.

The education division had been formed in 1970 to give specialist attention

EXHIBIT 1   *Crestlight Paper Company: Education Division Market and Sales by Product (£000s)*

	Market Estimates		Sales	
	1978	1977	1978	1977
Special paper	3,600	3,050	696	560
Reproduction supplies	2,200	1,850	401	337
Reproduction equipment	1,300	1,100	363	311
Total	7,100	6,000	1,460	1,208

to the increasing demand from the education sector for special paper and reproduction supplies and equipment. Nine years later the division carried a range of 1,000 items and sold directly to local education authorities (LEAs), central supplies departments (who usually supplied several authorities), universities, polytechnics, and some large schools. Several education wholesalers were also supplied. Some of these carried a much broader line of education supplies than Crestlight—including, for example, scientific apparatus—and had very active sales forces calling on similar direct customers.

Profit margins differed from order to order. The standard gross margin for direct supply to local education authorities and individual establishments was 40 percent of total sales value, while on sales to wholesalers and central purchasing stores the average margin was only 26 percent.

Learning from Wesley McFarlane

Wesley McFarlane was friendly and relaxed when Andrew moved in with him the following Monday. Tall and well dressed, he reminded Andrew of a trained athlete as he seemed to flow around the office without effort. Although he was only 52, he seemed to have welcomed the early retirement and gave no hint at all that he felt he had been moved out. Andrew rather gauchely tried to sound him out about the internal politics behind the move by asking him whether he minded moving at this stage in his career. Wesley came back without any hesitation, "Should have done it years ago. Sales management will never get you anywhere against the engineers and accountants, and a safe middle-of-the-road salary is a living death in Britain today." He then went on to outline to Andrew his plans for a partnership with his brother in a caravan sales agency south of London. Now that his three children were safely through school and launched on their own careers, he could turn his sales skills to his own advantage without family demands requiring him to draw too much out of the business at the wrong times. Wesley was so convincing with the detail of his own plans that he spent an hour explaining to Andrew the "ins" and "outs" of the caravan business. Andrew couldn't help but feel it more fascinating than selling school supplies.

EXHIBIT 2   *Map of Sales Territories*

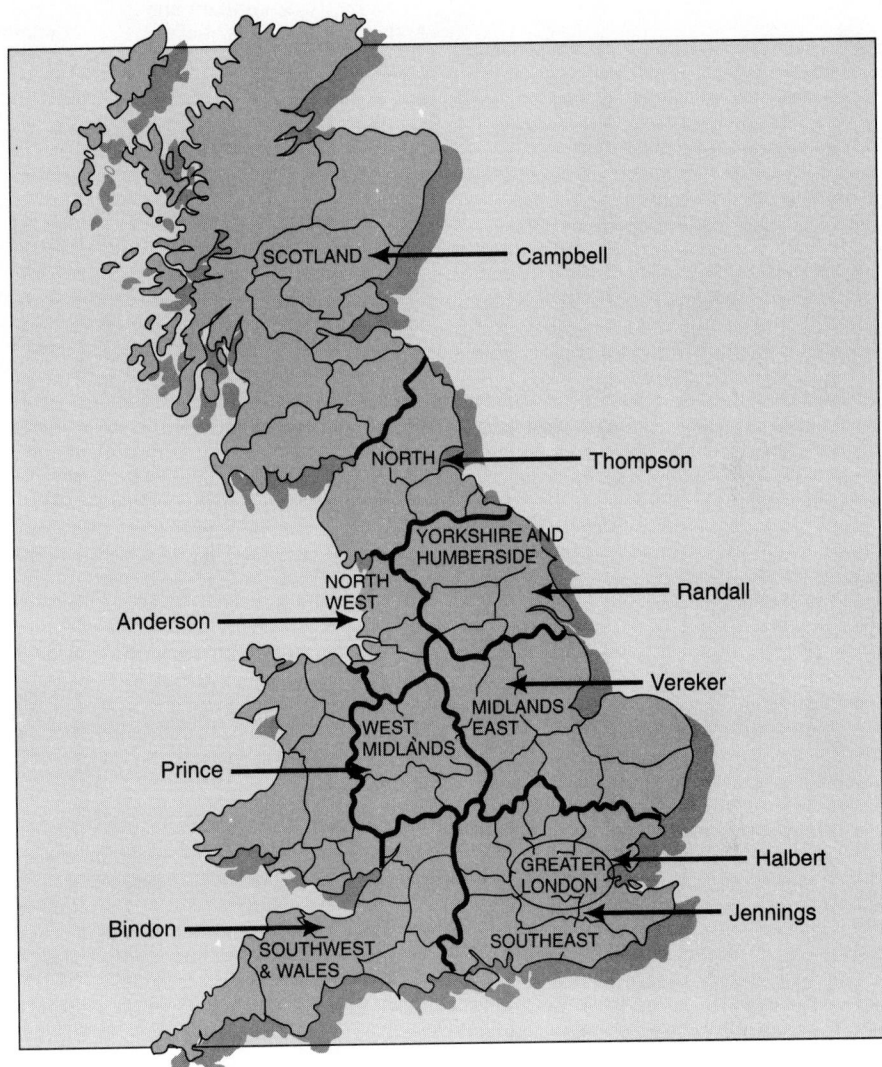

Wesley finally brought Andrew back to earth by starting on a comprehensive survey of the education division sales force. As Wesley talked, Andrew took his own brief notes and asked for photocopies of the annual sales figures and sales force and territory details that Wesley showed him. Exhibit 1 shows the divisional sales figures and Exhibits 2 to 6 the territory and sales force details and performance. Exhibit 7 sets out the notes on individual salesmen

EXHIBIT 3   *Sales Territory Details*

Territory	Salesman	Area ('000s sq km)	Secondary and Higher-Level Pupils 1978 (millions)	Estimated Potential Accounts	Home Base
1. Greater London	Halbert	1.6	1.60	570	Twickenham
2. South East	Jennings	25.6	2.27	1,060	Bromley
3. South West and Wales	Bindon	44.6	1.55	934	Cardiff
4. Midlands East	Vereker	28.2	1.18	653	Leicester
5. West Midlands	Prince	13.0	1.24	566	Solihull
6. North West	Anderson	7.3	1.65	699	Liverpool
7. Humberside	Randall	15.4	1.16	531	Bradford
8. North	Thompson	15.4	0.83	423	Newcastle
9. Scotland	Campbell	78.8	1.32	529	Glasgow
Total		229.9	12.80	5,965	

EXHIBIT 4   *Sales Force Details*

Salesman	Age	Year Joined Crestlight	Qualifications	Previous Experience	
1. Halbert, Russell	54	1965	—	Textile salesman	(10 years)
				Accounts clerk	(7 years)
2. Jennings, Frederick	42	1973	H.N.C.	Post office	
				Teleprinter salesman	(4 years)
				Equipment maintenance	(16 years)
3. Bindon, Harold V.	33	1971	B.A. (Geography)	Joined as sales trainee	
4. Vereker, John	29	1975	—	Head storeman	(3 years)
				Dispatch clerk	(3 years)
5. Prince, Alan	57	1976	—	Salesman, etc.	(35 years)
6. Anderson, Graham	37	1969	B. Tech.	Production scheduling	(5 years)
7. Randall, John	48	1951	—	Joined as clerk in original Crestlight unit. Appointed salesman 1964	
8. Thompson, Herbert	33	1975	B.Sc. (Metallurgy)	Wallpaper sales rep.	(4 years)
				Research technician	(2 years)
9. Campbell, Ian	43	1971	B.A. (English)	Teacher	(12 years)

EXHIBIT 5   *Sales Force Performance*

	1978				1977			
	Sales £('000s)	Accounts Sold	Gross Margin £('000s)	Calls Made	Sales £('000s)	Accounts Sold	Gross Margin £('000s)	Calls Made
Halbert	258	239	75	1,230	217	279	69	1,260
Jennings	239	509	79	1,168	198	539	69	1,194
Bindon	156	476	59	1,051	129	503	48	1,018
Vereker	112	353	41	1,409	98	356	36	1,290
Prince	154	413	55	1,196	123	382	43	1,185
Anderson	112	398	39	1,450	97	412	34	1,410
Randall	142	202	50	1,171	125	198	42	1,293
Thompson	123	364	47	1,220	101	323	39	1,163
Campbell	143	317	53	1,135	123	326	46	1,088
	£1,439		£498		£1,211		£426	

as Wesley pictured them—but, as Wesley said, Andrew would get a better picture by meeting them himself. He had, accordingly, arranged the next sales meeting for Wednesday, so that he could introduce the sales force to Andrew before he formally took over.

The remainder of Monday vanished rapidly as Wesley outlined his overall sales philosophy to Andrew:

Last year's sales of one and a half million were just above a 20 percent increase over 1977. Most of this represented price increases rather than volume and by my guess market penetration has gone up slightly from 19.5 percent. When I say "guess" I am basing this on my estimates of market size for the three product lines. These have been asked for each year for the annual plans and what I do is to identify all the competitors and place a sales figure against each. One or other of the salesmen is bound to have heard something about a competitor's sales levels, and I do some questioning around outside as well and check the competitors' annual reports and published estimates of educational purchasing. There are too many customers to build a figure up from their estimated annual order potential and industry figures don't coincide with our narrow line definitions.

They are all good men. There is not a bad egg among the nine and they work willingly if you don't push them too hard. Of course there are differences in sales performance, but these occur in all sales teams. Besides, you have to bear in mind the travel times some of them need to reach quite small accounts as well as the amount of work that has been done in the past to build up our accounts in a territory.

E X H I B I T 6   *Remuneration and Expenses—1978 Education Division Sales Force*

Name	Salary 31.12.78	Commissions 1978	Total Remuneration	Expenses 1978
Halbert	5,800	3,870	9,670	1,980
Jennings	4,800	3,585	8,385	2,810
Bindon	4,200	2,340	6,540	5,010
Vereker	3,800	1,680	5,480	3,820
Prince	4,900	2,310	7,210	2,600
Anderson	5,100	1,680	6,780	1,940
Randall	5,200	2,130	7,330	3,400
Thompson	4,000	1,845	5,845	3,200
Campbell	5,000	2,145	7,145	3,300
	42,800	21,585	64,385	28,060

These same factors have to be taken into account in territory sizes. I think we have them about right now. As you can see from the territory variation in numbers of secondary and higher level pupils, the range between smallest and largest is only a factor of two—which is, in fact, very small. But each salesman has plenty of potential to uncover, no matter what his territory size.

The basic salaries can't be adjusted very much. You have to keep the basic high enough to attract new reps, who might not make much commission for a while, and yet not so high that they have an easy time. Actually, I had been thinking about raising the commission rates. I think the carrot works a lot better than any pseudoanalytical target that tries to push from behind. Commission rates are only 1½ percent and if we raised them a further 1 percent instead of a salary increase this year, I think we would get five times as much back in gross margin.

Expenses are pretty much under control; I get the daily call reports and I know who they are entertaining and where they are travelling. Harold Bindon spends more time away from home than any of the others and his entertainment goes up as a result, but if life were too dreary we would have problems with that territory.

Tuesday rushed quickly past as Wesley and Andrew waded through the files for each of the product groups in the Crestlight education range. Eighty percent of the sales came from internal production in the other divisions but the remaining 20 percent included a very long list of products. In some of these cases, Wesley had been required as part of the agency agreement to provide quite detailed reports on the sales efforts and results.

The Sales Meeting

The Wednesday meeting got underway in the conference room with a great deal of joking and laughter. As Andrew came in, Wesley was called away to

EXHIBIT 7   *Wesley McFarlane's Comments on Salesmen*

Russell Halbert	Our star saleman. Very experienced. Knows central area. Reacts well to new ideas and well liked by customers. Has a smooth, competent air about him.
Frederick Jennings	Very sound man, systematic and conscientious and well dressed. Moved across from equipment side, so knows the technical aspects. Had some marital problems last year but apparently straightened them out.
Harold Bindon	Very large area but really gets round it. Presents himself well. Sales coming along nicely. Could go a long way in the company.
John Vereker	Sales not really very high. Young man with a lot to learn. Probably as a young man about town is taking time off for other things.
Alan Prince	Grandad of the team. An old sales lag. Joined only 3 years ago. Will not readily adopt new approaches, but you cannot teach an old dog new tricks. Will not be around for more than five years. No really formal education, so unlikely to make general impact on buyers in the education area. Nevertheless, doing quite acceptably.
Graham Anderson	Has a degree, but very disappointing sales results. Technically competent and extremely conscientious in covering his territory. A good worker and a rather engaging personality.
John Randall	Bright and attractive personality. Good saleman type. Always thinking up new ideas. A bit of a troublemaker. Fairly lazy and sales below what they might be. A good pep talk should move him along.
Herbert Thompson	Only been with us a few years, but keen to perform. Will take time to develop the polish of the true salesman, but the material is there. Needs guidance from sales manager about sales technique.
Ian Campbell	Very solid and unexciting. Always quiet at sales meetings. Suspect he will never make an outstanding salesman. Knows the Scottish educational buying scene very well. A chess player at competition level as a hobby.

the telephone, but the salesmen knew all about the management change and introduced themselves in ones and twos before drifting towards the table with coffee cups in hand. Wesley took the seat at the end of the long table and Andrew drew up a chair towards the other end, between John Randall and Ian Campbell.

Andrew could feel that Wesley was genuinely well liked and respected. He admired the way Wesley led the group smoothly through the agenda, starting with a discussion of the January sales figures and the effects that anticipation of a change in political party had had on educational spending. One foreign manufacturer of educational forms had been threatening to withdraw his line from Crestlight and this provoked a comparison of current buyers with those who had rejected the line. Wesley also had a spate of announcements concerning new items and replacements in the line. Under "Other Business," a long discussion boiled up around order procedure problems that had stemmed from some abstruse ruling in the Department of Education.

As the meeting was drawing to a close, John Randall stood up and on behalf of the salesmen made a short farewell speech thanking Wesley for his years of leadership. Wesley acknowledged the round of applause, thanked them warmly and then everybody headed for the Three Feathers where Wesley had booked a table for lunch.

The lunch went on rather a long time with numerous rounds of drinks and a series of wild sales stories directed at Wesley. John Randall and John Vereker were the most vociferous. Randall elaborated at great length about a female purchasing officer from a local education authority who had him take her out until 3 A.M. every night for a week before placing an order for a gross of protractors—while Vereker seemed the authority on landladies' daughters. At one point, Andrew ventured a story about clam digging that had been told with much hilarity at the Rugby Club. It went reasonably well, but was quickly lost in the stream of wisecracks and competing comments.

Finally, about 2:30 P.M., Wesley looked at his watch and the group began to break up. Andrew and Wesley were separated by the salesmen as they said their farewells. What struck Andrew as strange was that although each salesman used his own words, their message was the same: "If I can be of any help in showing you the ropes, don't hesitate to ask."

Case 4-3
WENTWORTH INDUSTRIAL CLEANING SUPPLIES*

Wentworth Industrial Cleaning Supplies (WICS), located in Lincoln, Nebraska, is experiencing a slowdown in growth; sales of all WICS products have leveled off far below the volume expected by management. Although total sales volume has increased for the industry, WICS's share of this growth has not kept pace. J. Randall Griffith, vice president of marketing, has been directed to determine what factors are stunting growth and to institute a program that will facilitate further expansion.

Company and Industry Background

WICS is a division of Wentworth International, competing in the janitorial maintenance chemical market. According to trade association estimates, the total market is roughly $2.5 billion in 1992. Exhibit 1 shows the nature of this market. Four segments comprise the institutional maintenance chemical market, which consists of approximately 2,000 manufacturers providing both national and private labels.

Total industry sales volume in dollars of janitorial supplies is approximately $1.3 billion. Exhibit 2 shows the breakdown by product type for the janitorial market. WICS addresses 75 percent of the market's product needs with a line of high quality products. The composition of WICS's product line is as follows:

Special purpose cleaners	46%
Air fresheners	9
General purpose cleaners	16
Disinfectants	15
Other	14

The janitorial maintenance chemical market is highly fragmented; no one firm, including WICS, has more than 10 percent market share. Agate and Marshfield Chemical sell directly to the end-user, while Lynx, Lexington Labs, and WICS utilize a distributor network. Most of WICS's competitors utilize only one channel of distribution; only Organic Labs and Swanson sell both ways. Most private-label products move through distributors. Sanitary supply distributors (SSDs) deliver 65 percent of end-user dollars, while direct-to-end-

---

*Joan Russler and Jeffrey Forbes, MBAs—Marketing, University of Wisconsin-Madison, assisted in the preparation of this case.

EXHIBIT 1   *Institutional Maintenance Chemical Market*

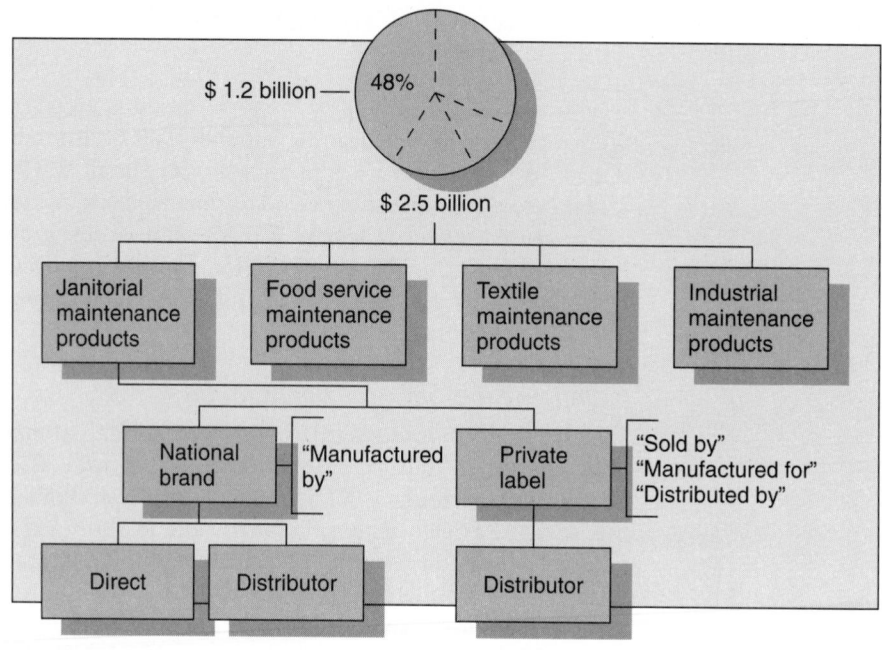

user dollar sales are 35 percent (Exhibit 3).[1] The following shows the sales breakdown by target market by type of distribution:

Distributor Sales

Retail	20%
Industrial	18
Health care	18
Schools	11
Building supply contractors	10
Restaurants	3
Hotels	3
Other	17

Direct Sales

Retail	47%
Building supply contractors	35
Health care	15
Hotels	2
Restaurants	1

[1]Includes paper supply distributors that carry janitorial supplies.

EXHIBIT 2   *WICS "Served" Portion of the Janitorial Maintenance Chemical Market*

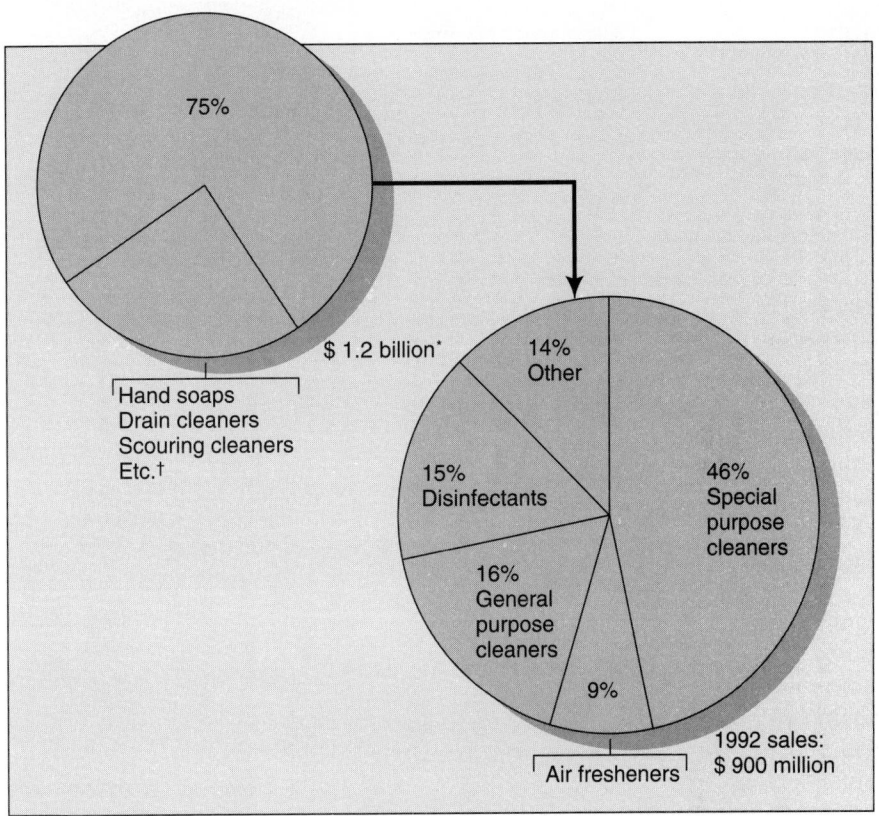

75%

$ 1.2 billion*

Hand soaps
Drain cleaners
Scouring cleaners
Etc.†

14%
Other

15%
Disinfectants

16%
General
purpose
cleaners

46%
Special
purpose
cleaners

9%

Air fresheners

1992 sales:
$ 900 million

*End-user dollars.

†Includes some general purpose cleaners and air fresheners that WICS does not manufacture.

Trade association data plus information from other sources estimate the number of SSDs to be between 5,000 and 6,000. The following shows the sales volume breakdown for the SSDs based on an average 5,500:

Size in Sales Volume

Less than $100,000	1,210
$100,000–$500,000	2,475
$500,000–$1,000,000	1,375
More than $1,000,000	440
Total	5,500

EXHIBIT 3   *Janitorial Maintenance Chemical Market (end-user dollars)*

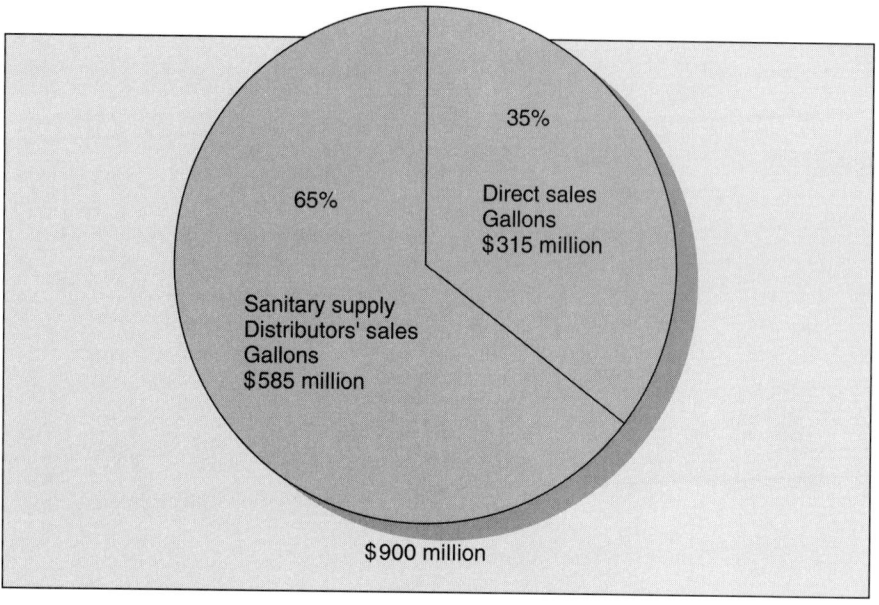

35%

Direct sales
Gallons
$315 million

65%

Sanitary supply
Distributors' sales
Gallons
$585 million

$900 million

According to a recent analysis of end-users, WICS provides cleaning supplies for approximately 20,000 customers. WICS's sales force is expected to call on these accounts as well as prospect for new business. These 20,000 end-users receive product from the SSDs who supply cleaning supplies manufactured by WICS and others as well. About one third of the average SSDs total sales is accounted for by WICS's products. An exception is the paper supply distributor, where WICS's products account for an average of 10 percent of sales.

The typical SSD carries other related items. In fact, according to a survey conducted by an independent firm, SSDs almost always carry a private-label line of cleaning supplies plus one to two additional branded products besides the WICS line. This survey revealed that 60 percent of the SSDs carry a private-label line along with WICS and one other national brand. Forty percent carry two national labels and WICS and a private label. The private label may be a regional label or the SSD's own label.

WICS places almost total reliance on selling through the SSDs, although a small amount of sales (less than 10 percent) are made direct. WICS sells its janitorial maintenance products through roughly 400 distributors, who in turn "see" 65 percent of the end-user dollar market. Thus 65 percent of sales in the total janitorial maintenance market are made through SSDs (35 percent

EXHIBIT 4   *WICS's Access to the Market*

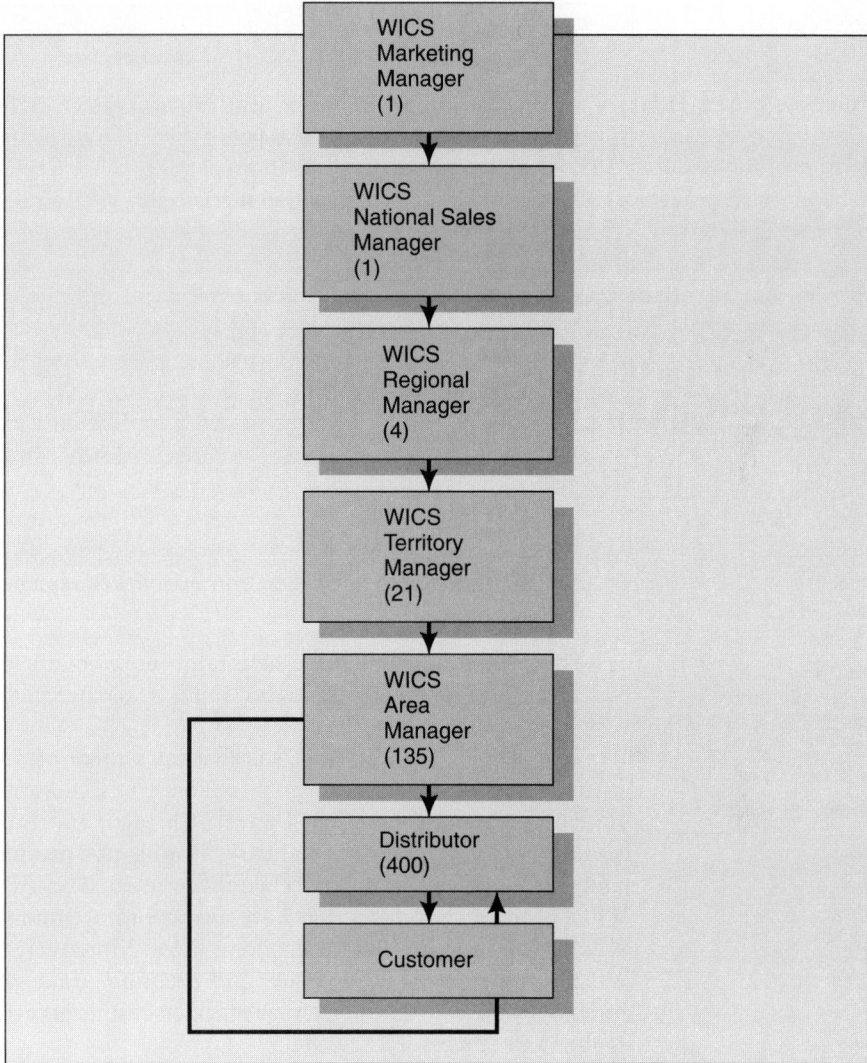

are direct sales); and the 400 SSDs used by WICS provided 65 percent coverage. The market seen by each distributor, referred to as his or her *window* on the market, is a function of the following:

Product lines carried (paper versus chemical).

Customer base (type and size).

EXHIBIT 5   *End-User Product Coverage*

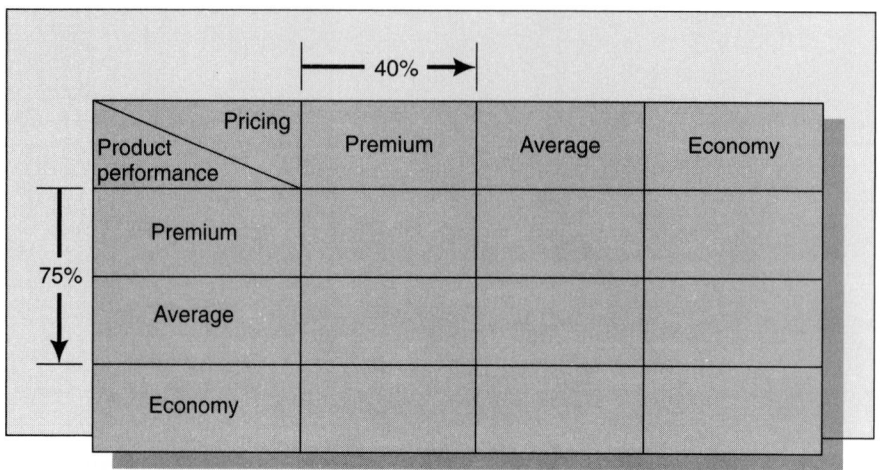

Nature of business (specialization by market versus specialization by sales function).

The combination of these factors produces end-user market coverage of 42 percent (65 percent distributor sales × 65 percent coverage). WICS has very limited direct sales.

To reach its market, WICS uses a sales force of 135 area managers, 21 territory managers, and 4 regional managers (Exhibit 4). Regional managers are located in San Francisco, Denver, Chicago, and Boston. Although WICS is viewed as a giant in the industry, it does not produce a complete line of janitorial chemicals. Janitorial chemicals are rated based on their performance. WICS produces products that have average to premium performance ratings; WICS has no products in the economy class. Moreover, due to various factors, WICS's coverage in the average and premium classes is not complete. The emphasis on premium and average products results in providing only 75 percent of the market's product needs.

To provide high distributor margins and extensive sales support, WICS charges premium prices. Recent estimates reveal that only 40 percent of the served market is willing to pay these premium prices. The impact of WICS's limited product line coupled with its premium prices is evident in Exhibit 5.

An overall description of WICS's marketing program shows that it has focused on market development. Distributors receive high margins (30 to 40 percent) and sales costs are high (10 to 15 percent) due to emphasis on selling technical benefits, demonstrations, and cold calls. Area managers call on prospective end-users to develop the market for the SSD. By comparison, WICS's

E X H I B I T   6   *Allocation of Area Manager Duties**

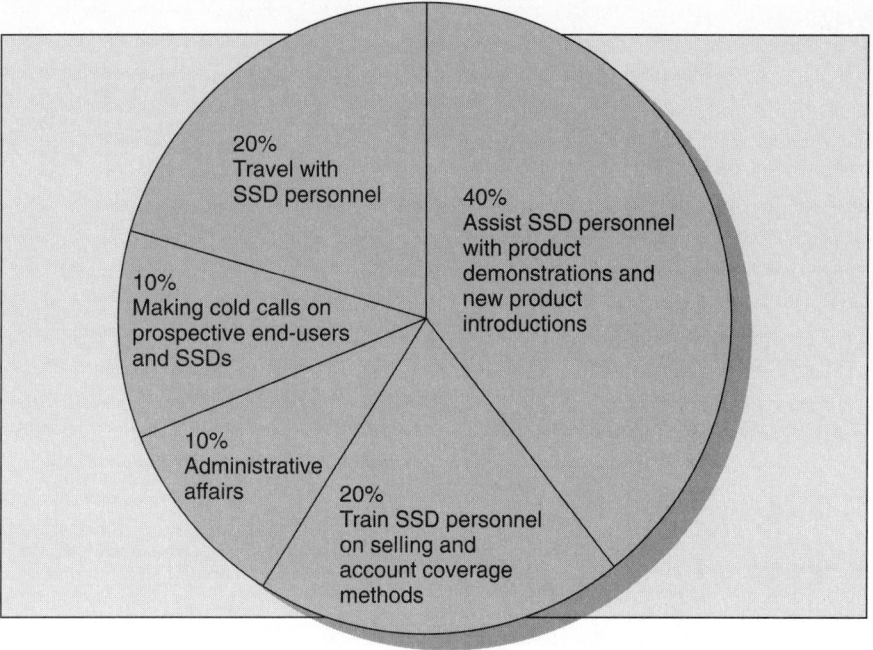

*Based on an analysis of call reports.

competitors offer SSDs low margins (15 to 20 percent) and incur low sales costs (5 to 8 percent).

Griffith recently received a memo from Steve Shenken, WICS's national sales manager, reporting on a study of the effectiveness of SSDs. Territory managers evaluated each SSD in their respective regions on a basis of reach (advertising and promotional programs) and frequency of sales calls. The composite report indicated distributors as a whole were doing an excellent job servicing present accounts. In other words, 400 SSDs provide WICS with a sizable share of the market.

Area managers (AMs) represent WICS in distributor relations. The AMs' "prime focus is to sell and service existing key end-user accounts and selected new target accounts in their assigned territories." According to a recent study, maintenance of current accounts comprises approximately 80 percent of the AMs' time (Exhibit 6). In addition to handling old accounts, the AM makes cold calls on prospective distributors as directed by the territory manager. However, the number of cold calls made monthly has decreased substantially in the past year since the major SSDs now carry WICS products. A study of

E X H I B I T 7   *Wentworth Industrial Cleaning Supplies Position Description*

Date: January 1, 1983	Position:	Area Manager, Maint. Prods.
Approved by: (1) _____	Incumbent:	135 Positions Nationally
(2) _____		
(3) _____	Division:	Janitorial Maintenance Products Division
		Reports to: Territory Manager, Janitorial Maintenance Products Division

POSITION PURPOSE:

To sell and service user accounts and authorized distributors in an assigned territory to assure that territory sales objectives are attained or exceeded.

DIMENSIONS:

Annual sales:	$300 M (average)
Number of distributors:	4 (average)
Number of distributor salesmen:	12 (average)
Annual expense budget:	$4.2 M (average)
Company assets controlled or affected:	$8 M (average)

NATURE AND SCOPE

This position reports to a territory manager, janitorial maintenance products. Each district is subdivided into sales territories that are either assigned to an individual member of the district or to a team effort, based on market and/or manpower requirements.

The janitorial maintenance products division is responsible for developing and marketing a broad line of chemical products for building maintenance purposes.

The incumbent's prime focus is to sell and service existing key user accounts and selected new target accounts in his assigned territory. He multiples his personal sales results by spending a major portion of his time working with distributor sales personnel, selling WICS maintenance products and systems to key accounts such as commercial, industrial, institutional, governmental accounts, and contract cleaners. When working alone, he sells key user accounts through an authorized distributor as specified by the user customer.

The incumbent plans, schedules, and manages his selling time for maximum sales productivity. He interviews decision makers and/or people who influence the buying decision. He identifies and evaluates customer needs through careful observation, listening and questioning techniques to assure proper recommendations. He plans sales strategy to include long-term/quick-sell objectives and develops personalized user presentations to meet individual sales situations, utilizing product literature, manuals, spot demonstrations, and sales aids to reinforce presentations. This position sells systems of maintenance to major volume user accounts through the use of surveys and proposals, test programs, and other advanced sales techniques. He develops effective closing techniques for maximum sales effectiveness. This position trains custodial personnel in product usage techniques through the use of product demonstrations and/or audiovisual training to assure customer satisfaction. He follows up promptly on customer leads and inquiries. He services customer and distributor complaints or problems and provides technical support as required. On a predetermined frequency basis, he surveys and sells assigned local accounts currently being sold on national contract. He represents the division in local custodial clinics and trade shows as required. He maintains an adequate current supply of literature, forms, and samples and maintains assigned equipment and sales tools in a business-like condition.

The incumbent is responsible for training, developing, and motivating distributor sales personnel. This is accomplished by frequent on-the-job training in areas of product knowledge, selling skills, and demonstration techniques. He sells distributor management and assists distributors to maintain an adequate and balanced inventory of the full product line. He introduces marketing plans and sells new products and sales promotions to distributor management. He participates in distributor sales meetings to launch new products or sales promotions, or for training and motivational purposes. He keeps abreast of pertinent competitive activities, product performance, new maintenance techniques, and other problems and opportunities in the territory. Periodically, he communicates Wentworth growth objectives versus distributor progress to distributor management (i.e., sales coverage, volume and product sales, etc.) He assists the distributor to maintain a current and adequate supply of product literature, price lists, and sales aids.

The incumbent prepares daily sales reports, weekly reports, travel schedules, weekly expense reports, and the like, and maintains territory and customer records. He maintains close communication with his immediate supervisor concerning products, sales, distributor and shipping problems.

He controls travel and business expenses with economy and sound judgment. He handles and maintains assigned company equipment and territory records in a business-like manner.

Major challenges to this position include maintaining established major users, selling prospective new target accounts, and strengthening distribution and sales coverage to attain or exceed sales objectives.

The incumbent operates within divisional policies, procedures, and objectives. He consults with his immediate supervisor for recommendations and/or approval concerning distributor additions or terminations, exceptions to approved selling procedures, and selling the headquarters level of national or regional accounts.

Internally, he consults with the editing office concerning distributor shipments, credit, and so forth. Externally, he works closely with distributor personnel to increase sales and sales coverage and with user accounts to sell new or additional products.

The effectiveness of this position is measured by the ability of the incumbent to attain or exceed territory sales objectives.

This position requires an incumbent with an in-depth and professional knowledge of user account selling techniques, product line, and janitorial maintenance products distributors, and a minimum of supervision.

PRINCIPAL ACCOUNTABILITES

1. Sell and service key user accounts to assure attainment of territory sales objectives.
2. Sell, train, develop, and motivate assigned distributors to assure attainment of product sales, distribution, and sales coverage objectives.
3. Plan, schedule, and manage personal selling efforts to assure maximum sales productivity.
4. Plan and develop professional sales techniques to assure maximum effectiveness.
5. Train custodial personnel in the use of Wentworth products and systems to assure customer satisfaction.
6. Maintain a close awareness of territory and market activities to keep the immediate supervisor abreast of problems and opportunities.
7. Perform administrative responsibilities to conduct an efficient territory operation.
8. Control travel and selling expenses to contribute toward profitable territory operation.

AM and SSD attitudes, conducted by MGH Associates, management consultants, is presented in Appendixes A and B. Some of the sales management staff question the use of AM time; however, there has been no indication that formal changes will be made in the future regarding sales force organization and directives. The AM job description has seen few revisions, if any, during the firm's past 10 years of rapid growth (Exhibit 7).

Area managers are compensated with a straight salary, enhanced periodically by various incentive programs and performance bonuses. Incentive programs generally require that AMs attain a certain sales level by a specified date. For example, the "Christmas Program" necessitated that AMs achieve fourth-quarter quotas by November 15; on completion of this objective, the AM received a gift of his or her choice, such as a color television. To date, management considers the Zone Glory Cup the most effective incentive program. The Glory Cup is an annual competition among areas within territories, which entails meeting or exceeding sales objectives by a specified date. An all-expense-paid vacation at a plush resort for area, territory, and region managers and their "legal" spouses is the prize for the winning team. However, management at WICS believes that prestige is the prime motivator in this competition and the underlying reason for the program's success.

In a recent meeting, Terry Luther, executive vice president of the WICS division of Wentworth International, expressed his concern to Griffith about WICS's mediocre performance. Luther indicated corporate cash flow expectations from WICS were not being met and that a plan was needed from Griffith concerning how WICS could improve its overall operating performance. Griffith was quite aware that Wentworth International would make personnel changes to meet corporate objectives and that selling off divisions not able to meet corporate expectations was not unlikely. Griffith informed Luther that an action plan would be developed and be on his desk within 30 days.

Griffith's first step was to approve an earlier request made by Mike Toner, sales and distributor relations manager, for a study of sales force and distributor attitudes and opinions (Appendixes A and B). Next, the following memo was sent, discussing Griffith's assignment from Luther:

Intra-Office Memorandum

To: Steve Shenken, National Sales Manager
     Caitlin Smith, Manager—Sales Analysis
     Ryan Michaels, Manager—Sales Training
     Calla Hart, Manager—Special Sales Program
     Charlotte Webber, Senior Product Manager
     Mike Toner, Sales and Distributor Relations Manager

From: Randall Griffith, Vice President—Marketing

Subject: WICS Performance Review

   As you all know, our performance has not met corporate expectations. To rectify this situation, before we all lose our jobs, we need to meet to discuss ways for improving our market performance.
   At our next meeting, I want each of you to develop proposals for your areas of responsibility. These proposals need not be detailed at this time. For the moment, I am seeking ideas, not final solutions.

Staff reaction to Griffith's memo was one of frustration and anger. Several managers thought they had already complied with Griffith's request. One person commented, "I've told Randy numerous times what we need to do to turn the division around, and all he does is nod his head. Why go through this 'wheel-spinning' exercise again?" Another said, "The only time old J. R. listens to us is when the top brass leans on him for results." Despite staff reaction, the meeting would be held, and everybody would have suggestions for consideration.

To provide adequate time, Griffith scheduled an all-day meeting to be held at Wentworth's nearby lodge, located on Lake Woebegone. Griffith started the meeting by reviewing past performance. Next, he asked each manager to outline his or her proposal. First to speak was Steve Shenken, who indicated that Mike Toner would present a proposal combining both of their ideas.

Shenken also said he would listen to all sales force proposals and try to combine the best parts into an overall plan.

Mike Toner's proposal

Toner's proposal was rather basic. If improving market was WICS's objective, then more SSDs are needed in all territories. According to Toner:

> Each area manager serves, on the average, four SSDs. Since we can only get so much business out of a SSD, then to increase sales we need more SSDs. I suggest that each area manager add two more distributors. Of course, this move will require that we either add more area managers or that we hire and train a special group to call on new end-users and new distributors. It's difficult to attract new SSDs unless we show them a group of prospective end-users who are ready to buy WICS's products. Now, I have not made any estimates of how many more people are needed, but we do know that present AMs do not have enough time to adequately seek new business.

After Toner presented this proposal, Griffith asked if the existing AMs could not be motivated to apply more effort toward securing new business. Calla Hart thought the AMs could do more and that her proposal, if adopted, would alleviate the need for expansion of the AMs and SSDs.

Calla Hart's proposal

As expected, Hart's proposal revolved around her extensive experience with WICS's incentive programs. This satisfactory experience led Calla to suggest the following:

> If I thought that the AMs and the SSDs were working at full capacity, I would not propose more incentive programs. But they are not! We can motivate the AMs to secure more new business, and we can get more new business from our distributors. We all know that the SSDs are content to sit back and wait for the AMs to hand them new business. Well, let's make it worthwhile to the SSDs by including them in our incentive programs. For the AMs I suggest that we provide quarterly incentives much like our Christmas Program. AMs who achieve their quotas by the 15th of the second month of the quarter would receive a gift.
>
> In addition, we need to develop a program for recognizing new end-user sales. Paying bonuses for obtaining new end-user accounts would be one approach. For example, let's reward the AM from each territory who secures the highest percentage increase in new end-user accounts. At the same time, we need to reward the distributor from each territory who achieves the highest percentage increase in new end-user sales dollars. And, let's recognize these top producers each quarter and at year end as well. Our incentive programs work. We know that, so let's expand their application to new sales.
>
> Finally, on a different note, I support establishing quotas for our distributors. We have quotas for our sales force, and we enforce them. AMs who do not make quotas do not stay around very long. Why not the same pro-

cedures for some of our SSDs? We all know that there are some distributors who need to be replaced. Likewise, I have not made any cost estimates but feel that we are just searching for new ideas.

Griffith thanked Hart for her comments. He wondered whether applying more pressure to the distributors was the most suitable approach. He agreed with Hart that WICS's incentive programs seemed to be very popular but questioned if other techniques might not work. Griffith then asked Ryan Michaels for his comments.

Ryan Michaels's proposal

During his short time with WICS, Michaels has gained respect as being very thorough and analytical. He is not willing to accept as evidence such comments as, "We know it works," as a reason for doing something. Determining the value of sales training, Michaels's area of assignment, has caused him considerable concern. He knows it is useful, but how useful is the question he is trying to answer. According to Michaels, WICS needs to examine the basic selling duties of the area managers:

> Before we recruit more AMs and SSDs, or try to motivate them to obtain more new business with incentive programs, we need to examine their job activities. I favor doing a job analysis of the area manager. Some evidence that I have seen indicates that job descriptions are outmoded. AMs do not perform the activities detailed in the job descriptions. For example, most AMs spend very little time calling on prospective end-users. Accompanying distributor sales reps on daily calls does not lead to new end-user business. Possibly the AMs could better spend their time doing new account development work. But before we make any decisions concerning time allocation, we need to conduct a job analysis. And, while we are collecting data, let's ask the AMs what rewards are important to them. How do they value promotions, pay increases, recognition, and so forth? Maybe the AMs do not want more contests.

Griffith agreed that the job descriptions were out of date. He also contended this is typical and nothing to be concerned about in the short run. The idea of finding out what rewards AMs value intrigued Griffith. Next, Griffith asked Charlotte Webber for her reactions to WICS's market share problem.

Charlotte Webber's proposal

Webber's proposal was more strategic in nature than the previous suggestions. Her experience as a product manager led her to consider product-oriented solutions and to suggest the following:

> I think we can increase market share and sales volume through the expansion of current lines and the addition of a full line of economy-based products. We can expand our present premium and average lines to cover 100 percent of the product class by adding air fresheners and general purpose cleaners. In

addition we must introduce the economy-based products to counter competition.

The proposed plan would not be costly because we could use our existing distributor network. If additional SSDs are necessary, we can select those in the $500,000 to $1,000,000 sales volume range. I feel that through these extensions and an increased number of SSDs we can address 75 percent of the SSD end-user dollars.

Griffith agreed that line extensions were a viable means of achieving some corporate goals. He expressed concern over entry into the low-quality segment of the market due to WICS's present customer perceptions of the company as a high-quality producer. Griffith turned to Caitlin Smith for additional suggestions on how to increase market share.

Caitlin Smith's proposal

Smith's proposal came as no surprise to those attending the meeting. Her position in sales analysis made her critically aware of WICS's high cost of sales. It was only recently, however, that she developed a plan incorporating market share and cost of sales. Her views were accurate, but often given little weight due to her inexperience. According to Smith:

Our cost of sales are currently running at 10 to 15 percent, while our competitors' costs average 5 to 8 percent. As many of you know I am in favor of changing the job description of the area manager and the sales presentation. These changes are necessary due to our products' stage in the life cycle and customer service level preferences. Recently I have become convinced that there is another means of reducing sales costs. By reducing prices we could increase sales volume and reduce the cost of sales. This strategy would also increase penetration and market share.

Griffith conceded that price reductions were a possibility but expressed concern over the possibility of weakening consumer perceptions of WICS as a high-quality manufacturer. He also questioned Smith's assumption that the industrial cleaning supplies industry was presently in the mature stage of the product life cycle.

Following these comments, Griffith thanked the participants for their input and adjourned the meeting. On retiring to his room, he reflected on the suggestions presented during the meeting and his own beliefs. He knew he must begin to formulate an action plan immediately since the 30-day deadline was drawing near.

CONCLUSIONS OF STUDY OF AREA MANAGER ATTITUDES

MGH Associates, management consultants, was retained by WICS to investigate attitudes and opinions of field personnel and sanitary supply distributors. Initially, MGH conducted lengthy interviews with selected individuals, followed by the administration of a comprehensive questionnaire. The results below identify role expectations and attitudes toward their reasonableness.

Territory Manager's Role Expectations

MGH Associates's interviews included territory managers because the territory manager is really the only management level contact the distributor has.

The territory manager interprets his or her role to be that of an overseer, to assure that WICS objectives are achieved, that quotas are met.

The territory manager interprets his or her role to include:

- Training the area managers to
    Sell WICS products.
    Train and motivate the distributor sales force.
- Coordinating area manager activities with headquarters in Lincoln.
- Hiring and firing area managers.
- Striving for new product commitments from the distributors.
- Acting as "referee" for competition between distributors.
- "Building the book" for the adding or deleting of distributors.
- Submitting the "study" to the regional manager, who writes a proposal based on the territory manager's "study." It is submitted to corporate management where the final decision is made.

Area Manager's Role Expectations

The following is the area manager's view of the role he or she believes WICS management expects to be performed:

- Multiply sales effort through distributor's sales force (listed first because it was consistently mentioned first).
- Teach and motivate the distributor's sales force to sell WICS products.
- Introduce new products to the market through
    Direct calls on end-users.
    Distributors.
- Keep margins high to keep distributors happy. If they are happy, they will push WICS.

- Follow through on direct sales responsibilities.
- Collect information for management.
- Fulfill responsibilities relating to incentives.
    New gallon sales.
    Repeat gallon sales.
    Demonstrations.
    30, 35, 40? calls/week.
    Major account calls.
    Cold calls—"to develop business the distributor is reluctant to go after."

Area Manager's Role Problems

The area manager's perception of what management expects does not imply that the area manager feels that management's approach is working. In general, the sales force appears frustrated by a sales role they see as ineffective:

- A sales role that stresses:
    New gallon sales.
    Cold calls on end-users.
    Product demonstrations.
    New product introduction.
- "Checking the boxes" rather than being "creatively productive."
    15 demos.
    10 cold calls
    5 distributor training sessions.
- Incentives stress selling techniques that may not be the most productive ways to sell.
    Emphasis is on new gallon sales over repeat gallon sales. Incentives weight new gallons over repeat gallons (two to one).
    Emphasis to "demonstrate as often as possible" for the points. Demonstrate to show you are a "regular guy" who gets his or her hands dirty, not necessarily to show product benefits.
- Bonus incentives appear to be a "carrot" only for those who don't regularly make bonus, that is, "hit 106 for maximum bonus and minimum quota increase."
- The sales role gives the area manager little ability to impact his or her own success to
    Change distribution.
    Move distributor outside his or her window.
- The area manager describes his or her role as:
    A "lackey."
    A "chaffeur."
    A "caretaker of old business."

Area Manager's Role: Making Cold Calls

One of the causes of area manager frustration is the general ineffectiveness of their cold calls sales role:

- The area manager makes cold calls on end-users not presently sold by the WICS distributor, with the difficult objective of moving these accounts to the WICS distributor.

- If the area manager succeeds in moving this account over to WICS products, chances are small that the distributor will keep the business.
  Without a major portion of the account's total purchases, the distributor cannot afford to continue to call on the account.
  > Distributor sales rep is on commission.
  > After five calls, will stop calling if purchases have not begun to increase.

- The distributor that lost the account will try extremely hard to get back the business. This may mean giving the product away to keep control of the account—maintain majority of the account's purchases. Past experience indicates it is very difficult to move distributors outside their "window."

APPENDIX

B:

CONCLUSIONS OF STUDY OF WICS SANITARY SUPPLY DISTRIBUTOR ATTITUDES

WICS Distributor's Role Expectations

The following is the WICS distributor's role as outlined by WICS management and sales force.

- Act as an extension of the WICS sales force.
- Push and promote WICS product line in a *specified area.*
  > Sell WICS over other brands.
  > Always sell the premium benefits of WICS products to the end-user, instead of distributor's private label.
  > Be aware that the WICS line could be lost if private label sales grow too large.
- Actively market new WICS products.

Distributor's Role Problems

Distributors have been angered by WICS's attempt to run their businesses ("WICS is trying to tell me what to do").

- WICS makes demands—"uses pressure tactics."
    Distributors say they are told "our way or no way."
    Distributors feel they are forced to carry products they don't want.
        High minimum buy-ins.
        "Won't see area manager if we don't carry the new product."
    Distributors say WICS management doesn't "realize we make
    our living selling all our products—not just WICS."
- Communication is poor with WICS management.
    One way—"Our opinions never reach Lincoln."
- "WICS uses the distributor as a testing ground for new products."
    Distributor is not told what to expect.
    After 14-week blitz, "You never hear about the product again."
    The distributor sales force is not trained to sell to, and cannot afford
    to call on, certain segments of the market.
- Growth takes the distributor into new geographical market areas, and
    WICS may elect not to go/grow with the distributor.
    New branch in different city.
    Growth may take distributor sales personnel out of area manager's
    district.
        Receives no support from WICS.
    Worst case—distributor sales rep's territory is completely outside
    district.
        No WICS representative at any accounts.
        Prefer to sell other than WICS.
- WICS does not realize that a distributor's total business extends beyond
    "its own backyard" in many markets.

Distributor's Role Selling Costs

Distributors have shown concern over the high cost of selling WICS products.
Sales costs are approximately 45 percent of the total operating costs.

- "WICS products are basically no better than anyone else's."
- Yet WICS asks distributors to switch competitor's accounts over to WICS
    products.
    Price advantage is very rare.
    A problem must exist.
    A demonstration is required.
- All these make the "problem-solving" sale time-consuming and costly.
- Result: When WICS product is sold, it is easy for competitive WICS dis-
    tributors to cut price to try to get the business.
    They have very low sales costs.
- Required action: Original distributor must cut margin to keep the business.
    This frustrates distributor salespeople.
    Causes them to sell private label

Case 4-4
PURITAN DRUG COMPANY*

On May 1, 1984, David Thomas transferred to the Syracuse Division of the Puritan Drug Company as divisional sales manager. Prior to his transfer, Thomas served as assistant to the vice president of sales in the company's New York headquarters location.

At the conclusion of Thomas' first month-end sales meeting held on June 6, 1984, Harvey Brooks, a salesman in one of the division's rural territories, informed Thomas of his wish to retire, effective the following month. Thomas was surprised by Brooks' announcement because Robert Jackson, the division manager, informed him that Brooks had recently requested and received a deferment of his retirement until he reached his 66th birthday in July 1985. Brooks' sole explanation was that he had "changed his mind."

Brooks' retirement posed a significant territorial reassignment problem for Thomas.

Background of the Syracuse Division

David Thomas became the divisional sales manager at the age of 29. He had joined Puritan Drug as a sales trainee after his graduation from Stanford University in 1978. From 1978 to 1980 he worked as a salesman. In the fall of 1980, the sales manager of the company made Thomas one of his assistants. Thomas assisted the sales manager in arranging special sales promotions of the lines of different manufacturers.

Thomas' predecessor in Syracuse, Harry L. Schultz, had served as divisional sales manager for 15 years before his death in April 1984. "H. L.," as Schultz was called, had also worked as a salesman for the drug wholesale house that merged with Puritan Drug in 1964 and became its Syracuse Division. Although Thomas had made Schultz's acquaintance in the course of business, he did not know Schultz well. Over the past month many members of the divisional sales force often expressed their admiration and affection for Schultz. Several sales reps made a point of telling Thomas that "Old H. L." knew every druggist in 12 counties by their first name. Schultz, in fact, had died of a heart attack while trout fishing with the president of the Syracuse Pharmacists' Association. Robert Jackson remarked that most of the druggists in town attended Schultz's funeral.

The Syracuse Division of Puritan Drug was one of 74 wholesale drug divisions in the United States owned by the firm. Each division acted as a functionally autonomous unit maintaining its own warehouse, sales, buying, and accounting departments. While the divisional manager was responsible for the performance of the division, there were a number of line functions performed by the regional and national offices of Puritan Drug. As divisional sales manager, for example, David Thomas maintained a relationship with the regional office in Albany, which was responsible for assisting him in implementing marketing policies established by the central office in New York.

As a wholesaler, the Syracuse Division sold to retail druggists a broad product line of approximately 18,000 items. The product line consisted of about anything and everything sold through drugstores except fresh food, tobacco products, newspapers, and magazines. In the Syracuse trading area, Puritan Drug competed with two other wholesalers; one carried substantially the same line of products as Puritan Drug, and the other carried a more limited line of drug products.

The Syracuse Division operated as a profitable family-owned wholesale drug house before its merger with Puritan Drug in 1964. While the division operated profitably since 1964, it had not shown a profit on sales equal to the average for the other wholesale drug divisions of Puritan Drug. From 1973 to 1984 the net sales of the division rose each year. However, because competitors did not make available their sales figures, it was impossible to ascertain whether this increase in sales represented a change in the competitive situation or merely a general trend of increasing business volume in the Syracuse trading area. While Schultz was of the opinion that the increase had been at the expense of competitors, the Albany office maintained that since the trend of increase was less than that of other divisions in the northern New York region, the Syracuse Divison may have actually lost ground competitively. A new technique for calculating the potential wholesale purchasing power of retail drugstores, adopted shortly before Thomas' transfer, indicated that the share of the wholesale drug market controlled by the Syracuse Division was below both the median and the mean for other Puritan Drug divisions.

Only a handful of the division's current work force was employed by the family-owned firm prior to its merger with Puritan Drug in 1964. H. L. Schultz was the one remaining executive whose employment in the Syracuse Division antedated the merger; only two sales reps, Harvey Brooks and Clifford Nelson, had sold for the predecessor company.

Many of the company executives and sales reps, although not employed by the predecessor company, nevertheless had employment histories with Puritan Drug going back to the 1960s and 1970s. Of those employees hired prior to 1974, only Robert Jackson, the division manager, had an undergraduate degree, earned at a local YMCA evening college. The more recently hired employees were, without exception, university or pharmacy college graduates. None of the younger employees were promoted when recent vacancies occurred for the jobs of divisional warehouse operations manager and divisional merchandise manager in Syracuse. Two of the younger employees, however, had recently been transferred to similar positions in other divisions.

The Syracuse Division Sales Force

From the time Thomas assumed Schultz's duties in early May, he had devoted four days a week to the task of traveling through each sales territory with the sales rep who covered it. He had made no changes in the practices or procedures of the sales force. Brooks' retirement request provided the first occasion where Thomas could make a nonroutine decision.

When Thomas took charge of the Syracuse Division sales force, it consisted of nine sales reps and four trainees. Four of the sales reps (Frederick Taylor, Edward Harrington, Grace Howard, and Linda Donnelly) had joined the company under the sales training program for college graduates initiated early in the 1970s. The other five sales reps had been with the company many years. Harvey Brooks and Clifford Nelson were the most senior in service. William Murray joined the company as a warehouse employee in 1960 at the age of 19. He became a sales rep in 1965. Walter Miller joined Puritan Drug as a sales rep in 1965 when the wholesale drug firm that he had previously worked for went out of business. Miller, who was 48 years old, had been a wholesale drug sales rep since the age of 20. Albert Simpson came to Puritan Drug after working as a missionary salesman for a manufacturer. Simpson, who joined the company in 1968 at age 26, had earlier served as an officer in the Army Medical Corps.

The four sales trainees graduated from college in June 1983. When Thomas arrived in Syracuse, they were in the last phase of their 12-month training program and were spending much of their time traveling with the experienced sales reps. Thomas believed that Schultz hired the trainees to cover anticipated turnover of sales reps and trainees and to implement the New York office's policy of getting more intensive coverage of each market area. The trainees expected to receive territory assignments, either in the Syracuse Division or elsewhere, on the completion of their training period at the end of June 1984.

Thomas had not seen very much of the sales reps as a group. His acquaintance with them had been formed by the one month-end sales meeting he attended and through his travels with them through their territories.

Walter Miller

Thomas was of the opinion that Walter Miller was a very easy-going, even-tempered person. He seemed to be very popular with the other sales reps and with his customers. Thomas thought that Miller liked him because he had commented to Thomas several times that his suggestions had been very helpful.

Harvey Brooks

Harvey Brooks had not been particularly friendly. Thomas observed that Brooks was well liked because of his good humor and friendly manner with everyone.

Thomas did notice, however, that Brooks intimated that the sales manager should defer to Brooks' age, experience, and judgment. Brooks and his wife lived in the town of Oswego.

On June 4, 1984, Thomas traveled with Brooks, and they visited five of Brooks' accounts. Thomas filed a routine report with the Albany office on the sales rep's field work:

Points requiring attention: Not using merchandising equipment; not following weekly sales plan. Pharmaceutical business going to competitors because of lack of interest. Too much time spent on idle chatter. Only shows druggists what "he thinks they will buy." Tends to sell easy items instead of profitable ones.

Steps taken for correction: Explained shortcomings and demonstrated how larger, more profitable orders could be obtained by following sales plan—did just that by getting the biggest order ever written for Carthage account.

Remarks: Old-time "personality." Should do terrific volume if trained on new merchandising techniques.

On a similar form completed by H. L. Schultz on the basis of his travels with Brooks on March 3, 1984, the following comments were made:

Points requiring attention: Not getting pharmaceutical business. Not following promotion plans.

Steps taken for correction: Told him about these things.

Remarks: Brooks made this territory—can sell anything he sets his mind to—a real drummer—very popular with his customers.

Grace Howard

Grace Howard (age 29) was the oldest of the sales reps who had passed through the formal sales training program. Thomas considered her earnest and conscientious. Howard had increased her sales each year. Although Thomas did not consider Howard to be the "sales rep type," he noted that Howard was quite successful in using the merchandising techniques that Thomas wanted to implement.

William Murray

William Murray handled many of the big accounts in downtown Syracuse. Thomas believed that Murray was an excellent sales rep who considered himself "very smooth." Thomas had been surprised at the affront Murray had taken when he had offered a few suggestions to improve Murray's selling technique. William Murray and his wife were good friends of the Jacksons, as well as the merchandise and operations managers and their wives. Thomas suspected that Murray had expected to be Schultz's successor.

Clifford Nelson

Clifford Nelson appeared to Thomas to be an earnest and conscientious sales rep. He had been amiable, but not cordial to Thomas. Thomas' report on Nelson's calls on 10 accounts on June 5, 1984, contained the following statements:

Points requiring attention: Rushing calls. Gets want book and tries to sell case lots on wanted items. Carries all merchandising equipment, but doesn't use it.

Steps taken for correction: Suggested change in routing; longer, better-planned calls; conducted presentation demonstration.

Remarks: Hard-working, conscientious, good salesman, but needs to be brought up-to-date on merchandising methods.

Schultz's comments on his observations of Nelson on March 4, 1984, were:

Points requiring attention: Uses the want book on the basis of most sales. Not pushing promotions.

Steps taken for correction: Discussed shortcomings.

Remarks: Nelson really knows how to sell—visits every customer each week. Hard worker—very loyal—even pushes goods with very low commission.

On the day Thomas traveled with Nelson, the sales rep suggested that Thomas have dinner at the Nelsons' home. Thomas accepted the invitation, but at the end of the day Nelson took him to a restaurant in Watertown instead, explaining that he did not want to inconvenience his wife because his two daughters were home from college on vacation.

Albert Simpson

Albert Simpson caused Thomas considerable concern. Simpson continually complained about sales management procedures, commission rates, the "lousy service of the warehouse people," and similar matters at the sales meeting. Thomas believed that while most of his complaints were valid, the matters were usually trivial, and that the other sales reps did not complain about any of these matters. Thomas mentioned his difficulties with Simpson to Robert Jackson, the district manager. Jackson replied that Simpson had been very friendly with Schultz. Simpson seemed quite popular with his customers.

Frederick Taylor

Frederick Taylor was, in Thomas' opinion, the most ambitious, aggressive, and argumentative sales rep in the division. He had been employed by the company since his graduation from the University of Rochester in 1980, first as a trainee, and then as a sales rep. Taylor had substantially increased the sales volume of his territory. He persuaded Schultz to assign him six inactive hospital accounts in July 1982. Within six months, he was able to generate sales to these accounts in excess of $50,000. While the other sales reps considered Taylor "cocky" and a "big spender," Thomas regarded Taylor's attitude as one of independence. If Taylor agreed with a sales plan, he worked hard to achieve its objectives; if he did not agree, he would not cooperate. Thomas thought that he had been successful in working with Taylor.

Linda Donnelly

Linda Donnelly impressed Thomas as being unsure of herself, confused, and overworked. Thomas attributed these difficulties to Donnelly's attempts to serve too many accounts in too large a territory. Donnelly was very receptive to Thomas' suggestions on how to improve her work. Thomas believed that, at age 24, Donnelly would improve with proper guidance. Donnelly had raised her sales to a point enabling her to move from salary to commissions in March 1984.

Edward Harrington

Edward Harrington (age 25) was the only sales rep who continued to work on a salary basis. His sales volume was insufficient to sustain the income of $1,500 a month, the company minimum for sales reps with more than one year's experience. Harrington was very apologetic about being on a salary. Thomas believed that Harrington's determination to "make good" would be realized through his conscientiousness. When he was assigned the territory in 1982, it consisted largely of uncontacted accounts. The volume of sales in the territory tripled over the past two years. Thomas felt that Harrington appreciated all the help given and that, in time, Harrington would be an excellent salesman.

Commission and Turnover Rates at Puritan Drug

Sales commission rates were paid to the sales force as follows:

Brooks and Nelson	2.375%
Miller and Donnelly	2.25
Murray and Simpson	2.125
Howard and Taylor	2

Expense accounts amounted to about .75 percent of sales. Thomas explained the differences in commission rates in terms of the differential product commissions set by the company. Higher commission rates were given on items the company wished to "push," such as pharmaceuticals and calendar promotion items.

While all four trainees seemed to be good prospects, they were somewhat of an unknown quantity to Thomas. He had held training conferences with them, and thought they performed rather poorly. He was concerned that Schultz had neglected their training, yet the reps were eager for assigned territories. They indicated this desire to Thomas at every possible opportunity.

The turnover of the Syracuse Division sales force had been quite low among the senior sales reps. Only six of the graduates of the sales training program had left the division since 1979. Two were promoted to department heads in other Puritan Drug divisions. The remaining four left to work for drug manufacturers. Drug manufacturers valued sales reps with wholesaling experience, and wholesalers who competed with Puritan Drug did not offer any training programs. Consequently, there were many opportunities for a sales rep who left Puritan Drug.

Sales Management at Puritan Drug

Throughout the month of May, Thomas devoted considerable thought to improving the sales performance of the Syracuse Division. He had accepted the transfer to this job at the urging of Richard Topping, vice president in charge of sales and his prior boss. Thomas was one of a dozen young employees whom Topping had brought into the New York office as assistants to the top sales executives. None of these young assistants remained in the New York office for more than three years. Topping had made a policy of offering them field assignments so that they could "show their stuff."

Thomas had observed the performance records of other divisional sales managers while he worked in New York. He knew that some sales managers had achieved substantial improvements on the past performances of their divisions. Thomas believed that the sales performance of his own division could be enhanced by improving the sales management plan. He also knew that the share of the Syracuse market for wholesale purchases of retail drugstores[1] held by Puritan Drug was 20.05 percent, compared to a 48 percent share for some of the other divisions.

Thomas remembered that Topping had regularly focused his staff's attention on the qualitative aspects of sales policy. Thomas had assisted Topping in implementing merchandising plans to utilize the sales reps' efforts to minimize the handling cost of their sales, and to maximize the gross margin.

The company promoted a three-step sales plan for increased profitability:

1. Sales of larger average value per line of the order were encouraged because the cost of processing and filling each line of an order was practically constant.

---

[1]The New York market analysis section calculated the potential wholesale sales for retail drugstores. This market estimate, called the PWPP (potential wholesale purchasing power), was calculated for each county by adjusting retail drugstore sales to an estimate of the purchases of goods from wholesalers.

2. Sales of larger total value were encouraged because the delivery cost for orders having a total weight between 20 and 100 pounds was practically constant.

3. Because some manufacturers offered margins considerably larger than others, sales of higher margin items were encouraged. Sales commissions varied with the margins available to Puritan Drug on the products the sales reps sold.

The headquarters office also sought to increase the effectiveness of Puritan Drug promotions by setting up a sales calendar. The sales calendar coordinated the activities of all Puritan Drug divisions so that during a given calendar period, every company account could be solicited for those specific items which yielded attractive margins. The sales calendar required that the sales reps in each division follow a fairly prescribed pattern in selling to each individual account. The divisional sales managers were responsible for the coordination of the activities of their sales reps. Thomas believed that his predecessor had never really accepted the sales patterns prescribed by the New York office.

The national office also required each division to keep uniform sales and market analysis records. In the New York office, Thomas had developed a familiarity with the uses of these records. He inherited from Schultz a carefully maintained system of sales department records.

The division trading area formed the basis of the sales and market analysis record system. The economics of selling costs, transportation costs of delivery, and sales reps' traveling expenses determined the limits of the trading area. Thomas knew from his own experience, however, that delineation of trading areas was heavily influenced by tradition, geography, number of sales reps, number of possible sales contacts, estimated market potential, competition, and agreements with adjacent Puritan Drug divisions. The Rochester and Albany trading areas bordered the Syracuse Division on the east, south, and west; Canada bordered the division in the north. (A map of this division is included as Exhibit 1.)

Since his arrival, Thomas had formed the opinion that the present territories had been established without careful regard for the number of stores in the area, the sales potential, or the travel involved. Although he had not yet studied any one territory carefully, Thomas suspected that all his sales reps skimmed the cream from many of their accounts. He believed that they simply did not have adequate time to do a thorough selling job in each store. Exhibit 2 provides information on sales and sales potential by county. Exhibits 3 and 4 provide selected data on individual territory assignments and performance.

Sales Territories of Harvey Brooks and Clifford Nelson

Harvey Brooks' sales territory included accounts scattered through small towns in four rural counties northeast of Syracuse (see Exhibit 5). Brooks originally developed the accounts for the predecessor company. At the time he undertook

EXHIBIT 1   *Syracuse Division Trading Area in Upstate New York—Salesmen's Assignments*

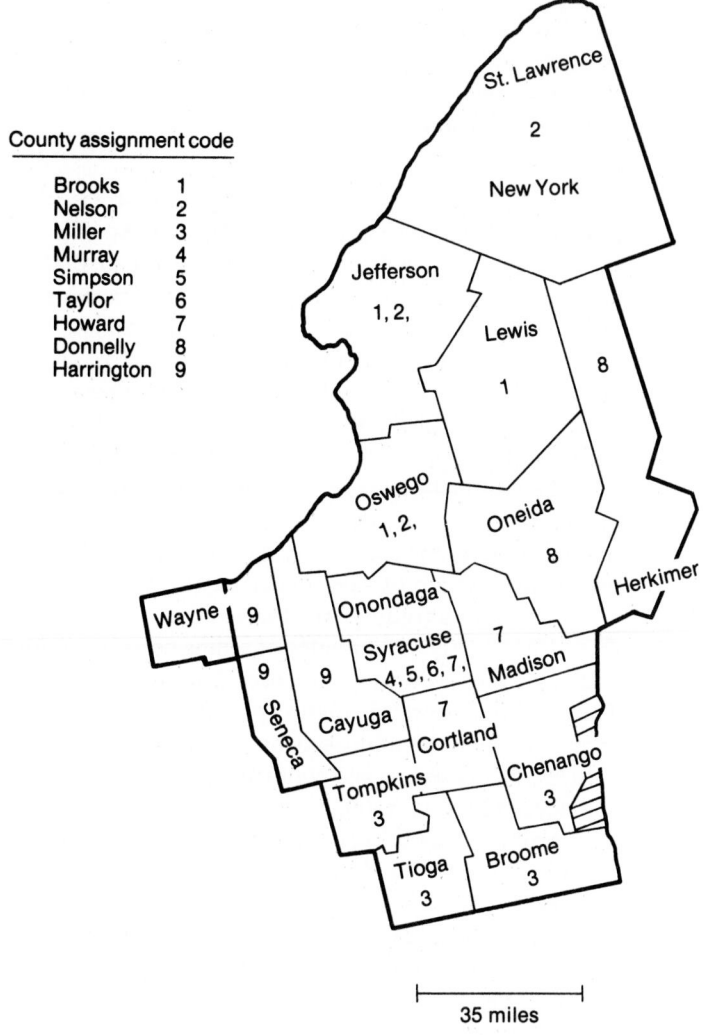

County assignment code

Brooks	1
Nelson	2
Miller	3
Murray	4
Simpson	5
Taylor	6
Howard	7
Donnelly	8
Harrington	9

35 miles

this task in 1954, a competing service wholesaler had established a mail-order business with the area's rural druggists. Brooks "took to the road" to build sales with personal service. He had been hired specifically for this job because he was a native of the area and an experienced "drummer."

In 1959, Clifford Nelson, a friend of Brooks, became a division sales rep. At the suggestion of Brooks, he covered other accounts in the same four-county area. Nelson previously had been a sales rep for a proprietary medicine firm.

EXHIBIT 2   Selected Data on Sales and Sales Potentials, by Counties

County	Salesman* Code	Population (000s)	Percent of Division	Retailers				Potential Wholesale Purchasing Power (000s)	Percent of Division PWPP	Sales† (000s)	Sales Percent of PWPP	Hospitals			Miscellaneous Sales (000s)
				Sold	Inactive Accounts	Accounts Not Sold	Total					Sold	Not Sold	Sales (000s)	
St. Lawrence	2	117.2	6.3%	23	1	2	26	$ 2,725	4.4%	$ 1,020	37.4%	2	4	$ 20	$ 15
Jefferson	1,2	90.2	4.9	34	—	—	34	3,265	5.3	918	28.2	—	2	10	—
Lewis	1	24.8	1.3	8	—	—	8	653	1.0	215	32.2	—	1	—	8
Herkimer	8	69.3	3.7	10	6	1	17	1,560	2.5	245	15.7	—	2	—	—
Oswego	1,2	97.3	5.3	25	1	—	26	3,350	5.5	933	27.1	1	2	—	25
Oneida	8	285.4	15.5	46	14	12	72	8,700	14.2	838	10.5	—	13	—	18
Wayne	9	76.6	4.1	4	—	1	5	618	1.0	138	22.3	—	—	—	—
Cayuga	9	75.6	4.1	12	4	—	16	1,403	2.3	253	18.0	2	—	10	68
Onondaga	4,5,6,7	474.8	25.8	98	9	13	120	19,118	31.2	5,415	28.7	6	9	270	480
Madison	7	59.7	3.2	12	2	3	17	3,125	5.1	653	20.9	—	2	—	—
Seneca	9	34.4	1.9	6	1	3	10	1,395	2.3	210	15.0	2	1	15	60
Cortland	7	45.4	2.5	6	2	1	9	1,275	2.1	403	31.5	—	2	—	—
Chenango	3	48.2	2.6	4	2	6	12	1,420	2.3	158	11.1	—	3	—	—
Tompkins	3	75.7	4.1	9	1	4	14	2,038	3.3	303	16.2	—	5	—	—
Tioga	3	46.2	2.5	4	—	7	11	805	1.3	200	24.8	—	—	—	—
Broome	3	225.3	12.2	22	2	13	37	9,925	16.2	633	6.4	—	8	—	45
Totals		1,846.6	100.0%	323	45	66	434	$61,375	100.0%	$12,562	20.5%	15	54	$325	$719

*County assignment code: Brooks —1 Murray —4 Howard —7
Nelson —2 Simpson —5 Donnelly —8
Miller —3 Taylor —6 Harington —9

†Excludes miscellaneous sales, sales to hospitals, and house sales.

EXHIBIT 3   *Selected Data on Sales Rep's Territory Assignments by County*

Sales Rep	County	Sales 1984*	Active† Accounts	PWPP‡	Assigned† Accounts
Miller	Chenango	$ 154,755	4	$ 1,417	15
	Tompkins	332,250	9	2,038	19
	Tioga	199,195	4	805	11
	Broome	675,750	22	9,928	45
Total		1,361,950	39	14,188	90
Brooks	Jefferson	365,085	16	2,265	18
	Lewis	215,985	8	653	9
	Oswego	924,650	25	2,675	28
Total		1,150,720	49	5,593	55
Howard	Onondaga	572,543	14	2,275	14
	Madison	652,125	12	3,125	19
	Cortland	402,500	6	1,275	11
Total		1,627,168	32	6,675	44
Murray	Onondaga	1,890,383	33	5,563	44
Total		1,890,383	33	5,563	44
Nelson	St. Lawrence	1,020,440	25	2,725	32
	Jefferson	556,298	20	1,000	20
	Oswego	6,950	1	675	1
Total		1,583,688	46	4,400	53
Simpson	Onondaga	1,834,815	29	7,520	48
Total		1,834,815	29	7,520	48
Taylor	Onondaga	1,595,183	28	3,760	29
Total		1,595,183	28	3,760	29
Donnelly	Herkimer	242,650	10	1,560	19
	Oneida	937,500	46	8,700	85
Total		1,180,150	56	10,260	104
Harrington	Wayne	136,000	4	618	5
	Cayuga	317,500	14	1,403	18
	Seneca	271,950	8	1,395	13
Total		725,450	26	3,416	36
Hospitals	Taylor (Syracuse)	270,000			
	Nelson/ Harrington	55,000			
House accounts		$ 1,322,530			
Total division sales		$14,951,910			

*The figure by sales rep includes sales to chain and independent drugstores and to miscellaneous accounts, but does not include sales to hospitals or house accounts indicated at the foot of the table.

Includes hospitals and other recognized drug outlets in the territory.

‡No potential is calculated for hospitals or miscellaneous sales. However, where a county is divided among several sales reps, the potential sales figure for each rep is obtained by allocating the county potential in proportion to the total *number* of potential drugstore and miscellaneous accounts in that county assigned to that rep.

E X H I B I T   4   *Summary Data on Sales Reps' Performance*

I	1984 Sales (000s)	Percent of Total Sales	1984 PWPP* (000s)	Percent of Total PWPP	Sales Percent of PWPP	1984 Active Accounts† No.	Percent	1984 Assigned Accounts† No.	Percent	Active Accounts Percent of Assigned	1984 Sales per Active Account	PWPP per Assigned Account†	1984 Commissions
Miller	$ 1,363	10.2%	$14,188	23.2%	9.6%	39	11.5%	90	17.9%	43.4%	$35,000	$157,750	$30,675
Brooks	1,505	11.3	5,593	9.1	27.0	49	14.5	55	10.9	89.0	30,750	101,500	35,725
Murray	1,890	14.2	5,563	9.1	34.0	33	9.8	44	8.8	75.0	57,250	126,250	40,200
Nelson	1,585d	11.9	4,400	7.2	36.0	46	13.6	53	10.5	85.0	34,500	83,000	38,500
Simpson	1,835	13.8	7,520	12.2	24.5	29	8.6	48	9.5	60.5	63,375	156,750	39,000
Subtotal	$ 8,178	61.4%	$37,264	60.8%	22.0%	196	58.0%	290	57.6%	67.2%	$58,450	$128,500	
II													
Howard	$ 1,628	12.2%	$ 6,675	10.9%	24.4%	32	9.5%	44	8.7%	72.7%	$51,900	$151,500	$33,000
Taylor	1,594§	12.0	3,760	6.1	42.4	28	8.3	29	5.8	96.5	66,750	129,500	31,900
Donnelly	1,180	8.9	10,260	16.7	11.5	56	16.5	104	20.7	53.8	21,050	98,750	26,550
Harrington	725§	5.5	3,415	5.5	21.3	26	7.7	36	7.2	72.3	27,875	95,000	18,000
Subtotal	$ 5,128	38.6%	$24,110	39.2%	21.3%	142	42.0%	213	42.4%	66.7%	$36,188	$113,250	
Total	$13,306§	100.0%	$61,374	100.0%	21.7	338	100.0%	503	100.0%	67.0%	$39,325	$122,000	

Hospital sales by:
Taylor $ 270
Nelson   30
Harrington   25
House sales: 1,322
Grand total $14,953

*No potential is calculated for hospital or miscellaneous sales. However, where a county is divided among several sales reps the potential sales figure for each rep is obtained by allocating the county potential in proportion to the total *number* of potential drugstore and miscellaneous accounts in that county assigned to that rep.

†Includes hospitals and other recognized drug outlets in the territory.

‡Understated since hospitals and miscellaneous accounts are included in the assigned accounts listed but not in the potential.

§Excluding hospital sales.

Exhibit 5   *Counties Sold by Brooks and Nelson*

He was seven years younger than Brooks. Since 1955, Brooks and Nelson each had had a number of accounts in the four-county area. (The list of their accounts appears as Exhibits 6 and 7.) Thomas noticed that the commission incomes Brooks and Nelson received had been stable over the years.

A Visit from Clifford Nelson

On the morning of June 9, three days after the June sales meeting, Thomas saw Clifford Nelson come in the front door of the Syracuse Division offices.

EXHIBIT 6   *Accounts Sold by Harvey Brooks, by Counties, with 1984 Purchases*

Jefferson County			Oswego County			Lewis County		
Adams Center	D	$ 8,925	Calosse	D	$ 4,273	Beaver Falls	D	$ 9,525
(Alexandria Bay)	D	45,750	Central Square	D	4,643	Croghan	D	61,493
(Alexandria Bay)	D	39,475	Constantia	M	180	Harrisville	D	46,290
Bellville	D	5,250	Cleveland	M	975	Lowville	D	59,220
(Carthage)	D	152,500	(Fulton)	D	37,800	Lowville	D	10,785
Chaumont	D	1,510	(Fulton)	D	61,275	Lyons Falls	D	15,060
(Clayton)	D	26,575	(Fulton)	D	69,500	Port Leydon	D	5,813
(Clayton)	D	41,000	(Fulton)	D	96,000	Turin	M	7,800
Deferiet	D	923	Hannibal	D	9,725	County total:		$215,986
Dexter	D	29,175	Hastings	M	9,600	Territory total: $1,505,724		
Ellisburg	D	590	Lacona	M	1,155			
LaFargeville	D	1,305	Mexico	D	39,750			
Plessis	D	2,200	Oswego	D	30,188			
Redwood	M	270	(Oswego)	D	51,900			
Rodman	D	8,025	(Oswego)	D	60,250			
Sackets Harbor	D	1,613	(Oswego)	D	102,500			
County total:		$365,086	(Oswego)	D	109,750			
			(Oswego)	D	56,075			
			Oswego	H	38			
			Parish	M	12,900			
			Phoenix	D	24,325			
			(Pulaski)	D	21,875			
			(Pulaski)	D	72,700			
			Sandy Creek	D	35,325			
			West Monroe	D	11,950			
			County total:		$924,652			

Code: D = Independent drugstore; M = miscellaneous account; H = Hospital.

Note: Accounts in parentheses are those indicated by Nelson as the ones he wanted from Brooks. These accounts total $1,044,963 (87.7 percent of Brooks' sales in Jefferson County, 80 percent in Oswego County, or 69.4 percent of the territory total). Added to Nelson's 1983 sales, this would increase his volume 65 percent to $2,658,018. Brooks' old territory would be left with $460,758 in sales.

Although Nelson passed within 30 feet of Thomas' desk, he did not appear to notice Thomas. Nelson walked through the office area directly to the partitioned space where Robert Jackson's private office was located. Twenty minutes later, Nelson emerged from the division manager's office and made his way to Thomas' desk.

"Hi there, young fellah!" he shouted as he approached.

"Howdy, Cliff. Sit down and chat awhile," Thomas replied. "What got you out of bed so early?" he asked, knowing that Nelson must have risen at 6 o'clock to make the drive to Syracuse from his home in Watertown.

E X H I B I T 7   *Accounts Sold by Clifford Nelson, by Counties, with 1984 Purchases*

St. Lawrence County			Jefferson County			Oswego County		
Canton	D	$ 98,100	Adams	C	$ 4,713	Pulaski	C	$6,825
Edwards	D	5,040	Carthage	C	5,325			
Edwards	M	14,138	Evans Mills	D	5,525			
Gouverneur	D	1,695	Philadelphia	D	9,450			
Gouverneur	D	70,373	Watertown	D	75,500			
Gouverneur	D	123,898	Watertown	D	11,850			
Heuvelton	D	810	Watertown	D	22,000			
Massena	D	84,443	Watertown	D	76,700			
Massena	D	25,478	Watertown	D	46,100			
Massena	C	18,360	Watertown	D	65,750			
Massena	C	16,688	Watertown	D	95,500			
Massena	H	285	Watertown	D	57,500			
Madrid	D	10,740	Watertown	D	24,250			
Morristown	D	20,483	Watertown	D	2,135			
Norfolk	D	22,463	Watertown	D	28,300			
Norwood	D	23,543	Watertown	C	9,075			
Ogdensburg	D	60,675	Watertown	C	14,925			
Ogdensburg	D	169,163	Watertown	M	1,700			
Ogdensburg	D	54,023	Watertown	H	315			
Ogdensburg	D	25,350	Watertown	H	9,000			
Ogdensburg	M	1,118	County total:		$565,613			
Ogdensburg	H	19,898						
Potsdam	D	115,830						
Potsdam	C	55,283						
Potsdam Falls	D	2,753						
County total:		$1,040,630						
Territorial total: $1,613,068								

Code: D = Independent drugstore; C = Chain drugstores; M = Miscellaneous account; H = Hospital.

Nelson squeezed his bulky frame into the armchair next to the desk. "It's a shame Harvey is retiring," he said. "I never thought he could stand to give it up. I never knew anyone who enjoyed selling as much as Harvey—except maybe me." Nelson continued praising Brooks and telling anecdotes which illustrated his point until Thomas began to wonder whether Nelson thought that he was biased in some way against the retiring sales rep. Thomas recalled that he had made some critical remarks about Brooks to Jackson, but he could not recall any discussion of Brooks' shortcomings with the man himself, or any of the other sales reps. Nelson ended his remarks by saying, "Old H. L.

always said that Harvey was the best damn wholesale drug salesman he'd ever known."

There was a brief silence, as Thomas did not realize that Nelson was finished. Finally Thomas said, "You know, Cliff, I think we ought to have a testimonial dinner for Harvey at the July sales meeting."

Nelson made no comment on Thomas' suggestion; instead, he went on to say, "None of these green trainees will ever be able to take Harvey's place. Those druggists up there are old-timers. They would resent being high pressured by some kid blown up to twice his size with college degrees. No sir! You've got to sell 'em right in those country stores."

Thomas questioned whether Nelson's opinion of the adaptability of the younger, college-educated sales reps was justified by the available evidence. He recalled that several of them with rural territories performed better against their May sales quotas than either Brooks or Nelson. Thomas was proud of his self-restraint when he commented, "Selling in a rural territory is certainly different."

"That's right, Dave. I wanted to make sure you understood these things before I told you." Nelson was nervously massaging his double chin between his thumb and forefinger.

Thomas looked at him with a quizzical expression. "Told me what?"

"I have just been talking to Robert Jackson. Well, I was talking to him about an understanding between Harvey and me. We always agreed that if anything should happen to the other, or he should retire, or something—well, we agreed that the one who remained should get to take over his choice of the other's accounts. We told H. L. about this and he said, 'Boys, what's OK by you is OK by me. You two developed that territory and you deserve to be rewarded for it.' Well, yes sir, that's the way it was."

Without pausing, Nelson went on, "I just told Jackson about it. He said that he remembered talking about the whole thing with H. L. 'Yes,' he said, 'Tell Thomas about it,' he said, 'Tell Thomas about it.' Harvey and I went over his accounts on Sunday. I went over his list of accounts with him and checked the ones that I want. Here is the list with the accounts all checked off.[2] I already know nearly all the proprietors. You'll see that—"

"Wait a minute, Cliff! Wait a minute!" Thomas interrupted. "You've lost me completely. In the first place, if there is any assignment of accounts to be made I'll do it. It will be done on a basis that is fair to the sales reps concerned, and profitable to the company. You know that."

"Dave, I'm only asking for what is fair," Nelson's face was flushed. Thomas noticed that the man he had always believed to be deliberately confident and self-possessed was now so agitated that it was difficult for him to speak. "I don't want my territory chopped up and handed to some green kid!"

Thomas noticed that everybody in the office was now watching Nelson.

---

[2]Nelson's selected accounts are the accounts in parentheses in Exhibit 6.

"Calm down, Cliff," he whispered to the sales rep, indicating with a nod of his head that others were watching.

"Don't talk to me that way!" replied Nelson. "I don't care. A man with 25 years' service deserves some consideration!"

"You're absolutely right, Cliff. You're absolutely right." As Thomas repeated his words, Nelson settled back in his chair. The typewriters started clattering again.

"Now, first of all, Cliff," as Thomas tried to return the conversation to a friendly basis. "Where did you get the idea that your territory was going to be 'chopped up'?"

"You said so yourself. You said it at the sales meeting the other day when you made that speech about how you were going to boost sales in Syracuse," Nelson emphasized his words by pounding the side of the desk with his masonic ring.

Thomas reflected for a moment. He recalled his speech at the sales meeting called, "How We Can Do a Better Job for Puritan Drug." The speech was a restatement of the merchandising policy of the New York office. He had mentioned that getting more profitable business would require that a larger percentage of the purchases of each account would have to come to Puritan Drug; that receiving a larger share of the business from each store would require more selling time in each store; and that greater concentration on each account would require reorganization of the sales territories. He realized that his future plans entailed reorganization of the territories. He had not anticipated, however, Nelson's reaction.

Finally, Thomas said, "I do plan to make some territorial changes—not right away—at least not until I have looked things over pretty darn carefully. Of course, you understand that our first duty is to make greater profits for the company. Some of our territories would be a great deal more profitable if they were organized and handled in a different manner."

"What are you going to do about Harvey's territory?" asked Nelson.

Since Thomas had not yet looked over the information about the territory, he was anxious not to commit himself to any course of action relating to it. "Well, I just haven't had a chance to study the situation yet," he replied. "If I could make the territory more profitable by reorganizing it, I guess that is what they would expect me to do."

"What about the promises the company made to me about letting me choose the accounts I want?" Nelson asked.

"You don't mean the company's promise; you mean Schultz's promise," Thomas corrected him.

"Well, if Schultz wasn't 'the company,' I don't see how you figure that you are!" Nelson's face resumed its flush.

"OK, Cliff. How about giving me a chance to look over the situation. You know that I want to do the right thing. Let me go over the list of the accounts you want. In a few days I can talk intelligently about the matter." Thomas felt that there was no point in carrying the discussion further.

"All right, Dave," said Nelson, rising. The two men walked toward the front entrance of the office. As they reached the top of the steps leading to the front door, Nelson turned to Thomas and offered his hand. "Look, Dave, I'm sorry I got so mad. You just can't imagine what this means to me. I know you'll see it my way when you know the whole story." Nelson's voice sounded strained.

Thomas watched the older man leave. He felt embarrassed, realizing that Nelson's parting words had been overheard by several manufacturers' representatives standing nearby.

A Conversation with the Division Manager

Thomas decided he would immediately discuss his conversation with Nelson with Jackson. He walked over to Jackson's office, and hesitated upon reaching the doorway. Jackson looked up, and indicated with a gesture that Thomas should take a seat.

Thomas sat down and waited for Jackson to speak. Jackson was occupied for the moment unwrapping a cigar. After a few moments of silence, Thomas opened the conversation. "Clifford Nelson just stopped by to speak to me."

"Yeah?" said Jackson, removing bitten flakes of tobacco from the end of his tongue.

"He said something about getting some of Harvey Brooks' accounts when Harvey retired," Thomas said in a deliberately questioning manner.

"Yeah."

Thomas continued, "Well, this idea of his was based on a promise that he said H. L. had made."

"Yeah. He told me that, too."

"Did Schultz make such a promise?" Thomas inquired.

"Hell, I don't know. It sounds like him." Jackson tilted back in his swivel chair.

"What shall I do about it?"

"Don't ask me; you're the sales manager." Jackson paused, holding his cigar away from his lips as if he were about to speak. Just as Thomas was about to say something, Jackson lurched forward to flick the ashes from his cigar into his ash tray. "Look here, Dave. I don't want any morale problems around here. You're the first of the 'wonder boys' to be put in charge of a department in this division. I don't want you to do anything to mess up the morale. We never had any morale problems when Schultz was around. We don't want anything like that in this division."

Thomas was momentarily bewildered. He knew from the way that Jackson used the phrase "wonder boys" that he was referring to the managers brought into the organization by Richard Topping.

Jackson went on, "Why the devil did you tell the reps that you were going to reassign the sales territories without even telling me?"

"But you were there when I said it."

"Said what?"

"Well, at the sales meeting, that one of the ways we were going to get more business was to reorganize the sales territory," Thomas replied.

"I certainly don't remember anything like that, Dave, you gave a good inspirational talk, but I sure can't remember anything about reassigning territories."

"Actually, I just mentioned the reorganization of territories in passing," Thomas smiled.

"I'll be damned. That sort of thing is always happening. Here everybody is frothing at the mouth about something that they think we are going to do and we haven't the slightest idea why they think we're going to do it. You know, probably the real reason Harvey Brooks is retiring, instead of staying on as he planned, was this fear of sales territory reorganization. Both he and Nelson know that their retirement pension is based on earnings from their last five years of active employment. Now that I think of it, three or four of the other sales reps have stopped during the last couple of days to tell me what a fine job they were doing. They probably had this territory reassignment stuff on their minds, too."

Jackson's cigar was no longer burning. He began groping under the papers on his desk for a match. Thomas took advantage of this pause in the conversation. "Mr. Jackson, I think there are some real advantages to be won by adjusting the sales territories. I think—"

"You still think that after today?" the division manager asked in a sarcastic tone.

"Why, yes! The profit made on sales to an individual account is related closely to delivery expense. The larger the total proportion of the account's business we get, the more profit we make because the delivery expense remains more or less constant."

"Look, Dave, you college computer types always have everything figured out, but sometimes that doesn't count. Morale is the important thing. The sales reps won't tolerate having their territories changed. I know that you have four trainees that you'd like to put out on territories. If you put them out on parts of the territories belonging to some of the more experienced reps—bam! God knows how many of our good sales reps would be left. I've never had any trouble with sales force morale since I've been manager of this division. Old Schultz, bless his soul, never let me down. He wasn't any damn Ph.D., but he could handle sales reps. Don't get off on the wrong foot with them, Dave. With the labor situation in the warehouse being what it is, I've just got too much on my mind. I don't want you creating more problems than I can handle. How 'bout it, boy!"

Jackson ground out his half-smoked cigar, looking steadily at Thomas.

Thomas was extremely upset with the division manager's implication that he lacked concern for sales rep morale. He had always thought of himself as very considerate. He realized that at the moment his foremost desire was to get away from Jackson.

Thomas rose from his chair, saying, "Mr. Jackson, you can count on me. I know you are right about this morale business."

"Atta boy," said the division manager. "It does us a lot of good to talk like this once in a while. Now, see if you can make peace with the sales reps. I want you to handle everything yourself."

"Well, thanks a lot," said Thomas, as he backed out of the office door.

As he walked through the office, he saw two manufacturers' representatives with whom he had appointments. His schedule of appointments that day prohibited him from doing more than gathering the material pertaining to the Nelson and Brooks territories.

Thomas Goes Home

Thomas left the office shortly after 5 o'clock to drive to a suburb of Syracuse. It was a particularly hot and humid day. Pre-Fourth of July traffic lengthened the drive home by nearly 20 minutes. When he finally turned into his own driveway, he felt as though his skin were caked with grime and perspiration. He got out of the car and walked around to the terrace at the rear of the house. Beth, his wife, was sitting in a deck chair, working on some papers.

"Hello Dave. You're late," she said, looking up with a smile.

"I know it. Even the traffic was bad today." He dropped his suit coat on a glass-topped table and sprawled out full length on a chaise lounge. "I'm exhausted. And, boy, I am disgusted with myself."

"Bad day?"

"Awful. You just can't imagine how discouraging it is trying to get this job organized. You would think it would be obvious to everyone that what ails the Syracuse Division is the organization of the sales force," said Thomas, arranging a pillow under his head.

"I didn't realize that you thought anything was wrong with the Syracuse Division."

"Well, what I mean is that we now get only 20 percent of the potential wholesale business. If I could organize the sales force my way—well, God knows, maybe we could get 40 percent of the business. That is what the New York office watches for. The sales manager who increases his division's share of the market gets the promotions when they come along. I know Topping transferred me to this division because he knew these possibilities existed."

"I don't understand. Is Mr. Topping still your boss, or is Mr. Jackson?"

"Beth, it's terribly discouraging. While Jackson is my boss, I'll never get anywhere in Puritan Drug unless Topping and the other people in New York promote me."

"Don't you like Mr. Jackson?"

"I had a run-in with him today."

"You didn't!" she said as she laid her papers aside.

Thomas didn't anticipate his wife's reaction. He gazed up at the awning as if he did not notice her intent expression. "We didn't argue particularly.

He just—well, he doesn't know too much about sales management. He put his foot down on my plans to reorganize the territories."

"I can't understand why you would go and get yourself into a fight with your boss when you haven't even been here two months."

"Honest, Beth, I didn't have any fight. Everything is OK. He just—well, do you want me to be a divisional sales manager all my life?"

"You're tired," she said sympathetically. "Why don't you go up and shower."

"That sounds wonderful," he said, raising himself from the chaise lounge.

An Unexpected Caller

Thomas had just stepped out of the shower when he heard his wife calling to him. "Dave, Fred Taylor is here to see you."

"Tell him I'll be down in just a minute. Offer him a drink, Beth."

As he dressed, Thomas wondered why Fred Taylor had chosen the dinner hour to call. During the month since he had moved into his new home, no other sales rep had ever dropped by uninvited.

When Thomas came downstairs, he found Taylor sitting on the living room couch, a gin and tonic in his hand.

"Hello, Fred," said Thomas, crossing the room with his right hand extended. "You look as if you had a hot day. Why don't you take off your coat? If we go out to the terrace, you may get a chance to cool off."

"Thanks, Dave," the visitor said as they moved out to the terrace. "I'm sorry to barge in this way, but I thought it was important."

"Well, what's on your mind?" asked Thomas as they sat down.

"I heard about what happened at the office today. I thought I'd come over and tell you that we stand behind you 100 percent."

Thomas was perplexed by Taylor's words. He realized that Taylor probably was referring to his meeting with Nelson. Thomas said, "I'm not sure what you mean, Fred."

"I heard that you and Nelson had it out this morning about changing the sales territories," Taylor replied.

Thomas smiled. Two thoughts entered his mind. He was amused at the proportions that the brief morning conversation had assumed. At the same time, he was curious to know how Taylor, who had presumably been in the field selling, had heard about the incident so quickly. Without hesitation he asked, "Where did you hear about this, Fred?"

"Bill Murray told me! He was down at the warehouse with Walter Miller when I stopped off to pick up a special narcotics order for a customer. They are all excited about this territory business. Murray said Nelson came out to his house at lunch time and told him about it. Everybody figured that you were going to change the territories when you started traveling around with each of the reps, especially after what you said at the sales meeting."

"Well, the reason I went on the road with each of the reps, Fred," said Thomas, "was so that I could learn more about their selling problems while, at the same time, meet the customers."

Taylor smiled, "Sure, but when you started filling out a rating sheet on each account, I couldn't help thinking you had some reason for it."

Thomas realized that Taylor had spoken with irony in his voice, but he thought it was better to let the matter pass. Since he was planning to use the information he had gathered for the reorganization of the sales territories, he decided that he would be frank with Taylor. To find out what the young sales rep's reaction might be to territorial changes, he said, "Fred, I've thought a lot about making some changes in the territories—"

Taylor interrupted him. "That's terrific. I'm sure glad to hear that. I don't like to speak ill of the dead, but old Schultz really gave the trainees the short end of the stick when he put us on territories. He either gave us a territory of uncontacted accounts where it was like beating our heads against a stone wall. Some of us actually quit, like the two guys who trained with me. Or, Schultz gave us replacement territories where some of the best accounts had been handed over to the older reps. Well, I know for a fact that when I took over my territory from Mike Green, Bill Murray and Albert Simpson got 12 of Green's best accounts. And, damn it, I got more sales out of what was left than Green ever did; Murray and Simpson's total sales didn't go up. It took me a while, but I had the laugh at every sales meeting when our monthly sales figures were announced."

"Is that right?" said Thomas.

"Damn right! And I wasn't the only one. That's why those old duffers are so down on the four of us that have come with the division since the mid-1970s. We've beaten them at their own game."

"Do you think that Harrington and Howard and Donnelly feel the same way?" asked Thomas.

"Think, hell! I know it! That's all we ever talk about. If you reorganize those territories and give us back the accounts that Schultz took away, you'll see some real sales records. Take, for example, the Medical Arts Pharmacy out by Mercy Hospital. Bill Murray got that one away from my territory and he calls there only once a week. If I could get that one back, I'd get in there three times a week, and get five times as much business."

Thomas had to raise his hands in a gesture of protest. "Don't you have enough accounts already, Fred, to keep you busy?"

"Dave, I spend 50 hours a week on the road and I love it; but I know damn well that if I put some of the time I spend in the 'two-by-four' stores into some of those big juicy accounts like Medical Arts Pharmacy, I'd do even more business."

Thomas commented, "I'm not particularly anxious to argue now, but if you start putting time into Medical Arts Pharmacy, what's going to happen to your sales to the two-by-four stores?"

Taylor quickly replied, "Those druggists all know me. They'd go right on buying."

Thomas did not agree with Taylor. He thought that Taylor realized this.

After a moment of silence, Taylor rose from his chair, saying, "I'd better scoot home. My family will be furious with me for being late when we have plans for the weekend."

The two men walked to Taylor's car. As Taylor climbed into his car, he said, "Dave, don't forget what I said. Harrington, Howard, Donnelly, and I stand behind you 100 percent. You won't ever hear us talk about going over to a competitor!"

"Who's talking about that?" asked Thomas.

"Well," said Taylor as he started the motor and shifted into gear, "I don't want to tell tales out of school."

"Sure," Thomas said quickly. "I'm sorry I asked. So long, Fred. I'll see you soon."

Case Index

General Index